Java

Rheinwerk Computing

The Rheinwerk Computing series from Rheinwerk Publishing offers new and established professionals comprehensive guidance to enrich their skillsets and enhance their career prospects. Our publications are written by leading experts in the fields of programming, administration, security, analytics, and more. Each book is detailed and hands-on to help readers develop essential, practical skills that they can apply to their daily work. For further information, please visit our website: *www.rheinwerk-computing.com*.

Philip Ackermann
JavaScript: The Comprehensive Guide
2022, 982 pages, paperback and e-book
www.rheinwerk-computing.com/5554

Sebastian Springer
Node.js: The Comprehensive Guide
2022, 834 pages, paperback and e-book
www.rheinwerk-computing.com/5556

Johannes Ernesti, Peter Kaiser
Python 3: The Comprehensive Guide
2022, 1036 pages, paperback and e-book
www.rheinwerk-computing.com/5566

Bernd Öggl, Michael Kofler
Git: Project Management for Developers and DevOps Teams
2023, 407 pages, paperback and e-book
www.rheinwerk-computing.com/5555

Bernd Öggl, Michael Kofler
Docker: Practical Guide for Developers and DevOps Teams
2023, approx. 496 pp, paperback and e-book
www.rheinwerk-computing.com/5650

Christian Ullenboom

Java

The Comprehensive Guide

Rheinwerk
Computing

Editor Hareem Shafi
German Edition Editors Anne Scheibe, Almut Poll
Translation Winema Language Services, Inc.
Copyeditor Yvette Chin
Technical Reviewer Dirk Evers
Illustration Leo Leowald, Germany
Cover Design Graham Geary
Photo Credit iStockphoto: 1332719560/© zxvisual; Shutterstock: 190908608/© picoStudio
Layout Design Vera Brauner
Production Graham Geary
Typesetting III-satz, Germany
Printed and bound in Canada, on paper from sustainable sources

ISBN 978-1-4932-2295-7
© 2023 by Rheinwerk Publishing, Inc., Boston (MA)
1st edition 2023
16th German edition published 2022 by Rheinwerk Verlag, Bonn, Germany

Library of Congress Cataloging-in-Publication Data
Names: Ullenboom, Christian, author.
Title: Java : the comprehensive guide / by Christian Ullenboom.
Description: 1st edition. | Bonn ; Boston : Rheinwerk Publishing/SAP Press,
  2022. | Includes bibliographical references and index.
Identifiers: LCCN 2022029163 | ISBN 9781493222957 (hardcover) | ISBN
  9781493222964 (ebook)
Subjects: LCSH: Java (Computer program language) | Computer programming.
Classification: LCC QA76.73.J38 U45 2022 | DDC 005.13/3--dc23/eng/20220812
LC record available at https://lccn.loc.gov/2022029163

Contents at a Glance

Dear Reader,

The first iteration of the book that you now hold in your hands was published for German readers in 2003. Today, that bestselling guide is in its 16th edition in Germany. What does it mean to write 16 editions of a book? Consider: reading your work repeatedly over the course of 20 years; expanding, rewriting, and refining, until you know the text like the back of your hand; evaluating changes to the topic area and sorting through hundreds of pages of text to implement the minutest updates to the Java language; reading, reviewing, and testing code snippets; and, of course, working through 16 editions of editor feedback and critique.

In many ways, this translation is a 17th edition, built on years of previous work. Christian Ullenboom has honed his manuscript once again, making key updates to ensure that this guide is the best resource for both new Java programmers and experienced professionals. And he's done this in a new language, to bring his decades of knowledge to English readers. I'm certain that you will find his expertise invaluable.

What did you think about *Java: The Comprehensive Guide*? Your comments and suggestions are the most useful tools to help us make our books the best they can be. Please feel free to contact me and share any praise or criticism you may have.

Thank you for purchasing a book from SAP PRESS!

Hareem Shafi
Editor, SAP PRESS

hareems@rheinwerk-publishing.com
www.rheinwerk-computing.com
Rheinwerk Publishing · Boston, MA

Contents

4   Arrays and Their Areas of Use

5   Handling Characters and Strings   287

6 Writing Custom Classes 369

7   Object-Oriented Relationship   427

9   There Must Be Exceptions

10   Nested Types

11   Special Types of Java SE

12 Generics<T>

13   Lambda Expressions and Functional Programming

14   Architecture, Design, and Applied Object Orientation

15   Java Platform Module System

16   The Class Library

18   Introduction to Data Structures and Algorithms   909

21 Bits and Bytes, Mathematics and Money 1011

22   Testing with JUnit

23 The Tools of the JDK

1091

Preface

"Some people think they are polite just because they still use words at all and not fists."
—*Friedrich Hebbel (1813–1863)*

In the beginning was the Word. Much later, on May 23, 1995, at SunWorld in San Francisco, the head of Sun Microsystems's then Science Office, John Gage, and Netscape co-founder Marc Andreessen introduced the new Java programming language with its integration into the Netscape web browser. This event was the beginning of the triumphal procession of a language that offers elegant ways to program on any platform and to express your thoughts in an object-oriented (OO) way. The possibilities of the language and its libraries are nothing new in themselves but have been packaged so well that Java is pleasant and fluid for programming. Java is now one of the most popular programming languages on the planet. In its 23 chapters, this book deals with the Java technology with an intense focus on the Java programming language. Important topics include object-oriented programming (OOP), designing classes, and the structure of Java's standard libraries.

Target Group

The chapters of this book are designed for beginners to the Java programming language as well as for advanced users. Basic knowledge of a structured programming language such as C, Python, JavaScript, or Visual Basic and knowledge of OOP are helpful because the book doesn't explicitly address computer architectures or what programming actually is. So, if you've already programmed in any language, this book is for you!

What This Book Is Not

This book shouldn't be taken as a programming book for beginners. If you have never programmed before and associate the word "translation" primarily with "interpreting," you should start with a basic tutorial or follow one along in parallel. Many areas in the life of an industrial programmer are covered in this book to a general depth, but this book cannot replace the *Java Language Specification (JLS)*, available at *https://docs.oracle.com/javase/specs*.

Java technologies have exploded in recent years, so that their initial manageability has given way to strong specialization. Today, covering everything in one book isn't possible, and we certainly won't aim for that goal with this one. A book that deals specifically with the graphical user interface (GUI) JavaFX or Swing—both parts of standard Java—could be as extensive as the book you're holding in your hands. Other special topics include OO analysis/design, Unified Modeling Language (UML), parallel or distributed programming, Enterprise JavaBeans (EJBs), database connectivity, object-relational mapping, web services, dynamic web pages, and many other topics. For all those topics, special-purpose books may be required to satisfy your curiosity.

This Java book trains you on the syntax of the programming language, the handling of important standard libraries, development tools and development environments, OO analysis and design, design patterns, and program conventions. But this book can't help you impress the cool IT geeks at a party. Sorry.

My Life and Java, Or "Why a Java Book?"

My involvement with Java started over 20 years ago and is related to a compulsory university course. In 1997, our project group dealt with an OO dialog specification. A state machine had to be programmed, and the question of which programming language to use came up. Since I wanted to introduce Java to the seminar's participants, I prepared a set of slides for our presentation. Parallel to the slides, the professor expected an elaboration in the form of a seminar paper. Working with Java was fun and something completely different from what I had been used to until then. Before Java, I had coded in Assembler for about 10 years; then later, I used the high-level languages Pascal and C, and mainly built compilers. I tried and tested code, wrote down my experiences, and learned about Java and its libraries. The work grew with my experience. During time in this group project, a fellow student approached me to give a Java training as a speaker. I felt like doing it but didn't have any documents. So, I kept writing training materials for the course. When the professor asked for the seminar paper at the end of the group project, the preliminary manuscript of the current book was already so extensive that this introduction more or less became the seminar paper.

That was in 1997, and of course, I could have stopped writing immediately after I turned in the paper. But to this day, I still enjoy Java and look forward to each new version. And I am not alone in my optimism: The forecasts for Java remain promising because the use of Java is now as established as that of COBOL in banking and insurance. That's why people keep talking about Java being "the new COBOL."

After about two decades, I now consider this book to be a multifaceted Java resource for ambitious developers who want to look behind the scenes. Its level of detail is not reached by any other book about the basics of Java in English—at least that I know of! I have enjoyed extending the book, even if many topics are hardly addressed in a normal Java course.

Software and Versions

The basis for this book is *Java Platform Standard Edition (Java SE)* version 17 using the free OpenJDK implementation, which is a kind of *Java Development Kit (JDK)*. The JDK essentially consists of a compiler and a runtime environment—the *Java virtual machine (JVM)*—and is available for the Windows, macOS, Linux, and Solaris platforms.

A graphical development interface, called an *integrated development environment (IDE)*, is not part of the JDK. While I don't advocate relying on one vendor (because vendors appeal to different groups of developers), this book introduces *IntelliJ* development environments in slightly greater detail. Our sample programs can basically be entered into any other development environment or text editor—such as Microsoft Visual Studio Code (VS Code) or vi—and compiled on the command line. However, pure text editors are outdated in development, and a graphical command-line approach simplifies program creation.

Which Java Version to Use

Since Oracle (then still led by Sun) introduced the Java programming language in 1995 with version 1.0, the version spiral has inexorably turned. A new version is released every 6 months, and every 2 years, a Long-Term-Support-Release (LTS), with updates for a longer period of time, is released. The latest LTS is Java 17. Especially for authors writing books about Java, the question arises as to which Java version the text should be based on and which libraries should be described. In this book, we always describe the capabilities of the latest version, which was Java 18 at the time of this writing. For the didactics of OOP, the version question is fortunately irrelevant.

The examples in this book are consistently based on Java 17.

Using This Book to Learn

This book is ideal for self-study. The first chapter is for warming up. If you don't have a development environment installed on your computer, you should first install the JDK from Oracle. Because the JDK only installs command-line tools, every developer should install a graphical IDE because an IDE makes the development of Java programs much more comfortable. An IDE provides several advantages over the raw command line, such as the following:

- Editing, compiling, and running a Java program are quick and easy with a keystroke or mouse click.
- An editor should highlight the syntax of Java in color (*syntax highlighting*).

- A context-sensitive help shows the parameters for methods and at the same time provides access to the application programming interface (API) documentation.

- Other benefits such as a GUI builder, project management, and debugging are added but don't play any role in this book.

In software development, the documentation of API interfaces is essential. Documentation can usually be viewed from the development environment with the touch of a button or found online. Chapter 1 also provides URLs for the available documentation.

Everything really starts with Chapter 2, and from then, we'll go step by step. Anyone with knowledge of JavaScript, C, C#, or C++ can easily skim Chapter 2. Those more familiar with OOP in C# or C++ can quickly read Chapter 3 and then jump on. Chapter 6 and Chapter 7 form the OO center of the book: These chapters teach the OO concepts of *class*, *method*, *association*, *inheritance*, and *dynamic binding*. After Chapter 7, the basic OO training is complete, and with Chapter 15, you'll have been introduced to all the basics of Java.

Personal Learning Strategies

If using this book in self-study, a successful learning strategy can be described. The key to understanding, as is so often the case, is the psychology of learning, which examines the reading conditions under which a text can be optimally understood. The method I'd like to present is called the *PQ4R method*, which stands for the following steps:

- *Preview*: First, you should get an initial overview of the chapter, for example, by browsing the table of contents and skipping the pages of individual chapters. Look at the figures and tables a little longer, as they already give away the content and make you want to read the text.

- *Questions*: Each chapter attempts to convey a thematic block. Before reading, you should consider the questions you want the chapter to answer.

- *Read*: Here we go—you must read the text. Unless you've borrowed a library book, you should highlight passages you think are important with lots of color and add notes in the margins. The same applies to new terms. Everyone should be able to answer the previously asked questions. If new questions arise, store them in your memory!

- *Reflect*: Whether motivated or not—an interesting finding from another study— anyone can learn. Success depends only on how deeply the knowledge is processed (called *elaborative processing*). In this process, topics must be linked to other topics. Think about how the statements fit with the other parts. Now is also a good time for practical exercises. For the examples given in this book, you should think of your own examples. If we describe an if statement using age as an example, an idea of your own could be something like an if statement on your height.

- *Recite*: At this point, you should be able to answer the questions posed earlier, without the text. For me, writing is a good way to reflect on what I know, but everyone should restate content in their own way. Great fun can be had by reflecting about all the keywords and their meanings, the relationship between abstract classes and interfaces, etc. while taking a shower.

Tip [+]

Explaining out loud helps with many types of problem solving—just chat up the toaster. Even nicer is learning with someone and explaining procedures to each other. An interesting visualization technique is the mind map, which can be used to organize the content.

- *Review*: Now, go through the chapter again and see if you've understood everything without further questions. Some "quick" explanations may have turned out to be wrong. Perhaps, the text doesn't clarify everything either. Then, a note directed to me (*ullenboom@gmail.com*) will be very welcome.

The PQ4R method facilitates the acquisition of knowledge. However, like all learned things, if you don't refresh your knowledge regularly, you'll forget it. The PQ4R method should therefore be given an additional "R" for long-term success: "R" for "repeat" or "refresh." As a rule, people over-read something at the beginning and pay little attention to details. Later, when more background knowledge is available, even basic things can appear in a new light and fit into the overall picture. Readers should therefore pick up the book again and again and turn its pages.

Focusing on the Essentials

Some sections are written for experienced programmers or computer scientists. Newcomers may need to stray from the sequential path of chapters at some points since some chapters may require more background information and familiarity with programming languages. Comparisons with other programming languages are intended for loosening up and comparison and aren't necessary for the understanding of Java.

Special Sections

The Java universe is rich in subtlety and often confuses newcomers. For this reason, the book weights knowledge in two ways. First, boxes set off from the text provide specialized and advanced information. Furthermore, some headings end in an asterisk (*), which means that this section can be skipped without the reader missing anything essential for later chapters.

Tasks

With this book and a trusted development environment, you can develop your first programs. However, reading is not enough to learn a new programming language. If you want to learn a programming language, you must practice and speak it like a foreign language.

Accompanying this book are practice exercises available online at *https://tutego.de/ javabuch/aufgaben/index_en.html*. At that site, you'll find links to complete solutions. The site is updated periodically with new tasks and solutions.

Structure of This Book

Chapter 1 highlights the special features of the Java language. In this chapter, I draw some comparisons with other popular OO languages. This chapter is not particularly technical and also describes the historical course of Java's evolution. The chapter isn't didactically structured, so that some concepts aren't covered in depth until the later chapters; beginners should skim through it. We'll also show you how to obtain and install a JDK so that your first programs can be compiled and run. Learning will be more fun with a development environment, so an introduction to IDEs is provided as well.

Things really get going in **Chapter 2**. This chapter describes variables, types, and imperative language elements by describing statements and expressions that form the foundation of any program. Descriptions of case statements, loop types, and methods can also be found in this chapter. These features are still possible without much object orientation.

Things do actually become OO in **Chapter 3**. We'll first explore the classes available in the standard library and develop our own classes later because our focus is on the basic concepts first, such as the keyword new, references, the null reference, and reference comparisons. The standard library is so rich that, with predefined classes and this basic knowledge alone, many programs can be developed. The provided data structures can be used in many ways.

Several data types can be combined in an array, which is introduced in **Chapter 4**. Arrays also form the basis of some Java concepts such as variable argument lists and the extended for.

The reason behind many problems is the changed "handling of characters and strings," which we'll introduce in **Chapter 5**. In this chapter, the important types Character (the data type for single characters), String, and StringBuilder (data types for strings) will be introduced. Concerning strings, sometimes, parts must be cut out, recognized, and converted. A split(...) from the String class is possible, and the Scanner class can split strings into substrings using separators. Format objects put any output into the desired format, including the output of decimal numbers.

With this knowledge about object creation and references, the next step can take place: **Chapter 6** deals with writing custom classes. Using games and rooms, we'll model object properties. Important concepts such as constructors, static properties, and enumerations are described in this chapter.

Object relationships, that is, the associations between objects (also referred to as "uses-A relationships") and inheritance relationships are the subjects of **Chapter 7**. This chapter introduces "real" OOP and covers dynamic binding, abstract classes, and visibility.

Java supports several types, and besides classes, another important type is the interface. **Chapter 8** introduces this particular type as well as two other types: enumeration types and records.

Exceptions, which are discussed in **Chapter 9**, form an important backbone for all programs since errors can hardly be avoided. For this reason, the active support of their handling is advised since doing so forces a programmer to take care of errors and fix them.

Chapter 10 describes how classes can be nested within each other. This nesting can improve encapsulation because implementations can then also be local.

Chapter 11 describes classes that are central to the Java library, such as comparison classes, wrapper classes, and the Object class, which is the superclass of all Java classes.

Generics can be used to declare classes, interfaces, and methods with a kind of type placeholder, where the concrete type is defined later. **Chapter 12** provides insight into this technology.

Lambda expressions have been around since Java 8; they simplify functional programming in particular. We devote **Chapter 13** to language properties. In this chapter, you'll also learn about many standard types that are used in functional programming.

At this point, the foundations have been laid, and the remaining chapters build on the knowledge already acquired. **Chapter 14** introduces SOLID principles, shows applications of good OOP, and introduces *design patterns*. Based on various examples, this chapter demonstrates how interfaces and class hierarchies can be used effectively in Java. The key is to think small but to write big applications.

Chapter 15 describes how, in Java, individual components or systems of components can be used flexibly for other applications.

After the first 15 chapters, readers will be almost completely familiar with the Java language. However, since Java is not only a language but also a set of standard libraries, the second half of the book focuses on basic APIs. At the end of each chapter, a "Further Reading" section provides references to interesting online resources. At this point, readers can leave the sequential path and focus on individual topics since the remaining topics are usually not directly interdependent.

The Java library consists of over 4,000 classes, interfaces, enumerations, exceptions, and annotations. Chapter 16 provides an overview of the most important packages and picks out some classes from the library, such as loading classes. In this chapter, you'll also find classes for configuring applications or ways to run external programs.

Chapter 17 through **Chapter 22** provide an overview of selected Java SE APIs. **Chapter 17** provides an introduction to concurrent programming, while **Chapter 18** shows common data structures such as lists, sets, and associative memory in a practical way. **Chapter 19** provides an overview of how you can read from and write into files. If you want to use a relational database to store data, you'll find useful information in **Chapter 20**. **Chapter 21** introduces you to the Math class, which provides typical mathematical methods to perform trigonometric calculations, for example. With another class, you can generate random numbers. The chapter also covers the handling of arbitrarily long integers or floats.

Automatic testing of applications helps detect errors in code, especially if silly code changes are introduced subsequently and the program no longer behaves in accordance with the specification. **Chapter 22** introduces the concept of test cases and demonstrates how to execute test cases easily and automatically. In addition, this chapter focuses on the design of testable applications.

Finally, **Chapter 23** provides a brief overview of command-line tools like *javac* for compiling Java programs and *java* for starting the JVM and executing Java programs.

Conventions

The following conventions are used in this book:

- Newly introduced terms are *italicized*, and the index refers to that exact location. Furthermore, *file names, HTTP addresses, names of executable programs, program options*, and *file extensions* (*.txt*) are italicized.

- User interface (UI) terms are written in **bold**.

- Listings, methods, and other program elements are set in programming font. In some places, a bent arrow ⤴ has been placed after a listing line as a special character to mark a line break. So, the code from the next line still belongs to the previous one.

- Method names and constructors are always followed by a pair of parentheses to distinguish methods/constructors from object/class variables. Thus, when writing System.out and System.gc(), you can clearly see that the former is a class variable, and the latter is a method.

- If a method or constructor has a parameter, the type is enclosed in parentheses, for example, Math.abs(double a) or Point(int x, int y). Often the parameter name is also omitted, for example, "System.exit(int) exits the program with a return value." The Java API documentation does the same. If a method or constructor has a parameter list, but is not relevant in the text, it's abbreviated with ellipses, as in "...". For example: "The System.out.print(...) method converts the passed arguments to strings and prints them." Thus, an empty pair of parentheses means that a method or constructor really has no parameter list. To make the specification short and yet precise, you'll see some specifications in the text like getProperty(String key[, String def]), which is an abbreviation for getProperty(String key) and getProperty(String key, String def). Elsewhere, the ellipses (...) are also found when the implementation or screen outputs aren't further required for understanding.

- To specify a group of methods, the * identifier symbolizes a placeholder. For example, print*(...) stands for the methods println(...), print(...), and printf(...). From the context, you should clearly see which methods are meant.

- Long package names are sometimes abbreviated, so that com.tutego.island.game becomes c.t.i.g, for example.

- To indicate compiler errors or runtime errors in the program code, a line may contain a ☠. Thus, you can see at first glance that the line is not compiled or throws an exception at runtime due to a programming error, for example, the following code:

```
int p = new java.awt.Point();      // ☠ Compiler error: Type mismatch
```

- In case of compiler errors—as in the previous point—messages are usually printed by the *javac* compiler and partly by the Eclipse Java compiler. Errors are detected by both compilers; only the output differs in wording.

- Facebook is now called Meta, and Sun became Oracle in early 2010. The name "Sun" only appears in the book when discussing a technology initiated by Sun and that came onto the market when Sun was responsible for it. The younger generation will hardly remember Sun Microsystems, that's how long ago it was. In 2010, Apple released the first iPad, which was also quite a long time ago.

Program Listings

Entire program listings are structured in the following way:

```
class Candy {
}
```

Listing 1.1 Candy.java

The source code shown is located in the file *Candy.java*. If the type (class, enumeration, interface, or annotation) is in a package, the path specification is placed with the file name:

```
package com.tutego.island;
class Candy { }
```

Listing 1.2 com/tutego/island/Candy.java

To save space, the book often presents source code snippets. The complete source code is available on the internet (*www.rheinwerk-computing.com/5557*). If an excerpt of a file like *Person.java* is displayed, we'll indicate this editing in the caption, for example, in the following ways:

Listing 1.3 Person.java (Snippet)

Listing 1.4 Person.java, main(), Part 1

If sample programs are provided for certain classes, the class names of these programs generally end in Demo. Thus, for the DateFormat Java class, a sample program that demonstrates the functionality of the DateFormat class is named DateFormatDemo.

Application Programming Interface Documentation in This Book

Class/object variables, constructors, and methods are found in a special listing that makes it easy to find in the book and use as a reference work.

```
abstract class java.text.DateFormat
extends Format
implements Cloneable, Serializable
```

▶ Date parse(String source) throws ParseException
  Parses a date or time string.

The rectangle contains the fully qualified class or interface name (such as the DateFormat class in the java.text package) or the name of the annotation or enumeration type.

The following lines list the superclass (`DateFormat` inherits from `Format`) and the implemented interfaces (`DateFormat` implements `Cloneable` and `Serializable`). Since any class that doesn't have an explicit superclass automatically inherits from `Object`, this inheritance is not specified separately. Visibility is `public` unless otherwise specified, which is common for library methods. If an interface is described, the methods are automatically abstract and public, and the `abstract` and `public` keywords aren't additionally specified. The subsequent enumeration class/object variables are followed by constructors and methods. Unless otherwise specified, visibility is `public`. If errors are specified with `throws`, then they aren't `RuntimeExceptions` but only checked exceptions. *Deprecated* methods aren't listed but may be mentioned if no alternative exists.

Executable Programs

Executable programs on the command line can be recognized by a dollar sign at the beginning (even if other operating systems and command lines display a different prompt). The characters to be entered by the user are set in bold; the output isn't, as in the following example:

```
$ java Joke
Where do fish sleep? In the riverbed.
```

Acknowledgments

I was 9 years old when my parents opened the world of computers to me with the Commodore 64. Because I lacked a medium to save programs and data, I had no choice but to re-enter everything after rebooting—the way I learned how to program. To my parents, a big thanks for the computer, for the love, and for trusting me.

Thanks are due to Sun Microsystems, which began development on Java in 1991. Without Sun, there would be no Java, and without Java, there wouldn't be this book. Thanks also to Oracle, as the buyer of Sun, because perhaps without the acquisition Java would have been finished.

Java lives—maybe I should say, "survives"—through many free tools and an active open-source community. A big "thank you" goes to all developers who write and maintain the many great Java tools, libraries, and frameworks available today, such as Eclipse, Maven, JUnit, and Spring Tomcat. Without them, Java wouldn't be where it is today.

Finally, I would like to express my thanks to Rheinwerk Publishing for helping me publish this book. I'm grateful for the collaboration with my editor.

Resources for This Book

All sample programs are available for you to download from the book's website: Go to *www.rheinwerk-publishing.com/5557*. Click on the **Resources** tab to view downloadable files with a brief description of each file's content. Click the **Download** button to start the download process. Depending on the size of the file (and your internet connection), some time may be required for the download to complete.

Feedback

No matter how carefully we've gone through the chapters of this book, discrepancies are likely in over 1,100 pages, just as any software can have purely statistical errors. If you have any comments, suggestions, corrections, or questions about specific points or general didactics, please don't hesitate to email me at *ullenboom@gmail.com*. I'm always open to suggestions, praise, and reprimands.

Now, we're ready to explore life between the curly brackets and follow the Greek philosopher Plato, who said, "The beginning is the most important part of the work."

Chapter 1
Introduction

"We're producing information en masse today, just like cars used to be."
—John Naisbitt (1929–2021)

After 20 years, Java has finally established itself as a platform. Millions of software developers worldwide make their living with the language, billions of devices run Java programs (e.g., all Blu-ray players). Every week, Oracle's runtime environment is downloaded millions of times. In this chapter, we'll introduce you to Java, discuss its features, compare it to other programming languages, and explore its platforms and development environments.

Figure 1.1 Many Devices Speak Java

1.1 Historical Background

In the 1970s, when hippies were still dancing to the music of Jimi Hendrix, Bill Joy wanted to create a programming language that would combine all the advantages of *MESA*[1] and *C*. Joy, co-founder of Sun Microsystems, was initially unable to fulfill this

---

1 The MESA programming language was developed in the 1970s at *the Xerox Palo Alto Research Center* (Xerox PARC). It was used to program the *Xerox Alto*, the first computer with a complete GUI. The syntax of MESA has similarities with Algol and Pascal.

wish, and only in 1990s could he describe what a new object-oriented (OO) language might look like, in his article "Further." For Joy, its basic principles should be based on C++. Only later did he realize that C++ was unsuitable as a base language and too unwieldy for large programs.

At that time, James Gosling was working on the Standard Generalized Markup Language (*SGML*). He developed in C++ and wasn't happy with this language either. The new language *Oak* was born out of this displeasure. The name came to Gosling's mind when he looked out the window and saw an *oak* tree, but maybe that's just a legend, because Oak also stands for *Object Application Kernel*.

Patrick Naughton launched the Green project in December 1990, involving Gosling and Mike Sheridan. A remnant from the Green project is *Duke*, which became a well-known symbol.[2]

Figure 1.2 Duke: The Mascot for Java

The idea behind this project was to develop software for interactive television and other consumer electronics devices. Components of this project were the operating system Green-OS, Gosling's interpreter Oak, and some hardware components. Joy showed the members of the Green project his "Further" essay and started implementing a graphical user interface (GUI). Gosling wrote the original compiler in C, and then Naughton, Gosling, and Sheridan designed the runtime interpreter in C as well. Ultimately, the C++ language was never used. Oak ran its first programs in August 1991. Thus, the Green dream team developed a device called *7 ((Star Seven), introduced internally in the fall of 1992. Former Sun CEO Scott McNealy (who left the company after the Oracle acquisition in January 2010) was impressed with *7, and the team became First Person, Inc., in November of that year. Now, it was a matter of marketing *7.

In early 1993, the team heard that Time Warner was looking for a system for set-top boxes, which are electronic end-user devices that connect to a TV set. First Person turned its attention from the consumer market to set-top boxes. Unfortunately, Time Warner was later no longer interested, but First Person continued to develop. After many changes in direction, their development work focused on the *world wide web* (referred to as the *web* for short). The programming language was supposed to receive program code over the network, and faulty programs should not cause any damage. With this development, most concepts from C(++) could already be checked off—access

---

2 Duke looks a bit like a tooth and therefore could for an ad for a dentist. The design is by Joe Palrang.

via invalid pointers that wildly write to memory are one example. The members of the original project team realized that Oak had all the features required for use on the web—perfect, even though it had originally been developed for a completely different purpose. The Oak language was renamed *Java* in 1994 because the name Oak was already registered by *Oak Technology*. According to tradition, the decision for the name Java was made in a coffee shop. In Java, Patrick Naughton demonstrated a prototype of the *WebRunner* browser, said to have been created over a single weekend. After minor revisions by Jonathan Payne, the browser was christened *HotJava* and presented to the public in May at SunWorld '95.

At first, only a few users could make friends with HotJava. So, a truly fortunate moment occurred when Netscape decided to license the Java technology. Java was implemented in version 2.0 of *Netscape Navigator*, which had launched in December 1995. On January 23, 1996, Java Development Kit (JDK) 1.0 was released, which for the first time provided a way to program Java applications and web applets (with "applet" defined as "a mini-application"). Shortly before the completion of JDK 1.0, the remaining members of the Green team founded the company *JavaSoft*, beginning Java's triumphant progress.

[«]

Where Is the Sun? Oracle Acquires Sun Microsystems in 2010

Java was originally developed by Sun Microsystems, a company with a long history in operating systems and hardware. Sun has laid many foundations for modern IT systems, but many are only familiar with it through Java.

Sun Microsystems never really fared that well as a company. Known and respected for its products, Sun lacked the skill to turn its products and services into cash. After major revenue losses, Oracle Corporation acquired Sun Microsystems for $7.4 billion, along with all rights and patents for Java, MySQL, Solaris, OpenOffice, VirtualBox, and other products. Oracle has since discontinued some open-source projects, but the large and commercially viable ones are still in good shape.

1.2   On the Popularity of Java: The Key Features

Java is an OOP language characterized by several key features to make it universally applicable and interesting for companies as a robust programming language. Because Java enables OOP, developers can create modern and reusable software components.

In part, Java seems rather conservative, but that's because the designers of the Java language don't immediately incorporate everything that's hip at the moment. Java has always incorporated into the language core what had proven useful and good in other programming languages. However, Sun and later Oracle avoided including things in the language that were only used by a few programmers or that led to frequent errors.

In the early days, C++ stood as a role model, but today, Java is squinting at C# and scripting languages.

Let's now look at some central properties of Java and highlight a few key terms and modes of operation.

1.2.1 Bytecode

First, Java is a programming language like any other. But unlike conventional interpreters of a programming language, which usually generate machine code for a specific processor (for example, for x86 microprocessors or processors of the ARM architecture) and a specific platform (such as Linux or Windows), the Java compiler generates what's called *bytecode* from its source code files. This program code is binary and serves as the starting point for the virtual machine (VM) to run. Bytecode is comparable to microprocessor code for an imaginary processor, which knows statements like arithmetic operations, jumps, and more.

1.2.2 Executing the Bytecode via a Virtual Machine

For the program code of the virtual processor to be executed, a *runtime environment* called the *Java virtual machine (JVM)*, takes care of the bytecode after the program code is translated into bytecode.[3] The runtime environment (also called the *runtime interpreter*) loads the bytecode, checks it, and executes it in a controlled environment. The JVM provides an entire range of additional services, such as an automatic *garbage collector* that cleans up memory, and strong type checking under a well-defined memory and threading model.

1.2.3 Platform Independence

A central characteristic of Java is its *platform independence* or *operating system independence*. This flexibility is achieved through two key concepts: First, Java doesn't bind itself to a particular processor or architecture; instead, the compiler generates bytecode that a runtime environment then processes. Second, Java abstracts from the properties of a concrete operating system and creates, for example, an interface to the input/output system or an application programming interface (API) for GUIs. Developers always program against a Java API, but never against the API of the actual platform, such as the Windows or Unix API. The Java Runtime Environment maps calls to files for the respective system, for example, and is thus an intermediary between the Java programs and the actual operating system API.

---

3 The idea of the bytecode is pretty old. The company *Datapoint* created the PL/B programming language around 1970, which maps programs to bytecode. Also, the original implementation of UCSD-Pascal, which was created around the beginning of 1980, uses an intermediate code (*p-code* for short).

Platform-independent programming languages and runtime environments are standard today, and Java is no longer an exception. The top languages today are JavaScript, Python, Ruby, PHP, Kotlin, and C#, and all of them have a runtime environment, while some languages can also be compiled into native code. Platform independence is difficult because a programming language and a bytecode-producing compiler are only one part—the bigger part is the runtime environment and an extensive API. While C itself is a portable language, and ANSI C programs can be compiled by any C compiler on any operating system with a compiler, the problem is the libraries, which don't go beyond a few simple file operations.

1.2.4 Java as a Language, Runtime Environment, and Standard Library

Not only is Java a programming language; it's also a runtime system, which Oracle wants to make clear by using the term *Java platform*. The programming language and JVM are accompanied by a set of standard libraries for data structures, string processing, date/time processing, GUIs, input/output operations, background threads, network operations, and more. These libraries form the basis for higher-value services such as database connections and web services.

1.2.5 Object Orientation in Java

Java was designed as a language to make it easy to write large, bug-free applications. In C programs, statistically, an error is expected every 55 program lines. Even in large software packages (from 1 million lines of code), an error is found on average every 200 program lines, regardless of the underlying programming language. These errors must be addressed, although to date no comprehensive strategy has been found for software development on a large scale. Much work in computer science is concerned with how thousands of programmers can work together and design software over decades. This problem is not easy to solve and was heavily debated during the software crisis of the mid-1960s.

A runtime environment eliminates many problems of a technical nature. OOP attempts to better model the complexity of the software problem. The philosophy is that humans think in an OO way, and thus, a programming environment should reflect this human way of thinking. Just as in the real world, objects are connected and communicate in the world of software. Objects consist of *properties*, which describe things that an object "has" and "can" do. A car "has" wheels and a seat and "can" accelerate and brake. Objects are created from *classes*, which are descriptions for the structure of objects.

The Java language is not completely OO, as Smalltalk demonstrates. Primitive data types exist for numeric numbers or Unicode characters and aren't managed as objects. The reason for this kind of design is that, with separation, the compiler and runtime environment can better optimize programs. However, Microsoft's VM for the .NET platform and other modern programming languages show that good performance is possible even without this separation.

1.2.6 Java Is Widespread and Well Known

Regardless of the performance of a language, in the end, only business matters count: How quickly and cheaply can the system desired by your customer be built, and how stable and amenable to changes is it? In addition, some further questions include: What literature is available on the market? What training paths are available? Where can a team get a developer or consultant in an emergency? These points aren't necessarily front of mind for computer scientists when comparing languages, but these questions can be decisive for the success of a software platform. Almost every university teaches Java, and with Java, a job is certain. Conferences introduce new trends and create trends. This chain can't be broken, and even if a new super language called "Bali" emerged today, years would be required to create a comparable system. Mind you: This discussion says nothing about innovation or performance—only about market saturation, but that's what makes Java interesting for so many people.

Today, Java is the basis of many highly successful products, many of which run on the server side, for example, Facebook, LinkedIn, Twitter, Amazon, and eBay. On the client side, Java is less common, although the game Minecraft is an exception to the rule.

[»]

Java Developers Are Happy

Andrew Vos looked at the comments developers added to their programs through version control.[4] In doing so, he counted how many "bad" words like "omg" and "wtf" occur at check-in. His approach may not be statistically tidy, but in the projects he examined, Java developers are doing quite well and have little to swear about. The comments are amusing to read and provide different explanations, such as that JavaScript programmers really only swear about Internet Explorer, but not about the JavaScript language itself, and that Python programmers are too decent to swear.

1.2.7 Java Is Fast: Optimization and Just-In-Time Compilation

JVM version 1.0 started with a pure interpretation of the bytecode. This approach caused massive speed problems because, during interpretation, the work of a processor—recognizing, decoding, and executing a statement—must be repeated again in software, which takes a lot of time. Java programs of the first hour were therefore significantly slower than interpreted C(++) programs and earned Java the reputation of being a slow language.

---

4 *http://tutego.de/go/profanity*

The *just-in-time (JIT) compiler* technique[5] was a first step to addressing the problem. A JIT compiler accelerates the execution of programs by translating the bytecode (i.e., the program instructions of the VM) into the machine code for the respective platform at runtime. A translation at runtime has enormous optimization potential because the JVM naturally knows what kind of CPU is used and can generate the best possible machine code for that CPU. One example is the instruction set extension called *Streaming SIMD Extensions 2 (SSE2)* for x86 processors: If the JVM finds this processor type, SSE2 code can be generated; otherwise, not.

After translation, a program is available in the memory adapted to the architecture, which the physical processor executes quickly without interpretation. With this technique, the speed is equal to that of other translated languages. However, a good JIT doesn't translate everything; instead, the compiler uses various heuristics to determine whether a translation—which itself takes time—is worthwhile at all. The JVM therefore always starts with an interpretation and then switches to compiler mode when necessary. Thus, Java is basically a compiled language, but also an interpreted programming language—apart from the execution via hardware. The Java compiler in the JVM might be the most frequently run compiler overall. And the result is exceptionally good, as can be seen when comparing Java to other languages.

Sun's JIT compiler continued to improve and evolve into a family of VMs now known as *HotSpot*. One special feature is that HotSpot monitors execution at runtime and finds "hot" (i.e., critical) spots, such as loops with many repetitions. The JVM can then control translations and optimizations in a targeted manner. Optimizations include classics such as expression merging, but also many dynamic optimizations fall into this area that a static C++ compiler wouldn't understand because it lacks context.[6] In addition, the JVM can reload bytecode at any time, which is optimized in the same way since all parts that have been previously loaded. The newly introduced program code can even invalidate old optimizations and machine code, which the JVM then recompiles.

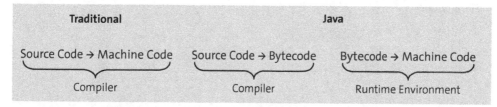

Figure 1.3 The Traditional Compiler and the Java Compiler with the Runtime Environment

---

5 This concept is also old: HP had JIT compilers for BASIC machines around 1970.
6 Dynamic method calls are usually extremely fast because the JVM knows the type hierarchy and can optimize aggressively. However, optimizations can be undone if the type hierarchy changes, for example, due to reloaded classes. The JVM also knows which program parts are executed concurrently and must be saved or whether synchronization can be omitted.

HotSpot, just like the runtime system, is published under the free GNU General Public License (GPL) license and can be viewed by everyone. The JVM is mainly programmed in C++, but for performance reasons, some parts are in machine code, which makes porting not so easy. The *Zero-Assembler Project* (*https://openjdk.java.net/projects/zero*) aims to realize HotSpot without machine code, so that porting is easy. The HotSpot VM has its own development and version numbers.

Completely new options are available with solutions like *GraalVM* (*https://www.graalvm.org*), which can mix JavaScript, Ruby, R, and Python in addition to Java. GraalVM can also compile native executables since the path via a classic runtime environment is no longer necessary.

1.2.8   Pointers and References

In Java, no pointers to memory areas exist, as they are known and feared from other programming languages. However, since an OOP language can't function without references, Java introduced *references*. A reference represents an object, and a variable stores this reference (called a *reference variable*). While programmers work only with references, the JVM associates the reference with a memory area; the access, called *dereferencing*, is indirect. References and memory blocks are therefore separated, which is quite flexible because Java can move an object in memory.

The object built in memory has a type that can't change, which is called the *object type*: A car remains a car and is not a laminating system. A reference in Java can take different types; we call this a *reference type*. For instance, a Java program can also view a car as a means of transportation.

[Ex]

Example*

The following program shows that tinkering is possible and easy in C++, and you can access private elements via pointer arithmetic.[7] For our purposes, consider this cautionary tale:

```
#include <cstring>
#include <iostream>
using namespace std;

class VeryUnsafe {
public:
  VeryUnsafe() { strcpy( password, "HaL9124f/aa" ); }
private:
  char password[ 100 ];
};
```

---

7 Even without a compiler, this can be tested online: *http://ideone.com*.

```
int main() {
  VeryUnsafe badguy;
  char *pass = reinterpret_cast<char*>( & badguy );
  cout << "Password: " << pass << endl;
}
```

This example demonstrates how problematic the use of pointers can be. The badguy pointer, which was initially intended as a reference to the VeryUnsafe class, mutates into a char pointer pass through the explicit type conversion. The characters can be read from the memory byte by byte without any problem, which also allows indirect access to the private data.

In Java, you cannot access arbitrary parts of the memory. Also, private variables are safe for now.[8] The compiler aborts with an error message—or the runtime system throws an exception—if the program tries to access a private variable.

1.2.9 Take Out the Trash, Garbage Collector!

In programming languages such as C(++), about half of the errors can be traced back to incorrect memory allocation. Working with objects and structures inevitably means creating and deleting them. However, the JVM independently takes care of managing these objects. As a result, objects don't need to be released; Java's *garbage collector* removes them. After explicitly building an object, Java's runtime system permanently monitors whether the object is still needed (i.e., still referenced). Conversely, garbage collecting also means that, if a secret reference still exists on an object, the garbage collector can't delete the object. Note that these *dangling references* are a nuisance and might only be found through longer debugging sessions.

The garbage collector is a concurrent thread in the background that finds and marks unreferenced objects and removes them from time to time. Thus, the garbage collector eliminates the need for manual memory queries. We should welcome this technology because many problems can disappear, such as memory leaks, where the release is "forgotten" and the utilized memory keeps swelling.

Automatic garbage collection is not without problems, since garbage collecting can strike whenever the system wants to do something time-critical, and interruptions aren't convenient. However, modern garbage collectors are good at detecting few active cycles and distributing the work evenly and also over several processor cores. But automatic garbage collection is nothing new, and these procedures have long been tried and tested. Even early programming languages such as LISP (1958) and Smalltalk (1972) included a garbage collector, and all modern programming languages (or their runtime environments) have automatic garbage collection.

---

8 However, this safety limitation is not entirely true. With *reflection*, you can access otherwise protected parts of memory if your security settings allow.

1.2.10 Exception Handling

Not everything can be planned. Sometimes, a network connection breaks down; sometimes, a file disappears; and sometimes, the divisor of an integer division process is 0. Java provides *exceptions* to deal with runtime errors. Exceptions are error objects that are generated at runtime to indicate an error and to interrupt the general flow of the program. These problem areas can be encapsulated by program constructs. The solution in many cases is cleaner than using return values and unreadable expressions in the program flow.

For speed reasons, C(++)[9] doesn't check the bounds of an array via *range checking* by default, which can cause many security problems. Incorrect access to the element $n + 1$ of an array of size n can cause two things: An access error occurs, or—much worse—other data is overridden during write access, and the error is no longer traceable.

Java's runtime system automatically checks the bounds of an array. These monitors can't be switched off, as the compilers of other programming languages sometimes allow. A clever runtime environment finds out whether no overrun is possible and then optimizes this query away; array checks are therefore no longer costly and don't automatically make themselves felt through poorer performance.

1.2.11 The Range of Libraries and Tools

Java has been around for so long now that there's a large number of tools, from development environments with supporting editors to good debuggers and build management tools. In addition to the standard libraries, other commercial or open-source libraries can be added. Whether writing PDF documents, reading Microsoft Excel documents, transferring data to SAP, or controlling the cash ejection at an ATM—Java libraries exist for all of these capabilities.

---

9 In C++, you could solve a variant with an overloaded operator.

New programming languages have a hard time keeping up. The number of programming languages has exploded in recent years, but they can't really attract the masses because they lack tools and libraries. More interesting are new languages based on the JVM because these programming languages still allow the use of the known tools and established libraries.

However, tools and libraries are sometimes what keep teams from switching to Java. Especially in game development, teams may have a lot of experience in C(++) and have spent years putting energy into gaming frameworks—the tools are simply there, but in Java, they aren't available (yet).

1.2.12   Comparably Simple Syntax

The syntax of Java is rather simple compared to languages like C++ or Perl and doesn't bristle with operators or complexity. Java inherited a simple and basic syntax from C, like the curly brackets, but avoided overloading the syntax with all sorts of things. Since programs are read more often than they're written, a syntax must be clear and consistent—the easier developers can see what's happening at first glance, the better.

> *"Always code as if the guy who ends up maintaining your code will be a violent psychopath who knows where you live."* —John Woods

There's no value to compactness in itself if programs are simply compact but the time required for a human to understand increases exponentially. The more compact the code, the longer decoding by humans will require. Even though the following Perl example from "The Fifth Obfuscated Perl Contest Results"[10] was deliberately designed as an unreadable program; anyone encountering at this program will get dizzy just looking at it:

```
#:: ::-| ::-| .-. :||-:: 0-| .-| ::||-| .:|-. :||
open(Q,$0);while(<Q>){if(/^#(.*)$/){for(split('-',$1)){$q=0;for(split){s/\|
/:..:/xg;s/:/../g;$Q=$_?length:$_;$q+=$q?$Q:$Q*20;}print chr($q);}}}print"\n";
#.: ::||-| .||-| :|||-| ::||-| ||-:: :|||-| .:|
```

A simpler syntax can be seen as both a curse (more typing) and a blessing (usually easier to understand). Java is rather "chatty" and in places abandons compactness. For example, in an inheritance relationship, Java is called with something like class Rum extends Drink; in Kotlin, you would write class Rum : Drink; in Ruby, class Rum < Drink.

1.2.13   Abandoning Controversial Concepts

Java could basically take over everything from different programming languages and be a super-language; however, the language's designers didn't do so and don't want

---

10 *https://en.wikipedia.org/wiki/Obfuscated_Perl_Contest*

that. Two capabilities of C(++) that were omitted in Java will be presented as examples in the following two sections.

In Java, No User-Defined Overloaded Operators Exist

When we use an operator such as the plus sign and use it to add expressions, we usually do so with known arithmetic quantities such as floats (floating point numbers) or integers. Since the same operator character is valid on different data types, such an operator is called *overloaded*. Operators like +, -, *, and / are overloaded for numbers just like the operators OR, AND, or XOR for integers and Boolean values. The comparison operators == and != are also overloaded because they can be used with all numbers, but also with truth values or object references. A conspicuously overloaded operator is the plus sign in strings. Strings can be easily created with a plus sign. Programmers use the word *concatenation* (rarely *catenation*) in this context. For the strings "Hello" + " " + "you there", "Hello you there" is the concatenation of the strings.

In Java, you cannot give new meanings to existing operators. Other programming languages might allow this redefinition, among them Python, C++, C#, and even ALGOL from 1968. For example, the plus sign might be used to add geometric point objects, divide fractions, or write a line to a file. If the objects represent mathematical constructs, operations named using short operator characters can be convenient—a matrix1.add(matrix2) with a longer method name is bulkier than a matrix1 + matrix2. Although user-defined overloaded operators are sometimes quite handy, the possibility might often provoke nonsensical uses. For this reason, the Java's designers didn't provide this option in Java, but some alternative languages on the JVM (e.g., Kotlin or Scala) allow it because it's a language constraint and not a VM constraint.

No Preprocessor for Text Replacements Exists*

Many C(++) programs include preprocessor directives, such as #define, #include, or #if, for including prototype definitions or for conditional compilation. Such preprocessor directives don't exist in Java. Without a preprocessor, a conditional compilation via #ifdef isn't possible either. Within statement blocks, in Java, you can instead formulate conditions of the type if (true) or if (false); using the -D switch on the command line, you can introduce variables that an if statement can then check at runtime via System.getProperty(...).

1.2.14 Java Is Open Source

The source code of the standard libraries has already been available since Java 1.0 (if installed with the JDK, this source code can be found in the root directory under the name *src.zip*), and anyone interested could look at the implementation. Although Sun disclosed the implementations at the time, neither the runtime environment nor the compiler or the libraries were under an accepted open-source license. Ten years after the first release of Java, there have been calls for Sun to place the entire Java platform under a more familiar type of license, such as the GPL or the Berkeley Source Distribution (BSD) license. At the same time, Jonathan Schwartz hinted at the JavaOne conference 2006 in San Francisco: "It's not a question of whether we'll open source Java, now the question is how." So if the question was "how" instead of "if," Rich Green announced the final release of Java as *OpenJDK*[11] under the open-source GPL 2 license during the opening speech of the JavaOne conference in May 2007. This event was preceded by the release of the compiler and VM at the end of 2006.

You'll find several statistics about the use of Java at *https://www.openhub.net/p/openjdk*, such as the following:

- More than 11 million lines of code in total have been written.
- Over 66,000 total commits have been made to the version control system since the inception of OpenJDK.
- About 70% of OpenJDK is Java code, about 10% C and C++.
- According to the *Constructive Cost Model (COCOMO)*, more than 3,600 years of development work have gone into the code.

Basically, with the OpenJDK, every developer can put together their own Java source code and publish any extensions. With the GPL license type, Java can find a place on Linux distributions that previously didn't want to integrate Java for licensing reasons.

1.2.15   What Java Is Less Suitable for

Java was designed as a programming language for general problems and covers large application areas (and is thus called a *general-purpose language*). However, some programming languages will be clearly better for a number of use cases. One example is in the area of scripting, where the constraint that every Java program requires at least one class and one method is rather annoying. Similarly, in the area of automated text processing, other programming languages can work more elegantly with regular expressions.

Also, when you have extremely machine- and platform-dependent requirements, things become cumbersome in Java. Java was designed to be platform-independent, so all methods should run on all systems. Extremely system-related properties, such as the clock frequency, are simply not visible, and security-relevant manipulations such as access to certain memory cells are also prohibited.

A few things Java can't do by default include the following:

- Clearing the screen on the text console, positioning the cursor, and setting colors
- Accessing low-level network protocols like ICMP
- Automating Microsoft Office

---

11   *http://openjdk.java.net*

- Reading images from a camera
- Accessing USB[12] or FireWire

With the disadvantage that Java can't access the hardware, the language can't be easily used for system programming. Driver software that addresses graphics, sound, or network cards can only be implemented in Java via workarounds. Exactly the same limitation applies to accessing the general functions of the operating system provided by Windows, Linux, or any other system. Typical system programming languages are C(++) or Go. Furthermore, since the JVM has a certain size, Java is not an option for microcontrollers so far.

Because of these limitations, note that Java can't replace a hardware-oriented language. But the language doesn't have to! Each language has its preferred terrain, and Java is a general-purpose application programming language; C(++) can still be used for hardware drivers, embedded systems, and VMs. The standard JVM is (so far still) written in C++ and is compiled using the garbage collector of the compiler or Microsoft Visual Studio Code (VS Code) and XCode. C and C++ will never disappear; these languages are like microbes in volcanic gas—they outlast all life. And just a microorganism becomes the food for other organisms, we can't get along without system-related languages like C(++) or Go.

If a Java program is nevertheless required to use system-related properties—which is problem free via the appropriate libraries—the *native call* of a system function, for example, is a good choice. Native methods are subroutines that aren't implemented in Java but in another programming language, often C(++). In some cases, an external program can also be called to manipulate the Windows registry or set file permissions, for example. However, ultimately, the solution must always be implemented anew for each platform.

1.3   Java versus Other Languages*

When dealing with the design of new programming languages or language extensions, other programming language constructs are often tested for their suitability and then incorporated into the concept if successful. Java is also an evolving language that has features of other languages.

1.3.1   Java and C(++)

Syntactically, Java is strongly based on C(++), for example, with the data types, operators, or parentheses, but hasn't adopted all the properties of C(++). In the historical chain, Java is often considered the successor to C++ (and the predecessor of C#), but the

---

12 Actually, support should exist for USB, but in this case—and unfortunately elsewhere too—Sun hasn't further pursued the project *JSR-80: Java USB API*.

Java programming language deliberately avoids problematic constructs such as pointers.

The class concept—and thus the OO approach—was significantly inspired by Simula and Smalltalk. The interfaces that provide an elegant means of class organization are based on Objective-C, where they are referred to as *protocols*. While Smalltalk manages all objects dynamically and while, in C++, the compiler combines everything into one big binary chunk, in Java, each type is a separate class file. All classes—optionally also from another computer via the network—are loaded by the JVM at runtime. Even method calls are possible via the network.[13] In summary, Java adopts known and proven concepts, and the language is certainly not a revolution; modern scripting languages are further along in this respect and also adopt concepts from functional programming languages.

1.3.2   Java and JavaScript

You should use the name "Java" with care. Not everything that has Java in its root word actually has to do with Java: JavaScript doesn't have much in common with Java, except for some similarities in imperative concepts. The JavaScript programming language was developed in 1995 by Netscape developer Brendan Eich. In 1997, the *European Computer Manufacturers Association (ECMA)* codified parts of JavaScript in the ECMA-262 standard and named the programming language *ECMAScript*. The current version is ECMAScript 2020. Popular browser vendors Google (Chrome), Microsoft (Edge), and Mozilla Foundation (Firefox) implement ECMAScript, but usually add extensions.

Java and JavaScript differ in many ways, just as keyholes and keystrokes have little to do with each other. The class usage is completely different with its prototype approach in JavaScript than in Java, and JavaScript can also be counted among the functional programming languages, which Java truly isn't.

1.3.3   A Word about Microsoft, Java, and J++

In the early days, Microsoft created some buzz around Java. With *Visual J++*, Microsoft provided its own Java compiler early on (as part of the *Microsoft Development Kit*) and its own fast runtime environment with the *Microsoft Java Virtual Machine (MSJVM)*. The only problem was that things like RMI and Java Native Interface (JNI) were intentionally missing—JNI was added in 1998. Against all standards, the J++ compiler introduced new keywords such as `multicast` and `delegate`. Microsoft also added some new methods and features, for example, *J/Direct*, to give the platform-independent programming language the Windows brand. With J/Direct, programmers could access functions of the Win32 API directly from Java and thus program pure Windows

---

13   This option is known as *Remote Method Invocation (RMI)*. Certain objects can communicate with each other via the network.

programs in Java. By integrating *DirectX*, the internet programming language Java was made multimedia capable, which, of course, led to the problem that applications built with J++ didn't necessarily run on other platforms. So, Sun sued Microsoft.

Since Sun hadn't been doing particularly well financially, Microsoft pumped a whopping $1.6 billion into the company in April 2004. Microsoft thus bought the end of antitrust problems and patent disputes. In January 2004, Microsoft stopped working on J++ because energy was flowing into the .NET framework and .NET languages. In the beginning, a Java version, *J#*, ran Java programs on the Microsoft .NET runtime environment CLR, but in early 2007, J# was also discontinued.

For a long time, Microsoft had almost completely withdrawn from Java development. Only rather small projects were pursued like the *Microsoft JDBC Driver for SQL Server*. But support for Java has become broad again:[14] Microsoft has joined the *Jakarta EE Working Group*, supports Java applications in *Microsoft Azure*, a cloud computing service,[15] and also provides an OpenJDK-based runtime environment.[16] Perhaps Microsoft will congratulate Oracle at some point, just as it congratulated Linux on its 20th birthday.[17]

1.3.4   Java and C#/.NET

Since C# appeared shortly after Java and after a dispute between Microsoft and Sun, and the languages were syntactically similar at the beginning, you might assume that Java was the godfather for the C# programming language.[18] But that was a long time ago. Meanwhile, C# has developed such strong momentum that Microsoft's programming language is much more innovative than Java. C# has become complex over the years, and Microsoft integrates elements into the programming language without much of a voting process, whereas, in the Java world, a gazillion people discuss and vote. At times, you might have the impression that Java can finally do what C# offers. From this point of view, Java today benefits from the experience gained in the C# world. The addition of lambda expressions to Java 8 also explicitly emphasized the adoption of C# syntax,[19] unlike the Microsoft documentation, which denies any similarity between C# and Java.

Oracle divides Java into the *Java Platform, Standard Edition (Java SE)* for "general" programs and *Jakarta EE*—formerly Java Platform, Enterprise Edition (Java EE)—as an extension for "large" enterprise systems. In contrast, Microsoft puts everything into a single framework called *.NET*. Bigger than the Java framework, .NET can be used to

---

14 *https://devblogs.microsoft.com/java*

15 *https://azure.microsoft.com/en-us/develop/java/*

16 *https://www.microsoft.com/openjdk*

17 *http://www.youtube.com/watch?v=ZA2kqAIOoZM*

18 Not a single word about Java exists in Microsoft documents. You'll only read about the fact that C# had other languages, such as C++, VB, and Delphi, as models.

19 *http://mail.openjdk.java.net/pipermail/lambda-dev/2011-September/003936.html*

program anything Windows can come up with. This feature is particularly noticeable in the GUI area, where the platform-independent Java has less to offer.

The current direction is *.NET Core*, an open-source alternative based on the "big" .NET framework, available for Windows, macOS, and Linux x64. All changes to the codebase can be reviewed at *https://github.com/dotnet/core*. Because existing .NET applications can't be migrated without customization, the adoption of .NET Core is not yet like that of .NET.

Somewhat cynically, note that Java is perhaps only alive because Microsoft has focused exclusively on Windows with .NET, but the world wanted something else. Microsoft waited too long with .NET Core because it didn't want to strengthen other platforms.

1.4 Further Development and Losses

In the ongoing evolution of Java, there were always phases in which development was rather slow, and then phases where many new features were added. From time to time, features were also removed, which is rather surprising, because backward compatibility plays a very big role at Oracle, and played a similar role earlier at Sun.

1.4.1 The Development of Java and Its Future Prospects

Twenty years ago, Java had two major advantages: simplicity compared to its predecessor C++ and the absence of "dangerous" syntactic constructs. As one of the language fathers, James Gosling (who left Sun after Oracle acquired it) wrote back in 1997:

> *"Java is a blue collar language. It's not PhD thesis material but a language for a job. Java feels very familiar to many different programmers because I had a very strong tendency to prefer things that had been used a lot over things that just sounded like a good idea."*[20]

The desire for a simple language still exists today; however, a lot has happened in the past 20 years, and Java has become significantly more complex. Significant language changes occurred in Java 5 (about 10 years after the introduction of Java) and in Java 8. The module system in Java 9 also presented new challenges.

In the trinity of the Java platform—with 1) Java as programming language, 2) the standard libraries, and 3) the JVM as runtime environment—great dynamism exists among the different programming languages running on the JVM. More and more apparent is the fact that developers who program in Java will continue to develop in Java but will also use a second programming language on the JVM. Thus, in addition to the Java programming language, various alternatives exist, such as *Kotlin (https://kotlinlang.org)*,

---

20 In the original: "Java is a blue collar language. It's not PhD thesis material but a language for a job" *(https://www.win.tue.nl/~evink/education/avp/pdf/feel-of-java.pdf)*.

Clojure (https://www.clojure.org), *Scala (https://www.scala-lang.org)*, *Groovy (https:// groovy-lang.org)*, *JRuby (https://www.jruby.org)*, or *Jython (https://www.jython.org)*, which all run on the JVM—different languages, same runtime environment. Scripting languages on the Java platform are quite popular; they establish a different syntax but use the JVM and libraries. Because these alternative programming languages are based on the JVM, they can use all Java libraries and therefore replace Java as a programming language in some areas. The fact that the alternative languages draw on the usual standard libraries works smoothly; however, the reverse, for example, using Scala libraries from within Jython, hasn't (yet) been standardized. This flexibility works better with the .NET platform, where it really doesn't matter whether you declare or use C# or VB.NET classes.

When the Sun acquisition was around the corner, Oracle was committed to Sun technologies. After the 2010 acquisition, the picture changed somewhat, and Oracle made more negative headlines, such as when it stopped supporting OpenSolaris, scaled back MySQL and considered it a threat to its own database, and was late in handing OpenOffice over to Apache. (LibreOffice had already taken on a life of its own.) Oracle also behaves quite differently than Sun when it comes to information policy and the support of user groups. By suing Google for copyright infringement in Android, Oracle didn't make any friends either. Android is considered proof that Java is indeed successful on the client side. When security gaps were discovered in Java, the company's reputation was again damaged. Overall, an assessment is likely to say, "Oracle has made an effort to meet the requirements."

Almost 10 years after the acquisition, new radical changes have occurred. For the first time, Oracle removed parts of the Java SE library, such as CORBA support, JAXB, JAX-RS (web services), applets, Java Web Start, and JavaFX. Furthermore, the JavaScript engine has now disappeared. Thus, the previously sacred mantra of backwards compatibility has been done away with—a current JVM can't run older Java software in every case.

1.4.2 Features, Enhancements, and Specification Requests

Java grows from version to version, so regular major increases in libraries occur as well as well-proportioned changes to the language and minimal changes to the JVM. Changes to the Java SE platform are categorized into features and enhancements. An *enhancement* is a small change that isn't worth mentioning—for example, a small function like isEmpty() has been added to the String class. These enhancements don't require much coordination and planning and are easily integrated by Oracle staff.

Features, on the other hand, are somewhat bigger in terms of implementation effort. In this case, the community might have been desperate for this functionality—they make this need clear by placing a feature request on Oracle's website, and then many people voted for this feature. Another peculiarity is how many features are planned because often a *Java Specification Request (JSR)* is created, which prescribes a certain planning order. Most changes to libraries are described by a JSR, and now hundreds of JSRs exist, as you can see at *https://jcp.org/en/jsr/overview*.

In the early days, the implementation was also the specification, but now, descriptive specifications for the Java compiler, the JVM, and various libraries are available, which is also true for Java as a whole. *Java SE* is a specification that implements, for example, the Oracle JDK and OpenJDK. The Oracle JDK is based on the OpenJDK, and the OpenJDK is licensed under the GPL license. OpenJDK is the reference implementation and thus defines the standard, which is important if certain properties aren't documented.

1.4.3   Applets

An understatement would be to attribute the widespread use of Java to the web. Java became popular in the mid-1990s through *applets*—Java programs executed by a browser. An HTML file referenced the applet, which was assigned a place on the web page, and the browser independently retrieved the class files and resources over the network and executed them in the JVM.

Over time, the importance of Java applets declined, due to a language that also appeared in 1995: JavaScript. Java applets first brought dynamism and moving graphics to what had been static web pages, but when the CSS (1996) and SVG (2001) web standards emerged, an increasing number of web developers turned to combining JavaScript with these standards. Java applets, justz like Flash or Silverlight, all have a problem: They require a browser plugin, which makes them unattractive for companies, since no customer should be excluded on the internet. In the past, when web standards weren't as advanced, Flash and Silverlight enabled building interactive web pages, but today, elaborate web applications are achievable with HTML5, CSS, and JavaScript.

A long time has passed since the early Netscape and Internet Explorer browsers integrated a JVM; at some point, these vendors removed it. For a while, Oracle shipped the *Java Plug-in* (spelled this way) to integrate its own JVM into browsers. However, modern browsers no longer support the Java Plug-in. Due to this lack of support from browsers—and the lack of good web standards—Oracle marked applets as deprecated in Java 9 and removed them completely in Java 10.

1.4.4   JavaFX

Rich Internet Applications (RIA) are graphically rich web applications that typically pull data from the internet. For many years, *Adobe Flash* dominated the field, almost 100%, and Microsoft played along for a time with Silverlight. Oracle, too, didn't want to leave the field to its competitors for strategic reasons. When it became apparent that applets were unpopular and too inflexible for complex GUI applications, Oracle released the *JavaFX platform* at the end of 2008 after a lengthy internal project phase. JavaFX is a completely new GUI stack and completely decoupled from Swing and the Abstract Windowing Toolkit (AWT).

In the first JavaFX version, the *JavaFX Script* programming language was part of JavaFX, but from version JavaFX 2 onwards, Oracle has changed directions: JavaFX is now a pure Java library, and the idiosyncratic JavaFX Script programming language is a thing of the past. However, with scripting languages on the JVM, a comparable "feel" is guaranteed.

For a while, it looked like JavaFX could inherit the GUI stack *AWT/Swing*. Swing is a GUI library that has been part of the standard since Java 1.2 (1998) but hasn't received any significant features for 10 years, although bugs are fixed regularly. But after the initial hype around JavaFX, Oracle pulled many developers away and put JavaFX on the sidelines. For Oracle, desktop technologies no longer play a role, which is why Oracle said goodbye to JavaFX altogether in 2018: As of Java 11, JavaFX is no longer integrated. Oracle has transferred JavaFX to the *OpenJFX* project (*https://openjfx.io/*), where it is being further developed as an open-source project—a mirror is located at *https:// github.com/teamfx*. For JavaFX fans, going open source was more of an advantage than a disadvantage because decoupling allows for more flexible further development. OpenJFX will then be a module like any other.

1.5   Java Platforms

The Java platform consists of projects that allow Java programs to run. At the moment, four platforms are distinguished: Java SE; Java Platform, Micro Edition (Java ME); Java Card; and Java EE/Jakarta EE.

1.5.1   Java Platform, Standard Edition

Java SE is a system environment for the development and execution of Java programs. Java SE contains everything needed to develop Java programs. Although the terminology is somewhat fuzzy, Java SE can be understood as a specification rather than an implementation. However, for Java programs to be compiled and executed, a concrete compiler, an interpreter, and the Java libraries must be installed on your computer. Different implementations of Java SE exist, such as OpenJDK.

Versions of Java Platform, Standard Edition

On May 23, 1995, Sun introduced Java to the general public for the first time. A lot has happened since then, and in each version, the Java library has been expanded. Nevertheless, hardly any incompatibilities exist from one version to the next, and almost 100% of what was compiled under Java n can also be compiled under Java $n + 1$ since only rarely have any compromises been made in bytecode compatibility.

Version	Date	Special Features
1.0	January 1995	First version. The following 1.0.x versions solve various security issues.
1.1	February 1997	New features in event handling, in the handling of Unicode files (reader/writer instead of only streams), database support via Java Database Connectivity (JDBC), nested classes, and standardized support for non-Java code (native code).
1.2	November 1998	No longer called JDK, but the *Java 2 Software Development Kit (SDK)*. *Swing* is the new library for GUIs, and a collection API for data structures and algorithms is available.
1.3	May 2000	Name services with the Java Naming and Directory Interface (JNDI) API, distributed programming with RMI/IIOP, and sound support.
1.4	February 2002	Interface for XML parser, logging, new IO system (NIO), regular expressions, and assertions.
5	September 2004	The Java SDK is named *JDK* again. New features include generic types, type-safe enumerations, extended `for`, autoboxing, and annotations.
6	End of 2006	Web services, script support, Java Compiler API, binding Java objects to XML documents, and system tray.
7	July 2011	Minor language changes, NIO2, first free version under the GPL.
8	March 2014	Language changes, lambda expressions, and stream APIs.
9	September 2017	Modularization of applications.
10	March 2018	Local variable declarations with `var`.
11	September 2018	Removal of the `java.ee` module.
12	March 2019	Compact number formatting, removal of various `finalize()` methods.
13	September 2019	Better Javadoc search functions.
14	March 2020	Switch expressions.
15	September 2020	Text blocks.
16	March 2021	Records and pattern matching with `instanceof`.
17	September 2021	Sealed classes.
18	March 2022	Many preview features.

Table 1.1 Innovations and Special Features in Various Java Versions

The product cycles show some jumps, especially since Java 9 was postponed twice.

Compatibility

Sun and now Oracle has placed great importance on *upward compatibility*; that is, a compiled Java program for version *n* can be executed by a JVM of version *n* + 1. In general, Java programs are upward compatible. Some breaks exist between Java 8 and Java 11, but few problems exist from Java 11 onwards.

Feature Release versus Time-Based Release

For 20 years, features determined the release of new Java versions: Developers put certain innovations on the wish list, and when all features were implemented and tested, the *general availability (GA)* took place. The main problem with this feature-based approach model was the delays associated with implementation issues. The Java 9 release was much discussed because it should definitely contain a module system.

Oracle responded to these issues and to the Java community's desire for more frequent releases with "JEP 322: Time-Based Release Versioning."[21] Four releases are planned per year:

- In March and September, major releases (such as Java 10, Java 11, Java 12, etc.) are published.

- Updates appear 1 month after a major release and then at 3-month intervals.

In other words: Updates occur every 6 months, which allows Oracle to further develop the language and libraries and to integrate new language features in our fast-moving IT world. If delays occur, these problems don't immediately stop the entire release. Java 10 was the first release on this schedule in March 2018.

Code Names, Name Changes, and Vendor Version Numbers

The first Java versions were Java 1.0, Java 1.1, and so on. With Java 5, the prefix "1." was dropped from the product's version identifier, so it was simply called Java 5, Java 6, etc. In developer versions, however, the notation with the "1." remained valid until Java 9.[22] In Java 10, a vendor identifier was added with *time-based release versioning*, so that alternatively to Java 10 and Java 11 also Java 18.3 and Java 18.9 were mentioned—in Java 12, Oracle dropped this *vendor version string* again.[23]

---

21 *http://openjdk.java.net/jeps/322*

22 See *http://docs.oracle.com/javase/1.5.0/docs/relnotes/version-5.0.html*.

23 See JDK-8211726 at *https://www.oracle.com/technetwork/java/javase/12-relnote-issues-5211422.html*.

1.5.2 Java Platform, Micro Edition: Java for the Little Ones

Java ME is a standard for resource-limited devices, such as PDAs, organizers, phones, and embedded systems with less than 1 MB of memory. The importance of Java ME lies in embedded devices, whereas systems like a Raspberry Pi are already powerful enough to run a normal JVM on them.

Android, a project initiated by Google and now in the hands of the *Open Handset Alliance*, almost completely displaced Java ME. Based on Java ME, Oracle specifies the *Java TV* runtime environment; however, these solutions are not in the spotlight.

1.5.3 Java for the Very, Very Little Ones

With *Java Card*, Oracle has defined a standard for Java-like programs on smart cards (such as SIM cards). However, Java's language standard is somewhat limited. The output of the Java compiler is a bytecode similar to the standard bytecode. This bytecode is then executed on the *Java Card Virtual Machine*, which is placed on the smart card. However, since vastly different memory requirements may exist for such a tiny system, the runtime environment is not comparable to the standard JVM. Java Card lacks threads and lacks automatic garbage collection. Differences also exist in the libraries. Not only are many well-known classes missing, but conversely, strong cryptographic algorithms are included in the package, and of course a package that allows the card application to communicate with the outside world is also included. In addition to the standard Java Card 3.0, editions exist, such as the *Classic Edition* and the *Connected Edition*. The Connected Edition no longer has many restrictions and also now has threads and automatic garbage collection.

With the standard Java Card, bringing programs onto cards from different manufacturers is easy—as long as the card complies with the standard. Before Java Card, this compliance was always a bit difficult because each map vendor used different APIs and tools, and the map was usually programmed in a dialect of C. Nowadays, Oracle doesn't pay much attention to Java Card.

1.5.4 Java for the Big Ones: Jakarta EE (Formerly Java Platform, Enterprise Edition)

Jakarta EE—formerly *Java Platform, Enterprise Edition (Java EE)*—is an add-on for Java SE and integrates the packages necessary for the development of enterprise applications. These packages include the component technology of *Enterprise JavaBeans (EJBs)*, *CDI* for dependency injection, *servlets*, *JSP*, *JSF* for dynamic web pages, the *JavaMail API*, and others. The implementation of the enterprise specification (*Eclipse GlassFish*, the reference implementation for Jakarta EE) is handled by an application server.

Over the past few years, parts of Jakarta EE have migrated to Java SE, such as JAX-WS (web services), JNDI (directory service), or JAXB (object XML mapping). These APIs are now standard and are no longer seen as just part of large enterprise applications. In Java 11, things took a step back again, and technologies such as JAB were removed from Java SE for development independently.

The first version of Jakarta EE dates back to 1999, when it was called *J2EE*. Some buzz around Jakarta EE has grown in recent years. For a long time, Sun, then Oracle defined the standard. Then, things went quiet, and Oracle failed to establish a lightweight alternative that optimally supported microservices and container virtualization. This lack strengthened alternative enterprise frameworks like *Spring* (Boot). Then, in September 2017, Oracle announced it was dropping Java EE—around the same time as the Java EE-8 release—leaving it in the hands of the Eclipse Foundation, which named it *Eclipse Enterprise for Java (EE4J)*. However, Oracle was against the use of the name "Java," so the final name is *Jakarta EE*. Today, the Eclipse Foundation is one of the most important organizations that further develop Java standards and solutions in a vendor-neutral manner.

1.5.5   Real-Time Java

While Java ME runs programs on devices with reduced memory and limited processing power, this says nothing about the responsiveness of the runtime environment to external events. When a sensor in the bumper of a car reports an impact, the runtime environment can't be stuck in a memory cleanup operation for 20 milliseconds before the event is processed and the airbag deploys. To close this gap, the Java community defined JSR 1, the *"Real-time Specification for Java" (RTSJ)*, early in 2001. (JSR 282 is the successor to RTSJ 1.1.)

Real-time applications are characterized by the fact that a maximum deterministic wait time may block the system from, for example, automatic garbage collection to respond to changes in sensors. A real-time system should guarantee a response time, which is something a normal VM can't do. The reason is two-fold: The time for automatic garbage collection is rather indefinite in normal runtime environments, and other actions of indefinite duration have been added. For instance, if Java loads a class, it does so at runtime, which can cause any number of additional dependencies and load cycles. Thus, before a method can be executed, hundreds of class files may be required, and loading can take an indeterminately long time.

With real-time capabilities, industrial systems can also be controlled with Java, and software from the aerospace, medical, telecommunications, and consumer electronics sectors can be implemented with Java. This area remained closed to Java for a long time and was a domain of C(++). For this to be possible in Java, the JVM and operating system must match. While a traditional JVM runs on more or less any operating system, the requirements for real-time Java are more stringent. The foundation is always an operating system with real-time capabilities, called a *Real-Time Operating System (RTOS)*, such as *Solaris 10, Realtime Linux, QNX, OS-9*, or *VxWorks*. A real-time JVM is based on this implementation of the real-time specification. Real-time Java (RT-Java) therefore also differs, for example, in that memory areas can be allocated and released directly (*scoped memory*), in that more thread priorities are available, and in that scheduling is clearly more in the hands of the developers. The development is different but takes place under the familiar tools such as integrated development environments (IDEs), test tools, and libraries. In recent years, however, excitement has abated around real-time Java.

1.6   Java Platform, Standard Edition, Implementations

The Java SE platform is basically just a specification and not an implementation. For programs to be compiled and executed, you'll need a real compiler, a runtime environment, and an implementation of the libraries. Different implementations from different manufacturers are available. If an implementation passes a series of tests called *Technology Compatibility Kit (TCK)*, they can refer to themselves as being "Java SE compatible."

1.6.1   OpenJDK

The free *OpenJDK* (*https://openjdk.java.net*) licensed under GPL is the reference implementation for Java SE. All developments take place in OpenJDK. Progress can be observed live, with hundreds of developers regularly fixing and extending the codebase. The sources for the OpenJDK can be found in the *GitHub* repository at *https://github.com/openjdk/jdk*. Many technologies that Oracle previously had only in the Oracle JDK have been transferred to the OpenJDK, such as *Java Flight Recorder, Java Mission Control, Application Class-Data Sharing*, and *Zero-Garbage-Collector (ZGC)*.

Binary Reference Implementation

Executables of Java SE reference implementations that are linked at *https://jdk.java.net/*. The web page *https://jdk.java.net/17/* lists Java 17 implementations for Linux/AArch64, Linux/x64, macOS/AArch64, macOS/x64, and Windows/x64 systems. These products are licensed under GLP v2 with the *Classpath Exception*.[24] (An alternative name for the reference implementation is *Oracle OpenJDK*.) Oracle itself has announced that it will no longer release updates for old versions when new Java versions are released.

OpenJDK Builds by Eclipse

Eclipse Adoptium (formerly *AdoptOpenJDK*) regularly releases builds of the OpenJDK, integrates other packages such as the JavaFX implementation OpenJFX, and integrates

---

24 *https://openjdk.java.net/legal/gplv2+ce.html*

alternative runtime environments such as *Eclipse OpenJ9*. Older versions are also provided with bug fixes. Supporters include Amazon, IBM/Red Hat, Microsoft, Pivotal, and many more. A version for different operating systems can be downloaded from the website at *https://adoptium.net/*. Eclipse Adoptium is currently one of the most popular distributions of OpenJDK.

Other OpenJDK Builds

The company Azul offers builds under the name *Zulu*, and a support contract can be set up at *https://www.azul.com/downloads/?package=jdk*. In addition to the Windows, Linux, and macOS platforms, Docker images are also available from Azul.

The *Red Hat build of OpenJDK* provides a Windows version of the OpenJDK in addition to Linux, available at *https://developers.redhat.com/products/openjdk/overview*. Integration with Linux is particularly good, and Red Hat still maintains security updates for older Java versions.

SAP provides builds for various operating systems and also a Docker image with *SapMachine* (*https://sap.github.io/SapMachine*).

Amazon Corretto (*https://aws.amazon.com/corretto/*) is used internally by Amazon in the cloud and is free of charge.

Alibaba Dragonwell (*http://github.com/alibaba/dragonwell8* and *https://github.com/alibaba/dragonwell11*) is an OpenJDK-derived implementation from Alibaba. Currently, only Linux is supported.

From BellSoft, the *Liberica JDK* (*https://bell-sw.com*) is available for a large number of different platforms, and a cooperation exists with VMware for Spring Native Applications.

Apple maintained a completely separate JVM for a long time until the company handed over the code to Oracle for OpenJDK. Google has also recently started using OpenJDK for Android.

1.6.2   Oracle JDK

You might be confused why Oracle provides the reference implementation on one side and yet another distribution on the other (the *Oracle JDK*). The Oracle JDK is the "official" version provided by Oracle's Java download site. A few small differences include the packaging (Oracle JDK has an installer while Oracle OpenJDK is just a ZIP file), the version identifier, and a few more modules.[25] The Oracle JDK is available under the Oracle No-Fee license and can be used privately as well as commercially. Oracle promises updates to the version at least until September 2024.

---

25 *https://blogs.oracle.com/java-platform-group/oracle-jdk-releases-for-java-11-and-later*

Long-Term Support

The semi-annual Java releases mean that versions are always out of date when a new version is released. For companies, problems may arise from having to keep up with the changes, which can create stress. For this reason, Oracle provides a Java version with Long-Term Support (LTS) and provides updates and security patches for this version. The LTS versions after Java 8 were Java 11 (September 2018) and currently Java 17 (September 2021). This version is useful for less agile companies. Oracle plans to maintain its Java SE 8 implementation for many years to come. The plan is to shorten the LTS cycle from 3 years to 2 years.

Oracle Java SE Subscription

Companies often want to hedge their bets; thus, Oracle also offers a *Java SE subscription*. With this offering, Oracle provides commercial support in case problems or errors arise in productive operation. Costs can add up quickly, but companies can be supported, which is especially useful for the older Java 8 version, which may be supported for several years to come. One disadvantage is that the subscription model is only available for the LTS versions, so companies are forced to make larger version jumps if they want the support. Other companies like Azul are cheaper and also provide support for non-LTS versions.

Oracle Certified System Configurations

An ideal, perfectly tested, and supported environment is considered an *Oracle Certified System Configuration*. This combination of operating system with installed service packs is described in detail on the company website, including for all previous versions.[26] Only 64-bit operating systems are supported; 32-bit systems are out.

Reporting bugs on non-certified platforms can quickly be followed by a "sorry, that's an unsupported platform, we won't look at that further." For Linux, for example, the Gentoo distribution is not on the list, so it would be "Not certified on Oracle VM." Java can still run there, but a fix may not be pursued in the case of an error. Solaris SPARC is also no longer a certified platform.

1.7   Installing the Java Development Kit

The following sections describe how you can install the Java SE JDK from Oracle. Downloads for Linux, macOS, and Windows are available at *https://www.oracle.com/java/technologies/downloads*.

---

26 *https://www.oracle.com/java/technologies/javase/products-doc-jdk17certconfig.html*

1.7.1 Installing Oracle JDK on Windows

The JDK is available at *https://www.oracle.com/java/technologies/downloads/#jdk17-windows* for Windows as an EXE file, an MSI installer, and as a ZIP archive:

- *https://download.oracle.com/java/17/latest/jdk-17_windows-x64_bin.zip*
- *https://download.oracle.com/java/17/latest/jdk-17_windows-x64_bin.exe*
- *https://download.oracle.com/java/17/latest/jdk-17_windows-x64_bin.msi*

The MSI can be installed easily, and no special settings are required. By default, the installation directory is *C:\Program Files\Java\jdk-17*. No prescribed location is required; you can choose any directory.

If you obtain the ZIP archive, you must first unpack it; one disadvantage of the ZIP variant is that the Java interpreter is not contained in the search path.

Programs and Directories in the Java Directory

By default, the installer installs Java 17 to the *C:\Program Files\Java\jdk-17* directory. The installer will include executable programs like the compiler and the interpreter as well as libraries and various source codes, but no Javadoc.

Directory/File	Meaning
bin	Development tools, including, among other things, the interpreter *java* and (with the JDK) the compiler *javac*.
conf	Configuration files; adjustments are rarely necessary here.
include	Files for binding Java to C(++) programs.
jmods	Java modules from the JDK, such as the base module.
legal	A set of copyright text files.
lib	Internal JDK tools.
lib/src.zip	An archive with the source code of the public libraries.
release	File with key-value pairs.

Table 1.2 Directory Structure

Testing the Installation

Once you've installed the JDK to your hard drive via the installer, the Java interpreter is contained in the search path, and thus, you can call the following:

```
$ java -version
java version "17" 2021-09-14 LTS
Java(TM) SE Runtime Environment (build 17+35-LTS-2724)
Java HotSpot(TM) 64-Bit Server VM (build 17+35-LTS-2724, mixed mode, sharing)
```

The call with java -version shows the installed version. If the screen output appears, the installation was successful, and the programs *java* (for the runtime environment) and *javac* (for compiling) can be used.

Setting the Search Path (for ZIP Installation)

If you've loaded the ZIP archive, you should include the *bin* directory *C:\Program Files\ Java\jdk-17\bin* in the search path since always specifying the complete path to the JDK installation every time you call it is inconvenient. To set these paths permanently, the environment variable PATH must be modified.

For the path information to be available after restarting the computer, you must modify different settings depending on the system. In Windows 10, look for **Edit environment variables for this account**. The **Environment Variables** dialog box opens. In the top, under **User Variables**, look for **Path**. Via **Edit…**, change the entry and add the JDK *bin* directory (*C:\Program Files\Java\jdk-17\bin*) to the path after a semicolon. Confirm this change by clicking **OK**.

If you now open a new command prompt, you can call *javac* for the Java compiler or *java* for the runtime environment.

Uninstalling the Java Development Kit

Whoever obtained the ZIP archive can simply delete the *Java* directory and thus uninstall Java. If you've set the PATH, you should delete it again from the system properties. If you've installed the JDK via the installer, you can uninstall the software as usual via **Add and Remove Programs**.

Java Development Kit Documentation

The main documentation page is located at *https://docs.oracle.com/en/java/javase/17*. The API documentation of the standard library and documentation of the tools aren't part of the JDK. This separation makes sense because otherwise the download would be unnecessarily large, and the documentation can also be viewed online. API descriptions can be viewed online at *https://docs.oracle.com/en/java/javase/17/docs/api/*.

1.8   Compiling and Testing the First Program

After describing the basic concepts of Java, let's consider the words of Dennis M. Ritchie:

> *"The only way to learn a new programming language is to write programs in it."*

In this section, we'll use the Java compiler and interpreter from the command line. If you want a proper development environment right away, you can easily skip this part and continue with other IDEs. The examples in this book are based on Windows.

The source code of a Java program can't be executed in this way alone. A special program, the *compiler* (also called *interpreter*), transforms the written program into another representation. In the case of Java, the compiler generates the DNA of each program—the bytecode.

1.8.1   A Square Numbers Program

Our first Java program will run a repetition of screen outputs that replicates a song for boring trips. The output should be the following:

```
99 bottles of beer on the wall, 99 bottles of beer. Take one down, pass it around,
98 bottles of beer on the wall, 98 bottles of beer. Take one down, pass it around,
97 bottles of beer on the wall, 97 bottles of beer. Take one down, pass it around,
96 bottles of beer on the wall, 96 bottles of beer. Take one down, pass it around,
[...]
3 bottles of beer on the wall, 3 bottles of beer. Take one down, pass it around,
2 bottles of beer on the wall, 2 bottles of beer. Take one down, pass it around,
1 last bottle of beer on the wall, 1 last bottle of beer.
```

For this example, put the *source code* in the document folder of the current user *%homepath%\Documents* (for example, *C:\Users\User\Documents*). The name of the source code file is *NinetyNineBottlesOfBeer.java*. Since the source code is pure text, you can create and edit it with any text editor.

For Windows users, the *Notepad* editor can be found under **Start · Programs · Accessories · Editor**. When saving with Notepad using **File · Save as**, the **File Name** field must have *NinetyNineBottlesOfBeer.java*, and **All files (*.*)** must be selected in the **Save as type** field so that the editor doesn't automatically assign the file extension *.txt*.

```java
/**
 * Prints a version of 99 Bottles of Beer
 * @version 2.0      18-01-2022
 * @author Christian Ullenboom
 */
public class NinetyNineBottlesOfBeer {
  public static void main( String[] args ) {
    for ( int i = 99; i > 1; i-- ) {
      System.out.print( i );
      System.out.print( " bottles of beer on the wall, " );
      System.out.print( i );
      System.out.println( " bottles of beer. Take one down, pass it around," );
    }
```

```
        System.out.println( "1 bottle of beer on the wall, 1 bottle of beer." );
    }
}
```

Listing 1.1 C:\Users\User\Documents\NinetyNineBottlesOfBeer.java

The entire program logic sits in the NinetyNineBottlesOfBeer class, which contains one method. All methods in an OOP language like Java must be placed in classes. A special subroutine called main(String[]) serves as an entry point for the JVM. The main(String[]) method performs a loop and produces the screen outputs.

1.8.2 The Compiler Run

Now, let's change to the command prompt (console) and navigate to the directory with the source code. If the source code file is available, the compiler translates it into byte-code. For our Java class in the *NinetyNineBottlesOfBeer.java* file, you would use the following path:

```
C:\Users\User\Documents>javac NinetyNineBottlesOfBeer.java
```

Provided that the program was free of errors, the compiler now creates the *NinetyNine-BottlesOfBeer.class* file, which contains the bytecode. When calling javac, the file to be translated must be specified completely, including its file extension. But wildcards are also possible: Thus, javac *.java translates all Java classes in the current directory. Although not important in Windows, case sensitivity should be respected.

Compiler Errors

If the compiler finds a syntactical error in a line, the compiler reports the error by specifying the file and the line number. Let's look at our program again and build in an error in line 9 in the main(...) method (the semicolon falls victim to the delete key).

In other words, the initial

```
System.out.print( i );
```

becomes

```
System.out.print( i )
```

The compiler run reports the following error:

```
C:\Users\User\Documents>javac NinetyNineBottlesOfBeer.java
        System.out.print( i )
                             ^
1 error
```

When the compiler can't perform a translation into Java bytecode due to a syntactic error, we call this a *compiler error* or a *translation error*. Even though the term "compiler error" sounds as if the compiler itself has an error, it's our program that has the error.

1.8.3 The Runtime Environment

The bytecode generated by the compiler isn't common machine code for a specific processor because Java was designed as a platform-independent programming language, so it doesn't cling to a physical processor—processors like Intel, AMD, or PowerPC CPUs can't do anything with this bytecode. Here is where a runtime environment comes in handy. This environment reads the bytecode file statement by statement and executes it on the actual microprocessor.

The *java* interpreter causes the program to be executed, with the following result:

```
C:\Users\User\Documents>java NinetyNineBottlesOfBeer
99 bottles of beer on the wall, 99 bottles of beer. Take one down, pass it around,
98 bottles of beer on the wall, 98 bottles of beer. Take one down, pass it around,
97 bottles of beer on the wall, 97 bottles of beer. Take one down, pass it around,
...
```

As an argument, the runtime environment java gets the name of the class that contains a main(...) method and is therefore considered executable. The specification must not be provided with the ending *.class* since in this case we are not referencing the file name, but the class name instead, as required.

Executing Single-File Source Code Programs Directly

If the entire program is in only one file (called *single-file source code programs*), the runtime environment can execute the program without a translation because the bytecode can be stored in the memory.[27] Note the file suffix *.java*:

```
C:\Users\User\Documents>java NinetyNineBottlesOfBeer.java
99 bottles of beer on the wall, 99 bottles of beer. Take one down, pass it around,
98 bottles of beer on the wall, 98 bottles of beer. Take one down, pass it around,
97 bottles of beer on the wall, 97 bottles of beer. Take one down, pass it around,
...
```

1.8.4 Common Compiler and Interpreter Issues

If we work on the command-line level (*shell*) without an IDE, various issues can occur. If the path to the compiler hasn't been set correctly, the command-line interpreter throws an error message in the following form:

---

27 *https://openjdk.java.net/jeps/330*

```
$ javac NinetyNineBottlesOfBeer.java
The command is either misspelled or could not be found.
Please check the spelling and the environment variable 'PATH'.
```

On Unix, the message is short as usual:

```
javac: Command not found
```

So, the solution in this case is to include *javac* in the search path, as described earlier.

If the compiler run was successful, you can call the interpreter via the *java* program. If you make a mistake in the name of the class or add the suffix *.class* to the class name, the interpreter will complain. When trying to bring the non-existent class Q to life, for instance, the interpreter writes the following message to the error channel:

```
C:\Users\User\Documents>java Q
Error: Could not find or load main class Q
Caused by: java.lang.ClassNotFoundException: Q
```

If the name of the class file is correct, but the main method doesn't have the signature public static void main(String[]), the Java interpreter can't find the method at which to begin program execution. For example, if you make a mistake with the main(...) method in NinetyNineBottlesOfBeer, the following error message will appear:

```
C:\Users\User\Documents>java NinetyNineBottlesOfBeer
Error: Main method not found in class NinetyNineBottlesOfBeer, please define the ma
in method as:
   public static void main(String[] args)
or a JavaFX application class must extend javafx.application.Application
```

Note

The Java compiler javac and the launcher for Java applications java have a -help switch that shows more information.

1.9   Development Environments

The JDK can be used to compile and execute Java programs on the command line, although this scenario is not pleasant for development. For this reason, different vendors have put effort in recent years to simplify Java development. Modern development environments offer the advantage over simple text editors in that they specifically help beginners to the language become acquainted with the appropriate syntax. IDEs, for example, now underline erroneous passages with curly lines much like modern word processors. In addition, the IDEs provide the necessary help during development, such as syntax highlighting, automatic code completion, access to version management, or even wizards to generate source code for GUIs or web service access with a just few entries. Regarding the distribution of Java IDEs in the wild, the top four are almost always the following IDEs:

1. IntelliJ IDEA
2. Eclipse IDE
3. VS Code
4. NetBeans

1.9.1   IntelliJ IDEA

JetBrains, a software company based in the Czech Republic, has proven that companies can still earn money with development environments. The Java development environment *IntelliJ IDEA* (*https://www.jetbrains.com/idea*) is available in two editions:

- A free, open-source basic version that covers everything needed for Java SE development is called *Community Edition*. The source code is available on GitHub for everyone.[28]

- The commercial *Ultimate Edition* is intended for Java Enterprise (supporting Jakarta EE, Spring, Micronaut, Quarkus, Helidon) development. It costs $499.00 in the first year, $399.00 in the second year, and $299.00 in subsequent years.[29]

The basic version already includes a GUI builder, support for test frameworks, and support for version management systems. The free community version doesn't provide support for frameworks like Spring or Jakarta EE, and in these cases, adopting the Ultimate Edition is advantageous. Extensions can partially upgrade the free community version in framework support.

JetBrains is a developer of the Kotlin programming language, which is why its support in IntelliJ is ideal. Students and teachers can apply for the Ultimate Edition and get it for free.[30] The differences between these editions are summarized at *https://www.jetbrains.com/idea/features/editions_comparison_matrix.html*.

Installing IntelliJ Community

The free Community Edition for Windows, macOS, and Linux can be downloaded from *https://www.jetbrains.com/idea/download*, as can the Ultimate Edition, which can be tested for 30 days.

After downloading, you must run the installation program. The process is self-explanatory.

---

28 *https://github.com/JetBrains/intellij-community*
29 *https://www.jetbrains.com/store/?fromMenu#commercial*
30 *https://www.jetbrains.com/community/education/#students*

Creating Your First Maven Project

After starting IntelliJ, you can import existing projects or create new ones. If IntelliJ is started after the installation, a dialog box with the **Create New Project** selection option appears. Several options are displayed on the left.

Two different approaches to creating projects exist:

- **Option 1: Simple Java project**

  For this option, select **Java** and then click **Next**. In the next window, do not select the checkbox and then click **Next** again. Then, name the project and click **Finish** to create the project. The desktop appears. In the area on the left, you'll see the project. If unfolded, you'll see the three directories *idea*, *out*, and *src*. While this approach is simple, we don't recommend this option because this type of project is limited.

- **Option 2: Maven project**

  If you select **Maven** (or later navigate to the menu path **File • New • Project**), a new dialog box opens. Do not activate **Create from Archetype**; instead, simply click **Next**. The dialog box changes, and now, you can enter a project name in the **Name** field.

  This step also suggests the part of the path under which IntelliJ stores the project, but the path can be changed. Click on the small arrow next to **Artifact Coordinates** to reveal more text fields, including setting central project properties, which are called *coordinates*:

  - **Group id**: The grouping name is comparable to the package name. It represents the company.
  - **Artifact id**: The name of the artifact (i.e., the product being built).
  - **Version**: The version number.

  The IDE will filled in these coordinates, but you can of course change them.

  Clicking **Finish** completes the project creation.

The Standard Directory Layout

A Java project needs a proper directory structure, and two approaches to organizing the files exist. The simplest form is to put sources, class files, and resources into one directory. But this mixture is not advantageous in practice.

In general, sources and the translated *class* files should be separate. Basically, directories could be named and organized in any way, but a common convention exists called the *Standard Directory Layout*.[31]

---

31 A complete description is available at *http://maven.apache.org/guides/introduction/introduction-to-the-standard-directory-layout.html*.

Directory	Contents
src/main/java	Sources
src/main/resources	Resources
src/test/java	Test cases
src/test/resources	Resources for test cases
src/site	Website
target	Result of a build
LICENSE.txt	License type of the project (e.g., Apache, BSD, GPL)
NOTICE.txt	References or dependencies to other projects
README.txt	Read me file

Table 1.3 The Standard Directory Layout and Common Files

Maven divides classes, test cases, and resources into various subdirectories. When the project is compiled, the generated class files end up in the *target/classes* directory.

[»]

Information

Building software and monitoring module dependencies are activities that should happen automatically, not manually. The free and open-source software *Apache Maven* has become something of a standard in this context. Maven can either be obtained from *https://maven.apache.org/* and used as a tool from the command line or can be nicely integrated via the development environment. All major IDEs support Maven out of the box.

To describe projects, Maven uses *Project Object Model (POM)* files. These files contain the entire configuration and project description, including the name and identifier of the project, its dependencies, its compiler settings, and its license.

The POM file is called *pom.xml* and is located in the root directory of an application—the file extension signals that this file is an XML file. A Java compiler and the tools no longer need to be called manually with Maven, as the entire control is ultimately carried out by Maven.

When you open the *pom.xml* file in IntelliJ, note how the generator has placed information about the coordinates and also introduced a properties XML element that determines the Java version number:

```
<project …>
  <modelVersion>4.0.0</modelVersion>
  <groupId>…</groupId>
```

```
<artifactId>…</artifactId>
<version>…</version>

<properties>
  <maven.compiler.target>17</maven.compiler.target>
  <maven.compiler.source>17</maven.compiler.source>
</properties>
</project>
```

You can manually add another subelement to the properties XML element for encoding, which should always be UTF-8:

```
<properties>
  <maven.compiler.target>17</maven.compiler.target>
  <maven.compiler.source>17</maven.compiler.source>
  <project.build.sourceEncoding>UTF-8</project.build.sourceEncoding>
</properties>
```

Tip   [+]

If the IDE doesn't set the version number, or sets it incorrectly, you can always add and change the version manually in *pom.xml*.

Adding a Class

If the context menu on the *src* folder is activated, select **New** and then **Java Class** to open a dialog box where you can enter the class name. Let's call the class NinetyNine-BottlesOfBeer and move on.

In the editor, let's complete our program:

```java
public class NinetyNineBottlesOfBeer {
  public static void main( String[] args ) {
    for ( int i = 99; i > 1; i-- ) {
      System.out.print( i );
      System.out.print( " bottles of beer on the wall, " );
      System.out.print( i );
      System.out.println( " bottles of beer. Take one down, pass it around," );
    }
    System.out.println( "1 last bottle of beer on the wall, 1 last bottle of beer."
);
  }
}
```

Translating and Executing

IntelliJ has no **Save** button and works automatically in the background. To run the program, click on the green triangle in the line with the `main` method and start the program.

1.9.2 Eclipse Integrated Development Environment

To replace the old *WebSphere* series and the *Visual Age for Java* environment, IBM developed *Eclipse* (*http://www.eclipse.org*). In November 2001, IBM released its IDE as open-source software, and later formed a consortium with the *Eclipse Foundation* to determine further development. Eclipse is licensed under the Common Public License and as open-source software is available to everyone free of charge. Four times a year, an update is published, and the releases are called YYYY-MM (where YYYY stands for the year and MM for the month).

Eclipse makes it possible to integrate tools as *plugins*. Many vendors have already adapted their products for Eclipse, and development is proceeding at a rapid pace worldwide.

Eclipse is a Java product with a native GUI that does its job quickly and smoothly. The working times are also so fast because Eclipse works with what's called an *incremental compiler*. When a user saves a Java source code file, the compiler automatically translates this file. This feature is called *autobuild*.

The driving force behind Eclipse was Erich Gamma, who went to Microsoft in 2011 and became team leader for VS Code, the new editor with a lean development environment. For web development, VS Code has quickly made friends, and Java development is also possible, although the refactoring capabilities still lag behind Eclipse or IntelliJ. However, VS Code may quickly catch up.

Eclipse Integrated Development Environment Packages and Installation

The Eclipse development environment is predominantly programmed in Java and requires at least Java version 8 to run.[32] Since parts like the GUI are implemented in C, Eclipse isn't 100% pure Java, and care must be taken when downloading to ensure you choose the appropriate system.

Two options for installation on Windows, Linux, and macOS are available:

- Via a native installer that loads components from the web and also includes a JVM
- Via an Eclipse package (a ZIP archive) that you can simply unpack and start

Eclipse is divided into different *packages*. For Java developers, the most important packages include the following:

---

32 Of course, Eclipse can also generate class files for Java 1.0; only the IDE itself requires at least Java 8.

- **Eclipse IDE for Java Developers**: The smallest version for developing Java SE applications. XML editor, Maven support, and a Git client are included in this package.

- **Eclipse IDE for Enterprise Java and Web Developers**: This version contains various extensions for the development of web applications and Java enterprise applications. This package includes editors for JavaScript and TypeScript, Jakarta Persistence, data tools, and more. This package is a good choice.

The packages are linked for download at *https://www.eclipse.org/downloads/packages*.

On the download page, you can find the current version as well as the latest releases. The main versions are called *Maintenance Packages*. In addition to these packages, *stable builds* are available, while the brave may consider *integration builds* and *nightly builds*, which offer glimpses of upcoming versions. By default, the labels of the development environment are in English, but with *Eclipse Language Packs*, translations for German, Spanish, Italian, Japanese, Chinese, and other languages are available as are individual updates for the subprojects (WST, JST). The latest releases and builds can be found at *http://download.eclipse.org/eclipse/downloads*. As of the Eclipse IDE 2021-12, you can develop with Java 17 without any problem and without any additional plugins.

1.9.3 NetBeans

NetBeans is another development environment that had been quite popular. The main development was performed by Sun Microsystems at that time, but when Oracle acquired Sun, development environments were not a big priority in the database company. Further developments did occur, but Oracle dragged on from version to version. Oracle eventually handed over the codebase to the Apache Foundation, thus parting ways with the IDE. The new home is *https://netbeans.apache.org*.

NetBeans provides convenient Java SE and Java Enterprise development capabilities with editors and wizards for creating GUIs and web applications. Its market share, however, is in the single-digit percentage range.

1.10 Further Reading

Sun published a small booklet entitled *Hello World(s)! From Code to Culture: A 10 Year Celebration of Java Technology* (*https://www.pearson.com/us/higher-education/program/Sun-Microsystems-Hello-World-s-From-Code-to-Culture-A-10-Year-Celebration-of-Java-Technology/PGM129811.html*), which provides information on the origins of Java. Further online information about the development team and the *7 project is provided by *http://tutego.de/go/star7* and *http://tutego.de/go/javasaga*. A version of the VM itself is available for history buffs at *http://tutego.de/go/javaarchive*.

Java is loved by many companies; top companies like LinkedIn, Netflix, eBay, Pinterest, Groupon, Spotify, Pandora, Square, Trivago, and TripAdvisor all rely on Java. A company that doesn't rely on Java is the exception rather than the rule.

Eclipse and IntelliJ are usually the standard tools for software development. If you use Eclipse, you can learn a lot of interesting things in the help resources at *http://tutego.de/go/eclipsehelp* and should evaluate various plugins as supplements. Mastering your IDE, especially its shortcuts, can make you a great software developer.

Chapter 2
Imperative Language Concepts

*"When I have conducted an opera a hundred times, it is time
I start learning it again."*
—Arturo Toscanini (1867–1957)

A program in Java isn't described in colloquial language; rather, a set of rules and a grammar define the syntax and semantics. In the following sections, we'll explore some smaller examples of Java programs to clear the way for larger programs.

2.1   Elements of the Java Programming Language

First, let's talk about the set of rules that govern the Java programming language (the grammar and the syntax) and look at the Unicode encoding, tokens, and identifiers, among other things. When naming a method, for example, you can choose from a large number of characters; the character set is called the *lexicon*.

The syntax of a Java program defines the tokens and thus forms the vocabulary. However, correctly written programs aren't necessarily correct. The term *semantics* therefore summarizes the meaning of a syntactically correct program. Semantics determines what the program does. The abstraction order is as follows: lexicon, syntax, and semantics. The compiler goes through these steps before it can generate the bytecode.

2.1.1 Tokens

A *token* is a lexical unit that provides the compiler with the building blocks of the program. Based on the grammar of a language, the compiler recognizes which sequences of characters form a token. For identifiers, for example, this recognition means "Take the next characters as long as a letter is followed only by letters or digits." For example, a number like 1982 forms a token by the following rule: "Read digits until no digit follows." For comments, the combinations /* and */ form a token.

Unfortunately, in C(++), an expression like *s/*t won't be parsed as expected. Only a space between the division sign and the asterisk "helps" the parser to recognize the desired division.

Whitespace

The compiler must be able to distinguish tokens from each other. For this reason, we use *separators*, which include *whitespace* characters such as spaces, tabs, line feeds, and form feeds. These characters have no other meaning than being separators. Thus, you can place any number of whitespace characters between the tokens—any number of spaces is valid between tokens. And since you don't have to be stingy with them, whitespace can clarify a section of a program tremendously. Programs are more readable when they are formatted with a lot of air.

Separators

In addition to the separators, 12 tokens are created from ASCII characters, which are defined as *separators*:

```
(   )   {   }   [   ]   ;   ,   .   ...   @   ::
```

However, the following is anything but good to read, although the compiler does accept it:

```
class _{static long _
(long __,long ___) {
return __==0 ?__+ 1:
___==0?_(__-1,1):_(__
-1,(__, ___-1)) ;  }
static  {int _=2 ,___
= 2;System.out.print(
"a("+ +','+___+ ")="+
_ (_, ___) ) ;System
.exit(1);}}//(C) Ulli
```

2.1.2 Text Encoding by Unicode Characters

Java encodes texts by means of *Unicode characters*. Each character is assigned a unique numerical value (*code point*), so that the capital "A," for example, is located at position 65. The Unicode character set includes the ISO-US-ASCII characters[1] from 0 to 127 (hexadecimal 0x00 to 0x7f, i.e., 7 bits) and the extended encoding according to ISO 8859-1 (Latin-1), which adds characters from 128 to 255. More details on Unicode are provided in Chapter 5.

2.1.3 Identifiers

For variables (and thus constants), methods, classes, and interfaces, *identifiers* are assigned to subsequently identify the corresponding modules in the program. Data is then available under variables. Methods are the subroutines in object-oriented programming (OOP) languages, and classes are the building blocks of object-oriented (OO) programs.

An identifier is a sequence of characters that can be almost arbitrarily long (the length is only theoretically fixed). These characters are elements from the Unicode character set, and each character is important for identification. Thus, an identifier that is 100 characters long must also always be specified correctly with all 100 characters. Some C and FORTRAN compilers are a bit more generous in this respect and evaluate only the first few digits.

Example

In the following Java program, the identifiers are set in bold:

```java
class Application {
  public static void main( String[] args ) {
    System.out.println( "Hello World" );
  }
}
```

String is set in bold because String is a class and not a built-in data type like int. While the String class is given preferential treatment in Java—and a plus sign can concatenate Strings together—it's still a class type.

Each Java identifier is a sequence of *Java letters* and *Java digits*,[2] where the identifier must start with a Java letter. Java letters include not only our Latin letters of the range "A" to "Z" (also "a" to "z") but also include many other characters from the Unicode

---

1 *https://en.wikipedia.org/wiki/ASCII*

2 Whether a character is a letter is determined by the static Character.isLetter(...) method; whether it's a valid identifier letter is indicated by the functions isJavaIdentifierStart(...) for the start letter and isJavaIdentifierPart(...) for the rest.

alphabet, such as the underscore, currency characters—like the characters for dollar ($), euro (€), and yen (¥)—and Greek and Arabic letters. Even if a large number of wild characters are possible as identifier letters, the programming should nevertheless be done with English identifier names. At this point, we should emphasize once again that Java is strictly case sensitive.

Table 2.1 lists some valid identifiers.

Valid Identifiers	Reason
Mami	Mami consists only of alphabetic characters and is therefore correct.
__RAPHAEL_IS_NICE__	Underscores are allowed.
Bóolêáñ	This identifier is correct, even though it contains accents.
α	The Greek alpha is a valid Java letter.
RECE$$ION	The dollar sign is a valid Java letter.
¥€$	Actually, these letters are also valid Java letters.

Table 2.1 Example Valid Identifiers in Java

Invalid identifiers, on the other hand, include the following:

Invalid Identifier	Reason
2plus2is4	The first symbol must be a Java letter and not a digit.
get your shots	Spaces aren't allowed in identifiers.
faster!	The exclamation mark, like many special characters, is invalid.
null class	The name is already occupied by Java. Null (case sensitive) or cláss would be possible.
_	A single underscore is considered a reserved keyword.

Table 2.2 Example Invalid Identifiers in Java

[»]

Note

In Java programs, identifier names are often formed from compound words of a description. For instance, in a sentence like "open file read only," the spaces are removed, and the words following the first word start with capital letters. Thus, the sample sentence becomes "openFileReadOnly." Linguists refer to a capital letter in the middle of words as *inner majuscule*. Programmers and IT-savvy people, on the other hand, like to talk about the *CamelCase notation*, because of two-humped camels.

Mixed case notation gets difficult with capitalized abbreviations, such as HTTP or URL; in these cases, the Java libraries aren't consistent so that class names such as HttpConnection or HTTPConnection are acceptable.

2.1.4   Literals

A literal is a constant expression. Several types of literals exist:

- The truth values true and false
- Integral literals for numbers such as 122
- Floating point literals such as 12.567 or 9.999E-2
- Character literals written in single quotes such as 'X' or '\n'.
- String literals for character strings written in double quotes such as "The rotation of earth 'really' makes my day."
- null stands for a special reference type.

Example   [Ex]

In the following Java program, the three literals are set in bold:

```
class Application {
  public static void main( String[] args ) {
    System.out.println( "Hello World" );
    System.out.println( 1 + 2.65 );
  }
}
```

2.1.5   (Reserved) Keywords

Certain words aren't allowed as identifiers because they're treated specially by the compiler as *keywords*. Keywords determine the "language" of a compiler, and you cannot add your own keywords when programming.

Example   [Ex]

Keywords are set in bold in the following listing:

```
class Application {
  public static void main( String[] args ) {
    System.out.println( "Hello World" );
  }
}
```

Keywords

The strings in Table 2.3 are keywords and therefore cannot be used as identifier names in Java.[3]

abstract	continue	for	new	switch
assert	default	goto†	package	synchronized
boolean	do	if	private	this
break	double	implements	protected	throw
byte	else	import	public	throws
case	enum	instanceof	return	transient
catch	extends	int	short	try
char	final	interface	static	void
class	finally	long	strictfp	volatile
const†	float	native	super	while
–				

Table 2.3 (Reserved) Keywords in Java

Although the words marked with † aren't currently used by Java, variables of this name can't be declared. We refer to these keywords as *reserved keywords* because they're reserved for future use. However, we don't foresee a time that goto will ever be used.

Restricted Identifiers and Literals

Inserting new keywords can break old program code. So, a few years ago,[4] Oracle added a new way to extend the syntax: *restricted identifiers*. var, yield, and record are examples of such restricted identifiers. In addition to the keywords, the literals true, false, and null are also not available for identifiers.

2.1.6 Summary of the Lexical Analysis

When the compiler translates Java programs, it starts with a lexical examination of the source code. We've already learned about the central elements, but let's summarize by looking at the following simple program:

```
class Application {
  public static void main( String[] args ) {
```

---

3 The JLS defines these keywords at *https://docs.oracle.com/javase/specs/jls/se17/html/jls-3.html#jls-3.9*.
4 Strictly speaking, as of Java 10.

```
    String text = "Hello World";
    System.out.println( text );
    System.out.println( 1 + 2.65 );
  }
}
```

The compiler will read over all comments, and the delimiters will take the compiler from token to token. The following tokens can be identified in the program:

Token Type	Example	Explanation
Identifiers	Application, main, String, args, text, System, out, println	Names for class, variable, method, and so on
Keyword	class, public, static, void	Reserved words
Literal	" Lumberjack Song", 1, 2.65	Constant values, like strings, numbers, and so on
Operator	=, +	Operator for assignments, calculations, and so on
Separator	(,), {, }, ;	Symbols that separate the tokens besides the separator character

Table 2.4 Tokens in Our Sample Program

2.1.7 Comments

Programming isn't only about expressing the correct algorithm in a language, but also about formulating our thoughts in an understandable way. This articulation is achieved, for example, by giving meaningful names to program elements such as classes, methods, and variables. Self-explanatory class names help considerably during development. But the solution concept and the algorithm don't necessarily become clearer even by the most beautiful variable names. For outsiders (and after months, perhaps yourselves) to quickly understand the solution concept and later extend or modify the program, you can write *comments* into the source code. They only help humans read the program and have no effect whatsoever on its processing.

Different Types of Comments

In Java, you can formulate comments in the following three ways:

- *Line comments*: These comments start with two slashes[5] (//) and comment out the rest of a line. The comment is valid from these characters until the end of the line, that is, until the newline character.

---

5 Incidentally, in C++, developers have reintroduced the line comment character // from the predecessor language BCPL, which had been removed from C.

- *Block comments*: Using /* */, you can comment out individual sections. The text in the block comment must not contain */ itself because block comments must not be nested.
- *Javadoc comments*: These comments are special block comments that contain Javadoc comments and are contained within /** */. For example, a Javadoc comment describes the method or the parameters from which the application programming interface (API) documentation can be generated later.

Let's look at an example where all three comment types appear:

```
/*
 * This source code is public domain.
 */
// Magic. Do not touch.
/**
 * @author Christian Ullenboom
 */
class DoYouHaveAnyCommentsToMake {      // TODO: Rename later
  // When I wrote this, only God and I understood what I was doing
  // Now, only God knows
  public static void main( String[] args /* Command line argument */ ) {
    System.out.println( "Sleeps all /*night*/ and he //works// all day" );
  }
}
```

For the compiler, a comment is a token, which is why 1/*2*/3 does not give the token 13, but the two tokens 1 and 3. But simply speaking, to the compiler, a file with comments looks the same as without, that is, like class DoYouHaveAnyCommentsToMake { public static void main(String[] args) { System.out.println("Sleeps all /*night*/ and he //works// all day");} }.

The console output is Sleeps all /*night*/ and he //works// all day and shows that no comments exist inside the string literals; the symbols /*, */, and // belong to the string.

The bytecode contains exactly the same—all comments are discarded by the compiler; no comments are included in the bytecode.

Comments with Style

All comments and remarks should be written in English to facilitate reading for project members from other countries.

Javadoc comments generally document the "what" and block comments document the "how."

For general comments, you should use the // characters, which offers two advantages:

- In editors that don't highlight comments or in a simple source code output on the command line, you can quickly see that a line beginning with // is a comment. Keeping track of a source text that is interrupted for several pages with the comment characters /* and */ is difficult. Line comments make it clear where comments start and where they end.

- The use of line comments is better suited for commenting out blocks of code during the development and debugging phases. If you use the block comments for program documentation, you'll be limited because you cannot nest comments of this type. Line comments can be nested more easily.

Pressing Ctrl+/ comments a line or block in and out of IntelliJ. But keep in mind that the forward slash / must be selected via the numeric keypad on your keyboard! If several lines are selected, the key combination comments out all selected lines with line comments. In a commented line, another press of Ctrl+/ takes back the comments of a line.

2.2 From Classes to Statements

Programs are sequences of operations that consist of *statements* at their core. These statements are assembled into larger building blocks, the *methods*, which in turn form *classes*. Classes themselves are collected in *packages*, and a collection of packages is delivered as a *Java archive*.

2.2.1 What Are Statements?

Java belongs to the imperative programming languages, in which the programmer specifies the processing steps of algorithms by means of *statements*. Statements may include the following elements:

- Expression statements, for example, for assignments or method calls
- Case distinctions, for example, via if
- Loops for repetitions, for example, using for or do-while

> **Note**
>
> The imperative command form is not at all natural for programming languages, and certainly other programming paradigms exist. Declarative programming languages follow an opposite philosophy, where the logic is in the foreground and no program flow is formulated. Well-known representatives of declarative programming include SQL, regular expressions, and (in general) functional and logical programming languages. A representative of the latter genre is the *Prolog* language in which the system

independently finds a solution to a problem description. The challenge is to describe the task precisely enough for the system to find a solution. In the SQL database language, you must describe what the result should look like. Then, the database management system (DBMS) can start working, but you don't control its internal processes.

2.2.2 Class Declaration

Programs are composed of statements. In Java, however, statements can't simply be written to a file and passed to the compiler. They must first be packed into a frame. This frame is referred to as a *compilation unit* and declares a class with its methods and variables.

The following lines of program code may seem a bit strange at first (we'll explain its elements in more detail later). The following file gets the (freely selectable) name *Application.java*:

```java
public class Application {

  public static void main( String[] args ) {
    // This is the beginning of our programs
    // Here we have space for our own statements
    // This is where our programs end
  }
}
```

Listing 2.1 src/main/java/Application.java

The two slashes // are followed by a line comment. This comment applies to a complete line up to its end and is used to add explanations to the source code lines to make the code more understandable.

Modern integrated development environments (IDEs) display keywords, literals, and comments in color. This color scheme can always be changed; in IntelliJ for example, you can change these settings via **File • Settings • Appearance & Behavior • Appearance • Theme**.

Java is an OOP language that doesn't permit program statements outside of classes. For this reason, the *Application.java* file declares an Application class with the class keyword to later specify a method with the program logic. The class name is an identifier and can basically be any name you like. However, one limitation exists: For a class declared with public, the class name must be the same as the file name.

The curly brackets of the class are followed by declarations of the methods (i.e., subroutines) that the class offers. A method is a collection of statements under one method name.

> **Naming Conventions** [«]
>
> All keywords in Java start with lowercase letters, and class names usually start with uppercase letters. Methods (like main) are lowercase, unlike in C# where they are capitalized.

2.2.3   The Journey Begins with main(String[])

The `public static void main(String[] args)` method is special for the runtime environment because, when the Java interpreter is called with a class name, this method is executed first.[6] Accordingly, exactly those statements inside the curly brackets are executed. If you mistakenly don't adhere to the syntax for the starting point, the interpreter can't start the program execution, and we've produced a semantic error although the method itself is correctly formed. Inside `main(String[])`, the parameter is named args. The name was chosen arbitrarily, but we'll always use args. We must comply with the keywords `public` and `static`.

The fact that errors are underlined with a curly line has become accepted in development environments as a visualization similar to spelling errors in word processors. IDEs provide a lot of hints in case of an error. An error in the source code is indicated with a curly red line, while warnings are underlined with a curly yellow line. In IntelliJ, pressing [F2] jumps to the error, while pressing [Shift]+[F2] goes backwards to the previous error.

2.2.4   The First Method Call: println(...)

Java has a large class library that allows developers to create files, open windows, access databases, call web services, and much more. At the bottom of the class library, methods will perform a desired operation.

A simple method is `println(...)`. This method outputs messages on the screen (the console). Inside the parentheses of `println(...)`, you can specify arguments.

For example, the `println(...)` method allows you to use *strings* as arguments, which then appear on the console. A string is a sequence of letters, digits, or special characters enclosed in double quotes. Let's implement[7] a complete Java class with a method call that outputs something to the screen via `println(...)`, with the following code:

---

6 However, not all the time. In a `static` block, you could also set a function call, but you shouldn't always assume you can. `static` blocks are executed when the classes are loaded into the virtual machine (VM). Other initializations are thus also already made.

7 The verb "to implement" derives from the Latin word *implere*, which means "to fulfill" and "to supplement."

```
class Application2 {

  public static void main( String[] args ) {
    // Start of program

    System.out.println( "Hello Javanese" );

    // End of program
  }
}
```

Listing 2.2 src/main/java/Application2.java

Why Isn't It Just Called println(...) for a Console Output?

Unlike many scripting languages, Java has no built-in methods that are just "there." Each method always "belongs" to a type. In this case, println(...) belongs to out, while out also belongs to something, namely, to the System class. Only through the complete notation does it become clear to the Java compiler and the runtime environment who or what is responsible for the output.

A string can contain escape sequences to represent special characters:

```
System.out.println( "'Hello' \"Javanese\"" );
```

The escape sequence \" places a double quote in a string. Single quotes don't need to be masked out in a string when enclosed in double quotes for a string. The statement results in the following screen output: 'Hello' "Javanese".

A line break can be inserted using \n:

```
System.out.println( "Hello\nJavanese" );
```

The output is the following:

```
Hello
Javanese
```

Note

The term *method* is the correct term for a subroutine in Java—the *Java Language Specification (JLS)* doesn't use the term *function*.

2.2.5   Atomic Statements and Statement Sequences

Method calls like the following are referred to as *atomic* (also *elementary*) *statements*:

- `System.out.println()`
- The *empty statement*, which consists only of a semicolon
- Variable declarations (which will be introduced later in Section 2.3.2)

These indivisible statements are assembled into *statement sequences*, which in turn form programs.

> **Example**
>
> Let's look at the following statement sequence:
>
> ```
> System.out.println( "Those who get up all wrinkled in the morning, " );
> System.out.println( "have the best opportunities to unfold during the day." )
> ;
> ;
> System.out.println();
> ;
> ```
>
> Empty statements (i.e., the lines with semicolons) generally exist only in the body of infinite loops.

The JVM executes each statement in the sequence one after the other in the specified order. However, statements can't just be placed anywhere, only in specific places, for example, within a method body.

2.2.6   More about print(...), println(...), and printf(...) for Screen Output

Most methods reveal what they do by their names, and for your own programs, using meaningful names makes sense. If Java's developers had simply called the output method `glubschi()` instead of `println()`, the meaning of the method would remain hidden. However, `println()`, by the root word "print," indicates that something is being "printed," that is, written to the screen. The suffix `ln` (short for *line*) means that a line feed character is output as well. In colloquial language, a new output starts in the next line. Besides `println(...)`, the library method `print(...)` doesn't append a line feed.

The `print*(...)` methods[8] can receive different arguments in parentheses. An argument is a value you are passing to the method when calling it. Even if you don't pass arguments to a method, a pair of parentheses must follow the method name when it's called. This inclusion must be absolutely consistent so you can clearly see that it's a method call and nothing else. Otherwise, it might be confused with variables.

---

8 Note this shorthand for methods starting with print (i.e., print(…) and println(…)).

Overloaded Methods

Java allows methods that have the same name but can be passed different things; we call these methods *overloaded*. The print*(...) methods, for example, are overloaded and accept types such as single characters, truth values, or numbers—or nothing at all—in addition to the String argument type.

```java
public class OverloadedPrintln {

  public static void main( String[] args ) {
    System.out.println( "Arrest the usual suspects!" );
    System.out.println( true );
    System.out.println( -273 );
    System.out.println();                    // Outputs an empty line
    System.out.println( 1.6180339887498948 );
  }
}
```

Listing 2.3 src/main/java/OverloadedPrintln.java

The output is the following:

```
Arrest the usual suspects!
true
-273

1.618033988749895
```

In the last line, you can easily see some problems with accuracy—we'll look at this phenomenon in more detail in Chapter 21, Section 21.2.

Variable Argument Lists

Java supports variable argument lists, which means that you can pass any number of arguments (or no argument at all) to certain methods. For example, the printf(...) method allows variable argument lists to prepare and output subsequent method arguments according to a formatting instruction—a string that must always be passed as the first argument, as in the following example:

```java
public class VarArgs {
  public static void main( String[] args ) {
    System.out.printf( "The curfew episode in season 10:%n" );
    System.out.printf( "%d channels, and nothing but %s.%n", 200, "cats" );
  }
}
```

Listing 2.4 src/main/java/VarArgs.java

The output of the program is the following:

```
The curfew episode in season 10:
200 channels, and nothing but cats.
```

The %n format specifiers sets a newline, %d is a format specifiers for an integer (%f would be the placeholder for a float), and %s is a placeholder for a string or something to be converted to a string. Other format specifiers will be introduced in Chapter 5, Section 5.5.

2.2.7   Application Programming Interface Documentation

The most important source of information for programmers is Oracle's official API documentation, where you'll learn, for example, that the println(...) method belongs to the PrintStream class. Several methods with the same name can be passed an integer, a float, a truth value, a character, or else a string as an argument.

The documentation is neither part of the JRE nor the JDK because the help is just too big for inclusion. Instead, you can read the documentation online at *https://docs.oracle.com/en/java/javase/17/docs/api/* or download it from the Oracle site at *https://www.oracle.com/java/technologies/downloads* and unpack it as a collection of HTML documents, as shown in Figure 2.1.

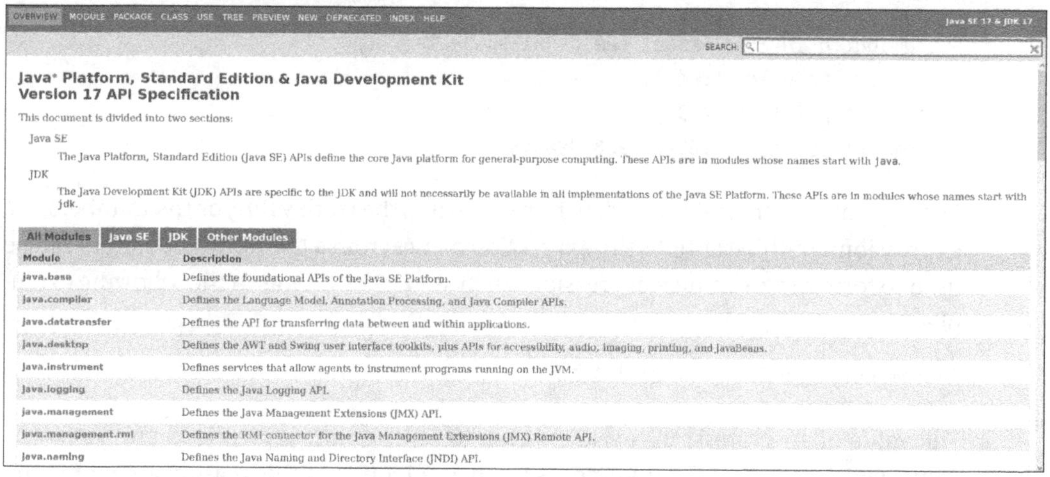

Figure 2.1 Online Documentation at Oracle

You can also access the API documentation from development environments, so searching the website isn't necessary.

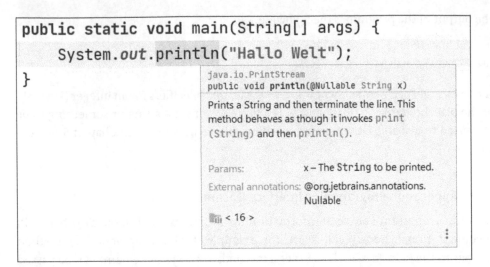

Figure 2.2 IntelliJ Displaying API Documentation in a Small Dialog Box via the Shortcut Ctrl+Q

2.2.8 Expressions

An *expression* produces a result when evaluated. In the example *Overloaded-Println.java*, shown in

Listing 2.3, the main(...) method contains the following:

```
System.out.println( "Arrest the usual suspects!" );
System.out.println( true );
System.out.println( -273 );
System.out.println( 1.6180339887498948 );
```

The arguments for println(...) such as the string, the truth value, or the numbers, are expressions. In this example, the expression comes from a literal, but operators can be used to form more complex expressions such as $(1 + 2) * 1.19$, as in the following example:

```
System.out.println( (1 + 2) * 1.19 );
```

The value of an expression is also referred to as its *result*. Expressions always have a value, which isn't true for statements (such as a loop). For this reason, an expression can exist in all places where a value is needed, for example, as an argument of println(...). This value is either a numeric value (from arithmetic expressions), a truth value (boolean), or a reference (such as from an object creation).

2.2.9 Expression Statements

A program is made out of statements. Certain expressions and method calls can also be used as statements if they are terminated with a semicolon, which is called an *expres-*

sion statement. For example, each method call with a semicolon forms an expression statement. Whether the method itself returns a return value or not doesn't matter.

```
System.out.println();        // println() has no return value (void)
Math.random();               // random() returns a float
```

The `Math.random()` method returns, as its result, a random value between 0 (inclusively so 0 is included) and 1 (exclusively, so 1 is never a selected value). Since nothing is done with the result of the expression, the return value is simply discarded. In the case of the random method, discarding the return value doesn't make sense because the method itself doesn't do anything else except for the calculation.

Besides method calls with terminating semicolons, other types of expression statements include assignments, for example. What all expression statements have in common is the final semicolon.[9]

> **Note**
>
> Not every expression can be an expression statement. For example, 1+2 is an expression, but 1+2; (with the expression terminated with a semicolon) isn't a valid statement. In JavaScript, these things are allowed, but not in Java.

2.2.10 First Insights into Object Orientation

In an OOP language, all methods are bound to specific objects (hence the term *object-oriented*). For example, let's consider the object `radio`: A radio plays music when the power switch is turned on and a station and volume are set. Thus, a radio provides certain services (operations), like `music on/off`, `louder/softer`. In addition, an object has a state, for example, the `volume` or the `year of construction`.

Note that, in OO languages, without exception, operations and states are always bound to objects or classes (more on this distinction follows in Chapter 3 and in Chapter 6). Calling a method on an object directs the request exactly to that particular object. If only the call `louder` exists in a Java program, the compiler doesn't know who to ask if there are, say, three `radio` objects. What if there's also a TV with the same operation? For this reason, you associate the object that can do something with an operation. A dot separates the object from its operation or state. Thus, `println(...)` belongs to an `out` object, which takes care of the screen output. The `out` object in turn belongs to the `System` class.

The runtime system provides two output channels: one for normal output and one to which you can direct errors. One advantage of this subdivision is that it enables you to separate errors from conventional outputs. The standard output goes to `System.out`,

---

9 The semicolon is also not used to separate statements, as in Pascal, but always terminates statements.

while the error output is directed to System.err. The print*(...) methods are the same for both out and err, which are of the same data type, as in the following example:

```
System.out.println( "This is a normal output" );
System.err.println( "This is an error output" );
```

Listing 2.5 src/main/java/SystemOutErr.java, main()

In this case, the object orientation becomes particularly clear once again. The out and err objects are two objects that can do the same thing, namely, output something via print*(...). But you cannot call the println() method without an explicit object referenced and expect the runtime environment to know whether the request goes to System.out or to System.err.

```
Run:     SystemOutErr ×                                          ⚙ —
 ▶  ↑    C:\Users\Christian\Dropbox\Software\jdk-17\bin\java.exe ...
 🔧  ↓    This is a normal output
         This is an error output
 ■  ⏸
 ⏻  ⏬    Process finished with exit code 0
```

Figure 2.3 IntelliJ Displays Normal Outputs and Error Outputs in Different Colors to Easily Distinguish Each Channel. The System.err Object Shouldn't Be Used to Turn Everything Red on the Screen!

2.2.11   Modifiers

The declaration of a class or method can contain one or several *modifiers* that may, for example, restrict its usage or synchronize parallel access.

Example

In the following program, two different modifiers occur in three places, which are set in bold:

```
public class Application {
  public static void main( String[] args ) {
    System.out.println( "Hello World" );
  }
}
```

The keyword public is a *visibility modifier* that determines whether or not the class or method is visible to the program code of other classes.

The keyword static allows you to call the method without forming an object of the class. In other words, without static, an object must be formed, and the method must be called via the concrete object. We'll only use static methods in the first two chapters of this book before introducing you to non-static methods starting in Chapter 3.

2.2.12 Grouping Statements with Blocks

A *block* summarizes a group of statements that are executed one after the other. Thus, a block is *a statement* that combines a sequence of statements into a new statement within curly brackets { }. In other words, the sequence of statements becomes a new statement when placed within curly brackets, thus combining multiple statements into a single block, as the following:

```
{
  Statement1;
  Statement2;
  ...
}
```

A block can be used wherever a single statement can be located. However, the new block has a special feature with regard to variables since it forms a local area for the statements located within it, including its (local) variables.

Code with Style

Lines enclosed in curly brackets are usually indented with whitespace. Usually, two whitespaces are used (as in this book) or four spaces. Many authors place the curly brackets on separate lines. A wealth of other code style advice focuses on ease of reading and understanding for humans. For instance, lines shouldn't be too long (80 to 100 characters is a good size), deep nesting should be avoided, and individual thematical units should be created using blank lines. The "Google Java Style Guide" at *https://google.github.io/styleguide/javaguide.html* provides some useful suggestions.

Empty Blocks

A block {} without a statement is referred to as an *empty block*. It behaves like an empty statement, that is, like a semicolon. In some cases, the empty block is indeed interchangeable with the semicolon, whereas in other cases the Java language forces a block to be empty if there are no instructions, instead of allowing a semicolon there as well.

Nested Blocks

Blocks can be as nested as you like, which results in inner blocks and outer blocks, as in the following example:

```
{                 // Start outer block
  {               // Start inner block
  }               // End inner block
}                 // End outer block
```

With empty blocks, the following code is fine in the static method main(...):

```
public static void main( String[] args ) {
  { System.out.println( "Hello Javanese" ); {{}}{{}{}}}
}
```

Blocks play an important role in grouping statements that are executed once or several times depending on conditions. In Section 2.5 and in Section 2.6, we'll come back to this topic in practice.

2.3   Data Types, Typing, Variables, and Assignments

As is typical for imperative programming languages, Java uses variables to store data. A variable is a reserved memory area and—depending on the content—occupies a fixed number of bytes. All variables (and also expressions) have a *type* that is known at translation time. The type is also called a *data type* because a variable contains a data value. Examples of simple data types are integers, floats, truth values, and characters. The type also determines the allowed operations because truth values can't be added, for example, whereas integers can. In contrast, floats can be added, but not linked via XOR. Since each variable has a fixed data type specified by the programmer, which is known at translation time and can't be changed subsequently, and since Java is quite careful about which operations are allowed and also knows the type of each expression at runtime at the latest, Java is considered both a *statically typed* and *strictly (strongly) typed* programming language.[10]

[»]

> **Note**
>
> In Java, the data type of a variable must be known at translation time. This requirement is referred to as *statically typed*. The opposite is *dynamic typing*, which is what JavaScript uses. In dynamic typing, the type of a variable can change at runtime, depending on what the variable contains.

---

10   While in the literature agreement generally exists on the terms *statically typed* and *dynamically typed*, different authors have different ideas about the terms *strictly (strongly) typed* and *weakly typed*.

Data types in Java fall into two categories:

- *Primitive types*: The primitive (simple) types are hard-coded data types in the Java language for numbers, Unicode characters, and truth values.

- *Reference types*: This data type can be used to manage object references to strings, data structures, or players' objects in a computer game, for example.

At the time, Sun decided on this categorization for a simple reason: Java was designed as a programming language to support small, weak devices. On these devices, the Java software, which was still interpreted at the beginning, had to run as quickly as possible. If the compiler distinguishes between primitive types and reference types, it can generate bytecode relatively easily that also distinguishes between those two types. This distinction also allows the runtime environment to execute the program code much more quickly and with a relatively simple compiler. This criterion was more important in the early days and is no longer important today because the runtime environment performs various optimizations.

Language Comparison with Smalltalk and .NET*

In Smalltalk, everything is an object, including the built-in language data types. For numbers, the base type Number has Integer, Float, and Fraction subtypes. Then, arithmetic operators, like +, -, *, /, //, and \\, (to list them all) exist, but these operators are only methods of the Number class.[11] For Java developers, method names like + or - are unusual, but in Smalltalk, they aren't. Syntactically, a 1 + 2 doesn't differ in Java and Smalltalk, but in Smalltalk, the addition is a message call of the Integer object 1 and of the + method with the argument 2, which in turn is an Integer object as well—the compiler builds the objects independently from the literals. An Integer class for integers has other methods like asCharacter and floor.[12] Note that this difference only impacts the semantic model on the language side; it has nothing to do with how later the runtime environment optimizes these particular message calls. By dividing Java into primitive data types and reference types, the language's creators accepted a break from the OO principle to optimize the interpreted runtime in the early 1990s—an optimization that is unnecessary from today's perspective.

.NET is more like Java: The compiler knows the built-in data types and gives them special treatment; they aren't method calls. Statements such as addition and subtraction can also be found in the bytecode (called the *Common Intermediate Language*, or CIL in .NET). But there's one more difference to Java: The compiler maps data types of .NET languages to .NET classes, and these classes have methods. In C#, the built-in float data type is identical to the Single data type (from the .NET System package), and whether developers write float f or Single f doesn't matter. However, Single (or float) has no mathematical operations compared to Smalltalk but does have a few

---

11   The documentation for GNU Smalltalk references is available at *http://www.gnu.org/software/ smalltalk/manual-base/html_node/Number_002darithmetic.html#Number_002darithmetic.*

12   *http://www.gnu.org/software/smalltalk/manual-base/html_node/Integer.html*

methods like ToString().[13] Consequently, in .NET, the built-in data types behave like objects: They have methods but have the same value semantics (for example, in method calls) as in Java and also look similar in bytecode, which gives them the same good performance.

The following sections deal with primitive data types. References are only used when objects come into play. We'll look at references in detail in Chapter 3, Section 3.7.1.

2.3.1   Overview of Primitive Data Types

In Java, two types of built-in primitive data types exist:

- *Arithmetic types*, for integers, such as integral types, floats, and Unicode characters
- *Truth values* for the states true and false

Table 2.5 provides an overview of these data types. We'll look at each data type in greater detail.

Type	Assignment (Value Range)
boolean	true or false
char	16-bit Unicode character (0x0000 … 0xFFFF)
byte	-2^7 to $2^7 - 1$ (−128 … 127)
short	-2^{15} to $2^{15} - 1$ (−32,768 … 32,767)
int	-2^{31} to $2^{31} - 1$ (−2,147,483,648 … 2,147,483,647)
long	-2^{63} to $2^{63} - 1$ (−9,223,372,036,854,775,808 … 9,223,372,036,854,775,807)
float	1.4×10^{-45} … 3.4×10^{38}
double	4.9×10^{-324} … 1.7×10^{308}

Table 2.5 Java Data Types and Their Value Ranges

Concerning integers, note that there's one positive number "less" than negative ones. This is due to the coding of two's complement.

For float and double, the display is somewhat abbreviated, and the sign is not specified since the smallest and largest numbers that can be represented can be both positive and negative. In other words, the value ranges don't differ—unlike with int, for example—depending on the sign.[14] Table 2.6 shows a slightly different representation.

---

13   *https://msdn.microsoft.com/en-us/library/system.int32*

14   There are still "special numbers" with floats, such as *plus* or *minus infinity*, but more on that in Chapter 21, Section 21.2.1.

Detailed Knowledge

Strictly speaking, the grammar of the Java language doesn't provide for negative number literals. For a number like -1.2 or -1, the minus is the unary operator and doesn't belong to the number. In the bytecode itself, the negative numbers are mapped again.

Type	Size	Format
Integers		
byte	8-bit	Two's complement
short	16-bit	Two's complement
int	32-bit	Two's complement
long	64-bit	Two's complement
Floats		
float	32-bit	IEEE 754
double	64-bit	IEEE 754
Other data types		
boolean	1-bit	true, false
char	16-bit	16-bit Unicode

Table 2.6 Java Data Types and Their Sizes and Formats

[»]

Note

Strings are treated preferentially but are merely references to objects and not a primitive data type.

Two main aspects distinguish the primitive data types:

- All data types have a fixed length that doesn't change under any circumstances. The disadvantage that the length of a data type can change in some high-level languages doesn't exist in Java. In C(++), this length always remains uncertain, and the move to 64-bit machines entails a lot of problems. The char data type is 16 bits long.

- The numeric data types byte, short, int, and long are signed, floating point values of type float and double. Unfortunately, their usage is not always practical, yet you should keep this fact in mind at all times. Problems arise when assigning the value 240 to a byte, for example, because 240 is outside the range of values that extends from –128 to 127. A char is basically an unsigned integer type.

To sort the numeric data types by size (let's leave char out of this scenario), you could build two lines for integers and floats, as in the following example:

```
byte < short < int < long
float < double
```

[»]

Note

The classes Byte, Integer, Long, Short, Character, Double, and Float declare the constants MAX_VALUE and MIN_VALUE, which specify the largest and smallest permissible values of the value range or the limits of the value ranges of each data type:

```
System.out.println( Byte.MIN_VALUE );        // -128
System.out.println( Byte.MAX_VALUE );        // 127
System.out.println( Character.MIN_VALUE );   // '\u0000'
System.out.println( Character.MAX_VALUE );   // '\uFFFF'
System.out.println( Double.MIN_VALUE );      // 4.9E-324
System.out.println( Double.MAX_VALUE );      // 1.7976931348623157E308
```

A separate class for each primitive data type with helper methods exists around that data type. For more information on these special classes, refer to Chapter 11, Section 11.5.

2.3.2   Variable Declarations

Variables can be used to store data that can be read and written by the program. To use variables, they must first be declared (defined[15]). The notation of a variable declaration

---

15   In C(++) "definition" and "declaration" mean something different. In Java, no such difference exists, and we therefore consider both terms as equivalent. The specification only uses the term *declarations*.

is always the same: The type name is followed by the name of the variable. The declaration is a statement and must therefore end with a semicolon. In Java, the compiler knows exactly the type of each variable and expression.

Let's declare a few (local) variables in the main(...) method to store the properties common to candies.

```
public class FirstVariable {

  public static void main( String[] args ) {
    String  name;
    int     quantity;
    double  price;
    boolean sticky;
    boolean chewy;
  }
}
```

Listing 2.6 src/main/java/FirstVariable.java

On the left, either a primitive type (like int) or a reference type (like string) is used. A declaration is not much more difficult since cryptic specifications common in C don't exist in Java.[16] A variable name (which is then an identifier) can contain all the letters and digits of the Unicode character set, except no digit should start the identifier. Also, the identifier name cannot be identical to any reserved keyword.

Declaring Multiple Variables Compactly

In the preceding listing, two variables (sticky and chewy) are of the same type. Whenever the variable type is the same, the declaration can be shortened with the variables separated by commas, as in the following example:

```
boolean sticky, chewy;
```

Variable Declaration with Value Initialization

In a declaration, a variable can be initialized with an initial value. The equal sign is followed by the value, which is often a literal.

```
public class Lollipop {

  public static void main( String[] args ) {
    String  name     = "Lollipop";
    int     quantity = 12;
    double  price    = 0.99;
```

---

16 In C, declarations like *char (*(*a[2])())[2]* are possible. Fortunately, the program cdecl is designed for "reading out" such definitions.

```
    boolean sticky   = false;
    boolean chewy    = false;
  }
}
```

Listing 2.7 src/main/java/Lollipop.java

As before, note that, when multiple variables of the same type are declared, a comma separates the identifiers. How you declare these variables also affects the initialization. For example, consider the following code:

```
boolean sticky     = true,
        chewy      = true;
String  person1    = "Silvio",
        person2    = "Ruby";
double  x, y,
        bodyHeight = 165 /* cm */;
```

The lines declare several variables at once. The variables x and y at the end remain uninitialized.

Calculating Interest: An Example of Variable Declaration, Initialization, and Output

Using the console output, we can now program a simple interest calculator. This program is supposed to output the interest on a given principal, at a given interest rate, after 1 year.

```
public class InterestRates {
  public static void main( String[] args ) {
    double capital       = 20000 /* Euro */;
    double interestRate = 3.6    /* percent */;
    double totalInterestRate = capital * interestRate / 100; // Year 1
    System.out.print( "Interest: " );
    System.out.println( totalInterestRate );   // 720.0
  }
}
```

Listing 2.8 src/main/java/InterestRates.java

[+]

> **Tip**
>
> Strings can be attached to each other with a plus sign. If a segment isn't a string, it will be converted to a string and then appended.
>
> ```
> System.out.println( "Interest: " + totalInterestRate );   // Interest: 720.0
> ```
>
> More examples follow in Section 2.4.11.

2.3.3   Automatic Type Detection with var

When variables are declared, the variable type can be replaced by var in some cases.

```
var name = "Lollipop";
var quantity = 12;
var price = 1;
var sticky = false;
var chewy = false;
```

Listing 2.9 src/main/java/VarLollipop.java (Snippet)

Note that, unlike our previous example, variable types such as string or int are no longer explicit in the code when declaring variables, only var. However, this omission doesn't mean that the compiler leaves the types open! The compiler absolutely needs information to the right of the equal sign to determine the type. This scenario is called *local-variable type inference*.

For this reason, a discrepancy exists in our program, namely, at var price = 1, which clearly demonstrates a problem with var. The variable is no longer a double as before, but 1 is an integer literal, so the Java compiler gives the variable price the type int.

The use of var is intended to help developers write shorter code, especially when the variable name already clearly indicates the type. If we find a text variable, the string type is obvious, just as length or size is an int or a prefix like is or has indicates a boolean variable.

But if var is used at the expense of comprehensibility, the abbreviation should not be used. The Java compiler also provides the following barriers:

- var is only possible if an initialization specifies a type. A declaration of the type var age; without initialization is not possible and leads to a compiler error.
- var can only be used with local variables. But variables can be declared in Java in other places, for instance, where using var isn't possible.

Language Comparison [«]

Java is relatively late with var.[17] Other statically typed languages have provided this option for a long time, for example, C++ with auto or C# with var. JavaScript also uses var, but in a completely different context: In JavaScript, variables aren't typed until runtime, and all operations aren't checked until execution time, whereas Java doesn't abandon type safety with var.

---

17 *http://openjdk.java.net/jeps/286*

2.3.4 Final Variables and the final Modifier

Variables can be declared with the `final` modifier so that exactly one assignment is possible. This additional keyword consequently prohibits further assignment to this variable, so that it can no longer be changed. A common use case for this modifier is to define constants, as in the following example:

```
int width = 40, height = 12;
final int area = width * height;
final int perimeter;
final var random = Math.random() * 100;
perimeter = width * 2 + height * 2;
area = 200;          // 💀 Compiler error
perimeter = 100;     // 💀 Compiler error
```

In the case of an attempted second assignment, compiler errors will occur.

Java allows *deferred initialization* for final values. Thus, assigning a value at the time of variable declaration isn't mandatory, as shown in our example, with the `perimeter` variable.

If variables are declared and initialized, `final` and `var` can be used together. Some programming languages provide their own keyword for this case (e.g., `val`), but Java doesn't.

> **Outlook**
>
> Object variables and class variables can also be final. However, the variables must then either be assigned in the declaration or in a deferred initialization in the constructor. We'll cover this topic in more detail in Chapter 6, Section 6.4.1. If final variables are inherited, subclasses can no longer overwrite this value either (which could be a problem, but perhaps also an advantage, for some constants).
>
> The `final` keyword has additional meanings in the context of inheritance. We'll look at that later in Section 2.7.2 as well.

2.3.5 Console Inputs

So far, you've learned about methods for output and `random()`. The `println(...)` methods "hang" on the `System.out` or `System.err` object, and `random()` "hangs" on the `Math` object.

The counterpart to `print*(...)` is a console input, with several different variants. The simplest variant involves the `java.util.Scanner` class. In Chapter 5, Section 5.10.2, we'll examine this class in much more detail. However, at this point, we just want to emphasize how strings, integers, and floats are read.

Reading Input of Type	Statement
String	String s = new java.util.Scanner(System.in).nextLine();
int	int i = new java.util.Scanner(System.in).nextInt();
double	double d = new java.util.Scanner(System.in).nextDouble();

Table 2.7 Reading a String or Integer and Float from the Console

Let's combine the three possibilities into one example. The next program will first read a string, then an integer, and finally a float.

```
public class SmallConversation {
  public static void main( String[] args ) {
    System.out.println( "Hey! What's your favorite candy?" );
    String name = new java.util.Scanner( System.in ).nextLine();

    System.out.printf( "How many %s candy can you eat?%n", name );
    int quantity = new java.util.Scanner( System.in ).nextInt();

    System.out.printf( "I see, %s. And how much did that cost?%n", quantity );
    double value = new java.util.Scanner( System.in ).nextDouble();

    System.out.printf( "%s? I see, I was guessing %s.%n",
                       value, value * 2 / 3 );
  }
}
```

Listing 2.10 src/main/java/SmallConversation.java

The conversation thus looks something like this:

```
Hey! What's your favorite candy?
Tootsie Roll
How many Tootsie Roll candy can you eat?
9
I see, 9. And how much did that cost?
6.90
6.9? I see, I was guessing 4.6000000000000005
```

The float must be entered in a localized manner. Floats often can't be represented quite precisely, hence the strange output.

The output via printf(...) can also write localized floats, with the format specifier %f and %g.

[+]
Dialog Input

If the input doesn't originate from the console, but from a separate dialog instead, a class from the Swing package can be helpful, as shown in the following example:

```
String input = javax.swing.JOptionPane.showInputDialog( "Input" );
```

2.3.6   Truth Values

The boolean data type describes a truth value that's either true or false. The strings true and false are reserved words and form literals along with constant strings and primitive data types. No other value is possible for truth values; in particular, numeric values aren't interpreted as truth values.

The boolean type is needed for conditions, branches, and loops, for example. As a rule, a truth value results from comparisons.

2.3.7   Integer Data Types

Java provides five integer data types: byte, short, char, int, and long, with fixed lengths of 1, 2, 4, and 8 bytes, respectively, which is an essential feature of Java. Integer types are always signed in Java (with the exception of char); no unsigned modifier exists, as in C(++).[18] Negative numbers are formed by prefixing them with a minus sign. A plus sign for positive characters is possible. int and long are the preferred types. byte rarely occurs, and short only in really rare cases, such as arrays with image data.

Integers Are by Default of the int Type

Looking at following code line, no error is seen on first sight:

```
System.out.println( 123456789012345 );        // ☠
```

Nevertheless, the compiler won't translate the line because it assumes an integer literal without explicit size specification as a 32-bit int. The line therefore results in a compiler error since our number isn't within the valid int value range of –2,147,483,648 to +2,147,483,647, but instead far outside (2,147,483,647 < 123,456,789,012,345). Thus, Java doesn't reserve as many bits as needed and doesn't automatically select the appropriate range of values.

Larger Integer Values with long

The Java compiler automatically considers any integer literal as int. If the value range of about +/–2 billion isn't sufficient, developers resort to the next higher data type, the

---

18   In Java, long and short form their own data type. They don't serve as modifiers as in C(++). So, a declaration like long int i is just as wrong as long long time_ago.

long data type. The fact that a number is long must be explicitly stated. For this purpose, an l or L is placed at the end of integer literals of the long type. To make the output of the number 123456789012345 valid, you must write the following:

```
System.out.println( 123456789012345L );
```

Tip   [+]

The lowercase "l" looks similar to the number one. For this reason, an uppercase "L" should always be used in length specifications.

Question   [«]

What will the following statement output?

```
System.out.println( 123456789 + 54321 );
```

The byte Data Type

A byte is a data type with a value range from –128 to +127. An initialization like

```
byte b = 200;                    // ☠
```

is therefore not allowed, since 200 > 127. Thus, all numbers from 128 to 255 (hexadecimal 0x80 to 0xFF) are dropped. In data processing, the Java byte isn't really useful because it has a sign, and especially in file processing, value ranges from 0 to 255 are required.

Java doesn't permit unsigned integers, but with an explicit type conversion number like 200 can be stored in a byte, for example, in the following code:

```
byte b = (byte) 200;
```

The Java compiler simply takes the bit assignment of 200 (0b00000000_00000000_00000000_11001000), cuts off the upper 3 bytes during type conversion and interprets the uppermost bit then set as a sign bit, as shown in the following output:

```
byte b = (byte) 200;
System.out.println( b );        // -56
```

More information about type conversion will follow in Section 2.4.10.

The short * Data Type

The short data type is rarely encountered. With its 2 bytes, this data type can represent a value range from –32,768 to +32,767. The sign "costs" 1 bit as with the other integers.

Thus, this data type has 16 bits, but only 15 bits are available for numbers. However, as with byte, an unsigned short can also be initialized in two ways:

```
short s = (short) 33000;
System.out.println( s );      // -32536
```

2.3.8 Underscores in Numbers

In some areas of application, numbers can get large rather quickly, for example, in the context of conversions. For instance, the System.currentTimeMillis() method returns the milliseconds that have passed since 1/1/1970, 00:00 according to the system clock. At 12:26:40 (UTC) on September 13, 2020, that's 1,600,000,000,000 milliseconds. How can we convert this number to days?

To convert a number of milliseconds into days, a division operation can be made. To convert milliseconds to seconds, we'll divide by 1,000; from seconds to minutes, divide by 60; from minutes to hours, divide by 60; and then for hours to days, the final division by 24. The product of 24 * 60 * 1,000 is 86,400,000. Let's write that down to make a calculation from the current time with the following code:

```
long currentMillis = System.currentTimeMillis();
long days = currentMillis / 86400000L;
System.out.println( days );    // 18530
```

86400000L is not particularly readable. Java provides the solution to make numeric literals more readable by means of an underscore. Instead of 86400000L, we can write:

```
long days = currentMillis / 86_400_000L;
```

The underscores make the blocks of 1,000 easy to read.[19]

Another solution is avoid using such a number at all and build it up by 24 * 60 * 60 * 1000L—this approach doesn't cost more runtime since this constant expression is fixed at translation time. In this case, building up the number is the better approach.

[Ex]

Example

The underscore notation is also helpful for literals in binary and hexadecimal representation since the underscores can also set off blocks, as in the following examples:

```
int  i = 0b01101001_01001101_11100101_01011110;
long l = 0x7fff_ffff_ffff_ffffL;
```

A literal starts with 0b in binary notation, with 0x in hexadecimal notation. More details follow in Chapter 21, Section 21.1.3.

---

19 For conversions between hours, minutes, etc., the TimeUnit class also helps with some static to*() methods.

The underscore can be used in any numeric literal, but two consecutive underscores aren't allowed, and it must not be located at the beginning.

> **Note**
>
> The underscores in literals are just an aid like spaces for indentation and won't be translated into the bytecode. In the class file, 0b01101001_01001101_11100101_01011110 and 0b01101001010011011110010101011110 look identical, especially because they are stored as the integer 1766712670 anyway.

2.3.9 Alphanumeric Characters

The alphanumeric data type char (from *character*) is 2 bytes in size and holds one Unicode character. A char is unsigned. The literals for characters are placed in single quotation marks. Language beginners often confuse the single quotation marks with the quotation marks of strings. The simple mnemonic rule is: one character—one quotation mark; several characters—two quotation marks.

> **Example**
>
> The correct quotation marks for characters and strings are shown in the following examples:
>
> ```
> char   c = 'a';
> String s = "Already barked today?";
> ```
>
> Since the compiler can automatically convert a char to an int, the expression int c = 'a'; is also valid.

2.3.10 The float and double Data Types

For floats (also called *floating point numbers*) of simple and increased precision, Java provides the data types float and double. These data types are described in the IEEE-754 standard and have a length of 4 bytes for float and 8 bytes for double. Float literals can have a pre-decimal part and a post-decimal part separated by a decimal point (no comma). A float literal doesn't require any digits before or after the decimal point, so the following code is also valid:

```
double d = 10.0 + 20. + .11;
```

Using only the dot is of course nonsense, whereas .0 is certainly allowed.

> **Note**
>
> The float data type is a bad joke with 4 bytes (i.e., 32 bits). The double data type is just fine with 64 bits. The IA32, x86-64, and Itanium processors support a "double extended" mode with 80 bits and thus offer better precision.

[»]

Note

The compiler doesn't report an error if a float can't be read precisely. No mistake exists in writing the following:

```
double pi =
  3.14159265358979323846264338327950288419716939937510582097494 4592;
```

The float * Data Type

By default, float literals are of the double type. A trailing f (or F) indicates to the compiler that the value is a float.

[Ex]

Example

Valid assignments for floats of the double and float types include the following:

```
double pi = 3.1415, delta = .001;
float  ratio  = 4.33F;
```

A d (or D) can also be added for the double data type, but this addition isn't necessary if literals for decimal numbers are in the source code; numbers like 3.1415 are automatically of the double type. However, while 1 + 2 + 4.0 first adds 1 and 2 as int, then converts the event to double, and then adds 4.0, the expression 1D + 2 + 4.0 would start right away with the float 1. Thus, 1D is also equal to 1. or 1.0.[20]

[»]

Question

What's the resulting output of the following lines of code?

```
System.out.println( 20000000000F == 20000000000F+1 );
System.out.println( 20000000000D == 20000000000D+1 );
```

[+]

Tip

What are the value ranges of float and double?[21]

---

20 A literal like 1D makes it clear why identifiers can't do anything with a digit: If a variable declaration like double 1D = 2; were allowed, then the compiler wouldn't know whether 1D stands for the literal or for the variable in println(1D).

21 For understanding, check out the output of System.out.println(Float.toHexString(20000000000F)); System.out.println(Float.toHexString(20000000000F + 1F)); System.out.println(Double.toHexString(20000000000D)); System.out.println(Double.toHexString(20000000000D + 1D));

Even More Precise Resolution for Floats*

No higher resolution or more precise data type for floats exists than `double`. The standard library provides the `BigDecimal` class for this task in `java.math`, which is described in more detail in Chapter 21, Section 21.6. This class is useful for data that should have particularly good accuracy, such as currencies.[22]

Language Comparison

In C#, the `decimal` data type has 128 bits (i.e., 16 bytes) and thus also offers enough precision to express a number like 0.00000000000000000000000001.

2.3.11 Good Names, Bad Names

For optimal readability and comprehensibility in the code, developers should consider some points when writing code:

- **A consistent naming schema is important**

  Is a numerator called `nu`, `num`, `nur`, or `numerator`? Also, we should write correct text and pay attention to spelling mistakes; otherwise, `necessaryConnection` easily becomes `nesesarryConnection`. Variables of similar notation, such as `counter` and `counters`, should be avoided.

- **Abstract identifiers should also be avoided**

  The declaration `int TEN = 10;` is absurd. A nonsensical idea is also the following: `boolean FALSE = true, TRUE = false;`. The program code would then work with `FALSE` and `TRUE`. Code written in this way would win top place in a contest for the most botched Java program.

- **Some Unicode characters can be included in identifiers, but they should be avoided**

  The statements `int ? = 4; int ? = 5; double ? = ? + ?;` are however correct.

- **O and O and 1 and l are easily confused**

  The combination "rn" is difficult to read and, depending on the character set, easily confused with "m."[23] Also valid—but bad—is: `int ínt, ìnt, înt; boolean bôôleañ;`.

Remark

Using unique names for your variables is vital. When vague names like `temp1`, `temp2`, etc. are used, how can you tell the difference between them?

---

22 Some programming languages have built-in data types for currencies, such as LotusScript with `Currency`, which covers an exceptionally large and accurate range of values with 8 bytes. Surprisingly, once in C#, the `currency` data type could be used for integer currencies.

23 Some software, like Mathematica, warns about variables with almost identical names.

If a designator name is chosen in an unfortunate way (pneumonoultramicroscopicsili-covolcanoconiosis is indeed a bit long), consistent renaming is still possible. Select **Refactor · Rename...** or press `Shift`+`F6`; the cursor must be on the identifier. At the same time, all references to the variable will change along with it.

2.3.12   No Automatic Initialization of Local Variables

The runtime environment—or the compiler—doesn't automatically initialize local variables with a null value or truth variants with `false`. Before reading, local variables must be initialized manually; otherwise, a compiler error will occur.[24]

In the following example, the two local variables `quantity` and `chewy` aren't automatically initialized, and so a compiler error occurs when `quantity` and `chewy` are attempted to be output. The reason is that initialization is necessary prior to the read access.

```
int      quantity;
boolean chewy;
System.out.println( quantity );     // ☠
// variable quantity might not have been initialized
quantity = 18;
if ( quantity >= 10 )                    // case distinction: if-then
  chewy = true;
System.out.println( chewy );  // ☠
// variable chewy might not have been initialized
```

Because assignments in conditional statements might not be executed, the compiler also reports an error with `System.out.println(chewy)` because it determines a program flow without an assignment. Since `chewy` is only set to the value `true` after the `if` query, write access to `chewy` would only occur, and subsequent read access would only be possible under the condition that `quantity` is greater than or equal to 10. But since the compiler assumes that other cases might exist, accessing an uninitialized variable would be an error.

Figure 2.4 IntelliJ Displaying Hints and Suggestions for Improvement When a Local Variable Isn't Initialized but Is Accessed

---

24 This behavior is different for object variables, static variables, and fields. By default, they are set to null (for references), 0 (for numbers), or `false`.

2.4 Expressions, Operands, and Operators

Let's start with some mathematical expressions and then illustrate how they are written in Java. A mathematical formula, such as the expression -27 * 9, consists of *operands* and *operators*. For example, an operand is a variable, a literal, or the return of a method call. In the case of a variable, the value is read from the variable and the calculation is performed with it.

The operators link the operands. Depending on the number of operands, the following types of operators are distinguished:

- An operator defined on exactly one operand is referred to as a *unary operator* (or *monadic operator*). The minus (negative sign) before an operand is a unary operator since it applies to exactly the following operand.

- The usual operators (plus, minus, multiply, and divide) by are *binary (dyadic) operators*.

- A question mark operator is used for conditional expressions, which have 3 characters.

Operators allow the connection of individual expressions to new expressions. Some operators are familiar from school, such as addition, comparison, assignment, and others. C(++) programmers will recognize many old friends.

2.4.1 Assignment Operator

In Java, the equal sign = is used for an *assignment*.[25] The assignment operator is a binary operator with the variable to be assigned on the left and an expression on the right.

Example

Let's look at some expressions with assignments:

```
int quantity = 12, total;
total = quantity * 2;
```

The multiplication calculates the product of 12 and 2 and stores the result in total. From all primitive variables that occur in the expression, the value is read and inserted into the expression.[26] This process is also called a *value operation* because the value of the variable is considered (and not its location or even its variable name).

---

25 Although the assignments look like mathematical equations, an important difference should be noted: The formula a = a + 1 can't be fulfilled mathematically—at least not in the decimal system without additional algebra—because no possible value of a satisfies a = a + 1. From a programming point of view, however, this expression is OK and increases the value of the variable a by one.

26 In some programming languages, value operations are specifically marked. For example, in LOGO, a value operation is written with a colon in front of the variable, as in :X + :Y.

Only after the expression has been evaluated does the assignment operator copy the result into the variable. If runtime errors occur, for example, due to a division by zero, no write access to the variable is possible.

[»] **Language Comparison**

The simple equals sign = is only used for assignment in Java, which is also the case in almost all programming languages. Rarely, a programming language uses a different symbol for the assignment, such as := in Pascal or <- in F# and R. To separate assignments from comparisons, Java follows the C(++) tradition and defines a binary comparison operator == with two equal signs. The comparison operator always returns the boolean result type, as in the following code:

```
int quantity = 1;
System.out.println( quantity == 1 );   // "true": Expression with comparison
System.out.println( quantity = 2 );    // "2": Expression with assignment
```

Assignments Are Also Expressions

Although assignments are often found as expression statements, assignments can be found anywhere an expression is allowed, for example, in a method call like print*(...):

```
int quantity = 1;                        // Declaration with initialization
quantity = 2;                            // Statement with assignment
System.out.println( quantity = 3 );  // Expression with assignment. Delivers 3.
```

Multiple Assignments in One Step

Assignments of the type a = b = c = 0; are allowed and are equivalent to the three statements c = 0; b = c; a = b;.

The explicit parentheses a = (b = (c = 0)) make it clear once again that assignments can be nested, and assignments like c = 0 are expressions that return a value. However, consider the following:

```
a = (b = c + d) + e;
```

This is a good simplification compared to the following:

```
b = c + d;
a = b + e;
```

In general, you should get by with one assignment per line.

The order of evaluation is shown in the following example:

```
int quantity = 10;
System.out.println( (quantity = 2) * quantity );  // 4
System.out.println( quantity );                    // 2
```

Nevertheless, code like this shouldn't occur in production.

2.4.2 Arithmetic Operators

An arithmetic operator links the operands with the operators addition (+), subtraction (-), multiplication (*), and division (/). In addition, the remainder operator (%) considers the remainder left when dividing. All operators are defined for integer values as well as for float values. The arithmetic operators are binary, and on the left and right sides, the types are numeric. The result type is also numeric.

Numeric Promotion

For expressions with different numeric data types, such as int and double, the compiler sets all operands to the more comprehensive type before applying the operation. Thus, before evaluating 1 + 2.0, the integer 1 is converted to a double, and then the addition operation is performed—the result has the double type again. This feature is called *numeric promotion*. For byte and short, a special rule applies in that they are first converted to int.[27] (Also, in Java bytecode, no arithmetic operations can occur on byte, short, and char). Then, the operation is executed, and the result type corresponds to the more comprehensive type.

The Division Operator

The binary operator / forms the quotient of the dividend and divisor. On its left is the dividend, and on the right, the divisor. Division operations are defined for integers and for floats. Integer division rounds to zero, and the result is not a float, so 1/3 provides the result 0 and not 0.333.... The data type of the result is determined by the operands and not the operator. If the result should be of the double type, at least one operand must also be a double.

```
System.out.println( 1.0 / 3 );      // 0.3333333333333333
System.out.println( 1   / 3.0 );    // 0.3333333333333333
System.out.println( 1   / 3 );      // 0
```

Division by Zero Penalty

In school, mathematics taught us that division by zero is not allowed. If we perform an integer division with the divisor 0 in Java, Java punishes us with an ArithmeticException. If the ArithmeticException isn't handled, the executing thread will end, and if the

---

27 *https://docs.oracle.com/javase/specs/jls/se17/html/jls-5.html#jls-5.6*

unchecked exception takes place in the main thread and isn't caught, the program will end. For floats, division by zero doesn't yield an exception, but +/– infinity instead, and 0.0/0.0 results in the special value, *not a number NaN* (described in more detail in Chapter 21, Section 21.2.1). Sometimes called a "non-number," NaN is generated by the processor when it cannot perform certain mathematical operations, such as division by zero.

[»]

Anecdote

On the guided missile cruiser *USS Yorktown*, a crew member accidentally entered the number zero. This attempt at division by zero resulted in an error propagated to the point where the software crashed, and the drive system stopped. The ship drifted in the water for several hours without propulsion.

The Remainder Operator %*

An integer division operator doesn't necessarily always tally smoothly, as in the case of 9 / 2. In this case, there is the remainder 1. This remainder is provided by the *remainder operator (%)*, often also referred to as *modulo*.[28] The operands can also be negative.

[Ex]

Example

```
System.out.println( 9 % 2 );              // 1
```

The division and the remainder are based on a simple formula in Java: $(int)(a/b) \times b + (a\%b) = a$.

[Ex]

Example

The equation is satisfied if we choose, say, a = 10 and b = 3. The following applies: (int)(10/3) = 3 and 10 % 3 results in 1. Then, 3 * 3 + 1 = 10.

As shown in this equation, with the remainder, the result is negative only if the dividend is negative; the result is positive only if the dividend is positive. It's easy to see that the result of the residual operation is always genuinely smaller than the value of the divisor. We have the same case as with integer division, that a divisor with the value 0 throws an ArithmeticException and leads to the result NaN for floats.

```
System.out.println( "+5 % +3 = " + (+5 % +3) );  // 2
System.out.println( "+5 / +3 = " + (+5 / +3) );  // 1
System.out.println( "+5 % -3 = " + (+5 % -3) );  // 2
```

---

28 Mathematicians distinguish between the two terms *remainder* and *modulo* because a modulo is not negative, while the remainder in Java is. But this distinction is not important for our purposes.

```
System.out.println( "+5 / -3 = " + (+5 / -3) );  // -1

System.out.println( "-5 % +3 = " + (-5 % +3) );  // -2
System.out.println( "-5 / +3 = " + (-5 / +3) );  // -1

System.out.println( "-5 % -3 = " + (-5 % -3) );  // -2
System.out.println( "-5 / -3 = " + (-5 / -3) );  //  1
```

Listing 2.11 src/main/java/RemainderAndDivDemo.java, main()

The fact that the first operand (*dividend*) defines the sign of the remainder and the second one (*divisor*) never does requires getting used to. In Chapter 21, Section 21.3.6, you'll learn about the floorMod(...) method, which works a little differently.

Note   [«]

If you want to use value % 2 == 1 to test whether value is an odd number, value must be positive because Java calculates -3 % 2 as -1. The test for odd numbers is only correct again with value % 2 != 0.

Remainder for Floats

The remainder operator is also applicable to floats, and the operands can again be negative.

Example   [Ex]

Test whether a double number is an integer after all: (d % 1) == 0.

If this expression is too crazy for you, you can alternatively use d == Math.rint(d).

Remainder for Floats and Math.IEEEremainder( )*

Using the formula mentioned earlier, you can easily calculate the result of a remainder operation even for floats. Note that the operator doesn't behave as it does under IEEE 754 because this standard specifies that the remainder operation calculates the remainder from a rounding division and not from a truncating one. Thus, the behavior wouldn't be analogous to the remainder for integers. However, Java defines the remainder for floats in the same way as it defines the remainder for integers. If you want remainder behavior as prescribed by IEEE 754, you can use the static library method Math.IEEEremainder(...).[29]

---

29 Some methods don't start with lowercase letters, although this situation is rare and only occurs in special cases. For instance, ieeeRemainder() simply didn't look nice to the authors.

You should also never expect an exception for the remainder operation on floats. Any errors are indicated with NaN, as described in the IEEE standard. Overflow or underflow may occur but can't be tested.

2.4.3 Unary Minus and Plus

Binary operators sit between two operands, while a unary operator takes on exactly one operand. The unary minus (operator for sign reversal), for example, reverses the sign of the operand. Thus, a positive value becomes negative, and a negative value becomes positive.

[Ex]

> **Example**
>
> Reverse the sign of a number: a = -a;
>
> An alternative is: a = -1 * a;

The unary plus is actually unnecessary; however, the Sun team included it to establish symmetry.[30]

[Ex]

> **Example**
>
> Minus and plus sit directly in front of the operand, and the compiler knows independently whether this is a unary or binary operator. The compiler also recognizes the following construction:
>
> int i = - - - 2 + - + 3;
>
> This expression results in the value -5. It's easier to understand the compiler if we include the operator order and mentally set the parentheses: -(-(-2)) + (-(+3)). On the other hand, the compiler doesn't recognize an expression like ---2+-+3 because the connected minus signs are interpreted as a decrement and not as a unary operator. So, the separators (spaces in this case) are significant.

2.4.4 Prefix or Postfix Increment and Decrement

Incrementing and decrementing variables is a common operation, for which the developers in the predecessor language C had also provided an operator. The practical operators ++ and -- abbreviate the program lines for increments and decrements:

```
quantity++;          // Abbreviation for quantity = quantity + 1
quantity--;          //                  quantity = quantity - 1
```

---

30 In the context of wrapper types, its use can be helpful because of the *unboxing* that takes place. More about on this topic later.

However, a local variable must be initialized upfront since a read access takes place before a write access. The ++/-- thus fulfills two tasks: Besides returning the value, it changes variables.

Note

Notice the post-increment in the name of the C++ programming language. The ++ is supposed to express that C++ is "C-with-one-up" (i.e., an improved C). Knowing about the postfix operator, however, this increase occurs only after being used—so C++ is also just C and the advantage follows later. One of the developers of Java, Bill Joy, once described Java as C++-- by which he meant C++ without the hard-to-maintain features.

Before or after?

The two operators return an expression and therefore return a value. However, subtle differences occur depending on where this operator is placed. In fact, the operator comes in two varieties: It can be placed before the variable, as in ++i (prefix notation), or after it, as in i++ (postfix notation). The prefix operator changes the variable before the expression is evaluated, while the postfix operator changes it after the expression is evaluated. In other words, if you use a prefix operator, the variable is first incremented or decremented, and then the value is supplied.

Example

Consider the following uses of prefix/postfix in an output statement:

Prefix Increment and Decrement	Postfix Increment and Decrement
| ```
int i = 10, j = 20;
System.out.println( ++i ); // 11
System.out.println( --j ); // 19
System.out.println( i ); // 11
System.out.println( j ); // 19
``` | ```
int i = 10, j = 20;
System.out.println( i++ ); // 10
System.out.println( j-- ); // 20
System.out.println( i ); // 11
System.out.println( j ); // 19
``` |

Table 2.8 Prefixes and Postfixes in an output statement

The possibility of increasing and decreasing variables can result in the following four variants:

	Prefix	Postfix
Increment	Pre-increment, ++i	Post-increment, i++
Decrement	Pre-decrement, --i	Post-decrement, i--

Table 2.9 Prefixes and Postfixes for Incrementing and Decrementing

[»]

> **Note**
>
> In Java, increment (++) and decrement (--) are allowed for all numeric data types, including float values:
>
> ```
> double price = 12;
> System.out.println( --price );              // 11.0
> price = 12.456;
> System.out.println( --price );              // 11.456
> ```

Some Oddities*

Finally, let's deal with a peculiarity of post-increment and pre-increment that shouldn't be imitated. Consider the following cases:

```
int i = 1;
i = ++i;
System.out.println( i ); // 2
int j = 1;
j = j++;
System.out.println( j ); // 1
```

The first case is not surprising because i = ++i increases the value 1 by 1, and then, 2 is assigned to the variable i. The situation with j is more sophisticated: The value of j is 1, and this value is remembered internally. Then, j++ increments the variable by 1. But the assignment sets j to the remembered value, which was 1. Thus, j = 1.

2.4.5   Assignment with Operation (Compound Assignment Operator)

In Java, assignments can be combined with numeric operators. For a binary operator (symbolically called #) in the expression a = a # (b), the *compound assignment operator* truncates the expression to a #= b.[31] Let's look at some examples.

Detailed Notation	Notation with Compound Assignment Operator
a = a + 2	a += 2
a = a - 10	a -= 10
a = a * -1	a *= -1
a = a / 10	a /= 10

Table 2.10 Detailed Variant and Short Notation with the Compound Assignment Operator

---

31 The abbreviation exists only in the program code, no compound assignment operator will exist in the bytecode.

While the prefix/postfix increment/decrement only increases/decreases by 1, compound operations in a relatively compact notation also allow larger increments/decrements, such as a+=2 or a-=10.

Example [Ex]

An assignment is always an expression, as in the following examples:

```
int a = 0;
System.out.println( a );        // 0
System.out.println( a = 2 );    // 2
System.out.println( a += 1 );   // 3
System.out.println( a );        // 3
```

Pay special attention to the automatic addition of parentheses for expressions like a *= 3 + 5, a = a * (3 + 5) and not, of course, the dot-before-dash rule a = a * 3 + 5.

Pun: A New Operator? [«]

The "sleepy operator" -=- is rarely used. Consider, for example, i -=- i. What is exactly happening here?

One-Time Evaluation for Array Access*

If the left side in the compound assignment operator is an array access (see Chapter 4, Section 4.1), the index calculation will be performed only once. This fact is important when using the prefix/postfix operator or method calls that have side effects, such as changing states like an enumerator.[32]

Example [Ex]

You can benefit from the compound assignment operator in array access because, first, the notation is short and, second, because the evaluation of the index occurs only once. Consider the following example:

```
int[] array1 = { 10, 90, 0 };
int i = 0;
array1[++i] = array1[++i] + 10;
System.out.println( Arrays.toString( array1 ) );  // [10, 10, 0]
int[] array2 = { 0, 90, 0 };
int j = 0;
array2[++j] += 10;
System.out.println( Arrays.toString( array2 ) );  // [0, 100, 0]
```

---

[32] More details are available in the JLS at *https://docs.oracle.com/javase/specs/jls/se17/html/jls-15.html#jls-15.26.2*.

2.4.6 Relational Operators and Equality Operators

Relational operators are *comparison operators* that compare expressions with each other, and the result is a truth value of the boolean type. The operators provided by Java for numerical comparisons include the following:

- Greater than (>)
- Less than (<)
- Greater than or equal to (≥)
- Less than or equal to (≤)

The special operator instanceof is for testing type relationships.

In addition, two comparison operators, called *equality operators*, are available in Java:

- Test for equality (==)
- Test for inequality (!=)

The fact that Java makes a distinction between equality operators and comparison operators is due to a slightly different precedence, but this order of precedence shouldn't concern you any further.

Like arithmetic operators, relational operators match their operands to a common type. If the types are reference types, only the comparison operators == and != are allowed. An exception is string, where + is also allowed.

Confusion Caused by == and =

The use of the relational operator == and the assignment operator = often causes problems for beginners because mathematics always knows only one equal sign for comparisons and assignments. Fortunately, the problem in Java isn't as drastic as in C(++), for example, because the types of the operators are different. The comparison operator always returns only the boolean value. However, assignments of numeric types result in a numeric type again. Thus, the following problem cannot occur:

```
int a = 10, b = 11;
boolean result1 = ( a = b );        // ☠ Compiler error
boolean result2 = ( a == b );
```

[Ex]

> **Example**
>
> For example, let's say the truth variable isExpensive should be true if the price is above 10:
>
> ```
> int price = 12;
> boolean isExpensive = price > 10;
> ```
>
> The evaluation sequence is as follows: First, the result of the comparison is calculated, and this truth value is then copied to isExpensive. Commonly, the expression on the

right is placed in parentheses, which can improve readability, as in the following example:

```
boolean isExpensive = (price > 10);
```

(Anti-)Style

In a comparison with ==, both operands can be swapped—if the two sides don't produce influencing side effects, such as state changes, for example. The result doesn't change because the comparison operator is commutative. Consequently, the following lines are semantically the same:

- `if ( worldExpoShanghaiCostInUSD == 58000000000L )`
- `if ( 58000000000L == worldExpoShanghaiCostInUSD )`

In an equality comparison between a variable and a literal, many developers with experience in the C programming language will put the constant on the left and the variable on the right. The reason for this style (called the *Yoda style*[33]) is to avoid mistakes. If an equal sign is missing in C, then `if(worldExpoShanghaiCostInUSD = 58000000000L)` can still be compiled as an assignment (although with a warning), whereas `if(58000000000L = worldExpoShanghaiCostInUSD)` cannot. The first incorrect version initializes a variable and always jumps to the `if` statement because in C every expression (here from the assignment, which is an expression) not equal to 0 is interpreted as true. This error is a logical error that the second notation prevents because it leads to a compiler error. In Java, this error can't happen unless the variable type is `boolean`, and then comparisons are also usually not written with `== false` or `== true`. In a nutshell, the Yoda notation shouldn't be used in Java.

2.4.7 Logical Operators: NOT, AND, OR, and XOR

The processing of program code is often linked to conditions. These conditions are often complex in their structure, with three operators being the most commonly used ones:

- **NOT (negation):** Turns the statement around; *true* becomes *false*, and *false* becomes *true*.

- **AND (conjunction):** Both statements must be true for the overall statement to be true.

---

33 Yoda is a character from *Star Wars* who uses a word order in his sentences that's unusual for us. Instead of building sentences with subject + verb + object (SVO), Yoda uses the object + subject + verb (OSV); object and subject are reversed, as are the operands from the example, so this expression would read "if 58000000000 equal to `worldExpoShanghaiCostInUSD` is" instead of the usual SVO reading "if `worldExpoShanghaiCostInUSD` is equal to 58000000000." In Arabic, this OSV position is common, so developers from the Arabic-speaking world might actually find this form natural. If that's not worth a study ...

- **OR (disjunction)**: One of the two statements must be true for the overall statement to be true.

> **Note**
>
> More than these three logical operators are actually not necessary to realize all possible logical operations. In mathematics, this is called *Boolean algebra*.

Logical operators are used to link truth values according to defined patterns. Logical operators operate only on `boolean` types, other types lead to compiler errors. Java provides the operators *NOT* (!), *AND* (&&), *OR* (||), and *XOR* (^). XOR is an operation that returns true only if exactly one of the two operands is `true`. If both operands are equal (i.e., either `true` or `false`), the result is `false`. XOR is also referred to as *exclusive OR*. The phrase "either ... or" captures this pretty well: It's either one or the other, but not both together. Example: "Do you want to either go to the movies or watch a DVD?" a ^ b is an abbreviation for (a && !b) || (!a && b).

boolean a	boolean b	! a	a && b	a || b	a ^ b
true	true	false	true	true	false
true	false	false	false	true	true
false	true	true	false	true	true
false	false	true	false	false	false

Table 2.11 Links of the Logical Operators NOT, AND, OR, and XOR

The logical operators always work on the `boolean` type. In Chapter 22, Section 22.1.1, we'll see that the same operations can be performed on any bit of an integer.

> **Outlook on Propositional Logic***
>
> Links of this kind are rather important in propositional logic or Boolean algebra. The terms AND, OR, and XOR, which are common for us, might also be known under different names. The AND link is called a *conjunction*, the OR link is called a *disjunction*, and the exclusive OR is called a *contravalence*. The three binary operators AND, OR, and XOR cover certain linkages, not all of which are possible. Propositional logic also features *implication* (if-then linkage) and *equivalence*.

2.4.8   Short-Circuit Operators

A logical expression only needs to be evaluated further if the final result can still change. If the result is already irrefutably fixed before the evaluation of all parts, the compiler shortens the program flow. The two operators && (AND) and || (OR) are useful for optimizing expressions:

- **AND**: If one of the two expressions is false, the expression can't be true. The result is false.

- **OR**: If at least one of the expressions is true, then the entire expression is also true.

Take, for example, `true || Math.random() > 0.5`. In this case, the method won't be called because the two operators && and || are *short-circuit operators*.[34] Thus, the characteristic of short-circuit operators is that they serve as shortcuts when the result of an expression is fixed; the remaining expressions are not evaluated.

Non-Short-Circuit Operators*

In some cases, a useful approach is for the runtime environment to evaluate all subexpressions. Perhaps, a method is intended to have side effects, such as state changes. For this reason, Java additionally provides the operators | and &, which don't work via a short-circuit and force an evaluation of all partial expressions. The result of the evaluation is the same as before.

The operation is documented by the following program, where you can easily see that a variable is incremented only when the non-short-circuit operator performs an evaluation.

```
int a = 0, b = 0, c = 0 , d = 0;
System.out.println( true || a++ == 0 );  // true, a not incremented
System.out.println( a );                 // 0
System.out.println( true | b++ == 0 );   // true, b incremented
System.out.println( b );                 // 1
System.out.println( false && c++ == 0 ); // false, c not incremented
System.out.println( c );                 // 0
System.out.println( false & d++ == 0 );  // false, d incremented
```

Listing 2.12 src/main/java/CircuitNotCircuitOperator.java, main()

No short-circuit operator can be used for XOR since both operands must always be evaluated before the result is fixed.

> **Note**
> Under certain conditions, omitting the short-circuit operator can be more performant because the compiler can avoid branches and jumps.

---

34 The JLS doesn't use this term! See also *https://docs.oracle.com/javase/specs/jls/se17/html/jls-15.html#jls-15.23.*

2.4.9   The Rank of Operators in Evaluation Order

The rule that multiplication and division operations take precedence over addition and subtraction operations is well known. Thus, the expression 1 + 2 × 3 results in 7 and not in 9.

> **Example**
>
> Even though expressions like a() + b() * c() form the product first, the evaluation order of binary operators dictates that the left operand must be evaluated first, which means that Java calls the a() method first.

Beyond addition and multiplication, a multitude of operators each have their own precedence rules.[35] For example, the multiplication operator has a higher priority and thus a different evaluation order than the plus operator.

The *ranking* of the operators (or *operator precedence*) is listed in Table 2.12, where the lambda arrow -> is omitted. The arithmetic type represents integers and floats, the integral type stands for char and integers, and the entry "primitive" stands for any primitive data types (i.e., also boolean).

Operator	Ranking	Type	Description
++, --	1	arithmetic	Increment and decrement
+, -	1	arithmetic	Unary plus and minus
~	1	integral	Bitwise complement
!	1	boolean	Logical complement
(Type)	1	any	Cast
*, /, %	2	arithmetic	Multiplication, division, and remainder
+, -	3	arithmetic	Binary operator for addition and subtraction
+	3	String	String concatenation
<<	4	integral	Shift to the left
>>	4	integral	Right shift with sign extension
>>>	4	integral	Right shift without sign extension
<, <=, >, >=	5	arithmetic	Numerical comparisons

Table 2.12 Operators with Ranking Order in Java (Operator Ranking Order)

---

35 Some (old) programming languages like APL don't follow any precedence rules. They evaluate expressions strictly from right to left, or vice versa.

Operator	Ranking	Type	Description
instanceof	5	object	Type comparison
==, !=	6	primitive	Equality/inequality of values
==, !=	6	object	Equal/inequal references
&	7	integral	Bitwise AND
&	7	boolean	Logical AND
^	8	integral	Bitwise XOR
^	8	boolean	Logical XOR
|	9	integral	Bitwise OR
|	9	boolean	Logical OR
&&	10	boolean	Logical conditional AND, short-circuit
||	11	boolean	Logical conditional OR, short-circuit
? :	12	any	Condition operator
=	13	any	Assignment
*=, /=, %=, +=, =, <<=, >>=, >>>=, &=, ^=, |=	14	arithmetic	Assignment with operation
+=	14	String	Assignment with string concatenation

Table 2.12 Operators with Ranking Order in Java (Operator Ranking Order) (Cont.)

The rule that multiplication and division operations take precedence over addition and subtraction operations is easy to remember. Also, note that the typical arithmetic operators (such as for addition and multiplication) by have a higher priority than comparison operations. But the evaluation becomes more complicated for numerous operators that may occur less frequently in the program.

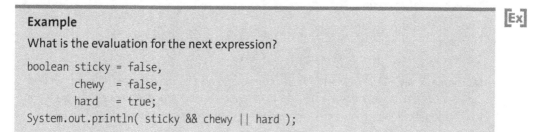

Example

What is the evaluation for the next expression?

```
boolean sticky = false,
        chewy  = false,
        hard   = true;
System.out.println( sticky && chewy || hard );
```

The result could be true or false depending on the ranking. But Table 2.11 shows that, in this example, the AND binds more strongly than the OR. Thus, the expression is read as (sticky && chewy) || hard and *not* as sticky && (chewy || hard) and thus evaluates to true.

Presumably, programmers implicitly know this order of precedence or have the table with rankings stuck to the monitor. But when reading through other people's code, it's inconvenient to need to consult the table that reveals whether the binary XOR or the binary AND binds more strongly.

[+]

Tip

All expressions that go beyond the simple rule about multiplication/division taking precedence over addition/subtraction should be placed in parentheses. Since unary operators also bind rather strongly, parentheses can be omitted in their cases.

Left and Right Associativity*

Mathematical commutativity and associativity apply to the operators + and *. In other words, operands can basically be rearranged without affecting the result. In division, you can additionally distinguish between *left and right associativity*, which is clearly illustrated by the example A / B / C. In this case, Java evaluates the expression from left to right, as (A / B) / C. Therefore, the division operator is left-associative. Parentheses are useful in this context because, if the compiler evaluates the expression to A / (B / C), this evaluation would be equivalent to A * C / B. In Java, most operators are left-associative, with some exceptions, such as assignments of the type A = B = C, which the compiler evaluates to A = (B = C).

[»]

Note

Mathematical associativity is of course endangered if calculation errors are involved due to overflows or non-representability. Consider, for example, the following code:

```
float a = -16777217F;
float b =  16777216F;
float c =  1F;
System.out.println( a + b + c );    // 1.0
System.out.println( a + (b + c) );  // 0.0
```

Mathematically, –16,777,217 + 16,777,216 equals –1, and –1 plus +1 equals 0. In the second case, –16.777.217 + (16.777.216 + 1) = –16.777.217 + 16.777.217 = 0. But Java evaluates a + b to 0 by constraining float, and thus, for 0 plus c, the output is 1 instead of 0.

2.4.10 Typecasting (Casting)

Java is a statically typed language, but the language isn't so strongly typed that it is obstructive. Thus, the compiler translates the following lines without any problem:

```
int  anInt = 1;
long long1 = 1;
long long2 = anInt;
```

Strictly speaking, a compiler could reject the last two lines if the typing is strong because the literal 1 is of type int and not 1L (i.e., long). Furthermore, in long2 = anInt, the variable anInt is of type int instead of the desired data type long.

Types of Casting

So, in practice, data types must be converted, which is referred to as *typecasting* (or *casting* for short). Java distinguishes between two types of typecasting:

- **Automatic (implicit) typecasting**
  Data of a smaller data type is automatically (implicitly) matched to the larger one. The compiler makes this adjustment independently. For this reason, our first example works with something like long2 = anInt.

- **Explicit typecasting**
  A larger type can be assigned to a smaller type, with possible loss of information.

Typecasting exists for primitive data types and for reference types. While the following paragraphs describe some adaptations for simple data types, Chapter 6, Section 6.1.4, covers type compatibility for references.

Automatic Adjustment of the Size

Values of the byte and short data types are automatically converted to the int data type during arithmetic operations. If an operand is of data type long, then all operands are extended to long. However, if short or byte is required as the result, then you must specify this data type change with an explicit typecast. Only the least significant bits of the result value are passed. Java generally performs typecasting automatically.

From Type	To Type
byte	short, int, long, float, double
short	int, long, float, double
char	int, long, float, double
int	long, float, double

Table 2.13 Implicit Typecasting

From Type	To Type
long	float, double
float	double

Table 2.13 Implicit Typecasting (Cont.)

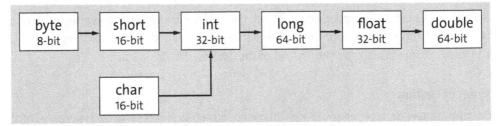

Figure 2.5 Graphical Representation of Automatic Typecasting

The adjustment is called a *widening conversion* because it automatically expands the range of values. The boolean type doesn't appear in this list since it cannot be converted to any other primitive type.

> **Note**
>
> The fact that a long can be converted to a double, which also applies to a conversion from int to float might be regarded as a bug in the Java language because information is lost during this shortening process. A double can't use the 64 bits for integers as "efficiently" as a long. Consider, for example, the following code:
>
> ```
> System.out.println( Long.MAX_VALUE ); // 9223372036854775807
> double d = Long.MAX_VALUE;
> System.out.printf( "%.0f%n", d );      // 9223372036854776000
> System.out.println( (long) d );        // 9223372036854775807
> ```
>
> However, the implicit type conversion should be entirely without loss.

> **Note**
>
> Although in terms of data type size, a char (16 bit) lies between byte (8 bit) and int (32 bit), the type doesn't appear anywhere in the right-hand column of Table 2.13 because char can't store a sign. The other data types (byte, short, int, long, float, and double) all have a sign. For this reason, the following code can't work:
>
> ```
> byte b = 'b';
> char c = b;    // ☠ Type mismatch: cannot convert from byte to char
> ```

Explicit Typecasting

The explicit conversion narrows a type, so this operation is referred to as a *narrowing conversion*. The desired type for typecasting is placed in parentheses before the data type to be converted. You must be clear that information can be lost with any explicit typecasting.

Example

When converting a float into an integer, the entire decimal part disappears, as in the following code:

```
int n = (int) 3.1415;                    // n = 3
```

Typecasting has a very high priority. Therefore, the expression may need to be parenthesized.

Example

In the following example, the assignment to n misses the mark:

```
int n = (int) 1.0315 + 2.1;
int m = (int)(1.0315 + 2.1);             // that is correct
```

```
int n = 3.1415;
    Add cast to 'int'
    Change type of 'n' to 'double'
                                    ...
                                    int n = (int) 3.1415;
                                    ...

                                    Press 'Tab' from proposal table or click for focus
```

Figure 2.6 If the Type of an Expression Doesn't Fit, Press Ctrl+1

Typecasting from Floats to Integers

Explicit typecasting from double and float to an integer type can, of course, result in a loss of precision as well as a limitation of the value range. When converting floats, Java uses rounding to zero, so it simply truncates the decimal part.

Example

The following example shows explicit typecasting from a float to an int:

```
System.out.println( (int) +12.34 );      //  12
System.out.println( (int) +67.89 );      //  67
System.out.println( (int) -12.34 );      // -12
System.out.println( (int) -67.89 );      // -67
int r = (int)(Math.random() * 5 );       // 0 <= r <= 4
```

Automatic Typecasting for Calculations with byte and short to int*

An operation of the `int` type with `int` returns the result type `int`, and `long` with `long` returns a `long`.

```
int    int1  = 1, int2 = 2;
int    int3  = int1 + int2;
long   long1 = 1, long2 = 2;
long   long3 = long1 + long2;
```

Listing 2.13 src/main/java/AutoConvert.java, main()

These lines will be compiled by the compiler as expected. And so, it seems intuitive that the same is true for the data types `short` and `byte`. The following code still works:

```
short short1 = 1, short2 = 2;
byte  byte1  = 1, byte2  = 2;
```

However, the following code does not:

```
short short3 = short1 + short2;  // ☠
// Type mismatch: cannot convert from int to short
byte  byte3 = byte1 + byte2;     // ☠
// Type mismatch: cannot convert from int to byte
```

You cannot add two `short` or `byte` numbers without explicit typecasting. The correct version of the code is the following:

```
short short3 = (short)( short1 + short2 );
byte  byte3  = (byte)( byte1 + byte2 );
```

The reason for this limitation can be found in the Java compiler. When integer expressions of type less than `int` are bound to an operator, the compiler arbitrarily adjusts the type to `int`. The addition of the two numbers in the example thus doesn't work with `short` or `byte` values, but with `int` values; internally in the bytecode it is realized in the same way.

Consequently, all integer operations with `short` and `byte` automatically lead to the result type `int`. And this leads to a problem with the assignment from the example because if the `int` type is on the right-hand side and the smaller type `byte` or `short` is on the left-hand side, the compiler must report an error. We can enforce this conversion using explicit typecasting.

We simply must accept that the compiler makes this adjustment. `int` and `int` remain `int`; `long` and `long` remain `long`. When an `int` dances with a `long`, the result type becomes `long`. If the operator works on a `short` or `byte`, the result is automatically `int`.

[+]

Tip

Small types like short and byte often lead to problems. If not intentionally used in large arrays and memory space is not an absolute criterion, int turns out to be the best choice because Java doesn't excel in particularly intuitive type conversions. For example, consider what happens with the unary minus and plus signs in the following code:

```
byte b = 0;
b = -b;              // ☠ Cannot convert from int to byte
b = +b;              // ☠ Cannot convert from int to byte
```

The compiler reports an error because the expression on the right is converted to an int by the unary operator, which is always true for the types byte, short, and char.[36]

No Typecasting between Simple Types and Reference Types

General conversions between simple types and reference types don't exist. For example, the following statements are false.

```
String s = (String) 1;      // ☠ Cannot cast from int to String
int i = (int) "1";          // ☠ Cannot cast from String to int
```

Listing 2.14 src/main/java/TypecastPrimRef.java, main() (Snippet)

[«]

Trickery with Boxing*

Sometimes, things look like typecasting when actually a technique called *autoboxing* is being used. Chapter 11, Section 11.5, goes into more detail, but for now, consider the following code:

```
Long lông = (Long) 2L;      // Alternative: Long lông = 2L;
System.out.println( (Boolean) true );
((Integer)2).toString();
```

Listing 2.15 src/main/java/TypecastPrimRef.java, main() (Snippet)

Typecasting Methods

In the case of explicit typecasting of integers, Java truncates the higher-order bytes. When converting from long (8 bytes) to int (4 bytes), the upper 4 bytes are dropped. If these four upper bytes are 0x00—we consider only the positive integers—then there's no loss of information. If we want to convert from long to int, but the loss of information should be reported, the static Math method int toIntExact(long value) can be used. With this method, an exception will be raised if the conversion entails data loss.

---

[36] *https://docs.oracle.com/javase/specs/jls/se17/html/jls-5.html#jls-5.6*

When converting floats to integers, the truncation of decimal places always occurs. The Math class has methods that can also round numbers, such as the two static Math methods int round(float) and long round(double). Chapter 21, Section 21.3.4, provides detailed information about the Math class.

Typecasting with the Compound Assignment Operator*

The compound assignment operator does a little more than resolve E1 #= E2 to E1 = (E1) # (E2), where # represents a binary operator. Interestingly, the type of E1 also comes into play because the expression E1 # E2 is set to the data type of E1 before the assignment, so the expression E1 #= E2, will become E1 = (*type of E1*)((E1) # (E2)).

[Ex]

> **Example**
>
> The compound assignment operator is supposed to add an integer to a float, as in the following example:
>
> ```
> int total = 1973;
> total += 30.2;
> ```
>
> The use of the compound assignment operator is fine because the interpreter carries out an implicit typecasting, so the meaning is total = (int)(total + 30.2). So much for Java being an intuitive and simple programming language.

2.4.11 Overloaded Plus for Strings

Although in Java nearly all operators refer to primitive data types, the plus operator is also used in another area. This overloaded plus sign was introduced in Java because the concatenation of strings is often needed. Objects of the String type can be connected to other strings and data types by the plus operator. If contiguous parts do not all take the String data type, they will automatically be converted to a string. The result type is always String.

[Ex]

> **Example**
>
> Let's put five pieces together to make a string:
>
> ```
> String s = '"' + "Extreme Salt Liquorice" + '"' + " above the age of " + 18;
> //        char  String                      char  String                  int
> System.out.println( s ); // "Extreme Salt Liquorice" above the age of 18
> ```

String concatenation is strictly from left to right and is of course not commutative like numeric addition.

If an expression consists of several parts, the evaluation order must be observed; otherwise, unwanted compositions will occur. For example, "The song: " + 90 + 9 + " Bottles of Beer" ends up with "The song: 909 Bottles of Beer" because the compiler starts the conversion to strings when it has recognized an expression as a String object. In other words, the compiler switches from "+ adds numbers" to "+ concatenates strings."

Let's look at the evaluation sequence of the plus operator with an example.

```
System.out.println( 1 + 2 );                   // 3
System.out.println( "1" + 2 + 3 );             // 123
System.out.println( 1 + 2 + "3" );             // 33
System.out.println( 1 + 2 + "3" + 4 + 5 );     // 3345
System.out.println( 1 + 2 + "3" + (4 + 5) );   // 339
System.out.println( 1 + 2 + "3" + (4 + 5) + 6 ); // 3396
```

Listing 2.16 src/main/java/PlusString.java, main()

Note

The plus operator for strings proceeds strictly from left to right and sometimes causes problems with embedded arithmetic expressions. In this context, parenthesizing can help, as in the following example:

```
int quantity = 10;
String s = "You have " + (quantity == 12 ? "a dozen" : quantity);
System.out.println( s ); // You have 10
```

If the expression around the condition operator were not parenthesized, then the plus operator would append the 1 to the string, and the > operator would occur. That operator, however, expects compatible data types, which aren't given in our case as the string would be on the left and the integer 2 on the right.

---

char Character in Concatenation

Only a string in double quotes is a string, and only then does the plus operator unfold its special effect. Java converts a single character in single quotes to an int according to the rules of typecasting in calculations, and additions are integer additions.

```
System.out.println( '0' + 2 );     // 50, because the ASCII value of '0' is 48
System.out.println( 'A' + 'a' );   // 162, because 'A'=65, 'a'=97
```

2.4.12   Operators Missing*

Some programming languages have a power operator (such as **), which doesn't exist in Java. Since no pointer operations exist in Java, the operator characters known in C(++) for referencing (&) and de-referencing (*) don't exist. Likewise, a sizeof is unnecessary since the runtime system and the compiler always know the size of classes and the primitive data types always have a fixed length.

Script languages like Perl or Python not only offer simple data types; they also define lists or associative memories, for example. Operators are automatically associated, for example, to query the data structures for values or to insert elements. In addition, many scripting languages allow you to check strings against regular expressions, such as Perl with the =~ and !~ operators.

For testing references for identity, Java provides the == operator. Some programming languages additionally provide a === operator so that with one operator a test for equality and with the other a test for identity is possible. We'll look at identity and the == operator in more detail in Chapter 3, Section 3.7.1.

2.5 Conditional Statements or Case Distinctions

Control structures are used in a programming language to execute specific program parts under certain conditions. Java provides the if and if-else statements as well as the switch statement for executing various parts of the program. Besides branching, loops are used to execute program parts multiple times. The significant part in the phrase "control structures" is the word "structure" because the structure should be obvious by just looking at it. Without loops and "high-level" control structures, only if/ thens and jumps, the logic of the program was not obvious, and the result was called *spaghetti code*. Although a general jump via goto isn't possible in Java, the language still has a special jump variant. In loops, continue and break allow defined jump destinations.

2.5.1 Branching with the if Statement

The if statement consists of the keyword if, which is necessarily followed by an expression of the type boolean in parentheses. This expression is followed by a statement, which is often a block statement.

For example, let's use an if statement to test if a user has guessed a random number correctly:

```
public class WhatsYourNumber {

  public static void main( String[] args ) {
    int number = (int) (Math.random() * 5 + 1);

    System.out.println( "What number do I have in mind between 1 and 5?" );
    int guess = new java.util.Scanner( System.in ).nextInt();

    if ( number == guess ) {
      System.out.println( "Good guess!" );
    }
```

```
      System.out.println( "Restart the program and guess again!" );
   }
}
```

Listing 2.17 src/main/java/WhatsYourNumber.java

The processing of the output statement depends on the expression in if, in the following ways:

- If the result of the expression is true (number == guess evaluates to true), the following statement (i.e., the console output with "Good guess!") is executed.
- If the result of the expression is false (number == guess evaluates to false), the statement is skipped, and the program continues with the first statement after the if statement.

Comparison of Programming Languages

In Java, the test expression for the condition of the if statement must always be of the boolean type. The same applies to loop conditions. Other programming languages such as JavaScript, C(++), or PHP evaluate a numeric expression to true if the result of the expression is not 0. Thus, if (10) is also valid in those languages, which would correspond to if (true) in Java. In PHP or JavaScript, an empty string or array is also "falsy."

---

if Queries and Blocks

After the if and the condition, the compiler expects a statement. A {} block is a special statement, as in our example. If only one statement is to be executed depending on the condition, the statement can be set directly without a block. The following variants are therefore identical:

Explicit Parenthesizing of the Statement	Without Parenthesizing the Statement

`if ( number == guess ) {`
`  System.out.println( "Super!" );`
`}`
	`if ( number == guess )`
	`  System.out.println( "Super!" );`

A program error occurs when the {} block is missing, but several statements still need to be evaluated depending on the condition. Let's look at an example: An if statement is supposed to test whether the guessed number was equal to the random number, and then if it was, assign a new random number to the number variable and return an output. First, let's consider the semantically incorrect variant:

```
if ( number == guess )
  number = (int)(Math.random()*5 + 1); System.out.println( "Good guess!" );
```

The implementation is semantically incorrect since the output always appears regardless of the test. The compiler assigns only the next statement to the case distinction, even if the appearance suggests otherwise.[37] This is a great risk for programmers who want to visually create relationships that don't exist in reality. The compiler interprets the statements in the following context, where the indentation reflects the actual execution:

```
if ( number == guess )
  number = (int) (Math.random() * 5 + 1);
System.out.println( "Good guess!" );
```

For our desired logic of executing both statements together depending on the condition, you'll need to use a block, as in the following example:

```
if ( number == guess ) {
  number = (int) (Math.random() * 5 + 1);
  System.out.println( "Good guess!" );
}
```

Basically, putting statements in blocks—even if there is only one statement in the block—is therefore not wrong.

[+]

Tip

Indentations don't change the semantics of the program! Indentations can only severely disrupt comprehension. For the program to be correct, you must use a block and put the statements together. Developers should consistently use indentation to clarify dependencies, and furthermore, only one statement should exist in a line.

Compound Conditions

The previous queries were quite simple, but much more complex conditions will occur in practice. Commonly used logical operators include && (AND), || (OR), and ! (NOT).

For example, to test whether

- a guessed number is either equal to the random number guess OR
- a certain number of trials has already been exceeded (trials greater than 10),

then we would write the compound condition in the following way:

```
if ( number == guess || trials > 10 )
```

If the logically linked expressions are more complex, the individual conditions should be placed in parentheses to support readability since not everyone immediately has access to the precedence rules for the operators found in Table 2.11.

---

37 In the Python programming language, indentation determines affiliation.

2.5.2   Choosing the Alternative with an if-else Statement

If the condition is met, the `if` branch is run through. But how can it be programmed that, in the reverse case (i.e., if the condition isn't true), program code is also executed?

One solution is to write a second `if` statement with a negated condition:

```
if ( number == guess )
  System.out.println( "Good guess!" );
if ( number != guess )
  System.out.printf( "Well, not true, I thought %s!", number );
```

However, a better solution is available: In addition to the one-sided alternative, a two-sided approach can be used. The optional keyword `else` with the appended statement causes the alternative to be executed if the `if` test is false.

If the user in our little game doesn't guess the number correctly, we want to output the random number to the user.

```
public class GuessTheNumber {

  public static void main( String[] args ) {
    int number = (int) (Math.random() * 5 + 1);

    System.out.println( "What number do I have in mind between 1 and 5?" );
    int guess = new java.util.Scanner( System.in ).nextInt();

    if ( number == guess )
      System.out.println( "Good guess!" );
    else
      System.out.printf( "Well, not true, I thought %d!", number );
  }
}
```

Listing 2.18 src/main/java/GuessTheNumber.java

If the expression `number == guess` is true, the first statement is executed; otherwise, the second statement is executed. In this way, you can assure that a statement will be executed in every case.

The Dangling else Problem

For branches with `else`, a well-known problem is called the *dangling-else problem*. Which statement does the `else` belong to?

```
if ( expression1 )
  if ( expression2 )
    statement1;
```

```
else
  statement2;
```

The indentation suggests that `else` is the alternative to the first `if` statement, which is, however, incorrect. The semantics of Java (and also almost all other programming languages) is defined in such a way that `else` belongs to the innermost `if`. Therefore, the only programming tip for this case is to parenthesize the `if` statements:

```
if ( expression1 ) {
  if ( expression2 ) {
    statement1;
  }
}
else {
  statement2;
}
```

These parentheses prevent confusion from arising in the first place. If `else` always belongs to the innermost `if` but this is not what you want, use curly brackets as shown earlier or add an empty statement in the `else` branch:

```
if ( x >= 0 )
  if ( x != 0 )
    System.out.println( "x really greater than zero" );
  else
    ; // x is equal to zero
else
  System.out.println( "x really less than zero" );
```

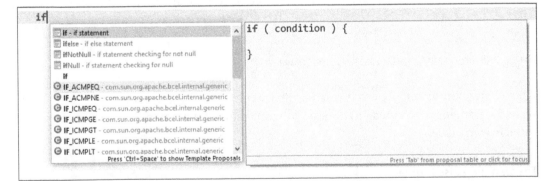

Figure 2.7 Pressing Ctrl+Space after the if Allows You to Create an if Statement with a Block

The Evil Semicolon

At this point, note that a novice programmer will probably write a semicolon after the closing parenthesis of the `if` statement. However, doing so results in a completely different execution sequence. Consider the following example:

```
int age = 29;
if ( age < 0 ) ;                // ☠ logical error
  System.out.println( "Alright, still in the womb" );
if ( age > 150 ) ;              // ☠ logical error
  System.out.println( "I see, a new Moses" );
```

The semicolon causes the empty statement to be executed depending on the condition and always produces the output "Alright, still in the womb" and "I see, a new Moses" regardless of the content of the age variable. This result is certainly not our intention. The example should be regarded as a caution against writing only more than one statement in each line; the empty statement with the semicolon is a statement in itself.

If an if statement is followed by two statements that aren't combined by a block statement, then the one following else statement is reported as an error because the associated if branch is missing because the if branch ends after the first statement without else. Consider the following example:

```
int age = 29;
if ( age < 0 )
  ;
System.out.println( "Alright, still in the womb" );
else if ( age > 150 ) ;        // ☠ Compiler error message: 'else' without 'if'
  System.out.println( "I see, a new Moses" );
```

Multiple Branching or Nested Alternatives

if statements for program guidance occur quite often in programs, even more often than for checking a variable for a certain value. For this purpose, if and if-else statements are often nested (cascaded). If a variable matches a value, then a statement is executed; otherwise, the variable is tested with a different value, and so on.

[Ex]

Example

Cascaded if statements help you assign, for example, a days variable matching the month (preassigned month variable) and the information if the year is a leap year (preassigned boolean variable isLeapYear):

```
int month = 2; boolean isLeapYear = false; int days;
if ( month == 4 )
  days = 30;
else if ( month == 6 )
  days = 30;
else if ( month == 9 )
  days = 30;
else if ( month == 11 )
  days = 30;
```

```
else if ( month == 2 )
  if ( isLeapYear )        // Special treatment in case of leap year
    days = 29;
  else
    days = 28;
else
  days = 31;
```

In this small program, semantic indentations are used; actually, the statements would move further and further to the right with each else.

The indented branches are also called *accumulated if statements* (or an *if cascade*) because each else statement in turn contains other if statements until all queries have been made.

Let's apply this principle to our number guessing game. Perhaps, we want to give the user a hint whether the entered number was smaller or larger than the target number.

```java
public class GuessTheNumber2 {

  public static void main( String[] args ) {
    int number = (int) (Math.random() * 5 + 1);

    System.out.println( "What number do I have in mind between 1 and 5?" );
    int guess = new java.util.Scanner( System.in ).nextInt();

    if ( number == guess )
      System.out.println( "Good guess!" );
    else if ( number > guess )
      System.out.println( "Nope, my number is larger than yours!" );
    else // number < guess
      System.out.println( "Nope, my number is smaller than yours!" );
  }
}
```

Listing 2.19 src/main/java/GuessTheNumber2.java

2.5.3   The Condition Operator

In Java, a single operator can use three operands, called the *conditional operator*. This operator allows you to make the value of an expression dependent on a condition without the use of an if statement. Operands are separated by ? and : and use the following syntax:

Condition **?** *Expression if condition is true* **:** *Expression if condition is false*

Example [Ex]

Determining the maximum is a good way to illustrate the use of the condition operator:

```
max = ( a > b ) ? a : b;
```

The value of the max variable is set depending on the condition a > b. The expression corresponds to the following if statement:

```
if ( a > b ) max = a; else max = b;
```

Three expressions occur in the conditional operator, which makes it a ternary operator—from the Latin *ternarius* ("consisting of three").[38] The first expression (in our case, the comparison a > b) must be of the boolean type. If the condition is met, then the variable is assigned the value of the second expression; otherwise, the max variable will be assigned the value of the third expression.

The condition operator can be used if the second and third operands are of a numeric type, Boolean type, or reference type. Calling methods that return void isn't allowed. So, it's not a compact syntax to simply call any two methods depending on a condition without if because there's always a result with the condition operator. We can do all sorts of things with it, such as outputting it directly.

Example [Ex]

To output the maximum of a and b directly, you would use the following code:

```
System.out.println( ( a > b ) ? a : b );
```

With if-else, this case is only possible with temporary variables or with two println(...) statements.

Examples

- The maximum or minimum of two numbers is given by the expressions a > b ? a : b or a < b ? a : b, respectively.
- The absolute value of a number returns x >= 0 ? x : -x.[39]
- An expression is supposed to convert a number n, which lies between 0 and 15, into a hexadecimal number: (char)((n < 10) ? ('0' + n) : ('a' − 10 + n)).

---

38 The conditional operator is the only ternary operator in Java. In other programming languages there are more: Python, for example, allows array slicing with array[start : stop], where array, start, stop are three operands. Python goes even further and array[start : stop : step] is a quaternary operator. So in communication we should always say "conditional operator," and not simply "ternary operator," because that may be ambiguous.

39 Because of two's complement, arithmetic can be problematic in ways that can't be avoided. Chapter 21, Section 21.3.2, covers this topic again in the context of Math.abs(...).

Nested Application of the Condition Operator*

Using the condition operator can quickly lead to unreadable programs, and therefore, you should use it with care.[40] You must use sufficient parenthesizing to make sure that the expressions are also evaluated in the intended order. Unlike most operators, the condition operator is right-associative (the assignment is also right-associative).

The following two expressions are therefore equivalent:

```
b1 ? a1 : b2 ? a2 : a3
b1 ? a1 : ( b2 ? a2 : a3 )
```

[Ex]

Example

To write an expression that returns –1, 0, or 1 for a number n depending on the sign, you can use a nested condition operator, for example, in the following code:

```
int sign = (n < 0) ? -1 : (n > 0) ? 1 : 0;
```

However, line breaks after the colons make sense and clarify the nested conditional expressions:

```
int sign = (n < 0) ? -1 :
           (n > 0) ? 1 :
              0;
```

The Condition Operator Is Not an L-Value*

The condition operator returns an expression as a result, which can be then used on the right side of an assignment. Since the resulting expression occurs on the right, it's called the *R-Value*. It can't be used on the left-hand side of an assignment (L-Value) in such a way that it selects a variable to which a value is assigned.[41]

[Ex]

Example

The following application of the condition operator isn't possible in Java:

```
boolean up = false, down = false;
int direction = 12;
((direction >= 0) ? up : down) = true; // 💀 Compiler error
```

However, the condition operator can select a reference, and then a method call is valid.

---

40 In C(++), unintentional multiple evaluation in macros can lead to hard-to-find errors. There are no macros in Java, so this can't happen to us.

41 In C(++), this problem can be solved via *((condition) ? &a : &b) = expression; by using pointers.

2.5.4 The Switch Statement Provides an Alternative

A shorthand form for specially constructed, accumulated if statements is provided by switch. In a switch block, a number of different jump targets are each marked with case. The switch statement allows the selection of the following elements:

- Integers
- Wrapper types (for more information, refer to Chapter 11, Section 11.5)
- Enumerations (enum)
- Strings

Internal Affairs [«]

The bytecode contains only one switch variant for integers. For strings, enumerations, and wrapper objects, the compiler applies tricks to reduce them to integer-based switch constructions.

switch for Integers (and Also chars)

A simple calculator for four binary operators can be quickly implemented with switch. We'll use the charAt(0) method to access the first character from a string input to get a char.

```java
public class Calculator {

  public static void main( String[] args ) {
    double x = new java.util.Scanner( System.in ).nextDouble();
    char operator = new java.util.Scanner( System.in ).nextLine().charAt( 0 );
    double y = new java.util.Scanner( System.in ).nextDouble();

    switch ( operator ) {
      case '+':
        System.out.println( x + y );
        break;
      case '-':
        System.out.println( x - y );
        break;
      case '*':
        System.out.println( x * y );
        break;
      case '/':
        System.out.println( x / y );
        break;
    }
```

```
    }
}
```

Listing 2.20 src/main/java/Calculator.java

The runtime environment searches for a *jump label* (also called a *jump target*), which is a constant that matches the expression specified in switch. If a hit is made, all statements following case are executed until an (optional) break terminates the execution. (Without break, the execution continues automatically in the next case block; more on this topic later in this section, when we discuss fall-through without a break.) If no constant of a case block matches the switch expression, no statements in the switch block will be executed for the time being. The case constants must be different; otherwise, a compiler error will arise.

The switch statement has some limitations, such as the following:

- The JVM can execute switch only on expressions of the int data type. Elements of data type byte, char, and short are thus allowed since the compiler automatically adjusts the type to int. Likewise, the enumerations and the wrapper objects Character, Byte, Short, and Integer are possible since Java automatically takes the values. More on this topic will follow in Chapter 11, Section 11.5. The data types boolean, long, float, and double can't be used. Although enumerations and strings are also possible as switch expression types, internally, they are mapped to integers. Apart from that, general objects aren't allowed.

- The values listed after case must be constant. Dynamic expressions, such as returns from method calls, aren't possible.

- No range specifications are possible, which would be useful for ages, for example, to define the ranges 0-18, 19-60, 61-99. The only solution in this context would be accumulated if statements.

> **[»]**
>
> **Note**
>
> The specification for case must be constant but may well come from a constant (final variable):
>
> ```
> final char PLUS = '+';
> switch ( operator ) {
>     case PLUS:
>     ...
> }
> ```

Covering Everything Else with default

If a program part should be processed only when no match with any other case constant is made, you can use the special jump label default. For example, in the case of an unknown operator, if your program should output an error message, you would write the following code:

```
switch ( operator ) {
  case '+':
    System.out.println( x + y );
    break;
  case '-':
    System.out.println( x - y );
    break;
  case '*':
    System.out.println( x * y );
    break;
  case '/':
    System.out.println( x / y );
    break;
  default:
    System.err.println( "Unknown operator " + operator );
}
```

The use of default is to detect incorrectly entered operators because the statements after default are always executed if no case constant was equal to the switch expression. default can also appear between the case blocks, but this is less clear and thus not recommended for general applications. Thus, the default program part would be processed even if a case part preceding the default has no break. Only one default is allowed.

Note

Of course, the compiler can't know whether all the values you use are covered by a case block. A default can help to find errors faster if a number arrives at switch for which the program doesn't store any operations. If you don't use default, an unhandled value will otherwise remain without consequences.

With enumerations, the situation is different again because, in this case, the quantity is countable. Code analysis can determine if as many case blocks exist as constants. IntelliJ, for example, can report on this metric.

switch Has Fall-Through without a Break

Up to now, we've put a break statement in the last line. Without a break, all subsequent statements would be executed after a match. They would thus run into a new section until a break or the end of switch has been reached. This scenario is comparable to a toy ball falling through from top to bottom and this thus referred to as *fall-through*. A common programming error is to forget the break, which is why an intended fall-through should always be specified as a comment.

This fall-through enables you to always execute the same instruction for different values. The following example implements a small parser for simple date values. The parser should handle three different dates, for example:

- "18 12": Year in short form and month
- "2018 12": Year and month
- "12": Month only (The current year should be applied implicitly.)

```java
public class SimpleYearMonthParser {

  public static void main( String[] args ) {

    String date = "17 12";

    int month = 0, year = 0;
    java.util.Scanner scanner = new java.util.Scanner( date );

    switch ( date.length() ) {
      case 5:  // YY MM
        year = 2000;
        // Fall-through
      case 7: // YYYY MM
        year += scanner.nextInt();
        // Fall-through
      case 2: // MM
        month = scanner.nextInt();
        if ( year == 0 )
          year = java.time.Year.now().getValue();
        break;
      default :
        System.err.println( "Wrong format" );
    }

    System.out.println( "month=" + month + ", year=" + year );
  }
}
```

Listing 2.21 src/main/java/SimpleYearMonthParser.java

In this example, a case statement determines the structure via the length. If the length is 5, the year is shortened, and we initialize the year with 2000 to read the year in the following step with the help of the scanner. We also would come to this step directly if the length of the input had been 7 (i.e., if the year had been 4 digits long). This section of code clarifies the year portion, but we still need to parse the months. If we come directly over a string of length 2, and no year is set before, we'll retrieve the current year via java.time.Year.now().getValue(); otherwise, we won't overwrite the variable.

What should the reader take away from this example? Actually, nothing but shake your head because the solution is hard to understand. Fall-through is really only useful for summarizing multiple case blocks.

Language Comparison*

[«]

Although a missing break can lead to annoying programming errors, the developers of Java adopted this behavior from its syntactic predecessor, C. An interesting alternative solution would be to turn the behavior around exactly and explicitly require the fall-through, for example, with a keyword. An interesting development in this regard is available: Java inherits this property from C(++), and C(++) in turn inherits fall-through from the programming language B. One of the "inventors" of B is Ken Thompson, who now works at Google and is involved in the new programming language Go. In Go, developers must explicitly use a fallthrough statement when forwarding one case block to the next. The same applies to the new Swift programming language; in this case, too, you can find fallthrough statements. Even in C++, since the C++17 standard, the standard [[fallthrough]] attribute[42] instructs a compiler not to display a warning if fall-through occurs.

Stack Case Labels

If several case blocks are placed one below the other to map areas, we call them *stack case labels*. Let's say a variable hour stands for an hour in the day, and we want to determine if it's now afternoon rest time, evening rest time, or working time. Consider the following example:

```
int hour = 12;

switch ( hour ) {
  // Night rest from 10 p.m. to 6 a.m.
  case 10:
  case 11:
  case 12: case 0:
  case 1:
  case 2:
  case 3:
  case 4:
  case 5:
```

---

42 *http://en.cppreference.com/w/cpp/language/attributes*

```
      System.out.println( "Night rest" );
      break;

  // Afternoon rest from 1 to 3 p.m.
  case 1:
  case 2:
      System.out.println( "Afternoon rest" );
      break;

  default :
      System.out.println( "Work" );
      break;
}
```

Listing 2.22 src/main/java/RestOrWork.java (Snippet)

case blocks can be summarized even more compactly and separated with commas. For instance, the example can be rewritten in the following way:

```
int hour = 12;
switch ( hour ) {
  // Night rest from 10 p.m. to 6 a.m.
  case 10, 11, 12, 0, 1, 2, 3, 4, 5:
      System.out.println( "Night rest" );
      break;

  // Afternoon rest from 1 to 3 p.m.
  case 1, 2:
      System.out.println( "Afternoon rest" );
      break;

  default:
      System.out.println( "Work" );
      break;
}
```

Single or multiple range specifications, such as 22 - 24, or 22 - 24, 0 - 5, are not permitted in Java!

switch on Strings

Besides the option to use switch on integers, a switch statement on string objects is also possible.

```
String input = javax.swing.JOptionPane.showInputDialog( "Input" );

switch ( input.toLowerCase() ) {
  case "cookies":
    System.out.println( "I like cookies." );
    break;
  case "cake":
    System.out.println( "I like cake." );
    break;
  case "chocolate":
  case "liquorice":
    System.out.println( "Hm. Yummy too." );
    break;
  default:
    System.out.printf( "Can you really eat %s?", input );
    break;
}
```

Listing 2.23 src/main/java/SweetsLover.java, main()

Although direct string comparisons are possible, regular expression checks unfortunately aren't, something that's provided in particular by scripting languages like Ruby or Perl.

As with switch with integers, the strings in the String-case branch can come from final variables. For example, if string COOKIES = "cookies"; is predefined, case COOKIES is allowed.

2.5.5   Switch Expressions

The switch keyword can be used in Java for statements and expressions. In total, switch can appear in four forms.

Statement/Expression	Java Version	Syntax	Fall-Through	Complete Coverage
Statement	1.0	:	Yes	No
Statement	14	->	No	No
Expression	14	:	Yes	Yes
Expression	14	->	No	Yes

Table 2.14 Four Types of Switch

We've already looked at the first type extensively, so let's look at the other variants now.

Simplified switch Statement, No Fall-Through, No Full Coverage

In the simplified switch statement, no colon exists after the label or default, but instead, you would use a ->. This use of -> has nothing to do with lambda expressions, even if the symbols are the same. The arrow is either followed by an expression, a block in curly brackets, or a throw statement that throws an exception. Implicitly, a break terminates each branch, so no more fall-through occurs.

[Ex]

> **Example**
>
> A variable operator is assigned with an operator character. A switch statement with arrow notation is to give an output for + and -.
>
> ```
> String operator = "+";
> switch ( operator ) {
>   case "+" -> System.out.println( "Plus" );
>   case "-" -> { String minus = "Minus"; System.out.println( minus ); }
> }
> ```

Because blocks must always be set for multiple statements, a local variable also doesn't step out of scope. A default can be set but isn't mandatory. The switch doesn't need to cover every possibility, which doesn't work for int-numbers and strings anyway.

[Ex]

> **Example**
>
> A variable operator is assigned with an operator character. A switch statement with arrow notation should always provide an output.
>
> ```
> String operator = "+";
> switch ( operator ) {
>   case "+" -> System.out.println( "Plus" );
>   case "-" -> System.out.println( "Minus" );
>   default  -> System.out.println( "Unknown operator" );
> }
> ```

With simplified switch statements, multiple labels that have the same handling are possible. Commas separate the labels.

[Ex]

> **Example**
>
> The operators * and × are treated in the same way:
>
> ```
> String operator = "+";
> switch ( operator ) {
>   case "+"       -> System.out.println( "Plus" );
>   case "*", "x" -> System.out.println( "Multiplied by" );
> }
> ```

Switch Expressions, No Fall-Through, Full Coverage

Traditionally, case distinctions are found with switch as a statement, and statements return nothing.

Example

A string writtenOperator will be initialized directly with an expression determined by the switch expression.

```
String operator = "+";
String writtenOperator = (switch ( operator ) {
  case "+" -> "Plus";
  case "-" -> "Minus";
  default  -> "Unknown operator";
} ).toUpperCase();
System.out.println( writtenOperator );
```

Expressions must always return results, and consequently, switch must always make a path to a value. The usual case is default as shown, but in some special cases (e.g., with enumerations), the compiler can check that all possibilities have been covered.

Example

In the case of enumerations, such as the days of the week in the DayOfWeek enum, the compiler can check for complete coverage:

```
DayOfWeek today = LocalDate.now().getDayOfWeek();
System.out.println( switch ( today ) {
  case MONDAY, TUESDAY, WEDNESDAY, THURSDAY, FRIDAY -> "Work";
  case SATURDAY, SUNDAY -> "Party";
} );
```

If no simple expression exists to the right of the arrow, but instead you write a block, this block must also return a result. For this purpose, the new keyword yield is used, followed by an expression. A block must have a yield or throw an unchecked exception.

Example

In a block, yield returns an expression for the switch expression:

```
String operator = "+";
System.out.println( switch ( operator ) {
  case "+" -> "Plus";
  case "-" -> { String minus = "Minus"; yield minus; }
  default  -> throw new IllegalArgumentException( "Unknown operator" );
} );
```

Switch Expression with the Colon Syntax, with Fall-Through, Full Coverage

The colon syntax can also be used as an expression. With a colon, fall-through is also possible again. A yield is mandatory; otherwise, an unchecked exception must be triggered. The syntax contains a source of error with fall-through, so this variant is perhaps the worst.

Example

Traditional colon switch syntax as an expression with yield.

```
String operator = "+";
System.out.println( switch ( operator ) {
  case "+" : yield "Plus";
  case "*" : System.out.println( "Asterisk" );
  case "×" : yield "Multiplied by";
  default  : throw new IllegalArgumentException( "Unknown operator" );
} );
```

2.6 Always the Same with Loops

Loops are used to process certain statements over and over again. A loop includes a *loop condition* and the loop's *body*. The loop condition, a Boolean expression, decides under which condition the repetition is executed. Depending on the loop condition, the body can be executed several times. For this purpose, the loop condition is checked in each loop pass. The result decides whether the body is traversed another time (true) or the loop is terminated (false). Java provides four types of loops.

Loop Type	Syntax
while loop	**while** (*condition*) *statement*
do-while loop	**do** *statement* **while** (*condition*);
Simple for loop	**for** (*initialization*; *condition*; *for-statement*) *statement*
extended for loop (also referred to as *for-each loop*)	**for** (*variable type* variable : *collection*) *statement*

Table 2.15 Four Loop Types in Java

The first three types of loops will be described in the following sections, while the extended for loop is necessary only for collections and therefore is described later in the context of arrays (see Chapter 4, Section 4.2) and dynamic data structures (see Chapter 18, Section 18.1.6).

2.6.1   The while Loop

The while loop is a *rejecting loop* that checks the loop condition before each loop entry. If a condition is true, the program executes the body; otherwise, it terminates the loop. As with if, the type of the condition for while loops must be boolean.[43]

Before each loop pass, the expression is re-evaluated, and if the result is true, the body will be executed. The loop is finished when the result is false. If the condition isn't true even before the first entry into the body, the body won't be traversed at all.

Example [Ex]

In the following example, an integer should be divided by 2 until the division results in 0:

```java
int number = 1234;
while ( number > 0 ) {
  number /= 2;
  System.out.println( number );
}
```

Listing 2.24 src/main/java/WhileLoop.java, main()

Note [«]

If everything interesting is performed within the loop header, a statement must still follow. This scenario is the appropriate use of the empty statement ; or the empty block {}.

```java
while ( Files.notExists( Paths.get( "dump.bin" ) ) )
  ;
```

If the file doesn't exist, notExists(...) returns true, the loop continues and is immediately followed by a new existence test. If the file exists, the return is false, which initiates the end of the loop. A quick tip at this point: Instead of going directly to the next file test, you should implement a short delay.

Endless Loops

If the condition of a while loop is always true, then the loop is endless. As a consequence, the loop is repeated endlessly, as in the following example:

```java
public class WhileTrue {
  public static void main( String[] args ) {
    while ( true ) {
```

---

43 We addressed earlier the issue with if. In C(++), you could write while (i), which would be while (i != 0) in Java.

```
        // over and over again
    }
  }
}
```

Listing 2.25 src/main/java/WhileTrue.java

Endless loops usually mean the end for a program. But help is available! You can escape from this endless loop with break, which we'll describe in more detail in Section 2.6.5. Strictly speaking, however, uncaught exceptions or System.exit(int) also terminate a program.

Figure 2.8 Console View with the Red Button for Terminating Programs

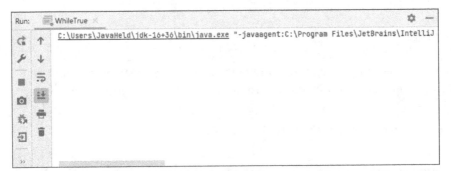

Figure 2.9 In the Development Environment, Programs Can Be Terminated from the Outside. IntelliJ Provides a Square Red Button to Terminate Any Running Program after Activation.

Fun

If a variable is decremented in a loop, the special "operator" --> can be used. For example, if the numbers from 12 to 1 are to be listed, this "goes-down-to operator" can be used:

```
int month = 12;
while ( month  -->  0 )
  System.out.println( month + 1 );
```

What's behind this?[44]

---

44 This approach is just a slightly little different way of writing month -- > 0, where the postfix decrement is used.

2.6.2 The do-while Loop

This loop type is an assuming loop because do-while doesn't check the loop condition until after each loop pass. Before it comes to the first test, the body has already been run through once. The loop type helps perfectly with our number guessing game because there is at least one pass with an input, and only if the user enters a wrong number should the body be traversed again.

```java
public class TheFinalGuess {

  public static void main( String[] args ) {
    int number = (int) (Math.random() * 5 + 1);
    int guess;

    do {
      System.out.println( "What number do I have in mind between 1 and 5?" );
      guess = new java.util.Scanner( System.in ).nextInt();

      if ( number == guess )
        System.out.println( "Good guess!" );
      else if ( number > guess )
        System.out.println( "Nope, my number is larger than yours!" );
      else // number < guess
        System.out.println( "Nope, my number is smaller than yours!" );
    }
    while ( number != guess );
  }
}
```

Listing 2.26 src/main/java/TheFinalGuess.java

Make sure you pay attention to the semicolon after the while statement. If the condition returns a true, the body will be executed again.[45] Otherwise, the loop is terminated, and the program continues with the next statement after the loop. One interesting detail is that you now must declare the guess variable outside the do-while block because a variable declared in the loop block isn't visible to the retest in while. Also, the compiler knows that the do-while block is run at least once, and guess will be initialized in any case; accessing uninitialized variables is forbidden and considered an error by the compiler.

---

45 This scenario is different in Pascal and Delphi where a loop of the repeat ... until condition type (the counterpart of Java's do-while) runs until the condition becomes true, and then terminates. If the condition isn't fulfilled (i.e., false), the process continues with a repetition. In Java, if the condition isn't met, the end of the loop passes; so, Java is just the opposite of Pascal or Delphi. However, the loop of type while condition ... do in Pascal and Delphi corresponds exactly to a while loop in Java.

Equivalence of a while and a do-while loop*

The do-while loop is used less often than the while loop. Nevertheless, the two can be merged. Let's look at the first case by replacing a while loop with a do-while loop, as in the following syntax:

```
while ( expression )
  Statement
```

Let's look at what's happening: Depending on the expression, the body will be executed. Since a test comes first, the do-while loop would already be one block execution further. Thus, in a first step, you'll query whether the condition is true or not via an if statement. If yes, then the program code will run in a do-while loop. The equivalent do-while loop uses the following syntax:

```
if ( expression )
  do
    Statement
  while ( expression ) ;
```

Let's consider the second case by replacing the do-while loop with a while loop, as in the following syntax:

```
do
  Statement
while ( expression ) ;
```

Since the statements are executed first and then the test, for the while variant, you'll simply write the expressions before the test. In this way, you can ensure that they are processed at least once:

```
Statement
while ( expression )
  Statement
```

2.6.3   The for Loop

The for loop is a special variant of a while loop and is typically used for counting. Just like while loops, for loops are dismissive: The body won't be executed until the condition is true.

> **Example**
>
> You can output the numbers from 1 to 10 on the screen.
>
> ```
> for ( int i = 1; i <= 10; i++ )             // i is loop counter
>   System.out.println( i );
> ```
>
> **Listing 2.27** src/main/java/ForLoop.java, main()

A closer look at the loop shows various segments:

- **Initialization of the loop**
  The first part of the for loop is an expression like i = 1, which is executed exactly once before the loop is executed. The expression initializes the variable i, but the result then is discarded. If an error occurs in the evaluation, the processing is interrupted, and the loop can't be executed completely. The first part can declare and initialize local variables. This count variable is then no longer valid outside of the block.[46] No local variable should share the same name. The first part can also be empty.

- **Loop test/loop condition**
  The middle part, such as i <= 10, is tested before passing through the loop body (i.e., before each loop entry). If the expression returns false, the loop won't be executed, or it won't be executed again and will be terminated instead. The result must be of type boolean, as in a while loop. The middle test part can be missing in the for loop, which makes it like an implicit true.

- **Loop increment through a for-statement**
  The last part, such as i++, is always executed at the end of each loop pass, but before the next loop entry. The result isn't used any further. If the condition of the test returns true, then the next time the body is entered, the changed value is in the body. The last part may also be missing.

Looking at our earlier example, the following evaluation sequence is performed:

1. Initialize i with 1.

2. Test whether i <= 10 is true.

3. If the result is true, then execute the block; otherwise, the end of the loop has been reached.

4. Increase i by 1.

5. Go to step 2.

Loop Counter

If the for loop is used to run through a variable, the *loop counter* is called either a *count variable* or *run variable*.

The initialization and the correct query at the end are important. The loop can run through once too often, leading to incorrect results. This kind of error in a query is also called an *off-by-one error*. For example, if instead of <= you use the operator <, then the

---

46 Unlike C++, the behavior is clearly defined, and no back and forth occurs. In C++, compiler builders once implemented the variant so that the variable was valid only in the block, others interpreted the language specification so that it remained valid outside. The current C++ definition now dictates that the variable is no longer valid outside the block. However, since old program code still exists, many compiler builders have included an option to determine the behavior of local variables.

loop runs only to 9. Another name for the loop error is *fencepost-error*. Consider the number of posts needed for a 100-meter fence so that all posts are spaced apart by 10 meters: Do you need 9, 10, or 11 fence posts?

When to Use a for and When to Use a while Loop?

Since the while and for loops are similar, you may wonder when to use one over the other. Unfortunately, the compact for loop can tempt you to overload. Some programmers like to pack everything into the loop head, and the body is just an empty statement. This bad style should be avoided.

for loops should be used whenever a variable is increased by a constant amount. If no loop variable occurs in the loop that's incremented or decremented, a while loop should be used. A do-while loop should be used if the termination condition can't be evaluated until the end of a loop pass. Also, the for loop should be used where all three expressions in the loop head refer to the same variable. Disjointed expressions in the loop header should be avoided.

Using write access to the loop variable in the body is a bad idea if the variable also modified in the head at the same time—this approach is hard to comprehend and can easily lead to endless loops.

The for loop isn't fixed to a particular type, even though using for loops for incrementing suggests the implicit type int. The initialization part can preassign anything, whether int, double, or a reference variable. The condition can test anything imaginable, but the result must be a boolean.

A for Loop Doesn't Have to Be a Counting Loop

The for loop shows compactly all essential information in the loop head but isn't limited to counting up values. Rather, a good option is a variable whose state is changed in each iteration and with the termination somehow dependent on the variable.

An Endless Loop with for

Since all three expressions in the head of the for loop are optional, they can be omitted. If no loop condition is specified in the for loop, the expression is always true. For instance, the notation

```
for ( ; ; );
```

is equivalent to

```
for ( ; true; );
```

The separating semicolons in for are required. No initialization and no evaluation of the update expression follows, which in turn is semantically equivalent to the following statement:

```
while ( true );
```

All three variables declare an endless loop.

> **Tip**
>
> The *Motor Industry Software Reliability Association (MISRA)* guidelines for the C programming language recommend the notation for(;;) for endless loops.

[+]

Nested Loops

Loops, especially for for loops, can be nested. Syntactically, this nesting is logical since any statements can reside within the loop body. To output five lines of asterisks, with one extra asterisk appearing in each subsequent line, you can write the following code.

```java
for ( int i = 1; i <= 5; i++ ) {
  for ( int j = 1; j <= i; j++ )
    System.out.print( '*' );
  System.out.println();
}
```

Listing 2.28 src/main/java/Superstar.java, main()

A special element in this example is the dependence of the loop counter j on i. The code produces the following output:

```
*
**
***
****
*****
```

The parent loop is called the *outer* loop, and the child is the *inner* loop. In our example, the outer loop with i counts the rows, and the inner loop outputs the asterisks to a line, so it's responsible for the column.

Since loops can be nested arbitrarily deep, you must pay special attention to the runtime. The inner loops are always executed with their passes as often as the outer loop is passed through.

Positioning for Loops and Expression Statements behind Each Other with a Comma*

A comma can be inserted in the first and last part of a for loop to place several expression statements one after the other. In this way, you can declare either several variables of the same type, as we've already done, or you can write several expressions next to each other, but no arbitrary statements or even other loops.

Using the variables i and j, you can build a small multiplication table in the following way:

```
for ( int i = 1, j = 9; i <= j; i++, j-- )
  System.out.printf( "%d * %d = %d%n", i, j, i*j );
```

The following output should result:

```
1 * 9 = 9
2 * 8 = 16
3 * 7 = 21
4 * 6 = 24
5 * 5 = 25
```

Another example with a more complex condition would be initializing starting value for the variables x and y before the loop is run. Then, we want the program to increment x and y and execute the loop as long as x or y remains less than 10:

```
double x, y;
for ( x = Math.random(), y = Math.random(), x++, y++;
      x < 10 || y < 10;
      x += Math.random(), y += Math.random() ) {
  // …
}
```

[+]

Tip

Complicated for loops become more readable by placing the three for parts on separate lines.

2.6.4   Loop Conditions and Comparisons with ==*

Loop termination conditions can look quite different from each other. In counting, the loop termination condition is often the comparison to a final value. Often at this point, an absolute comparison is written with ==, which can become problematic for two reasons.

[»]

Question

The following program counts to 10, right?

```
int input = new java.util.Scanner( System.in ).nextInt();
for ( int i = input; i != 11; i++ )
  System.out.println( i );
```

If the value of the variable i is smaller than 11, no problem occurs when counting because then the loop ends at 11 at the latest, and the loop terminates. However, if the value comes from an unknown source and is genuinely greater than 11, the condition is equally true, and the loop body will run through for quite a long time—to be precise, until you start again at 0 due to an overflow and then also end up at 11 on termination. Our intention was certainly different. The loop should only count as long as i is less than 11 and not simply not equal to 11. Therefore, the following code is a better fit:

```java
int input = new java.util.Scanner( System.in ).nextInt();
for ( int i = input; i < 11; i++ )  // Counts always only up to 10 or not at all
  System.out.println( i );
```

Now, the interpreter doesn't run on endlessly for numbers greater than 11 but instead stops the loop immediately without a pass.

Calculation Inaccuracies Aren't the Programmer's Friend

The second problem arises with floats. Demanding real comparisons can be quite problematic, as in the following example:

```java
double d = 0.0;
while ( d != 1.0 ) {            // Warning! Problematic comparison!
  d += 0.1;
  System.out.println( d );
}
```

If you let the program segment run, you'll see the loop quickly overshoots the target, as in the following output:

```
0.1
0.2
0.30000000000000004
0.4
0.5
0.6
0.7
0.7999999999999999
0.8999999999999999
0.9999999999999999
1.0999999999999999
1.2
1.3
```

And so on to infinity.

The reason for this problem is that the number 0.1 can't be exactly represented, and each addition operation leads to an accumulation of small inaccuracies.

For float values, therefore, a good idea is to always work with the relational operators <, >, <=, and >=.

A second possibility (besides the true less than/greater than comparison) is to define an allowed deviation (a *delta*). Mathematicians denote the deviation of two values with the Greek lowercase letter epsilon. To compare two floats while considering a tolerance in an equality comparison, you can simply write the following code:

```
if ( Math.abs(x - y) <= epsilon )
  ...
```

The epsilon is the allowed deviation. `Math.abs(x)` calculates the absolute value of a number x.

How to Write Range Specifications*

For range specifications of the type a >= 23 && a <= 42, we recommend including the lower value in the comparison, but not the value for the upper limit (that is, including lower limits and excluding upper limits). For our example, where a is to remain in the interval, the following is better: a >= 23 && a < 43. This recommendation applies to both floats and integers. The reasoning behind this approach is plausible when you consider the following points:

- The size of the interval is the difference of the limits.
- If the interval is empty, the interval limits are the same.
- The left lower limit is never greater than the right upper limit.

[»]

> **Note**
>
> The standard library also uses this convention throughout, for example, in the case of `substring(...)` for `string` objects or `subList(...)` for lists or when specifying array index values.

Our suggestions can be adopted for normal loops with comparisons. Thus, a loop with ten passes looks better when written in the following way:

```
for ( i = 0; i < 10; i++ )          // Better
```

In contrast, the following code, although semantically equivalent, is not recommended:

```
for ( i = 0; i <= 9; i++ )          // Not so good
for ( i = 1; i <= 10; i++ )         // Not so good either
```

2.6.5   Loop Termination with break and back to Test with continue

A break statement within a for, while, or do-while loop terminates the loop pass, and processing continues at the first statement after the loop. The fact that an endless loop can be terminated via break is useful when a condition occurs that determines the end of the loop. Let's apply this principle to our number guessing game next.

```java
public class GuessWhat {

  public static void main( String[] args ) {
    int number = (int) (Math.random() * 5 + 1);

    while ( true ) {
      System.out.println( "What number do I have in mind between 1 and 5?" );
      int guess = new java.util.Scanner( System.in ).nextInt();

      if ( number == guess ) {
        System.out.println( "Good guess!" );
        break;                      // End of loop
      }
      else if ( number > guess )
        System.out.println( "Nope, my number is larger than yours!" );
      else if ( number < guess )
        System.out.println( "Nope, my number is smaller than yours!" );
    }
  }
}
```

Listing 2.29 src/main/java/GuessWhat.java

The case distinction determines whether the user must guess again in another loop pass or whether the guess was correct; then, the break statement will end the loop.

> **Tip**   [+]
>
> Since a small break quickly disappears in the program text, but its significance is great, a small note should be placed on this statement.

Flags or break

break can be used easily to break out of a loop prematurely without using flags:

```java
boolean endFlag = false;
do {
  if ( condition ) {
    …
```

```
    endFlag = true;
  }
} while ( OtherCondition && ! endFlag );
```

Instead, you should simply follow this syntax:

```
do {
  if ( condition ) {
    …
    break;
  }
} while ( OtherCondition );
```

The second alternative is no longer semantically identical with the first one if there are additional statements in the loop body after the if statement.

New Run with continue

Within a for, while, or do-while loop, you can use a continue statement, which doesn't end the loop like break but instead returns to the loop head. After evaluating the continuation for statement, the next step is to check again whether the loop should be run through further. A frequent use of continue is in loops, which repeatedly fetch and test values in the body until they are suitable for further processing.

Let's look again at our guessing game example. So far, the user has been told to enter only numbers between 1 and 5 (inclusive), but if he enters -1234567, nothing different occurs. Let's change this by prepending a test that returns to the input prompt if the value range is wrong. In this case, continue helps you get back to the beginning of the block, which starts with a new prompt.

```
public class GuessRight {

  public static void main( String[] args ) {
    int number = (int) (Math.random() * 5 + 1);
    while ( true ) {
      System.out.println( "What number do I have in mind between 1 and 5?" );
      int guess = new java.util.Scanner( System.in ).nextInt();

      if ( guess < 1 || guess > 5 ) {
        System.out.println( "Only numbers between 1 and 5!" );
        continue;
      }

      if ( number == guess ) {
        System.out.println( "Good guess!" );
        break;                       // End of loop
```

```
      }
      else if ( number > guess )
        System.out.println( "Nope, my number is larger than yours!" );
      else if ( number < guess )
        System.out.println( "Nope, my number is smaller than yours!" );
    }
  }
}
```

Listing 2.30 src/main/java/GuessRight.java

However, some program sections are more readable without continue. A continue at the end of an if query can be made much clearer by an else part. The following syntax is a bad example:

```
while ( condition ) {        // Sweetened by continue
  if ( OtherCondition ) {
    // Code, Code, Code
    continue;
  }
  // More beautiful code
}
```

A much clearer example would follow this syntax:

```
while ( condition ) {
  if ( OtherCondition ) {
    // Code, Code, Code
```

```
  }
  else {
    // More beautiful code
  }
}
```

2.6.6   break and continue with Labels*

Although the keyword goto appears in the list of reserved words, Java doesn't allow arbitrary jumps, and goto lacks functionality. However, in Java, statements (or a block, which represents a special statement) can be labeled. One reason for introducing labels is that break or continue can be ambiguous. Consider the following points:

- If you have two nested loops, a break in the inner loop would only terminate the inner loop. However, what if the outer loop also should be terminated? The same applies to continue if the outer loop is to be continued, but not the inner loop.

- Not only do loops use the break keyword, but also the switch statement. What if a loop contains a switch statement, but the local case branch shouldn't be terminated via break, while the entire loop should be terminated with break?

Java language designers decided to introduce labels so that break and continue can either leave or pass through the labeled statement again. Used incorrectly, you might get spaghetti code as from the world of unstructured programming languages. But as responsible Java programmers, you shouldn't misuse this feature, of course.

break with a Label for loops

Let's look at a first example with a *label*, in which break not only breaks out of the inner devil's loop, but out of the outer one as well. Labels are defined by ending an identifier with a colon and placing it before a statement, thus labeling the statement like a loop.

```
heaven:
while ( true ) {
  hell:
  while ( true )
    break /* continue */ heaven;
  // System.out.println( "hell" );
}
System.out.println( "heaven" );
```

Listing 2.31 src/main/java/BreakAndContinueWithLabels.java, main()

A break without a label in the inner while loop only terminates the inner repetition, and a continue would lead to the continuation of this inner while loop. Our example shows the use of a label after the keywords break and continue. The example doesn't use the hell label, and the line with the output "hell" is deliberately commented out, because it isn't accessible and would otherwise lead to a compiler error. The fact that the statement isn't reachable is clear because, with break heaven, the program would never get to the next statement after the inner loop, and thus a console output wouldn't be reachable.

If we put break hell in the inner loop instead of break heaven, things change:

```
heaven:
while ( true ) {
  hell:
  while ( true )
    break /* continue */ hell;
  System.out.println( "hell" );
}
// System.out.println( "heaven" );
```

In this scenario, the "heaven" output is not attainable and must be commented out. The break hell in the inner loop acts like a simple break without a label, and the running program continuously results in screen outputs of the text "hell."

Note [«]

Labels can be defined before all statements (including before blocks). In our first case, we've put the label before the while(true) loop. Interestingly, a break with a label can exit not only a loop and case, but also a exit a simple block, as in the following:

```
label:
{
  ...
  break label;
  ...
}
```

Thus, the break label corresponds to a goto to the end of the block. A break cannot be replaced by continue because continue needs a loop in any case. Furthermore, a normal break without a label wouldn't be valid and couldn't leave the block.

Puzzle [«]

Why does the compiler interpret the following without complaint?

```
class WithoutComplaint {
  static void main( String[] args ) {
    http://www.tutego.de/
    System.out.print( "IT training institute" );
  }
}
```

Listing 2.32 src/main/java/WithoutComplaint.java

Terminating switch with break and a Label

Since break has multiple functions in the Java language, ambiguity occurs when break is used in the case block of a switch statement.

In the following example, a loop passes through a string. The access to a character in the string is realized by the string object method charAt(int); the length of a string is returned by length(). C, G, A, and T are the allowed characters in the string. To create statistics about the number of individual letters, a switch statement increments the correct variables c, g, a, and t by 1 each time a hit occurs. If an unallowed character exists in the string, the loop will be terminated. This scenario is where the label takes center stage.

```java
// cytosine [C], guanine [G], adenine [A] or thymine [T]
String dnaBases = "CGCAGTTCTTCGGXAC";
int a = 0, g = 0, c = 0, t = 0;

loop:
for ( int i = 0; i < dnaBases.length(); i++ ) {
  switch ( dnaBases.charAt( i ) ) {
    case 'A', 'a':
      a++;
      break;
    case 'C', 'c':
      c++;
      break;
    case 'G', 'g':
      g++;
      break;
    case 'T', 't':
      t++;
      break;
    default:
      System.err.println( "Unknown nucleotide " + dnaBases.charAt( i ) );
      break loop;
  }
}

System.out.printf( "Total: A=%d, G=%d, C=%d, T=%d%n", a, g, c, t );
```

Listing 2.33 src/main/java/SwitchBreak.java, main()

[»] **Puzzle**

If the following code were contained in the main(…) method, would the compiler interpret it? What would be the output? Pay close attention to the spaces!

```
int val = 2;
switch ( val ) {
  case 1:
    System.out.println( 1 );
  case2:
    System.out.println( 2 );
  default:
    System.out.println( 3 );
}
```

2.7 Methods of a Class

In OOP, objects interact with each other at runtime and send messages to each other as requests to do something. These requests result in a method call containing statements that are then executed. In Java, the offer of an object with regard to what it "can do" is expressed by means of methods.

You've already learned about several methods with the frequently used `println(...)` in our examples. This method is a method of the `out` object. Another program section now sends a message to the `out` object to execute the `println(...)` method. In the following descriptions, we won't look further into the active part of the message sending process; we'll simply say that a method is "called."

Three reasons exist for declaring methods:

- Recurring program parts shouldn't be programmed again and again but instead provided in one place. Changes to functionality can then be made more easily if the code is grouped together locally.

- Complex programs are broken down into small subprograms so that the complexity of the program is broken down as well. This organization makes it easier to see the control flow.

- The operations of a class, that is, the offerings of an object, are the reasons for method declarations in an OOP language. However, other reasons also speak in favor of methods, which we'll describe in this section.

2.7.1 Components of a Method

A method is composed of several components: the *method head* (*head* for short) and the *method body* (*body* for short). The head consists of a *return type* (also called a *result type*), the *method name*, and an optional *parameter list*.

Let's consider the well-known static main(String[]) method in the following example:

```
public static void main( String[] args ) {
  System.out.println( "What happened to you? Did you run here?" );
}
```

This code has the following components:

- The static method doesn't return anything, so the "return type" is void. At this point, note that void is not a type in Java; void simply means "free," "the void," or "cavity."
- The method name is main.
- The parameter list is String[] args.
- The body consists only of the screen output.

[»]
Naming Conventions

Like variable names, method names start with lowercase letters and are written in mixed case. Identifiers should not be named like keywords.[47]

The Signature of a Method

The method name and the parameter list determine the *signature* of a method; the return type and exceptions are not part of a method signature.[48] The parameter list is described by the number, order, and types of parameters. Only one method of the same signature can exist in a class; otherwise, the compiler will report an error. Since the methods void main(String[] args) and String main(String[] arguments) have the same signature (main, String[])—the names of the parameters don't matter—they can't be declared together in one class. (Later in this section, we'll show you how subclasses do allow certain special cases.)

[»]
Duck Typing

Scripting languages in particular (such as JavaScript, Python, or Ruby) allow for method declarations without a parameter type, so methods can be called with different argument types, as in the following code:

```
printSum( a, b ) print a + b
```

---

47 This naming mistake can lead to surprises with some libraries (i.e., JUnit). In Java 1.4, for example, the assert keyword was introduced, which JUnit chose as the method name. Countless lines of program code then had to be converted from assert() to assertTrue().

48 To be precise, type parameters are also part of the signature. We'll cover type parameters in Chapter 11.

Due to the unspecified parameter type, the method can be called with integers, floats, or strings. The runtime environment is tasked with recognizing this dynamic type and with executing the addition on the concrete type. This approach isn't possible in Java where the type must be known to the compiler. Programming languages that check the presence of methods or operators on the type only at runtime use what's called *duck typing*. The term comes from a poem by James Whitcomb Riley: "When I see a bird that walks like a duck and swims like a duck and quacks like a duck, I call that bird a duck." Applied to our case, if the parameters a and b support the operation "add," then the values can be added.

2.7.2 Signature Description in the Java Application Programming Interface Documentation

In the Java API documentation, all methods with their return values and parameters (including possible exceptions) are exactly defined. Let's look at the documentation of the static method max(int, int) of the Math class.

---

max

```
public static int max(int a,
                      int b)
```

Returns the greater of two int values. That is, the result is the argument closer to the value of Integer.MAX_VALUE. If the arguments have the same value, the result is that same value.

Parameters:

a - an argument.

b - another argument.

Returns:

the larger of a and b.

Figure 2.10 The Online API Documentation for Math.max()

The help information shown in Figure 2.10 provides details about the complete signature of the method. The return type is an int, the static method is called max, and it expects exactly two int numbers. We've concealed the keywords public and static (which are called *modifiers*). The keyword public specifies the visibility and who can use this method. Let's look a bit more closely at these keywords:

- In the case of public, anyone can use this method. The opposite is private in which only the object itself can use this method. This distinction is useful when methods are intended to reduce complexity and solve sub-problems. Private methods are usually not displayed in the help because they are an implementation detail.

- The static keyword indicates that the method can be used with the class name, that is, no instance of an object is required.

Other Modifiers and Exceptions*

Many methods that have other modifiers and an extended signature. Another example from the API documentation is shown in Figure 2.11. The visibility of this method is protected, which means that only derived classes and classes in the same directory (the same package) can use this method. An additional modifier is final, which in inheritance doesn't allow the subclass to overwrite the method and give it new program code. Finally, the throws keyword is followed by an exception. This exception tells you something about errors that might be caused by the method and what the programmer must take care of. In connection with inheritance, we'll discuss protected and final later. Chapter 9 is devoted to exceptions. Based on "Since: 1.1" in the documentation, we can note that the method has existed since Java 1.1. The information can also be bound to the class.

---

implAccept

```
protected final void implAccept(Socket s)
                    throws IOException
```

Subclasses of ServerSocket use this method to override accept() to return their own subclass of socket. So a FooServerSocket will typically hand this method a newly created, unbound, FooSocket. On return from implAccept the FooSocket will be connected to a client.

The behavior of this method is unspecified when invoked with a socket that is not newly created and unbound. Any socket options set on the given socket prior to invoking this method may or may not be preserved when the connection is accepted. It may not be possible to accept a connection when this socket has a SocketImpl of one type and the given socket has a SocketImpl of a completely different type.

Implementation Note:

An instance of this class using a system-default SocketImpl can accept a connection with a Socket using a SocketImpl of the same type: IOException is thrown if the Socket is using a custom SocketImpl. An instance of this class using a custom SocketImpl cannot accept a connection with a Socket using a system-default SocketImpl.

Parameters:

s - the Socket

Throws:

IllegalBlockingModeException - if this socket has an associated channel, and the channel is in non-blocking mode

IOException - if an I/O error occurs when waiting for a connection, or if it is not possible for this socket to accept a connection with the given socket

Since:

1.1

Figure 2.11 Extract from the API Documentation for the java.net.ServerSocket Class

2.7.3 Calling a Method

Since a method is always associated with a class or object, the owner of a method must be specified when the method is called. In the case of System.out.println(), println() is a method of the out object. If we form the maximum of two floats via the Math.max(a, b) call, then max(...) is a (static) method of the Math class. For the caller, who is offering this method, and who is also receiving this message, is apparent. What the caller does not see is how the method works. The method call branches to the program code, but the caller doesn't know what happens since only the result is used.

The called method is identified by its name. The parameter list is enclosed by a pair of parentheses. These parentheses must be included even if the method doesn't contain any parameters at all. The number and types of the passed values must match the declaration of the method. For instance, `Math.max(...)` requires exactly two parameters, and if the number is correct or the types are not correct, a compiler error will occur.[49]

Wanting Something versus Nothing, Giving Nothing versus Something

A method like `System.out.println()` returns nothing as the result of a "calculation." The static methods `Math.max(...)` and `Math.random()` are different since they do return results. In summary, four different types of methods exist.

Method	Without Return Value	With Return Value
Without parameter	`System.out.println()`	`Math.random()`
With parameter	`System.out.println(4)`	`Math.max(12, 33)`

Table 2.16 Methods with Return Values

The following sections describe these four cases in the following order:

- Methods without parameters and without returns
- Methods with parameters and without returns
- Methods without parameters and with returns
- Methods with parameters and with returns

2.7.4 Declaring Methods without Parameters

The simplest method has no return value and no parameters. The program code is enclosed in curly brackets behind the head and thus forms the body of the method. If the method returns nothing, then `void` is written before the method name. If the method returns something, the type of the return is written instead of `void`.

Let's write a static method with no return and no parameters that outputs something to the screen next.

```java
class FriendlyGreeter {
  static void greet() {
    System.out.println( "Good morning, and in case I don't see ya, "
                      + "good afternoon, good evening, and good night!" );
  }

  public static void main( String[] args ) {
    greet();
  }
}
```

Listing 2.34 src/main/java/FriendlyGreeter.java

---

49 In contrast, with JavaScript, you can pass more arguments, and no error will occur.

Custom methods can, of course, be named like library methods because they belong to different classes. So, instead of greet(), we could also have used the name println(), but we probably shouldn't do this to avoid confusion.

[+]

> **Tip**
>
> Assigning a method name is not so easy. For example, let's write a method that copies a file. Spontaneously, two words come to mind that want to be combined into a method name: "file" and "copy." But in which combination? Should it be copy-File(...) or fileCopy(...)? When this conflict arises, the verb should lead the action, so we'd choose copyFile(...). Method names should always begin with the activity word, followed by the "what," the object.

Pressing ⟨Ctrl⟩ while clicking on an identifier makes IntelliJ jump to the declaration; so, the custom code becomes a navigable web page.

2.7.5   Static Methods (Class Methods)

So far, we've only worked with static methods (also called *class methods*). The special thing about static methods is that they aren't bound to an object and can therefore always be called without an explicitly created object. Thus, static methods belong to classes in themselves and aren't associated with special objects. You can see this independence from the call of our static method greet()—no object is required to which the method is bound. This approach is possible because the method is declared as static, and within the class, all methods can be called simply by their names without any qualifier.

Static methods must be explicitly identified with the static keyword. If the static modifier is missing, you can declare an object method with it, but you can only call the method if you've previously created an object.

But we'll save this topic for Chapter 3. However, the error message should not scare you. If you omit static from the greet() declaration and call the static main(...) method now (without building an object), then the no-longer static method greet() returns the compiler error "Cannot make a static reference to the non-static method greet() from the type FriendlyGreeter."

If the static method is declared in the same class as the caller—in our case, main(...) and greet() in FriendlyGreeter—the call is unique with the name of the method alone. However, if the method declaration and method call are in different classes, the caller must name the class; you encountered this potential problem before, with calls like Math.random(...).

Declaration	Usage

```class FriendlyGreeter {```
 ```static void greet() {```
 ``` System.out.println("Hey!");```
 ```}```
 ```}```
	```class FriendlyGreeterCaller {```
	 ``` public static void main(String[] args)```
	 ``` {```
	 ``` FriendlyGreeter.greet();```
	 ``` }```
	 ```}```

2.7.6 Parameters, Arguments, and Value Transfers

Values can be passed to a method that are then included in the method's operation. For example, the println(2001) method has been passed a value, thus becoming a *parameterized method*.

Example

[Ex]

Consider the following method declaration printMax(double, double), which prints the larger of the two passed values on the screen:

```
static void printMax( double a, double b ) {
  if ( a > b )
    System.out.println( a );
  else
    System.out.println( b );
}
```

Formal parameters are used to address the values passed to methods. From our static method printMax(double a, double b), a and b are the formal parameters of the parameter list. Each parameter is listed separated by a comma, and the type must be specified for each parameter; a shortened form in the otherwise usual variable declaration (such as double a, b) is not possible. Each parameter variable of a method declaration must of course have a different name; otherwise, no restrictions exist.

Arguments (Current Parameters)

The caller of the method must specify an argument for each parameter. The parameters declared in the method head are ultimately local variables in the method body. When called, the runtime environment initializes the local variables with the arguments passed to the method. If we call our parameterized method with printMax(10, 20), for example, the literals 10 and 20 are *arguments* (current parameters of the method). When the method is called, the runtime environment places the arguments in the local variables, thus copying the value 10 to the parameter variable a and copying 20 to the parameter variable b. Within the method body, thus, access to the values passed from outside is available.

The end of the method block automatically means the end for the parameter variables. The caller also doesn't know what the internal parameter variables are called. A type conversion from int to double is done automatically by the compiler in our case. The arguments must match in type, of course, and the known rules for typecasting apply.

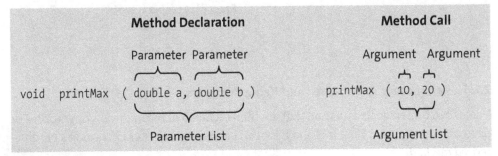

Figure 2.12 The Terms "Parameter" and "Argument"

Value Transfer via Call by Value

When a method is called, Java has a specific procedure in which each argument is passed to a parameter variable. This technique is called a *parameter passing mechanism*. Many programming languages have a wide range of confusing options. Java knows only a simple mechanism of *value passing* (*call by value*, sometimes also called *copy by value*). An example of method invocation makes this clear:

```
int i = 2;
printMax( 10, i );          // 10 goes in a and 2 goes in b
```

Our called method printMax(double a, double b) first gets 10 copied into the variable a and then gets the contents of the variable i (2 in our example) copied into b. In no case does the caller pass information about the memory area of i to the method. The moment the method is called, the runtime environment queries the assignment of i and uses it to initialize the parameter variable b. If printMax(...) changes its variable b internally, only the local variable b is changed (thus overwriting 2).

However, the change in the method has no consequence for the external i, which remains at 2. This type of call is also called *copy by value*. Only the value is passed (copied), and no reference is made to the variable.[50]

Evaluation of the Argument List from Left to Right*

In a method call, all arguments are evaluated first and then passed to the method. Thus, sub-methods can be evaluated, and assignments can be made. Errors then lead to an aborted method call. All expressions are evaluated up to the error.

---

50 In contrast, references in C++ are passed.

Question

What is the output of the following lines?

```
int i = 1;
System.out.println( Math.max( i++, --i ) );
```

2.7.7   Ending Methods Prematurely with return

If a method runs to the end, then the method is finished, and it goes back to the caller. However, depending on a condition, a method can be terminated before the end of the flow with a return statement. This approach is useful for methods that want to exit prematurely depending on parameters. Imagine that a hidden return automatically exists before the end of the method. An unnecessary return at the end of the method body should thus not be written.

Example

A static method printSqrt(double) is supposed to print the root of a number on the screen. For numbers less than zero, a message appears, and the method is exited. Otherwise, the root calculation is performed.

```
static void printSqrt( double d ) {
  if ( d < 0 ) {
    System.out.println( "There is no true square root of a negative number!"
);
    return;
  }
  System.out.println( Math.sqrt( d ) );
}
```

Listing 2.35 src/main/java/PrintSqrt.java, printSqrt()

Of course, the implementation would also have been possible with an else statement.

2.7.8   Unreachable Source Code for Methods*

If source code follows directly after a return statement, the code is not reachable in the sense of not executable. return always terminates the method and returns to the caller. If source code still exists after the return, the compiler will report an error, as in the following example:

```
public static void main( String[] args ) {
  int i = 1;
  return;
```

```
    i = 2;                  // ☠ Unreachable code!
}
```

Attempting to reduce a statement to the only most necessary code (the semicolon) can sometimes lead to amusing results, as in the following example:

```
public static void main( String[] args ) {
  ;return;;              // ☠
}
```

This example contains two null statements: one before the return and one after it. But the second semicolon after the return is not allowed because it represents an unreachable statement.

[+]

Tip

In some cases, a return in the middle of a method is desirable. For example, if a method should not be traversed entirely in the test phase, but instead should be terminated in the middle, you can use a statement such as if (true) return;.

2.7.9 Methods with Returns

For methods to return values to the caller, two things must be true:

- A method declaration gets a return type not equal to void.

- A return statement returns a value.

[Ex]

Example

Let's look at a static method that returns random numbers from 0 to less than 100:

```
static double largerRandom() {
  return Math.random() * 100;
}
```

If the expression is missing and only a simple return is available, the compiler will report a program error that an expression is needed or the method should not return anything.

[+]

Tip

Although some programmers like to parenthesize every expression, doing so isn't necessary. Parentheses are only intended to make complex expressions more readable. Parenthesized expressions otherwise only remind you of a method call, and this possibility of confusion should not exist with return values.

What Other Programming Languages Can Do*

Although multiple parameters can be declared, only one value at most can be returned to the caller. In the Python programming language, multiple values can also be returned via what's called a *tuple*. In Java, a tuple can be replicated by using a returned collection.

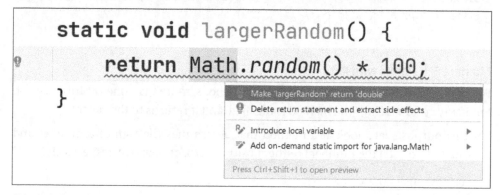

```
static void largerRandom() {
    return Math.random() * 100;
}
```

Make 'largerRandom' return 'double'
Delete return statement and extract side effects
Introduce local variable   ▶
Add on-demand static import for 'java.lang.Math'   ▶
Press Ctrl+Shift+I to open preview

Figure 2.13 IntelliJ Detects If a Return Type Is Missing and Suggests a Suitable Type When Pressing Ctrl+Enter

Returns Depending on Input

Static methods like Math.max(...) return a result depending on the arguments. For the caller, the implementation doesn't matter; it just abstracts and uses the method instead of an expression.

Example

A static method can calculate the mean value and return it, as in the following example:

```
static double avg( double x, double y ) {
  return (x + y) / 2;
}
```

Using Returns*

The return value doesn't need to be used at the call position. If your method calculates the average of two numbers, not using the return value is a programming error. This problem frequently arises with String methods, which don't modify String objects, but instead return new String objects.

[Ex] **Example**

Ignoring the return for a String method is a semantic program error, not a syntactic compiler error. Consider the following example:

```
String s = "Ja";
System.out.println( s.concat( "va" ) ); // Java
s.concat( "va" );                        // Return ignored, error!
System.out.println( s );                 // Ja
```

Multiple Exit Points with Returns

For methods with a return value, as for void methods, more than one return can exist. But if any return is "hit," the method is finished, and it returns to the caller.

For this purpose, let's look at a method that determines the sign of a number and returns +1, 0, or –1 if the number is either positive, zero, or negative, respectively:

```
static int sign( int value ) {
  if ( value < 0 )
    return -1;
  else if ( value > 0 )
    return +1;
  else
    return 0;
}
```

On closer inspection, notice how, in no case, can another test be performed when a return terminates the method. The program code can be rewritten because, in if statements with further else-if alternatives and return, the semantics is the same as though else-if is replaced by a simple if. An equivalent sign(int) method can be used in the following way:

```
static int sign( int value ) {
  if ( value < 0 )
    return -1;
  if ( value > 0 )
    return +1;
  return 0;
}
```

Compact Bodies with Boolean Returns

If the return is a truth value, the implementation can often be truncated if an expression is evaluated beforehand that directly determines the return value. Certain constructs can be written more compactly.

Construct with Case Distinction	Truncation

if (condition)
  return true;
else
  return false;
	return condition;

if (condition)
  return false;
else
  return true;
	return ! condition;

return condition ? true : false;	return condition;
return condition ? false : true;	return ! condition;

Table 2.17 Code Optimizations

Cheating without Return Doesn't Work

Every conceivable program flow of a method with a return must end with a return value;. The compiler has a keen eye and notices when a program path doesn't lead to a return completion.

Example

The static method isLastBitSet(int) is supposed to return 0 if the last bit of an integer is not set. It should return 1 if the last bit is set. This bit test is performed using the AND operator, as in the following example:

```
static int isLastBitSet( int i ) {      // ☠ Compiler error
  switch ( i & 1 ) {
    case 0: return 0;
    case 1: return 1;
  }
}
```

Although a bit can only be set or not set—there's no possible state in between—the method can't be interpreted, and you'll see an error like "This method must return a result of type int."

Although something might be obvious to the user, a compiler might opt out when it doesn't understand the meaning of some code. The same would be true for a week method that returns a day of the week as a string with an integer argument (0 to 6). With the cases 0 = Monday to 6 = Sunday, in our eyes then, a weekday cannot be 99. But the compiler doesn't understand the method and also doesn't know that the allowable value range. This problem can easily be fixed with a default.

[Ex]

Example

The static method posOrNeg(double) is supposed to return a string with the information whether the passed float is positive or negative, as in the following example:

```
static String posOrNeg( double d ) {   // ☠ Compiler error
  if ( d >= 0 )
    return "pos";

  if ( d < 0 )
    return "neg";
}
```

Surprisingly, this program code is also buggy because, although it obviously returns the appropriate string for positive or negative numbers, one case is not covered by this method. Again, the compiler can't recognize that the second expression should be a negation of the first. But additionally, in Java, some special values aren't numbers; the number d can also be a NaN, for instance, the square root of a negative number. This particular value isn't checked by posOrNeg(double). As a solution for the simple case without NaN, you can simply make an else out of the second if and the query; omit the statement; or write it compactly with the condition operator in the method body: return d >= 0 ? "pos" : "neg";.

Methods that return an error value such as 1 are often implemented in such a way that the error value is always automatically returned at the end. Then, the method is exited in the middle if the end is suitable.

Case Distinctions with the Exclusion Principle*

A method named between(a, x, b) is supposed to test whether a value x lies between a (lower limit) and b (upper limit). With methods of this type, you must pay attention to and document whether the test should be performed on genuinely less than (<) or on less than or equal to (<=). In this example, we also want to consider at equality between the two values.

Two solutions for the implementation exist, with most programmers leaning towards the first solution. The first solution is to use a mathematical equation. We'd like to write a <= x <= b, but this construction is not allowed in Java.[51] Thus, we must make an AND comparison; for instance, if a <= x && x <= b, then return true. In terms of a complete method, you would write the following code:

```
static boolean between( int a, int x, int b ) {
  return a <= x && x <= b;
}
```

---

51 In contrast, this construction is possible in the Python programming language.

The second implementation shows that the problem can be solved by the exclusion principle even without an AND comparison, as in the following example:

```
static boolean between( int a, int x, int b ) {
  if ( x < a )
    return false;

  if ( x <= b )
    return true;

  return false;
}
```

With nested queries, the code can be rewritten in the following way:

```
static boolean between( int a, int x, int b ) {
  if ( a <= x )
    if ( x <= b )
      return true;

  return false;
}
```

Whether programmers use the variant with the AND operator or the nested if is generally a matter of taste, but the most readable solution should win out, which in this case would be the one with the AND.

2.7.10 Overloading Methods

A method is characterized by *return value, name, parameters,* and possibly the *exception errors* it may throw. Java allows you to keep the name of the method and to use other parameters. A method is called *overloaded* if that method appears several times under the same name but with different parameter lists. This overloading is possible in two ways:

- A method has the same name but differs in the *number of parameters.*
- A method has the same name but has distinguishable *parameter types* for the compiler.

The first case is widely used. The name of a method should describe its task but not specifically mention the types of parameters it uses. This approach is common in other languages, but not in Java. For example, let's look at the static method max(...) provided in the Math class. This method is declared with the parameter types int, long, float, and double, which is much nicer than, say, the separate methods maxInt(...) and maxDouble(...).

[Ex]

Example

You could declare the static method avg(...) for two and three parameters in the following way:

```
static double avg( int x, int y ) {
  return (x + y) / 2.;
}
static double avg( double x, double y ) {
  return (x + y) / 2;
}
static double avg( double x, double y, double z ) {
  return (x + y + z) / 3;
}
static double avg( int x, int y, int z ) {
  return (x + y + z) / 3.;
}
```

[»]

Note

You cannot declare two methods with the same method name and the same parameter list, but different return types, within a single class:

```
static double largerRandom() { return Math.random() * 100; }
static int largerRandom() { return (int)(Math.random() * 100); } ☠
```

The compiler cannot make any selection at all if the code said something like System.out.println(largerRandom());.

print(...) und println(...) Are Overloaded*

The well-known print(...) and println(...) methods are overloaded methods, generally declared in the following way:

```
class PrintStream {
  ...
  void print( int    arg ) { ... }
  void print( String arg ) { ... }
  void print( double arg ) { ... }
  ...
}
```

If now the print(...) method is called with any object type, then the best fitting method is selected. This selection process works even for arbitrary objects, as described in Chapter 7, Section 7.5.2.

Negative Examples and Smart People*

Often, the Java library also follows the strategy of using identical names and different types, which is an extremely ugly and bad style. However, some exceptions exist. The following three methods can be found in the graphics library:

- draw**String**(**String** str, int x, int y)
- draw**Chars**(**char[]** data, int offset, int length, int x, int y)
- draw**Bytes**(**byte[]** data, int offset, int length, int x, int y)

Another example can be found in the DataOutputStream class. In this class, the methods are called writeInt(...), writeChar(...), and so on. Although we would decry these method names at first glance, this naming makes sense. An object of type DataOutput-Stream writes primitive values to a data stream. If the overloaded methods write(byte), write(short), write(int), write(long), and write(char) existed in DataOutputStream and we feed them with write(21), we have a problem. Java's typecasting would automatically adjust the data, and the data stream would contain more data than we want because write(21) doesn't call write(short) to write 2 bytes. Instead, it calls write(int) and thus writes 4 bytes. So, to keep track of the bytes written, explicit labeling of data types is worthwhile in some cases.

Language Comparison   [«]

Overloaded methods aren't a given in other programming languages. For example, C# and C++ allow overloaded methods; however, JavaScript, PHP, and C do not. In languages without overloaded methods, an array of arguments is passed to the method or function. Thus, the typing of the individual elements can be a problem, as is the restriction to a certain number of parameters.

2.7.11   Scope

Variables can be declared in any block and in any class.[52] Each variable has a *scope* (also referred to as a *validity range*). Only in its scope can the Java program access the variable; outside the scope, it can't. In other words, the variable is valid in the block and in the deeper nested blocks. Read access is only allowed if the variable has also been initialized. The scope directly determines the *lifetime* of the variable. A variable is "alive" only in the block in which it was declared. In this block, the variable is local.

Let's look at an example with two static methods:

```
public class Scope {

  public static void main( String[] args ) {
```

---

[52] These variables are called *object variables* or *class variables*, discussed in more detail in Chapter 6, Section 6.1.1.

```
   int foo = 0;

   {
     int bar = 0;              // bar is valid only in this block
     System.out.println( bar );
     System.out.println( foo );
   }

   System.out.println( foo );
   System.out.println( bar ); // ☠ Error: bar cannot be resolved
 }

 static void qux() {
   int foo, baz;              // foo has nothing in common with foo from main()

   {
     int baz;                 // ☠ Error: Duplicate local variable baz
   }
 }
}
```

Listing 2.36 src/main/java/Scope.java

Blocks can be built at any time. Outside the block, declared variables are invalid. After completion of the inner block (which declares bar), access to bar is no longer possible. Access to foo is still allowed within the static method main(...). But this foo is a different foo than the one in the static method qux(). A variable in the block is valid until the block is terminated by a closing curly bracket.

Inside a block, variable names can't be chosen in the same way as names of local variables of an outer block or as the names for the parameters of a method. You can see this limitation in the second static method using the baz declaration in our example. Although other programming languages (C++, for example) provide a syntax to access an overwritten local variable of a higher block, the Java language development team decided against it. Identical names in the inner and outer blocks are not allowed, which is a good thing, too, and minimizes potential sources of error. The parameters declared in methods are also local variables and belong to the method block.

[»]

Note

The scope is even more complex because inherited members from the superclasses, for example, are also included.

2.7.12 Default Values for Unlisted Arguments*

Overloaded methods can be used effectively if preinitialized values should be used, in case of non-existing arguments. So, if a parameter isn't occupied, a default value must be inserted. To achieve this insertion, we simply overload the method and call the other method with the default value appropriately. (The C# and C++ languages enable optional arguments in the language's grammar, which is something not possible in Java.)

Example

Let's use two overloaded static methods, tax(double cost, double taxRate) and tax(double cost), to calculate taxes. In this example, the tax rate should automatically be 19%, the German VAT rate, when the static method tax (double cost) is called but the tax rate isn't explicitly given; in the other case, we can choose taxRate arbitrarily.

```
static double tax( double cost, double taxRate ) {
  return cost * taxRate / 100.0;
}
static double tax( double cost ) {
  return tax( cost, 19.0 );   // instead of cost * 19.0 / 100;
}
```

2.7.13 Recursive Methods*

Let's start our introduction to recursion with a short example. On the way through the forest, you encounter a fairy. She says, "You have three wishes." Great situation. To end all unhappiness in the world, you avoid egocentric wish fulfillment, and aim for a socialist one: "I want peace for all, health, and prosperity for everyone." And poof, that's how it was, and everyone lived happily ever....

Some readers may slap their foreheads and say, "Nonsense! Self-replicating flowers, Pokémon Deoxys, and a life partner who tolerates my crankiness in the morning." Fortunately, we can solve this dilemma with recursion. The idea is simple—and already tested in our dreams—namely, formulating the last wish as "three more free wishes."

Example

Consider the following small wish method:

```
static void fairy() {
  wish();
  wish();
  fairy();
}
```

By calling the fairy() method all the time, we have an infinite number of free wishes. Thus, *recursion* is calling the own method we are in. Recursion can also work via a detour, at which point it's no longer called *direct recursion*, but *indirect recursion*. Recursion is an everyday phenomenon, which we also know from the microphone/speaker feedback or from looking into the mirror with a mirror.

Infinite Recursions

Let's now replace our fantasy program (whose runtime and memory requirements are also difficult to calculate) with Java methods.

[Ex]

Example

Consider the following example of endless recursion:

```java
static void down( int n ) {
  System.out.print( n + ", " );
  down( n - 1 );
}
```

Listing 2.37 src/main/java/EndlessRecursion.java, down()

If we call down(10), the number 10 is printed on the screen and then down(9) is called. If we continue the example, an endless output will eventually terminates with a StackOverflowError:

```
10, 9, 8, 7, 6, 5, 4, 3, 2, 1, 0, -1, -2, …
```

Aborting the Recursion

At this point, we realize that recursion is basically something infinite. However, this infinite range is unfavorable for programs. Therefore, you must formulate a termination condition similar to loops and then no longer start a recursion call. The termination condition is written as a case distinction that checks the argument and terminates processing with return, as in the following example:

```java
static void down1( int n ) {
  if ( n <= 0 )                // End of recursion
    return;

  System.out.print( n + ", " );
  down1( n - 1 );
}
```

Listing 2.38 src/main/java/Recursion.java, down1()

The static down1(int) method now calls down1(n - 1) only as long as n is greater than zero. This condition is called the *termination condition* of a recursion.

Different Types of Recursion

A characteristic of our previous programs was no statement existed after the call of the recursion, but the method was terminated with the call. This type of recursion, called *final recursion*, is relatively simple to understand. Recursions where instructions exist after the method call are a bit more complex. Let's consider two methods, the first of which is known and the second is new. Pay close attention to the position of print(...).

```java
static void down1( int n ) {
  if ( n <= 0 )   // End of recursion
    return;

  System.out.print( n + ", " );

  down1( n - 1 );
}

static void down2( int n ) {
  if ( n <= 0 )   // End of recursion
    return;

  down2( n - 1 );
  System.out.print( n + ", " );
}
```

Listing 2.39 src/main/java/Recursion.java, down1() und down2()

The difference is that down1(int) first outputs the number n and then recursively calls down1(int) so that a call to down1(10) outputs:

10, 9, 8, 7, 6, 5, 4, 3, 2, 1,

However, the method down2(int) first descends lower and lower, and the recursion must be finished until the first print(...) occurs. Therefore, unlike down1(...), the static method down2(10) outputs the numbers in ascending order:

1, 2, 3, 4, 5, 6, 7, 8, 9, 10,

This process is obvious if we look at the sequence of events. When calling down2(10), the comparison of n with zero is wrong, so down2(9) is called again without output—without output because print(...) is placed after the method call. The program goes recursively deeper until n equals zero. Then, the last method ends with return, and the output continues after the down2(int), the caller. The print(...) is the next instruction. Since we are now still deeply nested, print(n) outputs the number 1. Then, the method down2(int) is terminated again (an invisible return not written directly), which jumps back to the caller. This caller is again the method down2(int), but with the assignment n

= 2. This process continues until the program returns to the caller that called down(10), for example, the static main(...) method. Now, the trick is that each method has its own local variable.

The key combination ⌈Ctrl⌉+⌈Alt⌉+⌈H⌉ displays the call hierarchy so you can see what is calling a method. So, in the calls of down2(int), down2(int) as well as main(...) appear again because of the recursive call.

Recursion and the Stack and the Danger of a StackOverflowError*

From the example, you've seen how the call of down2(10) leads to the call of down2(9). And down2(10) can only be terminated when down2(9) has been completely processed. down2(10) is "open," so to speak, until the tail of child calls is finished. Now, of course, when a method call is made, the runtime environment must remember where to continue after the method call. For this task, the environment uses a *call stack* (or simply *stack*). For example, when down2(9) is called, the stack is filled with the return address that leads back to the context of down2(10). In each context, the old local variables are available again.

If no termination condition exists for a recursion, more and more return addresses will be added to the stack until the stack runs out of space. Then, the JVM generates a java.lang.StackOverflowError at runtime, and the program (thread) terminates. Usually, the StackOverflowError indicates a programming error, but some programs may need a really big stack and the usual stack size might just be too small.

Changing Stack Sizes*

The Oracle JVM uses different stack sizes for different operating systems. The stack size can be changed via a JVM switch[53] called -Xss:n (or in a slightly longer notation -XX:ThreadStackSize=n). To set the stack size to 2 MiB (2,048 KiB), you must write the following command:

```
$ java -Xss:2048 MyApplication
```

The stack size thus applies to all threads in the JVM, which of course can lead to memory problems with large stacks and many threads. Conversely, memory can also be saved if the system uses very many threads, and the stack size is reduced.

2.7.14 Towers of Hanoi*

The legend of the Towers of Hanoi is said to have been first published by Ed Lucas in the French magazine *Cosmo* in 1890.[54] According to legend, long ago, three pillars stood in

---

53 *https://docs.oracle.com/en/java/javase/16/docs/specs/man/java.html*

54 In this context, we adhere to a tradition by C. H. A. Koster from the book *Top-Down Programming with Elan* by Ellis Horwood (publisher Ellis Horwood Ltd, ISBN 0139249370, 1987).

the temple of Hanoi. The first was made of copper; the second, of silver; and the third, of gold. One hundred discs were stacked on the copper column. Each disc had a hole in the middle and were made of porphyry.[55] The disc with the largest circumference was on the bottom, and all the smaller discs were on top. An old monk set himself the task of moving the tower of discs from the copper column to the gold column. However, only one disc could be moved in a single step and, moreover, under the condition that a larger disc could never be moved onto a smaller one. The monk quickly realized that he had to use the silver pillar; so, he sat down at a table, made a plan, thought it over, and came to a decision. He could solve his problem in three steps. The next day, the monk tacked the solution on the temple door:

- If the tower consists of more than one disc, ask your oldest disciple to move a tower of $(N - 1)$ discs from the first to the third column using the second column.

- Carry the first disc yourself from one column to another.

- If the tower consists of more than one disc, ask your oldest disciple to move a tower of $(N - 1)$ discs from the third to the other column using the first column.

And so, the old monk called his oldest disciple and told him to shift the tower of 99 discs from the copper pillar to the gold pillar using the silver pillar and to report the completion to him. According to legend, the end of the world occurs when the monk finishes his work. Well, so much for the story. Let's say you want to program an algorithm for rearranging these discs in Java; a recursive solution is quite simple. The following program carries out these movements across the three pegs:

```java
class TowerOfHanoi {

  static void move( int n, String fromPeg, String toPeg, String usingPeg ) {

    if ( n > 1 ) {
      move( n - 1, fromPeg, usingPeg, toPeg );
      System.out.printf( "Move disc %d from %s to %s.%n", n, fromPeg, toPeg );
      move( n - 1, usingPeg, toPeg, fromPeg );
    }
    else
      System.out.printf( "Move disc %d from %s to %s.%n", n, fromPeg, toPeg );
  }

  public static void main( String[] args ) {
    move( 4, "copper peg", "gold peg", "silver peg" );
  }
}
```

Listing 2.40 src/main/java/TowerOfHanoi.java

---

55 A rock of volcanic origin. Special properties of porphyry include its high breaking strength, high resistance to physico-chemical agents, and high rolling and sliding friction.

If we start the program with four discs, we'll get the following output:

```
Move disc 1 from copper peg to silver peg.
Move disc 2 from copper peg to gold peg.
Move disc 1 from silver peg to gold peg.
Move disc 3 from copper peg to silver peg.
Move disc 1 from gold peg to copper peg.
Move disc 2 from gold peg to silver peg.
Move disc 1 from copper peg to silver peg.
Move disc 4 from copper peg to gold peg.
Move disc 1 from silver peg to gold peg.
Move disc 2 from silver peg to copper peg.
Move disc 1 from gold peg to copper peg.
Move disc 3 from silver peg to gold peg.
Move disc 1 from copper peg to silver peg.
Move disc 2 from copper peg to gold peg.
Move disc 1 from silver peg to gold peg.
```

Already with four slices, we have 15 movements. Even if our processor worked with many millions of operations per second, a computer would need thousands of geological ages to process 100 discs. This example makes one thing clear: Many things can be calculated in principle, but such an algorithm may not always be practical.

2.8   Further Reading

The all-encompassing source is the JLS, which can be found online at *https://docs.ora-cle.com/javase/specs*. Although some of the information is somewhat scattered, the JLS should help you expel all doubts.

The Dutch painter M.C. Escher (1898–1972) also made recursion famous in paintings. Pictures and information about his life can be found, for example, at *https://en.wikipe-dia.org/wiki/M._C._Escher*.

At the start of a project, developers should establish *code conventions*. A good source of information has already been mentioned: *https://google.github.io/styleguide/javagu-ide.html*. Early on, developers should get familiar with proper indentation and using whitespace.

Chapter 3
Classes and Objects

*"Nothing is more fairly distributed than common sense: no one thinks
he needs more of it than he already has."*
—René Descartes (1596–1650)

Java is an object-oriented programming language and this chapter focuses on objects
that are created by a blueprint (the class). Objects are addressed via references and
through references objects can be passed on to other places and can be compared.

3.1 Object-Oriented Programming

A book about Java programming must unite several parts:

- First, basic programming according to the imperative principle (variables, operators, case distinction, loops, and simple static methods) in a new grammar for Java
- Then, the object orientation (objects, classes, inheritance, interfaces) and extended possibilities of the Java language (exceptions, generics, lambda expressions)
- Finally, the libraries (string processing, input/output, etc.)

This chapter focuses on the paradigm of object orientation and demonstrates the syntax, such as how classes are implemented in Java and how class/object variables and methods are used.

> **Note**
>
> Java, of course, is not the first object-oriented (OO) language, nor was C++. Classically, Smalltalk and especially Simula-67 from 1967 are considered the progenitors of all OO languages. The concepts they introduced are still relevant today, including the four generally accepted principles of object-oriented programming (OOP): *abstraction, encapsulation, inheritance,* and *polymorphism.*[1]

[«]

---

1 Rest assured, all four basic pillars will be described in detail in the following chapters!

3.1.1   Why Object-Oriented Programming at All?

Since people perceive the world in objects, the analysis of systems is also often already modeled in an OO way. But with procedural systems that have only subroutines as a means of expression, mapping OO design into a programming language becomes difficult, and inevitably, a break will occur. Over time, documentation and implementation will diverge; the software then becomes difficult to maintain and extend. A better approach, therefore, is to think in an OO way and then use an OOP language to map these ideas.

[»]

Note

Bad code can be written in any language.

The objects mapped in the software have three important characteristics:

- Every object has an identity.
- Every object has a state.
- Every object has a behavior.

These three properties have important consequences: First, the identity of the object remains the same during its lifetime until its death and cannot change. Second, the data and the program code to manipulate that data are treated as belonging together. In procedural systems, you'll often find scenarios like a large memory area that can be accessed by all its subroutines in some way or other. For objects, this statement is not true since objects logically manage their own data and monitor the manipulation of that data.

So, OO software development is about modeling in objects and then programming. Design takes a central position in this process; large systems are decomposed and described in ever finer detail. The statement of the French writer François Duc de La Rochefoucauld (1613–1680) fits well here:

"Those who spend too much time on small things become incapable of great things."

3.1.2   When I Think of Java, I Think of Reusability

With each new project, you may notice similar problems have already been solved in previous projects. Of course, problems that have already been solved shouldn't be reimplemented; instead, repetitive parts should be reused as best as possible in different contexts. The goal is the best possible reuse of components.

The reusability of program parts has existed since before OOP languages came into being; however, OOP languages facilitate the programming of reusable software components. Thus, the many thousands of classes in the library are examples of how developers won't be constantly bothered about the implementation of data structures, for example, or the buffering of data streams.

Even though Java is an OOP language, being OO doesn't guarantee fancy design and ideal reusability. An OO language facilitates OOP, but OOP can also be achieved in a simple programming language such as C. In Java, programs are also possible that consist of only one class and accommodate 5,000 lines of program code with static methods. Bjarne Stroustrup (the creator of C++, also called Stumpy by his friends) aptly said this about comparing C and C++:

> "C makes it easy to shoot yourself in the foot, C++ makes it harder, but when you do, it blows away your whole leg."[2]

In the spirit of our didactic approach, this chapter will first use some classes from the standard library. We'll start with the Point class, which represents two-dimensional points. In a second step, we'll then program our own classes. Next, we'll focus on the concept of abstraction in Java, namely, how groups of related classes are designed.

3.2 Members of a Class

Classes are an important feature of OOP languages. A class defines a new type, describes the properties of the objects, and thus specifies the blueprint.

Each object is an *instance* of a class.

A class essentially declares two things:

- Attributes (what the object has)
- Operations (what the object can do)

Attributes and operations are also referred to as the *members* of an object. Which members a class should actually have is determined in the analysis and design phase. We won't describe this decision in this book; for us, the class descriptions are already available.

The operations of a class are implemented by the Java programming language through *methods*. The attributes of an object define its states, and they are implemented by class/object variables also referred to as *fields*.[3]

Note

The term "object-oriented programming" contains the term "object" but not the term "class," which we've used quite a bit. So, why isn't OOP called "class-based programming" instead? The reason is that class declarations aren't mandatory for OO pro-

[«]

---

2 Or as Bertrand Meyer put it, *"Do not replace legacy software by lega-c++ software."*
3 We won't use the term "field" in this context because it is a reserved word for arrays.

grams. Another approach is *prototype-based object-oriented programming*. In this case, JavaScript is the best-known representative; only objects exist, which are concatenated with a kind of base type, the *prototype*.

To approach a class, let's use a fun *first-person* approach (*object approach*), which is also used in the analysis and design phase. In this first-person approach, we put ourselves in the object and say "I am..." for the class, "I have..." for the attributes, and "I can..." for the operations. Readers should test this thought experiment on the human, car, worm, and cake classes.

Before we delve into custom classes, let's first explore some classes from the standard library. A simple class is Point, which describes a point on a two-dimensional plane by the coordinates x and y and provides some operations to modify point objects. Let's test a point again with the object approach.

Concept	Explanation
Class name	I am a **point**.
Attribute	I have an **x** and a **y** coordinate.
Operation	I can **move** myself and **set my position**.

Table 3.1 OOP Terms and Their Meanings

Regarding the point, in Oracle's application programming interface (API) documentation (*https://docs.oracle.com/en/java/javase/17/docs/api/java.desktop/java/awt/Point.html*), you can read that it defines the object variables x and y, has a setLocation(...) method (among other things), and offers a constructor that takes two integers.

3.3 Natural Modeling Using Unified Modeling Language*

For the representation of a class, program code can be used (i.e., either text or a graphical notation). One of the available graphical description types is the Unified Modeling Language (UML). Graphic illustrations are much easier for people to understand and provide a broader overview.

In the first section of a UML diagram, you can read the attributes of an object; in the second section, its operations. The + before the members, as shown in Figure 3.1, indicates that they are public, and anyone can use them. Compared to Java, the type specification is reversed: First comes the name of the variable, then the type or (in the case of methods) the type of the return value. Other programming languages such as TypeScript or Kotlin also use this "flipped" type specification in the code.

```
┌─────────────────────────────────────────┐
│            java::awt::Point              │
├─────────────────────────────────────────┤
│ + x : int                                │
│ + y : int                                │
├─────────────────────────────────────────┤
│ + Point()                                │
│ + Point(p : Point)                       │
│ + Point(x : int, y : int)                │
│ + getX() : double                        │
│ + getY() : double                        │
│ + getLocation() : Point                  │
│ + setLocation(p : Point)                 │
│ + setLocation(x : int, y : int)          │
│ + setLocation(x : double, y : double)    │
│ + move(x : int, y : int)                 │
│ + translate(dx : int, dy : int)          │
│ + equals(obj : Object) : boolean         │
│ + toString() : String                    │
└─────────────────────────────────────────┘
```

Figure 3.1 The java.awt.Point Class in a UML Representation

UML defines various diagram types that can describe different views of the software. Different diagrams are important for the individual phases in software design. Let's take a brief look at four diagrams and their areas of use.

- **Use cases diagram**
  A *use cases diagram* is usually created during the requirements phase and describes business processes by showing how people—or existing programs—interact with the system. The acting persons or active systems are called *actors* and are indicated in the diagram as small people. Use cases then describe the interaction with the system.

- **Class diagram**
  For a static view of a program's design, the *class diagram* is one of the most important diagram types. On one hand, a class diagram represents the elements of the class (i.e., its attributes and operations), and on the other hand, the relationships among the classes. Class diagrams are used most frequently in this book, especially to show association and inheritance to other classes. Classes are represented as rectangles in such a diagram, and the relationships between classes are indicated by lines.

- **Object diagram**
  At first glance, a class diagram and an object diagram are quite similar. The main difference is that an *object diagram* visualizes the assignment of attributes (i.e., the object states). For this purpose, *instance specifications* are used, which include the relationships the object has with other objects at runtime. For example, if a class diagram describes a person, one rectangle appears in the diagram. If this person has friends at runtime (i.e., has associations to other person objects), then a great many people can be associated in an object diagram, while a class diagram can't represent this instance.

■ **Sequence diagram**

The *sequence diagram* represents the dynamic behavior of objects. Thus, this diagram shows the order in which operations are called and when new objects are created. The individual objects are given a vertical lifeline, and horizontal lines between the lifelines of the objects describe the operations or object creations. Thus, the diagram is read from top to bottom.

Since the class diagram and object diagram tend to describe the structure of software, these models are also called *structure diagrams* (along with package diagrams, component diagrams, composition structure diagrams, and distribution diagrams). A use case diagram and a sequence diagram tend to show dynamic behavior and are therefore referred to as *behavior diagrams*. Other behavior diagrams include state diagrams, activity diagrams, interaction overview diagrams, communication diagrams, and timing diagrams. In UML, however, capturing the central statements of the system in a diagram is the goal, and thus, diagram types can be mixed without any problem.

In this book, you'll find mostly class diagrams.

3.4   Creating New Objects

A class describes what an object should look like. Expressed in a set or element relation, objects correspond to elements, and classes correspond to sets in which the objects are contained as elements. These objects have members that can be used. If a point represents coordinates, ways to query and change these states will be available.

In the following sections, we'll examine how instances of the Point class can be created at runtime and how the members of the Point objects can be accessed.

3.4.1   Creating an Instance of a Class Using the new Keyword

Objects must always be explicitly created in Java. For this purpose, the language defines the new keyword.

[Ex]

Example

The Java library declares the Point type for points. The following code will create a Point object:

```
new java.awt.Point();
```

Basically, new is something like a unary operator. The new keyword is followed by the name of the class of which an instance is to be created. The class name is fully qualified here because Point is in a java.awt package. (A package is a group of related classes; in

Section 3.6.3, you'll see how developers can also abbreviate this notation.) The class name is followed by a pair of parentheses for the *constructor call*. This call is a kind of method call that can be used to pass values for the initialization of the fresh object.

If Java's memory management can reserve free memory for the object to be created and if the constructor can be passed through validly, the new expression subsequently returns a *reference* to the fresh object to the program. If we don't remember this reference, automatic garbage collection can release the object.

3.4.2   Declaring Reference Variables

The result of new is a reference to the new object. The reference is usually held in a *reference variable* in order to be able to access properties of the object later.

Example

Let's declare the variable p of type java.awt.Point. The p variable then takes the reference from the new object created via new, as in the following example:

```
java.awt.Point p;
p = new java.awt.Point();
```

The declaration and initialization of a reference variable can be combined (also a local reference variable is uninitialized at the beginning like a local variable of a primitive type) in the following example:

```
java.awt.Point p = new java.awt.Point();
```

The types must be compatible, of course, and a Point object won't pass as a String. Thus, attempting to assign a point object to an int or string variable will result in a compiler error. Consider the following examples:

```
int     p = new java.awt.Point(); // 💀 Type mismatch: cannot convert from
                                  // Point to int
String s = new java.awt.Point(); // 💀 Type mismatch: cannot convert from
                                  // Point to String
```

So, a variable stores either a simple value (variable of type int, boolean, double, etc.) or a reference to an object. Ultimately, the reference is internally a pointer to a memory area but isn't visible to Java developers in this way.

Reference types are available in four designs: *class types*, *interface types*, *array types* (also called *field types*), and *type variables* (a special generic type). Our case represents an example of a class type.

```
new java.awt.Point();
```

⊙ Assign statement to new local variable (Ctrl+2, L)
▫ Assign statement to new field (Ctrl+2, F)
✖ Remove
✎ Return the allocated object
⊙ Extract to local variable (replace all occurrences)
⊙ Extract to local variable
@ Add @SuppressWarnings 'unused' to 'main()'
⊙ Extract to constant

```
import java.awt.Point;

public class T
{
...
Point point = new java.awt.Point();
...
```

Press 'Tab' from proposal table or click for focus

Figure 3.2 Pressing Ctrl+1 Allows You to Create Either a New Local Variable or an Object Variable for the Expression

3.4.3   Let's Get to the Point: Accessing Object Variables and Methods

The variables declared in a class are called *object variables* or *instance variables*. Each created object has its own set of object variables,[4] which make up the state of the object.

The dot operator allows you to access the states or call methods on objects. The dot is located between an expression that provides a reference and the object member. The API documentation describes which members exactly are provided by a class—if an object doesn't have a member, the compiler will prohibit its use.

```
java.awt.Point p = new java.awt.Point();
p.
```

○ x : int - Point
○ y : int - Point
⊙ clone() : Object - Point2D
⊙ distance(Point2D pt) : double - Point2D
⊙ distance(double px, double py) : double - Point2D
⊙ distanceSq(Point2D pt) : double - Point2D
⊙ distanceSq(double px, double py) : double - Point2D
⊙ equals(Object obj) : boolean - Point
⊙ getClass() : Class<?> - Object
⊙ getLocation() : Point - Point
⊙ getX() : double - Point
⊙ getY() : double - Point
⊙ hashCode() : int - Point2D
⊙ move(int x, int y) : void - Point
⊙ notify() : void - Object

Press 'Ctrl+Space' to show Template Proposals

The X coordinate of this Point. If no X coordinate is set it will default to 0.
Since:
> 1.0
See Also:
> getLocation()
> move(int, int)
@serial

Press 'Tab' from proposal table or click for focus

Figure 3.3 Ctrl+Space Displays the Possible Members of a Reference. Pressing Enter Selects the Member and, Especially for Methods, Places the Cursor between the Pair of Parentheses.

---

4 In some cases, several objects will share one variable, called *static variables*. We'll look at this case in more detail later in Chapter 6, Section 6.3.

Example

The p variable references a `java.awt.Point` object. The object variables x and y are supposed to be initialized, as in the following example:

```
java.awt.Point p = new java.awt.Point();
p.x = 1;
p.y = 2 + p.x;
```

A method call is just as simple as an access to class or object variables. The expression with the reference is followed by the method name after the dot.

Door and Playing Piece on the Game Board

At first glance, point objects appear to be mathematical constructs, but they can be used universally. Anything that has a position in two-dimensional space can be represented by a point object. The point stores x and y for us, and if we didn't have any point objects, we'd always have to store x and y separately.

Let's now put a playing piece and a door on a game board. Of course, the two objects have positions. Without objects, the storage of these coordinates would perhaps look like the following example:

```
int playerX;
int playerY;
int doorX;
int doorY;
```

Modeling x and y separately isn't ideal since a much better abstraction is available by using the Point class, which also provides several useful methods.

Without Abstraction, Only the Bare Data	Encapsulation of the States in an Object
int playerX; int playerY;	java.awt.Point player;
int doorX; int doorY;	java.awt.Point door;

Table 3.2 Objects Encapsulate States

The following example creates two points representing the x/y coordinates of a playing piece and a door on a game board. Once the points have been created, the coordinates are set, and a test is carried out to see how far apart the playing piece and the door in the following example:

```
class PlayerAndDoorAsPoints {

  public static void main( String[] args ) {
    java.awt.Point player = new java.awt.Point();
    player.x = player.y = 10;

    java.awt.Point door = new java.awt.Point();
    door.setLocation( 10, 100 );

    System.out.println( player.distance( door ) );   // 90.0
  }
}
```

Listing 3.1 PlayerAndDoorAsPoints.java

In the first case, we are explicitly assigning the variables x and y of the game. In the second case, we won't directly set the objects' states via the variables but instead change these states via the setLocation(...) method. The two objects have their own coordinates and won't get in each other's way.

Figure 3.4 UML Diagram Showing the Dependency between a Class and java.awt.Point with a Dashed Line. Attributes and Operations of the Point Object Are Not Shown.

toString()

The toString() method returns a String object as the result to reveal the state of the point. This method is special in that every object has a toString() method—however, the output is not useful in every case.

```
class PointToStringDemo {

  public static void main( String[] args ) {
    java.awt.Point player = new java.awt.Point();
    java.awt.Point door   = new java.awt.Point();
    door.setLocation( 10, 100 );

    System.out.println( player.toString() ); // java.awt.Point[x=0,y=0]
    System.out.println( door );                   // java.awt.Point[x=10,y=100]
  }
}
```

Listing 3.2 PointToStringDemo.java

> **Tip**
>
> Instead of explicitly calling println(obj.toString()) for the output, println(obj)
> works as well. This method is useful because the signature println(Object) accepts any
> object as an argument and automatically calls the toString() method on that object.

After the Dot, Life Goes On

As you've seen, the toString() method returns a String object as a result, as in the following code:

```
java.awt.Point  p = new java.awt.Point();
String          s = p.toString();
System.out.println( s );                         // java.awt.Point[x=0,y=0]
```

The String object itself has methods too. One String object method is length(), which returns the length of the string, as in the following example:

```
System.out.println( s.length() );                // 23
```

You can combine the request of the String object and its length into a single expression, which is referred to as *cascaded calls*, as in the following example:

```
java.awt.Point  p = new java.awt.Point();
System.out.println( p.toString().length() );   // 23
```

Object Creation without Variable Assignment

When using object members, the type to the left of the point must always be a reference. Whether the reference comes from a variable or is created on-the-fly does not matter. Consider the following example:

```
java.awt.Point  p = new java.awt.Point();
System.out.println( p.toString().length() );                 // 23
```

The following code does exactly the same thing:

```
System.out.println( new java.awt.Point().toString().length() ); // 23
```

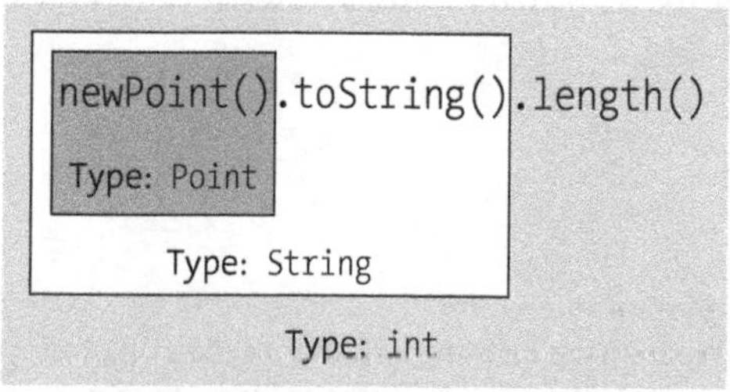

Figure 3.5 Each Nesting Results in a New Type

Basically, the following statement also works:

```
new java.awt.Point().x = 1;
```

However, this last option doesn't make sense in this context because, although the object is created and an object variable is set, the object is then fair game again for automatic garbage collection.

[Ex] Example

You can use the `File` object to determine the size of a file with the following code:

```
long size = new java.io.File( "file.txt" ).length();
```

The return value of the `File` method `length()` is the length of the file in bytes.

3.4.4   The Connection between new, the Heap, and the Garbage Collector

If a runtime system receives a request to create an object via `new`, it reserves enough memory to accommodate all object members and management information. A `Point` object stores coordinates in two `int` values so at least 2 × 4 bytes are needed. The Java runtime environment obtains the memory space from the *heap*. The heap grows from a starting size to the maximum size allowed so that a Java program can't grab arbitrary amounts of memory from the operating system, which would probably cause the machine to crash. In the HotSpot Java virtual machine (JVM), the heap is $1/64$ of main memory at startup and then grows to the maximum size of $1/4$ of main memory.[5]

[»] Note

Only a few special cases in Java exist where new objects aren't created via `new`. Thus, the `newInstance()` method, based on native code, creates a new object from the `Constructor` object. Also, `clone()` can create a new object as a copy of another object. With string concatenation via +, you don't see a `new`, but the compiler will build internal code to create a new `String` object.

If the system can't provide enough memory for a new object, automatic garbage collection tries to clear away everything unused in a final rescue operation. If still not enough free memory is available, the runtime environment will generate an `OutOfMemoryError` and terminate the entire program.[6]

---

5 *https://docs.oracle.com/en/java/javase/17/gctuning/ergonomics.html*
6 However, this particular exception can also be intercepted, which is important for server operation because if a buffer can't be created, for example, the whole JVM should not stop immediately.

Heap and Stack

The JVM specification provides for five different *runtime data areas*.[7] In addition to *heap memory*, let's take a quick look at *stack memory*. The Java Runtime Environment (JRE) uses it for local variables, for example. Also, Java uses the stack when calling methods with parameters. The arguments go on the stack before the method call, and the called method can access the values by reading or writing through the stack. With endless recursive method calls, the maximum stack size will be reached at some point, and an exception of type `java.lang.StackOverflowError` will occur. Since a JVM stack is associated with each thread, the end of the thread has come, with other threads continuing without impact.

Automatic Garbage Collection: It's Gone

Let's consider the following scenario:

```
java.awt.Point binariumLocation;
binariumLocation = new java.awt.Point( 50, 9 );
binariumLocation = new java.awt.Point( 51, 7 );
```

In this code, we're declaring a `Point` variable, building an instance, and assigning the variable. Then, we create a new `Point` object and override the variable. But what about the first point?

If the object is no longer referenced by the program, the automatic garbage collector notices and releases the reserved memory.[8] Automatic garbage collection regularly tests whether the objects on the heap are still needed. If they aren't needed, the object hunter deletes them. So, a kind of graveyard atmosphere always exists around the heap, and once the last reference has been taken from the object, it's already dead. Several garbage collection algorithms exist, and each JVM vendor has its own procedures.

3.4.5   Overview of Point Methods

A few methods of the `Point` class have already been mentioned, and the API documentation naturally enumerates all methods:

```
class java.awt.Point
```

The more interesting methods include the following:

▶ `double getX()`

▶ `double getY()`
   Returns the *x* or *y* coordinate.

---

7   Section 2.5 of the JVM specification, available at *https://docs.oracle.com/javase/specs/jvms/se17/html/jvms-2.html#jvms-2.5*.

8   With the `java` switch `-verbose:gc` set, a console output will always be produced when the garbage collector detects objects that are no longer referenced and clears them away.

▶ void setLocation(double x, double y)

Sets the *x* and the *y* coordinates at the same time. The coordinates are rounded and stored in integers.

▶ boolean equals(Object obj)

Checks if another point has the same coordinates. If so, the return is true; otherwise, it's false. If something other than a point is passed, the compiler won't find fault with this, but the result will always be false.

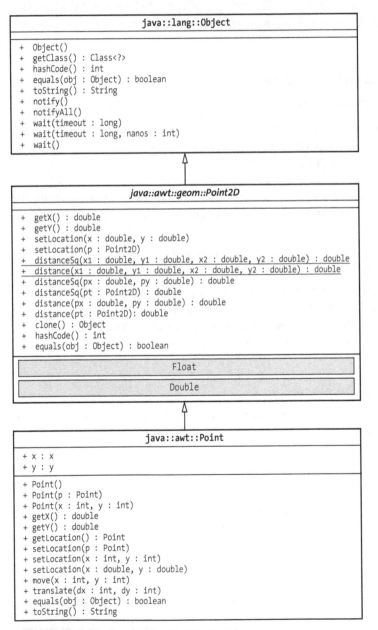

Figure 3.6 Inheritance Hierarchy in Point2D

[«]

3

> **Note**
>
> You may be surprised that a Point stores the coordinates as int, but the getX() and getY() methods return a double, and setLocation(double, double) takes the coordinates as double, rounds them, and stores them as int, thus losing precision. The reason relates to inheritance, which will be discussed in more detail in Chapter 7, Section 7.2. Point inherits from Point2D, and there's already double getX(), double getY(), and setLocation(double, double); the Point subclass can't simply turn double into int.

A Few Words about Inheritance and the API Documentation*

Not only does a class have its own members, it always inherits some members from its parents as well. In the case of Point, the superclass is Point2D—according to the API documentation. Even Point2D inherits from Object, the magic class that all Java classes have as a superclass. We'll devote Chapter 7, Section 7.2, to inheritance later, but right now, you must understand that the superclass passes object variables and methods to subclasses. Inherited object variables and methods are only briefly listed in the API documentation of a class in the block "Methods inherited from..." and are quickly forgotten. Therefore, developers must look not only at the methods of the class itself, but also at its inherited methods. So, for Point, we need to not just understand the methods of Point themselves, but also the methods from Point2D and Object.

Let's look at some methods of the superclass. The class declaration of Point contains an extends Point2D, which makes it explicitly clear that a superclass exists.[9]

```
class java.awt.Point
extends Point2D
```

▶ static double distance(double x1, double y1, double x2, double y2)
  Calculates the distance between the given points according to Euclidean distance.

▶ double distance(double x, double y)
  Calculates the distance of the current point to the specified coordinates.

▶ double distance(Point2D pt)
  Calculates the distance of the current point to the coordinates of the passed point.

Are Two Points the Same?

The equals(...) method tells you whether two points are equal, and its use is pretty simple. Let's imagine managing the coordinates for a player, a door, and a snake and

---

9 However, the class declaration is not yet complete since an implements Serializable is missing, but we are not concerned about this for now.

then test whether the player is "on" the door and whether the snake is "on" the player's position.

```java
class PointEqualsDemo {

  public static void main( String[] args ) {
    java.awt.Point player = new java.awt.Point();
    player.x = player.y = 10;

    java.awt.Point door = new java.awt.Point();
    door.setLocation( 10, 10 );

    System.out.println( player.equals( door ) );    // true
    System.out.println( door.equals( player ) );    // true

    java.awt.Point snake = new java.awt.Point();
    snake.setLocation( 20, 22 );


    System.out.println( snake.equals( door ) );    // false
  }
}
```

Listing 3.3 PointEqualsDemo.java

Since player and door have the same coordinates, equals(...) returns true. Whether we have the distance from the player to the door calculated or the distance from the door to the player—the result with equals(...) should always be symmetrical.

Another test option results from distance(...) because, if the distance between points is zero, then the points naturally lie on top of each other and thus have no distance.

```java
class Distances {

  public static void main( String[] args ) {
    java.awt.Point player = new java.awt.Point();
    player.setLocation( 10, 10 );
    java.awt.Point door = new java.awt.Point();
    door.setLocation( 10, 10 );
    java.awt.Point snake = new java.awt.Point();
    snake.setLocation( 20, 10 );

    System.out.println( player.distance( door ) );            // 0.0
    System.out.println( player.distance( snake ) );           // 10.0
    System.out.println( player.distance( snake.x, snake.y ) ); // 10.0
```

```
  }
}
```
Listing 3.4 Distances.java

Player, door, and snake are again represented as Point objects and preassigned with positions. For the player, we then call the distance(...) method and pass the reference to the door and the snake.

3.4.6   Using Constructors

When objects are created with new, a constructor gets called. A constructor has the task of putting an object into a start state, for example, initializing the object variables. A constructor is a good approach to initialization because a constructor is always called first, even before any other method is called. The initialization in the constructor makes sure that the new object has a meaningful initial state:

```
class java.awt.Point
extends Point2D
```

Three constructors can be found in the API documentation for Point:

▶ Point()
   Creates a point with the coordinates (0, 0).

▶ Point(int x, int y)
   Creates a new point and initializes it with the values from x and y.

▶ Point(Point p)
   Creates a new point and initializes it with the coordinates the passed point has as well. This kind of constructor is called a *copy constructor*.

A constructor without arguments is at *parameterless constructor*, sometimes also referred to as a *no-arg constructor*. Each class can have at most one parameterless constructor. You can also have a class that doesn't declare a parameterless constructor, only constructors with parameters (i.e., parameterized constructors).

Example   [Ex]

The following three variants create a Point object with the same coordinates (1, 2). Note that java.awt.Point has been abbreviated to Point:

```
Point p = new Point(); p.setLocation( 1, 2 );
Point q = new Point( 1, 2 );
Point r = new Point( q );
```

The parameterless constructor is written first, while the second and third constructors are parameterized constructors.

3.5   ZZZZZnake

A classic computer game is *Snake*. On the screen is a player, a snake, some gold, and a door. The door and the gold are fixed, the player can be moved, and the snake moves independently towards the player. You must try to move the player to the gold and then to the door. If the snake catches you before you achieve these goals, you're unlucky, and it's game over.

This game may sound complex at first glance, but you already have all the building blocks to program this game:

- Player, Snake, Gold, and Door are Point objects preconfigured with coordinates.
- A loop runs through all coordinates. If a player, the door, the snake, or gold has been "hit," a symbolic representation of the figure is displayed.
- You'll test three conditions for the game status: 1) Has the player collected the gold and is standing on the door? (You've won the game.) 2) Does the snake bite the player? (You've lost the game.) 3) Does the player collect gold?
- The Scanner enables you to respond to keystrokes and move the player around the board.
- The snake must move in the direction of the player. While the player can only move horizontally or vertically, the snake can move diagonally.

The corresponding source code for this game follows:

```java
public class ZZZZZnake {

  public static void main( String[] args ) {
    java.awt.Point playerPosition = new java.awt.Point( 10, 9 );
    java.awt.Point snakePosition  = new java.awt.Point( 30, 2 );
    java.awt.Point goldPosition   = new java.awt.Point( 6, 6 );
    java.awt.Point doorPosition   = new java.awt.Point( 0, 5 );
    boolean rich = false;

    while ( true ) {
      // Draw grid and symbols

      for ( int y = 0; y < 10; y++ ) {
        for ( int x = 0; x < 40; x++ ) {
          java.awt.Point p = new java.awt.Point( x, y );
          if ( playerPosition.equals( p ) )
            System.out.print( '&' );
          else if ( snakePosition.equals( p ) )
            System.out.print( 'S' );
          else if ( goldPosition.equals( p ) )
            System.out.print( '$' );
```

```java
        else if ( doorPosition.equals( p ) )
          System.out.print( '#' );
        else System.out.print( '.' );
      }
      System.out.println();
    }

    // Determine status

    if ( rich && playerPosition.equals( doorPosition ) ) {
      System.out.println( "You won!" );
      return;
    }
    if ( playerPosition.equals( snakePosition ) ) {
      System.out.println( "SSSSSS. You were bitten by the snake!" );
      return;
    }
    if ( playerPosition.equals( goldPosition ) ) {
      rich = true;
      goldPosition.setLocation( -1, -1 );
    }

    // Console input and change player position
    // Keep playing field between 0/0.. 39/9
     switch ( new java.util.Scanner( System.in ).next() ) {
     case "u" /* p */ -> playerPosition.y = Math.max( 0, playerPosition.y - 1 );
     case "d" /* own */ -> playerPosition.y = Math.min( 9, playerPosition.y + 1 );
     case "l" /* eft */ -> playerPosition.x = Math.max( 0, playerPosition.x - 1 );
     case "r" /* ight */ -> playerPosition.x = Math.min( 39, playerPosition.x + 1 );
     }

    // Snake moves towards the player

    if ( playerPosition.x < snakePosition.x )
      snakePosition.x--;
    else if ( playerPosition.x > snakePosition.x )
      snakePosition.x++;
    if ( playerPosition.y < snakePosition.y )
      snakePosition.y--;
    else if ( playerPosition.y > snakePosition.y )
      snakePosition.y++;
    } // end while
  }
}
```

Listing 3.5 ZZZZZnake.java

The Point members in use include the following:

- The object states x, y: The player and the snake can be moved, and the coordinates must be reset.
- The setLocation(...) method: Once the gold has been collected, you set the coordinates so that the coordinate from the gold is no longer on our grid.
- The equals(...) method: Tests if a point is on top of another point.

[»] **Extension**

If you're interested in a little more programming on this task, consider the following enhancements:

- Player, snake, gold, and door should be set to random coordinates.
- Instead of just one piece of gold, there should be two pieces.
- Instead of one snake, there should be two snakes.
- With two snakes and two pieces of gold, things can get a little tight for the player. Let's give the player a head start of 5 moves at the beginning without the snakes moving.
- For advanced developers: The program, which is so far only contained in the main method, should be split into different methods.

3.6 Tying Packages, Imports, and Compilation Units

The class library of Java is rather extensive, with thousands of types, and covers everything developers of platform-independent programs need as a basis. The class library includes data structures, classes for date/time calculation, file processing, and more. Most types are implemented in Java itself (and the source code is usually directly available from the development environment), but some parts are implemented natively, for example, when reading from a file.

When you program your own classes, they supplement the standard library, so to speak; the bottom line is that creating your own classes increases the number of possible types a program can use.

3.6.1 Java Packages

A *package* is a group of thematically related types. Packages can be arranged in hierarchies so that one package can contain another package—similar to the directory structure of a file system. Examples of packages include the following:

- java.awt
- java.util

- com.google
- org.apache.commons.math3.fraction
- com.tutego.insel

The Java standard library classes are located in packages starting with java and javax. Google uses the com.google root; the Apache Foundation publishes Java code at org.apache. In this way, you can read from the outside which types your own class depends on.

3.6.2   Packages in the Standard Library

The logical grouping and hierarchy can be observed easily in the Java library. The Java standard library starts with the java root; some types are in javax. This package contains other packages, such as awt, math, and util. For example, java.math contains the classes BigInteger and BigDecimal because working with arbitrarily large integers and floats is part of mathematics. A point and a polygon, represented by the Point and Polygon classes, are part of the graphical user interface (GUI) package, which is the java.awt package.

If someone put custom classes in packages with the prefix java, for example, java.tutego, a program author might cause confusion since you could no longer easily see whether the package was a component of each distribution. For this reason, the prefix java is forbidden for custom packages.

Classes that are in a package starting with javax can be part of the Java SE like javax.swing, but these classes don't necessarily have to be part of the Java SE; more on this topic will follow in Chapter 16.

3.6.3   Full Qualification and Import Declaration

To use the Point class, which is located in the java.awt package, outside of the java.awt package (which is almost always the case), you must make this known to the compiler with the entire package specification. For this purpose, the class name alone isn't sufficient because the class name might be ambiguous and a class declaration might exist in different packages.

Types can't be uniquely identified until you specify their package. A dot separates packages, so you'll write java.awt and java.util instead of just awt or util. With an innumerable number of packages and classes worldwide, uniqueness would not be feasible at all if we didn't write it this way. A type with the same name may be in different packages, for example, java.**util**.List and java.**awt**.List or java.**util**.Date and java.**sql**.Date. Therefore, only the package and the type together form a unique identifier.

To enable the compiler to precisely assign a class to a package, two options are available: First, types can be fully qualified, as we've been doing up to now. An alternative and more practical approach is to make the compiler aware of the types in the package through an import declaration.

Full Qualificataion	Import Declaration
| ```java
class AwtWithoutImport {
 public static void main(String[] args){
 java.awt.Point p =
  new java.awt.Point();

 java.awt.Polygon t =
  new java.awt.Polygon();
 t.addPoint( 10, 10 );
 t.addPoint( 10, 20 );
 t.addPoint( 20, 10 );

 System.out.println( p );
 System.out.println( t.contains(15,↩
15) );
 }
}
```<br>Listing 3.6: AwtWithoutImport.java | ```java
import java.awt.Point;
import java.awt.Polygon;

class AwtWithImport {
 public static void main(String[] args){
 Point p = new Point();


 Polygon t = new Polygon();

 t.addPoint( 10, 10 );
 t.addPoint( 10, 20 );
 t.addPoint( 20, 10 );

 System.out.println( p );
 System.out.println( t.contains(15,↩
15) );
 }
}
```<br>Listing 3.7: AwtWithImport.java |

Table 3.3 Type Access via Full Qualification and with an import Declaration

The source code on the left uses the full qualification approach, and each reference to a type costs more writing effort; on the right, the import declaration only mentions the class name and "swaps out" the package specification to an import. All types named with import are remembered by the compiler for this file in a data structure. When the compiler arrives at the line with Point p = new Point();, it finds the Point type in its data structure and can assign the type to the java.awt package, thus again providing the indispensable qualification.

Note

The types from java.lang are automatically imported, and thus, import java.lang.String; isn't needed.

3.6.4 Reaching All Types of a Package with Type-Import-on-Demand

If a Java class accesses several other types of the same package, the number of import declarations can become large. In our example, we're only using two classes from java.awt (Point and Polygon), but you can easily imagine what happens when additional windows, labels, buttons, sliders, and more are included from the GUI package. In this case, an asterisk * is allowed as the last member in an import declaration:

```
import java.awt.*;
import java.math.*;
```

With this syntax, the compiler knows all the types in the java.awt and java.math packages, so the compiler can map the package for the Point and Polygon classes as well as the package for the BigInteger class.

Note

The * is only allowed on the last hierarchy level and always applies to all types in this package. The following examples are syntactically incorrect:

```
import *;           // 💀 Syntax error on token "*", Identifier expected
import java.awt.Po*; // 💀 Syntax error on token "*", delete this token
```

A declaration like import java.*; is syntactically correct but has no effect because no type declarations exist in the package java, only subpackages.

The import declaration refers only to a directory (assuming that the packages are mapped to the file system) and doesn't include subdirectories.

Although the * does shorten the number of individual import declarations, there are two things to keep in mind:

- If two different packages contain a type with the same name, for example, Date in both java.util and java.sql or List in both java.awt and java.util, an interpretation error will occur when the type is used because the compiler doesn't understand the meaning. Full qualification will solve the problem.

- The number of import declarations tells you something about the degree of complexity. The more import declarations you use the greater the dependencies on other classes, which is generally a red flag. Although graphical tools can show dependencies accurately, import * could obscure the full scope of dependency.

Best Practice

Development environments usually set the import declarations automatically and usually cascade the blocks. Therefore, the * should be used sparingly because it "pollutes" the namespace by many types and increases the risk of collision.

3.6.5   Hierarchical Structures across Packages and Mirroring in the File System

The classes belonging to a package are usually located[10] in the same directory. The name of the package is the same as the name of the directory (and vice versa, of course). Instead of the directory separator (such as "/" or "\"), a dot is used.

Let's assume the following directory structure with a helper class:

com/tutego/insel/printer/DatePrinter.class

In this case, the package name is com.tutego.insel.printer, and thus the directory name is *com/tutego/insel/printer*. Umlauts and special characters should be avoided, because they always cause trouble in the file system. Identifiers should always be in English anyway.

The Structure of Package Names

Basically, a package name can be arbitrary, but hierarchies usually consist of inverted domain names. Thus, the domain of the website *http://tutego.com* becomes com.tutego. This naming ensures that classes remain unique worldwide. A package name is usually written entirely in lowercase.

3.6.6   The Package Declaration

To place the DatePrinter class in a com.tutego.insel.printer package, two things must be true:

- The package must be physically located in a directory (i.e., *com/tutego/insel/printer*).
- The source code contains a package declaration at the top.

The package declaration must be located at the very start; otherwise, an interpretation error will occur (of course, comments can be placed before the package declaration):

```
package com.tutego.insel.printer;

import java.time.LocalDate;
import java.time.format.*;

public class DatePrinter {
  public static void printCurrentDate() {
    DateTimeFormatter fmt =
  DateTimeFormatter.ofLocalizedDate( FormatStyle.MEDIUM );
```

---

10 I wrote "usually" because the package structure doesn't necessarily need to be mapped to directories. Packages could be read from a database by the class loader, for example. In the following sections, however, we always want to start from directories.

```
    System.out.println( LocalDate.now().format( fmt ) );
  }
}
```

Listing 3.6 src/main/java/com/tutego/insel/printer/DatePrinter.java

The package declaration is followed by the import declaration(s) and the type declaration(s) as usual.

To use the class, you have two options, as you already know: either the full qualification or an import declaration. The following code is an example of the first variant.

```
public class DatePrinterUser1 {
  public static void main( String[] args ) {
    com.tutego.insel.printer.DatePrinter.printCurrentDate();
  }
}
```

Listing 3.7 src/main/java/DatePrinterUser1.java

The following code is an example of the second variant, with the import declaration:

```
import com.tutego.insel.printer.DatePrinter;

public class DatePrinterUser2 {
  public static void main( String[] args ) {
    DatePrinter.printCurrentDate();
  }
}
```

Listing 3.8 src/main/java/DatePrinterUser2.java

Tip

A development environment takes a lot of work off your hands, so you'll rarely notice file operations like creating directories, for example. A modern integrated development environment (IDE) also takes care of moving types to other packages, the associated changes to the file system, and adjustments to the import and package declarations for you.

3.6.7   Unnamed Package (Default Package)

An *unnamed package* or *default package* contains a class without a package specification. A best practice is to always organize your own classes in packages. Doing so enables finer visibility, and conflicts with other companies and other programmers can be avoided. Big problems could arise if 1) every company were messy and put all their classes in unnamed packages and then 2) tried to swap out libraries. Conflicts would essentially be preprogrammed.

A class located in the package can import any other visible class from other packages, but not classes from the unnamed package. Let's assume Sugar is in the unnamed package and Chocolate in the com.tutego package:

Sugar.class
com/tutego/insel/Chocolate.class

The Chocolate class can't use Sugar because classes from the unnamed package are not visible to subpackages. Only other classes in the unnamed package can use classes in the unnamed package.

If Sugar was in a package (or even in a superpackage!), Chocolate could import Sugar:

com/Sugar.class
com/tutego/insel/Chocolate.class

3.6.8   Compilation Unit

A *.java* file is a *compilation unit* that consists of three (optional) segments in the following order:

1. The package declaration
2. The import declaration(s)
3. The declaration(s)

Thus, a compilation unit consists of, at most, one package declaration (not necessary if the type is in the default package), any number of import declarations, and any number of type declarations. The compiler translates each type of compilation unit into its own *.class* file. A package is ultimately a collection of compilation units. Usually, the compilation unit is a source code file; in general, the lines of code could also come from a database or be generated at runtime.

3.6.9   Static Import*

The import declaration informs the compiler about the packages, so that a type no longer needs to be fully qualified if it's explicitly listed in the import section or if the package of the type is named via *.

If a class specifies static methods or constants, its members are always addressed by the type name. Java provides a *static import* as an option to use the static methods or variables immediately without prefixed type names. So, while the normal import names the types to the compiler, a static import makes class members known to the compiler, thus going one level deeper.

Example [Ex]

Import the static variable out from System statically for the screen output with the following code:

```
import static java.lang.System.out;
```

With the otherwise usual output via System.out.print*(...), the class name can be omitted after the static import so that you only need out.print*(...).

Let's include several static members in the following example of a static import:

```
package com.tutego.insel.oop;

import static java.lang.System.out;
import static javax.swing.JOptionPane.showInputDialog;
import static java.lang.Integer.parseInt;
import static java.lang.Math.max;
import static java.lang.Math.min;

class StaticImport {

  public static void main( String[] args ) {
    int i = parseInt( showInputDialog( "First number" ) );
    int j = parseInt( showInputDialog( "Second number" ) );
    out.printf( "%d is greater than or equal to %d.%n",
            max(i, j), min(i, j) );
  }
}
```

Listing 3.9 src/main/java/com/tutego/insel/oop/StaticImport.java

Importing Multiple Types Statically

The following static import imports the static max(...)/min(...) methods:

```
import static java.lang.Math.max;
import static java.lang.Math.min;
```

If you require more static methods, the wildcard variant goes beyond the individual enumeration, as in the following example:

```
import static java.lang.Math.*;
```

Best Practice [«]

Even if Java provides this wildcard option, you should use it in moderation. The possibility of static imports is useful when classes want to use constants, but you run the risk, with a missing type name, that where the member actually comes from will become invisible, as well as what dependency it is based on. Problems also arise with methods that have names that are homonyms: A method from its own class can overlay statically imported methods. So, if later in the custom class—or superclass—a method is included that has the same signature as a statically imported method, a compiler error will not arise, but the semantics will change because then the new custom method will be used instead of the statically imported one.

3.7   Using References, Diversity, Identity, and Equality

In Java, null is an incredibly special reference that can trigger a large number of problems. But you can't do without it, and the following section will demonstrate its importance. After this discussion, we'll look at how object comparisons work and the difference between identity and equivalence.

3.7.1   null References and the Question of Philosophy

In Java, three special references exist: null, this, and super. (We'll defer descriptions of this and super to Chapter 6, Section 6.1.4.) The special literal null can be used to initialize reference variables. The null reference is typeless and thus can be assigned to any reference variable and passed to any method that awaits an object.[11]

Example

The declaration and initialization of two object variables with null is shown in the following example:

```
Point  p = null;
String s = null;
System.out.println( p );   // null
```

The console output in the last line briefly returns "null," which is actually a string representation of the null type.

Since null is typeless, and there's only one null, null can be type-matched to any type. Thus, for example, (String) null == null && (Point) null == null returns the result true. The null literal is intended for references only and can't be converted to any primitive type such as the integer 0.[12]

A whole lot can be done with null. The main purpose is to indicate uninitialized reference variables (i.e., to express that a reference variable doesn't reference any object). In

---

11   null thus behaves as though it were a subtype of any other type.
12   C(++) and Java differ in this regard.

lists or trees, for example, null indicates the absence of a valid successor or, in a graphical dialog box, that the user has aborted the dialog process. In these cases, null is a valid indicator, not an error.

> **Note**
>
> For a local variable initialized with null, the shortcut with var does not work. A compiler error would arise with the following example:
>
> `var text = null;  // ☠ Cannot infer type: variable initializer is 'null'`

Nothing Works on null except NullPointerException

Since null doesn't hide an object, you cannot call a method or query an object variable from null. The compiler knows the type of each expression, but only the runtime environment (i.e., the JVM) knows what's being referenced. When attempting to access a member of an object via the null reference, the JVM throws a NullPointerException.[13] Consider the following example:

```
package com.tutego.insel.oop;              // 1
public class NullPointer {                 // 2
  public static void main( String[] args ) {  // 3
    java.awt.Point p = null;               // 4
    String        s = null;                // 5
    p.setLocation( 1, 2 );                 // 6
    s.length();                            // 7
  }                                        // 8
}                                          // 9
```

Listing 3.10 src/main/java/com/tutego/insel/oop/NullPointer.java

Notice how we have a NullPointerException at runtime because the program terminates at p.setLocation(...) with the following output:

```
Exception in thread "main" java.lang.NullPointerException: Cannot invoke "java.a
wt.Point.setLocation(int, int)" because "p" is null
at com.tutego.insel.oop.NullPointer.main(NullPointer.java:6)
```

In the error message, the runtime environment tells you that the error, the NullPointerException, is in line 6. To correct the error, you have two options. First, you must either initialize the variables, that is, assign an object as in the following example:

---

13 The name is reminiscent of pointers. Although we aren't dealing with pointers in Java, but with references, it's called NullPointerException and not NullReferenceException. This distinction is a reminder that a reference identifies an object, and a reference to an object is a pointer. The .NET framework is more consistent in this regard and calls the exception NullReferenceException.

```
p = new java.awt.Point();
s = "";
```

Alternatively, before accessing the members, you can perform a test to determine whether object variables point to something or are null and, depending on the outcome of the test, allow access to the member or not.

[»]

null in Other Programming Languages*

Is Java a purely OOP language? No, because Java distinguishes between primitive types and reference types. Let's assume for a moment that primitive types don't exist. Would Java then be a pure OOP language, where each reference references a pure object? The answer is still "no" because null is something that enables you to initialize reference variables, but doesn't represent an object and has no methods. This scenario can cause a NullPointerException when de-referencing.

Other programming languages have different approaches to solving the problem, and null referencing isn't possible. For example, in Ruby, everything is always an object. Where Java uses null to express "unassigned," Ruby does so with nil. The subtle difference is that nil is an instance of the class NilClass (strictly speaking, a singleton that exists only once in the system). nil also has some public methods like to_s (like Java's toString()), which then returns an empty string. With nil, no NullPointerException exists anymore, but of course, an error can still arise if a method is called on this object of type NilClass that doesn't exist. In Objective-C, the standard language for iOS programs (so far), you have the null object nil. Usually, nothing happens when a message is sent to the nil object; the message is simply ignored.

3.7.2   Everything to null? Testing References

With the comparison operator == or the test for inequality via !=, you can easily determine whether a reference variable really references an object or not, for example, through the following code:

```
if ( object == null )
  // variable references nothing, but is correctly initialized with null
else
  // variable references an object
```

null Test and Short-Circuit Operators

At this point, let's come back to the usual logical short-circuit operators and the logical non-short-circuit operators. The former evaluates operands only from left to right until the result of the operation is fixed. At first glance, whether all subexpressions are evaluated or not doesn't seem to matter. In some expressions, however, this evaluation is important. In the following example, the variable s is of type String, and the program should output the string length when a string is entered:

```
String s = javax.swing.JOptionPane.showInputDialog( "Input a string" );
if ( s != null && ! s.isEmpty() )
  System.out.println( "Length of string: " + s.length() );
else
  System.out.println( "Dialog canceled or no input given" );
```

Listing 3.11 src/main/java/NullCheck.java, main

The return value of showInputDialog(...) is null if the user cancels the dialog. Our program should take this possibility into account. Therefore, the if condition tests whether s references an object at all and, if so, additionally whether the string is nonempty. After that evaluation follows an output.

This notation occurs frequently, and the AND operator for linking must be a short-circuit operator since it's explicit in this case that the length is determined only if the s variable references a String object at all and is not null. Otherwise, you'd get a NullPointerException on s.isEmpty() if every subexpression was evaluated and s was null.

The Luck of Others: null Coalescing Operator*

Since null occurs far too often, but null references must be avoided, you may see a lot of code like o != null ? o : non_null_o. Various programming languages, including JavaScript, Kotlin, Objective-C, PHP, and Swift provide a shortcut for this construct called the *null coalescing operator*. Sometimes written as ?? or as ?:, in our example, the null coalescing operator is written as o ?? non_null_o. This construct is especially nice with sequential tests of the type o ?? p ?? q ?? r, where it says something like, "Return the first non-null reference." Java doesn't provide such an operator.

3.7.3 Assignments with References

A reference allows access to a referenced object, and a reference variable stores a reference. Multiple reference variables may store the same reference, similar to an object being addressed under different names—just as a person might be addressed as "Boss" by her co-workers, she might be called "Honey" by her husband. This nicknaming is also referred to as an *alias*.

Example

Let's say you want to address a point object under an alternative variable name. Consider the following example:

```
Point p = new Point();
Point q = p;
```

A point object is created and referenced with the variable p. The second line now stores the same reference in the variable q. After that, p and q reference the same object. For

---

better understanding, what's important here is how often new occurs because that tells you how many objects the JVM will create. Since only one new exists in the two lines, only one point is created.

If two object variables reference the same object, a natural consequence is that object states can be read and modified via two paths. If the same person is consistently called "Boss" in the company and "Honey" at home, everyone is happy.

Let's continue with our example using point objects. If p and q point to the same point object, changes via p can also be observed via the q variable, as in the following example.

```java
public static void main( String[] args ) {
  Point p = new Point();
  Point q = p;
  p.x = 10;
  System.out.println( q.x ); // 10
  q.y = 5;
  System.out.println( p.y ); // 5
}
```

Listing 3.12 ItsTheSame.java, main

3.7.4   Methods with Reference Types as Parameters

The fact that the same object can be addressed via two names (i.e., via two different variables) can be observed in methods. A method that receives an object reference via the parameter can access the passed object. As a result, the method can change this object with the provided methods or access the object variables.

In the following example, we'll declare two methods. The first method, initializePosition(Point), is supposed to initialize a given point with random coordinates. Two Point objects are later passed to the method in main(...): one for the player and one for the snake. The second method, printScreen(Point, Point), prints the playing field on the screen and then prints a & when the coordinate hits a player and an S when it hits the snake. If the player and the snake happen to meet, the snake "wins."

```java
package com.tutego.insel.oop;
import java.awt.Point;

public class DrawPlayerAndSnake {

  static void initializePosition( Point p ) {
    int randomX = (int)(Math.random() * 40); // 0 <= x < 40
    int randomY = (int)(Math.random() * 10); // 0 <= y < 10
    p.setLocation( randomX, randomY );
  }

  static void printScreen( Point playerPosition,
                           Point snakePosition ) {
    for ( int y = 0; y < 10; y++ ) {
      for ( int x = 0; x < 40; x++ ) {
        if ( snakePosition.distanceSq( x, y ) == 0 )
          System.out.print( 'S' );
        else if ( playerPosition.distanceSq( x, y ) == 0 )
          System.out.print( '&' );
        else System.out.print( '.' );
      }
      System.out.println();
    }
  }

  public static void main( String[] args ) {
    Point playerPosition = new Point();
    Point snakePosition  = new Point();
    System.out.println( playerPosition );
    System.out.println( snakePosition );
    initializePosition( playerPosition );
    initializePosition( snakePosition );
    System.out.println( playerPosition );
    System.out.println( snakePosition );
    printScreen( playerPosition, snakePosition );
  }
}
```

Listing 3.13 src/main/java/com/tutego/insel/oop/DrawPlayerAndSnake.java

The code should produce the following output:

```
java.awt.Point[x=0,y=0]
java.awt.Point[x=0,y=0]
java.awt.Point[x=38,y=1]
java.awt.Point[x=19,y=8]
........................................
.................................&.
........................................
........................................
........................................
........................................
........................................
........................................
...................S....................
........................................
```

The moment main(...) calls the static method initializePosition(Point), we have two names for the Point object: playerPosition and p. However, this double naming is only inside the JVM because initializePosition(Point) knows the object only via p but doesn't know the playerPosition variable. With main(...), the reverse is true: Only the variable name playerPosition is known in main(...), but it has no idea about the name p. The Point method distanceSq(int, int) returns the squared distance from the current point to the passed coordinates.

[»]

Note

The name of a parameter variable may well be the same as the name of the argument variable, which wouldn't change the semantics. The namespaces are completely separate, and misunderstandings don't exist because both the calling method and the called method have completely separate local variables.

Value Transfer and Reference Transfer via Call by Value

Primitive variables are always copied by value (*call by value*). The same applies to references, which are to be understood as a kind of pointer, which are basically only integers. For this reason, the following static method has no side effects:

```
package com.tutego.insel.oop;
import java.awt.Point;

public class JavaIsAlwaysCallByValue {

  static void clear( Point p ) {
    System.out.println( p );  // java.awt.Point[x=10,y=20]
```

```
  p = new Point();
  System.out.println( p );  // java.awt.Point[x=0,y=0]
}

public static void main( String[] args ) {
  Point p = new Point( 10, 20 );
  clear( p );
  System.out.println( p );  // java.awt.Point[x=10,y=20]
  }
}
```

Listing 3.14 JavaIsAlwaysCallByValue.java

After assigning p = new Point() in the clear(Point) method, the parameter variable p references another point object, and the reference passed to the method is thus lost. Of course, this change isn't visible from outside because the parameter variable p of clear(...) is only a temporary alternative name for the p from main; a reassignment to the clear-p doesn't change the reference from the main-p. As a result, the caller of clear(...), which is main(...), has no new object under it. If you want to initialize the point with null, you must access the states of the passed object directly, for instance, in the following way:

```
static void clear( Point p ) {
  p.x = p.y = 0;
}
```

Call by Reference Doesn't Exist in Java: A Look at C and C++*

In C++, another way to pass arguments is called *call by reference*. A swap(...) function is a good example of the usefulness of call by reference:

```
void swap( int& a, int& b ) { int tmp = a; a = b; b = tmp; }
```

Pointers and references are something different in C++, which easily confuses beginners to the language. In C++ and also in C, a comparable swap(...) function could also have been implemented with pointers:

```
void swap( int *a, int *b ) { int tmp = *a; *a = *b; *b = tmp; }
```

The implementation provides a reference to the argument in C(++).

Final Declared Reference Parameter and the Missing const

As we've seen, final variables tell a programmer that variables must not be rewritten. Local variables, parameter variables, object variables, and class variables can be final. In any case, new assignments are taboo. Whether the parameter variable is of a primitive type or a reference type does not matter. Thus, with a method declaration of the following type, an assignment to p and also to value would be forbidden:

```
public void clear( final Point p, final int value )
```

If the parameter variable isn't final and is a reference type, we'd lose the reference to the original object with an assignment, which would make little sense, as we saw in the previous example. Parameter variables declared final make it clear in the program code that changing the reference variable doesn't make any sense, and the compiler forbids an assignment. In the case of our clear(...) method, the initialization would have been noticed directly as a compiler error. Consider the following example:

```
static void clear( final Point p ) {
  p = new Point();      // 💀 Cannot assign a value to final variable 'p'
}
```

Let's recap: If a parameter is declared final, no assignments are possible. However, final doesn't prohibit changes to objects, and therefore, final could be understood as "definitive." With the reference of the object, you can very well change the state, as we did in the previous sample program.

Therefore, final doesn't fulfill the task of preventing write access to objects. A method with passed references can therefore modify objects if, for example, set*(...) methods or variables can be accessed. Thus, the documentation must always explicitly describe when the method modifies the state of an object.

In C++, the addition const for parameters enables the compiler to recognize that object states shouldn't be changed. A program is called *const-correct* if it never modifies a constant object. This const is an extension of the object type in C++, which doesn't exist in Java. Although Java's developers have reserved the const keyword, it's not used yet.

3.7.5   Identity of Objects

The comparison operators == and != are defined for all data types in such a way that they test the complete correspondence of two values. With primitive data types, this correspondence is easy to see, and with reference types, it's basically the same. (Remember: references can be understood as pointers, which are integers.) The == operator tests references to see if they match (i.e., reference the same object). The != operator tests the opposite (i.e., whether they do not match), so the references aren't equal. Accordingly, the test says something about the identity of the referenced objects, but nothing about whether two different objects may have the same content. The content of the objects doesn't matter for == and !=.

[Ex]

Example

The following example shows two objects with three different point variables (p, q, and r) and illustrates the meaning of ==:

```
Point p = new Point( 10, 10 );
Point q = p;
Point r = new Point( 10, 10 );
System.out.println( p == q ); // true, because p and q reference the
                              // same object
System.out.println( p == r ); // false, because p and r reference two
                              // different point objects that happen to have
                              // the same coordinates
```

Since p and q reference the same object, the comparison returns true. p and r reference different objects, but they happen to have the same content. But how is the compiler supposed to know when two point objects are equal in content? Is it because a point is characterized by the object variables x and y? The runtime environment might hastily compare the assignment of each object variable, but this approach doesn't always correspond to the correct comparison we desire. For example, a point object could additionally record the number of method calls, which may not be taken into account in a comparison based on the location of two points.

3.7.6 Equivalence and the equals(...) Method

The universal solution is to let the class determine when objects are equal (i.e., have the same value). For this purpose, each class can implement a method called equals(...), and with its help, each instance of this class can compare itself with any other object. The classes always decide, according to the use case, which object variables they refer to for an equality test, and equals(...) returns true if the desired states (object variables) match.

[Ex]

Example

Two non-identical point objects with the same content can be compared via == and equals(...), as in the following example:

```
Point p = new Point( 10, 10 );
Point q = new Point( 10, 10 );
System.out.println( p == q );        // false
System.out.println( p.equals(q) ); // true, since symmetrically also
                                     // q.equals(p)
```

Only equals(...) tests content equivalence in this case.

Accordingly, due to the different meanings, we must carefully distinguish the concepts of *identity* and *equivalence* (also *equality*) of objects. For this reason, Table 3.4 shows a summary.

	Tested with	Implementation
Identity of the references	== or !=	Nothing to do
Equivalence of states	equals(…) or ! equals(…)	Depending on the class

Table 3.4 Identity and Equivamlence of Objects

equals(…) Implementation of Point*

The Point class declares equals(...), as described in the API documentation. Let's look at an implementation for an idea of how it works next.

```
public class Point … {

  public int x;
  public int y;
  …
  public boolean equals( Object obj ) {
    …
    Point pt = (Point) obj;
      return (x == pt.x) && (y == pt.y);   // (*)
    …
  }
}
```

Listing 3.15 java/awt/Point.java (Snippet)

Although some things are new in this example, we recognize the comparison in line (*). In this case, the Point object compares its own object variables with the object variables of the point object passed as argument to equals(...).

There's Always an equals(…): The Object Superclass and Its Equals*

Every class has a equals(...) method because of the universal superclass Object (see Chapter 7; for details). Thus, if a class doesn't specify its own equals(...) method, it inherits an implementation from the Object class, as in the following example:

```
public class Object {
  public boolean equals( Object obj ) {
    return ( this == obj );
```

```
  }
  ...
}
```

Listing 3.16 java/lang/Object.java (Snippet)

In this case, the equivalence is mapped to the identity of the references, but no comparison of content occurs. This equivalence is the only thing the given implementation can do because, if the references are identical, the objects are naturally the same. The only thing is that the base class `Object` doesn't "know" anything about is states.

Language Comparison

Programming languages generally provide their own operators for identity comparison and equivalence testing. `==` and `equals(...)` in Java is analogous to `is` and `==` in Python and `===` and `==` in Swift.

3.8   Further Reading

In this chapter, the topic of object orientation was introduced rather quickly, which doesn't mean that OOP is easy. The road to good design is rocky and leads through many Java projects. Reading other programs and studying design patterns can be immensely helpful. Readers should also get comfortable with UML to sketch design ideas. An interesting approach is taken by PlantUML (*https://plantuml.com/*) with a text syntax that the tool converts into graphics.

Chapter 4
Arrays and Their Areas of Use

"Those who fall out of line form the beginning of a new line."
—Erhard Horst Bellermann (1937–)[1]

In the programs you saw in previous chapters, variables stored exactly one value. In this chapter, we will see that there can be a collection of values behind a variable. We call these simple collections *arrays*.

4.1 Simple Field Work

An *array* is a special data type that combines several values into one unit, like a display case in which the compartments are numbered consecutively. The elements are addressed via an integer index. Each compartment (for Smurfs, for example) always takes values of the same type (only Smurfs, no Pokémon). Normally, the compartments of an array (its elements) are located one after the other in memory, but this implementation detail on the virtual machine (VM) is not visible to programmers.

---

1 *https://ebellermann.wordpress.com*

Each array contains values of only one specific data type or basic type, namely, the following:

- Elementary data types (like int, byte, long, etc.)
- Reference types
- Reference types of other arrays to form multidimensional arrays

4.1.1   Basic Components

Working with arrays requires you to learn three new things:

1. Declaring array variables
2. Initializing array variables as well as allocating space
3. Accessing arrays, with both read and write access

[Ex]

Example

1. Declare a variable named prices that references an array:

   ```
   double[] prices;
   ```

2. Initialize the variable with an array object of size 10:

   ```
   prices = new double[ 10 ];
   ```

3. Assign a random number to the first element and assign twice the value of the first element to the second element:

   ```
   prices[ 0 ] = Math.random();
   prices[ 1 ] = prices[ 0 ] * 2;
   ```

Note how square brackets are used in several places: once to declare the type, then to build the array, then to write to arrays and to read from arrays. We'll now describe these three elements in more detail.

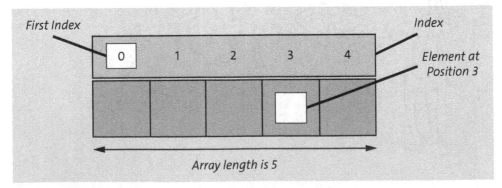

Figure 4.1 Terms of an Array

4.1.2 Declaring Array Variables

Declaring an array variable is similar to an ordinary declaration except that the characters [and] are placed after the data type. Let's use the prices variable again, which is intended to store prices, as defined in the following way:

```
double[] prices;
```

The declaration has two types of information at its core: that it "is an array" and that it will "store elements of type int."

Tip [+]

The square brackets are tokens, so whitespace isn't mandatory for separation. Another valid example is the following:

```
double[]prices;
```

Placing the square brackets before the variable is also syntactically valid but not at all recommended:

```
double []prices;  // Violation of the usual Java style guide
```

Note [«]

The square brackets can also be placed after the identifier name when declaring an array variable, but the declaration is slightly different in this case. This difference becomes apparent when more than one variable is declared, as in the following example:

```
double []prices,
      matrix[], threeDimMatrix[][];
```

This code corresponds to the following declaration:

```
double prices[], matrix[][], threeDimMatrix[][][];
```

The following example is more neatly written:

```
double[]     prices;
double[][]   matrix;
double[][][] threeDimMatrix;
```

To avoid errors of this kind, each line should contain only one declaration of a type. In any case, according to pure Java doctrine, the brackets should be placed after the type identifier, as Java creator James Gosling intended.

Arrays with Non-Primitive Elements

The data type of the array elements doesn't have to be a primitive data type. An array of object references can also be declared. This array then only stores references to actual objects. The size of the array in memory is therefore calculated from the length of the array multiplied by the memory requirement of a reference variable. Only the array object itself is created, not the objects the array will store simply because the compiler wouldn't even know which constructor to call.

[Ex]

Example

The following example declares two array variables:

```
String[] names;
Point[]  locations;
```

4.1.3   Creating Array Objects with new

Creating the array reference variable alone doesn't create an array of a specific length. In Java, the creation of the array is as dynamic as the nature of object creation. An array must be created using the new keyword because arrays are also objects.[2] The length of the array is specified in square brackets, which can be any integer value or even a variable. Even 0 is possible. Later, the size of the array cannot be changed.

[Ex]

Example

The following example creates an array of ten elements:

```
double[] prices;
prices = new double[ 10 ];
```

The array declaration can also occur together with the initialization, as in the following example:

```
double[] prices = new double[ 10 ];
```

The Java virtual machine (JVM) initializes the arrays by default, for instance, with 0, 0.0 or false for primitive values and with null for references.

Arrays Are Pretty Normal Objects

Several indications prove that arrays are objects, namely, the following:

- A special type of the new notation creates a copy of the array class; new always reminds us that an object is being built at runtime.

- An array object has an object variable named length, and methods are declared on the array object, such as clone() and everything that java.long.Object has.

---

2 Programming languages such as C(++) provide shortcuts such as int array[100] when creating arrays. In Java, this expression would cause a compiler error.

- The == and != operators follow their meaning as it relates to objects: These operators only compare whether two variables reference the same array object, but in no case do these operators evaluate the contents of the arrays (although `Arrays.equals(...)` can).

Access to array elements via the square brackets `[]` can be understood as a hidden call via secret methods like `array.get(index)`. The `[]` operator isn't provided for other objects.

4.1.4   Arrays with { contents }

The previous declarations of array variables don't create an array object that can store the individual array elements. However, if the entries are to be assigned values directly, a shortcut in Java can automatically create an array object and assign values to it at the same time.

Example [Ex]

Consider the following example of a value assignment of an array during its initialization:

```
double[] prices  = { 2.99, 3.10, 4.40 + 0.90 };
String[] names = {
    "Caramellos," "Gummi Fish."
    "Starbursts".toUpperCase(),    // STARBURSTS
    new StringBuilder( "M" ).append( '&' ).append( 'M' ).toString() // M&M
};
```

In this case, an array of suitable size is created, and the elements named in the enumeration are copied into the array. Dynamic calculations at runtime are possible because the values don't need to be fixed.

Note [«]

Empty arrays without contents are also allowed. The arrays are initialized but have no elements, and their `length` is 0, as in the following examples:

```
String[] names = {};
```

or

```
double[] prices = new int[0]
```

You can place a comma before the closing curly bracket, so that `double[] prices = { 2, 3, };` is valid. This syntax simplifies adding elements but doesn't produce any empty element. Even the following is possible in Java: `double[] prices = { , };`.

[»]

Note

The declaration of an array variable with initialization doesn't work with var, as in the following example:

```
var prices = { 2, 3 };  // ☠ Array initializer is not allowed here
```

4.1.5 Reading the Length of an Array via the Object Variable Length

The number of elements an array can store is called its *size* or *length* and is stored for each array object in the freely accessible object variable length, which is a public-final-int variable whose value is either positive or null. The size can't be changed subsequently.

[Ex]

Example

The following code creates an array and then outputs its length:

```
int[] prices = { 2, 3, 5, 7, 7 + 4 };
System.out.println( prices.length );           // 5
```

Array Lengths Are Final

The object variable attribute length of an array isn't only public and of type int, but of course also final. Write access isn't allowed because a dynamic enlargement of an array isn't possible; write access leads to a translation error.

[»]

Note

Other containers also have a length, which is usually requested via a method. Beginners often are confused when, for example, the length of a string is queried via a length() method, the number of elements in an array via the length attribute, and in the ArrayList data structure via size().

4.1.6 Accessing the Elements via the Index

The elements of an array are accessed using the square brackets [] placed after the reference to the array object. In Java, an array starts at index 0 (and not at a freely selectable lower limit as in Pascal). Since the elements of an array are numbered starting at 0, the last valid index is 1 less than the length of the array. Thus, for an array a of length n, the valid range is a [0] to a[n - 1].

Since the variables are accessed via an index, these variables are also called *indexed variables*.

> **Example**
>
> The following example accesses the first and last characters from the array:
>
> ```
> char[] name  = { 'C', 'h', 'r', 'i', 's' };
> char  first = name[ 0 ];                    // C
> char  last  = name[ name.length - 1 ];      // s
> ```

> **Example**
>
> The following example runs the entire array with prices and outputs the positions starting at 1:
>
> ```
> double[] prices = { 2, 3, 5, 7, 11 };
> for ( int i = 0; i < prices.length; i++ ) // Index: 0 <= i < 5 =
>                                            // prices.length
>   System.out.printf( "%d %s%n", i + 1, prices[ i ] );
> ```

Calculating the Arithmetic Mean of Prices

Instead of just running an array and outputting the values, our next program will calculate and output the arithmetic mean of prices.

```java
public class PrintTheAverage {

  public static void main( String[] args ) {
    double[] numbers = { 1.9, 7.8, 2.4, 9.3 };

    double sum = 0;

    for ( int i = 0; i < numbers.length; i++ )
      sum += numbers[ i ];

    double avg = sum / numbers.length;

    System.out.println( avg );  // 5.35
  }
}
```

Listing 4.1 src/main/java/com/tutego/insel/array/PrintTheAverage.java

The array must have at least one element; otherwise, an exception will occur when dividing by 0.

On the Type of the Index*

Inside the square brackets is a positive integer expression of type int, which must be computable at runtime. long values, boolean, floats, or references aren't possible; however, int enables the use of more than two billion elements. With regard to floats, the question of the access technique would remain. In this case, we would have to reduce the value to an interval.

[»]

> **Note**
>
> The index of an array must be of type int, and this also includes type conversions from byte, short, and char. An index of type char is favorable, for example, as a run variable, when arrays of characters are generated, as in the following example:
>
> ```
> char[] alphabet = new char[ 'z' - 'a' + 1 ]; // 'a' equals 97 and 'z' 122
> for ( char c = 'a'; c <= 'z'; c++ )
>   alphabet[ c - 'a' ] = c;            // alphabet[0]='a', alphabet[1]='b', etc.
> ```
>
> Strictly speaking, in this case, we're also dealing with index values of the type int because the char values are still calculated beforehand.

Strings Are Not Arrays*

An array of char characters has a completely different type than a String object. While square brackets are allowed for arrays, the String class doesn't provide access to characters via []. However, the String class provides a constructor so that a String object can be created from an array of characters. All characters of the array are copied, and then afterwards, the array and string have no more connection. Thus, if the array later changes, the string won't automatically change with it. Nor can it since strings are immutable.

4.1.7   Typical Array Errors

Errors may occur when accessing an element of an array. First, the array object may be missing, which means the referencing will fail.

[Ex]

> **Example**
>
> The compiler doesn't notice the following error, and the penalty is a NullPointerException at runtime.[3] Consider the following example:
>
> ```
> String[] names = null;
> names[ 0 ] = 1;     // ☠ NullPointerException
> ```

---

3 However, the compiler will also complain when local variables haven't been initialized.

Other errors may be caused by the index. If the index is negative[4] or larger than the size of the array, then an `ArrayIndexOutOfBoundsException` will occur.[5] Each access to the array is tested at runtime, although the compiler may well find some errors.

Example

With the following access attempts, the compiler could theoretically sound an alarm, which the standard compiler wouldn't do because accessing the elements is syntactically fine even with an invalid index. Consider the following examples:

```
int[] array = new int[ 100 ];
array[ -10 ] = 1;    // ☠ error at runtime, not at compile time
array[ 100 ] = 1;    // ☠ error at runtime, not at compile time
```

If the `IndexOutOfBoundsException` isn't caught, the runtime system aborts the program with an error message. The fact that the array boundaries are checked is part of Java's security concept and can't be turned off. However, this check is no longer a major performance issue today since the runtime environment doesn't need to check every index to ensure that a block with array access is correct.

Gimmick: The Index and the Increment*

In Chapter 2, we looked at using i = i++ as an increment. The statement is treated the same way for an array access, as in the following example:

```
array[ i ] = i++;
```

At position `array[i]`, the value of i is saved, and then the assignment is made. When you construct a loop around an array, you can extend it during initialization, as in the following example:

```
int[] array = new int[ 4 ];
int i = 0;
while ( i < array.length )
  array[ i ] = i++;
```

The initialization results in 0, 1, 2, and 3. This use isn't recommended due to a lack of clarity.

---

4 Python or Perl behave quite differently. In those cases, a negative index is used to address a field element relative to the last array entry. Even in C, a negative index is quite possible and practical.

5 `ArrayIndexOutOfBoundsException` is a subclass of *https://docs.oracle.com/en/java/javase/17/docs/api/java.base/java/lang/IndexOutOfBoundsException.html*, which in turn is a subclass of Runtime-Exception, and consequently doesn't necessarily need to be caught as an exception, also called *unchecked exceptions*, a topic for Chapter 9, Section 9.1.2.

4.1.8   Passing Arrays to Methods

References to arrays can be passed to methods in the same way as references to normal objects. Earlier in Section 4.1.6, we determined the mean value of a number series. The logic for this calculation can be perfectly swapped out to a method, as in the following example:

```java
public class Avg1 {

  static double avg( double[] numbers ) {
    double sum = 0;

    for ( int i = 0; i < numbers.length; i++ )
      sum += numbers[ i ];

    return sum / numbers.length;
  }

  public static void main( String[] args ) {
    double[] prices = { 2, 3, 4 };
    System.out.println( avg( prices ) );              // 3.0
  }
}
```

Listing 4.2 src/main/java/com/tutego/insel/array/Avg1.java

Checking null References

References always entail the problem that they can be null. A call of avg(null) is syntactically valid. Therefore, an implementation should check for null and report a false argument, as in the following example:

```java
if ( numbers == null || numbers.length == 0 )
  throw new IllegalArgumentException( "Array null or empty" );
```

For further details on this topic, refer to Chapter 9.

4.1.9   Multiple Return Values*

When we write methods in Java, they can't have more than one return value when return is used. But if you need to return more than one value, you'll need another solution. Two possible options can be useful in these cases:

- Containers, such as arrays or other collections, can combine values and return them as return values.
- Special containers are passed in which the method places return values; a return statement is no longer necessary.

Let's consider a static method that returns the sum and the product as an array for two numbers next.

```java
static int[] productAndSum( int a, int b ) {
  return new int[]{ a * b, a + b };
}

public static void main( String[] args ) {
  System.out.println( productAndSum(9, 3)[ 1 ] );
}
```

Listing 4.3 src/main/java/com/tutego/insel/array/MultipleReturnValues.java (Snippet)

4.1.10   Preinitialized Arrays

If we want to create an array object in Java and initialize it with values right away, you can write something like the following code:

```java
double[] prices = { 2, 3, 5 };
```

Java doesn't allow you to initialize array contents after the variable declaration or to use the array even without a variable as argument, as in the following examples:

```java
prices = { 2.2, 3.9 };          // 💀 compiler error
avg( { 1.23, 4.94 } );          // 💀 compiler error
```

An attempt like this example will fail and trigger the compiler message "Array initializer is not allowed here."

Two possible approaches can solve this problem. The first approach includes the introduction of a new variable, in the following example, tmpprices:

```java
double[] prices;
double[] tmpprices = { 2 };
prices = tmpprices;
```

The second approach represents a variant of the new notation, which is extended by a pair of square brackets. The initial values of the array then follow in curly brackets. The size of the array corresponds exactly to the number of values. For the earlier examples, the notation would be the following:

```java
double[] prices;
prices = new double[]{ 2, 5, 7, 11, 13 };
```

The following notation is also quite handy for method calls when arrays are passed:

```java
avg( new double[]{ 1.23, 4.94, 9.33, 3.91, 6.34 } );
```

Since in this case an initialized array with values is passed to the method right away and no additional variable is used, this type of array is referred to as an *anonymous array*. Actually, other kinds of anonymous arrays also exist, as shown by `new int[ 2000 ].length`, but in this case, the array is not initialized with its own values.

The Truth about Array Initialization*

As nice as the compact initialization of array elements can be, this approach is also runtime and memory intensive. Since Java is a dynamic language, the concept of array initialization doesn't quite fit into the picture. For this reason, the initialization is performed only at runtime.

An array like

```
int[] weights = { 2, 3, 5, 7 };
```

is transformed by the Java compiler and treated in a similar way to the following:

```
int[] weights = new int[ 4 ];
weights[ 0 ] = 2;
weights[ 1 ] = 3;
weights[ 2 ] = 5;
weights[ 3 ] = 7;
```

Only after a moment's reflection does the extent of the implementation become apparent: First, the methods will have memory requirements. If the `weights` array is declared in a method and initialized with values, the assignment costs runtime because we have many access attempts, which are also all nicely secured by the index check. In addition, since the bytecode for a single method may only be of limited length due to various restrictions in the JVM, this space can quickly be exhausted for really large arrays. For this reason, we don't advise storing images or large tables in the program code, for example. In C, a popular approach was to use a program that turned a file into a sequence of array declarations. If doing so is really necessary in Java, consider the following points:

- You can use a static array (a class variable) so that the array only needs to be initialized once during the program run.
- If the values are in the byte range, you can convert these values to a string and then later convert the string into an array. This option is a clever way to easily accommodate binary data.

4.2 The Extended for Loop

`for` loops often traverse arrays or data structures. As earlier in Section 4.1.6, when calculating the mean value, we can use the following code:

```
double sum = 0;
for ( int i = 0; i < numbers.length; i++ )
  sum += numbers[ i ];
double arg = sum / numbers.length;
```

The only justification for the loop variable i is to serve as an index; only with i can the element be addressed at a certain place in the array.

Because complete iterations of arrays are frequent, the following shortcut can be used for such iterations:

```
for ( type identifier: Array )
  …
```

The extended form of the for loop detaches from the index and queries each element of the array. Think of this as passing through a set because the colon can be read as "in." To the right of the colon is always an array or, as we'll see later in this section, something of type Iterable, such as a data structure. On the left, a new local variable is declared that will later accept each element of the collection as it runs.

Let's now rewrite our program for calculating averages. The static method avg(...) should run with the extended for over the loop instead of incrementing the index itself. An exception indicates whether the array reference is null or the array contains no elements.

```
static double avg( double[] numbers ) {
  if ( numbers == null || numbers.length == 0 )
    throw new IllegalArgumentException( "Array null or empty" );

  double sum = 0;

  for ( double n : numbers )
    sum += n;

  return sum / numbers.length;
}
```

Listing 4.4 src/main/java/com/tutego/insel/array/Avg2.java, avg()

The for line is therefore to be read as "For each element n of type double in numbers do...." A variable for the loop index is no longer necessary.

4.2.1 Using Anonymous Arrays in the Extended for Loop

To the right of the colon, you can quickly build an array over which the extended for can then run, as in the following example:

```
for ( int weight : new int[]{ 2, 3, 5, 7, 11 } )
  System.out.println( weight );
```

This approach is convenient for running over a fixed set of values and also works for objects, such as strings, as in the following example:

```
for ( String name : new String[]{ "Butterfinger Crisp", "NutRageous" } )
  System.out.println( name );
```

[»]

Note

To the right of the colon, you can have an array or an object of type `Iterable`:

```
for ( String name : Arrays.asList( "Butterfinger Crisp", "NutRageous" ) )
  System.out.println( name );
```

`Arrays.asList(...)` doesn't create an array as a return but instead builds a collection from the variable argument list, which is of the special `Iterable` type; anything `Iterable` can run the extended `for` loop. We'll get back to this topic later in this section. Regardless of the extended `for`, using `Arrays.asList(...)` has another advantage, such as for actual-element-of queries, like the following example:

```
if ( Arrays.asList( 1, 2, 6, 7, 8, 10 ).contains( number ) )
  …
```

More about this method will follow in Section 4.6.

Internally, the compiler implements this extended `for` loop quite classically, so that the bytecode is the same for both variants. However, some disadvantages of this variant include the following:

- The extended `for` always runs through the entire array by default. A start index and an end index can't be set explicitly. The loop can be aborted using `break` so that a premature end of the loop is basically possible.
- The order is always "front to back."
- The step length is always 1.
- The index isn't visible.
- The loop returns an element but can't write to the array.

If other requirements exist, only a classic `for` loop can help.

4.2.2 Example: Searching Arrays with Strings

In our first example, we want a non-primitive array to reference strings and later check if any user input in the array exists. Case-insensitive string comparisons can be implemented with `equalsIgnoreCase(...)`, as in the following example:

```java
String[] validInputs = { "Banana", "Apple", "Cherry" };

String input = null;
boolean found = false;
while ( ! found ) {
  input = new Scanner( System.in ).nextLine();

  for ( String s : validInputs )
    if ( s.equalsIgnoreCase( input ) ) {
      found = true;
      break;
    }
}

System.out.println( "Yummy " + input );
```

Listing 4.5 src/main/java/com/tutego/insel/array/UserInputInStringArray.java, main()

To initialize the array, the program uses a compact variant that combines three things: the construction of an array object (with sufficient space for three references), the initialization of the array object with the three object references, and finally the initialization of the validInputs variable with the new array—all in a single statement.

For the search, the extended for is used, which is embedded in a loop that ends exactly when the found flag becomes true. If we never enter a correct string, the outer loop will never end. If we find an entry, the flag can be set, and break will exit the array loop prematurely.

4.2.3 Creating Random Player Positions

In the second example, five randomly initialized points are to be stored in an array. The points are supposed to represent players.

First, let's initialize an array with the following code:

```java
Point[] players = new Point[ 5 ];
```

The declaration creates space for five references to point objects, but not a single Point object is created. By default, the array elements are initialized with the null reference, so System.out.println(players[0]) would bring the output "null" to the screen. We don't want to leave it at null, so the individual array positions must be initialized with something like players[0] = new Point().

Random numbers are generated by the mathematical method Math.random(). However, since the static method returns floats between 0 (inclusive) and 1 (exclusive), the numbers are first manipulated by multiplication and then truncated.

In the final step, we'll output a grid on the screen where two nested loops traverse all x/y coordinates of the selected area and then set a & when the point hits a player.

Let's look at the complete program.

```java
Point[] players = new Point[ 5 ];

for ( int i = 0; i < players.length; i++ )
  players[ i ] = new Point( (int)(Math.random() * 40),
                            (int)(Math.random() * 10) );

for ( int y = 0; y < 10; y++ ) {
  for ( int x = 0; x < 40; x++ )
    if ( Arrays.asList( players ).contains( new Point(x,y) ) )
      System.out.print( '&' );
    else
      System.out.print( '.' );
  System.out.println();
}
```

Listing 4.6 src/main/java/com/tutego/insel/array/FivePlayers.java, main()

The expression `Arrays.asList(players).contains(new Point(x, y))` checks whether any point in the `players` array is equal to the point with x/y coordinates.

The program generates the following output:

```
........................................
...............&........................
&.......................................
........................................
........................................
.............................&..........
........................................
...&.................&..............
........................................
........................................
```

While the extended for loop is good for traversing arrays, it doesn't work for initialization because the extended for is only good for reading. Element initializations work for arrays only with `players[i]=...`, which requires a classic for loop with the index.

4.3   A Method with a Variable Number of Arguments

For many methods, you'll clearly see exactly how many arguments must be passed. For example, nothing may be passed to a `Math.random()` method, and exactly one argument is valid for `Math.sin(double)`.

4.3.1   System.out.printf(...) Accepts Any Number of Arguments

In some methods, the number of valid arguments is basically unlimited. An example is printf(String, ...), which expects a string first but is free to pass anything else. Valid calls of this method include the following examples.

Call	Variable Argument List
System.out.printf("%n")	Is empty.
System.out.printf("%s", "One")	Consists of only one element: One.
System.out.printf("%s,%s,%s", "1", "2", "3")	Consists of three elements: 1, 2, and 3.

Table 4.1 Valid Calls of printf(...)

To make the number of parameters arbitrary, Java provides methods with a *variable number of arguments*, called *varargs*. (In other programming languages these are called *variadic function*.) The method printf(formattingstring, arg1, args2, arg3, ...) is an example of a varargs method.

```
class java.io.PrintStream extends FilterOutputStream
implements Appendable, Closeable
```

▶ PrintStream printf(String format, **Object...** args)
Accepts an arbitrary list of arguments and formats it according to the given formatting string, format. The formatting string determines how many arguments are needed. However, the compiler doesn't evaluate the string, so it can't check its correctness (i.e., that the number is correct), even at compile time.

A method with a variable number of arguments uses the ellipsis (...) to clarify that any number of arguments can be specified, including the specification of no elements. However, the type isn't dropped in this case since it is also specified.

4.3.2   Finding the Average of Variable Arguments

Earlier in Section 4.1.6, we wrote a method—avg(double[] numbers)—to calculate the arithmetic mean of values. Let's now change the parameter type to avg(double...numbers) so that the method can be easily filled with variable arguments. Only a small change from [] to ... is required; otherwise, nothing changes in the implementation. Let's look at a completely programmed example next.

```
public class AvgVarArgs {

  static double avg( double... numbers ) { /* implementation as before */ }
```

```
public static void main( String[] args ) {
  System.out.println( avg(1, 2, 9, 3) );       // 3.75
  }
}
```

Listing 4.7 src/main/java/com/tutego/insel/array/AvgVarArgs.java (Snippet)

[»]

> **Note**
>
> If variable argument lists are defined in the signature, they may form only the last parameter; otherwise, the compiler can't determine which parameters are varargs and which are the next filled parameter. This limitation automatically implies that a maximum of one vararg can be used in the parameter list.

The Connection between Varargs and Arrays

A method with a vararg is basically a method with an array as a parameter type. The bytecode does not really say avg(double... numbers) but says instead avg(double[] numbers) with the additional info that numbers is a vararg. Thus, the compiler allows any number of arguments and not exclusively a double[] array as the argument.

The user can call a varargs method without explicitly defining an array for the arguments. They don't even notice that the compiler has created an array with four elements in the background. Thus, from

```
System.out.println( avg(1, 2, 9, 3) );
```

the compiler generates the following:

```
System.out.println( avg( new double[] { 1, 2, 9, 3 } ) );
```

It's easy to see from the notation that we can also pass an array manually:

```
double[] values = { 1, 2, 9, 3 };
System.out.println( avg( values ) );
```

[»]

> **Note**
>
> Since varargs are implemented as arrays, overloaded variants like avg(int... numbers) and avg(int[] numbers)—the first with a vararg and the second with an array—are not possible. In this case, a better approach is to always use a variant with varargs, which is more powerful. Some authors also write the initial method main(String[] args) with variable arguments, for instance, main(String... args). This expression is valid because an array exists in the bytecode.

4.3.3 Vararg Design Tips*

If a method has only one array parameter that is located at the end, you can replace it relatively easily by a vararg, which gives the caller the convenient possibility to use a more compact syntax. Some authors also write the entry method main(String[] args) with variable arguments, so that variable arguments can easily be passed to the main(...) method when testing.

If a minimum number of arguments must be guaranteed—for max(...), at least two—you should use a declaration like max(int first, int second, int... remaining).

For performance reasons, we recommend providing methods with frequent parameter list sizes as fixed methods, such as max(double, double), max(double, double, double), and max(double...). With this approach, the compiler always selects the appropriate method automatically, no temporary array objects are needed for two or three parameters, and automatic garbage collection doesn't have to clear anything away.

4.4 Multidimensional Arrays*

Java implements multidimensional arrays as arrays of arrays. Multidimensional arrays can be used, for example, for representing mathematical matrices or raster images. This section describes how you can initialize, build, and use objects for multidimensional arrays.

The following code declares a two-dimensional array matrix with space for a total of 32 cells, arranged in 4 rows and 8 columns:

```
int[][] matrix = new int[ 4 ][ 8 ];
```

Multidimensional arrays are basically arrays with arrays as elements and can be easily declared.

As with one-dimensional arrays, multidimensional arrays can be initialized immediately during their creation, as in the following example:

```
int[][] matrix3x2 = { {1, 2}, {2, 3}, {3, 4} };
int[][] triangle  = { {1}, {2, 3}, {4, 5, 6} };
```

The second case suggests that the array doesn't have to be rectangular. More on this topic in Section 4.4.1.

Individual elements are addressed by the expression matrix[i][j].[6] The access is achieved with as many pairs of parentheses as dimensions of the array.

---

6 The notation A[i,j], which is common in Pascal, is not supported in Java. Basically, the notation would be possible because Java, unlike C(++), allows the comma operator only in for loops.

[Ex]

Example

The structure of two-dimensional arrays (and access to them) is comparable to a matrix or table. Then, the entry in the array a[x][y] can be read in the following table:

```
a[0][0]  a[0][1]  a[0][2]  a[0][3]  a[0][4]  a[0][5]  ...
a[1][0]  a[1][1]  a[1][2]  a[1][3]  a[1][4]  a[1][5]
a[2][0]  a[2][1]  a[2][2]  a[2][3]  a[2][4]  a[2][5]
...
```

Next, let's take a letter definition like the following:

```java
char[][] letter = { { ' ', '#', ' ' },
                    { '#', ' ', '#' },
                    { '#', ' ', '#' },
                    { '#', ' ', '#' },
                    { ' ', '#', ' ' } };
```

In this case, we can apply length in two different ways:

- letter.length results in 5 because there are five lines.
- letter[0].length results in 3—just like letter[1].length and so on—because each sub-array has a size of 3.

To output the letters of our example multidimensional array to the screen, you can use two nested loops, as in the following example:

```java
for ( int line = 0; line < letter.length; line++ ) {
  for ( int column = 0; column < letter[line].length; column++ )
    System.out.print( letter[line][column] );
  System.out.println();
}
```

Let's summarize our knowledge into a program that asks a user for a number and then outputs this number in binary representation. The digits 0 and 1 are made up of several symbols and are rotated 90 degrees clockwise and placed one below the other so we don't have to deal with placing the letters horizontally next to each other.

```java
package com.tutego.insel.array;

import java.util.Scanner;

public class BinaryBanner {

  static void printLetter( char[][] letter ) {
    for ( int column = 0; column < letter[0].length; column++ ) {
```

```java
      for ( int line = letter.length - 1; line >= 0; line-- )
        System.out.print( letter[line][column] );
      System.out.println();
    }
    System.out.println();
  }

  static void printZero() {
    char[][] zero = { { ' ', '#', ' ' },
                      { '#', ' ', '#' },
                      { '#', ' ', '#' },
                      { '#', ' ', '#' },
                      { ' ', '#', ' ' } };
    printLetter( zero );
  }

  static void printOne() {
    char[][] one = { { ' ', '#' },
                     { '#', '#' },
                     { ' ', '#' },
                     { ' ', '#' },
                     { ' ', '#' } };
    printLetter( one );
  }

  public static void main( String[] args ) {
    int input  = new Scanner( System.in ).nextInt();
    String bin = Integer.toBinaryString( input );
    System.out.printf( "Banner for %s (binary %s):%n", input, bin );
    for ( int i = 0; i < bin.length(); i++ )
      switch ( bin.charAt( i ) ) {
        case '0' -> printZero();
        case '1' -> printOne();
      }
  }
}
```

Listing 4.8 src/main/java/com/tutego/insel/array/BinaryBanner.java

The printLetter(char[][]) method gets the two-dimensional array as its argument and runs differently than in the first case to implement the rotation. The input "2" results in the following output:

```
Banner for 2 (binary 10):
   #
#####

 ###
#   #
 ###
```

4.4.1 Nonrectangular Arrays*

Since multidimensional arrays are implemented as arrays of arrays in Java, these arrays don't necessarily have to be rectangular. Each row in the array can have its own size.

[Ex]

Example

The following example creates a triangular array with rows of length 1, 2, and 3:

```
int[][] triangle = new int[ 3 ][];
for ( int i = 0; i < 3; i++ )
    triangle[ i ] = new int[ i + 1 ];
```

Initializing the Sub-Arrays

When you declare a multidimensional array, hidden loops automatically create the inner arrays. Consider the following example:

```
int[][] a = new int[ 3 ][ 4 ];
```

In this case, the runtime environment creates the appropriate sub-arrays automatically. However, this creation does not occur with the following code:

```
int[][] a = new int[ 3 ][];
```

Instead, you must initialize the sub-arrays yourself before accessing the elements, as in the following example:

```
for ( int i = 0; i < a.length; i++ )
    a[ i ] = new int[ 4 ];
```

Note that `int[][] m = new int[][4];` doesn't work, of course!

[Ex]

Example

You can initialize a multidimensional array in several ways:

```
int[][] matrix3x2 = { {1,2}, {2,3}, {3,4} };
```

or

```
int[][] matrix3x2 = new int[][]{ {1,2}, {2,3}, {3,4} };
```

or

```
int[][] matrix3x2 = new int[][]{ new int[]{1,2}, new int[]{2,3},
  new int[]{3,4} };
```

Pascal's Triangle

The following example shows another application of non-rectangular arrays, in which Pascal's triangle is emulated. The triangle is structured in such a way that the elements under a number form exactly the sum of the two numbers directly above it. The edges are filled with ones.

```
              1
            1   1
          1   2   1
        1   3   3   1
      1   4   6   4   1
    1   5  10  10   5   1
  1   6  15  20  15   6   1
```

Listing 4.9 Pascal's Triangle

In the following implementation, an array with the appropriate length is dynamically requested for each level:

```java
class PascalsTriangle {

  public static void main( String[] args ) {
    int[][] triangle = new int[7][];

    for ( int row = 0; row < triangle.length; row++ ) {
      System.out.print( " ".repeat( 14 - 2 * row) );

      triangle[row] = new int[row + 1];

      for ( int col = 0; col <= row; col++ ) {
        if ( (col == 0) || (col == row) )
          triangle[row][col] = 1;
        else
          triangle[row][col] = triangle[row - 1][col - 1] +
                               triangle[row - 1][col];

        System.out.printf( "%3d ", triangle[row][col] );
      }
      System.out.println();
```

```
      }
    }
  }
}
```

Listing 4.10 src/main/java/com/tutego/insel/array/PascalsTriangle.java, main()

The `String` method `repeat(...)` generates the leading spaces so that the triangle is centered.

Other Areas of Use

With two-dimensional arrays, the management of symmetric matrices is simple since these matrices contain elements that are symmetric to the diagonal. Thus, either the upper or the lower triangular matrix can be omitted.[7]

[»]

> **Note**
>
> An unusual syntax in Java allows you to place the pair of square brackets after the method header for array returns, in contrast to the following code:
>
> `static int[] productAndSum( int a, int b )`
>
> Alternatively, you can write the following code:
>
> `static int productAndSum( int a, int b )[]`
>
> The latter approach is not recommended. Even something like `int[] transposeMatrix(int[][] m)[]` is possible but should be written as `int[][] transposeMatrix(int[][] matrix)`.

4.5   Library Support for Arrays

Arrays are objects, but they "can't do" much. In many other programming languages, such as JavaScript, the situation is quite different. In Java, the methods are swapped out, especially in `java.util.Arrays`.

4.5.1   Cloning Can Be Worthwhile: Propagating Arrays

To create a copy of an array with the same size and element type, you can use the object method `clone()`.[8]

---

7   The use of this efficient type of storage for adjacency matrices. An adjacency matrix represents a simple way to store graphs. This two-dimensional array contains information about the existing edges in the (directed) graph. If an edge exists from one node to the other, an entry is made in the cell: either true/false for, "Yes, the two are connected," or an integer value for a weighting (edge weight). This is particularly useful for non-directed graphs.

8   This method is valid because arrays internally implement the `Cloneable` interface. Thus, `System.out.println( new int[0] instanceof Cloneable);` returns `true`.

This method clones—in our case copies—the elements of an array object into a new array.

Example [Ex]

The following code finds out whether an array is sorted or not:

```
int[] numbers = { 1, 2, 99 };
int[] numbersClone = numbers.clone();
Arrays.sort( numbersClone );
System.out.println( Arrays.equals( numbers, numbersClone ) );  // true
```

Arrays.sort(...) will operate in-place, so it would change the original array if any sorting is done. For that reason we make a copy and sort that copy. The Arrays.equals(...) call returns true in this example because the arrays have the same sorted contents.

In the case of cloned object arrays, note that the copy is flat. References from the first array are copied by clone() into the new array, but the referenced objects themselves are not cloned. Thus, for multidimensional arrays, only the first dimension is copied, and sub-arrays are thus shared.

Example [Ex]

In the following example, two arrays reference the same Point object; the copy is flat but not deep:

```
Point[] pointArray1 = { new Point(1, 2), new Point(2, 3) };
Point[] pointArray2 = pointArray1.clone();
System.out.println( pointArray1[ 0 ] == pointArray2[ 0 ] );  // true
```

4.5.2 Why Can Arrays "Do" So Little?

Arrays have a length attribute and a clone() method as well as the usual methods inherited from Object—which is not much! While other Java SE-classes like String, Arrays, or System have a Javadoc and consequently appear in the application programming interface (API) documentation there is no such Javadoc for arrays. Since an infinite number of array types exists—[] can be placed after any type—an infinite number of class declarations is possible.

What arrays can do is described in the Java Language Specification (JLS). Each time a new method or change is made, the JLS would require adjustment, which is impractical. Of course, methods like sort(...) and indexOf(...) on array objects would be handy, but if too much has been integrated in the language, that's not good. Oracle also wants to keep the documentation of such methods out of the JLS, which is why the methods have moved to an extra class, Arrays.

[»]

Note

The length is always the capacity of the array and is not information about how many array elements are in use. For example, an array may be 10 elements in size, but we might only use the first 2 positions.

4.5.3 Copying Array Contents

Another useful static method is System.arraycopy(...). It can work in two ways:

- **On two already existing arrays**
  Part of an array is copied into another array. arraycopy(...) is suitable for implementing enlarging arrays by first creating a new larger array and then copying the old array contents into the new one.

- **On the same array**
  The method can be used to move elements of an array by certain positions. The areas may well overlap.

[Ex]

Example

The arraycopy(...) method can also copy within its own array. The following code moves all elements in the array one position to the left or right and saves the remaining element to the end or to the start.

```java
static void rotateLeft( int[] numbers ) {
  int first = numbers[ 0 ];
  System.arraycopy( numbers, 1, numbers, 0, numbers.length - 1 );
  numbers[ numbers.length - 1 ] = first;
}
static void rotateRight( int[] numbers ) {
  int last = numbers[ numbers.length - 1 ];
  System.arraycopy( numbers, 0, numbers, 1, numbers.length - 1 );
  numbers[ 0 ] = last;
}
public static void main( String[] args ) {
  int[] numbers = { 1, 2, 3, 4 };
  rotateLeft( numbers );    // [2, 3, 4, 1]
  rotateLeft( numbers );    // [3, 4, 1, 2]
  rotateRight( numbers );   // [2, 3, 4, 1]
}
```

Listing 4.11 src/main/java/com/tutego/insel/array/ArrayRollLeftRight.java (Snippet)

```
final class java.lang.System
```

▶ static void arraycopy(Object src, int srcPos, Object dest, int destPos, int length)
Copies length entries of the src array from position srcPos into an array named dest from position destPos. The type of the array doesn't matter, but both arrays must be of the same type in both cases. For large arrays, this method works more quickly than a separate copy loop.

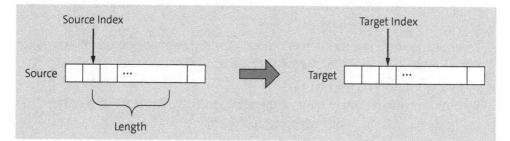

Figure 4.2 Copying the Elements from One Array to Another

4.6   Using the Arrays Class for Comparing, Filling, Searching, and Sorting

The java.util.Arrays class declares useful static methods for dealing with arrays, including options for comparing, sorting, and filling arrays, as well as conducting binary searches.

4.6.1   String Representation of an Array

Let's say we have a string array we want to output to the screen for debugging purposes.

```
String[] names = {
    "Butterfinger", "Dickmanns", "Fruitella", "Nutbar"
};
```

Listing 4.12 CandyNamesArraysToString, main()

An output with System.out.println(names) is out of the question because toString() is not meaningfully defined on the array object type. The static method Arrays.toString(...) returns the desired string representation of the array for different arrays. Let's compare the following two examples:

```
System.out.println( names );                // [Ljava.lang.String;@21b8d17c
System.out.println( Arrays.toString(names) ); // [Butterfinger, Dickmanns, …]
```

The use of Arrays.toString(...) doesn't necessarily spare you from a for loop that runs through the array and calls print*(...) on each element because the output is always of a specific format which starts with [, separates each element with commas and a space, and ends with].

The Arrays class declares the toString() method for different array types:

---

class java.util.**Arrays**

▶ static String toString(***[] a)
Returns a string representation of the array. The type specification *** stands for boolean, byte, char, short, int, long, float, double.

▶ static String toString(Object[] a)
Returns a string representation of the array. In the case of the object type, the method calls toString() on each object in the array.

▶ static String deepToString(Object[] a)
Also calls Arrays.toString(...) on each sub-array and not just toString() as with any other object.

4.6.2 Sorting

Various static Arrays.sort(…)/Arrays.parallelSort(…) methods allow sorting elements in the array. With primitive elements (but not boolean), no problems will arise because they follow a natural order.

[Ex]

Example

The following example sorts two arrays:

```
double[] profits = { -1.9, 3.1, 3.2, 3 };
String[] cities = { "Yuma", "Albuquerque", "Wichita" };
Arrays.sort( profits );
Arrays.sort( cities );
System.out.println( Arrays.toString( profits ) ); // [-1.9, 3.0, 3.1, 3.2]
System.out.println( Arrays.toString( cities ) );  // [
Albuquerque, Wichita, Yuma]
```

If the array consists of object references, the objects must be comparable. This comparison is accomplished either with an extra Comparator, or the classes implement the Comparable interface, such as String. Chapter 11, Section 11.4, describes these options in detail.

---

class java.util.**Arrays**

▶ static void sort(***[] a)

▶ static void sort(***[] a, int fromIndex, int toIndex)
Sorts the whole list of type *** (where *** stands for byte, char, short, int, long, float, or double) or a selected part. With specified limits, fromIndex is inclusive, and toIndex is exclusive. If the bounds are incorrect, the method throws an IllegalArgument Exception (in the case fromIndex > toIndex) or an ArrayIndexOutOfBoundsException (fromIndex < 0 or toIndex > a.length).

▶ static void sort(Object[] a)

▶ static void sort(Object[] a, int fromIndex, int toIndex)
Sorts an array of objects. The elements must implement Comparable.[9] In the method, no generic type parameter forces the elements to implement Comparable at translation time!

▶ static <T> void sort(T[] a, Comparator<? super T> c)
See Chapter 12 for information about type parameters.

▶ static <T> void sort(T[] a, int fromIndex, int toIndex, Comparator<? super T> c)
Sorts an array of objects with a given Comparator.

4.6.3   Parallel Sorting

Special sorting methods are intended for very large arrays. For parallelSort(...) methods, the library uses multiple threads to sort parts in parallel, which can increase speed. However, this is not a guarantee, because a performance advantage really only results with large arrays.

The algorithm is simple to understand: First, the array is partitioned into sub-arrays, which are sorted in parallel and then merged into a larger, sorted array. The process is also called *parallel sort-merge*.

4.6.4   Comparing Arrays of Primitives with Arrays.equals(...) and Arrays.deepEquals(...)*

The static method Arrays.equals(...) compares two arrays to check whether they have the same contents; for this purpose, the overloaded method is defined for all important types. If two arrays actually have the same contents, the method returns true; otherwise, false. Of course, both arrays must have the same number of elements; otherwise, the test is immediately over, and the result is false.

Example   [Ex]

Let's use the following code to compare three arrays:

---

9 This statement is not really true: If the array consists of no elements or only one element, there's nothing to compare. Consequently whether the object type is Comparable is not relevant.

```
int[] array1 = { 1, 2, 3, 4 };
int[] array2 = { 1, 2, 3, 4 };
int[] array3 = { 9, 9, 2, 3, 9 };
System.out.println( Arrays.equals( array1, array2 ) );                // true
System.out.println( Arrays.equals( array2, 1, 3, array3, 2, 4 ) );  // true
```

For arrays with nested referencing (arrays pointing to arrays), Arrays.equals(...) considers the inner array as an object reference and also compares it with equals(...). However, as a result, non-identical inner arrays referenced with the same elements are considered unequal. The static method deepEquals(...) also includes arrays with nested references in the comparison.

[Ex]

Example

The following example illustrates the difference between equals(...) and deep-Equals(...):

```
int[][] a1 = { { 0, 1 }, { 1, 0 } };
int[][] a2 = { { 0, 1 }, { 1, 0 } };
System.out.println( Arrays.equals( a1, a2 ) );      // false
System.out.println( Arrays.deepEquals( a1, a2 ) ); // true
System.out.println( a1[0] );                         // for example [I@10b62c9
System.out.println( a2[0] );                         // for example [I@82ba41
```

The last two console outputs show that the methods work differently. The arrays referenced by a1 and a2 contain the same elements, but are two different objects, so they aren't identical.

[»]

Note

As shown in the following example, deepEquals(...) can also compare one-dimensional arrays:

```
Object[] b1 = { "1", "2", "3" };
Object[] b2 = { "1", "2", "3" };
System.out.println( Arrays.deepEquals( b1, b2 ) ); // true
```

```
class java.util.Arrays
```

▶ static boolean equals(***[] a, ***[] a2)
Compares two arrays of the same type and returns true if the arrays are the same size and the elements are the same in pairs. *** represents boolean, byte, char, int, short, long, double, or float.

▶ `static boolean equals(***[] a, int aFromIndex, int aToIndex, ***[] b, int bFromIn-`
`dex, int bToIndex)`
Compares two arrays but stays in the selected sections.

4.6.5   Comparing Object Arrays Using Arrays.equals(...) and Arrays.deep-Equals(...)*

The `Arrays.equals(...)` method can also compare arrays with arbitrary objects. However, this approach doesn't use the identity check via `==` but instead checks for equivalence via `equals(...)`. A `Comparator` for comparisons is also possible; more on this topic is available in Chapter 11, Section 11.4.

> **Example**
>
> Do two string arrays contain the same words, where case doesn't matter?
>
> ```
> String[] words1 = { "normal", "is" , "boring" };
> String[] words2 = { "iS", "bOrinG" , "NoRmAL" };
> Arrays.sort( words1, String.CASE_INSENSITIVE_ORDER );
> Arrays.sort( words2, String.CASE_INSENSITIVE_ORDER );
> System.out.println(                              // true
>     Arrays.equals( words1, words2, String.CASE_INSENSITIVE_ORDER ) );
> ```

```
class java.util.Arrays
```

▶ `static boolean equals(Object[] a, Object[] b)`
Compares two arrays with object references. An object array may contain `null`. In this case, equivalence holds for all elements e1 from a and e2 from b at the same position: `e1==null ? e2==null : e1.equals(e2)`.

▶ `static boolean deepEquals(Object[] a, Object[] b)`
Returns `true` if the two arrays are equal as are all sub-arrays—recursively in the case of sub-object arrays.

▶ `static <T> boolean equals(T[] a, T[] b, Comparator<? super T> cmp)`
Compares two arrays with a `Comparator`, and `cmp.compare(a[i], b[i])` must be 0 for all pairs for both elements to be considered equal. We can ignore the `<? super T>` specification for now.

▶ `static <T> boolean equals(T[] a, int aFromIndex, int aToIndex, T[] b, int bFromIndex,`
`int bToIndex, Comparator<? super T> cmp)`
Compares sections of arrays with a `Comparator`.

4.6.6   Searching Differences Using Mismatch (...)*

Furthermore, you can use the following methods:

▶ int mismatch(***[] a, ***[] b)

▶ int mismatch(***[] a, int aFromIndex, int aToIndex, ***[] b, int bFromIndex, int bToIndex)

These methods return the index on the first element that's unequal. If both arrays are equal, the return value is -1.

For finding a mismatch in an array of objects, you can also use the following methods:

▶ int mismatch(Object[] a, Object[] b)

▶ int mismatch(Object[] a, int aFromIndex, int aToIndex, Object[] b, int bFromIndex, int bToIndex)

▶ <T> int mismatch(T[] a, T[] b, Comparator<? super T> cmp)

▶ <T> int mismatch(T[] a, int aFromIndex, int aToIndex, T[] b, int bFromIndex, int bToIndex, Comparator<? super T> cmp)

The first and second methods use equals(...) directly; the third and fourth use an external Comparator.

4.6.7   Filling Arrays*

Arrays.fill(...) fills an array with a fixed value. The start-end range can be specified optionally.

[Ex]

Example

Let's say we have a String array of length 6. The first half should be set with "Num Nums," and the remaining half, with "Orbit." Then, the array should be "shuffled" (i.e., mixed). Consider the following example:

```
String[] array = new String[ 6 ];
Arrays.fill( array, 0, array.length / 2, "Num Nums" );
Arrays.fill( array, array.length / 2, array.length, "Orbit" );
Collections.shuffle( Arrays.asList( array ) );
System.out.println( Arrays.toString( array ) );
```

No specific method exists to mix an array, but the Collections class can achieve this goal with lists, which provide a little detour (from array to list) to enable access to the shuffle(...) method.

class java.util.**Arrays**

▶ static void fill(***[] a, *** val)

▶ static void fill(***[] a, int fromIndex, int toIndex, *** val)
  Places the element val into the array. Possible types for *** are boolean, char, byte, short, int, long, double, or float or any objects via Object. For a range, fromIndex is inclusive, and toIndex is exclusive.

Besides the ability to fill an array with fixed values, an additional two methods are available: setAll(…) and parallelSetAll(…). These methods traverse a given array and call a specific method for each index used for initialization.

Example*

The following code fills a double array with random numbers:

```
double[] randoms = new double[ 10 ];
Arrays.setAll( randoms, v -> Math.random() );
System.out.println( Arrays.toString( randoms ) );
```

This example uses lambda expressions to describe the function. We'll return to this syntax in Chapter 13.

---

class java.util.**Arrays**

▶ static void setAll(int[] array, IntUnaryOperator generator)

▶ static void setAll(double[] array, IntToDoubleFunction generator)

▶ static void setAll(long[] array, IntToLongFunction generator)

▶ static <T> void setAll(T[] array, IntFunction<? extends T> generator)

▶ static void parallelSetAll(double[] array, IntToDoubleFunction generator)

▶ static void parallelSetAll(int[] array, IntUnaryOperator generator)

▶ static void parallelSetAll(long[] array, IntToLongFunction generator)

▶ static <T> void parallelSetAll(T[] array, IntFunction<? extends T> generator)
  Traverses a given array in its entirety, passing the index to the generator step by step. The generator maps the index to a value, which in turn is used for array initialization.

4.6.8   Copying Array Sections*

The Arrays class provides a set of copyOf(...) and copyOfRange(...) methods, which have an advantage over clone() in that they also allow range specifications and can make the new array larger. In the latter case, the method fills the array with null, false, or 0, depending on the type.

Example

Parts of string array names are to be transferred into new arrays:

```
String[] names = { "Big Hunk", "Mamba", "Charms", "Gushers" };
String[] slice1 = Arrays.copyOf( names, 2 );
System.out.println( Arrays.toString( slice1 ) ); // [Big Hunk, Mamba]
String[] slice2 = Arrays.copyOf( names, 5 );
System.out.println( Arrays.toString( slice2 ) );
// [Big Hunk, Mamba, Charms, Gushers, null]
String[] slice3 = Arrays.copyOfRange( names, 2, 4 );
System.out.println( Arrays.toString( slice3 ) ); // [Charms, Gushers]
String[] slice4 = Arrays.copyOfRange( names, 2, 5 );
System.out.println( Arrays.toString( slice4 ) ); // [Charms, Gushers, null]
```

---

class java.util.**Arrays**

▶ static ***[] copyOf(***[] original, int newLength)

▶ static ***[] copyOfRange(***[] original, int from, int to)

▶ static <T> T[] copyOf(T[] original, int newLength)

▶ static <T,U> T[] copyOf(U[] original, int newLength, Class<? extends T[]> newType)

▶ static <T> T[] copyOfRange(T[] original, int from, int to)

▶ static <T,U> T[] copyOfRange(U[] original, int from, int to,
  Class<? extends T[]> newType)

Creates a new array with the desired size or range from an existing array. As usual, the index from is inclusive, and to is exclusive. *** stands for boolean, byte, char, short, int, long, float, or double. The specifications in angle brackets are generics, which are presented in more detail in Chapter 12.

[Ex] **Example***

Let's look at a good example of copyOf(...) where the destination array is larger. The following code attaches two arrays to each other:

```
public static <T> T[] concat( T[] first, T[] second ) {
  T[] result = Arrays.copyOf( first, first.length + second.length );
  System.arraycopy( second, 0, result, first.length, second.length );

  return result;
}
```

This example uses generics (see Chapter 12, Section 12.2) to keep the type flexible. For a better understanding, think of T as type Object and mentally delete what is contained in the angle brackets.

4.6.9   Binary Search*

If the array is sorted, a binary search can be performed via `Arrays.binarySearch(...)`. If the array isn't sorted, the result is unpredictable. If `binarySearch(...)` finds the element, the return value is the index of the location; otherwise, the return value is negative.

Example [Ex]

The following example searches for an element in the sorted array:

```
int[] numbers = { 1, 10, 100, 1000 };
System.out.println( Arrays.binarySearch( numbers, 100 ) ); // 2
```

If the array isn't sorted in ascending order, an incorrect result is the consequence.

The method `binarySearch(...)` returns a coded position where an element could be inserted in case the element isn't in the array. So the index does not collide with a normal position of a find, which is always ≥ 0, the return is negative and coded as -**insertionPosition** - 1.

Example [Ex]

In the following example, element 101 does not exist in the array:

```
int[] numbers = { 1, 10, 100, 1000 };
System.out.println( Arrays.binarySearch( numbers, 101 ) ); // -4
```

The return is -4, because −4 = −3 − 1, which gives a possible insertion position of 3. This calculation is correct because 101 would go into the array in the following way: 1 (position 0), 10 (position 1), 100 (position 2), and finally 101 (position 3).

Tip [+]

Since the array must be sorted in `Arrays.binarySearch(...)`, a preceding call to `Arrays.sort(...)` can prepare the array for this sort operation. Consider the following example:

```
int[] numbers = { 10, 100, 1000, 1 };
Arrays.sort( numbers );
System.out.println( Arrays.toString( numbers  ) ); // [1, 10, 100, 1000]
System.out.println( Arrays.binarySearch( numbers, 100 ) );   // 2
```

Sorting is necessary only once and shouldn't be repeated unnecessarily.

```
class java.util.Arrays
```

▶ static int binarySearch(***[] a, *** key)
Searches for a key with the binary search. *** stands for byte, char, int, long, float, or double.

▶ static int binarySearch(Object[] a, Object key)
Searches for key using the binary search. The objects must implement the Comparable interface. Generally, this requirement means that the elements must be of the same type (i.e., strings and bouncy castle objects shouldn't be mixed).

▶ static <T> int binarySearch(T[] a, T key, Comparator<? super T> c)
Searches for an element in the object array using the binary search. The comparisons are carried out by the special comparison object c.

▶ static <T> int binarySearch(T[] a, int fromIndex, int toIndex,
T key, Comparator<? super T> c)
Restricts the binary search to ranges.

The API documentation of binarySearch(...) is a bit more difficult due to the use of generics (more on this topic in Chapter 12, Section 12.1.6). We'll also return to the static method binarySearch(...) for arbitrary lists in Chapter 18, Section 18.2.4. We'll also clarify the meaning of the Comparator and Comparable interfaces in detail in Chapter 11, Section 11.4.

4.6.10   Lexicographic Array Comparisons Using compare(...) and compareUnsigned(...)

Various int compare*(***[] a, ***[] b) methods can check arrays and test all pairs for order. The return already known from Comparator: If every a[i] == b[i], the return is 0. If an a[i] in the query sequence is less than b[i], the return is negative; if a a[i] is greater than b[i], the return is positive. The method is overloaded with a variant that selects a range in the array: compare(***[] a, int aFromIndex, int aToIndex, ***[] b, int bFromIndex, int bToIndex).

For byte, short, int, and long, several unsigned comparison method also exist:

■ int compareUnsigned(***[] a, ***[] b)

■ int compareUnsigned(***[] a, int aFromIndex, int aToIndex, ***[] b, int bFromIndex, int bToIndex)

Separate methods for objects exist, such as the following:

▶ static <T extends Comparable<? super T>> int compare(T[] a, T[] b)
Compares two object arrays, where the Comparator determines the order of the object pairs.

▶ static <T extends Comparable<? super T>> int compare(T[] a, int aFromIndex, int aToIndex, T[] b, int bFromIndex, int bToIndex)
Compares snippets.

▶ static <T> int compare(T[] a, T[] b, Comparator<? super T> cmp)

▶ static <T> int compare(T[] a, int aFromIndex, int aToIndex, T[] b, int bFromIndex, int bToIndex, Comparator<? super T> cmp)
Makes a comparison using an external Comparator object.

4.6.11   Arrays for Lists with Arrays.asList(…): Convenient for Searching and Comparing*

If the array is unsorted, binarySearch(...) won't work. The Arrays class doesn't have a method for this case. Consequently, a separate loop is needed. But another option is possible: The static method Arrays.asList(...) can decorate the array as a list of type java.util.List, which then provides handy methods like contains(…), equals(…), or subList(...). With these methods, more operations are possible on arrays, extending beyond the methods previously defined in the Arrays object itself.

Example

The following code tests whether the -? switch is set in the command line. The run-time environment passes the arguments passed in the command line as a string array to the main(String[] args) method:

```
if ( Arrays.asList( args ).contains( "-?" ) )
  …
```

Example

The following code tests whether sections of two arrays are equal:

```
// Index             0              1          2
String[] a = { "Asus",     "Elitegroup", "MSI" };
String[] b = { "Elitegroup", "MSI",       "Shuttle" };

System.out.println( Arrays.asList( a ).subList( 1, 3 ).
                equals( Arrays.asList( b ).subList( 0, 2 ) ) );  // true
```

In the case of subList(...), the start index is inclusive, and the end index is exclusive, which is the standard notation of ranges in Java, as in substring(...) or fill(...). Thus, in this example, entries 1 to 2 from a are compared with entries 0 to 1 from b.

class java.util.**Arrays**

▶ static <T> List<T> asList(T... a)
Returns a list of type T given an array of type T.

The static method `asList(...)` accepts either an array of objects (but not a primitive array!) or enumerated elements via the vararg.

[»]

Note

In the case of enumerated elements, no element or exactly one element is allowed as well. Consider the following example:

```
System.out.println( Arrays.asList() );              // []
System.out.println( Arrays.asList("Nuts") );        // [Nuts]
```

[»]

Note

A primitive array passed to `Arrays.asList(...)` doesn't return a list of primitive elements (no `list` is filled with primitive values). Consider the following example:

```
double[] prices = { 1.99, 2.19 };
System.out.println( Arrays.asList(prices).toString() ); // [[D@46f7f36a]
System.out.println( Arrays.toString(prices) );          // [1.99, 2.19]
```

The reason is simple: `Arrays.asList(...)` recognizes `prices` not as an array of objects, but as exactly one element of an enumeration. Thus, the static method places the array of primitives as one element in the list, and the `toString()` object method of a `java.util.List` object merely calls `toString()` on the array object, resulting in the cryptic output.

4.6.12   A Long Snake

Let's now use our newly acquired knowledge about arrays to enhance our snake game from Chapter 3, Section 3.5, to make the snake longer. Previously, the snake had no length, only a position on the board. Now, a program in an array should always memorize the snake's last position. For this purpose, the following changes are necessary:

- Instead of storing the position in a `Point` object, the last five positions are stored in `Point[] snakePositions`.

- If the player hits one of these five snake points, the game is lost. In the screen output, if a coordinate is equal to one of the snake points, we draw an "S." The test whether one of the snake coordinates hits a point p is performed with `Arrays.asList(snakePositions).contains(p)`.

Another point is that the snake moves, but the array of five points always stores only the last five movements—the old positions are discarded. The program realizes this functionality with a so called ring buffer (aka circular buffer)[10]—in addition to the posi-

---

10   *https://en.wikipedia.org/wiki/Circular_buffer*

tions, we'll manage an index pointing to the head. Each movement of the snake moves the index one position further until at the end of the array the index is at 0 again.

Some example possible points for the snake can be symbolically represented in the following way:

```
snakeIdx = 0
snakePositions = { [2,2], null, null, null, null }
snakeIdx = 1
snakePositions = { [2,2], [2,3], null, null, null }
...
snakeIdx = 4
snakePositions = { [2,2], [2,3], [3,3], [3,4], [4,4] }
snakeIdx = 0
snakePositions = { [5,5], [2,3], [3,3], [3,4], [4,4] }
```

Old positions are overridden and replaced by new ones.

Let's look at our game with these changes applied.

```java
package com.tutego.insel.array;

import java.awt.Point;
import java.util.Arrays;

public class LongerZZZZZnake {

  public static void main( String[] args ) {
    Point playerPosition   = new Point( 10, 9 );
    Point goldPosition     = new Point( 6, 6 );
    Point doorPosition     = new Point( 0, 5 );
    Point[] snakePositions = new Point[5];
    int snakeIdx = 0;
    snakePositions[ snakeIdx ] = new Point( 30, 2 );
    boolean rich = false;

    while ( true ) {
      if ( rich && playerPosition.equals( doorPosition ) ) {
        System.out.println( "You won!" );
        break;
      }
      if ( Arrays.asList( snakePositions ).contains( playerPosition ) ) {
        System.out.println( "SSSSSS. You were bitten by the snake!" );
        break;
      }
      if ( playerPosition.equals( goldPosition ) ) {
        rich = true;
        goldPosition.setLocation( -1, -1 );
```

```java
    }

    // Draw grid and symbols

    for ( int y = 0; y < 10; y++ ) {
      for ( int x = 0; x < 40; x++ ) {
        Point p = new Point( x, y );
        if ( playerPosition.equals( p ) )
          System.out.print( '&' );
        else if ( Arrays.asList( snakePositions ).contains( p ) )
          System.out.print( 'S' );
        else if ( goldPosition.equals( p ) )
          System.out.print( '$' );
        else if ( doorPosition.equals( p ) )
          System.out.print( '#' );
        else
          System.out.print( '.' );
      }
      System.out.println();
    }

    // Console input and change player position

    switch ( new java.util.Scanner( System.in ).next() ) {
      case "u" -> playerPosition.y = Math.max( 0, playerPosition.y - 1 );
      case "d" -> playerPosition.y = Math.min( 9, playerPosition.y + 1 );
      case "l" -> playerPosition.x = Math.max( 0, playerPosition.x - 1 );
      case "r" -> playerPosition.x = Math.min( 39, playerPosition.x + 1 );
    }

    // Snake moves towards the player

    Point snakeHead = new Point( snakePositions[snakeIdx].x,
                                 snakePositions[snakeIdx].y );

    if ( playerPosition.x < snakeHead.x )
      snakeHead.x--;
    else if ( playerPosition.x > snakeHead.x )
      snakeHead.x++;
    if ( playerPosition.y < snakeHead.y )
      snakeHead.y--;
    else if ( playerPosition.y > snakeHead.y )
      snakeHead.y++;

    snakeIdx = (snakeIdx + 1) % snakePositions.length;
```

```
      snakePositions[snakeIdx] = snakeHead;
    } // end while
  }
}
```

Listing 4.13 src/main/java/com/tutego/insel/array/LongerZZZZZnake.java

For more advanced work, try to enhance our game with the following goals:

- Replace the array with a dynamic data structure of type `ArrayList<Point>`.
- After every other step by the user, the length of the snake should grow by one.
- When the player collects a gold piece, the length of the snake should shrink by one.

4.7   The Entry Point for the Runtime System: main(...)

In Java classes, the special static method `main(...)` calls the runtime system in the specified main class (or start class) of the program.

4.7.1   Correct Declaration of the Start Method

For the JVM to start a Java program, you must use the special method `main(...)`. Since case sensitivity is relevant in Java, this method must be `main`, not `Main` or `MAIN`. Visibility must be set to `public`, and the method must be static because the JVM wants to call the method even without a copy of the class.

An array of `String` objects is accepted as a parameter. The parameters passed in the command line are stored in the array.

Two variants are available for declaring the start method:

- `public static void main( String[] args )`
- `public static void main( String... args )`

Incorrect Declarations

Only a method with the head `public static void main(String[] args)` is accepted as a start method. A method header like `public static void Main(String[] args)` is syntactically valid, but the JVM will not call this method to start. If the JVM doesn't find the start method, it issues an (internationalized) error message, such as the following example in English:

```
Error: Main method not found in class ***, please define the main method as:
    public static void main(String[] args)
or a JavaFX application class must extend javafx.application.Application
```

[»]

Note

In contrast to C(++), the first element of the argument array with index 0 doesn't contain the program name (i.e., the name of the main class), but the first program parameter of the command line.

4.7.2 Processing Command Line Arguments

A special variable for the number of arguments passed to the command line isn't necessary because the string array object tells us this information via `length`.

Let's write a program that accepts prices from the command line, sorts them, and finally outputs them one below the other:

```java
package com.tutego.insel.array;

import java.util.Arrays;

class SortNumbers {
  public static void main( String[] args ) {
    if ( args.length > 0 ) {
      double[] numbers = new double[ args.length ];
      for ( int i = 0; i < args.length; i++ )
        numbers[ i ] = Double.parseDouble( args[ i ] );
      Arrays.sort( numbers );
      for ( double number : numbers )
        System.out.println( number );
    }
  }
}
```

Listing 4.14 src/main/java/com/tutego/insel/array/SortNumbers.java

The program can be called on the command line as follows and results in the corresponding output:

```
$ java com.tutego.insel.array.SortNumbers 10.9 1.90 111.20
1.9
10.9
111.2
```

[»]

Library

For parsing command line arguments, the *Commons CLI* (*https://commons.apache.org/proper/commons-cli*) or *picocli* (*https://picocli.info*) libraries are especially useful.

In IntelliJ, by following the menu path **Run** · **Edit Configuration...**, a dialog box appears where the arguments can be set via the development environment (in the **Program Argument** text field).

4.7.3   The Return Type of main(...) and System.exit(int)*

The void return type of the start method main(...) is certainly worthy of discussion, since Java's developers could have also required that a program always return a status code to the calling program. However, they didn't opt for this requirement since Java programs are supposed to interact minimally with the surrounding operating system and because true platform independence is required, for example, in Java for programs on smartphones.

When a status code should be returned, the static method System.exit(status) is available; this method terminates an application. The argument passed to exit(int) is called the *status value* (also called an *exit status* or *exit code*) and is returned to the command line. The value is important for script programs because they can react to the success or failure of the Java program via this return value. A value of 0 indicates success by definition, and a value not equal to 0 indicates an error. The value range should be between 0 and 255. On the Unix command line, the return value of a program is available via $?; and in the Windows *cmd.exe*, via %ERRORLEVEL%, a kind of dynamic environment variable.

Let's look at an example of a Java program that returns the status value 42.

```
package com.tutego.insel.array;

public class SystemExitDemo {
  public static void main( String[] args ) {
    System.exit( 42 );
  }
}
```

Listing 4.15 src/main/java/com/tutego/insel/array/SystemExitDemo.java

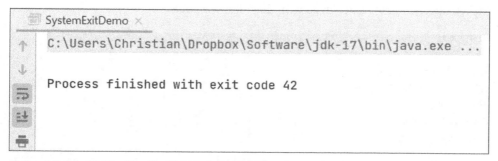

Figure 4.3 IntelliJ Displays the Exit Code in the Console Window

The following shell program first outputs the status value and also shows which case distinction the shell provides for status values:

```
@echo off
cd target\classes
java com.tutego.insel.array.SystemExitDemo
echo %ERRORLEVEL%
if errorlevel 10 (
    echo Exit code is above 10, exactly %ERRORLEVEL%.
)
```

Listing 4.16 showreturn.bat

The JVM starts the Java program and terminates the program via System.exit(int), which results in the variable %ERRORLEVEL% being assigned 42. The script first outputs the assignment of the variables. The Windows shell has a special variant for case distinctions with exit codes with if errorlevel value, which takes effect exactly when the current exit code is greater than or equal to the specified value. In our example, an output is shown if the exit code is greater than 10, and with 42, it is. Therefore, our small script will result in the following output:

```
>showreturn.bat
42
Error level is above 10, exactly 42
```

Keep in mind that %ERRORLEVEL% will naturally be overridden when commands follow. So, the following only outputs 0 because dir can be completed successfully and dir sets the exit code to 0 after execution:

```
java SystemExitDemo
dir
echo %ERRORLEVEL%
```

If calls exist between the call of the JVM and the evaluation of the variables, which might change the exit code, then storing the content of %ERRORLEVEL% temporarily makes sense and can be achieved with the following code:

```
@echo off
cd target\classes
java SystemExitDemo
SET EXITCODE=%ERRORLEVEL%
dir > NUL:
echo %ERRORLEVEL%
echo %EXITCODE%
```

Listing 4.17 showreturn2.bat

This code will result in the following output:

```
0
42
```

---

final class java.lang.**System**

▶ static void exit(int status)

Terminates the current JVM and returns the argument of the method as a state value. A value not equal to 0 indicates an error. So, the return value for the normal error-free exit is 0. A SecurityException is thrown if the calling code isn't allowed to exit the JVM. This scenario is especially true for programs in a container, such as a web server.

4.8   Further Reading

Arrays can be found as return and parameter types and indirectly in variable argument lists. As data structures they are less common, because the capabilities are very limited. Although all developers should study the Javadoc of the class java.util.Arrays (*https:// docs.oracle.com/en/java/javase/17/docs/api/java.base/java/util/Arrays.html*), it is more important in the long term to know dynamic data structures such as ArrayList or the *Stream types (*https://docs.oracle.com/en/java/javase/17/docs/api/java.base/java/util/ stream/package-summary.html*).

Chapter 5
Handling Characters and Strings

"Without difference, equality is no fun."
—Dieter Hildebrandt (1927–2013)

So far we've worked mainly with primitive data types and briefly with the object types String and Point. In this chapter we'll focus on single characters and sequences of characters, called *strings*. Strings can be declared mutable and immutable.

5.1 From ASCII via ISO-8859-1 to Unicode

The transmission of data has always played a central role in IT. As a result, different standards have emerged to capture different kinds of information. We'll cover these standards in this chapter.

5.1.1 ASCII

To enable the exchange of documents, the *American Standards Association* introduced a 7-bit encoding in 1963 called *American Standard Code for Information Interchange (ASCII)*.

ASCII places 128 characters in unique positions called *code points*. (Characters beyond the original 128 don't fit in 7 bits.) ASCII encodes 94 printable characters (letters, digits, and punctuation marks); 33 non-printable control characters (such as tabs and many other characters that have been useful in teleprinters but are no longer interesting today); and the space character, which does not count as a control character.

At the beginning of the ASCII alphabet, control characters exist at code points 0 through 31, followed by the space character at code point 32, and then all printable characters. At the last code point, 127, the delete control character ("DEL," formerly "rubout") ends the ASCII table.

The table shown in Figure 5.1 is from the original ASCII standard from 1968 and gives an overview of the code points of the characters.

USASCII code chart

b4 b3 b2 b1	Row	0 (000)	1 (001)	2 (010)	3 (011)	4 (100)	5 (101)	6 (110)	7 (111)
0 0 0 0	0	NUL	DLE	SP	0	@	P	`	p
0 0 0 1	1	SOH	DC1	!	1	A	Q	a	q
0 0 1 0	2	STX	DC2	"	2	B	R	b	r
0 0 1 1	3	ETX	DC3	#	3	C	S	c	s
0 1 0 0	4	EOT	DC4	$	4	D	T	d	t
0 1 0 1	5	ENQ	NAK	%	5	E	U	e	u
0 1 1 0	6	ACK	SYN	&	6	F	V	f	v
0 1 1 1	7	BEL	ETB	'	7	G	W	g	w
1 0 0 0	8	BS	CAN	(	8	H	X	h	x
1 0 0 1	9	HT	EM	)	9	I	Y	i	y
1 0 1 0	10	LF	SUB	*	:	J	Z	j	z
1 0 1 1	11	VT	ESC	+	;	K	[	k	{
1 1 0 0	12	FF	FS	,	<	L	\	l		
1 1 0 1	13	CR	GS	−	=	M	]	m	}
1 1 1 0	14	SO	RS	.	>	N	^	n	~
1 1 1 1	15	SI	US	/	?	O	_	o	DEL

Figure 5.1 The Original ASCII Table

5.1.2 ISO/IEC 8859-1

Over time, the ASCII standard has been updated several times, and some control characters were removed, but 7 bits could never accommodate all country-specific characters in natural languages. The German language uses umlauts, Russians use the Cyrillic alphabet, Greeks have alpha and beta, and so on. The solution, instead of 7-bit encoding, which can only accommodate 128 characters, was to simply use 8 bits, which then enabled the encoding of 256 characters. Since large parts of the world use the Latin alphabet, this encoding would naturally include all these letters with a large part of all diacritical characters (for example, ü, á, à, ó, â, Å, and Æ). Thus, a standardization committee created the *ISO/IEC 8859-1* standard in 1985, which describes 191 characters, making the encoding useful for a large number of languages such as German, Spanish, French, or Afrikaans. The characters from the ASCII alphabet kept their positions. Because of the Latin letters, the informal designation *Latin-1* has become established as an alternative to ISO/IEC 8859-1.

All characters from ISO/IEC 8859-1 are printable. Thus, all control characters, such as the tab or newline character, are *not* included. Of the 256 possible positions, 65 positions remain vacant because of ASCII, namely, the code points 0 to 31 (the control characters), the code point 127, and the code points from 128 to 159.

ISO 8859-1

Since wasting the available space doesn't make sense, an extension to the ISO/IEC 8859-1 standard, commonly known as *ISO 8859-1* (without IEC) was formulated. ISO 8859-1 contains all the characters from ISO/IEC 8859-1 as well as the control characters from the ASCII standard at code points 0 through 31 and code point 127. Thus, ASCII is completely contained in ISO 8859-1, but only the printable ASCII characters are in ISO/IEC 8859-1. The code points 128 to 159 are also defined in ISO 8859-1, although they're all quite unknown control characters (such as padding, start of a selection, no line break).

Windows-1252*

Because the characters at code points 128 to 159 are uninteresting control characters, Windows has overlaid these code points with letters and punctuation marks in what's called *Windows-1252* encoding. Code point 128, for example, is occupied by the € symbol, and at 153, you'll find the trademark (™) symbol. This reassignment of code points 128 through 159 has now also become established in the non-Windows world. Now, what is declared as ISO-8859-1 on the web can now contain the symbols from code points 128 to 159 from the Windows-1251 standard and is displayed by browsers in this way.

5.1.3   Unicode

Although Latin-1 included all the characters for most "major" languages, it lacked details such as Ő, ő, ű, or Ű for Hungarian; the complete Greek alphabet; Cyrillic letters; Chinese and Japanese characters; Indian script; mathematical characters; and much more. To solve this problem, the Unicode Consortium was formed with the task to encode every elementary character in the world and assign unique code points to them. Unicode thus contains all characters from ISO 8859-1, which simplifies the conversion of many documents. For example, "A" retains code point 65 from ISO 8859-1, which the letter in turn inherited from ASCII. But Unicode is much more powerful than ASCII or Latin-1: The current version of the Unicode standard defines about 150,000 characters.

Because of its many characters, specifying each character in decimal is difficult, so the hexadecimal specification has prevailed. The Unicode Standard uses the prefix "U+" followed by hexadecimal numbers. Thus, the letter "A" becomes U+0041. Basically, the range includes 1,114,112 possible code points, from U+0000 to U+10FFFF.

Unicode Tables on Windows*

On Windows, Microsoft includes the useful *charmap.exe* program for a character table that can be used to examine each font for its installed characters. In addition, a convenient feature of the character table is that it shows the position of a character in the Unicode table at the same time.

Under **Advanced View • Group by**, you can select Unicode sub-ranges in a new dialog box, such as currency characters or different languages. In the **Latin** subsection, for example, you'll find the characters from the French script (such as "Ç" with cedilla under U+00C7) and the Spanish script ("ñ" with tilde under U+00F1). Under **General Punctuation**, the inverted question mark can be found at U+00BF.

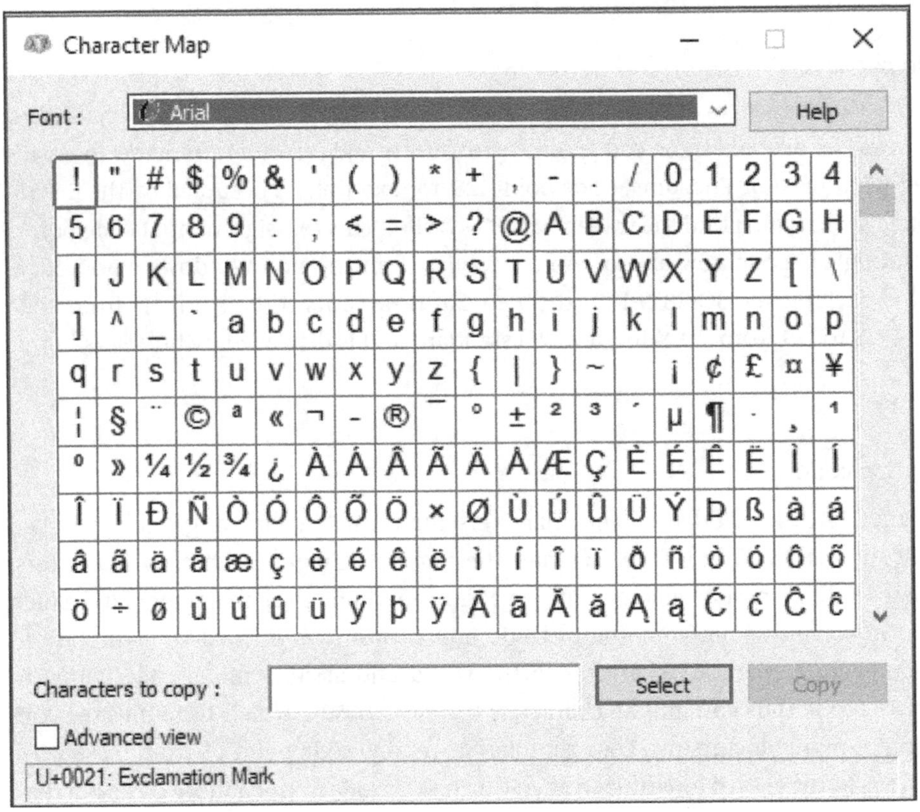

Figure 5.2 The Character Map Program on Windows

Displaying Unicode Characters*

The Unicode standard defines only the position of characters, not their graphical appearance. The graphical representation of a character is referred to as its *glyph*, or simply *character*. *Fonts* like Times New Roman or Arial contain representations for the glyphs. However, most fonts contain only subsets of all Unicode characters; many free fonts, for example, contain no Asian characters at all.

Also, the display of these characters—particularly on the console—is still a problem on some platforms. Support for the standard characters of the ASCII alphabet is less of a problem than the special characters defined by the Unicode standard. An attempt to output the smiley character in a standard output, for example, often fails due to the limited capability of the terminal or shell.

Note

Although Java internally encodes all strings to Unicode, it's inconvenient to choose class names that contain Unicode characters. Some file systems store the names in the old 8-bit ASCII character set, so parts of a Unicode character would be lost.

5.1.4   Unicode Character Encoding

Since there are about 150,000 characters in the current Unicode standard, 4 bytes (32 bits) are used to encode a character. A document containing Unicode characters thus has a memory requirement of 4 × (number of characters). When the characters are encoded in this way, it's called *UTF-32 encoding*.

For most texts, UTF-32 is wasteful because, if the text consists of only simple ASCII characters, 3 bytes are equal to 0. Let`s take the string "Erf" as an example; in UTF-32 this would be: U+000045U+000072U+000066, we can clearly see the zeros.

Therefore, we're looking for an encoding that can compactly encode the vast majority of texts but still allow the use of Unicode characters. The following two encodings are commonly used: *UTF-8* and *UTF-16*. UTF-8 encodes a character in either 1, 2, 3, or 4 bytes; in UTF-16, characters are encoded in either 2 bytes or 4 bytes. The example from Table 5.1 shows the encoding for the letters "A" and "ß"; for the Chinese character for "east"; and for a character from *Deseret*, a phonetic alphabet.

Glyph	A	ß	東	∂
Unicode code point	U+0041	U+00DF	U+6771	U+10400
UTF-32	00000041	000000DF	00006771	00010400
UTF-16	0041	00DF	6771	D801 DC00
UTF-8	41	C3 9F	E6 9D B1	F0 90 90 80

Table 5.1 Character Encoding in Various Versions of Unicode

When texts are exchanged, they're usually UTF-8 encoded. For websites, this UTF-8 is a good standard. UTF-16 is less common for documents but may be common as internal text representations. For example, the Java virtual machine (JVM) and the .NET runtime environment use UTF-16 internally.

5.1.5 Escape Sequences

To use certain special characters, such as a line break or a tab, in a string or char, you would use escape sequences.[1]

Characters	Meaning
\b	Backspace
\n	Line feed (newline)
\f	Page break (form feed)
\r	Carriage return
\t	Horizontal tab
\"	Double quotation mark
\'	Single quotation mark
\\	Backslash

Table 5.2 Escape Sequences

[Ex]

Example

The following example declares and initializes a char with simple characters and special characters:

```
char theLetterA  = 'a',
     doubleqoute = '"',
     singlequote = '\'',
     newline     = '\n';
```

The escape symbols are the same for strings. In this case, too, certain characters can be represented with escape sequences, as in the following example:

```
String s        = "Was she really 'chewing' a \"Tootsie Roll\"?";
String filename = "C:\\Documents\\Nevada\\Area-51.doc";
```

5.1.6 Notation for Unicode Characters and Unicode Escapes

Since the Java compiler processes all input as Unicode, it can process source code with German umlauts, Greek symbols, and Chinese characters. However, you should consider whether a program should directly contain Unicode characters because editors often have difficulties with Unicode characters—just like file systems.

---

1 Not all escape sequences originating from C are used in Java. For instance, Java lacks '\a' (alert), '\v' (vertical tab), and '\?' (question mark).

Unicode Escapes

Any Unicode character can be written for the compiler via *Unicode escapes*. The source code will then say \uxxxx, where x is a hexadecimal digit (i.e., 0 to 9, A to F, and a to f, inclusive). These six ASCII characters can describe a Unicode character and thus can be written in any ASCII text editor—no separate Unicode-capable editor is needed. Unicode characters for German special characters include the following:

Characters	Unicode
Ä, ä	\u00c4, \u00e4
Ö, ö	\u00d6, \u00f6
Ü, ü	\u00dc, \u00fc
ß	\u00df

Table 5.3 Special German Characters in Unicode

Tip

If you have special characters like umlauts on your keyboard, Unicode encodings shouldn't be used. As the author of source code, you shouldn't force readers to have a Unicode table at hand. The alternative display is therefore only worthwhile if the program text is to be deliberately made illegible. As a rule, however, identifiers should preferably be written in English, so that Unicode escapes occur only with strings.

Example

The following example displays the pi symbol and a smiley in a GUI dialog:

```
System.out.println( "Pi: \u03C0" );                        // Pi: π
javax.swing.JOptionPane.showMessageDialog( null, "\u263A" );
```

The popular smiley ☺ is defined in Unicode as \u263A (WHITE SMILING FACE) or as \u2639 (WHITE FROWNING FACE) ☹. The euro sign € can be found at \u20ac.

`System.out.println("\u0009");` will output a tab. The Unicode character \uffff isn't defined and can be used as an end symbol for strings.

Setting the Encoding of the Source Code*

If source code contains non-ASCII characters (such as umlauts), then this is of course a disadvantage compared to the \u notation, because it means that the file format plays a major role. It may happen that source code was stored in one character encoding (such as UTF-8), but another computer uses a different character encoding (perhaps

Latin-1) and wants to read the Java source code. This scenario can become a problem because, by default, the compiler reads the source code in the encoding it has itself since the encoding can't be read from a text file. If the source code is in a different format, the compiler unintentionally converts it to an incorrect, non-compliant Unicode format. To solve the problem, there's the following approach: The *javac* compiler can be given the encoding in which the source code is present with the -encoding switch. For example, if the source code is in UTF-8, but the Latin-1 encoding is set on the system with the compiler, then the -encoding UTF-8 switch must be set for the compiler. Additional details about this topic are available at *https://docs.oracle.com/en/java/javase/17/docs/specs/man/javac.html*. However, if there are different files in different formats, then the global setting won't help.

5.1.7 Java Versions Go Hand in Hand with the Unicode Standard*

In recent years, the Unicode standard has been extended, and Java has followed along with these extensions.

Java Version	Unicode Version	Number of Characters
1.0	1.1.5	34,233
1.1	2.0	38,950
1.1.7, 1.2, 1.3	2.1	38,952
1.4	3.0	49,259
5, 6	4.0	96,447
7	6.0	109,242
8	6.2	110,182
9	8	120,737
11	10	136,690
12	11	137,374
13	12.1	137,928
15	13	143,859

Table 5.4 Java Versions and Their Supported Unicode Standard

The Java versions from 1.0 to 1.4 used a Unicode standard that reserves 16 bits for each character. Thus, Java stores each character in 2 bytes and allows the encoding of more than 65,000 characters from the range U+0000 to U+FFFF. The range is also referred to as the *Basic Multilingual Plane (BMP)*. Java 5 supported the Unicode 4.0 standard for the first time, which requires 32 bits (i.e., 4 bytes) to map a character. But with the change to Unicode 4, the internal length for a char character was not increased, so that a char is still 2 bytes in size and the range is 0x0 to 0xFFFF. But, as a result, characters larger than 65,536 must be encoded differently somehow. The trick is to compose a "large" Unicode character from two chars. This pair of two 16-bit characters is called a *surrogate pair*. They form a Unicode 4.0 character in the *UTF-16 encoding*. These surrogate pairs increase the range of the BMP. If we had char as a real object, it could probably better hide internally how many bytes the storage really takes. But Java had to have primitive data types.

With the introduction of Unicode 4, not every character fits into the 16 bits of a char. Many methods therefore also assume an int for the full Unicode code point. In this book, however, this limit doesn't matter since Unicode characters from the higher ranges (for example, for the Phoenician script, which lies in the Unicode block U+10900 to U+1091F—i.e., shortly after 65,536, which can be mapped by 2 bytes) are only important for a small interest group.

Developer Frustration

The mapping of a character to a position is done by a table called a *code page*. However, because different mappings of characters to positions exist, problems may arise when exchanging documents. If one code page places the tilde (~) in position 161 and another code page places the ß character in position 161, conflicts are inevitable. Therefore, when text documents are exchanged, an indication must always be provided as to which format the texts are in. Unfortunately, however, operating systems don't always support such meta information. Thus, in XML or HTML documents, for example, the indication is written into the text itself. Unicode UTF-16 documents following a different convention: They start with the hex value 0xFEFF. This value is called the *Byte Order Mark (BOM)* and is intended to serve as an indicator for the byte order.

5.2   Data Types for Characters and Strings

The Java language and the Java library provide different data types, and developers must develop a sense of which data type is the right one. The following data types occur frequently:

- **char**: This primitive data type stores a Unicode character with 2 bytes. In Java, method calls on primitive data types aren't possible. Thus, a char can only store 1 character, but no queries are possible. Single quotes can be used to specify characters directly, such as 'H'.

- **Character**: A helper class with many static methods for querying the properties of characters.

- **String**: Combines several characters into one string. Anything in double quotes is a String object, for example, "Dick Dastardly". Once strings have been built, they can't be changed.

- **StringBuilder**: Stands for changeable strings. Single characters or character sequences can be appended, and characters (sequences) can be deleted or exchanged. The application programming interface (API) is less powerful than that of String. StringBuilder is more of an internal data type within methods and appears less as a parameter/return type.

5.3 The Character Class

char is a primitive data type and has no methods. For this reason, the Character class in the java.lang core package includes a large number of methods that are useful for dealing with single characters; many of these methods are static. This class includes methods for testing, such as whether a character is a digit, a letter, or a special character.

5.3.1 Is That So?

What all test methods have in common is that they start with the prefix is and return a boolean. In addition, methods are available for converting, for example, to uppercase or lowercase. The following list includes a few examples:

Expression	Result
Character.isDigit('0')	true
Character.isDigit('-')	false
Character.isLetter('ß')	true
Character.isLetter('0')	false
Character.isWhitespace(' ')	true
Character.isWhitespace('-')	false

Table 5.5 Results of Some is*() Methods

All these methods "know" about the properties of each Unicode character. Furthermore, the code point of each Unicode character is always the same, no matter whether a program is executed in Germany or Mongolia.

> **Note**
>
> The term "letter" not only describes well-known letters like "a" or "?." Unicode contains more than 100,000 characters, including hundreds of letters and numbers.

Testing Whether a String Consists Only of Digits

In the following example, we'll declare a method that will run through a string and test if the string consists only of digits. Although such functionality is useful in practice, Java Platform, Standard Edition (Java SE) doesn't provide a simple method for it.

```java
public class IsNumeric {

  /**
   * Returns {@code true} if the String contains only Unicode digits.
   * An empty string or {@code null} leads to {@code false}.
   *
   * @param  string Input String.
   * @return {@code true} if string is numeric, {@code false} otherwise.
   */
  public static boolean isNumeric( String string ) {
    if ( string == null || string.length() == 0 )
      return false;

    for ( int i = 0; i < string.length(); i++ )
      if ( ! Character.isDigit( string.charAt( i ) ) )
        return false;
    return true;
  }

  public static void main( String[] args ) {
    System.out.println( isNumeric( "1234" ) );  // true
    System.out.println( isNumeric( "12.4" ) );  // false
    System.out.println( isNumeric( "-123" ) );  // false
  }
}
```

Listing 5.1 src/main/java/com/tutego/insel/string/IsNumeric.java (Snippet)

Our method defines that null and an empty string aren't considered numeric. You can also specify that null should lead to an exception and that an empty string is definitely numeric. Conventions like these are up to the author of the library, and different utility libraries with such helper functions have different uses.

Our example uses two String methods: length() returns the length of a string, and charAt(int) returns the character at the desired position. A loop iterates over the string and tests each character with isDigit(...). If a character is not a digit, return false automatically exits the loop. If the loop runs successfully, a return true can report that each character was a digit.

Overview of the Most Important is*(...) Methods

```
final class java.lang.Character
implements Serializable, Comparable<Character>
```

▶ static boolean isDigit(char ch)
Is it a digit between 0 and 9?

▶ static boolean isLetter(char ch)
Is it a letter?

▶ static boolean isLetterOrDigit(char ch)
Is it an alphanumeric character?

▶ static boolean isLowerCase(char ch)

▶ static boolean isUpperCase(char ch)
Is it a lowercase letter or an uppercase letter?

▶ static boolean isWhiteSpace(char ch)
Is it a space, line feed, return, or tab (i.e., *whitespace*[2])?

[»] Choice of Words

In this book, *space* only refers to the " " character, which is generated by the *space bar*. This space is ASCII code 32, which in Unicode is \u0020. The term *whitespace*, on the other hand, stands for anything that creates whitespace (i.e., spaces, tabs, returns, etc.).

5.3.2 Converting Characters to Uppercase/Lowercase

To convert a character to uppercase/lowercase, the Character class declares the methods toUpperCase(...) and toLowerCase(...). The is*(...) methods that carry out the testing are often used when a string is traversed.

Our next example asks a user to enter a string. Valid letters should be converted to uppercase, and any whitespace should be replaced with an underscore. To run the input, we'll again use the String methods length() and charAt(int).

```
String input = new java.util.Scanner( System.in ).nextLine();

for ( int i = 0; i < input.length(); i++ ) {
  char c = input.charAt( i );
  if ( Character.isWhitespace( c ) )
    System.out.print( '_' );
```

---

2 It's called "whitespace" because the output character usually leaves the space white, but the position of the output still progresses.

```
else if ( Character.isLetter( c ) )
    System.out.print( Character.toUpperCase( c ) );
}
```

Listing 5.2 src/main/java/com/tutego/insel/string/UppercaseWriter.java (Snippet)

For example, for the input "honiara brotherhood guesthouse1," the output is "HONIA-RA_BROTHERHOOD_GUESTHOUSE." The "1" disappears because it's neither whitespace nor a letter.

```
final class java.lang.Character
implements Serializable, Comparable<Character>
```

▶ static char toUpperCase(char ch)

▶ static char toLowerCase(char ch)
The static methods return the matching uppercase or lowercase letter.

Note

The methods toUpperCase(...) and toLowerCase(...) exist twice: once as static methods on Character—in which case, they accept exactly one char as argument—and once as object methods on String objects.

Care should be taken with Character.toUpperCase('ß') because the result is "ß," unlike the String method "ß".toUpperCase(), returns the result "SS," that is, a string extended by one. Even though there's now an uppercase "ß" (Unicode U+00DF), Java still returns Unicode U+00DF, not U+1E9E, for Character.toUpperCase('ß').[3]

5.3.3   From Character to String

To convert a Unicode character to a string, you can use the overloaded static String method valueOf(char). A comparable method also exists in Character, namely, the static method toString(char). Both methods are limited in that the Unicode character can be only 2 bytes long. The static method Character.toString(int) creates a string for any Unicode character, and so, Character.toString(128123) results in a string with a ghost.

5.3.4   From char to int: From Character to Number*

When characters come from a user input, you are often required to convert them to numbers. The digit '5' is to become the numeric value 5. According to old hacker traditions,

---

3   Wikipedia summarizes the history of the uppercase ß at *https://en.wikipedia.org/wiki/%C3%9F#Development_of_a_capital_form*.

the solution was always to subtract the value of '0'. The ASCII zero '0' has the char value 48, and '1' then has the value 49, until '9' finally reaches 57. Logically, '5' - '0' = 53 - 48 = 5. The solution has the disadvantage of only working for ASCII digits.

For example, a neat Java solution is to convert a char to a string and then convert it via an Integer method, for example, in the following way:

```
char c = '5';
int  i = Integer.parseInt( String.valueOf(c) );  // 5
```

The parseInt(...) method is fully internationalized and also converts decimal numbers from other scripts, such as Hindi/Sanskrit:

```
System.out.println( Integer.parseInt( "४" ) );   // 5
```

This method works but isn't efficient for single characters in loops. Two other ways, using static methods from the Character class, are available.

The getNumericValue(...) Method

The Character method getNumericValue(char) returns the numeric value of a digit. Of course, this method has been internationalized too. Consider the following example:

```
int i = Character.getNumericValue( '5' );
System.out.println( i );                         // 5
System.out.println( Integer.parseInt( "४" ) );   // 5
```

The method is much more powerful because it knows the actual "value" of all Unicode characters, including, for example, also Roman numerals (I, II, III, IV, V, VI, VII, VIII, IX, X, XI, XII, L, C, D, and M), which are placed in the Unicode alphabet starting from \u2160:

```
System.out.println( Character.getNumericValue( '\u216f' ) ); // 1000
```

The Integer.parseInt(...) method can't handle \u216f, thus Integer.parseInt("\u216f") throws an exception.

The *digit(...) Methods

The Character class also has conversion methods for digits with respect to any base, and vice versa.

```
final class java.lang.Character
implements Serializable, Comparable<Character>
```

▶ static int digit(char ch, int radix)
Returns the numeric value that the character ch has under the base radix; common is base 10. For example, Character.digit('f', 16) is equal to 15. Any number system

with a base between Character.MIN_RADIX (2) and Character.MAX_RADIX (36) is allowed. If no conversion is possible, the return value is -1.

▶ static char forDigit(int digit, int radix)
   Converts a numeric value to a character. For example, Character.forDigit(6, 8) is "6," and Character.forDigit(12, 16) is "c."

Example

The following example converts a string of digits into an integer:

```
char[] chars = { '3', '4', '0' };
int result = 0;
for ( char c : chars ) {
  result = result * 10 + Character.digit( c, 10 );
  System.out.println( result );
}
```

The output is 3, 34, and 340.

5.4 Strings

A string is a collection of characters (data type char) that the runtime environment stores in the memory in an orderly fashion. The characters are taken from a character set that corresponds to the 16-bit Unicode standard in Java—with some workarounds, Unicode 4 with 32-bit characters is also possible.

Strings can be structured as char arrays, but arrays are not flexible. For this reason, Java provides three central classes that conveniently manage strings. These classes differ in two respects:

- If the strings are *immutable*, then they can't be changed after they have been created. In general, objects with unchangeable states are referred to as *immutable*. Alternatively, should the strings be permanently *mutable*?

- Are the operations on the strings secured against concurrent access from multiple threads?

	Manages Immutable Strings	Manages Mutable Strings
Thread safe	String	StringBuffer
Not thread safe	–	StringBuilder

Table 5.6 Three Classes that Manage Strings

301

The String class represents *immutable* strings. Therefore, a String is always thread-safe because synchronization is only necessary if there can be changes to the state. Objects of type String can be used to search for characters or substrings, and a string can be compared to another string, but characters in the string can't be modified. There are some methods that appear to make changes to strings, but they actually create new String objects that represent the modified strings. Thus, when two String objects are concatenated, the result is a third String object for the concatenated string.

[Ex]

Example

String objects themselves can't be modified, but of course, a reference can be set to another String object, as in the following example:

```
String s = "tutego";
s = "TUTEGO";
```

By "modify," we mean that statements can modify the state of an object, for example, by deleting the first character. Modifying the reference doesn't change the state of the object being referenced.

In contrast to String, the StringBuilder and StringBuffer classes represent dynamic, arbitrarily changeable character strings. The difference between these API-like classes is only that StringBuffer is protected from concurrent operations, whereas StringBuilder isn't. This distinction isn't necessary for Strings because, if objects can't be subsequently modified, parallel read access won't cause any problems.

CharSequence is the common interface of String, StringBuilder, and StringBuffer and is used multiple times in the library. Let's look at an example: The String class declares a contains(CharSequence s) method that tests whether the substring s occurs in the string. Now, what is the type of the variable s? We can pass instances of, say, String, StringBuilder, or StringBuffer because these instances are all of type CharSequences. We'll get into the type in a little more detail later in Section 5.5. At this point, it's sufficient to know that, wherever CharSequence is written, you can think of String, StringBuilder, or StringBuffer.

The three classes String, StringBuilder, and StringBuffer correspond to the ideal implementation of the object-oriented (OO) idea (we'll cover extensively in Chapter 6, Section 6.1.2): How exactly the strings are stored isn't revealed to the outside world. The OpenJDK implementation performs *string compression* by default for the String/StringBuilder/StringBuffer types.[4] In this process, the implementation creates a byte array containing the string in either Latin-1 or UTF-16 encoding, using one byte in the exclusive case of Latin-1 characters, thus reducing the memory requirement in half.

---

4 Described in *https://openjdk.java.net/jeps/254.*

So, the nice thing is that classes can relieve you from the tedious work of managing strings in arrays yourself, and you won't notice all the internal optimizations.

5.5   The String Class and Its Methods

The developers of Java have formed a symbiosis between String as a class and String as a "built-in" data type. Compared to other objects, this special treatment for String is evident in two aspects:

- The language allows the direct construction of String objects from String literals (strings in double quotes), such as "Dick Dastardly".

- The concatenation (of multiple strings with +, as in "Dick" + " " + "Dick Dastardly") is allowed, but the plus sign is not allowed for any other object type. For example, you can't add up two Point objects. So, with the plus sign on String objects, a special operator is defined on the String class; user-defined overloaded operators aren't possible in Java.

The String class provides exactly one constant, CASE_INSENSITIVE_ORDER of type Comparator<String>, a few constructors, some static methods, and some object methods. We'll explore these items next.

5.5.1   String Literals as String Objects for Constant Strings

To use strings, you must have an object of the String class. Note that, conveniently, anything enclosed in double quotes is automatically a String object. As a result, a dot for the method call can be placed right after the string literal.

> **Example**
>
> The code "Peanut butter".length() returns the length of the string. The result is 13. Whitespace and special characters are included in the count.

[Ex]

Only strings enclosed in double quotes are string literals and thus are preconstructed objects. However, this is not true for StringBuilder/StringBuffer, which must be created manually via new. When using string literals, you should explicitly refrain from creating String objects via new. The expression s = new String("String") doesn't make sense, but s = "String" is correct.

5.5.2   Concatenation with +

As we've seen in several examples, strings can be easily concatenated using +.

Example

If the segments have different data types during concatenation and one of them is String, all subsequent segments are automatically set to String. Consider the following example:

```
int quantity = 12;
double price = 0.99;
String s = "Quantity: " + quantity + ", price: " + price;
System.out.println( s );        // Quantity: 12, price: 0.99
```

5.5.3   Multiline Text Blocks with "″″″"

Strings with a newline occur repeatedly in programs, for example, in screen outputs or embedded HTML, XML, JSON, or SQL. Consider the following example:

```
String joke =
    "A teacher asked her student "Why are you doing math on the floor?"\n" +
    "The student answered, "You told us not to use any tables!"";
```

In the first string literal, \n represents the line break. The plus sign puts the two strings together. The Java compiler independently produces a larger string literal from the two constants.

Simple Text Blocks

To solve the problem more elegantly, Java provides text blocks,[5] which makes it easier to build multiline strings. Three double quotes (called the *opening delimiter*) introduce a text block, and three double quotes close a text block again (called the *closing delimiter*). When you use text blocks, we could rewrite the earlier example in the following way:

```
String joke = """
    A teacher asked her student "Why are you doing math on the floor?"
    The student answered, "You told us not to use any tables!"""";
System.out.println( joke );
```

A text block is always introduced with three double quotes, which must be followed by a line break. Thus, a text block always includes at least two lines of source code and can never be written on only one line.

After the introduction of a text block, the compiler appends a line break, LINE-FEED (shortened as LF; in Unicode, \u000A), to each line that isn't terminated with three

---

5 Standardized in JEP 378: Text Blocks (*https://openjdk.java.net/jeps/378*), text blocks were introduced in Java 15.

quotes. Our example only has one line break. If we had written the three quotation marks on the next line, we'd have two line breaks in the result:

```
String joke = """
        A teacher asked her student "Why are you doing math on the floor?"
        The student answered, "You told us not to use any tables!"
        """;
```

Placement determines whether the three quotes that close the text block are on a separate line (the resulting string ends with LF) or at the end of a string (the resulting string doesn't end with LF). When writing, the more symmetrical and prettier approach is having the beginning of a text block and the end of a text block each on a single line, but it's not always desirable to have a line break at the end.

Text blocks are an alternative notation for strings in double quotes. Later in the bytecode, how the string was created will not be evident. Text blocks can be used just like regular strings in all places where strings are required, for example, as arguments, as in the following example:

```
System.out.println( """
        A teacher asked her student "Why are you doing math on the floor?"
        The student answered, "You told us not to use any tables!"""" );
```

If a line break is useful in the source code within the text block (e.g., so that the line doesn't become too long), the line break in the resulting string can be prevented with a backslash, as in the following example:

```
System.out.println( """
        A teacher asked her student \
        "Why are you doing math on the floor?"
        The student answered, \
        "You told us not to use any tables!"""" );
```

The output is the same as before.

Formatting

Since text blocks are strings, you can concatenate text blocks with the + operator, as in the following example:

```
String teacher = "A teacher ";
String student = "The student ";
System.out.println(
    teacher + """
        asked her student "Why are you doing math on the floor?"
```

```
      """ +
   student + """
         answered, "You told us not to use any tables!"""" );
```

Notice how inserting variable contents isn't particularly elegant. However, the goal of text blocks is not necessarily to create something like string interpolation, as in Java-Script, for example.

Manipulating these strings is easier by using formatting strings, as the following example:

```
String teacher = "A teacher ";
String student = "The student ";
System.out.printf(
     """
         %s asked her student "Why are you doing math on the floor?"
         %s answered, "You told us not to use any tables!"""", teacher, student )
;
```

An alternative might be to write the following code:

```
String teacher = "A teacher ";
String student = "The student ";
String joke = String.format(
     """
     %s asked her student "Why are you doing math on the floor?"
     %s answered, "You told us not to use any tables!"""", teacher, student );
System.out.println( joke );
```

Another option is provided by the String method formatted(...):

```
String teacher = "A teacher ";
String student = "The student ";
String joke =
     """
     %s asked her student "Why are you doing math on the floor?"
     %s answered, "You told us not to use any tables!""""
         .formatted( teacher, student );
System.out.println( joke );
```

Meaning of Indentations

The indentation of the lines in a text block plays an essential role. The lines of a text block don't have to start at the beginning of the line, at position 0, but may be indented to the right and follow the usual conventions in the indentation of Java programs. When indenting, *incidental whitespace* should be excluded from the actual text block. In these cases, the Java compiler applies a small algorithm. The rule is that the line furthest to the left (the line with the three trailing quotation marks is one of them) determines the incidental whitespace that's truncated. Whether the whitespace character is a tab or space doesn't matter, even if it looks different on the screen! The *essential whitespace* remains to the right of this point.

Example 1

```
String joke2 = """
    Do we even need Halloween anymore?
      I've been wearing a mask and eating candy for 30 months...""";
System.out.println( joke2 );
```

Output 1:

```
Do we even need Halloween anymore?
  I've been wearing a mask and eating candy for 30 months...
```

Example 2

```
String joke2 = """
      Do we even need Halloween anymore?
    I've been wearing a mask and eating candy for 30 months...""";
System.out.println( joke2 );
```

Output 2:

```
  Do we even need Halloween anymore?
I've been wearing a mask and eating candy for 30 months...
```

Example 3

```
String joke2 = """
    Do we even need Halloween anymore?
    I've been wearing a mask and eating candy for 30 months...
    """;
System.out.println( joke2 );
```

Output 3:

```
  Do we even need Halloween anymore?
  I've been wearing a mask and eating candy for 30 months...
```

Escape Sequences

Finally, let's talk about a few rules. In the source code, an end of line could be indicated by different symbols in the text: CR (\u000D), CR-LF (\u000D\u000A), or LF (\u000A). The compiler performs what is called *normalization* so that, at the end, only one LF (\u000A) exists in the string.

Text blocks can contain all the escape sequences, including \n, \t, \', \", and \\. They are not raw strings, where the backslash (\) is taken as literal character, so the backslash must still be masked out. With \r, you can create a CR-LF sequence.

If single or double quotes occur in a string, they can be used without masking. However, a special case is when the double quote is right at the end before the three closing double quotes; in this case, masking is necessary.

```
String joke3 = """
    If you have 20 candy bars and eat 19 of them, what do you have?
    "Type 2 diabetes\"""";
System.out.println( joke3 );
```

If three quotation marks should appear in the output itself, one of the three quotation marks must be masked out to avoid being misinterpreted as a terminator. Consider how to obtain the following output:

```
1 "
2 ""
3 """
4 """"
5 """""
6 """"""
```

We would need to write the following code:

```
System.out.println( """
                    1 "
                    2 ""
                    3 ""\"
                    4 ""\""
                    5 ""\"""
                    6 ""\"""\"""" );
```

Such strings, however, are not particularly readable.

Another rule is that spaces are truncated from the end. Consider the following text block:

```
String s = """
1␣
""";
```

This text block becomes the string "1\u0002". The "open box" ␣ stands for blanks that otherwise wouldn't be seen in print.

If spaces must count at the end, you must introduce the escape sequence \s. This escape sequence is translated to a regular space (\u0020). For our earlier example, then, you could write the following code:

```
String s = """
        1      \s
        2  \s
        """;
```

Let's test your understanding with a task: What kind of string is created by the following code?

```
String joke2 = """
    Do we even need Halloween anymore?\s\
    I've been wearing a mask and eating candy for 30 months\
    ...
        """;
```

The result is a string that is equivalent to the following output:

```
"Do we even need Halloween anymore?
 I've been wearing a mask and eating candy for 30 months ...\n"
```

5.5.4 String Length and Testing for Empty Strings

String objects internally manage the string of characters they represent and provide a variety of methods to expose the properties of the object. You've already used one method, namely, length(). For String objects, length() is implemented to return the number of characters in the string (the length of the string). To find out if a string has no characters, the method isEmpty() can be used instead of length() == 0. The isBlank() method tests whether a string is empty or consists only of whitespace. In the context of this method, whitespace is any character where Character.isWhitespace(int) returns as true.

Statement	Result
"".length()	0
"".isEmpty()	true
" ".length()	1
" ".isEmpty()	false
" ".isBlank()	true
String s = null; s.length();	NullPointerException

Table 5.7 Results of the length(...), isEmpty(...), and isBlank(...) Methods

> **Note**
>
> From arrays, recall that `length` is an object variable. For `String`, `length()` is an object method and thus requires parentheses.

A Handy Helper Method: isNullOrEmpty(String)

For example, while the .NET framework provides the static member function `IsNullOr-Empty(String)`, which tests whether the passed reference is `null` or the string is empty, in Java, this evaluation must be tested separately. A separate static utility method comes in handy, as in the following example:

```java
/**
 * Checks if a String is {@code null} or empty ({@code ""}).
 *
 * <pre>
 * StringUtils.isNullOrEmpty(null)     == true
 * StringUtils.isNullOrEmpty(&quot;&quot;)    == true
 * StringUtils.isNullOrEmpty(&quot; &quot;)   == false
 * StringUtils.isNullOrEmpty(&quot;bob&quot;)  == false
 * StringUtils.isNullOrEmpty(&quot; bob &quot;) == false
 * </pre>
 *
 * @param str The String to check, may be {@code null}.
 * @return {@code true} if the String is empty or {@code null}, {@code false}
 * otherwise.
 */
public static boolean isNullOrEmpty( String str ) {
  return str == null || str.isEmpty();
}
```

Listing 5.3 src/main/java/com/tutego/insel/string/LengthAndEmptyDemo.java (Snippet)

This method, however, doesn't test whether the string consists of whitespace only.

5.5.5 Accessing a Specific Character with charAt(int)

Perhaps the most important method of the `String` class is `charAt(int index)`.[6] This method returns the corresponding character in a place called *index*. This method thus provides a way to traverse the characters of a string (along with the `length()` method).

---

6 The parameter type int reveals that strings can't be larger than `Integer.MAX_VALUE` (i.e., not longer than 2,147,483,647 characters).

If the index is less than zero or greater than or equal to the number of characters in the string, the method throws a `StringIndexOutOfBoundsException`[7] with the error location.

Example

The following code returns the first and last characters in the string s:

```
String s = "I'm not fat, just well-covered!";
char first = s.charAt( 0 );                        // 'I'
char last  = s.charAt( s.length() - 1 );           // '!'
```

[Ex]

You must remember that the count starts from 0. Therefore, you must subtract one digit from the length of the string. Since the comparison to the correct range occurs each time `charAt(int)` is accessed, you should consider whether the string should be copied once into its own character array instead (in case multiple access is expected).

Note*

Since Unicode characters can also be composed of 2 Java chars (the *surrogate pair*), an alternative method is available: `int codePointAt(int index)`. This method is slower than `charAt(...)` because a linear search must be performed. It isn't known in advance at which position a Unicode character is located from exactly one char or from two chars. In this book, we always assume Unicode characters that can be encoded in a char.

[«]

5.5.6   Searching for Contained Characters and Strings

The object method `contains(CharSequence)` tests whether a *substring* occurs in the string and returns `true` if it does. Case sensitivity is relevant. In the following program, we'll test whether a string contains one of the allowed names of candy:

```
static boolean containsCandyName( String text ) {
  text = text.toLowerCase();
  String[] candyNames = {
      "starburst", "snackers", "n&n", "cold tamales"
  };
  for ( String candyName : candyNames )
    if ( text.contains( candyName ) )
      return true;
  return false;
```

---

7 With 31 characters, this class name is already one of the longest and yet is surpassed by 5 characters by `TransformerFactoryConfigurationError`. However, in the Spring package (a collection of libraries for Enterprise Java development), you might encounter `JdbcUpdateAffectedIncorrectNumberOfRows-Exception`—not bad either.

```
}

public static void main( String[] args ) {
  String msg1 = "Starburst is so delicious.";
  System.out.println( containsCandyName( msg1 ) );  // true
  String msg2 = "I only like warm milk.";
  System.out.println( containsCandyName( msg2 ) );  // false
}
```

Listing 5.4 src/main/java/com/tutego/insel/string/ContainsCandyName.java (Snippet)

Returning Found Locations with indexOf(...)

The contains(...) method is *not* overloaded with a char, so we can't search for a single character unless the string consisted of only 1 character. However, this search is possible with the indexOf(...) method, which returns the location of a character or substring. If indexOf(...) finds nothing, it returns -1.

[Ex] **Example**

The following example searches a character with indexOf(...):

```
String s = "Ernest Gräfenberg";
int index1 = s.indexOf( 'e' );                 // 3
int index2 = s.indexOf( 'e', index1 + 1 );     // 11
int index3 = s.indexOf( 'e', 69696969 );       // -1
```

The assignment of index1 is 3 because, at code point 3, an 'e' occurs for the first time. The second method indexOf(...) continues searching with the second expression index1 + 1 (that is, starting at code point 4). The result is 11.

Like contains(...), the search is case sensitive. The characters in a string are numbered like array elements starting from 0. If the index argument is less than 0, this number is ignored, and the index is automatically set to 0.

[Ex] **Example**

If the character c describes an escape character, for example, a tab or a return, then processing can continue in the following way:

```
if ( "\b\t\n\f\r\"\\".indexOf(c) >= 0 ) {

  …

}
```

We couldn't use contains(...) because the parameter type is only CharSequence, not char.

The `indexOf(...)` method is parameterized not only with `char`, but also with `String`,[8] to search for entire strings and return the starting point.

Example   [Ex]

Call `indexOf(String, int)` with the search for a partial string:

```
String str = "I'll be ill if you remove the apostrophe.";
//            0123456789
String s = "ll";
int index = str.indexOf( s, str.indexOf(s) + 1 );        // 9
```

The next search position is calculated from the old finder position. The result is 9 because the substring "ll" appears there for the second time.

Searching from the End

Just as you can search a string starting at the beginning, you can also start at the end.

Example   [Ex]

In the following example, the `lastIndexOf(...)` method is used for this purpose:

```
String str = "May the Force be with you.";
int index  = str.lastIndexOf( 'o' );                     // 23
```

As with `indexOf(...)`, an overloaded version can search backwards from a certain position for the next occurrence of "o." In this case, you would write the following code:

```
index = str.lastIndexOf( 'o', index - 1 );               // 9
```

The parameters of the `char`-oriented methods `indexOf(...)` and `lastIndexOf(...)` are all of type `int` and not, as one might expect, of type `char` and `int`. The character to be searched is passed as the first `int` argument. The conversion of `char` to `int` is done automatically by the Java compiler, so this change isn't noticeable. Unfortunately, however, confusion in the order of arguments may occur: With `s.indexOf(start, c)` the first parameter `start` is interpreted as a character, and the desired character `c` is interpreted as the start position of the search.

Number of Substrings of a String*

So far, the Java library doesn't provide a direct method to determine the number of substrings in a string. However, such a method can be written quickly in the following way:

---

8 Of course, the `String` parameter type only allows objects of type `String`, and subclasses of `String` don't exist. However, other classes in Java can describe strings, such as `StringBuilder` or `String-Buffer`. These types don't support the `indexOf(...)` method, which is a pity because `indexOf(...)` could well have awaited a more general `CharSequence` type instead of `String`. (More details on this interface will follow in Section 5.7.)

```java
public class CountMatches {

  public static int frequency( String source, String part ) {
    if ( source == null || source.isEmpty() || part == null || part.isEmpty() )
      return 0;

    int count = 0;

    for ( int pos = 0; (pos = source.indexOf( part, pos )) != -1; count++ )
      pos += part.length();

    return count;
  }

  public static void main( String[] args ) {
    System.out.println( frequency( "cherry schnaps, schnitzel", "sch" ) );   // 2
    System.out.println( frequency( "cherry schnaps, schnitzel", "zel" ) );   // 1
    System.out.println( frequency( "cherry schnaps, schnitzel", "" ) );      // 0
  }
}
```

Listing 5.5 src/main/java/com/tutego/insel/string/CountMatches.java (Snippet)

The chosen implementation returns the number of non-overlapping substrings. The implementation would return the result "2" when calling frequency("aaaa", "aa") because, with pos += part.length(), the implementation always moves as many steps further to the right as the substring is long. Depending on the interpretation of the task—and other algorithms—the value "3" would also be a permitted return, but then the loop would always have to go only one position to the right.

5.5.7 The Hangman Game

The methods you've learned so far can solve an estimated 90% of all tasks in daily programming practice. In summary, so far, we covered the following methods:

- int charAt(int)
- int length()
- boolean equals(Object)
- boolean contains(CharSequence)
- int indexOf(char), int indexOf(String)

Let's now use these methods to make a little game, the famous Hangman game. The aim is to guess all the letters of a word. At the beginning, each letter is made unrecognizable by an underscore. The user starts guessing and gradually fills in the individual placeholders. If the player fails to guess the word after a fixed number of rounds, he has lost.

```
String hangmanWord = "alligatoralley";
String usedChars = "";

String guessedWord = "";
for ( int i = 0; i < hangmanWord.length(); i++ )
  guessedWord += "_";

for ( int guesses = 0; ; guesses++ ) {
  if ( guesses == 10 ) {
    System.out.printf(
      "Sorry, game over after 10 attempts! Speaking of which, the word was '%s'."
,
      hangmanWord );
    break;
  }

  System.out.printf(
      "Round %d. Previous guess: '%s'. What character do you choose?%n",
      guesses, guessedWord );
  char guessedChar = new java.util.Scanner( System.in ).next().charAt( 0 );

  if ( usedChars.indexOf( guessedChar ) >= 0 )
    System.out.printf( "'%c' you have entered before!%n", guessedChar );
  else {  //Character has not been used yet
    usedChars += guessedChar;
    hangmanWord.indexOf( c ) == -1
    if ( hangmanWord.indexOf( guessedChar ) >= 0 ) {
      guessedWord = "";
      for ( int i = 0; i < hangmanWord.length(); i++ )
        guessedWord += usedChars.indexOf( hangmanWord.charAt( i ) ) >= 0 ?
                        hangmanWord.charAt( i ) : "_";

      if ( guessedWord.contains( "_" ) )
        System.out.printf( "Good guess, |%s| can be found in the word. " +
                            "But there's something missing!%n", guessedChar );
      else {
        System.out.printf( "Congratulations, you have guessed the word '%s'!",
                            hangmanWord );
        break;
      }
    }
  }
}
```

```
    else
      System.out.printf( "Bad luck, %c does not occur in the word!%n",
                          guessedChar );
  }
}
```

Listing 5.6 src/main/java/com/tutego/insel/string/Hangman1.java, main(...)

The game starts with the following output:

```
Round 0. Previous guess: '_____'. What character do you choose?
```

The player types in a letter, such as "e," and then presses Enter. In turn, the program responds in the following way:

```
e
Good guess, 'e' can be found in the word. But there's something missing!
Round 1. Previous guess: '_____e_'. What character do you choose?
a
Good guess, 'a' can be found in the word. But there's something missing!
Round 2. Previous guess: 'a___a___a_e_'. What character do you choose?
```

This gameplay loop continues until the end of the game.

5.5.8   Good That We Have Compared

To compare strings, many possibilities and options are available, such as the following:

- The equals(...) method of the String class searches for absolute matches.
- The equalsIgnoreCase(...) method of the String class can be used for case-insensitive comparisons.
- The switch statement allows you to compare String objects with a list of jump targets. Internally, equals(...) performs the comparison.
- Whether a string starts or ends with a word is indicated by the String methods startsWith(...) and endsWith(...).
- For comparing individual sections, you can use the String method region-Matches(...), a method that can also work case insensitively.
- If a match to a regular expression is desired, the matches(...) method of String and the special classes Pattern and Matcher, which are specific to regular expressions, will help.

> [»] **Note**
> While the vast majority of scripting languages and also C# allow string comparisons via ==, the semantics for Java is unique: Comparison with == is only true if the two references are identical (i.e., two String objects are identical). == doesn't test equivalence.

The equals(...) Method

The String class overrides the equals(...) method inherited from the Object class to compare two strings. The method returns true if the strings are of equal length and if all characters match.

When comparing identities via ==, the result is usually different for strings than when comparing via equals(...). Consider the following example:

```
String input = javax.swing.JOptionPane.showInputDialog( "Password" );
String expected = "qwerty123";
System.out.println( input == expected );              // (1)
System.out.println( input.equals( expected ) );       // (2.1)
System.out.println( expected.equals( input ) );       // (2.2)
System.out.println( Objects.equals( expected, input ) ); // (3)
```

Assuming that input references the string qwerty123, the comparison (line 1) via == yields the value false since the String object returned by showInputDialog(...) is a completely different one than the present password qwerty123. Only the equals(...) comparison (lines 2.1 and 2.2) is correct in this case because the pure characters are compared, and they are equal. Basically, the variants (in lines 2.1 and 2.2) are the same since equals(...) is symmetric. But an advantage exists with line 2.2 because input can also be null, and so a NullPointerException won't be thrown, as with line 2.1. Objects.equals(...) is useful in this context because the method internally checks for null.

Note

In the equals(...) comparison, all characters play a role, even if they aren't visible. Thus, the following comparisons lead to false:

```
System.out.println( "\t".equals( "\n" ) );                 // false
System.out.println( "\t".equals( "\t " ) );                // false
System.out.println( "\u0000".equals( "\u0000\u0000" ) );  // false
```

The equalsIgnoreCase(...) Method

When you perform comparisons, equals(...) is case sensitive. With equalsIgnoreCase(...), the Java library provides an additional method that compares strings case insensitively; the test is done character by character.

Example

Let's compare two strings, one case sensitive and the other case-insensitive:

```
String str = "BOOMERANG";
boolean result1 = str.equals( "boomerang" );            // false
boolean result2 = str.equalsIgnoreCase( "BOOMerang" );  // true
```

[»]

Comparison of Methods

Let's assume we want to compare two strings regardless of case (ß is a letter only used in German).

```
String s = "Spaß", t = "SPASS";
System.out.println( s.toUpperCase().equals( t.toUpperCase() ) ); // true
System.out.println( t.toUpperCase().equals( s.toUpperCase() ) ); // true
System.out.println( s.toLowerCase().equals( t.toLowerCase() ) ); // false
System.out.println( t.toLowerCase().equals( s.toLowerCase() ) ); // false
System.out.println( s.equalsIgnoreCase( t ) );                   // false
System.out.println( t.equalsIgnoreCase( s ) );                   // false
```

With `equalsIgnoreCase(...)`, length is compared at the beginning. It's unequal, so the result is quickly determined. If the lengths are equal, all characters will be compared individually. `Character.toUpperCase('ß')` is also "ß" so far.

Lexicographic Comparisons with Greater/Less Relation

Like `equals(...)` and `equalsIgnoreCase(String)`, the methods `compareTo(String)` and `compareToIgnoreCase(String)` compare the current string with another string. Note, however, that the return value of `compareTo(String)` isn't a boolean, but an int. The result signals whether the argument is lexicographically less than, greater than, or equal to the `String` object. These distinctions are important in a sorting method, for example. The sorting algorithm must know how to sort two strings when comparing them.

[Ex]

Example

In the following example, we'll compare three strings in their lexicographic order. All comparisons show `true`:

```
System.out.println( "Justus".compareTo( "Bob" )    > 0 );
System.out.println( "Justus".compareTo( "Justus" ) == 0 );
System.out.println( "Justus".compareTo( "Peter" )  < 0 );
```

In the first case, since "Justus" is lexicographically greater than "Bob," the numeric return of the `compareTo(String)` method is greater than 0.

The comparison made by `compareTo(String)` is based only on the internal numeric encoding of the Unicode characters. Thus, `compareTo(...)` does not take into account specific regional features, such as the usual treatment of German umlauts. For this purpose, we'd need to use `Collator` classes.

compareToIgnoreCase(...) is for ordering (greater than, less than, equal to) while equals-IgnoreCase(...) is for testing the string equivalence: for both methods, case is irrelevant.

[«]

5

Note

The OpenJDK implements compareToIgnoreCase(...) with a Comparator<String>, which puts any two strings in order. The Comparator<String> is also accessible as a static variable named CASE_INSENSITIVE_ORDER, which is, for example, convenient for sorted sets where case isn't important. Comparators are introduced in more detail in Chapter 11, Section 11.4.

If the String Ends with …, Does It Start with …?

To determine whether a string starts with a certain string (let's call this a *prefix*), you can call the startsWith(...) method. A similar method exists for *suffixes*: endsWith(...), which checks if a string ends with a specific string of characters.

[Ex]

Example

The following code tests a filename extension with endsWith(String) and tests a salutation with startsWith(String):

```
String   filename   = "The best openings for beginners (in chess).TXT";
boolean  isTxt       = filename.toLowerCase().endsWith( ".txt" );    // true
String   email       = "Very honoured P. Ennis,\nThank you for your offer.";
boolean  isHonoured = email.toLowerCase().startsWith( "Dear" );    // false
```

The string is converted to lowercase before the request because no method of the type endsWithIgnoreCase(...) exists.

Comparing String Sections with regionMatches(…) *

An extension of the whole-or-nothing comparison methods is provided by regionMatches(...), which compares individual sections of one string with sections of another. If the first argument of regionMatches(...) assumes the truth value true, then case doesn't matter. As with equals*(...), the return value is a boolean.

[Ex]

Example

In the following example, the call of regionMatches(...) returns true:

```
String  s = "She's a straight lemonhead! ";
// Position: 0                17
boolean b = s.regionMatches( 17, "Make life! Take the lemons back!", 20, 5 );
// Position:                      0                     20
```

The method starts the comparison at the 17th character, that is, at the "l" in the string s, and at the 20th letters in the comparison string, which is also an "l." The counting of the characters starts again at 0. Five characters are compared from these two positions. In this example, comparing "lemon" and "lemon" returns as true.

[Ex] **Example**

In the following example, if the comparison should be case insensitive, the first argument of the overloaded method is true:

```
String  s = "She's a straight LEMONhead! ";
// Position: 0                17
boolean b =
 s.regionMatches( true, 17, "Make life! Take the LemOns back!", 20, 5 );
```

The String class can't perform a case-insensitive comparison for the startsWith(...) and endsWith(...) methods. Instead, you would use regionMatches(...).

[Ex] **Example**

To test if an email starts with a certain salutation, regardless of capitalization:

```
String startWith = "Dear ";
String email = "DEAR HAROLD, when is it time for sports again?";
boolean niceOpening = email.regionMatches( true,
                    0, startWith, 0, startWith.length() ); // true
```

5.5.9   Extracting String Sections

At this point, you've already used the most important method of the String class several times, namely, charAt(int index). However, this method is not the only method for accessing certain sections of a string.

Using substring(...) to Retrieve Sections of a String as a String

To retrieve a substring from a string, you can use the substring(...) method. This method exists in two variants, both of which return a new String object that corresponds to the desired section of the original.

[Ex] **Example**

In the following example, substring(int) returns a substring starting from an index to the end. The result is a new String object:

```
String s1 = "I think I am, therefore, I am. I think.";
// Position: 0                                31
String s2 = s1.substring( 31 );              // I think.
```

The index of `substring(int)` specifies the starting position (zero-based) from which characters are copied into the new substring. `substring(int)` returns the part from this character to the end of the original string. Thus, `s.substring(0)` is equal to `s` for any non-zero string `s`.

To specify a substring more precisely, you would use the second variant, `substring(int, int)`. Your arguments indicate the beginning and the end of the desired section.

[Ex]

Example

The following example cuts out a section of the string:

```
String twitter = "Instagram is just Twitter for people who go outside.";
//                0                 18     25
System.out.println( twitter.substring( 18, 25 ) );   // Twitter
```

While the start position is inclusive, the end position is exclusive. This specification is common in Java. In other words, at the end position, the character no longer belongs to the substring.

The `substring(int)` method is nothing more than a specialization of `substring(int, int)` because the first variant with the starting index can also be written as `s.substring(beginIndex, s.length())`.

[Ex]

Example

The following example converts the first character of a text to uppercase:

```
public static String firstToUpper( String ){
  if ( string.isEmpty() ) return "";
  return string.substring( 0, 1 ).toUpperCase().concat( string.substring( 1 )
  );
}
```

Note there is another solution, namely, the following:

```
return Character.toUpperCase( string.charAt( 0 ) ) + string.substring( 1 );
```

Of course, various index checks are now added—a StringIndexOutOfBoundsException[9] reports incorrect positional information as with charAt(int).

String before/after a Delimiter String*

The String class doesn't provide a simple library method for the case where a delimiter is given and a substring is requested before or after that delimiter.[10] Such a method would be useful, for example, for files where the dot separates the filename from the suffix. You can write two static utility methods, substringBefore(String string, String delimiter) and substringAfter(String string, String delimiter), which do exactly that. When applied, they look like this (ignore for a moment that the filename itself can also contain a dot):

- substringBefore("index.html", ".") returns "index".
- substringAfter("index.html", ".") returns "html".

The implementation of these methods is simple: In the first step, the methods search for the delimiter via indexOf(...). Then, they return the substring before or after this found delimiter string via substring(...). A few agreements: The delimiter isn't part of the return. And if the delimiter doesn't appear in the string, substringBefore(...) returns the entire string, while substringAfter(...) returns the empty string. String and delimiter must not be null. If so, a NullPointerException will follow, indicating the programming error. Programmed out, the two methods look as follows:

---

9   The API documentation discusses IndexOutOfBoundsException, but StringIndexOutOfBoundsException is a subclass of it.

10 Even XPath provides such functions with substring-before() and substring-after(). And Apache Commons Lang (*https://commons.apache.org/proper/commons-lang/*) also re-creates them in the org.apache.commons.lang.StringUtils class. With regular expressions or with a split(...) of String something like this problem can be solved theoretically, but the code isn't elegant either.

```java
public class StringUtils {

  /**
   * Returns the substring before the first occurrence of a delimiter.
   * The delimiter is not part of the result.
   *
   * @param string    to get a substring from.
   * @param delimiter String to search for.
   * @return          Substring before the first occurrence of the delimiter.
   */
  public static String substringBefore( String, String delimiter ) {
    int pos = string.indexOf( delimiter );

    return pos >= 0 ? string.substring( 0, pos ) : string;
  }

  /**
   * Returns the substring after the first occurrence of a delimiter.
   * The delimiter is not part of the result.
   *
   * @param string    to get a substring from.
   * @param delimiter String to search for.
   * @return          Substring after the first occurrence of the delimiter.
   */
  public static String substringAfter( String string, String delimiter ) {
    int pos = string.indexOf( delimiter );

    return pos >= 0 ? string.substring( pos + delimiter.length() ) : "";
  }
}
```

Listing 5.7 src/main/java/com/tutego/insel/string/StringUtils.java (Snippet)

Extracting Strings as an Array from the String via getChars(…)*

While charAt(int) returns only one character from the string, getChars(int srcBegin, int srcEnd, char[] dest, int dstBegin) copies multiple characters from a specified range of the string into a passed array.

Example   [Ex]

The following example copies parts of the string into an array:

```java
String s = "Blessing of the Throats";
char[] chars = new char[ 5 ];
int srcBegin = 7;
```

```
s.getChars( srcBegin, srcBegin + 5, chars, 0 );
System.out.println( new String(chars) );  // blessing
```

s.getChars(...) copies five characters from position 7 of the string s into the elements of the array char. The first character from the section is then in chars[0].

The method getChars(...) must of course again test whether the specified arguments are in the green range, that is, whether the start value isn't < 0 and whether the end value doesn't exceed the size of the string. If the arguments don't fit, the method throws a StringIndexOutOfBoundsException. In addition, if the start value is behind the end value, a StringIndexOutOfBoundsException will arise, which indicates how big a difference between the positions exists. The best approach is to calculate the end position from the start position, as was done in the earlier example. If all characters fit into the array, the implementation of the getChars(...) method uses System.arraycopy(...) to copy the characters from the internal array of the String object to the destination you've specified.

For accessing the complete contents of a string as an array of characters, you can use the toCharArray() method. Internally, the method also works with getChars(...). As a destination array, toCharArray() just creates a new array, which we then get back.

[»]

Note

The following code can be used to iterate over a string:

```
String string = "Clones are people two.";
for ( char c : string.toCharArray() )
  System.out.println( c );
```

This solution comes at a price, however, because simply creating a new char[] object for the pass costs memory and computation time for memory allocation and garbage collection. Therefore, this variant isn't recommended. Alternatively, chars() can be used, which returns a stream of characters for the string, but then works without an explicit for loop; we'll describe the Stream API in Chapter 18, Section 18.4.

Other Options for Decomposition

Two other ways exist for extracting certain parts from a string. One option is split (...), which allows you to split a string using a regular expression. You could also use the lines() method, which returns a stream of lines that were separated by line breaks.

[Ex]

Example

A string consists of several lines. The following example cuts off the whitespace at the beginning and end of each line and then output all lines:

```
String text = " I wouldn't lie to you. \n Well...that's a lie. \t ";
text.lines().forEach( line -> System.out.println( line.trim() ) );
```

This example draws on lambda expressions, which are the subject of Chapter 13.

5.5.10 Appending Strings, Merging Strings, Case Sensitivity, and Whitespace

Although String objects themselves are immutable, the String class provides methods that take out or add parts of a string. Of course, these changes aren't made to the String object itself on which the method is called, but the method returns a reference to a new String object with modified contents.

Appending to Strings

To append another string to a string, two obvious possibilities are available:

- Using the String method concat(String)
- Using the plus operator (which is more flexible since non-strings are first converted to strings)

Later, we'll show you how the StringBuilder/StringBuffer classes can take it even further and provide overloaded append(...) methods for different data types.

Example

The following code appends the current time (with deleted nanoseconds) to the end of a string:

```
String s1 = "Current time: ";
String s2 = LocalTime.now().withNano(0).toString();
String s3 = s1.concat( s2 ); // Current time: 12:53:14
```

Similarly, you can write the following code:

```
String s4 = "Current time: " + LocalTime.now().withNano(0).toString();
```

This code can even shortened because the plus operator automatically calls toString() on objects:

```
String s5 = "Current time: " + LocalTime.now().withNano(0);
```

concat(String) creates an internal array, copies the two strings into it via getChars(...), and returns the resulting string with a String constructor.

Merging Multiple Strings

Two overloaded class methods related to join(...) can join multiple strings and put a separator string between the links. These methods differ in terms of their parameter lists: One receives the links directly via a vararg, while the other receives them via `Iterable`:

▶ `static String join(CharSequence delimiter, CharSequence... elements)`

▶ `static String join(CharSequence delimiter, Iterable<? extends CharSequence> elements)`

The arguments must be strings and can't be common objects that are automatically converted to strings. In addition, the links must not be `null`.

Example

The following example puts words together with a space to form a sentence:

```
String[] words = { "I", "programmed", "you", "to", "believe", "that." };
String s = String.join( " ", words );
```

The delimiter string must not be `null` but can be empty.

No comparable method exists in `StringBuilder`/`StringBuffer`, but a small `StringJoiner` class can do the actual work of `join(...)`.

Case Sensitivity

The `Character` class declares some static methods that convert single characters to uppercase/lowercase. We can save the loop that does this for each character using the methods `toUpperCase(...)` and `toLowerCase(...)` from the `String` class.

What's interesting about both methods is that they observe some language-dependent subtleties. For example, that there is not really a capital "ß" in German, because "ß" becomes "SS." To take country-specific features into account, the `to*Case(...)` methods can additionally be fed with a `Locale` object (which represent a linguistic region).

Note

Some conversions to uppercase/lowercase may result in different strings depending on the local language.

The specification of a `Locale` for the two `to****Case(...)` methods is especially important for Turkish-language applications, as in the following example:

```
System.out.println( "TITANIK".toLowerCase() );                    // titanik
System.out.println( "TITANIK".toLowerCase( new Locale( "tr" ) ) ); // tıtanık
```

Note the subtle difference: In the second result string, the "i" has no dot!

Note

The parameterless methods `toUpperCase()` and `toLowerCase()` can select a locale according to the locale settings of the operating system. In the following example, `toLowerCase()` is modified by a locale:

```
public String toLowerCase() {
  return toLowerCase( Locale.getDefault() );
}
```

Thus, you should keep in mind that the default setting isn't necessarily the best.

Removing Whitespace

In a user input or in a configuration file, commonly whitespace (such as spaces or tabs) may exist before or after the important part of a text.

These whitespaces should be removed before processing. The `String` class provides `trim()`, `strip()`, `stripLeading()`, and `stripTrailing()` for this purpose. Let's look at their differences.

Method	Removes...
`trim()`	All code points less than or equal to the space U+0020 at the beginning and at the end of the string.
`strip()`	All characters at the beginning and at the end of the string that are whitespace characters according to the definition of `Character.isWhitespace(int)`.
`stripLeading()`	Like `strip()`, but only at the beginning of the string.
`stripTrailing()`	Like `strip()`, but only at the end of the string.

Table 5.8 Differences between trim() and strip*()

None of these four methods can remove whitespace in the middle of a string.

Example

The following example removes spaces and similar fill characters at the beginning and end of a string:

```
String s = " \tTalk to the hand.\n \t ";
System.out.println( "'" + s.trim() + "'" ); // 'Talk to the hand.'
```

[Ex]

Example

The following example tests if a string is empty with all whitespace subtracted:

```
boolean isBlank = "".equals( s.trim() );
```

An alternative is to write the following:

```
boolean isBlank = s.trim().isEmpty();
```

5.5.11 Searched, Found, and Replaced

Since String objects are immutable, a change method can only return a new string with the changes.

```
final class java.lang.String
implements Serializable, Comparable<String>, CharSequence
```

In Java, four methods can perform search and replace actions:

▶ String replace(char oldChar, char newChar)
Replaces all occurrences of the oldChar character with newChar.

▶ String replace(CharSequence target, CharSequence replacement)
One character string is replaced with another character string.

▶ String replaceAll(String regex, String replacement)
Replaces all strings described by a regular expression.

▶ String replaceFirst(String regex, String replacement)
Replaces the first string described by a regular expression.

Replacing without Regular Expressions

The replace(char, char) method replaces single characters.

[Ex]

Example

The following example changes the letter "o" occurring in a string to "u":

```
String s1 = "Honolulu";
String s2 = s1.replace( 'o', 'u' );          // s2 = "Hunululu"
```

The String object named s1 doesn't get changed. Only a new String object with the content Hunululu is created and returned by replace(...).

If something must be replaced, replace(...) internally creates a new char array, performs the replacements, and converts the internal character array to a String object that represents the return. If there's nothing to replace, we'll get back the same String object that made the request. The `replace(...)` method always replaces all characters. We must write ourselves a variant that replaces only the first character.

A second overloaded variant, `replace(CharSequence, CharSequence)`, searches for all occurring strings and replaces them with another string. The replacement string can also be empty, in which case the characters in the result will be deleted.

Example

In the following example, for the string s, "wristwatches" should be replaced by "watches":

```
String s = "Which wristwatches are Swiss wristwatches?";
System.out.println( s.replace( "wristwatches", "watches" ) );
```

The result is: "Which watches are Swiss watches?"

Searching and Replacing with Regular Expressions*

The methods `replaceAll(...)` and `replaceFirst(...)` search in strings using regular expressions and make replacements. `replaceFirst(...)`, as the name suggests, replaces only the first occurrence.

Example

In the following example, more than two spaces in a row should be compressed to one space:

```
String s = "A  proper  copper    coffee pot.";
System.out.println( s.replaceAll( " +", " " ) );
// A proper copper coffee pot.
System.out.println( s.replaceFirst( " +", " " ) );
// A proper  copper    coffee pot.
```

Because the search string is always a regular expression and special characters like "." or "+" have a special role, `replaceAll(...)` and `replaceFirst(...)` aren't directly suitable for general replacement tasks; instead, the `replace(...)` method is more suitable and also faster.

Example

For string replacement, you can juxtapose `replace(...)` and `replaceAll(...)`, as in the following example:

```
String s = """
    I'm Watt. \
    What's your name? \
```

```
    Watt's my name. \
    Yes, what's your name?""";
System.out.println( s.replace( ".", "!" ) );
```

The call replaces all dots with exclamation marks, so the result would be the following:

I'm Watt! What's your name? Watt's my name! Yes, what's your name?

Using s.replaceAll(".", "!") won't be successful, since the following string will be the result:

!!

The dot (.) stands for any character in regular expressions. Only when a backslash (\) masks out the dot (since the backslash is used in escape sequences in strings, this character itself must also be masked out), a statement like s.replaceAll("\\.", "!") returns the desired result. The static method Pattern.quote(String) masks out the pattern special characters for you, so that s.replaceAll(Pattern.quote("."), "!") works fine. The API documentation *https://docs.oracle.com/en/java/javase/17/docs/api/java.base/java/util/regex/Pattern.html* provides some small examples in addition to the full documentation.

5.5.12   Creating String Objects with Constructors and from Repeats*

The String class has various methods that build new String objects, especially because String objects are immutable. These methods include substring(...), join(...), and format(...).

Building New String Objects with Constructors

If the string isn't present as a string literal, new String objects can be built using the various constructors of the String class. Most constructors are intended for special cases and don't occur in normal Java programs. With a quick overview, the function is self-explanatory:

```
final class java.lang.String
implements CharSequence, Comparable<String>, Serializable
```

▶ String()
   Creates a new object without characters (the empty string "").

▶ String(String string)
   Creates a new object with a copy of string. Basically, the constructor is unnecessary since String objects are *immutable*.

▶ String(char[] value)
   String(char[] value, int offset, int length)

▶ String(int[] codePoints, int offset, int count)
  String(byte[] bytes)
  String(byte[] bytes, int offset, int length)
  String(byte[] bytes, String charsetName) throws UnsupportedEncodingException

▶ String(byte[] bytes, Charset charset)
  String(byte[] bytes, int offset, int length, String charsetName)
  throws UnsupportedEncodingException
  String(byte[] bytes, int offset, int length, Charset charset)
  String(StringBuffer buffer)

▶ String(StringBuilder builder)

In particular, the constructors are only necessary if a String object is to be built from a foreign representation such as a StringBuilder, StringBuffer, char[], or byte[] or parts (substring or sub-array) of them.

Example

The following example tests whether two strings—regardless of case—represent anagrams, that is, the two strings have the same letters:

```
String a1 = "iPad", a2 = "Paid";
char[] a1chars = a1.toCharArray();
char[] a2chars = a2.toCharArray();
Arrays.sort( a1chars );
Arrays.sort( a2chars );
boolean isAnangram =
 new String(a1chars).equalsIgnoreCase(new String(a2chars));
System.out.println( isAnangram );        // true
```

The Arrays.sort(...) method sorts an array, in this case, the char array. If case sensitivity is relevant, Arrays.equals(char[], char[]) can be used.

On the Constructor Call New String(String)

One constructor easily leads to confusion—the constructor that adopts another string. Thus, the following two lines result in the reference to a String object:

```
String rudi = "There is no spoon";
String rudi = new String( "There is no spoon" );
```

The second solution unnecessarily creates an additional String object because the literal is already a full-fledged String object. The constructor is basically unnecessary.

Strings in the Constant Pool

The JVM automatically creates a corresponding String object for each string literal. This creation happens once at most for each constant string, no matter how often the JVM uses it in the course of the program and which classes reference the string. This String object "lives" in an area called the *constant pool*.[11]

Note

Let's assume that the following statement is contained in one class A and in another class B:

```
System.out.println( "tutego" );
```

We can execute the following code:

```
int len = "tutego".length();
```

Then, the string "tutego" exists as a String object only once in the runtime environment.

For constant values, the compiler performs optimizations, such as computing constant expressions the same way. Not only does it insert the result 3 for expressions like 1 + 2, but the compiler also joins broken constant string parts concatenated with plus to form a string.

Example

The first and second declarations look the same in the bytecode:

```
String s =
 "Operating systems are like underwear-nobody really wants to look at them.";
String s = "Operating systems are like underwear" +
           '-' + "nobody really wants to look at them.";
```

The compiler automatically merges the strings[12] into one large string, so no concatenation is necessary at runtime. The compiler always "calculates" constant expressions directly itself.

Empty Strings or Null Strings

The statements both reference String objects that don't contain any characters:

```
String s = "";
String s = new String();
```

However, the second notation creates a new String object, while in the first case the string literal is in the constant pool.

---

11 The Java library implements the Gang of Four's *flyweight pattern* in this case.

12 By the way, the quote is from Bill Joy (his full name is William Nelson Joy), who co-founded Sun Microsystems. He was involved in the development of an impressive number of tools and technologies, such as the Unix kernel, TCP/IP ("Edison of the internet"), the NFS file system, Java, SPARC processors, and the vi editor.

We call a string without characters an *empty string* or a *null string*. Unfortunately, the last term is chosen somewhat unfortunately, so we won't use it in the book because the term *null string* can easily be confused with the term null reference. But while access to a null string might be unproblematic, de-references on the null reference inevitably lead to a NullPointerException, as in the following example:

```
String s = null;
System.out.println( s );        // Output: null
s.length();                     // ☠ NullPointerException
```

print*(null) results in the console output "null," and no exception arises because the case distinction in print*(Object) and print*(String) consider the null reference as a special case.[13] Accessing s via s.length(), on the other hand, leads to the unpopular NullPointerException.

Generating Strings from Repetitions

The useful object method repeat(int count) multiplies a string.

Example [Ex]

The following code repeats the string s three times:

```
String s = "tu";
System.out.println( s.repeat( 3 ) );     // tututu
```

5.6   Mutable Strings with StringBuilder and StringBuffer

Strings stored in String objects in the Java virtual machine share a property in that their contents can't be modified. The object of the classes StringBuilder and StringBuffer, to which changes can be made, behave differently. The changes subsequently affect the StringBuilder/StringBuffer object itself, and no newly created object is returned as a result, as for example with the plus operator and the concat(String) method for conventional String objects. But apart from that difference, the implementation of String objects and StringBuilder/StringBuffer objects is similar. In both cases, the classes use an internal character array.

The StringBuilder class provides the same methods as StringBuffer but isn't synchronized. In concurrent programs, the internal data structure of the StringBuilder object can therefore become inconsistent. StringBuilder works a bit more quickly because the implementation doesn't need to take care of concurrent access. Nowadays, however,

---

13   In the implementation of PrintStream—the origin of the print*(…) methods—you will find the special handling of null: public void print(String s) { if (s == null) s = "null"; write(s); }

the difference is no longer significant; that is, non-parallel access to a StringBuffer is equally fast.

StringBuilder and StringBuffer can be quickly explained: A constructor builds the objects and modification methods like append(...), and the toString() method returns the result as a string.

[»]

Note

Because of the symmetrical API of StringBuffer and StringBuilder, we'll only refer to the methods of StringBuilder in the following sections.

5.6.1 Creating StringBuilder Objects

You can use various constructors to build StringBuilder objects:

```
final class java.lang.StringBuilder
implements Appendable, CharSequence, Comparable<StringBuilder>, Serializable
```

▶ StringBuilder()
Creates a new object that contains the empty character line and has space for (initially) up to 16 characters. Subsequent insert operations fill in the buffer and automatically increase it further.

▶ StringBuilder(int length)
Similar to the previous constructor, but the initial capacity of the object is sufficient for the specified number of characters. Ideally, you should set the size so that it's close to the final size of the dynamic string.

▶ StringBuilder(String str)
Builds an object that contains a copy of the characters from str. In addition, the constructor already plans space for 16 more characters.

▶ StringBuilder(CharSequence seq)
Creates a new object from a CharSequence. Thus, the strings of other StringBuilder objects can also become the basis of this object.

Since only String objects are supported directly by the language, you can only use the explicit call of a constructor to create StringBuilder objects. All string literals in quotes are already instances of the String class.

[»]

Note

Neither in the String class nor in StringBuilder does a constructor exist that explicitly allows a char as a parameter to build a string from the given character. Nevertheless, StringBuilder has a constructor that accepts an int, where the passed integer specifies the internal starting size of the buffer. If we call the constructor with a char—for example, a '*'—the compiler automatically converts the character to an int. The resulting object doesn't contain any character but has only an initial capacity of 42 characters, since 42 is the ASCII code of the asterisk. Consequently, the only correct way to build a mutable string filled with the starting character c is new String-Builder(Character.toString(c)) or new StringBuilder().append(c).

5.6.2   Converting StringBuilder to Other String Formats

StringBuilder is usually used internally in methods but rarely appears as a parameter or return type. From the constructors of the classes, notice how a StringBuilder is built for a String parameter type, for example, but the way back is missing.

```
final class java.lang.StringBuilder
implements Appendable, CharSequence, Comparable<StringBuilder>, Serializable
```

▶ String toString()
Creates a String object from the current string.

▶ void getChars(int srcBegin, int srcEnd, char[] dst, int dstBegin)
Copies a desired section into a char array.

5.6.3   Requesting Characters or Strings

The familiar request methods from String can also be found in StringBuilder. Thus, charAt(int) and getChars(...) behave identically for instances of both classes. Also, substring(int start) and substring(int start, int end) are known from the String class as well. If only these methods are necessary, a StringBuilder is also unnecessary, and a String object is sufficient.

5.6.4   Appending Data

The most common use of StringBuilder objects is to join texts from data of different types. For this purpose, the classes declare a number of append(...) methods that are overloaded with different data types. The append(...) methods of StringBuilder return a StringBuilder. The append(...) methods always append data to the end and increase the internal space—an internal array—if necessary. They don't create a new String-Builder object. Let's use this information for a custom enumerate(...) method that traverses a string array and generates a screen enumeration.

```
public static String enumerate( String... lines ) {
  if ( lines == null || lines.length == 0 )
    return "";
```

```
  StringBuilder sb = new StringBuilder();

for ( int i = 0; i < lines.length; i++ ) {
   sb.append( i + 1 );
   sb.append( ". " );
   sb.append( lines[i] ).append( System.lineSeparator() );
}

  return sb.toString().trim();
}
```

Listing 5.8 src/main/java/com/tutego/insel/string/Enumerator.java, enumerate(...)

A call of enumerate("It's your choice to take this personally.", "Life is effort. I'll stop when I die!") returns a string that looks like the following output:

```
1. It's your choice to take this personally.
2. Life is effort. I'll stop when I die!
```

The summary lists all append(...) methods:

```
final class java.lang.StringBuilder
implements Appendable, CharSequence, Comparable<StringBuilder>, Serializable
```

▶ StringBuilder append(boolean b)

▶ StringBuilder append(char c)

▶ StringBuilder append(char[] str)

▶ StringBuilder append(char[] str, int offset, int len)

▶ StringBuilder append(CharSequence s)

▶ StringBuilder append(CharSequence s, int start, int end)

▶ StringBuilder append(double d)

▶ StringBuilder append(float f)

▶ StringBuilder append(int i)

▶ StringBuilder append(long lng)

▶ StringBuilder append(Object obj)

▶ StringBuilder append(String str)

▶ StringBuilder append(StringBuilder sb)

The methods append(char), append(CharSequence), and append(CharSequence, int, int) are required by the interface Appendable.

Particularly useful in practice is append(CharSequence, int, int), which allows you to append parts of String, StringBuilder, and StringBuffer objects.

Note   [«]

Each append(...) method modifies the StringBuilder and returns a reference to it. This scenario has a great advantage in that calls of the append(...) methods can be easily cascaded, as in the following example:

```
StringBuilder sb = new StringBuilder( "George Peppard" ).append(',');
sb.append(" Mr. T, ").append("Dirk Benedict, ").append("Dwight Schultz");
```

The evaluation is from left to right, so the result is "George Peppard, Mr. T, Dirk Benedict, Dwight Schultz".

Tip   [+]

Using the plus operator inside append(...) strings is counterproductive. For example, sb.append(", " + value) would be better written as sb.append(", ").append(value).

5.6.5   Setting, Deleting, and Reversing Characters and Strings

Since characters can be modified in a StringBuilder, other modification methods besides the append(...) methods can be used that are missing in the String class.

Setting Individual Characters

```
final class java.lang.StringBuilder
implements Appendable, CharSequence, Comparable<StringBuilder>, Serializable
```

▶ void setCharAt(int index, char ch)
  Replaces index with the ch character and overrides the old character.

Example   [Ex]

The following example changes the first character in the StringBuilder to an uppercase letter:

```
StringBuilder sb = new StringBuilder( "save water, shower together" );
char upperCharacter = Character.toUpperCase( sb.charAt(0) );
sb.setCharAt( 0, upperCharacter );
```

The first argument 0 in setCharAt(int, char) represents the position of the character to be set.

Inserting Strings

Various insert (...) methods insert the string representation of a value in a specific position, which is similar to the overloaded append(...) method:

```
final class java.lang.StringBuilder
implements Appendable, CharSequence, Comparable<StringBuilder>, Serializable
```

▶ StringBuilder insert(int offset, boolean b)

▶ StringBuilder insert(int offset, char c)

▶ StringBuilder insert(int offset, char[] str)

▶ StringBuilder insert(int index, char[] str, int offset, int len)

▶ StringBuilder insert(int dstOffset, CharSequence s)

▶ StringBuilder insert(int dstOffset, CharSequence s, int start, int end)

▶ StringBuilder insert(int offset, double d)

▶ StringBuilder insert(int offset, float f)

▶ StringBuilder insert(int offset, int i)

▶ StringBuilder insert(int offset, long l)

▶ StringBuilder insert(int offset, Object obj)

▶ StringBuilder insert(int offset, String str)

For char arrays, insert(...) is available in a modified way: insert(int index, char[] str, int offset, int len). In this case, the method doesn't transfer the complete array into the StringBuilder, only a section.

Deleting Single Characters and Character Ranges

A sequence of characters can be deleted via delete(int start, int end). Similarly, deleteCharAt(int index) deletes only one character. In both cases, an incorrect index is penalized by a StringIndexOutOfBoundsException.

Replacing Character Ranges

The replace(int start, int end, String str) method first deletes the characters between start and end and then inserts the new string str starting from start. As always, the end positions are exclusive; that is, they specify the first character after the section to be changed.

[Ex]
Example
The following example replaces the substring at positions 4 and 5 (that is, up to and excluding 6):

```
StringBuilder sb = new StringBuilder( "Sub-XX-Sens-O-Matic" );
//                                         0123456
System.out.println( sb.replace( 4, 6, "Etha" ) ) ;  // Sub-Etha-Sens-O-Matic
```

Reversing Strings

Another method, reverse(), reverses the string.

Example [Ex]

The following example tests whether s string is a palindrome, regardless of case. Palindromes read the same from the beginning as from the end, such as "racecar":

```
boolean isPalindrome =
  new StringBuilder( s ).reverse().toString().equalsIgnoreCase( s );
```

5.6.6   Length and Capacity of a StringBuilder Object*

As with a string, the length and the number of characters contained can be queried via the length () method. However, StringBuilder objects also have an internal buffer size, which can be queried via capacity() and is set in the constructor as described. In this buffer, which is rather an array of type char, changes, such as cutting or appending characters, are made. While length() specifies the number of characters, capacity() is always greater than or equal to length() and tells us something about how many more characters the buffer can store without needing a new, larger internal array.

Example [Ex]

```
StringBuilder sb = new StringBuilder( "www.tutego.de" );
System.out.println( sb.length() );                   // 13
System.out.println( sb.capacity() );                 // 29
```

For the length query, sb.length() returns 13, but sb.capacity() returns 13 + 16 = 29.

The start size should be initialized with the expected size to avoid internal zooming later, which costs more computing time. If the StringBuilder has a large internal buffer, but is short on characters in the long run, it can be shrunk to a smaller size with trimToSize().

Changing the Length

If the StringBuilder is supposed to store more data, setLength(int) changes the length to a specified number of characters. The parameter is the new length. If it's smaller than length(), the rest of the string will simply be truncated, but this approach doesn't change the size of the internal buffer.

[Ex]

> **Example**
>
> The following example concatenates all strings in an array with a separator and truncates the last separator at the end:
>
> ```
> String[] elements = { "Manila", "Cebu", "Ipil" };
> String separator = ", ";
> StringBuilder sb = new StringBuilder();
> for ( String elem : elements )
>   sb.append( elem ).append( separator );
> sb.setLength( sb.length() - separator.length() );
> System.out.println( sb );          // Manila, Cebu, Ipil
> ```

If setLength(int) is greater, the buffer increases, and the method fills the remaining characters with null characters \0000. The ensureCapacity(int) method requires that the internal buffer is sufficient for a certain number of characters. If necessary, the method creates a new, enlarged char array but doesn't change the string represented by the StringBuilder object.

5.6.7 Comparison of StringBuilder Instances and Strings with StringBuilder

The well-known equals(...) method can be used to compare Strings. However, this method is not implemented in StringBuilder as expected. In addition, other methods can make comparisons without regard to case.

equals(...) for the String Class

The String class implements the equals(Object) method so that a string can be compared to another string. However, equals(Object) of String compares only String/String pairs. The method doesn't start the comparison until the argument is also of type String. Thus, the compiler allows all passes also of type StringBuilder at equals(Object), but at runtime the result is always false, because a StringBuilder simply isn't of type String. Whether the strings are the same or not is irrelevant.

contentEquals(...) for the String

A common method for comparing one string with either another string or with String-Builder is contentEquals(CharSequence). This method returns true if the string and the CharSequence have the same character content. (Recall that String, StringBuilder, and StringBuffer are classes of type CharSequence.) The internal length of the buffer doesn't matter. If the argument is null, a NullPointerException gets thrown.

Example

The following example compares a `string` with a `StringBuilder`:

```
String       s  = "Cognition Amplifier";
StringBuilder sb = new StringBuilder( "Cognition Amplifier" );
System.out.println( s.equals(sb) );                    // false
System.out.println( s.equals(sb.toString()) );         // true
System.out.println( s.contentEquals(sb) );             // true
```

No Own equals(...) for StringBuilder

To compare two `StringBuilder` objects with each other, you *cannot* use the `equals(...)` method. For the usual method inherited from `Object`, only object references are compared. In other words, `StringBuilder` doesn't override the `equals(...)` method. Thus, if two different `StringBuilder` objects with the same content are compared with `equals(...)`, the result is always `false`.

Example

To implement the content comparison of two `StringBuilder` objects, you can first convert them to strings with `toString()` and then compare them using `String` methods, as in the following example:

```
StringBuilder sb1 = new StringBuilder( "The Ocean Cleanup" );
StringBuilder sb2 = new StringBuilder( "The Ocean Cleanup" );
System.out.println( sb1.equals( sb2 ) );                      // false
System.out.println( sb1.toString().equals( sb2.toString() ) ); // true
System.out.println( sb1.toString().contentEquals( sb2 ) );    // true
```

You'll learn about another option in the following section.

Lexicographic Comparisons (StringBuilder is Comparable)

`StringBuilder` allows lexicographic comparisons via the `int compareTo(StringBuilder another)` method. (`StringBuilder` implements the interface `Comparable<StringBuilder>`.) Thus, `String` and `StringBuilder` both realize an ordering (see the section on lexicographic comparisons in Section 5.5.8).

One side effect is that, for equal strings, the return of `compareTo(...)` is 0. This approach, however, is much better than converting the `StringBuilder` to a string first.

The `compareTo(...)` method of `StringBuilder` performs the comparison only with other `StringBuilder` objects. The static method `compare(CharSequence, CharSequence)` in `CharSequence` is more flexible in this respect. With this method, a lexicographic comparison of all conceivable `CharSequence` instances is possible.

[Ex]

Example

These are proper ways to compare two StringBuilder instances:

```
StringBuilder sb1 = new StringBuilder( "The Ocean Cleanup" );
StringBuilder sb2 = new StringBuilder( "The Ocean Cleanup" );
System.out.println( sb1.compareTo( sb2 ) == 0 );              // true
System.out.println( CharSequence.compare( sb1, sb2 ) == 0 );  // true
```

5.6.8 hashCode() with StringBuilder*

Our previous discussion shows that an equals(...) method that compares the content of StringBuilder objects wouldn't be bad. Nevertheless, a problem exists regarding when exactly StringBuilder objects should be considered equal. This question is interesting because StringBuilder objects are not only determined by their content, but also by the sizes of their internal buffers, that is, by their capacities. Should equals(...) return true if the contents are equal, or only if the contents and buffer size are equal? Since every developer has different views on equivalence, the default test for identical object references remains the only one. A similar reasoning applies to the hashCode() method, which returns the same, ideally unique, numeric value for all objects with the same content. The String class has a hashCode() method, but StringBuilder inherits the implementation from the Object class unchanged. In other words, the classes themselves don't provide an implementation.

5.7 CharSequence as Base Type

So far, you've learned how the classes String, StringBuilder, and StringBuffer can store and pass strings. A string is a value object and an important tool in programs since immutable string values are represented by it, while StringBuilder/StringBuffer comprise mutable strings.

But what happens when a substring is required where it shouldn't matter whether the original is a String, StringBuffer, or StringBuilder object? And what if read-only access is to be allowed so that changes are excluded? One solution is to expect everything to be a String object (and the Java library does this). But then the program parts that use StringBuilder/StringBuffer internally must first construct a new string, and that costs resources.

Fortunately, the String and StringBuilder/StringBuffer classes have a common base type: CharSequence. This type represents an immutable, read-only sequence of characters. (Interfaces, base types, and their implementation are described further in Chapter 8, Section 8.1.) Methods therefore no longer must decide on concrete classes but can simply accept a CharSequence object as an argument or pass it on as a return. As a return,

CharSequence isn't especially useful; in this context, String is more practical. A String and a StringBuilder/StringBuffer object have many more methods than CharSequence, but as a parameter type, CharSequence is well suited if more functionality isn't needed.

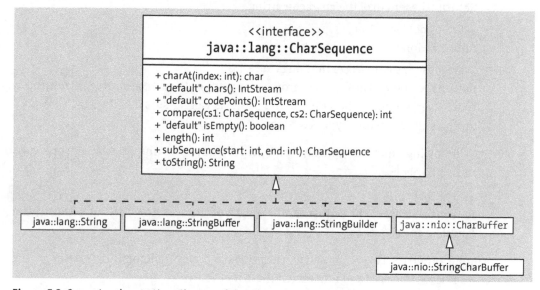

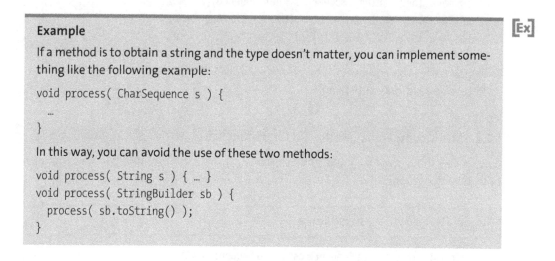

Figure 5.3 Some Implementing Classes of the CharSequence Interface

Example

If a method is to obtain a string and the type doesn't matter, you can implement something like the following example:

```
void process( CharSequence s ) {
  …
}
```

In this way, you can avoid the use of these two methods:

```
void process( String s ) { … }
void process( StringBuilder sb ) {
  process( sb.toString() );
}
```

5.7.1   Basic Operations of the Interface

The CharSequence interface makes three methods mandatory for the implementing classes:

```
interface java.lang.CharSequence
```

▶ `char charAt(int index)`
Returns the character at the `index` position.

▶ `int length()`
Returns the length of the character string.

▶ `default boolean isEmpty()`
Abbreviation for the test `length() == 0`.

▶ `CharSequence subSequence(int start, int end)`
Returns a new `CharSequence` from `start` to `end`. `subSequence(...)` returns a `CharSequence` object. The effect is the same as calling `substring(begin, end)` on a string; only the return type is different.

The following method already present anyway via the absolute superclass `java.lang.Object`:

▶ `String toString()`
Returns a string of the sequence. The length of the `toString()` string is exactly the length of the sequence.

Among others, `String/StringBuilder/StringBuffer` are implementing classes of the `CharSequence` interface and implement these methods:

```
class java.lang.String implements CharSequence, …
class java.lang.StringBuilder implements CharSequence, …
class java.lang.StringBuffer implements CharSequence, …
```

▶ `CharSequence subSequence(int beginIndex, int endIndex)`
Returns a read-only substring.

5.7.2 Static compare(…) Method in CharSequence

`CharSequence` has the static method `compare(...)`, which compares two `CharSequence` objects lexicographically:

```
interface java.lang.CharSequence
```

▶ `static int compare(CharSequence cs1, CharSequence cs2)`
Compares the two strings lexicographically.

This static method has an advantage in that now all combinations of `CharBuffer`, `Segment`, `String`, `StringBuffer`, and `StringBuilder` can be checked with this one method. Furthermore, if the comparison results in 0, you also know that the strings contain the same characters.

5.7.3   Default Methods in the CharSequence Interface*

This interface has two default methods:

interface java.lang.**CharSequence**

▶ default IntStream chars()

▶ default IntStream codePoints()

The importance of default and interfaces in general is discussed in Chapter 7. At this point, we just want to emphasize the advantage that chars() can be used to run over the characters. However, this method has nothing to do with the extended for, but with a different programming idiom.

Example

The following example runs over a string and outputs each character:

```
"Drama is life with the dull bits left out.".chars().forEach( c ->
  System.out.print( (char) c )
);
```

Syntactically, this example uses lambda expressions, which are introduced in detail in Chapter 13.

5.8   Converting Primitives and Strings

Before a data type can be output to the screen, sent to the printer, or stored in an ASCII file, the Java program must convert it to a string. For example, if we output the number 7 without conversion, we wouldn't see a "7" on the screen, but your computer may beep, depending on the implementation. Conversion is also important the other way round: If a user specifies his or her age in a dialog, this value is always a string at first. In a second step, the application must convert this value to an integer to implement an age query, for example.

5.8.1   Converting Different Types to String Representations

Overloaded static String.valueOf(...) methods return the string representation of a primitive value or object.

Example

The following example shows some conversions of data types to strings:

```
String s1 = String.valueOf( 10 );              // 10
String s2 = String.valueOf( Math.PI );         // 3.141592653589793
String s3 = String.valueOf( 1 < 2 );           // true
```

The valueOf(...) method is overloaded, and in total, an implementation exists for each primitive data type:

```
final class java.lang.String
implements CharSequence, Comparable<String>, Serializable
```

▶ static String valueOf(boolean b)

▶ static String valueOf(char c)

▶ static String valueOf(double d)

▶ static String valueOf(float f)

▶ static String valueOf(int i)

▶ static String valueOf(long l)
   Returns the string representation of the primitive elements.

▶ static String valueOf(char[] data)

▶ static String valueOf(char[] data, int offset, int count)
   Returns a String object from the char array or a section of the char array.

The valueOf(Object) Method

You can pass any object to the valueOf(Object) method.

[Ex]
Example

The following example shows some conversions of objects to strings:

```
String r = String.valueOf( new java.awt.Point() );  // java.awt.Point[x=0,y=0]
String s = String.valueOf( java.nio.file.Paths.get( "." ) ); // .
String t = String.valueOf( java.time.LocalTime.now() ); // 09:48:28.047834
```

Since each object has a toString() method, valueOf(Object) simply delegates to it.

```
public static String valueOf( Object obj ) {
    return (obj == null) ? "null" : obj.toString();}
```

Listing 5.9 java/lang/String.java, valueOf()

The implementation of valueOf(Object obj) simply asks the obj object itself for the string conversion. The special handling tests whether null was passed and then returns a valid string with the content "null". Since `String.valueOf(null)` returns "null," an output like `System.out.println(null)` also outputs the string `null` to the console because `println(Object)` internally calls `String.valueOf(…)`. Likewise, `System.out.println(null + "0")` produces the output "null0" since `null` is a link in the addition chain.

```
final class java.lang.String
implements CharSequence, Comparable<String>, Serializable
```

▶ static String valueOf(Object obj)

If `obj` is not equal to `bull`, the `obj.toString()` method returns, otherwise it returns "null."

5.8.2 Converting String Contents to a Primitive Value

Parsing a string—for example, "123" from a user input for the integer 123—isn't the responsibility of the `String` class, but of special classes that exist for each primitive data type. The classes listed in Table 5.9 declare static `parse*(string)` methods.

Class	Conversion Method	Return Type
java.lang.Boolean	parseBoolean(String s)	boolean
java.lang.Byte	parseByte(String s)	byte
java.lang.Short	parseShort(String s)	short
java.lang.Integer	parseInt(String s)	int
java.lang.Long	parseLong(String s)	long
java.lang.Double	parseDouble(String s)	double
java.lang.Float	parseFloat(String s)	float

Table 5.9 Methods for Converting a String to a Primitive Type

For each primitive type, what's called a *wrapper class* is available with `parse*(string)` conversion methods. Chapter 11, Section 11.5, explains the meaning of these classes in more detail. At this point, we only briefly consider the conversion functionality.

Example with Double.parseDouble(String)

Let's use the `Double.parseDouble(String)` method in an example. The user is asked for a float in a graphical dialog box, and the sine and cosine of this number should then be output to the screen.

```
String s = javax.swing.JOptionPane.showInputDialog( "Input floating decimal" );
double value = Double.parseDouble( s );
System.out.println( "Sine:   " + Math.sin( value ) );
System.out.println( "Cosine: " + Math.cos( value ) );
```

Listing 5.10 src/main/java/com/tutego/insel/string/SineAndCosine.java (Snippet)

parse*(String) and Potential NumberFormatException Errors

If a parse*(String) method can't perform a conversion because a string like "1lala2lö" cannot be converted, it throws a NumberFormatException. This problem also arises when parseDouble(String) receives a comma instead of a period as decimal separator. For the static method parseBoolean(String), case is irrelevant.

[»]

> **Note**
>
> This NumberFormatException error can serve as a test to determine whether a string contains a number or not, because *no* check method like Integer.isInteger(String) is available. An alternative is to use a regular expression and test against it, for instance, in the following example:
>
> ```
> stringWithNumber.matches("\\p{Digit}+")
> ```

parse*(...) and the Behavior with Plus, Minus, and Space Characters

If a string represents negative numbers, the string starts with a "-"; positive numbers may also start with a "+." The static conversion method Integer.parseInt(String) doesn't truncate spaces and would report a parser error if, for example, the string ended with a space. (The creator of the Java library, however, thought differently with Float.parseFloat(...) and Double.parseDouble(...), because the string is automatically trimmed before parsing.)

[Ex]

> **Example**
>
> The following example truncates spaces from the string and converts it to an integer:
>
> ```
> String s = " 1234   ".trim();          // s = "1234"
> int i = Integer.parseInt( s );         // i = 1234
> ```

What appears as the result in a String.valueOf(...)—and this is also what System.out.print*(...) is based on, for example—can parse*(...) back into the same value.

Localized parse*(String)

The parse*(...) methods aren't localized, so they can only convert English formatted strings into primitive values. With integers, this method is no problem, but with floats, a big problem arises because parseDouble("1,3") leads to NumberFormatException, while parseDouble("1.3") doesn't. Two approaches to solving this problem are available. One is to convert the decimal separator to a point beforehand, as in the following example:

```
String s = "3,1";
double d = Double.parseDouble( s.replace( ',', '.' ) );            // 3.1
```

However, this solution isn't good. Rather, a much better approach is to draw on classes that allow localized parsing, such as scanners (we'll return to this class in Section 5.10.2):

```
String s = "3,1";
double d = new Scanner( s ).useLocale( Locale.GERMANY ).nextDouble(); // 3.1
```

5.8.3   String Representation in Binary, Hex, and Octal Formats*

In addition to the overloaded static String.valueOf(primitive) methods, which return a number from a string representation in the familiar decimal system, and the reverse parse*(...) methods of the wrapper classes, other methods can convert and parse strings into the following number systems:

- Binary (base 2)
- Octals (base 8)
- Hexadecimal (base 16)
- Any base (up to 36)

The methods aren't found in the String class, but together with methods for parsing in the Integer and Long classes.

Building String Representations

On one hand, general class methods toString(int i, int radix) are available for any radix in the classes Integer and Long. On the other hand, special methods exist for the radixes 2, 8, and 16.

```
final class java.lang.Integer
extends Number
implements Comparable<Integer>, Serializable
```

- ▶ static String toBinaryString(int i)
- ▶ static String toOctalString(int i)
- ▶ static String toHexString(int i)
  Creates a binary representation (base 2), octal number representation (base 8), or hexadecimal representation (base 16) of the unsigned number.
- ▶ static String toString(int i, int radix)
  Creates a string representation of the number to the specified base.

```
final class java.lang.Long
extends Number
implements Comparable<Long>, Serializable
```

▶ static String toBinaryString(long i)

▶ static String toOctalString(long i)

▶ static String toHexString(long i)
  Creates a binary representation (base 2), octal number representation (base 8), or hexadecimal representation (base 16) of the unsigned number.

▶ static String toString(long i, int radix)
  Creates a string representation of the number to the specified base.

Negative numbers get a negative sign with the toString(...) methods, which isn't true for the other methods mentioned.

The parameter type is int or long and not byte, which leads to outputs that must be taken into consideration. In the same way, leading zeros aren't output.

Statement	Result
Integer.toHexString(15)	f
Integer.toHexString(16)	10
Integer.toHexString(127)	7f
Integer.toHexString(128)	80
Integer.toHexString(255)	ff
Integer.toHexString(256)	100
Integer.toHexString(-1)	ffffffff
Long.toHexString(-1)	ffffffffffffffff

Table 5.10 Examples of the toHexString() Method

If the number is negative, it's treated unsigned, and 2^{32} (for integer) and 2^{64} (for long) are added.

Output with printf(...)—or formatting with String.format(...)—provides an alternative, as described in detail in Section 5.11.1.

[»]

Note

A conversion with toHexString(x) isn't the same with negative numbers as with toString(x, 16), as shown in the following example:

```
System.out.println( Integer.toHexString( -10 ) );  // fffffff6
System.out.println( Integer.toString( -10, 16 ) ); // -a
```

In this case, toHexString(...) applies what is given as a remark in the Java documentation, namely, that for negative numbers the unsigned number is taken (i.e., 10) and then 2^{32} is added, which isn't the case with toString(...) and an arbitrary radix.

Parsing Strings with radix

A method for converting a string to an integer for a given base can be found in the Integer and Long classes. Only the Integer and Long classes contain support for a base that is also not equal to 10:

```
final class java.lang.Integer
extends Number
implements Comparable<Integer>, Serializable
```

▶ static int parseInt(String s)

▶ static int parseInt(String s, int radix)

```
final class java.lang.Long
extends Number
implements Comparable<Long>, Serializable
```

▶ static long parseLong(String s)

▶ static long parseLong(String s, int radix)

Some use cases include the following:

Conversion Call	Result
parseInt("0", 10)	0
parseInt("473", 10)	473
parseInt("-0", 10)	0
parseInt("-FF", 16)	-255
parseInt("1100110", 2)	102
parseInt("2147483647", 10)	2147483647
parseInt("-2147483648", 10)	-2147483648
parseInt("2147483648", 10)	☠ throws NumberFormatException

Table 5.11 Examples of Integer.parseInt(...) with Different Number Bases

Conversion Call	Result
parseInt("99", 8)	☠ throws NumberFormatException
parseInt("Papa", 10)	☠ throws NumberFormatException
parseInt("Papa", 27)	500050

Table 5.11 Examples of Integer.parseInt(...) with Different Number Bases (Cont.)

[Ex]

Example

The radix goes up to 36 (that is, 10 digits and 26 lowercase letters). With radix 36, for example, integer IDs can be represented more compactly as text than if they were decimal. Consider the following example:

```
String string = Long.toString( 2656437647773L, 36 );
System.out.println( string );   // xwcmdz8d
long 1 = Long.parseLong( string, 36 );
System.out.println( 1 ); // 2656437647773
```

[»]

Puzzle

What is the result of the expression Long.parseLong("" + 1 / 0., 35)?

Parsing Binary, Octal, and Hexadecimal Numbers

In the case of string conversions, special methods like toHexString(...) exist for the standard bases 2, 8, and 16, but they don't exist for parsing. A hexadecimal number is processed by parseInt(s, 16) because a method like parseHex(String) isn't available.

[»]

Note

The parseInt(...) and parseLong(...) methods don't behave as expected with string representations of negative numbers. Consider the following example:

```
int i = Integer.parseInt( "7fffffff", 16 ); // 2147483647
int j = Integer.parseInt( "80000000", 16 ); // ☠ NumberFormatException
```

0x7fffffff is the largest positive int number that can be represented. However, instead of returning the value -2,147,483,648 at 0x80000000, it returns a NumberFormatException. The Java API documentation also provides this example but doesn't make this behavior particularly clear. With negative numbers and parseInt(...)/parseLong(...), a minus must also be specified as a sign. So, the parse*(...) methods aren't reverse methods to, say, toHexString(...), but always to toString(...). Consider the following example:

```
System.out.println( Integer.toString( -2147483648, 16 ) ); // -80000000
System.out.println( Integer.parseInt( "-80000000", 16 ) ); // -2147483648
```

5.8.4   parse*(...) and print*() Methods in DatatypeConverter*

The java.util.HexFormat class helps with the task of producing and parsing hexadecimal strings.

[Ex]

Example

Convert a byte array to a hexadecimal string representation.

```
byte[] bytes = { 1, 2, 3, (byte) 254, (byte) 255 };
HexFormat = HexFormat.ofDelimiter( " " ).withPrefix( "#" );
String hex = hexFormat.formatHex( bytes );
System.out.println( hex );
```

5.9   Concatenating Strings

To generate a new string from partial strings, Java provides the following options:

- The plus operator for involved String objects
- The concat(String) method of the String class
- The StringBuilder and StringBuffer classes with their append(...) methods
- A join(...) method for the String class or the helper class java.util.StringJoiner for joining parts with a common separator
- Using format(...) of String or the helper class java.util.Formatter

In addition, a few methods and types can also be referred to as concatenations:

- Two special append*(...) methods for appending strings in the course of a replacement in the context of regular expressions
- A special StringWriter with append(...) and write(...) methods

[+]

Tip

The newly built StringBuilder should ideally get the appropriate buffer size in the constructor right away. However, the JVM itself also tries to optimize concatenation.

5.9.1   Concatenating Strings with StringJoiner

To concatenate strings into one large result using a common separator, String provides the convenient helper method join(...). This method is based on a small class named StringJoiner, which can also be used directly.

[Ex]

Example

Let's say we have an array that contains prices that should be concatenated into one large string. The segments should be separated with semicolons and spaces, "USD" should be placed in front of each price, and prices should use 2 decimal places with a dot as the decimal separator. Consider the following example:

```
double[] prices = { 1.90, 2.49 };
StringJoiner joiner = new StringJoiner( "; " );
for ( double price : prices )
  joiner.add( String.format( Locale.ENGLISH, "USD %.2f", price ) );
System.out.println( joiner );                    // USD 1.90; USD 2.49
```

Note that the static format(...) method is localized with English formatting.

The delimiter (which can of course also be an empty string "") is placed between each element that has been added. The add(CharSequence) method used in the example accepts a join string of type CharSequence and returns the current StringJoiner, so that the add(...) calls can be cascaded. The merge(StringJoiner) method can be used to integrate the content of another StringJoiner.

Concatenating with Infixes, Prefixes, and Suffixes

Not only the separator itself can be specified, but also a start character and end character.

[Ex]

Example

The output should start with a "{" and end with a "}" as in the following example:

```
StringJoiner joiner = new StringJoiner( ", ", "{", "}" );
```

Nothing Given to Concatenate

Sometimes, the StringJoiner isn't given anything to join. In this case, it will still use a prefix and suffix, as in the following example:

```
StringJoiner joiner = new StringJoiner( ", ", "{", "}" );
System.out.println( joiner.toString() ); // {}
```

If this behavior isn't desirable, setEmptyValue(CharSequence) specifies a substitute that comes into play exactly when no add(...) has added anything to the StringJoiner, as in the following example:

```
StringJoiner joiner = new StringJoiner( ", ", "{", "}" ).setEmptyValue("-");
System.out.println( joiner.toString() ); // -
```

In summary, the class provides two constructors and five methods:

---
class java.util.**StringJoiner**

▶ StringJoiner(CharSequence delimiter)

▶ StringJoiner(CharSequence delimiter, CharSequence prefix, CharSequence suffix)

▶ StringJoiner add(CharSequence newElement)

▶ StringJoiner merge(StringJoiner other)

▶ StringJoiner setEmptyValue(CharSequence emptyValue)

▶ int length()

▶ String toString()

Note

Actually, the StringJoiner class is quite weak, and even String.join(...) allows to accept strings as a collection of type Iterable, which StringJoiner, the implementation of String.join(…), does not allow itself.

5.10 Decomposing Strings

The Java library provides some classes and methods that allow us to break large strings into smaller ones according to certain patterns. In this context, the terms *token* and *delimiter* are worth mentioning: A token is a part of a string which is separated from other tokens by certain *delimiters*. Let's take the sentence "Modern music is playing instruments according to notes" (Peter Sellers) as an example. If we choose spaces as separators, the individual tokens will be "Modern," "Music," etc.

The Java library provides a number of options for string decomposition. The first two from this list are presented in the following sections:

- split(…) of String: Splits using a delimiter described by a regular expression.
- lines() of String: Returns a Stream<String> of lines.
- Scanner: nice class to traverse an input, also line by line.
- StringTokenizer: Delimiters are only single characters.
- BreakIterator: Finds character, word, line, or sentence boundaries.
- Matcher: In connection with the Pattern class, Matcher decomposes strings using regular expressions.

The methods and classes are, generally speaking, the counterparts of the concatenation options. For instance, split(...) is opposed to join(...), and StringTokenizer is opposed to StringJoiner.

5.10.1 Splitting Strings via split(...)

The object method split (...) of a String object splits its own string into substrings. The separators are completely arbitrary and described as a regular expression. The return is an array or an iterable with substrings.

[Ex]

> **Example**
>
> The following example decomposes a domain name into its component parts:
>
> ```
> String path = "www.tutego.com";
> String[] segs = path.split( Pattern.quote( "." ) );
> System.out.println( Arrays.toString(segs) ); // [www, tutego, com]
> ```
>
> Since the dot as a separator is a special character for regular expressions, it must be appropriately commented out with the backslash. This is done by the static method Pattern.quote(String), which returns a "disarmed" regex string. Otherwise, split(".") returns an array of length 0 on each string.

A common separator is \s, which is whitespace.

[Ex]

> **Example**
>
> The following example counts the number of words in a sentence:
>
> ```
> String = "So just listen now to my musical doodle.";
> int wordCount = string.split( "(\\s|\\p{Punct})+" ).length;
> System.out.println( wordCount );       // 8
> ```
>
> The separator is either whitespace or a punctuation mark. Alternatively, the expression "[\\s\\p{Punct}]+" can be used.

```
final class java.lang.String
implements CharSequence, Comparable<String>, Serializable
```

▶ String[] split(String regex)
Splits the current string with the regular expression.

▶ String[] split(String regex, int limit)
Splits the current string with the regular expression but returns a maximum limited number of substrings.

5.10.2 Yes We Can, Yes We Scan: The Scanner Class

The java.util.Scanner class can split a string into tokens and read simple files line by line. In the decomposition, a regular expression can describe the delimiter. This feature makes Scanner more flexible than a StringTokenizer, which only allows single characters as separators.

Building a Scanner

To build a Scanner object, the class provides several constructors that take the strings to be parsed from various sources, such as a String, a data stream (when reading from the command line, this data stream is System.in), a Path object, or various other input sources. If the source is of type Closeable, like a Writer, the Scanner should be closed via close(), which forwards the close() to the Closeable object. You do not need to call close() when the source is a String.

```
final class java.util.Scanner
implements Iterator<String>, Closeable
```

▶ Scanner(String source)

▶ Scanner(Path source) throws IOException

▶ Scanner(Path source, String charsetName) throws IOException

▶ Scanner(Path source, Charset charset) throws IOException

▶ Scanner(File source) throws FileNotFoundException

▶ Scanner(File source, String charsetName) throws FileNotFoundException

▶ Scanner(File source, Charset charset) throws IOException

▶ Scanner(InputStream source)

▶ Scanner(InputStream source, String charsetName)

▶ Scanner(InputStream source, Charset charset)

▶ Scanner(Readable source)

▶ Scanner(ReadableByteChannel source)

▶ Scanner(ReadableByteChannel source, String charsetName)

▶ Scanner(ReadableByteChannel source, Charset charset)

Reading a File Line by Line

Once the Scanner object has been created, the pair hasNextLine() and nextLine() can be used to easily read a file line by line.

A program is supposed to read a file and reverse the lines in such a way that the last line of the file is at the top and the first line of the file is at the bottom. The result on the console should be a string with no whitespace at the beginning and end.

```
InputStream resource =
 ReverseFile.class.getResourceAsStream( "EastOfJava.txt" );
try ( Scanner input = new Scanner( resource ) ) {
```

```
  StringBuilder result = new StringBuilder();
  while ( input.hasNextLine() )
    result.insert( 0, input.nextLine() + System.lineSeparator() );
  System.out.println( result.toString().trim() );
}
```

Listing 5.11 src/main/java/com/tutego/insel/string/ReverseFile.java (Snippet)

The construction with try (...) { ... } is called *try with resources* and automatically closes the file after its use. The handling of exceptions and the special use of try are both explained in more detail in Chapter 9, Section 9.6. Also, the encoding should always be specified, which in our case is ISO 8859-1 (i.e., Latin-1). The encoding string necessary for the Scanner constructor comes from a constant from StandardCharsets.

```
final class java.util.Scanner
implements Iterator<String>, Closeable
```

▶ boolean hasNextLine()
Returns true if a next line can be read.

▶ String nextLine()
Returns the next line.

[+]
> **Tip**
> If we initialize a Scanner with a string, this string can be decomposed line by line by the scanner. The string method lines() is an alternative; the result is a stream of lines. We'll discuss streams in more detail in Chapter 16.

Next, Please

After creating the Scanner object, the next() method returns the next string if a hasNext() returns true. (These methods are then also methods of the Iterator interface, where remove() isn't implemented.)

[Ex]
> **Example**
> In the following example, a String s will be read from the standard input:
> ```
> Scanner scanner = new Scanner( System.in );
> String s = scanner.next();
> ```
> Important: The Scanner shouldn't be closed in this case!

In addition to the next() method, which returns only a string, Scanner provides various next<type>() methods, which read the next token and convert it into a desired format, for example, into a double with nextDouble(). With the same number of has-Next<type>() methods, you can query whether another token of this type follows.

Example

Let's look at the individual next*() and hasNext*() methods with the following example:

```
Scanner scanner = new Scanner( "tutego 12 1973 12,03 True 123456789000" );
System.out.println( scanner.hasNext() );        // true
System.out.println( scanner.next() );           // tutego
System.out.println( scanner.hasNextByte() );    // true
System.out.println( scanner.nextByte() );       // 12
System.out.println( scanner.hasNextInt() );     // true
System.out.println( scanner.nextInt() );        // 1973
System.out.println( scanner.hasNextDouble() );  // true
System.out.println( scanner.nextDouble() );     // 12.03
System.out.println( scanner.hasNextBoolean() ); // true
System.out.println( scanner.nextBoolean() );    // true
System.out.println( scanner.hasNextLong() );    // true
System.out.println( scanner.nextLong() );       // 123456789000
System.out.println( scanner.hasNext() );        // false
```

Listing 5.12 src/main/java/com/tutego/insel/string/ScannerDemo.java, main()

If not all tokens are interesting, they'll be skipped by Scanner skip(Pattern pattern) or Scanner skip(String pattern), while separators will be ignored.

```
final class java.util.Scanner
implements Iterator<String>, Closeable
```

▶ boolean hasNext()

▶ boolean hasNextBigDecimal()

▶ boolean hasNextBigInteger()

▶ boolean hasNextBigInteger(int radix)

▶ boolean hasNextBoolean()

▶ boolean hasNextByte()

▶ boolean hasNextByte(int radix)

▶ boolean hasNextDouble()

▶ boolean hasNextFloat()

▶ boolean hasNextInt()

▶ boolean hasNextInt(int radix)

▶ boolean hasNextLong()

▶ boolean hasNextLong(int radix)

▶ boolean hasNextShort()

▶ boolean hasNextShort(int radix)
  Returns true if a token of the requested type can be read.

▶ String next()

▶ BigDecimal nextBigDecimal()

▶ BigInteger nextBigInteger()

▶ BigInteger nextBigInteger(int radix)

▶ boolean nextBoolean()

▶ byte nextByte()

▶ byte nextByte(int radix)

▶ double nextDouble()

▶ float nextFloat()

▶ int nextInt()

▶ int nextInt(int radix)

▶ long nextLong()

▶ long nextLong(int radix)

▶ short nextShort()

▶ short nextShort(int radix)
  Returns the next token.

The useRadix(int) method changes the base for numbers, and radix() queries it.

5.11   Formatting Outputs

Again and again, numbers, dates, and text must be formatted in a variety of ways. Java provides various solutions for formatting, such as the following:

- The format(...) and printf(...) methods enable formatted outputs.

- Formatting via Format classes: General formatting behavior is fixed in an abstract Format class. Concrete subclasses, such as NumberFormat and DateFormat, take care of specific data formats.

- Conversion of a string according to a given mask with a MaskFormatter

The Format classes not only provide country- and language-dependent output via format(...), but also the reverse way to split strings back into types like double or date. Any string generated by the Format object can also be read again with the parser.

5.11.1 Formatting and Outputting via format()

The String class provides a way to format strings according to a default with the static method format(...).

Example [Ex]

Build the String "Hey Patrick, I thought of something funnier than 24... 25!":

```
String s =
 String.format( "Hey %s, I thought of something funnier than %d... %d!",
                 "Patrick", 24, 24+1 );
System.out.println( s );
```

The first string passed to format(...) is called the *format string*. In addition to characters to be output, it contains additional *format specifiers* to tell the formatter how to format the argument. %s stands for an unformatted output of a string. The format string is followed by a vararg (or alternatively the array directly) containing the values referred to by the format specifiers.

Specifier	Stands for ...	Specifier	Stands for ...
%n	New line	%b	Boolean
%%	Percentage sign	%s	String
%c	Unicode character	%d	Decimal number
%x	Hexadecimal notation	%t	Date and time
%f	Float	%e	Scientific notation

Table 5.12 The Most Important Format Specifiers

Tip [+]

The line feed is dependent on the operating system, but %n is a good means of obtaining this line feed character (or string). However, instead of using String.format("%n") to query the separator, System.lineSeparator() is a better solution.

```
final class java.lang.String
implements CharSequence, Comparable<String>, Serializable
```

▶ static String format(String format, Object... args)
 Returns a formatted string from the string and arguments.

▶ static String format(Locale l, String format, Object... args)
Returns a formatted string consisting of the desired language, the string, and the arguments.

Internally, java.util.Formatter (no java.text.Format objects exist) are at work, which can also be used directly; the documentation is also placed there.

System.out.printf(…)

If a string formatted with String.format(...) should be output immediately, System.out.print(String.format(format, args)); doesn't need to be used. Conveniently, the format(...) method known from String is also contained in the PrintWriter and PrintStream classes for formatting and for outputs. (The System.out object is of type PrintStream.) However, since the method name format(...) isn't really consistent with the other print*(...) methods, the developers have made the format(...) methods also available under the name printf(...). (The implementation of printf(...) is a simple redirect to the format(...) method.) Also, with printf(...) a locale is possible as first argument.

[Ex]

Example

The following example outputs the numbers from 0 to 15 in hexadecimal format:

```
for ( int i = 0x0; i <= 0xf; i++ )
  System.out.printf( "%x%n", i );  // 0 1 2 … e f
```

Pimp My String with Format Specifiers*

The number of format specifiers is so large and their further parameterization so diverse that a look into the API documentation is definitely necessary. The most important specifiers are:

- %n results in the line feed character(s), each related to the current platform. This notation is preferable to a hard \n, which may or may not be the line feed character of the current platform.

- %% returns the percentage sign itself, just as \\ masks out the backslash in a string.

- %s returns a string, where null leads to the output "null." %S capitalizes the output.

- %b writes a Boolean, namely, the value true or false. The output is always false for null and true for other types like Integer or String. %B capitalizes the string.

- %c writes a character, where the types wrapper types Character, Byte, and Short are allowed. %C writes the character in uppercase.

- For numeric integer outputs with %d (decimal), %x (hexadecimal), and %o (octal), the wrapper types Byte, Short, Integer, Long, and BigInteger are allowed; %X capitalizes the hexadecimal letters.

- For floats with %f or %e (%E), %g (%G), and %a (%A), the wrapper types Float, Double, and BigDecimal are additionally allowed. The standard precision for %e, %E, and %f is six decimal places.

- In case of date/time specifications with %t or %T, the following are allowed: Long, Calendar, and Date. %t requires additional information, as you'll see in the next example.

- The hash code is written by %h or %H. If the value is null, the result is also the string with the content "null."

Additional flags, for example, for length specifications and the number of decimal places, are possible, as shown in the following example:

```
PrintStream o = System.out;

int i = 123;
o.printf( "|%d|%d|%n" ,        i, -i );      // |123|-123|
o.printf( "|%5d|%5d|%n" ,      i, -i );      // |  123| -123|
o.printf( "|%-5d|%-5d|%n" ,    i, -i );      // |123  |-123 |
o.printf( "|%+-5d|%+-5d|%n" ,  i, -i );      // |+123 |-123 |
o.printf( "|%05d|%05d|%n%n",   i, -i );      // |00123|-0123|

o.printf( "|%X|%x|%X|%n", 0xabc, 0xabc, -0xabc ); // |ABC|abc|FFFFF544|
o.printf( "|%04x|%#x|%n%n", 0xabc, 0xabc ); // |0abc|0xabc|

double d = 12345.678;
o.printf( "|%f|%f|%n" ,         d, -d );  // |12345,678000|-12345,678000|
o.printf( "|%+f|%+f|%n" ,       d, -d );  // |+12345,678000|-12345,678000|
o.printf( "|% f|% f|%n" ,       d, -d );  // | 12345,678000|-12345,678000|
o.printf( "|%.2f|%.2f|%n" ,     d, -d );  // |12345,68|-12345,68|
o.printf( "|%,.2f|%,.2f|%n" ,   d, -d );  // |12.345,68|-12.345,68|
o.printf( "|%(.2f|%(.2f|%n",    d, -d );  // |12345,68|(12345,68)|
o.printf( "|%10.2f|%10.2f|%n" , d, -d );  // |  12345,68| -12345,68|
o.printf( "|%010.2f|%010.2f|%n%n",d,-d);  // |0012345,68|-012345,68|

String s = "Gobbledygook";
o.printf( "|%s|%n", s );                  // |Gobbledygook|
o.printf( "|%S|%n", s );                  // |GOBBLEDYGOOK|
o.printf( "|%20s|%n", s );                // |        Gobbledygook|
o.printf( "|%-20s|%n", s );               // |Gobbledygook        |
o.printf( "|%7s|%n", s );                 // |Gobbledygook|
o.printf( "|%.7s|%n", s );                // |Gobbled|
o.printf( "|%20.7s|%n%n", s );            // |             Gobbled|
```

```
Date t = new Date();
o.printf( "%tT%n", t );                          // 18:19:20
o.printf( "%tD%n", t );                          // 09/13/21
```

Listing 5.13 src/main/java/com/tutego/insel/string/PrintfDemo.java, main()

In the case of floats, these values are rounded according to the RoundingMode.HALF_UP. Thus, for example, System.out.printf("%.1f", 0.45); returns the output "0.5."

Some flags can be read from the examples, especially for floats. A comma controls whether the thousands separators are used. A + indicates whether a sign always appears, and a space indicates whether a space is then left empty for positive characters. An opening parenthesis doesn't place a minus for negative numbers, but places instead negative numbers in parentheses.

[+]

> **Tip**
>
> If format(...) or printf(...) is called without a locale, the default language of the operating system is used. Compare the following examples:
>
> ```
> double bitcoinPrice = ThreadLocalRandom.current().nextDouble( 50_000 );
> System.out.printf( "%.2f%n", bitcoinPrice );
> System.out.printf( Locale.ENGLISH, "%.2f%n", bitcoinPrice );
> ```
>
> The following outputs would result:
>
> 46714,42
> 46714.42

Format Specifier for Date Values

From our earlier example, note that %t doesn't simply output the time but always expects another suffix that specifies exactly which date/time part is actually desired. Table 5.13 contains the most important suffixes, and more can be found in the API documentation. All outputs take into account the given Locale environment.

Symbol	Description
%tA, %ta	Full/abbreviated name of the day of the week
%tB, %tb	Full/abbreviated name of the name of the month
%tC	2-digit century (00–99)
%te, %td	Numeric day of the month without or with leading zeros (1–31 or 01–31)
%tk, %tl	Hour specification related to 24 or 12 hours (0–23, 1–12)

Table 5.13 Suffixes for Date Values

Symbol	Description
%tH, %tI	2-digit hour information related to 24 or 12 hours (00–23, 01–12)
%tj	Day of the year (001–366)
%tM	2-digit minute specification (00–59)
%tm	2-digit month specification (usually 01–12)
%tS	2-digit second specification (00–59)
%tY	4-digit year specification
%ty	The last 2 digits of the year (00–99)
%tZ	Abbreviated time zone
%tz	Time zone with shift related to GMT
%tR	Hours and minutes in the %tH:%tM format
%tT	Hours/minutes/seconds in the %tH:%tM:%tS format
%tD	Date in the %tm/%td/%ty format
%tF	ISO-8601 format %tY-%tm-%td
%tc	Complete date with time in the format %ta %tb %td %tT %tZ %tY

Table 5.13 Suffixes for Date Values (Cont.)

Allowed data types are long, Long, Calendar, and Date, and implementations of TemporalAccessor include DayOfWeek, Instant, LocalDate, LocalDateTime, LocalTime, Month, MonthDay, OffsetDateTime, OffsetTime, Year, YearMonth, ZonedDateTime, and ZoneOffset.

Position Specifications

The formatting string can contain a position specification of the type *Position*$, where then 1$ refers to the first argument, 2$ to the second and so on. (Note here that the numbering doesn't start at zero).

Example

Output the day and month of March 12, 2025:

```
LocalDate date = LocalDate.of( 2022, Month.MARCH, 12 );
System.out.printf( Locale.ENGLISH, "%te. %1$tb%n", date );  // 12. Mar
System.out.printf( Locale.FRENCH, "%te. %1$tb%n", date );   // 12. mars
```

The first statement creates a date object from year, month, and day.

The position specification in the format string enables two things:

- If, as in the example, the same argument is used more than once, you don't need to specify it more than once. Thus, `printf("`**`%te. %tb%n`**`", t, t)` repeats the argument t, which avoids specifying a position. Instead of this solution, you could also write %te. **%1$**tb%n, thus explicitly prescribing the position 1 for the second argument as well.

- The order of the passed arguments usually always remains the same, but the format string can put the arguments in different positions.

The second point is important for localized editions. Let's look at an example: A screen output is supposed to output the first and last name in different languages. However, the order of the parts of the name can be different, and the first name doesn't always precede the last name in every language. In English, the welcome text would read "Hello Christian Ullenboom," but in another language it could be "nuqneH Ullenboom Christian."

```
Object[] formatArgs = { "Christian", "Ullenboom" };

String germanFormat = "Hello %1$s %2$s";
System.out.printf( englishFormat, formatArgs );
System.out.println();

String bwatutiFormat = "nuqneH %2$s %1$s";
System.out.printf( bwatutiFormat, formatArgs );
```

Listing 5.14 src/main/java/com/tutego/insel/string/FormatPosition.java, main()

The calling order for first name/last name is always the same, but the format string, which comes from an external configuration file or database, for example, can change this order to match the local language.

[+]   **Tip**

If a subsequent format element references the preceding argument, a < can be set:

```
LocalDate d1 = LocalDate.of( 1973, Month.MARCH, 1 );
LocalDate d2 = LocalDate.of( 1966, 4, 23 );
System.out.printf( Locale.ENGLISH,
                   "%te. %<tb %<ty  -  %2$te. %<tb %<ty%n", d1, d2 );
//                     1. Mar 73  -  23. Apr 66
```

The specifications for month and year reference the preceding items in each case. Thus, d1 and d2 need to be specified only once.

5.12   Further Reading

For more information, take a look at the API documentation of the String, String-Builder, Scanner and Formatter classes and also explore regular expressions (Pattern and Matcher classes), which can be used to elegantly answer questions about matching as well as about the position of substrings.

When large amounts of data are processed as strings, the question of optimization is quite relevant. The default implementation of the JDK only uses a simple search algorithm, which is rather inefficient for large patterns and search strings. In the field of search algorithms, however, computer science has produced interesting approaches in recent decades, for example, the optimal mismatch algorithm. However, the complete Unicode standard with 32 bits poses a certain problem. Enterprise libraries, for example, for parsing XML or JSON, don't necessarily support the current Unicode standard with its hundreds of thousands of characters.

Chapter 6

Writing Custom Classes

"The law is the abstract expression of the general will being in and of itself."
—*Georg Wilhelm Friedrich Hegel (1770–1831)*

In the preceding chapters, you learned a lot about object orientation, but our discussion was more from the user point of view. You've seen how objects can be built, and we've also implemented simple classes with static methods. Now is the time to round out your knowledge of object-oriented programming (OOP) and build your own *custom data types*.

> **Note**
>
> We'll illustrate the concepts of object orientation with a program based on the *Drug Wars* game. John Dell developed this MS-DOS-based game in the early 1980s to demonstrate a core principle of economics: buy low and sell high. With easy-to-understand rules, *Drug Wars* can be played in a web browser at the following websites:
>
> - *https://classicreload.com/drug-wars.html* (first version)
> - *https://archive.org/details/DruglordV2.0SW1992FantasyWareInc.Simulation* (extended version)
>
> In our examples, we'll switch from hard drugs to soft drugs and use candy. We'll call our game *Jawbreaker*.

6.1 Declaring Custom Classes with Members

The declaration of a class is introduced by the class keyword. In the body of the class, you can declare the following elements:

- Object and class variables
- Methods
- Constructors
- Class initializers as well as instance initializers
- Nested types, such as classes, records, interfaces, and enumerations

6.1.1   Minimum Class

Our focus on candy is represented by the Candy class.

```
package com.tutego.insel.game.c.v1
class Candy { }
```

Listing 6.1 src/main/java/com/tutego/insel/game/c/v1/Candy.java

Figure 6.1 Unified Modeling Language (UML) Diagram of the Candy Class as Just an Outlined Box

The Candy class has a constructor generated by the compiler, and new Candy() creates a instance from this blueprint. Details about the constructor will follow in Section 6.5.3. We'll omit visibility modifiers (such as public) for now and then focus on them more closely in Section 6.2.

> **[»]   Code Abbreviations in this Book**
>
> As in previous chapters, the package and import declarations are omitted from our code snippets, so that the code can be a little shorter.

6.1.2   Declaring Object Variables

This class Candy { } class has no object variables and therefore can't store any states. Let's give the candy three object variables: one for the name (type String), a second for the price (type int), and a third for the number of candies (type int).

```
class Candy {
  String name;
  int    price;
  int    quantity;
}
```

Listing 6.2 src/main/java/com/tutego/insel/game/c/v2/Candy.java (Snippet)

> **[»]   Note**
>
> You can't use var with object variables and must therefore specify the data types.

A second class, Application, creates two instances of a candy in its static main(...) method, describes the object variables, and reads them.

```
Candy lollipop = new Candy();
lollipop.name = "Lollipop";
lollipop.price = 12;
lollipop.quantity = 2;

Candy licorice = new Candy();
licorice.name = "Licorice";
licorice.price = 22;

System.out.printf( "%s, %d × %d = %d%n", // Lollipop, 2 × 12 = 24
                   lollipop.name, lollipop.quantity, lollipop.price,
                   lollipop.quantity * lollipop.price );
System.out.printf( "%s, %d × %d = %d%n", // Licorice, 0 × 22 = 0
                   licorice.name, licorice.quantity, licorice.price,
                   licorice.quantity * licorice.price );
```

Listing 6.3 src/main/java/com/tutego/insel/game/c/v2/Application.java (Snippet)

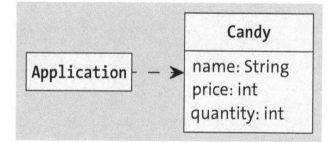

Figure 6.2 UML Class Diagram Showing the Dependencies of Application and Candy

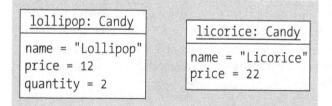

Figure 6.3 UML Object Diagram Showing the Two Candy Instances

When two files are open in the editor, then that's the point at which keyboard junkies may want to quickly switch between editors. In IntelliJ, the shortcuts are `Ctrl`+`Tab` and `Ctrl`+`Shift`+`Tab`.

> **Note**
>
> No special naming convention exist for object variables. Thus, although you can prefix local variables (such as f or _) to distinguish them, even Eclipse has moved away from this convention. Basically, object variables can also be named like methods, but this approach is unusual because variable names are generally nouns, while methods are verbs. Furthermore, identifiers cannot be identical to keywords.

Initializing Object Variables

Unlike local variables, the JVM initializes all object variables with a default value—the same is true for class variables, which we'll describe in Section 6.3. The following values are the defaults:

- 0 for numeric values and char
- false for boolean
- null for reference variables

If you don't like these default values, your variables can be assigned values, as in the following example:

```
class Candy {
  String name;
  int    price;
  int    quantity = 1;
}
```

The expression new Candy().quantity == 1 would therefore return true.

> **Design Tip**
>
> You may find yourself walking a tightrope when using simple data types or when referencing other objects. If Candy stores the price, an int (or double) is problematic because Candy would also have to perform a validation so that the price never becomes negative; however, this behavior does not fit in with the definition of what candy is or what it does! The general OOP rule is: For data that needs to be validated and may also be related to other object variables, create a new data type.

Validity Range, Visibility, and Lifetime

Local variables begin their lifecycles the moment they are declared and initialized. If the block ends, the local variable is no longer valid, and it can no longer be used because it has disappeared from the visibility area. This lifecycle is different for object variables. An object variable lives from the moment the object has been built via new and continues living until the garbage collector clears the object away. However, the variable is always visible and valid in the entire object and in all blocks.[1]

6.1.3   Declaring Methods

Object variables are joined by methods that usually operate on object variables. Let's give the candy two methods:

- `totalPrice()`: Calculates the total price as the product of quantity and price.
- `resetQuantity()`: Resets the quantity to 1.

Unlike our previous static methods, these three methods for Candy will be object methods, so they will *not* carry the `static` modifier.

```java
class Candy {
  String name;
  int    price;
  int    quantity = 1;

  int totalPrice() {
    return price * quantity;
  }

  void resetQuantity() {
    quantity = 1;
  }
}
```

Listing 6.4 src/main/java/com/tutego/insel/game/c/v3/Candy.java (Snippet)

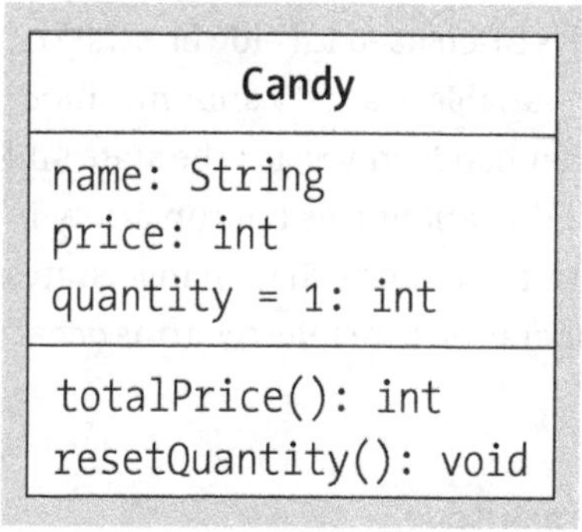

Candy
name: String price: int quantity = 1: int
totalPrice(): int resetQuantity(): void

Figure 6.4 UML Class Diagram of Candy with Three Object Variables and Two Methods

---

1 This coverage doesn't apply to static methods and static initialization blocks, which will be introduced later in Section 6.3.

The `totalPrice()` method builds the price as a product of price and quantity and returns the result. `resetQuantity()` resets the product quantity to 1.

Let's test our methods by creating some candy.

```
Candy lollipop = new Candy();
lollipop.name = "Lollipop";
lollipop.price = 12;
lollipop.quantity = 2;
System.out.println( lollipop.totalPrice() ); // 24
lollipop.resetQuantity();
System.out.println( lollipop.totalPrice() ); // 12
```

Listing 6.5 src/main/java/com/tutego/insel/game/c/v3/Application.java (Snippet)

Pressing [Ctrl]+[F12] activates a window with an overview. To navigate quickly in the compilation unit, a small text field allows you to search, and the cursor keys allow you to navigate. Pressing [Enter] transports you to the selected entry.

[+]

Java Virtual Machine (JVM): Internal Information*

Each object has its own object states, but not each object also has the code for the methods duplicated because the code doesn't change for each object. Internally, methods exist only once and use a reference to the object data on which they can operate.

Method Calls and Side Effects

All the variables and methods of a class are visible in the class itself. In other words, within a class, the object variables and methods are used by their names. Thus, the `totalPrice(...)` method directly accesses the necessary object variables `price` and `quantity` to execute the program logic. This shorthand is often used for side effects. The `resetQuantity()` method explicitly changes the object variable `quantity` and thus modifies the state of the object. `totalPrice(...)`, on the other hand, only reads the state and doesn't modify it. Methods that change states should document this appropriately in the application programming interface (API) description. Methods that change states are also called *mutators*; methods that perform read operations are referred to as *accessor methods*.

Object-Oriented and Procedural Programming in Comparison

Developers from the procedural world have internalized a different model of thinking, so at this point, we'd like to clarify the special nature of object orientation once again. While in good OO modeling, the objects always have states and behaviors at the same time, in the procedural world, only memory areas are referenced; the data and the behavior aren't connected. This separation becomes problematic when a procedural way of thinking is mapped into Java programs. Let's look at an example: The CandyData class is a pure data container for the state, but behavior is not declared.

```
class CandyData {
  String name;
  int    price;
  int    quantity = 1;
}
```

Listing 6.6 src/main/java/com/tutego/insel/nonoop/CandyData.java (Snippet)

Now, instead of attaching the methods neatly to the class, as in this first example, in the procedural world, a subroutine would get exactly one data object and request or change states from it.

```
class CandyFunctions {
  static int totalPrice( CandyData candy ) {
    return candy.price * candy.quantity;
  }
}
```

Listing 6.7 src/main/java/com/tutego/insel/nonoop/CandyFunctions.java (Snippet)

Since the subroutines are now no longer bound to objects, the methods can be static. However, methods (whether static or not) in the CandyData class would be just as wrong if they were passed a CandyData object.

This non-OO approach is easy to see in calls. As shown in Table 6.1, the incorrect way is on the left, and on the right, you'll see the correct, OO-modeled way.

Procedural Programming	OOP
CandyData lollipop = new CandyData(); lollipop.price = 12; int p = CandyFunctions.**totalPrice(lollipop)**;	Candy lollipop = new Candy(); lollipop.price = 12; int p = **lollipop.totalPrice()**;

Table 6.1 Procedural Programming and OOP Compared

An indication of problematic OO modeling is therefore when objects are passed to external methods instead of the methods themselves being set to the objects.

6.1.4 Shadowed Variables

If a method introduces a new variable, the same variable name can't be used again in an inner block.

Example

The following code in a main(...) method causes a compiler error:

```java
public static void main( String[] args ) {
  int args = 1;      // ☠ Duplicate local variable args
}
```

However, when a variable leaves a block, its name is free again. The following code is therefore allowed:

```java
for ( int i = 0; i < 10; i++ )
  System.out.println( i );
for ( int i = 0; i < 10; i++ )
  System.out.println( i );
```

Basically, no problem arises if a local variable/parameter variable has the same name as an object variable. In this case, we speak of a *shadowed variable*.[2] The compiler will then use the local variable and no longer use the object variable.

Example

In the following example, the local price variable in totalPrice() hides the object variable price:

```java
class Candy {
  int price;
  int quantity = 1;

  int totalPrice() {
    int price = quantity;
    price *= price * quantity;
    return price;
  }
}
```

We have two price variables in our example, but any access to price in the method automatically references the local variable and not the object variable.

Shadowed variables are useful because, without such a concept, a newly inserted object variable could quickly break many methods that also happen to use the same name in the body.[3]

---

2 *https://docs.oracle.com/javase/specs/jls/se17/html/jls-6.html#jls-6.4*
3 Almost all programming languages have shadowed variables, but one exception is TypeScript.

But what if we want to use a local variable simultaneously with an object variable of the same name?

6.1.5 The this Reference

In each object method and constructor,[4] a reference named this is available, which references the own instance. This reference enables you to implement elegant solutions, as the following examples show:

- The this reference solves the problem that may arise when parameters or local variables shadow object variables.

- If a method returns the this reference to the current object, methods of the class can easily be placed one behind the other.

- The this reference can give another method a reference to ourselves.

Using Shadowed Object Variables

If a local variable has the same name as an object variable, the former shadows the latter, as described in the previous section. Far from a tragedy, shadowing only becomes a problem if access to the object variable specifically is required at a later stage.

However, this limitation doesn't mean that the object variable can no longer be accessed. The this reference points to the current object, and thus access to object members is also possible at any time. In the following example, a local price variable is introduced again, but access to the object variable is achieved via this.price:

```
class Candy {
  int price;
  int quantity = 1;

  int totalPrice() {
    int price = quantity * this.price;
    return price;
  }
}
```

Listing 6.8 src/main/java/com/tutego/insel/game/c/v4/Candy.java (Snippet)

Using this for Setters

Common elements used with this include methods or constructors that initialize states. Developers like to name parameter variables in the same way as the copied variables to express a strong affiliation. So, let's write a setName(String) method with the following code:

---

4 As well as in instance initializers, but the code ends up in the constructor.

```
class Candy {
  String name;

  public void setName( String name ) {
    this.name = name;
  }
}
```

The object passed to setName(String) is to initialize the object variable name. Thus, this.name accesses the object variable directly, so the assignment this.name = name initializes the object variable with the argument.

Using this for Cascaded Methods*

The append(...) methods on StringBuilder return the this reference so the following can be written:

```
StringBuilder sb = new StringBuilder();
sb.append( "'Ding Dong' or " ).append( "'Boom Boom'" ).append( '?' );
```

Each append(...) changes the internal state and returns the StringBuilder object on which it is called, so we can append methods in a cascaded manner. This flowing style is called fluent API.

Let's use this cascaded approach and program a different implementation of the Candy class so that the name(String) and price(int) methods assign the name and the price. Both methods return their own Candy object via the this reference:

```
class Candy {
  String name;
  int    price;

  Candy name( String name ) {
    this.name = name;
    return this;
  }

  String name() {
    return name;
  }

  Candy price( int price ) {
    this.price = price;
    return this;
  }
```

```
  int price() {
    return price;
  }
}
```

Listing 6.9 src/main/java/com/tutego/insel/game/c/v5/Candy.java (Snippet)

Let's create a Candy and cascade the methods next.

```
Candy candy = new Candy().name( "Nerds Candy" ).price( 80 );
System.out.printf( "%s %d%n", candy.name(), candy.price() ); // Nerds Candy 80
```

Listing 6.10 src/main/java/com/tutego/insel/game/c/v5/Application.java (Snippet)

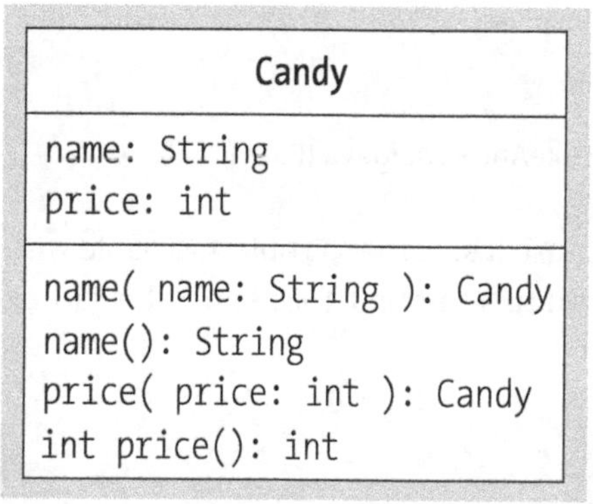

Candy
name: String price: int
name(name: String): Candy name(): String price(price: int): Candy int price(): int

Figure 6.5 UML Class Diagram for Candy with the Fluent API

The new Candy() expression returns a reference that we immediately use for the method call. Since name(...) returns an object reference of type Candy, .price(...) is possible directly behind it.

Thus, cascading name("Nerds Candy").price(80) causes the name and price to be set, and the next method call in the chain receives a reference to the same object via this, but with a changed internal state.

Examples of this type can be found in a few places in the Java library. Referred to as *builders*, this type usually consists only of the methods for write operations.

> **Note**
>
> The Candy name(String) method is convenient with its return but violates JavaBeans conventions (Section 6.2.6 for details) for two reasons: Setters must not have a return and must always start with set. JavaBeans are therefore not "compatible" with this compact builder notation.

Passing Oneself via this

If object A wants to communicate to another object B so that B "knows" the other object A, the this reference is particularly useful. Let's demonstrate this use case with an example: The two classes Luke and Darth represent two people, with Luke having an object variable dad for his father.

```
class Luke {
  Darth dad;
}

class Darth {
  void revealTruthTo( Luke son ) {
    son.dad = this;
  }
}
```

Listing 6.11 src/main/java/com/tutego/insel/oop/LukeAndVader.java (Part 1)

The revealTruthTo(Luke) method is exciting because it sets the dad object variable with the this reference on the passed Luke object. With this method, Luke knows his father, which can be tested in the following class:

```
Luke luke = new Luke();
Darth vader = new Darth();
System.out.println( luke.dad ); // null
vader.revealTruthTo( luke );
System.out.println( luke.dad ); // com.tutego.insel.oop.Darth@01234567
```

Listing 6.12 src/main/java/com/tutego/insel/oop/LukeAndVader.java (Part 2)

[»]

> **Note**
>
> In static methods, the this reference isn't available because we don't reference a concrete object in class methods.

6.2   Privacy and Visibility

Within a class, all methods and object/class variables are visible to the methods. You must ensure that the data and methods of a class are protected from external access or explicitly marked as publicly visible to others in turn. Different kinds of visibilities include the following:

- Public
- Protected

- Package-visible
- Private

Keywords are available for three visibilities, called *visibility modifiers*. In this section, we'll describe the visibilities public, private, and package-visible (without modifiers, also called *package-private*); we'll return to protected in Chapter 7, Section 7.2.

6.2.1 For the Public: public

The visibility modifier public on classes, constructors, methods, and other class parts specifies that all these distinguished elements are externally visible to everyone. Whether the user is in the same or in a different package doesn't matter.

If the class is public but a member is private, a foreign class still can't access the member. And if a member is public but the class is private, then another class can't "get" that member in the first place.

6.2.2 Not Public: Passwords Are private

The visibility modifier private prohibits all externally accessing classes from accessing members. This control would be important for a class that wants to store passwords, for example. For this task, you would declare a public Password class with a private object variable, named password. A public assign(String, String) method allows you to change the password (i.e., if the old password becomes known), and another public method check(String) checks the password. At the beginning, the password is the empty string.

```java
public class Password {

  private String password = "";

  public void assign( String oldPassword, String newPassword ) {
    if ( password.equals(oldPassword) && newPassword != null ) {
      password = newPassword;

      System.out.println( "Password set" );
    }
    else
      System.out.println( "Password could not be set" );
  }

  public boolean check( String passwordToCheck ) {
    return password.equals( passwordToCheck );
  }
}
```

Listing 6.13 src/main/java/com/tutego/insel/oop/Password.java (Snippet)

Notice how public object methods can access the private element of their class quite naturally.

Password
-password: String = ""
+assign(oldPassword: String, newPassword: String): void +check(passwordToCheck: String): boolean

Figure 6.6 UML Diagram Showing Private Members (Minus Signs) and Public Members (Plus Signs)

A second class, PasswordDemo, now wants to access the password from outside.

```
Password pwd = new Password();
pwd.assign( "", "earlyAlzheimers" );
pwd.assign( "earlyAlzheimers", "Z1ON0101" );
pwd.assign( "Z1ON0101", "P@$$wOrd" );
// System.out.println( pwd.password );
// The field Password.password is not visible
```

Listing 6.14 src/main/java/com/tutego/insel/oop/PasswordDemo.java (Snippet)

The Password class contains the private string password, which can't be referenced. The compiler detects and reports violations at translation or during runtime.

However, sometimes, a better approach would be if the compiler didn't tell you that the element was private, but instead simply reported that the specific element doesn't exist.

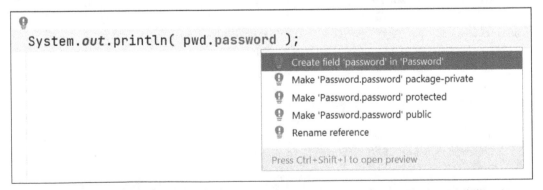

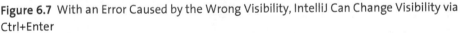

Figure 6.7 With an Error Caused by the Wrong Visibility, IntelliJ Can Change Visibility via Ctrl+Enter

6.2.3   Why Not Free Methods and Variables for All?

Private methods and variables are primarily used to provide classes with modularization options that don't need to be visible from the outside. For structuring purposes, subtasks are divided into methods, which, however, must never be called from the outside alone. Since the implementation is hidden and the programmer can see only one access method, this approach is sometimes called *data hiding*. Who would give a stranger their credit card PIN, for example? Or let's consider a radio playing music: From the outside, the radio perhaps provides methods like on(), off(), volumeUp(), and playMusic(), but the physical processes that make a radio play music at all are a completely different matter that ordinary users of a radio aren't interested in.

6.2.4   private Is Not Quite Private: It Depends on Who Sees It*

Private members are private only to other classes, but not to their own, even if the objects are different. Thus, this special case enables access to a private member of another object via a reference variable, as in the following example:

```java
public class Candy {
  private String name;

  public void setName( String name ) {
    this.name = name;
  }

  public boolean hasSameName( Candy that ) {
    return this.name.equals( that.name );
  }
}
```

Listing 6.15 src/main/java/com/tutego/insel/game/c/v6/Candy (Snippet)

The hasSameName(Candy) method of the Candy class is passed a reference to another candy in that. hasSameName(...) compares the string of its own object variable (this.name) with that of the object variable (that.name). Although this wouldn't be necessary, its use nicely illustrates the distinction between the current object (the own object) and the foreign object. At this point, note that access to that.name is allowed even though name is private. However, this access is allowed because the hasSameName(Candy) method is declared in the Candy class and the parameter is also of type Candy. However, with subclasses (see Chapter 7, Section 7.2.1), this access doesn't work. Private states and methods are thus protected against attacks from outside the declaring class.

6.2.5   Declaring Access Methods for Object Variables

Object variables are a great and necessary thing. However, you should always consider whether the user of an object should access the object's states directly or whether this access is a problem. For instance, consider the following points concerning access:

- For some variables, value ranges exist that must be adhered to. The age of a player can't be less than zero, and people more than 200 years old are found only in the Bible. When making age private, an access method like setAge(int) can use a range check to transfer only certain values to the object variable and reject the rest. The public method getAge() then gives access to the variable.

- Dependencies associated with some variables exist. For example, if a player has an age, the player class can simultaneously declare a truth variable for the age of majority. Of course, now a dependency exists. If the player is older than 18, the truth variable should be set to true. This dependency can't really be enforced with two public variables. However, a setAge(int) method can maintain this consistency for private object variables.

- If access methods are available, debug breakpoints can easily be set in those methods. Also, the methods can be extended to log the access or to check the rights of the caller.

- The secrecy principle applies to classes. Their internal operations should be kept secret by private (helper) methods, which also applies to variables and variable types. For example, if developers wanted to change their internal object variable from char to string and thus manage strings of any length, a major problem arises since an object would need to be inserted at each occurrence. If we wanted to introduce two variables—a char so that the old software currently in use can get by without changing it and a new string—we'd have a consistency problem.

- The caller doesn't always need to be provided with all the features in detail. Let's say a user would like to have *higher-order services* provided by the object, so that access to the lower object variables may not be necessary at all.

6.2.6   Setters and Getters according to the JavaBeans Specification

From these examples, we hope you see the good reasons for privatizing object variables and providing public methods for reading and writing. Because these methods access object variables, they're also called *access methods*. For each object variable, a write and a read method is declared, for which a fixed naming scheme (according to JavaBeans conventions) is followed. Access methods make a *property* accessible. For example, the following applies to a name property and a string type:

- String getName(): The method has no parameter list, and the return type is String.
- void setName(String name): The method has no return, but exactly one parameter.

The get*() methods are referred to as *getters*; the set*(...) methods, as *setters*. The methods are public, and the type of the getter return must be the same as the parameter type of the setter.

For boolean object variables, instead of get*(), you may (and in some cases must) use is*(). Since program development is usually done with English identifier names, unattractive identifier names such as getLiebe(), isGlücklich(), or set 顔文字 (String 顔文字) don't appear.

> **Language Comparison**
>
> In Java, methods that return a boolean always begin with the prefix is, while in Ruby a question mark concludes the method name. Thus, "".empty? returns true and "java".equal? "ruby" returns false.[5] This common convention in Ruby shows that other programming languages might be more generous with the allowed identifiers.

Access Methods for the Candy

The following example declares a setter and getter for each of three members (name, price, and quantity). The object variables are private, and the setters contain validation tests, for example, to check that the name of a candy isn't null or empty.

```java
public class Candy {
  private String name;
  private int price;
  private int quantity = 1;

  public void setName( String name ) {
    if ( name != null && !name.trim().isEmpty() )
      this.name = name;
  }

  public String getName() {
    return name;
  }

  public void setPrice( int price ) {
    if ( price > 0 )
      this.price = price;
  }
```

---

5 Parentheses in method calls are optional. Moreover, the following convention applies: In Java, the == operator tests identity, and equals() tests equivalence. In Ruby, the reverse is true: == tests for equivalence, and equal? tests for identity. In addition, in Ruby, the eq? method tests whether two objects have the same values and are of the same type.

```
  public int getPrice() {
    return price;
  }

  public void setQuantity( int quantity ) {
    if ( quantity >= 1 )
      this.quantity = quantity;
  }

  public int getQuantity() {
    return quantity;
  }
}
```

Listing 6.16 src/main/java/com/tutego/insel/game/c/v7/Candy (Snippet)

Instead of turning a deaf ear to invalid values, you can alternatively log or report unwanted values as exceptions, for example.

Let's write a little more code because of the method calls:

```
Candy lollipop = new Candy();
lollipop.setPrice( 12 );
System.out.println( lollipop.getPrice() * lollipop.getQuantity() ); // 12
```

Listing 6.17 src/main/java/com/tutego/insel/game/c/v7/Application.java (Snippet)

If a change is necessary during later development of the program, for example, if the price should now be stored internally as a double after all, only the internal implementation of the getters and setters must be adapted, not the API (i.e., the "interface").

Any modern development environment can generate setters and getters automatically. In IntelliJ, you can press [Alt]+[Insert] and then select **Getter or Setter** or **Getter and Setter** in the context menu. The second option works only for exactly one object variable: If your cursor is positioned on the variable, selecting **Refactor · Encapsulate Field...** from the context menu enables you to generate setters and getters and also to convert the direct access to an object variable into method calls.

6.2.7 Package-Visibility

The public and private visibilities are extremes along the spectrum of visibility. If no explicit visibility modifier is stated, *package-visibility* applies. With this level of visibility, classes can be seen only by other classes in the same package. The same rule applies to the members: Only types in the same package can see each other's package-visible members.

Let's look at some examples using four classes distributed over two packages:

```
com.tutego.insel.protecteda.Sugar
com.tutego.insel.protectedb.Caramels
com.tutego.insel.protecteda.Milk
com.tutego.insel.protectedb.Cholocate
```

Example 1

Two classes (Sugar and Caramels) are in different packages. The Sugar class is non-public and, without a visibility modifier, is thus only package-visible:

```
package com.tutego.insel.protecteda;
class Sugar { }
```

The Caramels class wants to reference Sugar but cannot because of the "invisibility" of Sugar. A compiler error is the result.

```
package com.tutego.insel.protectedb;
class Caramels {
  com.tutego.insel.protecteda.Sugar sugar;
  // 'com.tutego.insel.protecteda.Sugar' is not public in
  // 'com.tutego.insel.protecteda'. Cannot be accessed from outside package
}
```

Listing 6.18 src/main/java/com/tutego/insel/protectedb/Caramels.java

Of course, an import declaration wouldn't work either.

Example 2

For example, if the Milk class is public, but one of its members is a type from another package that is only package-visible. Thus, access won't be possible. The same limitation applies to the static CALORIES variable in the Milk class, which isn't public.

```
public class Milk {
  static final int CALORIES = 122;
}
```

Listing 6.19 src/main/java/com/tutego/insel/protecteda/Milk.java

And, finally, let's look at the Chocolate class.

```
package com.tutego.insel.protectedb;
import com.tutego.insel.protecteda.Milk;
class Chocolate {
  int calories = Milk.CALORIES;
```

6

```
//  'CALORIES' is not public in 'com.tutego.insel.protecteda.Milk'.
//  Cannot be accessed from outside package
}
```

Listing 6.20 src/main/java/com/tutego/insel/protectedb/Chocolate.java

The Chocolate class "sees" the Milk class but doesn't "see" the package-visible variable because com.tutego.insel.protecteda and com.tutego.insel.protectedb are two different packages.

In other words, to go to a specific room (type) of a house (package), finding a way to the house isn't sufficient because the room must also be accessible. If the house can't be found at all, you don't need to think about the room in that house in the first place.

Package-visible members are particularly useful because you can use them to form groups of types that know parts of each other's inner workings. Access to these parts from outside the package is then prohibited, similar to private. Let's look an example with our Candy class: If this class uses a helper class internally with database access for valid product names, this package-visible helper class remains invisible outside of the package.

6.2.8   Visibility Summary

In Java, four visibilities are available, and three visibility modifiers exist for them:

- Public types and members are declared by the public modifier. The types are visible everywhere, so any class and subclass from any other package can access public members. The methods and variables declared with public are visible wherever the class is visible. With an invisible class, the members are also invisible. In Java, however, because of the Java Platform Module System (JPMS), one restriction is that public types must also be exported; otherwise, they'll still be invisible to other modules.

- The private modifier is more rare in type declarations since it can only be used when multiple types are declared in a compilation unit (i.e., a file). The type that determines the file name can't be private, but other types (and cascaded classes) are allowed to be invisible—only the visible type can then use them. The methods and variables declared with private are only visible within their own class. An exception is cascaded classes, which can also access private members of the outer class. When a class is extended, the private elements aren't visible to subclasses.

- While private and public represent extremes, package visibility lies in between. This default visibility comes without modifiers. Package-visible types and members are visible only to classes from the same package, that is, neither to classes nor to subclasses of other packages.

- The visibility modifier protected has a dual function: First, this modifier has the same meaning as package visibility, and second, it frees the elements for subclasses. Whether the subclasses come from your own package (in which case the default visibility would be sufficient) or from another package doesn't matter. A combination of `private protected` can be used to make the members visible only to the subclasses and not immediately to the classes from the same package.[6]

Member	Sees Own Class	Sees Class in the Same Package	Sees Subclass in Other Package	Sees Class in Other Package
public	Yes	Yes	Yes	Yes
protected	Yes	Yes	Yes	No
Package-visible	Yes	Yes	No	No
private	Yes	No	No	No

Table 6.2 Who Sees Which Members at Which Visibility?

The use of visibility levels via the keywords `public`, `private`, and `protected` and the default "package-visible" without an explicit keyword should be done thoughtfully. OOP is characterized by thoughtful use of classes and their relationships. The most restrictive description is best; that is, never more publicity than is necessary should be provided. This approach helps to minimize dependencies and makes later changes to internal elements more easy.

Visibility in the Unified Modeling Language*

For the visibility of attributes and operations, UML provides various symbols that are placed in front of the respective member.

Symbol	Visibility
+	Public
−	Private
#	Protected
~	Package-visible

Table 6.3 UML Symbols for the Visibility of Attributes and Operations

---

6 The *Java Programmers' FAQ* (*http://tutego.de/go/privateprotected*) states: "It first appeared in [Java Development Kit (JDK)] 1.0 FCS (it hadn't been in the betas). Then it was removed in JDK 1.0.1. It was an ugly hack syntax-wise, and it didn't fit consistently with the other access modifiers. It never worked properly: in the versions of the JDK before it was removed, calls to private protected methods were not dynamically bound, as they should have been. It added little capability to the language. It's always a bad idea to reuse existing keywords with a different meaning. Using two of them together only compounds the sin. The official story is that it was a bug. That's not the full story. Private protected was put in because it was championed by a strong advocate. It was pulled out when he was overruled by popular acclamation."

[»]

Note

The lack of a visibility modifier in a UML diagram doesn't mean that it's "package-visible," just that the visibility hasn't been defined yet.

Order of Members in Classes*

The various elements of a class must be placed in one class. While the order doesn't matter, a common convention is to divide a class into the following order:

- Class variables
- Object variables
- Constructors
- Static methods
- Setters/getters
- Any object methods

Within a block, the information is often sorted with respect to its access rights. At the beginning, you'll see visible members, and then further down, private ones. The public part is placed at the beginning to provide a quick overview. The second part is then only interesting for the inheriting classes, and the last part describes protected information for developers alone. However, the order can be easily broken up by placing private methods before or after public ones to keep related parts together as well.

[»]

Code Style

Source code should always be indented with spaces instead of tabs. Two or four spaces are often encountered. Many developers like to put the opening curly bracket for the beginning of a block at the end of the line or put it alone in the next line. In all modern development environments, a code formatter can automatically correct the source code.

The `Ctrl`+`Alt`+`L` shortcut activates autoformatting. Minute details like indentations or the placement of spaces can be set under **File • Settings...**, then in the dialog box under **Editor • Code Style • Java**.

6.3   One for All: Static Methods and Class Variables

Object variables are closely related to their objects. When an object is created, its own set of instance variables together represent the state of the object. If an object method changes the value of a instance variable in an object, this change has no effect on the data of the other objects; each object stores an individual assignment. However, in some situations, states or methods are not directly associated with an individual object, but instead with the class—the "blueprint" of the objects.

Java supports this type of affiliation through *static members*. Since these members don't belong to any object (thus unlike object members), you can also call them *class members*. Static members have static methods and static variables, a few of which we've already encountered.

Static Methods	Static Variables
`Math.random()` returns a random number.	`System.out` references an output stream for standard console output.
`Math.sin(...)` calculates the sine.	`Math.PI` determines the number 3.1415…
`Integer.parseInt(...)` converts a string to an integer.	`Integer.MAX_VALUE` is the largest representable `int` integer.
`JOptionPane.showInputDialog(...)` shows an input dialog box.	`Font.MONOSPACED` stands for a font with a fixed width.
`Color.HSBtoRGB(...)` converts colors from the HSB color space to the RGB color space.*	`MediaSize.ISO.A4` defines the size of an A4 page, namely, 210 mm × 297 mm.
*Yes, the method starts with a capital letter, which is unusual.	

Table 6.4 Examples of Static Methods and Static Variables

These members aren't assigned to a concrete object, but rather to the class. The sine method is an example of a static method of the `Math` class, and `MAX_VALUE` is a class variable of the `Integer` class, while `out` is a class variable of the `System` class. None of these members are bound to any individual object but are, so to speak, "cross-object" members.

6.3.1   Why Static Members Are Useful

Static members have an advantage over object members in that the program they express won't use any state of the object. Let's look again at the static methods from the `Math` class. If they were object methods, they would usually use an object state. The static methods would have no parameters and take their working values not from the arguments, but from the internal state of the object. But no `Math` method does that. To calculate the sine of an angle, you don't need a specific math object. On the other hand, a method like `setPrice(int)` of a candy could be non-static since prices should be set individually for each candy and in no case will all candies always have the same price.

Static methods are thus more common than static variables since static methods derive their working values exclusively from parameters. Static variables are primarily used as constants.

6.3.2 Static Members with static

To implement static members in Java, you must add the static keyword before declaring a variable or a method. For access, you'll simply use the class name instead of the reference variable. Let's declare a static method and a static variable for a new class called City, with the following members:

- The constant KANDY_HERSHEY_DISTANCE represents the distance between two cities.
- The distance(...) method returns the distance between two cities given by their city names.

```java
public class City {

  public static int KANDY_HERSHEY_DISTANCE = 124;

  public String name;

  public static int distance( String cityName1, String cityName2 ) {
    if ( cityName1.equalsIgnoreCase( cityName2 )) return 0;
    if ( (cityName1.equalsIgnoreCase( "kandy" ) &&
          cityName2.equalsIgnoreCase( "hershey" )) ||
         (cityName1.equalsIgnoreCase( "hershey" ) &&
          cityName2.equalsIgnoreCase( "kandy" )) )
      return KANDY_HERSHEY_DISTANCE;
    return -1;
  }
}
```

Listing 6.21 src/main/java/com/tutego/insel/game/c/v8/City.java (Snippet)

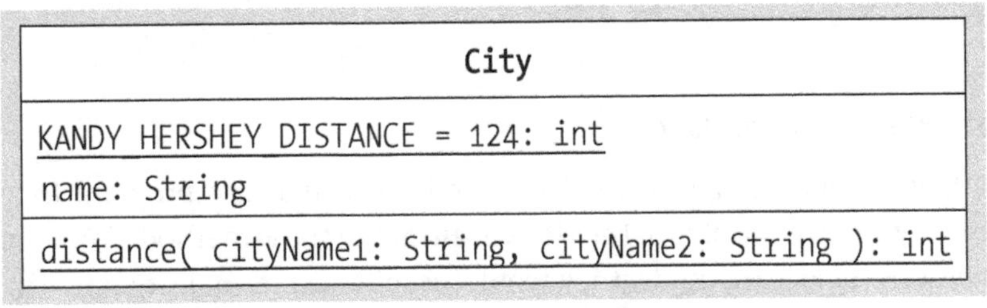

City
KANDY_HERSHEY_DISTANCE = 124: int
name: String
distance(cityName1: String, cityName2: String): int

Figure 6.8 UML Diagram with Static Members Underlined

These static members are addressed with the class name City, as in the following example:

```java
System.out.println( City.KANDY_HERSHEY_DISTANCE );        // 124
City.KANDY_HERSHEY_DISTANCE = 120;
System.out.println( City.KANDY_HERSHEY_DISTANCE );        // 120
```

```
System.out.println( City.distance( "Kandy", "Hershey" ) );      // 124
System.out.println( City.distance( "Neijiangs", "hershey" ) ); // -1
System.out.println( City.distance( "kandy", "kandy" ) );        // 0
```

Listing 6.22 src/main/java/com/tutego/insel/game/c/v8/Application.java (Snippet)

IntelliJ displays static members in italics by default.

> **Tip**
>
> If a class declares only static members, there's nothing wrong with specifying a private constructor to prevent the external construction of objects. Section 6.5.1 describes constructors in more detail and also explains other use cases for private constructors.

Validity Range, Visibility, and Lifetime

For static and non-static variables, you can observe significant differences over their lifetimes. An object variable starts its life via new and ends with automatic garbage collection. A static variable, on the other hand, begins its life the moment the runtime environment loads and initializes the class. The life of static variables ends when the JVM removes and cleans up the class. Access to static variables is always permitted in all blocks since, in object methods, the static variable "was already there earlier" than the object itself because new presupposes the loaded class definition, which prepares the static variables. Static variables can quickly cause memory problems when developers forget that they are referencing large object trees. And these variables stay in the memory as long as the class itself, which might be until the end of the application.

6.3.3 Using Static Members via References?*

If a class has a class member, the member can also be addressed like an object variable by reference. Thus, two options are available if an object instance exists and the class has a class variable. Let's stick to our example with the City class. To access KANDY_HERSHEY_DISTANCE, we can write the following code:

```
System.out.println( City.KANDY_HERSHEY_DISTANCE );      // good
City kandy = new City();
System.out.println( kandy.KANDY_HERSHEY_DISTANCE );     // bad
```

You should never write access to static members via an object reference because programmers won't know whether the member is static or non-static. But knowing if a member is static or not is important. For this reason, you should always address static members by their class name.

[»]

Note

For static access, the reference doesn't matter and can be `null`. If competing in a contest for the worst Java program, you could write:

`System.out.println( ((City) null).KANDY_HERSHEY_DISTANCE );`

Since `null` is type-less, it can be converted to any other type. The constant can then then be accessed via the `City` type. The expression `City.KANDY_HERSHEY_DISTANCE` is not only shorter, but also cleaner.

Figure 6.9 Figure 6.9: IntelliJ Message when Static Members Are Accessed by Reference with Refactoring

6.3.4   Why Case Sensitivity Is Important*

The default naming convention suggests that class names should be assigned with uppercase letters, and variable/method names, with lowercase letters (unless the variable describes a constant). If you encounter a code fragment like `Math.random()`, you'll immediately know that `random()` must be a static method because it's preceded by an identifier that is capitalized. This code therefore doesn't indicate a reference but instead a class name. For this reason, you should avoid capitalizing the names of objects in your programs.

The following example clearly demonstrates why reference variables should start with lowercase letters and why class names should start with uppercase letters:

```
String StringModifier = "What is the Matrix?";
String t = StringModifier.trim();
```

The `trim()` method is non-static, as the code suggests by capitalizing the variables.

The same problem arises if you name classes with lowercase letters, which can also be confusing. Consider the following example:

```
class city {
  static void distance() { }
}
```

Now, someone could write `city.distance()`, and a programmer would assume that `city` was a reference variable because it's lowercase and that `distance()` was an object method. This example clearly illustrates why sticking to these uppercase/lowercase conventions is important.

6.3.5   Static Variables for Data Exchange*

Each instance of a class can access its static members. Since a static variable exists only once per class, multiple objects can share a variable. With this knowledge, you can allow the exchange of information beyond an object's boundaries. In our next example, we'll write a constructor to count the number of objects created; a static method later returns the number of instances built up to that point.

```java
public class Rollercoaster {

  private static int numberOfInstances;

  {
    numberOfInstances++;
  }

  public static int getNumberOfInstances() {
    return numberOfInstances;
  }

  public static void main( String[] args ) {
    new Rollercoaster();
    new Rollercoaster();

    System.out.println( Rollercoaster.getNumberOfInstances() ); // 2
  }
}
```

Listing 6.23 src/main/java/com/tutego/insel/oop/Rollercoaster.java (Snippet)

The static variable numberOfInstances is incremented for each new instance via the constructor. The constructor isn't written out directly, but an instance initializer is used (Section 6.6.1) since the compiler automatically copies the code into each constructor. With this approach, developers can easily add new constructors for the Rollercoaster later without always having to keep the increment of the static variables in mind.

> **Note**
>
> Concurrent access to static variables can cause problems. For this reason, you must use special synchronization mechanisms—which aren't used in this example, however. Static reference variables can also quickly lead to memory problems since they can store objects for a long time. Deployment must be well thought out.

Figure 6.10 Synchronization Is Necessary: Don't Grab Static Variables at the Same Time

6.3.6   Static Members and Object Members*

As mentioned earlier, you can also use static members via an object reference. However, let's review how object members and static members can be mixed. Remember that our first programs consisted of the static main(...) method, but our other methods also had to be static. This inclusion makes sense because a static method—without an explicit specification of a calling object—can only call other static methods. Also, how should a static method call an object method if no associated object exists? Conversely, however, any object method can call any static method directly, which is the same with object variables. A static method can't address its own object variables because no implicit object whose members could be accessed exists.

this References and Static Members

Also, using the this reference isn't possible for static members.[7] So, if a static method cannot use a this reference, what object should this point to?

```
class InStaticNoThis {

  String name;

  void printName() {
    System.out.println( name );
  }

  public static void main( String[] args ) {
    name = "Amanda";   // 💀 Cannot make a static reference to the
                       // non-static field name
    printName();  // 💀 Cannot make a static reference to the non-static method
```

---

7   By the way, the same is true for the super reference, which we'll describe in Chapter 7, Section 7.2.6.

```
                    // printName() from the type InStaticNoThis
   System.out.println( this ); // 💀 Cannot use this in a static context
 }
}
```

Listing 6.24 src/main/java/com/tutego/insel/oop/InStaticNoThis.java (Snippet)

this isn't allowed in the static initialization block either (Section 6.6.2).

6.4   Constants and Enumerations

Some variables will change (such as a loop counter), and some won't when a program is running. Unchanging variables include, for example, the start time of the daily news or the dimensions of an A4 page. The values shouldn't be repeated in the source code but instead should be addressed by their names. For this purpose, variables are declared to which constant value can be assigned; these constants are then referred to as *symbolic constants*.

In Java, you can declare constants in two ways:

- As self-defined public static final variables.
- As enumerations via enum (which internally are also only public final static values)

6.4.1   Constants via Static Final Variables

Let's consider again the City class and the static variable:

```
public class City {

  private static int KANDY_HERSHEY_DISTANCE = 124;
  …
}
```

This variable can be changed by anyone who has access to the City class.

Static variables are also used to declare symbolic constants. To keep the variables unchanging, the final modifier is used. In this way, the compiler is informed that a value may only be assigned to this variable once. For variables, this modifier means they are constants; any rewrite would be an error. Usually, constants are public, but of course, they can be private if only used in the class to which they belong.

```
public class City {

  private static final int KANDY_HERSHEY_DISTANCE = 124;
  …
}
```

Now, the variable KANDY_HERSHEY_DISTANCE can only be read, but not modified at a later stage. Accessing a static final variable looks the same as accessing other static variables.

[+]

Tip

If numbers like 124 are in the source code without obvious meaning, these numbers are often called *magic numbers*. The task is to define these values as constants and to name them in a meaningful way. So, if you need the distance between the two cities Kandy and Hershey in the code, don't write 124. Instead, write KANDY_HERSHEY_DIS-TANCE. A common practice is to capitalize the names of constants throughout to emphasize their importance.

6.4.2   Type-Unsafe Enumerations

Constants are an invaluable way to make source code more expressive and clear, which is important because source code is read more often than it is written. Often, constants are found for mathematical constants or size constraints.

Constants are special when used as elements of an enumeration. Enumerations are reminiscent of completed sets, such as:

- Days of the week (i.e., Monday, Tuesday, etc.)
- Months of a year (i.e., January, February, etc.)
- Font styles (i.e., bold, italic, etc.)
- Predefined line patterns (i.e., solid, dashed, etc.)

For example, the days of the week and also the months of the year are provided by the java.util.Calendar class via public static int constants.

[Ex]

Example

If a couple finds out in June that they are expecting a baby, when might they need to buy diapers?

```
int month = Calendar.JUNE;
int conception = (month + 9) % 12;
System.out.println( conception );   // 2
```

Let's look at example of a CandyType class, which is supposed to declare constants for the texture of a candy:

```
public class CandyType {
  private CandyType() { }

  public static final int OTHER    = 0;
  public static final int CARAMELS = 1;
```

```
  public static final int CHOCOLATE = CARAMELS + 1;
  public static final int GUMMIES   = CHOCOLATE * 2;
}
```

Listing 6.25 src/main/java/com/tutego/insel/game/c/v9/CandyType.java (Snippet)

For their assignments, we recommend choosing constants relative to their predecessors to simplify the insertion in the middle, as shown with the CHOCOLATE and GUMMIES variables. This class has a private constructor, which prevents it from being created externally via new. For constructors, Section 6.5.

Problem with the Data Type int as a Constant Type

Simple constant types—as in our case int—entail several disadvantages. Suppose the Candy class were to store the type of candy as an integer.

```
public class Candy {
  public int price;
  public int candyType;
}
```

Listing 6.26 src/main/java/com/tutego/insel/game/c/v9/CandyType.java (Snippet)

The first disadvantage is that the constants don't necessarily have to be applied by everyone and developers may use the values directly.

```
Candy candy = new Candy();
candy.candyType = CandyType.CARAMELS;              // :)
candy.candyType = 1;                               // :-|
candy.candyType = Cursor.DEFAULT_CURSOR            // :-@
                + GridBagConstraints.PAGE_END / Character.LETTER_NUMBER;
candy.price = CandyType.CARAMELS ^ CandyType.GUMMIES; // :-O
```

Listing 6.27 src/main/java/com/tutego/insel/game/c/v9/Application.java (Snippet)

The next problem occurs as soon as the assignment of a constant later changes. This change won't happen with a constant like Math.PI, but it could happen with the candy type if a new snack is inserted later. This new entry could mess up the whole logic, if for example CARAMELS becomes 2 instead of 1, but compiled programs still compare the candy type with 1.

> **Note**
>
> Integers do have an advantage, however, when enumerations are combined, such as a candy that's both caramel and chocolate. This combination can be represented by CARAMELS + CHOCOLATE, which works well if each constant takes exactly 1 unique bit. Thus, if the values of the constants are 1, 2, 4, 8, 16, and so on, they can be added and we get a combination of different enumerations.

Let's summarize: Constants are just names for values, and in the evaluation, the value remains. No one can prohibit transmitting these values directly. With strings as values of the constants, we don't get closer to the solution either.

A good way to get away from integers or strings is to use objects of a class as constants. For this task, you don't need to resort to custom class declarations, but Java provides its own language constructs.

6.4.3   Enumeration Types: Type-Safe Enumerations with enum

To give enumeration constants their own type rather than being integers or strings, Java provides a language construct via the enum keyword. The notation for enumerations is somewhat reminiscent of the declaration of classes and variables, except that the enum keyword is used instead of class, that the variables are automatically static and public, and that no type is specified. Java itself declares many enumeration types, such as for days of the week, but we want to introduce an *enumeration* type named CandyType for the type of candy.

```
public enum CandyType {
  CARAMELS, CHOCOLATE, GUMMIES, OTHER
}
```

Listing 6.28 src/main/java/com/tutego/insel/game/c/va/CandyType.java (Snippet)

Constant names are usually capitalized, just as static variables used as constants are capitalized.

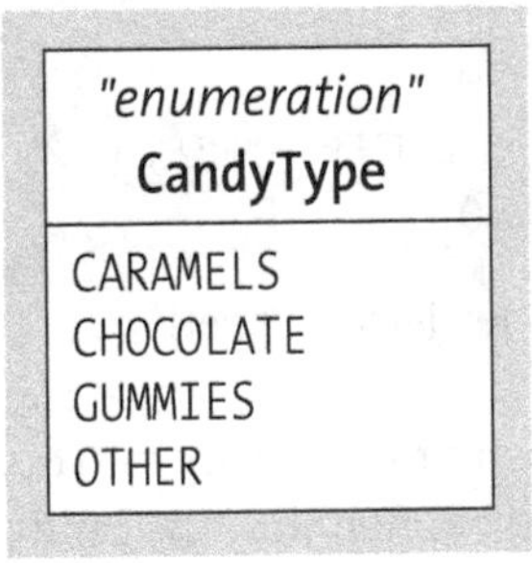

Figure 6.11 An Enumeration in UML Expressed Using the Stereotype

Using Enumerations

To understand how enumeration types can be used, let's look at how the compiler implements them. Internally, the compiler creates a normal class, in our case, CandyType. All enumeration elements are static variables (constants) of the enumeration type. Consider the following example:

```
public class CandyType {
  public static final CandyType CARAMELS   = new CandyType( … );
  public static final CandyType CHOCOLATE = new CandyType( … );
  …
}
```

When the class is loaded, four CandyType objects are created, and the static variables CARAMELS, CHOCOLATE, GUMMIES, and OTHER are initialized. Now, you can easily use these enumerations because they're addressed like any other static variable, as in the following example:

```
CandyType amedei = CandyType.CHOCOLATE;
```

Behind the enumerations are objects that can be further processed just like other objects, as in the following example:

```
if ( amedei == CandyType.CHOCOLATE )
  System.out.println( "Whew, that's expensive!" );
```

Also, enum constants implement the toString() method, which returns the name of the constant.

Enumeration Comparisons via ==

As the implementation of the enumeration types shows, one object is constructed for each constant, which are called *singletons* (i.e., objects that are created only once). We can't build our own new enumeration objects because the class only declares a private constructor. Accessing this object is like accessing a static variable. Comparing two constants thus amounts to comparing static reference variables, for which the comparison via == is perfectly correct. An equals(…) isn't necessary.

Example

The following method determines if a candy is unknown (OTHER):

```
public static boolean isUnknownCandyType( CandyType type ) {
  return type == CandyType.OTHER;
}
```

enum constants in switch

Enum constants can be used in switch statements.[8] Let's initialize a variable of type CandyType and use a case distinction with the enumeration for a test on two candy types; we'll use three alternative notations.

---

8 This use is possible because enum constants internally have integers as identifiers, which the compiler uses for the enumeration. This concept is similar to what the compiler does with switch on strings.

```
CandyType werther = CandyType.CARAMELS;
switch ( werther ) {
  case CARAMELS:
  case CHOCOLATE: System.out.println( "caramel/chocolate" );
}
switch ( werther ) {
  case CARAMELS, CHOCOLATE: System.out.println( "caramel/chocolate" );
}
switch ( werther ) {
  case CARAMELS, CHOCOLATE -> System.out.println( "caramel/chocolate" );
}
```

Listing 6.29 src/main/java/com/tutego/insel/game/c/va/Application.java (Snippet)

With `case`, a `CandyType.CARAMELS` qualification isn't possible and would lead to a compiler error. The reason is that with, `switch (werther)`, the type `CandyType` is already determined via the variable `werther`. The type of the `switch` variable cannot be different from the type of the variable in `case`.

Enumeration Type References Can Be Null

The fact that the enumerations are only objects has an important consequence. Let's first look at the variable declaration `type` of the enumeration type, which is initialized with a reference, in the following example:

```
CandyType type = CandyType.CARAMELS;
```

The `type` variable stores a reference to the `CandyType.CARAMELS` object. The unpleasant thing about reference variables, however, is that they can also be assigned `null`, which isn't an element of the enumeration in this sense, as in the following example:

```
CandyType type = null;
```

If such a `null` reference ends up in a `switch`, a `NullPointerException` will be thrown because hidden in the `switch` is an access to the ordinal number stored in the `Enum` object.

Methods that take elements of an enumeration—that is, object references—should generally test for `null` and throw an exception to indicate the erroneous part; the given helper method `Objects.requireNonNull(...)` can handle this check. Consider the following example:

```
public class Candy {

  private CandyType type;
```

```
public void setType( CandyType type ) {
  this.type = Objects.requireNonNull( type, "CandyType can't be null" );
}

public CandyType getCandyType() {
  return type;
}
}
```

Listing 6.30 src/main/java/com/tutego/insel/game/c/va/Candy.java (Snippet)

Declaring Enumeration Types as Nested Types*

New enumeration types can also be placed inside other type declarations; in this case, we're speaking of *nested types*. In other words, CandyType can also be declared within another class or some other interface. If the nested enumeration is public, anyone can use it. However, a nest enum follows the same visibilities as classes since enumerations are nothing more than classes generated by the compiler. Enumerations within types are always implicitly static, so the static keyword isn't needed.

Example

A type named CandyType is nested in Candy in the following example:

```
public class Candy {
  public /* static */ enum CandyType {
    CARAMELS, CHOCOLATE, GUMMIES, OTHER
  }
}
```

Static Imports of Enumerations*

The enum constants are static variables and can be addressed in different ways. Let's take CandyType again in its own compilation unit.

```
package com.tutego.insel.game.enums;

public enum CandyType {
  CARAMELS, CHOCOLATE, GUMMIES, OTHER
}
```

Listing 6.31 src/main/java/com/tutego/insel/game/enums/CandyType.java

The CandyType enumeration is located in the com.tutego.insel.game.enums package. To access a constant like CARAMELS, different import variants can be used.

Import Declaration	Access
import com.tutego.insel.game.enums.CandyType	CandyType.CARAMELS
import com.tutego.insel.game.enums.*	CandyType.CARAMELS
import static com.tutego.insel.game.enums.CandyType.*	CARAMELS

Table 6.5 Import Declarations and Access Variants: Top-Level Enum

Let's add a nested enumeration of the Candy class in the package in our next example:

```
package com.tutego.insel.game.enums;

public class Candy {
  public enum CandyType {
    CARAMELS, CHOCOLATE, GUMMIES, OTHER
  }
}
```

Listing 6.32 src/main/java/com/tutego/insel/game/enums/CandyType.java

Import Declaration	Access
import com.tutego.insel.game.enums.Candy	Candy.CandyType.CARAMELS
import com.tutego.insel.game.enums.Candy.CandyType	CandyType.CARAMELS
import static com.tutego.insel.game.enums.Candy.CandyType.*	CARAMELS

Table 6.6 Import Declarations and Access Variants: Nested Enum

Standard Methods of Enumeration Types*

The created enumeration objects get a number of additional members by default. They override toString(), hashCode(), and equals(...) from Object and additionally implement Serializable and Comparable[9] but not Cloneable since enumeration objects can't be cloned. The toString() method returns the name of the constant so that Candy-Type.CARAMELS.toString().equals("CARAMELS") is true. In addition, each enumeration object inherits from the special class Enum. Chapter 8, Section 8.2, explores this topic in more detail.

---

9 The order of the constants is the order in which they are written.

6.5   Creating and Destroying Objects

If a program creates objects via the new keyword, the memory management of the run-time system reserves memory on the system heap. Then, the object states are initialized. If the object is no longer referenced, the *automatic garbage collector* cleans up at certain intervals and returns the memory to the runtime system.

6.5.1   Writing Constructors

When a program creates a new object via new, a constructor is automatically called for initialization. Every class must have a constructor in Java. Either the compiler automatically creates a constructor, or you'll create your own. With your own constructor, you can set up an object with an initial, user-defined state after its creation. This approach may be necessary for classes that contain variables because they wouldn't make sense without prior assignment or initialization.

Constructor Declarations

Constructor declarations contain special initializations and look similar to method declarations—and also use the familiar visibilities, parameter lists, and overloading—but two distinct differences should be considered:

- Constructors always have the same name as the class.
- Constructor declarations don't have a return type—not even void.

Example

If our Candy class is to get a constructor, we must write the following code:

```
class Candy {
  Candy() { }                    // Constructor of Candy class
}
```

A constructor that has no parameters is called a *parameterless constructor*, a *no-arg constructor*, or a *nullary constructor*.

Call Sequence

The fact that the constructor is called during initialization and thus before an external method call can be demonstrated with a small example:

```
class Candy {
  Candy() {
    System.out.println( "2 inside the constructor" );
  }
```

```
  void eat() {
    System.out.println( "4 eating" );
  }

  public static void main( String[] args ) {
    System.out.println( "1 before the constructor call" );
    Candy d = new Candy ();
    System.out.println( "3 after the constructor call" );
    d.eat();
    System.out.println( "5 tummy ache" );
  }
}
```

Listing 6.33 src/main/java/com/tutego/insel/game/c/vb/Candy.java (Snippet)

The call order will be output on the screen in the following sequence:

```
1 before the constructor call
2 inside the constructor
3 after the constructor call
4 eating
5 tummy ache
```

[»]

> **Note**
> UML knows attributes and operations but not constructors in the Java sense. In a UML diagram, constructors are labeled like operations, which are just named like the class.

6.5.2   Relationship of Method and Constructor

Methods and constructors have a number of things in common, such as the following:

- They have program code.
- They have an (optional) parameter list.
- They can have modifiers.
- They can access object variables and can use this.

Another difference, mentioned earlier, is that methods have a return type (even if it's only void), but constructors don't. Two other differences concern syntax and semantics.

Constructors always carry the name of their class, and since class names are capitalized by convention, constructors are always capitalized as well, whereas methods are usually always lowercase. In addition, methods are usually verbs that instruct the object to do something; class names are nouns, not verbs.

The program code of a constructor is automatically called by the JVM exactly once after the creation of an object, namely, as the first method before all other methods. Methods can be called any number of times and are under the control of the user. Constructors can't be called again at a later time on an already existing object to reinitialize the object. The constructor call is implicitly and automatically linked to new and can't be understood separately from new.

In summary, a constructor is a kind of special method for initializing an object.

Java Virtual Machine: Internal Information

A Java compiler converts constructors as void methods called <init>.

6.5.3   The Default Constructor

If you don't specify a constructor at all in your class, the compiler automatically creates one because there must always be a constructor. The Java Language Specification (JLS) calls this required constructor the *default constructor*.

Consider the following code:

```
class Candy { }
```

The compiler turns it into a version that's identical in bytecode, such as the following:

```
class Candy {
  Candy() { }
}
```

The given constructor always has the same visibility as the class. If the class is package-visible, so is the constructor. And if the public/private/protected[10] modifiers set the type visibility, the automatically introduced constructor will also be public/private/protected.

Default Constructor or Parameterless Constructor

Whether a parameterless constructor was created by the compiler or developer is an implementation detail that is irrelevant to users of the class. For this reason, whether we create a parameterless constructor ourselves or whether we let the compiler generate a given constructor for us doesn't matter: In the bytecode, this difference in authorship can no longer be distinguished and is also irrelevant to the user of the class. Even a generated Javadoc API documentation for public class C1 {} and public class C2 { public C2(){} } would be structurally the same.

---

10   Only internal types can be private or protected.

Thus, the default constructor is always a parameterless constructor. Even if the compiler creates a default constructor, specifying your own parameterless constructor, even if the body is empty, can be useful in some cases. One reason is to document it with Javadoc; another reason is to choose the visibility explicitly, for example, if the class is public but the constructor is supposed to be private. More on this topic next.

Private Constructors

A constructor can be private, which prevents an instance of this class from being formed externally. What appears to be rather limited at first glance turns out to be quite clever if intended to deliberately prevent the creation of instances. This limitation makes sense for *utility classes*, which are classes that have only static methods and are thus helper classes. Numerous examples of these helper classes already exist, for example, Math. Why should instances be used in this case, which isn't necessary for calling max(...)? So, the creation of objects can be successfully prevented with a private constructor.

6.5.4   Parameterized and Overloaded Constructors

The default constructor has no parameters, which is why we called it a *parameterless constructor*. However, like a method, a constructor can also have a parameter list: Then, the constructor is called a *parameterized constructor* or a *general constructor*. Constructors can be overloaded like methods; that is, they can be declared with different parameter lists.

Let's implement the following requirement: A City object must always be created with a name. Optionally, a number of inhabitants can be transferred as well.

```
public class City {
  private String name;
  private int     population;

  public City( String name ) {
    setName( name );
  }

  public City( String name, int population ) {
    setName( name );
    setPopulation( population );
  }

  public void setName( String name ) {
    this.name = Objects.requireNonNull( name );
  }
```

```
  public String getName() {
    return name;
  }

  public void setPopulation( int population ) {
    if ( population >= 0 )
      this.population = population;
  }

  public int getPopulation() {
    return population;
  }
}
```

Listing 6.34 src/main/java/com/tutego/insel/game/c/vc/City.java (Snippet)

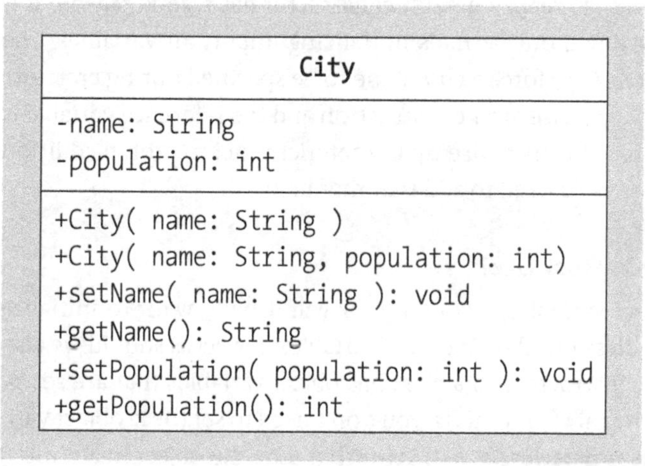

```
                          City
  -name: String
  -population: int

  +City( name: String )
  +City( name: String, population: int)
  +setName( name: String ): void
  +getName(): String
  +setPopulation( population: int ): void
  +getPopulation(): int
```

Figure 6.12 UML Diagram for City with Two Constructors

This use case may look like the following code:

```
City kandy = new City( "Kandy" );
System.out.printf( "%s %d%n",
                   kandy.getName(), kandy.getPopulation() );   // Kandy 0
City hershey = new City( "Hershey", 10_200 );
System.out.printf( "%s %d%n",
                   hershey.getName(), hershey.getPopulation() );
                                                      // Hershey 10200
```

Listing 6.35 src/main/java/com/tutego/insel/game/c/vc/Application.java (Snippet)

Parameterized constructors connect the initialization to the setters, so to speak. The object variables could be assigned directly, but we want to pass the values to be set to the setters because this way the setter can validate right away, and the constructor is freed from the validation task. As we'll discuss in Chapter 14, Section 14.1, we need to follow the rule Don't Repeat Yourself (DRY)! It's certainly a matter of taste whether a negative population number should simply be ignored during setting or whether it should create an exception, but that's another question.

When Does the Compiler Not Insert a Given Constructor?

If at least one constructor has been implemented by us, the compiler will no longer create a default constructor. Thus, you would have only parameterized constructors—as in our example earlier—trying to create an object for our City class simply with the parameterless constructor via new City() will result in a compiler error since no default constructor is generated by the compiler:

```
City city = new City();      // Cannot resolve constructor 'City()'
```

The fact that the compiler doesn't create a default constructor has a good reason: If it did, an object could be created without perhaps initializing important variables. The parameterized constructors of a City force a city name to be specified during creation, so that a name has been set in any case after construction and the reference variable is not null by default. To allow developers to use a parameterless constructor in addition to parameterized constructors, we'd need to add that manually.

What Does a Useful Constructor Look Like?

If an object has a set of object variables, a constructor will usually want to initialize these states. If we have an endless number of object variables in a class, should we also write an endless number of constructors? If a class has object variables that are set by set*(...) methods and read by get*() methods, you don't need to set these object variables in the constructor. A parameterless constructor that puts the object in an initial state is appropriate; then its states can be changed with the access methods, which is the recommended approach according to JavaBeans conventions. Constructors that cover the most common initialization scenarios are certainly also practical. The object of the java.awt.Point class can be created with the parameterless constructor, but you can also use a parameterized constructor, which would immediately set the coordinate values; so, all values are given before the first access.

6.5.5   Copy Constructors

A constructor is extraordinarily handy if it accepts a type-identical object via its parameter and takes the initial values for its own state from this object. Such a constructor is called a *copy constructor*.

Let's look at an example: The Candy class gets a constructor that accepts another candy. In this way, an already initialized Candy object can be passed to the constructor as a template for a new candy. The parameterized constructor can read all (or selectively chosen) object variables of an existing candy and transfer them to the newly created candy. The implementation resembles the following code:

```java
public class Candy {
  public String name;
  public int    price;

  public Candy() {
  }

  public Candy( Candy other ) {
    this.name  = other.name;
    this.price = other.price;
  }
}
```

Listing 6.36 src/main/java/com/tutego/insel/game/c/vd/Candy.java (Snippet)

Let's test this code in the following way:

```java
Candy sugarDaddy = new Candy();
sugarDaddy.name = "Sugar Daddy Caramel Pops";
sugarDaddy.price = 20;

Candy caramelPops = new Candy( sugarDaddy );
System.out.printf( "%s %d%n",                    // Sugar Daddy Caramel Pops 20
                  caramelPops.name, caramelPops.price );
```

Listing 6.37 src/main/java/com/tutego/insel/game/c/vd/Application.java (Snippet)

The main(...) method creates a new candy named sugarDaddy with the parameterless constructor and then initializes a new candy named caramelPops with the values of sugarDaddy. This template is referred to as a *prototype*.

> **Note**
>
> If the Candy class were to declare a second constructor, Candy(Object) in addition to the parameterized constructor Candy(Candy), at first glance, a conflict arises when used by new Candy(sugarDaddy) because both constructors would match. The Java compiler solves this possible confusion by always calling the most specific constructor, that is, Candy(Candy) and not Candy(Object). This preference is also true for new Candy(null)—again, the constructor Candy(Candy) is used. While this question isn't so significant for everyday life, candidates for the *Oracle Certified Professional Java Programmer* certification must be prepared for such a question. For the rest, the same principle applies to the methods.

6.5.6   Calling Another Constructor of the Same Class via this(...)

Sometimes, different constructors are provided, but only one constructor hides the actual initialization of the object. Let's change the City class a bit so that an object can once be initialized via a constructor City(String name, int population) and once via a copy constructor City(City other).

```java
public class City {
  public String name;
  public int     population;

  public City( String name, int population ) {
    this.name = name.trim();
    this.population = Math.max( 0, population );
  }

  public City( City other ) {
    this.name = other.name.trim();
    this.population = Math.max( 0, other.population );
  }
}
```

Listing 6.38 src/main/java/com/tutego/insel/game/c/ve/City.java (Snippet)

Notice how both constructors perform three tasks: removing the whitespace from the name, ensuring that the population isn't negative, and initializing the object variables name and population. In the end, however, notice that the code is almost identical. The following elements occur three times each: assignment of object variables, whitespace removal, and range check.

A smarter approach would be if the City(City) constructor called the City(String, int) constructor of its own class. Then, the same program code wouldn't need to repeat several times. Java allows such constructor redirecting via the this keyword:

```java
public class City {
  public String name;
  public int     population;

  public City( String name, int population ) {
    this.name = name.trim();
    this.population = Math.max( 0, population );
  }

  public City( City other ) {
    this( other.name, other.population );
  }
```

```
public City() {
  this( "Undefined", 0 );
  }
}
```

Listing 6.39 src/main/java/com/tutego/insel/game/c/vf/City.java (Snippet)

One advantage over the previous solution is that one central location needs to be revised if changes arise. This advantage can already be seen in trim(): Previously, the trimming was included in every constructor, but after the change, trimming was included only locally in one place. Let's suppose we implemented ten constructors for every conceivable case in exactly this style. If we need to initialize something in each constructor at once, the program code—such as a call of the init(...) method—must be inserted into each of the constructors. We can simply get around this problem by moving the work to a special constructor. Now, if the program changes in such a way that additional program code must be executed everywhere when initializing, then we change one line in the concrete constructor that is used by all. As a result, only a little modification work is required of us, which is a great advantage from a software point of view. Everywhere in Java libraries, this technique can be recognized.

> **Note**
>
> The this keyword is assigned two functions in Java: First, this is a reference to the current object, and second, when used with parentheses, this represents a redirect to another constructor of the same class. Using the class name as a method call, that is, writing City(other.name, other.population) instead of this(other.name, other.population) doesn't work syntactically because you could actually have a capitalized method City(...), which, however, has nothing to do with the constructor.

Constraints of this(...)*

When calling another constructor using this(...), you must keep in mind two important constraints:

- The call of this(...) must be the first statement of the constructor.
- No object members can be accessed before calling this(...) in the constructor. Thus, an object variable may not be passed as an argument to this(...), nor may another object method of the class be called to calculate the argument, for example. Only access to static variables (such as final variables that are constants) or calling static methods is allowed.

The first constraint states that creating an object is always the first thing a constructor must do. Nothing can be executed before initialization. The second limitation relates to the fact that the object variables aren't initialized until *after* the call of this(...), so accessing them wouldn't make any sense since the values would generally be null.

Example:

```
class CottonCandy {

  static        int CALORIES = 630;
  /*non-static*/ int calories = 630;

  CottonCandy() {
    // this( calories );   ?
    this( CALORIES );
  }

  CottonCandy( int calories ) {
  this.calories = calories;
  }
}
```

Listing 6.40 src/main/java/com/tutego/insel/oop/CottonCandy.java (Snippet)

Since object variables haven't yet been initialized up to a certain point (which we'll describe in Section 6.6), the compiler won't let us access them—only static variables are allowed as passing parameters. For this reason, the this(calories) call isn't valid because calories is an object variable. The compiler error reads: "Cannot reference CottonCandy.calories' before supertype constructor has been called." The expression this(CALORIES) is fine, however, because CALORIES is a static variable.

6.5.7   Immutable Objects and Wither Methods

Objects whose states can't be changed are referred to as *immutable*. These classes don't declare public variables in this case, nor do they declare methods with side effects that could modify these states. Consequently, for immutable objects, setters don't exist at all, and getters only maybe exist.

Different ways are available for objects to get their values, and parameterized constructors are good for this task. Assignments can be passed in the constructor call and thus written directly into final variables quite easily. The Java library contains a number of such classes that have no parameterless constructor and some parameterized classes that await values. The values passed in the constructor initialize the object, and the object retains these values throughout its lifetime. These classes include, for example, Integer, Double, Color, File, or Font.

Immutable objects that also implement the equals(...) method are called *value objects*.

Assigning Final Values from the Constructor

A final variable can be assigned a value only once. This limitation doesn't necessarily mean that the variable must be assigned a value at the declaration location—that assignment can also happen later. For example, a constructor may describe final object variables. The pair of final variable and initializing constructor is a frequently used idiom when variable values won't be changed later. Thus, in our next example, the name variable is final because it's set only once via the constructor and then only read.

```java
public class City {
  public final String name;
  public City( String name ) { this.name = name; }
  public String getName() { return name; }
}
```

Listing 6.41 src/main/java/com/tutego/insel/game/c/vg/City.java (Snippet)

Java Style

Whenever the assignment no longer changes, except for direct initialization in place or in the constructor, developers should use final variables.

Wither Methods

Even though objects can't be changed with setters, you can generally create new objects with changed states. For example, consider the String class with the methods trim() and toUpperCase()—the results are new strings, not changes to the original string.

To change state variables, you can generally use *wither methods*. These methods are similar to setters, except that they don't change any state of the current object but instead result in a new object with the changed state.

Getter	Setter	Wither
Type getXXX()	void setXXX(*Type* xxx)	*ImmutableType* withXXX(*Type* xxx)

Table 6.7 Naming Convention of the Getter, Setter, and Wither Methods for Property xxx

In the Java library, some data types have wither methods, generally temporal data types, such as LocalDate, LocalTime, etc.

Let's consider another example: A city has a name and a number of inhabitants. The instances are supposed to be immutable.

```java
public class City {
  public final String name;
  public final int    population;
```

```
  public City( String name, int population ) {
    this.name = name;
    this.population = population;
  }

  public City withName( String name ) {
    return new City( name, population );
  }

  public City withPopulation( int population ) {
    return new City( name, population );
  }
}
```

Listing 6.42 src/main/java/com/tutego/insel/game/c/vh/City.java (Snippet)

The object variables can be public because their values can't be changed from the outside, so we can do without unnecessary getters, as in the following example:

```
City almostKandy = new City( "H", 100 );
City kandy = almostKandy.withPopulation( 10_200 ).withName( "Hershey" );
System.out.printf( "%s %d", kandy.name, kandy.population ); // Hershey 10200
```

Listing 6.43 src/main/java/com/tutego/insel/game/c/vh/Application.java, main()

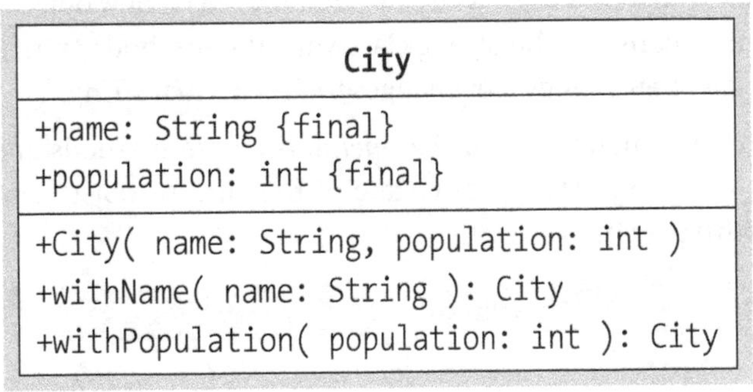

City
+name: String {final} +population: int {final}
+City(name: String, population: int) +withName(name: String): City +withPopulation(population: int): City

Figure 6.13 City with Wither Methods

6.5.8   We Don't Miss You: The Garbage Collector

Fortunately, when programming in Java, you're relieved of the tedious task of freeing memory from objects. If an object is no longer referenced, the garbage collector[11] finds

---

11 Automatic garbage collection has a long tradition in LISP and in Smalltalk, but Visual Basic also uses a garbage collector. Even the Commodore 64's BASIC language used garbage collection for strings that were no longer needed.

this object and takes care of everything else, which of course simplifies the development process. The use of automatic garbage collection prevents two major problems:

- An object might be deleted, but the reference still exists (*dangling pointer*).
- No pointer points to a specific object, but the object still exists in memory (*memory leak*).

[«]   6

Note

Constructors are special code blocks that the runtime environment always calls in the course of object creation. Languages such as C++, PHP, Python, and Swift are also familiar with the concept of a destructor, which is a special code block called whenever an object is no longer needed.

Java doesn't know general destructors, instead offering a special language construct so that resources can be closed automatically (see Chapter 9, Section 9.6).

The General Mode of Operation of the Garbage Collector

Automatic garbage collection might seem an ominous thing that cleverly manages objects. But how does a garbage collector work? The garbage collector is implemented as an independent thread with low priority. This feature manages the root objects from which the entire mesh of living objects (the *object graph*) can be accessed. This object graph includes the root of the thread group tree and the local variables of all active method calls (the stack of all threads). At regular intervals, the garbage collector marks objects that aren't needed and removes them.

Thanks to *HotSpot* technology, the creation of objects on Oracle's JVM happens rather quickly. HotSpot uses a generation-oriented garbage collection that exploits the fact that two groups of objects exist with significantly different lifetimes. Most objects die young, but the few that survive grow rather old. The strategy in this context is that objects are created in a "kindergarten" that is routinely searched for dead objects and is limited in size. Surviving objects graduate from kindergarten after some time and then move into another generation in memory that is rarely searched by the garbage collector. In this way, the garbage collector follows the philosophy of Joseph von Auffenberg, who said: "Improvements must succeed in time; in a storm, you can no longer mend your sails." Thus, automatic garbage collection cleans continuously; it doesn't just start working when the memory is already full, at which point it's too late.

Manual Nulling and Memory Leaks

In the following scenario, the garbage collector will remove the unneeded object after the reference variable reference when the runtime environment exits the inner block, as in the following example:

```
{
  {
    Candy reference = new Candy();
  }
  // Object after candy is free for garbage collection
}
```

In foreign programs, you'll sometimes encounter statements like the following:

```
reference = null;
```

These statements are often unnecessary because, as in the case of our block, the garbage collector knows when the last reference was taken from the object. The situation is different if the lifetime of the variable is longer, such as for an object variable or even a static variable or when the variable referenced in an array. If the referenced object is then no longer needed, the variable (or array entry) should be set to null; otherwise, the garbage collector wouldn't clear the object away due to the heavy referencing. While automatic garbage collection finds every object that is no longer referenced, it doesn't have the fortune-telling ability to detect memory leaks caused by unused but still referenced objects.

6.6 Class and Object Initialization*

An important feature of good programming languages is their ability not to create uninitialized states. For local variables, the compiler pays attention to the assignment (i.e., whether a value has already been assigned a value) before the first read access. For object variables and class variables, we've found so far that the variables are automatically assigned 0, null, false, or their own value. Let's now explore exactly how this works.

6.6.1 Initializing Object Variables

If the compiler sees a class with object or class variables, then these variables must be initialized at some point. If they're simply declared and not initialized with a value, the virtual machine controls the default. The case gets more exciting when the variables are explicitly assigned a value (which can also be 0). Then, the compiler automatically generates some additional lines because—to put it simply—no code is allowed outside constructors and methods.

Let's consider this scenario first with an object variable.

```
class Joystick {

  int numberOfButtons = 6;
```

```
Joystick() { }

Joystick( int numberOfButtons ) {
  this.numberOfButtons = numberOfButtons;
}

Joystick( String producer ) { }
}
```

Listing 6.44 src/main/java/com/tutego/insel/oop/Joystick.java (Snippet)

The numberOfButtons variable is assigned 6. However, the compiler builds code that sets the initialization in each constructor, as in the following example:

```
class Joystick {

  int numberOfButtons;

  Joystick() {
    numberOfButtons = 6;
  }

  Joystick( int numberOfButtons ) {
    this.numberOfButtons = 6;
    this.numberOfButtons = numberOfButtons;
  }

  Joystick( String producer ) {
    numberOfButtons = 6;
  }
}
```

Note how the variable is actually not initialized until the constructor is called. The assignment is located in the first line. This potential trap arises because the order of assignment, for example, is problematic.

Manual Nulling

Strictly speaking, the runtime environment initializes each object and class variable first with 0, null, or false and later with a value. For this reason, you don't need to manually null a variable, as in the following examples:

```
class Candy {
  String name  = null;          // unnecessary
  int    price = 0;             // unnecessary
}
```

The compiler would only additionally insert the initialization name = null; price = 0; into each constructor. For this reason, the following code is no masterpiece either:

```java
class Candy {
  int price = 0;
  Candy( int price ) { this.price = price; }
}
```

The initial assignment of 0 for price is constantly overridden.

6.6.2   Static Blocks as Class Initializers

A kind of constructor for the class object itself (and not for the instance of the class) is a static block that can be put into a class once or several times. Each block is executed exactly when the class is loaded into the virtual machine by the class loader.[12] The block is called *class initializer* or *static initialization block*.

```java
class StaticBlock {

  static {
    System.out.println( "Two fish are in a tank." );
  }

  public static void main( String[] args ) {
    System.out.println( "'How do you drive this thing?'" );
  }

  static {
    System.out.print( "One says, " );
  }
}
```

Listing 6.45 src/main/java/com/tutego/insel/oop/StaticBlock.java (Snippet)

When the class loader loads the StaticBlock class, it first executes the first static block and then the second static block. Since the StaticBlock class also contains main(...), the virtual machine then executes the startup method so that the following output is displayed on the screen:

```
Two fish are in a tank.
One says, 'How do you drive this thing?'
```

---

12   Usually, this class loading happens only once during a program run. However, under certain circumstances—if a separate class loader for the class exists, for example—a class can also be removed from the memory and then reloaded via a different class loader. Then, the static blocks are executed again.

6.6.3   Initializing Class Variables

Finally, the question remains where class variables should be initialized. This initialization makes no sense in the constructor since no objects need to be created for class variables. For this purpose, you can use the static{} block, which is executed whenever the class loader has loaded a class into the runtime environment. So, for a static initialization, the compiler will again insert something:

What We Write	What the Compiler Generates
```class Beer { static String isFreeFor = "Homer"; }```	```class Beer { static String isFreeFor; static { isFreeFor = "Homer"; } }```

Table 6.8 How the Compiler Realizes Initialized Static Variables

Class initializers aren't completely harmless because, if the code throws an exception, a hard java.lang.ExceptionInitializerError will be thrown. You can test this fact by changing the code shown earlier in the following way:

```
static String isFreeFor = "Homer".substring( -1 );
```

Then, call the code from the main program with the following statement:

```
System.out.println( Beer.isFreeFor );
```

6.6.4   Compiled Assignments of the Class Variables

If variables are final, then the variable may only have a single assignment. Whether the values are calculated at runtime is not related to final at first. In the following example, the variable is a constant that is known at compile time:

```
public class Finance {
  public static final int TAX = 19;
}
```

If another type accesses the TAX variable, this access isn't coded in the source code as a direct variable access Finance.TAX, but the compiler has inserted the literal 19 directly at each call position. This change is an optimization the compiler can make according to the Java Language Specification. In this context, these expressions are called *compile-time constant expressions*, if the following statements are true:

- The data type is a primitive or String.
- The expression can be calculated by the compiler.

Inserting the constant values is convenient but causes problems if the final class variable is changed later in the code. Then, also each class that had referenced the constant must be translated. If the dependent classes aren't recompiled, the old value will still be compiled into them.

The solution is to recompile the related classes and get into the habit of recompiling everything when a constant is changed. Another approach transforms the final variable into a subsequently initialized form, as in the following example:

```
public class Finance {
  public static final int TAX = Integer.valueOf( 19 );
}
```

The initialization takes place in the static initializer, and the constant with the literal 19 has disappeared for the time being. So, the compiler won't find a constant 19 when accessing Finance.TAX and therefore can't include the literal at the call positions. In the class file, the Finance.TAX reference will be present, and changing the constants won't force a new translation of the classes.

6.6.5 Instance Initializer

In addition to constructors, the Java language's creators provided another way to initialize objects. This option becomes especially important for anonymous inner classes, that is, classes that are located in another class.

An instance initializer is a constructor without a name. This kind of constructor consists of only a pair of curly brackets in a class declaration and resembles a static initialization block but without the static keyword.

```
public class JavaInitializers {

  static {
    System.out.println( "static initializer" );
  }

  {
    System.out.println( "instance initializer" );
  }

  JavaInitializers() {
   System.out.println( "constructor" );
  }

  public static void main( String[] args ) {
    new JavaInitializers();
```

```
    new JavaInitializers();
  }
}
```

Listing 6.46 src/main/java/com/tutego/insel/oop/JavaInitializers.java (Snippet)

The following output is generated:

```
static initializer
instance initializer
constructor
instance initializer
constructor
```

The static initializer is processed only once, namely, exactly when the class is loaded. The constructor and instance initializer are processed for each construction of an instance. The program code from the instance initializer is processed before the actual program code in the constructor.

Simplifying Constructors with Instance Initializers

Instance initializers can be used to perform initialization work during object creation. Program code can be placed in the blocks that would otherwise have to be copied into each constructor or otherwise centralized in a separate method. With the instance initializer, the program code can be simplified because the common part can be placed in this block, and you can thus avoid code duplication in your source code. However, this technique has several disadvantages compared to a regular initialization method, such as the following:

- Although the duplication is no longer present in the source code, duplication again occurs in the class file. This duplication arises because the compiler copies all the statements of the instance initializer into each constructor. This disadvantage can be avoided if a method is declared and called instead of the instance initializer.

- Instance initializers are quickly overlooked. Looking at the constructor then no longer tells you what it all does since scattered instance initializers can change or add initializations. Initialization thus doesn't contribute to clarity.

- Another shortcoming is that the initialization is only performed for new objects (i.e., with new). If objects are to be reused, a private method like initialize(...), which initializes the object as if freshly created, isn't too bad. A method can always be called, and thus the object states are like new.

- The API documentation doesn't list instance initializers, so the constructors must explain the task.

Multiple Instance Initializers

Multiple instance initializers can appear in one class. They are traversed in order, namely, before the actual constructor. The reason lies in the realization of the implementation: The program code of the instance initializers is placed at the beginning of all constructors. Object variables have already been initialized. Consider the following example:

```java
class WhoIsAustin {

  String austinPowers = "Mike Myers";

  {
    System.out.println( "1 " + austinPowers );
  }

  WhoIsAustin() {
    System.out.println( "2 " + austinPowers );
  }
}
```

This code is thus converted by the compiler into the following:

```java
class WhoIsAustin {

  String austinPowers;

  WhoIsAustin() {
    austinPowers = "Mike Myers";
    System.out.println( "1 " + austinPowers );
    System.out.println( "2 " + austinPowers );
  }
}
```

Listing 6.47 src/main/java/com/tutego/insel/oop/WhoIsAustin.java (Snippet)

Finally, note that, before accessing an object variable in the instance initializer, this variable must be declared in the program and thus known to the compiler. The following code is thus correct:

```java
class WhoIsDrEvil {

  String drEvil = "Mike Myers";

  {
```

```
    System.out.println( drEvil );
  }
}
```

The following code will result in an error:

```
class WhoIsDrEvil {

  {
    System.out.println( drEvil );        // ☠ Compiler error
  }

  String drEvil = "Mike Myers";
}
```

This limitation is rather unusual because if putting the print statement in the con-structor would be allowed.

Note

Instance initializers don't replace constructors! They're rarely used and are rather intended for inner anonymous classes, a concept which will be introduced later in Chapter 10, Section 10.5.

6.6.6   Setting Final Values in the Constructor and Static Blocks

As the examples in the previous section have shown, object variables are first set in the constructor, and then static variables are set in a `static` block. We must now bring this fact together with final variables, which leads us to the fact that they are also assigned in constructors or in initialization blocks. Unlike non-final variables, final variables must be set in any case, and only exactly one write access is possible.

Initializing a Constant with File Content

This procedure can also be used to specify "variable" constants whose assignment is only determined at runtime. You can also put values into a file and use them to assign the final static constant variable. Thus, changing the constants doesn't force a recompilation of the Java program.

In the following example, a file in the classpath is supposed to contain the calorie count for popcorn:

582

Listing 6.48 src/main/resources/calories.txt

The Popcorn class reads the value from the file in a static block and assigns the final static constant CALORIES.

```java
public class Popcorn {

  public final static int CALORIES;

  static {
    try ( Scanner scanner = new Scanner(
        Popcorn.class.getResourceAsStream( "/calories.txt" ) ) ) {
      CALORIES = scanner.nextInt();
    }
  }

  public static void main( String[] args ) {
    System.out.printf( "%d cal", CALORIES );  // 582 cal
  }
}
```

Listing 6.49 src/main/java/com/tutego/insel/oop/Popcorn.java (Snippet)

In this example, several classes work together to read a number. At the beginning, the Class object provides access to the file in the classpath; Popcorn.class is the notation to refer to the Class object of our own class. The getResourceAsStream(...) method is an object method of the Class object and returns a data stream to the file contents the Scanner class uses as an input source for reading. The object method nextInt() then reads an integer from the file.

6.7 Conclusion

We've built our first classes in this chapter from a UML diagram or modeling. However, classes don't stand alone but are related to other classes. Read on to find out how these relationships are implemented in Java.

Chapter 7
Object-Oriented Relationship

"It's harder to get out of a bad relationship than a good one."
—*Whitney Houston (1963–2012)*

Objects don't live in isolation but exist in relationships with other objects. In this chapter, we'll look at the object relationships and type relationships that objects and classes/interfaces can have. Basically, two simple types of relationships exist: An object is related to another object by reference, or a class inherits from another class so that the objects can inherit members from the superclass. In this respect, this chapter considers associations for object links and inheritance relationships. In addition, this chapter describes abstract classes and interfaces, which are special inheritance relationships because they can prescribe behaviors for subclasses.

7.1   Associations between Objects

An important feature of object-oriented (OO) systems is collaboration because an object should do only one thing really well and, if necessary, call in another object that specializes in a different task. For this purpose, an object "knows" other objects and can pass on requests. This connection is called an *association* and is the most important tool in the construction of object associations.

7.1.1   Association Types

In the case of associations, a distinction must be made between whether only one side is aware of the other or whether navigation is possible in both directions:

- A *unidirectional relationship* goes only one way (a person has an address, but the address doesn't "know" the person).

- A *bidirectional relationship* goes both ways (a company knows its employees, and the employees know their company). A bidirectional relationship is obviously a great advantage since the application can traverse the association in any direction.

In addition, relationships can be defined by their *multiplicity*, which indicates with how many objects one side has or can have a relationship. This corresponds to the concept of *cardinality* in databases. Common relationships are 1-to-1 relationships and 1-to-n relationships. Furthermore, you can describe whether a part is existence-dependent or can exist on its own.

Figure 7.1 Unidirectional Relationship

7.1.2   Unidirectional 1-to-1 Relationship

In this section, we'll introduce a new class for a player (Player); the player should be located in a city and also be able to travel to a new city.

```
class Player {
  private City location;
  void travelTo( City newLocation ) { this.location = newLocation; }
  City currentLocation() { return location; }
}
```

Listing 7.1 src/main/java/com/tutego/insel/game/c/vi/Player.java, Player

To allow a player to reference the current location, the Player class has a private object variable of type City. The city has only one name.

```
class City {
  private final String name;
  public City( String name ) { this.name = name; }
  @Override public String toString() { return name; }
}
```

Listing 7.2 src/main/java/com/tutego/insel/game/c/vi/City.java, Player

The following references must be set at runtime:

```
City candyTown  = new City( "Candy Town" );
Player pillLady = new Player();
pillLady.travelTo( candyTown );
```

```
System.out.println( pillLady.currentLocation() ); // Candy Town
pillLady.travelTo( new City( "Giant City" ) );
System.out.println( pillLady.currentLocation() ); // Giant City
```

Listing 7.3 src/main/java/com/tutego/insel/game/c/vi/Application.java, main

Associations in the Unified Modeling Language

Unified Modeling Language (UML) represents associations by means of a line between the involved classes. If an association has a direction, an arrow at the end of the association indicates the direction of this flow, as shown in Figure 7.2. If no arrows exist, the direction hasn't yet been specified more precisely and doesn't automatically mean that the relationship is bidirectional.

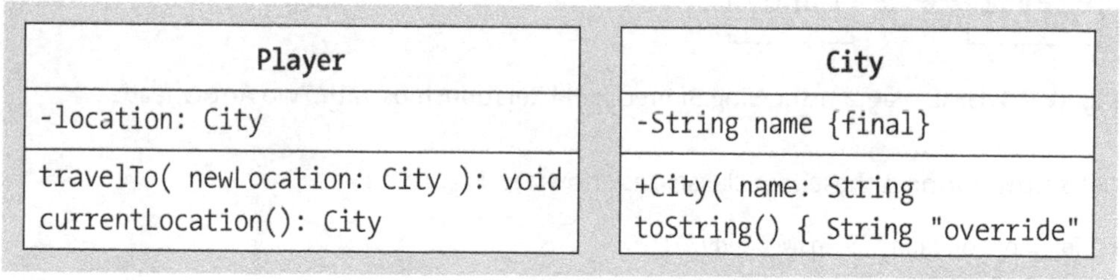

Player
-location: City
travelTo(newLocation: City): void
currentLocation(): City
City
-String name {final}
+City(name: String
toString() { String "override"

Figure 7.2 UML Diagram of Association via Attributes

Player
travelTo(newLocation: City): void
currentLocation(): City
location
City
-String name {final}
+City(name: String
toString() { String "override"

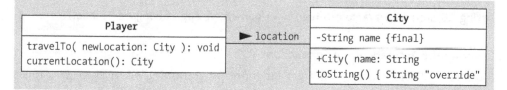

Figure 7.3 UML Diagram of Directed Association

The multiplicity is specified as "lower limit..upper limit," such as "1..4," for example. In addition, in UML, a role can specify which task the relationship has for one side. Roles are important for *reflexive associations* (also referred to as *circular* or *recursive associations*) when a type points to itself. A popular example is the `person` type with the `boss` and `employee` roles.

7.1.3 Becoming Friends: Bidirectional 1-to-1 Relationships

Directed associations are quite easy to implement in Java, as shown in our earlier example. Two-sided associations also appear simple at first glance since only the opposite side must be extended by a reference variable. Let's start with a scenario where the player has a candy and the candy "knows" which player is eating it, as shown in Figure 7.3.

```
class Player {
  Candy candy;
}
```

Listing 7.4 src/main/java/com/tutego/insel/game/c/vj/Player.java, Player

```
class Candy {
  Player player;
}
```

Listing 7.5 src/main/java/com/tutego/insel/game/c/vj/Candy.java, Candy

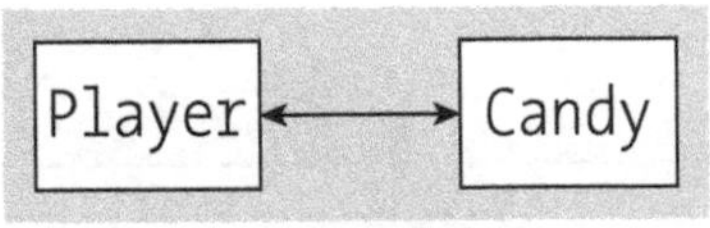

Figure 7.4 UML Diagram Showing Bidirectional Relationships with Two Arrowheads

Let's now connect these two classes, as shown in Figure 7.4.

```
Candy cottonCandy   = new Candy();
Player pillLady     = new Player();
pillLady.candy      = cottonCandy;
cottonCandy.player = pillLady;
```

Listing 7.6 src/main/java/com/tutego/insel/game/c/vj/Application.java (Snippet)

Ensuring the Accuracy of the Connections

Bidirectional relationships require a bit more programming effort since you must ensure that both sides have a valid reference. This requirement is important because, if the association is broken on one side, for example, by setting the reference to null, the other side must also break the reference. Consider the following example:

```
player.candy = null; // player doesn't want any more candy
```

If the player chooses a new candy, then the old candy must also "forget" the player, and vice versa. If the candy changes players, the former player must also delete the candy.

```
Candy cottonCandy   = new Candy();
Player pillLady     = new Player();
pillLady.candy      = cottonCandy;
cottonCandy.player = pillLady;

Candy babyRuth   = new Candy();
pillLady.candy   = babyRuth;
```

Listing 7.7 src/main/java/com/tutego/insel/game/c/vj/Application.java (Snippet)

In this scenario, we have a problem: The player has chosen a new candy, but if we asked the candy cottonCandy, it would still point to pillLady. However, this scenario isn't not acceptable in 1-to-1 relationships.

The root of the evil lies in the directly accessible variables. Variables can't maintain consistency conditions so you must implement consistency through methods. Methods can perform multiple operations, as in a transaction and can transition from one correct state to the next. For this reason, resolving or resetting relationships is best done with methods, such as setCandy(...) and setPlayer(...).

7.1.4   Unidirectional 1-to-n Relationships

Whenever an object needs to reference multiple other objects, a simple reference variable of the other side's type is no longer sufficient. Several approaches enable an object to reference more than one other object.

Relationship to a Small Manageable Number of Objects

If the number of associated objects is fixed and manageable, then multiple variables can be used.

Example

A player has a candy in his left and right pocket in the following example:

```
class Player {
  Candy candyLeftPocket, candyRightPocket;
}
```

If an object is meant to store more than a fixed number of references, the solution using multiple variables is no longer viable, especially if the referenced objects have no special status. What makes sense is to consider the person's right and left arms separately, but if a player has 10 pockets for candy, the variables should certainly not be called pocketCandy1, pocketCandy2, pocketCandy3, and so on.

Data Structures (Containers)

For example, if a player is carrying any number of candies, *data structures* take center stage. We'll use a special container on the first side that stores the references. This key step hands over the responsibility of who stores the references.

Relationship to a Large Known Number of Objects

The keyboard of a cell phone has a fixed number of keys, and a table has a fixed number of legs. For collections of this type, an array is well suited especially because the number of elements is known in advance, and thus, elements can be addressed via an index.

Example

One player can store 10 candies in the following example:

```
class Player {
  Candy[] candies = new Candy[ 10 ];
}
```

For other relationships, where the number of referenced objects is dynamic, an array is not an elegant solution because manual enlargements or reductions of the array are laborious.

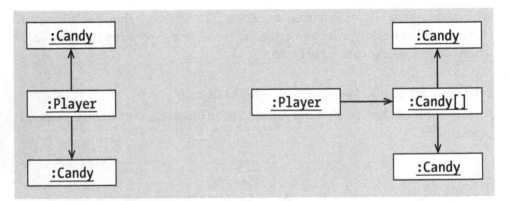

Figure 7.5 The Player Takes over Storage or an Array

Relationship to an Unknown Number of Objects with the Dynamic Data Structure ArrayList

For example, if a player should be able to carry multiple pieces of candy or you want any number of players in a city, arrays are impractical. Instead, a dynamic data structure like java.util.ArrayList makes more sense. We'll deal with these data structures and algorithms in more detail in Chapter 18, Section 18.1, but four methods of the Array-List, which stores elements of type E in a list (sequence), can be introduced at this point:

- boolean add(E e) adds an object e of type E to the list.
- E get(int index) returns the element at position index.
- E remove(int index) deletes the element at position index.
- int size() returns the number of elements in the list.

Furthermore, a list can be placed to the right of the colon of the augmented for loop so that the list can be easily run through.

The Player Is Hungry for Many Sweets

When a player should only have one candy, the following code is sufficient:

```
class Player {
  Candy candy;
}
```

With a data structure, the player can easily store multiple candies, as in the following example:

```
class Player {
  ArrayList candies = new ArrayList();
}
```

Previously, the player had a reference variable of type Candy; now, the player has a reference variable of type ArrayList. Interestingly, no direct 1-to-n relationship exists in the Player because the player still stores only one reference. This reference no longer points to *a* candy, but to *a* container, and the one container can store any number of candies for the player.

Quick Start in Generics

Java is a typed programming language, which means that every variable and expression has a type that the compiler knows and that doesn't change at runtime. For example, a count variable is of type int, a distance between two points could be of type double, and a coordinate pair could be of type Point. However, some gaps in typing exist. Take, for example, a list of candies, declared in the following way:

```
List candies;
```

Although the variable candies is now typed with List, which is better than nothing, what kind of objects the list stores exactly is unclear. Does the container hold candies, unicorns, or rusty boats? A useful approach is to not only have the list itself as the type, but to go inside the list, so to speak, and look closely at what the list actually references. This visibility is exactly the task of *generics*. An ArrayList is a *generic* type and can carry additional type information, which is placed in angle brackets after the type name, the actual "main type," as in the following example:

```
ArrayList<Candy> candies = new ArrayList<Candy>();
```

The information in angle brackets says that the ArrayList should only store Candy instances instead of other things like sausages or vaccination certificates.[1]

With generics, application programming interface (API) designers have a tool for prescribing types even more precisely. The developers of the List type can thus require the user to specify the element type. This requirement allows developers to tell the

---

1 This notation can also be slightly abbreviated to `ArrayList<Candy> candies = new ArrayList<>();`, which is not important now.

compiler more precisely what types they are using and allows the compiler to perform more accurate tests. You can opt not to specify this "secondary type," but omitting this secondary type would lead to a compiler warning and therefore isn't recommended. The more accurate your type specifications are, the better for everyone.

Generic types will appear sporadically in the following chapters, such as Comparable, for example, which helps to compare objects. The details of generics are the subject of Chapter 12, but we just want to emphasize that a list enable the player to correctly store any number of candies. At this point, we simply want to point out that users must enter a type in angle brackets.

Let's expand our program a little more. The player should be able to buy and eat the candies. So, let's first look at the declaration of Candy, which has a name and a calorie count.

```java
public class Candy {
  public final String name;
  public final int calories;
  public Candy( String name, int calories ) {
    this.name     = Objects.requireNonNull( name );
    this.calories = calories;
  }
  @Override public String toString() { return name + ", " + calories; }
}
```

Listing 7.8 src/main/java/com/tutego/insel/game/c/vk/Candy.java, Candy

The player can buy a candy, eat it, and output a list of all the candies. The three methods all access the private variable, candies, as in the following example:

```java
public class Player {
  private final ArrayList<Candy> candies = new ArrayList<Candy>();

  public void buy( Candy newCandy ) {
    candies.add( Objects.requireNonNull( newCandy ) );
  }

  public boolean eat( String name ) {
    for ( int i = 0; i < candies.size(); i++ )
      if ( candies.get( i ).name.equals( name ) ) {
        candies.remove( i );
        return true;
      }
    return false;
  }
```

```
public void listCandies() {
  int sum = 0;
  for ( Candy candy : candies ) {
    System.out.println( candy );
    sum += candy.calories;
  }
  System.out.printf( "Total calories: %d%n", sum );
}
}
```

Listing 7.9 src/main/java/com/tutego/insel/game/c/vk/Player.java, Player

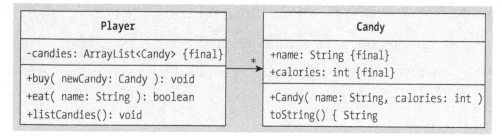

Figure 7.6 UML Diagram where the Player References Any Number of Candies

The data structure itself is private, and no access is possible from the outside. Only methods can access the data structure. Let's look more closely at our three methods next:

- buy(Candy) inserts a new candy into the ArrayList. The test method Objects.requireNonNull(...) will throw a NullPointerException if buy(null) is called by mistake because null is not a valid choice from the list.

- The eat(String) method runs over the list with an index, searches the list to see if a candy with the same name occurs, and uses the list method remove(int) to delete the candy at that point. If a candy could be found and deleted, eat(...) returns true; otherwise, false.

- listCandies() uses a nice language feature: the extended for loop to run through all the candies in the list. In the extended for loop, not only an array is allowed to the right of the colon, but also a data structure such as an ArrayList. In the body of our loop, the toString() representation of each Candy object is output to the screen, the calories extracted and totaled. After the loop, the total calories are also displayed on the screen.

Our small sample program can be thus programmed in the following way:

```
Player reese = new Player();
reese.buy( new Candy( "Kitty Katty", 200 ) );
reese.buy( new Candy( "P&Ps", 250 ) );
```

```
reese.buy( new Candy( "Snackers", 300 ) );
reese.buy( new Candy( "Snackers", 300 ) );
reese.buy( new Candy( "Bubba Hubba", 350 ) );
reese.listCandies();
System.out.println( reese.eat( "Chick-o-Stick" ) );
System.out.println( reese.eat( "Kitty Katty" ) );
reese.listCandies();
reese.buy( new Candy( "Kitty Katty", 200 ) );
reese.buy( new Candy( "Kitty Katty", 200 ) );
System.out.println( reese.eat( "Kitty Katty" ) );
reese.listCandies();
```

Listing 7.10 src/main/java/com/tutego/insel/game/c/vk/Application.java, main

This program returns the following screen output:

```
Kitty Katty, 200
P&Ps, 250
Snackers, 300
Snackers, 300
Bubba Hubba, 350
Total calories: 1400
false
true
P&Ps, 250
Snackers, 300
Snackers, 300
Bubba Hubba, 350
Total calories: 1200
true
P&Ps, 250
Snackers, 300
Snackers, 300
Bubba Hubba, 350
Kitty Katty, 200
Total calories: 1400
```

7.2   Inheritance

From childhood, we've learned to relate objects with each other. Associations map the "has" relationship between objects: A teddy bear has two arms, a table has four legs, and a dog has fur.

Besides the association of objects, another kind of relationship exists: the is-a-kind-of relationship. This relationship is also familiar from everyday life, such as in the following cases:

- Apples and pears are types of fruit.
- People and seagulls are living beings.
- Humans and bats are mammals.
- Airwaves and Wrigley's are chewing gum brands.

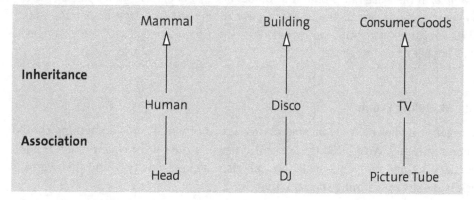

Figure 7.7 Examples of Inheritance and Association

What is special about the is-a-kind-of relationship is the fact that the group specifies certain characteristics for all elements of the group.[2] Fruit can be eaten raw, buildings have a surface, mammals are warm-blooded animals, and so on. What we're talking about is generalization[3] and specialization.[4]

Programming languages express grouping and hierarchy formation via inheritance. Inheritance is based on the idea that parents pass on traits to their children. Inheritance binds classes tightly together. By means of this close connection, you can see that classes are in a sense interchangeable. A program can express, "Give me any piece of fruit" and then might return an apple or a pear.

7.2.1   Inheritance in Java

Java arranges types in hierarchical relations in which they form is-a-kind-of relationships. A newly declared class extends another class via the extends keyword. The former class then becomes the *subclass* (also called *a child class* or *extension class*). The class

---

2 Semantic networks are an explanatory model for knowledge representation in cognitive psychology. Properties belong to categories that are hierarchically connected by is-a-kind-of relationships. Information that's not stored with a specific concept can be retrieved from a higher-level concept.

3 "All generalizations are false, including this one" (Mark Twain).

4 A similar distinction also exists in linguistics where the generic term of a concept is called a *hypernym* and the subordinate term of a concept is called a *hyponym*.

from which the subclass inherits is called the *superclass* (also called the *parent class*). The terms *ancestor* and *descendant* are also used by some authors.

The inheritance mechanism transfers all visible members of the superclass to the subclass. Thus, a superclass transmits members, and the subclass inherits them.

[»]

> **Note**
>
> In Java, only subtypes of classes can be declared. Restrictions on primitive types—for example, in the value range or in the number of decimal places—aren't possible. The Ada programming language allows subtypes of primitive types, for example, and subtypes are common in XML schema, where xs:short or xs:unsignedByte, for example, are subtypes of xs:integer.

7.2.2   Modeling Events

In our game, a player should be able to travel to another city, and something should happen randomly. We'll build these event types in a *class hierarchy*, where a general superclass defines an event—which we can also call an "activity"—and then various subclasses exist for defining special activities.

Base Class for All Commonalities

The base class (superclass) will be called Event, and since each event has an identifier and a duration, the class receives the object variables about and duration.

```
class Event {
  String about;
  int    duration;
}
```

Listing 7.11 src/main/java/com/tutego/insel/game/c/vl/Event.java, Event

Two Subclasses

An example of an event might be a nap, which should be modeled as a subclass. The Nap class extends Event and doesn't add anything.

```
class Nap extends Event { }
```

Listing 7.12 src/main/java/com/tutego/insel/game/c/vl/Nap.java, Nap

Syntactically, inheritance is described by the extends keyword. The declaration of the Nap class carries the appendix extends Event.

Besides Nap, let's create another subclass of Event: Workout. A separate object variable is added to this class.

```java
public class Workout extends Event {
  int caloriesBurned;
}
```

Listing 7.13 src/main/java/com/tutego/insel/game/c/vl/Workout.java, Workout

The three classes Event, Nap, and Workout can be represented in a UML diagram, where inheritance is indicated by an arrow pointing towards the superclass.

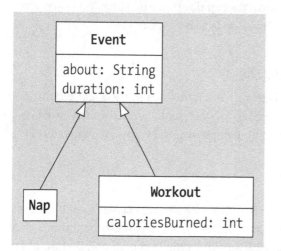

Figure 7.8 Nap and Workout Classes as Two Subclasses of the Event Class

Subclasses Inherit Members and Have Tight Coupling

The Nap and Workout classes inherit the about and duration object variables from the superclass and can easily access them in their own methods and constructors. The inherited members retain their visibility, so a public member remains public. Private members aren't visible to other classes, so they aren't visible to subclasses either; thus, they don't inherit private members. If the type of variables or the implementation of a method changes in the superclass, the subclass will also receive this change. For this reason, coupling by means of inheritance is tight because the subclasses are at the mercy of changes of the superclasses since superclasses know nothing about subclasses.

Our small sample program shows that the client basically doesn't know why a type "has" something and from which (base) class the members originate.

```java
Workout walking = new Workout();
walking.about = "Go for a run";      // Access inherited object variable
walking.duration = 30;               // Access inherited object variable
walking.caloriesBurned = 200;        // Access own object variable
```

```
Nap sleeping = new Nap();
sleeping.about = "Recreational sleep";   // Access inherited object variable
sleeping.duration = 60;                  // Access inherited object variable
```

Listing 7.14 src/main/java/com/tutego/insel/game/c/vl/Application.java, main

The is-a-kind-of-hierarchy doesn't need to stop at one level. You could also imagine a subclass named PowerNap under Nap, to define specialization of Nap. PowerNap may perhaps additionally contain things that normal sleep doesn't. And since Nap is an Event, and since PowerNap is a subclass of Nap, a PowerNap is also a type of Event.

7.2.3 The Implicit Base Class java.lang.Object

If no explicit extends keyword is added after a class name—as in the Event example—the class automatically inherits from java.lang.Object, which is an implicit base class. Thus, without an explicit superclass, the following two declarations are equivalent:

```
class Event
class Event extends Object
```

All classes thus directly or indirectly have the java.lang.Object class as their base class and inherit a number of methods, such as toString(). For this reason, methods that don't originate from the own classes always appear in the keyboard completion of an integrated development environment (IDE), as shown in Figure 7.9.

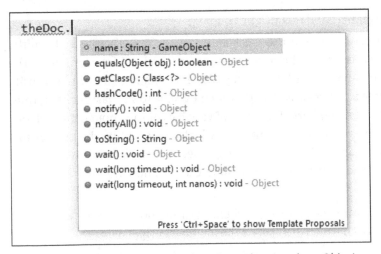

Figure 7.9 Methods from the Absolute Superclass java.lang.Object

7.2.4 Single and Multiple Inheritance*

In Java, only *single inheritance* is allowed in a direct way. So, after the extends keyword, only one class can be placed. Other object-oriented programming (OOP) languages (such as C++,[5] Python, Perl, or Eiffel) allow multiple inheritance and can combine several classes into a new class. But why does Java (along with some other languages such as C#, Objective-C, Simula, Ruby, or Delphi) not offer multiple inheritance at the class level?

Let's suppose the classes O1 and O2 both declare a public method f(), and U is a class that inherits from O1 and O2. If the method call f() exists in U, which of the two methods is meant won't be clear. In C++, the scope operator (::) solves this problem in such a way that the developer always specifies from which superclass the function is to be addressed.

An additional problem is called the *diamond problem* (also referred to as the *rhombus problem*). Two classes, K1 and K2, inherit a field x from a superclass O. A subclass U inherits from classes K1 and K2. Can the field x be accessed in U? Actually, the field exists only once, and thus, you have no reason to worry. Nevertheless, this scenario poses a problem because the compiler has "forgotten" that x hasn't changed in the subclasses K1 and K2. With single inheritance, this dilemma doesn't even arise.

Debate continues about whether the lack of multiple inheritance limits Java. No, this lack doesn't really limit Java. Although Java doesn't allow multiple superclasses, you can still implement multiple interfaces and thus adopt different types. (We'll deal with interfaces in more detail in Chapter 8, Section 8.1.)

7.2.5   Do Children See Everything? The Protected Visibility

A subclass inherits all visible members. We already know public, package-visible, and private. The result is:

- If the members are public in the superclass, the subclasses will also see the members. In general, everyone sees them.

- If the superclass has package-visible members, the subclass sees the members only if the classes are in the same package. Thus, package-visible members remain private for subclasses even if the classes are in a different package.

- Inheritance can be restricted by private. Then, no other class sees the members: neither foreign classes nor subclasses.

Thus, for public, package-visible, and private members, subclasses have no special status; they don't see "more" as a result. Only protected gives subclasses "more."

Language Comparison

The Eiffel programming language has an interesting feature: If a new class has inherit {NONE} *superclass*, the class inherits from the named superclass, but the members are private in the new class and aren't available to other subclasses of this new class.

---

5 Bjarne Stroustrup didn't introduce multiple inheritance until C++ 2.0 (1985–1987).

The protected Keyword

In addition to these three visibilities, a fourth visibility option is added: protected. This visibility includes (strangely enough) two members:

- protected members are inherited by all subclasses.
- Classes that are in the same package can see all protected members because protected is an extension of package visibility.

Thus, if other classes are in the same package and members are protected, the visibility for them is public. For other non-subclasses in other packages, the protected members are private. Thus, the order of visibility can be described in the following way:

public > protected > package-visible > private

> **Design Tip**
>
> If a member is protected in a class, that member is visible in all subclasses, regardless of which package the subclass is in. For example, if A has a protected variable and B inherits from A and C inherits from B, then C will also see the protected variable. This scenario is usually a problem for object variables because an implementation detail can quickly leak out, and the code becomes fragile. Consequently, protected variables should be omitted.

7.2.6   Constructors in Inheritance and super(...)

Although constructors have some similarities with methods (i.e., they can be overloaded or throw exceptions), constructors aren't inherited, unlike methods. Thus, a subclass must specify entirely new constructors because the constructors of the superclass can't be used to create an object of the subclass. Whether this scenario is pure object orientation is debatable; in the Python scripting language, for example, constructors are also inherited. In Java, constructors actually belong to the static part of a class.

In Java, a subclass automatically collects all visible members of the superclass, but the initialization of the individual members in a hierarchy is still the task of the constructors in the hierarchy. To ensure this initialization, Java automatically calls the parameterless constructor of the superclass in the constructor of any class (except java.lang.Object) so that the superclass can initialize "its" object variables. Whether the constructor in the subclass is parameterized or not doesn't matter; any constructor in the subclass must call a constructor in the superclass.

An Example with Constructor Redirection

Let's take another look at constructor chaining with the following example:

```
class Event { }
class Nap extends Event { }
```

Since we don't have explicit constructors, the compiler inserts them, and since Event inherits from java.lang.Object, the runtime environment sees the classes in the following way:

```
class Event {
  Event() { }
}

class Nap extends Event {
  Nap() { }
}
```

Looking for the super Call

The fact that every constructor of a class automatically calls the parameterless constructor of the superclass can also be formulated explicitly—the necessary keyword is super and forms the super() call; the parentheses are reminiscent of a method call. Since the compiler automatically inserts super() as the first statement in the constructor, you don't need to write this statement manually. So, whether you place super(...) in the constructor manually or let the compiler put one in, for the runtime environment, the preceding notation and the following notation are completely the same:

```
class Event extends Object {
  Event() {
    super();        // Calls parameterless constructor of Object
  }
}

class Nap extends Event {
  Nap() {
    super();        // Calls parameterless constructor of Event
  }
}
```

Note

super(...) must always be the first statement in the constructor. When building new objects, the runtime environment in the constructor therefore first runs through the hierarchy to java.lang.Object and starts the initialization process there from top to bottom. If the Java virtual machine (JVM) returns to its own constructor after initializing the superclass by calling super(), all superclass constructors have already initialized their states. Thus, you can later assume fully initialized variables of all base types in your own constructor.

---

super() Also for Parameterized Constructors

All constructors (both parameterless and parameterized) call the parameterless constructor of the superclass via super(...) by default. Let's look at a class for making music that assumes the musical instrument in the parameterized constructor.

```java
public class MusicMaking extends Event {
  public final String instrument;
  public MusicMaking( String instrument ) { this.instrument = instrument; }
}
```

Listing 7.15 src/main/java/com/tutego/insel/game/c/vl/MusicMaking.java, MusicMaking

A parameterless constructor does not exist, only a parameterized one, which also automatically calls the parameterless constructor of the base class Event. This superI(...)-call can be explicitly written out in the following way:

```java
public MusicMaking( String instrument ) {
  super();   // Automatically calls the parameterless constructor of Event
  this.instrument = instrument;
}
```

Of course, super(...) must be first again.

Filling super(...) with Arguments

Sometimes, not only do you need to address the parameterless constructor from the subclass, but you may need to address another (parameterized) constructor of the superclass. For this purpose, you can use super(...) with arguments. In other words, the call of super(...) can be parameterized, so that a parameterized constructor is called instead of the parameterless constructor. Reasons for this option include the following:

- A parameterized constructor of the subclass passes the arguments to the superclass; the parameterless constructor shouldn't be called because the superclass constructor should accept and process the object variables.

- If you don't find a parameterless constructor in the superclass, you must call a special parameterized constructor in the subclass using super(argument).

Let's go through an inheritance hierarchy step by step so that we can understand why a super(...) with parameter is necessary.

First, let's return to the MusicMaking class and its parameterized constructor.

```java
public class MusicMaking extends Event {
  public final String instrument;
  public MusicMaking( String instrument ) { this.instrument = instrument; }
}
```

Listing 7.16 src/main/java/com/tutego/insel/game/c/vl/MusicMaking.java, MusicMaking

If a `MusicMakingAndRecording` class extends the `MusicMaking` class for a special kind of music jam, the following compiler error will be thrown:

```
public class MusicMakingAndRecording extends MusicMaking {}// ☠
                                                // Compiler error
```

The error message of the compiler is "There is no default constructor available in 'com.tutego.insel.game.vl.MusicMaking'."

The reason is simple: `MusicMakingAndRecording` contains a default constructor generated by the compiler that looks for a parameterless constructor in `MusicMaking` with `super(...)`—but that constructor doesn't exist.

You must therefore either create a parameterless constructor in the superclass (which of course isn't possible for non-modifiable classes) or use `super(...)` in `MusicMakingAndRecording` in such a way that it calls the parameterized constructor of the superclass with a single argument, which might look like the following example:

```
public class MusicMakingAndRecording extends MusicMaking {
  public MusicMakingAndRecording() {
    super( "Guitar" );
  }
  …
}
```

Listing 7.17 src/main/java/com/tutego/insel/game/c/vl/MusicMakingAndRecording.java (Snippet)

Whether `MusicMakingAndRecording` has a parameterless or a parameterized constructor doesn't matter: In both cases, you must pass a value to the constructor of the direct superclass with `super(...)`.

Often, subclasses simply pass the passed constructor argument to the superclass constructor, as in the following example:

```
public class MusicMakingAndRecording extends MusicMaking {
  public MusicMakingAndRecording() {
    super( "Guitar" );
  }

  public MusicMakingAndRecording( String instrument ) {
    super( instrument );
  }
}
```

Listing 7.18 src/main/java/com/tutego/insel/game/c/vl/MusicMakingAndRecording.java, MusicMakingAndRecording

The this(...)-and-super(...) Conflict*

this(...) and super(...) have one thing in common: Both want to be the first statement of a constructor. Sometimes, a parameterized call of the constructor of the base class occurs with super(...), and at the same time, a this(...) with parameters tries to perform all the initializations in a central constructor. But unfortunately, doing both isn't possible. The solution is to dispense with this(...) and put the common program code in a private method, which is then called after the super call.

Summary: Constructors and Methods

Methods and constructors have some signature similarities, but also have some important differences, such as the return value or the use of this and super. Table 7.1 summarizes the differences and similarities:[6]

Usage	Constructors	Methods
Modifier	Visibility public, protected, package-visible, and private. *Cannot* be abstract, final, native, static, or synchronized.	Visibility public, protected, package-visible, and private. Can be abstract, final, native, static, or synchronized.
Return	No return type, not even void.	Return type or void.
Identifier name	Same name as the class. Starts with an uppercase letter by convention.	Any. Starts with a lowercase letter by convention.
this	this is a reference in object methods and constructors that references the current instance.	
this(…)	this(...) references another constructor of the same class. If this(...) is used, it must be in the first line.	Not allowed in methods.
super	super is a reference with the namespace of the superclass and can be used to call overridden object methods.	
super(…)	super(...) calls a constructor of the superclass. If used, it must be the first statement.	Not allowed in methods.
Inheritance	Constructors aren't inherited.	Visible methods are inherited.

Table 7.1 Constructors and Methods Compared

---

6 Strangely, synchronized isn't allowed, but a constructor is implicitly synchronized.

7.3   Types in Hierarchies

Inheritance involves some new aspects in terms of the compatibility of types. This section deals with the question of which types are compatible and how a type can be tested at runtime.

7.3.1   Automatic and Explicit Typecasting

Let's recap which types we've created so far: We modeled the Nap and Workout classes as subclasses of Event. The custom superclass Event itself doesn't extend an explicit superclass, so implicitly java.lang.Object is the superclass. Event has two object variables (about and duration), which are inherited by Nap and Workout, and Workout has the additional variable caloriesBurned for the "burned" calories.

Is-a-Type-of Relationships and Automatic Typecasting

An interesting property associated with the is-a-type-of relationship can be seen when looking at the relationships between types. We can break down these relationships in the following way:

- An event is an Event.
- A Nap is a Nap.
- A Workout is a Workout.
- A Nap is an Event.
- A Workout is an Event.
- An Event is a java.lang.Object.
- A Nap is a java.lang.Object.
- A Workout is a java.lang.Object.

Let's code these relationships in Java next.

```
Nap     napAsNap     = new Nap();
Event   napAsEvent   = new Nap();
Object  napAsObject  = new Nap();

Workout workoutAsWorkout = new Workout();
Event   workoutAsEvent   = new Workout();
Object  workoutAsObject  = new Workout();
```

Listing 7.19 src/main/java/com/tutego/insel/game/c/vl/TypeSuptype.java (Snippet)

Therefore, whenever a type is required, a subtype is also allowed. The compiler performs an implicit typecasting. We'll look at this principle, called the *Liskov substitution principle*, in Section 7.3.2.

What Do the Compiler and Runtime Environment Know about Our Program?

The compiler and runtime environment have different views of the program and know different things. By using new, only two types of objects exist at runtime: Nap and Workout, even if we have the following code:

```
Event workoutAsEvent = new Workout();
```

In this case, workoutAsEvent references a workout object at runtime. But the compiler "forgets" the relationship and thinks workoutAsEvent is just a simple Event.

Figure 7.10 The Compiler Only Sees a Section and Draws Its Own Conclusions

However, in the Event class, only about and duration are declared; no caloriesBurned object variable has been defined, although the actual Workout object does have a caloriesBurned, of course. But we can't access caloriesBurned for now in the following example:

```
System.out.println( workoutAsEvent.about );
System.out.println( workoutAsEvent.caloriesBurned );
// Cannot resolve symbol 'caloriesBurned'
```

You can write this code more restrictively in the following way:

```
System.out.println( workoutAsObject.about );
// Cannot resolve symbol 'about'
```

In this case, a complete Workout object still exists behind the reference variable workoutAsObject, but neither caloriesBurned nor about/duration can be used; only the capabilities from java.lang.Object remain.

> **Terminology**
>
> In Java, two type systems are at work: that of the compiler and that of the runtime environment. To distinguish the type that the compiler knows from the type that the JVM knows, we'll use the terms *reference type* and *object type*, respectively. Consider the following example:
>
> ```
> Event event    = new Workout()
> // ^^^^           ^^^^^^^
> // Reference type    Object type
> ```
>
> In this example, Event is the reference type, and Workout is the object type. (Memory aid: new builds objects that are in memory, and the compiler stores a reference in a reference variable.) The compiler sees only the reference type, not the object type. Put more simply: The compiler is only interested in the left-hand side of a construction like Event e = new Workout(), namely, (Event e), while the runtime environment is only interested in the right-hand side, namely, e = new Workout().

Explicit Type Conversion

This type restriction also applies elsewhere. If a variable of type Room is declared, we can't initialize the variable with a "smaller" type, as in the following example:

```
Event    event  = new Workout();    // Workout is object type at runtime
Workout  running = event;           // ☠
// Incompatible types. Found: '[…].Event', required: '[…].Workout'
```

During runtime, even if event references a Workout, you can't initialize running with it. The compiler knows event only under the "smaller" type Event, which isn't sufficient for initializing the "larger" Workout type.

However, you can make the object behind event a full-fledged Workout (with calories spent) for a compiler by an explicit typecasting.

```
Event    event  = new Workout();
Workout  running = (Workout) event;
System.out.println( running.caloriesBurned );
```

Listing 7.20 src/main/java/com/tutego/insel/game/c/vl/TypeSuptype.java (Snippet)

Impossible Matching and ClassCastException

However, explicit typecasting only works if event does actually reference a Workout object. The compiler can be coaxed into an invalid typecasting, and thus, the following incorrect code is also translated into bytecode without errors being raised:

```
Event    event   = new Nap();
Workout  running = (Workout) event; // 💀 ClassCastException
System.out.println( running.caloriesBurned );
```

Listing 7.21 src/main/java/com/tutego/insel/game/c/vl/TypeSuptype.java (Snippet)

The compiler goes along with this nonsense, but not the JVM; at runtime, this object results in a ClassCastException, with the following message:

```
Exception in thread "main" java.lang.ClassCastException: class [
…].Nap cannot be cast to class […].Workout ([…].Nap and [
…].Workout are in unnamed module of loader 'app')
    at …
```

> **Note**
>
> In programming, restricting the type may be relevant. If you use var, then the type of the variable will automatically be the type on the right. For example, let's say we write the following code:
>
> ```
> Event event = new Nap()
> ```
>
> In this case, we've specifically chosen the Nap type for event. Note that, when you declare a variable with var, the new variable gets exactly the type of the right-hand side.
>
> ```
> var event = new Nap();
> ```
>
> In this case, event is a Nap, so it has and can do more than an Event.

7.3.2 The Substitution Principle

Let's suppose you need to find out how long two events (Nap and Workout) last in total. A first attempt would probably involve declaring three methods that can be called with all combinations of Nap and Workout:

```
int totalDuration( Nap event1, Nap event2 ) {
  return event1.duration + event2.duration;
}
int totalDuration( Workout event1, Nap event2 ) {
  return event1.duration + event2.duration;
}
int totalDuration( Workout event1, Workout event2 ) {
  return event1.duration + event2.duration;
}
```

Notice how the bodies of these methods are identical. In this case, inheritance can help you generalize the code. To illustrate this advantage, let's consider two real-life scenarios:

- When we pack a suitcase, different things go into it. We don't have a special suitcase for shoes, then a second suitcase for the shirts, a third suitcase for the headphones we keep losing, and so on.

- Let's imagine some friends come back famished after a hike and ask, "Do you have anything to eat?" When we're hungry, all that matters is something edible. Therefore, we can offer ice cream, but also offer grilled grasshoppers and *hákarl* (fermented Icelandic shark), because it's all edible.

This starting point leads to an important concept in object orientation: "If you want a little, you can get a lot." More precisely, if subclasses like Nap or Workout extend the superclass Event, you can also pass a Nap or Workout object wherever something of type Event is requested since both are of type Event and specificity resides with the subclass. Also, you can pass other subclasses of Event and Nap since subclasses also carry the "gene" Event. All these things would be of type Event, and therefore, all are type compatible.

In the next example, we'll use a method called totalDuration(Event... events) that takes a variable argument list of Event objects and calculates the total of all durations. The method doesn't care about the object type at all because, if the method awaits an Event, we could pass an object exactly of the object type Event, but also Nap or Workout. Each event basically has the object variables about and duration since all subclasses inherit the members and subclasses can't "conjure away" the members.

```
public class TotalDuration {
  public static int totalDuration( Event... events ) {
    int sum = 0;
    for ( Event event : events )
      sum += event.duration;
    return sum;
  }

  public static void main( String[] args ) {
    Workout running = new Workout();
    running.duration = 50;
    Event sleeping = new Nap();
    sleeping.duration = 40;
    System.out.println( totalDuration( running, sleeping ) );
  }
}
```

Listing 7.22 src/main/java/com/tutego/insel/game/c/vl/TotalDuration.java, TotalDuration

With Event, we've created a base class that teaches some basic functionality (in our case, the object variables about and duration) to all its subclasses. Thus, the base class provides a common denominator, such as common object variables or methods that each subclass will have—we can not specify that certain object variables/methods go to certain subclasses. This type relationship is much more flexible than writing special methods for the concrete types Nap and Workout. If new Event types appear later in an application, totalDuration(Event...) can handle them as a matter of course, and you won't have to touch the "algorithm" again.

When an object of a subclass appears instead of the object itself is called *substitution*. The principle was formulated by Professor Barbara Liskov[7] and is therefore referred to as the *Liskov substitution principle.*

Countless other examples exist in the Java library. The println(Object) method is such an example. The method accepts any object because the parameter type is Object. Substitution means that you can put any object there since all classes are derived from Object.

7.3.3   Testing Types with the instanceof Operator

In the previous example, the totalDuration(...) method could be passed a variable number of Events objects, and thus, the method can access anything that has an Event. If we pass "more" (that is, if we pass concrete subclasses), then the method doesn't know this additional information. Now and then, you'll need to know the concrete

---

7 *Discover* magazine ranks Liskov among the 50 most important women in science.

type, and the relational operator instanceof helps you check instances for their relationships to reference types. This operator determines, during runtime, whether a reference is unequal to null and of a particular type. The operator is binary and thus has two operands.

Let's look at an example that doesn't add anything of type Nap when calculating a total:

```java
public static int totalDurationOfNoNapEvents( Event... events ) {
  int sum = 0;
  for ( Event event : events )
    if ( ! (event instanceof Nap) )
      sum += event.duration;
  return sum;
}
```

Listing 7.23 src/main/java/com/tutego/insel/game/c/vl/TotalDuration.java, totalDurationOfNoNapEvents

> **Note**
>
> The instanceof operator tests an object for its hierarchy. For example, o instanceof Object is true for every object o because every object is always a child of java.lang.Object. In this context, the programming language Smalltalk makes a distinction using two messages: isMemberOf (exactly) and isKindOf (like Java's instanceof). To test the exact type, you can use the Class object, as in the expression o.getClass() == Object.class, which tests whether o is exactly an Object object.

instanceof, Reference Types, and Object Types

Basically, the compiler can already know some types, but the test is really performed at runtime. Let's formulate an example to illustrate that instanceof really needs to run the test at runtime. In all cases, the object is a Workout at runtime, only the reference type differs in the following example:

```java
Workout wo1 = new Workout();
System.out.println( wo1 instanceof Workout );      // true
System.out.println( wo1 instanceof Event );        // true
System.out.println( wo1 instanceof Object );       // true

Event wo2 = new Workout();
System.out.println( wo2 instanceof Workout );      // true
System.out.println( wo2 instanceof Event );        // true
System.out.println( wo2 instanceof Object );       // true
System.out.println( wo2 instanceof Nap );          // false
```

```
Object wo3 = new Workout();
System.out.println( wo3 instanceof Workout );        // true
System.out.println( wo3 instanceof Event );          // true
System.out.println( wo3 instanceof Object );         // true
System.out.println( wo3 instanceof Nap );            // false
System.out.println( wo3 instanceof String );         // false
```

Listing 7.24 src/main/java/com/tutego/insel/game/c/vl/InstanceofDemo.java, main

No Arbitrary Type Tests with instanceof

However, the compiler doesn't let everything through. If two types aren't in the type hierarchy at all, the compiler rejects the test because the inheritance relationships are already incompatible, as in the following example:

```
System.out.println( "Aye-aye" instanceof Event );
// Inconvertible types; cannot cast 'java.lang.String' to '[…].Event'
```

The expression is incorrect because StringBuilder is not a base class for String.

> **Note**
>
> You can use instanceof to control the program flow based on the actual types, for example, with code like if(reference instanceof type) A else B. As a rule, however, the control logic of this type generally indicates a design problem that can often be solved in a different way. Dynamic binding is one such solution, which we'll discuss later in Section 7.5.

instanceof and null

An instanceof test with a reference that's null always returns false, as in the following example:

```
String ref = null;
System.out.println( ref instanceof String );        // false
System.out.println( ref instanceof Object );         // false
```

This test result makes sense because null doesn't correspond to any concrete object.

> **Tip**
>
> Because instanceof contains a null test, you should avoid writing the following code:
>
> ```
> if ( s != null && s instanceof String )
> ```
>
> Instead, you should always use a more simplified type of notation, as in the following example:
>
> ```
> if ( s instanceof String )
> ```

7.3.4 Pattern Matching for instanceof

The Java compiler and runtime environment have different, but powerful, type systems. While the runtime environment always knows the precise object type, the compiler only knows the reference type, which can be a base type of the object type. For example, if a reference variable is of type Object and a String is referenced at runtime, then the object type is String, and the compiler doesn't know the type, only that it's somehow an Object.

Sometimes, a switch must be programmed in the code that takes the actual object type into account. At runtime, the object type can be tested with the instanceof operator. A common case distinction in programs is to first test the exact type with instanceof or with getClass() and then match a reference variable to a subtype.

Let's look at an example. This method should receive two Event parameters, and if these events are of type Workout, the number of calories consumed should be extracted and compared. One variant of this program could be as follows:

```java
static boolean burnedSameCalories( Event event1, Event event2 ) {
  if ( !(event1 instanceof Workout && event2 instanceof Workout) )
    return false;
  Workout workout1 = (Workout) event1;
  Workout workout2 = (Workout) event2;
  return workout1.caloriesBurned == workout2.caloriesBurned;
}
```

Listing 7.25 src/main/java/com/tutego/island/game/c/vl/PatternMatchingInstanceOf.java (Snippet)

This solution approach works according to the fail-fast method. Early on, the code tests whether the two events are of the Workout type at all. If not, the method is exited with false. Then, if both Event objects are of type Workout, explicit typecasting takes place, and the calories are extracted and compared.

Another implementation variant is not to leave the method in the case distinction, but instead making the comparison in the body of the case distinction account for special Workout objects:

```java
static boolean burnedSameCalories( Event event1, Event event2 ) {
  if ( event1 instanceof Workout && event2 instanceof Workout ) {
    Workout workout1 = (Workout) event1;
    Workout workout2 = (Workout) event2;
    return workout1.caloriesBurned == workout2.caloriesBurned;
  }
  return false;
}
```

In both cases, you can easily see in the code that first an instanceof test is performed, and then a new variable is declared, which is derived from another expression (in this case, a variable) by a type conversion.

Such cases are fairly common. For this reason, after the type to be tested for instanceof, an identifier for a new variable can be initialized exactly when the instanceof test is true. In Java, this language feature is called *pattern matching for instanceof*.[8] The pattern is exactly this instanceof test, and the variable is called the *pattern variable*. The pattern variable is only set if the test was successful. Otherwise, the variable won't be initialized and won't available for access.

With two pattern variables, let's formulate our program to be a little more concise:

```java
static boolean burnedSameCalories( Event event1, Event event2 ) {
  if ( event1 instanceof Workout workout1 &&
 event2 instanceof Workout workout2 )
    return workout1.caloriesBurned == workout2.caloriesBurned;
  return false;
}
```

This example shows that, in the body of the case distinction, the initialized variables workout1 and workout2 can be accessed.

However, the other branch is also possible, namely, that in case of unsuitable types, the method will be exited:

```java
static boolean burnedSameCalories( Event event1, Event event2 ) {
  if ( !(event1 instanceof Workout workout1 &&
 event2 instanceof Workout workout2) )
    return false;
  return workout1.caloriesBurned == workout2.caloriesBurned;
}
```

With this solution approach, notice how the variables remain declared for the remaining code block.

The compiler can track quite precisely at which point a pattern variable is valid and initialized, which allows another variant:

```java
static boolean burnedSameCalories( Event event1, Event event2 ) {
  return    event1 instanceof Workout workout1 &&
 event2 instanceof Workout workout2
        && workout1.caloriesBurned == workout2.caloriesBurned;
}
```

---

8 This feature was introduced in Java 16 as part of "JEP 394: Pattern Matching for instanceof", *https://openjdk.org/jeps/394*.

Now is where *flow scoping* takes place. The evaluation of the operands with the && operator occurs from left to right. Since the AND operator used in this case works as a short-circuit method, as many parts are evaluated until the answer is fixed (i.e., terminated earlier if an operand is `false`). However, because the pattern variables were already introduced at the beginning, after two valid type checks, the compiler knows that for the third expression—the comparison—two variables `workout1` and `workout2` of type `Workout` exist.

7.4 Overriding Methods

We've seen that a subclass inherits the visible members of its superclass through inheritance. The subclass can now in turn add methods. In this context, overloaded methods, that is, methods that have the same name as another method from a superclass but have a different number of parameters or different parameter types, count as completely normal, added methods.

7.4.1 Providing Methods in Subclasses with a New Behavior

The methods are the offer of an object and the interface to the outside. First and foremost, it's a what, but not a how. Subclasses must unconditionally be able to do the same as their superclass, but the how may differ. In such a case, the subclass can *override* a method of the superclass. If the subclass implements the method anew, it says: "I can do it better." The *overriding method* of the subclass can thus specialize the program code and use members that aren't known in the superclass. The *overridden method* of the superclass is then out of the race for the time being, and a method call on an object of the subclass would get caught in the overridden method.

For a method to override another method, the subclass must have a method with the same method name and the exact same parameter list (i.e., the same signature). The name of the parameter variable is irrelevant. If the return type is `void` or a primitive type, the type must be the same in the overriding method. For reference types, the return type may vary somewhat, which we'll discuss in more detail in Section 7.8.2.

> **Note**
>
> Generally, we speak of overridden methods, but not of overridden object/class variables, since variables aren't overridden. They are only *covered*.[9] Object variables are also not dynamically bound, a virtue that will be explained in more detail in Section 7.8.5.

---

9 Strictly speaking, the JLS distinguishes between "shadowing" and "hiding." Interested readers can learn more at *https://docs.oracle.com/javase/specs/jls/se17/html/jls-6.html#jls-6.4*.

Overriding toString()

The absolute base class `java.lang.Object` transmits a `toString()` method to all subclasses, which outputs an object identifier, mostly for debugging purposes.

```java
public String toString() {
  return getClass().getName() + "@" + Integer.toHexString(hashCode());
}
```

Listing 7.26 java/lang/Object.java, toString()

The method returns the name of the class followed by a @ and a hexadecimal identifier. The `Event` class without its own `toString()` is supposed to test the effect.

```java
class Event {
  String about;
  int    duration;
}
```

Listing 7.27 src/main/java/com/tutego/insel/game/c/vm/Event.java, Event

On an `Event` object, `toString()` returns a somewhat cryptic identifier.

```java
Event e = new Event();
String s = e.toString();
System.out.println( s ); // com.tutego.insel.game.vm.Event@1a2b3c4d
```

Listing 7.28 src/main/java/com/tutego/insel/game/c/vm/Application.java (Snippet)

So, overriding `toString()` in the subclasses is a good idea. A textual object identifier should include the name of the class and the states of an object. For a `Workout` that has an (inherited) about and duration as well as caloriesBurned, this code can be written in the following way:

```java
public class Workout extends Event {
  int caloriesBurned;

  @Override public String toString() {
    return String.format( "%s[about=%s, duration=%d, caloriesBurned=%d]",
                          getClass().getSimpleName(),
                          about, duration, caloriesBurned );
  }
}
```

Listing 7.29 src/main/java/com/tutego/insel/game/c/vm/Workout.java, Workout

The `getClass().getSimpleName()` expression is taken over by the implementation from the `Object` class, and thus the class name is received dynamically, which means you don't need to hard-code the class name as a string. This approach is useful especially if the class name changes later.

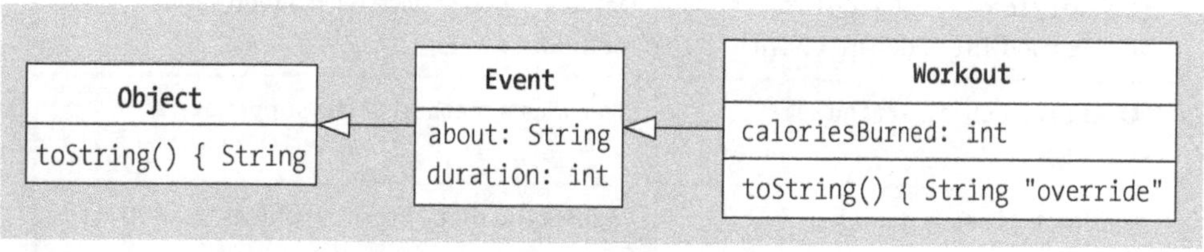

Figure 7.11 Workout as a Subclass of Event and Has Its Own toString(). The UML Stereotype Identifies the Override.

Let's look at the test next.

```
Workout running = new Workout();
running.about = "Go for a run";
running.duration = 60;
running.caloriesBurned = 250;
System.out.println( running );
```

Listing 7.30 src/main/java/com/tutego/insel/game/c/vm/Application.java (Snippet)

Remember: A `println(Object)` on any object calls the `toString()` method from that object. The following result is output:

```
Workout[about=Go for a run, duration=60, caloriesBurned=250]
```

Side Note on Annotations

So far, you've used numerous modifiers, such as `static` or `public`. A special feature of these modifiers is that they don't affect the program control but still represent important additional information. For instance, modifiers introduce semantics into your code. This information is referred to as *metadata*. The `static` and `public` modifiers are metadata for the compiler, but with a little imagination, you can easily imagine metadata that's not evaluated by the compiler but by a Java library. For example, just as `public` tells the compiler that an element is visible to everyone, on the other hand, special metadata can be attached to an element to express that the element can only take on certain ranges of values.

Java provides a built-in capability for metadata, called *annotations*. Consider annotations like custom modifiers. Although you cannot invent a new visibility, you can still provide additional information to the compiler, to specific tools, or to the runtime environment through annotations. Let's look at a few examples of annotations and use cases.

Annotation	Explanation
@WebService class Calculator { **@WebMethod** int add(int x, int y) ...	Defines a web service with a web service method.
@Override public String toString()...	Overrides a method of the superclass.
@XmlRoot class Person { ...	Enables the mapping of an object to an XML file.

Table 7.2 Examples of Annotations and Their Use Cases

Annotations can be used like additional modifiers, but they are distinguished by a preceding @ character. (The @ character, meaning "at," is also a good abbreviation for *annotation type*.) For this reason, the order doesn't matter, so that you can, for example, write either of the following lines of code:

- **@Override** public String toString()
- public **@Override** String toString()

However, a common practice is to place annotations at the beginning. When annotations are placed on types, the annotation usually gets its own line.

Annotation types are the declarations, much like a class type. If attached to an element, an annotation is called a *concrete annotation*. So, while Override itself is the annotation type, @Override before toString() is a concrete annotation.

The @Override Annotation

Our sample class Workout uses the annotation @Override for the toString() method and makes it clear in this way that the toString() method of the class overrides the method of the supertype. The @Override annotation doesn't mean that this method must be overridden in subclasses, only that it overrides a method itself. Annotations are additional modifiers that are either checked by the compiler or can be queried later. Although you don't need to use the @Override annotation, it has two advantages:

- Although the runtime environment knows that a method is being overridden, code should also give a programmer all the necessary information about what is happening. A method being overridden is something significant enough that it should be documented in the code.

- In addition, the compiler checks whether we are actually overriding a method from the superclass. For example, if we made a mistake in the method name and thus unintentionally added a new method to the subclass, the compiler would report this as an error based on its knowledge of @Override. Simple typos like tostring() will be quickly noticed. Overloaded methods and overridden methods are different: An overloaded method only "happens" to share a name with the original method but otherwise has no relation to the logic. Thus, @Override helps developers to really override methods and not accidentally overload methods with the wrong parameters.

final Parameters in Inheritance*

If a method is overridden, then the types of the parameter list are the determining factors, not the names. Also, whether the parameter variables are final or not doesn't matter. Consider this additional information for the particular method. A subclass can therefore arbitrarily add or remove the final. Old libraries can thus be easily reused.

7.4.2 With super to the Parents

When you override a method, you're opting for an entirely new implementation. But what if the functionality as a whole was good and only one little thing was missing? In the case of the overridden toString() method, the subclass realizes a completely new implementation and doesn't refer to the logic of the superclass.

If a subclass wants to say, "What my parents can do isn't so bad after all," you can use the special reference super to access members in the superclass namespace. (Of course, the object behind super and this is the same, only the namespace is different.) In this way, subclasses can still do something of their own, but the realization from the parent class is still available.

In our game, Event had no toString(), which we'll change next.

```java
class Event {
  String about;
  int    duration;

  @Override public String toString() {
    return String.format( "%s[about=%s, duration=%d]",
                          getClass().getSimpleName(),
                          about, duration );
  }
}
```

Listing 7.31 src/main/java/com/tutego/insel/game/c/vn/Event.java, Event

The Workout subclass extends Event and should override toString() because Workout has an additional object variable: caloriesBurned. However, if toString() is overridden in Workout, toString() must also take care of the inherited members (i.e., about and duration). This situation is undesirable because if, for example, an object variable is added or deleted in the Event superclass, all toString() methods of all subclasses must be changed if the subclasses want to include all assignments of the object variables in the string identifier, which is inconvenient. Generally speaking, a subclass shouldn't take responsibility for the superclass.

One solution to the problem is to simply access the toString() method of the Event superclass in toString() of a subclass like Workout and then include the possible states from the base type:

```java
public class Workout extends Event {
  int caloriesBurned;

  @Override public String toString() {
    return String.format( "%s[caloriesBurned=%d]",
                          super.toString(),
                          caloriesBurned );
  }
}
```

Listing 7.32 src/main/java/com/tutego/insel/game/c/vn/Event.java (Snippet)

If instead of super.toString(), only toString() existed in the body, the method call would lead to an endless recursion. For this reason, this code doesn't work without a super reference.

The following test shows the result:

```java
Workout running = new Workout();
running.about = "Go for a run";
running.duration = 60;
running.caloriesBurned = 250;
System.out.println( running );
```

Listing 7.33 src/main/java/com/tutego/insel/game/c/vn/Application.java (Snippet)

The result is the following output:

```
Workout[about=Go for a run, duration=60][caloriesBurned=250]
```

Properties of the super Reference*

In overridden methods, the super reference can be usefully deployed, but other applications also exist. An interesting scenario is when methods of the superclass should be called instead of the custom overridden methods. Thus, the following example makes it clear that, in any case, the toString() method of the Object superclass should be called and not its overridden custom variant:

```java
public class ToStringFromSuper {

  public ToStringFromSuper() {
```

```
    System.out.println( super.toString() );   // Call toString() object
  }

  @Override
  public String toString() {
    return "(._.)";
  }

  public static void main( String[] args ) {
    new ToStringFromSuper();        // ToStringFromSuper@3e25a5
  }
}
```

Listing 7.34 src/main/java/com/tutego/insel/oop/ToStringFromSuper.java

Of course, you can only use super if the method has a valid visibility in the superclass. Therefore, you cannot break the principle of secrecy with this construct.

A concatenation of super keywords at a deeper inheritance hierarchy isn't possible. super must be followed by an object member and thus applies to an overridden method or an overridden object variable. Code like super.super.lol() are therefore always invalid. A subclass receives all members of its superclasses as a unit and doesn't distinguish from which hierarchy something originates.

7.5   Testing Dynamic Bindings

With regard to inheritance, in a form of is-a-type-of relationship, subclasses are always also of the same type as their superclasses. The visible methods that superclasses have thus also exist in the subclasses. The advantage of specialization is that the superclass specifies a simple implementation, and a subclass can override it. We saw this specialization earlier with toString(). However, not only is specialization interesting from a design perspective but also in terms of inheritance. If a superclass provides a visible method, you always know that all subclasses will have that method, whether they override the method or not. As you'll see in a moment, this inheritance leads to one of the most important constructs in OOP languages.

7.5.1   Bound to toString()

Since each class inherits members from java.lang.Object, the toString() method can be called on any object. In our examples, the Object, Event, and Workout classes all have their own toString() methods. Event overrides the toString() of Object, while Workout overrides the toString() method of Event.

Now, let's look at an interesting scenario where the toString() method is called but the reference type and the object type are different.

```
Workout ww = new Workout();
ww.about = "Running";
ww.duration = 100;
ww.caloriesBurned = 300;
System.out.println( ww.toString() );

Event ew = new Workout();
ew.about = "Running";
ew.duration = 100;
System.out.println( ew.toString() );

Object ow = new Workout();
System.out.println( ow.toString() );
```

Listing 7.35 src/main/java/com/tutego/insel/game/c/vn/DynamicBinding.java, main

The toString() method is called three times, where the object type always remains the same (Workout), but the reference type is always different (Workout, Event, or Object).

Now is time for the most exciting question in OOP: What happens in the toString() method call?

The answer is the following output:

```
Workout[about=Running, duration=100][caloriesBurned=300]
Workout[about=Running, duration=100][caloriesBurned=0]
Workout[about=null, duration=0][caloriesBurned=0]
```

This output is easy to understand if you consider that two type systems are at work, and the compiler doesn't have the same knowledge as the runtime environment. The crucial thing is that the runtime environment looks at the object type when calling a method, not at the reference type—the same behavior as instanceof. Since the variable type agreed to in the program doesn't indicate which implementation of the toString() method is called, we call this scenario *late dynamic binding* (or *dynamic binding* for short). Only at runtime (which is late in comparison to translation time) does the runtime environment dynamically select the appropriate object method and match the actual type of the calling object. The JVM knows that a Workout object exists behind each of the three variables, so it calls the toString() method from Workout.

[»]

Language Comparison

Dynamic binding is automatic in Java and can't be controlled or switched off by a modifier. In C++, functions—the term "method" is not used in C++—are not dynamically bound without explicit indication. If you want to bind functions dynamically in C++, you must explicitly place the keyword virtual in front of the function; the result is a *virtual function*.

What's important is that a method is overridden. Let's assume that there's no toString() in Object, but only an implementation in the Nap and Workout subclasses. We wouldn't benefit from that in any way! We therefore explicitly use the commonality that Event, Workout, and other subclasses inherit toString() from Object. Without the superclass, no connective link would exist, and consequently, the superclass always provides a method that subclasses can override. If we were to create a new subclass of Object and not override toString(), the runtime environment would find toString() in Object, but the method would exist in any case—either the original method or the overridden variant.

Terminology

Dynamic binding is often also referred to as *polymorphism*, and a dynamically bound call is then referred to as a *polymorphic call*. This meaning is fine in the context of Java; however, in the world of programming languages "polymorphism" can designate many different things, such as parametric polymorphism (which in Java is called *generics*).

7.5.2   Implementing System.out.println(Object)

Let's look at a program that makes dynamic binding even more obvious. The print*(...) methods are overloaded to accept any object and then output the string representation.

```
public void println( Object x ) {
  String s = String.valueOf( x );
  // String s - (obj == null) ? "null" : obj.toString();
  synchronized ( this ) {
    print( s );
    newLine();
  }
}
```

Listing 7.36 java/io/PrintStream.java, println() (Snippet)

The println(Object) method consists of three parts: First, the string representation of an object is requested, which is where the dynamically bound call can be found. Then, this string is passed to print(String), and finally, newLine() produces the line break.

The compiler has no idea at all what x is, and x can be anything because everything is a java.lang.Object. Statically, nothing can be read from the argument x, and so the runtime environment must decide which class the method call will go to—the miracle of dynamic binding.

IntelliJ displays a type hierarchy when you press Ctrl + H, by default showing superclasses and known subclasses.

7.6   Final Classes and Final Methods

So far, we've encountered the final modifier only in connection with variables. In that case, final means that the variable may only be written once, during initialization. But final also acts as a modifier for classes and methods.

7.6.1   Final Classes

If a class isn't supposed to form subclasses, classes are provided with the final modifier. This limitation prevents subclasses from subsequently changing members. An attempt to inherit from a final class would result in a compiler error. Although OO reuse is thus limited, this limitation is accepted for security reasons. For example, simply overriding a password check should never be possible. A number of final classes exist in the Java library, some of which you've already seen, such as the following:

- String and StringBuilder
- Integer, Double, etc. (as wrapper classes)
- Math
- System and Locale
- Color

[+] **Tip**

Declaring a protected member in a class as final makes little sense since no subclass could then use this method or variable. For this reason, the member should be package-visible (protected contains "package-visible") or private or public.

7.6.2   Non-Overridable (final) Methods

The Event class stores a duration and is supposed to receive an additional format() method, which returns a string representation of this duration according to the ISO-8601 standard.

```java
public class Event {
  public int duration;

  /**
   * @return a string representation of this event duration using ISO-8601.
   */
  public String format() {
    return Duration.ofMinutes( duration ).toString();
  }
}
```

Listing 7.37 src/main/java/com/tutego/insel/game/c/vo/Event.java, Event

466

The format is described via the Javadoc, so callers should be able to rely on the duration always being formatted according to ISO-8601.

For example, the string can be built in the following way:

```
Event flight = new Event();
flight.duration = 6 /* h */ * 60 + 12 /* min */;
System.out.println( flight.format() ); // PT6H12M
```

The SportsEvent subclass now finds this notation too hard to read and thus represents it differently:

```
public class SportsEvent extends Event {
  @Override public String format() {
    return duration + " minutes";
  }
}
```

The result is as expected:

```
Event tongaVsSamoa = new SportsEvent();
tongaVsSamoa.duration = 90;
System.out.println( tongaVsSamoa.format() ); // 90 minutes
```

The problem in this situation is a violation of the Liskov substitution principle. A subclass must not break the "contract," and if the base type promises a certain format, then subclasses must adhere to this format. One approach to solving this problem is to prohibit subclasses from overwriting a method. This limitation is achieved by using the final modifier in the method declaration, as in the following example:

```
final public String format() {
  return Duration.ofMinutes( duration ).toString();
}
```

If you add the final modifier to the format() method in Event, the compiler reports the following error for the SportEvent subclass:

```
'format()' cannot override 'format()' in [
...].Event'; overridden method is final
```

Since method calls are always bound dynamically, a caller can no longer unintentionally end up in the subclass because final methods prevent this call from happening.

Note

[«]

Private methods can also be final, but private methods can't be overridden anyway (as described in Section 7.4.1), so final is superfluous.

7.7 Abstract Classes and Abstract Methods

A class shouldn't always be programmed out immediately, for example, if the super-class wants to specify methods for the subclasses but doesn't know how to implement them. In Java, two concepts enable this scenario: *abstract classes* and *interfaces*. While `final` basically closes the class and makes subclasses impossible, abstract classes are the opposite: Without subclasses, abstract classes are useless.

Consequently, the following three scenarios are possible:

Class Type	Meaning
Normal non-abstract and non-final class	A subclass can be created but doesn't have to be.
Final class	A subclass can't be created.
Abstract class	A subclass must be created.

Table 7.3 Class Types Compared

7.7.1 Abstract Classes

So far, you could form an object from each class via `new`. However, making instances isn't always useful; for example, an instance should be prohibited if a class should exist only as a superclass in an inheritance hierarchy.

This superclass can then express is-a-kind-of relationships to serve as a modeling class and thus specify signatures for its subclasses. A superclass has specifications for the subclass. In other words, all subclasses inherit the methods of the superclass. An instance of the superclass itself doesn't need to exist at all.

To express this scenario in Java, let's place the `abstract` modifier before the type decla-ration of the superclass. No instances of this class can then be formed, and any attempt to create an object would result in a compiler error. Apart from this limitation, abstract classes behave just like normal classes, contain the same members, and can also inherit from other classes themselves. Abstract classes are the opposite of *concrete classes*.

Now, let's make the `Event` class abstract to act as a superclass for all events since direct instances of the `Event` class aren't necessary.

```
abstract class Event {
  String about;
  int    duration;
}
```

Listing 7.38 src/main/java/com/tutego/insel/game/c/vp/Event.java, Event

With the now abstract class Event, you can express that it is a general class for which no concrete objects exist or could be formed. An attempt results in the following compiler error:

```
Event flight = new Event(); // 'Event' is abstract; cannot be instantiated
```

The meaning behind this error is simple: No general and unspecified events occur in the real world, only specific subtypes of events, such as a nap, a soccer game, or eating candy. Thus, making an instance of the Event class makes no sense. The class should only appear in the hierarchy and categorize events, so to speak, and give them properties.

> **Tip**
>
> You can also use abstract classes to prevent an instance of a class from being formed. However, the abstract modifier shouldn't be used for this purpose. A better approach is to set the visibility of the constructor to private or protected.

Base Type Abstract Class

Abstract classes are always used in conjunction with inheritance. Abstract superclasses are general, and subclasses must further specialize the base type. A class will extend the abstract class, and from this class—if the subclass isn't abstract itself—an instance can be created.

Also, with abstract classes, the is-a-kind-of relationship still applies, so that Nap and Workout can be written for the Event subclasses in the following way:

```
Event    sleep   = new Nap();
Event    running = new Workout();
Event[] events   = { new Nap(), new Nap(), new Workout(), new Nap() };
```

Listing 7.39 src/main/java/com/tutego/insel/game/c/vp/Application.java (Snippet)

The Event[] events declaration only identifies the type of the array regardless of whether the Event class is abstract or not. The array contains references to subclasses of Event.

> **Note**
>
> Abstract classes can, of course, in turn have abstract subclasses. Consider the following examples:
>
> ```
> abstract class Event { }
> abstract class Hackathon extends Event { }
> ```
>
> Note that no instance can be created from Hackathon via new.

7.7.2   Abstract Methods

The `abstract` modifier before the `class` keyword introduces the declaration of an abstract class. But a method can also be abstract. In this context, an abstract method simply specifies its signature, and a subclass implements that method at some point. The abstract class is thus responsible for the method head, while the implementation is done elsewhere—clear separation between "What can I do?" and "How do I do it?" While the superclass expresses that it *can do* something via the declaration of the abstract method, the subclasses realize *what* the code for that behavior looks like. Put simply, abstract methods express that they have no idea about the implementation and that the subclasses must take care of the behavior. Of course, the whole thing must be written within the scope of the specification.

Since an abstract class can contain abstract methods, but need not, we can distinguish among the following kinds of classes and methods:

- **Pure (pure) abstract classes**: The abstract class contains only abstract methods.
- **Partially abstract classes**: The class is abstract but also contains concrete implementations (i.e., non-abstract methods). This approach provides a framework for subclasses to use.

An Event May Occur on the Journey

In our little game, let's say we want the player to be able to change cities. During the journey, unfortunately, various events may occur, for instance:

- The player could be mugged and have his candy stolen.
- The player might get hungry, and then he eats some sweets.
- By some lucky coincidence, the player can be given more candy.

These events are all random, and maybe nothing happens at all during the trip.

For one event, we've already declared a class. Now, an abstract method for program code should be declared in the `Event` superclass, which can be then executed when the event occurs. For the individual events to have access to the player, the current player is passed to the method. This approach allows the event methods to fall back on the player. In this sense, the player is considered a *context object*.

Let's consider our abstract method for these events:

```java
abstract class Event {
  String about;
  int    duration;

  abstract void process( Player player );
}
```

Listing 7.40 src/main/java/com/tutego/insel/game/c/vq/Event.java, Event

Since abstract methods are always without implementation, we used a semicolon in curly brackets instead of specifying the method body. If at least one method is abstract, then automatically the whole class is. Therefore, you must explicitly write the abstract keyword before the class name. If you forget the abstract keyword for such a class, you'll trigger a compiler error. A class with an abstract method must be abstract; otherwise, anyone could construct an instance and call that method. If you try to create an instance of an abstract class, you'll also get a compiler error. Of course, an abstract class can have non-abstract members, as Event shows with the object variables about and duration. Concrete methods are also allowed, but we don't need them in this case. (Recall that we programmed a toString() method earlier in Section 7.5.1.)

Basically, you could also have an empty body and then hope that the subclasses override the method. But making a method abstract should be a deliberate design decision because, after all, it's unclear what exactly is supposed to happen in any particular event. Each event is a little different, and you cannot provide a certain implementation now. Abstract methods express that this implementation must be mandatory.

Transmitting Abstract Methods

When you inherit abstract methods from a class, two options become available:

- You can override all abstract methods and implement them. Then, the subclass no longer needs to be abstract (although it can still be). Normal instances of the subclass can still be made.

- You don't override the abstract method, so it will be inherited normally. In other words, an abstract method remains in our class, and the class must again be abstract.

Let's return to the example: The abstract method from the superclass should be implemented (differently) by each subclass because each event does something different to the players. Let's start with the mugging event. In this process, the player loses all the candy.

```
class Mugging extends Event {
  @Override void process( Player player ) {
    player.candy.quantity = 0;
  }
}
```

Listing 7.41 src/main/java/com/tutego/insel/game/c/vqi/Mugging.java (Snippet)

The gift event would be much nicer: The player is given a random number of new candies:

```
class Gift extends Event {
  @Override void process( Player player ) {
    player.candy.quantity += ThreadLocalRandom.current().nextInt( 1, 10 );
  }
}
```

Listing 7.42 src/main/java/com/tutego/insel/game/c/vq/Gift.java (Snippet)

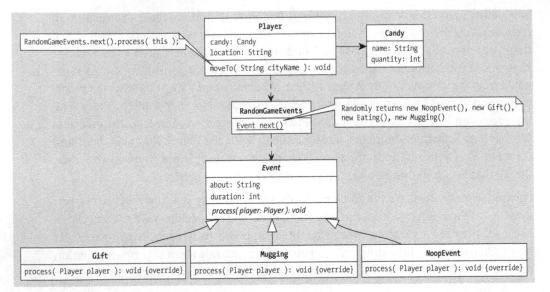

Figure 7.12 UML Diagram Showing the Names of Abstract Classes as Italicized. Subclasses Override the Abstract Method of the Superclass.

In our test program, we'll initialize the player, give them a candy, then mug them, and then give them a gift.

```java
Candy liquorice = new Candy();
liquorice.quantity = 10;
liquorice.name = "Salty candy shell";
Player peter = new Player();
peter.candy = liquorice;

Event mugging = new Mugging();
Event gift    = new Gift();

System.out.println( peter.candy.quantity ); // 10
mugging.process( peter );
System.out.println( peter.candy.quantity ); // 0
gift.process( peter );
System.out.println( peter.candy.quantity ); // 7
```

Listing 7.43 src/main/java/com/tutego/insel/game/c/vq/Playground.java, main

From the output, you can easily see how event handling affects the player `peter` and changes the number of candies.

Note

Once methods exist with a body in a class, they can't be abstractly overridden later. Once an implementation is in place, a method implementation cannot be "required" again. For example, toString() exists in Object and can't be overridden abstractly in Event, for instance, to dictate to the Gift or Mugging subclasses that they must override toString().

If a class doesn't implement all inherited abstract methods, the class itself must be abstract again. If our subclass of an abstract base class isn't abstract, IntelliJ provides the shortcut `Alt`+`Enter`, which either makes the current class abstract or implements all inherited abstract methods with a dummy body.

The beauty of abstract methods is that they can be implemented by concrete classes in any case. So, polymorphic method calls can always take place.

Played to the End

So far, we haven't implemented the change in the cities behavior, and the previous example was only intended to clarify type relationships. Now, let's expand our game in such a way that the player can change cities and then some random things can happen.

First, once again, the three Event subclasses that now receive a console output.

```java
class Mugging extends Event {
  @Override void process( Player player ) {
    System.out.println( "Damn it! Someone steals all your sweets." );
    player.candy.quantity = 0;
  }
}
```

Listing 7.44 src/main/java/com/tutego/insel/game/c/vq/Mugging.java, Mugging

```java
class Gift extends Event {
  @Override void process( Player player ) {
    System.out.println( "Lucky you! Someone gives you sweets." );
    player.candy.quantity += ThreadLocalRandom.current().nextInt( 1, 10 );
  }
}
```

Listing 7.45 src/main/java/com/tutego/insel/game/c/vq/Gift.java, Gift

```java
class Eating extends Event {
  @Override void process( Player player ) {
    System.out.println( "You're hungry and you eat some of your sweets." );
```

```
    player.candy.quantity *= Math.random();
  }
}
```

Listing 7.46 src/main/java/com/tutego/insel/game/c/vq/Eating.java, Eating

What's new is an Event subclass that does nothing. We refer to such objects as *null objects*.

```
class NoopEvent extends Event {
  @Override void process( Player player ) { }
}
```

Listing 7.47 src/main/java/com/tutego/insel/game/c/vq/NoopEvent.java, NoopEvent

Since the events can occur randomly, a static random() method is supposed to return a random event.

```
class RandomGameEvents {
  private RandomGameEvents() {}
  static Event next() {
    double random = Math.random();
    if ( random < 0.5 ) return new NoopEvent();    // 0.0 <= random < 0.5
    if ( random < 0.8 ) return new Gift();          // 0.5 <= random < 0.8
    if ( random < 0.9 ) return new Eating();        // 0.8 <= random < 0.9
    return new Mugging();                           // 0.9 <= random < 1.0
  }
}
```

Listing 7.48 src/main/java/com/tutego/insel/game/c/vq/RandomGameEvents.java, RandomGameEvents

In this method, notice how the events aren't equally probable. Nothing should happen while traveling 50% of the time, 30% of the time the player should receive a gift, 10% of the time the player is hungry, and 10% of the time the player is mugged.

The Candy class is thus simplified and contains only a name and a quantity, as in the following example:

```
public class Candy {
  String name;
  int     quantity;
}
```

Listing 7.49 src/main/java/com/tutego/insel/game/c/vq/Candy.java, Candy

Things get interesting when the player travel to a new destination, as in the following example:

```java
class Player {
  Candy   candy;
  String location;

  void moveTo( String cityName ) {
    if ( location.equalsIgnoreCase( cityName ) ) {
      System.out.println( "You're already there! (O_)" );
      return;
    }
    RandomGameEvents.next().process( this );
    location = cityName;
  }
}
```

Listing 7.50 src/main/java/com/tutego/insel/game/c/vq/Player.java, Player

The moveTo(String) method is passed an arbitrary city name, and if the player is already in that city, the journey is unnecessary. The interesting part follows when the journey begins: A random event is determined, and the player is passed to the process(Player) method.

```java
Candy liquorice = new Candy();
liquorice.quantity = 10;
liquorice.name = "Salty candy shell";
Player peter = new Player();
peter.candy = liquorice;
peter.location = "Dallas";

System.out.println( "Enter the destination where you want to travel. "
                  + "An empty input will end the game." );
while ( true ) {
  System.out.printf( "You're currently in %s and hold %d '%s'%n",
                    peter.location, peter.candy.quantity, peter.candy.name );
  System.out.print( "Destination: " );
  String input = new Scanner( System.in ).nextLine();
  if ( input.trim().isEmpty() ) break;
  peter.moveTo( input );
}
```

Listing 7.51 src/main/java/com/tutego/insel/game/c/vq/Application.java, main

The actual main program is not big now. A candy is built like the player, and the infinite loop is entered. The program asks for input, and if no input exists, the loop ends, and the program is over. If the input wasn't empty, this input is a destination, and Peter travels to this place, with all the surprises that follow.

Why?

Abstract methods are a particularly important language feature because they promise that an implementation will exist later. This ability is often used by frameworks: A library declares an abstract class with an abstract method, and you implement that method, create an instance of that implementation, and pass the object back to the framework. The framework now knows that the method must have been implemented and can call it. Without dynamic binding, nothing like this would work at all.

7.8   Further Information on Overriding and Dynamic Binding

After those basics, let's now look at some special features and other terms.

7.8.1   No Dynamic Binding for Private, Static, and final Methods

When a private, static, or final method is not overridden, such a method is excluded from dynamic binding. If a method in the subclass has the same name as a private method in the superclass, this doesn't matter to the compiler, which is good because private implementations are secret and hidden anyway. The subclass shouldn't know anything about the private methods in the superclass. Instead of *overriding* a method, we call this *covering* or *concealing* in this context.

The fact that private, static, and final methods aren't overridden is an important contribution to security. Indeed, if subclasses could override internal private methods, we would violate the inner workings of the superclass. In other words, private methods aren't visible in the subclasses and are therefore not overridden. Otherwise, private implementations could be changed subsequently, and superclasses would no longer be sure to use only their own methods.

7.8.2   Covariant Return Types

If a method with a reference type overrides another as a return, the overriding method can use, as its return type, any subtype of the return type of the overridden method. This explanation sounds more complicated than it is, so let's consider a quick example.

```
class Event {}
class Workout extends Event {}

class Calendar {
  Event first() { return new Event(); }
}

class WorkoutCalendar extends Calendar {
```

```
//  @Override Event first() {
  @Override Workout first() {
    return new Workout();
  }
}
```

Listing 7.52 src/main/java/com/tutego/insel/game/c/vr/Application.java, main

The Calendar class declares the first() method and returns an Event. The Calendar subclass WorkoutCalendar overrides the first() method and could of course use the Event return type, but it returns a subtype of Event, namely, Workout. Referred to as *covariant return type*, this option can be quite convenient because developers can often do without explicit typecasting.

> **Note**
> What is strange in this context is that modified access rights have always existed in Java. A subclass can extend visibility. Also, for exceptions, a subclass can create more specific exceptions or completely different exceptions than the superclass method.

7.8.3   Array Types and Covariance*

The statement "If you want a little, you can get a lot" also applies to arrays because, if Sub class is a subclass of Super class, Sub[] is also a subtype of Super[]. This feature is called *covariance*. Since Object is the base class of all objects, an Object array can also store all other objects.

Let's explore covariance by building a static set(...) method that simply places an element in the first position in the array.

```
public static void setFirst( Object[] array, Object element ) {
  array[ 0 ] = element;
}
```

Listing 7.53 src/main/java/com/tutego/insel/oop/ArrayCovariance.java, set()

Covariance isn't a problem when reading state but is potentially dangerous when writing a state. Let's see what happens with different array and element types in the following example:

```
Object[] objectArray = new Object[ 1 ];
String[] stringArray = new String[ 1 ];
System.out.println( stringArray instanceof String[] );  // true
System.out.println( stringArray instanceof Object[] );  // true
```

```
setFirst( stringArray, "Life won't wait" );      // 1
setFirst( objectArray, "Yes you can" );          // 2

setFirst( stringArray, new Object() );           // 3 ☠
// Exception in thread "main" java.lang.ArrayStoreException: java.lang.Object
setFirst( stringArray, new StringBuilder( "Set clear targets" ) ); // 4 ☠
// Exception in thread "main" java.lang.ArrayStoreException: java.lang.StringBuilder
```

Listing 7.54 src/main/java/com/tutego/insel/oop/ArrayCovariance.java, main

Let's recap: In line 1, the string can be stored in a String array. The call in line 2 also works because a String can also be stored in an Object array since String is a subclass of Object.

Now, we face a dilemma: The array needs to store a reference whose type isn't compatible. This problem is shown by lines 3 and 4 in the setFirst(...) call. At compile time, everything seemed fine, but during runtime, an ArrayStoreException is thrown, with the following message:

```
Exception in thread "main" java.lang.ArrayStoreException: java.lang.Object/
StringBuilder
```

We deserve this punishment, however, because a pure Object or StringBuilder object can't be stored in a String array.

To summarize, Java's type system can't check this subtlety at translation time. Only at runtime is a test possible, with the bitter result of an ArrayStoreException. This scenario is somewhat different with generics where comparable constructs are forbidden in inheritance relationships.

7.8.4   Dynamic Binding even with Constructor Calls*

The fact that a subclass constructor calls the superclass constructor can interfere with the initialization of variables in the subclass. Let's first consider the following code:

```
public class KingOfDenmark extends HardCandy {
  String type = "I am King of Denmark";
}
```

Now, where does the type variable get initialized? We know that initializations are always done in the constructor, but we have a super() in the constructor at the same time. Since the Java Language Specification (JLS) prohibits code before super(), the assignment must follow after the superclass call. The problem now is that a superclass constructor is called before variables in the subclass are initialized. If the superclass now manages to access the subclass variables, the value that gets set later will be missing. The access actually succeeds, but only by trickery because a superclass (say Hard-Candy) can't access the variables of the subclass. However, within the superclass, you can call exactly that method of the subclass that overrides the subclass from the super-class. Since method calls are dynamically bound, a method can read the value, as in the following example:

```java
class HardCandy {
  HardCandy() {
    printType();
  }
  void printType() {
    System.out.println( "I do not know yet :-(" );
  }
}


public class KingOfDenmark extends HardCandy {

  String type = "I am King of Denmark";

  @Override
  void printType() {
    System.out.println( type );
  }

  public static void main( String[] args ) {
    HardCandy candy = new HardCandy();
    candy.printType();

    KingOfDenmark = new KingOfDenmark();
    kingOfDenmark.printType();
  }
}
```

Listing 7.55 src/main/java/com/tutego/insel/oop/KingOfDenmark.java

The result is the following output:

```
I do not know yet :-(
I do not know yet :-(
null
I am King of Denmark
```

A special characteristic of this program is the fact that overridden methods—here printType()—are bound dynamically. This binding already exists even if the object hasn't been fully initialized. Therefore, the constructor of the HardCandy superclass doesn't call the printType() method of HardCandy, but instead calls the printType() method of KingOfDenmark.

In this example, when a KingOfDenmark object is created, KingOfDenmark calls the constructor of HardCandy via super(). This constructor in turn calls the printType() method in KingOfDenmark but doesn't find a string because this data won't be set until after super(). Let's write a constructor for KingOfDenmark explicitly to clarify things:

```java
public class KingOfDenmark extends HardCandy {

  String type = "I am King of Denmark";

  KingOfDenmark() {
    super();
    type = "I am King of Denmark";
  }
  …
}
```

As a consequence, dynamically bound method calls via the this reference are potentially harmful in constructors and should therefore be avoided by having the constructor call only private (or final) methods since these methods aren't dynamically bound. If the constructor calls a private (final) method in its class, then the method stays that private (final).

7.8.5 No Dynamic Binding for Covered Object Variables*

Let's say Canadian champion eater "Furious Pete"[10] eats everything in record time; let's immortalize his pizza-eating feats in a Java program. The PizzaEater superclass represents the average eater, taking an estimated 900 seconds for a 12" pizza. FuriousPete is a specialization and can eat a 12" pizza in 32 seconds.

```java
class PizzaEater {

  int consumptionTime = 900 /* Seconds */;

  void eat() {
    System.out.printf( "I eat a pizza in %d seconds%n", consumptionTime );
  }
}

public class FuriousPete extends PizzaEater {
```

---

10 *https://guinnessworldrecords.com/news/2016/4/competitive-eater-challenged-to-fastest-time-to-eat-a-12%E2%80%99%E2%80%99-pizza-record-guinnes-426366*

```java
int consumptionTime = 32 /* Seconds */;

@Override void eat() {
  System.out.println( consumptionTime );                        // 32
  System.out.println( super.consumptionTime );                  // 900
  System.out.println( this.consumptionTime );                   // 32
  System.out.println( ((PizzaEater) this).consumptionTime ); // 900
}

public static void main( String[] args ) {
  new FuriousPete().eat();
}
}
```

Listing 7.56 src/main/java/com/tutego/insel/oop/FuriousPete.java

The PizzaEater superclass declares a consumptionTime object variable, and the subclass also declares an object variable with the same name. (In Java, having the same name for an object variable enables it to shadow another object variable of the same name.)

The subclass can come one level higher with super.consumptionTime. The reference super, like this, is a special reference and can be used in the same way, except that super goes into the namespace of the superclass. A concatenation of super keywords in a deeper inheritance hierarchy isn't possible. super must be directly followed by an object member, and code like super.super.consumptionTime are thus always invalid.

For method calls, the runtime system always binds dynamically, which isn't the case for access to object variables. In this case, the compiler determines the class from which the object variable should be taken. Our program achieves this behavior with the following statement:

```java
System.out.println( ((PizzaEater) this).consumptionTime );     // 900
```

The output 900 is identical to System.out.println(super.consumptionTime). The this reference has the type FuriousPete in its context. But if we convert the type to the PizzaEater base type, we'll get exactly the assignment of consumptionTime from the base class of our hierarchy. An explicit typecasting in the direction of a supertype is also never necessary for dynamically bound method calls; the runtime environment decides independently where the call goes. In the eat() methods of FuriousPete, then, the following lines are identical:

```java
((PizzaEater) this).eat();
eat();
```

In this case, this scenario is a recursion.

7.9   A Programming Task

Good OO modeling isn't easy and requires a lot of practice. Many developers start "modeling" in the code way too early, but doing so isn't a good idea because you'll often need rebuild the code, which ultimately costs time. Starting with a neat design makes sense, and you should be clear: "Which class has which responsibilities, and who talks to whom?" To document the design, UML diagrams are helpful, and for this purpose, we recommend reviewing documentation on the internet or picking up a book like *UML Distilled: A Brief Guide to the Standard Object Modeling Language* by Martin Fowler. Starting the design with boxes and lines on paper or on a whiteboard can also be extremely useful.

In the previous two chapters, we laid the foundation for our Jawbreaker game, which you are welcome to finish. Let's briefly summary some of its basic rules:

- At the beginning, the player has $2,000 in cash and $0 in debt.
- In the original game, drugs like cocaine, heroin, etc. were used. Put in your favorite candy instead. The player can buy and sell these in his city.
- The prices of drugs ($) in the original game ranged in values, for instance, cocaine costs 15,000–30,000, heroin costs 5,000–14,000, and so on. Prices should fluctuate randomly, and drug prices may decrease/increase as the player travels. Set your own price ranges for the candies.
- A player can carry a maximum of 100 products. (All products have the same weight.)
- A player can travel to various neighborhoods, such as the "Bronx," "Central Park," "Manhattan," and so on.
- A player can't travel to the city he is currently in.
- One trip lasts one day. During the trip, random events may happen, such as the following:
  - The player's money can be stolen by a stranger.
  - During a trip, the player can find drugs now and then.
  - Depending on the distance to the selected city, a trip may cost more or less money.
- In the Bronx—but only there—you can program 1) a bank for deposits/withdrawals, 2) a *stash* for securing drugs, and 3) a *loan shark* for lending money.
  - The player can borrow money from the loan shark only if he has no debts.
  - Debt interest is 10% per day.
  - Savings interest is 5.5% per day.
- After 30 days, the game is over. Then, profits and debts are offset to calculate a final score.

You're invited to add more rules to the game. A text interface can also be implemented using Java thanks to an open-source library like *https://github.com/mabe02/lanterna*.

Chapter 8

Interfaces, Enumerations, Sealed Classes, Records

"Education comes not from reading, but from thinking about what you read."
—Carl Hilty (1833–1909)

Classes are the most important types in the Java language, but they aren't the only types; you'll also encounter interfaces, enumeration types, records, and annotation types. Annotation types (which you'll learn more about in Chapter 11, Section 11.7) are a topic related to reflection and don't play a role in this chapter, which instead focuses on the other three types.

8.1 Interfaces

Interfaces are a good complement to abstract classes/methods, which we covered in Chapter 7, Section 7.7. In object-oriented (OO) design, you must separate the "what" from the "how." Abstract methods, like interfaces, say something about the "what," but only concrete implementations realize the "how."

8.1.1 Interfaces Are New Types

Because Java only knows single inheritance, providing classes with more than one type is difficult. However, since a class can accept several types in general OO modeling, we can use the concept of the *interface*. A class can then inherit from another class and implement any number of interfaces and in this way obtain additional types.

Like a class, an interface is a type, and the two have many things in common, the only difference being the intention. An interface may contain the following elements:

- Abstract methods
- Private and public concrete methods (also known as *default methods*)
- Private and public static methods
- Constants (i.e., static variables)
- Nested types (you'll learn more about these in Chapter 10), such as enumerations

An interface must not declare a constructor. This rule is obvious because instances of interfaces can't be created, only instances of the concrete implementing classes. Also, an interface can't declare object variables; every variable is automatically a class variable.

Class inheritance is always linear. For instance, `Candy` inherits from `Object`, `Workout` inherits from `Event`, and `Event` inherits from `Object`; from the subclasses, a direct path to the superclass can be traversed. Since multiple inheritance is not possible in Java, you can't say in one place, for example, that a `Candy` is an `Object` but should additionally take the type `Buyable` because it can also have a price. A class can't inherit from multiple types; you can't do that with single inheritance. This limitation is a disadvantage because, in practice, a class often needs to appear under different "views," which is where *interfaces* can help.

8.1.2   Declaring Interfaces

The declaration of an interface is reminiscent of an abstract class. One difference is that, instead of `class`, the keyword `interface` is used, as in the following example:

```
interface Buyable {
}
```

The interface can then be implemented by classes.

8.1.3   Abstract Methods in Interfaces

The most important elements in interfaces are abstract methods. In an abstract class, an abstract method has no implementation but declares only the head of a method with modifiers; the return type; and the signature but without body). Thus, only one rule is declared, while the implementation of an object method is done subsequently by a class.[1]

Let's say certain things need be "buyable" in a game; they have a price. A `Buyable` interface is supposed to prescribe the `price()` method to all classes.

```
interface Buyable {
  double price();
}
```

Listing 8.1 src/main/java/com/tutego/insel/game/i/v1/Buyable.java, Buyable

As object methods in interfaces are abstract and public by default, the `abstract` and `public` modifiers are redundant and can be omitted. The operations declared by the

---

1 Or a lambda expression, but more on that topic later in Chapter 13.

interfaces are terminated with a semicolon, as with abstract methods. Implementation is possible, as we'll discuss later in Section 8.1.14.

> **Note**
>
> The name of an interface often ends in -ble (i.e., Accessible, Adjustable, or Runnable). The name doesn't usually start with a prefix like "I," although the Eclipse developers use this naming convention, which is also common in .NET.

8.1.4 Implementing Interfaces

If a class wants to use an interface, the implements keyword follows the class name which in turn is followed by the name of the interface. The expression then is: "Classes are inherited, and interfaces are implemented."

Let's say a player can buy a bike for his trip. Bikes are buyable and should implement the Buyable interface, as shown in Figure 8.1. Each bike should always have a unit price of 199.

```java
public class Bike implements Buyable {
  @Override public double price() {
    return 199;
  }
}
```

Listing 8.2 src/main/java/com/tutego/insel/game/i/v1/Bike.java, Bike

The @Override annotation again indicates an overridden method (in this case, the implemented method of an interface).

> **Note**
>
> If the operations declared in interfaces are public, the implemented methods in the classes must also always be public. protected isn't allowed as visibility. And private interface methods are not visible in implementing classes anyway.

Bike is a class that has no explicit superclass, so Object extends it. Thus, no problem arises if a class extends another class and additionally implements an interface.

In the following example, a visit to a museum is an event that is buyable:

```java
class MuseumVisit extends Event implements Buyable {
  int price;
  MuseumVisit( int price ) { this.price = price; }
```

```
@Override public double price() {
  return price;
}
}
```

Listing 8.3 src/main/java/com/tutego/insel/game/i/v1/MuseumVisit.java, MuseumVisit

So, as desired in our case, the class extends another class and additionally implements operations from an interface. A little hint: For the examples we use a simplified version of the Event class: `abstract class Event {}`.

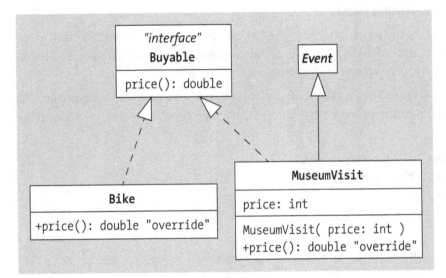

Figure 8.1 UML Diagram of the Buyable Interface and the Bike and MuseumVisit Implementations

The following type relationships now apply, which can also be tested with `instanceof`:

- Event is an Event.
- Event is an Object.
- MuseumVisit is a MuseumVisit.
- MuseumVisit is an Event.
- MuseumVisit is an Object.
- MuseumVisit is a Buyable.
- Bike is a Bike.
- Bike is a Buyable.
- Bike is an Object.

If a method requires an object of a certain type, many options are available.

Method Requires Type	Is a Valid Argument Type
Object	Object, Event, MuseumVisit, Bike, Buyable
Event	Event, MuseumVisit
Buyable	Buyable, Bike, MuseumVisit
Bike	Bike
MuseumVisit	MuseumVisit

Table 8.1 What Methods Can Get When They Require Certain Types

To summarize, when a specific type like Bike or MuseumVisit is required, we have a few options. With base types, usually several variants exist—if you want a little, you can get a lot.

If a class doesn't implement all operations from the interfaces, it thus inherits abstract methods and must itself be marked as abstract again.

IntelliJ displays the type hierarchy when you press Ctrl + H .

8.1.5 A Polymorphism Example with Interfaces

Although interfaces don't "do" anything at first glance; programmers like to inherit something so they can save implementation work. Interfaces are enormously important inventions. Interfaces can be used to describe vastly different views of an object. Each interface enables a new view of the object, a kind of role. If a class implements diverse interfaces, its instances can appear in different roles. In this case, again the substitution principle becomes important, for example, where a powerful object is used as an argument of a method. However, depending on the context, the parameter type of a method may be only the small interface.

With Bike or MuseumVisit, you have two classes that implement Buyable. Thus, two classes exist that have a common type and a common price() method.

```
Buyable hercules = new Bike();
Buyable binarium = new MuseumVisit( 8 );
System.out.println( hercules.price() );  // 199.0
System.out.println( binarium.price() );  // 8.0
```

Listing 8.4 src/main/java/com/tutego/insel/game/i/v1/Application.java, main

For Buyable, let's write a static method calculateSum(...) that calculates the price of a collection of objects available for purchase. To allow calculateSum(...) to take any number of arguments, but at least one, you can implement the method via a vararg.

```
class PriceUtils {

  static double calculateSum( Buyable first, Buyable... more ) {
    double result = first.price();

    for ( Buyable buyable : more )
      result += buyable.price();

    return result;
  }
}
```

Listing 8.5 src/main/java/com/tutego/insel/game/i/v1/PriceUtils.java, PriceUtils

This method assumes some things are buyable, not caring what exactly the Buyable types are. What matters is the fact that the elements implement the Buyable interface.

The dynamic binding occurs in the first expression, first.price(). Also, later we're calling the price() method on each object that implements Buyable. By totaling the different values, you can calculate the total price of the elements from the parameter list. This method can be called in the following way:

```
Bike hercules = new Bike();
MuseumVisit binarium = new MuseumVisit( 8 );
Buyable winora = new Bike();
Buyable mimomenta = new MuseumVisit( 12 );
double sum = PriceUtils.calculateSum( hercules, binarium, winora, mimomenta );
System.out.println( sum );      // 418.0
```

Listing 8.6 src/main/java/com/tutego/insel/game/i/v1/PriceUtilsDemo.java, main

[+]

Tip

As mentioned earlier, the type of a variable should always be the smallest necessary type. Interfaces as variable types aren't excluded. Developers who declare all their variables to be of an interface type apply the concept of *programming against interfaces*. Thus, they don't bind to a specific implementation, but to a base type.

In summary, in the context of interfaces, pure dynamic binding for method calls is possible.

8.1.6 Multiple Inheritance with Interfaces

A class can't have more than one base class, regardless of whether the former is abstract or not. The reason is that multiple inheritance can lead to a problem: that a class inherits the same method from two superclasses and then doesn't know which method to include. The situation is different for interfaces; a class can implement any number of interfaces because no code comes from an interface—only a rule for implementation. In the worst case, the rule for implementing an operation exists several times.

> **Terminology** [«]
>
> When some developers say Java has multiple inheritance and others say Java doesn't have multiple inheritance, both parties are right. In *class inheritance*, also called *implementation inheritance*, no two superclasses are allowed. In *interface inheritance*, a class may very well have multiple base types. Typically, the term *multiple inheritance* isn't used in Java because it traditionally refers to class inheritance.

Let's write a new class named Flight, defined in the following way:

1. The class represents an event, so Flight can be a subclass of Event.

2. Flights are buyable, the class can implement the interface Buyable and thus the method price().

3. You need to compare the airfare of a flight with the airfares of other flights. A suitable interface for this task already exists in the Java library: java.lang.Comparable. The Comparable interface requires our Flight to implement the int compareTo(Flight) method. The return value of the method shows how one fare relates to the other fare. We'll define that the cheaper flight is placed "before" a more expensive one. In programming terms, if our own flight is "smaller" than the other, compareTo(...) returns a negative result. If our flight is "bigger," that is, more expensive, compareTo(...) returns a positive result; otherwise, the return value is 0. We'll define the Double.compare(double, double) method to achieve this task. (Actually, together with the Comparable method we should also override equals(...) and hashCode() from Object, but our current example omits this part.[2])

The resulting implementation should appear as follows:

```
class Flight extends Event implements Buyable, Comparable<Flight> {
  final double ticketPrice;

  Flight( int ticketPrice ) { this.ticketPrice = ticketPrice; }
```

---

2 If compareTo(...) returns 0 for two equal objects, equals(...) should also return true. But if equals(...) isn't overridden, the method implemented in Object only performs a reference comparison. Thus, for two objects that are basically the same, the default implementation equals(...) would return false. The same is true for hashCode(): Two equal objects must also have the same hash value.

```
@Override public double price() {
  return ticketPrice;
}

@Override public int compareTo( Flight other ) {
  return Double.compare( ticketPrice, other.ticketPrice );
}
}
```

Listing 8.7 src/main/java/com/tutego/insel/game/i/v1/Flight.java, Flight

This implementation uses generics with Comparable<Magazine>, which you'll learn about in more detail in Chapter 12, Section 12.1.6, but let's use them now. In the background, Comparable now knows exactly with which other type the comparison should take place.

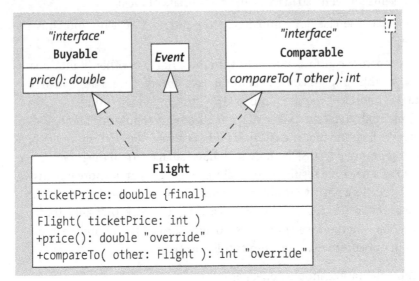

Figure 8.2 The Flight Class with Various Supertypes

This "multiple inheritance" provides Flight with entirely different types, as tested in the following example:

```
Flight londonToDurban = new Flight( 1200 );
System.out.println( londonToDurban instanceof Flight );     // true
System.out.println( londonToDurban instanceof Event );      // true
System.out.println( londonToDurban instanceof Object );     // true
System.out.println( londonToDurban instanceof Buyable );    // true
System.out.println( londonToDurban instanceof Comparable ); // true
```

Listing 8.8 src/main/java/com/tutego/insel/game/i/v1/FlightDemo.java, main()

490

Our Flight can now be passed exactly where a Flight, Event, Object, Buyable (PriceUtils.calculateSum(...)), or Comparable is required.

Thus, Comparable enables you to compare two flights in the following way:

```
Flight londonToDurban    = new Flight( 1200 );
Flight dortmundToBrussels = new Flight( 200 );
System.out.println( londonToDurban.compareTo( londonToDurban ) );         // 0
System.out.println( londonToDurban.compareTo( dortmundToBrussels ) );   // 1
System.out.println( dortmundToBrussels.compareTo( londonToDurban ) );   //-1
System.out.println( dortmundToBrussels.compareTo( dortmundToBrussels ) );// 0
```

Listing 8.9 src/main/java/com/tutego/insel/game/i/v1/FlightComparison.java, main()

Just as the calculateSum(...) method doesn't care what Buyable objects are specifically passed, which enables sorting, a particularly useful use case for Comparable. A sorting method doesn't care what exactly objects it must sort, as long as the objects say whether they are located before or after another object. Consider the following example:

```
Flight londonToDurban      = new Flight( 1200 );
Flight dortmundToBrussels   = new Flight( 200 );
Flight berlinToNairobi      = new Flight( 1500 );
Flight duesseldorfToWindhoek = new Flight( 1400 );
Flight[] flights = {
  londonToDurban, dortmundToBrussels, berlinToNairobi, duesseldorfToWindhoek
};
Arrays.sort( flights );
for ( Flight flight : flights )
  System.out.print( (int) flight.price() + " "); // 200 1200 1400 1500
```

Listing 8.10 src/main/java/com/tutego/insel/game/i/v1/FlightComparison.java, main()

The static method Arrays.sort(...) expects an array whose elements are Comparable. The sorting algorithm makes comparisons via compareTo(...) but doesn't need to know anything else about the objects.

Our flights with the types Flight, Event, Object, Buyable, and Comparable can therefore be used flexibly in different contexts. Thus, you don't need to write a special sorting method that can only sort flights or a method for calculating a total that works only on flights. Instead, you can model different application scenarios, each with different interfaces that expect different things from the object.

8.1.7 No Risk of Collision with Multiple Inheritance*

With the multiple inheritance of classes, the danger arises that two superclasses might inherit the same method with two different implementations to their subclasses. The subclass would then not know which logic it inherits, and thus, special syntax would be needed in Java to resolve this dilemma. The designers of the Java language didn't want to enable multiple inheritance.

The problem doesn't exist with interfaces because, even if two implementing interfaces were to prescribe the same operation, two different implementations of application logic wouldn't exist. The implementing class gets the request to realize the operation twice, so to speak. Let's say a politician must combine two different things: he must be likeable, but he must also act assertively. You could model this logic in the following way:

```java
interface Likeable {
  void act();
}

interface Assertive {
  void act();
}

public class Politician implements Likeable, Assertive {
  @Override public void act() {
    // Implementation
  }
}
```

Listing 8.11 src/main/java/com/tutego/insel/oop/Politician.java

Two interfaces prescribe the same operation. A class implements these two interfaces and must satisfy both specifications, as shown in Figure 8.3.

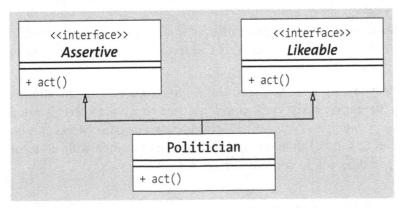

Figure 8.3 A Class Inheriting the Same Operation from Two Interfaces

[«]

> **Note**
>
> A return type isn't part of the signature of a method in Java. If a class implements two
> interfaces and the signatures of the operations from the interfaces are the same, the
> return types must also be the same. Problems in implementation arise if the signatures
> of the methods from the interfaces are the same (i.e., same method name and same
> parameter list), but the return types aren't type-compatible. The reason is simple: A
> class can't implement two methods with the same signature but different return
> types. If `Assertive` had a `boolean act()`, `Politician` would then have to implement
> `void act()` and `boolean act()` at the same time, which isn't possible.

8

8.1.8 Extending Interfaces: Subinterfaces

A *subinterface* is an extension of another interface. As is the case with inheritance, this
extension is created via the `extends` keyword. Consider the following example, which
evaluates the how smelly something is:

```
interface Disgusting {
  double disgustingValue();
}

interface Stinky extends Disgusting {
  double olf();
}
```

The interface models smells that are particularly repulsive. In addition, the stinky
source should indicate the strength of stinkiness in units of "olf." A class that now
implements `Stinky` must implement the abstract methods from both interfaces—thus
the `disgustingValue()` method from `Disgusting` as well as the operation `olf()` specified
in `Stinky` itself. Without implementing both methods, an implementing class will have
to be abstract.

[+]

> **Tip**
>
> A subinterface can "override" an operation of the super-interface. While at first glance,
> this overriding feature doesn't make much sense, two purposes are served:
>
> - In the subinterface, the application programming interface (API) documentation
>   can be specified.[3]
> - Because of covariant returns, an operation in the subinterface can receive a more
>   special return type.

---

3 Refer to `java.util.Collection` and `java.util.Set`.

8.1.9   Constant Declarations for Interfaces

Interfaces can't have object variables and consequently can't store states, but they may declare named constants.

[Ex]

> **Example**
>
> Let's say our Buyable interface needs to declare a constant for a maximum price. You could write the following code:
>
> ```
> interface Buyable {
>   /* public static final */ int MAX_PRICE = 10_000_000;
>   double price();
> }
> ```

All class variables of an interface (object variables don't exist in the interface) are always implicitly public static final. This scenario prevents the variable from being reassigned. You can still set these three modifiers, but since these modifiers are already implied, you should omit them. Other modifiers aren't allowed anyway.

While the class variable may be final, this keyword doesn't prevent object manipulation. Manipulation is possible because, even if the variables themselves don't allow any change after initialization, mutably referenced objects may later change.

[Ex]

> **Example and Tip**
>
> In the following example, the Volcano interface references a mutable StringBuilder object:
>
> ```
> interface Volcano {
>   StringBuilder EYJAFJALLAJÖKULL = new StringBuilder( "Eyjafjallajökull" );
> }
> ```
>
> Since EYJAFJALLAJÖKULL is a public StringBuilder variable and since StringBuilder is a mutable container, a statement like Volcano.EYJAFJALLAJÖKULL.replace(0, Volcano.EYJAFJALLAJÖKULL.length(), "Vesuvius"); modifies the contents, which absolutely contradicts the idea of a constant. A better approach is to always reference immutable objects, such as strings. Arrays in which elements can be exchanged are problematic as well are all mutable objects such as StringBuilder or ArrayList.

8.1.10   Subsequent Implementation of Interfaces*

If a class doesn't implement a particular interface, it can't participate in dynamic binding through that interface, even if the class has a method through which an interface abstracts. For example, if the non-final class FIFA has a public method price(), but doesn't implement Buyable with a method of the same name, you would use a trick. By creating a new class, you can bring in an existing method from the class and bring in the method from the interface into the type hierarchy, as in the following example:

```
class FIFA {
  public double price() { … }
}

interface Buyable {
  double price();
}

class FIFAisBuyable extends FIFA implements Buyable { }
```

A new FIFAisBuyable subclass inherits from the FIFA class and implements the Buyable interface, so that the compiler unifies the existing price() method with default interface. Now, FIFAisBuyable can be used as Buyable and behind it is the implementation of FIFA. As a subclass, all visible members of the superclass are also retained. However, this solution doesn't us if a FIFA object is received from elsewhere.

8.1.11 Static Programmed Methods in Interfaces

As a rule, an interface declares operations (i.e., abstract object methods), which a class must implement later. The interface method implemented in a class can be overridden again later, so it participates in dynamic binding in a normal manner. The interface can't declare an object state because object variables are taboo in interfaces—every declared variable is automatically static (i.e., a class variable).

Static methods are allowed in interfaces and can be placed next to constants as utility methods. Thus, you can write static class methods and static interface methods; neither would be dynamically bound.

Example [Ex]

In Section 8.1.2, we declared a Buyable interface. The idea behind this interface is that anything that can be bought implements this interface and has a price. Additionally, a constant exists to codify a maximum price. Consider the following example:

```
interface Buyable {
  int MAX_PRICE = 10_000_000;
  double price();
}
```

A static isValidPrice(double) method can now be added to check whether a purchase price is within the valid range, as shown in the following example:

```
interface Buyable {
  int MAX_PRICE = 10_000_000;
```

```
  static boolean isValidPrice( double price ) {
    return price >= 0 && price < MAX_PRICE;
  }
  double price();
}
```

The `Buyable.isValidPrice(123)` call is then possible from the outside.

All declared members are `public` by default but can also be private. Implicitly, constants are always static. Static methods must carry the `static` modifier; otherwise, they are considered abstract methods.

[»]

Note

Static interface methods enable a new way of declaring the `main(...)` method:

```
interface HelloWorldInInterfaces {
  static void main( String[] args ) {
    System.out.println( "A different Hello World!" );
  }
}
```

The `interface` keyword is four characters longer than `class` but saving `public` and a separator results in a shortening of three characters—again, a new way to haggle over length.

Access to a static interface method is possible only through the name of the interface, or the members can be imported statically. For static methods of classes, access by reference is basically allowed too (although undesirable), such as via `new Integer(12).MAX_VALUE`. However, you cannot use this approach with the static methods of interfaces. For example, if `Car` implements the `Buyable` interface, `new Car().isValidPrice(123)` would result in a compiler error. Even `Car.isValidPrice(123)` is false, which is a bit surprising since static methods are usually inherited.

Let's summarize the allowed members of an interface:

	Variable	Method
Object	No, not allowed	Yes, usually abstract
Class	Yes, as a constant	Yes, always with implementation

Table 8.2 Allowed Members of an Interface

Interface methods can have implementations, so they don't have to be abstract.

> **Design**
>
> An interface with only static methods is an indication of a design problem and should be replaced by a final class with a private constructor. Interfaces are always intended as specifications for implementation. If only static methods occur in an interface, the interface doesn't fulfill its purpose of providing specifications that can be implemented differently.

8.1.12 Extending and Modifying Interfaces

Once interfaces have been declared and spread across a large application, changes are difficult to make because they quickly break compatibility. Changing the name of a parameter variable is not a problem. But if an interface gets a new operation, then a compiler error will arise if not all implementing classes implement this new method. So, framework developers are careful about how they modify interfaces, and they are in control of how far compatibility is broken.

> **History Lesson**
>
> Changing interfaces subsequently (i.e., when many classes already implement the interface) is a bad idea. If the interface renews itself, for example, if only one operation is added or a parameter type changes, then suddenly all implementing classes are broken. Sun itself risked this fragility with the `java.sql.Connection` interface. During the transition from Java 5 to Java 6, the interface was extended, and no driver implementations could be compiled anymore.

Code Compatibility and Binary Compatibility*

If you insert a constant (`public static final` variable) in an interface or change the name of a parameter, for the implementing classes, no compiler error will arise. In this case, these changes are *code compatible*.

If you add a new operation to an interface, however, a compiler error for all implementing classes will immediately arise. However, if you were to just recompile the interface into bytecode, the code will operate just fine at runtime because, if an interface gets a new method, no problem arises for the JVM at all. The JVM works on the class files themselves and doesn't care if a class dutifully implements all the methods of the interface; it only resolves method references. If an interface suddenly dictates "more," the JVM has no problem with that.

So, while almost all interface changes lead to compiler errors, some changes are fine for the JVM. We refer to this compatibility as *binary compatibility*. For example, if the interface is modified, recompiled, and placed in the module path, the following tasks are fine:

- Adding new methods in the interface
- Having the interface inherit from an additional interface
- Adding or deleting a throws exception
- Changing the last parameter type from T[] to T...
- Adding new constants (i.e., static variables)

However, some changes aren't binary compatible and will result in a JVM error, such as the following:

- Changing the method name
- Changing parameter types and reordering the parameters
- Adding or removing a formal parameter

Strategies for Changing Interfaces

When an interface hasn't been widely used, changes are easier to make. For example, if the name of an operation is poorly chosen, refactoring in the integrated development environment (IDE) will change the name in the interface as well as any identifiers in the implementing classes. What's more problematic is when external users rely on the interface. Then, clients also must make adjustments, or developers simply must make do without "cosmetic changes" like changing the method name.

If operations are added, a convention has been established that is often encountered in the Java universe: If an interface is to be extended by operations, a new interface comes into being that extends the old one and whose name ends in "2." Thus, java.awt.LayoutManager2 is an example from the area of graphical interfaces, and Attributes2, EntityResolver2, and Locator2 are examples in XML processing.[4]

Default methods are another way to extend interfaces at a later time. These methods extend an interface but bring with them ready-made implementations so that subclasses don't necessarily have to provide an implementation. Let's look at how to use default methods next.

8.1.13 Default Methods

After an interface has been propagated, you should still be able to add operations. Developers should be allowed to introduce new operations without requiring subclasses to implement these methods. For this to be possible, the interface must have a

---

4 A look at the API of the Eclipse framework shows that this pattern has been applied dozens of times (*http://help.eclipse.org/oxygen/topic/org.eclipse.platform.doc.isv/reference/api/index.html?overviewsummary*).

default implementation. In this way, the problem of "mandatory implementation" is solved because, if an implementation already exists, the implementing classes have nothing to complain about and can override the default behavior if needed. Oracle calls these methods *default methods* in interfaces with predefined implementations.[5] Interfaces with default methods are called *extended interfaces*.

As far as the syntax is concerned, a default method differs from the conventional implicitly abstract method declaration in two aspects:

- The declaration of a default method starts with the `default` keyword.[6]
- Instead of a semicolon, a block with the implementation in curly brackets marks the end of the declaration for a default method. We call the implementation of the default method the *default code*.

Apart from these differences, extended interfaces behave like normal interfaces. A class that implements an interface inherits all operations, whether abstract methods or default methods. If the class should be non-abstract, it must implement all abstract methods inherited from the interface. A class can override the default methods but doesn't have to because a pre-implementation is already given in the default method of the interface.

Note

Extended interfaces put "code" into an interface, but this insertion was also possible previously, for example, by having an implicit public and static variable reference an implementation, as in the following example:

```
interface Comparators {
  Comparator<String> TRIM_COMPARATOR = new Comparator<String>() {
    @Override public int compare( String s1, String s2 ) {
      return s1.trim().compareTo( s2.trim() );
    } };
}
```

In this case, the implementation uses an inner anonymous class, a concept that is explored in more detail in Chapter 10, Section 10.5.

---

5 The name changed several times during the planning for this feature. At the beginning, the name for this feature was "defender methods," then for a long time, "virtual extension methods."

6 Initially, `default` was supposed to be placed behind the method header, but Java's developers wanted to make `default` look like a modifier. Since modifiers are located at the beginning, `default` also moved to the front. Actually, a modifier isn't even necessary because, if you have an implementation (i.e., a code block) in {}, it's clear that that code will become a default method. But Java's developers wanted explicit documentation, just as `abstract` is used—actually, this modifier for methods wouldn't be necessary either because no code block exists when a method is abstract.

8.1.14   Declaring and Using Extended Interfaces

Let's implement all these concepts in an example. For events, a lifecycle should be made possible. Defined by start() and finish() methods, the lifecycle is provided as an interface that can be implemented by events. So, let's start with version 1 of this interface:

```java
interface EventLifecycle {
  void start();
  void finish();
}
```

Listing 8.12 src/main/java/com/tutego/insel/game/i/v2/EventLifecycle.java, EventLifecycle

The Event class implements the interface when written in the following way:

```java
abstract class Event implements EventLifecycle {
  String about;
  int duration;

  abstract void process();

  @Override public void start() { }
  @Override public void finish() { }
}
```

Listing 8.13 src/main/java/com/tutego/insel/game/i/v2/EventLifecycle.java, EventLifecycle

The class overwrites the two methods empty so the Event subclasses like Nap or Workout are free to decide whether to override the empty methods again or not.

A subclass can then be quickly written in the following way:

```java
class Nap extends Event {
  @Override void process() {
    System.out.println( "Yaaaawn" );
  }
}
```

Listing 8.14 src/main/java/com/tutego/insel/game/i/v2/Nap.java, Nap

The longer the software lives, the more design mistakes come to the fore. Converting an entire architecture is a mammoth task, although simple changes like renaming can be quickly accomplished via refactoring. Let's assume that we receive a change request for our interface because merely reporting the start and end doesn't suffice. To enable pausing an event, a new method should be added to the interface: pause(). What are the consequences of the new pause() method in EventLifecycle?

```
interface EventLifecycle {
  void start();
  void finish();
  void pause();
}
```

That would be a problem! Suddenly, an error concerning Nap would arise, and you'd see the following message:

```
Class 'Nap' must either be declared abstract or implement abstract method 'pause
()' in 'EventLifecycle'
```

Adding methods in interfaces is difficult because then all implementing classes must be changed. In this case, default methods play perfectly into our hands because you can extend the interface but pass along an empty default implementation. Thus, subclasses don't have to implement the pause() method, but they can, as version 2 of our now extended EventLifecycle interface shows:

```
interface EventLifecycle {
  void start();
  void finish();
  default void pause() {}
}
```

Classes that have already used EventLifecycle won't notice the change, which has an advantage: The interface can evolve, but everything remains binary compatible, and nothing needs to be recompiled. Existing code can draw on the new method, which is automatically present with the "empty" implementation. Furthermore, default methods behave like other methods of interfaces: Dynamic binding will continue to be kept when implementing classes override the methods. For example, if an implementation like Workout does something when you pause, Workout overrides the method and stops calorie consumption, for example. A nap, on the other hand, has nothing to pause and can live well with the default code in pause(). The procedure is somewhat comparable to normal, non-final methods: They can be overridden, but overriding them isn't necessary.

Note [«]

Instead of the empty block, the body could also include the expression throw new UnsupportedOperationException ("Not yet implemented"); to announce that no implementation exists. Thus, an added default method doesn't lead to a compiler error, but during runtime, methods that are not overridden lead to an exception. Basically, this scenario is the opposite of the default code has been achieved because no logic is executed by default—triggering an exception to report an error is not considered logic.

Context of the Default Methods

Default methods behave like methods in abstract classes and can call all methods of the interface (including inherited methods).[7] The methods are later bound dynamically at runtime.

Let's examine an interface named Buyable for buyable objects next:

```
interface Buyable {
  double price();
}
```

Unfortunately, the interface doesn't prescribe whether things are purchasable at all. A method like hasPrice() would be quite good in Buyable. But what would be the default implementation? You can resort to price() and test if the return is a valid price, which is true if the price is greater than 0. Consider the following example:

```
interface Buyable {
  double price();
  default boolean hasPrice() { return price() > 0; }
}
```

If classes implement the Buyable interface, they must implement price() because the method is not a default method. However, these subclasses are free to override has-Price(), fill it with their own logic, and thus not use the default implementation. If implementing classes don't choose a new implementation, they get the default code and inherit a concrete hasPrice() method. In that case, a call of hasPrice() gets passed internally to price() and then to the class that implements Buyable and the price() method. The calls are dynamically bound and end up with the actual implementation.

> **Note**
>
> An interface can also declare the methods of the absolute superclass java.lang.Object, for example, to add a description with Javadoc. However, you *cannot* preset methods like toString() or hashCode() using default code.

In addition to the option to draw on methods of the custom interface, the this reference is also available. The this reference is especially important because it allows the default code to delegate to utility methods and pass a reference to itself. For example, if you've already implemented a hasPrice(Buyable) method in a PriceUtils utility class, the default code could consist of simple delegation through the following code:

```
class PriceUtils {
  public static boolean hasPrice( Buyable b ) { return b.price() > 0; }
}
```

---

7 And at the same time, the well-known template design pattern can be implemented.

```
interface Buyable {
  double price();
  default boolean hasPrice() { return PriceUtils.hasPrice( this ); }
}
```

The fact that the PriceUtils.hasPrice(Buyable) method provides the Buyable type for the parameter and the default code with this refers to just such a Buyable object is of course no coincidence, but deliberately chosen. The type of the this reference at run-time corresponds to that of the class that implemented the interface and whose object instance was created.

If the default methods have additional parameters, these parameters can also be passed on to the static method, as in the following example:

```
class PriceUtils {
  public static boolean hasPrice( Buyable b ) { return b.price() > 0; }
  public static double priceOr( Buyable b, double defaultPrice ) {
    if ( b != null && b.price() > 0 )
      return b.price();
    return defaultPrice;
  }
}
interface Buyable {
  double price();
  default boolean hasPrice() { return PriceUtils.hasPrice( this ); }
  default double priceOr( double defaultPrice ) {
   return PriceUtils.priceOr( this, defaultPrice );
  }
}
```

Since interfaces can contain static utility methods with implementation, the default code can delegate to these static methods. However, you should consider whether most of the code should really be placed in an interface or whether a better choice would be to move it into a package-visible implementation. We recommend swapping out the implementation so that interfaces don't become too code heavy. If the Java Development Kit (JDK) uses default code, a static method is always available in a utility class.

8.1.15 Public and Private Interface Methods

Static and default methods don't necessarily have to be public; they can also be private. This is good because it prevents code duplication; private methods can be used to swap out parts of the program within the interface. Private methods remain in the interface and aren't inherited by the implementing classes.

8.1.16 Extended Interfaces, Multiple Inheritance, and Ambiguities*

Default methods had to be introduced to subsequently equip interfaces with new operations without significant compiler errors. The ideal situation is when new default methods are added and define default behaviors, thus avoiding compiler errors for implementing classes or errors for interfaces that extend extended interfaces.

Extended interfaces with default code normally participate in OO modeling, can be inherited and overridden, and are dynamically bound. Some special cases exist, however, that we should examine, for example, the following cases:

- A class inherits a method from a superclass but at the same time receives default code for the same method from an interface.
- A class of two extended interfaces is offered different implementations.

Let's go through some different cases.

Overriding Default Code

An interface can extend other interfaces and provide new default code. In other words, default methods can override other default methods from super-interfaces and implement them with new behaviors.

Let's introduce an interface named `Priced` with a default method, shown in the following example:

```
interface Priced {
  default boolean hasPrice() { return true; }
}
```

Another interface can override the default method, as in the following example:

```
interface NotPriced extends Priced {
  @Override default boolean hasPrice() { return false; }
}
public class TrueLove implements NotPriced {
  public static void main( String[] args ){
    System.out.println( new TrueLove().hasPrice() );         // false
  }
}
```

When the `TrueLove` class implements the `NotPriced` interface, everything is fine, and no conflict arises. The inheritance relation is linear (`TrueLove` → `NotPriced` → `Priced`).

Class Implementation Takes Precedence over Default Methods

If a class implements an interface and also inherits it from a superclass, the following can happen: The interface has default code for a method, and the superclass also inherits the same method with code. Then, the subclass gets an implementation from two sides. First, the compiler must decide whether something like this is syntactically correct at all, which is confirmed with the following code:

```java
interface Priced {
  default boolean hasPrice() { return true; }
}
class Unsaleable {
  public boolean hasPrice() { return false; }
}
public class TrueLove extends Unsaleable implements Priced {
  public static void main( String[] args ) {
    System.out.println( new TrueLove().hasPrice() );   // false
  }
}
```

TrueLove inherits the hasPrice() implementation from the Unsaleable superclass and also from the extended Priced interface. The code compiles and results in the output false, which means the class with the code "wins" against the default code. This functionality can be easily seen in the order class … extends … implements…. In this case, extends is located at the beginning, so methods from implementations have a higher priority than the methods from extended interfaces.

Addressing Default Methods from Special Super-Interfaces*

A subclass can override a concrete method of the superclass but can still access the implementation of the overridden method. However, the call must be made via super; otherwise, a method call will be called recursively.

Default methods can also override other default methods from super-interfaces and implement them with new behavior. But just like normal methods, default methods can use super to draw on a default behavior from the parent type.

For an example, let's use our well-known interface Buyable and a new extended interface PeanutsBuyable. Consider the following example:

```java
interface Buyable {
  double price();
  default boolean hasPrice() { return price() > 0; }
}
interface PeanutsBuyable extends Buyable {
  @Override default boolean hasPrice() {
    return Buyable.super.hasPrice() && price() < 50_000_000;
  }
}
```

In the `Buyable` interface, the default code of `hasPrice()` says that everything greater than 0 has a price. `PeanutsBuyable`, on the other hand, uses an extended definition and therefore reimplements the default behavior. According to the famous statement of a former Deutsche Bank CEO[8] everything priced under 50 million is "peanuts" and can be bought without any problem, causing no pain, at least for Deutsche Bank. In the implementation of `hasPrice()`, `PeanutsBuyable` resorts to the default code of `Buyable` to get a decision on the price from the supertype and becomes even more specialized with the AND operation.

Inheriting Default Code for a Method from Multiple Interfaces*

If a class from two extended interfaces is offered the same default code, a compiler error will arise. The following `RockAndRoll` class illustrates this dilemma:

```
interface Sex {
  default boolean hasPrice() { return false; }
}
interface Drugs {
  default boolean hasPrice() { return true; }
}
public class RockAndRoll implements Sex, Drugs { } // ☠ Compiler error
```

Even if both implementations were identical, the compiler would have to reject this code because the code could change at any time.

Solving the Multiple Inheritance Problem via super

The `RockAndRoll` class can't be simply translated because the class gets code from two sources. However, the problem can be easily solved by overriding the `hasPrice()` method in `RockAndRoll` and then delegating it to a method.

```
interface Sex {
  default boolean hasPrice() { return false; }
}
interface Drugs {
  default boolean hasPrice() { return true; }
}
public class RockAndRoll implements Sex, Drugs {
  @Override public boolean hasPrice() { return Sex.super.hasPrice(); }
}
```

Listing 8.15 src/main/java/com/tutego/insel/oop/RockAndRoll.java

---

8 *https://en.wikipedia.org/wiki/Hilmar_Kopper#Controversy*

In the body of the hasPrice() method, you can't simply write hasPrice() because doing so would create a recursive call. Also, you can't write Drugs.hasPrice() because this syntax is reserved for calling static methods. For this reason, super comes into play with the following new notation: Drugs.super.hasPrice(); the same is true for the interface Sex.

Abstract Overridden Interface Operations Take Away Default Methods

Default methods have the interesting language feature in that subtypes can change the status from "has implementation" to "has no default implementation." Consider the following example:

```
interface Priced {
  default boolean hasPrice() { return false; }
}
interface Buyable extends Priced {
  @Override boolean hasPrice();
}
```

The Priced interface provides a default method. Buyable extends the Priced interface but overwrites the method—but not with code! This approach makes the hasPrice() method abstract again in Buyable. Thus, an abstract method may well override a default method. In this case, classes that implement Buyable still need to implement a has-Price() method if they don't want to be abstract themselves. An interesting Java feature is that the implementation of a default method in a subtype can be "taken away" again. This change isn't possible with visibility, for example: Once a method is public, a subclass can't restrict its visibility.

With default methods, the behavior of the compiler has a great advantage: Certain changes to the super-interface are allowed and have no effect on the subtypes. Let's assume that hasPrice() didn't exist previously in Priced, but only abstractly in Buyable. Default code is merely a nice gesture, after all, and should be easily integrated it into Priced without any problem. In other words, developers can include such a default method in the base type without a problem and without causing errors in the subtypes. Supertypes can therefore be changed without touching the lower subtypes. However, the annotation @Override can subsequently be set to the subinterface for documentation purposes.

Not only can a subinterface "take away" the default methods, but an abstract can also take away default methods, as in the following example:

```
abstract class Food implements Priced {
  @Override public abstract double price();
}
```

The Priced interface brings a default method, but the abstract Food class takes it away again, so extending Food classes must implement price() in any case if they don't want to be abstract themselves.

8.1.17   Creating Building Blocks with Default Methods*

Default methods provide library designers with an entire new set of options. Currently, we're not sure what Java's developers will do with default methods and which direction the Java API will take. In any case, the question will arise as to whether a default implementation moves into an interface as default code or, as before, a default implementation is provided as an abstract class from which, in turn, other classes derive. As an example, let's consider data structures: A Collection interface prescribes a default behavior, AbstractCollection, which specifies an implementation as much as possible, and subclasses like ArrayList then again build on top of this base implementation. Extended interfaces can reduce hierarchies because an abstract base implementation can be dispensed with. On the other hand, an abstract class can introduce states via object variables, which is something an interface can't do.

Default methods can do something else as well—serve as building blocks for classes. A class can implement multiple interfaces with default methods and thus basically inherits basic functionality from different places. In other programming languages, this feature is known as *mixin* or *trait*. This approach is different from multiple inheritance, which isn't allowed in Java. Let's take a closer look at this difference now.

Using Default Methods for Developing Traits

What is the core concept of object-oriented programming (OOP)? Without hesitation, you might answer with classes, encapsulation, and abstraction. Classes and class relationships are the framework of any Java program. In the context of inheritance, subclasses are specializations, and the Liskov substitution principle applies (see Chapter 7, Section 7.3.2). Thus, if a type is required, you can also pass a subtype. With perfect inheritance, a subclass specializes in behavior but doesn't inherit from a class simply because it has useful functionality. But why not, actually? The first thing to note is that inheritance often violates the is-a-kind-of relationship because of its usefulness. Second, Java only allows single inheritance with only a single superclass. If a class provides something useful like logging and our class inherits from it, it can't simultaneously inherit from another class, for example, to record states in configuration data. An unfortunate inheritance thus obstructs a later extension. So, the problem with "functionality inheritance" is that we can only commit once.

If a class simply needs a certain functionality, where should that functionality come from if not from the superclass? Actually, only one variant is obvious in this case: The class can access other objects by means of delegation. If a point with color shouldn't inherit from java.awt.Point, a color point can simply reference a point in an internal variable. This is a solution, but then not ideal if there is an is-a-kind-of relationship. And interfaces were specifically introduced so that a class has multiple types. Abstractions over interfaces and superclasses are important, and delegation doesn't help in this case. What we need is a technique to put a program block into a class—basically something like multiple inheritance, but different because the blocks don't appear as complete types; the block itself is only an implant and not interesting on its own. What is more, an object can't be created by this block type.

The closest thing to these building blocks are abstract classes, which would be classes, and thus, users could only inherit from that building block once. Extended interfaces enable completely new options: They form the building blocks from which classes can access additional functionality.[9] These building blocks are useful because they allow an algorithm to be put into an extra compilation unit and reused more easily. For example, let's assume you have two extended interfaces: PersistentPreference and Logged. The first extended interface is supposed to write key-value pairs to the central configuration using store(), while get() should read these pairs, as in the following example:

```
import java.util.prefs.Preferences;
interface PersistentPreference {
  default void store( String key, String value ) {
    Preferences.userRoot().put( key, value );
  }
  default String get( String key ) {
    return Preferences.userRoot().get( key, "" );
  }
}
```

The second extended interface is Logged, which provides with the following three compact logger methods:

```
import java.util.logging.*;
interface Logged {
  default void error( String message ) {
    Logger.getLogger( getClass().getName() ).log( Level.SEVERE, message );
  }
  default void warn( String message ) {
    Logger.getLogger( getClass().getName() ).log( Level.WARNING, message );
  }
  default void info( String message ) {
    Logger.getLogger( getClass().getName() ).log( Level.INFO, message );
  }
}
```

9 See, for instance, *http://scg.unibe.ch/archive/papers/Scha02aTraitsPlusGlue2002.pdf.*

A class can now incorporate these building blocks in the following way:

```
class Player implements PersistentPreference, Logged {
  // …
}
```

The methods are now part of Player and can also be overridden by subclasses. Our next task is to change the implementation of store() in Player so that the key always starts with player. The question you should answer is whether store() from Player can access the store() from the extended interface.

State in the Building Blocks?

Not every desirable module is possible with extended interfaces. One reason is that the interfaces can't introduce a state. For example, let's take a container as a data structure that stores and manages elements. You can't easily implement a block for a container because a container manages children, which requires an object variable for the state. Interfaces have only static variables, which are visible to everybody. Even if the interface referenced a modifiable data structure, every user of the container module would be affected by these changes. Since no state is available, no constructors for interfaces can be used, and consequently no constructors exist for such blocks. Where there is no state, there is nothing to initialize. If a default method needs a state, that method must request that state by itself. A technique that Java Language Architect at Oracle Brian Goetz calls a "virtual field pattern"[10] can be used in this case, which we'll explore in the following example.

If a container references a set of objects that are sortable, you can implement a Sortable block with a sort() method. The Comparable interface is not supposed to implement the class directly because only the referenced elements are sortable, but not objects of the class itself. Furthermore, a new sort() method is to be added to Sortable. For sorting to succeed, the implementation must somehow get to the data, which is where a trick comes into play: Although sort() is a default method, the extended interface Sortable has an abstract getValues() method that must be implemented by the class and that passes the data to the sorter. In the source code, the following code would be used:

```
import java.util.*;
interface Sortable<T extends Comparable<?>> {
  T[] getValues();
  void setValues( T[] values );
  default void sort() {
    T[] values = getValues();
    Arrays.sort( values );
```

---

10 *https://mail.openjdk.java.net/pipermail/lambda-dev/2012-July/005171.html*

```
    setValues( values );
  }
}
```

Listing 8.16 src/main/java/com/tutego/insel/oop/SortableDemo.java (Part 1)

To summarize, for sort() to access the data, Sortable expects a getValues() method from the implementing classes, and for the data to be written back after sorting, it expects a second method: setValues(...). The trick is that the later implementation of Sortable with the two methods provides the sorter access to the data, but also includes access to any other piece of code since the methods are public. This perhaps unintentionally leaves a "bad taste."

Let's say RandomValues is supposed to be one user of Sortable; this class internally generates random numbers.

```
class RandomValues implements Sortable<Integer> {
  private final List<Integer> values = new ArrayList<>();
  public RandomValues() {
    Random r = new Random();
    for ( int i = r.nextInt( 20 ) + 1; i > 0; i-- )
      values.add( r.nextInt(10000) );
  }
  @Override public Integer[] getValues() {
    return values.toArray( new Integer[values.size()] );
  }

  @Override public void setValues( Integer[] values ) {
    this.values.clear();
    Collections.addAll( this.values, values );
  }
}
```

Listing 8.17 src/main/java/com/tutego/insel/oop/SortableDemo.java (Part 2)

The previous part prepared the types, and the last part of the demo concludes with the following example code:

```
public class SortableDemo {
  public static void main( String[] args ) {
    RandomValues r = new RandomValues();
    System.out.println( Arrays.toString( r.getValues() ) );
    r.sort();
    System.out.println( Arrays.toString( r.getValues() ) );
  }
}
```

Listing 8.18 src/main/java/com/tutego/insel/oop/SortableDemo.java (Part 3)

When the demo program is called, the console displays the following example output:

```
[2732, 4568, 4708, 4302, 4315, 5946, 2004]
[2004, 2732, 4302, 4315, 4568, 4708, 5946]
```

As interesting as this option is, one problem has already been addressed: Each method in an interface is either `public` or `private`. What would be nice is if the data access method was `protected` and thus only visible to the implementing class, but that doesn't work.

Summary

What we did in the last few examples of building blocks was to include a default behavior in classes without requiring access to the base class, which exists only once, and without the class delegating to helper classes. In this way of working, subclasses can override and specialize methods in any case. Thus, you're dealing with common classes and with extended interfaces that don't form independent entities themselves. In practice, some cases will exist where either an abstract class or an extended interface comes into question for an implementation of a problem.

You should then remember the differences between abstract classes and interfaces once again: An abstract class can have object variables and methods of all visibilities and also set them final so that they can no longer be overridden. An interface, on the other hand, is designed with no state and only contain purely virtual and public methods to allow the implementation to be overridden.

8.1.18   Marker Interfaces*

Interfaces without methods are also possible, and these empty interfaces are referred to as *marker interfaces*. They're useful because you can easily use `instanceof` to check whether an object takes an intended type.

The Java library already contains some marker interfaces, such as following:

- `java.util.RandomAccess`: A data structure provides quick access via an index.
- `java.rmi.Remote`: Identifies interfaces whose operations can be called from the outside.
- `java.lang.Cloneable`: Ensures that the `clone()` method of `Object` can be called.
- `java.util.EventListener`: This type is implemented by many listeners in the Java library.
- `java.io.Serializable`: States of an object can be written to a data stream (more on this topic will follow in Chapter 19).

[»]   **Note**

Since annotations were made a tool of the language, marker interfaces are not generally encountered in new libraries.

8.1.19   (Abstract) Classes and Interfaces in Comparison

An abstract class and an interface with abstract methods are similar: Both prescribe operations to their subclasses or the classes that must be implemented. However, one important difference is that any number of interfaces can be implemented, but only one class—whether abstract or not—can be extended. Furthermore, abstract classes are usually useful for refactoring or during the design phase, when commonalities can be easily swapped out to a superclass. Abstract classes can also contain object states, but interfaces can't.

During design, the basic idea for interfaces still applies: When regulating behavior, an interface is golden. For basic implementations, abstract classes come into play, often ending in Abstract in the Java library.

Binding How, Where, and What Dynamically

Where the call "ends up" is different depending on whether the method is included in a concrete class, an abstract class, and an interface. Let's explore this topic with the following method:

```
void fun( T t ) {
  t.m();
}
```

If the method requests an argument of type T and calls the method m() on the parameter variable t, the following statements are true:

- If T is a final class, the method m() of T is always called since there can be no subclasses that override m().
- If T is a non-final class and m() is a final method, exactly m() is called because no subclass can override m().
- If T is a non-final class and m() is not a final method, subclasses of T could override m(), and t.m() would then dynamically call the overridden method.
- If T is an abstract class and m() is an abstract method, a subclass implementation of m() is called in each case.
- If T is an interface and m() is not a default implementation, an implementation m() of an implementing class is called in any case.
- If T is an interface and m() is a default implementation, t.m() may end up with the default implementation or with an overridden version of an implementing class.

8.2   Enumeration Types

Each enumeration type inherits from the special class Enum. For this next example, let's define some countries:

```
public enum Country {
  GERMANY, UK, CHINA
}
```

Listing 8.19 src/main/java/com/tutego/insel/enums/v1/Country.java (Snippet)

The compiler translates this code into an enumeration class that resembles the following code:

```
public class Country extends Enum {

  public static final Country GERMANY = new Country( "GERMANY", 0 );
  public static final Country UK      = new Country( "UK",      1 );
  // other constants...

  private Country( String s, int i ) {
    super( s, i );
  }

  // other methods...
}
```

8.2.1   Methods on Enum Objects

Each enumeration element is an object that automatically has some default methods coming from the superclass `java.lang.Enum`. On one hand, these default methods overwrite the methods from `java.lang.Object`. On the other hand, some new object methods and some static methods are also added, as shown in Figure 8.4.

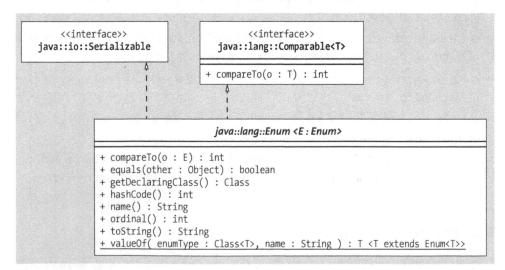

Figure 8.4 Type Relationship of Enum

String Representation

The name of the constant is returned by the `name()` method, which is joined by the familiar `toString()` method, which calls `name()` by default but can be overridden. The `name()` method can't be overridden. Consider the following example:

```
System.out.println( Country.GERMANY.toString() );          // GERMANY
System.out.println( Country.GERMANY.name() );              // GERMANY
```

Listing 8.20 src/main/java/com/tutego/insel/enums/v1/CountyDemo.java (Snippet)

From the Enumeration Element Name to the Enum Object

The enumeration class generated by the compiler provides a static `valueOf(String)` method that returns the enumeration element matching the `name()` representation. If `valueOf(String)` receives a string for which no enumeration element exists, an `IllegalArgumentException` will follow. In addition, another static method, `Enum.valueOf(Class<T> enumType, String name)`, originates from the `Enum` superclass.

The following example illustrates the conversion of a string to its corresponding `Enum` object:

```
Country germany1 = Country.valueOf( "GERMANY" );
Country germany2 = Enum.valueOf( Country.class, "GERMANY" );
System.out.println( germany1 );    // GERMANY
System.out.println( germany2 );    // GERMANY
```

Listing 8.21 src/main/java/com/tutego/insel/enums/v1/CountyDemo.java (Snippet)

> **Note**
>
> While the `Enum.valueOf(Class, String)` method exists only once, the compiler generates a `valueOf(String)` method for each enumeration type; since the method has been generated by the compiler, the method doesn't appear in the Javadoc. `Enum.valueOf(...)` is slightly more dynamic in use because that makes the method parameterizable with the `Class` object. Consider the following example:
>
> ```
> String name = "GERMANY";
> Class<Country> enumClass = Country.class;
> Enum<Country> anEnum = Enum.valueOf( enumClass, name );
> ```
>
> The data in angle brackets are part of generics (i.e., type specifications); Chapter 12 will explain generics in greater detail.

```
abstract class java.lang.Enum<E extends Enum<E>>
implements Comparable<E>, Serializable
```

▶ final String name()

Returns the name of the constant. Since the method—like many others of the class—is final, the name can't be changed.

▶ String toString()

Returns the name of the constant. This method calls name() by default but can be overridden because it isn't final.

▶ static <T extends Enum<T>> T valueOf(Class<T> enumType, String s)

Enables searching Enum objects for a constant name and Enum class. This method returns the Enum object for the given string or throws an IllegalArgumentException if no Enum object can be assigned to the string.

Enumerating All Constants of the Class

A useful static method is values(), which returns an array of all enumerations of the enumeration type. This method is useful for extended for loops, which are supposed to enumerate all constants. An alternative with the same result is the Class method getEnumConstants().

```
for ( Country c : Country.values() ) System.out.printf( "%s ", c );
System.out.printf( "%n%s%n", Arrays.asList( Country.class.getEnumConstants() ) );
```

Listing 8.22 src/main/java/com/tutego/insel/enums/v1/CountyDemo.java (Snippet)

The result is the following output:

```
GERMANY UK CHINA
[GERMANY, UK, CHINA]
```

Ordinal Number, Order

From the Enum superclass, each enumeration inherits a protected parameterized constructor that expects the name of the constant and an associated counter. Thus, each element of the enumeration becomes an object of the base type Enum, which stores a name and an ID, the *ordinal number*. Of course, you can also ask for its name and counter.

[Ex]
> **Example**
>
> The following example is a method that returns the ordinal number of an element of the enumeration or returns "-1" if the constant doesn't exist:
>
> ```
> static int getOrdinal( String name ) {
>   try { return Country.valueOf( name ).ordinal(); }
>   catch ( IllegalArgumentException e ) { return -1; }
> }
> ```
>
> **Listing 8.23** src/main/java/com/tutego/insel/enums/v1/CountyDemo.java (Snippet)

> Thus, `getOrdinal("UK") = 1` and `getOrdinal("ENGLAND") == -1`.

The ordinal number specifies the position in the declaration and is also the ordering criteria of the `compareTo(...)` method. The ordinal number can't be changed and always represents the order of the declared constants.

```
abstract class java.lang.Enum<E extends Enum<E>>
implements Comparable<E>, Serializable
```

▶ `final int ordinal()`
Returns the ID associated with the constant. In general, this ordinal number isn't important, but special data structures like `EnumSet` or `EnumMap` use this unique ID. The order of the numbers is given by the order in which they are specified.

▶ `final boolean equals(Object other)`
The `Enum` superclass overrides `equals(...)` with the logic as in `Object` (i.e., the comparison of the references) to mark it as `final`.

▶ `protected final Object clone() throws CloneNotSupportedException`
The `clone()` method is `final protected` and can therefore neither be overridden nor called from outside. In this way, no instances of the `Enum` objects could compromise the identity of every object of the enum. Basically, however, custom implementations of `clone()` are allowed to provide the `this` reference.

▶ `final int compareTo(E o)`
Since the `Enum` class implements the `Comparable` interface, the `compareTo(...)` method is also available. Its comparisons are based on the ordinal numbers. Comparisons are only allowed within an `Enum` type.

▶ `final Class<E> getDeclaringClass()`
Returns the `Class` object from the enumeration class for a concrete `Enum`. Warning: If applied to the enumeration class itself, the method will return `null`. Only on the elements of the enumeration does the method provide a value that makes sense. So, `Country.class.getDeclaringClass()` would be `null`, but `Country.UK.getDeclaringClass()` would return `Class<Country>`.

Note
In the `Class` object, the `getEnumConstants()` method is interesting because, like `values()`, this method also returns an array with all entries. However, the advantage of using the `Class` object is that it's general: The call of the static `values()` method is always associated with the class; `getEnumConstants()` works with any `Class` object; and even if it's not supposed to represent an enumeration class, the return is `null`.

8.2.2   Enumerations with Custom Methods, Constructors, and Initializers*

Since an enum type is a special kind of class declaration, it can also declare object/class variables, methods, static or object initializers, and constructors. Each enumeration automatically has methods like name() and ordinal(), and developers can also add their own.

Country with an Additional Class Method

An enumeration type can have static methods. These methods can access static members of the enumeration type and, for example, select constants. values() is one such given static method that returns an array of all enumeration elements.

Example

The following example declares an enumeration named Country and two static methods so that Country.getDefault() returns GERMANY and Country.random() returns a randomly chosen country:

```
public enum Country {
  GERMANY, UK, CHINA;
  public static Country getDefault() { return GERMANY; }
  public static Country random() { return values()[
  (int)(Math.random()*3 ) ]; }
}
```

Additional Static Initializers

Blocks of the type static { ... } are allowed in the body of an enumeration type. When the runtime environment of a class loads, it initializes all static variables one after the other or executes the static blocks. The enumerations are static variables and are initialized upon loading. If the static initializer is located after the constants, it too will be called later than the constructors, which may want to access static variables initialized by the static block. Consider the following example:

```
public enum Country {

  GERMANY, UK, CHINA;

  {
    System.out.println( "Object initializer" );
  }

  static {
    System.out.println( "Class initializer" );
  }
```

```
  private Country() {
    System.out.println( "Constructor" );
  }

  public static void main( String[] args ) {
    System.out.println( GERMANY );
  }
}
```

Listing 8.24 src/main/java/com/tutego/insel/enums/v2/Country.java (Snippet)

The result is the following output:

```
Object initializer
Constructor
Object initializer
Constructor
Object initializer
Constructor
Class initializer
GERMANY
```

Both execution and output depend on the order of declaration, and any rearrangement results in a change of behavior. Now, programmers might try to place potential static blocks at the beginning (i.e., before the constants), but readers should test the result. We'll return to constructors later in this section.

Country with Additional Object Method

Let's provide an enumeration named Country with a method that returns the ISO-3166-2 country code of the respective enumeration element. Consider the following example:

```
public enum Country {

  GERMANY, UK, CHINA;

  public String getISO3Country() {
    return switch ( this ) {
      case GERMANY -> "DEU";
      case UK -> "GBR";
      default -> "CHN";
    };
  }
}
```

Listing 8.25 src/main/java/com/tutego/insel/enums/v3/Country.java (Snippet)

The getISO3Country() method can now be called on the enumeration, in the following way:

```
System.out.println( Country.CHINA.getISO3Country() ); // CHN
```

Note that the switch statement is permitted on enumerations, which is quite useful. Let's write a small demo program next:

```
Country c = Country.GERMANY;

switch ( c ) {
  case GERMANY -> {
    System.out.println( "A beer?" );
    System.out.println( c.getISO3Country() ); // DEU
  }
  default -> System.out.println( "Different country" );
}
```

Listing 8.26 src/main/java/com/tutego/insel/enums/v3/CountryEnumDemo.java (Snippet)

enum with Custom Constructors

Besides the first variant for getISO3Country(), let's say we need to use a second implementation and add constructors to solve the same problem but in a different way. Consider the following example:

```
public enum Country {

  GERMANY( "DEU" ),
  UK( "GBR" ),
  CHINA( "CHN" );

  private final String iso3Country;

  Country( String iso3Country ) {
    this.iso3Country = iso3Country;
  }

  public String getISO3Country() {
    return iso3Country;
  }
}
```

Listing 8.27 src/main/java/com/tutego/insel/enums/v4/Country.java (Snippet)

When constants are declared, an argument for the constructor is passed in parentheses. The constructor stores the string in the internal variable iso3Country, which is then referenced by getISO3Country().

> **Note**
>
> Constructors of enumeration types are always automatically private and can't have any other visibility. This limitation is logical because calling constructors from outside should not be possible. The methods may well have different visibilities.

enum with Overridden Methods

In the enumeration type, not only can methods be added, but also overridden. Let's start with a localized and overloaded method toString() for a new enumeration containing weekdays.

```java
public enum WeekdayInternational {

  SUNDAY, MONDAY, TUESDAY, WEDNESDAY, THURSDAY, FRIDAY, SATURDAY;

  @Override
  public String toString() {
    return toString( Locale.getDefault() );
  }

  public String toString( Locale l ) {
    return new SimpleDateFormat( "", l ).getDateFormatSymbols()
                                  .getWeekdays()[ ordinal() + 1 ];
  }
}
```

Listing 8.28 src/main/java/com/tutego/insel/enums/WeekdayInternational.java (Snippet)

The first method gets overridden from within our Object superclass, while the second one is added as an overloaded method. An example will clarify the call and the functionality:

```java
System.out.println( WeekdayInternational.SATURDAY );
// Saturday
System.out.println( WeekdayInternational.SATURDAY.toString() );
// Saturday
System.out.println( WeekdayInternational.SATURDAY.toString(Locale.FRANCE) );
// samedi
System.out.println( WeekdayInternational.SATURDAY.toString(Locale.ITALY) );
// sabato
```

Listing 8.29 src/main/java/com/tutego/insel/enums/WeekdayInternationalDemo.java (Snippet)

At this point, however, the possibilities of the enum syntax don't end. Similar to the syntax of inner anonymous classes that allow methods to be overridden, enumeration types provide a comparable syntax for specifically overriding methods for a specific constant.

Let's assume that a game has its own currency, the Pono dollar. Now, this currency should be related to a reference currency, the euro; let's make the exchange rate simply 1:2 in the following example:

```java
public enum GameCurrency {

  EURO() {
    @Override public double convertTo( GameCurrency targetCurrency, double value
  ) {
      return targetCurrency == EURO ? value : value / 2;
    }
  },
  PONODOLLAR() {
    @Override public double convertTo( GameCurrency targetCurrency, double value
  ) {
      return targetCurrency == PONODOLLAR ? value : value * 2;
    }
  };

  public abstract double convertTo( GameCurrency targetCurrency, double value );
}
```

Listing 8.30 src/main/java/com/tutego/insel/enums/GameCurrency.java (Snippet)

The interesting part is the declaration of the abstract convertTo(...) method and the local implementation for each constant. (Of course, you don't need to make every method in enum abstract; it can also be concrete. Then, not every enum element must implement the abstract method.)

The following static import for the enumeration can be used to quickly illustrate its usage and functionality:

```java
System.out.println( EURO.convertTo( EURO, 12 ) );              // 12.0
System.out.println( EURO.convertTo( PONODOLLAR, 12 ) );        //  6.0
System.out.println( PONODOLLAR.convertTo( EURO, 12 ) );        // 24.0
System.out.println( PONODOLLAR.convertTo( PONODOLLAR, 12 ) ); // 12.0
```

Listing 8.31 src/main/java/com/tutego/insel/enums/GameCurrencyDemo.java (Snippet)

enum Can Implement Interfaces

The API documentation of `Enum` indicates that the abstract class implements two interfaces: `Comparable` and `Serializable`. Each constant declared in `enum` is a subclass of `Enum`, so each constant is always comparable and serializable by default. Besides these default interfaces, an `enum` can implement other interfaces. This feature is particularly useful because this way it prescribes a certain behavior for all enumeration elements, and each enumeration element then provides these operations. The operations of the interface can be implemented in two ways: `enum` itself implements the operations of the interface in the body, or the individual enumeration elements each implement the implementations differently. Often, the elements themselves may provide different implementations.

Our next example of `enum` (`DefaultIcons`) implements the `Icon` interface for graphical icons. Since the icons all have the same dimensions, the `Icon` operations `getIconWidth()` and `getIconHeight()` are always the same and are implemented only once; the actual `paintIcon(...)` implementations (which are only hinted at here) differ.

```java
public enum DefaultIcons implements Icon {

  WARNING {
    @Override public void paintIcon( Component c, Graphics g, int x, int y ) {
      // g.draw*()
    } },
  ERROR {
    @Override public void paintIcon( Component c, Graphics g, int x, int y ) {
      // g.draw*()
    } };

  @Override public int getIconWidth() { return 16; }

  @Override public int getIconHeight() { return 16; }
}
```

Listing 8.32 src/main/java/com/tutego/insel/enums/DefaultIcons.java (Snippet)

The `DefaultIcons.ERROR` access provides an object that is, among other things, of type `Icon` and can be passed in all places where an `Icon` is desired.

8.3   Sealed Classes and Interfaces

Before we dive into the topic of sealed classes, let's briefly review the properties of the types we've discussed so far.

Type	Instance Count	Subclasses Possible	Behavior Customizable	States Mutable
Regular class declaration	Any	Yes	Possible	Yes
Class with abstract method	Any	Must	Possible	Yes
Class with final method	Any	Yes	Yes, except for the final method	Yes
Final class	Any	No	No	Yes
Enumeration type	Fixed	No	Yes	No

Table 8.3 Possibilities and Limitations of the Different Types in Java

This table clearly shows that the individual types always differ in some way or other—in one type something is forbidden; in another type, that same thing might be explicitly necessary.

In the case of enumerations, no instances can be created directly as the objects are created internally. As many instances exist as there are elements in the enumeration type. Explicit subclasses of enumeration types are generally not possible, but indirect subclasses are. For this purpose, let's first introduce an abstract method in the enumeration type (or implement an interface) that can then implement the individual enumeration elements. In this sense, any number of subclasses can be created from non-final regular classes, but only a limited number from enumeration types, and only internally; the subclasses themselves aren't visible at all because they're hidden. Also, enumeration types cannot store mutable states; they must remain constants.

Let's suppose we want to determine if the result of an operation was valid or invalid. This result can be expressed using an enumeration type in the following way:

```
enum Result {
  Failure, Success
}
```

The following method could return something of type `Result`:

```
public class Baking {
  static Result cake() { return Failure or Success }
}
```

Callers know they can expect only two types of `Result`s: either `Failure` or `Success`. Anything else is impossible and, no other `Result` types can be added.

But now a request could arrive that a state should be stored as well, one that, for example, can remember message or that errors should have an error code. These scenarios immediately disqualify enumeration types, while classes come into play. You would thus write the following alternative code:

```
abstract class Result {
  Object body;
}
class Success extends Result { }
class Failure extends Result {
  final int errorCode;
}
```

This implementation enables you to store the state. Let's return to the cake() method:

```
Result cake() { … }
```

Again, the method returns Result, but the receiver has a problem because, besides Success or Failure, any number of subclasses of the Result class could be created and returned by cake().

What we're looking for is a way to limit the number of possible subclasses but still, in principle, allow any number of instances that can have different states. This scenario is where sealed classes take center stage.

8.3.1   Sealed Classes and Interfaces

With sealed classes, we know in advance which classes they extend. The compiler can use these classes to perform certain checks, such as checks for completeness with switch, as with enum.

Sealed classes are non-final and list the permitted subclasses via permits, as in the following example:

```
abstract sealed class Result permits Failure, Success {
  final Object body;
  public Result( Object body ) { this.body = body;   }
}
```

Listing 8.33 src/main/java/com/tutego/insel/sealed/Result.java, Result

Whether the superclass is abstract or not doesn't matter for permits. In our case, we don't need any direct Result instances. permits is a bit like a softened final. With final, no subclasses can exist at all, while with permits at least a few special subclasses can exist.

Our example only has the two subclasses Failure and Success. The subclasses are final in our example so that new types won't appear subsequently; in a moment, we'll explore some alternatives.

```java
final class Success extends Result {
  Success( Object body ) { super( body ); }
}
```

Listing 8.34 src/main/java/com/tutego/insel/sealed/Success.java, Success

```java
final class Failure extends Result {
  final int errorCode;
  Failure( int errorCode, Object body ) {
    super( body );
    this.errorCode = errorCode;
  }
}
```

Listing 8.35 src/main/java/com/tutego/insel/sealed/Failure.java, Failure

A method like cake() can only create instances of Success and Failure, for instance, in the following code:

```java
public class Baking {
  static Result cake() {
    return Math.random() > 0.5 ? new Success( "Yummy" )
                              : new Failure( 29, "Burned" );
  }
}
```

Listing 8.36 src/main/java/com/tutego/insel/sealed/Baking.java, Baking

The recipient knows, as with the enumeration types before, that only Success or Failure is possible:

```java
var result = Baking.cake();
if ( result instanceof Success )
  System.out.println( "Success: " + result.body );
else
  System.out.println( "Failure: " + result.body );
```

Listing 8.37 src/main/java/com/tutego/insel/sealed/OperationDemo.java, main()

In case discrimination, we only have two cases to distinguish between in our case. We'd have a big problem if a third Result subclass suddenly moved in because it would be treated like a Failure in the existing code.

Outcook

Outlook

With sealed classes, exactly how many subclasses there are is known in advance. "JEP 406: Pattern Matching for switch"[11] paves the way for a new feature that did not ultimately make it into Java 17. The idea therefore is to rewrite the following code:

```
if ( result instanceof Success success ) …
else if ( result instanceof Failure failure ) …
else throw …
```

Instead, you would write the following code:

```
switch ( result ) {
  case Success success -> …
  case Failure failure -> …
}
```

The compiler knows that only two concrete types exist, and therefore, no default branch is necessary.

In addition to classes, interfaces can also enumerate their permitted implementations; we'll explore another example in Section 8.4.

8.3.2 Subclasses Are Final, Sealed, and Non-Sealed

A subclass of a sealed superclass must be either final, sealed, or non-sealed. Recall from our earlier examples of final that final classes prohibit further subclasses. However, a subclass can itself be sealed and thus explicitly list new subclasses.

The non-sealed modifier is a bit exotic because this keyword is the only (contextual) keyword that contains a hyphen. This modifier means that the seal is removed, and now, any number of subclasses can exist. In mathematics, commutative operations describe operations where the arguments of the operation can be swapped without changing the result. Addition and multiplication are commutative; subtraction and division aren't. We can map these associations in the following ways:

```
abstract sealed class BinaryOperation
        permits Commutative, Noncommutative { }
abstract sealed class Commutative extends BinaryOperation
        permits Addition, Multiplication { }
final class Addition extends Commutative { }
final class Multiplication extends Commutative { }
non-sealed class Noncommutative extends BinaryOperation { }
class Subtraction extends Noncommutative { }
```

Listing 8.38 src/main/java/com/tutego/insel/sealed/BinaryOperation.java (Snippet)

---

11 *https://openjdk.java.net/jeps/406*

For commutative operations, only instances of `addition` and `multiplication` are permitted, and no subclasses can be created. However, you can create any subclass from `Noncommutative`.

8.3.3   Abbreviated Notations

As we discuss in this section, `permits` isn't used in two special cases.

Subclasses in the Same Compilation Unit

The `permits` keyword can be omitted if the subclasses reside in the same compilation unit. Consider the following example:

```
public sealed class State { }
final class Open extends State { }
final class Closed extends State { }
```

Listing 8.39 src/main/java/com/tutego/insel/sealed/State.java (Snippet)

Nested Types

In Java, type declarations can be placed inside other type declarations to express a tight binding of types. This topic will be the subject of Chapter 10, Section 10.1, but let's look at a preview:

```
public sealed class Feeling {
  public enum Scale {
    Not_at_all, A_little, Moderately, Quite_a_lot, Extremely
  }

  public final Scale scale;

  protected Feeling( Scale scale ) { this.scale =
Objects.requireNonNull( scale ); }

  public static final class Friendly extends Feeling {
    public Friendly( Scale scale ) { super( scale ); }
  }
  public static final class Tense extends Feeling {
    public Tense( Scale scale ) { super( scale ); }
  }
  public static final class Active extends Feeling {
    public Active( Scale scale ) { super( scale ); }
  }
}
```

Listing 8.40 src/main/java/com/tutego/insel/sealed/Feeling.java, Feeling

The following example uses types:

```
Feeling active = new Feeling.Active( Feeling.Scale.Moderately );
System.out.println( active.scale );
```

8.4   Records

Besides classes, interfaces, and enumeration types, another data type is available: *records*.[12] As with classes, objects can be created from records via new, but unlike classes, record objects are basically immutable, at least the direct fields of the record. In terms of syntax, little code is required to combine multiple data elements into a lightweight data structure; the specification refers to this code as *nominal tuples*.

8.4.1   Simple Records

The syntax in the declaration is also a little different from that of classes. First, the new record keyword is used, followed by the name of the data type, and then instead of the usual curly bracket, a parenthesis. The *record components* with their types and names follow in parentheses—optionally, these parameters can be annotated. The notation with parentheses is reminiscent of a constructor parameter list, which is exactly how records are instantiated later. The closing parenthesis is followed by a block in curly brackets. The body of the block can be empty.

In our first example, a record named Location is supposed to store geographic coordinates.

```
public record Location(  // Name
    double latitude,      // Components in header
    double longitude
) { }                    // Body
```

Listing 8.41 src/main/java/com/tutego/insel/records/v1/Location.java, Location

The Location record thus has two components: latitude and longitude. Almost all identifiers are valid, but clone, finalize, getClass, hashCode, notify, notifyAll, toString, and wait can't be the names of the component.

The declaration of a record is compact, and the compiler creates a single constructor automatically. While regular classes have a default constructor, records have a *canonical constructor*, which initializes all states. At least this one canonical constructor exists, but others can be added. Its visibility is automatically that of the record; since in our example the Location record is public, the constructor is also public.

---

12   Records have been around since Java 16. Oracle documents the motivation for it and its history at *https://openjdk.java.net/jeps/395*.

In addition, the compiler generates a number of methods. On one hand, with query methods, the notation of the getter doesn't come into play. On the other hand, an access method is called like the component name. Mutation methods are absent because the states of a record are immutable.

Each record automatically inherits from the java.lang.Record superclass, which documents how equals(...), hashCode(), and toString() should behave for each record. Similar to enumeration types, an inheritance relationship to java.lang.Enum also exists. A record can't extend any other class or record.

Consider the following example of using these methods:

```
Location manila = new Location( 14.60416, 120.98222 );
System.out.printf( "latitude=%f, longitude=%f%n",
                  manila.latitude(), manila.longitude() );
System.out.println( manila );


Location location1 = new Location( 14.60416, 120.98222 );
System.out.println( location1.equals( manila ) );
Location location2 = new Location( 14, 120 );
System.out.println( location2.equals( manila ) );
```

Listing 8.42 src/main/java/com/tutego/insel/records/v1/LocationDemo.java, LocationDemo

The result is the following output:

```
latitude=14,604160, longitude=120,982220
Location[latitude=14.60416, longitude=120.98222]
true
false
```

Records are objects that are identified by their values. Equivalence is therefore of importance, not identity. For this reason, each record has an equals(...) implementation, where referenced subelements must also have an equals(...) that makes sense.

> **[»]**
>
> **Note**
>
> Decoupling from internal states isn't possible since records aren't made for that functionality. Storing two int values in one long would not be possible with a record, as shown in the following example:
>
> ```
> class Coordinate {
>   private final long value;
>   Coordinate( int x, int y ) { value = (((long) x) << 32) | (y &
> 0xffffffffL); }
>   int x() { return (int) (value >> 32); }
> ```

```
    int y() { return (int) value;}
}
```

Externally, a constructor and also access methods exist, but the internal mapping of a record is quite different.

8.4.2   Records with Methods

Our Location record was set up simply. The fact that the state is in the foreground of a record can be seen from the declaration of its states at the top. But records can do a bit more than hold states: They can declare object methods and static methods in the body.[13] Our next example demonstrates this feature:

```java
public record Location(
    double latitude,
    double longitude
) {

  Point2D.Double toPoint() {
    return new Point2D.Double( longitude, latitude );
  }

  Location withLatitude( double latitude ) {
    return new Location( longitude, latitude );
  }

  Location withLongitude( double longitude ) {
    return new Location( longitude, latitude );
  }

  @Override public double longitude() {
    System.out.println( "Access" + longitude );
    return longitude;
  }

  @Override public String toString() {
    return latitude + "," + longitude;
  }

  static boolean isValid( double latitude, double longitude ) {
    return     ( -90 <= latitude  && latitude  <= +90)
```

---

13   Native methods are prohibited in records.

```
                && (-180 <= longitude && longitude <= +180);
  }
}
```

Listing 8.43 src/main/java/com/tutego/insel/records/v2/Location.java, Location

The first method, toPoint(), converts the coordinates and returns them as a Point2D object, by directly accessing the—private and final—object variables that are automatically set in the canonical constructor. Within a record, direct access to the state variables is also possible. The wither methods withLatitude(double) and withLongitude(double) show a way to "change" states for immutable types, namely by creating a new immutable Location object with the changed states. Withers are common with immutable data types, and they are prominent with the Date-Time API. Furthermore, the example shows that the access methods can also be overridden. The toString() method can be overridden as well. Static methods are also not a problem, but a record may of course not have any abstract methods; neither can a record be abstract since the data type is final. Consider the following example:

```
Location manila = new Location( 14.60416, 120.98222 );
System.out.println( manila.toPoint() );
System.out.println( manila.withLatitude( 14 ) );
System.out.println( manila.withLongitude( 120 ) );
System.out.println( manila.longitude() );
System.out.println( manila );
System.out.println( Location.isValid( 15, 120 ) );
System.out.println( Location.isValid( 200, 0 ) );
```

The result is the following output:

```
Point2D.Double[120.98222, 14.60416]
120.98222,14.0
120.0,14.60416
Access120.98222
120.98222
14.60416,120.98222
true
false
```

Listing 8.44 src/main/java/com/tutego/insel/records/v2/LocationDemo.java, LocationDemo

8.4.3   Customizing Record Constructors

Records automatically have a constructor in which the state variables are initialized. Let's look at record Location(double latitude, double longitude) { } again. The constructor generated by the compiler will automatically read this.latitude = latitude; this.longitude = longitude;.

You can include code in the constructor to validate or normalize the parameters, for example. In this case, you must distinguish between the following two notations:

```java
public record Location(
    double latitude,
    double longitude
) {

// -- Variant 1 ----------------------------------------
  public Location {
    if ( ! isValid( latitude, longitude ) )
      throw new IllegalArgumentException( "Invalid range" );
  }


// -- Variant 2 ----------------------------------------
//  public Location( double latitude, double longitude ) {
//     if ( ! isValid( latitude, longitude ) )
//       throw new IllegalArgumentException( "Invalid range" );
//     this.latitude = latitude;
//     this.longitude = longitude;
//  }

  private static boolean isValid( double latitude, double longitude ) {
    return    ( -90 <= latitude  && latitude  <= +90)
           && (-180 <= longitude && longitude <= +180);
  }
}
```

Listing 8.45 src/main/java/com/tutego/insel/records/v3/Location.java, Location

With the second constructor, you can directly access, modify, and save the parameter variables. Note that the assignments this.latitude = latitude; this.longitude = longitude; take place in any case; otherwise, a compiler error will arise because final variables must always be initialized in the constructor. In the first compact notation, the compiler automatically puts the initialization into the bytecode. One more rule applies: The visibility of the custom constructor must be at least the same as that of the record.

Let's consider the following demo of our record next:

```java
System.out.println( new Location( 14.60416, 120.98222 ) );
try {
  System.out.println( new Location( -1000, +1000 ) );
```

```
}
catch ( Exception e ) {
  e.printStackTrace();
}
```

Listing 8.46 src/main/java/com/tutego/insel/records/v3/LocationDemo.java, LocationDemo

The following result is output:

```
Location[latitude=14.60416, longitude=120.98222]
java.lang.IllegalArgumentException: Invalid range
  at com.tutego.insel.records.v3.Location.<init>(Location.java:12)
  at com.tutego.insel.records.v3.LocationDemo.main(LocationDemo.java:9)
```

8.4.4 Adding Constructors

Records always have a canonical constructor that accepts all record components. This constructor cannot be removed. You can add more overloaded constructors, and of course, static creator methods are an alternative as well.

Let's consider the following small application example with three constructors and a static factory method fromPoint(...):

```
public record Location(
    double latitude,
    double longitude
) {

  public Location( double latitude, double longitude ) {
    this.latitude = latitude;
    this.longitude = longitude;
  }

  public Location( Point point ) {
    this( point.y, point.x );
  }

  public Location() {
    this( 0, 0 );
  }

  public static Location fromPoint( Point point ) {
    return new Location( point.y, point.x );
  }
}
```

Listing 8.47 src/main/java/com/tutego/insel/records/v4/Location.java, Location

If you write your own constructor, it's important that it calls the canonical constructor. Consider the following example:

```java
public Location( Point point ) {    // ☠ this.latitude = point.y;
  this.longitude = point.x;
}
```

In this case, you'll get a compiler error of the type: "Non-canonical record constructor must delegate to another constructor."

8.4.5 Sealed Interfaces and Records

Records go well with sealed interfaces because records are automatically final. For example, GeoJSON[14] is an open format to express geographic data in JavaScript Object Notation (JSON). For example, we have primitives, such as points, lines, and polygons. Our next program should list the permitted subclasses through the GeoJSONshape interface, which are GeoJSONpoint and GeoJSONline as examples:

```java
sealed interface GeoJSONshape
    permits GeoJSONpoint, GeoJSONline {
  record Coordinate(int x, int y) {
    @Override public String toString() { return '[' + x + "," + y + ']'; }
  }
}
```

Listing 8.48 src/main/java/com/tutego/insel/sealed/GeoJSONshape.java, GeoJSONshape

A GeoJSONline record with the record components x and y is declared as a nested type. Two records implement the interface. A point consists of exactly one coordinate.

```java
record GeoJSONpoint(Coordinate coordinate) implements GeoJSONshape { }
```

Listing 8.49 src/main/java/com/tutego/insel/sealed/GeoJSONpoint.java, GeoJSONpoint

A line consists of a collection of coordinates. A particularly useful approach is to use a vararg, as in the following example:

```java
record GeoJSONline(Coordinate... coordinates) implements GeoJSONshape { }
```

Listing 8.50 src/main/java/com/tutego/insel/sealed/GeoJSONline.java, GeoJSONline

Perhaps our program shouldn't write a complete GeoJSON document, but only the subtrees for points and lines. We would write the following code:

---

14 *https://en.wikipedia.org/wiki/GeoJSON* provides some insight.

```
static void printGeoJSONcoordinates( GeoJSONshape shape ) {
  Objects.requireNonNull( shape );
  System.out.print( "\"coordinates\": " );
  if ( shape instanceof GeoJSONpoint point )
    System.out.printf( "{ \"type\": \"Point\", \"coordinates\": %s }%n",
                       point.coordinate() );
  else if ( shape instanceof GeoJSONline line )
    System.out.printf( "{ \"type\": \"LineString\", \"coordinates\": [
%s ] }%n",
                          Arrays.stream( line.coordinates() )
                                .map( GeoJSONshape.Coordinate::toString )
                                .collect( Collectors.joining( "," ) ) );
  else
    throw new IllegalStateException( "Unknown shape " + shape.getClass() );
}
```

Listing 8.51 src/main/java/com/tutego/insel/sealed/GeoJSONwriter.java,
printGeoJSONcoordinates()

This method would be used in the following way:

```
GeoJSONpoint point = new GeoJSONpoint( new Coordinate( 10, 20 ) );
GeoJSONline poly = new GeoJSONline( new Coordinate( 20, 30 ),
                                    new Coordinate( 50, 90 ) );
GeoJSONwriter.printGeoJSONcoordinates( point );
GeoJSONwriter.printGeoJSONcoordinates( poly );
```

Listing 8.52 src/main/java/com/tutego/insel/sealed/GeoJSONdemo.java, main()

The result is the following output:

```
"coordinates": { "type": "Point", "coordinates": 101,20] }
"coordinates": { "type": "LineString", "coordinates": [ 111,30],141,90] ] }
```

8.4.6   Records: Summary

Records are used for the simple aggregation of values, not for creating inheritance relationships; arguably, however, a record can implement interfaces, as we've just seen.

In the best case, records are immutable down to the last link. That the component type itself can also be a record can come in handy sometimes. Consider the following examples:

```
record City(String name, double population, int area, Location center) {}
```

Listing 8.53 src/main/java/com/tutego/insel/records/v3/City.java, City

```
City city = new City( "Gothic", 234534, 8374, new Location( 14, 120 ) );
System.out.println( city.center() ); // Location[latitude=14.0, longitude=
120.0]
```

Listing 8.54 src/main/java/com/tutego/insel/records/v3/CityWithLocation.java,
CityWithLocation

Note

Although records have immutable components, these components can be changeable.
A record Line(Point from, Point to) {} is not "deeply" immutable; the points themselves can't be replaced by new Point objects, but the coordinates, and thus indirectly
the record, can be changed:

```
Line line = new Line( new Point(), new Point() );
line.from().setLocation( 1,1 );
System.out.println(line); // Line[from=[…]Point[x=1,y=1], to=[…]Point[x=0,y=
0]]
```

The whole concept of immutability depends on the fact that only primitive values or
other immutable data types are referenced and not mutable objects.

Chapter 9
There Must Be Exceptions

"Why not make exceptions the rule when exceptions prove the rule?"
—Georg-Wilhelm Exler

Program errors are inevitable: Inputs could be wrong, files could disappear, and network connections could collapse. A special challenge is presented by unexpected errors, but Java offers the elegant technique to catch exceptions, so that programs can rescue themselves from almost any situation.

In early programming languages, no way existed for routines to indicate a failure except via a return value—in the C programming language, this limitation is still the case today. Two problems arise with this reliance on return values:

- The error code is often a "magic" value like -1, NULL, or 0. However, a zero can also indicate correctness, which is arbitrary. Querying these values is mandatory, and an assumption might creep in like, "This will always succeed, an error is impossible." If the program then fails to recognize this error and continues, nasty surprises can arise.

- Queries of return values interrupt the program flow, which isn't pleasant, especially since the return value, if it doesn't indicate an error, may further be used. The return value is thus overloaded in the broadest sense since it indicates two states. Often, cascaded if queries arise along with the error queries, making the source code difficult to read. Then, the actual algorithm in the code moves further and further to the right.

Example [Ex]

The Java library doesn't set a good example for the delete(), mkdir(), mkdirs(), and renameTo(...) methods of the File class. Instead of using an exception to indicate that the operation failed, these methods return false, which is unfortunate because many developers forgo testing, resulting in bugs that are difficult to find later.

9.1 Fencing In Problem Areas

When using exceptions, the program code isn't interrupted by querying the return status. A specially distinguished program piece monitors proper execution and calls special program code for handling in case of an error.

9.1.1   Exceptions in Java with try and catch

The monitored program area (block) is introduced by the try keyword. The try block is usually[1] followed by a catch block containing the program code that handles the exception, as briefly outlined in the following way:

```
try {
  // Program code that can execute an exception
}
catch (… ) {
  // Program code to handle the exception
}
// It continues as normal because the exception was handled
```

Errors lead to exceptions, and these exceptions are handled by a catch block. The catch is followed by the program block that is executed when an exception occurs to catch the error. The error can be handled, reported on the command line, or written to a logger, for example. Whether an error really occurs at runtime isn't actually known, but if it does occur, handling is in place.

After error handling, the program may struggle to continue after the point where the error occurred. Also, you cannot really determine in retrospect exactly where the error occurred if multiple exception-triggering locations exist within a single, large try block in Java. Other programming languages certainly allow multiple exception triggering, however.

Figure 9.1 Playing Field for the Error Gremlin: catch Blocks

9.1.2   Checked and Unchecked Exceptions

Java distinguishes between two groups of exceptions: checked and unchecked exceptions.

---

1   In some cases, also a finally block, so that the construction then becomes a try-finally block.

- *Checked exceptions* must be handled by either catching or redirecting them. They can be triggered by methods or constructors in case of an error and are usually found in input/output operations.
- *Unchecked exceptions* don't necessarily need to be caught. However, if the exceptions occur and aren't caught, the executing thread will end.

Occurrence of Unchecked Exceptions (RuntimeException) in the Java Library

Some types of exceptions can potentially occur in many program locations, such as an integer division by zero[2] or invalid index values when accessing array elements. If such exceptions occur while the program is running, they're usually based on a reasoning error by the programmer, and the program shouldn't normally attempt to catch and handle the thrown exception thrown. Therefore, in the Java application programming interface (API), a subclass of Exception, the RuntimeException class, identifies programming errors that need to be fixed. The name "RuntimeException" is oddly chosen, however, since all exceptions are always generated, thrown, and handled at runtime. But this name expresses that the compiler isn't interested in these exceptions, but rather the Java virtual machine (JVM) at runtime is.

> **Note**
>
> A useful approach might be to consider a RuntimeException as a self-blame error. With proper checking of value ranges, for example, many RuntimeExceptions wouldn't arise.

9.1.3 A NumberFormatException (Unchecked Exception)

You learned about the Integer.parseInt(...) method earlier in Chapter 3, Section 3.6.9, and Chapter 5, Section 5.8. This method converts a number given as a string into a decimal number. Consider the following example:

```java
int vatRate = Integer.parseInt( "19" );
```

In this example, conversion is possible, and the method performs the conversion without exception. The situation is different if the string doesn't represent a number, for instance, in the following example:

```java
package com.tutego.insel.exception;            /* 1 */
public class MissNumberFormatException {       /* 2 */
  public static int getVatRate() {             /* 3 */
    return Integer.parseInt( "19%" );          /* 4 */
  }                                            /* 5 */
  public static void main( String[] args ) {   /* 6 */
```

---

2 Floating point divisions by 0.0 result in either ± infinity or not a number (NaN).

```
    System.out.println( getVatRate() );        /* 7 */
  }                                             /* 8 */
}                                               /* 9 */
```

The execution of the program terminates with an exception and the JVM automatically issues the following message:

```
Exception in thread "main" java.lang.NumberFormatException: For input string: "1
9%"
  at java.base/java.lang.NumberFormatException.forInputString(
    NumberFormatException.java:65)
  at java.base/java.lang.Integer.parseInt(Integer.java:652)
  at java.base/java.lang.Integer.parseInt(Integer.java:770)
  at c.t.i.e.MissNumberFormatException.getVatRate(MissNumberFormatException.java
:4)
  at e.t.i.e.MissNumberFormatException.main(MissNumberFormatException.java:7)
```

Listing 9.1 src/main/java/com/tutego/insel/exception/MissNumberFormatException.java

In the first line, notice how a java.lang.NumberFormatException has been thrown. The last line indicates the location in the program that led to the exception. (You've observed a similar error output, the NullPointerException, in Chapter 3, Section 3.7.1.)

```
C:\Users\Christian\Dropbox\Software\jdk-17\bin\java.exe ...
Exception in thread "main" java.lang.NumberFormatException Create breakpoint : For input string: "19%"
 at java.base/java.lang.NumberFormatException.forInputString(NumberFormatException.java:67)
 at java.base/java.lang.Integer.parseInt(Integer.java:668)
 at java.base/java.lang.Integer.parseInt(Integer.java:786)
 at com.tutego.insel.exception.MissNumberFormatException.getVatRate(MissNumberFormatException.java:4)
 at com.tutego.insel.exception.MissNumberFormatException.main(MissNumberFormatException.java:7)
```

Figure 9.2 IntelliJ Displays an Exception in Red in the Output Window. Conveniently, Error Messages Behave like Hyperlinks: One Click, and the Integrated Development Environment (IDE) Shows the Line That Threw the Exception.

Catching a NumberFormatException

A poor solution to an exception would be if a program simply terminates and the JVM ends. Exceptions should rather be caught and reported. To catch exceptions, you must know exactly what kind of exception is being thrown. Our case is easy to understand because the exception has already appeared and can be clearly assigned to a reason. The Java documentation also mention this NumberFormatException at the parseInt(…) method. Because the caught exception isn't handled, the program terminates, but the NumberFormatException now remains to be caught.

To catch this exception, we'll revisit the try-catch concept again.

```
String stringToConvert = "19%";
int vat = 19;
try {
  vat = Integer.parseInt( stringToConvert );
}
catch ( NumberFormatException e ) {
  System.err.printf( "'%s' cannot be converted to a number!%n",
    stringToConvert );
}
System.out.printf( "Moving on to VAT=%d%n", vat );
```

Listing 9.2 src/main/java/com/tutego/insel/exception/CatchNumberFormatException.java, main()

The entire result is the following output:

```
'19%' cannot be converted to a number!
Moving on to VAT=19
```

Because the string isn't a number, `Integer.parseInt("19%")` results in a `NumberFormatException`, which we'll handle so that we can then continue with the console output.

The try statement is followed by a block called a *try block*, which we'll use in combination with a catch clause. The code `catch(NumberFormatException e)` declares an *exception handler* to catch everything of exception type `NumberFormatException`. The variable e is an *exception parameter*. Since exceptions are objects, the variable e references this exception object. The use of var is not allowed in this context, so you cannot write catch (var e).

9.1.4 Appending a Date/Timestamp to a Text File (Checked Exception)

Let's write a second program with exception handling that appends the current date/timestamp as text in a text file. The `LocalDateTime.now()` expression returns such a date/timestamp. The `Files.writeString(...)` method allows you to write to files. In this case, you would write the following lines:

```
String content = LocalDateTime.now() + "\n";
Files.writeString( Path.of( "timestamps.txt" ),
                   content, StandardOpenOption.APPEND );
```

These lines can't be compiled in this way, and thus, a compiler error is thrown. The reason for the error is `Files.writeString(...)` because this method can throw an `IOException`, which is a checked exception. In other words, we must face the fact that this exception might be thrown and prepare handling for this case.

Documented Exceptions in the Javadoc

An exception doesn't really come as a surprise, and developers must be prepared that for negative consequences if they pass something wrong to methods or constructors. In the best case, the API documentation explains which inputs are valid and which ones are not. The "interface" of a method also includes the behavior in the event of an error. The API documentation should describe exactly what exception—or what response in the case of special return values—can be expected if the method receives invalid values. The Javadoc for `Files.writeString(...)` provides this information, as shown in Figure 9.3.

```
writeString

public static Path writeString(Path path,
                               CharSequence csq,
                               OpenOption... options)
                        throws IOException

Write a CharSequence to a file. Characters are encoded into bytes using the UTF-8 charset.

This method is equivalent to: writeString(path, csq, StandardCharsets.UTF_8, options).

Parameters:
path - the path to the file
csq - the CharSequence to be written
options - options specifying how the file is opened
Returns:
the path
Throws:
IllegalArgumentException - if options contains an invalid combination of options
IOException - if an I/O error occurs writing to or creating the file, or the text cannot be encoded using the specified charset
UnsupportedOperationException - if an unsupported option is specified
SecurityException - In the case of the default provider, and a security manager is installed, the checkWrite method is invoked to check write access to the file. The checkDelete
method is invoked to check delete access if the file is opened with the DELETE_ON_CLOSE option.
Since:
11
```

Figure 9.3 The Javadoc Documents All Possible Exceptions.

The description "IOException - if an I/O error occurs writing to or creating the file, or the text cannot be encoded using the specified charset" is perhaps a bit vague, failing to explain why exactly the error occurred. But no matter, you must treat the error anyway. Note also that `IOException` may not be the only error on our list. `IllegalArgument-Exception`, `UnsupportedOperationException`, and `SecurityException` may arise, but nothing forces us to catch these errors, which is exactly the difference between a checked exception and an unchecked exception.

try-catch Handling

Since `Files.writeString(...)` might throw an `IOException`, which is a checked exception that must be handled, two possible solutions are available: First, you could use `try-catch` to handle the error; second, you could use `throws` to pass the error to the caller.

Let's solve the problem in our program with the `IOException` first by means of a direct `try-catch` handling, in the following example:

```
public class TimestampWriter {
  public static void writeTimestamp() {
    String content = LocalDateTime.now().toString();
    try {
      Files.writeString( Path.of( "timestamps.txt" ),
                         content, StandardOpenOption.APPEND );
    }
    catch ( IOException e ) {
      e.printStackTrace();
    }
  }

  public static void main( String[] args ) {
    writeTimestamp();
  }
}
```

Listing 9.3 src/main/java/com/tutego/insel/exception/TimestampWriter.java (Snippet)

Once we've caught the error, the error is gone, and everything continues as normal.

Stack Trace

The virtual machine remembers which method called which other method in a stack, and this information is referred to as *stack trace*. Thus, if the static main(...) method calls the writeTimestamp() method which in turn calls writeString(...), the stack at the time of writeString(...) would resemble the following list:

```
writeString
writeTimestamp
main
```

A stack trace is useful in case of an error because, with one, you can read that writeString(...) threw the exception and not some other method.

Stack traces are often logged in the program. A method already contained in the catch block is quite helpful in this context: e.printStackTrace(). By default, this method sets the stack trace to the System.err channel.

9.1.5 Repeating Canceled Sections*

No language-supported way in Java is present for exceptions to return to the point that threw the exception. However, this return is often desirable, for example, when an incorrect entry must be repeated.

Let's ask for a string on the console and try to convert it to a number. Of course, something can go wrong in the process. If a user enters a string that doesn't represent a number, parseInt(...) will throw a NumberFormatException. If that exception occurs, we want to repeat the input, as defined in the following code:

```
int number;
while ( true ) {
  try {
    System.out.println( "Please enter number:" );
    String input = new java.util.Scanner( System.in ).nextLine();
    number = Integer.parseInt( input );
    break;
  }
  catch ( NumberFormatException e ) {
    System.err.println( "That was not a number!" );
  }
}
System.out.printf( "%d is a %s number%n", number,
                   Math.random() > 0.5 ? "wonderful" : "boring" );
```

Listing 9.4 src/main/java/com/tutego/insel/exception/ContinueInput.java, main()

The chosen solution is simple: We'll program the entire part in an infinite loop. If the problematic passage passes without exception, we'll end the loop via break. If a Number-FormatException occurs, then break won't be executed, and the program flow will return to the infinite loop.

Incidentally, you could write new java.util.Scanner(System.in).nextInt() to read our integers, but if the method doesn't receive a number, an InputMismatchException will be thrown, which is also an unchecked exception.

9.1.6 Empty catch Blocks

Java requires that exceptions be handled (or routed up) in a catch but doesn't specify what has to happen in catch blocks. These blocks can include a useful handling or can simply be empty. An empty catch block is usually not particularly useful because then the exception is suppressed clandestinely. (This scenario would be comparable to ignored status return values in C functions.)

A minimal error output via System.err.println(e) is recommended, or you can use the more informative e.printStackTrace(...) for an Exception e or the logging of this exception. Even better is an active response because the output itself doesn't handle this exception! In the catch block, a perfectly legitimate option is to throw other exceptions in turn, thus transforming the exception and passing it upwards.

[«]

Note*

As with `Thread.sleep(...)`, if the `InterruptedException` really doesn't matter, the block can of course be empty, but few useful examples of this choice exist. When the block is empty, a comment often helps to make clear that the omission is purposeful.

9.1.7 Catching Multiple Exceptions

In multiple places, a program block may throw an exception. For example, in the following lines, something has been written twice:

```
try {
 Path p = Path.of( "timestamps.txt" );
 Files.writeString( p, LocalDateTime.now() + "\n", StandardOpenOption.APPEND );
 Files.writeString( p, LocalDateTime.now() + "\n", StandardOpenOption.APPEND );
}
catch ( IOException e ) { … }
```

If more than one place raises the *same* exception type, in exception handling later, tracing which of the two statements caused the exception can be difficult. If this information is important, two separate `try` blocks should be used: either two blocks in sequence or one block nested within another.

The situation is different when *different* exceptions are thrown, such as an `IOException` and, for example, a `NumberFormatException`.

In this context, several things might occur:

- All exceptions are caught.
- Some exceptions are caught; others are redirected to the caller.
- All exceptions are passed upwards to the caller.

In the next example, an integer should be read from the command line and the same number of date/timestamps should be written to a text file.

```
Path path = Path.of( "timestamps.txt" );
try {
  int count = new Scanner( System.in ).nextInt();
  for ( int i = 0; i < count; i++ ) {
    Files.writeString( path, LocalDateTime.now() + "\n",
                       StandardOpenOption.APPEND );
  }
}
catch ( InputMismatchException e ) {
  System.err.println( "Input was not an integer" );
}
```

```
catch ( IOException e ) {
  System.err.println( "Error when writing to the file" );
}
```

Listing 9.5 src/main/java/com/tutego/insel/exception/UserInputTimestampWriter.java
(Snippet)

IOException is a checked exception, and thus, handling is mandatory. InputMismatchException is an unchecked exception and wouldn't necessarily need to be handled, but if
something like 12ABC is parsed, the program will crash with a stack trace, which should
be avoided. Some exceptions may arise when writing to the file. You must anticipate
these potential problems and therefore write the problem sections in a try block.

If an exception then occurs in the try block, the catch part will catch it. In our code,
notice how a try block can have several catch clauses associated with it that each catch
different types of exceptions.

9.1.8   Combining Identical catch Blocks with Multi-Catch

If a program draws on sections that can fail, situations quickly arise in more complex
processes in which different exceptions can occur. We recommend writing the program code in one big try block, and then responding via catch blocks to all the possible
exceptions that kept the block from running completely through.

Often, a phenomenon occurs that the called program parts raise different exception
types, but the exception handling looks the same. To avoid source code duplication,
the program code should be summarized. In Java, multiple exceptions can be handled
in the same way; this notation is called *multi-catch*. In this modified variant of catch, no
longer are you anticipating just one exception, but rather a collection of exceptions
separated by |. (The vertical line is an OR operator and is therefore also used in this case
because exceptions can also be understood as in an OR connection.) The exception
variable is implicitly final.

```
Path path = Path.of( "timestamps.txt" );
try {
  int count = new Scanner( System.in ).nextInt();
  for ( int i = 0; i < count; i++ ) {
    Files.writeString( path, LocalDateTime.now() + "\n",
                       StandardOpenOption.APPEND );
  }
}
catch ( InputMismatchException | IOException e ) {
  System.err.println( "Program error" );
  e.printStackTrace();
}
```

Listing 9.6 src/main/java/com/tutego/insel/exception/UserInputTimestampWriterMulti-
Catch.java (Snippet)

9.2   Redirecting Exceptions and throws at the Head of Methods/Constructors

Besides "sectioning off" problematic blocks by means of a try block with an appended catch block for handling, you can respond to exceptions in another way: redirecting them to the caller.

Unchecked exceptions that haven't been caught will automatically be passed to the caller, and if they aren't caught, the thread will the end. If only the main thread exists, the JVM will terminate the program.

9.2.1   throws in Constructors and Methods

To pass exceptions to the caller, a throws clause is introduced in the head of the relevant method or constructor. This clause indicates that a particular exception isn't handled by the method or constructor, but instead the exception is passed to the calling entity. If an exception occurs in the method or constructor, the processing ends, the exception isn't handled locally, but the caller must take care of the exception.

Let's rewrite our writeTimestamp() method so that it will no longer handle the exceptions itself, but instead pass them upwards.

```java
public class TimestampWriter2 {
  public static void writeTimestamp() throws IOException {
    String content = LocalDateTime.now() + "\n";
    Files.writeString( Path.of( "timestamps.txt" ),
                       content, StandardOpenOption.APPEND );
  }

  public static void main( String[] args ) {
    try {
      writeTimestamp();
    }
    catch ( IOException e ) { e.printStackTrace(); }
  }
}
```

Listing 9.7 src/main/java/com/tutego/insel/exception/TimestampWriter2.java (Snippet)

Now, main(...) must deal with IOException. Note that main(...) could also have its own throws clause; in that case, the JVM would pass the buck. Redirecting upwards is quite common because often a method or constructor can't handle the exception at all and continue as if nothing had happened.

> **[+] Tip**
>
> Rarely are unchecked exceptions included in throws. However, deliberate unchecked exceptions should definitely show up in the Javadoc.

9.3   The Class Hierarchy of Exceptions

An exception is an object whose type is directly or indirectly derived from java.lang.Throwable. (The naming with -able suggests an interface, but Throwable is a non-abstract class.) You'll have direct little interaction with Throwable but rather will interact with the direct subclass Exception or the exception classes derived from Exception.

9.3.1   Members of the Exception Object

The exception object passed to you in the catch clause is rich with information. In this way, you can find out which exception is actually involved and what error message is called. The stack trace can also be queried and output, as in the following example:

```
try {
  Integer.parseInt( "19%" );
}
catch ( NumberFormatException e ) {
  String name = e.getClass().getName();
  String msg  = e.getMessage();
  String s    = e.toString();

  System.out.println( name );// java.lang.NumberFormatException
  System.out.println( msg ); // For input string: "19%"
  System.out.println( s ); // java.lang.NumberFormatException: For input
                           // string: "19%"

  e.printStackTrace();
}
```

Listing 9.8 src/main/java/com/tutego/insel/exception/
NumberFormatExceptionElements.java, main()

In the last case, with e.printStackTrace(), in the System.err error channel, you'll get the same output as the one the virtual machine raises if the exception isn't caught. Consider the following example:

```
java.lang.NumberFormatException
For input string: "19%"
java.lang.NumberFormatException: For input string: "19%"
```

```
java.lang.NumberFormatException: For input string: "19%"
 at java.base/java.lang.NumberFormatException.forInputString(
   NumberFormatException.java:65)
 at java.base/java.lang.Integer.parseInt(Integer.java:652)
 at java.base/java.lang.Integer.parseInt(Integer.java:770)
 at c.t.i.e.NumberFormatExceptionElements.main(NumberFormatExceptionElements.java:7)
```

The output consists of the class name of the exception, the message, and the stack trace. printStackTrace(...) is parameterized and can also be sent to an output channel.

9.3.2   Base Type Throwable

All exceptions are subclasses of Throwable. From Throwable, the hierarchy of exception types branches to java.lang.Exception and java.lang.Error. The classes that emerge from Error won't be pursued further in this book since these exceptions are so serious that they usually aren't caught and handled by programmers. Throwable inherits a number of useful methods that are shown in Figure 9.4, which also summarizes the inheritance relationships once again.

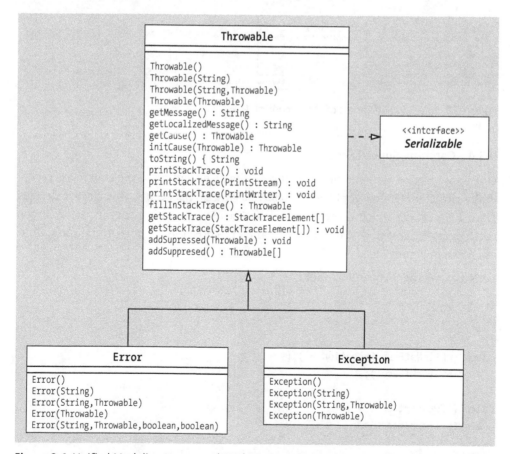

Figure 9.4 Unified Modeling Language (UML) Diagram of the Important Throwable Superclass

9.3.3 The Exception Hierarchy

In the library, all exception classes are derived from java.lang.Exception. Exceptions are errors or exceptional situations that you should handle. The Exception class then divides again into further subclasses or subhierarchies. Figure 9.5 shows some subclasses of the Exception class.

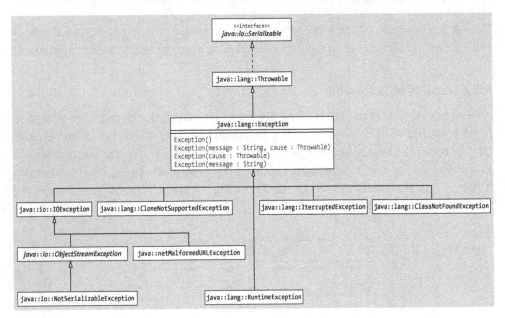

Figure 9.5 Selected Subclasses of the Exception Class

9.3.4 Catching Super-Exceptions

One consequence of hierarchies is that catching an exception of the superclass is generally sufficient. For example, if a FileNotFoundException occurs, this class is derived from IOException, which means that FileNotFoundException is a specialization. If you catch every IOException, you also handle the FileNotFoundException at the same time, as shown in Figure 9.6.

Let's assume the following handling:

```
try {
  …
}
catch ( FileNotFoundException e ) {
  e.printStackTrace();
}
catch ( IOException e ) {
  e.printStackTrace();
}
```

Since the handling in the catch blocks is identical, catch (IOException e) can catch the FileNotFoundException at the same time, as in the following example:

```
try {
  …
}
catch ( IOException e ) {
  e.printStackTrace();
}
```

Even if the exception is caught via a superclass, the exception can basically be identified again later via instanceof. For instance, you could write the following code:

```
catch ( IOException e ) {
  if ( e instanceof FileNotFoundException )
    System.err.println( "File does not exist!" );
  else
    System.err.println( "General input/output error!" );
}
```

However, for reasons of clarity, this technique shouldn't be used often.

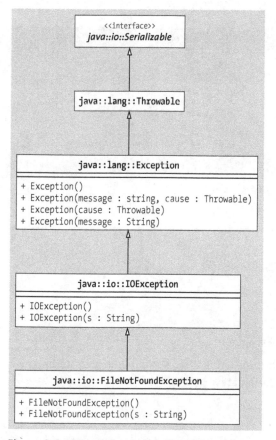

Figure 9.6 IOException in the Class Diagram

9.3.5   Already Caught?

The Java compiler checks whether exceptions may have already been caught in the chain and reports an error if catch blocks aren't reachable. As mentioned earlier, File-NotFoundException is a special IOException, and a catch(IOException e) can catch exceptions of type FileNotFoundException right away. Consider the following example:

```
try {
   …
}
catch ( IOException e ) { // catch IOException and all subclasses
}
```

Of course, a FileNotFoundException can still be caught as its own type, but you must note the order of the catch blocks. The order is absolutely relevant; the type tests start at the top and then continue through to the bottom. If an early catch already catches exceptions of a certain type, for example, a catch on IOException catches all input/output errors, a subsequent catch on the FileNotFoundException is false.

Let's suppose a try block can throw a FileNotFoundException and an IOException. Then, the handling shown on the left in Table 9.1 is correct, but the example on the right is incorrect.

Correct	With Compiler Error

try {
…
}
catch (FileNotFoundException e) {
}
catch (IOException e) {
}
	try {
	…
	}
	catch (IOException e) {
	}
	catch (FileNotFoundException e) { // ☠
	}

Table 9.1 The Order of the Catch Blocks Matters

> **Note**
> The following example using *multi-catch* is incorrect:
>
> ```
> try {
>    new RandomAccessFile( "", "" );
> }
> catch ( FileNotFoundException | IOException | Exception e ) { }
> ```
>
> The Java compiler reports an error of the type "Alternatives in a multi-catch statement cannot be related by subclassing" and terminates.

Set checks are performed by the compiler even without *multi-catch*, and thus the following example is also incorrect for the same reasons:

```
try { new RandomAccessFile( "", "" ); }
catch ( Exception e ) { }
catch ( IOException e ) { }
catch ( FileNotFoundException e ) { }
```

While reordering these lines will correct the errors, the order doesn't matter with multi-catch.

9.3.6 Procedure of an Exceptional Situation

The runtime system generates an exception object if an error is to be displayed via an exception. Then, the processing of the program lines is immediately interrupted, and the runtime system independently moves to the first catch clause (or jumps further to the caller in case of a throws or an unchecked exception). If the first catch clause doesn't match the type of exception encountered, all remaining catch clauses will be checked one after another, and the first matching clause is jumped to (or selected). First, something is tried (that's why it's called *try*), and if an Exception object is *thrown* in the program section because of an error, the object can be *caught* at some point. Since the first matching catch clause is always selected, the last catch clause must never be first in the example since it matches any IOException, and FileNotFoundException is a subclass of IOException. All other statements in the catch blocks would then not be executed; the compiler would recognize this problem and issue an error.

9.3.7 No General Catching!

If a program block throws an IOException, a MalformedURLException, and a FileNotFoundException and the three exceptions should be handled in the same way, a catch (IOException e) catches both the FileNotFoundException and the MalformedURLException type at the same time since both are subclasses of IOException. Thus, one block handles all three exception types, which is pretty useful.

Now, however, some exceptions may coexist in an inheritance relationship, such as InputMismatchException and IOException. Let's recall again the example of the UserInputTimestampWriterMultiCatch class, shown in Figure 9.6, where we used the following multi-catch:

```
try {
    …
}
catch ( InputMismatchException | IOException e ) {
    …
}
```

Since `InputMismatchException` and `IOException` are subclasses of `Exception`, you can also write the following code:

```
try {
  …
}
catch ( Exception e ) {
  …
}
```

The solution chosen in this case, to run up the exception hierarchy until a common superclass is found, isn't ideal. For what works well for exception types that are as well in the hierarchy (like `MalformedURLException`, which is an `IOException`), `catch(Exception e)` is dangerous because it catches much more and handles everything in its exception handling. If, for example, a `null` reference appears through an uninitialized variable with reference type and a `NullPointerException` occurs, this reference would also be caught by mistake, although the program error has nothing to do with the `InputMismatch-Exception` or `IOException`. Consider the following example:

```
try {
  Point p = null;
  p.x = 2;          // ☠ NullPointerException
  int i = 0;
  int x = 12 / i;   // ☠ Integer division by 0

  something can throw InputMismatchException...
  something can throw IOException...
}
catch ( Exception e ) { Handling }
```

A `NullPointerException` and the `ArithmeticException` shouldn't be handled. The central problem in this case is that these exceptions are unchecked exceptions of type `Runti-meException`, and `RuntimeException` is a subclass of `Exception`. If you catch all `Exception` types, everything will be caught—including `RuntimeException` as well. You cannot always catch all non-runtime exceptions, which would work if `RuntimeException` wasn't a subclass of `Exception`, such as a `Throwable`, but designers of the Java language did not model it that way.

If main(String[]) Redirects Everything

If exception handling in a main program doesn't matter at all, you can also redirect all exceptions to the runtime environment, which will then terminate the program—terminate the thread, to be precise—in the event of an error.

```
public static void main( String[] args ) throws Exception {
  Files.writeString( Path.of( "timestamps.txt" ),
                     LocalDateTime.now() + "\n",
                     StandardOpenOption.APPEND );
}
```

Listing 9.9 src/main/java/com/tutego/insel/exception/IDontCare.java, main()

This approach works because all exceptions are derived from the Exception[3] class. If the exception isn't caught anywhere else, a runtime error message will be issued because the Exception object has landed at the interpreter (i.e., at the virtual machine) at the outermost call level. Of course, this style isn't recommended (although used in this book to keep programs short) because exceptions should be handled in any case.

9.3.8 Known RuntimeException Classes

The Java API as a whole provides a large number of RuntimeException classes, and more are coming. Table 9.2 lists some known exception types and shows which operations throw which exceptions. In this collection of exceptions, we're anticipating several special APIs we'll introduce later in this book.

Subclass of RuntimeException	What Triggers the Error
ArithmeticException	Integer division by 0.
ArrayIndexOutOfBoundsException	Index bounds were disregarded, for example, by (new int[0])[1]. An ArrayIndexOutOfBoundsException is a subclass of IndexOutOfBoundsException along with StringIndexOutOfBoundsException.
ClassCastException	Typecasting isn't possible at runtime. Thus, String s = (String) new Object(); throws a ClassCastException with the message "java.lang. Object cannot be cast to java.lang.String."
EmptyStackException	The stack is empty. new java.util.Stack().pop() provokes the error.
IllegalArgumentException	A commonly used exception used by methods to report false arguments. Integer.parseInt("tutego") throws a NumberFormatException, a subclass of IllegalArgumentException.

Table 9.2 RuntimeException Classes

---

3 More specifically, all exceptions in Java are derived from the Exception superclass Throwable.

Subclass of RuntimeException	What Triggers the Error
`IllegalMonitorStateException`	A thread wants to wait but doesn't have the monitor, for example, `new String().wait();`.
`NullPointerException`	Reports one of the most common programming errors, for example, by `((String) null).length()`.
`UnsupportedOperationException`	Operations aren't permitted, for example, by `java.util.Arrays.asList(args).add("jv")`.

Table 9.2 RuntimeException Classes (Cont.)

9.3.9   Interception Is Possible, but Not Mandatory

A `RuntimeException` can be caught in the code but doesn't have to be. Since the compiler doesn't insist on interception, exceptions thrown from `RuntimeException` are also called *unchecked exceptions*, while all others are referred to as *checked exceptions*. Also, a `RuntimeException` doesn't necessarily need to be specified on `throws` in the method signature, although some authors do for documentation purposes.

Conveniently, an unchecked exception can surface like a *bubble* along the chain of method calls and eventually be caught by a block that takes care of it. If a `RuntimeException` occurs at runtime and a `try-catch` doesn't occur at some point in the call hierarchy, the JVM terminates the executing thread. So, if an action called in `main(...)` throws a `RuntimeException`, that's the end for this main program.

[+]

Style

You don't specify a `RuntimeException` in the method header, which should be documented in the Javadoc.

9.4   Final Handling Using finally

In addition to `catch`, another block can be used with `try`, namely, `finally`. This block is used for final handling and is well suited for sharing resources.

In the following examples, we'll read the dimensions of a GIF image and learn how to close the file correctly. The GIF graphic format is quite simple and well documented, for example, at *https://www.fileformat.info/format/gif/egff.htm*. At that site, you can learn how to read dimensions in the header of a GIF file because the first bytes `'G'`, `'I'`, `'F'`, `'8'`, `'7'` (or `'9'`), `'a'` are followed by the width of the image in 2 bytes at positions 6 and 7 and its height at positions 8 and 9.

```
  Offset: 00 01 02 03 04 05 06 07 08 09 0A 0B 0C 0D 0E 0F
00000000: 47 49 46 38 39 61 54 00 AC 00 F7 00 00 00 00 00   GIF89aT.,.w.....
00000010: FF FF FF FE FE FE E9 0B 30 26 0C 0D 6B 10 16 A9   ...~~~i.0&..k..)
00000020: 10 22 E4 0C 2E DF 0D 2C BA B4 B5 FF FB FC FF FC   ."d.._.,:45.{|.|
00000030: FD FC F9 FA A1 93 98 09 01 04 FD FB FC FF F9 FD   }|yz!.....}{|.y}
00000040: FA F7 F9 FF F5 FC FD F7 FC FF F8 FF FF FB FF FF   zwy.u|}w|.x..{..
00000050: FD FF F4 EF F5 4E 3C 52 0D 0B 0E 71 6C 75 80 7F   }.touN<R...qlu..
00000060: 81 5E 55 69 FA F8 FF FC FB FF 03 02 07 58 55 74   .^Uizx.|{....XUt
```

Figure 9.7 The First Bytes of a GIF Image in the HEX Editor

9.4.1 The Ignorant Version

In the first variant, let's simply write down the algorithm and not care about error handling. In our example, possible exceptions are redirected to the JVM by the static main(...) method.

```java
import java.io.*;

public class ReadGifSizeIgnoringExceptions {

  public static void main( String[] args ) throws IOException {
    RandomAccessFile raf = new RandomAccessFile( "duke.gif", "r" );
    raf.seek( 6 );

    System.out.printf( "%s x %s Pixel%n", raf.read() + raf.read() * 256,
                                          raf.read() + raf.read() * 256 );
  }
}
```

Listing 9.10 src/main/java/com/tutego/insel/exception/ReadGifSizeIgnoring-Exceptions.java

In the class, we haven't yet considered one small thing: closing the data stream. The program ends with reading the bytes, but the closing step via close() is missing. (The program is small, and the JVM releases all native operating system resources after the program ends. However, since our Java program can run longer, a good practice is to close resources after completing file operations.)

Let's add the following line after the console output:

```java
...
System.out.printf( "%s x %s Pixel%n", raf.read() + raf.read() * 256,
                                      raf.read() + raf.read() * 256 );
raf.close();
```

close() in turn can also throw an IOException, but fact that has already been announced via throws in the main signature. Of course, you can abbreviate throws File-NotFoundException, IOException back to throws IOException.

9.4.2   The Well-Intentioned Attempt

The fact that, in our case, a program terminates the main thread and thus also the JVM as soon as a file isn't available is a bit harsh. For this reason, we'll formulate a try-catch to properly catch and document the exception. Consider the following example:

```
import java.io.*;

public class ReadGifSizeCatchingExceptions {

  public static void main( String[] args ) {
    try {
      RandomAccessFile raf = new RandomAccessFile( "duke.gif", "r" );
      raf.seek( 6 );

      System.out.printf( "%s x %s Pixel%n", raf.read() + raf.read() * 256,
                                            raf.read() + raf.read() * 256 );
      raf.close();
    }
    catch ( FileNotFoundException e ) {
      System.err.println( "File does not exist!" );
    }
    catch ( IOException e ) {
      System.err.println( "General input/output error!" );
    }
  }
}
```

Listing 9.11 src/main/java/com/tutego/insel/exception/ReadGifSizeCatching-Exceptions.java

But is everything OK with this solution or have we missed something?

9.4.3   From Now On, Closing Is Part of the Agenda

Let's assume that opening doesn't result in an exception but that accessing a byte unexpectedly does. read() is aborted, and the JVM directs us to the exception block, which prints a message. The problem is that the program hasn't closed the data stream. You might be tempted to write a close() in the catch branch as well, but doing so would be source code duplication, which must be avoided. In this case, a finally block comes into play.

finally blocks always come after catch blocks, and their most important property is that the program code in the finally block is always executed, regardless of whether an exception occurred or not and the routine went through smoothly. We need the finally block for the purpose of resource sharing. Since finally is always executed, the file will be closed (and the internal file handle released) if all went well—and likewise in the case of an exception. Consider the following example:

```java
RandomAccessFile raf = null;

try {
  raf = new RandomAccessFile( "duke.gif", "r" );
  raf.seek( 6 );

  System.out.printf( "%s x %s Pixel%n", raf.read() + raf.read() * 256,
                                        raf.read() + raf.read() * 256 );
}
catch ( FileNotFoundException e ) {
  System.err.println( "File does not exist!" );
}
catch ( IOException e ) {
  System.err.println( "General input/output error!" );
}
finally {
  if ( raf != null )
    try { raf.close(); } catch ( IOException e ) { }
}
```

Listing 9.12 src/main/java/com/tutego/insel/exception/ReadGifSize.java, main()

Since close() can throw an IOException, the call itself must be wrapped with a try-catch. This scenario leads to somewhat daunting constructions like try-catch-finally-try-catch (TCFTC). Another drawback is that the raf variable must now be declared outside the try block. As a local variable, this variable gives it a larger radius—larger than it should be. This problem can be solved with an extra block even if that doesn't look as pretty. The special language construct *try with resources* solves this elegantly; more information on this topic will follow in Section 9.6.1.

> **Note** [«]
>
> Local variables declared in a try block aren't visible in the appended catch or finally block.

9.4.4   Summary

One or more catch blocks can optionally be followed by a finally block. The runtime environment always executes the statements in the finally block, regardless of whether an exception occurred or the statements in the try block passed optimally. Thus, the finally block is executed in any case—let's leave System.exit(int) or system errors aside at this point—even if a return, break, or continue in the try block exists or a statement raises a new exception. The program code in the finally block doesn't even know if an exception occurred previously or if everything went smoothly. If this information is of interest, a statement at the end of the try block would have to assign a flag, which an expression in the finally block can then test.

Statements in the finally block are always useful if some operations must always be executed. A typical use case is for the sharing of resources, especially the closing of files.

Note

A finalizer for objects exists but has nothing to do with finally. A finalizer is a special method that is called whenever the garbage collector clears away an object. Finalizers have become obsolete.

9.4.5   A try without a catch, but a try-finally

A try block always catches exceptions, but appending a catch block to handle them isn't mandatory; instead, throws can simply pass the exceptions upwards. Only a construction of the type try {} without catch is invalid, whereas a try block without catch but with finally is absolutely legitimate. This construction is fairly common and important in Java, for instance, when no exception should be handled and instead the program code should always be processed independently of possible exceptions. A typical example is the sharing of resources.

Let's return to our program to determine the size of a GIF image. If no rescue is available when the IO error occurs, we should pass the exception to the caller, but make sure you don't forget to release the resources requested in the method, as in the following example:

```
import java.io.*;

public class ReadGifSizeWithTryFinally {

  public static void printGifSize( String filename ) throws IOException {
    RandomAccessFile raf = new RandomAccessFile( filename, "r" );

    try {
      raf.seek( 6 );
```

```
      System.out.printf( "%s x %s Pixel%n", raf.read() + raf.read() * 256,
                                    raf.read() + raf.read() * 256 );
    }
    finally {
      raf.close();
    }
  }

  public static void main( String[] args ) throws IOException {
    printGifSize( "duke.gif" );
  }
}
```

Listing 9.13 src/main/java/com/tutego/insel/exception/ReadGifSizeWithTryFinally.java

Instead of catching the IOException from close() itself in the finally block, you can also pass it upwards in this implementation when an exception is thrown upon closing. In the *ReadGifSize.java* example from Listing 9.12, for example, we had written the following code:

```
if ( raf != null )
  try { raf.close(); } catch ( IOException e ) { }
```

An IOException on close() would quietly bog down because the handler is empty. With *ReadGifSizeWithTryFinally.java*, a possible exception is redirected upwards upon closing, but not with *ReadGifSize.java* because, in that case, the program flow is completely different. For yet another reason, the semantics are different, and therefore, this style isn't recommended if exceptions can be thrown in the finally block as in *ReadGifSizeWithTryFinally.java*.

Important: Java Behavior with Multiple Exceptions

If an exception occurs in the try block and the finally block raises an exception at the same time, the exception in the try block will be ignored—this scenario is referred to as a *suppressed exception*. Consider the following example:

```
try {
  throw new Error();
}
finally {
  System.out.println( "Let's be naughty: " + 1/0 );
}
```

The ArithmeticException, which isn't interesting in this context, comes to the caller due to a division by zero, but the much more important hard Error has been suppressed.

In our example, if an exception occurs in the try block and also in the finally block during closing, then the closing exception overrides any other exception. However, the exception in the try block is usually more important and shouldn't disappear. To solve the problem, another language tool is available, which we'll discuss in Section 9.6.

9.5   Triggering Custom Exceptions

So far, exceptions have only been caught, but not generated. In this section, we'll show you how custom exceptions can be thrown. On one hand, exceptions may arise when the JVM is provoked, for example, in the case of an integer division by 0, or can be generated explicitly by using throw.

9.5.1   Triggering Exceptions via throw

If a method or a constructor itself is supposed to throw an exception, an exception object must first be created, and then, exception handling is triggered. In the lexicon, the throw keyword signals an exception, and processing stops at that point.

The exception type in the following example is IllegalArgumentException, which indicates an incorrect argument:

```
Player( int age ) {
  if ( age <= 0 )
    throw new IllegalArgumentException(
        "No age <= 0 allowed, age must be positive or 0" );

  this.age = age;
}
```

Listing 9.14 com/tutego/insel/exception/v1/Player.java (Constructor)

In this example, note that negative age transfers or those with 0 aren't permitted and cause an exception. In the first step, new creates the exception object via a parameterized constructor. The IllegalArgumentException class provides such a constructor that accepts a string to convey more detailed reasons for an exception. The API contains information about which parameters declare the individual exception classes. After creating the exception object, throw terminates local processing, and the JVM looks for a catch that handles the exception.

[»]

Note

A throws IllegalArgumentException on the constructor is unnecessary in this example because IllegalArgumentException is a RuntimeException that needn't be specified via a throws in the method signature.

Let's consider another example where players with a negative age are initialized.

```java
try {
  Player d = new Player( -100 );
  System.out.println( d );
}
catch ( IllegalArgumentException e ) {
  e.printStackTrace();
}
```

Listing 9.15 src/main/java/com/tutego/insel/exception/v1/Player.java, main()

This scenario causes an exception, and the stack trace output by printStackTrace()
reads the following message:

```
Exception in thread "main" java.lang.IllegalArgumentException: No age <=
 0 allowed, age must be positive or 0
 at com.tutego.insel.exception.v1.Player.<init>(Player.java:9)
 at com.tutego.insel.exception.v1.Player.main(Player.java:28)
```

> **Note**
>
> If a constructor throws an exception, usage like the following example is problematic:
>
> ```java
> Player p = null;
> try {
>   p = new Player( v );
> }
> catch ( IllegalArgumentException e ) { }
> p.getAge();    // BOOM: ☠ NullPointerException
> ```
>
> The exception won't result in an object if v is negative. Thus, p remains preset with null. A NullPointerException follows in the BOOM line. The program code that expects the object, but perhaps calculates with a null, should be included in the try block. But usually such exceptions represent programming errors and aren't caught.

Since the IllegalArgumentException is a RuntimeException, a try-catch is technically not
necessary as in the following example:

```java
public static void main( String[] args ) {
  Player d = new Player( -100 );
}
```

The runtime exception wouldn't necessarily need to be caught, but the effect would be
that the exception wouldn't be handled, and the program would terminate.

```
class java.lang.IllegalArgumentException
extends RuntimeException
```

▶ IllegalArgumentException()
Creates a new exception without specifying the error.

▶ IllegalArgumentException(String s)
Creates a new exception object with a detailed error specification.

9.5.2   Knowing and Using Existing Runtime Exception Types

The Java API provides a large number of exception classes, and declaring separate exception classes for each case isn't necessary. Many standard cases, such as incorrect arguments or incorrect program states, cover standard exception classes.

[»]

> **Note**
>
> Developers should never write throw new Exception() or even throw new Throwable(), but always use concrete subclasses.

Let's briefly explore some standard runtime exception subclasses of the java.lang package next.

IllegalArgumentException

The IllegalArgumentException indicates that a parameter hasn't been specified correctly. This exception type can thus only be found in constructors or methods that have been passed incorrect arguments. Often, the reason is a disregarding of the value range. If the values are basically correct, this exception type must not be triggered. A few more details about this topic will follow in Section 9.5.3.

IllegalStateException

Objects usually have states. If operations need to be performed, but the states aren't correct, the method can throw an IllegalStateException, indicating that the operation isn't possible in the current state. If the condition were correct, the exception wouldn't occur. Static methods should not have an IllegalStateException.[4]

UnsupportedOperationException

If classes implement interfaces or put into effect abstract methods of superclasses, an implementation must always exist, even if the subclass can't or doesn't actually want to implement the operation. Instead of just leaving the body of the method empty and

---

4 In the .NET framework, a similar exception exists, the System.InvalidOperationException. In Java, however, the name captures the problem a bit better.

letting a potential caller think the method is executing something, these methods should throw an UnsupportedOperationException. The API documentation flags the abstract methods the subclasses may not want to implement as *optional operations*, as shown in Figure 9.8.

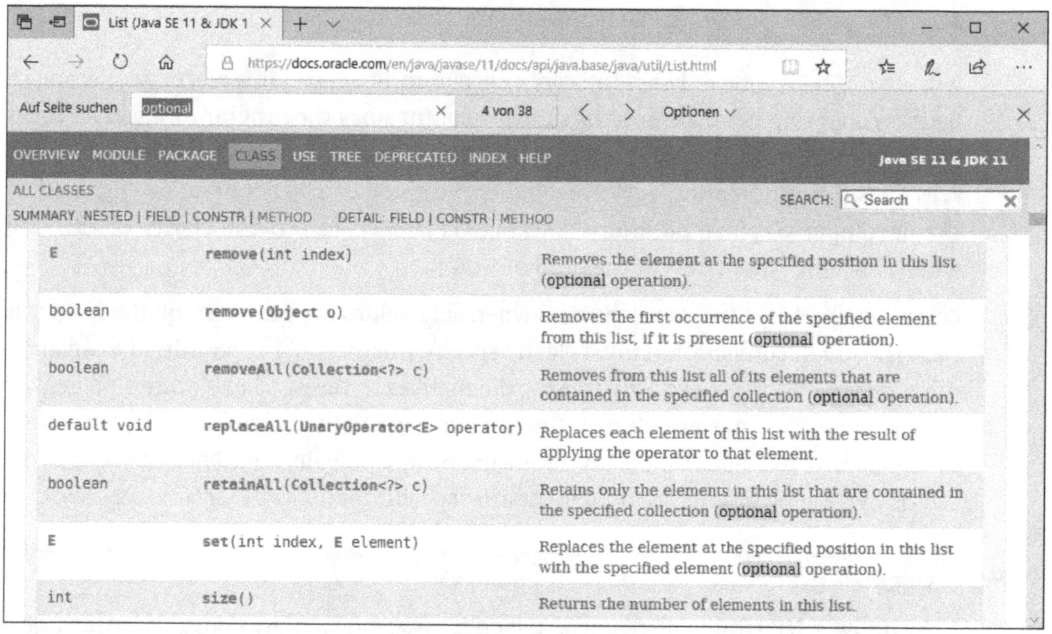

Figure 9.8 Optional Operations in the java.util.List Interface

Unfortunately, a javax.naming.OperationNotSupportedException also exists but shouldn't be used. This exception is specifically intended for name services and is not also a RuntimeException.

IndexOutOfBoundsException

An IndexOutOfBoundsException is thrown automatically by the JVM if, for example, a program disregards the bounds of an array. You can use this exception type yourselves whenever you have index access, such as access to a line in a file, but the index is in the wrong range. IndexOutOfBoundsException has the subclasses ArrayIndexOutOfBoundsException and StringIndexOutOfBoundsException. Usually, however, programmers don't use these types. Inconsistencies exist in the use of IllegalArgumentException and IndexOutOfBoundsException. For example, if the index is wrong, some authors choose the first exception type, while others use the second one. Basically, both are valid. However, the IndexOutOfBoundsException is more concrete and indicates more of an implementation detail. The parameterized constructor IndexOutOfBoundsException(int) takes the wrong index in the integer parameter. The index should always be reported to simplify troubleshooting.

Throwing a Custom NullPointerException?

A `NullPointerException` is one of the most common exceptions. The JVM triggers this exception for something like the following code example:

```
String s = null;
s.length();          // ☠ NullPointerException
```

A `NullPointerException` always indicates a programming error in a piece of code, and so usually, querying these exceptions serves no point since the programming error must be fixed. Programmers rarely throw a `NullPointerException` by themselves because the JVM does that automatically. However, this exception can be deliberately triggered by the developer when an additional message is needed to provide clarity or early on when checking parameters at the head of a method.

Often, this `NullPointerException` arises when null values are passed to methods. In this case, the API documentation must clearly specify whether null is permitted as an argument or not. If not, it's perfectly fine for the method to throw a `NullPointerException` if null was passed by mistake after all. Checking for null to then throw an `IllegalArgumentException`, for example, isn't really necessary. However, again, an `IllegalArgumentException` is more general and less implementation specific than a `NullPointerException`.

> **Note**
>
> To throw a `NullPointerException`, a simple `throw null;` is also possible instead of `throw new NullPointerException();`. However, since a custom `NullPointerException` is rare without an additional error message, this idiom isn't really useful.

To summarize, a `NullPointerException` is thrown in the following cases:

- When you call an object method on a null object
- During read or write access to an object state on a null object
- When you access the array length via `length` on an array that's null, as in `int[] a = null; print(a.length);`
- In an element access to an array that's null, like in `int[] a = null; a[0]++;`
- With `throw null`

9.5.3   Testing Parameters and Good Error Messages

An `IllegalArgumentException` is a valuable exception that indicates an internal exception, namely, that a method was called with incorrect arguments. Ideally, a method should check all parameters for their correct range of values and operate according to the *fail-fast principle*, that is, report an exception as quickly as possible instead of ignoring or delaying errors. For example, if a person's age can't be negative in `setAge(int)`, an `IllegalArgumentException` is a good choice. If in addition the exception string is meaningful, this exception can help immensely when troubleshooting the error: One tip is to specify a meaningful message.

Negative Example

If the value range is wrong when forming a substring or if the index is too large for array access, a `StringIndexOutOfBoundsException` or `ArrayIndexOutOfBoundsException` will occur. Consider the following example:

```
System.out.println( "Oracle-Paul".substring( 0, 20 ) );  // ☠
```

This code returns the following output:

```
java.lang.StringIndexOutOfBoundsException: begin 0, end 20, length 11
```

Then, let's say we write the following code:

```
System.out.println( "Oracle-Paul".toCharArray()[20] );   // ☠
```

The result is the following output:

```
java.lang.ArrayIndexOutOfBoundsException: Index 20 out of bounds for length 11
```

Since testing parameters can turn into a big `if-throws` party, introducing a helper class with static methods like `isNull(...)`, `isFalse(...)`, and `isInRange(...)` makes sense, which will then throw an `IllegalArgumentException` if just the parameter isn't correct.[5] The Java standard library provides various `check*(...)` methods in the `Objects` class.

null Checks

For `null` checks, the method `Objects.requireNonNull(reference)` is useful, which throws a `NullPointerException` whenever `reference` is `null`. Optionally, the error message can be specified as the second argument.

Tool Support

Another approach involves checks by external code check programs. Google, for example, uses parameter annotations, such as `@Nonnull` or `@Nullable`, in its numerous Java libraries.[6] Static analysis tools (now integrated in development environments) or external tools such as SonarLint (*https://www.sonarlint.org*) and *FindBugs* (*findbugs.source-forge.net/*) can check for cases in which the method is called with `null`. However, these tests don't take place at runtime.

---

5 You don't need to write these helper methods yourselves since the open-source landscape already provides something comparable with the `org.apache.commons.lang.Validate` class from the Apache Commons Lang (*http://commons.apache.org/proper/commons-lang*) or with `com.google.common.base.Preconditions` from Google Guava (*http://github.com/google/guava*); in any case, good parameter validation is a must for public methods of libraries.

6 These parameter annotations were defined in Java Specification Request (JSR) 305 "Annotations for Software Defect Detection." Java 7 was originally supposed to support this feature, but this idea has been dropped.

9.5.4   Declaring New Exception Classes

Custom exceptions are always direct (or indirect) subclasses of Exception. (Custom exceptions can also be subclasses of Throwable, but this choice is not common.) Custom Exception classes usually provide two constructors: a parameterless constructor and a constructor parameterized with a string to accept and store an error message.

To declare a new exception type for the Player class from Listing 9.15, let's extend RuntimeException to PlayerException next.

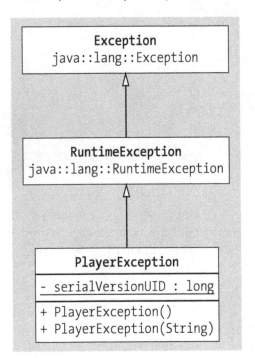

Figure 9.9 UML Diagram for PlayerException

```
package com.tutego.insel.exception.v2;

public class PlayerException extends RuntimeException {

  public PlayerException() { }

  public PlayerException( String s ) {
    super( s );
  }
}
```

Listing 9.16 src/main/java/com/tutego/insel/exception/v2/PlayerException.java

Let's revisit the initialization with age. Instead of the IllegalArgumentException, the constructor throws our more specialized PlayerException in case of an error.

```
if ( age <= 0 )
  throw new PlayerException(
        "No age <= 0 allowed, age must be positive or 0" );
```

Listing 9.17 src/main/java/com/tutego/insel/exception/v2/Player.java (Snippet)

In the main program, you can respond to the PlayerException by catching the exception explicitly with try-catch or by passing it on to the caller—after all, our exception is a RuntimeException and would not need to be caught directly. Consider the following example:

```
Exception in thread "main" c.t.i.e.v2.PlayerException: No age <=
 0 allowed, age must be positive or 0
 at com.tutego.insel.exception.v2.Player.<init>(Player.java:9)
 at com.tutego.insel.exception.v2.Player.main(Player.java:16)
```

> **Tip**
>
> Creating subclasses of Exception is always a good idea. If you didn't create any subclasses, but instead directly indicated an exception via throw new Exception(), you couldn't distinguish this exception from other exceptions later on. The reason is that the hierarchy creation supports specialization in case of multiple catch clauses as well as a distinction using instanceof. If the exceptions are exactly of the Exception type, you'd always have to catch your exceptions with catch(Exception e) and thus get all other exceptions caught as well, which could then lack meaningful distinctions. However, developers shouldn't use exception hierarchies too much; in many cases, a standard exception is sufficient.

9.5.5 Custom Exceptions as Subclasses of Exception or RuntimeException?

Java isn't alone with regard to exception handling. All modern programming languages have these language tools. However, one thing makes Java stand out: the distinction between checked and unchecked exceptions. Thus, when designing custom exception classes, the question arises whether or not they should be a subclass of RuntimeException.

Some aids to decision making include the following considerations:

■ Let's look at how the Java API deploys *checked* and *unchecked exceptions*. In general, unchecked exceptions signal programming errors that need to be fixed. A good example is NullPointerException, ClassCastException, or ArrayIndexOutOfBoundsException. No question, exceptions of this type are programming errors that need to be fixed. A `catch` would be unnecessary since this kind of exception simply doesn't occur in correct code. The situation is different for checked exceptions. These exceptions indicate errors that may simply occur under certain circumstances. An `IOException` may not be too bad because the file may not exist. However, when making this distinction, note that the JVM is the entity that throws the exception, not a method.

- Should the application be able to "recover" from the exception or not? If a program error occurs due to a `RuntimeException`, the application shouldn't "crash" but should continue working in a way that makes sense. Things are different with checked exceptions, which usually indicate that the error can be corrected, and the program can then be continued normally.

- A module can work internally with `RuntimeExceptions`, while an API designer modeling interfaces to systems can make good use of checked exceptions. This flexibility is one of the reasons why modern frameworks like *Jakarta EE* (formerly Java EE) or *Spring* rely almost exclusively on `RuntimeException`: If an error does exist, then handling something and simply correcting it might be difficult. If, for example, an internal module shows an exception during database access, the entire operation must be aborted, and nothing can be saved. What happens with the `NullPointerException` on a small scale also applies on a large scale: The exception is a real problem, and the program simply can't continue.

- Checked exceptions can report if the caller doesn't comply with the method contract. The `FileNotFoundException` is such an example.[7] If the program had asked for the existence of the file beforehand via the `Files` method `exists(...)`, you wouldn't have seen this exception. (The special case that the file was still there during the test, but then deleted in the background, should also not be neglected.) The caller is at fault, so to speak, and receives a checked exception because it doesn't comply with the general conditions. In the case of an unchecked exception, the caller is not to blame for the problem, but instead a programming error exists. Because checked exceptions appear in the Javadoc, what happens if a developer doesn't comply with the preconditions of the method should be clear. According to this philosophy, the `NumberFormatException` should actually be a checked exception that triggers `Integer.parseInt(...)`. In this case, the developer has fed the method `parseInt(...)` with an incorrect value, thus violating the method contract. A checked exception would be correct in the context of this philosophy. On the other hand, one could argue that ignoring the correct parameters is an internal error because it's the caller's job to ensure the correct parameters are used, and so `parseInt(...)` can exit with a `RuntimeException`.

- The distinction between *internal errors* and *external errors* allows for a division into checked and unchecked exceptions. Programming errors with exceptions (like `Null-`

---

7 A reaction like "File not found. Should I fake it? (Y/N)" is not smart either.

PointerException or ClassCastException) can be avoided because as programmers we can control our source code and remove the errors. But with external errors, you have no choice. The network can suddenly collapse and give you a SocketException and an IOException. These problems are out of our hands and can't be prevented even by the most careful programming. This, of course, weakens the argument of the previous bullet point: You can query whether a file exists to avoid a FileNotFoundException, but if the hard drive suddenly catches fire, we are sure to get an IOException because Java programs aren't created like this: "Ask if the hard drive is ready, and then read." So if the error isn't inside the program, but outside, checked exceptions can be used.

- Checked exceptions in method signatures require the user to be aware of a specific API. Changing the exception type at a later stage is problematic since all catch or throws clauses would have to be modified. RuntimeExceptions are more flexible in this context. In agile program development, if the type of checked exceptions in the lifecycle of a software changes frequently, many changes may be required, which of course cost time and money.

The first point leads to some decisions in the Java API that plague developers but are consistent, such as the InterruptedException. Each Thread.sleep(...) to put a thread to sleep must catch an InterruptedException. This exception can occur when a thread sends an interrupt from outside. Because this event is not an error by any means, InterruptedException is a checked exception, even though we often find it annoying and rarely need to respond to InterruptedException. When creating a URL, the malformedURLException is also annoying, but if the input comes from a dialog box, the protocol may simply be wrong.[8]

Checked exceptions are annoying to many developers, which leads to a problem when the exceptions are simply caught but nothing happens, such as with an empty catch block. However, the exception should perhaps run upwards. The problem is less common with a RuntimeException, which is usually handled at the correct central location.

If we look closely at our previous list, another fact quickly becomes clear—that today there's a lot of uncertainty about the correct Exception base class. While the compiler forces you to handle a checked exception, nothing can prevent you from doing the same for an unchecked exception. Integer.parseInt(...) and NumberFormatException are good examples: The compiler doesn't force you to perform a test, but you do so anyway. If developers are consistent and check exceptions independently, then the compiler generally doesn't need to perform the test. For this reason, some developers pursue a radical strategy and design all exceptions as RuntimeExceptions. The distinction as to whether an application should then "recover" or not is up to the viewer and

---

8 One luxury would be to have a check at compile time because if, for example, new URL("http://de.tutego") is in the code, the exception can't exist. But we are far away from necessary try-catch blocks, depending on what the compiler can decide statically.

is only pure convention. With this all-is-unchecked version, Java would then be on par with C#, C++, Python, Groovy, and others.[9]

[»] **Special Returns or Exceptions?**

An exception isn't always necessary, but when necessary, a return should be issued like null or "-1." When an exception should be thrown isn't always easy to know and depends on the context. For example, let's say a method reads a file and performs a search. If a certain substring isn't present, should the method throw an exception or not? The following criteria are important to keep in mind:

- If the document must have an identifier in the first line and the test checks for this identifier, then a log error exists if the identifier isn't present.
- Within the document, a simple text search takes place. A search term can be contained but doesn't have to be.

In the first case, an exception fits because an internal error exists. If the identifier must be in the file, but isn't, then this error must not be dropped, and an exception demonstrates this fact perfectly. Whether the exception should be checked or unchecked is different matter. In the second case, an exception is inappropriate because if the search string isn't contained in the document isn't an error—that can happen. This same is true with indexOf(...) or matches(...) of String—after all, the methods wouldn't throw any exceptions if there was no match.

9.5.6 Catching and Redirecting Exceptions*

The exception that's caught by a catch block can be triggered anew with another throw, which is referred to as a *rethrow*. An example will illustrate how this process works. A helper method named createUriFromHost(String) prefixes a host name with "http://" and returns the result as a URI object. Thus, createUriFromHost("tutego.de") returns a URI with *http://tutego.de*. But if the host name is wrong, the constructor of the URI class will throw an exception.

```
public class Rethrow {

  public static URI createUriFromHost( String host ) throws URISyntaxException {
    try {
      return new URI( "http://" + host );
    }
    catch ( URISyntaxException e ) {
      System.err.println( "Wrong URI! " + e.getMessage() );
```

---

9 But one thing is for sure: Java father James Gosling disagrees: *http://www.artima.com/intv/solid.html*.

```
      throw e;
    }
  }

  public static void main( String[] args ) {
    try {
      createUriFromHost( "tutego.de" );
      createUriFromHost( "%" );
    }
    catch ( URISyntaxException e ) {
      e.printStackTrace();
    }
  }
}
```

Listing 9.18 src/main/java/com/tutego/insel/exception/Rethrow.java (Snippet)

The URI class tests strings more accurately than the URL class, which is why we'll use URI in this example. The exceptions are also somewhat different: URISyntaxException is the exception on URI; MalformedURLException is the exception on URL. We'll provoke exactly this exception by passing a "http://%" to the constructor, which is obviously an incorrect URI. Our method will catch the URISyntaxException, report the error on the standard error output, and then pass it on because our method can't really handle the problem. The method can only report, which is an advantage if the caller doesn't do that.

The result is the following output:

```
Wrong URI! Malformed escape pair at index 7: http://%
java.net.URISyntaxException: Malformed escape pair at index 7: http://%
  at java.base/java.net.URI$Parser.fail(URI.java:2974)
  at java.base/java.net.URI$Parser.scanEscape(URI.java:3102)
  ...
  at java.base/java.net.URI.<init>(URI.java:623)
  at com.tutego.insel.exception.Rethrow.createUriFromHost(Rethrow.java:9)
  at com.tutego.insel.exception.Rethrow.main(Rethrow.java:20)
```

9.5.7 Changing the Call Stack of Exceptions*

If you catch an exception e in exception handling and then redirect just that exception via throw e, you must be aware that the exception e also redirects the call stack. Let's return to our previous example:

```
Help! Malformed escape pair at index 7: http://%
java.net.URISyntaxException: Malformed escape pair at index 7: http://%
 at java.base/java.net.URI$Parser.fail(URI.java:2915)
  ...
```

```
at java.base/java.net.URI.<init>(URI.java:600)
at com.tutego.insel.exception.Rethrow.createUriFromHost(Rethrow.java:9)
at com.tutego.insel.exception.Rethrow.main(Rethrow.java:20)
```

The main(...) method catches the exception of createUriFromHost(...), but this method isn't located at the top of the call stack. The exception didn't come from createUriFromHost(...) itself, but from fail(...), so fail(...) is located on top. If this scenario not desired, you can correct the code because the base class for all exceptions (Throwable) provides the fillInStackTrace() method, which can be used to refill the call stack. Our well-known method createUriFromHost(...) is supposed to fall back on fillInStackTrace(), as in the following example:

```
public static URI createUriFromHost( String host ) throws URISyntaxException {
  try {
    return new URI( "http://" + host );
  }
  catch ( URISyntaxException e ) {
    System.err.println( "Help! " + e.getMessage() );
    e.fillInStackTrace();
    throw e;
  }
}
```

Listing 9.19 src/main/java/com/tutego/insel/exception/RethrowFillInStackTrace.java, createUriFromHost()

If the URISyntaxException occurs in createUriFromHost(...), our method will catch it. Originally, in e, the call stack is stored with the fail(...) method at the top; however, fillInStackTrace() first clears the whole stack trace and refills it with the path that the current thread takes to the method, which calls fillInStackTrace(), that is, createUriFromHost(...). For this reason, the console output also starts with our method:

```
Help! Malformed escape pair at index 7: http://%
java.net.URISyntaxException: Malformed escape pair at index 7: http://%
 at com.….RethrowFillInStackTrace.createUriFromHost(RethrowFillInStackTrace.java
:12)
 at com.….RethrowFillInStackTrace.main(RethrowFillInStackTrace.java:20)
```

9.5.8   Nested Exceptions*

The reason for an exception may be that an embedded part fails, which is comparable to a transaction: If one part of the chain contains an error, the entire part can't be executed. The same is true with exceptions. Let's suppose you have a foo() method that throws an exception named HellException if it fails. Now, if the foo() method calls a bar() subroutine that performs an input/output operation, for example, and it fails, the IOException will be the cause of the HellException. So, mentioning the failure of the subtask when naming the reason for one's own failure makes sense (again proof of how "human" programming can be).

A *nested exception* stores a reference to another exception. When an exception object is created, the *cause* can be passed as an argument in two possible constructors of the Throwable class:

```
class java.lang.Throwable
implements Serializable
```

▶ Throwable(Throwable cause)

▶ Throwable(String message, Throwable cause)

The reason for the exception is queried by the Throwable getCause() method.

Since constructors aren't inherited in Java, subclasses often provide constructors to assume the reason. At least Exception does that and thus has four producers:

```
class java.lang.Exception
extends Throwable
```

▶ Exception()

▶ Exception(String message)

▶ Exception(String message, Throwable cause)

▶ Exception(Throwable cause)

Some deeper subclasses then also have these constructor types with Throwable parameters, like IOException, SQLException, or ClassNotFoundException, while others don't, like PrinterException, for example. Custom subclasses can also use initCause (Throwable) to specify a nested exception exactly once.

Wrapping Checked Exceptions in Unchecked Exceptions

In modern frameworks, the use of exceptions that don't need to be checked (i.e., instances of RuntimeException) has become increasingly common. Known exceptions to be checked are wrapped in RuntimeException objects (a kind of exception wrapper), which store the reference to the throwing non-RuntimeException.

Let's consider an example. The following three lines specify whether the web page for a URL is available:

```
HttpURLConnection.setFollowRedirects( false );
HttpURLConnection con = (HttpURLConnection)(new URL( url ).openConnection());
boolean available = con.getResponseCode() == HttpURLConnection.HTTP_OK;
```

Since the constructor of URL can throw a MalformedURLException and since network access can throw an IOException, these two exceptions must either be handled or passed on to the caller. (MalformedURLException is a special IOException, which shortens the program a bit.) Let's create a variant in which we wrap the checked exceptions in a RuntimeException so that a utility method is available, and thus, the caller doesn't have to deal with any exceptions for a long time:

```java
public static boolean isAvailable( String url ) {
  try {
    HttpURLConnection.setFollowRedirects( false );
    HttpURLConnection con =
 (HttpURLConnection)(new URL( url ).openConnection());
    return con.getResponseCode() == HttpURLConnection.HTTP_OK;
  }
  catch ( IOException e ) {
    throw new RuntimeException( e );
  }
}


public static void main( String[] args ) {
  System.out.println( isAvailable( "http://caliginous.junk/" ) ); // false
  System.out.println( isAvailable( "http://www.tutego.com/" ) ); // true
  System.out.println( isAvailable( "pigeon://germany/dortmund/huelshof/28/
" ) ); // ☠
}
```

Listing 9.20 src/main/java/com/tutego/insel/exception/NestedException.java, NestedException

The last line causes an exception because the "pigeon" protocol doesn't exist. But the program aborts already before that, namely, at the first URL, because no connection to the server is possible. The result is the following output:

```
Exception in thread "main" java.lang.RuntimeException: java.net.UnknownHostExcep
tion: caliginous.junk
 at c.t.i.e.NestedException.isAvailable(NestedException.java:15)
 at c.t.i.e.NestedException.main(NestedException.java:23)
Caused by: java.net.UnknownHostException: caliginous.junk
 at java.base/sun.nio.ch.NioSocketImpl.connect(NioSocketImpl.java:567)
 at java.base/java.net.Socket.connect(Socket.java:633)
 …
java.base/java.net.HttpURLConnection.getResponseCode(HttpURLConnection.java:529)
 at c.t.i.e.NestedException.isAvailable(NestedException.java:12)
 ... 1 more
```

In practice, with large stack traces and a scenario where intercepting and repackaging occurs, deciphering the history from the output is almost impossible since various parts are repeated and then abbreviated again.

Note

Instead of using the parameterized constructor `new RuntimeException(e)`, you could have used `initCause(...)`, as in the following example:

```
catch ( IOException e ) {
  RuntimeException e2 = new RuntimeException();
  e2.initCause( e );
  throw e2;
}
```

However, one important difference to note: Without the parameterized constructor and with `initCause(...)`, no automatic call of `fillInStackTrace()` will occur, so the stack trace looks different.

UncheckedIOException

Exceptions in input/output operations are traditionally reported in Java via a checked exception of type `IOException`. With frameworks, this scenario is sometimes a bit annoying, so you can use a kind of wrapper class in the `java.io` package that embeds a checked `IOException` in an unchecked `UncheckedIOException`.

```
class java.io.UncheckedIOException
extends RuntimeException
```

▶ `UncheckedIOException(IOException cause)`
  Wraps cause.

▶ `UncheckedIOException(String message, IOException cause)`
  Wraps cause with an additional message.

So far, the Java library makes use of this exception type in only one place, that is, in `lines()` of the `BufferedReader` class. In this way, in the Stream API, the checked exceptions won't get in the way.

9.6   try with Resources (Automatic Resource Management)

Java has an automatic garbage collection capability that detects objects that are no longer referenced and automatically frees their memory. Now, the garbage collector refers exclusively to the memory, but many other resources exist, such as the following:

- File system resources like files
- Network resources like socket connections
- Database connections
- Natively bound resources of the graphics subsystem
- Synchronization objects

In these contexts, after the work has been done, so that resources can be released, cleanup is vital, such as closing files and database connections.

With the try-catch-finally construct, you've seen how to release resources. A relatively large amount of source code must be written, and three aspects of try-catch-finally must be considered:

- If a variable is to be accessible in finally, it must be declared outside the try block, which provides it with greater visibility than necessary.
- Closing a resource often entails an additional try-catch.
- An exception thrown in finally (for example, on close()) overrides the exception thrown in the try block.

9.6.1 try with Resources

To simplify the closing of resources, a special variant of the try statement can be used: *try with resources*. This language construct can be used to automatically close *resource types* that implement the java.lang.AutoCloseable interface. Input/output classes like Scanner, InputStream, Writer, and RandomAccessFile implement this interface and can be used directly. Because try with resources serves the *Automatic Resource Management (ARM)* functionality, this special try block is also called *ARM block*.

Let's put this idea into practice: In our previous program ReadGifSizeWithTryFinally, we had to close the RandomAccessFile with a lot of code. Using try with resources makes this closing step much easier.

```java
public static void main( String[] args ) {
  try ( RandomAccessFile raf = new RandomAccessFile( "duke.gif", "r" ) ) {
    raf.seek( 6 );
    System.out.printf( "%s x %s Pixel%n", raf.read() + raf.read() * 256,
                                          raf.read() + raf.read() * 256 );
  }
  catch ( IOException e ) {
    System.err.println( "Input/output error!" );
  }
}
```

Listing 9.21 src/main/java/com/tutego/insel/exception/ReadGifSizeTryWithResources.java

Previously, we set a block directly after the try keyword, but try with resources uses its own extended syntax: try is followed by a resource specification in parentheses instead of the direct {} block, and only then does the {} block follow—so, in this case, try (…) {…} instead of try {…}.

The resource specification consists of a set of parentheses and a list of resources. The resources are final variables of the AutoCloseable type, and these final variables will be automatically closed later. The variables can be initialized with an equal sign directly with an expression, such as with a constructor or method call. Using var is permitted.

The local variable declared in try is only valid in the block and is automatically released, regardless of whether the ARM block was processed correctly or whether an exception occurred during processing. The compiler inserts all necessary checks.

> **Note**
>
> If close() isn't called on a variable of type AutoCloseable, or if close() isn't used in a try with resources scenario, the Java compiler will issue a warning. The warning disappears with the annotation @SuppressWarnings("resource").

9.6.2   The AutoCloseable Interface

try with resources closes resources that "match" the AutoCloseable type. For this reason, let's take a closer look at the following interface:

```java
package java.lang;

public interface AutoCloseable {
  void close() throws Exception;
}
```

Listing 9.22 java/lang/AutoCloseable.java

Exceptions

What is noticeable about close() is that this method can throw a general Exception. To compare, the input/output classes throw an IOException when they fail, but different classes can throw different exceptions on close() or not throw anything at all.

Type	Signature
java.io.Scanner	close() // without exception
javax.sound.sampled.Line	close() // without exception
java.io.RandomAccessFile	close() throws IOException
java.sql.Connection	close() throws SQLException

Table 9.3 Some Types That Implement or Extend AutoCloseable

If a class implements the interface, the exception on throws can be omitted. Take the Scanner class for example: the close() method and no other Scanner method doesn't throw any IO exception but instead Scanner catches exceptions internally, stores the last exception and makes the last exception accessible later via the ioException() method.

9.6.3   Exceptions to close()

When try is used with resources, the one exception declared on close() persists. The method doesn't spirit away possible thrown exceptions, and either a catching catch is needed, or the exception must be passed upwards.

Of course, it's a bit strange that the compiler reports an error in the code but that error isn't visible at all. However, you should get used to this behavior because the closing instruction is always present in the bytecode. If close() raises a checked exception that isn't handled, a compiler error will occur regardless of whether the compiler generates the close() statement or you explicitly put the close() in.

[Ex]

Example

The close() method of BufferedReader throws an IOException, so the following method can't be interpreted:

```
void no() {
    try ( Reader r = new BufferedReader(null) ) { }    // ☠ Compiler error
}
```

The expression new BufferedReader(null) needs *no* handling because the constructor doesn't throw an exception. Only the unhandled exception of close() results in "exception thrown from implicit call to close() on resource variable 'r'."

The advantage of try with resources is that the associated catch can catch the exception from close(). Consider the following example:

```
try ( RandomAccessFile raf = new RandomAccessFile( "duke.gif", "r" ) ) {
    raf.seek( 6 );
}
catch ( IOException e ) {
    System.err.println( "Input/output error!" );
}
```

With try with resources, the compiler independently places a close() in the bytecode, which throws an IOException in the example—catch catches that too.

Scanner, for example, doesn't throw an exception on close(), so no catch block needs to follow.

```
InputStream in = ClassLoader.getSystemResourceAsStream( "EastOfJava.txt" );
try ( Scanner res = new Scanner( in ) ) {
  System.out.println( res.nextLine() );
}
```

Listing 9.23 src/main/java/com/tutego/insel/exception/ScannerTryWithResources.java (Snippet)

A catch block isn't mandatory because none of the methods throws a checked exception—neither getSystemResourceAsStream(...), new Scanner(InputStream), nextLine(), nor the close() that calls try with resources automatically. The situation is different if the resource is a RandomAccessFile or classic data stream (InputStream/OutputStream/Reader/Writer) because, in these cases, the close() method declares an IOException.

9.6.4   Types That Are AutoCloseable and Closeable

In the Java library, there is a second interface named Closeable. But the close() method declares a throws IOException, so this Closeable is only used with IO-resources and Closable with every resource that can be released, such as a graphics object. Closeable extends AutoCloseable because closing input/output resources is a special way to close general resources.

Who Is AutoCloseable?

Since all classes that implement Closeable are also automatically of type AutoCloseable, a number of types are eligible in this context. But basically these classes are from the java.io package, like RandomAccessFile, Channel, Reader, and Writer implementations; FileLock and XMLDecoder; and a few more exotics like URLClassLoader or ImageOutputStream. Types from the java.sql package are also among the beneficiaries. Classes from the threading area, where for example a lock could be released again, or graphics applications, where the graphics context must be released again, do not implement AutoCloseable.

> **Note**
>
> Some streams must remain open. This rule applies, for example, to System.in, an InputStream provided by the system. Even wrapped in a Scanner, a close() on the Scanner will become a close() on the InputStream, and a re-read from System.in will be acknowledged with a "java.io.IOException: Stream closed." So, a try (Scanner in = new Scanner(System.in)) { ... } isn't a good idea.

9.6.5   Using Multiple Resources

The previous examples demonstrate the use of exactly one resource. However, multiple types are also possible, separated by semicolons:

```
try ( InputStream  in  = Files.newInputStream( srcPath );
      OutputStream out = Files.newOutputStream( destPath ) ) {
  ...
}
```

Furthermore, nested streams are possible because a resource can reference a previous resource, as in the following example:

```
try ( InputStream fis = Files.newInputStream( srcPath );
      InputStream bis = new BufferedInputStream( fis ) ) {
  ...
}
```

This model is often used for decorators in a decorator design pattern.

[»]

Note

The separation is created with a semicolon, and each segment can declare a different type, such as InputStream/OutputStream. Consequently, the resource types don't need to be the same, and even if they are, the type must always be rewritten, so for example:

```
try ( InputStream in1 = …; InputStream in2 = … )
```

The following code is invalid:

```
try ( InputStream in1 = …, in2 = … )    // ☠ Compiler error
```

At the end of the resource collection, you may—but don't need to—place a semicolon, just as array initializations may have commas at the end:

```
int[] array = { 1, 2, };
//                    ^ comma optional
try ( InputStream in = Files.newInputStream( path ); ) { … }
//                                                 ^ semicolon optional
try ( InputStream  in  = Files.newInputStream( src );
      OutputStream out = Files.newOutputStream( dest ); ) { … }
//                                                      ^ semicolon optional
```

Whether this style is acceptable everyone must decide for themselves—there's no useless sign in Java.

Closing Order

Resources are closed in the reverse order of how they were opened.

[Ex]

Example

First in, then out is initialized. Finally, out is closed, then in in the following example:

```
try ( InputStream  in  = Files.newInputStream( srcPath );
      OutputStream out = Files.newOutputStream( destPath ) ) {

  …

}
```

During the creation in the chain, if an exception occurs, only the resource that was opened will be closed. So, in the previous example, if an exception occurs during the first initialization of in, the assignment of out won't start at all and therefore it won't be closed either. (Internally, the compiler implements this scenario as nested try-catch-finally blocks).

try with Resources on null Resources

A close() is not always called at the end of a try-with-resources block. A close attempt may only occur if the resource is not null.

Example

The following code block compiles the code and prints its results as an output in the console:

```
try ( Scanner scanner1 = null; Scanner scanner2 = null ) {
  System.out.println( "Ok" );
}
```

With constructors, an object is always given, but some factory calls may return null. For those cases, it's quite convenient that try-with-resources then does nothing to avoid a NullPointerException on close().

9.6.6   Suppressed Exceptions*

Although the compiler automatically places a call of close() in a finally block in the case of try with resources, its use isn't quite that simple. Two exceptions may arise that require some special attention:

- Only an exception in the try block, basically unproblematic
- Exception with close(), also rather unproblematic. But there will be multiple close() calls if not only one resource was used, which is inconvenient.
- Even worse: Exception in the try block and then also exception(s) on close(). That's a big problem!

One exception alone is not a problem, but two exceptions at once pose a big problem because a program block can only report exactly one exception and not a sequence of exceptions. For this reason, several issues must be addressed if both the try block and close() throw an exception:

- Which exception is more important? The exception in the try block or the one from the close()?
- Should the exception from close() perhaps always be hidden and only the one from the try block ever get to the user?
- If both exceptions are equally important, how should they be reported?

How did Java engineers decide? An exception on close() must not disappear in case of a concurrent occurrence of an exception in the try block under any circumstances.[10] So how do you report both exceptions? Here's a trick: Because the exception in the try block is more important, it represents the "main" exception, and the close() exception piggybacks on top as extra information.

This behavior will be shown in the next example. To better control exceptions, a custom AutoCloseable implementation should throw an exception in close().

```
public class NotCloseable implements AutoCloseable {
  @Override public void close() {
    throw new UnsupportedOperationException( "I do not like close()" ); // ☠
  }
}
```

Listing 9.24 src/main/java/com/tutego/insel/exception/NotCloseable.java (Snippet)

Now, let's use the NotCloseable class as a resource:

```
public class SuppressedClosed {
  public static void main( String[] args ) {
    try ( NotCloseable res = new NotCloseable() ) {
      throw new NullPointerException();          // ☠
    }
  }
}
```

Listing 9.25 src/main/java/com/tutego/insel/exception/SuppressedClosed.java (Snippet)

NotCloseable throws an exception in the close() that arrives at the try with resources. Without catch, the JVM aborts the thread, and the result on the console is:

```
Exception in thread "main" java.lang.NullPointerException
 at com.tutego.insel.exception.SuppressedClosed.main(SuppressedClosed.java:6)
 Suppressed: java.lang.UnsupportedOperationException: I do not like close()
   at com.tutego.insel.exception.NotCloseable.close(NotCloseable.java:4)
   at com.tutego.insel.exception.SuppressedClosed.main(SuppressedClosed.java:7)
```

---

10 In an early prototype, the exception was swallowed completely.

The main exception is the NullPointerException. The interesting line starts with Suppressed: because the close() exception is referenced there. However, for the caller, the
exception of the failed try block doesn't come directly from close() but is wrapped in
the main exception and must be requested separately.

For comparison, if we comment out throw new NullPointerException(), only the close()
exception will remain, and the console will show the following message:

```
Exception in thread "main" java.lang.UnsupportedOperationException: I do not lik
e close()
  at com.tutego.insel.exception.NotCloseable.close(NotCloseable.java:4)
  at com.tutego.insel.exception.SuppressedClosed.main(SuppressedClosed.java:7)
```

So, the exception isn't placed somewhere else; it's the "main exception." The important
thing is that more than one exception may arise when closing. Let's simulate this again
by adding one line to our example:

```
try ( NotCloseable res1 = new NotCloseable();
      NotCloseable res2 = new NotCloseable() ) {
    throw new NullPointerException();
}
```

Listing 9.26 src/main/java/com/tutego/insel/exception/SuppressedClosed2.java (Snippet)

When called, the result is the following output:

```
Exception in thread "main" java.lang.NullPointerException
  at com.tutego.insel.exception.SuppressedClosed2.main(SuppressedClosed2.java:7)
  Suppressed: java.lang.UnsupportedOperationException: I do not like close()
    at com.tutego.insel.exception.NotCloseable.close(NotCloseable.java:4)
    at com.tutego.insel.exception.SuppressedClosed2.main(SuppressedClosed2.java:8)
  Suppressed: java.lang.UnsupportedOperationException: I do not like close()
    at com.tutego.insel.exception.NotCloseable.close(NotCloseable.java:4)
    at com.tutego.insel.exception.SuppressedClosed2.main(SuppressedClosed2.java:8)
```

Any suppressed close() exception will show up.

Implementation

In Section 9.4, the behavior that an exception in finally suppresses an exception in
the try block was introduced. The compiler places close() in a finally block when
implementing try with resources. However, exceptions in the finally block shouldn't
conceal a potential main exception. Therefore, the implementation from the compiler
catches every possible exception in the try block as well as the close() exception and
appends this close exception, if any, to the main exception.

Special Methods in Throwable*

To allow a normal exception to piggyback on the suppressed `close()` exceptions, two special methods exist in the base class `Throwable`:

```
final class java.lang.Throwable
```

▶ `final Throwable[] getSuppressed()`
Returns all suppressed exceptions. The `printStackTrace(...)` method shows all suppressed exceptions and accesses `getSuppressed()`. For users, rarely will use cases exist for this method.

▶ `final void addSuppressed(Throwable exception)`
Adds a new suppressed exception. Usually, the `finally` block from the `try` with resources calls the method, but you can also use the method itself to report on more than one exception. The Java library itself uses this feature in only few places currently.

In addition to the two methods, a `protected` constructor can determine whether suppressed exceptions should exist at all or whether they could swallowed completely. If so, then even `printStackTrace(...)` won't show them anymore.

[»]

A Glance beyond the Horizon

In C++, destructors are available to execute arbitrary statements when an object is released. The closing of resources can also be implemented in this case. C# uses the special keyword `using` instead of `try`, uses types implementing the `IDisposable` interface, and uses a `Dispose()` method instead of `close()`. (In Java, the interface was originally also supposed to be called `Disposable` instead of `AutoCloseable`.) In Python, 2.5, a *context management protocol* was implemented via the keyword `with` so that Python automatically calls `__enter__()` when entering a block and the `__exit__()` method when exiting. This feature is interesting in that two methods are available. With Java, you only have `close()` when exiting the block, but no method exists for entering a block.

9.7   Special Features of Exception Handling*

A few surprises lurk in exception handling, which we'll describe separately in this section.

9.7.1   Return Values for Thrown Exceptions

If the method promises a return, the compiler checks whether each program flow leads to a return value. However, you must clarify the statement "Every method with a result type not equal to `void` must have a `return` statement." Only in one special case is the method not required to have a return statement, namely, exactly if the throw statement terminates processing before the end of the method, as in the following example:

```
class Windows10KeyGenerator {
  public String generateKey() {
    throw new UnsupportedOperationException();
  }
}
```

Looking at generateKey() reveals that, despite an announced return value, no return statement can be found in the body. The processing is thus aborted by an exception before the return. If the compiler can see that a method throws an exception and the return statement is unreachable, then everything after throw is unreachable and no further statements may follow.

generateKey() doesn't need to announce this exception with throws because UnsupportedOperationException is a RuntimeException.

9.7.2   Exceptions and Returns Disappear: The Duo return and finally

One unusual phenomenon in Java exception handling occurs with a return statement inside a finally block. First, a return in the finally block "overrides" the return value of a return in the try block. Consider the following example:

```
static String getIsbn() {
  try {
    return "3821829877";
  }
  finally {
    return "";
  }
}
```

The caller always receives an empty string.

The following program is also interesting:

```
public static int fun() {
  while ( true ) {
    try {
      return 0;
    }
    finally {
      break;
    }
  }
```

```
  return 1;
}
```

In this case, the output to the console is 1. The break in finally lets the runtime environment exit the loop and ignore the return value.

Another curiosity is the exception. The runtime environment does *not* pass an exception thrown in the try block to the caller when a return statement is issued in the finally block, but simply offers the return.

For example, the following method throws a RuntimeException, but the caller of the method will never see this exception:

```
static void translucentVsBillyButcher() {
  try {
    throw new RuntimeException();
  }
  finally {
    return;
  }
}
```

If you remove the line that contains the return, the behavior of the runtime environment will be as expected.

IntelliJ marks finally and return with "'finally' block cannot complete normally" and "'return' inside 'finally' block," respectively, to indicate the problem. With the annotation @SuppressWarnings("finally"), you can turn off this hint.

9.7.3   throws on Overridden Methods

An important rule must be followed when overriding methods: Overridden methods in a subclass must *not* throw *more* exceptions than already listed in the throws part of the superclass. Doing so would violate the substitution principle Thus, a method of the subclass can only perform the following tasks:

- Trigger the same exceptions as the higher-level class
- Use a subclass of the exception in the base class
- Omit exceptions

For this purpose, consider the following constructed example for the previous two cases where ProtocolException as a subclass of IOException:

```
public class SubRandomAccessFile extends RandomAccessFile {
  public SubRandomAccessFile( File file, String mode ) throws FileNotFoundException {
    super( file, mode );
  }
```

```
  @Override
  public long length() {
    try {
      return super.length();
    }
    catch ( IOException e ) {
      return 0;
    }
  }
  @Override
  public void write( int b ) throws ProtocolException {
    try {
      super.write( b );
    }
    catch ( IOException e ) {
      throw new ProtocolException();
    }
  }

  @Override
  public void close() {
  }
}
```

Listing 9.27 src/main/java/com/tutego/insel/exception/SubRandomAccessFile.java (Snippet)

The methods length(), write(...), and close() throw an IOException in RandomAccess-File. Our subclass SubRandomAccessFile overrides length() and omits the exception in the signature. This problem has some consequences in usage. For example, you might use the class as SubRandomAccessFile of the type, as in the following example:

```
SubRandomAccessFile raf = …
raf.length();
```

In this case, length() will no longer need to catch an exception and must not be caught either because a try-catch on an IOException leads to a compiler error.

Consider the reverse scenario. If raf is of the type of the base class RandomAccessFile, the exception must be caught in any case, as in the following example:

```
RandomAccessFile raf = …;
try {
  raf.length();
}
catch ( IOException e ) { }
```

This case shows the difficulty of omitting the exceptions for overridden methods.

For the write(...) method, throws lists the exception type ProtocolException as a subclass of IOException. Of course, simply leaving super.write(...) in write(...) is not enough, which would only throw a more general IOException, but not the promised more specific ProtocolException. Therefore, you can intercept the super.write(...) in the body of the method and create the more specific ProtocolException.

[»]

Design

Accordingly, if an overridden subclass method can't add checked exceptions, the base type design must be such that subclasses can report necessary exceptions.

[»]

Note

If a subclass implements its own constructor that then calls super(...) for a constructor that throws an exception, the subclass constructor must also report this exception because the new constructor can't catch the exception. So, in our example, the following code would be forbidden:

```
public SubRandomAccessFile( File file, String mode ) {
  try {
    super( file, mode );
  } catch ( Exception e ) { }
}
```

The reason is quite simple: If the superclass constructor throws an exception, the object isn't fully initialized. Furthermore, if the constructor of the subclass then catches the exception, perhaps the subclass would inherit not fully initialized members of the superclass and thus is an incomplete object, which is undesirable.

9.7.4   Unreachable catch Clauses

If code in a try block throws an exception and a catch clause for it is available, the catch clause is referred to as *reachable*. In addition, this catch clause must not be preceded by another catch that catches this exception. For example, if you provide catch(Exception e) as the first catch statement, it naturally handles all exceptions. In consequence, catch clauses must always be sorted from special to general exception types (anything else would also be prevented by the compiler).

If you create a RandomAccessFile object and then use readLine(), a FileNotFoundException must be caught by the constructor and an IOException by readLine(). Since a FileNotFoundException is a specialization (i.e., a subclass of IOException), a catch(IOException e) would already suffice. Consequently, if the catch for the FileNotFoundException is placed behind it in the source code, that part will never be executed, as the compiler rightly notes.

Exaggerated throws Clauses

A method compiles even if it specifies too many or too general exceptions in its throws clause. Consider the following example:

```
void openFile() throws FileNotFoundException,
                       IOException,
                       InterruptedException {
  try ( RandomAccessFile r = new RandomAccessFile( "", "" ) ) { }
}
```

Listing 9.28 src/main/java/com/tutego/insel/exception/TooManyExceptions.java, openFile()

Our openFile() method calls the constructor of RandomAccessFile, which as we know can lead to a FileNotFoundException. The openFile() method, however, gives the more general superclass IOException in addition to FileNotFoundException and reports another checked exception with InterruptedException, which the body doesn't trigger at all. Nevertheless, the compiler does let it through.

When calling such methods in try blocks, the exceptions declared too much must be caught in the catch clauses, even if they can't actually be reached:

```
try {
  openFile();
}
catch ( IOException e ) { }
catch ( InterruptedException e ) { }
```

Listing 9.29 src/main/java/com/tutego/insel/exception/TooManyExceptions.java, useFile()

The point is that this problem may well happen later in an extension of a method, such as an InterruptedException, and then the callers are already prepared for this eventuality.

9.8   Hard Errors: Error*

Classes derived from java.lang.Error represent hard errors related to the JVM. In contrast, classes derived from Exception react differently since they represent general program errors. Some examples of concrete Error classes include the following:

- AnnotationFormatError
- AssertionError
- AWTError

- `CoderMalfunctionError`[11]
- `FactoryConfigurationError` (XML error)
- `IOError`
- `LinkageError` (with many subclasses)
- `ThreadDeath` and `TransformerFactoryConfigurationError` (XML error)
- `VirtualMachineError` (with subclasses `InternalError`, `OutOfMemoryError`, `StackOverflowError`, and `UnknownError`)

In the case of `ThreadDeath`, you can deduce that not all `Error` classes end in "Error" because this exception may not be an error in the strict sense because the JVM triggers `ThreadDeath` whenever the program wants to terminate a thread with `stop()`.

Since an `Error` indicates "abnormal" behavior, operations that can throw such an error also need not sit in a `try` block or be passed upwards with `throws`. (`Error` errors count as unchecked exceptions, although `Error` isn't a subclass of `RuntimeException`!) However, you *can* catch these errors because `Error` classes are subclasses of `Throwable` and therefore can be handled in the same way. In this respect, a catch is legitimate, and a `finally` is also correct. Whether catching is useful is another question, however, because if the JVM indicates an error, how you respond to the error in a way that makes sense is still open. What should you do in case of a `LinkageError`? However, catching an `OutOfMemoryError` in certain parts of the program can be beneficial. Separate subclasses of `Error` shouldn't be applied. Fortunately, though, these classes are just subclasses of `Throwable` and not of `Exception`, so a `catch(Exception e)` won't accidentally catch things like `ThreadDeath`, which don't really need to be handled.

9.9   Assertions*

One connotation of the term *assertion* suggests what it is about: *assurances*. Assertions formulate statements that must always be true if the code runs correctly. If a condition isn't met, an exception will follow, indicating that something must have gone wrong in the program. The use of assertions in code promotes documentation for the valid program state.

You can distinguish between the following types of assertions:

- *Precondition*: A state that must always be true prior to an operation
- *Postcondition*: A state that must always be true after an operation

Formulating correct states is an essential element of *design by contract*, a development method that involves establishing a "contract" about what a program must do. Bertrand Meyer, also the inventor of the Eiffel programming language, coined the term.

---

[11]   The funniest error class, in my opinion, for some developers, this error could be triggered on any method.

9.9.1   Using Assertions in Custom Programs

Java programs use the `assert` statement for assertions in the source code. Two variants exist, one with notifications and one without:

```
assert AssertConditionExpression;
assert AssertConditionExpression : MessageExpression;
```

`AssertConditionExpression` stands for a predicate that's evaluated at runtime. The expression isn't in parentheses because it's not a method call.

9.9.2   Enabling Assertions and Runtime Errors

Assertions are always contained in the class file because the compiler always maps them to bytecode. However, assertions are ignored at runtime by default because they are disabled. Thus, speed during program execution is not negatively affected. To enable assertions, the runtime environment must be started with the switch -ea (which stands for "enable assertions").

If assertions are enabled and the JVM evaluates the result of the `assert` statements as true, the runtime environment will continue processing normally. If the evaluation results in `false`, the program is terminated with a `java.lang.AssertionError`.

Let's recall the two variants:

```
assert AssertConditionExpression;
assert AssertConditionExpression : MessageExpression;
```

The optional second parameter, `MessageExpression`, is a text that appears as a message in the error message during stack trace. The exceptions thrown in Java are of type `Error` and not of type `Exception` and therefore shouldn't be caught because a condition that isn't fulfilled is a programming error.

> **Note**
>
> By default, the JVM ignores assertions during execution, and activation occurs only on command. A procedure without condition checks is rather the normal case. Consequently, expressions in `assert` statements must not have any side effects. Consider the following example:
>
> ```
> assert counter-- == 0;
> ```
>
> This statement isn't a good idea because decreasing the variables is a side effect that only happens if the JVM also has assertions enabled. However, this statement can also be used as a trick to force assertions during execution. In the static initializer of a class, for instance, we can write the following code:

```
boolean assertEnabled = false;
assert assertEnabled = true;
if ( ! assertEnabled )
  throw new RuntimeException( "Assertions must be activated" );
```

Example

A separate static method subAndSqrt(double, double) determines the difference of two numbers and calculates the square root from the result. Of course, every developer knows that the square root of negative numbers isn't allowed, but this calculation would pass in Java, with the result as NaN. If any part of the program then calls the subAndSqrt(double, double) method with an incorrect pair of numbers and the result is NaN, an assert error must occur because an internal program error must be corrected.

Consider the following example:

```
public class AssertKeyword {

  public static double subAndSqrt( double a, double b ) {
    double result = Math.sqrt( a - b );

    assert ! Double.isNaN( result ) : "Calculation result is NaN";

    return result;
  }

  public static void main( String[] args ) {
    System.out.println( "Sqrt(10-2)=" + subAndSqrt(10, 2) );
    System.out.println( "Sqrt(2-10)=" + subAndSqrt(2, 10) );
  }
}
```

Listing 9.30 src/main/java/com/tutego/insel/assertion/AssertKeyword.java (Snippet)

Let's call the program with the -ea switch:

```
$ java -ea com.tutego.insel.assertion.AssertKeyword
```

The result is the following output:

```
Sqrt(10-2)=2.8284271247461903
Exception in thread "main" java.lang.AssertionError: Calculation result is NaN
  at com.tutego.insel.assertion.AssertKeyword.subAndSqrt(AssertKeyword.java:8)
  at com.tutego.insel.assertion.AssertKeyword.main(AssertKeyword.java:15)
```

9.9.3   Enabling or Disabling Assertions More Detailed

Assertions don't need to be set globally for an entire program but can also be declared in a more detailed way, for example, for a class or a package. By using a clever variation of -ea (enable assertions) and -da (disable assertions), you can control exactly what the runtime environment should check.

[Ex]

Example

The following example enables assertions for the com.tutego.App class:

```
$ java -ea:com.tutego.App  ClassWithMain
```

The following example enables assertions for the default package (as indicated by the ellipses):

```
$ java -ea:...  ClassWithMain
```

The following example enables assertions for the com.tutego package including all subpackages (as indicated by the ellipses as well):

```
$ java -ea:com.tutego....  ClassWithMain
```

The following example enables assertions for the com.tutego package including all subpackages but disables assertions for the App class in the com.tutego package:

```
$ java -ea:com.tutego.... -da:com.tutego.App  ClassWithMain
```

9.10   Conclusion

Individual program architects may use exceptions differently, and generally two camps can be found: those who work with checked exceptions and those modeling primarily with unchecked exceptions. For this reason, this aspect must be learned along with each new library and framework, just like which articles go with specific nouns in a language like English. However, a sensible strategy is essential. At a minimum, exceptions should be logged. When testing, you should ensure that the method isn't only given nice input values, but also false arguments, so that the exceptions expected with false inputs can also be tested.

Chapter 10
Nested Types

"Utility is part of the beauty."
—Albrecht Dürer (1471–1528)

Java allows you to define a type declaration within another type declaration, creating a *nested type*. In this chapter you'll learn about nested types and how to use them.

10.1 Nested Classes, Interfaces, and Enumerations

So far, you've learned about classes, interfaces enumerations, and records that were declared either alone in the file or together with other types in a file (i.e., a compilation unit). In addition, however, you can include a type declaration in another type declaration. This option makes sense when the motivation is to hide even more details, for instance, local type declarations that don't need more visibility.

This same principle applies for local variables: These variables are only visible to the method, not to the entire class. Nested types show a close dependency, and thus, a nested type is only useful in conjunction with the outer type.

[Ex]

Example

A class declaration named In is placed in the class Out. Thus, In is a class nested in Out, as shown in the following example:

```
class Out {
  class In {
  }
}
```

If a type declaration is placed inside another type declaration, we speak of a nested type. Not only class declarations can be put in other class declarations: Interface declarations or enumeration types are allowed in class declarations as are class declarations in interface declarations; other combinations are valid. Nested types can be static or non-static.

The Java Language Specification (JLS) describes four types of nested types.

Type of Nesting	Example with Nested Classes
Static nested type	```class Out { static class In {} }```
Inner type (non-static nested type)	```class Out { class In { } }```
Local (inner) type	```class Out { Out() { class In { } } }```
Anonymous inner class	```class Out { Out() { Runnable r = new Runnable(){ public void run() { } }; } }```

Table 10.1 The Four Types of Nested Types

The non-static nested types are called *inner types*. The special thing about inner types is that they always have a reference to their outer types. A nested (non-)static class is also referred to as a *member class*.

The opposite of nested types are *top-level types*, which is what we've been dealing with all along so far. The runtime environment knows only top-level types, and nested types eventually become just "normal" class files.

10.2   Static Nested Types

The simplest variant of a nested class or interface is placed in the type like a static property and is called a *static nested type*. These nested types can do the same as "normal" types, but they form a small subpackage with its own namespace. In particular, no outer class objects are needed to create instances of static nested classes following this pattern. (The other inner types we'll get to know are all non-static and need a reference to the outer object.)

Let's declare SquirrelNutCaramel as an outer class and Peanut as a static nested class.

```java
public class SquirrelNutCaramel {

  static String name = "Squirrel Nut Caramel";
  int invented = 1890;

  static class Peanut {
    void print() {
      System.out.println( name );
      // System.out.println( invented );
    }
  }

  public static void main( String[] args ) {
    Peanut peanut = new Peanut();  // or SquirrelNutCaramel.Peanut peanut = …
    peanut.print();
  }
}
```

Listing 10.1 src/main/java/com/tutego/insel/nested/Lamp.java, Lamp

The static nested class Peanut has access to all other static members of the outer class SquirrelNutCaramel (in our case, to the name variable). Access to object variables isn't possible from the static nested class because the nested class is considered a separate class that's located in the same package, and this access wouldn't be possible in the construction. For example, if you write the following code:

```java
System.out.println( invented );
```

The compiler will answer this access attempt with an error message: "Non-static field 'invented' cannot be referenced from a static context."

Access from outside to static nested classes can succeed with the notation Outer-Type.NestedType; the dot is thus used in the same way access to static members is formed, using packages as namespaces. A static nested class must have a different name than its outer class.

10.2.1   Modifiers and Visibility

The allowed modifiers include abstract, final, and some visibility modifiers. Normal top-level classes may be package-visible or public; nested classes may also be public or package-visible, or alternatively protected or private. A private static nested class should be understood like a normal private static variable: This class be seen by the enclosing outer class but cannot be seen by other top-level classes. protected with static nested types allows for slightly more efficient bytecode for the compiler but is otherwise not in use.

10.2.2   Records as Containers

In Java, if a method should have more than one return value, you must use a data structure. In this regard, records are quite suitable to act as small containers. Consider the following example:

```java
public class MinMaxDemo {
  public record MinMax(int min, int max) {}

  public static MinMax minMax( int... values ) {
    IntSummaryStatistics stats = IntStream.of( values ).summaryStatistics();
    return new MinMax( stats.getMin(), stats.getMax() );
  }
}
```

Listing 10.2 src/main/java/com/tutego/insel/nested/MinMaxDemo.java, MinMaxDemo

The implementation of the actual functionality is moved to a Java method. (More information on streams follows in Chapter 18, Section 18.4.)

10.2.3   Implementing Static Nested Types*

The compiler generates normal class files from nested types, but these class files are equipped with what's called *synthetic methods*. For nested types, the compiler generates new names according to the pattern OuterType$NestedType. Note how the dollar sign separates the names of outer tape and nested type. The corresponding *.class* file on your hard drive will then use this name, which is also called the *binary name* of the nested type. Using this name is important, for example, when loading manually.

10.3 Non-Static Nested Types

A non-static nested type is an inner type that is comparable to an object property. Let's declare an inner class named Room in House with the following example code:

```
class AlmondJoy {

  String name = "Almond Joy";
  private int introduced = 1946;

  class Coconut {
    void print() {
      System.out.println( name );
      System.out.println( introduced );
    }
  }
}
```

Listing 10.3 src/main/java/com/tutego/insel/nested/AlmondJoy.java (Snippet)

An instance of the Coconut class has access to all members of AlmondJoy, including its private members.

10.3.1 Creating Instances of Inner Classes

To create an instance of Coconut, an instance of the outer class must exist first. One important difference in this regard relates to the static nested classes: Static nested types can exist even without an object of the outer class, as discussed in Section 10.2.

In a constructor or in an object method of the outer class, an instance of the inner class can be created simply via the new keyword. If you are coming from outside the outer class (or from a static block of the outer class) and you want to create instances of the inner class, for non-static nested classes, you must ensure that an instance of the outer class is available. Java prescribes a special form for the creation via new, which has the following general format:

reference.**new** InnerClass(…)

In this syntax, reference is a reference of the type of the outer class. To create an object in the static main(String[]) method of the house, you can write the following code:

```
AlmondJoy almondJoy = new AlmondJoy();
Coconut coconut = almondJoy.new Coconut();
```

Listing 10.4 src/main/java/com/tutego/insel/nested/AlmondJoy.java, main()

This code can even be reduced to one line:

```
Coconut coconut = new AlmondJoy().new Coconut();
```

10.3.2   The this Reference

If an inner class In wants to access the this reference of its surrounding class Out, you must write Out.this. If variables of the inner class overlap variables of the outer class, you would write Out.this.property to access the members of the outer class Out.

```
class FurnishedHouse {

  String s = "House";

  class Room {
    String s = "Room";

    class Chair {
      String s = "Chair";

      void print() {
        System.out.println( s );                      // Chair
        System.out.println( this.s );                 // Chair
        System.out.println( Chair.this.s );           // Chair
        System.out.println( Room.this.s );            // Room
        System.out.println( FurnishedHouse.this.s );  // House
      }
    }
  }

  public static void main( String[] args ) {
    new FurnishedHouse().new Room().new Chair().print();
  }
}
```

Listing 10.5 src/main/java/com/tutego/insel/nested/FurnishedHouse.java, FurnishedHouse

[»]

Note

Non-static nested classes can be nested arbitrarily, but since the name is unique, you can always get to the particular property via classname.this.

Considering our earlier examples, objects for the inner classes Room and Chair can be created in the following ways:

```
FurnishedHouse h            = new FurnishedHouse(); //
  Instance of FurnishedHouse
FurnishedHouse.Room r       = h.new Room();         // Instance of Room in h
FurnishedHouse.Room.Chair c = r.new Chair();        // Instance of Chair in r
c.print();                                          // Method of Chair
```

The qualification with the dot in FurnishedHouse.Room.Chair doesn't automatically mean that FurnishedHouse is a package with the Room subpackage in which the Chair class exists. The double use of the dot doesn't really improve readability, and you risk creating confusion between inner classes and packages. For this reason, a naming convention should be followed: Class names should start with uppercase letters; package names, with lowercase letters.

10.3.3 Class Files Generated by the Compiler*

For our House and Room example, the compiler creates the *House.class* and *House$Room.class* files. For the inner class to access the object variables of the outer class, the compiler automatically generates a reference to the associated object of the outer class in each instance of the inner class. As a result, the inner class can also access object variables of the outer class. For the inner class, you'll have the *House$Room.class* file with the following code:

```
class House$Room {

  final House this$0;

  House$Room( House house ) {
    this$0 = house;
  }
  ...
}
```

The this$0 variable references the House.this instance (i.e., the associated outer class). The constructors of the inner class get an additional parameter of type House to initialize the this$0 variable. Since you don't get to see the constructors anyway, it's irrelevant.

10.4 Local Classes

Local classes are also inner classes, but these classes aren't simply set like a property in the body of a class. Instead, you'll directly define local classes in statement blocks consisting of methods, constructors, and initialization blocks. Local interfaces aren't possible.

10.4.1   Example with a Custom Declaration

In the following example, the main(...) method declares an inner class named Snowden
with a constructor that accesses the final variable PRISM:

```java
public class NSA {

  public static void main( String[] args ) {
    final int PRISM = 1;
    int tempora = 2;
    tempora++;                              // (*)

    class Snowden {
      Snowden() {
        System.out.println( PRISM );
//        System.out.println( tempora ); // ☠ Commented out a compiler error
      }
    }
    new Snowden();
  }
}
```

Listing 10.6 src/main/java/com/tutego/insel/nested/NSA.java, NSA

In this case, the declaration of the local class Snowden is used like a statement. A visibility
modifier is invalid for local classes, and the class must not declare class methods and
general static variables. (Final constants are permitted.)

Any local class can access methods of the outer class. Additionally, a local class can
access local variables and parameters, but only if the variables are final. In this context,
final variables don't necessarily require the presence of the final modifier to be final. If
no write access is available to variables, they are *effectively final*. The PRISM variable is
explicitly marked with the final modifier, so the inner class can access it. tempora isn't
final (tempora++ is a write access), and therefore, a read access in the inner class at
println(tempora) leads to a compiler error. This scenario is tested in the example: If the
line (*) is commented out with tempora++;, then tempora is effectively final, and Snowden
can access tempora.

If the inner class is in a static method, the inner class cannot call object methods of the
outer class.

10.4.2   Using a Local Class for a Timer

To make these examples a bit more concrete for real-life situations, let's look at how a
timer can perform repetitive tasks. The Java library already provides everything you
need. Our task is to create an instance of java.util.Timer() and to pass an instance of
the TimerTask type to the scheduleAtFixedRate(...) object method. The TimerTask class

prescribes an abstract method run(), in which the concurrent program code to be processed regularly is placed.

Let's use this feature for a program that reminds us, immediately and then at regular intervals, to exercise.

```
public class SportReminder {
  public static void main( String[] args ) {
    class SportReminderTask extends TimerTask {
      @Override public void run() {
        System.out.println( "Come on, you candy-ass!" );
      }
    }
    new Timer().scheduleAtFixedRate( new SportReminderTask(),
                                     0 /* ms delay */,
                                     1000 /* ms period */ );
  }
}
```

Listing 10.7 src/main/java/com/tutego/insel/nested/SportReminder.java, SportReminder

Our SportReminderTask class, which extends TimerTask, is declared directly in main(...). The generated object follows later in scheduleAtFixedRate(...), and the timer runs to remind us every second of the importance of exercise. The advantage of the local class declaration is that no one else can see the local class except main(...).

10.5 Anonymous Inner Classes

Anonymous classes go one step further than local classes: These inner classes have no names and always automatically create an object; class declaration and object creation are combined into one language construct. The general notation is as follows:

```
new ClassOrInterface() { /* Members of the inner class */ }
```

New methods and object variables can be declared, and methods can be overridden in the block of curly brackets. new is followed by the name of a class or interface, with the following options:

- new *Class name(Optional Arguments)* { ... }: If new is followed by a class type, then the anonymous class is a subclass of Class name. Possible arguments for the constructor of the base class can be specified (which might be necessary, for example, if the superclass doesn't declare a parameterless constructor).

- new *Interface name()* { ... }: If new is followed by the name of an interface, then the anonymous class inherits from Object and implements the given interface. If the anonymous class doesn't implement the operations of the interface, then you have an error. This situation wouldn't help us at all because then you'd have an abstract inner class from which no object can be created.

For anonymous inner classes, one restriction is that no additional extends or implements specifications are possible. Likewise, custom constructors are not possible (but instance initializers are), and only object methods and final static variables are allowed.

10.5.1   Using an Anonymous Inner Class for the Timer

In Listing 10.7, we declared a new local class for the timer, but strictly speaking, we only had to use the class once, namely, to create an instance and pass scheduleAtFixedRate(...). This scenario is perfect for anonymous inner classes. For instance, you could write the following code:

```
class SportReminderTask extends TimerTask {
  @Override public void run() { … }
}
new Timer().scheduleAtFixedRate( new SportReminderTask(), … );
```

These statements would be changed into the following code:

```
new Timer().scheduleAtFixedRate( new TimerTask() {
                                @Override public void run() {
                                    System.out.println( "Come on, you candy-
ass" );
                                }
                              },
                              0 /* ms delay */,
                              1000 /* ms period */);
```

Listing 10.8 src/main/java/com/tutego/insel/nested/ShorterSportReminder.java, main()

So, in essence, we've converted new SportReminderTask() to new TimerTask() { ... }. Nothing is left of the SportReminderTask class name; the object is anonymous.

> **Note**
>
> An anonymous class can override methods of the superclass, implement operations from interfaces, and even provide new members. Consider the following example:
>
> ```
> String s = new Object() {
>   String quote( String s ) {
>     return String.format( "'%s'", s );
>   }
> }.quote( "Cora" );
> System.out.println( s );  // 'Cora'
> ```
>
> **Listing 10.9** src/main/java/com/tutego/insel/nested/ObjectWithQuote.java, main()

The newly declared anonymous type has a quote(String) method that can be called directly. Without this direct call, however, the quote(...) method is invisible because the type is anonymous, and so only the methods of the superclass (Object, in our case) or the interface are known.

10.5.2 Implementing Anonymous Inner Classes*

The compiler also generates a normal class file for anonymous inner classes. As you've seen for a "normal" nested class, the Java compiler chooses the notation Outer-Class$InnerClass. Of course, this notation doesn't work for anonymous inner classes because we lack the name of the inner class. The compiler therefore chooses the following notation for class names: InnerToStringDate$1. If you have more than one inner class, $2, $3, and so on will follow accordingly.

Exceptions in Anonymous Inner Classes

In a stack trace, the generated class name appears in case of an exception. Let's say, for example, that the declaration is embedded in a main(...) method of class T:

```
new Object() { String nuro() { throw new IllegalStateException(); } }.nuro();
```

Thus, in the execution, you'll see the following output:

```
Exception in thread "main" java.lang.IllegalStateException
  at T$1.nuro(T.java:6)
  at T.main(T.java:6)
```

10.5.3 Constructors of Anonymous Inner Classes

The compiler converts anonymous classes into normal class files. Each class can declare its own constructor, and even for anonymous classes, you should be able to put initialization code in there.

Let's write an inner class that is a subclass of java.awt.Point. This inner class is supposed to override the toString() method.

```
Point p = new Point( 10, 12 ) {
  @Override public String toString() {
    return "(" + x + "," + y + ")";
  }
};

System.out.println( p );    // (10,12)
```

Listing 10.10 src/main/java/com/tutego/insel/nested/InnerToStringPoint.java, main()

Thus, the anonymous subclass is initialized by the normal constructor of Point.

Instance Initialization Blocks for Anonymous Inner Classes

However, since anonymous classes have no name, we'll need to find some way for constructors to address them. In this case, *instance initialization blocks* (i.e., blocks in curly brackets directly within a class) can help, as described in Chapter 6, Section 6.6.5. Instance initializers don't actually exist in the bytecode, but the compiler automatically puts the program code into each constructor. Although anonymous classes can't have a direct constructor, program code does get into the constructor of the bytecode file via the instance initializer.

Let's look at an example: The anonymous class is a subclass of Point and initializes a point with random coordinates in the constructor. From this special point object, we can then read the coordinates again.

```java
java.awt.Point p = new java.awt.Point() {
  {
    x = (int)(Math.random() * 1000); y = (int)(Math.random() * 1000);
  }
};

System.out.println( p.getLocation() );  // java.awt.Point[…]

System.out.println( new java.awt.Point( -1, 0 ) {{
  y = (int)(Math.random() * 1000);
}}.getLocation() );                      // java.awt.Point[x=-1,y=…]
```

Listing 10.11 src/main/java/com/tutego/insel/nested/AnonymousAndInside.java, main()

> [»]
> **Language**
> Because of the two curly brackets, this variant is also called *double brace initialization*.

The double brace initialization is compact if, for example, data structures or hierarchical objects are to be initialized.

> [Ex]
> **Example***
> Let's create a nested map—that's an associative memory. This map again contains another associative memory at one point, as shown in the following example:
>
> ```java
> Map<String,Object> map = new HashMap<String,Object>() {{
>   put( "name", "Donald" );
>   put( "address", new HashMap<String,Object>() {{
>     put( "street", "1313 Webfoot Street" );
> ```

```
    put( "city", "Duckburg" );
  }} );
}};
```

Warning

The double brace initialization is not quite "cheap" since an additional class file is generated in the file system for the subclass. In addition, the inner class holds a reference to the outer class. Furthermore, some problems may arise with equals(...) because, with the double brace initialization, you're creating a subclass that may no longer be validly compared with equals(...). The Class objects are now no longer identical.) All in all, this rather speaks against using this design. The Map type provides a better option with the use of static of(...)/entry(...) methods.

10

Not at All super()*

Inside an "anonymous constructor," super(...) can't be used to call the superclass constructor. This limitation is because a super(...) is automatically inserted into the initialization block. The parameters for the desired variant of the (overloaded) superclass constructor are specified at the beginning of the declaration of the anonymous class, as demonstrated by the following example:

```
System.out.println( new java.awt.Point( -1, 0 ) {{
  y = (int)(Math.random() * 1000);
}}.getLocation() );                        // java.awt.Point[x=-1,y=…]
```

[Ex]

Example

Let's initialize a BigDecimal object that can store integers of any size. In the constructor of the anonymous subclass, you can then output the value using the inherited toString() method, as shown in the following example:

```
new java.math.BigDecimal( "12345678901234567890" ) {{
  System.out.println( toString() );
}};
```

10.5.4   Accessing Local Variables from Local and Anonymous Classes*

Local and anonymous classes can have read access to the local variables and parameters of the enclosing method, but only if the variable is final. Of course, local and inner classes can't change these variables because final prohibits a second write access.

If a change is necessary, two tricks might be pretty useful:

- Using a final array of length 1 to store the result
- Using `Atomic*` classes from the `java.util.concurrent.atomic` package to store elements of a primitive type or a reference

Consider the following example:

```
public static void main( String[] args ) {
  final int[] result1 = { 0 };
  final String[] result2 = { null };
  final AtomicInteger result3 = new AtomicInteger();
  final AtomicReference<String> result4 = new AtomicReference<>();

  System.out.println( result1[0] );     // 0
  System.out.println( result2[0] );     // null
  System.out.println( result3.get() );  // 0
  System.out.println( result4.get() );  // null

  new Object() {{
    result1[0] = 1;
    result2[0] = "snort wasabi hot sauce";
    result3.set( 1 );
    result4.set( "skateboard in bowling lanes" );
  }};

  System.out.println( result1[0] );     // 1
  System.out.println( result2[0] );     // snort wasabi hot sauce
  System.out.println( result3.get() );  // 1
  System.out.println( result4.get() );  // skateboard in bowling lanes
}
```

Listing 10.12 src/main/java/com/tutego/insel/nested/ModifyLocalVariable.java, main()

The `Atomic*` classes are actually designed for performing atomic write and change operations but can be useful in this scenario.

10.5.5   Nested Classes Access Private Members

The outer enclosing class can access private members of the nested class, as shown in the following example:

```
public class NotSoPrivate {

  private static class Family { private String dad, mom; }
```

```
  public static void main( String[] args ) {
    class Node { private Node next; }

    Node n = new Node();
    n.next = new Node();

    Family ullenboom = new Family();
    ullenboom.dad = "Heinz";
    ullenboom.mom = "Eva";
  }
}
```

Listing 10.13 src/main/java/com/tutego/insel/nested/NotSoPrivate.java, NotSoPrivate

An Outsider class defined in the same compilation unit (i.e., the same file) can't access NotSoPrivate.Family, and of course, no class from another compilation unit has access either.

10.6   Nests

Nested classes have a special feature for private members, namely, that the outer type can access private members of the nested class. Similarly, the nested class can access private members of the outer class. This scenario leads to a special type of implementation in Java bytecode, which must share private members with other classes because, at the virtual machine level, only top-level classes exist.

Java provides *nests*[1] to enable the mapping of nesting in the resulting bytecode. Three new object methods are available in the library for Class: getNestHost(), isNestmateOf(Class), and getNestMembers().

```
package com.tutego.insel.nested;

public class OuterNest {

  public static class In1 {
    private void intern1() {
      new OuterNest().new In2().intern2();
    }
  }

  public class In2 {
    private void intern2() {
      new In1().intern1w();
```

---

[1] See JEP 181: "Nest-Based Access Control," *https://openjdk.java.net/jeps/181.*

```
    }
  }

  public static void main( String[] args ) {
    for ( Class<?> clazz : OuterNest.class.getNestMembers() ) {
      System.out.printf( "%s %b%n", clazz, clazz.isNestmateOf( OuterNest.class )
);
    }
  }
}
```

Listing 10.14 src/main/java/com/tutego/insel/nested/OuterNest.java

The following output is shown on the console:

```
class com.tutego.insel.nested.OuterNest true
class com.tutego.insel.nested.OuterNest$In1 true
class com.tutego.insel.nested.OuterNest$In2 true
```

10.7   Conclusion

Nested types, especially anonymous inner classes, for implementing functional interfaces have become less important with the introduction of lambda expressions. Chapter 13 goes into further detail on this topic.

Chapter 11
Special Types of Java SE

"Following advice means shifting responsibility."
— Johannes Urzidil (1896–1970)

When we program with Java Platform, Standard Edition (Java SE), we often unconsciously use types from the standard library. This connection often goes entirely unnoticed because, for instance, the java.lang package is imported automatically—and thus types like String or Object are always included. On the other hand, some things happen behind the scenes, such as the following behaviors:

- If a superclass doesn't extend its own class, it automatically inherits from java.lang.Object.

- If a primitive data type is given but an object type is desired, the compiler converts the simple data type to a wrapper object in a process is referred to as *boxing*.

- If you concatenate strings using +, the compiler—at least up to Java 8—automatically creates a java.lang.StringBuilder, concatenates the segments using append(...), and then returns a new String with toString(). With no other reference type does the compiler allow "addition," only comparisons with == or !=.

- With extended for loops, the compiler expects either an array or something of type Iterable. From these objects, the compiler queries the iterator and independently walks through the collection.

- For try with resources, the compiler expects an AutoCloseable and calls the close() method on these objects in the finally block.

- When declaring an enumeration type with enum, the compiler generates a class derived from java.lang.Enum. For records, the Java compiler automatically extends a java.lang.Record superclass. You aren't allowed to create subclasses of Enum or Record since the compiler forbids it.

This chapter introduces different types that are favored in some way or have a special position in Java because they are ubiquitous, such as the following:

- The Object base class
- Comparison objects
- Wrapper classes
- Enumerations and the Iterable and Iterator interfaces
- Enumeration types (enum) and the special class Enum

Some types are included in the java.lang package since these types are so elementary.

11.1   Object Is the Mother of All Classes

As shown in Figure 11.1, java.lang.Object is the topmost of all parent classes. Consequently, this class plays a special role since all other classes are automatically subclasses and inherit or overwrite the methods.

java::lang::Object
+ equals(obj : Object) : boolean
+ getClass() : Class
+ hashCode() : int
+ notify()
+ notifyAll()
+ toString() : String
+ wait()
+ wait(timeout : long)
+ wait(timeout : long, nanos : int)

Figure 11.1 Unified Modeling Language (UML) Diagram of Object, the Absolute Base Class

11.1.1   Class Objects

While it's true that every object is an instance of a class, what is a class really? In a language like C++, classes don't exist at runtime, and the compiler translates the class structure into an executable program. An absolute contrast to this approach is Smalltalk: This runtime environment manages classes as objects. The idea of representing classes as objects is also adopted by Java—classes are objects of type java.lang.Class.

```
class java.lang.Object
```

▶ final Class<? extends Object> getClass()
Returns the reference to the class object that created the object. The Class object is always unique in the Java virtual machine (JVM). Thus, a call of x.getClass() from different instances x of type X always returns the same Class<X> object, and the instance of the Class can be safely checked using ==.

[Ex]   **Example**

The getName() object method of a Class object returns the name of the class, as in the following example:

```
System.out.println( "Klaviklack".getClass().getName() ); // java.lang.String
```

Class Literals

A *class literal* is an expression with the structure *datatype*.class, where datatype is a class, interface, array, or primitive type. Consider the following examples:

- `String.class`
- `Integer.class`
- `int.class` (which isn't identical to `Integer.class`)

The type of the expression is always `Class`. For primitive types, writing *primitive-Type*.class returns the same result as *wrapperType*.`TYPE`. For instance, `Integer.TYPE` is therefore identical with `int.class`. Class objects play a role especially in dynamic queries via *reflection*. At runtime, any classes can be loaded, objects can be created, and methods can be called.

11.1.2   Object Identification with toString()

Each object should identify itself with a string via the `toString()` method and return the content of the relevant object variable as a string.

[Ex]

Example

The `Point` class implements `toString()` so that the return string contains the coordinates. Consider the following example:

```
System.out.println( new java.awt.Point() );   // java.awt.Point[x=0,y=0]
```

One nice thing is that `toString()` is automatically called when the `print*(...)` methods are called with an object reference as argument. Similarly, this is also true for the string operator + with an object reference as operand, as in the following example:

```java
public class Player {
  String name;
  int     age;

  @Override
  public String toString() {
    return getClass().getName() + "[name=" + name + ",age=" + age + "]";
  }
}
```

Listing 11.1 src/main/java/com/tutego/insel/object/tostring/Player.java, Player

The result is the following output:

```java
Player tinkerbelle = new Player();
tinkerbelle.name   = "Tinkerbelle";
tinkerbelle.age    = 32;
System.out.println( tinkerbelle.toString() );
System.out.println( tinkerbelle );
```

Listing 11.2 src/main/java/com/tutego/insel/object/tostring/PlayerToStringDemo.java, main()

is thus:

```
com.tutego.insel.object.tostring.Player[name=Tinkerbelle,age=32]
com.tutego.insel.object.tostring.Player[name=Tinkerbelle,age=32]
```

In your own implementations, you must ensure that the visibility is public because toString() is publicly specified in the Object superclass and you can't restrict visibility in the subclass. Although the specification doesn't clearly state that toString() must not return null, the empty string "" is definitely better. The @Override annotation makes the override clear.

[!]

Warning

Some creative programmers use the toString() representation for object comparisons. For instance, if you have two Point objects (p and q) and p.toString(). equals(q.toString()), then both points are equal. But relying on the return of toString() for this comparison is highly dangerous for several reasons: Obviously, toString() doesn't need to be overridden. Second, toString() doesn't necessarily need to represent all elements, and the output could be abbreviated. Third, of course, objects can be equal even if their string representations aren't equal, which is the case with URL objects, for example. The only permitted case for such a construction would be String/StringBuilder/StringBuffer/CharSequence, which explicitly deals with strings. In addition to erroneous behavior, often a massive performance problem arises. equals(...) usually takes shortcuts, so that, for example, obj.equals(obj) immediately returns true or that, in the case of data structures, the objects are first tested for the same length before elements are compared.

JDK Standard Implementation

New classes should override toString(). If not, the program will arrive at the default implementation in Object, where only the class name and the less meaningful hash value are bound together hexadecimally, as in the following example:

```
public String toString() {
  return getClass().getName() + "@" + Integer.toHexString(hashCode());
}
```

Let's learn more about the method:

```
class java.lang.Object
```

▶ String toString()
Returns a string representation of the object consisting of class name and hash value.

While the hash value itself says little, for classes that don't override toString() and hashCode() methods, a difference in the hash value is a first indication that the two references aren't identical.

Example

In the following example, an object of class A {} is created, and toString() returns its ID:

```
class A {}
A a = new A();
System.out.println( "1. " + a + ", 2. " + a + ", 3. " + new A() );
```

The output could be as follows:

1. Main$1A@**4554617c**, 2. Main$1A@**4554617c**, 3. Main$1A@**74a14482**

With multiple calls of toString() on one instance (output 1 and 2), the return remains constant. When the program is restarted, the hash value may look different.

Having the toString() Method Generated

While the toString() method is good for debugging, typing the methods manually is rather annoying. Two solutions simplify the implementation of the toString() method:

- By default, IntelliJ can generate a toString() method for selected object variables via the context menu. By the way, the same is true for equals(...) and hashCode().
- The states are read automatically via reflection. In this case, Apache Commons Lang (*https://commons.apache.org/proper/commons-lang/*) leads onto the right path.

11.1.3 Object Equivalence with equals(...) and Identity

Whether two references represent the same object is determined by the comparison operator ==, while != checks the opposite. The operators test against identity but know nothing of possible content equivalence. Our earlier example with strings illustrates this fact quite well: A comparison with firstname == "Christian" generally has an incorrect, unintended effect, although the expression is syntactically correct. At this point, the comparison of content should take place, evaluating whether all characters of the string match. An equals(...) method should check objects for equivalence. Thus, the String object has an implementation that compares strings character by character, as in the following example:

```
String firstname = "Christian";
if ( "Christian".equals( firstname ) )
    ...
class java.lang.Object
```

► boolean equals(Object o)

Tests if the other object is the same as your own. Equivalence is defined differently by each class, but the base class compares only the references o == this.

equals(...) Implementation from Object and Subclasses

The default implementation from the absolute superclass Object can't know anything about the equivalence of special objects and only tests the references.

```
public boolean equals( Object obj ) {
  return  this == obj;
}
```

Listing 11.3 java/lang/Object.java, equals()

If a class doesn't override equals(Object), the result of o1.equals(o2) is equivalent to o1 == o2. Subclasses override this method to make a content comparison with their states. The method is well-served in subclasses because each class needs different logic to determine when an object is equal to another object.

Not every class implements its own equals(Object) method, so the runtime environment may inadvertently end up with Object and its reference comparison. This scenario has unexpected consequences, and this misconception unfortunately occurs with instances of the StringBuilder and StringBuffer classes that don't implement their own equals(...). (We described this issue in detail in Chapter 5, Section 5.5.8.)

Overriding the equals(...) Method

You must be careful when using self-declared methods because the signature is important in this context. The method must accept an Object and return boolean. If this signature is used incorrectly, overloading will occur (instead of the overriding of the method), and if the return isn't equal to boolean, a second method with the same signature will be created, which isn't permitted in Java (because Java doesn't permit covariant parameter types yet). To minimize the problem, the @Override annotation should be appended to equals(Object).

The use of the equals(Object) method has some requirements, such as the following:

- If the comparison is called equals(null), the result is always false.
- If a this is involved, a shortcut can be used, and true can be returned.
- The argument may be of type Object, but nevertheless, we're always comparing concrete types. The equals(Object) method of a class X will therefore only compare objects of type X. An intriguing question is whether equals(Object) in class X should also take subclasses of X into consideration.
- An implementation of equals(Object) should always involve an implementation of hashCode() because if two objects are equal according to equals(...), the hash values

must also be equal. However, with an inherited hashCode() method from Object this is not fulfilled in all cases, since presumably with equal objects hashCode() nevertheless returns different results.

Note

The data type for the parameter in the equals(Object) method is always Object and never anything else; otherwise, equals(...) won't be overridden but instead overloaded. Thus, the following notation for a class named Candy is incorrect:

```
public class Candy {
  public int price;
  public boolean equals( Candy that ) { return this.price == that.price; }
}
```

In the words of computer scientists, Java doesn't yet support covariant parameter types, but it does support covariant return types. For this reason, a good practice is to set the @Override annotation because it raises an alarm if we think we're overriding a method but actually aren't.

Basic Structure of the equals(...) Method

The previous list only captures the preliminary work until the actual comparison starts. Then, the comparison is a matter of comparing the state of one's own object with the state of another object. In general, we can distinguish between *tests of primitive values*, *tests of arrays*, and *tests of reference types*:

- For boolean and all primitive integer values, a simple == comparison is possible. In a == comparison of floats, a problem occurs due to the special value: not a number (NaN). This value bypasses the conversion to an integer bit pattern. Basically, a test using the static compareTo(...) methods in the wrapper classes could also help in this case, in which compareTo(...) == 0 is used to check for equality.

- For the comparison of arrays, Arrays.equals(array1, array2) is a good choice.

- For the comparison of references, the comparison is passed to the objects, making sure that the reference variables are null. The useful helper method Objects.equals(obj1, obj2) takes care of this comparison.

Tip

Of course, you could fall back on the object method equals(...) from the numeric wrapper classes, but doing so would involve the constant creation of new objects for each primitive comparison. This approach costs an unnecessary amount of time because equals(...) and also hashCode() methods must be fast since they are often called during operations in data structures.

Example of a custom equals(...) Method

The first two requirements are easy to meet, and an example of Candy with the object variables price and quantity can be quickly implemented:

```
@Override
public boolean equals( Object o ) {
  if ( o == null )
    return false;

  if ( o == this )
    return true;

  Candy that = (Candy) o;

  return    this.price == that.price
         && this.quantity == that.quantity;
}
```

This solution seems obvious but leads to a ClassCastException at least for a non-Candy object. The problem can be solved quickly in the following way:

```
if ( ! (o instanceof Candy) )
  return false;
```

Now, we are on the safe side, but has the goal been achieved?

[»]

> **Note**
>
> The equals(...) method always returns false for non-matching types and doesn't throw an exception.

The Problem of Symmetry*

While the listed implementation works well for final classes, the symmetry is broken for subclasses. Why? Quite simply, instanceof tests types in the hierarchy and will return true even if the argument passed to equals(...) is a subclass of Candy. This subclass will have the same object variables as the superclass; thus, from the point of view of Candy, everything is fine. Let's assume two variables (candy and toxicWaste) have the types Candy and ToxicWaste (a fictitious subclass of Candy), respectively. If both objects are equal, candy.equals(toxicWaste) returns true. Let's turn the tables and ask what toxicWaste.equals(candy) will return. While we haven't implemented ToxicWaste, we assume that there's an equals(...) method there, implemented using the same instanceof schema as Candy. Then, a test will run o instanceof ToxicWaste and result in false. However, this terminates the case distinction with return false . Let's summarize:

```
candy.equals( toxicWaste ) == true
toxicWaste.equals( candy ) == false
```

This inconsistency is not acceptable, and to resolve it, you must not use instanceof but instead should ask if the type is exact. This check can be done via getClass() and a simple reference comparison.[1] As a result, the following code is correct:

```java
public class Candy {

  int price;
  int quantity;

  @Override
  public boolean equals( Object o ) {
    if ( o == null )
      return false;

    if ( o == this )
      return true;

    if ( o.getClass() != getClass() )
      return false;

    Candy that = (Candy) o;

    return    this.price == that.price
           && this.quantity == that.quantity;
  }

  @Override
  public int hashCode() {
    return 31 * price + quantity;
  }
}
```

Listing 11.4 src/main/java/com/tutego/insel/object/Candy.java, Candy

You'll learn more about the hashCode() method in Section 11.1.5. We've only included it here for the sake of completeness since equals(...) and hashCode() should always go hand in hand.

---

1 Class objects don't need to be compared via equals(...) because Class objects don't have their own equals(...). Instead, these objects only inherit the implementation of Object, in which case, only a reference comparison takes place.

Specifying a new equals(...) for extended classes makes sense so that the new object variables will also be included in the test. For hashCode() methods, you'll need to use a similar strategy.

Records and equals(...)/hashCode()

Records have an automatically implemented equals(...) method. Primitive elements are implemented using the static equals(...) methods of the appropriate wrapper classes, and for references, the automatic implementation falls back on Objects.equals(...). For hashCode(), the vararg method Objects.hash(...) returns the hashcode across all record components.

Once the Same, Always the Same*

Another aspect of equals(...)[2] should be noted: If the object is never changed, the result must remain the same throughout the lifecycle of the object. One small problem arises in equals(...) of the URL class, which compares whether two URL addresses that point to the same resource. According to the documentation:

> *"Two URL objects are equal if they have the same protocol, reference equivalent hosts, have the same port number on the host, and the same file and fragment of the file."*

Host names are considered equal if either both point to the same IP address or, if an IP address can't be resolved, both host names are equal (case-insensitive) or null. However, since behind the URLs *http://tutego.com/* and *http://www.tutego.com/* ultimately exists *http://www.tutego.de/*, equals(...) will return true in the following example:

```
URL url1 = new URL( "http://tutego.com/" );
URL url2 = new URL( "http://www.tutego.com/" );
System.out.println( url1.equals( url2 ) );                // true
```

Listing 11.5 src/main/java/com/tutego/insel/object/UrlEquals.java, main()

Dynamically mapping host names to IP address of computers can be problematic for several reasons:

- The (human) reader intuitively expects something else.
- If no network connection is available, no name resolution can be performed, and the comparison will return false. However, the return shouldn't depend on whether or not a network connection exists.
- The fact that the two URLs point to the same server could change at runtime.

---

2 A correct implementation of the equals(...) method forms an equivalence relation. If you leave out the null reference, the statement becomes reflexive, symmetric, and transitive. Those terms are used by mathematicians and are explained by detail in the Javadoc.

11.1.4   Cloning an Object Using clone()*

Two ways to replicate an object are available:

- A constructor (also called a *copy constructor*) that takes an existing object as a template, creates a new object, and copies the states
- A public clone() method

The application programming interface (API) documentation describes what each class can provide.

> **Example**
>
> The following example creates a Point object and then clones it:
>
> ```
> java.awt.Point p = new java.awt.Point( 12, 23 );
> java.awt.Point q = (java.awt.Point) p.clone();
> System.out.println( q );              // java.awt.Point[x=12,y=23]
> ```
>
> More than 300 classes in the Java library support a clone() method that returns a new instance with the same state. An overridden method can customize the return type thanks to covariant return types. However, the clone() method at java.awt.Point use just the return type Object.

Array objects provide clone() by default. However, if the arrays store non-primitive values, clone() will return only a flat copy, which means that the new array object (the clone) references the exact same objects as the original and doesn't clone the entries themselves.

clone() from java.lang.Object

Since clone() isn't automatically supported, the question is how you can implement clone() for your classes with the least effort. Simply calling clone() doesn't work, however, because the method is protected, so the method is not visible for now.

```
class java.lang.Object
```

- ▶ protected Object clone() throws CloneNotSupportedException
  Returns a copy of the object.

A Custom clone() Method

Custom classes override the protected method clone() of the Object superclass and make it public. Two options can be considered for implementation:

- You could manually create a new object, copy all object variables, and return the reference to the new object.

- The runtime system should create a copy by itself, and we return that copy. The second solution shortens development time and is also more exciting.

To get the system to clone an object, two tasks must be performed:

- A super.clone() call triggers the clone() method from Object, causing the runtime environment to create a new object and copy the object variables. The method copies the data of the current object element by element into the new one. The method is protected in the superclass, but that's the trick: Only subclasses can call clone(); classes outside the inheritance hierarchy cannot.

- The class implements the marker interface Cloneable. If a clone() is called externally on an object whose class doesn't implement Cloneable, the result is a CloneNotSupportedException. Of course, Object does *not* implement the Cloneable interface itself because otherwise classes would already have this type automatically, which would be pointless.

clone() returns a reference to the new object, but if no free memory is available, an OutOfMemoryError is thrown.

Let's say that players need to be cloned for a game. You could write the following code:

```
package com.tutego.insel.object;

public class Player implements Cloneable {

  public String name;
  public int    age;

  @Override
  public Player clone() {
    try {
      return (Player) super.clone();
    }
    catch ( CloneNotSupportedException e ) {
      // Can't really happen due to Cloneable
      throw new InternalError();
    }
  }
}
```

Listing 11.6 src/main/java/com/tutego/insel/object/Player.java

Since covariant return types are possible in Java, clone() returns not just Object, but the Player subtype, as shown in Figure 11.2. Let's test the class in the following way:

```
Player susi = new Player();
susi.age  = 29;
susi.name = "Susi";
Player dolly = susi.clone();
System.out.println( dolly.name + " is " + dolly.age ); // Susi is 29
```

Listing 11.7 src/main/java/com/tutego/insel/object/PlayerCloneDemo.java, main()

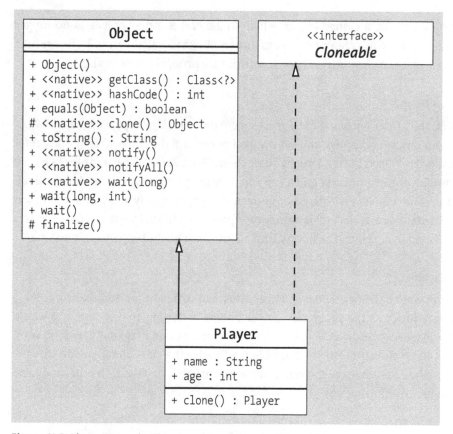

Figure 11.2 Player Extends Object and Implements Cloneable

Note

If you inherit from a class with an implemented clone() method, which itself works with super.clone(), you'll also get your own states copied.

clone() and equals(...)

The clone() method and the equals(...) method are related, as are the equals(...) and hashCode() methods. If the clone() method is overridden, equals(...) should also be adjusted because, without an overridden equals(...), the following code will be inherited from Object:

```
public boolean equals( Object obj ) {
  return  this == obj;
}
```

Listing 11.8 java/lang/Object.java, equals()

However, as a result, a cloned object, which in general is a new object, is no longer equals(...)-equal to its creator because of its new object identity. Formally, this results in o.clone().equals(o) == false. These semantics are probably undesirable.

Shallow or Deep?

By default, the clone() method of the system creates a *shallow copy*. For child objects, only the references are copied, and the original object and the copy subsequently refer to the same child objects (they actually share them). For example, if an employee has an object variable for an employer and a copy of an employee is created, the clone will reference the same employer. With an employer, this copying may still be coherent, but for data structures, a *deep copy* is sometimes preferred. In this variant, all subobjects are also cloned recursively. The library implementation behind Object can't do that.

No Clones, Please!

If you don't want either a shallow or a deep copy, but instead want to inherit a clone() implementation from the superclass, you can prevent cloning. In this case, you would override clone() but throw a CloneNotSupportedException signaling that you don't want the object to be cloned. However, a problem will arise if a class already overrides the clone() method and changes the signature in the process. In Object, the method head is written in the following way:

```
public class Object {
  ...
  protected native Object clone() throws CloneNotSupportedException;
  ...
}
```

Listing 11.9 java/lang/Object.java (Snippet)

The method is native, which means the method not implemented in Java, but in the system language. The visibility is protected because only subclasses should see the methods. A subclass overrides clone() and usually omits the throws CloneNotSupportedException. Visibility is usually raised to public.

For Point2D (from which Point inherits the clone() method), we can write the following:

```
public abstract class Point2D implements Cloneable {
  ...
  public Object clone()
  ...
}
```

Listing 11.10 java/awt/geom/Point2D.java (Snippet)

```
public class Point extends Point2D implements java.io.Serializable {
  ...
}
```

Listing 11.11 java/awt/Point.java (Snippet)

If a class inherits a clone() method from which throws CloneNotSupportedException has been removed, it can't reintroduce the exception—subclasses can omit throws clauses but can't add them. The following code is therefore *not* possible:

```
public class PointSubclass extends java.awt.Point {
  @Override // from Point2D
  public Object clone() throws CloneNotSupportedException // ☠ Compiler error!
  ...
}
```

Since the signature can no longer store an exception clause, you must use a trick and wrap the CloneNotSupportedException in a runtime exception, as in the following example:

```
public class ColoredPoint extends java.awt.Point {

  public int rgb;

  @Override               // from Point2D
  public Object clone() {
    throw new RuntimeException( new CloneNotSupportedException() );
  }
}
```

Listing 11.12 src/main/java/com/tutego/insel/object/ColoredPoint.java, ColoredPoint

An attempt at cloning leads to something like the following output:

```
Exception in thread "main" java.lang.RuntimeException:
java.lang.CloneNotSupportedException
  at com.tutego.insel.object.ColoredPoint.clone(ColoredPoint.java:10)
```

```
  at …
Caused by: java.lang.CloneNotSupportedException
  ... 2 more
```

Technically, wrapping the `CloneNotSupportedException` in a `RuntimeException` solves our problem; however, you should be aware that you're now "disabling" a behavior that was previously permitted. Subclasses shouldn't take away any behaviors.

11.1.5   Returning Hash Values via hashCode()*

The `hashCode()` method is supposed to return an integer number (both positive and negative) for each object that is unique and identifies the object. The integer is called a *hashcode* or a *hash value*, and `hashCode()` is the implementation of a *hash function*. Hash values are necessary if the objects are placed in special data structures that work according to the hashing procedure. Data structures with hashing algorithms provide efficient access to their elements. The `java.util.HashMap` class implements such a data structure.

```
class java.lang.Object
```

▶ `int hashCode()`
   Returns the hash value of an object. The base class `Object` implements the method natively.

Player with Hash Function

In the following example, the `Player` class is supposed to override the `hashCode()` method from `Object`. To successfully store the objects in an associative memory, `equals(...)` is also required, which is also implemented by the `Player` class in the following example:

```java
package com.tutego.insel.object.hashcode;

public class Player {

  String name;
  int    age;
  double weight;

  /**
   * Returns a hash code value for this {@code Player} object.
   *
   * @return A hash code value for this object.
   *
```

```
 * @see java.lang.Object#equals(java.lang.Object)
 * @see java.util.HashMap
 */
@Override public int hashCode() {
  int result = 31 + age;
  result = 31 * result + ((name == null) ? 0 : name.hashCode());
  long temp = Double.doubleToLongBits( weight );
  result = 31 * result + (int) (temp ^ (temp >>> 32));

  return result;
}

/**
 * Determines whether two players are equal. Two instances of
 * {@code Player} are equal if the values of their {@code name}, {@code age}
 * and {@code weight} member fields are the same.
 *
 * @param that    an object to be compared with this {@code Player}
 *
 * @return {@code true} if the object to be compared is an instance of
 *         {@code Player} and has the same values; {@code false} otherwise.
 */
@Override
public boolean equals( Object that ) {
  if ( this == that )
    return true;

  if ( that == null )
    return false;

  if ( getClass() != that.getClass() )
    return false;

  Player other = (Player) that;

  if ( age != other.age )
    return false;

  if ( Double.compare( weight, other.weight ) != 0 )
    return false;

  if ( ! Objects.equals( name, other.name ) )
    return false;
```

```
    return true;
  }
}
```

Listing 11.13 src/main/java/com/tutego/insel/object/hashcode/Player.java

We can test the class with something like the following lines:

```
Player bruceWants = new Player();
bruceWants.name = "Bruce Wants";
bruceWants.age = 32;
bruceWants.weight = 70.3;

Player bruceLii = new Player();
bruceLii.name = "Bruce Lii";
bruceLii.age = 32;
bruceLii.weight = 70.3;

System.out.println( bruceWants.hashCode() );                    // -340931147
System.out.println( bruceLii.hashCode() );                      // 301931244
System.out.println( System.identityHashCode( bruceWants ) );    // 1671711
System.out.println( System.identityHashCode( bruceLii ) );      // 11394033
System.out.println( bruceLii.equals( bruceWants ) );            // false

bruceWants.name = "Bruce Lii";
System.out.println( bruceWants.hashCode() );                    // 301931244
System.out.println( bruceLii.equals( bruceWants ) );            // true
```

Listing 11.14 src/main/java/com/tutego/insel/object/hashcode/PlayerHashcodeDemo.java, main()

The static method System.identityHashCode(...) returns the hashcode for an object as it would be returned by the default implementation of Object if we hadn't overridden it.

[»]

Note

Since the hashcode can be negative, expressions like array[o.hashCode() % array. length()] are problematic. If o.hashCode() is negative, the result of the remainder is also negative, and the consequence is an ArrayIndexOutOfBoundsException.

IntelliJ can automatically generate the hashCode() and equals(...) methods, so you don't need to write them by hand.

Deep or Shallow Comparisons/Hash Values

If an object references subobjects, for example, a person references a String object for the name (no primitive data types), the equals(...) and hashCode() methods pass the comparison and calculation of the hashcode to the referenced subobject (provided the reference isn't null). The following snippet of our equals(...) method illustrates this point:

```
if ( name == null )
  if ( ((Player)that).name != null )
    return false;
else if ( !name.equals( ((Player)that).name ) )
  return false;
```

Listing 11.15 src/main/java/com/tutego/insel/object/hashcode/Player.java, equals() (Snippet)

Accordingly, one task of the String class (name is of type String) is to perform the equivalence test. Thus, two individuals can be equals(...)-equal without any problem, even if they reference two non-identical but equals(...)-equal String objects.

This delegation to the referenced subobject can be read with hashCode() too, as in the following example:

```
result = 31 * result + ((name == null) ? 0 : name.hashCode());
```

Listing 11.16 src/main/java/com/tutego/insel/object/hashcode/Player.java, hashCode() (Snippet)

In rare cases, an equals(...) method or hashCode() method of a class doesn't delegate the comparison or hashcode calculation to the child objects but instead implements the comparison or calculation operation itself.

hashCode() Methods of the Wrapper Classes

Each wrapper class declares a static hashCode(...) method that you can use to compute the hash value of a primitive element. (Section 11.5 provides further details about this topic.) Consequently, to calculate the hash value of an entire object, all the individual hash values must be calculated and then concatenated to form an integer, in the following way:

```
int h1 = WrapperClass.hashCode( value1 );
int h2 = WrapperClass.hashCode( value2 );
int h3 = WrapperClass.hashCode( value3 );
...
```

Generators often use the following pattern to link the hash values, which is a good starting point:

```
int result = h1;
result = 31 * result + h2;
result = 31 * result + h3;
...
```

If you use the static hashCode(...) methods of the wrapper classes, you only need to work with the data type int and don't need to know how the hash value is calculated from a double, for example. However, calculating a hash value may come up, so here's the implementation:

Class	Class Method, Static int	Implementation
Boolean	hashCode(boolean value)	value ? 1231 : 1237
Byte	hashCode(byte value)	(int)value
Short	hashCode(short value)	(int)value
Integer	hashCode(int value)	value
Long	hashCode(long value)	(int)(value ^ (value >>> 32))
Float	hashCode(float value)	floatToIntBits(value)
Double	hashCode(double value)	(int)(doubleToLongBits(value) ^ (doubleToLongBits(value) >>> 32));
Character	hashCode(char value)	(int)value

Table 11.1 Static hashCode(...) Methods and Their Implementations

equals(...) and hashCode() Calculation for (Multidimensional) Arrays

Multidimensional arrays represent a special case with regard to equals(...)/hashCode(). Multidimensional arrays are nothing more than arrays of arrays. The first array for the first dimension references sub-arrays for the second dimension. This implementation becomes important when a question arises as to how these references of the first dimension should be considered with regard to equals(...). In this case, the question is whether the sub-arrays of two arrays are only identical or are also the same. (We addressed this issue in more detail in Chapter 4, Section 4.6.)

If your class contains an array and that should be considered in an equals(...), then three variants are possible for handling this array. Comparing arrays yourself via == as if they were primitive values is fine if the identity of the arrays is desired in the comparison. While many classes override the equals(...) method of Object, arrays are objects too but they don't provide their own equals(...) method. The result of an arrays1.equals (arrays2) call would therefore be an identity comparison. A real content comparison is possible with methods of the Arrays utility class. However, two methods could be used in this case:

- `Arrays.equals(Object[] a, Object[] a2)` goes through each element of a. In the case of multidimensional arrays, each reference to a sub-array is considered and tested to determine whether it's identical to the second array a2. Thus, if two equal but non-identical main arrays have identical sub-arrays, `Arrays.equals(...)` will return true. However, it will retur `false` if the sub-arrays are not identical.

- If the equality of the sub-arrays plays a role, `Arrays.deepEquals(...)` is the appropriate method because this method always queries the sub-arrays with `equals(...)`.

A comparable issue exists when you calculate the hash value. The `Arrays` class provides the `Arrays.hashCode(...)` and `Arrays.deepHashCode(...)` methods to calculate the hash value of an entire array. The first method asks each sub-element for the hash value via the `hashCode()` method provided by `Object`.

Let's assume we have a multidimensional array. Then, the sub-element is also an array. `Arrays.hashCode(...)` will then, as mentioned, only call the `hashCode()` method on the array object, while `Arrays.deepHashCode(...)` will also descend into the sub-array and call `Arrays.deepHashCode(...)` on all sub-arrays until an `equals(...)` comparison is possible on a non-array.

What does this mean for our `equals(…)`/`hashCode()` method? The IntelliJ IDE generates the following code for a two-dimensional `char` array, which uses `Arrays.deep*(...)`:

```java
char[][] chessboard = new char[8][8];

  @Override public boolean equals( Object o ) {
    if ( this == o )
      return true;
    if ( !(o instanceof Chess) )
      return false;

    Chess chess = (Chess) o;

    return Arrays.deepEquals( chessboard, chess.chessboard );
  }

  @Override public int hashCode() {
    return Arrays.deepHashCode( chessboard );
  }
}
```

Listing 11.17 src/main/java/com/tutego/insel/object/hashcode/Chess.java, Chess

Hash Value of a float

Depending on the data types, the calculations always look slightly different. While integers can be put directly into an integer expression for the hash value, in the case of double, the static conversion methods `Double.doubleToLongBits(double)` and `Float.floatToIntBits(float)` are in use.

The data types `double` and `float` have another specialty since `Double.NaN` and `Float.NaN` and the sign of 0 have to be considered (as described in detail in Chapter 21, Section 21.2.1).

In conclusion, if x = +0.0 and y = -0.0, then x == y, but `Double.doubleToLongBits(x) != Double.doubleToLongBits(y)`.

If x = y = `Double.NaN`, then x != y, but `Double.doubleToLongBits(x) == Double.doubleToLongBits(y)`.

If we *don't* want to treat the two zeros differently, but instead want to value them as the same, the following is a common idiom:

```
x == 0.0 ? 0L : Double.doubleToLongBits( x )
```

`Double.doubleToLongBits(0.0)` returns "0," but calling `Double.doubleToLongBits(-0.0)` returns "–9.223.372.036.854.775.808."

Equals, the Zero, and Hashing

Objects with equivalent contents according to the `equals(...)` method must get the same hash value.

The two methods `hashCode()` and `equals(...)` are related. Usually when one method is implemented, an implementation of the other method is also necessary because, in the case of equivalence, the hash values must of course also match, which can be written formally in the following way:

```
x.equals( y ) => x.hashCode() == y.hashCode()
```

This statement captures how the hash value for `Point` objects should be calculated from their coordinates. Two point objects that are identical in content have the same coordinates and thus have the same hash value.

If objects have the same hash value but aren't the same (called a *collision*), we have a case where equivalence does not hold in the equation. In other words, don't assume that, if the hash values of two objects are equal, that the objects are also equal. The probability of equivalence may be high, but this scenario doesn't necessarily guarantee that the two objects are truly equal.

11.1.6   System.identityHashCode(...) and the Problem of Non-Unique Object References*

The equality of objects can be redefined with the `equals(...)` method. If `equals(...)` is newly implemented, then this implementation usually also applies to the `hashCode()` method, which should also be overwritten.

The default implementation of Object now operates in the following way: Different hash values are calculated even for objects that take the same values, which is another reason why you should override hashCode(). But what does hashCode() of Object actually return? This object ID uniquely identifies the object. The original ID is lost when hashCode() is reimplemented. But if you're interested in the original hashCode() value, you can use System.identityHashCode(...).

Note [«]

Although the hash values for two equals(...)-equals objects are the same, identity-HashCode() usually returns different values:

```
Point p = new Point( 0, 0 );
Point q = new Point( 0, 0 );
System.out.println( System.identityHashCode(p) ); // e. g. 16032330
System.out.println( System.identityHashCode(q) ); // e. g. 13288040
System.out.println( p.hashCode() );                // 0
System.out.println( q.hashCode() );                // 0
```

If hashCode() isn't overridden, then the hash value matches the identityHashCode(...).

Example [Ex]

Some classes don't override hashCode(), and thus, identityHashCode(...) is equal to the hash value. This scenario arises, for example, with the StringBuilder class, as shown in the following example:

```
StringBuilder sb1 = new StringBuilder(), sb2 = new StringBuilder();
System.out.printf( "%d %d%n", System.identityHashCode(sb1), sb1.hashCode() );
// for example 1829164700 1829164700
System.out.printf( "%d %d%n", System.identityHashCode(sb2), sb2.hashCode() );
// for example 460141958 460141958
```

This static method identityHashCode(...) returns the original identifier of the objects. At first glance, these identifiers may look like unique IDs, but may not be. You may indeed have two different objects in the memory for which the result of System.identityHashCode(...) is the same.

11.1.7 Synchronization*

Threads can communicate with each other and share data in the process. Threads can also wait for certain conditions to occur, for example, new input data. The Object class declares a total of five versions of the wait(...), notify(), and notifyAll() methods for thread termination synchronization.

11.2   Weak References and Cleaners

References to objects around us in everyday life are called *strong references* because automatic garbage collection would never release a used object. However, in addition to strong references, with *weak references*, the garbage collector will remove the objects. What sounds crazy at first becomes interesting when implementing caching data structures: If an object is in the cache, that's fine and access is fast; if the object is not in the cache, that's fine too, but access takes a little longer. Thus, you can use weak references to create cached objects that automatic garbage collection is allowed to clear up when memory is running low.

Thus, weak references interact with automatic garbage collection in a simple way, through a few types for in the `java.base` module in the `java.lang.ref` package. Special containers can reference an object but still can be emptied by automatic garbage collection, such as the following:

- `SoftReference<T>`: A container for *softly reachable* objects. These objects are released late by the garbage collector when the JVM approaches an `OutOfMemoryError`.

- `WeakReference<T>`: A container for *weakly reachable* objects. These objects are released by the garbage collector relatively early in the first garbage collection.

- `PhantomReference<T>`: A container that's always empty but is used to keep track of when the garbage collector separates from an object.

- `Reference<T>`: Abstract base class for "reference objects" of `PhantomReference`, `SoftReference`, and `WeakReference`.

The containers themselves aren't removed by the garbage collector and end up in a `ReferenceQueue<T>`. The queue can be used to determine which `Reference` containers are empty and can be removed from a data structure, for example. Empty containers are useless and can't be recycled.

Another type in the package is `Cleaner`. An operation (of type `Cleaner.Cleanable`) can be registered to a `Cleaner`, which will be called whenever the automatic garbage collection strikes and the object is no longer accessible. Internally, the class uses `PhantomReference`.

[Ex]

Example

Let's create a point and register a `Cleaner`. Then, we'll stimulate the garbage collector by using too much memory space, which will trigger the `Cleaner`.

```
Point p = new Point( 1, 2 );
Cleaner.create().register( p, () -> System.out.println( "point is gone" ) );
p = null;
new byte[ (int) Runtime.getRuntime().freeMemory() ].clone();
```

Listing 11.18 src/main/java/com/tutego/insel/lang/ref/CleanerDemo, main()

The register(Object obj, Runnable action) method receives the object to watch in the first parameter and then a Runnable, calling the run() method whenever the Cleaner cleans up. With our need for memory, therefore, a console output of "Point is gone!" is likely. In no case may the cleanup operation reference p again. This example also uses a lambda expression (with the arrow) to shorten the code a little. More on this topic will follow in Chapter 13.

11.3   The java.util.Objects Utility Class

The Objects class contains some static utility functions. These functions primarily perform null tests to avoid a subsequent NullPointerException when object methods are called.

11.3.1   Built-In Null Tests for equals(…)/hashCode()

For example, if the object variable name of a person is null, then name.hashCode() can't simply be called without a NullPointerException following the call. Three methods of Objects perform null tests before being passed to the Object method: equals(…), hash-Code(), and toString(). An additional helper method works with comparators, which you'll learn more about in Section 11.4.

```
class java.util.Objects
```

▶ static boolean equals(Object a, Object b)
Returns true if both arguments are either null or if a.equals(b) also returns true; otherwise, this method returns false. That Objects.equals(null, null) returns true makes sense, and thus, the method saves you from some manual testing.

▶ static int hashCode(Object o)
Returns 0 if o is null; otherwise, o.hashCode().

▶ static int hash(Object… values)
Calls hashCode() on each object in the values collection and concatenates it to a new hash value. The implementation is simply a return Arrays.hashCode(values). Using the method is rather expensive due to the construction of the varargs array and possible boxing operations for primitive values.

▶ static <T> int compare(T a, T b, Comparator<? super T> c)
Returns 0 if a and b are both either null or the Comparator declares the objects a and b to be equal. If a and b are both not null, the return is c.compare(a, b). If only a or b is null, the result depends on the Comparator and the order of the parameters.

Example

Let's recall the overridden hashCode() method for a player (described in Section 11.1.5), where the player name should go into the hash value.

```
result = 31 * result + ((name == null) ? 0 : name.hashCode());
```

Listing 11.19 src/main/java/com/tutego/insel/object/hashcode/Player.java, hashCode() (Snippet)

With Objects.hashCode(Object), the null test can be omitted because the static method already performs it. Consider the following example:

```
result = 31 * result + Objects.hashCode( name );
```

11.3.2   Objects.toString(...)

Another static method is Objects.toString(Object). This method exists in the class for symmetry reasons since toString() is one of the standard methods of the Object class. The method doesn't need to be used because a corresponding method already exists with String.valueOf(...).

```
class java.util.Objects
```

▶ static String toString(Object o)
  Returns the string "null" if the argument is null; otherwise, o.toString().

Note

The String.valueOf(...) method is overloaded and better suited for primitive arguments than Objects.toString(Object), which always requires wrapper objects to be created first. Although String.valueOf(3.14) and Objects.toString(3.14) look the same, in the second case, a wrapper double object comes into play.

11.3.3   null Checks with Built-In Exception Handling

In the preceding methods, null is treated as a special case, and exceptions are avoided. For example, Objects.toString(null) or Objects.hashCode(null) are fine and "work around" null. This flexibility is not always useful, however, because traditionally you want to avoid null as an argument and in returns. Therefore, a good practice is to first test in a method body to determine whether the arguments are non-null, unless null is absolutely desired.

For tests that check whether references are non-null, Objects provides a couple of requireNonNull*(...) methods to carry out null checks and throw a NullPointerException

if an error occurs. These tests are useful for constructors and setters that should initialize values but want to prevent null from being passed through.

Example

The setName(...) method is supposed to prohibit a name argument equal to null. Consider the following example:

```
public void setName( String name ) {
  this.name = Objects.requireNonNull( name );
}
```

Alternatively, the following error message is possible:

```
public void setName( String name ) {
  this.name = Objects.requireNonNull( name, "Name must not be null" );
}
class java.util.Objects
```

▶ static <T> T requireNonNull(T obj)
Throws a NullPointerException if obj is null. Otherwise, the obj is the return. The
declaration is generic and to be understood in such a way that the parameter type is
the same as the return type.

▶ static <T> T requireNonNull(T obj, String message)
Like requireNonNull(obj), except that the NullPointerException message is determined.

▶ static <T> T requireNonNull(T obj, Supplier<String> messageSupplier)
Like requireNonNull(obj, message), but the message comes from messageSupplier.
This is useful for messages that are more expensive to build because the Supplier
defers the cost of creating the string until a NullPointerException actually occurs
because only then is the message necessary.

▶ static <T> T requireNonNullElse(T obj, T defaultObj)
Returns the first object that's not null. defaultObj must not be null; otherwise, a
NullPointerException will follow. Implemented as return (obj != null) ? obj :
requireNonNull (defaultObj, "defaultObj");.

▶ static <T> T requireNonNullElseGet(T obj, Supplier<? extends T> supplier)
Returns the first object that isn't null. If obj is null, the method gets the reference
from the supplier, which then must not return null; otherwise, a NullPointerException
will follow.

11.3.4   Tests for null

Behind isNull(Object o) and nonNull(Object o), a simple test is available for o == null or
o != null.

> class java.util.**Objects**

▶ static boolean isNull(Object obj)
▶ static boolean nonNull(Object obj)
  Returns true if obj is null or non-null; otherwise, false.

In normal program code, developers won't use these methods, but these methods are useful for method references so that, for example, stream.filter(Objects::nonNull) can be read. We'll return to method references in Chapter 13, Section 13.2, and Chapter 18, Section 18.4.

11.3.5   Checking Index-Related Program Arguments for Correctness

In Chapter 9, Section 9.1.2, we highlighted the need to check value ranges and throw exceptions, such as IllegalArgumentException or IndexOutOfBoundsException, in case of errors to prevent incorrect values from sneaking into the object.

Other methods from Objects check valid value ranges of index-based methods and throw an IndexOutOfBoundsException in case of an error.

> class java.util.**Objects**

▶ static int checkIndex(int index, int length)
▶ static long checkIndex(long index, long length)
▶ static int checkFromToIndex(int fromIndex, int toIndex, int length)
▶ static long checkFromToIndex(long fromIndex, long toIndex, long length)
▶ static int checkFromIndexSize(int fromIndex, int size, int length)
▶ static long checkFromIndexSize(long fromIndex, long size, long length)

[Ex]

Example

The following example is an implementation of the get(int) method in java.util.ArrayList:

```
public E get(int index) {
  Objects.checkIndex(index, size);
  return elementData(index);
}
```

The private elementData(int index) method directly accesses the internal array with elementData[index], which could be larger, however, because the implementation of ArrayList has a certain buffer size. Therefore, prior index-verification is necessary.

11.4 Comparing Objects and Establishing Order

The Object method equals(Object) provides information about whether two objects have the same state but says nothing about which object is "bigger" or "smaller." However, in many applications, the order of objects plays a role. This need is obvious in sorting operations, but also in simpler questions, such as finding the largest or smallest item in a collection. If objects are to be compared in Java, these objects must always be arranged in a certain order. The system can never decide on its own, and often, multiple criteria determine a sort order. For example, why is one candy "smaller" than another candy? Perhaps one candy has 20 calories and the other has 600 calories, or maybe because they have different weights?

11.4.1 Naturally Ordered or Not?

In Java, two different functional interfaces (in two different packages) for determining the order are available:

- Comparable
  When a class implements Comparable, objects can compare themselves with other objects. Since the classes generally implement only one sorting criterion, *natural ordering* is implemented in this case.

- Comparator
  An implementing class called Comparator takes two objects and compares them. A Comparator for candy could, for example, compare according to calories or weight or use a completely different logic. The implementation of Comparable would not make sense because in this case only one criterion can be implemented ("natural" order), but candies follow no natural order.[3]

To summarize, while Comparable usually implements only one ordering criterion, many extra classes of the Comparator type may exist, each defining different orders.

Comparable and Comparator in the Java Application Programming Interface

An implementation of Comparable can be found exactly where a natural ordering is obvious, such as with the following types:

- BigDecimal, BigInteger, Byte, Character, Double, Float, Integer, Long, and Short
- Date, Calendar, LocalTime, and LocalDate
- String, StringBuilder, and StringBuffer
- File and URI
- Enum
- TimeUnit

---

3 In the 10th century, the Grand Vizier Abdul Kassem Ismael always took his entire library of 117,000 volumes with him. Four hundred camels were trained to transport the works in alphabetical order.

The API documentation contains only a little information on `java.text.Collator` and its subclass, `Comparator`.

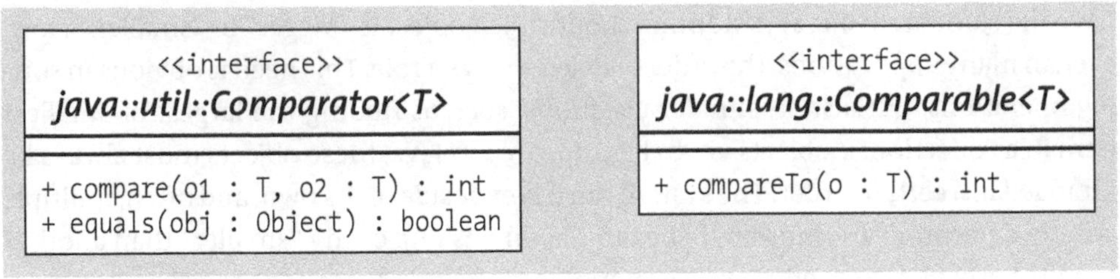

<<interface>> **java::util::Comparator\<T>**
+ compare(o1 : T, o2 : T) : int + equals(obj : Object) : boolean

<<interface>> **java::lang::Comparable\<T>**
+ compareTo(o : T) : int

Figure 11.3 Simplified UML Diagram of Comparator and Comparable

> [»]
>
> **Note**
>
> Since two ways exist to define an ordering with `Comparator` and `Comparable`, the Java API often provides two methods when an ordering is needed: one with a `Comparator` (then no requirement is placed on the elements) and one without a `Comparator` (but then the elements must implement the `Comparable` interface). If a variant with natural order is missing, a `Comparator` can be queried at any time with `Comparator.natu-ralOrder()`, which falls back on the `Comparable` method `compareTo(...)`.

11.4.2 compare*() Method of the Comparable and Comparator Interfaces

The functional interface `Comparable` originates from the `java.lang` package and declares a `compareTo(...)` method:

```
interface java.lang.Comparable<T>
```

▶ int compareTo(T o)
  Compares itself with another object.

The functional interface `Comparator` comes from the `java.util` package (not from `java.lang` like `Comparable`, shown in Figure 11.3) and declares an abstract method:

```
interface java.util.Comparator<T>
```

▶ int compare(T o1, T o2)
  Compares two arguments for their order.

> [»]
>
> **Note***
>
> In addition to `compare(...)`, `Comparator` also declares the `boolean equals (object obj)` known from `Object`. This method doesn't need to be implemented because `Object`

already provides an implementation. The method is in the interface only so that the API documentation explains that equals(...) only tests whether two Comparator objects are equal.

11.4.3   Return Values Encode the Order

The return value of compare(...) for Comparator or compareTo(...) for Comparable may be less than 0 (negative), equal to 0, or greater than 0 (positive) and thus determines the order of the objects—referred to as a *three-way comparison*. Let's assume you have two objects o1 and o2 whose classes implement Comparable. Then, the following agreement rules apply:

o1.compareTo(o2) < 0	↔	o1 is "smaller than" o2.
o1.compareTo(o2) == 0	↔	o1 is "equal to" o2.
o1.compareTo(o2) > 0	↔	o1 is "greater than" o2.

An external Comparator (symbolically called comp) behaves similarly:

comp.compare(o1, o2) < 0	↔	o1 is "smaller than" o2.
comp.compare(o1, o2) == 0	↔	o1 is "equal to" o2.
comp.compare(o1, o2) > 0	↔	o1 is "greater than" o2.

Example

In the following example, LocalTime represents time values, and the class implements Comparable:

```
LocalTime elevenses = LocalTime.of( 11, 0 );
LocalTime lunchtime = LocalTime.of( 12, 0 );
System.out.println( elevenses.compareTo( lunchtime ) );  // -1
System.out.println( lunchtime.compareTo( elevenses ) );  // 1
```

11.4.4   Sorting Candy by Calories Using a Sample Comparator

Let's say we need to sort candies by their calories and thus need to write a Comparator for this purpose—that candies are Comparable isn't appropriate because no natural order exists for candies.

Therefore, an external Comparator object should decide which Candy object is "bigger" by the number of its calories. Fewer calories mean the candy is "smaller."

The following Candy record stores calorie values:

```
public record Candy(int calories) {}
```

Listing 11.20 Listing 11.20: src/main/java/com/tutego/insel/util/Candy.java, Candy

A candy built by new Candy(100) should be "smaller" than new Candy(623). For this purpose, the candy Comparator must use the calories, and no other criteria exist.

```
class CandyCaloriesComparator implements Comparator<Candy> {
  @Override public int compare( Candy candy1, Candy candy2 ) {
    return Integer.compare( candy1.calories(), candy2.calories() );
  }
}
```

Listing 11.21 src/main/java/com/tutego/insel/util/CandyCaloriesComparator.java, CandyKcalComparator

All wrapper classes have compare(...) methods for a three-way comparison. This construction is shorter than instructions like the following:

```
int v1 = candy1.calories(), v2 = candy2.calories();
if ( v1 < v2 ) return -1;
else if ( v1 > v2 ) return 1;
return 0;
```

[+]
Design Tip

A comparator can basically have a state, for example for the language, if strings are included in the comparison. A stateless comparator can be programmed with an enum or written compactly with a lambda expression.

Many places in libraries will require ordering, such as when searching for the maximum element or sorting a list. Collections.max(...), for example, finds the largest element of a list, while Arrays.sort(...) sorts an array.

Let's consider an example illustrating how the Comparator object can do many things, for example, find the largest or smallest element in a collection or sort a data structure. Let's sort an array of candy. The candy with the fewest calories should be placed in front.

```
Candy[] candies = { new Candy( 100 ), new Candy( 623 ), new Candy( 123 ) };
Arrays.sort( candies, new CandyCaloriesComparator() );
System.out.println( candies[ 0 ].calories() );     // 100
```

Listing 11.22 src/main/java/com/tutego/insel/util/CandyCaloriesComparatorDemo.java (Snippet)

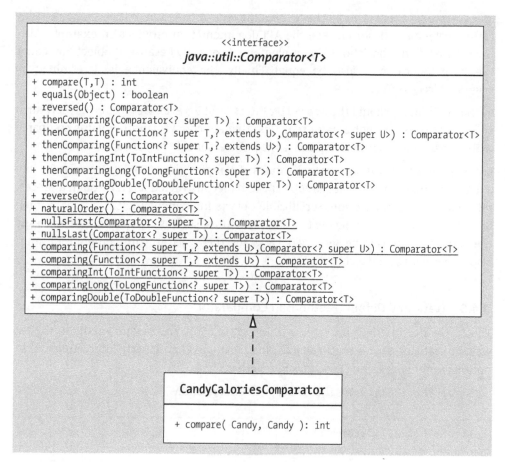

Figure 11.4 The Custom Comparator Must Merely Override compare(...) from the Interface

The sorting method always draws on the Comparator for the pairs to compare and then asks for the order. If you include a println(...) in your compare(...) method, you can watch the sort algorithm at work.

11.4.5 Tips for Comparator and Comparable Implementations

If objects should be compared with a Comparator, but null values should be sorted out beforehand, the static method int compare(T a, T b, Comparator<? super T> c) from the Objects class is useful. The method returns 0 if a and b are both either null or the comparator declares the objects a and b to be equal. If a and b are both not null, the return is c.compare(a, b). If only a or b is null, the return depends on the Comparator and the order of the parameters.

For implementations of Comparable, in addition to an implementation of compareTo(...), the appropriate implementation in equals(...) is also important. This implementation consistent only if e1.compareTo(e2) == 0 returns the same result as e1.equals(e2), where e1 and e2 have the same type. A violation of this rule can quickly cause problems with sorted sets; the API documentation provides an example. Also, the hashCode() method should be implemented correctly because, if objects are equal, the hash values must also be equal. Finally, the equivalence is determined by equals(…)/compareTo(…).

e.compareTo(null) should throw a NullPointerException even if e.equals(null) returns false. null is usually not greater than, less than, or equal to another value compared with compareTo(...)so an exception is the only reasonable response.

Java supports *serialization*, where the states of complex objects are written serially into a data stream. From this data, an object can be reconstructed later, through a process referred to as *deserialization*. Serializable objects implement the Serializable interface. If a Comparator is connected to a data structure—such as a TreeSet or TreeMap—and the data structure is to be serialized. However, the Comparator implementation must also implement Serializable.

11.4.6   Static and Default Methods in Comparator

The Comparator interface provides a whole set of static and default methods. (By the way, no static or default methods exist in Comparable.) Particularly interesting are the options for linking several Comparators together.

Let's start with the methods that are easy to understand:

```
interface java.util.Comparator<T>
```

▶ static <T extends Comparable<? super T>> Comparator<T> naturalOrder()
Returns a Comparator that uses the natural order of objects, which means int compare(Comparable<Object> c1, Comparable<Object> c2) is implemented as return c1.compareTo(c2);.

▶ static <T extends Comparable<? super T>> Comparator<T> reverseOrder()
The static method returns a Comparator that uses the natural order like naturalOrder() but reverses the order and thus corresponds to Collections.reverseOrder(). Basically, this method is a Comparator with a compare(Comparable<Object> c1, Comparable<Object> c2) method that returns c2.compareTo(c1).

▶ default Comparator<T> reversed()
Returns a new Comparator for this current Comparator that reverses the order. Corresponds to Collections.reverseOrder(this).

▶ static <T> Comparator<T> nullsFirst(Comparator<? super T> comparator) and static <T> Comparator<T> nullsLast(Comparator<? super T> comparator)
For a given Comparator, these methods return a new Comparator for comparisons with null and places null either before or after the other values in order.

Sequence of Comparators

Often, the ordering criterion is composed of several conditions, as the sorting in a phone book shows. First, you might sort by last name, then follows with sorting by first name. To achieve this goal with a Comparator object, either all individual comparators must be packed into a new Comparator object, or individual Comparators must be bound together to form a "super"-Comparator. The second solution is of course the recommended approach because it increases reusability, and individual Comparators can then be easily used for other contexts. A useful method is available in Comparator for exactly such a stringing:

```
interface java.util.Comparator<T>
```

▶ default Comparator<T> thenComparing(Comparator<? super T> other)
First applies its own Comparator and, if it shows states as being equal, then applies the other Comparator, other. In other words, if the current Comparator returns the result 0, the second passed Comparator must answer the question about the order.

Let's now use these thenComparing(...) methods from Comparator in an example that sorts a list of names by last name and then by first name.

```java
public class ComparatorThenComparingDemo {

  record Candy(int calories, String name) {
    @Override public String toString() {
      return name + "/" + calories;
    }
  }

  static final Comparator<Candy> CANDY_CALORIES_COMPARATOR =
      new Comparator<Candy>() {
        public int compare( Candy c1, Candy c2 ) {
          return Integer.compare( c1.calories(), c2.calories() );
        }
      };

  static final Comparator<Candy> CANDY_NAME_COMPARATOR =
      new Comparator<Candy>() {
        public int compare( Candy p1, Candy p2 ) {
          return p1.name.compareTo( p2.name() );
        }
      };

  public static void main( String[] args ) {
    List<Candy> candies = Arrays.asList(
```

```
        new Candy( 230, "Special Dark Chocolate" ), new Candy( 230, "Milk
Chocolate Bar" ),
        new Candy( 60, "Tootsie Pop" ), new Candy( 280, "Snickers Bar" ) );

    candies.sort( CANDY_CALORIES_COMPARATOR );
    System.out.println( candies );

    candies.sort( CANDY_NAME_COMPARATOR );
    System.out.println( candies );

    candies.sort( CANDY_CALORIES_COMPARATOR.thenComparing( CANDY_NAME_
COMPARATOR ) );
    System.out.println( candies );
  }
}
```

Listing 11.23 src/main/java/com/tutego/insel/util/ComparatorThenComparingDemo.java
(Snippet)

The result is the following output:

```
[Tootsie Pop/60, Special Dark Chocolate/230, Milk Chocolate Bar/
230, Snickers Bar/280]
[Milk Chocolate Bar/230, Snickers Bar/280, Special Dark Chocolate/
230, Tootsie Pop/60]
[Tootsie Pop/60, Milk Chocolate Bar/230, Special Dark Chocolate/
230, Snickers Bar/280]
```

With lambda expressions, as described in Chapter 13, the whole thing can be written in
a slightly more compact way.

Extracting a Comparison Value and Making Comparisons*

The remaining methods in Comparator all provide the special capability of taking certain function objects that extract the "key" for the comparisons and then reference the
key for the comparison. With the syntax of the method references, you can formulate
quite compact Comparator objects.

Let's look the related methods next:

```
interface java.util.Comparator<T>
```

▶ static <T,U> Comparator<T> comparing(Function<? super T,? extends U> keyExtractor,
  Comparator<? super U> keyComparator)

- ▶ static <T,U extends Comparable<? super U>> Comparator<T> comparing(Function<? super T, ? extends U> keyExtractor)
- ▶ static <T> Comparator<T> comparingInt(ToIntFunction<? super T> keyExtractor)
- ▶ static <T> Comparator<T> comparingLong(ToLongFunction<? super T> keyExtractor)
- ▶ static<T> Comparator<T> comparingDouble(ToDoubleFunction<? super T> keyExtractor)
- ▶ default <U extends Comparable<? super U>> Comparator<T> thenComparing(Function<? super T,? extends U> keyExtractor)
- ▶ default <U> Comparator<T> thenComparing(Function<? super T,? extends U> keyExtractor, Comparator<? super U> keyComparator)
- ▶ default Comparator<T> thenComparingDouble(ToDoubleFunction<? super T> keyExtractor)
- ▶ default Comparator<T> thenComparingInt(ToIntFunction<? super T> keyExtractor)
- ▶ default Comparator<T> thenComparingLong(ToLongFunction<? super T> keyExtractor)

Example

Our example to compare candies can be formulated in a different way: You can use lambda expression syntax or alternatively an even more compact method reference; we'll return to this topic in detail in Chapter 13. Consider the following example:

```
Comparator<Candy> comp = Comparator.comparingInt( candy -
> candy.calories() );
// Comparator<Candy> comp = Comparator.comparingInt( Candy::calories );
candies.sort( Comparator.comparingInt( Candy::calories )
                    .thenComparing( Candy::name ) );
```

Listing 11.24 src/main/java/com/tutego/insel/util/ComparatorDemo.java (Snippet)

11.5   Wrapper Classes and Autoboxing

The class library provides special classes for each primitive data type like int, double, or char. These *wrapper classes* (also called *envelope classes*) fulfill three important tasks:

- Wrapper classes provide static helper methods for converting a primitive data type to a string (called *formatting*) and from the string back to a primitive data type (called *parsing*).
- The data structures such as lists and sets that are used in Java can only store references. Thus, the problem arises of how to add primitive data types to these containers. Wrapper objects encapsulate a simple primitive value in an object so that a reference exists that can be stored in a prebuilt data structure, for example.
- The wrapper type is important for generics. For example, if a special function maps an integer to a float, an implementation with Function<**int, double**> isn't correct—

it must be Function<**Integer,Double**>. Primitive data types don't exist even with generics; wrapper types are always used instead.

Wrapper classes exist for all primitive data types, as listed in Table 11.2.

Wrapper Class	Primitive Type
Byte	byte
Short	short
Integer	int
Long	long
Double	double
Float	float
Boolean	boolean
Character	char

Table 11.2 Wrapper Classes and Primitive Data Types

> **Note**
>
> For void, which isn't a data type, the class Void exists. This class declares only the constant TYPE of type Class<Void> and is more relevant for reflection (reading properties of a class).

In this section, we'll first look at creating wrapper objects then explore the methods that appear in all wrapper classes. Finally, we'll introduce you to individual methods of each wrapper class. (Note that we covered the Character class in Chapter 5, Section 5.3, when we talked about characters and strings.)

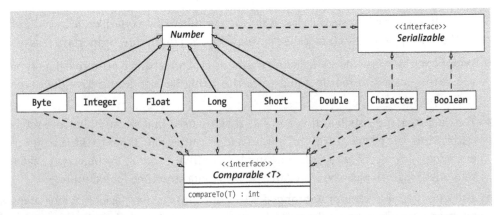

Figure 11.5 Essential Type Relationships of Wrapper Classes: Character Doesn't Extend Number

11.5.1   Creating Wrapper Objects

Wrapper objects can be created in two ways:

- Via static valueOf(...) methods, which are passed a primitive expression or a string.
- Via boxing: From a primitive value, the compiler automatically generates valueOf(...) method calls that return the wrapper object.

Example

The following example creates some wrapper objects:

```
Integer  int1 = Integer.valueOf( "30" );   // valueOf()
Long     lng1 = Long.valueOf( 0xCOBOL );   // valueOf()
Double   dobl = Double.valueOf( 12.3 );    // valueOf()
Boolean  bool = true;                      // Boxing
Integer  int2 = 42;                        // Boxing
Long     lng2 = 42L;                       // Boxing
```

Let's compare and contrast these two ways of creating wrapper classes:

- Boxing is the shortest variant in terms of writing effort, and generally the best, because this option is the most compact. (Boxing isn't without its problems, however, as Section 11.5.12 describes.) Since boxing accesses the valueOf(...) methods, the two variants are semantically identical and differ only in the program code (but are not different in the bytecode).

- Compared to a constructor, a static valueOf(...) method for creating objects has an advantage: Unlike new and the constructor, a static method doesn't always have to create objects anew but can also use preconstructed objects. And that's exactly what valueOf(...) does with the four classes Byte, Short, Integer, and Long: If the integers come from the value range –128 to +127, valueOf(...) uses prepared objects from a cache. Of course, this approach only works because callers of valueOf(...) obtain an *immutable* object—a wrapper object can't be changed after its creation.

Note

In the wrapper class Integer, three static overloaded methods exist: getInteger(String), getInteger(String, int), and getInteger(String, Integer). These methods can be easily confused with the valueOf(String) method by language novices because of the same return and parameters. However, the getInteger(String) methods read an environment variable and thus have a completely different task than valueOf(String). In the wrapper class Boolean, the method getBoolean(String) has the same feature that it read an environment variable. The other wrapper classes don't have methods for reading environment variables.

Wrapper Objects Are Immutable

Once a wrapper object has been created, the value stored in the wrapper object can't be changed afterwards. To ensure this immutability, concrete wrapper classes are all final. These wrapper classes are intended only to serve as wrappers and not as complete data types. Since the value can't be changed (it's immutable), objects with this property are also called *value objects*. To increase the content of an Integer object io by 1, for example, you must reference a new object. Consider the following example:

```
Integer io = Integer.valueOf( 12 );
io = Integer.valueOf( io.intValue() + 1 );
```

The variable io references a second Integer object at the end, and the value of the first io object with 12 remains untouched, which is essentially the same as using the data type String. When the string s = "Co"; s = s + "ra"; is called, the reference variable s is also only assigned a new object, but the string itself doesn't change.

11.5.2 Conversions to a String Representation

All wrapper classes provide static toString(value) methods for converting the primitive element to a string.

```
String s1 = Integer.toString( 1234567891 ),
       s2 = Long.toString( 123456789123L ),
       s3 = Float.toString( 12.345678912f ),
       s4 = Double.toString( 12.345678912 ),
       s5 = Boolean.toString( true );
System.out.println( s1 );  // 1234567891
System.out.println( s2 );  // 123456789123
System.out.println( s3 );  // 12.345679
System.out.println( s4 );  // 12.345678912
System.out.println( s5 );  // true
```

Listing 11.25 src/main/java/com/tutego/insel/wrapper/WrapperToString.java, main()

[+]

> **Tip**
>
> The following statement is a Java-specific idiom[4] for conversion as well:
>
> ```
> String s = "" + number;
> ```

The string always appears in the English written variant. For example, decimal numbers have a period instead of a comma.

---

4 A JavaScript idiom is to make a number out of a string using the expression s - 0, if the variable s is a string representation of a number.

> **Note**
>
> When displaying numbers, country-specific formatting is often useful. You can access these formatting options via `printf(...)`. Another option is to use a `Locale` specification for the language as the first parameter. Consider the following examples:
>
> ```
> System.out.printf( Locale.GERMANY, "%f%n", 1000000. );   // 1000000,000000
> System.out.printf( Locale.ENGLISH, "%f%n", 1234.567 );   // 1234.567000
> System.out.printf( Locale.CHINA, "%,.3f%n", 1234.567 );  // 1,234.567
> ```
>
> The format specifier for floats is `%f`. The additional specification with `,.3f` in the last case leads to the thousands separator and three decimal places.

toString(...) as Object and Class Method

If a wrapper object is present, the object method `toString()` returns the string representation of the value stored by the wrapper object. Having identically named `toString(...)` static methods and an object method `toString()` shouldn't cause confusion; while the class method pulls the working value for conversion from the argument, the object method uses the stored value in the wrapper object.

Statements that go over the wrapper object exclusively for conversion, such as `Integer.valueOf(v).toString()`, can be easily rewritten as `Integer.toString(v)`. In addition, the overloaded static method `String.valueOf(v)` is also useful, which—precisely because it is overloaded—is declared for all possible data types. However, `valueOf(v)` internally also uses only `WrapperClass.toString(v)`.

11.5.3 Parsing from a String Representation

Wrapper classes provide static `parse*(...)` methods to convert a string to a primitive data type. The string can be preceded by a minus for negative numbers, but a plus for positive numbers is also allowed. These methods were introduced in Chapter 5, Section 5.8.2.

11.5.4 The Number Base Class for Numeric Wrapper Objects

All numeric wrapper classes can provide the stored value in any other numeric type. Like `doubleValue()` and `intValue()`, the method names consist of the name of the desired type and `Value`. Technically, the wrapper classes `Byte`, `Short`, `Integer`, `Long`, `Float`, and `Double` of the `Number`[5] class override `*Value()` methods.[6]

---

5 In addition, `BigDecimal` and `BigInteger` extend the `Number` class and thus also have the `*Value()` methods. `AtomicInteger` and `AtomicLong` also extend `Number` but aren't immutable like other classes.

6 Only the `byteValue()` and `shortValue()` methods aren't abstract and needn't be overridden. These methods call `intValue()` and convert the value to `byte` and `short` via a type conversion.

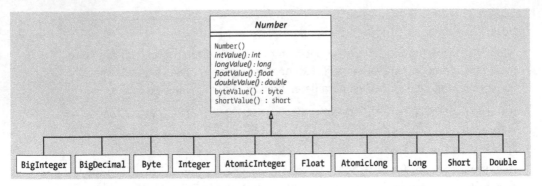

Figure 11.6 UML Diagram of Number

```
abstract class java.lang.Number
implements Serializable
```

▶ byte byteValue()
  Returns the value of the number as byte.

▶ abstract double doubleValue()
  Returns the value of the number as double.

▶ abstract float floatValue()
  Returns the value of the number as float.

▶ abstract int intValue()
  Returns the value of the number as int.

▶ abstract long longValue()
  Returns the value of the number as long.

▶ short shortValue()
  Returns the value of the number as short.

[»]

Note

If the operand types are different in the condition operator, an automatic adjustment will take place, as in the following examples:

```
boolean b = true;
System.out.println( b ? 1 : 0.1 );   // 1.0
System.out.println( !b ? 1 : 0.1 );  // 0.1
```

The result type is double, so that the integer 1 is output as "1.0" (i.e., a float). The compiler makes the same adjustment for wrapper types that it unboxes and converts, as in the following examples:

```
Integer i = 1;
Double  d = 0.1;
```

```
System.out.println( b ? i : d );    // 1.0
System.out.println( !b ? i : d );   // 0.1
```

While this output is actually clear, misunderstandings can occur if the result isn't simply output but cached as a reference to the resulting wrapper object. Since the type in the example is either `Integer` or `Double`, the result type can only be the `Number` supertype. Consider the following examples:

```
Number n1 = b ? i : d;
System.out.println( n1 );           // 1.0
System.out.println( n1 == i );      // false
```

The program logic and output are, of course, exactly the same as before, but developers might assume that the compiler doesn't perform a conversion, but instead references either the original `Integer` or `Double` object; however, the compiler doesn't. The n1 variable in this case references an `Integer`-unboxed, double-converted `Double` object, and so the references of n1 and i are not identical at all.

If the compiler is really to return the original objects, either the `Integer` or the `Double` object must be explicitly set to `Number`, so that unboxing is thus switched off and the condition operator assumes that only arbitrary references exist that aren't to be interpreted, as in the following examples:

```
Number n2 = b ? (Number) i : d;     // or Number n2 = b ? i : (Number) d;
System.out.println( n2 );           // 1
System.out.println( n2 == i );      // true
```

11.5.5 Performing Comparisons with compare*(...), compareTo(...), equals(...), and Hash Values

If we have two integers 1 and 2 in front of us, saying that 1 is smaller than 2 is a trivial task. With floats, this comparison is a bit more complicated because "special numbers" exist like infinity or a negative 0 and a positive 0. To ensure that comparing two values always follows the same schema, two kinds of methods in wrapper classes can tell you whether two values are less than, greater than, or equal to each other:

- On one hand, the object method `compareTo(...)` is found in the wrapper classes. This method isn't in the class by chance because wrapper classes implement the `Comparable` interface (as described in Section 11.4.)

- Wrapper classes also have static `compare(x, y)` and sometimes `compareUnsigned(x, y)` methods.

The return value of these methods is an `int`, which encodes whether a value is greater than, less than, or equal to.

Example

The following example tests several different values:

```
System.out.println( Integer.compare(1, 2) );        // -1
System.out.println( Integer.compare(1, 1) );        //  0
System.out.println( Integer.compare(2, 1) );        //  1

System.out.println( Double.compare(2.0, 2.1) );     // -1
System.out.println( Double.compare(Double.NaN, 0) ); //  1

System.out.println( Boolean.compare(true, false) ); //  1
System.out.println( Boolean.compare(false, true) ); // -1
```

Listing 11.26 src/main/java/com/tutego/insel/wrapper/CompareToDemo.java, main()

A true is "greater" than a false.

Table 11.3 summarizes the methods of the wrapper classes.

Class	Method from Comparable	Static Method compare*(...)
Byte	int compareTo(Byte aByte)	int compare[Unsigned](byte x, byte y)
Short	int compareTo(Short aShort)	int compare[Unsigned](short x, short y)
Float	int compareTo(Float aFloat)	int compare(float f1, float f2)
Double	int compareTo(Double aDouble)	int compare(double d1, double d2)
Integer	int compareTo(Integer aInteger)	int compare(int x, int y)
Long	int compareTo(Long aLong)	int compare(long x, long y)
Character	int compareTo(Character aChar)	int compare[Unsigned](char x, char y)
Boolean	int compareTo(Boolean aBoolean)	int compare(boolean x, boolean y)

Table 11.3 Methods of Wrapper Classes

The implementation of a static WrapperClass.compare(...) method is equivalent to WrapperClass.valueOf(x).compareTo(WrapperClass.valueOf(y)), only the second variant is slower and also longer in spelling.

Equal Test via equals(...)

All wrapper classes override the equals(...) method from the Object base class. This scenario allows you to test whether two wrapper objects have the same value, even if the wrapper objects aren't identical.

Example [Ex]

Let's consider the results of some equal tests:

```
Boolean.TRUE.equals( Boolean.TRUE )                    true
Integer.valueOf( 1 ).equals( Integer.valueOf( 1 ) )   true
Integer.valueOf( 1 ).equals( Integer.valueOf( 2 ) )   false
Integer.valueOf( 1 ).equals( Long.valueOf( 1 ) )      false
Integer.valueOf( 1 ).equals( 1L )                      false
```

Note that the parameter type of equals(...) is always Object, but the types must be identical; otherwise, the comparison will automatically return false. This fact is shown by the penultimate and the final examples. The equals(...) method from lines 4 and 5 rejects any comparison with a non-integer, and a long is just not an integer. Boxing is used in the last line, so the program code looks shorter but corresponds to the code from the penultimate line.

The object method equals(...) of wrapper classes is also a short alternative to wrapperObject.compareTo(anotherWrapperObject) == 0.

Outlook [«]

The fact that wrapper classes implement equals(...) is good because, in this way, wrapper objects can be easily placed and retrieved in data structures like an ArrayList. Furthermore, the fact that wrapper objects are also Comparable is also great for data structures like TreeSet, which—without externally given Comparator classes for comparisons—expect a natural ordering of the elements.

Hash Values

The hash value of an object maps the state to a compact integer. If two objects have unequal hash values, the objects must also be unequal (at least if the calculation is correct). To determine the hash value, each class declares the int hashCode() method via the superclass java.lang.Object. All wrapper classes override this method. In addition, static methods are available, so you can easily calculate the hash value even without a wrapper object.

Example

The following example calculates a hashcode via the object method and static method:

```
Double d = 12.12;
System.out.println( d.hashCode() );            // -469813427
System.out.println( Double.hashCode( 12.12 ) ); // -469813427
```

The value itself is irrelevant.

For the calculation of hash values and their meanings for data structures, Section 11.1.5.

11.5.6   Static Reduction Methods in Wrapper Classes

In the numeric wrapper classes Integer, Long, Float, and Double, you'll find three methods, sum(...), max(...), and min(...), that do exactly as they promise.

```
final class java.lang.Integer|Long|Float|Double
extends Number
implements Comparable<Integer>
```

▶ static *Type* sum(*Type* a, *Type* b)
Calculates and returns the total of two values, corresponding to a simple *a* + *b*. The *Type* specification stands for the corresponding primitive (type byte, short, int, long, float, or double), for example, in int sum(int a, int b).

▶ static *Type* min(*Type* a, *Type* b)
Returns the minimum of the two numbers.

▶ static *Type* max(*Type* a, *Type* b)
Returns the maximum of the two numbers.

Furthermore, the Boolean classes provide three methods for three Boolean operations:

```
final class java.lang.Boolean
implements Comparable<Boolean>, Serializable
```

▶ static boolean logicalAnd(boolean a, boolean b)
Returns a && b.

▶ static boolean logicalOr(boolean a, boolean b)
Returns a || b.

▶ static boolean logicalXor(boolean a, boolean b)
Returns a ^ b.

These methods aren't exciting in themselves. For sums (addition), the + operator does just as well (and is located behind the sum(...) methods anyway), and so nobody will get the idea to write i = Integer.sum(i, 1) instead of i++. For the maximum/minimum values, the Math class also already provides the corresponding methods min(a, b) and max(a, b). The reason we mention these methods is because they're quite interesting in the context of functional programming and because they can reduce two values to one.

11.5.7 Constants for the Size of a Primitive Type*

All wrapper classes have an int constant named SIZE for the number of bits and an int constant named BYTES, which is assigned the size of the associated primitive data type.

Wrapper Class	SIZE Assignment	BYTES Assignment
Byte	8	1
Short	16	2
Integer	32	4
Long	64	8
Float	32	4
Double	64	8
Character	16	2

Table 11.4 BYTES and SIZE Constants in Wrapper Classes

The assignments are basically clear to every developer, it's rather intended for tools or generic libraries.

11.5.8 Handling Unsigned Numbers*

All integer data types (except for char) are always signed, and Java is unlikely to ever introduce new data types to distinguish between positive and negative numbers, as C# and C(++) do, for example. Developers must live with the fact that a byte is always between –128 and +127 and not between 0 and 255. Even if the language doesn't introduce new types, the Java API helps with methods in wrapper classes.

toUnsigned*(...) Methods

The first type of methods interprets a bit pattern as an unsigned number. For example, if a byte is assigned the bit pattern 11111111, this value doesn't stand for "255" but instead for "–1." The static conversion toUnsigned*(...) methods of the wrapper class can help interpret the bit pattern without a sign bit, thus requiring a change to a next higher data type. This change is obvious because, in the case of 11111111, a `byte` can't store the number 255 because of the restriction to the range of –127 to 128, whereas `int` can.

Byte	`static int toUnsignedInt(byte x)`
	`static long toUnsignedLong(byte x)`
Short	`static int toUnsignedInt(short x)`
	`static long toUnsignedLong(short x)`
Integer	`static long toUnsignedLong(int x)`

Table 11.5 toUnsigned*(…) Methods in Byte, Short, and Integer

Obviously, `long` doesn't provide such a method because no built-in data type exists that is greater than `long`.

toUnsignedString(…) and parseUnsignedString(…)

What `Long` does provide, however, and also `Integer`, are conversions to string representations and also parse methods:

Integer	`static String toUnsignedString(int i)`
	`static String toUnsignedString(int i, int radix)`
	`static int parseUnsignedInt(String s)`
	`static int parseUnsignedInt(String s, int radix)`
Long	`static String toUnsignedString(long i)`
	`static String toUnsignedString(long i, int radix)`
	`static long parseUnsignedLong(String s)`
	`static long parseUnsignedLong(String s, int radix)`

Table 11.6 Creating and Parsing String Representations of Unsigned Numbers

The `parse*(...)` methods throw a `NumberFormatException` if the format is wrong.

Comparison, Division, and Remainder

Finally, a third group of methods are more mathematical: static methods for comparing, dividing, and residual value creation.

Integer	static int compareUnsigned(int x, int y)
	static int divideUnsigned(int dividend, int divisor)
	static int remainderUnsigned(int dividend, int divisor)
Long	static int compareUnsigned(long x, long y)
	static long divideUnsigned(long dividend, long divisor)
	static long remainderUnsigned(long dividend, long divisor)

Table 11.7 Mathematical Methods

11.5.9   The Integer and Long Classes

The Integer class encapsulates the value of an integer of type int in an object and provides the following elements:

- Constants
- Static methods to convert to a string and back
- Other helper methods of a mathematical nature

To turn the string into a number, you can use Integer.parseInt(String).

Example

The following example converts the integer 38,317, which is a string, into an integer:

```
String number = "38317";
int integer = 0;
try {
  integer = Integer.parseInt( number );
}
catch ( NumberFormatException e ) {
  System.err.println( "Error converting " + number );
}
System.out.println( integer );
```

The NumberFormatException is an unchecked exception (see Chapter 9, Section 9.1.3, for more details). So, you don't need to enclose it in a try block.

The static method Integer.parseInt(String) converts a string to int, and the reverse method Integer.toString(int) returns a String. Other variants with different bases were described in detail in Chapter 5, Section 5.8.2.

```
final class java.lang.Integer
extends Number
implements Comparable<Integer>
```

▶ static int parseInt(String s)
Generates the corresponding number from the string. The base is 10.

▶ static int parseInt(String s, int radix)
Generates the number with the given base.

▶ static String toString(int i)
Converts the integer to a string and returns it.

parseInt(...) doesn't permit country-specific thousands separators, such as the period in Germany versus the comma in certain English-speaking countries.

Integer and Long are basically identical APIs, except that the smaller data type int is replaced by long.

11.5.10   The Double and Float Classes for Floats

Like the other wrapper classes, the Double and Float classes have dual functionality: On one hand, they encapsulate a float as an object and on the other hand, they provide static utility methods. We'll return to mathematical object and class methods in more detail in Chapter 21, Section 21.2.

11.5.11   The Boolean Class

The Boolean class encapsulates the boolean data type.

Creating Boolean Objects

Besides the constructor and factory methods, Boolean declares two constants: TRUE and FALSE.

```
final class java.lang.Boolean
implements Serializable, Comparable<Boolean>
```

▶ static final Boolean FALSE
▶ static final Boolean TRUE
Constants for truth values.

▶ Boolean(boolean value)
Creates a new Boolean object. This constructor shouldn't be used; instead, Boolean.TRUE or Boolean.FALSE should be used. Boolean objects are immutable, and a new Boolean(value) is unnecessary.

▶ `Boolean(String s)`
Parses the string and returns a new `Boolean` object.

▶ `static Boolean valueOf(String s)`
Parses the string and returns the wrapper types `Boolean.TRUE` or `Boolean.FALSE`. The static method has an advantage over the `Boolean(boolean)` constructor in that it always returns the same immutable object `Boolean.TRUE` or `Boolean.FALSE` instead of creating new objects. For this reason, you'll rarely need to call the constructor to always create new `Boolean` objects.

▶ `static boolean parseBoolean(String s)`
Parses the string and returns either `true` or `false`.

The `Boolean(String name)` constructor or the two static methods `valueOf(String name)` and `parseBoolean(String name)` accept strings and perform the test `name != null && name.equalsIgnoreCase("true")` in the Java Development Kit (JDK). Thus, on one hand, case is unimportant, and on the other hand, things like " false " (with spaces), "false," or "easter eggs" automatically return `false`, where "TRUE" or "True" then return `true`.

Tip

If every developer used only the constants `Boolean.TRUE` and `Boolean.FALSE`, comparisons with `==` or `!=` would be OK for only two objects. However, since a constructor exists for `Boolean` objects (although it's quite debatable why constructors exist for wrapper classes at all), the safest bet is `boolean1.equals(boolean2)`. You just can't know if a library method like `Boolean isNice()` draws on the two constants or instead creates new `Boolean` objects.

[+]

Converting Boolean to an Integer

The primitive type `boolean` can't be converted to another primitive type via a type conversion. However, in practice, you may need `true` to be mapped to 1 and `false` to 0. The usual approach to achieve this mapping is the following statement:

```
int val = aBoolean ? 1 : 0;
```

11.5.12   Autoboxing: Boxing and Unboxing

Autoboxing is a feature of Java where primitive data types and wrapper types are converted into each other on demand. Consider the following example:

```
int     primInt = 4711;
Integer wrapInt = primInt;
// stands for wrapInt = Integer.valueOf(primInt)   (1)
primInt = wrapInt;
// stands for  primInt = wrapInt.intValue()        (2)
```

The statement in (1) is called *boxing* and automatically creates a wrapper object if necessary. Notation (2) is called *unboxing* and stands for obtaining the element from the wrapper object. As a result, wherever the compiler expects a primitive element, but a wrapper object is present, the value from the wrapper is used with a matching *Value(...) method. The compiler will generate the code automatically; nothing of the autoboxing will be obvious later in the bytecode.

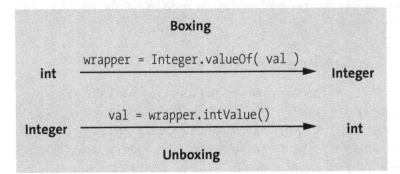

Figure 11.7 Autoboxing of int/Integer

The Operators ++ and --*

The compiler converts according to fixed rules, and also the operators ++, -- are permitted. Consider the following examples:

```
Integer i = 12;
i = i + 1;                  // (1)
i++;                        // (2)
System.out.println( i );    // 14
```

Importantly, neither (1) nor (2) change the original integer object with the 12 (because all wrapper objects are immutable), but i only references other Integer objects for 13 and 14.

[»]

> **Note**
>
> In loops, although valid, you shouldn't write the following code due to excessive object generation:
>
> ```
> for ( Double d = 1.0; d < 100; d *= 1.5 )    // double is better, not Double
>     System.out.println( d );
> ```

Boxing for Dynamic Data Structures (Outlook)

Autoboxing is convenient when "primitive" elements need to be stored in data structures, as in the following examples:

```
ArrayList<Double> list = new ArrayList<Double>();
list.add( Math.sin(Math.PI / 4) );    // Boxing with boolean add(Double)
double d = list.get( 0 );             // Unboxing with Double get(int)
```

Unfortunately, the type of the list actually must be set with the wrapper type `Double` and not with the primitive type `double`. (But maybe that limitation will change at some point.) In any case, autoboxing makes these processes a little more bearable.

No Conversion of the null Reference to 0

During unboxing, the compiler or runtime environment doesn't perform a conversion from `null` to 0. In other words, in the following attempted assignment, no compiler error arises, but a `NullPointerException` is thrown at runtime:

```
int n = (Integer) null;  // ☠ java.lang.NullPointerException at runtime
```

> **Note**
>
> In `switch` blocks, the following types are permitted `int`, enumerations, and strings. For integers, the compiler automatically performs conversions and unboxing to `int`. However, the risk of a `NullPointerException` is real during unboxing. Consider the following example:
>
> ```
> Integer integer = null;
> switch ( integer ) { } // ☠ NullPointerException at runtime
> ```

Autoboxing for Arrays?

Since primitive data types and wrapper objects are automatically converted by autoboxing, the difference isn't that noticeable in practice. With arrays, however, the difference becomes obvious because Java can't perform automatic conversions. Even if, for example, `char` and `character` are automatically converted into each other, arrays just aren't convertible. Consider the following array initialization of the type `char`:

```
Character[] chars = { 'S', 'h', 'a' };
```

This code contains boxing three times from `char` to `character` on the right, and an automatic conversion at the element level is valid, so that the following statement is of course fine:

```
char first = chars[ 0 ];
```

However, a type cast of array objects is incorrect:

```
char[] sha = chars;    // ☠ Compiler error!
```

So, the types char[] and character[] are two completely different types, and a transition isn't possible (not to mention the problems with null references). Thus, in practice, it's necessary to convert between the different types, and unfortunately, the Java standard library doesn't provide methods for this task.[7]

More Problems than Solutions Due to Autoboxing? (Part 1)*

A number of irregularities are associated with autoboxing that you'll need to be aware of to avoid mistakes. One irregularity is related to unboxing, which the compiler performs whenever an expression expects a primitive value. If no primitive element is expected, no unboxing will be performed. Consider the following examples:

```
Double d1 = Double.valueOf( 1 );
Double d2 = Double.valueOf( 1 );

System.out.println( d1 >= d2 );     // true
System.out.println( d1 <= d2 );     // true
System.out.println( d1 == d2 );     // false
System.out.println( d1 == d2-0 );   // true
```

Listing 11.27 src/main/java/com/tutego/insel/wrapper/Autoboxing.java (Snippet)

The comparison with == is a reference comparison. Since no unboxing occurs on primitive values, we are essentially comparing only primitive values. If the compiler sees two reference variables in front of it, no reason exists for unboxing, even if they are wrapper types. Therefore, for two different Integer objects, this identity comparison must always be false. This scenario is of course problematic because the old mathematical rule "from i <= j and i >= j follows automatically i == j" is no longer valid. If the different Integer objects for the same values didn't exist, this problem wouldn't exist either. The minus-null trick enables you to achieve an unboxing so that two numbers will be compared again. Alternatively, an explicit typecasting to int or access to the object method intValue() for deliberate unpacking will help too.

More Problems than Solutions Due to Autoboxing? (Part 2)*

An interesting fact to know is what exactly happens now when boxing converts a number into a wrapper object. At that moment, the constructor isn't called but instead the static valueOf(...) method. Consider the following examples:

```
Integer n1 = new Integer( 10 );
Integer n2 = Integer.valueOf( 10 );
```

---

7 This gap is filled by the open-source library *Apache Commons Lang* (*http://commons.apache.org/proper/commons-lang*) with its ArrayUtils class, which performs the conversions with the toObject(...) and toPrimitive(...) methods.

```
Integer n3 = 10;                      // Integer.valueOf( 10 );
Integer n4 = 10;                      // Integer.valueOf( 10 );
System.out.println( n1 == n2 );   // false
System.out.println( n2 == n3 );   // true
System.out.println( n1 == n3 );   // false
System.out.println( n3 == n4 );   // true
```

Listing 11.28 src/main/java/com/tutego/insel/wrapper/Autoboxing.java (Snippet)

In this example, we're comparing the identity of the wrapper objects four times. What's noticeable is that some comparisons are incorrect, which is no wonder and can be quickly explained by `new` (because in these cases the runtime environment always creates new objects). The identical objects (n2, n3, n4) are conspicuous; they are created by the subsequent `valueOf(int)` during the boxing process. The puzzle is solved via the Javadoc or with a look into the implementation created by Oracle. Integer objects created via boxing originate from a pool. Using the pool, the JDK tries to solve the problem with `==` to determine that selected wrapper objects are really identical, and `==` behaves with wrapper references as `==` does with primitive values.

Since not any number of wrapper objects can come from a pool, the identity of the objects created via boxing is valid only in a selected value range between −128 and +127 (i.e., in the value range of 1 byte). Consider the following examples:

```
Integer j1 = 2;
Integer j2 = 2;
System.out.println( j1 == j2 );   // true
Integer k1 = 127;
Integer k2 = 127;
System.out.println( k1 == k2 );   // true
Integer l1 = 128;
Integer l2 = 128;
System.out.println( l1 == l2 );   // false
Integer m1 = 1000;
Integer m2 = 1000;
System.out.println( m1 == m2 );   // false
```

Listing 11.29 src/main/java/com/tutego/insel/wrapper/Autoboxing.java (Snippet)

As mentioned earlier, even for wrapper objects, the comparison with `==` is always a reference comparison. Because 2 and 127 are within the value range between −128 and +127, the corresponding `Integer` objects come from the pool. This same isn't true for values between 128 and 1,000, which are always new objects. Thus, the `==` comparison also returns `false`.

[»]

Final Question

What output comes onto the screen? Does anything change when i and j are at 222?

```
Integer i = 1, j = 1;
boolean b = (i <= j && j <= i && i != j);
System.out.println( b );
```

11.6   Iterator, Iterable*

In many programs, not only does the individual data play a role, but also collections of this data are meaningful. For example, arrays are collections as are standard data structures like ArrayList, HashSet, or files. A collection is mainly characterized by methods that add and remove data and check for the presence of elements. Of course, each of these mutable data structures has a specific API, but in the spirit of good object-oriented (OO) modeling, describing this behavior in interfaces is desirable.

Two interfaces stand out in particular:

- Iterator: Provides a way to run through collections step by step.
- Iterable: Provides such an Iterator, so it's an Iterator producer.

11.6.1   The Iterator Interface

An *iterator* is a data provider that must have a method to return the subsequent element. Then, a second method is required to provide information about whether the data provider provides any other elements. For this purpose, the Java API declares an Iterator interface with two operations.

	Do You Have More?	Give Me the Next One!
Iterator	hasNext()	next()

Table 11.8 Two Central Methods of the Iterator

[Ex]

Example

The process of *iteration* always uses the following syntax:

```
while ( iterator.hasNext() )
  process( iterator.next() );
```

The hasNext() method determines whether a next element exists at all and, if so, whether next() may ask for the next element. Each time you call next(), you'll get another element of the data structure. This process allows the iterator to run through a data provider (usually a data structure) element by element. Random access is not possible. If hasNext() returns false but we're still asking for an element with next(), we'll get a NoSuchElementException.

```
interface java.util.Iterator<E>
```

▶ boolean hasNext()

Returns true if the iteration provides more elements.

▶ E next()

Returns the next element in the enumeration and moves the position. A NoSuchElementException is through if no more elements exist.

Basically, the method that returns the next element could also return null by definition, indicating that no more elements are left, and hasNext() could be omitted. However, then, null can't be a valid iterator value, which would be awkward.

The Iterator interface doesn't itself extend another interface.[8] The declaration is generic since what the iterator returns is always of a known type.

For the Iterator, the Only Way is Forward

Unlike the index of an array, the iterator doesn't permit you to read an object again (next() automatically proceeds to the next element), nor can you jump ahead or go back and forth. An iterator can be illustrated by a data stream: To visit an element twice,

---

8 Concrete enumerators (and iterators) can't be serialized automatically; the implementing classes must implement the Serializable interface for this purpose.

for example, to traverse a data structure from right to left again, you must create a new Iterator object again or memorize the elements in between. Only with lists and sorted data structures is the order of the elements predictable. Basically, the implementation of the data structure and the iterator decides in which order the elements are issued. If the data is sorted, the iterator will also respect the order. (The documentation describes the details.)

[»]

Note

In Java, an iterator isn't placed on an element but between elements instead. The has-Next() method tells you whether a next element exists, and next() returns it and con-tinues setting the internal position. No concept of the current element can be queried again and again; next() is stateful. At the beginning of the iteration, the iterator is located before the first element.

Executing Code on Remaining Elements of an Iterator

In the Iterator interface, a default method forEachRemaining(Consumer<? super E> action) can execute an arbitrary code snippet—transported via a Consumer—on each element. The implementation of the default method can be written in three lines:

```
default void forEachRemaining( Consumer<? super E> action ) {
  Objects.requireNonNull( action );
  while ( hasNext() )
    action.accept( next() );
}
```

Listing 11.30 java.util.Iterator.java, forEachRemaining()

Using this method, an external iteration can be converted to an internal iteration via a custom loop, and lambda expressions can shorten the interface implementation (as described in Chapter 13).

[Ex]

Example

The following example outputs each argument of the console input:

```
new Scanner( System.in ).forEachRemaining( System.out::println );
interface java.util.Iterator<E>
```

▶ default void forEachRemaining(Consumer<? super E> action)
Executes action on each upcoming element of the iterator up to the last element.

> **Note**
>
> Each `Collection` data structure provides an `Iterator` with `iterator()`, on which in turn a call of `forEachRemaining(...)` is possible. However, the Stream API provides a more flexible alternative for processing program code, which is also useful when the stream comes from other sources, such as arrays.

«

Optional: Deleting Elements via Iterator

The `Iterator` method `next()` is a read-only method and doesn't change the underlying data structure. But the `Iterator` interface also provides a `remove()` method that can remove the last object supplied by `next()` from the data collection.

Since this operation doesn't always make sense (for example, with immutable data structures or when an iterator reads files line by line), this operation is marked as optional in the API documentation. Thus, a concrete iterator doesn't have to support an erase operation and might simply do nothing or throw an `UnsupportedOperationException`.

```
interface java.util.Iterator<E>
```

▶ `default void remove()`
  Deletes the last object supplied by `next()` from the underlying collection. The operation doesn't have to be provided by iterators and throws an `UnsupportedOperation Exception("remove")` if not otherwise overridden.

11.6.2   The Supplier of the Iterator

Iterators play an especially important role in Java and occur thousands of times in the JDK. The only question is: Where does an iterator come from so that a collection can be run? Data providers must offer a method to supply iterators.

First Example

The `iterator()` method of `Path` returns an `Iterator<Path>` via the path elements. Consider the following example:

```
Iterator<Path> iterator = Paths.get( "/chris/brain/java/20" ).iterator();
while ( iterator.hasNext() )
  System.out.println( iterator.next() );
```

This expression returns four lines with "chris," "brain," "java," and "20."

Second Example

Data structures such as lists and sets also declare an `iterator()` method:

```
Iterator<Integer> iter = new TreeSet<>( Arrays.asList( 4, 2, 9 ) ).iterator();
```

The output would be sorted as 2, 4 ,and 9 with the while loop from earlier.

Third Example

The `Scanner` class implements `Iterator<String>` so that the familiar pair of `hasNext()`/`next()` can run over the tokens, as in the following example:

```
Iterator<String> iterator = new Scanner( "Dog Cat Mouse" );
```

The output consists of three lines with the loop shown earlier.

So, in the first and second case, it's the call of `iterator()` that gets us an `Iterator`, while in the third case it's a class that is itself an `Iterator` with a constructor.

11.6.3   The Iterable Interface

An `iterator()` method that returns an `Iterator` can often be found in data structures. There's a reason for that: The classes with `iterator()` method implement a `java.lang.Iterable` interface that prescribes the `iterator()` operation. The `TreeSet` we used in the example implements `Iterable` in the same way that `Path` implements it.

```
interface java.lang.Iterable<T>
```

▶ `Iterator<T> iterator()`
   Returns a `java.util.iterator` which iterates over all elements of type T.

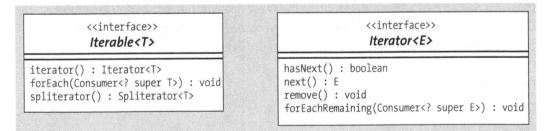

Figure 11.8 UML Diagram of Iterable and Iterator

11.6.4   Extended for and Iterable

So far, we've used the extended `for` in small examples where the goal was to run an array of elements.

```
for ( String s : new String[]{ "T. Noah", "S. Colbert", "J. Oliver" } )
  System.out.printf( "%s is great.%n", s );
```

Listing 11.31 src/main/java/com/tutego/insel/iterable/SimpleIterable.java, main()

Not only does the extended for loop traverse arrays but everything of type Iterable. Since many data structure classes in particular implement this interface, the extended for can be used to virtually iterate through result sets, as in the following example:

```
for ( String s : Arrays.asList( "T. Noah", "S. Colbert", "J. Oliver" ) )
  System.out.printf( "%s is great.%n", s );
```

11.6.5   Internal Iteration

The Iterable interface provides two methods with default implementation. The interesting method is forEach(...), while the spliterator() method is not that interesting at this point.

```
interface java.util.Iterable<T>
```

▶ default void forEach(Consumer<? super T> action)
  Fetches the iterator, runs over all elements, and then calls the consumer to which the element gets passed.

The forEach(...) method implements what's called *internal iteration*. With this feature, you don't need to formulate a loop with the pair hasNext()/next(), but forEach(...) can accomplish the same goal.

Example

The following example runs over the first prime numbers and outputs them:

```
Consumer<Integer> consumer = new Consumer<Integer>() {
  public void accept( Integer e ) { System.out.printf( "Prime: %d%n", e ); }
};
Arrays.asList( 2, 3, 5, 7, 11, 13, 17, 19, 23, 29, 31 )
      .forEach( consumer );
```

The Arrays.asList(...) call returns a java.util.List and is Iterable.

What looks like a lot of code written can be drastically shortened using lambda expressions, as in the following example:

```
Arrays.asList( 2, 3, 5, 7, 11, 13, 17, 19, 23, 29, 31 )
      .forEach( e -> System.out.printf( "Prime: %d%n", e ) );
```

This compact notation is the subject of Chapter 13.

11.6.6   Implementing a Custom Iterable*

For our own objects to be placed right after the colon from the extended for, the corresponding class must implement the Iterable interface and thus provide an iterator() method. iterator() must return a matching Iterator, which in turn must implement the hasNext() and next() methods (to specify the next element in the enumeration and indicate the end).

Our next example consists of a class that implements Iterable and can decompose the words in a sentence. The basic implementation is StringTokenizer, which returns the next subsequences via nextToken() and reports via hasMoreTokens() whether further tokens can be read.

Let's start with the first part, the WordIterable class, which must first implement Iterable to be positioned on the right side of the dot. Then, this instance must return an Iterator via iterator() that runs over all words. This iterator can be implemented as its own class, but we'll implement the WordIterable class to embody both Iterable and Iterator at the same time; therefore, only one instance is needed. One drawback of this approach is that you can't have multiple different Iterator instances for one WordIterable.

```java
class WordIterable implements Iterable<String>, Iterator<String> {

  private StringTokenizer tokenizer;

  public WordIterable( String s ) {
    tokenizer = new StringTokenizer( s );
  }

  // Method from interface Iterable

  @Override public Iterator<String> iterator() {
    return this;
  }

  // Methods from interface Iterator

  @Override public boolean hasNext() {
    return tokenizer.hasMoreTokens();
  }

  @Override public String next() {
    if ( hasNext() )
      return tokenizer.nextToken();
    throw new NoSuchElementException();
  }
}
```

Listing 11.32 src/main/java/com/tutego/insel/iterable/WordIterable.java (Snippet)

Consider the following example:

```
String s = "Even miracles take a little time.";
for ( String word : new WordIterable(s) )
  System.out.println( word );
```

Listing 11.33 src/main/java/com/tutego/insel/iterable/WordIterableDemo.java, main()

The extended for loop is rebuilt internally by the Java compiler in the following way:

```
{
  String word; Iterator<String> iterator = new WordIterable(s ).iterator();
  while ( iterator.hasNext() ) {
    word = iterator.next();
    System.out.println( word );
    }
  word = null;
  iterator = null;
}
```

11.7   Annotations in Java Platform, Standard Edition

In Section 11.1, you learned about annotations as custom modifiers. In the process, you encountered @Override several times. Annotations are only recognized by the compiler and are also only valid on methods.

11.7.1   Places for Annotations

Annotations can be set in declarations of the following elements:

- Types (i.e., classes, interfaces, enumerations, and other annotation types)
- Members (i.e., constructors, methods, and class/object variables)

For example, an annotation of a type can be set for the following elements:

- Variable declarations
- new keyword
- Typecasting
- The implements clause
- The throws clause for methods

Annotations in type usage are called *type annotations* for short. This form allows even further testing of external tools in particular. Java comes with some annotation types, but so far, these annotation types are used exclusively for declarations, like the well-known @Override. Predefined type annotations are not yet contained in Java SE.

[+]

Outlook

An example of an external library is the *Checker Framework* (*https://checkerframe-work.org/*), which provides a large number of annotation types and a property checking tool. This library can be used to write the following code, for example:

```
@NonNull Object ref = new Object();
public int compareTo(@NonNull String other) { … }
boolean lessThan(double[] arr1, double @SameLen("#1") [] arr2) { … }
```

Another example is *Jakarta Bean Validation* (*https://beanvalidation.org/*), which can be used to write, for example, the following code:

```
Optional<@Past LocalDate> getBirthday() { … }
@Min(value = 18) @Max(value = 150) int age;
```

11.7.2   Annotation Types from java.lang

The `java.lang` package declares five annotation types, and `@Override` has often appeared in this book already.

Annotation Type	Effect
@Override	The annotated method overrides a method from the superclass or implements a method of an interface.
@Deprecated	The marked element is obsolete and should no longer be used.
@SuppressWarnings	Suppresses certain compiler warnings.
@SafeVarargs	Special marking for methods with variable argument count and generic argument type.
@FunctionalInterface	For interfaces that have only exactly one (abstract) method.

Table 11.9 Annotations from the java.lang Package

The five annotations have special semantics for the compiler or the runtime system. Java SE declares other annotation types in other packages (such as the `java.lang.annotation` and `javax.annotation` packages), which aren't relevant in this context. In addition, some special technology-specific annotation types exist for XML object mapping or web service declarations, for example.

11.7.3   @Deprecated

The `@Deprecated` annotation does the same job as the Javadoc tag `@deprecated`. Marked elements are considered obsolete, expressing that the developer should use alternatives.

> **Example**
>
> In the following example, the `fubar()` method is marked as deprecated:
>
> ```
> @Deprecated
> public void fubar() { … }
> ```
>
> If any program section calls `fubar()`, the compiler outputs a simple message.

The translation with the `-Xlint:deprecation` switch provides the exact warnings; at the moment, `-deprecation` provides the same output.

An element can also be marked as obsolete via a Javadoc tag. One difference remains: The Javadoc tag can only be evaluated by Javadoc (or another doclet), while annotations can be evaluated by other tools.

11.7.4   Annotations with Additional Information

The annotations `@Override` and `@Deprecated` belong to the class of marker annotations because no additional specifications are necessary (or permitted). In addition, a *single-value annotation* gets exactly one additional piece of information, in contrast to a full annotation with arbitrary key-value pairs.

Notation of Annotations	Function
`@AnnotationType`	(Marker) annotation
`@AnnotationType( value )`	Annotation with exactly one value
`@AnnotationType( key1=value1, key2=value2, … )`	Annotation with key-value pairs

Table 11.10 Annotations with and without Additional Information

The parentheses are optional in marker annotations.

11.7.5   @SuppressWarnings

The `@SuppressWarnings` annotation controls compiler warnings. Different values determine more precisely which indications are suppressed. For example, if a program uses generically declared data types but doesn't use generics, a warning will occur. Let's take the following program code:

```
ArrayList list;
list = new ArrayList();
list.add( "SuppressWarnings" );
```

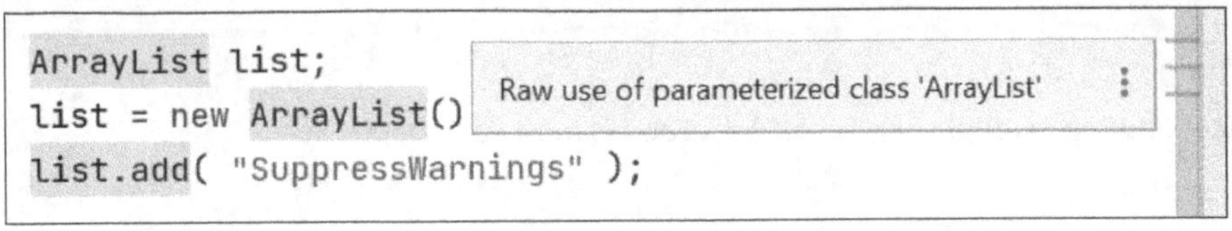

```
ArrayList list;
list = new ArrayList()        Raw use of parameterized class 'ArrayList'        ⋮
list.add( "SuppressWarnings" );
```

Figure 11.9 Warnings in Eclipse

The javac compiler reports rather ambiguously via the command line:

```
Note: ABC.java uses unchecked or unsafe operations.
Note: Recompile with -Xlint:unchecked for details.
```

With the -Xlint switch set, you can then call the object more precisely:

```
warning: [rawtypes] found raw type: ArrayList
    ArrayList list;
    ^
  missing type arguments for generic class ArrayList<E>
  where E is a type-variable:
    E extends Object declared in class ArrayList

warning: [
unchecked] unchecked call to add(E) as a member of the raw type ArrayList
    list.add( "SuppressWarnings" );
            ^
  where E is a type-variable:
    E extends Object declared in class ArrayList
3 warnings
```

Two different types of warnings occur:

- The ArrayList class is declared as a generic type, which is how the type should be parameterized, for example, with ArrayList<String>.

- The third line uses add(...), a method that could get a more precise type parameter via generics. Since we haven't specified a type, a warning will follow.

Warnings can be turned off using the @SuppressWarnings annotation. As a special modifier, this annotation can be appended to a variable declaration, a method declaration, or a class declaration. The range is ascending. If you want to disable all warnings for old code quickly and painlessly, you can add @SuppressWarnings("all") to the class declaration.

[Ex]   **Example**

In the following example, the compiler should not output any messages for the class:

```
@SuppressWarnings( "all" )
public class SuppressAllWarnings {

  public static void main( String[] args ) {
    java.util.ArrayList list1 = new java.util.ArrayList();
    list1.add( "SuppressWarnings" );

    java.util.ArrayList list2 = new java.util.ArrayList();
  }
}
```

Listing 11.34 src/main/java/com/tutego/insel/annotation/SuppressAllWarnings.java

Instead of suppressing every warning with @SuppressWarnings("all"), a better strategy is to be selective in the following ways:

- Using @SuppressWarnings("rawtypes") for ArrayList list and list = new ArrayList()
- Using @SuppressWarnings("unchecked") for list.add("...")

Since two identical modifiers aren't permitted—and @SuppressWarnings twice is also not permitted—a special array notation is chosen.

Example

The compiler should not provide messages for the non-generic used ArrayList and its methods:

```
@SuppressWarnings( { "rawtypes", "unchecked" } )
public static void main( String[] args ) {
  ArrayList list = new ArrayList();
  list.add( "SuppressWarnings" );
}
```

We briefly mentioned that the @SuppressWarnings annotation can also be used for variable declarations. For our example, however, this option is of little help if, for example, all warnings are switched off when the list is declared. Consider the following example:

```
@SuppressWarnings( "all" ) ArrayList list;
list = new ArrayList();           // Warning: ArrayList is a raw type …
list.add( "SuppressWarnings" );  // Warning: Type safety …
```

@SuppressWarnings("all") applies only to the one ArrayList list declaration and not to subsequent statements that do something with the list. Therefore, for clarity, our example places the annotation on the same line.

Note

The `@SuppressWarnings("xyz")` notation is just a shortcut for `@SuppressWarnings({"xzy"})`, which in turn is just a shortcut of `@SuppressWarnings(value={"xzy"})`.

In addition to the `rawtype` and `unchecked` identifiers that come from generics, others aren't particularly well documented. This lack of documentation stems from the fact that messages during program translation belong to the compiler infrastructure and not to the runtime environment, and thus not to the traditional Java API. Basically, the compiler can perform code analysis of any complexity and raise an alarm in case of suspected errors. But keep in mind that these are only warnings: If you do everything right as a programmer, you won't see the messages. Nevertheless, understanding these warning is relevant because the compiler will sometimes note something that a developer wants to use deliberately, in which case it's necessary to turn off these messages.

11.8   Further Reading

The API documentation of the standard classes from the `java.lang` package is immensely helpful and should be studied completely: *https://docs.oracle.com/en/java/javase/17/docs/api/java.base/java/lang/package-summary.html*.

Chapter 12

Generics<T>

"Earthly happiness means: Misfortune does not visit us too regularly."
—Karl Gutzkow (1811–1878)

In this chapter, you'll learn about generics, which make your code more stable by providing the compiler with more type information.

12.1 Introduction to Java Generics

Generics are among the most complex language constructs in Java. Because of this complexity, we'll approach generics in two steps: first from the user's side and then from the application programming interface (API) designer's side. Taking advantage of generically declared types is rather easy, so let's pick this low-hanging fruit first.

12.1.1 Man versus Machine: Type Checking of the Compiler and the Runtime Environment

An important feature of Java is that the compiler checks the types and thus knows which members are present and which aren't. In this way, Java differs from dynamic programming languages such as Python or PHP, which perform this type check later during runtime.

In Java, two instances check the types, and they're both smart in different ways. First, the Java virtual machine (JVM) has absolute type intelligence when running your application and performing the ultimate check to ensure that no objects have been assigned to the wrong types. Then, the compiler performs a few useful checks but is sometimes a bit too gullible and follows the developer blindly. An incorrect explicit type conversion causes the JVM to throw an exception.

Let's look at an example, which at this point still looks uncomplicated:

```
Object o = "String";
String s = (String) o;
```

Via explicit type casting, Object o is sold to the compiler as a String. This scenario is fine because o actually references a String object. Problems arise if the type *can't* be converted to String, even when we instruct the compiler to perform type casting, as in the following example:

```
Object o = Integer.valueOf( 42 );        // or with Autoboxing: Object o = 42;
String s = (String) o;
```

The compiler accepts the type casting, and no error arises at translation time. However, this adaptation clearly can't be carried out by the JVM. For this reason, a ClassCast-Exception arises at runtime since an Integer can't be converted to a String.

Generics is about giving the compiler more information about types and avoiding ClassCastException errors.

12.1.2 Rockets

Our previous examples were all about players and candies. Let's imagine that a player has a *rocket* for traveling, which can be loaded. Since we can't know exactly what the rocket carries, we'll make a base type that represents all possible object types. In our first example, we'll start with the most general base type Object, so that the user can transport everything with his rocket.[1]

```
public class Rocket {
  private Object value;
  public Rocket() {}
  public Rocket( Object value ) { this.value = value; }
  public void set( Object value ) { this.value = value; }
  public Object get() { return value; }
  public boolean isEmpty() { return value == null; }
  public void empty() { value = null; }
}
```

Listing 12.1 src/main/java/com/tutego/insel/nongeneric/Rocket.java, Rocket

In this example, we have a standard constructor as well as a parameterized constructor. Objects can be placed into the rocket via set(...) and read again via the access method get(). Let's provide a player with two rockets, one on the right and one on the left:

```
public class Player {
  public String name;
  public Rocket rightRocket;
  public Rocket leftRocket;
}
```

Listing 12.2 src/main/java/com/tutego/insel/nongeneric/Player.java, Player

---

1 Primitive data types can be stored via wrapper objects.

Now, since our player has a rocket, let's quickly write an example method. Our player `michael` can transport numbers in each rocket. Then, we'll determine which in which rocket he hides the bigger number.

```
Player michael = new Player();
michael.name = "Omar Arnold";
Rocket rocket = new Rocket();
Long aBigNumber = 111111111111111L;
rocket.set( aBigNumber );                          // (1)
michael.leftRocket  = rocket;
michael.rightRocket = new Rocket( 2222222222222222222L );

System.out.println( michael.name + " transports " +
              michael.leftRocket.get() + " and " + michael.rightRocket.get() );

Long val1 = (Long) michael.leftRocket.get();   // (2)
Long val2 = (Long) michael.rightRocket.get();

System.out.println( val1.compareTo( val2 ) > 0 ? "left" : "right" );
```

Listing 12.3 src/main/java/com/tutego/insel/nongeneric/PlayerRocketDemo.java, main()

The example has no particular pitfalls; however, two unattractive things stand out. Both of these problems stem from the fact that the Rocket class was declared with the Object type to store the contents of the rocket in such a general way that the rocket can take on anything. Consider the following points:

- During initialization, a good practice would be to say that the rocket can only take on a certain type (i.e., Long). If such a restriction were possible, then in line (1) really only Long objects could be placed in the rocket and nothing else (such as Integer objects, for example).

- When extracting in line (2) the contents of the rockets via get(), you must remember what you put in. If data structures require special types, then this requirement should also be documented. But if the compiler knew that Long is stored in the rocket in any case, then type casting could be omitted, and the program code would be shorter. Also, the compiler could warn us if you tried to retrieve Long from the rocket as an Integer, but we'd need to pass this knowledge to the compiler! If a Long object exists in the rocket, but we expect it to be an Integer (and set an explicit type casting to Integer), the compiler won't report an error. However, at runtime, a nasty Class-CastException will arise instead.

Long story short: The compiler doesn't sufficiently consider type safety in our example. Explicit type casting is usually messy and should be avoided. But how can we make our rockets type-safe?

One solution would be to declare a new class for each type to be stored in the rocket, so once a RocketLong for the long data type, then perhaps RocketInteger for int, Rocket-String for string, and so on. The problem with this approach is code must be copied, and the repeated code is almost identical. This solution isn't smart since you can't write a new class for each data type while keeping the logic unchanged. Ideally, we'd write a little code to still get type safety at compile time but not type safety at runtime where a ClassCastException might surprise us. In general, we could keep the type free (i.e., "generic") when declaring it, and as soon as we use the rocket, we could make the compiler pay attention to this now specified type and ensure correctness of use.

The solution to this problem is called *generics*.[2] This feature offers developers completely new ways to program data structures and algorithms that are independent of a data type and are thus "generic."

12.1.3   Declaring Generic Types

To convert Rocket into a *generic type*, you must insert a type proxy (called a *type parameter*) in the right places where the Object occurred; the type parameter is represented by a *type variable*. The name of the type variable must be specified in the class declaration.

The following example shows the syntax for the generic type of Rocket:

```
public class Rocket<T> {
  private T value;
  public Rocket() {}
  public Rocket( T value ) { this.value = value; }
  public void set( T value ) { this.value = value; }
  public T get() { return value; }
  public boolean isEmpty() { return value == null; }
  public void empty() { value = null; }
}
```

Listing 12.4 src/main/java/com/tutego/insel/generic/Rocket.java, Rocket

At this point, we've defined the type variable T and now can use it instead of Object in the Rocket class.

For generic types, the specification of the type variable appears only once, at the beginning of the class declaration and enclosed in angle brackets after the class name. Simply put, the type parameter can be used wherever a conventional type existed. Some limitations exist, however, because of *raw types*, which we'll describe in detail in Section 12.2.4.

In our example, we can directly replace Object with T, and the generic class is ready.

---

2 In C++, these types of classes are referred to as *parameterized classes* or *templates*.

Naming Conventions [«]

Type parameters are usually single capital letters like T (for "type"), E (for "element"), K (for "key"), or V (for "value"). These letters are just placeholders and not real types. The following code is possible but absolutely not recommended:

```
public class Rocket<Elf> {
  private Elf value;
  public void set( Elf value ) { this.value = value; }
  public Elf get() { return value; }
}
```

Elf looks much more like a real class type than like a type parameter, and in this construction, not only are elves allowed in the class, but all types.

Not only can a class or interface be declared generically, so can a record. Thus, an immutable alternative to making the Rocket class generic is shown in the following example:

```
public record Rocket<T>(
    T value
) {
  public boolean isEmpty() { return value == null; }
}
```

Listing 12.5 src/main/java/com/tutego/insel/records/Rocket.java, Rocket

Other Areas of Use for Generics

In a number of examples, memory structures like our rocket make sense not only for a data type Long, but basically for all types, anywhere that the implementation is (relatively) independent of the type of the elements. This flexibility applies, for example, to a sorting algorithm that uses the order of elements. If one element is greater than, less than, or equal to another, the algorithm need only use that order. The type doesn't matter—whether they are numbers of type Long, Double, or even carrots or customers. The algorithm itself simply won't be affected by the type. The most common use of generics are for containers that are made type safe.

History Lesson [«]

The idea of introducing generics into Java is older and goes back to the *Pizza* project or *GJ* subproject (A Generic Java Language Extension) by Martin Odersky (who is also the creator of the Scala programming language), Gilad Bracha, David Stoutamire, and Philip Wadler. GJ then became the basis of Java Specification Request (JSR) 14, "Add Generic Types To The Java Programming Language."[3]

---

3 *https://www.cs.purdue.edu/homes/hosking/352/generics.pdf*

12.1.4   Using Generics

To use our new Rocket class, you'll specify it along with type arguments, which creates *parameterized types*.

```
Rocket<Integer>  intRocket    = new Rocket<Integer>();
Rocket<String>   stringRocket = new Rocket<String>();
```

Listing 12.6 src/main/java/com/tutego/insel/generic/RocketPlayer.java, main(), Part 1

A concrete type is always enclosed in angle brackets after the class/interface name.[4] The rocket intRocket is an instance of a generic type with the concrete type argument Integer. This rocket can now officially contain only Integer values.

Figure 12.1 Rocket<Integer>: For Integer Only

The stringRocket rocket, on the other hand, contains only strings. The compiler also checks this consistency, and type casting is no longer needed.

```
intRocket.set( 1 );
int x = intRocket.get();          // No more type casting needed
stringRocket.set( "Sesquipedalian" );
String s = stringRocket.get();
```

Listing 12.7 src/main/java/com/tutego/insel/generic/RocketPlayer.java, main(), Part 2

As developers, we've thus made it clear in the program code that the rockets contain an Integer and nothing else. Because program code is read more often than written, you should always put as much information as possible about the context in the program

---

4 That XML is also enclosed in angle brackets and is considered large and bloated isn't something parallel to Java's generics.

code. Readability may suffer somewhat since, especially for instantiation, the type must be specified both on the right and on the left, and the syntax can become long with nested generics. But as we'll discuss in Section 12.1.5, this code can be abbreviated.

The beauty of type safety is that all members are checked with the specified type. For example, when we access the element from `intRocket` via `get()`, the element is of type `Integer` (and through unboxing equals `int`), and `set(...)` also allows only an `Integer`. Thus, the program code is more robust and, by eliminating type casting, also shorter and more readable.

No Primitives

Type arguments in Java can be classes, interfaces, enumerations, or arrays of classes, interfaces, or enumerations, but not primitive data types. This limits the number of options, but since autoboxing is available, this limitation is tolerable. Furthermore, if null exists in the `Rocket<Integer>`, unboxing at runtime will result in `NullPointerException`.

Term	Example
Generic type	Rocket<T>
Formal type parameter	T
Parameterized type	Rocket<Long>
Actual type parameter	Long
Raw type	Rocket

Table 12.1 Summary of Generics Terms

Nested Generics

If a generic type like `Rocket<T>` is given, no restriction exists on `T` for now. Thus, `T` isn't limited to simple class or interface types but can again be a generic type. This breadth is logical because each generic type is an independent type that can be used (almost) like any other type, as in the following example:

```
Rocket<Rocket<String>> rocketOfRockets = new Rocket<Rocket<String>>();
rocketOfRockets.set( new Rocket<String>() );
rocketOfRockets.get().set( "Inner Rocket<String>" );
System.out.println( rocketOfRockets.get().get() ); // Inner Rocket<String>
```

Listing 12.8 src/main/java/com/tutego/insel/generic/RocketPlayer.java, main(), Part 3

In this case, the rocket contains an "inner rocket" that stores a string named `"Inner Rocket<String>"`. With similar constructions, you can quickly see how helpful generics can be to the compiler (and to us). Without generics, all the rockets would look the same.

Precise with Generics	Imprecise without Generics
Rocket<String> stringRocket;	Rocket stringRocket;
Rocket<Integer> intRocket;	Rocket intRocket;
Rocket<Rocket<String>> rocketOfRockets;	Rocket rocketOfRockets;

Table 12.2 Clarification through Generics

Only a well-chosen name and precise documentation can help with non-generically declared variables. Before the introduction of generics, developers used block comments to indicate type information, for example, in Rocket/*<string>*/ stringRocket.

No Arrays of Parameterized Types

The following statement prepares a single rocket with an array of strings:

```
Rocket<String[]> rocketForArray = new Rocket<String[]>();
```

But can an array of multiple rockets be declared, each containing strings? Yes. However, while the declaration is still possible, the initialization is invalid, as in the following example:

```
Rocket<String>[] arrayOfRocket;
arrayOfRocket = new Rocket<String>[2];  // ☠ Compiler error
```

The reason for this error is hidden in the implementation in bytecode, and the best solution is to use the convenient data structures available from the java.util package. For developers, a List<Rocket<String>> is more useful than a Rocket<String>[] anyway and the performance is almost the same. However, since arrays are automatically used by the compiler with variable argument lists, there's a problem if the parameter variable is a type variable. For signatures like f(T... params) the @SafeVarargs annotation helps to suppress the compiler message.

12.1.5 Diamonds Are Forever

When initializing a variable whose type is generic, notice that the actual type parameter must be specified twice. With nested generics, the extra work is inconvenient. Consider a list containing Maps, where the associative memory connects date values with Strings, as in the following example:

```
List<Map<Date,String>> listOfMaps;
listOfMaps = new ArrayList<Map<Date,String>>();
```

The actual type parameter Map<Date, String> is placed once on the side of the variable declaration and once after the new keyword.

The Diamond Operator

If the compiler has all the available type information, generic type arguments can be omitted after new, and only a pair of angle brackets remains.

> **Example**
>
> You should avoid writing the following code:
>
> List<**Map<Date,String>**> listOfMaps = new ArrayList<**Map<Date,String>**>();
>
> Instead, you should write the following code:
>
> List<**Map<Date,String>**> listOfMaps = new ArrayList<>();
>
> You should avoid writing the following code:
>
> Rocket<**Rocket<String>**> rocketOfRockets = new Rocket<**Rocket<String>**>();
>
> Instead, you should write the following code:
>
> Rocket<**Rocket<String>**> rocketOfRockets = new Rocket<>();

The fact that the compiler can infer the types from the context goes back to a compiler feature called *type inference*, which we'll encounter again in Section 12.1.7. Because of the appearance of the angle brackets <>, the type represented by the angle brackets is also referred to as the *diamond type*. The pair of angle brackets <> is also called the *diamond operator*. This construction is an operator because it identifies the type and thus is also referred to as the *diamond type inference operator*.

Areas of Use of the Diamond

In our example, the diamond replaces the entire actual type parameter, Map<Date,String>. You cannot use this operator for nested generics. Consequently, new ArrayList<Map<>>() fails. Also, the new diamond operator is permitted only with new. Thus, an incorrect usage would be to include the diamond operator on the left side of a variable declaration as well as on the right side in the creation of the instance. A declaration like List<> listOfMaps; would thus cause a compiler error because the compiler couldn't derive any types on each subsequent use.

Since the diamond is used with new, you can always use it when instances are created, with a few exceptions that we'll cover in the following subsection. Our next example, which doesn't make any sense, shows four areas of use:

```java
import java.util.*;

public class WhereToUseTheDiamond {

  public static List<String> foo( List<String> list ) {
    return new ArrayList<>();
  }
```

```
public static void main( String[] args ) {
  List<String> list = new ArrayList<>();
  list = new ArrayList<>();
  foo( new ArrayList<>( list ) );
 }
}
```

In this example, the diamond operator is used in four areas:

- In declarations and initializations of class/object variables and local variables
- During initialization of class/object variables and local variables/parameter variables
- As an argument in method/constructor calls
- As method returns

Without question, the first and second cases are the most useful. In almost all these cases, the diamond operator can make your code more concise. Especially in the first case, nothing speaks fundamentally against its use, but concerning the other three areas, you must carefully consider whether the readability of your program code might suffer. For example, if a data structure is initialized in the middle of a method via list = new ArrayList<>(), but the variable declaration isn't on the same page of the screen, sometimes, a reader may miss which types are exactly contained in the list.

Using the Diamond Operator Isn't Always Possible

In some situations, the type derivation doesn't work as expected. Often, this inconsistency stems from the use of the diamond operator in method calls or calls that build on each other. Thus, in these cases, we recommend doing away with the diamond operators, in addition for reasons of code readability.

[Ex]
> **Example**
>
> For the compiler, the following statement is an unsolvable case:
>
> List<String> list = new ArrayList<>().subList(0, 1);
>
> Using the diamond operator isn't possible, as shown in this example, because the compiler reports a "Type mismatch: cannot convert from List<Object> to List<String>." Type inference is complex,[5] and fortunately, developers don't need to bother about its

---

5 To test the diamond operator, Java's developers wrote a tool that runs through the Java Development Kit (JDK) and checks which generically used occurrence of new could be simplified by the diamond operator. (Approximately 5,000 places were found.) Not every team has accepted every permitted conversion towards the diamond operator. For example, the team that maintains Java security libraries wanted to continue to maintain the explicit notation of generics in assignments. When this feature was built into Java 7, two algorithms were available for type selection: simple and complex. The complex approach includes the argument type in addition to the type information provided by an assignment. Initially, the team used the simple algorithm, but later chose the complex approach, which relies on algorithms that the compiler also uses in other places.

> internal processes. An explicit type specification solves the problem, for example, new
> ArrayList<**String**>().subList(0, 1).

Diamond Operator versus var

The diamond operator and var have similar tasks but differ in the source of the information. In the case of the diamond, for example, the left side of an assignment gives the compiler information about what type is referred to on the right side of the assignment. With var, on the other hand, the reverse is true: The right side has the context, and therefore the variable type can be omitted on the left. Consider the following examples:

```
List<String> list1 = new ArrayList<>();   // List<String>
var list2 = new ArrayList<String>();       // ArrayList<String>
var list3 = new ArrayList<>();             // ArrayList<Object>
```

In the final case, no compiler error arises. However, nothing is known about the actual type parameter, which is why Object applies.

To abbreviate the code, you have two options: var for the "left side" or the diamond operator for the "right side."

12.1.6   Generic Interfaces

An interface can be declared as a generic type in the same way as a class. Let's look at the java.lang.Comparable interface and at a snippet of java.util.Set (which is an interface that prescribes operations for set operations; more on this topic will follow in Chapter 18, Section 18.2).

Comparable Interface	Set Interface
```public interface Comparable<T> { int compareTo(T o); }```	```public interface Set<E> extends Collection<E> { boolean add(E e); int size(); boolean isEmpty(); boolean contains(Object o); Iterator<E> iterator(); Object[] toArray(); <T> T[] toArray(T[] a); ... }```

Table 12.3 Generic Declaration of the Comparable and Set Interfaces

693

As mentioned earlier, the methods access the type variables T and E. In the case of Set, notice how Set itself extends a generically declared interface.

When using generic interfaces, the following two usage patterns can be derived:

- A non-generic type resolves generics during implementation.
- A generic class type implements a generic interface and passes the parameter variable.

Non-Generic Type Resolves Generics during Implementation

In the first case, a class implements the generically declared interface and specifies a concrete type. For example, all numeric wrapper classes implement Comparable, and the type argument is exactly the type of the wrapper. Consider the following example:

```
public final class Integer extends Number implements Comparable<Integer> {
  public int compareTo( Integer anotherInteger ) { … }

  …
}
```

Listing 12.9 java/lang/Integer.java (Snippet)

This usage frees the Integer class from generics for the user.

[+]
> **Tip**
> Complex generic types can be greatly simplified with custom type declarations. For example, instead of writing HashMap<String,List<Integer>> over and over again, you can use the following shortcut:
>
> class StringToIntListMap extends HashMap<String,List<Integer>> {}

Generic Class Type Implements Generic Interface and Passes on the Parameter Variable

The Set interface prescribes operations for sets. For example, one class that implements Set is HashSet. The following example shows the header of the type declaration:

```
public class HashSet<E>
    extends AbstractSet<E>
    implements Set<E>, Cloneable, java.io.Serializable
```

Notice how Set declares the type variable E, and this type "propagates" to HashSet, i.e. the implementation does not determine a type. However, the class Properties shows that it can be done differently:

```
public class Properties
    extends Hashtable<Object,Object>
```

> **Note**
>
> In some situations, void is also used as an actual type parameter. For example, if interface I<T> { T foo(); } declares a type variable T without returning anything when I is implemented, then the actual type parameter can be Void. Consider the following example:
>
> ```java
> class C implements I<Void> {
>   @Override public Void foo() { return null; }
> }
> ```
>
> However, void and Void are different because, with Void, a return is required, which makes return null necessary.

12.1.7   Generic Methods/Constructors and Type Inference

The generic constructions we've covered so far can be summarized in the following ways:

- class classname**<T>** { ... }
- interface interfacename<T>**{ ... }**

A type variable specified in the class or interface declaration can be accessed in all non-static members of the type.

> **Example**
>
> The following example code will result in an error:
>
>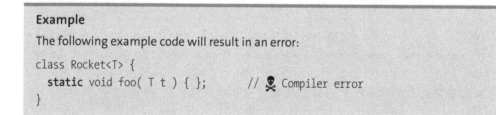
> ```java
> class Rocket<T> {
>   static void foo( T t ) { };          // 💀 Compiler error
> }
> ```

However, some complications arise in the following scenarios:

- When (static) methods want to use their own type variables
- When different (static) methods want to use different type variables

A class can be declared without generics but have *generic methods*. In general, each constructor, object method, and class method can declare one or more type parameters. The type variables are then no longer located at the class, but at the method/constructor declaration and are "local" to the method or constructor. The general format for declaring a generic method is as follows:

```java
modifier <type variable(s)> return type method name(parameter) throws clause
```

Quite by Chance One or the Other Argument

Generic methods are particularly useful for utility classes that provide only static methods but don't exist as objects themselves. The following example illustrates this scenario using a random() method:

```java
public class GenericMethods {

  public static <T> T random( T m, T n ) {
    return Math.random() > 0.5 ? m : n;
  }

  public static void main( String[] args ) {
    String s = random( "Woo-Hoo!", "D'Oh!" );
    System.out.println( s );
  }
}
```

Listing 12.10 src/main/java/com/tutego/insel/generic/GenericMethods.java, GenericMethods

In this case, <T> T random(T m, T n) declares a generic method, where the return type and parameter type are determined by a type variable T. The specification of <T> with the class name has been omitted with this syntax and has been moved to the declaration of the method.

> **Note**
>
> Of course, a class can be declared as a generic type and a method contained in it can be declared as a generic method with different type. In this case, the type variables should be named differently to avoid confusing the reader. In the following example, T in sit(...) doesn't refer to the parameter variable of the Lupilu class, but does refer to the parameter value of the method:
>
> ```java
> interface Lupilu<T> { <T> void sit( T val ); }  // Confusing
> interface Lupilu<T> { <V> void sit( V val ); }  // Better
> ```

The Compiler in Search of Commonalities

The type (which is important for the return) is automatically derived by the compiler from the context (i.e., from the arguments). This feature is called *type inference*, which has far-reaching consequences.

When declaring <T> T random(T m, T n), at first glance, you may think that the variable types m and n must absolutely be equal. But this requirement isn't true because, with types, the compiler goes up the type hierarchy until it finds a common type.

Call	Identified Types	Common Basic Types
random("Food", 1)	String, Integer	Object, Serializable, Comparable
random(1L, 1D)	Long, Double	Object, Number, Comparable
random(new Point(), new StringBuilder())	Point, StringBuilder	Object, Serializable, Cloneable

Table 12.4 Common Base Types

Note that Object always belongs in the group, which is not surprising.

In the case of random(...), the valid return types are at the intersection of types. Accordingly, String and Integer are permitted for the parameter types, as in the following examples:

```
Object       s1 = random( "Quack", 1 );
Serializable s2 = random( "Quack", 1 );
Comparable   s3 = random( "Quack", 1 );
```

Scarce Factory Methods

The diamond operator can abbreviate variable declarations with the initialization of a reference variable. In the following example, the generic type String must be specified twice:

```
Rocket<String> r = new Rocket<String>();
```

Instead, the diamond operator (<>) permits the following example statement:

```
Rocket<String> r = new Rocket<>();
```

The type inference provides an alternative solution if we build creator methods by ourselves. Let's give our Rocket class a factory method, as shown in the following example:

```
public static <T> Rocket<T> newInstance() {
  return new Rocket<T>();
}
```

Thus, the following alternative is possible:

```
Rocket<String> r = Rocket.newInstance();
```

From the result type Rocket<String>, the compiler derives the actual type parameter String for the rocket. Although we can't significantly reduce the effort for writing a simple type like String, the code will definitely become shorter for nested data structures. If the rocket needs to store an associative memory that associates a string with a list of numbers, a compact way of writing this is shown in the following example:

```
Rocket<Map<String,List<Integer>>> r = Rocket.newInstance();
```

Generic Methods with Explicit Actual Type Parameter*

In some situations, the compiler can't infer the correct type from the context by means of type inference. For example, if the argument of the static method `Arrays.asList(...)` is an array, then the explicit type argument is necessary because the compiler can't tell if the array itself is one element of the return list or if the array is the vararg conversion and all elements of the array go into the return list. Consider the following example:

```
List<String> list11 = Arrays.asList( new String[] { "A", "B" } );
List<String> list12 =
  Arrays.asList( "A", "B" );  // Parameter is defined as vararg
System.out.println( list11 );   // [A, B]
System.out.println( list12 );   // [A, B]
List<String> list21 = Arrays.<String>asList( new String[] { "A", "B" } );
List<String> list22 = Arrays.<String>asList( "A", "B" );
System.out.println( list21 );   // [A, B]
System.out.println( list22 );   // [A, B]
List<String[]> list31 = Arrays.<String[]>asList( new String[] { "A", "B" } );
// List<String[]> list32 = Arrays.<String[]>asList( "A", "B" );
System.out.println( list31 );   // [[Ljava.lang.String;@69b332]
```

First, note that the results for `list11`, `list12`, `list21`, and `list22` are identical. The compiler automatically converts a vararg as an array and passes the array to the `asList(...)` method. Therefore, in the bytecode, the calls look the same. For `list21` and `list22`, the actual type parameter is explicitly specified in each case, but doing so is not really necessary since the result is like `list11` and `list12`, respectively. But the actual type parameter `String` makes it clear that the elements in the array (the vararg arguments) are strings.

Things get really exciting with `list31`. First, let's consider the problem: `new String[]{"A", "B"}` is the argument of a vararg method, which is ambiguous because this array could be the first element of the vararg array automatically built by the compiler (in which case it would be an array within an array). Alternatively, the default internal conversion may apply—the Java compiler interprets the passed array as the vararg conversion. This ambiguity is solved by `<String[]>` since, in that case, it's clear that the string array we've created must be the only element of a new vararg array. Furthermore, `Arrays.<String[]> asList(...)` indicates that the type of the array elements is `String[]`. For this reason, the last variable declaration doesn't work either because, for `asList("A", "B")`, the element type is `String`, but not `String[]`.

The syntax takes some getting used to, but in practice, explicit specifications are rarely needed.

12.2 Implementing Generics, Type Erasure, and Raw Types

To understand generics and learn what information is available at runtime, let's now look at how the compiler translates generics into bytecode.

12.2.1 Implementation Options

In general, two ways to implement generic types exist:

- **Heterogeneous variant**:
  Individual code is generated for each type (such as String, Integer, or Point, which results in three class files). This variant is also called *code specialization*.

- **Homogeneous translation**
  From the parameterized class, a class is created that only uses Object, for example, instead of the type parameter. For the actual type parameter, the compiler places type castings into the statements.

Java uses homogeneous translation, and the compiler generates only one class file. Multiple instances of the class don't exist, either in bytecode or in memory.

12.2.2 Type Erasure

Recall that Java has two type systems: one in the compiler and one in the Java Runtime Environment (JRE). Although generic type information exists in the bytecode—in what's called *signature attributes*—the JVM can generally do little with generics. Therefore, the Java compiler must rewrite the bytecode so that the JVM can process it.

This rewriting process is referred to as *type erasure*. Think of it as dropping everything enclosed in angle brackets and making every type variable an Object.[6]

With Generics	After Type Erasure
| ```
public class Rocket<T> {
  private T value;
  public void set( T value ) {
    this.value = value; }

  public T get() { return vale; }
}
``` | ```
public class Rocket {
  private Object value;
  public void set( Object value ) {
    this.value = value; }

  public Object get() { return value;
  }
}
``` |

Table 12.5 Generic Class before and after Type Erasure

---

6 If *bounds* are involved—a type restriction that will be introduced later in Section —a more precise type is used instead of Object.

Thus, after the type erasure, the program code corresponds exactly to what you would have programmed without generics. The erasure is also performed in the code that uses the generic:

With Generics	After Type Erasure

`Rocket<Integer> r =`
`  new Rocket<Integer>( 1 );`
`r.set( 1 );`
`Integer i = r.get();`
	`Rocket r = new Rocket( 1 );`
	`r.set( 1 );`
	`Integer i = (Integer) r.get();`

Table 12.6 Using Generic Classes before and after Type Erasure

In the `r.get()` expression, the compiler inserts exactly the explicit type casting we inserted manually in our first example.

This type erasure is somewhat disappointing but has historical reasons. Planned for a future Java version are *reified generics*, that is, generic information that is also completely accessible at runtime.

[»]

Java Generics and C++ Templates

Java generics go far beyond what C++ templates offer in terms of type descriptions. In C++, any type argument can be used, which leads to incredible error messages. Thus, the C++ compiler performs rather a simple substitution. But due to the heterogeneous implementation, the C++ compiler generates different (and wonderfully optimized) machine code for each template type used. In the case of Java, the heterogeneous variant would result in a great many similar classes that differ only in a few type conversions. Anyway, since in Java only references are possible as type variables (and no primitive types), no special optimization is possible at this point. However, code specialization makes other things doable in C++ that are impossible in Java, for example, template metaprogramming. In this case, the compiler is used as a kind of interpreter for recursive template calls to generate optimal program code later, which is essentially functional programming with a compiler.

12.2.3   Problems with Type Erasure

Due to type erasure, some things in the code simply aren't possible; let's look at a few examples.

No New T()

Since type erasure in declarations such as `Rocket<T>` replaces the parameter variable with `Object`, the following *can't* be written inside the `Rocket` class, for example, to create a new type `T` transport:

Planned: With Generics (Compiler Error!)	Consequence of the Type Erasure

```class Rocket<T> {```
``` T newRocketContent() {```
```   return new T(); } // ☠```
```}```
	```class Rocket<T> {```
	``` Object newRocketContent() {```
	``` return new Object(); }```
	```}```

Table 12.7 Why new T() Can't Work: Only a new Object() Would Be Created

As the caller of `newRocketContent()`, however, we don't always expect a ridiculous `Object`, but an object of type T.

No instanceof

The `instanceof` operator is invalid for parameterized types, even though its use would be handy, for example, to make case distinctions based on the actual types:

```
void printType( Rocket<?> p ) {
  if ( p instanceof Rocket<Number> )        // ☠ illegal generic type for instanceof
    System.out.println( "Rocket with Number" );
  else if ( p instanceof Rocket<String> )  // ☠ illegal generic type for instanceof
    System.out.println( "Rocket with String" );
}
```

The compiler rightly reports an error—not just a warning—because the Rocket<String> and Rocket<Number> types don't exist at runtime; only type-erased Rocket objects exist. After the type erasure, code would be created that wouldn't make any sense:

```
void printType( Rocket r ) {
  if ( r instanceof Rocket )
    …
  else if ( r instanceof Rocket )
    …
}
```

No Typecasting to a Parameterized Type

Typecastings like the following example are illegal:

```
Rocket<String> r = (Rocket<String>) new Rocket<Integer>(); // ☠ Compiler error
```

With generics, the compiler tests the types, and the type erasure makes the actual type parameter disappear. Thus, the compiler would generate the following code:

```
Rocket r = (Rocket) new Rocket();
```

No .class for Generic Types and No Class Objects with Actual Type Parameter at Runtime

A .class placed after a type returns the Class for the object of the respective type:

```
Class<Object> objectClass = Object.class;
Class<String> stringClass = String.class;
```

Class itself is declared as a generic type.

For generic types, .class isn't permitted. Note that the following code is still valid (with a warning):

```
Class<Rocket> rocketClass = Rocket.class;
```

But the following code is no longer valid:

```
Class<Rocket<String>> rocketClass = Rocket<String>.class;    // 💀 Compiler error
```

The reason for this error is the type erasure itself: All Class objects for a type are the same and have no information about the actual type parameter at runtime. Consider the following example:

```
Rocket<String>  r1 = new Rocket<String>();
Rocket<Integer> r2 = new Rocket<Integer>();
System.out.println( r1.getClass() == r2.getClass() );       // true
```

All instances of generic types are represented by the same Class object at runtime. So, behind Rocket<String> and Rocket<Integer>, only Rocket exists. In a nutshell, everything in angle brackets disappears at runtime.

No Generic Exceptions

Basically, a construction like class MyClass<T> extends SuperClass is allowed. But the compiler includes a special rule that prevents a generic class from extending Throwable (Exception and Error are subclasses of Throwable). Consider the following example:

```
class MyException<T> extends Exception { }   // 💀 Compiler error
```

If this statement were permitted, the source code could perhaps contain the following expressions:

```
try { }
catch ( MyException<Type1> e ) { }
catch ( MyException<Type2> e ) { }
```

However, type erasure would result in two identical catch blocks, which isn't allowed.

No Static Members

Static members aren't connected to individual objects, but to classes. For example, Rocket can appear once as a parameterized type Rocket<String> and once as Rocket <Integer>—that is, as two instances. But can Rocket also declare a static method that accesses the type parameter of the class? No. The following static method in Rocket, would get the error message for T: "Cannot make a static reference to the non-static type T":

```
public static boolean isEmpty( T value ) { return value == null; }   // ☠
```

Static variables and the parameters/returns of static methods aren't bound to an instance. A type variable, however, as we've used so far, is always associated with the instance. The T for the value isn't set until we connect Rocket<String> or Rocket<Integer> to an instance, for example. With Rocket.isEmpty(""); for example, the compiler can't know what type is meant, since no instances are necessary for static method calls. In other words, a parameterized type has never been specified. Using code like Rocket<String>.isEmpty("") will result in a compiler error because this syntax isn't allowed.

Static generic methods are of course possible: As discussed earlier, they then have their own type variables.

No Overloading with Type Variables

If after the type erasure only Object comes out, of course, no method can be parameterized once with a type variable and once with Object. This overloading is not permitted.

```
public class Rocket<T> {
  public T value;
  public void set( T value ) { this.value = value; }
  public void set( Object value ) { this.value = value; }   // ☠ Compiler error!
}
```

The compiler returns the warning "Method set(T) has the same erasure set(Object) as another method in type Rocket<T>".

If the type is more specific, such as String, the situation is different again.

Arrays of Generic Classes Can't Be Created

The compiler also restricts the use of generics in arrays. The following statement is valid but results in a warning:

```
Rocket[] rockets = new Rocket[1];
```

Further, the line (2)of the following example results in the compiler error "Cannot create a generic array of Rocket<String>":

```
Rocket<String>[] rockets;                      // (1)
rockets = new Rocket<String>[1];               // (2) ☠ Compiler error
```

This example can't be used in a type-safe way, but three quick solutions are conceivable:

- Don't use generics at all and append a @SuppressWarnings("unchecked") to the array variable.

- Replace the type with a wildcard, resulting in something like Rocket<?>[] rockets = new Rocket<?>[1];. Wildcards are placeholders that we'll describe in more detail in Section 12.5.3.

- Switch directly to Collection API data structures, where a Collection <String> rockets = new ArrayList<>(); doesn't cause any problem.

In summary, array variables of generic types can be declared , as shown in line(1), but array objects can't be created, as shown in line (2). With the following trick, you can create the array:

```
class RocketFullOfMoney extends Rocket<BigInteger> {}
Rocket<BigInteger>[] rockets = new RocketFullOfMoney[1];
```

This approach not ideal, because you must create an extra temporary class Rocket-FullOfMoney. But it's common in the Java world.

12.2.4   Raw Types

Generically declared types don't necessarily need to be parameterized, but in general, you should give the compiler as much type information as possible. The following example of a generically declared Rocket<T> class is perfectly legal:

```
Rocket r = new Rocket();        // Dangerous, as we'll see momentarily
r.set( "What's the phone number of NASA? 10 9 8 7 6 5 4 3 2 1." );
String content = (String) r.get();
```

A generic type that isn't used as a parameterized type (i.e., without an actual type parameter) is referred to as a *raw type*. In our example, Rocket is the raw type of Rocket<T>. With a raw type, the compiler can no longer check type conformity because the raw type is the type used after the type erasure. Thus, get() returns Object, and set(Object) can accept anything.

If a compiler encounters program code that doesn't use a generic type as a parameterized type, warnings will be issued because the compiler wants the type to be used generically, as shown in Figure 12.2.

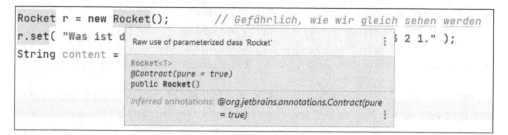

Figure 12.2 Development Environments Warn about Raw Types by Default

Also, with `set(...)`, the compiler issues a warning because it recognizes that type safety is in danger. The `set(...)` method is designed to accept an argument of the type with which it was parameterized. If the concrete type is missing due to the use of the raw type, `Object` will remain, and the compiler will issue a warning for the methods otherwise specified with a type. Consider the following example:

```
p.set( "Type safety: The method set(Object) belongs to the " +
       "raw type Rocket. References to generic type " +
       "Rocket<T> should be parameterized" );
```

The note states that the rocket should have been typed. If we don't pay attention to this warning, we can quickly run into problems, as in the following example:

```
Rocket<String> r1 = new Rocket<>();
Rocket r2 = r1;                      // Compiler warning
r2.set( new java.util.Date() );      // Compiler warning
String string = r1.get();            // ☠ ClassCastException at runtime
System.out.println( string );
```

The compiler doesn't issue an error but does issue some warnings. The third line is highly problematic because you could wrap an arbitrary number of objects via our non-parameterized rocket. But since the object behind r2 and the type-erased r1 are identical, we now have a type problem that leads to a `ClassCastException` at runtime:

```
Exception in thread "main" java.lang.ClassCastException: java.util.Date ↩
cannot be cast to java.lang.String
```

So, our only recommendation is to avoid raw types in new programs since their use can lead to exceptions that only become apparent at runtime.

Type Castings

A raw type can be automatically converted to a more special form, with warnings from the compiler, of course. Consider the following example:

```
Rocket r = new Rocket();              // (1) Warning
r.set( "Get enough sleep" );          // (2) Warning
Rocket<Point> stringRocket = r;       // (3) Warning
Point result = stringRocket.get();    // (4) ClassCastException at runtime
```

In the case of the r variable, used via the raw type in line (2), the compiler doesn't check any types in set(...) at all because the compiler never recognized the existence of these types.

Line (3) sells the raw type to the compiler as a parameterized type. Explicit type casting isn't necessary because type castings are only valid between "real" types (like Object to Rocket), not from Rocket to Rocket<String> since Rocket<String> is the same Class type (Section 12.2.3).

The statement in line (4) doesn't fetch a String type from the rocket but also doesn't result in an error at translation time. This statement, however, will cause a problem in internal type casting at runtime. So, the wrong type can get into the rocket via this "raw-not-raw" backdoor.

SuppressWarnings Annotation

In rare cases, converting to the type is necessary. Let's look at cast(Object) as an example:

```
public <T> T cast( Object obj ) {
  return (T) obj; //
 Compiler warning: Type safety: Unchecked cast from Object to T
}
```

If the cast can't be avoided, you can set a @SuppressWarnings annotation to give the compiler the type to keep it happy, as in the following example:

```
@SuppressWarnings("unchecked")
public <T> T cast( Object obj ) {
  return (T) obj;
}
```

Ultimately, generics provide ways to make source code more secure. You shouldn't break that security with raw types.

12.3 Restricting Types via Bounds

For generic specifications, the types can be further restricted. This limitation is useful because an arbitrary type is often too general. Our declaration of random(...) didn't impose any restrictions on the types:

```
public static <T> T random( T m, T n ) {
  return Math.random() > 0.5 ? m : n;
}
```

Thus, the following is possible:

```
Object o1 = new Object();
Object o2 = new Point();
System.out.println( random( o1, o2 ) );
```

Since the type is arbitrary, objects can be passed that may make little sense, especially when they're combined.

12.3.1 Simple Restrictions with extends

When you declare a generic type, you can specify that the later parameterized type extends a specific class or implements a concrete interface. For example, if our static random(...) method should accept only objects of type CharSequence (i.e., strings like String and StringBuffer/StringBuilder), we must write that requirement into the declaration, as in the following example:

```
public class Bounds {

  public static <T extends CharSequence> T random( T m, T n ) {
    return Math.random() > 0.5 ? m : n;
  }

  public static void main( String[] args ) {
    String random1 = random( "Shi", "Kar" );
    System.out.println( random1 );

    CharSequence random2 = random( "Ushi", new StringBuilder("Taka") );
    System.out.println( random2 );
  }
}
```

Listing 12.11 src/main/java/com/tutego/insel/generic/Bounds.java, Bounds

A call with two strings is correctly let through by the compiler, just as with String and StringBuilder, where the return type is then only CharSequence.

A mistake can be easily provoked because only one Point needs to be passed to the random(...) method, and Point is not of type CharSequence. Thus, the following statement is incorrect:

```
System.out.println( random( "", new Point() ) ); // ☠ Compiler error
                                                  // "Bound mismatch"
```

This statement leads to the error message: "Bound mismatch: The generic method random(T, T) of type Bounds is not applicable for the arguments (String, Point). The inferred type Serializable is not a valid substitute for the bounded parameter <T extends CharSequence>."

The compiler engages in type inference; that is, it checks which types the "" and Point arguments have in common and comes up with Serializable. However, the type doesn't help because our intention was to use CharSequences.

Type Restriction for Common Methods

A type restriction like <T extends CharSequence> is interesting because you can see that a concrete actual type parameter (say String or StringBuffer) has at least the methods of the CharSequence interface. This restriction is logical because, if the type is restricted, the compiler can ensure that the concrete types implement the prescribed interface (or extend the class), and in this way, the compiler can thus ensure that the methods exist.

Let's suppose we want to implement a type-safe max(...) that should return the larger of two values. Comparisons are easy to make if the objects implement Comparable because compareTo(...) returns a value that indicates which object is smaller, larger, or equal according to the defined metric.

```
public static <T extends Comparable<T>> T max( T m, T n ) {
  return m.compareTo( n ) > 0 ? m : n;
}
```

Listing 12.12 src/main/java/com/tutego/insel/generic/BondageBounds.java, max()

The use of this method is simple, as in the following example:

```
System.out.println( max( "cinema", "reading" ) );          // cinema/reading
System.out.println( max( 12, 100 ) );                      // 100
```

> **Note**
> With the type not bound, you can only use the methods of Object, that is, methods like equals(...), hashCode( ), and toString().

Let's look at an error case. Intuitively, you can assume that anything of type Comparable is a valid argument type for max(...). But this assumption is not precise because we're writing <T extends Comparable<T>> T max(T m, T n), which means that the *common* type for m and n must be Comparable according to the type inference, instead of just *either one of them*. For instance, the compiler rejects the following statement with an error:

```
System.out.println( max( 12L, 100F ) );
// ☠ Compiler error "incompatible mismatch"
```

After boxing, the compiler derives the common type Number from Long 12 and Float 100. (Remember: The compiler goes up the type hierarchy until a common type is found that can be used for T, in this case, Number.) But Number isn't of type Comparable, and so the following error message appears:

```
error: method max in class … cannot be applied to given types;
    System.out.println( max( 12L, 100F ) );
                        ^
  required: V,V
  found: long,float
  reason: inference variable V has incompatible bounds
    equality constraints: Long,Float
    lower bounds: Float,Long
  where V is a type-variable:
    V extends Comparable<V> declared in method <V>max(V,V)
```

> **Note** [«]
>
> <T extends Comparable<T>> is a *recursive type bound*. This construction rarely occurs and won't be discussed further. If you're interested in this topic, *http://tutego.de/go/getthistrick* will provide further guidance. For example, the max(...) method can be mistakenly called via the following expression:
>
> ```
> static <T extends Comparable/*Missing*/> T max( T m, T n ) { … }
> ```
>
> The compiler will issue the warning "Comparable is a raw type. References to generic type Comparable<T> should be parameterized." If you ignore this warning, max(12L, 100F) can indeed be called, but also a ClassCastException will be thrown with the error message "java.lang. Float cannot be cast to java.lang.Long."

12.3.2   Other Supertypes with &

If the concrete type should fit several types, further supertypes can be added using an ampersand (&). However, note that only one class inheritance specification can take place. In other words, only one extends can be used since Java doesn't support multiple inheritance (see Chapter 7, Section 7.2.4) at the class level. The rest must be implemented through interfaces. For a class C and interfaces I1 to In, the general notation is T extends C & I1 & I2 & … & In.

Let's assume a fictitious superclass Endeavour and the interfaces Serializable and Comparable.[7] Then, the following declarations are basically permitted:

- <T extends Endeavour>
- <T extends Serializable & Comparable>

---

7 Comparable gets a type parameter itself, which the example omits for reasons of clarity.

- <T extends Endeavour & Serializable>
- <T extends Endeavour & Comparable & Serializable>

Syntactically wrong would be <T extends Endeavour & T extends Comparable> because the extends keyword may occur only once.

12.4   Type Parameters in the throws Clause*

In Section 12.2.3, you learned how type erasure makes a construction like class MyException<T> extends Exception impossible. However, a type parameter is permitted in the throws clause. This use opens up interesting options for classes that can throw checked or unchecked exceptions, depending on the use case.

12.4.1   Declaring a Class with Type Variable <E extends Exception>

For our next example, the CharIterable interface should be implemented by classes that provide a stream of characters. CharIterable is a generic interface type with a formal type parameter that must later be a subclass of Exception. Consider the following example:

```
public interface CharIterable<E extends Exception> {
  boolean hasNext() throws E;
  char    next()    throws E;
}
```

Listing 12.13 src/main/java/com/tutego/insel/generic/CharIterable.java, CharIterable

Characters can originate from a file, an internet resource, or a string, for example, but the usage always looks the same:

```
while ( iter.hasNext() )
  System.out.print( iter.next() );
```

12.4.2   Parameterized Type for Type Variable <E extends Exception>

Let's move on to the classes that implement CharIterable so that users can run off characters with the loop we just created. The declaration of the CharIterable<E extends Exception> interface contains a type variable restricted to Exception, which allows, for example, the following implementations:

- class StringIterable implements CharIterable<**RuntimeException**>
- class WebIterable implements CharIterable<**IOException**>

In the case of StringIterable, if the characters come from a string, no input/output exception is expected. For this reason, the actual type parameter is RuntimeException.

However, when reading from files or internet resources, IOExceptions may occur, so WebIterable chooses the actual type parameter (IOException).

Sample Implementations for the Parameterized Type

Let's implement the two classes StringIterable and WebIterable. Since StringIterable chooses the actual type parameter RuntimeException when implementing the interface, we'll write a throws RuntimeException, although the throws clause is again optional and can be omitted. Consider the following example:

```java
public class StringIterable implements CharIterable<RuntimeException> {

  private final String string;
  private int    pos;

  public StringIterable( String string ) {
    this.string = string;
  }

  @Override public boolean hasNext() {
    return pos < string.length();
  }

  @Override public char next() {
    return string.charAt( pos++ );
  }
}
```

Listing 12.14 src/main/java/com/tutego/insel/generic/StringIterable.java, StringIterable

With WebIterable, things look different. In this case, the actual type parameter is IOException, and thus a throws IOException is required at the method signature.

```java
public class WebIterable implements CharIterable<IOException> {

  private final Reader reader;

  public WebIterable( String url ) throws IOException {
    reader = new InputStreamReader( new URL( url ).openStream() ) ;
  }

  @Override public boolean hasNext() throws IOException {
    return reader.ready();
  }

  @Override public char next() throws IOException {
```

```
    return (char) reader.read();
  }
}
```

Listing 12.15 src/main/java/com/tutego/insel/generic/WebIterable.java, WebIterable

Using StringIterable and WebIterable

The following example shows that exception handling isn't necessary when running a string but is required when reading characters from the web:

```
StringIterable iter1 = new StringIterable( "Shasha" );   // try is unnecessary
while ( iter1.hasNext() )
  System.out.print( iter1.next() );


System.out.println();


try {
  WebIterable iter2 = new WebIterable( "http://tutego.de/javabuch/aufgaben/
bond.txt" );
  while ( iter2.hasNext() )
    System.out.print( iter2.next() );
}
catch ( IOException e ) {
  e.printStackTrace();
}
```

Listing 12.16 src/main/java/com/tutego/insel/generic/CharReadableExample.java, main()

Instead of `StringIterable iter1 = new StringIterable...` you could of course have written `CharIterable <RuntimeException> iter1...` and similarly `CharIterable<IOException> iter2` instead of `WebIterable iter2`.

Summary

These examples clearly show that the actual type parameter `RuntimeException` disables even such elementary things as checked exceptions. Some peculiarities of the compiler are that it permits things like `throws E` and that `E` can then be a checked or unchecked exception. With this peculiarity, however, we can declare `CharIterable` in the following way:

```
public interface CharIterable<E extends Exception> {
  boolean hasNext() throws E;
  char    next()    throws E;
}
```

This approach is particularly useful because our use case makes it clear that unchecked exceptions, as in the case of string traversal with StringIterable, are quite possible; checked exceptions, after all, always require a bit more effort.

Application Programming Interface Design of the Scanner Class

Scanner represents a class where the Java API designers didn't want checked exceptions on next() methods. The Scanner class can split normal strings where next() can't throw an IOException. But Scanner can also get an input stream, and then input/output exceptions are quite possible.

So, what should you do? Either always trigger an IOExeption for the next() methods or never? If the next() methods don't throw an exception (this is the design at the moment), the errors that can occur when reading from the data stream fall by the wayside. However, if the next() methods declared a throws IOException, this would be annoying when splitting pure strings—and the developers didn't want that. As a result, the IOException gets dropped in next() and must be explicitly requested via the ioException() method. This is contrary to the idea of always using checked exceptions for input/output errors. By the way, it's the same with PrintWriter: The write(...) and print*(...) methods don't throw an IOException, but developers ask later via check-Error() whether any problems arose. You may consider whether Scanner<E extends Exception> and methods like next() throws E would solve the problem.

12.5   Inheritance and Invariance with Generics

Inheritance and substitution are commonplace concepts for Java developers, so their extension to generics isn't surprising. The toString() method, for example, is called naturally on all objects, and the call is dynamically bound. Similarly, String.toString(Object o) lets you pass any object, and the static method calls the object method toString().

12.5.1   Arrays Are Covariant

Let's take the hierarchy of the wrapper classes as an example. Of course, Object is at the top. The numeric wrapper classes all extend the abstract Number class. Under these wrapper classes are, for example, Integer, Double, and the other numeric wrappers. No headaches should arise in the following example code:

```
Number number = Integer.valueOf( 10 );
number = Double.valueOf( 1.1 );
```

First, number points to an Integer, then to a Double object.

But what's the situation with arrays? Since a Number array is the base type of a Double array, we could have the following statements:

```
Number[] numbers = new Double[ 100 ];
numbers[ 0 ] = 1.1;
```

The fact that an array of type Double[] is a subtype of Number[] and that Object[] is above all non-primitive fields is referred to as *covariance*. But how can this concept be applied to generics?

12.5.2 Generics Aren't Covariant, but Invariant

You can write the following code:

```
Set<String> set = new HashSet<String>();
```

A HashSet with Strings is a type of Set with Strings. However, a HashSet with Strings isn't a HashSet with Objects. Thus, the following statement would be wrong:

```
HashSet<Object> set = new HashSet<String>();          // 💀 Compiler error!
```

Generics aren't covariant; they're *invariant*. This feature isn't intuitive at first glance, but an example can quickly set us straight. Let's stay with our Rocket example and with wrapper classes. Even though Number is the superclass of Integer, Rocket<Number> is not a supertype of Rocket<Integer>. If it were, the following code would be possible and cause a problem at runtime:

```
Rocket<Number> r;
r = new Rocket<Integer>();          // Is this OK?
r.set( 2.2 );
```

The argument 2.2 is about autoboxing a Double and thus seems to fit Number. However, Double shouldn't be permitted at all since we created a rocket for Integer with Rocket<Integer>, and a Double isn't permitted in the Integer rocket. From this example, it follows that the derivation relationship between types isn't transmitted to generic classes. So, a Rocket<Number> isn't a superclass that permits all conceivable numeric types in the rocket. The compiler immediately grumbles at the following attempt:

```
Rocket<Number> r;
r = new Rocket<Integer>();
// 💀 Type mismatch: cannot convert from Rocket<Integer>  // to Rocket<Number>
```

The compiler can't be misled even by the following alternative notation:

```
Rocket<Integer> r1 = new Rocket<>();
Rocket<Number> r2 = r1; // 💀 Type mismatch: cannot convert
                        // from Rocket<Integer> to Rocket<Number>
```

> **Note**
>
> In the case of read-only immutable objects, no reason exists for covariance. Let's assume that the following declaration is correct:
>
> ```
> Rocket<Number> r = new Rocket<Integer>( 1 );
> Number n = r.get();
> ```
>
> Then, `p.set(2.2)` isn't OK, for example, because `Double` isn't compatible with `Integer`. However, if the object was initialized via a constructor, for example, no objection arises to reading from it with a base type, (i.e., `Number` in this case). However, Java can't tell if a type is immutable and therefore can't make such exceptions for generics. The compiler always assumes both read and write access.

12.5.3   Wildcards with ?

Let's write a method named `isOneRocketEmpty(...)` that gets a variable number of rockets; what the rockets are carrying shouldn't matter. The method should also test if a rocket is empty. For this example, you might write the following method call:

```
Rocket<String>  r1 = new Rocket<>( "Bad-Bank" );
Rocket<Integer> r2 = new Rocket<>( 1500000 );
System.out.println( isOneRocketEmpty( r1, r2 ) );                    // false
```

For the method head, we might try to write the following code:

```
public static boolean isOneRocketEmpty( Rocket<Object>... rockets )
```

But stop! Since `Rocket<Object>` doesn't include rockets with all types, but only hits exactly one rocket containing an `Object` object, this parameterization isn't useful for `isOneRocketEmpty(...)`, as mentioned earlier. If that parameterization were possible, type safety would be jeopardized. If this method really accepted all contents for rockets, a value with the wrong type could easily be foisted onto a rocket. When `isOneRocketEmpty(...)` is called with a `Rocket<String>` then, because of `isOneRocketEmpty(Rocket<Object>… rockets)`, the call of `set(12)` on the `Rocket` would also be valid. Now, suddenly instead of the desired contents of the rocket (`String`), an `Integer` would be placed in the rocket, which should not be valid!

If the type doesn't matter, think of the original type (raw type). One the drawback with raw types is that the compiler doesn't check anything at all, but we want some kind of checking. So, the `isOneRocketEmpty(...)` method should accept arbitrary rocket contents, but at the same time, we should forbid the method from putting the wrong things into the rocket. So, an `isOneRocketEmpty(Rocket... rockets)` isn't a good idea and also causes various warnings.

The solution is to use the *wildcard type (?)*, which then represents a family of types. If Rocket<Object> isn't the base type of all rocket contents, then the base type is Rocket<? >. Note that ? doesn't stand for Object but for an unknown type! This wildcard can now be used to implement isOneRocketEmpty(...).

```java
public static boolean isOneRocketEmpty( Rocket<?>... rockets ) {
  for ( Rocket<?> rocket : rockets )
    if ( rocket.isEmpty() )
      return true;

  return false;
}

public static void main( String[] args ) {
  Rocket<String>  r1 = new Rocket<>( "Bad-Bank" );
  Rocket<Integer> r2 = new Rocket<>( 1500000 );
  System.out.println( isOneRocketEmpty( r1, r2 ) );                      // false
  System.out.println( isOneRocketEmpty( r1, r2, new Rocket<Byte>() ) ); // true
}
```

Listing 12.17 src/main/java/com/tutego/insel/generic/RocketsEmpty.java

Calling isOneRocketEmpty() doesn't result in false if no rocket is passed, which you can assume at this point.

Mentally, you must strictly separate wildcards from type variables. Instantiations with wildcards aren't permitted since a wildcard doesn't stand for a concrete type but instead for a whole series of possible types. In addition, wildcards can't be used in methods like type variables, even if the type is arbitrary.

Correct Use with Type Variables	Incorrect Use with Wildcards (Compiler Error!)
Rocket<?> r = new Rocket<**Byte**>();	Rocket<?> r = new Rocket<**?**>();
static <T> T random(T m, T n) { ... }	static <?> ? random(? m, ? n) { ... }

Table 12.8 Using Wildcards Correctly

[+]   **Application Programming Interface Design**

In many places, a type variable could be used instead of ?, but if the type doesn't need to be caught, then no reason exists for using a type variable. Let's consider an example from the java.util.Collections class: The static method int frequency(Collection<?> c, Object o); determines how often an equivalent object o occurs in the collection c. The collection type isn't relevant and isn't used for the second parameter or for the return type.

Effects on Read/Write Operations

If we use a wildcard type, as in Rocket<?>, we don't know anything about the type, and the compiler will lose all information. For example, consider the following declarations:

```
Rocket<?>        r1 = new Rocket<Integer>();
```

or

```
Rocket<Integer>  r2 = new Rocket<Integer>();
Rocket<?>        r3 = r2;
```

Nothing is known about the real actual type parameters with r1 and r3. This lack of information has important implications for the methods you can call on Rocket, such as the following:

- Calling r1.get() is legal because everything the method will return is always an Object, even if it's null. Accordingly, the statement Object v = r1.get(); is correct.
- r1.set(value) isn't permitted because the compiler lacks the actual type parameters of r1 and can't check types. In r1, you cannot use a Double because Rocket should only store Integers. The only exception is null since null has any type. r1.set(null) is therefore a valid statement, which also means that objects created with <?> are not automatically immutable.

12.5.4 Bounded Wildcards

Specifying the actual type parameter as in Rocket<Integer> and the wildcard variant Rocket<?> represent two extremes. Rocket<Integer> rocket takes only integers; Rocket <?>, on the other hand, takes everything. But something must also exist in between, for example, to express that the rocket should only contain a number or a string.

For this reason, type restrictions with extends and super are possible. This results in three types of wildcards.

Wildcard	Name	Actual Type Parameter
?	Wildcard type	Is arbitrary
? extends *Type*	Upper-bounded wildcard type	Everything that extends Type (i.e., subtypes) and Type itself
? super *Type*	Lower-bounded wildcard type	All supertypes of Type and Type itself

Table 12.9 The Three Wildcard Types

A wildcard thus describes the feature of an actual type parameter. Consider the following notation:

`Rocket<? extends Number> r;`

All possible `Number` objects can be in the rocket p. Let's clarify `extends` and `super` with another example that shows what family of types is described by the syntax.

? Extends CharSequence	? super String
CharSequence	String
String	CharSequence
StringBuffer	Object
StringBuilder	
...	

Table 12.10 Some Included Types with extends and super

The first table row provides clear examples of `extends` and `super` including the specified type itself. In `<? extends CharSequence>`, `CharSequence` is exactly the upper bound of the wildcard, and in `<? super String>`, `String` is the lower bound of the wildcard. While the number of types with the lower bound is limited (the number of superclasses can't expand), the number of types with the upper bound is basically unknown since new subclasses can always be created.

Areas of Use

Each of these wildcard types has an area of use. The upper-bounded wildcard and the lower-bounded wildcard can be found in the sorting methods of data structures and algorithms, for instance.

Example	Meaning
`Rocket<?> p;`	Rockets with any content.
`Rocket<? extends Number> p;`	Rockets only with numbers, that is, subclasses of `Number`, like `Integer`, `Double`, `BigDecimal`, etc.
`Comparator<? super String> comp;`	`Comparator` that compares objects of type `String`, `Object`, or `CharSequence`, that is, supertypes of `String`. : For example, a `Comparator` that can compare `CharSequence` objects can also compare `String`s because inheritance makes a `String` a kind of `CharSequence`. All `<? super String>` comparator types can (somehow) compare strings.

Table 12.11 Examples of All Three Wildcard Types

Example with Upper-Bounded Wildcard Type

The upper-bounded wildcard is more common than the lower-bounded variant. For this reason, let's look at an example that clarifies the common use of the upper-bounded wildcard. Our Player had a right rocket and a left rocket. However, now the rockets shouldn't store any sort of things, only special game objects of the *Portable* type. Portable is an interface that prescribes a weight for the objects that are portable. Two types should be portable: Pen and Cup. You could implement the Portable interface in the following way:

```java
interface Portable {
  double getWeight();
  void    setWeight( double weight );
}

abstract class AbstractPortable implements Portable {

  private double weight;

  @Override public double getWeight() { return weight; }

  @Override public void setWeight( double weight ) { this.weight = weight; }

  @Override public String toString() { return getClass().getName() +
                                "[weight=" + weight + "]"; }
}
class Pen extends AbstractPortable { }

class Cup extends AbstractPortable { }
```

Listing 12.18 src/main/java/com/tutego/insel/generic/PortableDemo.java (Snippet)

To test whether the player is carrying too many things, an areLighterThan(...) method will check if the weight of a list of portable things stays below a given limit. Our first attempt at this method could look like the following statement:

```java
boolean areLighterThan( List<Portable> collection, double maxWeight )
```

Hang on! This method would again only accept Portable objects because covariance doesn't apply. If this method did work, then maybe a Pen can be added via collection.add(...), even if the passed list was declared with Cup. Then, the list would suddenly contain something wrong. Also, Portable is an interface, so the areLighterThan(...) method with a List<Portable> parameter type makes no sense at all. A reasonable notation is only possible with an upper-bounded wildcard type as in the following example:

```java
boolean areLighterThan( List<? extends Portable> list, double maxWeight )
```

In this way, the method accepts only lists of Portable objects. This limitation is necessary because Portable objects have a weight, and the weight property is required.

```java
class PortableUtils {

  public static boolean areLighterThan( List<? extends Portable> list,
                                        double maxWeight ) {
    double accumulatedWeight = 0.0;

    for ( Portable portable : list )
      accumulatedWeight += portable.getWeight();

    return accumulatedWeight < maxWeight;
  }
}

public class PortableDemo {

  public static void main( String[] args ) {
    Pen pen = new Pen();
    pen.setWeight( 10 );
    Cup cup = new Cup();
    cup.setWeight( 100 );
    System.out.println( PortableUtils.areLighterThan( Arrays.asList( pen, cup ),
                                                      10 ) ); //false
    System.out.println( PortableUtils.areLighterThan( Arrays.asList( pen, cup ),
                                                      120 ) );  //true

  }
}
```

Listing 12.19 src/main/java/com/tutego/insel/generic/PortableDemo.java (Snippet)

As described earlier, the List<? extends Portable> data structure declared with upper-bounded wildcards can only be read. This data structure cannot be changed.

12.5.5   Bounded Wildcard Types and Bounded Type Variables

Of course, a connection exists between bounded wildcard types and bounded type variables, and two variants are selectable in the declaration. Let's demonstrate these options with our areLighterThan(...) method. Originally, we declared our method in the following way:

```java
boolean areLighterThan( List<? extends Portable> list, double maxWeight )
```

You could also have declared a type parameter locally for the method in the following way:

```
<T extends Portable> boolean areLighterThan( List<T> list, double maxWeight )
```

Both variants serve the same purpose. However, the first option is preferable to the second.

> **Best Practice**
>
> Whenever the type parameter (such as T) appears only in the signature (the signature consists of the method name, the parameter list, and the exceptions) and no recourse for the T type exists in the method itself, you should choose the first variant, with the wildcard. This variant is shorter and also makes it more clear that this type won't appear again, for example, in a second parameter or the return.

Type parameters are a good way to create dependencies between the individual arguments including the return type. The next example includes some new methods to return the lightest object in a collection of rockets.

```java
public static <T extends Portable> T lightest( Collection<T> collection ) {
  Iterator<T> iterator = collection.iterator();
  T lightest = iterator.next();

  while ( iterator.hasNext() ) {
    T next = iterator.next();

    if ( next.getWeight() < lightest.getWeight() )
      lightest = next;
  }

  return lightest;
}
```

Listing 12.20 src/main/java/com/tutego/insel/generic/PortableDemo.java, PortableUtils

The compiler makes sure that the type of the return matches the type of the collection.

Waiving Bounded Wildcard Types in Returns

If you can use either bounded wildcard types or bounded type variables, bounded type variables are always preferable, unless the best practice in the box earlier applies. Wildcard types don't provide type information, and thus, letting the compiler give you a more precise type via type inference is generally preferable.

Let's assume we have a static method leftSublist(...) that returns a sublist from a list. The sublist starts at the first position and goes halfway down.

Our first attempt at this method is shown in the following example:

```java
public static List<?> leftSublist( List<? extends Portable> list ) {
  return list.subList( 0, list.size() / 2 );
}
```

The return type List<?> is the worst option we can choose because the caller of the method can do nothing at all with the return. The caller knows nothing about the contents of the list.

Let's try again with the following example:

```java
public static List<? extends Portable> leftSublist( List<?
 extends Portable> list )
```

This version is already slightly better because, in this variant, the recipient at least gets back the information that the list contains any portable things.

Even better, of course, is to rely on the compiler's type inference and return to the caller exactly the type with which it provided the parameter type. For this purpose, however, you must insert a type variable because, f a method declares parameters or a return with multiple wildcard types, the real type arguments are completely arbitrary and unrelated.

```java
public static <T extends Portable> List<T> leftSublist( List<T> list ) {
  return list.subList( 0, list.size() / 2 );
}
```

Listing 12.21 src/main/java/com/tutego/insel/generic/PortableDemo.java, PortableUtils

Now, the type of the list coming in is the same as the type of the list going out. With extends, the list can only be read-only.

> **Note**
>
> Especially in the Collections class from the Java standard API, many methods could also be written differently. For example, instead of <T extends E> boolean addAll(Collection<T> c), the authors chose boolean addAll(Collection<? extends E> c).

12.5.6   The PECS Principle

While types restricted with extends allow read operations, the opposite is true for super. In this case, reading isn't permitted, but writing is. A good mnemonic for this concept is the PECS principle, defined in the following way:

Producer = Extends, Consumer = Super (PECS)

Let's look at an example: A static method named `copyLighterThan(...)` should copy only those elements from one list to another that are lighter than a given upper limit.

Our first attempt at this method is shown in the following example:

```
public static void copyLighterThan( List<? extends Portable> src,
                                     List<?
 extends Portable> dest, double maxWeight ) {
  for ( Portable portable : src )
    if ( portable.getWeight() < maxWeight )
      dest.add( portable );            // ☠ Compiler error !!
}
```

At first glance, our code looks sound, but the program can't translate it. The problem is the `dest.add(portable)` statement. Recall that write operations cannot occur with an upper-bounded wildcard. This limitation makes sense because the `src` list can be a list of `Cup` objects, for example, and `dest` can be a list of `Pen` objects. Both are `Portable` but still incompatible since `Cups` can't be copied to `Pens`. So, what should be the type of the result list? Let's start with the source list. In this context, `List <? extends Portable>` is correct because the list can contain everything that's portable. But what are the requirements for the target list? What must the type look like so that everything of the `Portable` type, like `Cup` or `Pen` (or even still subclasses of `Cups` and `Pens`) can be stored? The answer is simple: any type above `Portable`! These types would include `Portable` itself and `Object`, that is, all supertypes. However, `Portable` is the lower-bounded wildcard type, which we write as `super`. The result is:

```
public static void copyLighterThan( List<? extends Portable> src,
                                     List<?
 super Portable> dest, double maxWeight ) {
  for ( Portable portable : src )
    if ( portable.getWeight() < maxWeight )
      dest.add( portable );
}
```

Listing 12.22 src/main/java/com/tutego/insel/generic/PortableDemo.java, PortableUtils

The following example calls our method:

```
List<? extends Portable> src = Arrays.asList( pen, cup );
List<? super Portable>   dest = new ArrayList<>();
PortableUtils.copyLighterThan( src, dest, 20 );
System.out.println( dest.size() ); // 1
Object result = dest.get( 0 );
System.out.println( result );      // com.tutego.insel.generic.Pen[weight=10.0]
```

Listing 12.23 src/main/java/com/tutego/insel/generic/PortableDemo.java, main() (Snippet)

The dest list is writable, but the readable type is only Object—the compiler doesn't know what is actually in the list. The compiler only knows that any supertypes of Portable might be included, and the most general type available is Object.

Wildcard Capture

The PECS principle has an important consequence that's particularly noticeable in list operations: A list parameterized with a wildcard can't be modified. But how can you write a method that reverses a list, for example? From the API design point of view, a reverse(...) method could be written in the following way:

```
public static void reverse( List<?> list );
```

Or the same method could be written in the following way:

```
public static <T> void reverse( List<T> list );
```

As mentioned earlier, we should opt for the wildcard notation for completely free types, but now, we're facing a dilemma.

```
public static <T> void reverse( List<?> list ) {
  for ( int i = 0; i < list.size() / 2; i++ ) {
    int j = list.size() - i - 1;
    ? tmp = list.get( i );                 // ☠ Compiler error
    list.set( i, list.get( j ) );
    list.set( j, tmp );
  }
}
```

We have no choice but to choose the variant with the type variable after all, so that we have access to the type T.

Since reverse(List<?> list) is now preferred by the API design, but reverse(List<T> list) is necessary in the implementation, the question arises how to combine both. reverse(List<?> list) can redirect to an internal reverse method, reverse_(List<T>). Although the methods have to be named differently, the mapping from a wildcard to a type variable works because of the so-called *wildcard capture*.

```
public class WildcardCapture {

  private static <T> void reverse_( List<T> list ) {
    for ( int i = 0; i < list.size() / 2; i++ ) {
      int j = list.size() - i - 1;
      T tmp = list.get( i );
      list.set( i, list.get( j ) );
      list.set( j, tmp );
```

```
    }
  }

  public static void reverse( List<?> list ) {
    reverse_( list );
  }
}
```

Listing 12.24 src/main/java/com/tutego/insel/generic/WildcardCapture, WildcardCapture

The compiler "catches" the unknown type of the list at reverse(list) and "fills" the type variable at reverse_(list).

12.6   Consequences of Type Erasure: Type Tokens, Arrays*

Type erasure is generally not such a big deal, but in special situations, that the type isn't present at runtime can be annoying.

12.6.1   Type Tokens

As you've seen, when a rocket has been declared with the type variable T, this T isn't really replaced by the actual type parameter like a search and replace in an office document. Instead, usually only Object is used. Consider the following example:

```
class Rocket<T> {
  T newRocketContent() { return new T(); } // 💀 Compiler error
}
```

So, the type erasure turns new T() into new Object(), which isn't worth anything. But how can a type still be created and type T be present at runtime?

The trick is to use a Class object for the type.

Actual Type Parameter	Class Object Represents Type Argument
String	String.class
Integer	Integer.class

Table 12.12 Transfer of Actual Type Parameters via Class objects

This Class object, which now represents the type, is referred to as the *type token*. Of course, that Class itself is declared as a generic type suits the situation, and two interesting methods have been "made generic" as well.

Example

The following example queries Class objects:

```
Class<String> clazz1 = String.class;
String newInstance = clazz1.getConstructor().newInstance();
Class<? extends String> clazz2 = newInstance.getClass();
System.out.println( clazz1.equals( clazz2 ) );  // true
```

First, the getConstructor() method uses the Class object to pick out the parameter-less constructor. Using the Constructor object, newInstance() then creates a new instance with the type represented by the Class object.

With a given object, getClass() can be used to query the associated Class object for the class:

```
class java.lang.Object
```

▶ final native Class<?> getClass()
  Returns Class object.

Note

The Class<?> return on getClass() isn't the best code, especially the general wildcard. Furthermore, this expression prevents the following statement from being written:

```
Class<String> clazz = "Simulatte.getClass();  //
```
☠ "Type mismatch" compiler error

Instead, the query should read:

```
Class<? extends String> clazz = "Simulatte".getClass();
```

Since Object isn't declared generically, getClass() can't provide more precise information.

Solutions with Type Tokens

To use type tokens, the Class object must be passed as an argument in a constructor or method. For example, you can create a newInstance() method that catches checked exceptions and reports them as RuntimeException in case errors arise.

The type of the Class object can be easily transferred to the return in the following way:

```
public static <T> T newInstance( Class<T> type ) {
  try {
    return type.getConstructor().newInstance();
  }
```

```
catch ( ReflectiveOperationException e ) {
  throw new RuntimeException( e );
}
}
```

ReflectiveOperationException is the superclass of ClassNotFoundException, IllegalAccessException, InstantiationException, InvocationTargetException, NoSuchFieldException, and NoSuchMethodException. Specifying this base type is useful because it saves typing—a lot that can go wrong with reflection, and countless checked exceptions exist.

12.6.2   Supertype Tokens

A Class object is a good way to represent a type, but one problem exists. The Class object itself can't represent generic types.

Actual Type Parameter	Class Object Represents Type Argument
String	String.class
Integer	Integer.class
Rocket<String>	Rocket<String>.class Does not work! ☠

Table 12.13 A Class Object Can't Describe a Generic Type

The real type can only be determined and captured with a lot of trickery. The Reflection API is used in this context, so we'll only briefly explore the class through an example.

```
public abstract class TypeRef<T> {

  public final Type type;

  protected TypeRef() {
    ParameterizedType superclass =
 (ParameterizedType) getClass().getGenericSuperclass();
    type = superclass.getActualTypeArguments()[0];
  }
}
```

Listing 12.25 src/main/java/com/tutego/insel/generic/TypeRef, TypeRef

The following example creates an anonymous subclass, thus making the type accessible:

```
TypeRef<Rocket<String>> ref1 = new TypeRef<>(){};
System.out.println( ref1.type ); //
 com.tutego.insel.generic.Rocket<java.lang.String>
```

```
TypeRef<Rocket<Byte>> ref2 = new TypeRef<>(){};
System.out.println( ref2.type ); //
 com.tutego.insel.generic.Rocket<java.lang.Byte>
```

Listing 12.26 src/main/java/com/tutego/insel/generic/TypeRefDemo, main()

In this way, you're allowed to capture the type argument via java.lang.reflect.Type, and ref1 is clearly different from ref2.

However, the type doesn't exist as a Class object, and operations like getConstructor(). newInstance() aren't possible on Type because the interface doesn't declare any methods at all and can only represent types.

12.6.3   Generics and Arrays

Type erasure is the reason why arrays can't be implemented in a way a developer might like to.[8] The following code, for instance, results in a compiler error:

```
class TwoBox<T> {
  T[] array = new T[ 2 ];    // ☠ Cannot create a generic array of T
  T[] getArray() { return array; }
}
```

The reason for this error can be easily seen if you consider code would be required for type erasure:

```
class TwoBox {
  Object[] array = new Object[ 2 ];            // (1)
  Object[] getArray() { return array; }
}
```

The caller would now want to use TwoBox parameterized, as in the following example:

```
TwoBox<String> twoStrings = new TwoBox<String>();
String[] stringArray = twoStrings.getArray();
```

At this point, let's think again about type erasure and what the compiler generates:

```
TwoBox twoStrings = new TwoBox();
String[] stringArray = (String[]) twoStrings.getArray(); // (2)
```

Now, while line (1) builds an Object array of length 2 and also getArray() passes this array out as an Object array, line (2) casts this Object array to a string array. But this step isn't possible because these two types aren't type compatible. Of course, an Object

---

8 A related bug is described by Oracle at *http://bugs.java.com/bugdatabase/view_bug.do?bug_id= 4888066*. Sun's response to a request to fix this issue was terse: "Someday, perhaps, but not now."

array can reference strings, but the array itself as an object is an `Object[]` and not a `String[]`.

Reflection Helps

The Java API provides a way to create arrays of a type via reflection:

```
T[] array = (T[]) Array.newInstance( clazz, 2 );
```

However, the `Class` type `clazz` must be known and passed as an additional parameter. The syntax `T.class` causes a compiler error because, via type erasure, it would always be `Object.class` anyway.

12.7   Further Reading

Generics are fortunately relatively easy for users to understand because all users must do is put a type in the angle brackets and they're done. Designers of Java libraries have a much harder time with generics because they must consider which types are actually needed for an operation and provide wildcards accordingly. For training purposes, we recommend reviewing the application of the generics for all methods in `java.util.Collections`.

The websites *http://gafter.blogspot.com/2006/12/super-type-tokens.html* and *https://www.artima.com/weblogs/viewpost.jsp?thread=206350* provide further information and use cases, but note that super type tokens are quite rare in the Java world.

Chapter 13

Lambda Expressions and Functional Programming

"Computer systems process what they are fed.
If crap comes in, crap comes out."
—André Kostolany (1906–1999)

The development from machine language (or Assembler) to high-level language illustrates the interesting history of parameterization. Even the first high-level languages allowed the parameterization of functions with different arguments. "Born" in 1996, several decades after the first high-level languages, Java provided parameterized subroutines from the start. Later, generics were added for the parameterization of a type. Functional programming made it possible to parameterize a behavior—a sorting method always works the same, but its behavior during comparisons is adjusted. This parameterization can be of a completely different quality than passing different values. With lambda expressions, parameterizing a behavior is quite simple.

13.1   Functional Interfaces and Lambda Expressions

Interfaces play an important role in Java because they prescribe an application programming interface (API) and represent a link between the implementation and the caller. To implement interfaces in general, you can use classes and records, and for certain interfaces, you can also use compact lambda expressions—the focus of this chapter.

13.1.1   Classes Implement Interfaces

Class declarations can exist in different places in your code—let's look at two ways.

Nested Classes as Code Transporters

Suppose we need to sort strings so that any whitespace at the beginning and the end is ignored in the comparison. For instance, " Newton " should equal "Newton". For specifications of this type, a `Comparator` must be passed to a sorting algorithm as a piece of code so that the algorithm can establish the correct order. In practice, you would write the following code:

```
public static void main( String[] args ) {
  class TrimComparator implements Comparator<String> {
    @Override public int compare( String s1, String s2 ) {
      return s1.trim().compareTo( s2.trim() );
    }
  }
  String[] words = { "M", "\nSkyfall", " Q", "\t\tAdele\t" };
  Arrays.sort( words, new TrimComparator() );
  System.out.println( Arrays.toString( words ) );
}
```

Listing 13.1 src/main/java/com/tutego/insel/lambda/TrimCompare.java, main()

The result is the following output:

```
[        Adele    , M,  Q,
Skyfall]
```

The `TrimComparator` contains the program code for the comparison logic in the `compare(...)` method. An object from `TrimComparator` is created and passed to `Arrays.sort(...)`. In the next sections we will see how we can make this code more compact.

Anonymous Inner Classes as Code Transporters

Classes contain program code, and objects of classes are passed to methods like `sort(...)` to get the program code where it needs to go. But this approach is rather inelegant. For the description of the program code, you'll need an extra class, which is a lot of typing. By using an anonymous inner class, the program code can be shortened a bit, however, as in the following example:

```
String[] words = { "M", "\nSkyfall", " Q", "\t\tAdele\t" };
Arrays.sort( words, new Comparator<String>() {
  @Override public int compare( String s1, String s2 ) {
    return s1.trim().compareTo( s2.trim() );
  } } );
System.out.println( Arrays.toString( words ) );
```

However, a lot of work is still required: We need to override a method and then create an object. For program authors, this task is annoying, and the JVM must deal with many superfluous class metadata. If the compiler knows that a `Comparator` is needed for `sort(...)`, and if a `Comparator` has only one method, why can't the compiler figure it out by itself and we can just write the core of the method, the statement `s1.trim().compareTo(s2.trim())`?

13.1.2 Lambda Expressions Implement Interfaces

Lambda expressions make passing program code to a method easier because this compact syntax can implement interfaces with an operation. Thus, our example can be rewritten in the following way:

```
String[] words = { "M", "\nSkyfall", " Q", "\t\tAdele\t" };
Comparator<String> c = (String s1, String s2) ->
                          { return s1.trim().compareTo( s2.trim() ); }
Arrays.sort( words, c );
System.out.println( Arrays.toString( words ) );
```

The expression in bold is a *lambda expression,* which is a compact way to implement interfaces with exactly one method: The Comparator interface has exactly one operation, compare(...).

A lambda expression and a method declaration look similar, but modifiers, the return type, the method name, and (potential) throws clauses are omitted from lambda expressions.

Method Declaration	Lambda Expression
public int compare (String s1, String s2)	(String s1, String s2) ->
{ return s1.trim().compareTo(s2.trim( )); }	{ return s1.trim().compareTo(s2.trim( )); }

Table 13.1 Comparison of the Method Declaration of an Interface with Its Lambda Expression

If you consider a lambda expression as an implementation of the interface, nothing about Comparator or compare(...) specifically requires mention—a lambda expression more or less just represents the Java code and leaves out information that that the compiler can infer from the context.

You can explicitly store the lambda expression in a variable, but even better, you can use it directly as an argument of Arrays.sort(...), as in the following example:

```
Arrays.sort( words,
         (String s1, String s2) -
> { return s1.trim().compareTo(s2.trim()); } );
```

Of course, this approach is nice and compact, much shorter than using anonymous classes. We can even get more concise with lambda expressions, as we'll see later in Section 13.1.4.

General Syntax for Lambda Expressions

All lambda expressions can be formulated in a syntax with the following general form:

```
( LambdaParameter ) -> { Statements }
```

Lambda parameters are, so to speak, the input values for the instructions. The parameter list is declared as known from methods or constructors, but no varargs are allowed in the "lambda parameter list". Further syntactic shortcuts are available, as we'll see later in Section 13.1.6, but for now, let's stick with this basic notation.

History

The Java term *lambda expression* goes back to the 1930s with lambda calculus (also written as *?-calculus*), which is a formal language for examining functions.

13.1.3   Functional Interfaces

Not every interface has a shortcut via a lambda expression, and a central condition governs when a lambda expression can be used.

Definition

Interfaces that have only one abstract method are called *functional interfaces*. A *function descriptor* describes this method. An abstract class with exactly one abstract method does *not* count as a functional interface.

Lambda expressions and functional interfaces have a special relationship because a lambda expression is an instance of the functional interface. Of course, types and exceptions must fit. One obvious limitation is that functional interfaces prescribe exactly one abstract method because, if more than one existed, a lambda expression would have to provide multiple implementations or somehow favor one method over the others.

Consequently, to create an object of a functional interface type, you have two options: You can choose the traditional way via creating classes that implement functional interfaces and then use new to create an object.

Alternatively, you can use compact lambda expressions. Modern integrated development environments (IDEs) can show you when compact lambda expressions can be used instead of anonymous inner classes, for example, and provide possible refactoring suggestions. Lambda expressions make you code more compact and, after a short learning curve, more readable.

Note

Functional interfaces must boil down to exactly one method to be implemented, even if several operations are prescribed from upper-level interfaces but condensed to one operation through the use of generics. Consider the following example:

```
interface I<S, T extends CharSequence> {
  void len( S text );
  void len( T text );
}
interface FI extends I<String, String> { }
```

`FI` is our functional interface with a unique `len(String)` operation. Static and default methods don't interfere in functional interfaces.

Multiple Functional Interfaces in the Java Standard Library

Java comes with a large number of interfaces that are characterized as functional interfaces. A small selection of interfaces includes the following:

- `interface Runnable { void run(); }`
- `interface Supplier<T> { T get(); }`
- `interface Consumer<T> { void accept(T t); }`
- `interface Comparator<T> { int compare(T o1, T o2); }`
- `interface ActionListener { void actionPerformed(ActionEvent e); }`

Many of these interfaces are located in the `java.util.function` package introduced in Java 8. Whether an interface has other static methods or default methods (i.e., interface methods with a given implementation) doesn't matter—all that matters is that the interface declares exactly one operation to be implemented.

Example

The parameter list can be empty, and the return can be `void`, as in the example of the `Runnable` interface, which has a `void run()` method, and thus, the following statement is the `Runnable` interface's corresponding lambda expression:

```
Runnable run = () -> {};
```

13.1.4   The Type of a Lambda Expression Depends on the Target Type

In Java, every expression has a type. The expressions 1 and 1*2 have types (namely int), just like "A" + "B" (type `String`) or `String.CASE_INSENSITIVE_ORDER` (type `Comparator<String>`). Lambda expressions also always have a type because a lambda expression is like an instance of a functional interface. However, compared to expressions such as 1*2, lambda expressions behave somewhat differently because the type of a lambda expression is determined exclusively from its context. Let's recall our earlier sort(...) method:

```
Arrays.sort( words, (String s1, String s2) -> { return … } );
```

No mention of the type Comparator can be found in the expression, but the compiler recognizes from the type of the second parameter of sort(...), which is from Comparator, whether or not the lambda expression matches the method of the Comparator.

Consequently, the type of a lambda expression depends on which functional interface it currently implements in the respective context. The compiler can't construct a lambda expression without knowledge of the *target type*, as shown in Figure 13.1.

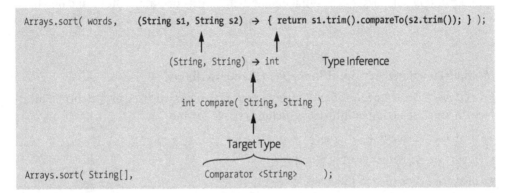

Figure 13.1 Type Inference of the Compiler

[Ex]   Example

Callable and Supplier are functional interfaces with methods that declare no parameter lists and return a reference; the code for the lambda expression looks the same, as shown in the following examples:

```
java.util.concurrent.Callable<String> c = () -> { return ""; };
java.util.function.Supplier<String>   s = () -> { return ""; };
```

Who Determines the Target Type?

Precisely because the type can't be read from the lambda expression, you can only use lambda expressions where sufficient type information is available, which includes, but isn't limited to, the following positions:

Context	Example
Variable declarations	Runnable run = () -> { };

Table 13.2 Positions Providing Context for Lambda Expressions

Context	Example
Assignments to declared variables	Runnable run; run = () -> { };
Arguments to methods or constructors	Arrays.sort(list, (s, t) -> { return 0; });

Method returns	Runnable boring() {
	  return () -> { };
	}

Array initializations	Runnable[] runnables = {
	  () -> { }, () -> { }
	};

Typecasting	Object o = (Runnable) () -> { };

Table 13.2 Positions Providing Context for Lambda Expressions (Cont.)

Thus, the use of a lambda expression is always possible if enough context information is available. This rule also applies to the condition operator—it can return a different lambda expression depending on the condition. Consider the following example:

```
Supplier<Double> randomNegOrPos = Math.random() > 0.5
                        ? () -> { return Math.random(); }
                        : () -> { return -Math.random(); };
```

> **Note** [«]
>
> A local variable declaration with var doesn't work with lambda expressions. A lambda expression requires placement on the left and var the type on the right.
>
> ```
> var o = () -> {};        // ☠ Lambda expression needs an explicit target-type
> ```

Parameter Types

In practice, the most common case is that the parameter types of methods specify the target type. The use of lambda expressions slightly changes the view on overloaded methods. Our example with () -> { return ""; } illustrates this change because it "fits" the target type Callable<String> as well as Supplier<String>. Let's assume we have the following two overloaded run(...) methods:

```
class OverloadedFuntionalInterfaceMethods {
  static <V> void run( Callable<V> callable ) { }
  static <V> void run( Supplier<V> callable ) { }
}
```

Let's go through calling the methods next:

```
Callable<String> c = () -> { return "Don't tell me how to eat donuts!"; };
Supplier<String> s = () -> { return "Don't tell me how to eat donuts!"; };
run( c );
run( s );
// run( () -> { return "Don't tell me how to eat donuts!"; } ); //
☠ Compiler error
run( (Callable<String>) () -> { return "Don't tell me how to eat donuts!"; } );
```

If you call run(c) or run(s), no problem arises because c and s are clearly typed. However, calling run(...) with the lambda expression doesn't work because the target type (either Callable or Supplier) is ambiguous. In this case, explicit typecasting can help.

[+]   **Application Programming Interface Design Tip**

From an API designer's point of view, overloaded methods are nice, of course, but from a user's point of view, type conversions are not nice. To avoid explicit typecasting, overloaded methods should be avoided if they have the parameter type of a functional interface. Instead, the methods can be named differently (which of course doesn't work for constructors). In our case, if the method is named runCallable(...) and runSupplier(...), no typecasting is needed anymore, and the compiler can infer the type.

Return Types

Type inference plays a significant role in lambda expressions. This influence is especially true on the return types, which don't appear in the declaration and for which no syntax exists at all. Instead, the compiler "infers" the appropriate return type. Consider the following example:

```
Comparator<String> c =
    (String s1, String s2) -> { return s1.trim().compareTo( s2.trim() ); };
```

In this case, string is explicitly provided as the parameter type of the Comparator method; the return type int, which is returned by the expression s1.trim().compareTo(s2.trim()), on the other hand, doesn't appear.

Sometimes, the compiler needs a little help: Let's use the functional interface Supplier<T> as an example, which declares a T get() method. For the assignment, you would write the following code:

```
Supplier<Long> two  = () -> { return 2; }       // ☠ Compiler error
```

However, this code isn't correct and leads to the compiler error "incompatible types: bad return type in lambda expression." In this case, 2 is a literal of type int, and the compiler can't adapt this value to long. Thus, you must write the following code:

```
Supplier<Long> two  = () -> { return 2L };
```

Alternatively, you could write the following:

```
Supplier<Long> two  = () -> { return (long) 2 };
```

Ultimately, no new rules apply to lambda expressions that don't already apply to method returns because even a method declaration like the following is criticized by the compiler:

```
Long two() { return 2; }      // ☠ Compiler error
```

However, because wrapper types are much more common with functional interfaces due to generics, these features occur more often than with method declarations.

Are Lambda Expressions Objects?

A lambda expression is an instance of a functional interface and occurs as an object. For objects, normally a natural is-a-kind-of relationship to java.lang.Object always exists. But if the context is missing, even the is-a-kind-of relationship to java.lang.Object is disturbed. In this case, then, the following code isn't correct:

```
Object o = () -> {};           // ☠ Compiler error
```

The compiler error is: "incompatible types: the target type must be a functional interface." Only an explicit type conversion can correct the error and specify the target type to the compiler, as shown in the following example:

```
Object r = (Runnable) () -> {};
```

Lambda expressions don't have their own types per se, and basically nothing changes for Java's type system. (Later Java versions may introduce changes to the type system, however.)

> **Note** [«]
>
> The fact that lambda expressions are objects is a feature that shouldn't be overused. Thus, the usual Object methods equals(Object), hashCode(), getClass(), and toString() as well as those for thread control are of no particular importance. You should never have a scenario where lambda expressions must be compared using == because the result is undefined according to the Java Language Specification (JLS).
>
> Real objects have an identity (an identity hashcode) that can be compared and tested with instanceof and that can be backed up with a synchronized block—none of these features apply to lambda expressions. Basically, the term "lambda expression" already captures something you should never forget: It's an expression, that is, something that's evaluated and produces a result.

13.1.5   @FunctionalInterface Annotations

Any interface with exactly one abstract method is suitable as a functional interface and thus suitable for a lambda expression. However, not every interface in the API that declares only an abstract method at the moment should also be used for lambda expressions. For example, further development of an interface with several (abstract) methods may be planned, but currently only one abstract method is available. The compiler can't know if an interface might evolve.

To indicate that an interface is intended as a functional interface, the annotation type FunctionalInterface exists in the java.lang package. This annotation indicates that the interface should have exactly one abstract method indefinitely and thus will continue to be a functional interface in the future.

[Ex]

Example

A custom functional interface should always be marked as FunctionalInterface, as in the following example:

```
@FunctionalInterface
public interface Buyable {
  double price();
}
```

The compiler checks whether the annotated interface contains exactly one abstract method and raises an error if it doesn't. For compatibility reasons, however, the compiler doesn't enforce this annotation for functional interfaces. Thus, you can easily rewrite nested classes that implement traditional interfaces with one method into lambda expressions. In other words, the annotation is not a prerequisite for using the interface in a lambda expression and serves only for documentation purposes. In Java Platform, Standard Edition (Java SE), however, all central functional interfaces are marked in this way.

[+]

Tip

Any interface marked with @FunctionalInterface gets an extra sentence in the Javadoc: "Functional Interface: This is a functional interface and can therefore be used as the assignment target for a lambda expression or method reference." This addition makes functional interfaces even more visible.

[»]

Note

The FunctionalInterface annotation type is also visible at runtime, which means that programs can also test whether an interface is annotated via reflection.[1]

---

1 This annotation type is itself annotated with @Documented @Retention(value=RUNTIME) @Target(value=TYPE).

13.1.6 Syntax for Lambda Expressions

Lambda expressions, like methods, have possible parameter and return values. The Java grammar for writing lambda expressions provides a few useful syntactic shortcuts.

Detailed Notation

Lambda expressions can be written in different ways since short versions exist for various constructions. However, one notation that always applies is the following:

```
( LambdaParameter ) -> { Statements }
```

Fully written out, the lambda parameter—like a method parameter—consists of several elements:

- The type
- The name
- Optional modifiers

The parameter name opens a new scope for a variable, where the parameter name must *not* override *any* other local variable names. Now, the lambda parameter variable behaves like a new variable from an inner block and not like a variable from an inner class where the visibility is different.

> **Example**
>
> The following results in a compiler error in the lambda expression because s has already been declared—the parameter variable from the lambda expression must be "fresh." Consider the following example:
>
> ```
> String s = "Donuts. Is there anything they can't do?";
> Comparator<String> c = (String s, String t) -> { … }; // ☠ Compiler error
> ```

Short Version 1: Type Inference (Implicit Type)

The Java compiler can read many types from context, which is called *type inference*. We covered this topic in Chapter 12, Section 12.1.5, when we discussed the diamond operator. With this operator, you can write something like the following code:

```
List<String> list = new ArrayList<>()
```

If enough type information is available to the compiler, then the compiler allows a short version for lambda expressions. The following declaration is valid:

```
Comparator<String> c =
  (String s1, String s2) -> { return s1.trim().compareTo( s2.trim() ); };
```

The compiler knows, thanks to type inference, that to the right of the equal sign an expression of type `Comparator<String>` must exist and that the `Comparator` method `compare(...)` has two parameters of type `String`. Therefore, the following shortcut works:

```
Comparator<String> c = (s1, s2) -
> { return s1.trim().compareTo( s2.trim() ); };
```

[»]

> **Note**
>
> The parameter list contains either explicitly declared parameter types or implicit inferred types. A mix of explicit and implicit isn't permitted, the compiler blocks something like (`string s1, s2`) or (`s1, string s2`) with an error message.

If the compiler can determine the types, parameter types are optional. But type inference isn't always possible, so the short version isn't always possible either. In addition, the explicit notation also increases readability: Short expressions aren't necessarily the most understandable ones.

[»]

> **Note**
>
> The compiler reads from the types whether all members are present. The types are provided either explicitly or implicitly. Consider the following example:
>
> ```
> Comparator<String> sc = (a, b) ->
>   { return Integer.compare( a.length(), b.length() ); };
> Comparator<BitSet> bc = (a, b) ->
>   { return Integer.compare( a.length(), b.length() ); };
> ```
>
> The `String` and `BitSet` classes both have the `length()` method, so the lambda expression is correct. The same lambda code in the source code can be used for two completely different classes that have nothing in common at all, except that they both happen to have a method called `length()`.

Short Version 2: The Lambda Body Is Either a Single Expression or a Block

If the body of a lambda expression consists of only a single expression, a shortened notation can make the block parentheses and the semicolon redundant. Thus, you could write the following code:

```
( LambdaParameter ) -> { return expression; }
```

But the following code is more concise:

```
( LambdaParameter ) -> expression
```

Lambda expressions with `return` statements in their bodies occur frequently since this construction corresponds to typical functions. Thus, the abbreviated syntax for lambda expressions only requires the expression, which then forms the return. Table 13.3 shows two examples.

Long Notation	Short Notation

`(s1, s2) ->`
`{ return s1.trim().compareTo(`
`s2.trim() ); }`
	`(s1, s2) ->`
	`s1.trim().compareTo( s2.trim() )`

`(a, b) -> { return a + b; }`	`(a, b) -> a + b`

Table 13.3 Long Notation and Short Notation

> **Note**
>
> Notations with the curly brackets and notations with the return expressions can't be mixed. Either you have a block of curly brackets and a `return`, or you have no brackets and no `return` keyword. Incorrect mixes, such as the following statements, result in errors:
>
> ```
> Comparator<String> c;
> c = (s1, s2) -> { s1.trim().compareTo( s2.trim() ) };     // ☠ Compiler error (1)
> c = (s1, s2) -> return s1.trim().compareTo( s2.trim() ); // ☠ Compiler error (2)
> ```
>
> If you used an explicit `return` in line (1), everything would be fine; if you omitted the `return` in line (2), the line would also be compilable.

void-compatible

Expressions can also evaluate to `void` in Java, so without problems a call like `System.out.println()` can be set in the compact notation without block. In other words, when lambda expressions are used with the short expression syntax, these expressions might return something but don't have to.

Long Notation	Short Notation
`() -> { System.out.println(); }`	`() -> System.out.println()`
`(s) -> { System.out.println(s); }`	`(s) -> System.out.println(s)`

Table 13.4 Long Notation and Short Notation

Whether lambda expressions have a return is expressed by two terms:

- **void compatible**

  The lambda body doesn't return a result, either because the block doesn't contain a return (or contains a return without a return value) or because a void expression is used in the short notation. So, the lambda expression () -> System.out.println() is void compatible, as is () -> {}.

- **Value compatible**
  The body terminates the lambda expression with a return statement that returns a value or consists of the compact notation with a return not equal to void.

A mixture of void compatible and value compatible isn't permitted and leads to a compiler error in the same way as with methods.[2]

Short Version 3: Single Identifier instead of Parameter List and Parentheses

The parentheses can be omitted if the parameter list fulfills the following prerequisites:

- Only a single identifier exists.
- The type is clear due to type inference.

Long Notation	Types Inferred	Fully Shortened
(String s) -> s.length()	(s) -> s.length()	s -> s.length()
(int i) -> Math.abs(i)	(i) -> Math.abs(i)	i -> Math.abs(i)

Table 13.5 Different Degree of Shortening

If all the short versions come together, about half the code can be saved. Thus, (int i) -> { return Math.abs(i); } will simply become i -> Math.abs(i).

> **[»]**
>
> **Note on the Syntax**
>
> Only in the case of exactly one lambda parameter can the parentheses be omitted; otherwise, ambiguities will exist for which complex rules are required for resolution. For example, in a notation like foo(k, v -> { ... }), whether foo declares two parameters is unclear. Is the second argument a lambda expression, or is it exactly one parameter, in which case a lambda expression is passed that itself declares two parameters? To avoid these problems, developers can see at a glance that foo(k, v -> { ... }) clearly represents two arguments and foo((k, v) -> { ... }) passes only one argument.

Short Version 4: Type Inference via var

In lambda expressions, var can also be used. However, a mixture of explicit types, implicit types, and var types isn't permitted. Consider the following examples:

---

2 Arguably, however, some exceptions exist, as with { throw new RuntimeException(); } where lambda expressions are both void compatible and value compatible.

```
Comparator<String> c0 = (var x, var y) -> 0;
Comparator<String> c1 = (x, var y) -> 0;          // ☠ implicit and var
Comparator<String> c2 = (var x, y) -> 0;          // ☠ var and implicit
Comparator<String> c3 = (int x, var y) -> 0;      // ☠ var and explicit
Comparator<String> c4 = (int x, y) -> 0;          // ☠ explicit and implicit
```

Actually, the use of var makes little sense when you can use implicit types.

Unused Parameters in Lambda Expressions

Sometimes, a lambda expression implements a functional interface, but not every parameter is of interest. For example, let's look at a functional interface from Java SE, somewhat simplified in the following way:

```
interface Consumer<T> { void accept( T t ); }
```

A consumer that outputs the argument in quotation marks could be written in the following way:

```
Consumer<String> printQuoted = s -> System.out.printf( "'%s'", s );
printQuoted.accept( "Chris" );  // 'Chris'
```

Now, what if a consumer doesn't want to access the argument at all, for example, because the current time is output, but the code must be present as a Consumer. In this case, you could write the following code:

```
Consumer<String> printNow =
  s -> System.out.print( System.currentTimeMillis() );
```

The variable s in the lambda parameter list is unused and a code checker might issue a warning such as "unused variable."

No special notation for unused parameters exists, nor can you omit the variable name and specify only the type.

13.1.7 The Environment of Lambda Expressions and Variable Accesses

A lambda expression "sees" its environment just like the rest of the code in the block. Object variables and class variables can be accessed via read and write access by lambda expressions without any problems.

Read Access to Final, Local, or Parameter Variables

A lambda expression has *read-only* access to local variables and method or exception parameters, and the variables must be (effectively) final. The fact that a variable is final does not have to be written with a modifier, but it must be *effectively final*. A variable is effectively final if it's no longer written to after initialization. The `final` modifier can then be omitted.

For example, if a lambda expression is in a loop, the expression can't access the loop counter because the counter changes on each iteration. (A different scenario occurs for a variable in an extended `for` loop, which can be accessed by a lambda expression.)

For example, let's say a user should be given the option, via an input, to specify whether string comparisons with our trimming `Comparator` should take place regardless of case.

```java
public static void main( String[] args ) {
  /*final*/ boolean ignoreCase = new Scanner( System.in ).nextBoolean();
  Comparator<String> c = (s1, s2) -> ignoreCase ?
        s1.trim().compareToIgnoreCase( s2.trim() ) :
        s1.trim().compareTo( s2.trim() );
  String[] words = { "M", "\nSkyfall", " Q", "\t\tAdele\t" };
  Arrays.sort( words, c );
  System.out.println( Arrays.toString( words ) );
}
```

Listing 13.2 src/main/java/com/tutego/insel/lambda/TrimIgnoreCaseCompare.java, main

Whether `ignoreCase` is set `final` by us or not doesn't matter because the variable is used as effectively final in this case. Of course, it's no harm to always put `final` in front as a modifier to make other programmers aware of this fact.

Newly inserted lambda expressions that access local variables or parameter variables can therefore lead to compiler errors in retrospect. The following segment is correct without a lambda expression:

```java
boolean ignoreCase = new Scanner( System.in ).nextBoolean();  // 1
...                                                           // 2
ignoreCase = true;                                            // 3
```

If a lambda expression that accesses `ignoreCase` is subsequently inserted between lines 1 and 3, a compiler error will occur. However, the error is not in line 3, but in the lambda expression because the `ignoreCase` variable is no longer effectively final after the change, which is required for use in the lambda expression.

Write Access to Local Variables or Parameter Variables?*

Lambda expressions can only read local variables but not write to them. The same applies to anonymous inner classes. (This limitation involves the location where variables are stored: Object variables and static variables are "living" on the heap, while local variables and parameters are "living" on the stack.) Now, when threads come into play, commonly, you'll have different threads use variables from the heap, and synchronization options are available for this task. However, a thread can't access local variables from another thread because one thread cannot access the stack memory of another thread.

The restriction that outer local variables can only be read by lambda expressions is in itself a good thing because this restriction minimizes errors during the concurrent execution of lambda expressions: If several threads process lambda expressions and describe a local variable, thread synchronization would otherwise be required.

Ultimately, not every programming language prohibits writing local variables from lambda expressions. In C#, a lambda expression can describe local variables, which then cease to "live" on the stack.

With containers like an array or with special Atomic* classes from the java.util.concurrent.atomic package, the problem can be solved. For example, if a lambda expression accesses the array boolean[] ignoreCase = new boolean[1];, the ignoreCase variable itself is final, but ignoreCase[0] = true; is permitted because this statement is a write access to the array, not to the ignoreCase variable. However, depending on the code, risk grows when multiple lambda expressions are executed in parallel. If, for example, a lambda expression can change an array's content and is executed in parallel, the access isn't synchronized, and the result may be "corrupt" because parallel access to variables must always be performed in a coordinated manner.

Implementation Details and Exceptions in Lambda Expressions*

When the developers of the compiler built a prototype for lambda expressions, they technically implemented them with nested classes—but only in the test phase because nested classes are complete classes for the JVM and resource heavy. Loading and initializing classes is relatively expensive and involve high overheads because of the many small lambda expressions.

Currently, the Java compiler converts lambda expressions with methods. If we apply the Java Development Kit (JDK) tool *javap* to the bytecode via the call javap -p TrimIgnoreCaseCompare, the following result occurs, somewhat abbreviated:

```
public class TrimIgnoreCaseCompare {
  public TrimIgnoreCaseCompare();
  public static void main(String[]);
  private static int lambda$0(boolean, String, String);
}
```

The body of the private static method lambda$0(...) contains the code block ignoreCase ? s1.trim() .... The JVM as the caller of the method passes the content of the ignoreCase variable. Since Java only has *call by value* as a parameter passing mechanism, a copy of the value of ignoreCase goes into the method. Even if the method were to change the parameter variable, the new assignment would never come out of the method.

The fact that lambda expressions are converted to methods is also clearly visible in stack trace exceptions. Let's have the Comparator use the following code to throw an ArithmeticException:

```
Comparator<String> c = (s1, s2) -> 1 / 0;
```

The execution then processes the following output:

```
Exception in thread "main" java.lang.ArithmeticException: / by zero
    at TrimIgnoreCaseCompare.lambda$0(TrimIgnoreCaseCompare.java:6)
    at java.base/java.util.TimSort.countRunAndMakeAscending(TimSort.java:355)
    at java.base/java.util.TimSort.sort(TimSort.java:220)
    at java.base/java.util.Arrays.sort(Arrays.java:1442)
    at TrimIgnoreCaseCompare.main(TrimIgnoreCaseCompare.java:8)
```

So, the lambda$0(...) method created by the compiler can be read easily.

Now, we've seen where the lambda expression code goes; however, we don't yet know how to call it. If you write Arrays.sort(words, (s1, s2) -> ...), the JVM must call the lambda$0(...) method for the lambda expression, which is still a long way to the method call. In this case, the compiler draws on a special bytecode: invokedynamic. One great advantage of this special bytecode is that the runtime environment has a lot of scope for optimization. Nested classes are just one possible technical implementation for lambda expressions: invokedynamic is the declarative variant, so to speak, and nested classes are the imperative, programmed play. Ultimately, the overhead with invokedynamic is low, and refactoring program code from nested classes to lambda expressions results in small bytecode files. From a performance point of view, lambda expressions and the implementation of functional interfaces and classes don't differ; rather, the optimization is to be found on the side of the JVM, which must deal with fewer class files. Conversely, the reverse is also true: When developers replace their old, existing implementation of functional interfaces with lambda expressions, the bytecode becomes more compact because a small invokedynamic is much shorter than complex new class files.

Namespaces

If an anonymous inner class declares variables inside the method, they are always "new." In other words, the new variables overlay existing local variables from the outer context. For example, the ignoreCase variable can be easily redeclared in the body of compare(...), as in the following example:

```
boolean ignoreCase = true;
Comparator<String> c = new Comparator<String>() {
  @Override public int compare( String s1, String s2 ) {
    boolean ignoreCase = false;          // absolutely OK
    return...
  }
};
```

In a lambda expression, this redeclaration isn't possible, and thus, the following code leads to an error message, "variable ignoreCase is already defined" from the compiler:

```
boolean ignoreCase = true;
Comparator<String> c = (s1, s2) -> {
  boolean ignoreCase = false;  // ☠ Compiler error
  return...
}
```

this References

A lambda expression also differs from an inner (anonymous) class with regard what the this reference points to:

- For the lambda expression, this always points to the object in which the lambda expression is embedded.
- With an inner class, this references the inner class, which is a completely new type.

The following example makes this clear:

```
class InnerVsLambdaThis {
  InnerVsLambdaThis() {
    Runnable lambdaRun = () -> System.out.println( this.getClass().getName() );
    Runnable innerRun  = new Runnable() {
      @Override public void run() { System.out.println( this.getClass().getName(
)); }
    };

    lambdaRun.run();       // InnerVsLambdaThis
    innerRun.run();        // InnerVsLambdaThis$1
  }
  public static void main( String[] args ) {
    new InnerVsLambdaThis();
  }
}
```

Listing 13.3 src/main/java/com/tutego/insel/lambda/InnerVsLambdaThis.java (Snippet)

First, we're using this in a lambda expression in the constructor of the InnerVsLamb-daThis class. In this way, this points to the newly built InnerVsLambdaThis object. For the inner class, this references another object, of type Runnable. Since an anonymous class has no name, it simply carries the identifier InnerVsLambdaThis$1.

Recursive Lambda Expressions

Lambda expressions can reference themselves. However, because this doesn't work for self-reference, a small detour is necessary. First, an object variable or a class variable must be declared, then a lambda expression must be assigned to this variable, and then the lambda expression can access this variable and start a recursive call. For the factorial calculation, you would write the following code:

```
public class RecursiveFactLambda {

  public static IntFunction<Integer> fact =
      n -> (n == 0) ? 1 : n * RecursiveFactLambda.fact.apply( n - 1 );

  public static void main( String[] args ) {
    System.out.println( fact.apply( 5 ) );   // 120
  }
}
```

Listing 13.4 src/main/java/com/tutego/insel/lambda/RecursiveFactLambda.java (Snippet)

IntFunction is a functional interface from the java.util.function package with a T apply(int i) operation. In this case, T is a generic return type, which we've assigned to Integer. By the way, writing n * fact.apply(n - 1) doesn't work because the compiler then reports: "Cannot reference a field before it is defined." fact could have been declared as a normal method just as well. The notation with lambda expressions does not offer great advantages in this case, especially since the term *anonymous method* doesn't really fit anymore because the lambda expression has a name, namely, fact.

Lambda Expressions Can't Fall Back on Their Own Default Methods

A functional interface may have only exactly one abstract method but may contain further static and default methods. If a class implements a functional interface, the method can fall back on default methods. Consider the following example:

```
class TruePredicate implements Predicate<Object> {
  @Override public boolean test( Object o ) {
    return negate().test( o );
  }
}
```

Listing 13.5 src/main/java/com/tutego/insel/lambda/InnerVsLambdaDefaultMethod.java (Snippet)

A lambda expression can't fall back on default methods, in the following example:

```
Predicate<Object> truePredicate = o -> negate().test( o ); // ☠ Compiler error
```

In practice, this problem is not a real problem, and it even prevents errors. Default methods fall back almost exclusively on abstract methods and "can do" nothing on their own, as can be easily seen in the negate() method of Predicate in the following example:

```
default Predicate<T> negate() {return (t) -> !test(t);}
```

Listing 13.6 java/util/function/Predicate.java (Snippet)

The method negate() calls test(…) again. If the negate method is called in the implementation of test(...), endless recursion will follow.

13.1.8 Exceptions in Lambda Expressions

Lambda expressions are implementations of functional interfaces, and so far, we haven't considered what happens when a block of code from a lambda expression throws an exception, especially who must catch it.

Exceptions in the Code Block of a Lambda Expression

In java.util.function, you'll find a functional interface named Predicate, the basic declaration of which follows:

```
public interface Predicate<T> { boolean test( T t ); }
```

A Predicate performs a test and returns true or false as a result. A lambda expression can implement this interface. Suppose you wanted to test whether a file has length 0, for example, to find inactive or unused files. Our first attempt will use the existing Files class, which provides the size(...) method, as in the following example:

```
Predicate<Path> isEmptyFile = path -> Files.size( path ) == 0;
// ☠ Compiler error
```

The problem now is that Files.size(...) throws an IOException that must be handled as a checked exception, *not* in the block containing the lambda expression as a whole, but by the code in the lambda expression itself, as dictated by the compiler. The following code is *not* a solution:

```
try {
  Predicate<Path> isEmptyFile = path -> Files.size( path ) == 0; // ☠
} catch ( IOException e ) { … }
```

Instead, you should write the following code:

```
Predicate<Path> isEmptyFile = path -> {
  try {
    return Files.size( path ) == 0;
  } catch ( IOException e ) { return false; }
};
```

The feature Java doesn't have is called *exception transparency*, and in this case, you can clearly see the difference between checked and unchecked exceptions. With exception transparency, no exception handling is necessary in the lambda expression and instead can be performed at a higher-level location.

However, since this feature is missing in Java, you must handle checked exceptions in your lambda expressions directly.

Functional Interfaces with a throws Clause

Unchecked exceptions can always occur and (if uncaught) will cause the thread to abort as usual. A throws clause on the methods/constructors isn't needed for that. But functional interfaces can declare a throws clause with checked exceptions, and the implementation of a functional interface can logically throw checked exceptions.

A declaration like Callable from the java.util.concurrent package can clarify this issue:

```
public interface Callable<V> {
  V call() throws Exception;
}
```

This code could be implemented via the following lambda expression:

```
Callable<Integer> randomDice = () -> (int)(Math.random() * 6) + 1;
```

Calling call() on a randomDice must be accompanied by exception handling since call() throws an Exception, as shown in the following example:

```
try {
  System.out.println( randomDice.call() );
  System.out.println( randomDice.call() );
}
catch ( Exception e ) { … }
```

Now, that the caller must handle the exception is clear. The declaration of the lambda expression contains no reference to the exception, which is different from what we described in the previous subsection.

> **Design Tip** [+]
>
> Exceptions in the methods of functional interfaces severely limit their usefulness, and therefore, none of the functional interfaces from, for example, `java.util.function` throws a checked exception. The reason is simple: Every method caller would otherwise have to either forward or handle the exception.[3]

To make the limitations and problems related to a `throws` clause a bit clearer, let's imagine that the `Predicate` functional interface contains a `throws Exception` at the operation (leaving aside the meaning of the `Exception` type itself). Consider the following example:

```
interface Predicate<T> { boolean test( T t ) throws Exception; } // What if?
```

The consequence would be that every caller of `test(...)` would now in turn get hold of the `Exception` and would have to catch it or forward it. If the `test(...)` caller directed the exception further up with a `throws exception`, we'd suddenly get a `throws Exception` in all places in the method signature, which is not desired in any case. For example, `Collection` (an interface that implements our familiar `ArrayList`) contains a declaration of `removeIf(Predicate filter)`; now, `removeIf(...)`—which ultimately calls `filter.test(...)`—would have to deal with the exception, and `removeIf(Predicate filter) throws Exception` is not a good idea.

From Checked to Unchecked

Checked exceptions aren't nice in lambda expressions. One solution is to wrap code that throws checked exceptions and embed the checked exception in an unchecked one. You might write something like the following code:

```
public class PredicateWithException {
  @FunctionalInterface
  public interface ExceptionalPredicate<T,E extends Exception> {
    boolean test( T t ) throws E;
  }
  public static <T> Predicate<T> asUncheckedPredicate(
                                  ExceptionalPredicate<T,Exception> predicate )
  {
    return t -> {
      try {
        return predicate.test( t );
      }
```

---

3 Some users of `Callable` are related to concurrency (hence, the `java.util.concurrent` package). But other than this context, no other usage exists in the Java library, apart from two examples from `javax.tools`. `java.util.function.Supplier` is a corresponding alternative without a `throws` clause.

```
      catch ( Exception e ) {
        throw new RuntimeException( e.getMessage(), e );
      }
    };
  }
  public static void main( String[] args )  {
    Predicate<Path> isEmptyFile =
      asUncheckedPredicate( path -> Files.size( path ) == 0 );
    System.out.println( isEmptyFile.test( Paths.get( "c:/" ) ) );
  }
}
```

Listing 13.7 src/main/java/com/tutego/insel/lambda/PredicateWithException.java (Snippet)

The ExceptionalPredicate interface is a predicate with an optional exception. In our own helper method asUncheckedPredicate(ExceptionalPredicate), we're taking an ExceptionalPredicate and wrapping it in a Predicate that is returned by the method. Checked exceptions are set into an unchecked exception of RuntimeException type. Thus, Predicate doesn't have to redirect a checked exception, which it can't do anyway according to the declaration.

The Java library itself doesn't provide any standard methods for embeddings of this kind. One internal method does something comparable. Consider the following example:

```
/**
 * Convert a Closeable to a Runnable by converting checked IOException
 * to UncheckedIOException
 */
private static Runnable asUncheckedRunnable( Closeable c ) {
  return () -> {
    try {
      c.close();
    }
    catch ( IOException e ) {
      throw new UncheckedIOException( e );
    }
  };
}
```

Listing 13.8 java.nio.file.Files.java, asUncheckedRunnable(…)

Now is where the UncheckedIOException class comes into play. This unchecked exception is used as a wrapper class for input/output errors. You'll find the UncheckedIOException, for example, with lines() of BufferedReader or Files, which returns a Stream<String> with lines—in this context, checked exceptions are only in the way.

13.1.9 Classes with an Abstract Method as a Functional Interface?*

When the developers of the Java language discussed lambda expressions, one question that arose was whether abstract classes with only one abstract method could also be used for lambda expressions.[4] The developers decided against it, among other things, because the JVM can make far-reaching optimizations when implementing interfaces. With classes, this limitation becomes difficult because a constructor does extensive initialization with side effects (not to mention the constructors of all superclasses) and could also throw exceptions. However, only the execution of an implementation of the functional interface is desired and no other code.

13.2 Method References

Lambda expressions are already quite short, but for certain calls, even more concise constructions are possible.

13.2.1 Motivation

The larger software systems become, the more important things like clarity, reusability, and documentation are. Earlier, we wrote an implementation for our string comparator, initially via an inner class, later via a lambda expression. In any case, we have written code. But what if a utility class already came with an implementation? Then, of course, the lambda expression could delegate to the existing implementation, and we'd save on code. Let's look at this topic through an example:

```java
class StringUtils {
  public static int trimCompare( String s1, String s2 ) {
    return s1.trim().compareTo( s2.trim() );
  }
}
public class TrimCompareWithDelegation {
  public static void main( String[] args ) {
    String[] words = { "A", "B", "a" };
    Arrays.sort( words,
               (String s1, String s2) -> StringUtils.trimCompare(s1, s2) );
    System.out.println( Arrays.toString( words ) );
  }
}
```

Listing 13.9 src/main/java/com/tutego/insel/lambda/TrimCompareWithDelegation.java (Snippet)

---

4 In the past, the concept *Single Abstract Method (SAM)* was used in this context.

13.2.2   Method References with ::

What is striking in the example is that the referenced method `int trimCompare(String, String)` is the same as `int compare(String, String)` from the parameter types and from the return type. Even if you omit the method name, it works like the method in `Comparator`. For exactly such cases, another syntactic shortening is thus available.

[»]

> **Definition**
>
> A *method reference* is a reference to a method, but the reference is made without a call. Syntactically, two colons separate the type name or reference on the left from the method name on the right.

Consider the following line:

```
Arrays.sort( words, (String s1, String s2) -
> StringUtils.trimCompare(s1, s2) );
```

This line can be shortened with a method reference in the following way:

```
Arrays.sort( words, StringUtils::trimCompare );
```

Now, we no longer have a lambda expression in the code, only a method reference. The sort method expects a method from the `Comparator` that takes two strings and returns an integer. The name of the class and the name of the method are irrelevant, so a method reference can be used at this point.

A method reference, like a lambda expression, is like in instance of a functional interface, but for an existing method of a known class. As usual, the context determines exactly what type the expression is.

[»]

> **Note**
>
> The same code for a method reference can result in completely different types—the context makes the difference. Consider the following examples:
>
> ```
> Comparator<String>                  c1 = StringUtils::trimCompare;
> BiFunction<String,String,Integer> c2 = StringUtils::trimCompare;
> ```

13.2.3   Variations of Method References

In the example, the `trimCompare(...)` method is static, and to the left of the colon is the name of a type. However, this use of method references is not the only use case—in total, three variants of method references exist.

Method Reference to a ...	Syntax for a Method Reference	Lambda Expression
Class method	`Type::classmethod`	`() -> Type.classmethod()`
		`(p1) -> Type.classmethod(p1)`
		`(p1[, p2[, …]]) -> Type.class-method([p1[, p2[, …]])`
Object method	`ref::objectmethod`	`() -> ref.objectmethod()`
		`(p1) -> ref.objectmethod(p1)`
		`([p1[, p2[, …]]) -> ref.object-method([p1[, p2[, …]])`
Object method of a type	`ObjectType::object-Method`	`(obj) -> obj.objectmethod()`
		`(obj, p1) -> obj.objectmethod(p1)`
		`(obj, p1, p2[, …]]) -> obj.object-method([p1[, p2[, …]])`

Table 13.6 Different Method References

Table 13.6 makes it clear that multiple parameters are permitted. Parameters don't appear in the notation for the method reference.

Method Reference to a Static Method

`System.currentTimeMillis()` returns a `long` with the milliseconds that have elapsed since 1/1/1970, 0 o'clock. The method can be used as a `Supplier`:

```
Supplier<Long> time = System::currentTimeMillis;
```

`Math.max(...)` is a static method that reduces two elements to the maximum, which is also what a `BiFunction` does. For this reason, the following code applies:

```
BiFunction<Integer, Integer, Integer> max = Math::max;
```

If a main method in the `JavaApplication` class is declared with `main(String... args)`, the method does match as a `Runnable`:

```
Runnable r = JavaApplication::main;
```

The scenario would be different for `main(String[])`, in which case a parameter is mandatory, but a vararg can also be empty.

Method Reference to an Object Method

System.out is a reference, and a method like println(...) can be bound to a Consumer. But println(...) also match to a Runnable because println() exists without a parameter list. Consider the following example:

```
Consumer<String> out = System.out::println;   // s -> System.out.println(s)
out.accept( "My cousin in Trinidad ..." );
Runnable out = System.out::println;            // () -> System.out.println()
out.run();
```

Method Reference to an Object Method of a Type

The string method isEmpty() returns true if the string is empty; otherwise, false. It's like a Predicate. Thus, you can use String::isEmpty instead of s -> s.isEmpty().

String::length is another example. This function maps a String to an int. In code, the function is Function<String,Integer> len = String::length.

To easily build a Comparator object, we can use *key extractors*, which require a function. Consider the following example in which the generics are abbreviated:

```
static <…> Comparator<…> comparing*(*Function<…> keyExtractor)
```

Suppose you have a Candy class and a calories() method. To access the data, you can use the method reference Candy::calories instead of c -> c.calories().

this and super Are Possible

Instead of choosing the name of a reference variable, this can also describe the object, and super is also possible. this is useful when you want to delegate the implementation of a functional interface to a method of your own class. For example, if a local trimCompare(...) method existed in the class where the lambda expression is also located, and if this method was to be used as a Comparator in Arrays.sort(...), you might write Arrays.sort(words, this::trimCompare).

Limitations

You cannot select a special (overloaded) method via the method reference. A specification like String::valueOf or Arrays::sort is relatively broad. For the latter, the compiler can select any one of the 18 matching overloaded methods, and thus, the compiler might select the wrong method. In this case, an explicit lambda expression must resolve any ambiguity. For generic types, for example, List<String>::length or also List::length can be used. Again, the compiler recognizes everything itself.

What's This All About?

For newcomers to the Java language, this language feature will seem like the greatest magic on earth, and even Java professionals will get shaky fingers here, either from fear or excitement. In the past, a lot of code had to be written explicitly in Java, but with these new method references, the compiler can do a lot by itself.

This feature is useful with the functional libraries at the Stream API (we'll cover this later in Chapter 18, Section 18.5). A brief glance is provided by the following example:

```
Object[] words = { " ", '3', null, "2", 1, "" };
Arrays.stream( words )                // " ", '3', null, "2", 1, ""
      .filter( Objects::nonNull )     // " ", '3', "2", 1, ""
      .map( Objects::toString )       // " ", "3", "2", "1", ""
      .map( String::trim )            // "", "3", "2", "1", ""
      .filter( s -> ! s.isEmpty() )   // "3", "2", "1"
      .map( Integer::parseInt )       // 3, 2, 1
      .sorted()                       // 1, 2, 3
      .forEach( System.out::println );// 1 2 3
```

13.3 Constructor References

To create an object, you use the new keyword. This keyword entails the call of a constructor, which can optionally be passed arguments. However, the Java API also declares types from which no direct objects can be created via new. Instead, factories are tasked with creating objects. These factories can be static or non-static methods.

Typical examples of constructors include the following:

- new StringBuilder("1") → StringBuilder
- new File("dir") → File
- new BigInteger(val) → BigInteger

Examples of factories include the following:

- LocalDate.of(2022, 02, 02) → LocalDate
- Paths.get("dir") → Path
- BigInteger.valueOf(val) → BigInteger

Both constructors and factories can be thought of as special functions that convert from one type to another, making them perfect for transformations. Let's contrast the following two examples:

Constructor	Method
new BigDecimal(12.2)	BigDecimal.valueOf(12.2)

Basically, mapping double → BigDecimal is performed in two ways: once via new and a constructor and once via the valueOf(double) method.

13.3.1 Writing Constructor References

Where method references can specify static methods and object methods, *constructor references* provide the ability to specify constructors so that they can be passed elsewhere as creators. This feature allows you to elegantly specify constructors as creators, even from a class that doesn't have any creator methods. As with method references, a functional interface plays a crucial role in this context. But this time the method of the functional interface, when called, causes the constructor call. Where syntactically for method references the method name is placed to the right of the colon, for constructor references, you would use a new.[5]

Constructor references with the library methods of the Stream API are useful.

Example

The Stream API can build a stream with three Double numbers, for instance. The floats are converted to BigDecimal objects, then calculated to the power of 20 before the return is output in the following example:

```
Stream.of( 12.5, 11.5, 9.5 )
    .map( BigDecimal::valueOf )
    .map( bigDecimal -> bigDecimal.pow( 20 ) )
    .forEach( System.out::println );
```

This notation is equivalent to the following code:

```
Stream.of( 12.5, 11.5, 9.5 )
    .map( BigDecimal::valueOf )
    .map( bigDecimal -> bigDecimal.pow( 20 ) )
    .forEach( System.out::println );
```

Put simply, the map(...) method expects a Function<Double,BigDecimal>—exactly the transformation that new and constructor perform as well as the method.

Example

Let's say we have the following custom functional interface:

```
interface DateFactory { Date create(); }
```

A constructor reference binds the constructor to the create() method of the functional interface in the following example:

```
DateFactory factory = Date::new;
System.out.print( factory.create() );
// for example, Fri Oct 06 22:34:24 CET 2017
```

The last two lines can also be summarized in the following way:

```
System.out.println( ((DateFactory)Date::new).create() );
```

---

5 Since new is a keyword, no method can be named new; so, the identifier is safe.

If only a parameterless constructor is to be called, the functional interface must have only one method that has no parameters and returns something. The return type of the method must of course match the class type. This rule applies to the DateFactory type from our earlier example. But you can also go a bit more generic, for example, with the existing functional interface Supplier, as we'll see momentarily in Section 13.3.2.

The Java API often contains parameters of the Class type, which are used as type specification to create objects via the Constructor of the Class with the newInstance() method. The use of Class can be replaced by a functional interface, and constructor references can be passed instead of Class objects.

13.3.2 Parameterless and Parameterized Constructors

With a parameterless constructor, the method has only one return. In contrast, with a parameterized constructor, the method of the functional interface must of course have a compatible parameter list, as illustrated in the following examples:

Constructor	Date()	Date(long t)

Compatible functional interface	`interface DateFactory {`
	`  Date create();`
	`}`
		`interface DateFactory {`
		`  Date create(long t);`
		`}`

Constructor reference	`DateFactory factory =` `  Date::new;`	`DateFactory factory =` `  Date::new;`
Call	`factory.create();`	`factory.create(1);`

Table 13.7 Standard and Parameterized Constructor with Corresponding Functional Interfaces

> **Note**
>
> If the type inference of the compiler reaches its limits, additional type information is required. In this case, the additional information is provided after the colon in square brackets, such as in Class::<Type1, Type2>new.

13.3.3 Useful Predefined Interfaces for Constructor References

The functional interface appropriate for a parameterless constructor must have a return and take no parameter. In contrast, the functional interface for a parameterized constructor must have a corresponding parameter list. Often, a constructor might parameterless or takes exactly one parameter. For these two cases, the Java API provides two practical (generically declared) functional interfaces.

Functional Interface	Functional Descriptor	Mapping	Matches...
Supplier<T>	T get()	() → T	Parameterless constructor
Function<T,R>	R apply(T t)	(T) → R	Simple parameterized constructor

Table 13.8 Existing Functional Interfaces as Creators

[Ex]

Example

The functional interface Supplier<T> has a T get() method that you can connect to the parameterless constructor of Date, as in the following example:

```
Supplier<Date> factory = Date::new;
System.out.print( factory.get() );
```

Using Supplier with the type parameter Date gives the parameterized type Supplier<Date>, while get() consequently returns the type Date. The factory.get() call leads to the call of the constructor.

[»]

Brain Teaser

A constructor can be a Supplier or a Function. Once again, checked exceptions are problematic. You should consider whether the constructor URI(String str) throws URISyntaxException can be addressed via URI::new.

13.4   Functional Programming

Functional programming makes it possible to parameterize a behavior—a sorting method always works the same, but its behavior during comparisons is different. This parameterization is on a different abstraction level than just passing simple values.

13.4.1   Code = Data

When you hear the term *data*, you might first think of numbers, bytes, strings, or even complex objects with states. In this chapter, we'll expand this view a little and direct it to program code. Java code, epitomized as a series of bytecodes, also consists of data.

Once you buy into this view that code equals data, then code can also be passed like data and can thus be transferred from one point to another, stored, and later referenced. This ability to transfer code makes customizing the behavior of algorithms easy.

Let's start with a few examples where program code is passed and accessed later:

- A thread executes program code in the background. The program code that the Java thread should execute is wrapped into an object of type Runnable (more precisely, set in a run() method). When the thread's turn arrives, the thread calls the run() method.

- Timer is a java.util class that can execute program code at specific times. The object method scheduleAtFixedRate(...) is passed an object of the type TimerTask, which contains the program code.

- To sort data, you can define your own sort order, which can be passed to the sorter as a Comparator. The Comparator declares a comparison method to which the sorter turns to put two objects in the desired order.

- If the user clicks a button on the interface, an action occurs. For example, in the graphical user interface (GUI) framework Swing—the program code in an object of the type ActionListener and is attached to the button JButton with addAction-Listener(...). If button activation occurs, the UI system processes the program code in the actionPerformed(...) method of the stored ActionListener.

To move program code from one place to another, the same mechanism is always used in Java: A class implements a (usually non-static) method that contains the program code to be executed. An object of this class is passed to another location, and the interested party then accesses the program code via the method. The fact that an object can contain more than one implementation, such as variables, constants, and constructors, is not relevant in this context. Let's now take a closer look at this mechanism by exploring its variants.

13.4.2 Programming Paradigms: Imperative or Declarative

In some way, a developer must describe the problem at hand as a program that the computer can eventually execute. In this context, different types of problem description are available, referred to as *programming paradigms*. So far, we've mostly dealt with imperative programming, which focuses on statements. In the English language, verbs have an imperative mood (i.e., the command form), which can be compared quite well with imperative programming because, in both cases, statements capture commands like "do this, do that." These "commands," through variables, case distinctions, and jumps, describe the program and the solution path.

While imperative programming is technically the oldest form of describing programs, it's not the only one. In contrast, declarative programming describes not the how to solve the problem, but the what, (that is, what is actually required), without getting bogged down in exact procedures. At first glance, this kind of programming sounds abstract, but you're already familiar with the principle if you've ever performed the following actions:

- Made a selection like "*.html" in the command line or in the File Explorer in Windows search field
- Written a database query with SQL
- Used an XML selection with XQuery
- Formulated a build script with Maven
- Described an XML transformation with Extensible Stylesheet Language Transformations (XSLT)

Let's stay with SQL for a moment to illustrate one point clearly. Of course, in the end, the CPU executes the processing of the tables and the evaluations of the results in a purely imperative way, but declarative programming is about the program description on a higher level of abstraction. Declarative programs are usually much shorter, and thus other advantages come into play, such as easier extensibility and comprehensibility. Since declarative programs often have a mathematical background, formally proving the correctness of the descriptions is also easier.

Declarative programming is a programming style, and a declarative description needs some kind of "runtime environment" because SQL cannot directly control a CPU, for example. But instead of dealing only with special use cases (such as database or XML queries), typical algorithms can also be formulated declaratively, using functional programming. Thus, imperative programs and functional programs are equally powerful in their capabilities.

13.4.3   Principles of Functional Programming

While imperative programming focuses on the sequence of statements and object-oriented programming (OOP) focuses on objects with states and behaviors, functional programming is characterized by other things.

Pure Functions without Side Effects

In mathematics, a *function* is a mapping from elements of a definition set to exactly one element of a target set, for example, `double zero = Math.sin(Math.PI);`. Similarly, `string JOHNANDEVE = "johnAndEve".toUpperCase()` is another example from an object-oriented (OO) point of view: A value comes in, and a value comes out.

Functions are called *pure functions*, if they fulfill the following two prerequisites:

- They always provide the same outputs for the same inputs.
- They have no side effects (i.e., don't modify any external state).

Consequently, `Math.sin(...)` is a pure function, but `System.out.println()` or `Math.random()` aren't. That their implementations do change states, for example, on the stack, and thus describe memory cells doesn't matter—what's important is the conceptual view. The API documentation should be good enough to name side effects.

An expression built from pure functions is called a *pure expression*. This kind of expression has a feature called *referential transparency* in computer sciences, namely, that the result of an expression can be substituted for the expression itself without the program exhibiting any different behavior. Instead of `Math.sin(Math.PI)`, the compiler can substitute the expression with 0, and the result would be the same. A compiler can perform various optimizations in the presence of referential transparency.

In OOP, you'll use methods to modify the states of objects. A radio should be louder? We can call `volumeUp()`, and the internal state `volume` is increased. Having states in objects is natural for OO software development.

OO developers get a funny feeling when they hear "functional programming" because it sounds like no states exist, which is a misconception. Conditions still exist; it's just that they are "elsewhere." For this purpose, let's look at `"john&Eve".toUpperCase()`. What is the condition in this case? Does `toUpperCase()` modify a state? The `String` method doesn't change the state of an existing `String` object. The basic gist is that the return of `toUpperCase()` is a new `String` object with the desired states. At the core of functional programming, functions get an object and also return an object, but these objects aren't changed and can (and even should) be immutable. To summarize, in object orientation, an operation with side effects results in a change to the object; in functional programming, an operation results in a new object with no change to the old object.

Functional libraries can be easily recognized by the fact that they request objects and return objects. For this reason, any method that returns `void` raises suspicion because the state must be obtained and stored somewhere else. This condition can cause problems when writing, so a backup is necessary for modern parallel access.

Nested Calls Instead of Statement Sequences

While imperative programs distinguish between statements and expressions, in functional programming languages, everything is an expression. In the functional world, the focus is on evaluations of expressions rather than on the sequential processing of statements.

Of course, developers of functional programs don't write everything nested into a single line, but they use several lines. Many functional programming languages provide an operator reminiscent of a variable assignment, but this operator is just a name, a symbol, for the expression—the context is again referential transparency. This approach is quite different from imperative programming languages, where the variable represents a memory area. In functional programming languages, identifiers only make complex nested expressions more readable.

In Java, only a few statements are also expressions, such as method calls with returns or assignments. Case distinctions and loops don't return a result—one reason why neither exist in these forms in functional programming languages. Even with the condition operator in Java, case distinctions with alternatives can be implemented, which is an expression. Repetitions can be implemented in functional programming languages via recursions. A typical example is the calculation of the factorial. The formula is $n! = 1 \times 2 \times 3 \times ... \times n$, and with loops and variables. In the imperative way, you would write the following code:

```java
public static int factorial( int n ) {
  int result = 1;
  for ( int i = 1; i <= n; i++ )
    result *= i;
  return result;
}
```

Clearly, the many assignments and the case distinction of the loop can be read, which are the typical indicators for imperative programs. The loop counter increases, so state comes into the program because the current index must be kept somewhere in the memory. The recursive variant is quite different. No assignments are made in the program, and the notation is reminiscent of a mathematical definition. Consider the following example:

```java
public static int factorial( int n ) {
  return n == 0 ? 1 : n * factorial( n - 1 );
}
```

Since the number of repetitions can be high and recursions traditionally use up the stack, optimizations are quite important. Many developers therefore look closely at optimizing *end-recursive methods*—the methods that ultimately call the method itself again. In this case, space can be saved on the stack. (The JVM can't do this so far and for Oracle engineers it has little priority.)

First-Order Functions and Higher-Order Functions

The two points mentioned so far can also be implemented in Java with discipline. However, one thing is not possible with Java that is common in functional programming languages: Functions have a completely different status—they are their own types.

[Ex]

Example

The following example assigns and executes some functions in JavaScript:

```javascript
function printVodka() { console.log("Vodka"); }
function printWhiskey() { console.log("Whiskey"); }
printDrink = Math.random() > 0.5 ? printVodka : printWhiskey;
printDrink();
```

In Java, only primitive types and reference types exist, and methods as such aren't types. Functions are values in functional programming languages and thus the following actions are possible:

- Functions can be assigned to variables.
- Functions can be passed to other functions.
- Functions can, in turn, return functions.

Thus, functional programming involves *higher-order functions*, which allows for the rather flexible composition of functions because functions can be easily passed on.

13.4.4   Imperative Programming and Functional Programming

Functional programming is a real alternative to imperative programming. Languages that fall into this paradigm are LISP (first introduced in 1958) and derivatives such as Clojure, Erlang, ML (and OCaml), F#, and Haskell. Java is not a functional programming language because it lacks the ability to use higher-order functions, but you can compensate for this disadvantage with some tricks.

Why Functional Programming Has a Hard Time

A list of the most popular programming languages[6] would show that purely functional programming languages aren't terribly popular. Functional programming is feared by many developers for several reasons:

- **Readability**
  Historically, LISP from 1958 represents the beginning of functional programming languages. This language is quite flexible, but awkward to read. Our factorial in LISP would be written as (defun factorial (n) (if (= n 1) 1 (* n (factorial (- n 1)))))). All those parentheses make a program difficult to read, and the expressions are in the prefix notation - n 1 instead of the usual notation n - 1. Other functional programming languages are different, but a certain prejudice persists that all functional programming languages are hard to read.

- **Terminology**
  Higher-order functions, idempotence, function, functor, predicate, arity, lambda, closure, currying, monoid, and monad—you might think that these terms from functional programming are only for mathematicians and computer scientists. These concepts scare many developers, who consequently don't engage with the paradigm.

- **Academic and mathematical**
  Functional programming also has something academic about it because this programming paradigm is often associated only with mathematical functions in the

---

6 For example, *http://www.tiobe.com/tiobe-index/* or *http://githut.info*.

minds of developers. Only a few will actually need to calculate factorials or Fibonacci numbers in programs, so programmers quickly put functional programming aside. But these prejudices are unfounded, and we recommend mentally detaching functional programming from mathematics because the vast majority of programs have nothing to do with mathematical functions in the true sense, but instead deal much more with formally described methods.

- **Performance and memory consumption**
  Without clever optimizations on the part of the compiler and the runtime environment, recursive calls in particular can lead to bulging stacks and poor runtimes.

- **Purely functional**
  Some functional programming languages called "pure" don't permit state changes. The development of input/output operations or simple random numbers is thus a big deal, which is no longer comprehensible for developers.

Functional Object-Oriented Languages Are Popular

In recent years, many OOP languages have gained support for functional programming, or new functional programming languages with pragmatic state changes have appeared. From our point of view today, a combination of both concepts looks promising for the future. Functional programming is a way of thinking that has certain advantages, especially in a world of parallel execution where state changes can quickly become a problem. Also, declarative programming shifts more responsibility to the framework, which can get better and better as it progresses through optimizations.

How to Program Functionally with Java?

Java doesn't allow you to pass methods as values—there are no values and no *first-class functions*. Since we can't pass functions, we must use a trick. Instead of passing functions, you would perform the following tasks:

1. Set the functionality into a method.
2. Set the method into a class.
3. Create an object of this class.
4. Pass this object as a kind of wrapper for the function.

To prevent a receiver from getting any object with any method, an interface is added as an intermediary: One side implements the interface and adheres to a contract, and the receiver gets something of the desired type and can call the method.

With this detour Java can also only go far, and the option has existed since Java 1.0. However, the code size is large, so the path was impractical. Now, however, lambda expressions are the perfect language tool because they make functional programs compact and easy to read, and the JVM has excellent optimization capabilities. Of course, Java can never do 100% of what a functional programming language can do (and enforces), but these capabilities are quite sufficient for practical use.

Thus, Java enables both OOP and functional programming, and developers can choose the path that's best for solving a problem. Of course, this ambiguity can also create problems because, whenever several possible solutions exist, disputes may arise as to which variant is the best. Indeed, conflicting opinions can prevail from developer to developer. But a functional approach has some undeniable advantages, which we'll focus on more closely next.

13.4.5 Comparator as an Example of Higher-Order Functions

Let's look again at our example from Section 13.1, string sorting, but this time from the perspective of a functional programmer. A Comparator is a simple "function" with two parameters and one return. This "function" (implemented as a method) is in turn passed to the sort(...) method. All these tasks are functionally programmed because we're programming functions and then passing them. Table 13.9 shows three examples (generics omitted).

Code	Meaning
`Comparator c1 = (s, t) -> …`	Implements a function via a lambda expression
`Arrays.sort(array, c1);`	Takes a "function" as an argument
`Comparator c2 = Collections.reverseOrder(c1);`	Accepts a "function" and also returns a function

Table 13.9 Examples of Functions in Transfer and as a Return

We've already established that functions can't be passed in Java, so we can help ourselves with the possibility of putting the functionality in a method, so that the function becomes an object with a method, which implements the logic. Lambda expressions or method/constructor references provide a compact syntax without the burden of having to write an extra class with a method.

The Comparator type is a functional interface and represents a special function with two parameters of the same type and an integer return. Other functional interfaces are a bit more flexible than Comparator, for example, interfaces that allow the return to be double or something else (instead of int).

13.4.6 Viewing Lambda Expressions as Mappings or Functions

Recall that lambda expressions can be formulated in the following general syntax:

```
( LambdaParameter ) -> { Statements }
```

The arrow clear shows that we're dealing with a lambda expression with functions that map something else. In the case of the Comparator, we have a mapping of two strings to an integer, which can be wrapped in a slightly more mathematical notation: (String, String) → int.

[Ex]

Example

Methods exist with and without returns and with and without parameters. The same is true with lambda expressions. shows a few examples in Java code with their mappings.

Lambda Expression	Mapping
(int a, int b) → a + b	(int, int) → int
(int a) → Math.abs(a)	(int) → int
(String s) → s.isEmpty()	(String) → boolean
(Collection c) → c.size()	(Collection) → int
() → Math.random()	() → double
(String s) → { System.out.print(s); }	(String) → void
() → {}	() → void

Table 13.10 Lambda Expressions and How They Map as Functions

[»]

Terminology: Function versus Method

The Java language definition doesn't know the term *function* and speaks only of *methods*. Methods are always bound to classes, which means that methods are always bound to a context. This binding is central to object orientation since methods have read and write access to object variables. Lambda expressions, on the other hand, implement functions that first obtain their working values purely from the parameters and don't depend on classes or objects. The idea behind functional programming languages is to get along without states, that is, to use functions in such a way that they deliver a result. Functions always return the same result for a specific parameter combination, regardless of the state of the surrounding overall program.

13.5   Functional Interfaces from the java.util.function Package

Functions implement mappings, and since different types of mappings exist, the Java standard library in the java.util.function package provides functional interfaces for the most common cases. Table 13.11 provides an overview.

Interface	Mapping
Consumer<T>	(T) →void
DoubleConsumer	(double) →void
BiConsumer<T,U>	(T, U) →void
Supplier<T>	() →T
BooleanSupplier	() →boolean
Predicate<T>	(T) →boolean
LongPredicate	(long) →boolean
BiPredicate<T,U>	(T, U) →boolean
Function<T,R>	(T) →R
LongToDoubleFunction	(long) →double
BiFunction<T,U,R>	(T, U) →R
UnaryOperator<T>	(T) →T
DoubleBinaryOperator	(double, double) →double

Table 13.11 Some Predefined Functional Interfaces

13.5.1   Blocks with Code and the Functional Interface Consumer

Instructions of code can be put into a method of an object and passed on in this way. This transfer is a common need for which the java.util.function package specifies a simple Consumer functional interface that represents a consumer. This consumer accepts and then "consumes" (consumes) data but returns nothing.

```
interface java.util.function.Consumer<T>
```

▶ void accept(T t)

Performs operations with the transfer t.

▶ default Consumer<T> andThen(Consumer<? super T> after)

Returns a new Consumer that first executes the current Consumer and then after.

The accept(...) method gets one argument—though of course the implementation doesn't have to use it—and doesn't return anything. Transformations aren't possible with the type because the consumer can only save the results via detours, and the interface isn't intended for that purpose. Consumer types are intended more as the end link of a chain, where, for example, data is written to a file that has been previously processed. These side effects are intentional, as they come after a chain of side-effect-free operations.

Consumer Type in the Application Programming Interface

In the Java API, the Consumer type usually shows up as an argument of a forEach(Consumer) method that runs data sources and calls accept(...) for each element. The method on the Iterable type is interesting because the important Collection data structures like ArrayList implement this interface. Thus, you can easily run over all the data and execute a piece of code for each element. Iterator also has a similar method, the forEachRemaining(Consumer) method where the word "remaining" clearly indicates that the Iterator may have already experienced a few next() calls, and therefore, the consumers don't necessarily catch the first elements.

[Ex]

Example

The following example outputs each element in a list to the console:

```
Arrays.asList( 1, 2, 3, 4 ).forEach( System.out::println );
```

Compared to a typical iteration, the functional variant is a little shorter in code, but otherwise, no difference exists. Also, forEach(...) does nothing else on Iterable other than fetching all elements via the Iterator.

Writing a Custom Wrapper Consumer

Consumers always represent code, and an API can now simply accept a block of code along the lines of doSomethingWith(myConsumer) to, for instance, process it in a background thread or execute it repeatedly. Furthermore, a block of code can be stopped after an allowed maximum duration, after a certain time interval, etc.

Let's write a Consumer wrapper that logs the execution time of another consumer.

```java
class Consumers {
  public static <T> Consumer<T> executionTimeLogger( Consumer<T> block ) {
    return t -> {
      long start = System.nanoTime();
      block.accept( t );
      long duration = System.nanoTime() - start;
      System.getLogger( "executionTime" ).log(
          System.Logger.Level.INFO, "Execution time (ns): {0}", duration );
    };
  }
}
```

Listing 13.10 src/main/java/com/tutego/insel/lambda/Consumers.java (Snippet)

The following call shows the usage of this method:

```java
Arrays.asList( 1, 2, 3, 4 )
      .forEach( executionTimeLogger( System.out::println ) );
```

The result is the following output:

```
1
Jan. 23, 2023 12:16:31 PM c.t.i.l.Consumers lambda$executionTimeLogger$0
INFO: Execution time (ns): 87.800
Jan. 23, 2023 12:16:31 PM c.t.i.l.Consumers lambda$executionTimeLogger$0
INFO: Execution time (ns): 25.100
Jan. 23, 2023 12:16:31 PM c.t.i.l.Consumers lambda$executionTimeLogger$0
INFO: Execution time (ns): 18.100
Jan. 23, 2023 12:16:31 PM c.t.i.l.Consumers lambda$executionTimeLogger$0
INFO: Execution time (ns): 13.200
2
3
4
```

What we've implemented is an example of the *execute-around-method pattern*, where you put something else around a block of code.

13.5.2 Supplier

A *supplier* (also called *provider*) is a factory and provides objects. In Java, the java.util.function package declares the Supplier functional interface for object providers:

```
interface java.util.function.Supplier<T>
```

▶ T get()
  Performs operations with the transfer t.

Supplier doesn't declare any other static or default methods. What's exactly returned by get() is a task of the implementation. The result might be new objects, the same objects always (singletons), or objects from a cache.

13.5.3 Predicates and java.util.function.Predicate

A predicate is a statement about an object that is true or false. The question "tutego".isEmpty() asks whether the string "tutego" is empty or not. While the result is "false", isEmpty is therefore a predicate because it can make a truth statement about an object (a string in our case).

Predicates as objects are flexible because objects can be passed to different places. Thus, a predicate can determine what should be deleted from a collection or whether at least one element is in a collection.

The java.util.function package[7] declares a flexible Predicate functional interface in the following way:

```
interface java.util.function.Predicate<T>
```

▶ boolean test(T t)
Performs a test on t and returns true if the criterion is met; otherwise, false.

[Ex]

Example

In the following example, the test of whether a character is a digit can now be performed differently by predicate objects:

```
Predicate<Character> isDigit =
   c -> Character.isDigit( c );  // short: Character::isDigit
System.out.println( isDigit.test('a') );  // false
```

If the Predicate interface had existed earlier in Java 1.0, no need would exist for the Character.isDigit(...) method. A Predicate<Character> could be used as a static variable in the Character class, so that a test would then be written as Character.IS_DIGIT.test(...) or as a return from a Predicate<Character> isDigit() method using Character.isDigit().test(...). In the future, the API may change so that statements on objects with truth returns will no longer be realized as methods with the classes (but instead will be offered as predicate objects). Fortunately, however, method references give you the flexibility to easily use existing methods as lambda expressions, and so we can return from methods to functions.

The Predicate Type in the Application Programming Interface

A few places in the Java API where Predicate objects are used include the following:

- As an argument for delete methods, to specify elements in collections that should be deleted or filtered
- In the default methods of the Predicate interface itself to link predicates
- In regular expressions, on a Pattern (asPredicate() and asMatchPredicate() return a Predicate for tests)
- In the Stream API, where objects are identified via a predicate as they pass through the stream, for example, to filter them out

[Ex]

Example

The following example deletes all characters that are digits from a list of arbitrary characters:

---

7 Be careful in these cases because javax.sql.rowset also has a Predicate interface.

```
Predicate<Character> isDigit = Character::isDigit;
List<Character> list = new ArrayList<>( Arrays.asList( 'a', '1' ) );
list.removeIf( isDigit );
```

In this way, the focus is not on the loop, but on the deletion.

Default Methods of Predicate

A number of default methods are provided by the Predicate functional interface:

```
interface java.util.function.Predicate<T>
```

▶ default Predicate<T> negate()
Returns a negation of the current predicate (implemented as return t -> ! test(t);).

▶ static <T> Predicate<T> not(Predicate<? super T> target)
Returns target.negate().

▶ default Predicate<T> and(Predicate<? super T> p)

▶ default Predicate<T> or(Predicate<? super T> p)
Links the current predicate to another predicate with a logical AND/OR.

▶ static <T> Predicate<T> isEqual(Object targetRef)
Returns a new predicate that performs an equivalence test with targetRef, basically
return ref -> Objects.equals(ref, targetRef).

Example

The following example deletes characters that are *not* digits from a list of characters:

```
Predicate<Character> isDigit = Character::isDigit;
Predicate<Character> isNotDigit = isDigit.negate();
List<Character> list = new ArrayList<>( Arrays.asList( 'a', '1' ) );
list.removeIf( isNotDigit );
// alternatively: list.removeIf( Predicate.not( isDigit ) );
```

13.5.4   Functions via the Functional Interface java.util.function.Function

Functions in the sense of functional programming can be of different types: with
parameter lists/returns or without. But functions are basically special forms, and the
functional interface java.util.function.Function is the most general function that
returns a result for an argument.

```
interface java.util.function.Function<T,R>
```

▶ R apply(T t)

Applies a function and provides a return to the input t.

Example

The following example is a function to determine the absolute value:

```
Function<Double,Double> abs = a -> Math.abs( a );   // alternativ Math::abs
System.out.println( abs.apply( -12. ) );            // 12.0
```

For functions, too, an area of tension arises for the API design. Basically, "functions" now no longer need to be provided as methods at all; classes could also offer them as Function objects. But since method references easily bridge from method names to objects, developers can work quite well with classic methods.

The Function Type in the Application Programming Interface

The Stream API is the biggest beneficiary of the Function type. A few examples exist in object comparisons (Comparator), in the concurrency package, and in associative memories. In the Stream API section, we'll explore many more examples.

Example

An associative memory is supposed to be implemented as a cache, which associates the content to file names. If no content for the key (the file name) exists yet, the file content should be read and put into the associative memory. Consider the following example:

```
class FileCache {
  private final Map<String,byte[]> map = new HashMap<>();
  public byte[] getContent( String filename ) {
    return map.computeIfAbsent( filename, file -> {
      try {
        return Files.readAllBytes( Paths.get( file ) );
      } catch ( IOException e ) { throw new UncheckedIOException( e ); }
    } );
  }
}
```

Listing 13.11 src/main/java/com/tutego/insel/lambda/FileCache.java (Snippet)

We'll return to this method in Chapter 18, Section 18.3; we just wanted to show you passing functions to other functions—in this case, a Function<String,byte[]) to computeIfAbsent(...). As soon as the getContent(String) call addresses the file cache, the method will ask the Map for a value, and if it has no value for the key, the lambda expression will return the content for the file name.

Getter Methods as Functions via Method References

Method references are among the most syntactically concise tools in the Java language. In combination with getters, a pattern can be read that's often seen in code. First, let's review Function and its use in method references, with the following example:

```
Function<String,String> func1a = (String s) -> s.toUpperCase();
Function<String,String> func1b = String::toUpperCase;
Function<Point,Double>  func2a = (Point p) -> p.getX();
Function<Point,Double>  func2b = Point::getX;
System.out.println( func1b.apply( "jocelyn" ) );         // JOCELYN
System.out.println( func2b.apply( new Point( 9, 0 ) ) ); // 9.0
```

The fact that Function matches the given method reference is incomprehensible at first glance since the signatures of toUpperCase() and getX() don't declare a parameter. Thus, these methods aren't functions in the usual sense (into which something goes and out of which something comes). However, we're dealing with a special case because the methods mentioned in the method reference fulfill the following prerequisites:

- The methods are non-static (i.e., Math::max).

- No reference is being used (i.e., System.out::print).

In this case, however, the compiler will call an object method on exactly the object passed as the first argument of the functional interface. (Please read this sentence twice!)

Thus, Function is a practical type in all scenarios in which states are somehow queried via getters, as is often the case with a Comparator, for example. In this scenario, a static method is quite useful, for instance, Comparator<...> Comparator.comparing(Function<...> keyExtractor. (Note that generics are omitted.)

> **Example** [Ex]
>
> The following example gets a list of packages accessible from the class loader and sorts them by name:
>
> ```
> List<Package> list = Arrays.asList( Package.getPackages() );
> Collections.sort( list, Comparator.comparing( Package::getName ) );
> System.out.println( list ); // [package java.io, … sun.util.locale …
> ```

Default Methods in Function

The functional interface prescribes only one apply(...) method but declares three additional default methods:

```
interface java.util.function.Function<T,R>
```

▶ static <T> Function<T,T> identity()

Returns a function that always returns the input as a result, implemented as return t -> t;.

▶ default <V> Function<T,V> andThen(Function<? super R,? extends V> after)

Corresponds to t -> after.apply(apply(t)).

▶ default <V> Function<V,R> compose(Function<? super V,? extends T> before)

Corresponds to v -> apply(before.apply(v)).

identity() seems pointless at first glance but serves a purpose if a Function is required in the API where nothing should change and the input should be the output.

The andThen(...) and compose(...) methods differ in the order in which the functions are called. The good thing is that the parameter names (before, after) make it clear what is called here and in what order.

[Ex]

Example

```
Function<String, String> f1 = s -> "~" + s + "~";
Function<String, String> f2 = s -> "<" + s + ">";
System.out.println( f1.andThen( f2 ).apply( ":)" ) ); // <~:)~>
System.out.println( f2.andThen( f1 ).apply( ":)" ) ); // ~<:)>~
System.out.println( f1.compose( f2 ).apply( ":)" ) ); // ~<:)>~
System.out.println( f2.compose( f1 ).apply( ":)" ) ); // <~:)~>
```

Function versus Consumer/Predicate

Basically, everything can be represented as a Function because of the following:

- A Consumer<T> can also be understood as Function<T,Void> (something goes in, but nothing comes out).
- A Predicate<T> can also be understood as Function<T,Boolean>.
- A Supplier<T> can also be understood as Function<Void,T>.

Nevertheless, these special types serve their purpose because the more accurate the type, the better.

Function is not a base type of Consumer or Supplier because "no return" or "no parameter" can't be expressed by a generic type, which would be possible with Function<T,R>.

UnaryOperator

Another interface in the java.util.function package specializes Function, namely, the UnaryOperator. A UnaryOperator is a special Function where the types for "input" and "output" are the same.

```
interface java.util.function.UnaryOperator<T>
extends Function<T,T>
```

▶ static <T> UnaryOperator<T> identity()
Returns the identity operator that maps all inputs to outputs.

Generic types make it clear that the type of the method parameter is the same as the result type. Except for identity(), no other functionality exists; the interface is used only for type declaration.

In some places in the Java library, this type also occurs, for example, in the replaceAll(UnaryOperator) method of List types.

Example

The following example doubles each entry in a list:

```
List<Integer> list = Arrays.asList( 1, 2, 3 );
list.replaceAll( e -> e * 2 );
System.out.println( list );  // [2, 4, 6]
```

13.5.5   I Take Two

"Bi" is a well-known Latin prefix for "two," which when applied to types from the java.util.function package means that two arguments can be passed instead of only one argument.

Type	Interface	Operation
Consumer	Consumer<T>	void accept(T t)
BiConsumer<T,U>	void accept(T t, U u)	
Function	Function<T,R>	R apply(T t)
BiFunction<T,U,R>	R apply(T t, U u)	
Predicate	Predicate<T>	boolean test(T t)
BiPredicate<T,U>	boolean test(T t, U u)	

Table 13.12 One- and Two-Argument Methods in Comparison

The "bi" types have no type relationship with non-"bi" types.

BiConsumer

The BiConsumer declares the accept(T, U) method with two parameters, each of which can carry different types. The main use of the type in the Java standard library is associative memories that pass keys and values to accept(...). For example, Map declares the following method:

```
interface java.util.Map<K,V>
```

▶ default void forEach(BiConsumer<? super K,? super V> action)
Runs through the associative memory and calls the accept(...) method from the passed BiConsumer on each key-value pair.

[Ex]
Example

The following example results in an output of temperatures of various cities:

```
Map<String,Integer> map = Map.of( "Manila", 25, "Dortmund", -5 );
map.forEach( (k, v) -> System.out.printf( "%d°C in %s%n", v, k ) );
```

A BiConsumer has a default method named andThen(...), just as the Consumer declares it for chaining.

```
interface java.util.function.BiConsumer<T,U>
```

▶ default BiConsumer<T,U> andThen(BiConsumer<? super T,? super U> after)
Links the current BiConsumer to after to form a new BiConsumer.

BiFunction and BinaryOperator

A BiFunction is a function with two arguments, while a regular Function accepts only one argument.

[Ex]
Example

The following example illustrates the use of Function and BiFunction with method references:

```
Function<Double,Double> sign = Math::abs;
BiFunction<Double,Double,Double> max = Math::max;
```

The Java library uses Function much more often than BiFunction. The most common use is in the standard library around associative memories, where a key and a value are passed to a BiFunction.

[Ex]
Example

The following example converts all associated values of a HashMap to uppercase:

```
Map<String,String> twitterNames = new HashMap<>();
twitterNames.put( "elonmusk", "Elon Musk" );
twitterNames.put( "jimmyfallon", "Jimmy Fallon" );
BiFunction<String, String, String> uppercaser = (k, v) -> v.toUpperCase();
twitterNames.replaceAll( uppercaser );
System.out.println( twitterNames );  // {elonmusk=ELON MUSK, …}
```

If the type is the same for a Function, the Java API provides the more special type UnaryOperator for these cases. If all three types of a BiFunction are the same, BinaryOperator can be used for comparison, in the following ways:

- interface UnaryOperator<T> extends Function<T,T>
- interface BinaryOperator<T> extends BiFunction<T,T,T>

13

Example

The following example illustrates the use of BiFunction and BinaryOperator:

```
BiFunction<Double,Double,Double> max1 = Math::max;
BinaryOperator<Double>               max2 = Math::max;
```

BinaryOperator plays a major role in what's called *reductions*, for example, when two values become one, as in Math.max(...). We'll return to this topic when we discuss the Stream API.

The BiFunction interface declares exactly one default method:

```
interface java.util.function.BiFunction<T,U,R>
extends Function<T,T>
```

▶ default <V> BiFunction<T,U,V> andThen(Function<? super R,? extends V> after)

BinaryOperator, on the other hand, has two static methods:

```
public interface java.util.function.BinaryOperator<T>
extends BiFunction<T,T,T>
```

▶ static <T> BinaryOperator<T> maxBy(Comparator<? super T> comparator)
▶ static <T> BinaryOperator<T> minBy(Comparator<? super T> comparator)
  Returns a BinaryOperator that returns the maximum/minimum with respect to a given comparator.

BiPredicate

A BiPredicate tests two arguments and condenses them to a truth value. Like Predicate, BiPredicate also declares three default methods and(...), or(...) and negate(...), although of course BiPredicate lacks a static isEqual(...) method like Predicate. For BiPredicate there's only one use in the Java standard library in a method for finding files. The use is rare, and besides, a predicate is always a function with boolean return, so that there's actually no compelling need for this interface.

[Ex]

Example

By the way, with Bi* and two arguments the specialization stop; no types like Tri*, Quad*, etc. exist. These types aren't necessary in practice because, on one hand, a reduction can often take place—for example, max(1, 2, 3) is equal to max(1, max(2, 3)). On the other hand, the parameter type can be a collection, as in Function<List<Integer>,Integer> max.

13.5.6 Functional Interfaces with Primitives

The functional interfaces presented so far are quite flexible due to the generic type parameters, but what is missing are signatures with primitives—Java has a "problem" in that generics only work with reference types, but not with primitive types. For this reason, four versions exist of almost all interfaces in the java.util.function package: a generic one for arbitrary references and then versions for the types int, long, and double. The designers of the API left wrapper types and support for certain primitive types out for performance reasons, so as to avoid boxing.

Table 13.13 provides an overview of functional interfaces, all of which have no inheritance relationships to other interfaces.

Functional Interface	Function Descriptor
*Supplier	
BooleanSupplier	boolean getAsBoolean()
IntSupplier	int getAsInt()
LongSupplier	long getAsLong()
DoubleSupplier	double getAsDouble()
*Consumer	
IntConsumer	void accept(int value)
LongConsumer	void accept(long value)

Table 13.13 Special Functional Interfaces for Primitive Values

Functional Interface	Function Descriptor
DoubleConsumer	void accept(double value)
ObjIntConsumer<T>	void accept(T t, int value)
ObjLongConsumer<T>	void accept(T t, long value)
ObjDoubleConsumer<T>	void accept(T t, double value)
*Predicate	
IntPredicate	boolean test(int value)
LongPredicate	boolean test(long value)
DoublePredicate	boolean test(double value)
*Function	
DoubleToIntFunction	int applyAsInt(double value)
IntToDoubleFunction	double applyAsDouble(int value)
LongToIntFunction	int applyAsInt(long value)
IntToLongFunction	long applyAsLong(int value)
DoubleToLongFunction	long applyAsLong(double value)
LongToDoubleFunction	double applyAsDouble(long value)
IntFunction<R>	R apply(int value)
LongFunction<R>	R apply(long value)
DoubleFunction<R>	R apply(double value)
ToIntFunction<T>	int applyAsInt(T t)
ToLongFunction<T>	long applyAsLong(T t)
ToDoubleFunction<T>	double applyAsDouble(T t)
ToIntBiFunction<T,U>	int applyAsInt(T t, U u)
ToLongBiFunction<T,U>	long applyAsLong(T t, U u)
ToDoubleBiFunction<T,U>	double applyAsDouble(T t, U u)
*Operator	
IntUnaryOperator	int applyAsInt(int operand)
LongUnaryOperator	long applyAsLong(long operand)

Table 13.13 Special Functional Interfaces for Primitive Values (Cont.)

13

Functional Interface	Function Descriptor
DoubleUnaryOperator	double applyAsDouble(double operand)
IntBinaryOperator	int applyAsInt(int left, int right)
LongBinaryOperator	long applyAsLong(long left, long right)
DoubleBinaryOperator	double applyAsDouble(double left, double right)

Table 13.13 Special Functional Interfaces for Primitive Values (Cont.)

Static and Default Methods

Some generically declared functional interface types have default methods or static methods, and similar methods can be found in the primitive functional interfaces:

- The *Consumer interfaces declare default *Consumer andThen(*Consumer after), but not the Obj*Consumer type, which don't have default methods; the * is a abbreviation for the prefix Int, Long and Double.
- The *Predicate interfaces declare the following methods:
  - default *Predicate negate()
  - default *Predicate and(*Predicate other)
  - default *Predicate or(*Predicate other)
- Each *UnaryOperator declares the following methods:
  - default *UnaryOperator andThen(*UnaryOperator after)
  - default *UnaryOperator compose(*UnaryOperator before)
  - static *UnaryOperator identity()
- BinaryOperator has two static methods, maxBy(...) and minBy(...), which don't exist in the primitive *BinaryOperator version because no Comparator is needed in primitive comparisons.
- The *Supplier interfaces don't declare static methods or default methods (just like Supplier).

13.6   Optional Is Not a Non-Starter

Java has one particular reference that can make a developer's hair stand on end and is a reason for long hours of debugging: the null reference. Actually, null merely says: "assigned, but not initialized." What makes null so problematic is the NullPointerException, which is thrown by referenced null expressions.

Example

[Ex]

Developers may forget to initialize the object variable `location` with an object, so `set-Location(...)` will fail, as shown in the following example:

```
class Place {
  private Point2D location;
  public void setLocation( double longitude, double latitude ) {
    location.setLocation( longitude, latitude );  // ☠ NullPointerException
  }
}
```

13.6.1 Using null

Errors of this type are relatively easy to detect through testing. But the real problem is that developers generally like to consider the typeless null[8] as a special magic value, and thus null can sometimes mean something else besides "not initialized." Consider the following points:

- If the API allows null in arguments for methods/constructors, null usually means "use a default value" or "if nothing given, then ignore."

- In method returns, null often stands for "nothing done" or "no return." In contrast, other methods in turn use the return null to encode that an operation was successfully performed and would otherwise return error objects, for example.[9]

Example 1

Let's look at the Javadoc documented method `getTask(out, fileManager, diagnosti-cListener, options, classes, compilationUnits)` in the `JavaCompiler` interface. This method is an example of several specific uses of null:

- `out` means "a writer for additional output from the compiler; use `system.err` *if null*."

- `fileManager` means "a file manager; *if null* use the compiler's standard file manager."

- `diagnosticListener` means "a diagnostic listener; *if null* use the compiler's default method for reporting diagnostics."

- `options` means "compiler options, **null** means no options."

- `classes` means "names of classes to be processed by annotation processing, **null** means no class names."

- `compilationUnits` means "the compilation units to compile, **null** means no compilation units."

---

8 Note that `null instanceof` *Type* is always `false`.

9 Fortunately, `null` is rarely used as an error identifier; those days are over. Exceptions are the better choice because errors are exceptions in the program.

All arguments can ultimately be null: for instance, getTask(null, null, null, null, null, null) is a correct call. The API isn't beautiful, and for such long parameter lists, a fine alternative is available, namely, the *builder pattern*. With this pattern, you could write new CompilationTask.Builder().out(...).fileManager(...).....build().

Example 2

The BufferedReader allows line-by-line reading from data sources, and readLine() returns null if no more lines need to be read.

Example 3

Much confusion about the API may exist in relation to the associative memory. An ordinary HashMap can get null as an associated value, but get(key) returns null even if no associated value exists. This scenario leads to an ambiguity since the return of get(...) doesn't reveal whether there's a mapping to null or whether the key doesn't exist. Consider the following example:

```
Map<Integer,String> map = new HashMap<>();
map.put( 0, null );
System.out.println( map.containsKey( 0 ) );       // true
System.out.println( map.containsValue( null ) ); // true
System.out.println( map.get( 0 ) );               // null
System.out.println( map.get( 1 ) );               // null
```

If the map can contain null values, there must always be a pair of the type if(map.containsKey(key)) followed by map.get(key). Ultimately, the best approach is for developers to do away with null in data structures.

Documenting null

To get null under control, several approaches are conceivable. First, you must consider whether you want to use null at all. If so, you should always document null as a potential return or valid parameter assignment in the API documentation. The only problem is not everyone reads the Javadoc. Thus, we'll need something more explicit. Annotations such as @Nullable and @NonNull, which aren't part of Java SE, can be added to the classpath and evaluated by static analysis tools like IntelliJ.

Of course, if null isn't permitted as a parameter, a method should perform a check and throw an exception. You can do this check explicitly via a test, for example, with if (param == null) throw new ... or indirectly via Objects.requireNonNull(param).

Alternatives to null

Since null has so many use cases and many programmers skip reading the Javadoc, you should consider alternatives to some uses of null. Sometimes, this substitution is easy, such as when the returns are collections. In this case, a good alternative to null is just an empty collection. This scenario is a special case of the *null object pattern*.

Errors that occur due to a `NullPointerException` could of course be completely avoided if you always properly tested for `null` references. But developers tend to forget `null` checks because they aren't aware or don't expect that a return can be `null`. What is required is a program construct that makes it explicit that such a value can't exist, so that `null` doesn't have to take on this role. If you can see in the code that a value is optional (i.e., can be present or not), the potential for errors would be reduced.

> **History**
>
> Tony Hoare is considered the "inventor" of the null reference. Today, he regrets it, calling the decision "my billion-dollar mistake."[10]

13.6.2 The Optional Type

The Java library provides a kind of container that may or may not contain an element. If the container contains an element, its value is never `null`. This container can be queried whether it contains an element or not. A `null` as identifier is therefore superfluous.

> **Example**
>
> Construction of various `Optional` objects and result of the methods:

```
Optional<String> opt1 = Optional.of( "Aitazaz Hassan Bangash" );
System.out.println( opt1.isPresent() );   // true
System.out.println( opt1.isEmpty() );     // false
System.out.println( opt1.get() );         // Aitazaz Hassan Bangash
Optional<String> opt2 = Optional.empty();
System.out.println( opt2.isPresent() );   // false
System.out.println( opt2.isEmpty() );     // true
// opt2.get() -> java.util.NoSuchElementException: No value present
Optional<String> opt3 = Optional.ofNullable( "Malala" );
System.out.println( opt3.isPresent() );   // true
System.out.println( opt3.isEmpty() );     // false
```

---

10 In Hoare's words: *"It was the invention of the null reference in 1965. At that time, I was designing the first comprehensive type system for references in an object oriented language (ALGOL W). My goal was to ensure that all use of references should be absolutely safe, with checking performed automatically by the compiler. But I couldn't resist the temptation to put in a null reference, simply because it was so easy to implement. This has led to innumerable errors, vulnerabilities, and system crashes, which have probably caused a billion dollars of pain and damage in the last forty years."* Further insights into his thinking are available at *https://www.infoq.com/presentations/Null-References-The-Billion-Dollar-Mistake-Tony-Hoare.*

```
System.out.println( opt3.get() );           // Malala
Optional<String> opt4 = Optional.ofNullable( null );
System.out.println( opt4.isPresent() );   // false
// opt4.get() -> java.util.NoSuchElementException: No value present
final class java.util.Optional<T>
```

▶ static <T> Optional<T> empty()
Returns an empty Optional object.

▶ boolean isPresent()
Returns true if this Optional object has a value, otherwise the return is false, as in the case of empty().

▶ boolean isEmpty()
Opposite of isPresent().

▶ static <T> Optional<T> of(T value)
Creates a new Optional object with a value that must not be null; otherwise, you'll get a NullPointerException, so getting null into the Optional object won't work.

▶ static <T> Optional<T> ofNullable(T value)
Returns an Optional object with the value if it's not null; if it is null, the return is Optional.empty().

▶ T get()
Returns the value. If the Optional object doesn't contain a value because it's isEmpty(), a NoSuchElementException will follow.

▶ T orElse(T other)
If a value is isPresent(), return the value; if it's isEmpty(), return other.

▶ Stream<T> stream()
Convert Optional to the Stream data type.

Furthermore, Optional overrides the equals(...), toString() and hashCode() methods and a few more methods that we'll explore later in this section.

[»]

Note

Using null internally, for example, has an advantage in that objects can be serialized. Optional does *not* implement Serializable, which is why object variables of type Optional aren't serializable. Thus, object variables of this type can't be transferred in the case of remote calls with Remote Method Invocation (RMI), for example. Also, mappings to XML or to databases are more cumbersome unless JavaBean properties are used instead of internal object variables.

Spouse or Not?

Optional is thus used to explicitly express in code whether a value is present or not. This rule is true on both sides: The creator must explicitly call of*(...), and the user must explicitly call isPresent(), isEmpty(), or get(). Both sides are aware that they're dealing with a value that's optional, that is, the value may or may not exist. Let's illustrate this concept in the following example, for a person who may have a spouse:

```
public class Person {
  private Person spouse;
  public void setSpouse( Person spouse ) {
    this.spouse = Objects.requireNonNull( spouse );
  }
  public void removeSpouse() {
    spouse = null;
  }
  public Optional<Person> getSpouse() {
    return Optional.ofNullable( spouse );
  }
}
```

Listing 13.12 src/main/java/com/tutego/insel/lang/Person.java (Snippet)

In this example, null is possible for the internal reference to the partner; however, this encoding isn't intended to reach the outside. For this reason, getSpouse() doesn't directly return the reference, but instead, Optional is used and expresses whether a person has a spouse or not. Also, with setSpouse(...), we can't accept null because null arguments should be avoided as much as possible. Optional isn't appropriate in this case because passing null would be an error. Additionally, of course, the Javadoc should document for setSpouse(...) that a null argument results in a NullPointerException. Therefore, Optional doesn't fit as a parameter type.

```
Person john = new Person();
System.out.println( john.getSpouse().isEmpty() );   // true
Person eve = new Person();
john.setSpouse( eve );
System.out.println( john.getSpouse().isPresent() ); // true
System.out.println( john.getSpouse().get() );       // com/.../Person
john.removeSpouse();
System.out.println( john.getSpouse().isEmpty() );   // true
```

Listing 13.13 src/main/java/com/tutego/insel/lang/OptionalDemo.java, main()

13.6.3   Starting Functional Interfaces with Optional

In addition to methods like of*(...) and isPresent() as well as isEmpty(), other methods are also based on functional interfaces:

```
final class java.lang.Optional<T>
```

▶ void ifPresent(Consumer<? super T> consumer)
If Optional represents a value, call the Consumer with that value; otherwise, do nothing.

▶ void ifPresentOrElse(Consumer<? super T> action, Runnable emptyAction)
If Optional represents a value, call the Consumer with that value; otherwise, execute emptyAction. Runnable must be used in this case as a type from java.lang because no interface in the java.util.function package lacks parameters and also doesn't return any values.

▶ Optional<T> filter(Predicate<? super T> predicate)
If Optional contains a value and the predicate Predicate is true on the value, the return is the own Optional (i.e., this); otherwise, the return is Optional.empty().

▶ <U> Optional<U> map(Function<? super T,? extends U> mapper)
If Optional represents a value, then apply the function and wrap the result (if the result isn't null) back into an Optional. If Optional is without value, then the return is Optional.empty(), which is also true if the function returns null.

▶ <U> Optional<U> flatMap(Function<? super T,Optional<U>> mapper)
Like map(...), except that the function returns Optional instead of a direct value. If the mapper function returns an empty Optional object, the result of flatMap(...) is also Optional.empty().

▶ Optional<T> or(Supplier<? extends Optional<? extends T>> supplier)
If Optional represents a value, return it. If Optional is empty, get the value from the other Optional.

▶ T orElseGet(Supplier<? extends T> other)
If Optional represents a value, return it; if Optional is empty, get the alternative value from the Supplier.

▶ <X extends Throwable> T orElseThrow(Supplier<? extends X> exceptionSupplier)
If Optional represents a value, return it; otherwise, use Supplier to fetch the exception object and trigger it.

▶ T orElseThrow()
Behaves like get().

[Ex]

Example

If Optional has no value, a NullPointerException should be thrown instead of the NoSuchElementException, as in the following example:

```
String s = optionalString.orElseThrow( NullPointerException::new );
```

Example of a NullPointerException-Safe Cascading of Calls with Optional

The two *map(...) methods are particularly interesting and enable an entirely new style of programming. Let's look at an example: The following two-liner outputs "MICROSOFT 6TO4 ADAPTER" (retrieved from my system) in the console:

```
String s = NetworkInterface.getByIndex( 2 ).getDisplayName().toUpperCase();
//                                          ^ null?           ^ null?
System.out.println( s );
```

However, the program code is far from ideal because `NetworkInterface.getByIn-dex(int)` can return `null` as can `getDisplayName()`. To get around this problem without a `NullPointerException`, you would write the following code:

```
NetworkInterface networkInterface = NetworkInterface.getByIndex( 2 );
if ( networkInterface != null ) {
  String displayName = networkInterface.getDisplayName();
  if ( displayName != null )
    System.out.println( displayName.toUpperCase() );
}
```

Not much is left of the elegance of our original two-liner. Let's integrate `Optional`, which would actually be a great return type for `getByIndex()` and `getDisplayName()`, in the following example:

```
Optional<NetworkInterface> networkInterface =
 Optional.ofNullable( NetworkInterface.getByIndex( 2 ) );
if ( networkInterface.isPresent() ) {
  Optional<String> name =
 Optional.ofNullable( networkInterface.get().getDisplayName() );
  if ( name.isPresent() )
    System.out.println( name.get().toUpperCase() );
}
```

With `Optional`, instead of `if`, you can take a lambda expression and place in `ifPresent(...)`, as in the following example:

```
Optional<NetworkInterface> networkInterface =
 Optional.ofNullable( NetworkInterface.getByIndex( 2 ) );
networkInterface.ifPresent( ni -> {
  Optional<String> displayName = Optional.ofNullable( ni.getDisplayName() );
  displayName.ifPresent( name -> {
    System.out.println( name.toUpperCase() );
  } );
} );
```

Now, if you remove the local variables `networkInterface` and `displayName`, you'll end up with the following code:

```
Optional.ofNullable( NetworkInterface.getByIndex( 2 ) ).ifPresent( ni -> {
  Optional.ofNullable( ni.getDisplayName() ).ifPresent( name -> {
    System.out.println( name.toUpperCase() );
  } );
} );
```

13

In terms of structure, this code is identical to the `if` query and can also be easily recognized by the indentation. Rewriting case distinctions with `Optional` and `ifPresent(...)` doesn't bring any advantage.

Thinking in terms of case distinctions doesn't help in this scenario either. Keep in mind that `NetworkInterface.getByIndex( 2 ).getDisplayName().toUpperCase()` is a chain of mappings. `NetworkInterface.getByIndex(int)` maps to `NetworkInterface`, `getDisplayName()` of `NetworkInterface` maps to `String`, and `toUpperCase()` maps from one `String` to another `String`. You can concatenate three mappings and thus express the following: If a mapping fails, then stop mapping. Here is where `Optional` and `map(...)` come into play. In code, you would write the following:

```
Optional<String> s = Optional.ofNullable( NetworkInterface.getByIndex( 2 ) )
                        .map( ni -> ni.getDisplayName() )
                        .map( name -> name.toUpperCase() );
s.ifPresent( System.out::println );
```

The `Optional` class helps us do two things: First, `map(...)` will map to an `Optional.empty()` when receiving a `null` reference, and second, concatenating empty `Optionals` isn't a problem. Nothing will happen—`Optional.empty().map(...)` does nothing, and the return is just an empty `Optional`. At the end of the chain, no `String` exists (as at the beginning of the example), but instead, we have `Optional<String>`.

Rewritten with method references and further shortened, the following code is both readable and safe from a `NullPointerException`:

```
Optional.ofNullable( NetworkInterface.getByIndex( 2 ) )
        .map( NetworkInterface::getDisplayName )
        .map( String::toUpperCase )
        .ifPresent( System.out::println );
```

This logic does away with external case distinctions and works only with optional mappings, and thus this code is a good example of functional programming.

13.6.4 Primitive-Optional with Special Optional* Classes

While references can be `null` and in this way indicate non-existence, this use isn't easy to apply to primitive data types. If a method returns a `boolean`, not much is left besides `true` and `false`, and an "unassigned" is then gladly wrapped again via a `boolean` and tested for `null`. Especially with integers you may encounter returns like -1,[11] as is the case in the following examples:

- If no more input is left for `InputStreams` read(...), -1 will be returned.

---

11 All constant declarations can be viewed at *http://docs.oracle.com/en/java/javase/17/docs/api/constant-values.html*.

- `indexOf(Object)` of `List` returns `-1` if the searched object isn't in the list and consequently no position can be referenced.
- With an unknown byte length of a MIDI file (type `MidiFileFormat`) the method `getByteLength()` has `-1` as return.

These magic values should be avoided, and therefore, the `Optional*` can be introduced.

As a generic type, `Optional` can encapsulate any type, and primitive values could be wrapped in wrappers. However, this approach isn't efficient, and so the Java library provides the special `Optional` types `OptionalInt`, `OptionalLong`, and `OptionalDouble` for the primitive types `int`, `long`, and `double`, respectively.

Let's explore the methods of the four `Optional*` classes, as listed in Table 13.14.

Optional<T>	OptionalInt	OptionalLong	OptionalDouble
static <T> Optional<T> empty()	static OptionalInt empty()	static OptionalLong empty()	static OptionalDouble empty()
T get()	int getAsInt()	long getAsLong()	double getAsDouble()
boolean isPresent() boolean isEmpty()			
static <T> Optional<T> of(T)	static OptionalInt of(int)	static OptionalLong of(long)	static OptionalDouble of(double)
static <T> Optional<T> ofNullable(T)	Not transferable		
T orElse(T)	int orElse(int)	long orElse(long)	double orElse (double)
Stream<T> stream()	IntStream stream()	LongStream stream()	DoubleStream stream()
boolean equals(Object)			
int hashCode()			
String toString()			
void ifPresent(Consumer<? super T>)	void ifPresent(IntConsumer)	void ifPresent(LongConsumer)	void ifPresent(DoubleConsumer)

Table 13.14 Comparison of Optional with the Primitive Optional* Classes. Parameter Variables Have Been Removed.

Optional<T>	OptionalInt	OptionalLong	OptionalDouble
Void ifPresentOrElse(Consumer<? super T>, Runnable)	void ifPresentOrElse(**IntConsumer**, Runnable)	void ifPresentOrElse(**LongConsumer**, Runnable)	void ifPresentOrElse(**DoubleConsumer**, Runnable)
T orElseGet(Supplier<? extends T>)	int orElseGet(**Int**Supplier)	long orElseGet(**LongSupplier**)	double orElseGet(**Double**Supplier)
<X extends Throwable> T orElseThrow(Supplier<? extends X>)	<X extends Throwable> **int** orElseThrow(Supplier<? extends X>)	<X extends Throwable> **long** orElseThrow(Supplier<? extends X>)	<X extends Throwable> **double** orElseThrow(Supplier<? extends X>)
Optional<T> filter(Predicate<? super T>)	Not available		
<U> Optional<U> flatMap(Function <? super T,Optional<U>>)			
<U> Optional<U> map(Function<? super T, ? extends U>)			

Table 13.14 Comparison of Optional with the Primitive Optional* Classes. Parameter Variables Have Been Removed. (Cont.)

The Optional method ofNullable(...) falls out in the primitive Optional classes. The optional types for the three primitive types have fewer methods overall, and Table 13.14 isn't quite complete.

[+]

> **Tip**
>
> The fact that the map*(...) methods are missing is impractical, but if transformations are desired, a stream can be requested with stream(), and the map*(...) methods can be called on the stream. The following example calculates the square root of an "optional number":
>
> ```
> OptionalDouble sqrt =
>   OptionalDouble.of( 16 ).stream().map( Math::sqrt ).findFirst();
> ```

> **Best Practice** [«]
>
> Optional* types are excellent as return types and are conceivable as parameter types, but they aren't attractive as internal object variables. Internally, null is an acceptable choice since this "type" is fast and saves memory. Optional is good for the outside world in the API but internally using null is ok.

13.7   What Is So Functional Now?

So far, much of this section has been spent introducing types from the java.util.function package, the functional interfaces developers can use to express mappings in Java. Now let's talk more generally about functional programming and its advantages.

13.7.1   Recyclability

First, functions provide an additional level of code reusability. Consider the following predicate:

```
Predicate<Path> exists = path -> Files.exists( path );
```

This exists predicate is relatively simple and also omits exception handling. But of course you could write something more complex. The point is that these predicates can be reused in all sorts of places, such as for filtering in lists or deleting items from lists. The predicate can be passed as a function or connected to new predicates, as in the following examples:

```
Predicate<Path> exists    = path -> Files.exists( path );
Predicate<Path> directory = path -> Files.isDirectory( path );
Predicate<Path> existsAndDirectory = exists.and( directory );
```

Methods like ifPresent(Predicate) or removeIf(Predicate) then take this predicate and perform operations. These small, mini-objects are easy to test, which minimizes errors in your code overall.

13.7.2   Stateless, Immutable

Functional programming is about getting by without external states. Pure functional programming languages are based on pure functions, and even in Java, not every method must change an external state. However, Java developers are accustomed to thinking in terms of states, which is not inherently wrong: A text document in memory is just as much an object graph as a graphical application with input fields. The goal of functional programming are operations on data structures and calculations that lack side effects.

Pure functions without states have several advantages, such as the following:

- Functions can be executed any number of times without changing system states.
- Functions can be executed in any order without the result becoming different.
- Functions are easier to test than extensive state changes.

These advantages are particularly appealing from the parallelization point of view because processors don't really get faster; we have more processor cores available. Pure functions allow libraries to distribute tasks across cores (such as searching and filtering) and parallelize these tasks. The less that state influences the game, the better because states require synchronization, which increases wait times.

Of course, a developer still must be careful because a lambda expression doesn't have to be pure and can have side effects. For this reason, you must know when a lambda expression may be concurrent and thus synchronization is needed.

[Ex]

Example

The Iterable interface declares a forEach(...) method, with a parameter of a functional interface type. In this case, a lambda expression is possible. However, a fundamental error would be for this lambda expression itself to interfere with the collection, as in the following case:

```
List<Integer> ints = new ArrayList<>( Arrays.asList( 1, 99, 2 ) );
ints.forEach( v -
> { System.out.println( ints + ", " + v); ints.set( v, 0 ); } );
```

The result is far from what was expected, which shows that lambda expressions can cause illegal side effects, as shown in the following output:

```
[1, 99, 2], 1
[1, 0, 2], 0
[0, 0, 2], 2
```

The avoidance of states, coupled with the *immutability* of values, can increase how easily a program can be comprehended since developers often have a hard time "replaying" the system in their minds with all the changes, especially if changes are happening concurrent. Our previous example illustrates this potential problem quite well. Understanding and debugging such systems is difficult. The fewer side effects, the easier a program is to understand. States make a program complex, not only in concurrent environments. If a method is pure, a developer only needs to understand the code of the method. If a method depends on the states of the object, a developer must understand the code of the entire class.

13.8   Further Reading

Programming functionally changes the design of Java programs fundamentally—away from methods with side effects to small functions that return objects with new states. The future will reveal novel patterns and best practices on how to develop in Java. Also, whether further concepts of functional programming will flow into Java and/or the JVM remain to be seen. So far, for example, immutability isn't a language construct but is guaranteed by the API if setters and write access to variables are absent. However, reflection can throw a wrench in the works as well. Approaches for upcoming Java versions in the area of *pattern matching* are presented by Brian Goetz at *https://www.youtube.com/watch?v=n3_8YcYKScw*. At *https://openjdk.java.net/jeps/406*, you'll find a project description, and in Java 17, pattern matching can even already be used with the --enable-preview switch. *Tail call optimization (TCO)* on the JVM side—something held dear in other functional programming languages—isn't currently implemented in the HotSpot JVM.

Java provides functional interfaces for the usual scenarios in the java.util.function package. But these interfaces may not be enough. For example, no available functional interface has three, four, five ... parameters. Some gaps are filled, for example, by *https://www.vavr.io*, which provides a new implementation of Optional in addition to immutable data structures and also provides a Try monad.

To delve even deeper into the functional programming mindset, we recommend developers look into pure functional programming languages like Haskell, where you must work without side effects. Somewhat easier for Java programmers is the ML language family, which also provides imperative elements such as while loops. For Java programmers, this mixing usually seems weird—the hip programming languages Scala or Kotlin combine OOP and functional programming almost perfectly. Java developers may benefit most from the functional approaches in the Stream API, which has already been briefly touched upon.

The implementation of lambda expressions was described only briefly in this chapter. Refer to *https://dzone.com/articles/hacking-lambda-expressions-in-java* for more details.

13

Chapter 14
Architecture, Design, and Applied Object Orientation

"One of the saddest things in life is that a man must do many good deeds to prove that he is capable, but need only commit one mistake to prove that he is no good."
—*George Bernard Shaw (1856–1950)*

While the examples from Chapter 2 through Chapter 13 essentially fit into a small `main(...)` method, in this chapter, you'll learn about a few best practices for decoupling types and mechanisms to distribute members among types.

Figure 14.1 Professional Architecture and SOLID Modeling Ensure Resilience

14.1 SOLID Modeling

If you want to write good object-oriented (OO) software, you should adhere to certain design principles. These best practices aren't mandatory, of course, but usually improve the design.

14.1.1   Three Rules

The first three rules are:

- **Don't Repeat Yourself (DRY)**
  Code duplication should be avoided, and duplicate code should be outsourced to methods. Furthermore, existing code—from your own libraries, from Java Platform, Standard Edition (Java SE) or open-source libraries—should be used.

- **Keep It Simple, Stupid (KISS)**
  More precisely, "keep it simple and foolproof." A problem should be solved in a simple and easy-to-understand way. For developers, this rule means you should write simple code, maybe only few lines of code, understandable at first sight.

- **You Ain't Gonna Need It (YAGNI)**
  This principle should remind you to write simple code and to program only what is expected to fulfill the requirement of the moment. YAGNI is central to *extreme programming (XP)* and the idea of "always implementing the simplest possible solution that works." Something may be programmed that never goes live later, which is a waste of time and money, but the code still needs to be documented, maintained, and tested.

14.1.2   SOLID

Michael Feathers used the acronym *SOLID* to capture five points that make a good OO design. The individual criteria themselves come from various authors.

S: Single Responsibility Principle

In somewhat flippant terms, this principle stands for "Do exactly one thing, but do it right." A type should have exactly one *responsibility*, so that, when changes are made, in the best case, only one place must be adjusted and not many places. The opposite is referred to as *God classes*, that is, classes that can do anything—an anti-pattern. Robert C. Martin, who describes the single responsibility principle in his book *Agile Software Development: Principles, Patterns, and Practices*, also says, "There should never be more than one reason to change a class." So what does this principle mean in practical terms?

Let's assume a person class stores a name, zip code, and age. Some requirements exist for zip codes and ages: In the US, a postal code consists only of digits and is 5 digits long. In general, an age is never a negative number and is limited and finite. However, these two validations are two different things, so a person class takes on responsibilities that in themselves have nothing to do with a person. Accordingly, the class will need to be adjusted in two places when the validation is changed; two reasons are more than one reason and consequently break the single responsibility principle.

If the modeling takes the single responsibility principle to an extreme, too many small types are created. This profusion of types doesn't help other code developers if responsibilities are no longer understandable due to this confusion.

O: Open–Closed Principle

Bertrand Meyer formulated in his 1988 book *Object-Oriented Software Construction* that modules must be both *open* (for extensions) and *closed* (for modifications). Where others use the term "module," Java developers should imagine a "type." A conventional class is closed to modification, especially with private states, but a subclass allows new states to be added without code changes to the superclass. Additionally, methods can be overridden to customize an implementation. However, a subclass must not give methods different semantics, which would otherwise break the object's cohesiveness.

L: Liskov Substitution Principle (LSP)

Barbara Liskov gave the 1987 lecture "Data Abstraction and Hierarchy" about the fact that replacing objects in programs with objects of a subtype should be possible without sacrificing correctness. Of course, for the replacement to work, the subtype must know what is "correct" so that methods do not realize an incorrect implementation that breaks the behavior. In other words, children must inherit and respect the behavior of their parents. This rule is not easy in Java because syntactic constructs such as preconditions, postconditions, and invariants don't exist; developers must therefore extract what is correct behavior purely from the Javadoc (i.e., the textual information).

I: Interface Segregation Principle

The interface segregation principle is attributed to Robert Cecil Martin when he worked on the printer system for Xerox. The central statement of this principle is "Many client-specific interfaces are better than one general interface." The *client* is the user of a Java type, and the term *interface* means the range of methods in general. In practical terms, some types have a lot of methods that thus make these types "general." If such objects are passed around, then the program places always get the entire object with all methods. However, the complete range of methods isn't always necessary, and sharing all the methods may even be dangerous. A better approach is to keep the application programming interface (API) small, allowing various entities only what is actually needed.

D: Dependency Inversion Principle

"Depend only on abstractions, not on specializations" is how Robert Cecil Martin put this principle.[1] This principle is best illustrated by a layered architecture: An upper layer

---

[1] The first version reads: "A. High-level modules shouldn't depend on low-level modules. Both should depend on abstractions. B. Abstractions shouldn't depend on details. Details should depend on abstractions."

draws on services from a deeper layer. However, the upper layer shouldn't cling to concrete types but instead should depend only on basic types, such as Java interfaces. In this context, the principle of *programming against interfaces* fits well.

The Big Picture

Like a Quentin Tarantino movie, everything is somehow connected in a grand design. However, design practices have focal points: The single responsibility principle takes on types and architecture at large. The open-closed principle is about types and their extensions. LSP is about inheritance and subtypes, and the interface segregation principle is about business logic and type dependencies.

14.1.3 Don't Be STUPID

Every "do" in SOLID is matched by a "don't" in *STUPID*. This acronym stands for the things you should avoid:

- **Singleton**
  A singleton is an object that can exist only once in the system. Such objects are always around, and they aren't bad in themselves. However, a problem arises when many developers write the singleton itself as a class, and then an implementation is quickly created that's difficult to test due to its global state. A better approach is to use frameworks that provide copies of objects for you to work with.

- **Tight coupling**
  The goal of good design is to reduce dependencies; the fewer modules/packages/types a piece of code draws on, the better. Specifically, the fewer `import` declarations are required, the better.

- **Untestability**
  If testing isn't thought through until after design and programming, it's often already too late—the result then is code that's difficult to test, especially if the coupling is too tight. A better approach is test-driven development (TDD), where testability affects the design. Designers and developers should consider in advance how a particular class and specific functionalities can be tested before moving on to intensive implementation.

- **Premature optimization**
  Developers think they have a sense of which parts of the program eat up performance and which parts are fast. But often they're wrong, wasting a lot of time optimizing the wrong spots. The best approach is to implement a simple solution according to KISS and then have a profiler—a software that measures the duration of code executions—show you exactly where rework is needed.

- **Undescriptive naming**
  Variable names like `one`, `z`, `l`, `myvariable`, `var1`, `val10`, `theInt`, `aDouble`, `_1bool`, and `button123` aren't particularly meaningful and must be avoided. A future reader of your code should immediately understand what a variable is about.

- **Duplications**

  Code copied exactly with minor changes must be avoided. Code duplicates can be found relatively well with the available tools and plugins for various integrated development environments (IDEs).

14.2 Architecture, Design, and Implementation

A long path must be traversed from customer's wish to the finished software. In between, you'll encounter requirements documents, test cases, the selection of an infrastructure, database choices, licensing issues, human vanity, and much, much more. Since this book focuses on software development, let's spend some time in the areas of architecture, design, and implementation.

The term *software architecture* isn't really straightforward, but it means the big picture (i.e., the fundamental decisions made in creating the software). Perhaps the best way to characterize architecture is as something that is costly and time-consuming to change once put in place. A well-known architecture pattern is the layer model, which divides software into several layers. The upper layer can only access services of the layer directly below it, but can't skip any layer, and the lower layer has no idea about higher layers.

In design, developers take care of mapping ideas to packages, classes, and interfaces. This process isn't unique, and so many options exist. Some options are bad because they affect readability, extensibility, or performance; others are better. But your choices always depend on context. Therefore, we'll look at some design patterns to help guide your choices in Section 14.3.

An implementation converts a design, perhaps codified in Unified Modeling Language (UML) models, into the source code of a programming language. The implementation combines a static model (i.e., which class inherits from which) and brings it together with the necessary dynamic behavior. Implementation issues might be discussed several times over, for example, when choosing the right data structure or realizing concurrency.

14.3 Design Patterns

In OO design, you've learned that classes should not be tightly coupled, but instead loosely coupled. This suggestion means classes shouldn't know too much about other classes, and interactions should be through well-defined interfaces so that classes can still be modified subsequently. Loose coupling has many advantages, including increasing reusability and making the program more change friendly.

Let's use an example to explain these features: Customer data must be stored in a data structure. For this data source, a graphical user interface (GUI), such as an input screen, displays and manages the data. When data is entered, deleted, and changed, these changes should be transferred to the data structure. (We'll describe the other way, from the data structure into the visualization, momentarily.) Although we already have a link between the input screen and the data structure, we must be careful not to get bogged down in the design because presumably the programming boils down to the two being tightly linked. Most likely, the GUI will somehow know about the data structure, and any change in the input screen will directly call methods of the concrete data structure, which is what we want to avoid. Moreover, we haven't considered what will happen if, as a result of further program versions, a graphical representation of the data is now drawn, for example, in the form of a bar chart. What happens if the content of the data structure is changed via another program location and then forces a rebuild of the screen display? In this scenario, we'll be caught in a tangle of method calls, and our program is no longer change-friendly. What happens if we now want to replace our homemade data structure with an SQL database?

14.3.1 Motivation for Design Patterns

Considerations about basic design criteria go way back. Prior to object-oriented programming (OOP), with structured programming, developers were happy to use various tools to build software more quickly and more easily. Assembler programmers were also happy to use structured programming to increase efficiency—after all, they only used subroutines because they could save a few bytes again. But after Assembler and structured programming, we've now arrived at object orientation, and no revolutionary programming paradigm has since emerged to replace object orientation. The software crisis has led to new concepts. Almost every development team realizes that OO isn't everything, but might be rather surprised after years of development work and say, "Uh-oh, it's all crap." As beautiful as OO can be, having 10,000 classes cavort in a class diagram is just as confusing as a Fortran program with 10,000 lines. Since good design was often sacrificed for a few milliseconds of runtime in the past, unsurprisingly, some programs are no longer readable. However, as illustrated by the typesetting program TeX (circa 1985), code lives longer than hardware, and the next generation of multi-core processors will soon be yearning for work in our desktop PCs.

Accordingly, a level above the individual classes and objects is missing because the objects themselves are not the problem, rather the coupling causes issues. The coupling is where rules that have become known as *design patterns* come in handy. These are tips from software designers who had noticed that many problems can be solved in a similar way. For this reason, they've established sets of rules with solution patterns that show an optimal reuse of components and ease of change. Design patterns run throughout the Java class library, and the best known are the observer, singleton, factory, and composite patterns.

14.3.2 Singleton

A *singleton* is a class of which there's only one instance in an application.[2] This limitation is useful for things that should only exist exactly once in an application, for instance, in the following examples:

- A graphical application has only one window.
- A console application has only one input/output stream each.
- All print jobs go into a printer maintenance queue.

Indisputably, unique objects must exist, but the way to achieve them is full of variation. Basically, a distinction can be made between the following two approaches:

- A framework takes care of the one-time construction of the object and then returns the object on request.
- You implement a singleton in Java code yourself.

The better solution is to use a framework, for instance, *CDI*, *Spring*, *Guice*, or *Jakarta EE* (formerly Java EE). But Java SE doesn't contain any of these frameworks, which is why we want to explicitly highlight them for demonstration.

The technical implementations are versatile; in Java, enumerations (enum) and normal classes are suitable for the implementation of singletons. In the following sections, we'll assume a scenario where an application wants to access configuration data centrally.

Singletons over Enumerations

A good way to use singletons are as enumerations—at first sight, an enumeration type doesn't seem to designed for singletons because an enumeration somehow implies more than one element. But the properties of enum are perfect for a singleton, and the library implements some tricks to also create the object only once if possible, such as when the enumeration is serialized over the wire and then deserialized and reconstructed. The idea is to provide exactly one element (often referred to as an INSTANCE) that will eventually become the only instance of the enumeration class, as well as the accompanying methods.

```java
public enum Configuration {
  INSTANCE;
  private final Properties props = new Properties( System.getProperties() );
  public String getVersion() {
    return "1.2";
  }
```

---

2 Only one instance per class loader, to put it a little more precisely.

```
  public String getUserDir() {
    return props.getProperty( "user.dir" );
  }
}
```

Listing 14.1 com/tutego/insel/pattern/singleton/Configuration.java, Configuration

In addition to the later public static INSTANCE variable, the Configuration type declares also an internal props variable, which can be used by the enumeration to store or request states there. We do this read only in the example via getUserDir().

A user accesses the enum members as usual in the following example:

```
System.out.println( Configuration.INSTANCE.getVersion() );  // 1.2
System.out.println( Configuration.INSTANCE.getUserDir() );  // C:\Users\...
```

Listing 14.2 com/tutego/insel/pattern/singleton/ConfigurationDemo.java, main()

14.3.3 Factory Methods

A *factory method* goes one step further than a singleton. This method doesn't generate exactly one instance but may generate several. However, the basic idea is that the user doesn't create a instance via a constructor, but generally via a static method. This approach has an advantage in that a static factory method can do the following things:

- Can return old objects from a cache
- Can move the creation process to subclasses
- Can return null

A constructor always creates an instance of its own class. A constructor can't return something like null because, with new, a new object is always created. Errors could only be displayed via an exception.

Many examples of factory methods exist in the Java library. A naming convention makes them easy to recognize: They're called getInstance() most of the time. A search in the API documentation reveals 90 such methods. Many of these methods are parameterized to specify exactly what objects the factory should produce. For example, let's consider some static factory methods of java.util.Calendar, such as the following:

- Calendar.getInstance()
- Calendar.getInstance(java.util.Locale)
- Calendar.getInstance(java.util.TimeZone)

The non-parameterized method returns a default Calendar object. However, Calendar is itself an abstract base class. Inside the getInstance(...) method, you'll find the following source code:

```
static Calendar getInstance() {
  …
  return new GregorianCalendar();
  …
}
```

Listing 14.3 java.util.Calender, getInstance()

In the body of the getInstance(…) factory method, the GregorianCalendar subclass is deliberately selected. This subclass extends Calendar and is possible because, by inheritance, the subclass GregorianCalendar is a Calendar. The caller of getInstance(…) doesn't see this precise type and receives a Calendar object as desired. This option enables getInstance(…) to test in which country the Java virtual machine (JVM) is running and, depending on that country, select the appropriate Calendar implementation.

14.3.4   Implementing the Observer Pattern with Listeners

Let's now explore the observer pattern. This pattern, with its origins in Smalltalk-80, is also known under the name *Model View Controller (MVC)*. Let's take a closer look at this pattern, which is an essential concept when programming GUIs with Swing.

Listeners allow for an implementation of the observer pattern. Event triggers send out special event objects, and interested parties log in and out of the triggers. The classes and interfaces involved follow a specific naming convention; * is used to represent an event name, such as Window, Click, etc.

Working with this pattern, you should keep in mind the following considerations:

- A class for the event objects is called *Event. The event objects can store information such as triggers, timestamps, and other data.

- The interested parties implement a Java interface called *Listener as a listener. You are free to choose any method name, but usually the *Event is passed to it. This interface can also prescribe multiple operations.

- The event trigger provides the add*Listener(*Listener) and remove*Listener(*Listener) methods to subscribe and unsubscribe interested parties. Whenever an event occurs, the trigger creates the event object *Event and informs each listener entered in the list about a call of the method from the listener.

An example will illustrate the types involved.

Radio Advertisements

Let's say a radio must broadcast AdEvent objects for advertising. The event objects will store the advertising slogan. Consider the following example:

```
package com.tutego.insel.pattern.listener;

import java.util.EventObject;

public class AdEvent extends EventObject {

  private final String slogan;

  public AdEvent( Object source, String slogan ) {
    super( source );
    this.slogan = slogan;
  }
  public String getSlogan() {
    return slogan;
  }
}
```

Listing 14.4 com/tutego/insel/pattern/listener/AdEvent.java

The AdEvent class extends the Java base class EventObject, a class that traditionally extends all event classes. The parameterized constructor of AdEvent takes the event trigger in the first parameter and passes it to the superclass constructor with super(source), which stores it and makes it available again with getSource(). The use of the base class isn't necessarily mandatory and has not been generically adapted over the years, so source is merely Object. The second parameter of the AdEvent constructor is our advertising.

The AdListener is the interface that interested parties implement, as shown in the following:

```
package com.tutego.insel.pattern.listener;

import java.util.EventListener;

interface AdListener extends EventListener {
  void advertisement( AdEvent e );
}
```

Listing 14.5 com/tutego/insel/pattern/listener/AdListener.java

Our AdListener implements the EventListener interface (a marker interface), which all Java listeners are supposed to implement. We'll specify only one advertisement(AdEvent) operation for concrete listeners. You must carefully consider whether the interface should carry @FunctionalInterface because, in the future, the event trigger might want to call another method to report something else, for example.

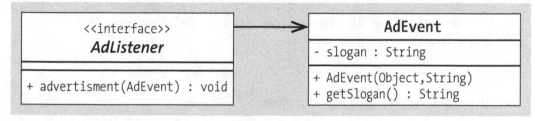

Figure 14.2 UML Class Diagram of AdListener Referencing AdEvent

The radio can now register and deregister interested parties and can send advertising messages via a timer. The exciting thing about this implementation is that the listeners aren't managed in their own data structure, but instead, a special listener class from the Swing package is used.

```java
package com.tutego.insel.pattern.listener;

import java.util.*;
import javax.swing.event.EventListenerList;

public class Radio {

  private final EventListenerList listeners = new EventListenerList();

  private final List<String> ads = List.of( "A Bite of Heaven.",
                                            "Bag the sweets and run.",
                                            "Chew on this, for a while.",
                                            "Taste the explosion." );

  public Radio() {
    new Timer().schedule( new TimerTask() {
      @Override public void run() {
        Collections.shuffle( ads );
        notifyAdvertisement( new AdEvent( this, ads.get(0) ) );
      }
    }, 0, 500 );
  }

  public void addAdListener( AdListener listener ) {
    listeners.add( AdListener.class, listener );
  }

  public void removeAdListener( AdListener listener ) {
    listeners.remove( AdListener.class, listener );
  }
```

```
protected synchronized void notifyAdvertisement( AdEvent event ) {
  for ( AdListener l : listeners.getListeners( AdListener.class ) )
    l.advertisement( event );
  }
}
```

Listing 14.6 com/tutego/insel/pattern/listener/Radio.java

This demo application uses the Radio object and implements a concrete listener, once via an inner anonymous class and once via a lambda expression.

```
Radio r = new Radio();
class ComplainingAdListener implements AdListener {
  @Override public void advertisement( AdEvent e ) {
    System.out.println( "Oh no, advertising again: " + e.getSlogan() );
  }
}
r.addAdListener( new ComplainingAdListener() );
r.addAdListener( e -> System.out.println( "I hear nothing" ) );
```

Listing 14.7 com/tutego/insel/pattern/listener/RadioDemo.java, main()

The Java API documentation contains some generic types:

```
class javax.swing.event.EventListenerList
```

▶ EventListenerList()
  Creates a container for listeners.
▶ <T extends EventListener> void add(Class<T> t, T l)
  Adds a listener l of type T.
▶ Object[] getListenerList()
  Returns an array of all listeners.
▶ <T extends EventListener> T[] getListeners(Class<T> t)
  Returns an array of all listeners of type t.
▶ int getListenerCount()
  Specifies the number of all listeners.
▶ int getListenerCount(Class<?> t)
  Specifies the number of listeners of type t.
▶ <T extends EventListener> void remove(Class<T> t, T l)
  Removes the listener l from the list.

14.4   Further Reading

Many developers focus only on the programming language and APIs and less on architecture and design. We recommend studying books and other literature focused on application design. Of particular note in this context is *Design Patterns. Elements of Reusable Object-Oriented Software* by Gamma, Helm, Johnson, and Vlissides (Addison-Wesley Professional, 1994).

14

Chapter 15
Java Platform Module System

"The whole is greater than the sum of its parts."
—*Aristotle (384–322 B.C.)*

After looking at the interaction of classes, in this chapter, you'll see how individual types or associations can be reused easily by other programs. We'll explore this topic with individual components and with a collection of classes that are bundled up into archives.

15.1 Class Loader and Module/Classpath

A *class loader* is responsible for loading the binary representation of a class from a background memory or main memory. From the data source (generally, the *.class* file), the class loader returns a byte array containing the information that's used in the second step to bring the class into the runtime system; this process is referred to as *linking*. Some class loaders are predefined, but you can write your own class loaders, for example, to get encrypted class files from a network or to load compressed *.class* files stored in databases.

15.1.1 Loading Classes per Request

To begin, let's consider a simple program with three classes:

```
package com.tutego.insel.tool;

public class HambachForest {
  public static void main( String[] args ) {
    boolean rweWantsToCutTrees = false;
    Forest hambachForest = new Forest();
    if ( rweWantsToCutTrees ) {
      Protest<Forest> p1 = new Protest<>();
      p1.believeIn = hambachForest;
    }
  }
}
```

```
class Forest { }

class Protest<T> {
  static java.awt.Rectangle MIN_BOUNDARY;
  T believeIn;
  java.time.LocalDate since;
}
```

When the runtime environment starts the HambachForest program, it must load a number of classes. This loading of classes is performed dynamically at runtime. What's immediately clear is that at least HambachForest must be loaded. And since the Java virtual machine (JVM) calls the static main(String[]) method and passes options, String must also be loaded. Invisibly, other referenced classes exist behind String. For example, Object is loaded because implicit in the class declaration of HambachForest is class HambachForest extends Object. Internally, the types entail many other types. String implements Serializable, CharSequence, and Comparable, so these three interfaces must also be loaded. Depending on which program paths are run, the program continues. However, you must understand that these class files are loaded as late in the process as possible.

Figure 15.1 Work When Loading Types: Loading the Guitarist Requires Loading the Amplifier, Etc.

15.1.2 Watching the Class Loader at Work

In our example, the runtime environment loads the classes independently (called *implicit class loading*). Classes can also be loaded by name using Class.forName(String), which is called *explicit class loading*.

To see which classes are loaded at all, the JVM can be given a switch at the start of the runtime environment: -verbose:class. Then, when running, the machine outputs all the types it loads. Continuing with our example, with the switch activated, the output is about 450 lines long. The following is an excerpt:

```
java -verbose:class com.tutego.insel.tool.HambachForest
[0.008s][info][class,load] java.lang.Object source: shared objects file
[0.008s][info][class,load] java.io.Serializable source: shared objects file
[0.008s][info][class,load] java.lang.Comparable source: shared objects file
[0.009s][info][class,load] java.lang.CharSequence source: shared objects file
[0.009s][info][
class,load] java.lang.constant.Constable source: shared objects file
...
[0.034s][info][class,load] sun.security.util.Debug source: shared objects file
[0.034s][info][class,load] com.tutego.insel.tool.HambachForest source: file:/C:/
.../target/classes/
[0.035s][info][
class,load] java.lang.PublicMethods$MethodList source: shared objects file
[0.035s][info][
class,load] java.lang.PublicMethods$Key source: shared objects file
[0.035s][info][class,load] java.lang.Void source: shared objects file
[0.035s][info][class,load] com.tutego.insel.tool.Forest source: file:/C:/.../
target/classes/
[0.035s][info][class,load] java.lang.Shutdown source: shared objects file
[0.035s][info][class,load] java.lang.Shutdown$Lock source: shared objects file
```

Notice that the Protest class doesn't get loaded. If we change the rweWantsToCutTrees variable to true, our Protest class will be loaded, and only one line will be added in the output! This scenario is surprising at first glance because the class references Rectangle and LocalDate. But both types aren't needed, so they aren't loaded. The class loader only obtains classes when they are needed for the program flow, not by the mere declaration as class/object variables. If we initialize LocalDate with, for example, LocalDate.now(), an impressive 200 class files will be added.

15.1.3   JMOD Files and JAR Files

The class loader obtains *.class* files not only from directories, but usually from containers. Thus, no directories need to be exchanged, only individual files. Container formats include JMOD (newly introduced in Java 9) and *Java Archive files (JAR files)*. When Java software is delivered, JAR or JMOD files are a good choice because these files are easier to use and save more space by passing along a compressed archive rather than a large file tree.

JAR Files

Collections of Java class files and resources are usually grouped into *JAR files*. These files are basically regular ZIP archives with a special directory named *META-INF* (for meta-files). The JDK comes with the *jar* tool in the *bin* directory for creating and extracting JAR files. In Chapter 23, Section 23.5, we'll return to this tool.

JAR files are treated by the runtime environment like directories of class files and resources. In addition, JAR files have an advantage in that they can be signed, and illegal changes are conspicuous. JAR files can contain module information, in which case they're called *modular JAR files.*

JMOD Files

The JMOD format is specifically for modules, and this format organizes types and resources. For reading and packing, you can use the *jmod* tool in the *bin* directory of the JDK.

JAR versus JMOD

Modules can be packed into JMOD and JAR containers. If a JAR isn't a modular JAR (i.e., it doesn't contain module information), some key information such as dependencies or a version will be missing. A JMOD is always a named module.

JMOD files aren't as flexible as JAR files because they can only be used at translation time and to link a runtime image. JMOD files can't be used at runtime like JAR files. The file format is proprietary.[1] The only advantage of JMOD is that native libraries can be integrated in a standardized way.

15.1.4   Where the Classes Come from: Search Locations and Special Class Loaders

In Java, a cascade of different class loaders is responsible for loading classes. In general, several class loaders work together in a chain in the following ways:

- First is the class loader for all "core" classes, the *Bootstrap class loader.* It loads central types like `Object` and `String` from the runtime library. If it doesn't find a desired class, the request continues.

- The *platform class loader* loads other classes from the distribution that aren't part of Java Platform, Standard Edition (Java SE).

- *Application class loader* (also *system class loader*): If a class wasn't found even by the platform class loader, the search follows via the user-defined class or module path.

For security reasons, the class loader always starts with the Bootstrap class loader for a new class and then passes on the request if it couldn't load the class itself. For this purpose, the class loaders are connected to each other. Each class loader has a parent class loader for this purpose. First, the parent may try to load the classes. If it can't, the work is passed on to the underlying class loader.

After the last class loader, you can install your own custom class loader. This custom class loader will also have a parent, usually embodied by the application class loader.

---

1 According to *http://openjdk.java.net/jeps/261*, a JAR file is a ZIP file.

Querying the Classpath

At runtime, the normal classpath is in the system property `java.class.path`. For example, if you output this property with `System.out.println(System.getProperty ("java.class.path"))`, a slightly shortened path will be output, as in the following example using a project in the author's file system:

`C:\Users\Christian\workspace\programs-on-the-island\target\`**test-classes**`;C:\Users\ Christian\workspace\programs-on-the-island\target\`**classes**`;C:\Users\Christian\.m2\ repository\org\apache\commons\commons-csv\1.5\`**commons-csv-1.5.jar**`;C:\Users\ Christian\.m2\repository\javax\xml\bind\jaxb-api\2.3.0\`**jaxb-api-2.3.0.jar**`;…`

The Maven directories *test-classes* and *classes* can be read, as well as the JAR data from the local Maven repository. The entries are separated by semicolons.

> **Note** [«]
>
> If the JVM is called via `java -jar`, the JVM only pays attention to the classes named in the JAR and ignores the classpath.

15

15.1.5   Setting the Search Path

Where to find the classes must be communicated to the JVM, and this practice is elementary for the delivery, which is also referred to as *deployment*. Java doesn't load classes until they are needed. For example, some program sequences are designed only for special conditions, and if a new type that isn't present is referenced late, this error will be noticed too late. Consequently, not only the sources for classes and resources of the application must be communicated to the compiler, but all types referenced by the program from, for example, open-source and commercial libraries.

If files must be retrieved from a directory or an external module in a Java project, the usual way is to specify these files in the search path. This specification is necessary for all JDK tools—most of the time, this specification occurs with the compiler and the runtime environment.

In Java, we can distinguish between a classpath and a module path.[2] The classpath is easy to set, but the module path is different.

Setting the Class/Module Path

You can include directories and JAR files in the classpath two ways:

- Via a switch
- Via an environment variable

---

2 Prior to Java 9, only JAR files and directories could be referenced in a classpath. Even if the classpath continued to exist from Java 9, it should be empty in the long run.

The -classpath Switch

Search locations can be specified flexibly, with the first variant supplying the class files or archives to an SDK tool via the -classpath switch (-cp for short):

```
$ java -classpath classpath1;classpath2 my.package.with.MainClass
```

The classpath contains root directories of packages and JAR files, which are archives of class files and resources.

[Ex]

Example

A JAR file named *library.jar* in the current directory, the resources under the *bin* directory, and all JAR files in the *lib* directory can be included in the classpath in the following way:

```
$ java -cp "library.jar;bin/.;lib/*" my.package.with.MainClass
```

On Windows, the separator is a semicolon; on Unix, you would use a colon. The asterisk represents *all* JAR files but *isn't a* common wildcard, like *parser*.jar.*[3] When operating system command lines see a *, they usually start their own processing. For this reason, the entire path specification must be enclosed in double quotation marks.

The CLASSPATH Environment Variable

An alternative to the -cp switch is to set the CLASSPATH environment variable with a string that specifies path information:

```
$ SET CLASSPATH=classpath1;classpath2
$ java my.package.with.MeinClass
```

The global nature of these variables is problematic, so local -cp specifications are better. Also, the -cp options "override" the entries in CLASSPATH. Finally, if neither CLASSPATH nor a -cp option is set, the classpath for the JVM consists only of the current directory, that is, ".".

[»]

Note

Directly extending the classpath in the development environment is unusual because usually Maven or Gradle projects determine the dependencies, and then the integrated development environment (IDE) automatically includes the paths to the Java files in the classpath.

---

3 More details are available about this topic at the now somewhat dusty site, *https://docs.oracle.com/javase/8/docs/technotes/tools/windows/classpath.html*

Classpath Hell

Delivering Java classes in JAR files is the usual way. But two problems arise with class-paths:

- By mistake, two JAR files with different versions can be in the classpath. Let's assume they are *parser-1.2.jar* and *parser-2.0.jar*, where application programming interface (API) and implementation have changed slightly in the new version. This difference may not be noticeable at first because no loading error is raised for the type since the type actually exists—the JVM takes the first type it finds. If a program uses the new API, but the loaded class is from the old JAR, an error occur will at runtime. In the case of duplicate JARs with different versions, a reordering in the classpath leads to a completely different result. Fortunately, this problem can be solved relatively quickly.

- Two Java libraries—let's call them *vw.jar* and *audi.jar*—each need another JAR to work. But while *vw.jar* needs the version *bosch-1.jar*, let's say *audi.jar* needs the version, *bosch-2.jar*. A problem arises because JARs are always global in the default classpath, but not hierarchical. Thus, no JAR can have a "local" sub-JAR.

Solutions to the second problem exist, in which new class loaders are drawn upon. OSGi—a specification describing a modular system–is well known but has lost momentum in the Java world.

15.2   Importing Modules

To import modules, Java provides the *Java Platform Module System (JPMS)*, known also by its project name *Jigsaw*.[4] Its focus is on strong encapsulation: Implementation details can keep a module secret. Even helper code within the module, even if public, must not leak out. Second, there's an abstraction of behavior via interfaces can implement internal classes from the module, whereby the concrete classes aren't known to the user. As a third point, explicit dependencies can make interactions with other modules clear. A graphical representation can help you keep track of usage relationships even in large architectures.

15.2.1   Who Sees Whom?

Classes, packages, and modules can be viewed as containers with different visibilities in the following ways:

- A type, whether a class or an interface, contains class/object variables and methods.
- A package contains types.

---

4 This change is the most important changes in Java 9 and led to many compatibility issues in the early days.

- A module contains packages.
- Private members in a type aren't visible in other types.
- Non-public types aren't visible in other packages.
- Non-exported packages aren't visible outside a module.

A module is defined by several elements:

1. By a name
2. By the specification of what it exports
3. By the specification of which modules it needs for its own job

A second aspect is interesting: A module should export something. If nothing is exported, nothing is visible to the outside. Everything you want outsiders to see must be listed in the module description because not all public types of the module are public by default; if they were, modules would have no advantages over JAR files. Thus, with the new modular system, you have an entirely different visibility. From the gang of four (public, private, package-visible, and protected), public has much finer grades because what is public is determined by the module. This visibility thus applies for the following items:

- Types the module exports for all
- Types for explicitly enumerated modules
- All types in the same module

The compiler and the JVM take care of visibility compliance, and even tricks with reflection are no longer possible if a module hasn't granted clearance.

Module Types

In this section, we'll take a closer look at three types of modules. When you write new modules, they are *named modules*. In addition, for compatibility reasons, *automatic modules* and *unnamed modules* can be used to integrate existing JAR files. The Java SE library is itself divided into modules that we call *platform modules*. The runtime environment displays all platform modules with a --list-modules switch. Using the switch before Java 9 will result in an error.

[Ex]

Example

The following example will list approximately 70 modules:

```
$ java --list-modules
java.base@17
java.compiler@17
java.datatransfer@17
java.desktop@17
java.instrument@17
```

```
java.logging@17
java.management@17
java.management.rmi@17
java.naming@17
...
jdk.unsupported.desktop@17
jdk.xml.dom@17
jdk.zipfs@17
```

The folder *C:\Program Files\Java\jdk-17\jmods* contains JMOD files.

15.2.2   Platform Modules and a JMOD Example

The command-line tool jmod shows what a module exports and needs. Let's take the Java Database Connectivity (JDBC) API for database connections as an example: The types are located in a separate module called java.sql. Consider the following example:

```
C:\Program Files\Java\jdk-17\bin>jmod describe ..\jmods\java.sql.jmod
java.sql@17
exports java.sql
exports javax.sql
requires java.base mandated
requires java.logging transitive
requires java.transaction.xa transitive
requires java.xml transitive
uses java.sql.Driver
platform windows-amd64
```

From this code, we can read the following information:

- The name.
- The packages that the module exports, namely, java.sql and javax.sql.
- The modules that java.sql needs. java.base is always included; in addition, other modules may be required.
- The message with uses is related to the service locator, which we can ignore for now.
- Information about the platform (windows-amd64) in which jmod is written (i.e., the assignment of the system property os.arch on the build server).

15.2.3   Using Internal Platform Features: --add-exports

When Sun started developing the Java libraries in the last century, a number of internal helper classes came along with the library. Many of these internal helper classes started with the package prefixes com.sun and sun. The types were always communicated as internal types, but among some developers, curiosity and interest were so great that the warnings from Sun/Oracle were ignored. The big bang happened in Java 9 because, since then, public is no longer automatically public for all classes outside the module. The internal classes are no longer exported, and thus, they are no longer usable.

Act 1: The Source Code

A compiler error occurs in the following example:

```
package com.tutego.insel.tool;

public class ShowRuntimeArguments {
  public static void main( String[] args ) throws Exception {
    System.out.println( java.util.Arrays.toString(
                        jdk.internal.misc.VM.getRuntimeArguments() ) );
  }
}
```

Listing 15.1 com/tutego/insel/tools/ShowRuntimeArguments.java

Our program draws on the VM class to query the actual occupancy of the command line. What we receive in the main(String[] args) method via args doesn't contain any JVM arguments.

Act 2: The Compiler Error

In the following example, the program can no longer be interpreted without compiler errors:

```
$ javac com/tutego/insel/tool/ShowRuntimeArguments.java
com\tutego\insel\tool\
ShowRuntimeArguments.java:6: error: package jdk.internal.misc is not visible
      jdk.internal.misc.VM.getRuntimeArguments() ) );
                   ^
  (package jdk.internal.misc is declared in module java.base, which does not exp
ort
it to the unnamed module)
1 error
```

The problem is documented by the compiler: jdk.internal.misc is not accessible for our program.

Act 3: The Magic Compiler Switch

Although the VM class itself is public and the getRuntimeArguments() method is also public, jdk.internal.misc hasn't been exported. As a result, access from our program isn't possible because the JVM implements access control. However, we can turn that control off. With the --add-exports switch, we provide the package jdk.internal.misc of our class from the java.base module. The general syntax is shown in the following example:

```
--add-exports <source-module>/<package>=<target-module>(,<target-module>)*
```

The specification must be set for the compiler and for the runtime environment. For our example, therefore, you would write the following code:

```
$ javac --add-exports java.base/jdk.internal.misc=ALL-UNNAMED com/tutego/insel/
tool/ShowRuntimeArguments.java
```

Act 4: The Cranky Java Virtual Machine

The program has been compiled, so let's run it. The result is the following output:

```
$ java com/tutego/insel/tool/ShowRuntimeArguments
Exception in thread "main" java.lang.IllegalAccessError: class
com.tutego.insel.tool.ShowRuntimeArguments (in unnamed module @0x4d591d15)
cannot access class jdk.internal.misc.VM (in module java.base) because module
java.base does not export jdk.internal.misc to unnamed module @0x4d591d15
    at
com.tutego.insel.tool.ShowRuntimeArguments.main(ShowRuntimeArguments.java:6)
```

Our program doesn't work! But the error message looks familiar.

Act 5: The Java Virtual Machine Wants What the Compiler Wants (The End)

To resolve this issue, we must set the same switch as for the compiler:

```
$ java --add-exports java.base/jdk.internal.misc=ALL-UNNAMED com/tutego/insel/
tool/ShowRuntimeArguments
```

The program is running, and the output is:

```
[--add-exports=java.base/jdk.internal.misc=ALL-UNNAMED]
```

A specification like java.base/jdk.internal.misc, where the module is in front and the package name is behind the /, can be encountered rather frequently. Behind the equal sign, either our package exists, which can see the types in jdk.internal.misc, or (as in our case) ALL-UNNAMED.

Finding Internal Types with jdeps

To determine if a program uses internal types, you can use the command-line program jdeps:

```
$ jdeps com/tutego/insel/tool/ShowRuntimeArguments.class
ShowRuntimeArguments.class -> java.base
 com.tutego.insel.tool  -> java.io            java.base
 com.tutego.insel.tool  -> java.lang          java.base
 com.tutego.insel.tool  -> java.util          java.base
 com.tutego.insel.tool  -> jdk.internal.misc  JDK internal API (java.base)
```

Unlike the Java compiler, the full file name (i.e., including *.class*) is necessary in this case. The "JDK internal API" message prepares you for the fact that trouble lies ahead.

In this way, you can examine a large codebase relatively easy, and developers can pro-actively get to the bottom of parts that have problematic dependencies.

15.2.4   Integrating New Modules

Every Java SE project is based on the java.se module, which entails various module dependencies, as shown in Figure 15.2.

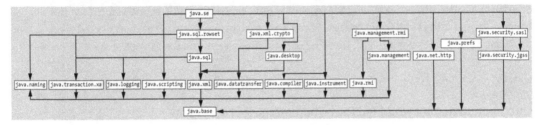

Figure 15.2 Module Dependencies of the java.se Module

> [»]
>
> **Note**
>
> Not all installed modules are included in the java.se module, such as the JDK modules and java.smartcardio. However, these modules are referenced in the module path by default, as the following "one-liner" shows:
>
> ```
> System.out.println(
>     ModuleLayer.boot().modules().stream()
>         .map( Module::getName ).sorted().collect( Collectors.joining( ", " )
> )
> );
> ```
>
> The result lists the following modules:
>
> java.base, java.compiler, java.datatransfer, java.desktop, java.instrument, j
> ava.logging, java.management, java.management.rmi, java.naming, java.net.http
> , java.prefs, java.rmi, java.scripting, java.security.jgss, java.security.sas
> l, java.smartcardio, java.sql, java.sql.rowset, java.transaction.xa, java.xml
> , java.xml.crypto, jdk.accessibility, jdk.attach, jdk.charsets, jdk.compiler,

```
jdk.crypto.cryptoki, jdk.crypto.ec, jdk.crypto.mscapi, jdk.dynalink, jdk.edi
tpad, jdk.httpserver, jdk.internal.ed, jdk.internal.jvmstat, jdk.internal.le,
jdk.internal.opt, jdk.jartool, jdk.javadoc, jdk.jconsole, jdk.jdeps, jdk.jdi
, jdk.jdwp.agent, jdk.jfr, jdk.jlink, jdk.jpackage, jdk.jshell, jdk.jsobject,
jdk.jstatd, jdk.localedata, jdk.management, jdk.management.agent, jdk.manage
ment.jfr, jdk.naming.dns, jdk.naming.rmi, jdk.net, jdk.nio.mapmode, jdk.rando
m, jdk.sctp, jdk.security.auth, jdk.security.jgss, jdk.unsupported, jdk.unsup
ported.desktop, jdk.xml.dom, jdk.zipfs
```

All these modules can be used directly without switches.

Adding and Opening New Modules to the Core Modules

If external modules must be added to core modules, you can use the `--add-modules` switch. Another switch is `--add-exports`, which opens all public types and members at translation or runtime.

15.3   Developing Custom Modules

To show you how to implement modules practically, let's create two new Maven Java projects, along with the necessary module info files.

15.3.1   Module com.tutego.candytester

Now, we'll create a new Maven project with the coordinates `com.tutego:candy-tester:1.0`. The project should contain the following simple class:

```
package com.tutego.insel.candy;

import java.util.*;

public class YummyTester {
  public static boolean testYumminess( String name ) {
    return List.of( "ding ding tong", "meiji", "balikutsa", "pez", "gumballs" )
            .contains( name.toLowerCase( Locale.ROOT ) );
  }
}
```

Listing 15.2 com/tutego/insel/candy/YummyTester.java

The Maven project has the following simple Project Object Model (POM) file:

```
<?xml version="1.0" encoding="UTF-8"?>
<project xmlns="http://maven.apache.org/POM/4.0.0"
        xmlns:xsi="http://www.w3.org/2001/XMLSchema-instance"
```

```
        xsi:schemaLocation="http://maven.apache.org/POM/4.0.0 http://
maven.apache.org/xsd/maven-4.0.0.xsd">
  <modelVersion>4.0.0</modelVersion>
  <groupId>com.tutego</groupId>
  <artifactId>candytester</artifactId>
  <version>1.0</version>
  <properties>
    <maven.compiler.source>17</maven.compiler.source>
    <maven.compiler.target>17</maven.compiler.target>
  </properties>
</project>
```

Listing 15.3 pom.xml

Note how no special information in the POM file indicates the module system.

15.3.2   Module Declaration with module-info.java and Exports

The module information is declared via a file called *module-info.java* (referred to as the *module info file*); annotations are not used. This central file is the main difference between a module and a simple JAR file. As soon as the special class file *module-info.class* is present in the module path, the runtime environment starts interpreting the project as a module.

Our project should have the following module info file:

```
module com.tutego.candytester {
  exports com.tutego.insel.candy;
}
```

Listing 15.4 module-info.java

After the `module` keyword, you'll add the name of the module, in this case, `com.tutego.candytester`. This name is followed by a block in curly brackets.

Usually, two keywords are prominent in the block: `exports` and `requires`. Since we don't need anything yet, and are only offering something, only `exports` is relevant. Although we'll need (`requires`) `java.base`, the default module doesn't need to be displayed.

Our `com.tutego.candytester` module exports only types "behind" the `com.tutego.insel.candy` package and no other packages, which don't exist in this example anyway.

15.3.3   Module com.tutego.main

Now, let's say a second module should use the functionality of the `com.tutego.candytester` module. Let's first create a new Maven project with the coordinates com.tutego:main:1.0. We'll enter a dependency in the POM file, as shown in the following example:

```xml
<?xml version="1.0" encoding="UTF-8"?>
<project xmlns="http://maven.apache.org/POM/4.0.0"
         xmlns:xsi="http://www.w3.org/2001/XMLSchema-instance"
         xsi:schemaLocation="http://maven.apache.org/POM/4.0.0 http://
maven.apache.org/xsd/maven-4.0.0.xsd">
  <modelVersion>4.0.0</modelVersion>
  <groupId>com.tutego</groupId>
  <artifactId>main</artifactId>
  <version>1.0</version>
  <properties>
    <maven.compiler.source>17</maven.compiler.source>
    <maven.compiler.target>17</maven.compiler.target>
  </properties>
  <dependencies>
    <dependency>
      <groupId>com.tutego</groupId>
      <artifactId>candytester</artifactId>
      <version>1.0</version>
      <scope>compile</scope>
    </dependency>
  </dependencies>
</project>
```

Listing 15.5 pom.xml

15.3.4 Module info File with requires

The second module info file looks as follows:

```java
module com.tutego.main {
  requires com.tutego.candytester;
  requires java.desktop;
}
```

Listing 15.6 module-info.java

The module has its own unique name: com.tutego.main. In addition, we have two module dependencies in this case. The requires keyword makes it clear that it requires two modules: com.tutego.candytester and java.desktop. The latter may be surprising because every Java program without a module system can use the graphical user interface (GUI) libraries of Java. However, if the module system has been activated, only the implicit java.base module is included, which, however, doesn't contain any GUI

827

elements (i.e., no XML, SQL, or other modules). A look at the Javadoc will help: *https:// docs.oracle.com/en/java/javase/17/docs/api/java.base/module-summary.html*

[»]

> **Information**
>
> A module `requires` another module but `exports` a package. You can easily be confused by the module name and package name.

15.3.5 Writing Module Inserters: Java Virtual Machine Switches -p and -m

Let's now add a main class that deploys `YummyTester`:

```
package com.tutego.insel.main;

import com.tutego.insel.candy.YummyTester;

public class Main {
  public static void main( String[] args ) {
    System.out.println( YummyTester.testYumminess( "Chris" ) ); // false
    JOptionPane.showMessageDialog( null, YummyTester.testYumminess( "Meiji" ) );
 // true
  }
}
```

Listing 15.7 com/tutego/insel/main/Main

When the JVM starts the program, it loads the main module and all dependent modules. IntelliJ generates the following (shortened) output:

```
$ java.exe -p C:\Users\Christian\workspace\main\target\classes;C:\Users\
Christian\workspace\candytester\target\classes -m com.tutego.main/
com.tutego.insel.main.Main
false
true
```

Two switches (`-p` and `-m`) are interesting in this context. In the following examples, the specification of the classpath is missing entirely:

- `-m modulepath…` or `--module-path modulepath…`
  List of directories separated by semicolons, containing modules.
- `-m module[/mainclass]` or `--module module[/mainclass]`
  Determines the *initial module* for the main class.

In these ways, you can also start the program yourself from the console.

15.3.6 Experiments with the Module Info File

Let's start experimenting with our two `module-info.java` files:

Module	Change	Result
`com.tutego.candy-tester` `com.tutego.main`	`requires java.base;`	The line is possible but unnecessary because `java.base` is always required (requires).
`com.tutego.candy-tester`	`// exports com.tutego.insel.ca ndy;`	Results in a compiler error: "Package 'com.tutego.insel.candy' is declared in module 'com.tutego.candytester', which does not export it to module 'com.tutego.main'."
`com.tutego.candy-tester`	`exports com.tutego.insel.ca ndy to god;`	Only the god module gets access to `com.tutego. island.greeter`. We aren't God, so the main module reports the same error as in the line before.
`com.tutego.candy-tester`	`exports com.tutego. insel.notexisting;`	Adding it results in a compiler error: "Package not found: com.tutego.insel.notexisting."
`com.tutego.main`	`// requires com.tutego.candy-tester;`	Compiler error "Package 'com.tutego.insel.candy' is declared in module 'com.tutego.candytester', but module 'com.tutego.main' does not read it."
`com.tutego.main`	`exports com.tutego.insel.ma in;`	No result because `com.tutego.insel.main` isn't required (requires) by any module.

Table 15.1 The Module Syntax and Its Effects

The statement with `exports com.tutego.island.candy to god` is referred to as a *qualified export*.

15.3.7 Automatic Modules

JAR files have played a central role in the Java system for 20 years; doing away with them from one day to the next would cause major problems. A look at *https://mvnre-pository.com/repos* reveals over 25 million artifacts. Although documentation and other files are included in these statistics, this figure illustrates how many JAR files are in circulation.

Now, two directions exist for the use of JAR files: You can put the JAR either in a classpath or in a module path. If a JAR is used in a module path and it has no module info file, an *automatic module* will be created. Except for one small limitation, this feature works for most existing Java libraries.

An automatic module has certain properties for its module name and for consequences with its dependencies, such as the following:

- Without a module info file, automatic modules don't have a self-selected name but instead are assigned a name by the system, which is derived from the file name.[5] To put it more simply, appended version numbers and the file extension are removed, and all non-alphanumeric characters are replaced with dots, but never two dots in a row. The version will still be recognized. The documentation provides the example of *foo-bar-1.2.3-SNAPSHOT.jar*, which leads to the module name `foo.bar` and version `1.2.3-SNAPSHOT`.

- Automatic modules always export all their packages. So, a dependency to this automatic module exists, the procurer can use all visible types and members.

- Automatic modules can read all other modules, even the unnamed ones.

At first glance, migration seems to be a simple task for the modular system: All JARs go into the module path, whether module info files exist or not. However, some JAR files are rejected by the JVM as automatic modules, namely, if they contain types of a package already in another included module. Modules must not contain *split packages* (i.e., containing the same package again). The migration then requires you complete one of the following tasks:

- Merging of the packages into one module
- Shifting types into different packages
- Using the classpath

15.3.8   Unnamed Modules

The JVM has a classpath on the outside, but internally, the classpath looks different. If JAR files are placed in the classpath, they are packaged into an *unnamed module*. Every JAR in the classpath—regardless of whether it contains a *modul-info.class* or not—goes into the unnamed module. Thus, we only have one unnamed module, so we are speaking in the singular, not in the plural.

"Unnamed" already indicates that the module has no name, and consequently, no dependency to JAR files can exist in the unnamed module, which makes the unnamed module different from automatic modules. An unnamed module has the same property

---

5 `Automatic-Module-Name` in the *META-INF* file is an alternative. More about this topic later in Chapter 23, Section 23.5.2.

as an automatic module in that it exports all packages. Furthermore, because it's part of the migration, an unnamed module also has access to all other modules.

15.3.9   Readability and Accessibility

The runtime environment sorts modules into a graph. The dependence of each modules leads to *readability*: If module A needs module B, module A *reads* module B, and B is *read by* A. This concept is elementary for the functioning of the module system because, in this way, errors are already excluded at translation time, such as cycles or identical packages in different modules. Readability is key to a *reliable configuration*.

The concept of *accessibility* goes one step further. If a module can basically read another module, it doesn't necessarily access all packages and types because only those types are visible that have been exported. Types that are both readable and reachable are referred to as *reachable* types.

The next question is which module type has access to which other module type. Table 15.2 summarizes some considerations about readability.

Module Type	Origin	Exports Packages	Access
Platform module	JDK	Explicitly	
Named modules	Container with module info in module path	Explicitly	Platform modules, other named modules, and automatic modules
Automatic modules	Container without module info in module path	All	Platform modules, other named modules, automatic modules, and unnamed module
Unnamed module	Class files and JAR files in the classpath	All	Platform modules, named modules, and automatic modules

Table 15.2 Readability of the Modules

The module info file is the most important part because this file turns a JAR into a modular JAR. If the module information is missing, a JAR remains a regular JAR as Java developers have known for over 20 years. The JAR file can be set in the new module path or in the known classpath, which results in four combinations.

	Module Path	Classpath
JAR with module information	Becomes named module	Becomes unnamed module
JAR without module information	Becomes automatic module	Becomes unnamed module

Table 15.3 JARs in the Path

JAR archives in the classpath are the known behavior, and using the module path is still rare.

15.3.10   Module Migration

Let's assume our monolithic application has no dependencies on external libraries and will be modularized. Then, the first step is to put the entire application into a large named module. Next, individual areas must be identified so that gradually the building blocks move into individual modules. This task isn't always easy, especially since cyclical dependencies are likely. Oracle developers had a lot of trouble with the modularization of the JDK.

The Problem with Automatic Modules

Traditionally, build tools like Maven or Gradle generated JAR files, and filenames are somehow generated. However, if these JAR files become automatic modules, the filename suddenly plays a major role, but the filename may never have been deliberately chosen. If a named module references an automatic module, two problems may arise: If the file name changes (let's leave the version number aside for the moment), the name of the automatic module also changes, and the dependency can no longer be resolved. The second problem is even bigger: Many Java libraries don't yet have module information, and consequently, developers must express the dependency on this automatic module via a derived name.

Take, for example, the popular open-source library *Google Guava*. Version 31.0.1-jre of a JAR file would have the filename *guava-31.0.1-jre.jar*. Consequently, the automatic module is named guava. A named module can express a dependency via required guava. If Google converts the library into a real Java module, the name will change. The plan is to use com.google.guava. But, if the name changes, all referencing in projects that now still use required guava will result in a compiler error. An alias would be a great idea, but this feature doesn't exist. Furthermore, the problem is not only in our code that references Guava, but also in *transitive dependencies*.

One solution may mitigate the problem: In the JAR manifest file, an Automatic-Module-Name entry can be set that "overrides" the automatic module name.

[Ex]

> **Example**
>
> Apache Commons Lang sets a name in the following way:[6]
>
> `Automatic-Module-Name: org.apache.commons.lang3`
>
> Guava doesn't set a module name.

---

6 *https://github.com/apache/commons-lang/blob/4753c6b4d4ddd17576b48f40922de12f8f5b2be7/pom.xml#L792*

Named modules that have dependencies on automatic modules are therefore problematic. We hope that the central Java libraries on which so many solutions rely will quickly introduce module information, which would be a *bottom-up* solution. This approach is the only promising option but will probably take a long time. Even though Java provides a module system, few Java libraries have module information; instead, `Automatic-Module-Name` is more common.

15.4 Further Reading

To learn more about the history of the modules, good insights are available in various presentations by the Java's creators at *https://openjdk.java.net/projects/jigsaw/*. The module system provides even more options, such as opening for reflection or transitive dependencies with `requires transitive`, so that a module co-determines another module for the user. Furthermore, `provide ... with` and the `uses` syntax is available for service loaders. If you have an interface I and an implementation C, you can specify that the module information `provides I with C`, while the service loader can supply the type C with `ServiceLoader.load(I.class)`. This approach works without the *META-INF/ services files* that were necessary prior to Java 9. In addition, JDK modules can be replaced by other modules, and classes can be "patched" by assigning them to other modules.

Even though the new module system is interesting, criticism stems from the fact it doesn't go far enough for some teams. One point of criticism is the version number, which currently is only ornamental. In general, little demand for the version number exists, and the more acerbic critics claim that the module system only exists because Oracle itself wanted to improve the modularization of its own JDK.

A few special books describe the topic in detail, such as *Java 9 Modularity: Patterns and Practices for Developing Maintainable Applications* by Sander Mak and Paul Bakker (O'Reilly Media, 2017).

Chapter 16
The Class Library

"What we need is some crazy people;
look where the normal ones have taken us."
—George Bernard Shaw (1856–1950)

In this chapter you'll learn about the Java class library.

16.1   The Java Class Philosophy

A programming language consists not only of a grammar, but also, as in the case of
Java, of a programming library. A platform-independent language—as many imagine C
or C++ to be—isn't really platform independent if different functions and programming models are used on each computer, which is exactly the weak point of C(++).
These algorithms, which aren't dependent on the operating system, can be applied
everywhere in the same way, but the result is realized in the end with inputs/outputs
or graphical user interfaces (GUIs). The Java library, on the other hand, tries to abstract
away from platform-specific features, and the developers have gone to great lengths to
put all the important methods into well-formed object-oriented (OO) classes and packages. These elements cover in particular the central areas of data structures, input and
output, graphics, and network programming.

16.1.1   Modules, Packages, and Types

At the top of the Java library are modules, which in turn consist of packages, which in turn contain types.

Modules of the Java SE

The *Java Platform, Standard Edition (Java SE)* application programming interface (API) consists of the following modules, all of which begin with the prefix java:

Module	Description
java.base	Fundamental types of Java SE
java.compiler	Java language model, annotation processing, and Java compiler API
java.datatransfer	The API for data transfer between applications, usually the clipboard
java.desktop	GUIs with Abstract Windowing Toolkit (AWT) and Swing, the *Accessibility* API, audio, printing, and JavaBeans
java.instrument	Instrumentalization is the modification of Java programs at runtime
java.logging	The *Logging* API
java.management	*Java Management Extensions (JMX)*
java.management.rmi	*Remote Method Invocation (RMI)* connector for remote access to the JMX beans
java.naming	The *Java Naming and Directory Interface (JNDI)* API
java.prefs	The *Preferences* API is used to store user preferences
java.rmi	Remote method calls with the RMI API
java.scripting	The *Scripting* API
java.security.jgss	Java binding of the *IETF Generic Security Services* API (GSS API)
java.security.sasl	Java support for *IETF Simple Authentication and Security Layer (SASL)*
java.sql	The JDBC API for accessing relational databases
java.sql.rowset	The *JDBC RowSet* API
java.xml	XML classes with the *Java API for XML Processing* (JAXP), *Streaming API for XML* (StAX), *Simple API for XML* (SAX), and *W3C Document Object Model* (DOM) API
java.xml.crypto	The API for XML cryptography

Table 16.1 Modules of the Java SE

The java.base module—the most important module—contains core classes such as Object and String, among others. This module is the only module that doesn't itself contain any dependency on other modules. Every other module, however, references at least java.base. The Javadoc contains a nice graphical representation, shown in Figure 16.1.

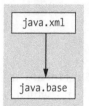

Figure 16.1 The java.xml Module Has a Dependency on the java.base Module

In some cases, more dependencies exist, such as with the java.desktop module, shown in Figure 16.2.

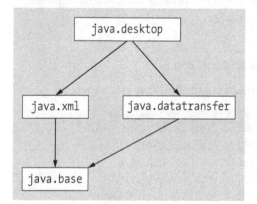

Figure 16.2 Dependencies of the java.desktop Module

The java.se Module

One special module is java.se, which doesn't declare its own packages or types but merely groups other modules together. The name for such a construction is *aggregator module*. The java.se module defines the API for the Java SE platform in this way, as shown in Figure 16.3.

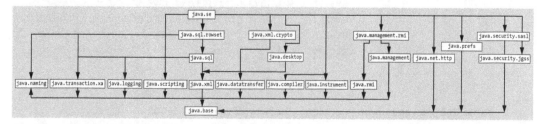

Figure 16.3 Dependencies of the java.se Module

> **Note**
>
> In the following sections, we won't discuss the Java SE types in terms of the module from which they originate. You only need to know in which module a type is located when building smaller subsets of Java SE.

Other Modules

Two other modules that also start with `java` but aren't part of the Java SE standard are `java.jnlp` for the Java Network Launch Protocol (JNLP) and `java.smartcardio`, which is the Java API for communication with smart cards according to the international standard ISO/IEC 7816-4.[1]

The Java Development Kit (JDK) is the standard implementation of Java SE. This implementation provides developers with more packages and classes, such as with an HTTP server or with Java tools like the Java compiler and the Javadoc tool. In this implementation, several modules will start with the prefix `jdk`.

16.1.2   Overview of the Packages of the Standard Library

The *Java 11 Core Java SE API* consists of the following modules and packages:

Modules	Packages Included
`java.base`	`java.io`, `java.lang`, `java.lang.annotation`, `java.lang.invoke`, `java.lang.module`, `java.lang.ref`, `java.lang.reflect`, `java.math`, `java.net`, `java.net.spi`, `java.nio`, `java.nio.channels`, `java.nio.channels.spi`, `java.nio.charset`, `java.nio.charset.spi`, `java.nio.file`, `java.nio.file.attribute`, `java.nio.file.spi`, `java.security`, `java.security.cert`, `java.security.interfaces`, `java.security.spec`, `java.text`, `java.text.spi`, `java.time`, `java.time.chrono`, `java.time.format`, `java.time.temporal`, `java.time.zone`, `java.util`, `java.util.concurrent`,
`java.base`	`java.util.concurrent.atomic`, `java.util.concurrent.locks`, `java.util.function`, `java.util.jar`, `java.util.regex`, `java.util.spi`, `java.util.stream`, `java.util.zip`, `javax.crypto`, `javax.crypto.interfaces`, `javax.crypto.spec`, `javax.net`, `javax.net.ssl`, `javax.security.auth`, `javax.security.auth.callback`, `javax.security.auth.login`, `javax.security.auth.spi`, `javax.security.auth.x500`, `javax.security.cert`

Table 16.2 Packages in the Modules of the Java 17 Core Java SE API

---

1 *https://en.wikipedia.org/wiki/ISO/IEC_7816*

Modules	Packages Included
java.compiler	javax.annotation.processing, javax.lang.model, javax.lang.model.element, javax.lang.model.type, javax.lang.model.util, javax.tools
java.datatransfer	java.awt.datatransfer
java.desktop	java.applet, java.awt, java.awt.color, java.awt.desktop, java.awt.dnd, java.awt.event, java.awt.font, java.awt.geom, java.awt.im, java.awt.im.spi, java.awt.image, java.awt.image.renderable, java.awt.print, java.beans, java.beans.beancontext, javax.accessibility, javax.imageio, javax.imageio.event, javax.imageio.metadata, javax.imageio.plugins.bmp, javax.imageio.plugins.jpeg, javax.imageio.plugins.tiff, javax.imageio.spi, javax.imageio.stream, javax.print, javax.print.attribute, javax.print.attribute.standard, javax.print.event, javax.sound.midi, javax.sound.midi.spi, javax.sound.sampled, javax.sound.sampled.spi, javax.swing, javax.swing.border, javax.swing.colorchooser, javax.swing.event, javax.swing.filechooser, javax.swing.plaf, javax.swing.plaf.basic, javax.swing.plaf.metal, javax.swing.plaf.multi, javax.swing.plaf.nimbus, javax.swing.plaf.synth, javax.swing.table, javax.swing.text, javax.swing.text.html, javax.swing.text.html.parser, javax.swing.text.rtf, javax.swing.tree, javax.swing.undo
java.instrument	java.lang.instrument
java.logging	java.util.logging
java.management	java.lang.management, javax.management, javax.management.loading, javax.management.modelmbean, javax.management.monitor, javax.management.openmbean, javax.management.relation, javax.management.remote, javax.management.timer
java.management.rmi	javax.management.remote.rmi
java.naming	javax.naming, javax.naming.directory, javax.naming.event javax.naming.ldapjavax.naming.spi
java.prefs	java.util.prefs
java.rmi	java.rmi, java.rmi.activation, java.rmi.dgc, java.rmi.registry, java.rmi.server, javax.rmi.ssl

Table 16.2 Packages in the Modules of the Java 17 Core Java SE API (Cont.)

Modules	Packages Included
java.scripting	javax.script
java.security.jgss	javax.security.auth.kerberos, org.ietf.jgss
java.security.sasl	javax.security.sasl
java.sql	java.sql, javax.sql, javax.transaction.xa
java.sql.rowset	javax.sql.rowset, javax.sql.rowset.serial, javax.sql.rowset.spi
java.xml	javax.xml, javax.xml.catalog, javax.xml.datatype, javax.xml.namespace, javax.xml.parsersjavax.xml.stream, javax.xml.stream.events, javax.xml.stream.util, javax.xml.transform, javax.xml.transform.dom, javax.xml.transform.sax, javax.xml.transform.stax, javax.xml.transform.stream, javax.xml.validation, javax.xml.xpath, org.w3c.dom, org.w3c.dom.bootstrap, org.w3c.dom.events, org.w3c.dom.ls, org.w3c.dom.ranges, org.w3c.dom.views, org.xml.sax, org.xml.sax.ext, org.xml.sax.helpers
java.xml.crypto	javax.xml.crypto, javax.xml.crypto.dom, javax.xml.crypto.dsig, javax.xml.crypto.dsig.dom, javax.xml.crypto.dsig.keyinfo, javax.xml.crypto.dsig.spec

Table 16.2 Packages in the Modules of the Java 17 Core Java SE API (Cont.)

Developers should be able to map the following packages according to their respective capabilities:

Package	Description
java.awt	The AWT package provides classes for graphics output and GUI usage.
java.awt.event	Interfaces for the various events in GUIs.
java.io java.nio	Input and output options. Files are represented as objects. Data streams allow sequential access to file contents.
java.lang	A package that's automatically included. Contains indispensable classes like string, thread, or wrapper classes.
java.net	Communication via networks. Provides classes for building client and server systems that can connect to the internet via TCP and IP, respectively.

Table 16.3 Important Packages in the Java SE

Package	Description
`java.text`	Support for internationalized programs. Provides classes for handling text and formatting dates and numbers.
`java.util`	Provides types for data structures, space and time, and parts of internationalization, as well as random numbers. Subpackages take care of regular expressions and concurrency.
`javax.swing`	Swing components for GUIs. This package has various subpackages.

Table 16.3 Important Packages in the Java SE (Cont.)

For a developer, you can't avoid studying the Java API documentation at *https://docs.oracle.com/en/java/javase/17/docs/api/index.html*.

Official Interface (java and javax Packages)

The list provided by the Java documentation represents the permitted access to the library. The types are basically designed to last forever, so developers can count on still being able to run their Java programs in 100 years. But who defines the API? In essence, three sources define APIs:

- Oracle developers put new packages and types into the API.
- The *Java Community Process (JCP)* adopts a new API. Then, Oracle is not acting alone, but instead, a group works out a new API and defines its interfaces.
- The *World Wide Web Consortium (W3C)* provides an API for XML Document Object Model (DOM), for example.

A good mnemonic is that anything starting with java or javax is a permitted API, and anything else can lead to non-portable Java programs. Some classes are supported that aren't part of the official API. These classes include, for example, various Swing classes for controlling the appearance of the interface.

Standard Extension API (javax Packages)

Some Java packages start with javax. Originally, these extension packages were intended to complement the core classes. Over time, however, many packages that initially had to be included have now migrated to the standard distribution, so that today, a fairly large proportion start with javax, but no longer represent extensions that need to be additionally installed. Sun didn't want to rename the packages at that time, so as not to make migration more difficult. If you notice a package name with javax in the source code today, therefore, you can no longer easily determine whether an external source must be included or whether the package is already part of the distribution (and since Java version).

Truly external packages include the following packages:

- The *Java Communications API* for serial and parallel interfaces
- The *Java Telephony API*
- Speech input/output with the *Java Speech API*
- *JavaSpaces* for shared memory of different runtime environments
- *JXTA* for establishing P2P networks

The bottom line is that developers are dealing with the following libraries:

- With the official Java API
- With APIs from Java Specification Request (JSR) extensions
- With unofficial libraries, such as open-source solutions, for example, to access PDF files or control ATMs

An important role is also played by types from the `jakarta` package, which is part of Jakarta EE (formerly Java EE) and semi-official.

16.2   Simple Time Measurement and Profiling*

In addition to the convenient classes for managing date values, two static methods provide simple ways to measure times for program sections:

```
final class java.lang.System
```

▶ `static long currentTimeMillis()`
Returns the milliseconds elapsed since 1/1/1970, 00:00:00 Coordinated Universal Time (UTC).

▶ `static long nanoTime()`
Returns the time from the most accurate system timer. This method has no reference point to any date.

The difference between two time values can be used to roughly estimate the execution times of programs.

[+]
Tip

The values of `nanoTime()` are always ascending, which isn't necessarily true for `currentTimeMillis()` because Java gets the time from the operating system. System times can change, for example, when a user adjusts the time. Differences of `currentTimeMillis()` timestamps are then completely wrong and could even be negative.

16.2.1   Profilers

Where the Java virtual machine (JVM) does waste clock cycles in a program is shown by a *profiler*. Optimization can then begin at those points. *Java Mission Control* is a powerful program of the JDK and integrates a free profiler. *Java VisualVM* is another free program that can be obtained from *https://visualvm.github.io/*. On the professional and commercial side, *JProfiler* (*https://www.ej-technologies.com/products/jprofiler/overview.html*) and *YourKit* (*https://www.yourkit.com/java/profiler*) are competitors. The *Ultimate Version* of IntelliJ also includes a profiler.

16.3   The Class Class

Let's suppose we want to write a class browser. This program should display all classes belonging to the running program and furthermore additional information, such as variable assignment, declared methods, constructors, and some information about the inheritance hierarchy. For this purpose, you'll need the library class, class. Instances of Class are objects that, for example, represent a Java class, record or a Java interface.

In this respect, Java differs from many conventional programming languages because the members of classes can be queried by the currently running program using the Class objects. The instances of Class are a restricted kind of meta-object[2]—containing the description of a Java type but revealing only selected information. Besides normal classes, interfaces are also represented by a Class object, and even arrays and primitive data types—instead of Class, the class name Type would probably have been more appropriate.

16.3.1   Obtaining a Class Object

First, for a given class, you must identify the associated Class object. Class objects themselves can only be created by the JVM. (We can't create instances because the constructor of Class is private.) To obtain a reference to a Class object, the following solutions are available:

- If an instance of the class is available, you can call the getClass() method of the object and get the Class instance of the associated class.

- Each type contains a static variable named .class of type Class, which references the associated Class instance.

- The ending .class is also permitted for primitive data types. The same Class object returns the static variable TYPE of the wrapper classes. Thus, int.class == Integer.TYPE is true.

---

2 True metaclasses are classes whose only instance in each case is the regular Java class. Then, for example, the regular class variables would actually be object variables in the metaclass.

- The class method Class.forName(String) can query a class, and you'll obtain the associated Class instance as a result. If the type hasn't been loaded yet, for-Name(String) searches for and binds the class. Because searching can go wrong, a ClassNotFoundException is possible.

- If you already have a Class object but are interested in its ancestors instead, you can simply get a Class object for the superclass via getSuperclass().

The following example shows three ways to obtain a Class object for java.util.Date:

```
Class<Date> c1 = java.util.Date.class;
System.out.println( c1 );          // class java.util.Date
Class<?> c2 = new java.util.Date().getClass();
 // or Class<? extends Date> c2 = …

System.out.println( c2 );          // class java.util.Date
try {
  Class<?> c3 = Class.forName( "java.util.Date" );
  System.out.println( c3 );        // class java.util.Date
}
catch ( ClassNotFoundException e ) { e.printStackTrace(); }
```

Listing 16.1 src/main/java/com/tutego/insel/meta/GetClassObject.java, main()

The variant with forName(String) is useful if the name of the desired class wasn't determined when the program was translated.

Otherwise, the previous technique is more catchy, and the compiler can check if the type exists. A full qualification is needed: Class.forName("Date") would only search for Date in the default package, and the return isn't a collection after all.

[Ex]
> **Example**
> Note that class objects for primitive elements aren't returned by forName(String). The two expressions Class.forName("boolean") and Class.forName(boolean.class.get-Name()) lead to a ClassNotFoundException.

```
class java.lang.Object
```

▶ final Class<? extends Object> getClass()
Returns the Class instance at runtime which represents the class of the object.

```
final class java.lang.Class<T>
implements Serializable, GenericDeclaration, Type, AnnotatedElement
```

▶ static Class<?> forName(String className) throws ClassNotFoundException
Returns the Class instance for the class, record or interface with the specified fully qualified name. If the type hasn't yet been required by the program, the class loader searches for and loads the class. The method never returns null. If the class couldn't be loaded and included, a ClassNotFoundException will occur. The alternative method, forName(String name, boolean initialize, ClassLoader loader), also allows loading with a desired class loader. The class name must always be fully qualified.

ClassNotFoundException and NoClassDefFoundError*

A ClassNotFoundException can be thrown by any of the following methods:

- forName(...) from Class
- loadClass(String name [, boolean resolve]) from ClassLoader
- findSystemClass(String name) from ClassLoader

An exception occurs whenever the class loader can't find the class by its class name. Thus, the trigger is when an application wants to load types dynamically, but those types aren't present.

In addition to ClassNotFoundException, the NoClassDefFoundError is a hard LinkageError that the JVM raises whenever it can't load a class referenced in the bytecode. For example, let's consider an expression like new MyClass(). When the JVM executes this code, it attempts to load the bytecode from MyClass. If the bytecode for MyClass has been removed after compilation, the JVM raises the NoClassDefFoundError due to the unsuccessful load attempt. Also, the error occurs if the MyClass class was found when loading the bytecode, but MyClass has a static initialization block that in turn references a class for which no class file exists.

While ClassNotFoundException is more common than NoClassDefFoundError, the exception is generally an indication that a Java Archive file (JAR file) is missing in the module path.

Problems after Applying an Obfuscator*

The fact that the compiler automatically generates bytecode according to this modified source code only leads to unexpected problems if you run an obfuscator over the program text, which subsequently modifies the bytecode and thus obscures the meaning of the program or the bytecode and renames types in the process. Obviously, an obfuscator must not rename types whose Class instances are requested.

Otherwise, the obfuscator must correctly replace the corresponding strings as well (but of course not replace all strings that happen to match class names).

16.3.2 A Class Is a Type

In Java, different types exist, and classes, records, interfaces, and enumeration types are represented by the JVM as Class objects. In the Reflection API, the Type interface represents all types and the only implementing class is Class. Below Type there are some subinterfaces:

- ParameterizedType represents generic types like List<T>.
- TypeVariable<D> represents, for example, T extends Comparable<? super T>.
- WildcardType represents ? super T.
- GenericArrayType represents something like T[].

The only method of Type is getTypeName(), and this method is just a default method that calls toString(). Type is the return of various methods in the Reflection API, such as getGenericSuperclass() and getGenericInterfaces() of the Class class, and many other methods listed in the Javadoc under **USE**.

16.4 The Utility Classes System and Members

In the java.lang.System class, methods exist for requesting and changing system variables, for redirecting the standard data streams, for determining the current time, for terminating the application, and for several other tasks. All methods are exclusively static, and an instance of System can't be created. In the java.lang.Runtime class, additional helper methods are available, such as for starting external programs or for requesting memory requirements. Unlike System, only one method is static in this class, namely the singleton method getRuntime(), which returns the instance of Runtime.

java::lang::System
+ err : PrintStream
+ in : InputStream
+ out : PrintStream
+ arraycopy(src : Object, srcPos : int, dest : Object, destPos : int, length : int)
+ clearProperty(key : String) : String
+ console() : Console
+ currentTimeMillis() : long
+ exit(status : int)
+ gc()
+ getProperties() : Properties
+ getProperty(key : String, def : String) : String
+ getProperty(key : String) : String
+ getSecurityManager() : SecurityManager
+ getenv(name: String) : String
+ getenv() : Map
+ identityHashCode(x : Object) : int
+ inheritedChannel() : Channel
+ load(filename : String)
+ loadLibrary(libname : String)
+ mapLibraryName(libname : String) : String
+ nanoTime() : long
+ runFinalization()
+ runFinalizersOnExit(Value : boolean)
+ setErr(err : PrintStream)
+ setIn(in : InputStream)
+ setOut(out : PrintStream)
+ setProperties(props : Properties)
+ setProperty(key : String, value : String) : String
+ setSecurityManager(s : SecurityManager)

java::lang::Runtime
+ addShutdownHook(hook : Thread)
+ availableProcessors() : int
+ exec(cmdarray : String[], envp : String[], dir : File) : Process
+ exec(command : String, envp : String[], dir File) : Process
+ exec(command : String) : Process
+ exec(cmdarray : String[]) : Process
+ exec(cmdarray : String[], envp : String[]) : Process
+ exec(command : String, envp : String[]) : Process
+ exit(status : int)
+ freeMemory() : long
+ gc()
+ getLocalizedInputStream(in : InputStream) : InputStream
+ getLocalizedOutputStream(out: OutputStream) : OutputStream
+ getRuntime() : Runtime
+ halt(status : int)
+ load(filename : String)
+ loadLibrary(libname : String)
+ maxMemory() : long
+ removeShutdownHook(hook : Thread) : boolean
+ runFinalization()
+ runFinalizersOnExit(value : boolean)
+ totalMemory() : long
+ traceInstructions(on : boolean)
+ traceMethodCalls(on : boolean)

Figure 16.4 Members of the System and Runtime Classes

> **Remark**
>
> All in all, the System and Runtime classes don't seem particularly orderly, as shown in Figure 16.4; you may think everything that doesn't fit elsewhere can be found in these two classes. Also, some methods of one class would be just as good in the other class.
>
> The fact that the static method System.arraycopy(...) for copying arrays isn't located in java.util.Arrays can only be explained historically. Furthermore, System.exit(int) redirects to Runtime.getRuntime().exit(int). Some methods are obsolete and distributed differently: The exec(...) of Runtime to start external processes is handled by a new class (ProcessBuilder), and the question about the memory state or the number of processors is answered by MBeans, such as ManagementFactory.getOperatingSystemMXBean().getAvailableProcessors(). But API design is like gambling: One rash action, and you've lost the farm.

16.4.1 Memory of the Java Virtual Machine

The Runtime object includes the following three methods that provide information about the memory of the JVM:

- maxMemory() returns the maximum number of bytes available for the JVM. The value can be set when calling the JVM with -Xmx in the command line.

- totalMemory() is what is currently used and can grow to maxMemory(). Basically, this memory limit can also shrink again. The following applies: maxMemory() > totalMemory().

- freeMemory() indicates the memory that is free for new objects and also provokes the automatic garbage collection process. The following applies: totalMemory() > freeMemory(). However, freeMemory() isn't the entire freely available memory area because the "share" of maxMemory() is still missing.

Two pieces of information are missing and therefore must be calculated:

- **Used memory:**
  ```
  long usedMemory = Runtime.getRuntime().totalMemory() -
  Runtime.getRuntime().freeMemory();
  ```
- **Free total memory:**
  ```
  long totalFreeMemory = Runtime.getRuntime().maxMemory() - usedMemory;
  ```

> **Example**
>
> The following example outputs information about the memory on a computer:
>
> ```
> long totalMemory    = Runtime.getRuntime().totalMemory();
> long freeMemory     = Runtime.getRuntime().freeMemory();
> long maxMemory      = Runtime.getRuntime().maxMemory();
> long usedMemory     = totalMemory - freeMemory;
> ```

16

```
long totalFreeMemory = maxMemory - usedMemory;

System.out.printf(
  "total=%d MiB, free=%d MiB, max=%d MiB, used=%d MiB, total free=%d MiB%n",
  totalMemory >> 20, freeMemory >> 20, maxMemory >> 20,
  usedMemory >> 20, totalFreeMemory >> 20 );
```

The result is the following output:

```
total=126 MiB, free=124 MiB, max=2016 MiB, used=1 MiB, total free=2014 MiB
```

16.4.2   Number of CPUs or Cores

The `Runtime` method `availableProcessors()` returns the number of logical processors or cores.

[Ex]

Example

Print the number of processors/cores:

```
System.out.println( Runtime.getRuntime().availableProcessors() );  // 4
```

16.4.3   System Properties of the Java Environment

The Java environment manages system properties, such as path separators or virtual machine versions in the `java.util.Properties` object. The static method `System.get-Properties()` queries these system properties and returns the filled `Properties` object. However, the `Properties` object isn't absolutely necessary for querying individual properties: `System.getProperty(...)` directly queries a property.

[Ex]

Example

The following example outputs the name of the operating system:

```
System.out.println( System.getProperty( "os.name" ) );  // e.g., Windows 10
```

The following example outputs all system properties on the screen:

```
System.getProperties().list( System.out );
```

An excerpt of the result is shown in the following output:

```
-- listing properties --
sun.desktop=windows
awt.toolkit=sun.awt.windows.WToolkit
java.specification.version=9
file.encoding.pkg=sun.io
sun.cpu.isalist=amd64
…
```

Table 16.4 shows a list of the important standard system properties.

Key	Meaning
java.version	Version of the Java Runtime Environment (JRE)
java.class.path	The current classpath
java.library.path	Path for native libraries
java.io.tmpdir	Path for temporary files
os.name	Name of the operating system
file.separator	Separator of the path segments, for example / (Unix) or \ (Windows)
path.separator	Separator for path specifications, such as : (Unix) or ; (Windows)
line.separator	Newline character (string)
user.name	Name of the logged-on user
user.home	Home directory of the user
user.dir	Current directory of the user

Table 16.4 Standard System Properties

16

Application Programming Interface Documentation

A few more keys are listed in the API documentation at System.getProperties(). Some variables are also accessible in other ways, such as through the File class.

```
final class java.lang.System
```

▶ static String getProperty(String key)
Returns the assignment of a system property. If the key is null or empty, a NullPointerException or an IllegalArgumentException, respectively, will occur.

▶ static String getProperty(String key, String def)
Returns the assignment of a system property. If the property isn't present, the method returns the string def, which is the default value. For the exceptions, the same applies as for getProperty(String).

▶ static String setProperty(String key, String value)
Reassigns a system property. The return is the previous assignment or null if no previous assignment exists.

▶ static String clearProperty(String key)
Deletes a system property from the list. The return is the previous assignment or null if no previous assignment exists.

▶ static Properties getProperties()

Returns a Properties object filled with the current system assignments.

16.4.4   Setting Custom Properties from the Console*

Properties can also be set from the console during the program startup. This approach is convenient for a configuration that controls, for example, the behavior of a program. On the command line, -D specifies the name of the property and, after an equal sign (without whitespace), its value. Consider the following example:

```
$ java -DLOG -DUSER=Chris -DSIZE=100 com.tutego.insel.lang.SetProperty
```

The LOG property is "simply exists" but with no assigned value. The next two properties, USER and SIZE, are associated with values that are first of type String and must be further processed by the program. This information doesn't appear with the argument list in the static main(String[]) method because it precedes the name of the class and is already processed by the JRE.

To read the properties, we'll use the familiar System.getProperty(...) method in the following example:

```
Optional<String> logProperty = ofNullable( System.getProperty( "LOG" ) );
Optional<String> user nameProperty = ofNullable( System.getProperty( "USER" ) );
Optional<String> sizeProperty = ofNullable( System.getProperty( "SIZE" ) );

System.out.println( logProperty.isPresent() );                           // true
user nameProperty.ifPresent( System.out::println );                      //
  Chris
sizeProperty.map( Integer::parseInt ).ifPresent( System.out::println ); // 100
System.out.println( System.getProperty( "DEBUG", "false" ) );            //
  false
```

Listing 16.2 com/tutego/insel/lang/SetProperty.java, main()

In return, you'll receive a string indicating the value via getProperty(String). If no property of that name exists at all, you'll get null instead. In this way, we can know if this value was set at all. So, a simple null test tells us whether logProperty is present or not. Instead of -DLOG, -DLOG= also returns the same result because the associated value is the empty string. Since all properties are of type String to begin with, user nameProperty is easy to output, and you'll get either null or the string specified after =. If the types aren't strings, they must be processed further, for example, with Integer.parseInt(), Double.parseDouble(), and so on. The System.getProperty(String, String) method, which is passed two arguments, is pretty useful in this case because the second argument represents a default value. Thus, a default value can always be assumed.

Boolean.getBoolean(String)

In the case of properties that are assigned truth values, the following statement can be written:

```
boolean b = Boolean.parseBoolean( System.getProperty( property ) );  // (*)
```

There's another variant for the truth values. The static method `Boolean.getBoolean(String)` searches for a property with the specified name in the system properties. Thus, the following is analogous to the line (*):

```
boolean b = Boolean.getBoolean( property );
```

You might be surprised to find this static method in the wrapper class `Boolean` because property access has nothing to do with wrapper objects and the class actually goes beyond its area of responsibility in this case.

Compared to a separate, direct `System` query, `getBoolean(String)` also has a disadvantage in that, when it returns `false`, you can't distinguish whether the property simply doesn't exist or whether the property is assigned the value `false`. Also, incorrectly set values like `-DP=false` always result in `false`.[3]

```
final class java.lang.Boolean
implements Serializable, Comparable<Boolean>
```

▶ `static boolean getBoolean(String name)`
  Reads a system property named `name` and returns `true` if the value of the property is equal to the string `"true"`. The return value is `false` if the value of the system property is `false`, if the property doesn't exist, or if the property is `null`.

16.4.5 Newline Characters and line.separator

To move from the end of one line to the beginning of the next, a *newline* is inserted. The character for a new line doesn't have to be a single character; several characters may also be necessary. Unfortunately for programmers, the number of characters for a newline sequence depends on the architecture, for instance:

- Unix, macOS: Line feed (LF for short), \n
- Windows: Carriage return (CR for short) and line feed

The control code for a carriage return is 13 (0x0D); the control code for a line feed is 10 (0x0A). Java also assigns its own escape sequences for these characters: \r for carriage returns and \n for line feeds. (The \f sequence is for a form feed, also called a "page feed," which doesn't play any role in line breaks).

---

3 This confusion is due to the implementation: `Boolean.valueOf("false")` returns `false` just like `Boolean.valueOf("")` or `Boolean.valueOf(null)`.

In Java, you can obtain a newline character or a newline string from the system in one of the following three ways:

- By calling `System.getProperty("line.separator")`
- By calling `System.lineSeparator()`
- You don't always have to query the character (or, strictly speaking, a possible string of characters) individually. If the character is part of a formatted output at the formatter, `String.format(...)` or `printf(...)`, the format specifier %n stands for exactly the newline string stored in the system.

16.4.6   Environment Variables of the Operating System

Almost every operating system uses the concept of *environment variables*; for example, PATH is known for the search path for applications on Windows and Unix. Java enables access to these system environment variables. Two static methods are used for this purpose:

---
final class java.lang.**System**

▶ static `Map<String, String> getEnv()`
Reads a set of `<string, string>` pairs with all system properties.

▶ static `String getEnv(String name)`
Reads a system property named name. If the property doesn't exist, the return will be null.

Variable Name	Description	Example
COMPUTERNAME	Name of the computer	*MOE*
HOMEDRIVE	Drive of the user directory	*C:*
HOMEPATH	Path of the user directory	*\Users\Christian*
OS	Name of the operating system*	*Windows_NT*
PATH	Search path	*C:\windows\SYSTEM32; C:\windows ...*
PATHEXT	File extensions that represent executable programs	*.COM;.EXE;.BAT;.CMD;.VBS;.VBE;.JS;. JSE;.WSF;.WSH;.MSC*
SYSTEMDRIVE	Drive of the operating system	*C:*
TEMP and also TMP	Temporary directory	*C:\Users\CHRIST~1\AppData\Local\ Temp*
USERDOMAIN	Domain of the user	*MOE*

Table 16.5 Selection of Some Environment Variables Available in Windows

Variable Name	Description	Example
USERNAME	Name of the user	*Christian*
USERPROFILE	Profile directory	*C:\Users\Christian*
WINDIR	Directory of the operating system	*C:\windows*

* The result differs from `System.getProperty("os.name")`, which already returns "Windows 10" for Windows 10.

Table 16.5 Selection of Some Environment Variables Available in Windows (Cont.)

Some variables are also accessible via the system properties, for instance, with `System.getProperties()`, `System.getProperty(...)`, and so on.

[Ex]

Example

The following example outputs the environment variables of the system:

```
Map<String,String> map = System.getenv();
map.forEach( (k, v) -> System.out.printf( "%s=%s%n", k, v ) );
```

16

16.5   The Languages of Different Countries

When developers start with console or GUI output, they often hardwire the output to a local language. If the language changes, the software can't handle other country-specific rules, for example, when formatting floats. Developing "multilingual" programs that provide localized outputs in different languages is not too difficult. Basically, you'll replace all language-dependent strings and formatting of data with code that takes into account country-specific output formats and rules. Java offers a solution for these cases: on one hand, you can define a language that then specifies rules according to which the Java API can automatically format data, and on the other hand, you can allow language-dependent parts to be swapped out to resource files.

16.5.1   Regional Languages via Locale Objects

In Java, `Locale` objects represent languages in geographic, political, or cultural regions. The language and the region must be separated because a region or a country doesn't always clearly specify the language. For Canada, in the province of Quebec, the French edition is relevant, which, of course, differs from the English edition. Each of these language-specific properties can be encapsulated in a special object. These `Locale` objects are then passed to a `Formatter` that's located behind `String.format(...)` and `printf(...)` or passed to a `Scanner`. These outputs are referred to as *locale sensitive*.

Building Locale Objects

Locale objects are always created with the name of the language and optionally with the name of the country or a region and variant. The Locale class provides three ways to build the objects:

- Using the Locale constructor (deprecated in Java 19)
- Using the nested Builder class of Locale uses the builder pattern to build new Locale objects
- Using the Locale method forLanguageTag(...) and a string identifier

Example

Country abbreviations are specified in the constructor of the Locale class, for example, for a language object for Great Britain or France. Consider the following examples:

```
Locale greatBritain = new Locale( "en", "GB" );
Locale french       = new Locale( "fr" );
```

In the second example, we don't care about the country. We're simply choosing French as the language, no matter what part of the world.

Languages are identified by 2-letter abbreviations from the ISO 639 code[4] (*ISO Language Code*), and country names are 2-letter abbreviations described in ISO 3166[5] (*ISO Country Code*).

Example

Three variants for building Locale.JAPANESE are found in the following example:

```
Locale loc1 = new Locale( "ja" );
Locale loc2 = new Locale.Builder().setLanguage( "ja" ).build();
Locale loc3 = Locale.forLanguageTag( "ja" );
final class java.util.Locale
implements Cloneable, Serializable
```

▶ Locale(String language)
Creates a new Locale object for the language given by the ISO-693 standard. Invalid identifiers aren't recognized.

▶ Locale(String language, String country)
Creates a Locale object for a language according to ISO 693 and a country according to the ISO 3166 standard.

---

4 *https://en.wikipedia.org/wiki/List_of_ISO_639-1_codes*
5 *https://en.wikipedia.org/wiki/ISO_3166-1*

▶ Locale(String language, String country, String variant)
Creates a Locale object for a language, a country, and a variant. variant is a vendor-dependent specification like "WIN" or "MAC."

The static Locale.getDefault() method returns the currently set language. For the running JVM, Locale.setDefault(Locale) can change the language.

The Locale class has more methods; developers should study the Javadoc for the Builder, for forLanguageTag(...) and the new extensions and filter methods.[6]

Constants for Some Languages

The Locale class has constants for commonly occurring languages, with an option for specifying countries. The constants for countries and languages include, for example, CANADA, CHINA, FRENCH, GERMAN, ITALIAN, KOREAN, TAIWAN, UK and US. Behind an abbreviation like Locale.UK, nothing else exists except for the initialization with new Locale("en", "GB").

Methods That Accept Instances of Locale

Locale objects are actually not interesting as objects—they do have methods, but more exciting is its use as a type for the identification of a language. Dozens of methods in the Java library accept Locale objects and adjust their behaviors based on them. Examples include printf(Locale, ...), format(Locale, ...), and toLowerCase(Locale).

Tip

If no variant of a format or parse method exists with a Locale object; the method usually doesn't support language-dependent behavior. The same limitation applies to objects that don't accept a Locale via a constructor or setter. Double.toString(...) is one such example, as is Double.parseDouble(...). In internationalized applications, these methods will rarely be found. Also, string concatenation with, for example, a float isn't permitted (because a Double method is called internally), and using String.format(...) is definitely a better option.

Methods of Locale*

Locale objects provide a number of methods that reveal the ISO-639 code of the country, for example.

Example

The following example outputs the Locale information accessible for languages in selected countries. The objects System.out and Locale.* are imported statically:

---

6 Oracle's Java tutorial describes these extensions at *http://docs.oracle.com/javase/tutorial/i18n/locale/index.html*.

```
out.println(GERMANY.getCountry());          // DE
out.println(GERMANY.getLanguage());         // de
out.println(GERMANY.getVariant());          //
out.println(GERMANY.getISO3Country());      // DEU
out.println(GERMANY.getISO3Language());     // deu
out.println(CANADA.getDisplayCountry());    // Canada
out.println(GERMANY.getDisplayLanguage());  // German
out.println(GERMANY.getDisplayName());      // German (Germany)
out.println(CANADA.getDisplayName());       // English (Canada)
out.println(GERMANY.getDisplayName(FRENCH)); // allemand (Allemagne)
out.println(CANADA.getDisplayName(FRENCH));  // anglais (Canada)
```

Listing 16.3 src/main/java/com/tutego/insel/locale/GermanyLocal.java, main()

Static methods also exist for querying `Locale` objects:

```
final class java.util.Locale
implements Cloneable, Serializable
```

▶ static Locale getDefault()
Returns the language preset by the JVM, which defaults to the operating system.

▶ static Locale[] getAvailableLocales()
Returns a list of all installed `Locale` objects. The field contains at least `Locale.US` and about 160 entries.

▶ static String[] getISOCountries()
Returns an array of all 2-letter ISO-3166 country codes.

▶ static Set<String> getISOCountries(Locale.IsoCountryCode type)
Returns a set with all ISO-3166 country codes, where the `IsoCountryCode` list determines the following: `PART1_ALPHA2` returns the code of 2 letters, `PART1_ALPHA3` of 3 letters, `PART3` of 4 letters.

On the other hand, other methods provide abbreviations according to ISO standards:

```
final class java.util.Locale
implements Cloneable, Serializable
```

▶ String getCountry()
Returns the country abbreviation according to the ISO-3166 2-letter code.

▶ String getLanguage()
Returns the abbreviation of the language in ISO-639 code.

▶ String getISO3Country()
Returns the ISO abbreviation of the country of these settings and throws a `MissingResourceException` if the ISO abbreviation isn't available.

▶ String getISO3Language()
Returns the ISO abbreviation of the language of these settings and throws a `MissingResourceException` if the ISO abbreviation isn't available.

▶ String getVariant()
Returns the abbreviation of the variant or an empty string.

These methods provide abbreviations, but they aren't intended for human-readable output. For various get*() methods, therefore, corresponding getDisplay*() methods exist:

```
final class java.util.Locale
implements Cloneable, Serializable
```

▶ String getDisplayCountry(Locale inLocale)
final String getDisplayCountry()
Returns the name of the country for screen outputs for a language or Loa-cale.getDefault().

▶ String getDisplayLanguage(Locale inLocale)
String getDisplayLanguage()
Returns the name of the screen output language for a given Locale or Locale.getDefault().

▶ String getDisplayName(Locale inLocale)
final String getDisplayName()
Returns the name of the settings for a language or Locale.getDefault().

▶ String getDisplayVariant(Locale inLocale)
final String getDisplayVariant()
Returns the name of the variant for a language or Locale.getDefault().

16.6   Overview of Important Date Classes

Because date calculations are convoluted entities, we can be grateful to the developers of Java for providing many classes for date calculation and formatting. The developers have kept the classes abstract enough to allow for local specifics like output formatting, parsing, time zones, or daylight saving time/winter time in different calendars.

Prior to Java 1.1, only the java.util.Date class was available for displaying and manipulating date values, and this class had to carry out several tasks:

- Creation of a date/time object from year, month, day, minute, and second
- Querying day, month, year, and so on with an accuracy of milliseconds
- Processing and output of date strings

Since the Date class wasn't quite bug-free and internationalized, new classes were introduced in JDK 1.1, namely, the following:

- Calendar takes on Date's task of converting between different date representations and time scales. The GregorianCalendar subclass is created directly.

- DateFormat breaks up date strings and formats the output. Date formats also depend on the country, which Java represents through Locale objects, and on a time zone, which is represented by the instances of the TimeZone class.

In Java 8, another date library was added with entirely new types. Finally, date and time can be represented separately:

- LocalDate, LocalTime, and LocalDateTime are the temporal classes for a date, for a time, and for a combination of date and time, respectively.

- Period and Duration represent intervals.

16.6.1   Unix Time: January 1, 1970

January 1, 1970, was a Thursday with groundbreaking changes: The British rejoiced that the age of majority dropped from 24 to 18, and as in every year, and people everywhere woke up to massive hangovers from the night before. For us, however, a technical innovation is of concern: The date of 1/1/1970, 0:00:00 UTC is also referred to as the *Unix epoch*, and a *Unix time* is described in relation to this time in terms of seconds. For example, 100,000,000 seconds after 1/1/1970 is March 3, 1973, at 09:46:40. The *Unix Billennium* was celebrated 1,000,000,000 seconds after Jan. 1, 1970, namely, on Sept. 9, 2001, at 01:46:40.

16.6.2   System.currentTimeMillis()

Unix time is also an important concept for us Java developers because many times in Java are relative to this date. The timestamp 0 refers to 1/1/1970 0:00:00 Greenwich Mean Time. The System.currentTimeMillis() method returns the past milliseconds—not seconds!—relative to 1/1/1970, 00:00 UTC, although your operating system's clock may not be that accurate. The number of milliseconds is represented in a long (i.e., in 64 bits), which will suffice for about 300 million years.

[!]

Warning

The values of currentTimeMillis() don't necessarily ascend because Java gets the time from the operating system, where the system time can change. A user can adjust the time, or a service such as the *Network Time Protocol (NTP)* takes over this task. Differences of currentTimeMillis() timestamps are then completely wrong and could even be negative. An alternative is nanoTime(), which has no reference point, is more precise, and is always ascending.[7]

---

7 *http://stackoverflow.com/questions/351565/system-currenttimemillis-vs-system-nanotime* goes into more details and provides links to internal implementations.

16.6.3   Simple Time Conversions via TimeUnit

A time duration in Java is often expressed in terms of milliseconds. 1,000 milliseconds correspond to 1 second, 1,000 × 60 milliseconds to 1 minute, and so on. However, all those large numbers aren't easy to read, which is why TimeUnit objects are used with their to*(...) methods for the purpose of conversion. Java declares the following constants in TimeUnit: NANOSECONDS, MICROSECONDS, MILLISECONDS, DAYS, HOURS, SECONDS, and MINUTES.

Each of the enumeration elements defines the conversion methods, for instance, toDays(…), toHours(…), toMicros(…), toMillis(…), toMinutes(…), toNanos(…), and toSeconds(…). These methods receive a long and return a long in the corresponding unit. In addition, two convert(...) methods convert from one unit to another.

Example

The following example converts 23,746,387 milliseconds to hours:

```
int v = 23_746_387;
System.out.println( TimeUnit.MILLISECONDS.toHours( v ) ); // 6
System.out.println( TimeUnit.HOURS.convert( v,
  TimeUnit.MILLISECONDS ) ); // 6
enum java.util.concurrent.TimeUnit
extends Enum<TimeUnit>
implements Serializable, Comparable<TimeUnit>
```

▶ NANOSECONDS, MICROSECONDS, MILLISECONDS, SECONDS, MINUTES, HOURS, DAYS
  TimeUnit **enumeration elements.**

▶ long toDays(long duration)

▶ long toHours(long duration)

▶ long toMicros(long duration)

▶ long toMillis(long duration)

▶ long toMinutes(long duration)

▶ long toNanos(long duration)

▶ long toSeconds(long duration)

▶ long convert(long sourceDuration, TimeUnit sourceUnit)
  Returns sourceUnit.to*(sourceDuration), where * represents the respective unit. For example, this method returns **HOURS**.convert(sourceDuration, sourceUnit), then sourceUnit.to**Hours**(1). The readability of this method isn't ideal, so the other methods should be preferred. Results may be truncated, not rounded. If an overflow occurs, no ArithmeticException will follow.

▶ long convert(Duration duration)

Converts the passed duration into the time unit that represents the current TimeUnit. For example, TimeUnit.MINUTES.convert(Duration.ofHours(12)) returns 720. Thus, for example, aunit.convert(Duration.ofNanos(n)) and aunit.convert(n, NANOSEC-ONDS) are the same.

16.7   Date-Time API

The java.time package is based on the standardized calendar system of ISO-8601, and this covers how a date is represented, including time, date and time, UTC, time intervals (duration/time span), and time zones. The implementation is based on the Gregorian calendar, although other calendar types are also conceivable. Java's calendar system can use other standards or implementations as well, including the *Unicode Common Locale Data Repository (CLDR)* for localizing days of the week or the *Time-Zone Database (TZDB)*, which documents all time zone changes since 1970.

16.7.1   Initial Overview

The central temporal types from the Date-Time API can be quickly documented:

Type	Description	Field(s)
LocalDate	Represents a common date	Years, months, and days
LocalTime	Represents a common time	Hours, minutes, seconds, and nanoseconds
LocalDateTime	Combination of date and time	Years, months, days, hours, minutes, seconds, and nanoseconds
Period	Duration between two Local-Dates	Years, months, and days
Year	Year only	Year
Month	Month only	Month
MonthDay	Month and day only	Month, day
OffsetTime	Time with time zone	Hours, minutes, seconds, nanoseconds, and zone offset
OffsetDateTime	Date and time with time zone as UTC offset	Year, month, day, hours, minutes, seconds, nanoseconds, and zone offsets

Table 16.6 All Temporal Classes from java.time

Type	Description	Field(s)
ZonedDateTime	Date and time with time zone as ID and offset	Year, month, day, hours, minutes, seconds, nanoseconds, and zone info
Instant	Time (continuous machine time)	Nanoseconds
Duration	Time interval between two instants	Seconds/nanoseconds

Table 16.6 All Temporal Classes from java.time (Cont.)

16.7.2   Human Time and Machine Time

Date and time, which we as humans understand in units such as days and minutes, is referred to as *human time*, while the continuous time of the computer, which has a resolution in the nanosecond range, is called *machine time*. The machine time begins at a time we call an *epoch*, namely, the Unix epoch.

From Chapter 7, Section 7.2.5, you learned how most classes are made for humans and that only Instant/Duration refers to machine time. LocalDate, LocalTime, and LocalDateTime represent human time without reference to a time zone, whereas ZonedDateTime does reference a time zone. When choosing the right time classes for a task, the first consideration is, of course, whether to represent human time or machine time. This choice is followed by questions about exactly which fields are needed and whether a time zone is relevant or not. For example, if the execution time is to be measured, you don't need to know on which date the measurement started and ended; in this case, Duration would be correct, unlike Period.

Example

Examples for explicit formatting and default formatting for the US locale:

```
LocalDate now = LocalDate.now();
System.out.println( now ); // e.g., 2023-01-31
System.out.printf( "%d. %s %d%n",
                    now.getDayOfMonth(), now.getMonth(), now.getYear() );
// e.g., 31. JANUARY 2023
LocalDate bdayMLKing = LocalDate.of( 1929, Month.JANUARY, 15 );
DateTimeFormatter formatter =
 DateTimeFormatter.ofLocalizedDate( FormatStyle.MEDIUM );
System.out.println( bdayMLKing.format( formatter ) ); // Jan 15, 1929
```

The getMonth() method on a LocalDate returns a java.time.Month object as the result, and these are enumerations. The toString() representation returns the constant in uppercase letters.

All classes are based on the ISO system by default. Other calendar systems, such as the Japanese calendar, are created using types from java.time.chrono, and of course, entirely new systems are also possible.

[Ex]

> **Example**
>
> Output for the Japanese calendar:
>
> ```
> ChronoLocalDate now = JapaneseChronology.INSTANCE.dateNow();
> System.out.println( now );                 // Japanese Reiwa 4-01-31
> ```

Package Overview

The types of the Date-Time API are distributed among different packages:

- java.time
  Contains the standard classes like LocalTime and Instant. All types are based on the ISO-8601 calendar system, commonly known as the "Gregorian calendar." This calendar is extended by the *Proleptic Gregorian Calendar*. This calendar is also valid for the time before 1582 (the introduction of this calendar), so that a consistent timeline can be used.

- java.time.chrono
  In this package, you'll find predefined alternative (i.e., non-ISO) calendar systems, such as the Japanese calendar, the Thai-Buddhist calendar, the Islamic calendar, and a few others.

- java.time.format
  Classes for formatting and parsing date and time, such as the DateTimeFormatter.

- java.time.zone
  Supporting classes for time zones, such as ZonedDateTime.

- java.time.temporal
  Deeper API that allows access and modification of individual fields of a date/time value.

Design Principles

Before we get into the individual classes, let's look at some design principles because all types of the Date-Time API follow recurring patterns. The first and most important property is that all objects are *immutable*; that is, they can't be changed. In contrast, with the "old" API, Date and the Calendar classes were mutable, with sometimes devastating consequences. If these objects are passed around and changed, incalculable side effects can occur. The classes of the new Date-Time API are immutable, and so the date/time classes like LocalTime or Instant are opposed to mutable types like Date or Calendar. All methods that look as if they permitted changes now instead create new objects with the desired changes. Side effects are therefore absent, and all types are thread safe.

Immutability is a design property as is the fact that null isn't permitted as an argument. In the Java API, null is often accepted because it expresses something optional, but the Date-Time API usually penalizes null with a NullPointerExcpetion. The fact that null isn't in use as an argument and not as a return benefits another property: The code can be mostly written with a fluent API (i.e., cascaded calls) since many methods return the this reference, as is known from StringBuilder.

Added to these more technical features is a consistent naming that is different from the naming of the well-known JavaBeans. So, no constructors and no setters exist (immutable classes don't need them), but instead, patterns adhere to many types from the Date-Time API:

Method	Class/Instance Method	Basic Meaning
now()	Static	Returns an object with current time/current date
of*()	Static	Creates new objects
from	Static	Creates new objects from other representations
parse*()	Static	Creates a new object from a string representation
format()	Instance	Formats and returns a string
get*()	Instance	Returns fields of an object
is*()	Instance	Queries the status of an object
with*()	Instance	Returns an instance of the object with a changed state
plus*()	Instance	Returns an instance of the object with a totaled state
minus*()	Instance	Returns an instance of the object with a reduced state
to*()	Instance	Converts an object to a new type
at*()	Instance	Combines this object with another object
*Into()	Instance	Combines an own object with another target object

Table 16.7 Name Patterns in the Date-Time API

You've already used the now() method in one of the first examples in this section, and this method returns the current date, for example. Other creator methods are prefixed with of, from, or with; no constructors exist. The methods of the with*() type assume the role of setters.

16.7.3   The LocalDate Date Class

A date (without a time zone) is represented by the LocalDate class. This class can be used to represent a birth date, for example.

A temporal object can be created using the static of (. . .) factory methods and derived via ofInstant(Instant instant, ZoneId zone) or from another temporal object. Interesting are the methods that work with a TemporalAdjuster.

Equipped with these objects, you can use various getters and query individual fields, such as getDayOfMonth(); getDayOfYear() (return int); getDayOfWeek(), which returns an enumeration of type DayOfWeek; and getMonth(), which returns an enumeration of type Month. Furthermore, other methods include long toEpochDay() and long toEpochSecond(LocalTime time, ZoneOffset offset).

[Ex]

Example

Find the next Saturday from now:

```
LocalDate today = LocalDate.now();
LocalDate nextSaturday =
 today.with( TemporalAdjusters.next(DayOfWeek.SATURDAY) );
System.out.printf( "Today is %s, and next Saturday is %s",
                   today, nextSaturday );
```

In addition, some methods return new LocalDate objects with minus*(...) or plus*(...) if, for example, a number of years should be returned with minusYear(long yearsToSubtract). By negating the sign, the opposite method can also be used. In other words, LocalDate.now().minusMonths(1) provides the same result as LocalDate.now().plusMonths(-1). The with*(...) methods reassign a field and return a modified new LocalDate object.

From a LocaleDate object, you can create other temporal objects: atTime(...), for example, returns LocalDateTime objects in which certain time fields are assigned. atTime(int hour, int minute) is such an example. With until(...), a time duration of the Period type can be returned. Two methods that provide a stream of LocalDate objects up to an endpoint are also interesting:

- Stream<LocalDate> datesUntil(LocalDate endExclusive)
- Stream<LocalDate> datesUntil(LocalDate endExclusive, Period step)

16.8   Logging with Java

Logging information about program states is important for reconstructing and understanding the flow and states of a program at a later time. A logging API can write messages to the console or to external storage, such as text files, XML files, and databases, or to distribute these messages via chat.

16.8.1   Logging Application Programming Interfaces

Regarding logging libraries and APIs, the Java world is unfortunately divided. Since the Java standard library didn't provide a logging API in its first versions, the open-source library *log4j* quickly filled this gap. This library is used in almost every major Java project today. When the Logging API moved into Java 1.4 with Java Specification Request (JSR) 47, the Java community was surprised to find that java.util.logging (*JUL*) was neither API-compatible with the popular Log4j nor as powerful as Log4j.[8]

Over the years, the picture has changed. While in the early day's developers relied exclusively on log4j, more and more projects are now using JUL. One of the reasons is that some developers want to avoid external dependencies (although this doesn't really work since almost every included Java library is based on log4j). Another reason is that for many projects JUL is simply sufficient. In practice, for larger projects, as a result, multiple logging configurations overcrowd their own programs, as each logging implementation is configured differently.

16.8.2   Logging with java.util.logging

The Java logging API can write a message that you can then use for maintenance or security checks. The API is simple:

```java
package com.tutego.insel.logging;

import static java.time.temporal.ChronoUnit.MILLIS;
import static java.time.Instant.now;
import java.time.Instant;
import java.util.logging.Level;
import java.util.logging.Logger;

public class JULDemo {

  private static final Logger log = Logger.getLogger( JULDemo.class.getName() );

  public static void main( String[] args ) {
    Instant start = now();
    log.info( "About to start" );

    try {
      log.log( Level.INFO, "Lets try to throw {0}", "null" );
      throw null;
    }
```

---

8 The standard logging API, on the other hand, provides only basics like hierarchical loggers. Standard logging doesn't come close to the power of log4j with its large number of writers in files, syslog/NT loggers, databases, and dispatch over the network.

```
    catch ( Exception e ) {
      log.log( Level.SEVERE, "Oh Oh", e );
    }
    log.info( () -
> String.format( "Runtime: %s ms", start.until(now(), MILLIS )) );
  }
}
```

Listing 16.4 src/main/java/com/tutego/insel/logging/CULDemo.java, JULDemo

When you run the example, the following warning appears on the console:

```
Jan. 24, 2022 7:47:46 PM com.tutego.insel.logging.JULDemo main
INFO: About to start
Jan. 24, 2022 7:47:46 PM com.tutego.insel.logging.JULDemo main
INFO: Lets try to throw null
Jan. 24, 2022 7:47:46 PM com.tutego.insel.logging.JULDemo main
SEVERE: Oh Oh
java.lang.NullPointerException: Cannot throw exception because "null" is null
at com.tutego.insel.logging.JULDemo.main(JULDemo.java:20)

Jan. 24, 2022 7:47:46 PM com.tutego.insel.logging.JULDemo main
INFO: Runtime: 35 ms
```

The Logger Object

The Logger object is a central element that can be retrieved via Logger.getAnonymousLogger() or via Logger.getLogger(String name), where name is usually assigned the fully qualified class name. Often, the Logger object is declared as a private static final variable in the class.

Logging with Log Level

Not every message is equally important. Some messages are useful for debugging or because of timing measurements, but exceptions in the catch branches are hugely important. To support different levels of detail, you can specify a *log level*. This level determines how "serious" the error or a message is, which is important later when errors are sorted according to their urgency. Log levels are declared as constants in the Level class[9] in the following ways:

- FINEST (smallest level)
- FINER
- FINE

---

9 Since the logging framework joined Java in version 1.4, it doesn't yet use typed enumerations, which have only been available since Java 5.

- CONFIG
- INFO
- WARNING
- SEVERE (highest level)

For the logging process itself, the Logger class provides the general method log(Level level, String msg) or a separate method for each level.

Level	Call via log(...)	Special Log Method
SEVERE	log(Level.SEVERE, msg)	severe(String msg)
WARNING	log(Level.WARNING, msg)	warning(String msg)
INFO	log(Level.INFO, msg)	info(String msg)
CONFIG	log(Level.CONFIG, msg)	config(String msg)
FINE	log(Level.FINE, msg)	fine(String msg)
FINER	log(Level.FINER, msg)	finer(String msg)
FINEST	log(Level.FINEST, msg)	finest(String msg)

Table 16.8 Log Levels and Methods

All these methods send a message of type String. If an exception and the associated stack trace must be logged, developers must use the following logger method, which is also used in the example:

▶ void log(Level level, String msg, Throwable thrown)

The variants of severe(...), warning(...), and so on are not overloaded with a Throwable parameter type.

16.9 Maven: Resolving Build Management and Dependencies

In Chapter 1, Section 1.9.1, we created a Maven project, but never really benefited from using Maven. Two things stand out:

1. Dependencies can be easily declared, and they are automatically downloaded by Maven, including all sub-dependencies. Maven's particular strength lies in resolving transitive dependencies.

2. During the build, Java source code alone doesn't make a project; the sources must be compiled, test cases must be run, and Javadoc should be generated. At the end, the final result is usually a compressed JAR file.

16.9.1   Dependency to Be Accepted

As an example, let's create a dependency on the small web framework *Spark* (*https://sparkjava.com*). Let's open the Project Object Model (POM) file *pom.xml* and add the code lines in bold for the dependency:

```
<project …>
  …
  <properties>
    <maven.compiler.target>17</maven.compiler.target>
    <maven.compiler.source>17</maven.compiler.source>
    <project.build.sourceEncoding>UTF-8</project.build.sourceEncoding>
  </properties>
  <dependencies>
    <dependency>
      <groupId>com.sparkjava</groupId>
      <artifactId>spark-core</artifactId>
      <version>2.9.3</version>
    </dependency>
  </dependencies>
</project>
```

Listing 16.5: pom.xml

All dependencies are located in a special XML element named <dependencies>. Below that element, you can then have any number of <dependency> blocks.

Now that everything is prepared, let's write the main program:

```
public class SparkServer {
  public static void main( String[] args ) {
    spark.Spark.get( "/hello", ( req, res ) -
> "Hello Browser " + req.userAgent() );
  }
}
```

Listing 16.5 src/main/java/SparkServer.java

When you start the program as usual, a web server starts as well, and you can read the output via the URL *http://localhost:4567/hello*. (You can ignore the logger outputs.)

16.9.2   Local and the Remote Repository

Resolving dependent JAR files takes longer the first time because Maven contacts a remote repository and always pulls the latest JAR files from that location and then stores these files locally. The extensive remote repository stores almost all versions of JAR files for many well-known open-source projects. The *Central Repository* can be found *https://repo.maven.apache.org/maven2/*.

The downloaded resources themselves aren't stored in the project but in a local repository located in the user's home directory and named *.m2*. In this way, all Maven projects share the same JAR files, and they don't have to be reobtained and updated on a project-by-project basis.

16.9.3 Lifecycles, Stages, and Maven Plugins

A Maven build consists of a three-stage lifecycle: `clean`, `default`, and `site`. Within this lifecycle are *stages*. For example, `default` contains the `compile` stage for translating the sources. Everything Maven runs are *plugins*, such as `compilers`, and many others that are listed at *https://maven.apache.org/plugins/*. A plugin can execute different *goals*. For example, the Javadoc plugin (described at *https://maven.apache.org/components/plugins/maven-javadoc-plugin/*) currently knows 16 goals. A goal can be accessed subsequently via the command line or via the integrated development environment (IDE).

For example, a JAR file is created via the `package` stage:

```
$ mvn package
```

The command-line tool must be called in the directory where the POM file is located.

16.10 Further Reading

The Java library provides a large number of classes and methods, but not always exactly what's required by the current project. Some problems, such as the structure and configuration of Java projects, object-relational mappers (*www.hibernate.org*), or command-line parsers, may require various commercial or open-source libraries and frameworks. With purchased products, licensing issues are obvious, but with open-source products, integration into one's own closed source project isn't always a given. Various types of licenses (*https://opensource.org/licenses*) for open-source software with always different specifications—whether the source code is changeable, whether derivatives must also be free, whether mixing with proprietary software possible—complicate the choice, and violations (*https://gpl-violations.org/*) are publicly denounced and unpleasant. Java developers should increasingly focus their attention on software under the Berkeley Source Distribution (BSD) license (the Apache license belongs in this group) and under the LGPL license for commercial distribution. The Apache group has assembled a nice collection of classes and methods named *Apache Commons* (*http://commons.apache.org*), and studying these sources are recommended for software developers. The website *https://www.openhub.net* is exceptionally well suited for this purpose and enables searching via specific keywords through more than 1 billion source code lines of various programming languages—amazing how many developers use profanities!

Chapter 17

Introduction to Concurrent Programming

"Because of the emergency here, people are going to try many different solutions in parallel."
—Raul Andino-Pavlovsky

Java supports *concurrent programming*, which allows several programs to be run simultaneously. In this chapter you'll learn how Java can use threads for running concurrent programs.

17.1 Concurrency and Parallelism

Computer systems solve problems in the real world, so we'll also stay in the real world in our approach to concurrent programming environments. As you go through the world, you notice many things happening at the same time: The sun is shining, mopeds and cars race down the street, the radio is playing. Some people are talking, maybe some are eating, and dogs are romping around on the lawn. Not only do these things happen simultaneously, but manifold dependencies exist between these events, such as in waiting situations: At the red light, some cars are waiting, while at the green light people are crossing the street—when the signal changes, these other things also change.

When many things happen simultaneously, we refer to an interacting system as *concurrent*. At the same time, processes can be executed *in parallel*. Some things only seem to happen in parallel, but in reality, they happen quickly one after the other. What we then perceive in these cases is called *quasi-parallelism*. If two people eat at the same time, for example, it is parallel, but if someone eats and breathes, it seems simultaneous from the outside, but isn't. Swallowing and breathing are generally sequential.[1] Let's transfer these concepts to software: The simultaneous processing of programs and use of resources is concurrent. Ultimately, depending on the technical conditions of the machine (i.e., hardware), this concurrency may actually be implemented by parallel processing—for example, across several processors or cores.

In Java, concurrent programs are implemented by threads, where each thread corresponds to a task. Ideally, the processing of the threads also happens in parallel if the

---

1 Let's leave toddlers out of it for a moment.

machine has multiple processors or cores. A program that is implemented concurrently can cut its working time in half with two processors or cores in parallel execution; however, work times don't have to be halved: It's still up to the operating system how it executes the threads.

Figure 17.1 Pit Stop: Perfect Use of the Time Window through Parallel Work

17.1.1 Multitasking, Processes, and Threads

A modern operating system gives the user the illusion that different programs are running simultaneously—operating systems support *multitasking* and are referred to as being *capable of multitasking*. When a program is executed, the operating system creates a *process*—all running programs consist of processes. A process is composed of the program code and the relevant data and has its own address space. Furthermore, resources such as open files or assigned interfaces are included. The management of the virtual memory of the operating system separates the address spaces of the individual processes. This separation prevents one process from corrupting the memory space of another process: A process doesn't see the memory area of another process. To enable processes to exchange data with each other, a special memory area is marked as *shared memory*. Programs running amok are possible but are stopped by the operating system.

This concurrency of processes is ensured by the operating system, which switches the processes every few milliseconds on single-processor machines. The part of the operating system that handles switching is called the *dispatcher*. For this reason, with a processor (with only one core), the program is concurrent, but not really parallel; instead, the operating system fools us into thinking it is concurrent by interleaving the processes. If multiple processors or processor cores are at work, the program parts are actually processed in parallel. The information about which processes get which computing time comes from the *scheduler*.

17.1.2   Threads and Processes

In modern operating systems, each process has at least one *thread* (or *execution thread*) that executes the program code. Strictly speaking then, processes are no longer executed concurrently, but only the threads. Within a process, multiple threads might all run together in the same address space, as shown in Figure 17.2. The individual threads of a process can access their public data among themselves.

Java Threads are Native Operating System Threads

Programming threads is easy in Java, and concurrent activities give the user the impression of simultaneity. All modern operating systems support threads directly, and so the Java virtual machine (JVM) usually maps thread management to the operating system. In this case, we're dealing with *native threads*. A 1-to-1 mapping allows for easy distribution on multi-core or multi-processor systems since the operating system takes care of thread management.

Whether or not the runtime environment uses native threads isn't contained in the JVM specification. The Java Language Specification also deliberately leaves the type of implementation free. What the language can guarantee, however, is a correctly interlocked execution. Problems can occur that readers familiar with databases know from transactions. You run the risk of competing access attempts on shared resources. To avoid this problem, a programmer can ensure mutual exclusion through synchronized program blocks. However, this approach also increases the risk of *deadlocks*, which a developer must avoid.

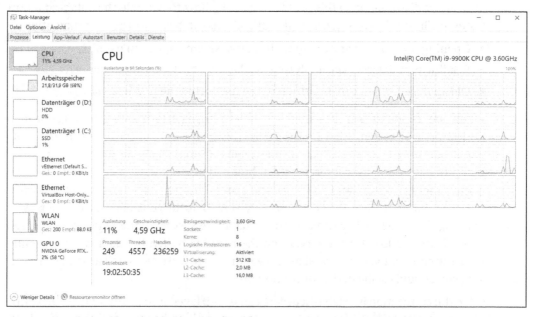

Figure 17.2 Windows Displaying the Number of Running Threads in the Task Manager

17.1.3   How Concurrent Programs Can Increase Speed

At first glance, why the concurrent execution of a program can increase speeds on a single-processor system isn't obvious. Therefore, let's consider a program that executes a sequence of statements. The program sequence visualizes a database report. First, a progress indicator window is displayed. The data is then analyzed, and the progress bar is continuously updated. Finally, the results are written to a file.

The steps of the program can be summarized in the following way:

1. Build a window.
2. Open the database from the network server and read the records.
3. Analyze the data and visualize the progress.
4. Open the file and write the created report.

What at first glance looks like a typical sequential program can be accelerated by clever concurrency and parallel processing.

To make this easier to understand, let's once again draw a comparison with processes. Let's assume that five users are logged on to a single-processor machine, typing source code in the editor and occasionally using the Java compiler. These users would probably not notice the load on the system created by other users because editor operations don't load the processor. When files are compiled and thus transferred from the background memory to the main memory, the processor is already better utilized, but this step doesn't happen regularly. Ideally, all users translate only when the others aren't · translating—in the worst case, of course, all users want to translate at the same time.

Let's apply distribution to this problem, namely, how to compile the database report faster. We'll start by considering which operations can be performed concurrently:

- Opening the window and opening the database can happen in parallel.
- Reading new datasets and analyzing old data can be done simultaneously.
- Old analyzed values can be written to the file during the new analysis.

When operations are truly executed in parallel, a huge performance gain can be seen in multiprocessor systems. But interestingly, this gain can be achieved even with only one processor because tasks can be executed simultaneously on different resources. When the graphical user interface (GUI) builds the window, it of course needs some computing time to do so. The file can be opened in parallel, whereby less processor power is required since the comparatively slow hard drive is addressed. The task of opening the database is passed on to the database server on the network. The speed depends on the load on the server and the network. When the data is subsequently read, the connection to the database server must of course be established. For this reason, you should establish the connection first.

Once the connection is established, data can be retrieved into a buffer via the network. The processor is not under load, but the server on the other side and the network do. Instead of the processor dozing off and getting bored, you better occupy the processor by having it analyze old data. For this purpose, we'll use two buffers: In one buffer, a thread loads the data, while a second thread analyzes the data in the other buffer. Then, the roles of the two buffers are exchanged. Now, the processor is busy. However, it will probably have finished its work before the new data has arrived over the network. In the meantime, the report data can be written to the report—a task that again puts the load on the hard drive and less on the processor.

From this example, you can see how concurrent modeling can improve performance by taking advantage of the wait times that occur during slow operations. Slow operations don't charge the processor, and the wait time for the processor to access a database over the network can be used for other activities. Table 17.1 summarizes these concepts.

Resource	Capacity Load
Main memory accesses	Processor
File operations	Hard drive
Database access	Network connection

Table 17.1 Resources That Can Work in Parallel

This example also demonstrates that concurrency must be well planned. Only when interleaved activities use different resources does this concurrency result in a speed advantage on single-processor systems. For this reason, a concurrently implemented sorting algorithm with one processor (core) isn't especially useful. The second problem is that additional synchronization requirements complicate programming. You must wait for the result of an operation so that you can proceed with the processing.

17.1.4   How Java Can Provide for Concurrency

For concurrent programs, the Java library provides a set of classes, interfaces, and enumerations, such as the following:

- Thread: Each running thread is an instance of this class.
- Runnable: Describes the program code that the JVM should execute concurrently.
- Lock: Used to mark critical sections where only one thread may be located.
- Condition: Threads can wait for the notification of other threads.

17.2   Generating Existing Threads and New Threads

In this section, we'll illustrate how the concurrent program code is packaged into a Runnable and presented to the thread for execution.

17.2.1   Main Thread

Every program code in Java always runs in a thread. When the JVM starts, it automatically creates a thread called the *main thread*. This thread processes the main(...) method. Everything you put in the main(...) method is processed by the main thread, which can be easily seen in a debugger.

Usually, other threads exist in the Java environment, which are started by the system via the help of libraries. When Java opens a window, for instance, a GUI thread is started in which related events are processed.

17.2.2   Who Am I?

In Java, a thread is represented by the java.lang.Thread class, which connects the Java side with the operating system side.

The Thread class uses the static method currentThread() to provide the object reference for the Thread instance that's currently executing the code. In this way, non-static Thread methods like toString() can be used.

[Ex]
Example

The following example calls toString() on the currently running thread:

```
public static void main( String[] args ) {
  System.out.println( Thread.currentThread() ); // Thread[main,5,main]
}
```

The string representation consists of the thread name, priority, and an associated thread group.

If repeated access to Thread.currentThread() in a loop is required, the result should be cached, because the call isn't cheap.

```
class java.lang.Thread
implements Runnable
```

▶ static Thread currentThread()
Returns the thread that executes the running part of the program.

17.2.3   Implementing the Runnable Interface

For the thread to know what to execute, you must give it code. These statements are packaged in a Runnable type command object and passed to the thread. When the thread is started, it processes the program lines from the command object concurrently with the rest of the program code. The functional interface Runnable prescribes only one run() method, as shown in Figure 17.3.

---

interface java.lang.**Runnable**

▶ void run()
  Implementing classes realize the operation and place there the program code to be executed concurrently.

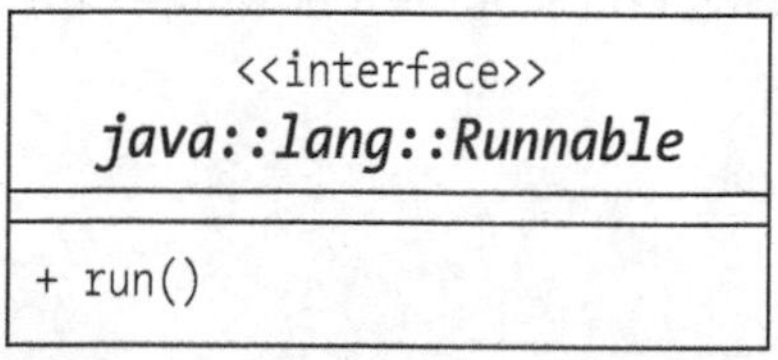

```
        <<interface>>
   java::lang::Runnable
```
```
+ run()
```

Figure 17.3 Unified Modeling Language (UML) Diagram of the Simple Runnable Interface

Now, let's specify two threads, one that outputs the current date and time 20 times and another one that simply outputs a number.

```
package com.tutego.insel.thread;

public class DateCommand implements Runnable {
  @Override public void run() {
    Stream.generate( LocalDateTime::now ).limit( 20 ).forEach( System.out::print
ln );
  }
}
```

Listing 17.1 src/main/java/com/tutego/insel/thread/DateCommand.java

```
package com.tutego.insel.thread;

class CounterCommand implements Runnable {
  @Override public void run() {
    IntStream.range( 0, 20 ).forEach( System.out::println );
  }
}
```

Listing 17.2 src/main/java/com/tutego/insel/thread/CounterCommand.java

Our concurrently executing program code in run() consists of a limited stream. In the first case, the program outputs 20 current date values, and in the other case, a loop counter.

17.2.4   Starting Thread with Runnable

Now, simply calling the run() method of a class directly is not enough because then nothing would be concurrent; we would simply execute a method sequentially. For the program code to run alongside the actual application, you must connect a Thread object to the Runnable and then explicitly start the thread. For this step, you'll pass a reference to the Runnable object to the constructor of the Thread class and call start(). Once start() has created a runtime environment for the thread, it internally calls the run() method exactly once by itself. If the thread is already running, a second call of the start() method throws an IllegalThreadStateException. Consider the following example:

```
Thread t1 = new Thread( new DateCommand() );
t1.start();

Thread t2 = new Thread( new CounterCommand() );
t2.start();
```

Listing 17.3 src/main/java/com/tutego/insel/thread/FirstThread.java, main()

When the program is started, something like the following example output may appear on your screen:

```
0
1
2
3
4
5
6
7
8
2017-02-17T13:40:35.315250400
2017-02-17T13:40:35.327260600
2017-02-17T13:40:35.327260600
2017-02-17T13:40:35.327260600
9
10
11
12
13
14
15
16
17
18
```

19
2017-02-17T13:40:35.327260600
...

In this output, you can see the interlocking of the two threads. Although the sequence is clearly defined within a thread by the loop, the operating system will determine when it's the turn of any specific thread. So, we're not surprised that the first line in this output comes from the counting thread, which is actually the second thread. This scenario clearly demonstrates the non-determinism[2] in threads. The output can be interpreted by the different runtimes required for the date and time output: Date processing requires many more objects and creating them takes time. But these needs are an internal matter, which must not play any role in the sequence. If you expect thread results in a specific order, you'll need to synchronize threads.

```
class java.lang.Thread
implements Runnable
```

▶ Thread(Runnable target)
Creates a new thread with a Runnable that specifies the program code to be executed concurrently.

▶ void start()
A new thread gets started in addition to the thread that calls the method. The new thread executes the run() method concurrently. Each thread can be started only once.

17.2.5 Parameterizing Runnable

The run() method of Runnable has no parameter list and no return. Therefore, the question is how information gets in and out of Runnable. The fact that run() has no parameter list is quickly explained by the fact that it is completely unknown which parameters exist at all.

Two simple ways exist to access parameters within run():

- If a class implements the Runnable interface, a constructor can remember the values in internal states. If the thread calls run(), the method can access the values.

- If a lambda expression implements the functional interface Runnable, the body can access local variables from the context.

Storing results from a background operation is more difficult than you might think at first glance. Concurrent write access is particularly dangerous, and therefore, synchronization mechanisms are needed. Basically, two options are conceivable in this case:

---

2 "Not predictable" in this context means that the point in time at which the scheduler carries out the context change is unknown.

- A Runnable implementation arrives at a result and stores it in its own state, which is later queried from the outside.

- run() writes to non-self-managed memory.

17.2.6 Extending the Thread Class*

Since the Thread class itself implements the Runnable interface and provides an empty run() method, you can also extend Thread to program your own concurrent activities.

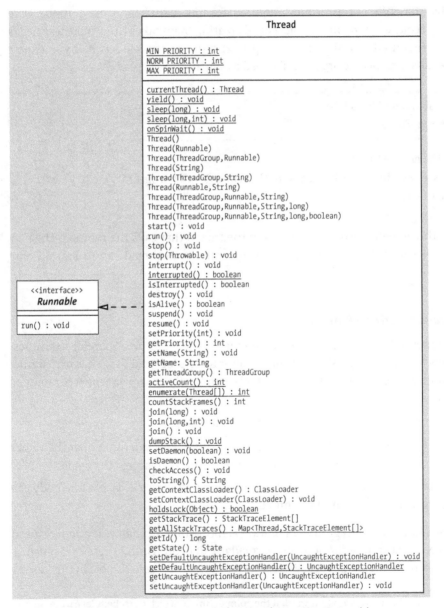

Figure 17.4 UML Diagram of the Thread Class Implementing Runnable

Then, you no longer need to add a Runnable instance to the constructor because, if our class is a subclass of Thread, calling the inherited start() method will suffice. Now, the program continues working directly, so it executes the next statement after start() a short time later. However, you should refrain using from this variant because the "executor" (i.e., the Thread) should be separated from the code to be executed (the Runnable).

---

class java.lang.**Thread**
implements Runnable

▶ void run()

This method in Thread has an empty body. Subclasses override run() so that it contains the program code to be executed concurrently.

Overriding start() and Self-Starters

You can also override the start() method, but doing so is rarely useful or necessary because then you'd have to write a call super.start() so that the thread actually starts. For us as thread users to avoid having to call the start() method first, a thread can also start itself. The constructor simply calls its own start() method for this purpose.

Instead of start(), Calling run()

run(), like start(), is a public method of the Thread class—Thread implements Runnable, so the run() method must be public. One programming mistake that beginners often make is when, instead of start(), they accidentally call run() on the Thread. What happens then? Almost exactly the same as with start(), the only difference being that the object method run() isn't processed concurrently with the rest of the program. The current thread processes the run() method sequentially until it finishes and the statements after the call take their turn. The error isn't always directly noticeable because the actions in run() do take place, just not concurrently.

Extending Thread or Implementing Runnable?

The best approach is to create Runnable objects that are then passed to the thread. Command objects of this type are quite flexible because simple Runnable objects can be easily passed and even executed by threads from a thread pool. One disadvantage of extending Thread is that single inheritance can be troublesome; if a class inherits from Thread, the extension is already "used up." But whether a class implements Runnable or extends Thread, one thing remains: a new class.

17.3   Thread Members and States

A thread has a whole set of states, such as a name and a priority, which can be queried and set. Not every property can be changed after startup so this section focuses on properties that can actually be changed.

17.3.1   The Name of a Thread

A thread has a large number of properties such as a state, a priority, and also a name. A name can be set with setName(...) and queried with getName():

```
class java.lang.Thread
implements Runnable
```

▶ Thread(String name)
Creates a new Thread object and sets the name. Useful for subclasses that call the constructor via super(name).

▶ Thread(Runnable target, String name)
Creates a new Thread object with a Runnable and sets the name.

▶ final String getName()
Returns the name of the thread. The name is specified in the constructor or assigned with setName(...). By default, the name is "Thread-x," where x is a unique number.

▶ final void setName(String name)
Changes the name of the thread.

17.3.2   The States of a Thread*

An instance of Thread will have a few conditions:

- *New*: The lifecycle of a Thread object starts with new, but the object doesn't run yet.
- *Running* and *ready*: Via start(), the thread gets into the state "ready" or "running." The thread always switches back and forth between the two states. If the thread is *running*, the scheduler has selected it for execution by the operating system; if *ready*, the thread is not currently running but will be considered by the scheduler for the next round until the scheduler allocates computing time to it again.
- *Waiting*: This state is achieved using special synchronization techniques or input/output functions—the thread dwells in a wait state.
- *Terminated*: After the activity of the Thread object has ended, the object can no longer be activated and is dead (i.e., terminated).

With a Sign of Life: State via Thread.State

The getState() method shows the current state of a thread. This method returns an object of the Thread.State enumeration type (the only enumeration in the java.lang package), which declares the following states:

State	Explanation
NEW	New thread, not yet started
RUNNABLE	Runs in the JVM.
BLOCKED	Waits for a MonitorLock when it wants to enter a synchronized block, for example.
WAITING	Waits for a notify(), for example.
TIMED_WAITING	Waits in a sleep(), for example.
TERMINATED	Execution is finished.

Table 17.2 States of a Thread

In addition, the isAlive() method inquires whether the thread has been started but isn't yet dead.

17.3.3   Sleepers Wanted

Sometimes, you'll find it necessary to pause a thread for a certain time. For this purpose, the methods of two classes are available:

- **The overloaded static method Thread.sleep(...)**
  Somewhat surprisingly, this method is not an instance method of a Thread object but is a static method. You can only send your own thread to sleep but you cannot simply put an external thread, whose reference you have, to sleep for a few seconds and thus stop it from executing.

- **The object method sleep(...) on a TimeUnit object**
  In addition, this method always references the executing thread. The advantage over sleep(...) is that, with this method, the time units are more visible.

Example

[Ex]

Let's say the executing thread needs to sleep for 2 seconds. We can achieve this goal with Thread.sleep(...) in the following way:

```
try {
  Thread.sleep( 2000 );
} catch ( InterruptedException e ) { }
```

Then, with `TimeUnit`, we can specify a sleep period in the following way:

```
try {
  TimeUnit.SECONDS.sleep( 2 );
} catch ( InterruptedException e ) { }
```

Sleep can be interrupted by an `InterruptedException`, for example, by `interrupt()`. The exception must be handled because it isn't a `RuntimeException`.

```
class java.lang.Thread
implements Runnable
```

▶ static void sleep(long millis) throws InterruptedException
The currently executing thread is put to sleep for `millis` milliseconds; a small inaccuracy is of course possible. If another thread interrupts the sleeping thread, an `InterruptedException` will be thrown prematurely.

▶ static void sleep(long millis, int nanos) throws InterruptedException
The currently executing thread is put to sleep for `millis` milliseconds and additionally for `nanos` nanoseconds. Unlike `sleep(long)`, an `IllegalArgumentException` will be thrown if the number of milliseconds is negative. This exception will also be thrown if the nanosecond count is not between 0 and 999,999.

[+]

Tip

To discourage developers from using an outdated API, a delay can be built in, which is quite nasty, but then the new API will quickly catch on.

```
enum java.util.concurrent.TimeUnit
extends Enum<TimeUnit>
implements Serializable, Comparable<TimeUnit>
```

▶ NANOSECONDS, MICROSECONDS, MILLISECONDS, SECONDS, MINUTES, HOURS, DAYS
Enumeration elements of `TimeUnit`

▶ void sleep(long timeout) throws InterruptedException
Executes a `Thread.sleep()` for the time unit.

[+]

Tip

To perform something task after a certain time, you don't need to start a separate thread and then put that thread into sleep mode. The Java API provides timers that are useful in these cases.

An overloaded `Thread.sleep(long, TimeUnit)` method would be a good idea, but this method doesn't exist.

17.3.4   When Threads Are Finished

Some threads run all the time because they implement server functions, for example. Other threads perform an operation once and are finished afterwards. Generally, a thread is finished when one of the following conditions is true:

- The `run()` method terminated without an error. If we program an infinite loop, it would potentially form a never-ending thread.
- A `RuntimeException` occurs in the `run()` method, which terminates the method. That doesn't end the other threads or the JVM in its entirety.
- The thread was canceled from the outside. The `stop()` method, which is basically problematic, can be used for this purpose. Its use isn't recommended, and it's also deprecated.
- The virtual machine is terminated and takes all threads to the grave with it.

17.3.5   Terminating a Thread Politely Using Interrupts

A thread is usually finished when the `run()` method has been properly executed to the end. However, if a `run()` method contains an infinite loop, such as a server waiting for incoming requests, the thread must be forced to surrender externally. We'll discuss the obvious possibility of using the `Thread` method `stop()` to stall a thread in Section 17.3.7.

However, if you don't want to terminate the thread from the outside, you can politely ask the thread to quit its job and thus come to an end. In this case, the thread would only have to check periodically whether someone from the outside has expressed the wish to abort.

The interrupt() and isInterrupted() Methods

The `interrupt()` method sets an internal flag from outside in a `Thread` object, which can then be queried periodically in the `run()` method via `isInterrupted()`.

The following program displays a message on the screen every half second. After 2 seconds, the interrupt request is reported via `interrupt()`. The otherwise infinitely running loop pays attention to this signal and aborts:

```
Runnable killingMeSoftly = () -> {
  System.out.println( "There is life before death." );

  while ( ! Thread.currentThread().isInterrupted() ) {
    System.out.println( "It runs, and runs, and runs, and runs." );
```

```
    try {
      Thread.sleep( 500 );
    }
    catch ( InterruptedException e ) {
      Thread.currentThread().interrupt();
      System.out.println( "Interruption in sleep()." );
    }
  } // end while

  System.out.println( "This is the end, beautiful friend." );
};

Thread t = new Thread( killingMeSoftly );
t.start();
Thread.sleep( 2000 );
t.interrupt();
```

Listing 17.4 src/main/java/com/tutego/insel/thread/ThreadusInterruptus.java, main(...)

The output nicely shows the sequence of operations:

```
There is life before death.
It runs, and runs, and runs, and runs.
It runs, and runs, and runs, and runs.
It runs, and runs, and runs, and runs.
It runs, and runs, and runs, and runs.
Interruption in sleep().
This is the end, beautiful friend.
```

[»]   **Note**

If inherited from Thread, the isInterrupted() and interrupt() methods are immediately accessible in the subclass.

The run() method in the thread is implemented in such a way that the loop is exited exactly when isInterrupted() returns true (i.e., the interrupt() method was called from outside for this thread instance). This step is exactly what happens in the main(...) method.

At first glance, the program is easy to understand, but let's focus on the interrupt() in the catch block. If this line were not there, the program would most likely not work. Why not? The secret is, if the output is only every half second, the thread is in the sleep(...) method almost all the time. So, interrupt() will probably find the thread just sleeping. The method sleep(...) doesn't like this interruption at all and reacts in the following way, which is well documented in the Javadoc:

1. `sleep(...)` throws an `InterruptedException` when interrupted with `interrupt()`, which is exactly the exception our `try-catch` block catches.

2. The method resets the interrupt flag. A query via `isInterrupted()` consequently reports no interruption.

In general, that the interrupt flag is reset is good because it has done its job. In our case, however, `interrupt()` must be called again because the termination flag must be set again so that `isInterrupted()` can determine the end in the `while` loop.

If you use the object method `isInterrupted()`, besides `sleep(...)`, the `Object` methods `join(...)` and `wait(...)` also clear the flag via `InterruptedException`.

Note

The methods `sleep(...)`, `wait(...)`, and `join(...)` all throw an `InterruptedException` if they are interrupted by the `interrupt()` method. In other words, `interrupt()` terminates these methods with the exception.

Summary: interrupted(), isInterrupted(), and interrupt()

These method names are rather confusing, so let's summarize their tasks again: The object method `interrupt()` sets a flag in a (different) `Thread` object to indicate that a request to terminate the thread was received. However, the thread isn't terminated, although the method name suggests it would. This flag can be queried with the object method `isInterrupted()`. Usually, this query is done inside a loop that determines whether the thread's activity should continue. The static method `interrupted()` is also a request method and tests the corresponding flag of the currently running thread, like `Thread.currentThread().isInterrupted()`, but in addition the method also clears the interrupt status, which `isInterrupted()` doesn't do. Two consecutive calls of `interrupted()` will therefore result in a `false` unless another interruption occurs in the meantime.

17.3.6   Unhandled Exceptions, Thread End, and UncaughtExceptionHandler

If an unhandled unchecked exception occurs during thread execution, the JVM terminates the thread. This termination won't be logged separately on the console; only the exception message will be displayed.

Example

In the following example, the JVM terminates the thread due to an uncaught exception, while the `main` thread continues to run:

```
Thread t = new Thread( () -> {
    System.out.println( Thread.currentThread() );
```

```
      System.out.println( 1 / 0 );
   }, "Waiting for the summer rain" );
t.start();
System.out.println( t.isAlive() );
Thread.sleep( 1000 );
System.out.println( Thread.currentThread() );
System.out.println( t.isAlive() );
```

The result is the following output:

```
true
Thread[Waiting for the summer rain,5,main]
Exception in thread "Waiting for the summer rain" java.lang.ArithmeticExcepti
on: / by zero
  at T.lambda$0(T.java:8)
  at java.base/java.lang.Thread.run(Thread.java:844)
Thread[main,5,main]
false
```

Setting UncaughtExceptionHandler

One reason for a thread to end is an unhandled exception, such as from an uncaught RuntimeException. To allow a controlled exit in this case, an UncaughtExceptionHandler can be appended to the thread, which will be notified whenever the thread ends because of an unhandled exception.

UncaughtExceptionHandler is a nested interface declared in Thread that imposes the operation void uncaughtException(Thread t, Throwable e). An implementation of the interface can be appended either to an individual thread or to all threads. Therefore, in case of a termination by unhandled exceptions, the JVM calls the uncaughtException(...) method. In this way, the application can still log the error passed by the JVM via throwable e.

```
class java.lang.Thread
implements Runnable
```

▶ void setUncaughtExceptionHandler(Thread.UncaughtExceptionHandler eh)
Sets the UncaughtExceptionHandler for the thread.

▶ Thread.UncaughtExceptionHandler getUncaughtExceptionHandler()
Returns the current UncaughtExceptionHandler.

▶ static void setDefaultUncaughtExceptionHandler(Thread.UncaughtExceptionHandler eh)
Sets the UncaughtExceptionHandler for all threads.

▶ static Thread.UncaughtExceptionHandler getDefaultUncaughtExceptionHandler()
Returns the assigned UncaughtExceptionHandler of all threads.

An UncaughtExceptionHandler set locally with setUncaughtExceptionHandler(...) overrides the entry for the setDefaultUncaughtExceptionHandler(...).

If the Thread Is to Report an Error

Since a thread operates concurrently, the run() method poorly reports exceptions or returns values synchronously. Who should listen to the method and at what point? A solution to the problem is using a listener who logs in to the thread and is informed whether the thread could do its job or not. Another solution is provided by Callable (see Chapter 5, Section 5.5.8), which can return a special error code or display an exception.

17.3.7   The stop() from the Outside and the Rescue with ThreadDeath*

If a thread doesn't listen to interrupt(), but instead for some reason urgently needs to be terminated, you must use the deprecated stop() method, even though we should avoid using a deprecated method. By the way, if you use native compilation with GraalVM, the method is not supported.[3]

The fact that this method is deprecated tells you to avoid using stop(). (Unfortunately, unlike most other outdated methods, no replacement can be easily recommended.) You can't override stop() either because it's final. When you terminate a thread from outside, you no longer give it a chance to leave its state consistently. In addition, the interruption can occur at any point, allowing requested resources to remain in a state of limbo.

```
class java.lang.Thread
implements Runnable
```

▶ final void stop()
   If the thread hasn't been started at all or if it has already been processed or terminated, the method will return immediately.

▶ Rendezvous with join(...) *

When you distribute tasks to several threads, a time will come when the results must be collected. However, the results can't be joined until all threads have finished executing. When they meet at a specific time, it's called a *rendezvous*.

Several strategies for waiting exist. First, you can use Callable and then wait synchronously for the end with get(). If you use Runnable, a thread can't pass direct results like a method to the outside because the run() method has the void result type. Moreover, since a concurrent thread works asynchronously, you don't even know when to expect the result.

---

3 *https://www.graalvm.org/22.1/reference-manual/native-image/Limitations/*

The transfer of values isn't a problem. Class variables and also object variables can help in this case because you can communicate through them. The only thing missing now is that waiting for the end of a thread's activity, which can be achieved with join(...) methods.

In the example shown in Listing 17.5, a thread places a result in the result variable. You can see the effects of join() if you include the line that's been commented out in the following example:

```
class JoinerRunnable implements Runnable {
  public int result;

  @Override public void run() {
    result = LocalDate.now().getDayOfYear();
  }
}

JoinerRunnable runnable = new JoinerRunnable();
Thread thread = new Thread( runnable );
thread.start();
// thread.join();
System.out.println( runnable.result );
```

Listing 17.5 src/main/java/com/tutego/insel/thread/JoinTheThread.java, main(...)

Without calling join(), the result will be 0 because starting the thread costs some time. During this time, we can output the object variable automatically initialized to 0. If we include join(), the run() method will be executed at the end, and the thread sets the result variable to the day of the year (value range 1 to 366), which is what will be displayed on the screen.

```
class java.lang.Thread
implements Runnable
```

▶ final void join() throws InterruptedException
The currently executed thread waits for the thread for which the method is called to finish.

▶ final void join(long millis) throws InterruptedException
Like join(), but this variant waits at most millis milliseconds. If the thread hasn't been completely terminated by then, the program will continue. In this way, you can try to wait for the thread within a certain period of time but otherwise continue. With millis is 0, this method has the same effect as join().

▶ final void join (long millis, int nanos) throws InterruptedException
Like join(long) but with a potentially more precise specification of the maximum wait time.

After a thread.join(long), the thread.isAlive() method is sometimes useful because it indicates whether thread is still actively working or has finished.

In TimeUnit, a helper method, timedJoin(...), allows you to work with durations more nicely.

```
class java.lang.TimeUnit
implements Runnable
```

▶ void timedJoin(Thread thread, long timeout) throws InterruptedException
Calculates milliseconds (ms) and nanoseconds (ns) from the TimeUnit and timeout and performs a join(ms, ns) on the thread.

Waiting for the Slowest

Large problems can be split up into several parts, and each subproblem can then be solved by a thread. This approach is a worthwhile investment, especially for multiprocessor systems. Finally, you can simply wait for the threads to finish and collect the result. Join(...) is well suited for this purpose.

Example

Let's say two threads are working on one problem. You must thus wait until both have completed their tasks. Then, for example, another thread could reuse the resources used by a and b, as in the following example:

```
Thread a = new Thread( runnableA );
Thread b = new Thread( runnableB );
a.start();
b.start();
a.join();
b.join();
```

Whose join() we call first doesn't matter since we must wait for the slowest thread anyway. If a thread is already finished, join() returns immediately.

17.3.8 Stopping and Resuming the Work*

To make one thread stop working for a certain time and still have another thread wake up the sleeping thread, you would have to implement that feature by yourself. Although two Thread methods—suspend() and resume()—can be used, this start-stop technique is deprecated because it's as problematic as stop(). In the future, these methods will be removed from Java Platform, Standard Edition (Java SE).

17.3.9   Priority*

Each thread has a priority, which indicates how much computing time a thread should receive in relation to other threads. The priority is a number between Thread.MIN_PRIORITY (1) and Thread.MAX_PRIORITY (10). The value allows the scheduler to identify which thread to give priority to when multiple threads are waiting for compute time. At its initialization, each thread gets the priority of the creating thread. Normally, the priority Thread.NORM_PRIORITY (5) is assigned.

The operating system (or the JVM) always takes threads out of the queue according to priority (hence *priority queue*). A thread with priority *N* is placed before all threads with importance less than *N*, but after threads with priority greater than or equal to *N*. Now, if a cooperative thread with priority *N* calls the yield() method, a thread with priority <= *N* also gets a chance to be executed.

The priority can be changed by calling setPriority(...) and queried with getPriority(). However, Java makes very weak assertions about the meaning and impact of thread priorities.

[»]

Example

In the following example, we're assigning the highest priority to thread t:

```
t.setPriority( Thread.MAX_PRIORITY );
class java.lang.Thread
implements Runnable
```

▶ final int getPriority()
Returns the priority of the thread.

▶ final void setPriority(int newPriority)
Sets the priority of the thread. The method returns an IllegalArgumentException if the priority isn't between MIN_PRIORITY (1) and MAX_PRIORITY (10).

Granularity and Precedence

The ten priority levels don't necessarily guarantee different code executions. Although you might assume that a thread with priority NORM_PRIORITY+1 executes program code more often than a thread with priority NORM_PRIORITY, the operating system may implement these preferences differently. Let's assume the platform implements only five priority levels. If 1 is the lowest level and 5 is the highest while the middle level is 3, probably NORM_PRIORITY and NORM_PRIORITY + 1 will be transformed to level 3 and therefore have the same priority. Thus, even with different priorities, you can't expect that a particular program part will necessarily run more quickly. In addition, some operating systems with schedulers don't support priorities or interpret them in unexpected ways.

17.4 Enter the Executor

A thread is always required for the concurrent execution of a Runnable. Although the concurrent processing of program code isn't possible without threads, the two are strongly connected in programming. Thus, ideally, the Runnable is somewhat separated from the actual processing thread. Several reasons exist for this suggestion:

- As early as during the creation of a Thread object, the Runnable object must be passed in the Thread constructor. You cannot create the Thread object, then later assign the Runnable object via a setter and then start the thread using start().

- If start() is called twice on the Thread object, the second call results in an exception. Thus, a created thread can't process a Runnable twice by calling start() twice. For this reason, a new Thread object is always needed for a new processing of a Runnable. In other words, an existing thread can't simply process a new Runnable.

- The thread starts processing the Runnable program code immediately after the call of start(). The implementation of the Runnable itself must be changed if the program code shouldn't be executed immediately, but instead later (at the next day's show) or repeatedly (always at Christmas).

An abstraction that separates the execution of the Runnable program code from the technical implementation (such as the threads) is desirable.

17.4.1 The Executor Interface

Instead of binding the Runnable directly to a thread and thus to its executor, an abstraction is available for all "processors." The Executor interface prescribes a method for this task:

```
interface java.util.concurrent.Executor
```

▶ void execute(Runnable command)
    Will be implemented later by classes that can process a Runnable.

Anyone who now processes commands via Runnable is an executor.

Concrete Executors

Two major implementations of this interface are available so far:

- ThreadPoolExecutor: The class creates a collection of threads, the *thread pool*. Execution requests are taken up by free threads.

- ScheduledThreadPoolExecutor: An extension of ThreadPoolExecutor to include the ability to execute commands at specific times or with specific repetitions.

The two classes have non-trivial constructors, and a utility class simplifies the construction of these special Executor objects.

---

class java.util.concurrent.**Executors**

▶ static ExecutorService newCachedThreadPool()
Returns a thread pool with growing size.

▶ static ExecutorService newFixedThreadPool(int nThreads)
Returns a thread pool with a maximum of nThreads. More on this topic follows in Section 17.4.2.

▶ static ScheduledExecutorService newSingleThreadScheduledExecutor()

▶ static ScheduledExecutorService newScheduledThreadPool(int corePoolSize)
Return special Executor objects to set repetitions. More on this topic follows in Section 17.4.7.

Over 20 methods are available in Executors. Our list shows only highlights some that will be relevant in the following sections.

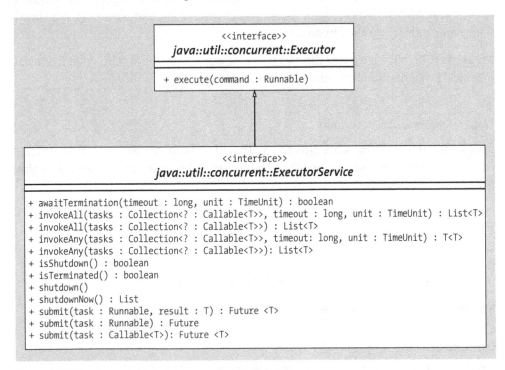

Figure 17.5 The ExecutorService Interface Extends Executor

ExecutorService is an interface that extends Executor (see Figure 1.5 with UML diagram).
Among other things, operations that shut down the executors can be found here. In the
case of thread pools, this interface is useful because otherwise the threads wouldn't be
terminated because they're waiting for new tasks.

[«]

Note

Of course, you can also write your own "executors," for example, one that lets the
Swing GUI thread execute a Runnable, as in the following example:

```
Executor executor = runnable -> SwingUtilities.invokeLater( runnable );
```

Alternatively, you can write something shorter:

```
Executor executor = SwingUtilities::invokeLater;
```

17.4.2   Happy as a Group: The Thread Pools

Time is required to build threads, for the operating system to manage them, and then
to tear them down again and take them out of the internal tables. For example, if a
server's goal is to answer a request directly without delay, the time to set up a thread
can be disruptive. Also associated with a thread are resources, such as stack memory,
that must be reserved by the operating system.

One optimization is to build threads and keep them alive in the pool, which can be
achieved in three steps:

1. If a request arrives to process a Runnable, a free thread is taken from the pool.

2. The thread processes the run() method of the Runnable.

3. After processing, the thread puts itself back into the pool.

Thread pools have an additional advantage in that they can limit workloads and parallel processing. If a thread pool manages only a fixed number of threads and all threads
are in progress, the system can reject new requests or force them to wait. This feature
effectively prevents denial-of-service attacks. For example, with a web server, if every
incoming connection opens a thread, a server can easily be bombarded with requests.

Executors.newCachedThreadPool(...)

An important static method of the Executors class is newCachedThreadPool(...). Behind
this method is a ThreadPoolExecutor constructor call. The result is an ExecutorService
object, that is, an implementation of the Executor interface with the execute(Runnable)
method. Consider the following example:

```
Runnable r1 = () -> {
  System.out.println( "1.1 " + Thread.currentThread().getName() );
  System.out.println( "1.2 " + Thread.currentThread().getName() );
};
```

```
Runnable r2 = () -> {
  System.out.println( "2.1 " + Thread.currentThread().getName() );
  System.out.println( "2.2 " + Thread.currentThread().getName() );
};
```

Listing 17.6 src/main/java/com/tutego/insel/thread/concurrent/
ThreadPoolDemo.java, main(), Part 1

Now, the thread pool can be obtained as ExecutorService, and the two command objects can be executed as Runnable via execute(...).

```
ExecutorService executor = Executors.newCachedThreadPool();

executor.execute( r1 );
executor.execute( r2 );

Thread.sleep( 500 );

executor.execute( r1 );
executor.execute( r2 );

executor.shutdown();
```

Listing 17.7 src/main/java/com/tutego/insel/thread/concurrent/
ThreadPoolDemo.java, main(), Part 2

The following output indicates the good reuse of the threads:

```
1.1 pool-1-thread-1
2.1 pool-1-thread-2
2.2 pool-1-thread-2
1.2 pool-1-thread-1
2.1 pool-1-thread-2
2.2 pool-1-thread-2
1.1 pool-1-thread-1
1.2 pool-1-thread-1
```

The name of the thread indicates that two threads from a thread pool named pool-1 are used in our case: thread-1 and thread-2. After executing the first two jobs (r1 and r2) and after the short wait, the threads pool-1-thread-1 and pool-1-thread-2 are free again, so r1 and r2 are processed by these two threads again. The following three operations to control the pool end can be useful:

```
interface java.util.concurrent.ExecutorService
extends Executor
```

▶ void shutdown()

Shuts down the thread pool. Running threads aren't terminated, but new requests aren't accepted.

▶ boolean isShutdown()

Determines if the Executor been shut down.

▶ List<Runnable> shutdownNow()

Currently running Runnables are encouraged to stop. The return is a list of Runnables to be terminated.

17.4.3 Threads with return via Callable

The concurrent thread can only return results via detours. In a separate class that extends Runnable, for example, a data structure can be passed in the constructor into which the thread places a calculated result. The data structure can then be examined by the caller for changes.

The Java library provides yet another option because, while run() in Runnable has void as return, call() transmits a return to another interface named Callable, as shown in Figure 17.6, and can also throw an exception. Let's look at some examples:

interface java.lang. **Runnable**	interface java.util.concurrent. **Callable<V>**
■ void run() This method contains the program code to be executed concurrently.	■ V call() throws Exception This method contains the program code to be executed concurrently and returns a type V return.

Table 17.3 Methods in Runnable and Callable

```
            <<interface>>
java::util::conurrent::Callable<V>
```
```
+ call() : V
```

Figure 17.6 The Simple Interface Callable with an Operation

Example: Sorting Fields via Callable

Let's implement an example that sorts a field. The sorting should be performed by a Callable in the background. When the operation is finished, the reference to the sorted field should be returned. Sorting is performed as usual by Arrays.sort(...).

```java
class SorterCallable implements Callable<byte[]> {
  private final byte[] b;
```

```
  SorterCallable( byte[] b ) {
    this.b = b;
  }

  @Override public byte[] call() {
    Arrays.sort( b );
    return b;
  }
}
```

Listing 17.8 src/main/java/com/tutego/insel/thread/concurrent/
SorterCallable.java, SorterCallable

Of course, creating the Callable object and calling call() yourself doesn't make much sense because a thread is supposed to do the job in the background. For this purpose, however, you don't need to use the Thread class itself, but instead, you can use an ExecutorService, available via Executors. newCachedThreadPool(). Consider the following example:

```
byte[] b = new byte[ 4000000 ];
new Random().nextBytes( b );
Callable<byte[]> c = new SorterCallable( b );
ExecutorService executor = Executors.newCachedThreadPool();
Future<byte[]> result = executor.submit( c );
```

Listing 17.9 src/main/java/com/tutego/insel/thread/concurrent/
CallableGetDemo.java, main() (Snippet)

ExecutorService provides a submit(Callable) method that accepts our Callable and selects a thread for processing. The return is a mysterious Future.

ExecutorService Executes: Callable and Runnable with Future

For reasons of symmetry, two submit(...) methods exist in addition to submit(Callable), which also accept a Runnable. Together, they add up to the following methods:

```
interface java.util.concurrent.ExecutorService
extends Executor
```

▶ <T> Future<T> submit(Callable<T> task)
ExecutorService is supposed to process the task and give access to the result via the return.

▶ Future<?> submit(Runnable task)
ExecutorService processes the Runnable and enables you to query, via the Future

object, whether the output has already been processed or not. get() returns null at the end.

▶ <T> Future<T> submit(Runnable task, T result)
   Like submit(task) but the get(...) query over Future returns result.

To convert a Runnable into a Callable, some auxiliary methods in the Executors class can be used. These methods include the static method callable(Runnable task), which returns a Callable<Object>, and the method callable(Runnable task, T result), which returns a Callable<T>.

17.4.4 Memories of the Future: The Future Return

Because the result arrives asynchronously, submit(Callable) returns a Future object that you can use to determine whether the result is already available or if the process still must wait. Actually, after a submit(...) is the best time to trigger other concurrent tasks, and then you can later collect the result using get(...). The programming pattern is always the same: first, pass work to ExecutorService, then do something else and come back later. However, since in our example we have nothing to do in the meantime but sort a byte field, we'll drop the Callable and immediately wait for the sorted field via get(), as shown in the following example:

```
byte[] b = new byte[ 4000000 ];
new Random().nextBytes( b );
Callable<byte[]> c = new SorterCallable( b );
ExecutorService executor = Executors.newCachedThreadPool();
Future<byte[]> result = executor.submit( c );
// Now other things can be done first, and later ...
try {
  byte[] bs = result.get();
  System.out.printf( "%d, %d, %d%n",
                     bs[0], bs[1], bs[bs.length - 1] ); // -128, -128, 127
}
catch ( InterruptedException | ExecutionException e ) {
  e.printStackTrace();
}
```

Listing 17.10 src/main/java/com/tutego/insel/thread/concurrent/ CallableGetDemo.java, main()

Since the field is sorted and the value range of a byte is small (−128 to +127), with 4,000,000 values, the smallest element of the random numbers is −128, and the largest, 127.

Let's look at the operations of the Future interface in detail next:

```
interface java.util.concurrent.Future<V>
```

▶ V get() throws InterruptedException, ExecutionException
Waits for the result and then returns it. This method blocks processing until the result is available. Exceptions may occur, for instance, CancellationException if the calculation was canceled, ExecutionException if the calculation threw an exception, or InterruptedException if the current thread was interrupted while waiting.

▶ V get(long timeout, TimeUnit unit)
throws InterruptedException, ExecutionException, TimeoutException
Waits a given time for the result and then returns the result. If a result doesn't arrive in the given duration, a TimeoutException will occur.

▶ boolean isDone()
Determines if the work has finished or was canceled.

▶ boolean cancel(boolean mayInterruptIfRunning)
Aborts the job.

▶ boolean isCancelled()
Determines if the job stopped before the end.

Waiting with Time Limit

Potentially infinite blocking isn't always desirable. For this case, the overloaded method of get(...) permits a parameterization with a wait time and time unit.

```
byte[] bs = result.get( 2, TimeUnit.SECONDS );
```

Listing 17.11 src/main/java/com/tutego/insel/thread/concurrent/CallableGetTimeUnit-Demo.java (Snippet)

If the result isn't available within 2 seconds, the method will throw a TimeoutException with, for instance, the following message:

```
java.util.concurrent.TimeoutException
    at java.util.concurrent.FutureTask$Sync.innerGet(FutureTask.java:228)
    at java.util.concurrent.FutureTask.get(FutureTask.java:91)
    at com.tutego.insel.thread.concurrent.CallableDemo.main(CallableDemo.java:27)
```

[»]

Note

Generally, enough time exists between sending the task and picking up the result so that no blocking wait situation occurs when picking the task up, which is perfect. What's unfavorable is if submit(...) is almost immediately followed by get(...), but the result isn't yet available because then Future can't help much. An interesting solution is provided by an implementation of Future (the CompletableFuture implementation), which puts tasks in a sequence. The idea is simple: To avoid wait times, when the result is calculated by one step, that result is directly forwarded to the next processing step.

Wrapping Callable or Runnable with FutureTask

Taking a closer look at the stack call we just made, the type java.util.concurrent.FutureTask catches our eye. The class implements Future, Runnable, and RunnableFuture and is used internally by the Java library when we use submit(...) to transfer something to the ExecutorService. In addition, we can use the type directly as a wrapper around a Callable or Runnable because some useful callback methods can be overridden, such as done() when a calculation is done.

Let's consider an example: A Callable returns the name of the user. A FutureTask wraps itself around this Callable, learns when the Callable is done, then modifies the user name, and also outputs a message.

```java
Callable<String> user name = () -> System.getProperty( "user.name" );
FutureTask<String> wrappedUser name = new FutureTask<>( user name ) {
  @Override protected void done() {
    try {
      System.out.printf( "done: isDone=%s, isCancelled=
%s%n", isDone(), isCancelled() );
      System.out.println( "done: get=" + get() );
    }
    catch ( InterruptedException | ExecutionException e ) { /* Ignore */ }
  }
  @Override protected void set( String v ) {
    System.out.println( "set: " + v );
    super.set( v.toUpperCase() );
  }
};
ExecutorService scheduler = Executors.newCachedThreadPool();
scheduler.submit( wrappedUser name );
System.out.println( "main: " + wrappedUser name.get() );
scheduler.shutdown();
```

Listing 17.12 src/main/java/com/tutego/insel/thread/concurrent/WrappedUser name.java (Snippet)

What's important about the usage is not to evaluate the return from the submit(...), which we normally do, but instead to query the passed FutureTask.

The outputs of the program are often a bit jumbled, as shown in the following example:

```
set: Christian
done: isDone=true, isCancelled=false
done: get=CHRISTIAN
main: CHRISTIAN
```

The order in the calls always follows a particular sequence: The FutureTask detects the completion of the Callable and calls set(...). Then, done() is executed.

17.4.5   Processing Multiple Callable Objects

The submit(Callable) method of the ExecutorService accepts and executes exactly one Callable:

- `<T> Future<T> submit(Callable<T> task)`

Of course, if an application needs to process multiple Callable objects, multiple calls of submit(Callable) may be required. But an ExecutorService can process multiple Callable objects by itself. Two alternative variants are available:

- All Callable objects in a list are executed, and the result is a list of Future objects.
- All Callable objects in a list will be executed, but the first one to finish will return the result.

At base are two methods, but since they are also given time constraints, four methods in total can be used:

```
interface java.util.concurrent.ExecutorService
extends Executor
```

▶ `<T> List<Future<T>> invokeAll(Collection<? extends Callable<T>> tasks)`
`throws InterruptedException`
Performs all tasks and returns a list of Future objects representing the results.

▶ `<T> List<Future<T>> invokeAll(Collection<? extends Callable<T>> tasks,`
`long timeout, TimeUnit unit) throws InterruptedException`
Executes all tasks and will return the results as a list of Future objects as long as the timeout time isn't exceeded in the given time unit.

▶ `<T> T invokeAny(Collection<? extends Callable<T>> tasks)`
`throws InterruptedException, ExecutionException`
Executes all tasks but returns the result of an executor that finishes first. Thus, get(...) will never have to wait.

▶ `<T> T invokeAny(Collection<? extends Callable<T>> tasks,long timeout, TimeUnit`
`unit)`

throws InterruptedException, ExecutionException, TimeoutException
Performs all tasks but is valid only for a limited time. The first result of a Callable object that finishes in time returns invokeAny(...).

Tip

The get(long timeout, TimeUnit unit) method of Future won't send an interrupt to the thread if it fails to produce a result in time. In contrast, one advantage of *Any(..., TimeUnit) methods is that they trigger an interrupt.

17.4.6   CompletionService and ExecutorCompletionService

The invokeAll(...) methods from the ExecutorService are useful for submitting multiple tasks concurrently and collecting the results later. However, the return is of type List<Future<T>>, and you won't be notified when a result is available. You could run the list over and over again and ask each Future object if it's done via isDone(), but this approach isn't an ideal solution.

java.util.concurrent.CompletionService is another Java interface (which doesn't extend any base type) that you can use to make a Callable or Runnable work and later sequentially collect the results that have been completed. The Java library contains an implementation of the interface, ExecutorCompletionService, which internally collects the completed results in a queue, and you can query the queue. Let's look at this interface through an example:

```
ExecutorService executor = Executors.newCachedThreadPool();
CompletionService<Integer> completionService =
  new ExecutorCompletionService<>( executor );
List.of( 4, 3, 2, 1 ).forEach( duration -> completionService.submit( () -> {
  TimeUnit.SECONDS.sleep( duration );
  return duration;
} ) );

for ( int i = 0; i < 4; i++ ) {
  try {
    System.out.println( completionService.take().get() );
  }
  catch ( InterruptedException | ExecutionException e ) {
    e.printStackTrace();
  }
}

executor.shutdown();
```

Listing 17.13 src/main/java/com/tutego/insel/thread/concurrent/ExecutorCompletion ServiceDemo.java (Snippet)

The `ExecutorCompletionService` type expects an executor in the constructor to execute the code. For our example, we'll use a thread pool. `CompletionService` has two submit(...) methods:

▶ Future<V> submit(Runnable task, V result)

▶ Future<V> submit(Callable<V> task)

Four `Callable` instances are sent that wait 4, 3, 2, and 1 seconds and return their wait times at the end. Of course, the first thing to finish is the `Callable` with return 1, then return 2, and so on.

Our program isn't interested in the returns because we're using the take() method. In total, `CompletionService` has three removal methods:

▶ Future<V> take()
Returns the result from the first completed task and removes it from the internal queue. If no result is available, the method will wait.

▶ Future<V> poll()
Returns the result from the first completed task and removes it from the internal queue. If no result is available, poll() won't wait but will instead return null.

▶ Future<V> poll (long timeout, TimeUnit unit)
If take() waits for a result, but one doesn't appear after the timeout expires, the method will return null, much like poll().

What the interface lacks is a method that returns the remaining number. Therefore, we'll need to introduce a counter as an extra variable in our code.

17.4.7 ScheduledExecutorService: Repetitive Tasks and Time Controls

The `ScheduledThreadPoolExecutor` class is another class besides `ThreadPoolExecutor` that implements the `Executor` and `ExecutorService` interfaces. However, the important interface also implemented by this class is `ScheduledExecutorService`, a direct subtype of `ExecutorService`. Several schedule*(...) operations are declared in this class, which can execute a `Runnable` or `Callable` at specific times and in repetition. (Although something similar exists with `java.util.Timer`, the `ScheduledThreadPoolExecutor` uses threads from the pool.)

`Executors` provide several static methods for producing readily configured `ScheduledExecutorService` objects, for example, newScheduledThreadPool(int corePoolSize).

The following example executes an output every 2 seconds after a start time delay of 1 second:

```
ScheduledExecutorService scheduler = Executors.newScheduledThreadPool( 1 );

scheduler.scheduleAtFixedRate(
    () -> System.out.println( "Tata" ),
```

```
    1 /* initial delay */,
    2 /* period */,
    TimeUnit.SECONDS );
```

Listing 17.14 src/main/java/com/tutego/insel/thread/concurrent/
ScheduledExecutorServiceDemo.java. main()

After the 1-second start delay, you'll see a "Tata" every other second.

17.4.8 Asynchronous Programming with CompletableFuture (CompletionStage)

One nice thing about Future objects is that they're processed in the background, and you can query them later to see if a result is already available. However, the Future interface lacks a method to automatically process a follow-up job after completion. For this purpose, the Java library provides a special subclass: CompletableFuture. This class implements the CompletionStage interface, which probably contains the largest number of operations throughout Java SE. The type's name expresses that it's concerned with the *completion* of *stages*.

Let's consider an example of a hard-drinking but brave pirate:

```java
package com.tutego.insel.thread.concurrent;

import java.time.LocalTime;
import java.util.concurrent.CompletableFuture;
import java.util.concurrent.TimeUnit;
import java.util.logging.Logger;

class Pirate {

  public static void main( String[] arg ) throws Throwable {

    System.setProperty( "java.util.logging.SimpleFormatter.format",
                        "-> %2$s: %5$s %6$s%n");

    String result =
      CompletableFuture.supplyAsync( Pirate::newName )
                    .thenApply( Pirate::swear )
                    .thenCombine( drinkRum(), Pirate::combinePirateAndDrinks
)
                    .thenCombine( drinkRum(), Pirate::combinePirateAndDrinks
)
                    .exceptionally( e -> "Pirate Guybrush did not survive"
                                    + "the death curse  '"
                                    + e.getCause().getMessage() + "'" )
```

```
                                     .get();
    System.out.println( result );
    // Pirate Guybrush swears and then drinks 10 bottles of rum and then drinks
    // 11 bottles of rum
    // Pirate Guybrush did not survive the death curse 'Avada Kedavra'
  }

  static String newName() {
    Logger.getGlobal().info( Thread.currentThread().getName() );
    return "Pirate Guybrush";
  }

  static String swear( String pirate ) {
    Logger.getGlobal().info( Thread.currentThread().getName() );
    if ( Math.random() < 0.4 )
      throw new IllegalStateException( "Avada Kedavra" );
    return pirate + " curses";
  }

  static CompletableFuture<Integer> drinkRum() throws InterruptedException {
    Logger.getGlobal().info( Thread.currentThread().getName() );
    TimeUnit.SECONDS.sleep( 1 );
    return CompletableFuture.supplyAsync( () -> LocalTime.now().getSecond() );
  }

  static String combinePirateAndDrinks( String pirate, int bottlesOfRum ) {
    Logger.getGlobal().info( Thread.currentThread().getName() );
    return pirate + " and then drinks " + bottlesOfRum + " bottles of rum";
  }
}
```

Listing 17.15 src/main/java/com/tutego/insel/thread/concurrent/Pirate.java

The following output doesn't contain an exception:

```
-> com.tutego.insel.thread.concurrent.Pirate drinkRum: main
-> com.tutego.insel.thread.concurrent.Pirate newName: ForkJoinPool.commonPool-
worker-1
-> com.tutego.insel.thread.concurrent.Pirate swear: ForkJoinPool.commonPool-
worker-1
-> com.tutego.insel.thread.concurrent.Pirate combinePirateAndDrinks: main
-> com.tutego.insel.thread.concurrent.Pirate drinkRum: main
-> com.tutego.insel.thread.concurrent.Pirate combinePirateAndDrinks: main
Pirate Guybrush curses and then drinks 18 bottles of rum and then drinks 19 bott
les of rum
```

Let's walk through the steps of this program:

1. `supplyAsync(…)`: First, you need to build the chain of sections either with the default constructor or with static methods. In our case, we used `supplyAsync(Supplier<U> supplier)`. This method takes a free thread from the `ForkJoinPool.commonPool()` and lets the thread process the `supplier`. The result can be retrieved via the return, which is a `CompletableFuture`.

2. `thenApply(…)`: Next, we apply `thenApply(Function<? super T,? extends U> fn)`, which is comparable to a `map(...)` operation of a stream.

3. `thenCombine(…)`: Things get interesting with `thenCombine(CompletionStage<? extends U> other, BiFunction<? super T,? super U,? extends V> fn)`. This method combines the result of its own `CompletionStage` via a bifunction (`combinePirateAndDrinks(...)`) with another `CompletionStage` (supplied by `drinkRum(...)`), which in our case we also build up again with `supplyAsync(...)`. Thus, we combine two independent CompletionStages and synchronize the result. From the output, you can easily see that drinkRum is already executed at the beginning, by the `thread[main,5,main]`, not by the `ForkJoinPool`, because it runs independently of the others.

4. `exceptionally(…)`: Several methods can handle possible exceptions during the processing chain. One of these methods is `exception(Function<Throwable,? extends T> fn)`, which catches an exception and returns a default value. Our handling takes out the reason from the internally redirected `java.util.concurrent.CompletionException` with `getCause()`, and so we obtain the `IllegalStateException` that was actually thrown.

The missing processing of `combinePirateAndDrinks(...)` in shown in output of the error case:

```
-> com.tutego.insel.thread.concurrent.Pirate newName: ForkJoinPool.commonPool-
worker-1
-> com.tutego.insel.thread.concurrent.Pirate drinkRum: main
-> com.tutego.insel.thread.concurrent.Pirate swear: ForkJoinPool.commonPool-
worker-1
-> com.tutego.insel.thread.concurrent.Pirate drinkRum: main
Pirate Guybrush did not survivethe death curse  'Avada Kedavra'
```

17.5 Further Reading

`CompletableFuture` is a complex data type, so reading the Javadoc about it is worthwhile. Also, the Javadoc of the `java.util.concurrent` package lists quite a few data types that are interesting. Ultimately, though, developers should try to let a framework handle concurrency, synchronization, and notification. The less you code yourself, the fewer mistakes you can make. An excellent book for that topic is *Java Concurrency in Practice* by Brian Goetz, et al. (Addison-Wesley Professional, 2006).

Chapter 18

Introduction to Data Structures and Algorithms

"Happiness is simply good health and a bad memory."
—Ernest Hemingway (1899–1961)

Algorithms[1] are a central topic in computer science. Their research and study occupy a significant place in that field. Algorithms can operate effectively with data only if the data is suitably structured. Even a simple example like a phone directory illustrates the importance of organizing data according to a schema: Searching for a cell phone number of a given name succeeds quickly, while searching for the name of a known number might be a tedious task. Data structures and algorithms are thus closely related, and the choice of the right data structure determines runtime efficiency; neither ever serves its purpose alone. Unfortunately, choosing the "right" data structure isn't as easy as it sounds, and a number of difficult problems in computer science remain unsolved because a suitable data organization hasn't been found.

The most important data structures, such as lists, sets, and associative memories, will be introduced in this chapter.

18.1 Lists

A list represents a sequence of data where the elements have a fixed order. The `java.util.List` interface prescribes behavior that all concrete lists must implement. Interesting implementations of the `list` interface include the following:

- `java.util.ArrayList`: A list based on an array
- `java.util.LinkedList`: A list by concatenated elements
- `java.util.concurrent.CopyOnWriteArrayList`: A fast list, optimal for frequent concurrent read access
- `java.util.Vector`: A synchronized list (This class is not deprecated but should no longer be used because all access is synchronized in a rather slow way.)

---

1 The word *algorithm* comes from the name of the Persian-Arab mathematician Ibn Mûsâ Al-Chwârismî from the 9th century.

The methods for accessing lists via the common List interface are always the same. Thus, each list allows point access via get(index), and each list can return all stored elements sequentially by means of an iterator. But the implementations of the interface List differ in properties such as performance, memory requirements, or safe concurrency.

Since all data structures can store any object derived from Object, the lists are not fixed to certain data types in general, but generics can specify these types more precisely.

18.1.1   First List Example

Lists have some important properties: They remember the order of the inserted elements, and elements can also appear twice. Let's apply these skills for a little memory game. The user specifies destination cities for a route, which the program stores in a list in the order originally entered. After entering a new destination on the route, the user must recite all the cities back in the correct order. Once this task is complete, the new city is added, and the process restarts. Basically, the game is infinite, but since no human can remember an infinite number of cities in a sequence, at some point, they'll answer incorrectly, which will terminate the program.

```
package com.tutego.insel.util.list;

import java.text.*;
import java.util.*;

public class MemorizeYourRoadTripRoute {
  public static void main( String[] args ) {
    List<String> cities = new ArrayList<>();

    while ( true ) {
      System.out.println( "What new city should be added?" );
      String newCity = new Scanner( System.in ).nextLine();
      cities.add( newCity );

      System.out.printf( "What is the overall route? (Hint: %d %s)%n",
                         cities.size(), cities.size() == 1 ?
 "city" : "cities" );

      for ( String city : cities ) {
        String guess = new Scanner( System.in ).nextLine();
        if ( ! city.equalsIgnoreCase( guess ) ) {
          System.out.printf( "%s is not correct, %s would be correct. Too bad!%n
",
                             guess, city );
```

```
        return;
      }
    }
    System.out.println( "Great, all cities in the right order!" );
  }
 }
}
```

Listing 18.1 src/main/java/com/tutego/insel/util/list/MemorizeYourRoadTripRoute.java

18.1.2 Selection Criterion ArrayList or LinkedList

An ArrayList stores elements in an internal array (the same is true for Vector). A LinkedList, on the other hand, stores the elements in a linked list and implements the linking with a separate helper object for each list element. Areas of use, for LinkedList and ArrayList, include the following scenarios:

- Since ArrayList uses an array internally, accessing a specific element by its position in the list is quite fast. When LinkedList must be searched in a more elaborate way, more time is required.

- However, the linked list has one clear advantage: When elements are deleted or inserted in the middle of the list, the linking of the helper objects only needs to be changed in one place. In an ArrayList, this change requires a lot of work, unless the element can be deleted at the end or (if the buffer size is large enough) inserted. If an element isn't to be inserted or deleted at the end, all subsequent list elements must be moved.

- With an ArrayList, the size of the internal array can become too small. Then, the run-time environment has no choice but to create a new, larger array object and copy all the elements to that array.

18.1.3 The List Interface

The List interface prescribes the general behavior for lists. Most of these methods are familiar from the Collection interface because List extends the Collection interface. Some methods have been added that reference the position of an element. (Set instances, which also implement Collection, don't use an index.)

Adding and Setting Elements

The add(...) method adds new elements to the list, where a position can determine the insertion point. The addAll(...) method adds foreign elements from another collection to the list. set(...) places an element in a specific position and overrides the original element (instead of moving it). The size() method names the number of elements in the data structure.

```java
List<String> list1 = new ArrayList<>();
list1.add( "Eva" );
list1.add( 0, "Charisma" );
list1.add( "Pallas" );

List<String> list2 = Arrays.asList( "Tina", "Wilhelmine" );
list1.addAll( 3, list2 );
list1.add( "XXX" );
list1.set( 5, "Eva" );

System.out.println( list1 );        // [
Charisma, Eva, Pallas, Tina, Wilhelmine, Eva]
System.out.println( list1.size() ); // 6
```

Listing 18.2 src/main/java/com/tutego/insel/util/list/ListDemo.java (Snippet)

Position Requests and Searches

Whether or not the collection is empty is determined by isEmtpy(). An element at a specific location can be queried by get(int). Whether elements are part of the collection is answered by contains(...) and containsAll(...). As with strings, indexOf(...) and lastIndexOf(...) return the find positions.

```java
boolean b = list1.contains( "Tina" );
System.out.println( b );            // true

b = list1.containsAll( Arrays.asList( "Tina", "Eva" ) );
System.out.println( b );            // true

Object o = list1.get( 1 );
System.out.println( o );            // Eva

int i = list1.indexOf( "Eva" );
System.out.println( i );            // 1

i = list1.lastIndexOf( "Eva" );
System.out.println( i );            // 5

System.out.println( list1.isEmpty() ); // false
```

Listing 18.3 src/main/java/com/tutego/insel/util/list/ListDemo.java (Snippet)

Lists or Arrays and Creating New Lists

Arrays can be derived from the lists, which is how intersections can be formed:

```java
String[] array = list1.toArray( new String[list1.size()] );
// alternative: String[] array = list1.toArray( String[]::new );

System.out.println( array[3] );      // "Tina"

List<String> list3 = new LinkedList<>( list1 );
System.out.println( list3 );              // [Charisma, Eva, Pallas, Tina,
                                          // Wilhelmine, Eva]
list3.retainAll( Arrays.asList( "Tina", "Eva" ) );
System.out.println( list3 );              // [Eva, Tina, Eva]
```

Listing 18.4 src/main/java/com/tutego/insel/util/list/ListDemo.java (Snippet)

Deleting Elements

Methods are also available for deleting elements. In this regard, the list provides over-loaded remove(...) methods: removeIf(...) and removeAll(...). The shortest way to delete everything from the list is clear().

```java
System.out.println( list1 );     // [Charisma, Eva, Pallas, Tina, Wilhelmine, Eva]
list1.remove( 1 );
System.out.println( list1 );     // [Charisma, Pallas, Tina, Wilhelmine, Eva]

list1.remove( "Wilhelmine" );
System.out.println( list1 );     // [Charisma, Pallas, Tina, Eva]

list1.removeAll( Arrays.asList( "Pallas", "Eva" ) );
System.out.println( list1 );     // [Charisma, Tina]

list1.clear();
System.out.println( list1 );     // []
```

Listing 18.5 src/main/java/com/tutego/insel/util/list/ListDemo.java (Snippet)

> **Note**
>
> The remove(int) method deletes an element at the given position. In contrast, remove(Object) searches for an object similar to equals and then deletes it but then doesn't search further for other occurrences. removeIf(...) and removeAll(...) always run completely over the entire data structure and look if an element satisfies the criterion for deletion, which may occur several times.

18

[Ex]

Example

The following example deletes all null references and whitespace strings from a list:

```
List<String> list = new ArrayList<>();
Collections.addAll( list, "1", "", " ", "two", null, "police" );
list.removeIf( e -> Objects.isNull( e ) || e.trim().isEmpty() );
System.out.println( list ); // [1, two, police]
```

Summary

The List interface (in addition to those from the extended Collection interface) includes the following methods:

```
interface java.util.List<E>
extends Collection<E>
```

▶ boolean add(E e)
Adds the element e to the end of the list (an optional operation).

▶ void add(int index, E element)
Inserts an object at the specified position in the list (an optional operation).

▶ boolean addAll(int index, Collection<? extends E> c)
Inserts all elements of the collection at the specified position in the list (an optional operation).

▶ void clear()
Deletes all elements from the set (an optional operation).

▶ boolean contains(Object o)
Returns true if the element o is in the list. (The comparison is done by equals(...), and it isn't a reference comparison.)

▶ boolean containsAll(Collection<?> c)
Returns true if all elements of the collection c are in the current list.

▶ static <E> List<E> copyOf (Collection<? extends E> coll)
Creates an unmodifiable copy.

▶ E get(int index)
Returns the element at the specified position in the list.

▶ int indexOf(Object o)
Returns the position of the first occurrence for o or -1 if no list element matches o in content (i.e., by equals(...) and not by reference). Unfortunately, no method is available that continues searching from a certain point, as provided by the String class. However, a sublist can be used for this task via subList(...), a method that is described a few lines later.

▶ boolean isEmpty()
Returns true if the list is empty.

▶ Iterator<E> iterator()
Returns the iterator. But the method calls listIterator() and returns a ListIterator object.

▶ int lastIndexOf(Object o)
Searches from the back of the list for the first occurrence of o and returns -1 if no list element matches o in content.

▶ ListIterator<E> listIterator()
Returns a list iterator for the entire list. A list iterator provides additional operations in contrast to the general container iterator.

▶ ListIterator<E> listIterator(int index)
Returns a list iterator that traverses the list starting at position index.

▶ E remove(int index)
Removes the element at the index position from the list.

▶ boolean remove(Object o)
Removes the first object in the list that is equals(...) equal to o. Returns true if an element was removed (an optional operation).

▶ boolean removeAll(Collection<?> c)
Deletes the elements from c in its own list (an optional operation).

▶ default boolean removeIf(Predicate<? super E> filter)
Removes all elements from the list for which the predicate is fulfilled.

▶ boolean retainAll(Collection<?> c)
Optional. Removes all objects from the list that don't appear in the collection c.

▶ default void replaceAll(UnaryOperator<E> operator)
Calls the operator on each element and writes back the result.

▶ E set(int index, E element)
Replaces the element at the index position with element (an optional operation).

▶ int size()
Returns the number of elements in the collection.

▶ List<E> subList(int fromIndex, int toIndex)
Returns the section of this list from position fromIndex (included) toIndex (not included). The returned list represents a view of a section of the original list. Changes to the partial list affect the entire list, and vice versa (as far as they affect the matching section).

▶ default void sort(Comparator<? super E> c)
Sorts the list, equivalent to Collections.sort(this, c).

▶ boolean equals(Object o)
Compares the list with another list. To do this, the method traverses both lists and

18

compares element by element; two list objects are equal if their elements are pair wise equal.

▶ int hashCode()

Returns the hash value of the list.

So what List adds to the Collection are the index-based methods:

- add(int index, E element)
- addAll(int index, Collection<? extends E> c)
- get(int index), indexOf(Object o)
- lastIndexOf(Object o)
- listIterator()
- listIterator(int index)
- remove(int index)
- set(int index, E element)
- subList(int fromIndex, int toIndex)

And additionally the two default methods replaceAll(...) and sort(...).

[»]

Note

The remove(...) method is overridden and deletes the following elements:

- An element that's searched for with equals(...)
- An element at a position given in remove(int)

Consider the following confusing example:

```
List<Integer> list = new ArrayList<>( Arrays.asList( 9, 8, 1, 7 ) );
Integer index = 1;
list.remove( index );
System.out.println( list );  // [9, 8, 7]
```

remove(Object) is called because Object is most similar to the argument type Integer. Thus, the Integer.valueOf(1) element disappears from the list. Unboxing doesn't take place, as expected, and therefore, the naming index and the object type in the example are deliberately misleading.

The following example more clearly represents what we meant:

```
list = new ArrayList<>( List.of( 9, 8, 1, 7 ) );
int realIndex = 1;
list.remove( realIndex );
System.out.println( list );  // [9, 1, 7]
```

Copying and Cutting

The list classes implement clone() and create a shallow copy rather than a deep copy. That is, the elements in the data structure are not themselves cloned; by the way, this is always true for clone() in general.

To delete a range, you can use subList(from, to).clear(). The subList technique immediately covers some other operations for which no special range variants exist, for example, indexOf(...) for searching in a part of the list.

18

Example

[Ex]

The following example creates a list, shortens it, and output the elements in backwards order:

```
List<String> list = new ArrayList<>(
    Arrays.asList( "0 1 2 3 4 5 6 7 8 9".split( " " ) ) );
list.subList( 2, list.size() - 2 ).clear();
System.out.println( list );                      // [0, 1, 8, 9]
for ( ListIterator<String> it = list.listIterator( list.size() );
      it.hasPrevious(); )
  System.out.print( it.previous() + " " );       // 9 8 1 0
```

Like many other methods of Collection data structures, subList(...) creates a view on the list, which means that changes to this sublist will result in changes to the original. The same is true for clear(), which you can use to delete a subset of the original list.

[»]

Note

The `removeRange(int, int)` method, which can be used for deleting, can't be used (directly) because this method is `protected`.[2] This limitation can be resolved, for example, in the following way:

```
class RemovableList<E> extends ArrayList<E> {
  @Override public void removeRange(int fromIndex, int toIndex) {
    super.removeRange(fromIndex, toIndex);
  }
}
```

Static Methods in List

The `List` interface declares a set of static methods that build an immutable list:

```
interface java.util.List<E>
extends Collection<E>
```

▶ static <E> List<E> copyOf(Collection<? extends E> coll)

▶ static <E> List<E> of()

▶ static <E> List<E> of(E... elements)

18.1.4   ArrayList

Each instance of the `ArrayList` class represents a variable length array. The elements are accessed efficiently via indexes, which `ArrayList` implies via the implementation of the `RandomAccess` marker interface (refer back to Chapter 8, Section 8.1.18 for more information).

Creating an ArrayList

To create an `ArrayList` object, three constructors are available:

```
class java.util.ArrayList<E>
extends AbstractList<E>
implements List<E>, RandomAccess, Cloneable, Serializable
```

---

2 In `AbstractList`, `removeRange(int, int)` is validly implemented with a `ListIterator`, so the method isn't abstract. The API documentation justifies this scenario by saying that `removeRange(...)` isn't part of the official interface of lists but is intended for the authors of new list implementations.

▶ `ArrayList()`

An empty list with an initial capacity of 10 elements is created. If more than 10 elements are inserted, the list size must increase.

▶ `ArrayList(int initialCapacity)`

A list with the internal size of `initialCapacity` elements is created.

▶ `ArrayList(Collection<? extends E> c)`

Copies all elements of the collection `c` into the new `ArrayList` object.

The Internal Operation of ArrayList *

The `ArrayList` object manage two sizes: first, the number of elements stored externally and, second, the internal size of the array. If the capacity of the array is greater than the number of elements, then elements can still be included without the list having to do anything. The number of elements in the list (i.e., its size) is returned by the `size()` method; the capacity of the underlying array is returned by `capacity()`.

The list will automatically increase in size if more elements are included than were originally planned for the place. This operation is called *resizing*. The `initialCapacity` size plays an important role with regard to working efficiently and should therefore be chosen appropriately. For this reason, let's first consider how a list works if its internal array is too small.

If an array stores 10 elements, but now an 11th is to be inserted, the runtime system must reserve a new memory area and copy each element of the old array into the new array. This operation costs time. For this reason alone, the constructor `ArrayList(int initialCapacity)` should be chosen because these constructors set an initial size. Knowledge of your data then helps determine the data structure. If no value has been preset, 10 elements are assumed. In many cases, this value is too small.

At this point, we've described creating a new array and copying elements, but we haven't said anything about the size of the new array. The `ArrayList` makes the internal array 1.5 times larger when expanded.

The internal size of an array can be changed via `ensureCapacity(int)`. Calling `ensureCapacity(int minimumCapacity)` causes the list to hold at least `minimumCapacity` elements in total without resizing.

18.1.5 LinkedList

The `LinkedList` class implements the `List` interface as a linked list and doesn't map the elements to an array. The implementation realizes the `LinkedList` as a doubly linked list in which each element has a predecessor and successor–excluding the first and last element. (Singly linked lists have only one successor, making it difficult to navigate in either direction.)

18

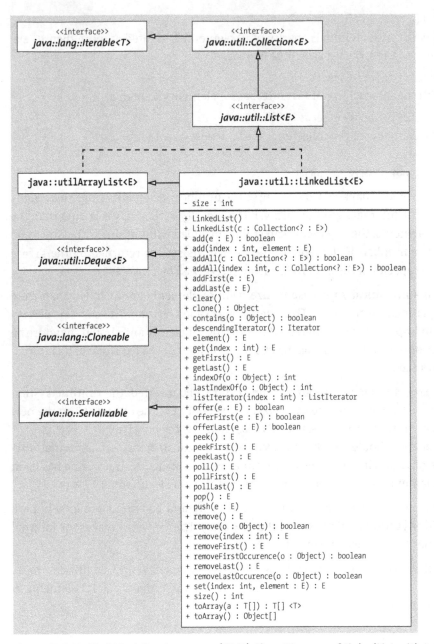

Figure 18.1 Unified Modeling Language (UML) Class Diagram of LinkedList with Inheritance Relationships

A LinkedList has other helper methods besides the given operations from the List interface, such as addFirst(...), addLast(...), getFirst(), getLast(), removeFirst(), and removeLast(). The implemented interfaces Queue and Deque are somewhat responsible for the existence of these methods.

```
class java.util.LinkedList<E>
extends AbstractSequentialList<E>
implements List<E>, Deque<E>, Cloneable, Serializable
```

▶ LinkedList()

Creates a new empty list.

▶ LinkedList(Collection<? extends E> c)

Copies all elements of the collection c into the new linked list.

18.1.6 The Array Adapter Arrays.asList(…)

Arrays of object references and dynamic data structures don't really go together, although they're needed together quite often. The Java library provides the static method Arrays.asList(...) to treat an existing array as a java.util.List. The parameter type is a vararg, which is, after all, internally mapped to an array. Thus, asList(...) can be used in two ways:

- Arrays.asList(array): The array variable is a reference to an array, and the result is a list containing the same elements as the array.

- Arrays.asList(e1, e2, e3): The elements e1, e2, and e3 are elements of the list.

The design pattern that the Java library applies to the static method is referred to as the *adapter design pattern*, which adapts the interface of one type to another interface of a different type.

[Ex]

Example

The following example determines the number of smileys :-) in a string:

```
String s = "Peter :-) Paul :-) Mary";
int i = Collections.frequency( Arrays.asList(s.split("\\s")), ":-)" );
System.out.println( i );    // 2
```

In String, no method is available for counting substrings.

[Ex]

Example

The following example outputs the largest element of an array:

```
Integer[] ints = { 3, 9, -1, 0 };
System.out.println( Collections.max( Arrays.asList( ints ) ) );
```

To determine the maximum, the utility class Arrays doesn't provide a method, so the max(...) method of Collections comes in handy. In addition, Arrays provides no way to replace array elements, whereas Collections does. But sorting and filling arrays is possible. In this case, asList() doesn't need to step in.

---

class java.util.**Arrays**

▶ public static <T> List<T> asList(T… a)

Provides access to an array via the List interface. Its variable arguments are quite convenient.

[»]

Note

Because of generics, the parameter type of asList(...) is an object array, but never a primitive array. In our previous example, the following code would compile:

```java
int[] ints = { 3, 9, -1, 0 };
Arrays.asList( ints );
```

However, the return of Arrays.asList(ints) is of type List<int[]>, which means the entire list consists of exactly one element, and that element is the primitive array. Fortunately, Collections.max(Arrays.asList(ints)) results in a compiler error because max(Collection<? extends T>) can't determine a maximum from a List<int[]>, that is, from a list of arrays. In contrast, with Arrays.asList(3, 9, -1, 0), the compiler already converts the varargs arguments directly into wrapper objects via autoboxing, which results in a list of Integer objects.

Internal Matters

The return of asList(...) isn't a concrete class type like ArrayList or LinkedList, but something unknown, which asList(...) returns as List. This list is just another view of the array.

Now, however, some room for interpretation about what exactly is possible with the return remains. In addition, we might need to know whether the list allows fast point access (RandomAccess implemented) or whether optional operations such as changes or even total reorganizations are conceivable. A look at the implementation reveals more. The result is an adapter that redirects list methods like get(index) or set(index, element) directly to the array. Since array lengths are final, modification methods such as remove(...) or add(...) result in an UnsupportedOperationException.

[»]

Note

If changes to the asList(...) return are desired, the result must be copied into a new data structure, in the following way:

```java
List<String> list = new ArrayList<>( Arrays.asList( "A", "B" ) );
list.add( "C" );
```

List.of(...)

An alternative to asList(...) are various static overloaded of(...) methods of the List interface. In these methods, too, any number of arguments can be passed. With asList(...), however, the underlying array may change, so that the list changes automatically. With List.of(...), the references passed will be copied. Also, no elements can be written back to the List.of(...) list, but they can be written to the asList(...) list.

18.1.7 ListIterator*

The ListIterator interface is an extension of Iterator. This interface adds other methods so that elements can also be inserted at the current position. The location is also called the *cursor*. You should conceive of the location of the cursor as always *between* the elements; at the start, the cursor is located *before* the first element. The remove() and set(e) methods aren't associated with cursor positions; they operate on the last element that was provided by next() or previous().

```
List<String> list = new ArrayList<>();
Collections.addAll( list, "b", "c", "d" );

ListIterator<String> it = list.listIterator();

it.add( "a" );                    // Add in front
System.out.println( list );       // [a, b, c, d]

it.next();                        // Position before
it.remove();                      // Delete element
System.out.println( list );       // [a, c, d]

it.next();                        // Position before
it.set( "C" );                    // Replace element
System.out.println( list );       // [a, C, d]

it = list.listIterator( 1 );      // New iterator with start pos. 1
it.add( "B" );                    // Add B
System.out.println( list );       // [a, B, C, d]

it = list.listIterator( list.size() );

it.previous();                    // One place forward
it.remove();                      // Delete last element
System.out.println( list );       // [a, B, C]
```

Listing 18.6 src/main/java/com/tutego/insel/util/list/ListIteratorDemo.java, main()

[+]

Tip

As shown in the following example, `ListIterator` can also process the elements backwards:

```
List<String> list = new ArrayList<String>();
Collections.addAll( list, "1", "2", "3", "4" );
for ( ListIterator<String> it = list.listIterator( list.size() );
      it.hasPrevious(); )
  System.out.print( it.previous() + " " ); // 4 3 2 1
interface ListIterator<E>
extends Iterator<E>
```

▶ boolean hasPrevious()

▶ boolean hasNext()
  Returns true if a preceding or following element exists.

▶ E previous()

▶ E next()
  Returns the previous or next element of the list or issues NoSuchElementException if the element doesn't exist. Then, the method sets the cursor position back or forward.

▶ int previousIndex()

▶ int nextIndex()
  Returns the index of the preceding or following element. If previousIndex() goes before the list, the method will return -1. If nextIndex() goes after the list, the method will return the length of the entire list.

▶ void remove()
  Removes the last element returned by next() or previous() (an optional operation).

▶ void add(E o)
  Inserts a new object in front of the current position in the list (an optional operation).

▶ void set(E o)
  Replaces the element returned last by next() or previous() (an optional operation).

18.1.8   Understanding toArray(...) of Collection: Recognizing Traps

The toArray() method of the Collection interface returns an array of objects by definition. You must understand both the type of the entries and the type of the array itself.

[Ex]

Example

The following application of toArray() transfers all the points of a collection into a new array:

```
ArrayList<Point> list = new ArrayList<>();
list.add( new Point(13, 43) );
list.add( new Point(9, 4) );
Object[] points = list.toArray();
```

With toArray(), we get an array with references to Point objects, but we can't simply write points[1].x to access the Point object variable because the points array has the declared element type Object. The explicit type conversion is missing, and only ((Point)points[1]).x is correct.

You might consider simply changing the type of the array from Object[] to Point[] since are Point instances in the array, after all, and then try the following incorrect code:

```
Point[] points = list.toArray();              // 💀 Compiler error
```

The compiler reports the error "Type mismatch: cannot convert from Object[] to Point[ ]" because the return value of toArray() is an Object[] and not a Point[]. Now, maybe we could fix this type problem with a typecasting to a Point[], perhaps in the following way:

```
Point[] points = (Point[]) list.toArray();   // 💀 Problem at runtime
```

While we no longer have a problem at compile time, at runtime, we'll get the message "java.lang.ClassCastException: class [Ljava.lang.Object; cannot be cast to class [Ljava.awt.Point;" even if only Point objects actually existed in the array.

Let's examine this programming error. What we did wrong is simple: We confused the type of the array with the types of the array elements. In the following code, we can assign anything to an array of object references:

```
Object[] os = new Object[ 3 ];
os[0] = new Point();
os[1] = "Which seat can I take?";
os[2] = LocalDate.now();
```

Notice that the type of the array is Object[], and the array elements are also of type Object. Behind the keyword new, which creates the array object, is the common super-type for allowed array elements. For Object[] arrays, the elements may be references for any objects. Clearly, an array can only hold object references that are compatible with the type for the array itself, that is, that refer to instances of the specified class or to copies of subclasses of that class. Consider the following example:

```
/* 1 */  Object[] os = new Point[ 3 ];
/* 2 */  os[0] = new Point();
/* 3 */  os[1] = LocalDate.now();             // 💀 ArrayStoreException
/* 4 */  os[2] = "Which seat can I take?";    // 💀 ArrayStoreException
```

Lines 3 and 4 are permitted by the compiler but lead to an ArrayStoreException at runtime.

Let's return to the toArray() method. Because the data structure to be read might contain anything, the type of the elements must be Object. We've just established that the element type of the array object returned as a result by the toArray() method must be at least as comprehensive. Since there's no more general (more comprehensive) type than Object, the type of the array is also Object[].This rule must be true, even if the elements of a data structure have a more special type in individual cases. A general implementation of toArray() has no choice but to create the array of type Object[] and the elements of type Object.

To summarize, we previously wrote Object[] os = new Point[3]; and saw that Object[] is a base type of Point[]. This fact is possible because Object is also a basic type of Point. The inheritance relationship of types carries over to the inheritance relationship of the arrays of those types, which is called *covariance*. However, if only an Object[] array is created—as by the parameterless toArray()—the result can't be casted to the Point[] type, even if each element is a Point.

The Solution to the Problem

Now, before we write a loop with a type conversion for every single array element or do a typecasting every time we access elements, we should consider the second toArray(T[]) method, which accepts a predefined array for the result as a parameter. With this method, the result array is of a more special type than Object[].

[Ex]

Example

The following example requests an array of type Point from the toArray() method:

```
List<Point> list = new ArrayList<>();
list.add( new Point(13,43) );
list.add( new Point(9,4) );
Point[] points = (Point[]) list.toArray( new Point[0] );
```

You'll get list items copied into an array, and the type of the array is Point[], matching the list items currently present. The parameter indicates the desired type, which in this case is the Point array.

[+]

Performance Tip

A best practice is to specify the size of the result array, that is, as large as the list, for toArray(T[]). Then, toArray(T[]) fills exactly this array and returns it instead of building a new array. Consider the following example:

```
ArrayList<Point> list = new ArrayList<>();
list.add( new Point(13,43) );
```

```
list.add( new Point(9,4) );
Point[] points = list.toArray( new Point[list.size()] );
// alternative Point[] points = list.toArray( Point[]::new );
```

Creating Arrays with Reflection*

Internally, the toArray(T[]) method uses *reflection* to dynamically create an array of the same type as the passed array. A method from java.lang.reflect.Array is used for this task:

▶ public static Object newInstance(Class<?> componentType, int length)

Example [Ex]

In the following example, we'll create a new array that has the same type as array. The new empty field should have space for len elements:

```
Object[] array = { new Point(-1, -1), new Point( 1, 1 ) };
int len = 100;
Object[] b = (Object[]) Array.newInstance(
                        array.getClass().getComponentType(), len);
```

The array.getClass() call returns a Class object for the array, such as an object representing the Point[] type. With array.getClass().getComponentType(), you'll get a Class object for the element type of the array (i.e., Point).

So, we dynamically do what new TYP[len] does, where new must have the element type set at compile time. Since the return value of newInstance() is a general Object, the conversion to a suitable array must finally take place.

If the passed array is large enough to store all the elements of the collection, toArray(T[]) copies the elements from the collection into the array. Incidentally, toArray(new Object[0]) is equivalent to calling toArray().

18.1.9 Managing Primitive Elements in Data Structures

Each Collection API data structure, even if used generically, accepts only references. Primitive data types don't accept the collections, which has the consequence that wrapper objects are necessary. (Via boxing, Java seems to insert primitive elements, but in reality, Java inserts wrapper objects.)

For instance, in the following code, two new Double objects are created and then moved into the list:

18

```
List<Double> list = new ArrayList<>();
list.add( 1.1 );
list.add( 2.2 );
```

When written differently and more clearly, you can truly see what is really happening:

```
List<Double> list = new ArrayList<>();
list.add( Double.valueOf(1.1) );
list.add( new Double(2.2) );
```

From the call of `Double.valueOf(...)`, the `new` usage can't be read, but the method is implemented as `Double valueOf(double d){ return new Double(d); }`.

Special Libraries

For performant applications and large amounts of primitive elements, using a class for the special data type makes sense. Instead of programming these special classes on their own, developers can use two implementations:

- *Eclipse Collections* (*https://www.eclipse.org/collections/*) include primitive collections and a comprehensive API.

- *fastutil* (*https://fastutil.di.unimi.it/*) provides extensions with data structures for numerous primitive elements and high-performance input/output classes.

18.2   Sets

A set is an (initially) unordered collection of elements. Each element may occur only once. For sets, the Java library provides the interface `java.util.Set`. Popular implementing classes include the following:

- `HashSet`: For fast set implementation by hashing method (based on `HashMap`).
- `TreeSet`: Sets are implemented by balanced binary trees that allow sorting.
- `LinkedHashSet`: Fast set implementation while maintaining insertion order.
- `EnumSet`: A special set exclusively for enumerations.
- `CopyOnWriteArraySet`: For fast, thread-safe data structures, optimized for many read operations but few write operations.

18.2.1   A First Example of a Set

Our next example program analyzes a text and recognizes cities that were previously entered into a data structure. All cities that appear in the text are collected and subsequently output.

```java
package com.tutego.insel.util.set;

import java.text.BreakIterator;
import java.util.*;

public class WhereHaveYouBeen {
  public static void main( String[] args ) {
    // Build set with cities

    Set<String> allCities = new HashSet<>();
    allCities.add( "Seattle" );
    allCities.add( "Denver" );
    allCities.add( "Manila" );
    allCities.add( "Seoul" );
    allCities.add( "Siquijor" );

    // Build set for visited cities

    Set<String> visitedCities = new TreeSet<>();

    // Parse sentence and break it into words. All cities found
    // include in new data structure
    String sentence = "From Seattle I drive to Denver and fly to Manila.";
    BreakIterator iter = BreakIterator.getWordInstance();
    iter.setText( sentence );

    for ( int first = iter.first(), last = iter.next();
          last != BreakIterator.DONE;
          first = last, last = iter.next() ) {
      String word = sentence.substring( first, last );
      if ( allCities.contains( word ) )
        visitedCities.add( word );
    }

    // Some statistics

    System.out.println( "Number of visited cities: " + visitedCities.size() );
    System.out.println( "Number of unvisited cities: " +
                        (allCities.size() - visitedCities.size()) );
    System.out.println( "Visited cities: " + String.join( ", ", visitedCities )
);
    Set<String> unvisitedCities = new TreeSet<>( allCities );
    unvisitedCities.removeAll( visitedCities );
    System.out.println( "Unvisited cities: " + String.join( ", ", unvisitedCitie
```

18

```
s ) );
  }
}
```

Listing 18.7 src/main/java/com/tutego/insel/util/set/WhereHaveYouBeen.java

A total of three sets occur in this program:

- allCities stores all possible cities. The choice falls on the HashSet type because the set doesn't need to be sorted, concurrency is not an issue, and HashSet provides a good access time.

- A TreeSet visitedCities memorizes the visited cities. This Set is also fast but has the advantage of keeping the elements sorted, which will help our later output.

- To determine all unvisited cities, the program calculates the difference set between all cities and visited cities. No method in the Set interface does this directly—in fact, no operation in Set has the return type Set or Collection. So, you can only use a method like removeAll(...), which removes the visited cities from the set of all cities to determine which cities haven't been visited yet. But a "problem" with the remove-All(...) method is its destructive nature: The elements are deleted from the set. However, because the original set shouldn't be changed, we'll copy all cities to a cache (unvisitedCities) and delete elements from this cache, leaving the original set untouched.

> **[»]**
>
> **Note**
> Regular expressions are an option for decomposing sentences and occur elsewhere in the book as well. However, the BreakIterator has an advantage in that it can correctly classify every single Unicode character.

18.2.2 Methods of the Set Interface

In addition to operations for requesting and inserting elements, a set class declares methods for intersecting and joining sets.

```
interface java.util.Set<E>
extends Collection<E>
```

▶ boolean add(E o)
Places o in the set if no equals-equals object exists in the set yet. Returns true on successful insertion.

▶ boolean addAll(Collection<? extends E> c)
Inserts all elements of c into the Set. If c is a different Set, addAll(...) stands for the

set union. In essence, this method is similar to for (E e : c) add(e);. The return is true if the collection has changed in any way.

▶ void clear()
Deletes the Set.

▶ boolean contains(Object o)
Determines if the element o is included in the set.

▶ boolean containsAll(Collection<?> c)
Determines if c a subset of Set.

▶ static <E> Set<E> copyOf (Collection<? extends E> coll)
Creates an unmodifiable copy.

▶ boolean isEmpty()
Determines if the Set empty.

▶ Iterator<E> iterator()
Returns an iterator for the Set.

▶ boolean remove(Object o)
Deletes o from the Set and returns true if the deletion was successful; otherwise, returns false if no equals-like object exists in the set.

▶ boolean removeAll(Collection<?> c)
Deletes all elements of the Collection from the Set and returns true on successful deletion.

▶ boolean retainAll(Collection<?> c)
The set *retains* all elements that are also contained in c—in other words, all elements of the current set that aren't also present in c are deleted. No change occurs to the data structure c. The own set is then the intersection with c, but c may contain many more elements.

▶ int size()
Returns the number of elements in the set.

▶ Object[] toArray()
First creates a new array to store all the elements of the set and then copies the elements into the array.

▶ <T> T[] toArray(T[] a)
If the passed array is large enough for all elements of the set, then all elements of the set are copied into the array, and a is returned. If the array is too small, a new array of type T is created, and all elements are copied from the set to the array and returned.

▶ default <T> T[] toArray(IntFunction<T[]> generator)
As documented in Collection.

In the Set interface, the equals(...) and hashCode() methods originating from Object are specified with their functionalities related to sets in the API documentation.

In addition, several static methods for creating immutable sets are available:

▶ static <E> Set<E> copyOf(Collection<? extends E> coll)

▶ static <E> Set<E> of()

▶ static <E> Set<E> of(E... elements)

> **Note**
>
> Elements stored in a Set must remain immutable. On one hand, they may not be retrievable after a change; on the other hand, elements may appear twice in the set in this way, which contradicts the philosophy of the interface.

Adding Another Element

If an element isn't yet contained in a set, add(...) inserts the element and returns true. If already present, add(...) does nothing and returns false. (This scenario is different for a Map because in that case put(...) overrides the key.) Whether an element to be added matches an existing element already in the set is determined by the equals(...) method, in which case equivalence matters instead of identity.

```
Set<Point> set = new HashSet<>();
Point p1 = new Point(), p2 = new Point();
System.out.println( set.add(p1) );        // true
System.out.println( set.add(p1) );        // false
System.out.println( set.add(p2) );        // false
System.out.println( set.contains(p1) );   // true
System.out.println( set.contains(p2) );   // true
```

Listing 18.8 src/main/java/com/tutego/insel/util/set/HashSetDoubleAdd.java, main()

18.2.3   HashSet

A java.util.HashSet class manages elements in a fast hash-based data structure. As a result, elements are quickly sorted and easily found. If sorting the elements in the HashSet is necessary, elements must be copied into a List or a TreeSet and then sorted.

```
class java.util.HashSet<E>
extends AbstractSet<E>
implements Set<E>, Cloneable, Serializable
```

▶ HashSet()
  Creates an empty HashSet object.

▶ HashSet(Collection<? extends E> c)
  Creates a new unsorted HashSet from the collection c.

▶ HashSet(int initialCapacity)

▶ HashSet(int initialCapacity, float loadFactor)

These two constructors are meant for optimization. HashSet is internally based on the HashMap.

18.2.4 TreeSet: The Sorted Set

The java.util.TreeSet class also implements the Set interface like HashSet but follows a different implementation strategy. A TreeSet always manages the items sorted.[3] If TreeSet saves a new element, TreeSet automatically inserts the element sorted into the data structure. This operation costs a little more time than a HashSet, but this kind of sorting is permanent. For this reason, outputting all elements in an orderly fashion later isn't time consuming. However, searching for a single element is somewhat slower than in the HashSet. But the term "slower" must be put into perspective: The search is logarithmic in time and therefore not really "slow." When inserting and deleting, a reorganization of the tree must be accepted for certain constellations, which worsens the insertion or deletion time. However, these costs also exist in re-hashing, but these costs can be avoided by using the appropriate starting size.

```
class java.util.TreeSet<E>
extends AbstractSet<E>
implements NavigableSet<E>, Cloneable, Serializable
```

▶ TreeSet()
Creates a new, empty TreeSet.

▶ TreeSet(Collection<? extends E> c)
Creates a new TreeSet from the given Collection.

▶ TreeSet(Comparator<? super E> c)
Creates an empty TreeSet with a given Comparator that does the comparisons for sorting the internal data structure.

▶ TreeSet(SortedSet<E> s)
Creates a new TreeSet and takes over all elements of s and also the sorting of s. (No constructor is available with NavigableSet.)

Example [Ex]

The following code tests whether a list of date values, each of which can occur only once in the list, is sorted in ascending order:

---

3 Internally, the items are kept in a balanced binary tree. For an introduction, see *https://en.wikipedia.org/wiki/Self-balancing_binary_search_tree*.

```
List<Instant> dates = List.of( Instant.ofEpochMilli( 2L ),
                               Instant.ofEpochMilli( 3L ) );
boolean isSorted = new ArrayList<>( new TreeSet<>( dates ) ).equals( dates );
```

If the constructor of TreeSet accepts another collection, the result is a sorted collection of all elements. This collection can in turn be passed into another constructor that accepts arbitrary Collection objects. Our example compares two List instances via equals(...), where lists have an order. If the order after sorting matches the order before sorting, the list was already sorted.

Of course, better implementations can be conceived. For example, you could use an iterator to run the collection and see if the next element is always greater than or equal to.

Significance of Sorting

Due to internal sorted storage, two particularly important conditions should be kept in mind:

- Comparing the elements must be possible. For example, if Player objects come into the TreeSet, but Player doesn't implement the Comparable interface, TreeSet throws an exception because TreeSet doesn't know what order the players should be in.

- The elements must be of the same type. How can a church object be compared with a vacuum cleaner object?

[Ex]

Example

In this example, words should be considered the same even if they differ in capitalization or have whitespace at the beginning and end. The following code sorts strings into a set (case-insensitive) and ignores whether the word was preceded or followed by whitespace:

```
Comparator<String> comparator =
  (s1, s2) -> String.CASE_INSENSITIVE_ORDER.compare( s1.trim(), s2.trim() );
Set<String> set = new TreeSet<>( comparator );
Collections.addAll( set, "xxx ", " XXX", "tang", " xXx", " QUEEN " );
System.out.println( set ); // [ QUEEN , tang, xxx ]
```

The equals(...) Method and the Comparison Methods

The equals(...) method plays a major role in many data structures. The TreeSet is different because it uses an external Comparator or the compareTo(...) method for classification if the elements are Comparable. If the compare method returns 0, the elements are equal, and equal elements aren't permitted in the set. equals(...) isn't used in this case, although of course the equals implementation should return true if compare(...) or compareTo(...) returns 0.

For example, let's use the Comparator from our previous example for String objects, which makes case-insensitive comparisons and ignores whitespace. Then, according to equals(...) the strings "xxx" and "XXX" are certainly not equal, but our own Comparator would indicate equivalence:

```
Comparator<String> comparator =
  (s1, s2) -> String.CASE_INSENSITIVE_ORDER.compare( s1.trim(), s2.trim() );
Set<String> set = new TreeSet<>( comparator );
set.add( "xxx " );
set.add( "XXX" );
System.out.println( set );                        // [xxx ]
System.out.println( set.contains( "  XXX   " ) ); // true
```

18.2.5 The Interfaces NavigableSet and SortedSet

TreeSet implements the interface NavigableSet and provides methods that return the next higher or next lower element for a given element. Thus, not only are the usual queries about set affiliation conceivable on sets, but also queries like "Give me the element that is greater than or equal to a given element."

The following example queues up three LocalDate objects in a TreeSet. The LocalDate class implements Comparable<LocalDate> because these objects have a natural order. The methods lower(…), ceiling(…), floor(…), and higher(…) select the requested object from the set.

```
NavigableSet<LocalDate> set = new TreeSet<>();
set.add( LocalDate.of( 2018, Month.MARCH, 10 ) );
set.add( LocalDate.of( 2018, Month.MARCH, 12 ) );
set.add( LocalDate.of( 2018, Month.MARCH, 14 ) );

LocalDate cal1 = set.lower( LocalDate.of( 2018, Month.MARCH, 12 ) );
System.out.printf( "%tF%n", cal1 );    // 2018-03-10

LocalDate cal2 = set.ceiling( LocalDate.of( 2018, Month.MARCH, 12 ) );
System.out.printf( "%tF%n", cal2 );    // 2018-03-12

LocalDate cal3 = set.floor( LocalDate.of( 2018, Month.MARCH, 12 ) );
System.out.printf( "%tF%n", cal3 );    // 2018-03-12

LocalDate cal4 = set.higher( LocalDate.of( 2018, Month.MARCH, 12 ) );
System.out.printf( "%tF%n", cal4 );    // 2018-03-14
```

Listing 18.9 src/main/java/com/tutego/insel/util/set/SortedSetDemo.java

18

A method like `tailSet(...)` is useful especially for date objects because it can return all time points after a specified start date.

`TreeSet` implements the `NavigableSet` interface, which in turn extends `SortedSet`—a historical legacy. In total, `NavigableSet` provides 15 operations, adding from `SortedSet` the methods `headSet(…)`, `tailSet(…)`, and `subSet(…)` with overloaded version of methods that allow the bounds to be exclusive or inclusive.

```
interface java.util.NavigableSet<E>
extends SortedSet<E>
```

▶ `NavigableSet<E> headSet(E toElement)`

▶ `NavigableSet<E> tailSet(E fromElement)`
Return a subset of elements that are genuinely smaller/larger than `toElement`/`fromElement`.

▶ `NavigableSet<E> headSet(E toElement, boolean inclusive)`

▶ `NavigableSet<E> tailSet(E fromElement, boolean inclusive)`
Compared to the upper methods, additionally determine whether the output element may belong to the result set.

▶ `NavigableSet<E> subSet(E fromElement, E toElement)`
Returns a subset in the desired range.

▶ `E pollFirst()`

▶ `E pollLast()`
Retrieves and removes the first or last element. The return is `null` if the set is empty.

▶ `E higher(E e)`

▶ `E lower(E e)`
Returns the subsequent or preceding element in the `Set` that's genuinely greater or less than `E`, respectively; otherwise, `null` is returned if no such element exists.

▶ `E ceiling(E e)`

▶ `E floor(E e)`
Returns the subsequent or preceding element in the `Set` that's greater than or less than or equal to `E`; otherwise, `null` is returned if no such element exists.

▶ `Iterator<E> descendingIterator()`
Returns the elements in reverse order.

From the `SortedSet` interface, `NavigableSet` basically inherits only three operations because `subSet(…)`, `headSet(…)`, and `tailSet(…)` are redefined with covariant return type in `NavigableSet`.

```
interface java.util.SortedSet<E>
extends Set<E>
```

▶ E first()

Returns the smallest element in the list.

▶ E last()

Returns the largest element.

▶ Comparator<? super E> comparator()

Returns the Comparator associated with the set. The return can be null if the objects can compare themselves via Comparable.

▶ SortedSet<E> subSet(E fromElement, E toElement)

▶ SortedSet<E> headSet(E toElement)

▶ SortedSet<E> tailSet(E fromElement)

Returns subsets as live views.

Unlike HashSet, the TreeSet iterator returns the elements sorted in ascending order. The two toArray(...) methods also benefit from this feature since they use the iterator to return a sorted array.

18.2.6   LinkedHashSet

A LinkedHashSet combines the order fidelity of a list with the high performance of set operations of HashSet. This class doesn't provide list methods like first() or get(int index) but is an implementation of the Set interface only, where the iterator returns the elements in the insertion order. Consider the following example:

```
Set<Integer> set = new LinkedHashSet<>(
  Arrays.asList( 9, 8, 7, 6, 9, 8 )
);

for ( Integer i : set )
  System.out.print( i + " " );        // 9 8 7 6

System.out.printf( "%n%s", set );   // [9, 8, 7, 6]
```

Listing 18.10 src/main/java/com/tutego/insel/util/set/LinkedHashSetDemo.java, main()

Since a Set can contain each element only once, as a result, you'll get each element only once, but at the same time, the order of insertion isn't lost. The iterator returns the elements according to the exact insertion order.

Example

The fact that a LinkedHashSet is a set that contains elements only once but behaves like a list when inserted is useful for deleting duplicate elements from a list, as in the following example code:

```
public static <T> List<T> removeDuplicate( List<T> list ) {
  return new ArrayList<>( new LinkedHashSet<>( list ) );
}
```

The result is a new list, and list itself isn't modified. For example, removeDuplicate(Arrays.asList(1,2,1,3,1,2,4)) results in the list [1, 2, 3, 4].

LinkedHashSet and Iterator

An iterator can be used to list each element of LinkedHashSet by order of insertion. The iterator of LinkedHashSet also supports the remove() method. You can use this method to delete the oldest entries and keep only the newest two elements in the following way:

```
LinkedHashSet<Integer> set = new LinkedHashSet<>();
set.addAll( Arrays.asList( 3, 2, 1, 6, 5, 4 ) );
System.out.println( set );  // [3, 2, 1, 6, 5, 4]
for ( Iterator<Integer> iter = set.iterator(); iter.hasNext(); ) {
  iter.next();
  if ( set.size() > 2 )
    iter.remove();
}
System.out.println( set );  // [5, 4]
```

18.3   Associative Memory

An associative memory associates a key with a value. Java provides the general interface Map for data structures of this kind with important operations like put(key, value) to create an association and get(key) to get an associated value.

18.3.1   The HashMap and TreeMap Classes and Static Map Methods

The Java library implements associative memory with a few classes, and we'll focus our attention on two important classes first:

- A quick implementation is the *hashtable*, which is implemented in Java by java.util.HashMap.[4] The key objects must be "hashable" (i.e., must implement equals(...) and hashCode() concretely). A special interface for the elements isn't necessary.

---

4 Prior to Java 1.2, java.util.Hashtable was used, but that class should no longer be used.

- In addition, the java.util.TreeMap class is somewhat slower in access but keeps all key objects always sorted. Elements are sorted into an internal binary tree. Keys can be put in order, which requires some preparation.

Example

Let's start with an associative memory to which we can add values, as in the following example:

```
Map<String,String> twitterNames = new HashMap<>();
twitterNames.put( "katyperry", "Katy Perry" );
twitterNames.put( "taylorswift13", "Taylor Swift" );
twitterNames.put( "Cristiano", "Cristiano Ronaldo" );
twitterNames.put( "ddlovato", " Demi Lovato" );
twitterNames.put( "KingJames", "LeBron James" );
```

The second HashMap is supposed to associate strings with numbers:

```
Map<String,Number> num = new HashMap<>();
num.put( "two", 2 );       // Boxing via Integer.valueOf(2)
num.put( "three", 3.0 );   // Boxing via Double.valueOf(3.0)
```

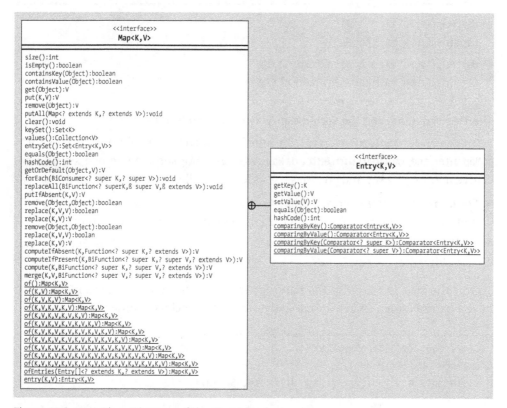

Figure 18.2 UML Class Diagram of the Map Interface

18

While hashCode() and equals(...) methods are essential for the key objects of the hashed associative memory but aren't necessary for tree-oriented methods—in these cases, only an order between the elements must be established, either with Comparable or Comparator.

An associative memory works fast only in one direction. For example, in the case of a phone directory, if a name has been associated with a number, the data structure can quickly answer the question of which phone number. The other direction takes much longer because no link exists in the other direction. The association is always one-sided. These classes are not prepared for reciprocal relationships.

The HashMap Class

The HashMap class is ideal for storing many elements unsorted and making them quickly available again via the keys. The internal hashing process is fast, but sorting the keys by a given criterion isn't possible. An iterator will also provide an arbitrary order for us.

```
class java.util.HashMap<K,V>
extends AbstractMap<K,V>
implements Map<K,V>, Cloneable, Serializable
```

▶ HashMap()
Creates a new hash table.

▶ HashMap(Map<? extends K,? extends V> m)
Creates a new hash table from another Map.

The TreeMap Class and the SortedMap/NavigableMap Interface

A TreeMap implements the NavigableMap interface, which in turn inherits from the SortedMap interface, which in turn extends Map. A NavigableMap sorts the elements of an associative memory by key and provides access to the smallest or largest element.

- Some methods from SortedMap like firstKey(), lastKey(), subMap(fromKey, toKey), and tailMap(fromKey, toKey) form partial views of the associative memory.
- Additional methods like NavigableMap: pollFirstEntry(), pollLastEntry(), and descendingMap() are available.

To sort the keys in a TreeMap, the same applies as for the TreeSet: The elements must have a natural order, or an external Comparator must specify the order.

```
class java.util.TreeMap<K,V>
extends AbstractMap<K,V>
implements NavigableMap<K,V>, Cloneable, Serializable
```

▶ TreeMap()

Creates a new TreeMap that expects a natural order from its elements.

▶ TreeMap(Comparator<? super K> comparator)

Creates a new TreeMap with a Comparator so that the elements don't need to have a natural order.

▶ TreeMap(Map<? extends K,? extends V> m)

Creates a TreeMap with sorted elements from m, which must have a natural order.

▶ TreeMap(SortedMap<K,? extends V> m)

Creates a TreeMap with sorted elements from m and also adopts the order from m.

To allow sorting, access is slightly slower than via HashMap, but hashing doesn't permit elements to be sorted.

Static Map Methods

The Map interface declares some static methods for building immutable Map objects:

```
interface java.util.Map<K, V>
```

▶ static <K, V> Map<K,V> copyOf(Map<? extends K,? extends V> map)

▶ static <K, V> Map<K,V> of()

▶ static <K, V> Map<K,V> of(K k1, V v1)

▶ static <K, V> Map<K,V> of(K k1, V v1, K k2, V v2)

▶ static <K, V> Map<K,V> of(K k1, V v1, K k2, V v2, K k3, V v3)

▶ static <K, V> Map<K,V> of(K k1, V v1, K k2, V v2, K k3, V v3, K k4, V v4)

▶ static <K, V> Map<K,V> of(K k1, V v1, K k2, V v2, K k3, V v3, K k4, V v4, K k5, V v5)

▶ static <K, V> Map<K,V> of(K k1, V v1, K k2, V v2, K k3, V v3, K k4, V v4, K k5, V v5, K k6, V v6)

▶ static <K, V> Map<K,V> of(K k1, V v1, K k2, V v2, K k3, V v3, K k4, V v4, K k5, V v5, K k6, V v6, K k7, V v7)

▶ static <K, V> Map<K,V> of(K k1, V v1, K k2, V v2, K k3, V v3, K k4, V v4, K k5, V v5, K k6, V v6, K k7, V v7, K k8, V v8)

▶ static <K, V> Map<K,V> of(K k1, V v1, K k2, V v2, K k3, V v3, K k4, V v4, K k5, V v5, K k6, V v6, K k7, V v7, K k8, V v8, K k9, V v9)

▶ static <K, V> Map<K,V> of(K k1, V v1, K k2, V v2, K k3, V v3, K k4, V v4, K k5, V v5, K k6, V v6, K k7, V v7, K k8, V v8, K k9, V v9, K k10, V v10)

▶ static <K, V> Map.Entry<K,V> entry(K k, V v)

▶ static <K, V> Map<K,V> ofEntries(Map.Entry<? extends K,? extends V>... entries)

18

18.3.2   Inserting and Querying the Associative Memory

We've said that the elements of the associative memory are pairs consisting of keys and their associated values. The retrieval of values is efficiently possible only via keys.

Inserting Data

To add key-value pairs, the put(key, value) method can be used. The first argument is the key, and the second argument is the value to be associated with the key.

> **Note Regarding null**
>
> In some implementations of the Map interface, the key or value can be null. In these cases, we recommend looking at the Javadoc of the individual classes. For HashMap, null is explicitly allowed as a key and a value; for ConcurrentHashMap, neither key nor value may be null.

```
interface java.util.Map<K, V>
```

▶ V put(K key, V value)
Stores the key and the value in the associative memory. If already an entry exists in the associative memory for this key, the old value will be overridden, and the previous value for the key will be returned (unlike from Set, where the operation would do nothing in this case). If the key is new, put(...) will return null. Thus, with put(key, value) == null, you can't clearly determine if put(...) overrides a value and the old value was null or if there wasn't any key-value pair in the associative memory in the first place.

▶ void putAll(Map<? extends K, ? extends V> m)
Inserts all key-value pairs from m into the current Map. This method also overrides existing keys under certain circumstances.

Traversing All Values

The default method forEach(java.util.function.BiConsumer) traverses all key-value pairs and calls a BiConsumer, which is a functional interface with a method that gets two parameters—key and value. The consumer can then evaluate the data.

> **Example**
>
> The following code creates a Map with two pairs and outputs them:
>
> ```
> Map<String, Integer> numbers = Map.of( "two", 2, "three", 3 );
> BiConsumer<String, Integer> action =
>     (key, value) -> System.out.println( key + "=" + value );
> numbers.forEach( action );
> ```

The result could be the following output:

```
three=3
two=2
```

or

```
two=2
three=3
```

The fact that the order is different might seem odd but is desired by design; Map isn't supposed to have a particular order. Incidentally, the same rule applies to Set.

Querying an Associated Value

To read an element again, Map declares the get(key) operation. The argument identifies the object to be found via the key by picking out the object from the data structure that's equal to the query object in the sense of equals(...). If the object doesn't exist, the return will be null. However, null can also be the value associated with a key since null is perfectly permitted as a value.

Example

[Ex]

The following example queries the associative memory after "two":

```
Map<String, Integer> numbers = Map.of( "two", 2, "three", 3 );
Integer number = numbers.get( "two" );
if ( number != null )
  System.out.println( number.intValue() );
```

The result will be a Number object. With generics, typecasting can be omitted if—as in our example—Integer objects were associated with the string. If the type hasn't been specified previously, typecasting is necessary.

18

```
interface java.util.Map<K,V>
```

▶ V get(Object key)
Returns the object associated with the corresponding key. If no object matches, the method will return null.

▶ default V getOrDefault(Object key, V defaultValue)
If an associated value exists for the key, that value will be returned; otherwise, the default value will be returned.

Does the Key Exist? Does the Value Exist?

With get(...), the presence of a key can't really be tested for sure because null can be associated with a key. This rule applies, for example, to HashMap, where null is permitted both as key and value. A safe alternative is provided by the containsKey(...) method, which returns true if a key occurs in the table.

In contrast to get(...) and containsKey(...), which allow finding a value given a key, you can also search only for values without a certain key. However, this search operation is much slower because all values must be traversed. The class provides contains-Value(...) for this purpose. We can also get all associated values from the Map without the keys.

```
interface java.util.Map<K,V>
```

▶ boolean containsKey(Object key)
   Returns true if the key occurs in the associative memory. HashMap performs the comparison for equivalence with equals(...). Accordingly, the object to be compared should suitably override this method from Object. hashCode() and equals(...) must be consistent with each other. The equivalence of two objects under equals(...) must also follow the equality of hashCode() in each case.

▶ boolean containsValue(Object value)
   Returns true if the associative memory contains one or more values that match the contents of the value object (i.e., via equals(...)).

18.4   The Stream API

Together with lambda expressions on the language side, an entire new library was implemented in Java 8 that makes processing datasets easy called the *Stream API*. At the core of the Stream API are operations to filter, map, and reduce the data in collections.

18.4.1   Declarative Programming

The Stream API is used in a functional style, and programs can thus be quite compact. The individual methods of the Stream API are all presented in detail in this section, each shown in the following example:

```
Object[] words = { " ", '3', null, "2", 1, "" };
Arrays.stream( words )                  // Creates new stream
      .filter( Objects::nonNull )       // Leave non-null references in the stream
      .map( Objects::toString )         // Convert objects to strings
      .map( String::trim )              // Truncate whitespace
      .filter( s -> ! s.isEmpty() )     // Leave non-empty elements in the stream
      .map( Integer::parseInt )         // Convert strings to integers
      .sorted()                         // Sort the integers
      .forEach( System.out::println );  // 1 2 3
```

While the classes from the Collection API implement optimal storage forms for data, the task of the Stream API is to conveniently query and aggregate the data. The Stream API emphasizes the *what*, not the *how*. Traversals and iterations don't occur in the code; instead, the Fluent API declaratively describes what the result should look like. The library ultimately implements the how. For example, an implementation can decide whether processing is sequential or parallel, whether the order is important, whether all data must be cached for sorting purposes, and so on.

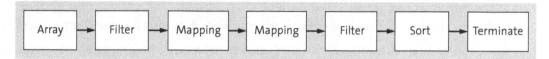

Figure 18.3 The Pipeline Principle for Streams from the Previous Example

18.4.2 Internal versus External Iteration

The first thing you notice about the Stream API is that the classic loop is missing. Usually, you would use loops to run through data and make queries on the elements. Traditional loops are always sequential and run from element to element, from beginning to end. The same rule is true for an iterator. The Stream API takes a different approach. With its help, the external iteration (controlled by loops from the developer) can be replaced by an internal iteration (the Stream API fetches data). For example, when forEach(...) requests data, the data source is tapped and the data retrieved, but not before.

One advantage is that we specify which data structure should be run through, but how this task is done internally can be determined and optimized by the implementation itself. If you write the loop yourself, the processing always runs element by element, while an internal iteration can also parallelize on its own and have partial problems computed by multiple execution units.

Note

Appended to various collections is a forEach(...) method that runs over all elements and calls a method on a passed consumer. However, the classic for loop (or even the extended for loop) isn't now obsolete. Besides being easy to write and debug, the usual loop still has some advantages. forEach(...) usually gets the executable code via a lambda expression, which has its limitations. For example, a lambda expression may not describe local variables (all local variables addressed by the lambda expression are effectively final) and may not throw checked exceptions. Inside a loop, neither is an issue. Incidentally, a break can be used for loop terminations, which doesn't exist in lambda expressions either (return in lambda corresponds to continue).

18.4.3   What Is a Stream?

A stream is a sequence of data (but not a data source per se) that stores data like a data structure. The data from the stream is processed through a chain of the following downstream processing steps:

- Filter
- Map
- Reduce

Processing along a chain is referred to as a *pipeline* and consists of three components:

- The pipeline starts with a data source, such as an array, a data structure, or a generator.
- Various processing steps follow, such as filtering (elements disappear from the stream) or mapping (a data type can also be converted into another data type). These changes along the way are called *intermediate operations*. The result of an intermediate operation is again a stream.
- At the end, the result is collected, and the result is no longer a stream. For example, a reduction would be the formation of a maximum or the concatenation of strings.

The actual data structure isn't changed; rather, at the end of the intermediate operations, a terminal operation asks for the result. An example terminal operation is forEach(...), which is located at the end of the chain and for which the stream stops.

Many terminal operations reduce the passing data to a value, unlike forEach(...), for example. This reduction occurs in methods for simply counting elements or for calculating totals and are called *reducing operations*. In the API, ready-made methods are available for standard reductions—for instance, calculating a total, maximum, or average—but general reductions are possible via your own functions, for example, calculating a product instead of the total.

Lazy Love

All intermediary operations are "lazy" because they postpone computations until they are needed. As shown in the first example, when the elements are taken from the array, they are passed to the next processing step in order. If the filter removes elements from the stream, they are gone and don't need to be considered in a later step. It is therefore not the case that the data physically exists multiple times in a data structure with all elements, for example.

In contrast to continuing operations, in terminal operations, a result must be present: These operations are "eager." Basically, everything is deferred until a value is needed, that is, until a terminal operation really wants to access the result.

State: Yes or No?

Intermediary operations may or may not have states. A filter operation, for example, has no state because, to accomplish its task, the program must look only at the current element, not at preceding ones. A sort operation, on the other hand, has a state: It "wants" all other elements to be saved because only knowing the current element isn't sufficient for sorting; knowledge of all preceding ones is needed too.

18.5 Creating a Stream

The `java.util.stream` package declares various types related to streams. At the center is a generically declared `Stream` interface for object streams. A copy is always generated from a data source. Numerous stream generators are available.

Type	Method	Return
`Collection<E>`	`stream()`	`Stream<E>`
`Arrays`	`stream(T[] array)` (static)	`Stream<T>`
	`stream(T[] array, int start, int end)` (static)	`Stream<T>`
`Stream`	`empty()` (static)	`Stream<T>`
	`of(T... values)` (static)	`Stream<T>`
	`of(T value)` (static)	`Stream<T>`
	`generate(Supplier<T> s)` (static)	`Stream<T>`
	`iterate(T seed, UnaryOperator<T> f)` (static)	`Stream<T>`
	`iterate(T seed, Predicate<? super T> hasNext, UnaryOperator<T> next)` (static)	`Stream<T>`
	`ofNullable(T t)` (static)	`Stream<T>`
`Optional<T>`	`Stream()`	`Stream<T>`
`Scanner`	`tokens()`	`Stream<String>`
`String`	`lines()`	`Stream<String>`
`Files`	`lines(Path path)`	`Stream<String>`
	`lines(Path path, Charset cs)`	`Stream<String>`

Table 18.1 Methods That Provide Stream Instances

18

Type	Method	Return
	list(Path dir)	Stream<Path>
	walk(Path start, FileVisitOption… options)	Stream<Path>
	walk(Path start, int maxDepth, FileVisitOption… options)	Stream<Path>
	find(Path start, int maxDepth, BiPredicate<Path,BasicFileAttri- butes> matcher, FileVisitOption… options)	Stream<Path>
BufferedReader	lines()	Stream<String>
Pattern	splitAsStream(CharSequence input)	Stream<String>
ZipFile	stream()	Stream<? extends ZipEntry>
JarFile	stream()	Stream<JarEntry>
	Stream<JarEntry>	versionedStream()

Table 18.1 Methods That Provide Stream Instances (Cont.)

The Stream.empty() method returns a stream without elements, as expected.

18.5.1   Stream.of*(…)

Stream has some factory methods for new streams, such as of(...). Several instance methods of other classes may also provide streams. The of(...) methods are implemented as static interface methods of Stream, and of(T... values) is just a facade for Arrays.stream(values). The method static <T> Stream<T> ofNullable(T t), if t == null, returns an empty stream, and if t != null, it returns a stream with exactly the element t. This method is useful for partial streams that are to be integrated.

[Ex]

> **Example**
>
> The following example produces a stream from the given integers, removes their signs, sorts the result, and then outputs the result:
>
> ```
> Stream.of( -4, 1, -2, 3 )
>     .map( Math::abs )
>     .sorted()
>     .forEach( System.out::println ); // 1 2 3 4
> ```

18.5.2 Stream.generate(...)

generate(...) produces elements from a Supplier; the stream is infinite.

Examples

[Ex]

The following example creates a stream of Fibonacci numbers[5]:

```
class FibSupplier implements Supplier<BigInteger> {
  private final Queue<BigInteger> fibs =
      new LinkedList<>( Arrays.asList( BigInteger.ZERO, BigInteger.ONE ) );
  @Override public BigInteger get() {
    fibs.offer( fibs.remove().add( fibs.peek() ) );
    return fibs.peek();
  }
};
Stream.generate( new FibSupplier() )
      .limit( 1000 ).forEach( System.out::println );
```

This implementation doesn't use a lambda expression but instead an old-fashioned class implementation since we need to remember the last two elements to determine the next element in the Fibonacci sequences. Thus, the implementation stores a LinkedList that's used as a Queue. When requesting a new Fibonacci number, we delete the first element from the queue (the head element) so that the second one slips in, and add the value to the remembered head element, resulting in the new Fibonacci number. We append the new element to the end in the second step and return it. Parallel access isn't allowed. The stream is initially infinitely large but is then limited to 1,000 elements via limit(...).

18.5.3 Stream.iterate(...)

The two static iterate(...) methods generate a stream from a start value and a function that produces the next element. In iterate(T seed, UnaryOperator<T> f) the stream is infinite; in the second method iterate(..., Predicate<? super T> hasNext, ...), a satisfied predicate terminates the stream and is reminiscent of a classic for loop. Termination via a predicate is quite flexible because, with the first iterate(...) method, the stream is infinite and thus is often followed by limit(...) or takeWhile(...) to limit the elements.

Example 1

[Ex]

The following example produces several permutations of a string:

```
UnaryOperator<String> shuffleOp = s -> {
  char[] chars = s.toCharArray();
  for ( int index = chars.length - 1; index > 0; index-- ) {
```

---

5 *https://en.wikipedia.org/wiki/Fibonacci_number*

```
      int rndIndex = ThreadLocalRandom.current().nextInt( index + 1 );
      if ( index == rndIndex ) continue;
      char c = chars[ rndIndex ];
      chars[ rndIndex ] = chars[ index ];
      chars[ index ] = c;
    }
  return new String( chars );
};
String text = "He's a very naughty boy! Now, go away!";
Stream.iterate( text, shuffleOp ).limit( 10 ).forEach( System.out::println );
```

The random integers don't come from a Random object this time, but from ThreadLocalRandom. This special class is connected to the current thread and can also provide single random numbers or a stream. With concurrency, this variant provides better performance.

Example 2

The following example creates an infinite stream of BigInteger objects starting at 10,000,000 and continues in units until, with high probability, a prime number appears. Then, the stream ends at that point:

```
Predicate<BigInteger> isNotPrime = i -> ! i.isProbablePrime( 10 );
UnaryOperator<BigInteger> incBigInt = i -> i.add( BigInteger.ONE );
Stream.iterate( BigInteger.valueOf( 10_000_000 ), isNotPrime, incBigInt )
      .forEach( System.out::println );
```

18.5.4   Parallel or Sequential Streams

A stream can be parallel or sequential. In other words, threads can perform certain operations concurrently, such as searching for an item. Stream returns true via isParallel() if a stream performs operations concurrently.

All Collection data structures can provide a potentially concurrent stream using the parallelStream() method.

Type	Method	Return
Collection	parallelStream()	Stream<E>
Collection	stream()	Stream<E>

Table 18.2 Querying Parallel and Non-Parallel Streams from Each Collection

Any parallel stream can be converted to a sequential stream using the Stream method, sequential(). Parallel streams use the fork-and-join framework internally, but not every stream should automatically be parallel. (Parallelization doesn't necessarily lead to performance improvements.) For example, if parallelization isn't possible, using threads serves little purpose.

18.6 Terminal Operations

As mentioned earlier in Section 18.4.3, operations can be intermediary or terminal. The Stream interface provides a total of 18 terminal operations, and the returns of these methods might be something like void or an array. For intermediary operations, returns are all new Stream instances. Let's look at the available terminal operations one by one.

> **Note** [«]
>
> Once a stream has been consumed, it can't be reused!

18.6.1 Number of Elements

Perhaps the simplest terminal operation is count(). This operation provides a long with the number of elements that exist in the stream.

```
interface java.util.stream.Stream<T>
extends BaseStream<T,Stream<T>>
```

▶ long count()

> **Example** [Ex]
>
> The following example determines how many elements an array of references has, apart from null:
>
> ```
> Object[] array = { null, 1, null, 2, 3 };
> long size = Stream.of( array )
>                 .filter( Objects::nonNull ).count();
> System.out.println( size );  // 3
> ```

18.6.2 And Now All: forEach*(...)

The Stream API provides two forEach*(...) methods to run the results:

```
interface java.util.stream.Stream<T>
extends BaseStream<T,Stream<T>>
```

▶ void forEach(Consumer<? super T> action)

▶ void forEachOrdered(Consumer<? super T> action)

A code block of the Consumer type is always passed. The functional interface Consumer has one parameter, and forEach*(...) passes element by element to the Consumer as it runs.

Running with forEach(...) is an implementation detail. The order isn't necessarily deterministic, which is especially noticeable in parallel streams. forEachOrdered(...) behaves differently, respecting the order of the stream source even if the stream is processed in parallel in between. However, sometimes, the stream framework doesn't use internal parallelization when forEachOrdered(...) queries the elements.

[Ex]

Example

In the first case, the output of the values is unordered (for example, rfAni); in the second case, ordered (Afrin):

```
"Afrin".chars().parallel().forEach( c -> System.out.print( (char) c ) );
System.out.println();
"Afrin".chars().parallel().forEachOrdered( c -
> System.out.print( (char) c ) );
```

18.6.3 Getting Individual Elements from the Stream

If the stream produces multiple data points in order, findFirst() returns the first element in the stream, whereas findAny() can return any element from the stream. The latter method is especially interesting for parallel operations, although which element is returned is completely open. Both methods have an advantage in that they are abbreviating operations and thus save you some work.

Since a stream of elements can be empty, the return of the following methods is always an Optional:

```
interface java.util.stream.Stream<T>
extends BaseStream<T,Stream<T>>
```

▶ Optional<T> findFirst()

▶ Optional<T> findAny()

[Ex]

Example

Example for both find*(…)-methods:

```
Consumer<Character> print = System.out::println;
List<Character> chars = List.of( '1', 'a', '2', 'b', '3', 'c' );
```

```
chars.parallelStream().findFirst().ifPresent( print ); // 1
chars.parallelStream().findAny().ifPresent( print );   // b
```

findFirst() always returns the first element 1, but findAny() could return any. In the output that result could be b, for example.

If other stateful operations are in between, an optimization with findAny() is sometimes invalid. So, stream.sorted().findAny() won't be able to bypass sorting.

18.6.4 Existence Tests with Predicates

Three methods determine whether the elements of a stream fulfill a condition:

```
interface java.util.stream.Stream<T>
extends BaseStream<T, Stream<T>>
```

▶ boolean anyMatch(Predicate<? super T> predicate)

▶ boolean allMatch(Predicate<? super T> predicate)

▶ boolean noneMatch(Predicate<? super T> predicate)

The condition is always formulated as a Predicate.

Example

For a stream with two strings, the following code tests whether either all, any, or none of the elements are empty:

```
System.out.println( Stream.of("", "").allMatch( String::isEmpty ) );  // true
System.out.println( Stream.of("", "a").anyMatch( String::isEmpty ) );  // true
System.out.println( Stream.of("", "a").noneMatch( String::isEmpty ) ); // false
```

18.6.5 Reducing a Stream to Its Smallest or Largest Element

A stream can consist of any number of elements, which can be reduced to one value by means of reduction functions. A well-known example is the Math.max(a, b) method, which maps two values to the maximum. These maximum/minimum methods also exist in the Stream:

```
interface java.util.stream.Stream<T>
extends BaseStream<T, Stream<T>>
```

▶ Optional<T> min(Comparator<? super T> comparator)

▶ Optional<T> max(Comparator<? super T> comparator)

Note that a Comparator must always be passed, and the methods never draw on the natural order. Helpful in this regard is a Comparator utility method that returns a natural Comparator. The methods return an Optional.empty() if the stream is empty.

[Ex]

> **Example**
>
> What's the largest number in the stream?
>
> ```
> System.out.println( Stream.of( 9, 3, 4, 11 ).max( Comparator.naturalOrder() )
> .
> get() );
> ```

Determining the minimum and maximum are just two examples of reduction. In general, each pair of values can be reduced to one value, for instance, with a minimum function.

Stream (4, 2, 3, 1)	Function Application	Result (Minimum)
4	-	4
2	*min*(4, 2)	2
3	*min*(2, 3)	2
1	*min*(2, 1)	1

Table 18.3 Minimum Calculation for the Stream via Reduction

In the first case, no function is applied, and the stream is not reduced. The individual element thus remains present.

18.6.6   Reducing a Stream with Its Own Functions

Java uses the functional interfaces BiFunction<T,U,R> or BinaryOperator<T> for reductions. (BinaryOperator<T> is a BiFunction<T,T,T> by inheritance.)

The Stream type declares three reduce(...) methods that use these functional interfaces. Note that this reduction function is associative, that is, $f(a, f(b, c)) = f(f(a, b), c)$ holds because arbitrary pairs can be formed and reduced, especially in concurrent processing.

```
interface java.util.stream.Stream<T>
extends BaseStream<T,Stream<T>>
```

▶ Optional<T> reduce(BinaryOperator<T> accumulator)
   Gradually reduces all pairs of values to one value using the accumulator. If the Stream

is empty, the `Optional.empty()` method returns. If only one element exists, that element forms the return.

▶ `T reduce(T identity, BinaryOperator<T> accumulator)`

Reduces the values, reducing the first element with `identity` over the `accumulator`. If the stream is empty, `identity` forms the return.

▶ `<U> U reduce(U identity, BiFunction<U,? super T,U> accumulator, BinaryOperator<U> combiner)`

The first two methods always return the element type `T` of the stream as the result type. With this method, the result type is not `T`, but `U`, since the `accumulator` maps the types (`U`, `T`) to `U`. The `combiner` is *only* necessary if two results are merged in parallel processing; otherwise, the `combiner` is superfluous. However, because the value must not be `null`; unfortunately, you must pass something, even if that value is unnecessary in later processing. The combiner is always invoked after the function.

Example

The following code tries to determine the largest element in a stream of positive numbers:

```
System.out.println( Stream.of( 9, 3, 4, 11 ).reduce( 0, Math::max ) );  // 11
```

Unlike the `max(...)` method of `Stream`, `reduce(...)` directly returns an `Integer` and not an `Optional` because if `Stream` is empty, `0` (the identity, here the neutral element) will be returned. This result is problematic because `0` is not the largest element of an empty stream.

Example

The following example reduces a stream of `Dimension` objects to the sum of their areas:

```
Dimension[] dims = { new Dimension( 10, 10 ), new Dimension( 100, 100 ) };
BiFunction<Integer, Dimension, Integer> accumulator =
    (area, dim) -> area + dim.height * dim.width;
BinaryOperator<Integer> combiner = Integer::sum;
System.out.println(
  Arrays.stream( dims ).reduce( 0, accumulator, combiner )
); // 10100
```

The result of a reduction is always a new value, where "value" can of course be anything: a number, a string, a date, and so on.

18.6.7   Writing Results to a Container, Part 1: collect(...)

While the reduce(...) methods always produce new values in each processing step due to the accumulator, the Stream method collect(...) can work somewhat differently. Simply put, collect(...) allows you to put data from a stream into a container (a data structure or even a string) and return that container.

```
interface java.util.stream.Stream<T>
extends BaseStream<T,Stream<T>>
```

▶ <R> R collect(Supplier<R> resultFactory, BiConsumer<R,? super T> accumulator, BiConsumer<R,R> combiner)

Collects the elements in a container. These three parameters all have different tasks:

- resultFactory: The Supplier sets up the container. This value is also the return type.

- Accumulator: The BiConsumer gets two arguments (the container and the element) and then must add the element to the container.

- combiner: The container is only necessary for parallel processing and is responsible for merging two containers.

[Ex]

Example

In the following example, four numbers of a stream should end up in the Linked-HashSet:

```
LinkedHashSet<Integer> set = Stream.of( 2, 3, 1, 4 )
        .collect(LinkedHashSet::new, LinkedHashSet::add, LinkedHashSet::addAll);
System.out.println( set );  // [2, 3, 1, 4]
```

For the general initialization of a LinkedHashSet, we still have a bit too much code. An easier approach is to add the elements with Collection.addAll(...).

As with reduce(...), the collect(...) method gets each element, but the latter method doesn't combine that element into a combination but set the elements usually in a container. For this reason, the used types aren't BinaryOperator/BiFunction (get something and return something) but BiConsumer (get something but return nothing). The condition is thus located in the container and not in the intermediate processing steps.

[Ex]

Example

A separate class makes this state keeping necessary, for example, when a stream of integers is queried for how many numbers were positive, negative, or zero. You could thus write the following collector:

```
class NegZeroPosCollector {
  public long neg, zero, pos;
  public void accept( int i ) {
    if ( i > 0 ) pos++; else if ( i < 0 ) neg++; else zero++;
  }

  public void combine( NegZeroPosCollector other ) {
    neg += other.neg; zero += other.zero; pos += other.pos;
  }
}
```

During usage, the collector must be built, and the accumulator and combiner must be specified in the following way:

```
NegZeroPosCollector col = Stream.of( 1, -2, 4, 0, 4 )
                             .collect( NegZeroPosCollector::new,
                                       NegZeroPosCollector::accept,
                                       NegZeroPosCollector::combine );
System.out.printf( "-:%d, 0:%d, +:%d", col.neg, col.zero, col.pos );
// -:1, 0:1, +:3
```

18.6.8 Writing Results to a Container, Part 2: Collector and Collectors

Two variants of the collect(...) method exist, and the second variant is defined in the following way:

```
interface java.util.stream.Stream<T>
extends BaseStream<T,Stream<T>>
```

▶ <R> R collect(Collector<? super T,R> collector)

A Collector combines supplier, accumulator, and combiner. The static Collector.of(...) method builds a Collector, which you can also pass to collect(Collector). Returning to our earlier example, you could write the following identical code:

```
.collect( Collector.of( LinkedHashSet::new,
                        LinkedHashSet::add, LinkedHashSet::addAll) );
```

The advantage of using Collector is that it combines three objects (actually, also a fourth one, Collector.Characteristics). This interface declares two static of(...) methods, as well as other methods, each of which queries the functions from the Collector. Some relevant methods include the accumulator(), characteristics(), combiner(), finisher(), and supplier() methods.

18

`Collector.Characteristics` is an enumeration type with three elements (CONCURRENT, IDENTITY_FINISH, and UNORDERED) that describe the properties of a `Collector`.

The Collectors Utility Class

For standard cases, you won't need to assemble a `Collector` with `Collector.of(...)`. Instead, you can use a utility class, `Collectors`, with almost 40 static methods, each of which returns `Collector` instances. These methods can be roughly grouped in the following way:

- `toSet()`, `toList()`, `to*Map(...)`, etc. for collections
- `toUnmodifiable*()` for unmodifiable collections where elements can't be added, deleted, or replaced.
- `groupingBy*(...)` and `partitioningBy(...)` for creating groups
- `averagingLong(...)`, among others, for simple returns
- String `Collectors` like `joining(...)`, which concatenate strings in a stream

[Ex]   **Example**

The following example combines several strings in a stream to create a single string:

```
String s = Stream.of( "192", "0", "0", "1" )
                  .collect( Collectors.joining(".") );
System.out.println( s );  // 192.0.0.1
```

The following example builds a set<string> with two start values:

```
Set<String> set = Stream.of( "a", "b" ).collect( Collectors.toSet() );
```

The following example builds a Map<Integer, String> consisting of two key-value pairs:

```
Map<Integer,String> map =
  Stream.of( "1=one", "2=two" )
        .collect( Collectors.toMap( k -> Integer.parseInt(k.split("=")[0]),
                                    v -> v.split("=")[1] ) );
final class java.util.stream.Collectors
```

▶ static <T> Collector<T,?,List<T>> toList()

▶ static <T> Collector<T,?,Set<T>> toSet()

We recommend closely studying the other methods in the Javadoc.

[»]   **Note**

A `Collector` is the only reasonable means to transfer stream elements into a container. Developers should avoid the side effects of any intermediary or terminal operations for two reasons: First, you would lose the advantage of functional programming (where operations have no side effects), and second, chaos could break out from the parallel processing of non-synchronized data structures. So, *no* alternative to the charming `Collectors.joining(".")` can be written in the following way:

```
StringBuilder res = new StringBuilder();
Stream.of( "192", "0", "0", "1" )
     .forEach( s ->
                res.append( res.length() == 0 ? "" : "." ).append( s ) );
System.out.print( res );
```

If a lambda expression requires write access to external variables, alarm bells should ring. Incidentally, the same rule applies to reductions. Although basically `forEach(...)` can write anything in a, for example, thread-safe atomic data type, a call to `reduce(...)` is very much preferred because this the functional style of programing.

Tip [+]

Since data of a stream is often written to a list at the end, the default method `toList()` can be used directly on the `Stream` type. Even though you might imagine an implementation using a `Collector`, the OpenJDK implementation is different, as shown in the following example:

```
default List<T> toList() {
  return (List<T>) Collections.unmodifiableList(
      new ArrayList<>( Arrays.asList( this.toArray() ) )
  );
}
```

18.6.9 Writing Results to a Container, Part 3: Groupings

Objects can often be divided into groups by the fact that referenced subobjects determine a category. Since this concept sounds terribly abstract, let's consider a few examples:

- Accounts have an account type, and we want to search for a listing of all accounts by account type. So, *n* accounts associated with an account type, all of which have the same account type.

- People may have a profession, and we want to search a list of all people by profession.

- Threads can be in different states (waiting, sleeping, etc.); what you're searching for is an association between a state and threads in that state.

To solve these problems with the Stream API, collect(...) can be used with a special Collector provided by the groupingBy*(...) methods of Collectors. We'll deal only with the simplest variant.

[Ex]

Example

The following example outputs all running threads:

```
Map<Thread.State, List<Thread>> map =
  Thread.getAllStackTraces().keySet().stream()
        .collect( Collectors.groupingBy( Thread::getState ) );
System.out.println( map.get( Thread.State.RUNNABLE ) );
```

First, Thread.getAllStackTraces().keySet() returns a set<threads> with all active threads. From this set, you can derive a stream and use a collector that groups by thread status. The result is an association between Thread.State and a List<Threads>.

The Collectors class uses a lot of Generics:

```
final class java.util.stream.Collectors
```

▶ static <T,K> Collector<T,?,Map<K,List<T>>> groupingBy(Function<? super T,? extends K> classifier)

▶ static <T,K,A,D> Collector<T,?,Map<K,D>> groupingBy(Function<? super T,? extends K> classifier, Collector<? super T,A,D> downstream)

▶ static <T,K,D,A,M extends Map<K,D>> Collector<T,?,M> groupingBy(Function<? super T,?
  extends K> classifier, Supplier<M> mapFactory, Collector<? super T,A,D> downstream)

▶ static <T,K> Collector<T,?,ConcurrentMap<K,List<T>>> groupingByConcurrent(Function<? super T,? extends K> classifier)

▶ static <T,K,A,D> Collector<T,?,ConcurrentMap<K,D>> groupingByConcurrent(Function<? super T,? extends K> classifier, Collector<? super T,A,D> downstream)

▶ static <T,K,A,D,M extends ConcurrentMap<K,D>> Collector<T,?,M>
  groupingByConcurrent(Function<? super T,? extends K> classifier, Supplier<M>
  mapFactory, Collector<? super T,A,D> downstream)

The function that extracts the key for the associative memory is the classifier in the API. This function must always be specified. We've looked at the simplest method—the first one—in an example; it always returns a Map of lists. The other methods can also return a Map with other data structures (or simple accumulated values instead of lists), which is the intention of downstream. Also, concrete Map implementations can be specified (such as TreeMap), as in the mapFactory. Otherwise, groupingBy(Function) would select a Map class for you.

Example

The following example collects the names of all threads by status:

```
Map<Thread.State, List<String>> map =
  Thread.getAllStackTraces().keySet().stream()
        .collect( Collectors.groupingBy(
              Thread::getState,
              Collectors.mapping( Thread::getName, Collectors.toList() ) ) );
System.out.println( map.get( Thread.State.RUNNABLE ) );
```

The following example builds an associative memory that doesn't associate the thread state with the threads themselves, but simply with the number of threads:

```
Map<Thread.State, Long> map =
  Thread.getAllStackTraces().keySet().stream()
        .collect( Collectors.groupingBy( Thread::getState,
                                         Collectors.counting() ) );
System.out.println( map.get( Thread.State.RUNNABLE ) );     /3 3
```

The following example associates each thread status with an average value of the priorities of threads of the same status:

```
Map<Thread.State,Double> map =
  Thread.getAllStackTraces().keySet().stream().collect(
    Collectors.groupingBy( Thread::getState,
                           Collectors.averagingInt(Thread::getPriority) ) );
        System.out.println( map.get( Thread.State.RUNNABLE ) ); // 7.25
        System.out.println( map.get( Thread.State.WAITING ) );  // 8.0
```

18.6.10 Transferring Stream Elements to an Array or an Iterator

Finally, let's consider the last three aggregating methods. Two `toArray(...)` methods of `Stream` transfer the stream's data into an array. `iterator()` on `Stream` in turn returns an `Iterator` with all the data (the method comes from the `BaseStream` supertype).

```
interface java.util.stream.Stream<T>
extends BaseStream<T,Stream<T>>
```

▶ `Object[] toArray()`

▶ `<A> A[] toArray(IntFunction<A[]> generator)`

▶ `Iterator<T> iterator()`

The two `toArray(...)` methods are necessary because, in the first case, the type the array is unclear—only `Object[]` is known to be true by default. The `IntFunction` is passed the size of the stream, and the result is usually an array of that size. Constructor references can come in handy in this context. Primitive arrays can never form a return—for this scenario, you would need to use special primitive stream classes.

[Ex]

Example

The following example puts all elements of a stream into a `String` array:

```
String[] strings = Stream.of( "well", "Hmm", "Like" ).toArray( String[
]::new );
```

18.7   Intermediary Operations

Not all terminal operations result in a new modified stream but instead may simply terminate the current stream. The situation is different for intermediary operations, which modify the stream, for example, by removing elements, mapping them to other values and types, or sorting elements. Each intermediary method returns a new stream object, as seen in Table 18.4.

Full Notation	Cascaded Notation

`Stream<Object> a =`
`  Stream.of(" ",'3',null,"2",1,"");`
`Stream<Object> b =`
`  a.filter(Objects::nonNull);`
`Stream<String> c =`
`  b.map(Objects::toString );`
`Stream<String> d =`
`  c.map(String::trim);`
`Stream<String> e = d.filter(s -`
`> !s.isEmpty());`
`Stream<Integer> f =`
`  e.map(Integer::parseInt);`
`Stream<Integer> g = f.sorted();`
`g.forEach(System.out::println);`
	`Stream`
	`  .of(" ",'3',null,"2",1,"")`
	`  .filter(Objects::nonNull)`
	`  .map(Objects::toString)`
	`  .map(String::trim)`
	`  .filter(s -> ! s.isEmpty())`
	`  .map(Integer::parseInt)`
	`  .sorted()`
	`  .forEach(System.out::println);`

Table 18.4 Detailed and Compact Writing in Comparison

[»]

Note

No current method may modify the current source; otherwise, the result is indeterminate. Changes occur only along the chain from one stream to the next, as discussed earlier in Section 18.6.8.

18.7.1 Element Previews

A simple intermediary operation is peek(...), which may view the current element during a pass.

```
interface java.util.stream.Stream<T>
extends BaseStream<T,Stream<T>>
```

▶ Stream<T> peek(Consumer<? super T> action)

[Ex]

Example

The following example looks in a stream before and after a sort:

```
System.out.println( Stream.of( 9, 4, 3 )
                           .peek( System.out::println ) // 9 4 3
                           .sorted()
                           .peek( System.out::println ) // 3 4 9
                           .collect( Collectors.toList() ) );
```

18.7.2 Filtering Elements

One of the most important stream methods is filter(...), which returns all elements in the stream that satisfy a criterion and ignores all others that don't satisfy that criterion.

```
interface java.util.stream.Stream<T>
extends BaseStream<T,Stream<T>>
```

▶ Stream<T> filter(Predicate<? super T> predicate)

[Ex]

Example

The following example outputs all the words that have any two vowels in a row:

```
Stream.of( "boot", "aha", "mouse" )
      .filter( Pattern.compile( "[aeiou]{2}" ).asPredicate() )
      .forEach( System.out::println );       // boot mouse
```

18.7.3 Stateful Intermediary Operations

The vast majority of intermediary operations can evaluate and modify elements directly on the fly, eliminating the need for memory-intensive intermediate storage. However, some intermediary operations have a state, such as the following operations:

18

- `limit(long)`: Limits the stream to a certain number of maximum elements
- `skip(long)`: Skips a number of elements
- `distinct()`: Deletes all duplicate elements
- `sorted(...)`: Sorts the stream

```
interface java.util.stream.Stream<T>
extends BaseStream<T,Stream<T>>
```

- `Stream<T> limit(long maxSize)`
- `Stream<T> skip(long n)`
- `Stream<T> distinct()`
- `Stream<T> sorted()`
- `Stream<T> sorted(Comparator<? super T> comparator)`

[Ex]

Example 1

The following example determines which word is the longest word in the list:

```
Stream.of( "Blessed", "are", "the", "cheesemakers" )
    .sorted( Comparator.comparing( String::length ).reversed() )
    .findFirst().ifPresent( System.out::println ); // cheesemakers
```

Alternatively, with `max(...)`, you could write the following code:

```
    .max( Comparator.comparing( String::length ) )
```

[Ex]

Example 2

The following example splits a string into substrings, maps each substring to the first character, and deletes duplicate elements from the stream:

```
List<String> list = Pattern.compile( " " ).splitAsStream( "Pu Po Aha La" )
    .map( s -> s.substring(0, 1) )
    .peek( System.out::println ) // P P A L
    .distinct()                  // \/\/\/
    .peek( System.out::println ) //   P A L
    .collect( Collectors.toList() );
System.out.print( list );                         // [P, A, L]
```

`peek(...)` makes it clear what the elements look like before and after applying `distinct()`.

> **Note**
>
> A method like skip(...) looks innocent at first glance, but its use can be quite heavy on memory usage and performance when parallel streams with order (such as sorting) come into play. With stream.parallel().sorted().skip(10000), all elements must still be sorted first so that the first 10,000 can be skipped. Sequential streams or streams without order (which are provided by the Stream method unordered()) are incomparably faster, but of course not possible in every case.

18.7.4   Prefix Operations

By a *prefix*, we mean a subsequence of a stream that starts at the first element. You can use limit(long) to generate a prefix yourself, but in general, the idea is to have a condition that all elements of a prefix stream must satisfy and to terminate the stream when the condition no longer applies to an element. Java declares the two methods take-While(...) and dropWhile(...) for this purpose, used in the following ways:

- default Stream<T> takeWhile(Predicate<? super T> predicate)
- default Stream<T> dropWhile(Predicate<? super T> predicate)

takeWhile(...) could be paraphrased as "take as long as predicate applies," while drop-While(...) means "drop as long as predicate applies."

> **Example**
>
> In the following example, the stream should end immediately upon arriving at the word "Tesla":
>
> ```
> new Scanner( "Am considering taking Tesla private at $420. Funding secured."
> )
>     .useDelimiter( "\\P{Alpha}+" ).tokens()
>     .takeWhile( s -> ! s.equalsIgnoreCase( "tesla" ) )
>     .forEach( System.out::println );  // Am considering taking
> ```

> **Example**
>
> In the following example, all empty strings or strings with whitespace should be skipped at the beginning:
>
> ```
> Stream.of( " ", "", "a", "", "b" )
>     .dropWhile( s -> s.trim().isEmpty() )
>     .forEach( System.out::println ); // "a", "", "b"
> ```

takeWhile(...) and dropWhile(...) can be used together: Thus, Stream.of(1, 2, -1, 3, 4, -1, 5, 6).dropWhile(i -> i > 0).skip(1).takeWhile(i -> i > 0).forEach(System.out::println); returns the output 3 4. The element that satisfies the predicate is itself the first element in the new stream. We can skip this element using skip(1).

> **Note**
>
> Prefixes are only useful for ordered streams. If streams are parallel, they must be put back in the right order for the prefix calculation, which can be a rather expensive operation.

18.7.5   Images

The ability to map elements in a stream to new elements is one of the most powerful tools of the Stream API. Three types of mapping methods can be distinguished in this context:

- The simplest variant is map(Function). The function gets the stream element as an argument and returns a result, which then goes into the stream. In this case, the type may change if the function doesn't give the same type as it takes. The function is applied to each element one by one, and the order of results follows the order of the stream.

- The three methods mapTo[Int|Long|Double]([int|long|double]Function) work like map(Function), except that the functions return a primitive value, and the result is a primitive stream.

- flatMap*(*Function) methods also replace elements in the stream, with the difference that the functions all return Stream objects themselves whose elements are then placed in the result stream. The term *flat* comes from the fact that the "inner" streams do not themselves all come as elements in the source stream (so to speak, a Stream<Stream>) but are "knocked flat." Application examples are usually scenarios like "*n* players associate *m* items; we search a stream of all items of all players." The function can return null if nothing is to be placed in the stream.

```
interface java.util.stream.Stream<T>
extends BaseStream<T,Stream<T>>
```

- <R> Stream<R> map(Function<? super T,? extends R> mapper)

- IntStream mapToInt(ToIntFunction<? super T> mapper)

- LongStream mapToLong(ToLongFunction<? super T> mapper)

- DoubleStream mapToDouble(ToDoubleFunction<? super T> mapper)

- <R> Stream<R> flatMap(Function<? super T,? extends Stream<? extends R>> mapper)

- `IntStream flatMapToInt(Function<? super T,? extends IntStream> mapper)`
- `LongStream flatMapToLong(Function<? super T,? extends LongStream> mapper)`
- `DoubleStream flatMapToDouble(Function<? super T,? extends DoubleStream> mapper)`

Example

The following example converts a string array with numbers into a `long` array:

```
String[] numbers = { "1", "2", "3" };
long[] parseInts =
 Stream.of( numbers ).mapToLong( Long::parseLong ).toArray();
```

Example

The `Locale.getAvailableLocales()` method returns an array of `Locale` objects supported by a system. In the following example, we're interested in all country codes:

```
Stream.of( Locale.getAvailableLocales() )
     .map( Locale::getCountry )
     .distinct()
     .forEach( System.out::println );
```

Via a `Locale` object, `DateFormatSymbols.getInstance(locale).getWeekdays()` retrieves the names of the weekdays. In the following example, we want all the days of the week of all installed areas as the result:

```
Stream.of( Locale.getAvailableLocales() )
     .flatMap( l -
> Stream.of( DateFormatSymbols.getInstance( l ).getWeekdays() ) )
     .filter( s -> ! s.isEmpty() )
     .distinct()
     .forEach( System.out::println );
```

Tip

The function passed to `flatMap(...)` must return a stream as a result or `null` if nothing should happen. Always supplying a stream is never wrong, and thus instead of `null`, you would have the function return an empty stream with `Stream.empty()`. Applications for these empty streams can be seen in the following scenario: In the API, let's say some methods return only `null` instead of arrays or collections, and we assume `result` is such a return (which can be `null` or an array). Then, you would use the `Stream` in the following way:

```
Stream<…> flatStream = Optional.ofNullable( result )
                             .map( Stream::of ).orElse( Stream.empty() );
```

The case distinction is whether the collection is null should be solved here functionally with Optional or with result != null ? result: Stream.empty(). The static Stream.of(...) is used in this case via a method reference and works for an array; for a stream from a collection, you must use result.stream().

Let's summarize with an example. The Class method getEnumConstants() returns an array of constants if the Class object represents an enumeration—otherwise, the array isn't empty, but null. (In this way, you can distinguish between whether Class object has no elements or isn't an enumeration type at all.) In the following example, we'll collect and output all constants from three Class objects:

```
Stream.of( Object.class, Thread.State.class, DayOfWeek.class )
      .flatMap( clazz -> Optional.ofNullable( clazz.getEnumConstants() )
                            .map( Stream::of ).orElse( Stream.empty() )
)
      .forEach( System.out::println );
```

null is often an uninvited guest, and the stream method ofNullable(...) can help you avoid errors. The following code gets all the coordinates into one stream:

```
Stream.of( null, new Point( 1, 2 ), null, new Point( 3, 4 ) )
      .flatMap( q -> Stream.of( q.x, q.y ) )
      .forEach( System.out::println );
```

With flatMap(...), a NullPointerException will be thrown. With filter(...), you could hide any null in advance, but another solution would be to write the following code:

```
Stream.of( null, new Point( 1, 2 ), null, new Point( 3, 4 ) )
      .flatMap( p -> Stream.ofNullable( p ).flatMap( q -
> Stream.of( q.x, q.y ) ) )
      .forEach( System.out::println );
```

18.8   Further Reading

Every programmer should know the basic data structures and their performance and memory characteristics. A good book to dive deeper into this topic is *Data Structures and Algorithms in Java* by Robert LaFore (Sams Publishing, 2002). The Stream API doesn't have many methods, but like SQL, the possible combinations are vast. Practice is the name of the game. But be careful! If an expression is no longer readable, simplify it, for example, by using classic loops. For practice, try to create separate tasks for each method of the Stream API. The book *Java 8 in Action: Lambdas, Streams, and functional-style Programming* by Raoul-Gariel Urma, Mario Fusco, and Alan Mycroft (Manning Publications, 2014) sheds light on functional programming and the Stream API.

Chapter 19
Files and Data Streams

"Quick-wittedness is any answer that is so clever
that the listener wishes he had given it."
—*Elbert Green Hubbard (1856–1915)*

Computers are so useful to us because they process data. The processing cycle begins with the *reading* of the data, includes *processing*, and ends with the *output* of the data. This is called the *IPO model* (input-process-output) in data processing systems. In the early days of IPO, inputs consisted of punch cards entered by system operators. Fortunately, those days are over. Nowadays, we store our data in *files*[1] and databases. Note that a file is only interesting in its context; otherwise, it contains no information, and therefore, the view of a file is important. A program also consists of data and is often represented as a file.

19.1 Old and New Worlds in java.io and java.nio

Whenever an application programming interface (API) doesn't behave as desired, we often say that it's "historically grown." This characterization is exactly what can be seen in file operations.

19.1.1 java.io Package with the File Class

The java.io package declares a central File class since Java 1.0, which stands for a file or directory in the current file system. File offers numerous file-oriented operations, such as creating, deleting, and renaming files; listing directories; and more.

File Problems

With File, everything is focused on one class, and that class can't really solve everyday problems. The following questions will remain:

- How can we copy a file easily and quickly?
- How can we move a file while keeping the semantics the same on different platforms?

---

1 The English word "file" originates from the Latin word *filum*, which referred to a collection of documents strung on a wire.

- How can we respond to a change in the file system so that a callback informs us immediately that file has changed?

- How can we simply traverse a directory recursively?

- How can we create and track a symbolic link?

- The File class has become a catch-all for all possible query methods like readability, modification dates, and so on. One problem with this development is that certain things aren't really identical on every system, such as file permissions, for example.

- How can we implement File operations that are abstracted and not only based on the local file system? Abstraction is desirable so that the same API also addresses a virtual file system in the main memory, addresses remote file systems such as FTP, or addresses a repository.

19.1.2   NIO.2 and the java.nio Package

An alternative to the java.io package, with its File class, is the java.nio.file package with further types, like the Path, Paths, Files, and FileSystem types. Those types are called NIO.2 types.

java.io.File or java.nio.* Types?

The File class is needed in only a few places these days and actually only for two reasons:

- Old APIs expect File objects as parameters. Bridges are available for linking APIs in this case, but the new NIO.2 types basically replace the File class entirely. In the long run, the File object should no longer be expected.

- File objects are still necessary if files are really to be represented on your own local file system and not independently of the file system like a ZIP file. A good example is Desktop with the open(File) method.

19.2   File Systems and Paths

At the center of NIO.2 are the FileSystem and Path types:

- FileSystem describes a data system and is an abstract class. This type is implemented by concrete file systems, such as the local file system or a ZIP archive. To access the current file system, the FileSystems class declares a static method: FileSystems.get-Default().

- Path represents a path to a file or directory, where paths can be relative or absolute. These methods are somewhat reminiscent of the old File class, but one big difference is that File itself represents the file or directory and declares query methods like isDirectory() or lastModified(). In contrast, Path represents only the path and provides only path-related methods. Modification methods aren't included; extra types like BasicFileAttributes for attributes must be used in these cases.

19.2.1   FileSystem and Path

A Path object can't be created via a constructor like File because the class is abstract. However, File and Path have a few things in common, for example, being immutable. The FileSystem object provides the corresponding getPath(...) method, and a FileSystem is retrieved from FileSystems via a factory method.

Example   [Ex]

The following example creates a Path object:

```
FileSystem fs = FileSystems.getDefault();
Path p = fs.getPath( "C:/Windows/Fonts/" );
```

With a shortcut, you can write the following code:

```
Path p = Paths.get( "C:/Windows/Fonts/" );
```

Since the expression FileSystems.getDefault().getPath(...) is a bit clumsy, three shorter options are available:

- Using the utility class Paths. A call of Paths.get(...) returns the Path (see Chapter 7, Section 7.1.2).
- Using the two static of(...) methods that exist in Path.
- A Path can also be derived from a File object with toPath().

---

final class java.nio.file.**Paths**

▶ static Path get(String first, String... more)
Creates a path from segments. For example, if the backslash \ is the path separator on your file system, then Paths.get("a", "b", "c ") is equal to Paths.get("a\b\c").

▶ static Path get(URI uri)
Creates a path from a URI.

---

final class java.nio.file.**Path**

▶ static Path of(String first, String... more)
▶ static Path of(URI uri)

Each Path object also has a getFileSystem() method, which you can use to get back to the FileSystem.

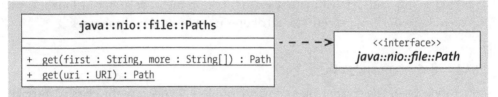

Figure 19.1 Dependencies of the Paths and Path Types

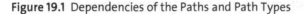

Note

The path string must not contain \u0000 in Java; otherwise, an exception will be thrown. Thus, Paths.get("my.php\u0000.jpg") leads to the exception "java.nio. file.InvalidPathException: Illegal char < > at index 6: my.php." This exception is an important security feature, for example, to protect a web server from accepting false files. The filename looks like a JPG file via "my.php\u0000.jpg".endsWith(".jpg"), but if everything after the null string were truncated (which some file systems do), a *my.php* file would suddenly be created.

Features of a Path

The Path type declares various get*(...) methods and an isAbsolute() method, which have some similarity to the methods from File, as shown in Figure 19.2. Listing 19.1 shows a few examples of usage.

```
Path p = Paths.get( "C:/Windows/Fonts/" );
System.out.println( p.toString() );                // C:\Windows\Fonts
System.out.println( p.isAbsolute() );              // true
System.out.println( p.getRoot() );                 // C:\
System.out.println( p.getParent() );               // C:\Windows
System.out.println( p.getNameCount() );            // 2
System.out.println( p.getName(p.getNameCount()-1) ); // Fonts
```

Listing 19.1 src/main/java/com/tutego/insel/nio2/FileSystemPathFileDemo1.java, main()

Methods such as getPath(), getRoot(), and getParent() all return Path objects from the components of a given path. Three methods will not result in a Path:

- toString() returns a string representation.
- toUri() returns a URI.
- toFile() returns a traditional File object.

Because Path stores a hierarchical list of names for the path, each segment of the path can be queried. This task of getName(int n) in turn returns a Path. The subpath(int beginIndex, int endIndex) method returns a Path with the segments of the specified range. Path implements the Iterable interface, which imposes an iterator() method, which in turn means that Path can appear to the right of the colon in the extended for.

<<interface>> *java::nio::file::Path*
+ *getFileSystem() : FileSystem* + *isAbsolute() : boolean* + *getRoot() : Path* + *getFileName() : Path* + *getParent() : Path* + *getNameCount() : int* + *getName(index : int) : Path* + *subpath(beginIndex : int, endIndex : int) : Path* + *startsWith(other : Path) : boolean* + *startsWith(other : String) : boolean* + *endsWith(other : Path) : boolean* + *endsWith(other : String) : boolean* + *normalize() : Path* + *resolve(other : Path) : Path* + *resolve(other : String) : Path* + *resolveSibling(other : Path) : Path* + *resolveSibling(other : String) : Path* + *relativize(other : Path) : Path* + *toUri() : URI* + *toAbsolutePath() : Path* + *toRealPath(options : LinkOption[]) : Path* + *toFile() : File* + *register(watcher : WatchService, events : WatchEvent.Kind<?>[], modifiers : WatchEvent.Modifier[]) : WatchKey* + *register(watcher : WatchService, events : WatchEvent.Kind<?>[]) : WatchKey* + *iterator() : Iterator<java.nio.file.Path>* + *compareTo(other : Path) : int* + *equals(other : Object) : boolean* + *hashCode() : int* + *toString() : String*

Figure 19.2 The Class Diagram of Path

The check methods startsWith(Path other) and endsWith(Path other), which determine whether the path starts or ends with a certain other path, are quite convenient. equals(...) is overridden from within Object. Since Path implements the Comparable<Path> interface, compareTo(Path) is implemented as well. The equals(...) method doesn't resolve the paths, but only looks at their names; the static method isSame-File(Path, Path) of the Files class performs this test and resolves relative references. Besides equals(...), Path also overrides hashCode().

```
interface java.nio.file.Path
extends Comparable<Path>, Iterable<Path>, Watchable
```

▶ String toString()

▶ File toFile()

▶ URI toUri()

▶ Path getFileName()

▶ Path getParent()

- ▶ Path getRoot()
- ▶ boolean isAbsolute()
- ▶ int getNameCount()
- ▶ Path getName(int index)
- ▶ Iterator<Path> iterator()
- ▶ Path subpath(int beginIndex, int endIndex)
- ▶ boolean endsWith(Path other)
- ▶ boolean endsWith(String other)
- ▶ boolean startsWith(Path other)
- ▶ boolean startsWith(String other)
- ▶ boolean equals(Object other)
- ▶ int compareTo(Path other)
- ▶ int hashCode()

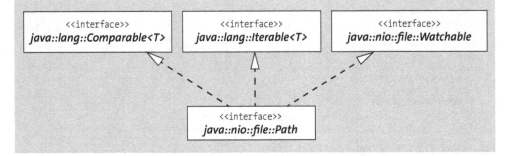

Figure 19.3 The Inheritance Relationship of Path

[»]

Note

The getFileName() method doesn't return a String but instead a Path object with only the file name with getNameCount() == 1. Therefore, using path.getFileName().endsWith(".xml") to check whether a filename like *trainings.xml* ends in ".xml" isn't helpful because endsWith(...) tests whether the last segment in the path (in this case, the complete filename without directory specification) has exactly this name. For example, path.getFileName().toString().endsWith(".xml") is valid as a solution.

[»]

Note

Different file systems have their own limitations and notations. Sometimes, the folder separator character is a "/" and sometimes a "\." Wikipedia[2] provides an overview of

---

2 *https://en.wikipedia.org/wiki/Path_(computing)#Representations_of_paths_by_operating_system_and_shell*

how different operating systems define separators or define the root directory. Java also accepts the slash as a folder separator on Windows.

Creating New Paths

The resolve*(...) methods create new paths from existing ones. These methods accept the parameter types String and Path.

[Ex]

Example

The following example joins a user directory with an image directory:

```
Path picturePath = Paths.get( System.getProperty("user.home") )
                    .resolve( "Pictures" )
                    .resolve( "Squid Game" );
System.out.println( picturePath ); // e.g., C:\Users\Chris\Pictures\Squid Game
```

The subdirectories can also be entered directly in get(...).

In the same folder as *Haldeman.jpg*, a new path for the file *nixon.tar* is requested:

```
Path haldeman = Paths.get( "d:/smoking gun tapes/Haldeman.jpg" );
Path nixon    = haldeman.resolveSibling( "nixon.tar" );
System.out.println( nixon );  // d:\smoking gun tapes\nixon.tar
```

An interesting method is also relativize(Path), which returns a relative path from a base specification that leads to another path.

19

[Ex]

Example

As shown in the following example, the relative path ..\Cursors leads from *c:/Windows/Fonts* to *c:/Windows/Cursors*:

```
System.out.println( Paths.get( "C:/Windows/Fonts" )
                    .relativize( Paths.get("C:/Windows/Cursors") )
); // ..\Cursors
interface java.nio.file.Path
extends Comparable<Path>, Iterable<Path>, Watchable
```

▶ Path relativize(Path other)

▶ Path resolve(Path other)

▶ Path resolve(String other)

▶ Path resolveSibling(Path other)

▶ Path resolveSibling(String other)

Normalization and Path Resolution

As with the `File` class, the `Path` class symbolizes a path but doesn't have to point to a concrete file or directory. For this reason, the methods we've described so far only provide information that can be inferred from the given name without resorting to the file system. Thus, for relative paths, the query methods provide little that's exciting. Consider the following example:

```
Path p = Paths.get( "../.." );
System.out.println( p.toString() );                 // ..\..
System.out.println( p.isAbsolute() );               // false
System.out.println( p.getRoot() );                  // null
System.out.println( p.getParent() );                // ..
System.out.println( p.getNameCount() );             // 2
System.out.println( p.getName(p.getNameCount()-1) ); // ..
```

Listing 19.2 src/main/java/com/tutego/insel/nio2/FileSystemPathFileDemo2.java, main()

To bring some order into relative path specifications, the `Path` class provides the `normalize()` method, which removes the references "." and ".." without accessing the file system. To resolve the relative addressing with access to the file system, the `Path` class provides the two methods, `toAbsolutePath()` or `toRealPath(...)`, as shown in the following example:

```
Path dotDotSlashDotDot = Paths.get( "../.." );
System.out.println( dotDotSlashDotDot.toAbsolutePath() );
// e.g., C:\Users\Christian\Dropbox\workspace\..\..

try {
  System.out.println( dotDotSlashDotDot.toRealPath( LinkOption.NOFOLLOW_
LINKS ) );
// e.g., C:\Users\Christian\

  System.out.println( Paths.get( "../?" ).toRealPath( LinkOption.NOFOLLOW_
LINKS ) );
}
catch ( IOException e ) {
  e.printStackTrace();
}
```

Listing 19.3 src/main/java/com/tutego/insel/nio2/RealAndAbsolutePath.java, main()

The first method `toAbsolutePath()` doesn't normalize; the method simply resolves the relative path to an absolute path. The resolution of ../.. is performed by `toRealPath(LinkOption...)`, where the (optional) argument expresses whether links should be followed or not.

> **Note**
>
> The toRealPath(...) method raises an exception when trying to resolve a path to a file
> that doesn't exist. For example, Paths.get("../?").toRealPath(…) links to
> "java.nio.file.NoSuchFileException," whether with or without LinkOption.NOFOLLOW_
> LINKS. In contrast, Paths.get("../0x").toAbsolutePath() doesn't result in an error.

```
interface java.nio.file.Path
extends Comparable<Path>, Iterable<Path>, Watchable
```

▶ Path normalize()

▶ Path toAbsolutePath()

▶ Path toRealPath(LinkOption… options)

Two other register(...) methods are available in Path, but these methods relate to registering a listener that reacts to changes in the file system.

19.2.2   The Files Utility Class

Since the Path class represents only paths (and not file information such as length or modification time) and since Path also doesn't provide a way to create and delete files, the Files class takes over these tasks.

A simple method is size(...), which returns the length of the file. Unlike java.io.File, almost all Files methods result in an IOException if problems occur with the input/output operations.

```
final class java.nio.file.Files
```

▶ static long size(Path path) throws IOException
  Returns the size of the file.

Easy Reading and Writing of Files

Through the methods readAllBytes(...), readAllLines(...), readString(...), lines(...), write(...), and writeString(...), Files can simply read a file's content or write strings or a byte field. Consider the following example:

```
URI uri = ListAllLines.class.getResource( "/lyrics.txt" ).toURI();
Path p = Paths.get( uri );
System.out.printf( "File '%s' with size of %d byte(s) with lines:%n",
                   p.getFileName(), Files.size( p ) );
int lineCnt = 1;
```

```
for ( String line : Files.readAllLines( p ) )
  System.out.println( lineCnt++ + ": " + line );
```

Listing 19.4 src/main/java/com/tutego/insel/nio2/ListAllLines.java, main()

---

final class java.nio.file.**Files**

▶ static byte[] readAllBytes(Path path) throws IOException
Reads the file completely into a byte field.

▶ static List<String> readAllLines(Path path) throws IOException

▶ static List<String> readAllLines(Path path, Charset cs) throws IOException
Reads the file line by line and provides a list of these lines. The specification of an encoding is optional; by default, the encoding is StandardCharsets.UTF_8.

▶ static String readString(Path path) throws IOException

▶ static String readString(Path path, Charset cs) throws IOException
Reads a file completely and returns the contents as a string. Without encoding, UTF-8 applies by default.

▶ static Path write(Path path, byte[] bytes, OpenOption… options) throws IOException
Writes a byte array to a file.

▶ static Path write(Path path, Iterable<? extends CharSequence> lines, OpenOption… options) throws IOException

▶ static Path write(Path path, Iterable<? extends CharSequence> lines, Charset cs, OpenOption… options) throws IOException
Writes all lines from the Iterable to a file. The encoding is optional but is StandardCharsets.UTF_8 unless otherwise specified.

▶ static Path writeString(Path path, CharSequence csq, OpenOption… options) throws IOException

▶ static Path writeString(Path path, CharSequence csq, Charset cs, OpenOption… options) throws IOException
Writes a string to the named file. The passed path is returned. Without encoding, UTF-8 applies by default.

The OpenOption enumeration is a vararg, and therefore, arguments aren't mandatory. StandardOpenOption is an enumeration of type OpenOption with constants like APPEND, CREATE, and so on.

[Ex] **Example**
The following example reads a UTF-8 encoded file:

```
String s = Files.readString( path );
```

Note

Even though an obvious choice might be to feed the Files method with a Path object representing an HTTP URI, this approach won't work. Thus, already the first line of the program returns an exception of the type "java.nio.file.FileSystemNotFoundException: Provider 'http' not installed." You can not treat a HTTP-URI as a Path object.

```
URI uri = new URI( "http://tutego.de/javabuch/aufgaben/bond.txt" );
Path path = Paths.get( uri );        // ☠
List<String> content = Files.readAllLines( path );
System.out.println( content );
```

A Stream of Lines

The previous Files methods read and write the complete content, which can become a memory problem. If the reading should be done line by line, Stream<String> is a good alternative instead of readAllLines(), in which each line is a String object, thus all lines are kept in the memory. Two methods provide a stream of lines:

```
final class java.nio.file.Files
```

▶ static Stream<String> lines(Path path)
▶ Stream<String> lines(Path path, Charset cs)
  Returns a stream of lines from a file. The specification of the encoding is optional, which is StandardCharsets.UTF_8 by default.

Copying Data Streams

In some cases, the data should not go directly from a file into a byte array or string list (or from a byte array or string collection into a file). Instead, you want data to move from a file into a data stream. In this case, two copy(...) methods are useful:

```
final class java.nio.file.Files
```

▶ static long copy(InputStream in, Path target, CopyOption... options)
  Empties the input stream and copies the data to the file. The number of bytes copied is the return value.
▶ static long copy(Path source, OutputStream out)
  Copies all data from the file to the output stream. The number of bytes copied is the return value.

19.3   Random Access Files

Files can be read and modified in two different ways: first, via a data stream that processes bytes as in a media stream and, second, via *random access*. While the data stream enforces a strict sequence, random access doesn't care because it can jump back and forth arbitrarily within a file and maintains a file pointer that you can set. Since we're dealing with files, the whole thing is then called a *random access file*, and the class that provides random access is java.io.RandomAccessFile.

19.3.1   Opening a RandomAccessFile for Reading and Writing

The class declares two constructors that use a file name or File object to create a RandomAccessFile object. In the constructor, the second parameter specifies a string for the access mode; this parameterized constructor can be used to open a file in read or write mode, as shown in Table 19.1. The specification avoids errors because a file opened for reading can't be overwritten by mistake.

Mode	Function
r	The file will be opened for reading. Attempting to write to this file is penalized with an exception. If the file doesn't exist, an error will be triggered.
rw	The file is opened for reading and writing. An existing file is opened, and the data can be appended without deleting the file. If the file doesn't exist, the file will be (re-)created, and its start size will be zero. If the file should be deleted, you must do so explicitly by using delete() from the File class itself.

Table 19.1 Two Modes for the Constructor of RandomAccessFile

In addition, an s or d can be appended to rw; these additions represent options for synchronizing the data with the file system when writing.

```
class java.io.RandomAccessFile
implements DataOutput, DataInput, Closeable
```

▶ RandomAccessFile(String name, String mode) throws FileNotFoundException

▶ RandomAccessFile(File file, String mode) throws FileNotFoundException
Opens the file. Whether the file is prepared for reading or writing is determined by the mode string with the valid assignments r or rw. If the mode is set incorrectly, an IllegalArgumentException will be raised. A FileNotFoundException will be raised if the file can't be opened.

▶ void close()
Closes an open file.

19.3.2   Reading from RandomAccessFile

To retrieve data from a file managed with `RandomAccessFile`, you can use one of the `read*(...)` methods. These methods directly read the byte field from the file or read several bytes combined to a primitive data type. `readChar()`, for example, reads 2 bytes in a row and combines them into a `char`.

```
class java.io.RandomAccessFile
implements DataOutput, DataInput, Closeable
```

▶ `int read() throws IOException`
Reads exactly 1 byte and returns this byte as `int`.

▶ `int read(byte[] b) throws IOException`
Reads the amount of `b.length()` bytes and stores this value in the `b` field.

▶ `int read(byte[] b, int off, int len) throws IOException`
Reads `len` bytes from the file and writes them to the `b` array starting at the position `off` in the array. The read size is always returned, even if less than `len` bytes were read.

▶ `final boolean readBoolean() throws IOException`

▶ `final byte readByte() throws IOException`

▶ `final short readShort() throws IOException`

▶ `final int readInt() throws IOException`

▶ `final long readLong() throws IOException`

▶ `final char readChar() throws IOException`

▶ `final double readDouble() throws IOException`

▶ `final float readFloat() throws IOException`
Reads a primitive data type.

▶ `final int readUnsignedByte() throws IOException`
Reads a byte interpreted as unsigned.

▶ `final int readUnsignedShort() throws IOException`
Reads two bytes interpreted as unsigned.

▶ `final void readFully(byte[] b) throws IOException`
Attempts to fill the entire buffer `b`.

▶ `final void readFully(byte[] b, int off, int len) throws IOException`
Reads `len` bytes and stores them in buffer `b` starting at index `off`.

Finally, the following two methods return a string:

■ `final String readLine() throws IOException`
Reads a line of text terminated by the end-of-line character \r or \n or a combination \r\n. The last line doesn't need to be terminated in this way because an end of file counts as an end of line. `readLine()` doesn't interpret characters as Unicode, but

simply takes the characters as ASCII bytes. (Without converting various code pages, such as from a file in an unfamiliar IBM format, readLine() won't read the correct corresponding Unicode lines. This byte-in-char conversion would have to be done manually.) Also, because RandomAccessFile doesn't buffer, line-by-line processing of ASCII files via readLine() isn't suitable for speed reasons, and the appropriate Scanner or BufferedReader class should be used.

- final String readUTF()
  Reads a modified UTF-encoded string and returns a Unicode string. A UTF string combines either 1, 2, or 3 bytes into a Unicode character. Later in this section, we'll describe UTF encoding in more detail.

Return -1 and EOFException*

The methods do not all return an error if the file has already been processed and no more data is present. In the case of int read(), int read(byte[]), or int read(byte[], int, int), a return value of -1 is the result, and no exception arises. The same behavior is true for readLine(). The method returns null at the end of the file. Other read methods may enforce a certain number of bytes, for example, readLong() with 8 bytes or readByte() for only 1 byte. Thus, in case of an end of file, an EOFException will follow. You'll rarely see other uses of EOFException in the Java library.

UTF-8 Encoding*

writeUTF(String) and readUTF() are two operations prescribed by the DataOutput and DataInput interfaces. In addition to RandomAccessFile, DataOutputStream implements the DataOutput interface, and DataInputStream implements the DataInput interface.

Java manages Unicode characters via the char data type, which is only 16 bits long.[3] In many regions, most characters come from the conventional 8 bits of the Latin-1 character set. If the characters were sent as Unicode (i.e., 2 bytes), half of the 16-bit data stream would essentially consist of zeros. For this reason, an alternative encoding can write each 16-bit Unicode character in a space-saving manner and is 1, 2, or 3 bytes long depending on the assignment. The coding of the characters depends on the assignment of the bits in the following ways:

- '\u0001' to '\u007F': The characters are written directly with 1 byte. Texts in European languages, most of which are written in 7-bit ASCII, can thus be written in a compact manner.
- '\u0080' to '\u07FF': The characters are encoded with 2 bytes.
- '\u0800' to '\uFFFF': The characters are coded with 3 bytes.

The encoding chosen by Java is based on UTF-8 and will be referred to simply as *UTF-8 encoding* in the following sections.

---

3 Java 5 starts supporting Unicode 4 with 32-bit characters, but strings with two chars are required for the implementation.

> **Note**
>
> If the strings were written using only the presented encoding, the character reader wouldn't know when the end of the string has been reached. Therefore, writeUTF(String) starts with a length identifier. For reading lines, readUTF() is advantageous because readLine() doesn't perform the correct Unicode conversion.

19.3.3   Writing with RandomAccessFile

RandomAccessFile implements the interfaces DataOutput and DataInput. Thus, the read*(...) methods are implemented, as we've presented so far, but a set of write methods is also available in the form write*(...). These methods are analogous to the reading methods we discussed earlier:

- write(byte[] b)
- write(int b)
- write(byte[] b, int off, int len)
- writeBoolean(boolean v)
- writeByte(int v)
- writeBytes(String s)
- writeChar(int v)
- writeChars(String s)
- writeDouble(double v)
- writeFloat(float v)
- writeInt(int v)
- writeLong(long v)
- writeShort(int v)
- writeUTF(String str)

The return type is void, and the methods can throw an IOException.

19.3.4   The Length of the RandomAccessFile

You can access the length of the file with two methods: one in write mode (modifying) and one in read mode.

```
class java.io.RandomAccessFile
implements DataOutput, DataInput, Closeable
```

▶ void setLength(long newLength) throws IOException

Sets the size of the file to newLength. If the file is smaller than newLength, the size will be increased with the unspecified data. If the file is larger than the length to be set, the file will be truncated. Thus, file contents can be easily deleted using setLength(0).

▶ long length() throws IOException

Returns the length of the file. Write access increases the value, and setLength() also modifies the length.

19.3.5   Back and Forth within the File

The reading methods we describe earlier automatically set the data pointer one position further. However, you can also manually set the data pointer to a self-selected location and use it to navigate through a file.

[Ex]

Example

The following example creates a file and sets the byte 0xFF to position 1,000:

```
try ( RandomAccessFile file = new RandomAccessFile("c:/test.bin", "rw" ) ) {
  file.seek( 999 );
  file.write( 0xFF );
}
```

Listing 19.5 src/main/java/com/tutego/insel/io/CreateBigFile.java, main()

Since skipBytes(int) can't put the file pointer "behind" the file, the solution works only with seek(long).

Any subsequent read or write access can then start at the position of the pointer. The following methods described relate to this file pointer and its position:

```
class java.io.RandomAccessFile
implements DataOutput, DataInput, Closeable
```

▶ long getFilePointer() throws IOException

Returns the current position of the file pointer. The first byte is at position zero.

▶ void seek(long pos) throws IOException

Sets the position of the file pointer to pos. This specification is absolute and therefore can't be negative. If negative, an exception will be thrown. file.seek(file .length()); sets the pointer to the end of the file.

▶ int skipBytes(int n) throws IOException

Unlike seek(), skipBytes() positions relatively. n is the number by which the file pointer is moved. If n is negative, no bytes will be skipped. A relative positioning with positive and negative n for a RandomAccessFile raf can be achieved using raf.seek(raf.getFilePointer() + n). But the total must not be negative; otherwise, seek() will throw an IOException. The return provides the bytes actually skipped, which doesn't have to be identical with n! Interestingly, seek(long) is parameterized with long, but skipBytes(int) is parameterized only with int.

If seek(long) sets the pointer further than is possible, the file is not automatically made larger. However, the file will change in size when data is written.

19.4   Base Classes for Input/Output

Different classes for reading and writing binary and character data are collected in the java.io package. For byte-oriented processing beyond text document, such as processing for PDF or MP3 files, other classes can work with HTML documents and configuration files. Separating binary data from character data is useful because, for example, when reading text files, they must always be converted to Unicode since Java internally encodes all characters in Unicode.

The stream classes from the java.io package are built around three central principles:

1. Some abstract base classes prescribe operations for inputs/outputs.

2. These abstract base classes exist once for Unicode characters and once for bytes.

3. The implementations of these abstract base classes either realize the concrete input to or output from a particular resource (such as a file or memory area) or are filters.

19.4.1   The Four Abstract Base Classes

Since classes for reading and writing Unicode characters and bytes must be separated, classes exist for input/output of bytes (or byte arrays), and classes exist for input/output of Unicode characters (arrays or strings), as shown in the following table:

Base Class	Bytes (or Byte Arrays)	Characters (or Character Arrays)
Input	InputStream	Reader
Output	OutputStream	Writer

Table 19.2 Base Classes for Input/Output

We refer to these four types as *IO stream classes*. These classes contain the expected methods like read(...) and write(...).

The InputStream and OutputStream classes form the base classes for all byte-oriented classes and thus serve as a link for methods that require an input and output object as parameters. Thus, an InputStream isn't only conceivable for files, but also for data coming through a network. The same applies to Reader and Writer; they are the abstract base classes for reading and writing Unicode characters and Unicode strings. The base classes specify abstract read(...) or write(...) methods, and the subclasses override the methods because only they know how something is actually read or written.

19.4.2 The Abstract Base Class OutputStream

Looking at the OutputStream, notice how all the essential operations related to writing are gathered in one place. The nice thing about all data streams is that special subclasses know how to implement exactly the prescribed functionality. In other words, a concrete stream of data writing to files or to a network connection knows how bytes should get into files or onto the network. At this point, Java has reached the end of its platform independence because, on such a deep level, only native methods can write the bytes.

```
abstract class java.io.OutputStream
implements Closeable, Flushable
```

▶ abstract void write(int b) throws IOException
Writes a single byte to the data stream.

▶ void write(byte[] b) throws IOException
Writes the bytes from the array to the stream.

▶ void write(byte[] b, int off, int len) throws IOException
Writes parts of the byte array, specifically len bytes from the position off, to the output stream.

▶ void close() throws IOException
Closes the data stream. This method is the only method from Closeable.

▶ void flush() throws IOException
Writes data still held in the buffer. This method is the only method from the Flushable interface.

▶ static OutputStream nullOutputStream()
Returns an OutputStream that discards all bytes.

The IOException isn't a RuntimeException and must be handled.

[Ex]

Example

The ByteArrayOutputStream class is a subclass of OutputStream and stores all data in an internal byte array. Let's write in some data using the three given methods:

```
byte[] bytes = { 'O', 'N', 'A', 'L', 'D' };
//                 0    1    2    3    4
ByteArrayOutputStream out = new ByteArrayOutputStream();
try {
```

```
  out.write( 'D' );           // write D
  out.write( bytes );         // write ONALD
  out.write( bytes, 1, 2 );   // write NA
  System.out.println( out.toString( StandardCharsets.ISO_8859_1.name() ) );
  }
catch ( IOException e ) {
  e.printStackTrace();
  }
```

About Concrete and Abstract Methods*

Two features can be seen in the methods of the OutputStream: First, only bytes are written, and second, not all methods are abstract and must be overridden by subclasses for concrete output streams. Only write(int) is abstract and elementary. This scenario is tricky because in fact the methods that write a byte array can be mapped to the method that writes a single byte. Let's look at the source code of the library:

```
public abstract void write(int b) throws IOException;

public void write(byte[] b) throws IOException {
  write(b, 0, b.length);
}

public void write(byte b[], int off, int len) throws IOException {
  if (b == null) {
    throw new NullPointerException();
  } else if ((off < 0) || (off > b.length) || (len < 0) ||
             ((off + len) > b.length) || ((off + len) < 0)) {
    throw new IndexOutOfBoundsException();
  } else if (len == 0) {
    return;
  }
  for (int i = 0 ; i < len ; i++) {
    write(b[off + i]);
  }
}
```

Listing 19.6 java/lang/OutputStream.java (Snippet)

From both concrete write(...) implementations, notice how they rather conveniently defer the work to other methods. But this implementation isn't ideal! Let's imagine that a file output stream overwrites only the one abstract method that is necessary. And let's further assume that our program now always writes large byte arrays, such as a 5 Megabyte file that's in the memory. Then, for each byte in the byte array, a loop

987

passes all the bytes to a presumably native method. If implemented in this way, we couldn't use the speed of the medium at all, especially since every file system provides functions that may transfer entire blocks. Fortunately, the implementation doesn't look like this because we forgot in the model that the subclass must implement the abstract method, but it can still override other methods as can the actual file-based streams.

Note

When a superclass calls an abstract method that later implements the subclass, this design pattern is called the *template pattern*.

At the same time, a question arises how an OutputStream, which prescribes the properties for all conceivable output streams, can know how a special output stream is closed with close(), for example, or knows to write its buffered bytes with flush()—the methods would have to be abstract, too! OutputStream simply provide an empty implementation. The advantage is that subclasses are not required to always override the methods but if they can, they should.

19.4.3   The Abstract Base Class InputStream

The counterpart of OutputStream is InputStream in which each binary input stream is represented by the abstract InputStream class. The console input System.in is of type InputStream. The class provides several read*(...) methods and is also slightly more complex than OutputStream.

```
abstract class java.io.InputStream
implements Closeable
```

▶ int available() throws IOException
   Returns the number of available characters in the data stream that can be read immediately, without blocking. (Blocking means the method waits until new data is available.)

▶ abstract int read() throws IOException
   Reads a byte from the data stream and returns it. The return value is -1 if the data stream doesn't provide any more data. If data is basically still available, the method will block. The return type is int because -1 (0xFFFFFF) indicates the end of the data stream and -1 as a byte (which would be 0xFF) couldn't be distinguished from a normal data point. Unfortunately, no constant for -1 exists in the Java API.[4]

---

4 You could use TT_EOF from the java.io.StreamTokenizer class. However, Oracle itself didn't want to commit to a constant and quickly closed the request: *https://bugs.java.com/bugdatabase/view_bug.do?bug_id=1204354*.

▶ int read(byte[] b) throws IOException
Reads up to b.length bytes from the data stream and puts them into the b array. The actual length of the bytes read is returned and needn't be b.length; fewer bytes may be read as well. In the base class InputStream, this method is simply implemented as return read(b, 0, b.length);.

▶ int read(byte[] b, int off, int len) throws IOException
Reads the data stream and puts the data into the byte array b, starting at the position off. In addition, len limits the maximum number of bytes to be read.

▶ int readNBytes(byte[] b, int off, int len) throws IOException
Attempts to read the number of len bytes from the data stream and put them into the byte array. In contrast to read(byte[], int, int), readNBytes(...) carries out several attempts to obtain the number of len data by accessing read(byte[], int, int).

▶ byte[] readNBytes(int len) throws IOException
Attempts to read the number of len bytes from the stream and put them into the return array. The array can be smaller than len if the end of the stream has been reached before.

▶ byte[] readAllBytes() throws IOException
Reads all remaining data from the data stream and returns an array with these bytes.

▶ long transferTo(OutputStream out) throws IOException
Reads all bytes from the data stream and writes them to out. If an exception occurs, we recommend closing both data streams.

▶ long skip(long n) throws IOException
Skips a number of characters. The return provides the bytes actually skipped, which doesn't have to be identical with n!

▶ boolean markSupported()
Returns a truth value indicating whether the stream permits memorizing and resetting positions. This marker is a pointer that can point to specific locations in the input file.

▶ void mark(int readlimit)
Memorizes the current position in the data stream. If markSupported() is true, readlimit bytes can be read afterwards, and jumping back to the marked position is possible.

▶ void reset() throws IOException
Jumps back to the position set with mark().

▶ void close() throws IOException
Closes the data stream. This operation is from the Closeable interface.

▶ static InputStream nullInputStream()
Returns an InputStream that doesn't read bytes.

19

Notice that all methods except mark(int) and markSupported() throw an IOException in case of an error. In the read(...) method, which reads multiple bytes, an array is always passed as a buffer into which the InputStream writes, but the same principle applies in the Reader. No method returns an array with the read data for two reasons: First, buffers are usually reused, and so you'd possibly have a large number of objects. Second, the data stream could be very large or even infinite.

[»]

Note

available() returns the number of bytes that can be read without blocking. ("Blocking" means that the method doesn't return immediately but waits until new data is available.) The return of available() says nothing about how many characters the InputStream can store in total. However, for FileInputStream, the available() method usually does return the file length, which is generally not the case for network streams.

19.4.4   The Abstract Base Class Writer

The abstract Writer class is the base type for all character-based writing classes.

```
abstract class java.io.Writer
implements Appendable, Closeable, Flushable
```

▶ void write(int c) throws IOException
Writes a single Unicode character. Only the low part (16 bits of the int) of the 32-bit integer is written.

▶ void write(char[] cbuf) throws IOException
Writes an array of characters.

▶ abstract void write(char[] cbuf, int off, int len) throws IOException
Writes len characters of the cbuf array starting from the position off.

▶ void write(String str) throws IOException
Writes the string str.

▶ void write(String str, int off, int len) throws IOException
Writes len characters of the str string starting from the position off.

▶ Writer append(char c) throws IOException
Appends a sign. Behaves like write(c), except that it returns an Appendable, as required by the Appendable interface. Writer is a suitable Appendable.

▶ Writer append(CharSequence csq) throws IOException
Appends a string. This method is an implementation from the Appendable interface.

▶ `Writer append(CharSequence csq, int start, int end) throws IOException`
Appends parts of a string. This method is an implementation from the `Appendable` interface.

▶ `abstract void flush() throws IOException`
Writes the internal buffer. Joins different `flush()` calls to form a chain based on the dependency of the objects. The method writes all data to the buffer. This method is an implementation from the `Flushable` interface.

▶ `abstract void close() throws IOException`
Writes the buffered stream and closes it. `Write(...)` or `flush()` calls executed after closing will cause an `IOException`. An additional `close()` won't throw an exception. This method is an implementation from the `Closeable` interface.

▶ `static Writer nullWriter()`
Returns a special `Writer` that discards all characters. The return is comparable to the Unix device */dev/null*.

A passed `null` reference always leads to an exception.

19.4.5   The Appendable Interface*

All `Writers` (and also the classes `PrintStream`, `CharBuffer`, `StringBuffer`, and `String-Builder`) implement the `Appendable` interface, which prescribes three methods:

```
interface java.io.Appendable
```

▶ `Appendable append(char c)`
Appends the character `c` to the current `Appendable` and returns the current object of type. `Appendable`.

▶ `Appendable append(CharSequence csq)`
Appends the string to this `Appendable` and returns it.

▶ `Appendable append(CharSequence csq, int start, int end)`
Appends a part of the string to this `Appendable` and returns it.

Covariant Return in Writer from Appendable

The `Writer` class demonstrates pretty well a covariant return type; that is, the return type of an overridden or implemented method can also be a subtype. And this is how `Writer` proceeds, which implements the `Appendable` interface. The `append(...)` method in `Writer` doesn't simply have the `Appendable` return type from the `Appendable` interface but fleshes it out to `Writer`, which is a subtype of `Appendable`. Consider the following example:

```
public Writer append( char c ) throws IOException {
  write( c );
  return this;
}
```

19.4.6   The Abstract Base Class Reader

The abstract class Reader can read characters from an input stream that provides characters. The only methods subclasses must implement are read (char[], int, int) and close(), which corresponds to the procedure for the Writer classes, which also must implement only write(char[], int, int) and close() in addition to flush(), which doesn't exist for read streams. Consequently, two abstract methods exist for the Reader class. However, the subclasses also reimplement other methods for reasons of speed.

```
abstract class java.io.Reader
implements Readable, Closeable
```

▶ protected Reader()
  Creates a new reader that synchronizes with itself.

▶ protected Reader(Object lock)
  Creates a new reader synchronized with the lock object.

▶ abstract int read(char[] cbuf, int off, int len) throws IOException
  Reads len characters into the cbuf buffer starting from location off. If len characters aren't present, the Reader will wait. The method returns the number of characters read or -1 if the end of the stream was reached.

▶ int read(CharBuffer target) throws IOException
  Reads characters into the CharBuffer. The method prescribes the Readable interface.

▶ int read() throws IOException
  This parameterless method reads the next character from the input stream and then waits when there's no character ready in the stream. The return value is an int in the range of 0 to 65,635 (0x0000 to 0xFFFF). But the reason the return value is int and not char can easily be explained by the fact that the method must encode the return value -1 (0xFFFFFFFF) if the data stream doesn't provide any more data.

▶ int read(char[] cbuf) throws IOException
  Reads characters from the stream and writes them to an array. The method waits until inputs are available. The return value is the number of characters read or -1 if the end of the data stream was reached.

▶ long transferTo(Writer out) throws IOException
  Reads all characters from this stream and writes them to out.

▶ abstract void close() throws IOException

Closes the stream. If a call of read(...), mark(int) or reset() follows, the methods throw an IOException. A doubly closed stream has no further effect.

▶ static Reader nullReader()

Returns a Reader that doesn't read characters.

Get Ready

In addition to these necessary methods, which are given with the Reader class, you can use other interesting methods to query for status and set positions. The ready() method returns true if a read(...) is possible without blocking the input. The default implementation of the abstract Reader class always returns false.

> **Note**
>
> Let's assume that the data stream is to be completely emptied until no more data is available, and the data stream has reached its end. We could write the following code:
>
> ```
> for ( int c; (c = reader.read()) != -1; )
>   System.out.println( (char) c );
> ```
>
> Another way to implement the solution differently might involve the following code:
>
> ```
> while ( reader.ready() )
>   System.out.println( (char) reader.read() );
> ```
>
> However, the semantics are quite different: In the second example, data is only read until either the data stream is empty or—and this is the point—blocking is necessary if, for example, no data is available via the network and we must wait for more data to arrive. In this case, we only get the data until the point when blocking starts, but not all the data.

```
abstract class java.io.Reader
implements Readable, Closeable
```

▶ boolean ready() throws IOException

Returns true if reading directly from the stream is possible. However, a false result does not always mean blocking is occurring.

> **Note**
>
> InputStream and Reader are similar, but an InputStream doesn't declare a ready() method. For this purpose, a method named available() in InputStream can tell you how many bytes can be read without blocking. Again, this method doesn't exist in the Reader.

19

Jumps and Markers

You can use the mark(int) method to mark a position at which the Reader is currently located. Calling the reset() method resets the input stream to this position. In other words, this location can be returned to at a later time. mark(int readAheadLimit) has an integer parameter (int, not long) that specifies how many characters may be read until the mark is no longer valid. The number is important because this value denotes the internal size of the buffer that must be applied for the stream.

Not every data stream supports this return. For example, the StringReader class supports marking a position, but the FileReader class doesn't. Thus, you should check upfront via markSupported() whether the marking process is supported in any given class. If the data stream doesn't support markers and you ignore this warning, an IOException will be raised because Reader implements mark(int) and reset() quite simply. You can override these methods if necessary.

```
public void mark( int readAheadLimit ) throws IOException {
  throw new IOException("mark() not supported");
}
public void reset() throws IOException {
  throw new IOException("reset() not supported");
}
```

Listing 19.7 java/io/Reader.java (Snippet)

Consequently, markSupported() also returns false in the Reader class.

```
abstract class java.io.Reader
implements Readable, Closeable
```

▶ long skip(long n) throws IOException
Skips n characters. Blocks until characters are present. Returns the number of characters actually skipped.

▶ boolean markSupported()
Determines if the stream supports the mark() operation.

▶ void mark(int readAheadLimit) throws IOException
Marks a position in the stream. The parameter determines after how many characters the marker becomes invalid; in other words, the parameter specifies the buffer size.

▶ void reset() throws IOException
If a marker exists, the stream starts at the marker. If the position hasn't been set before, then an IOException with the string "Stream not marked" will be thrown. The API documentation leaves how the method should react if more than readAheadLimit characters have been read in the meantime open with the remark "might fail."

Reader implements the already known Closeable interface with the close() method. Just as a Writer implements the Appendable interface, a Reader implements the Readable interface and thus the operation, int read(CharBuffer target) throws IOException.

19.4.7   The Interfaces Closeable, AutoCloseable, and Flushable

Two special interfaces, Closeable and Flushable, prescribe methods that implement all resources to be closed and/or write data out of an internal buffer.

Closeable

All read and write stream classes that can be closed implement Closeable. In Java Platform, Standard Edition (Java SE), these are all Reader/Writer and InputStream/OutputStream classes as well as other classes like java.net.Socket.

```
interface java.io.Closeable
extends AutoClosable
```

▶ void close() throws IOException
  Closes the data stream. Closing a closed stream once again has no consequences.

The Closeable interface extends java.**lang**.AutoCloseable (see Chapter 9, Section 9.6.2) so that anything that implements Closeable is thus of type AutoCloseable and can be used as a variable with a try with resources.

```
interface java.lang.AutoClosable
```

▶ void close() throws Exception
  Closes the data stream. Closing a closed stream once again has no consequences.

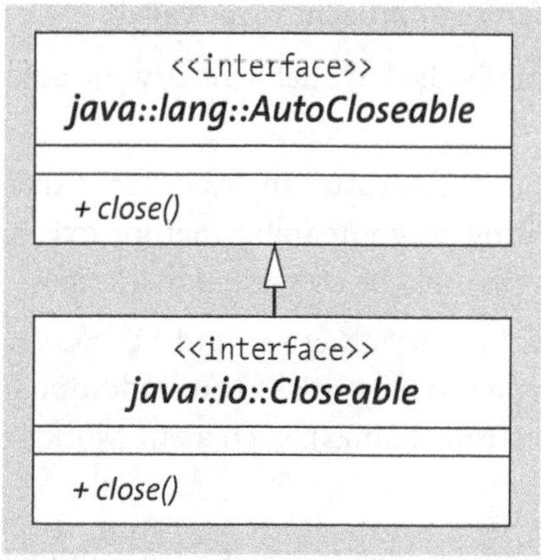

Figure 19.4 Unified Modeling Class (UML) Class Diagram Showing the Inheritance Relationship between Closeable and AutoCloseable

> **Note**
>
> Each InputStream, OutputStream, Reader, and Writer implement close() and, along with close(), also implement the constraint to handle a checked IOException. With an input stream, the exception is almost worthless and can actually be ignored. With an output stream, the exception is already much more valuable because the task of close() doesn't only consist of closing a resource, but also of writing buffered data upfront. Thus, a close() is often an indirect write(...), and in this context, you must know whether all residual data has been written correctly. The exception shouldn't be ignored under any circumstances, and the catch block must not simply be left empty. Logging is the least you can do in this context.

Flushable

Flushable is only found in writing classes and is especially important for classes that buffer data:

interface java.io.**Flushable**

▶ void flush() throws IOException
   Writes buffered data to the stream.

The base classes Writer and OutputStream implement this interface, as does Formatter.

19.5   Reading from Files and Writing to Files

To read data from files or write data to files, a stream class is needed that manages the mapping of the abstract methods of Reader, Writer, InputStream, and OutputStream to files. To carry out such implementations, three different approaches are available:

- The Files utility class provides some new*(...) methods that enable read/write data streams for character- and byte-oriented files.

- A Class object provides getResourceAsStream(...) and returns an InputStream that reads bytes from files in the module path. For writing, no comparable method exists. If Unicode characters must be read, the InputStream must be converted to a Reader.

- The special classes FileInputStream, FileReader, FileOutputStream, and FileWriter are stream classes that map read(…)/write(…) methods to files. Thus, additional classes exist for special sources and targets (also called sinks), such as network or database connections.

Each of these variants has its own advantages and disadvantages, so we'll briefly describe the individual options and distinguish them from each other next.

19.5.1   Obtaining Byte-Oriented Data Streams via Files

The Files class provides methods that directly provide the input/output stream. Let's start with the byte-oriented stream classes:

```
final abstract java.nio.file.Files
```

▶ static OutputStream newOutputStream(Path path, OpenOption… options)
throws IOException
Creates a file and provides the output stream to the file.

▶ static InputStream newInputStream(Path path, OpenOption… options)
throws IOException
Opens the file and provides an input stream for reading.

Since the OpenOption is a vararg and can therefore be omitted, the program code is short. (An even shorter version would lack the correct error handling, however.)

Example: Write a Small PPM Graphic File

The PPM format is a simple graphics format. This format starts with an identifier, followed by the dimensions and finally the ARGB values for representing pixel colors.

```
try ( OutputStream out =
 Files.newOutputStream( Paths.get( "littlepic.tmp.ppm" ) ) ) {
  out.write( "P3 1 1 255 255 0 0".getBytes( StandardCharsets.ISO_8859_1 ) );
}
catch ( IOException e ) {
  e.printStackTrace();
}
```

Listing 19.8 src/main/java/com/tutego/insel/stream/WriteTinyPPM.java, main()

PPM files can be converted online, for example, via *https://convertio.co/ppm-jpg/*.

19.5.2   Obtaining Character-Oriented Data Streams via Files

In addition to the static Files methods newOutputStream(...) and newInputStream(...), two additional methods return character-oriented streams (i.e., Reader/Writer):

```
final abstract java.nio.file.Files
```

▶ static BufferedReader newBufferedReader(Path path, Charset cs)
throws IOException

▶ static BufferedWriter newBufferedWriter(Path path, Charset cs, OpenOption… options)

19

```
throws IOException
```
Provides an input/output stream that reads Unicode characters. The Charset object determines the character encoding of the texts so that the text is correctly converted to Unicode.

▶ static BufferedReader newBufferedReader(Path path)
```
throws IOException
```
Corresponds to newBufferedReader(path, StandardCharsets.UTF_8).

▶ static BufferedWriter newBufferedWriter(Path path, OpenOption... options)
```
throws IOException
```
Corresponds to Files.newBufferedWriter(path, StandardCharsets.UTF_8, options).

BufferedReader and BufferedWriter are subclasses of Reader/Writer that cache files in the internal buffer for optimization purposes.

newBufferedWriter(…)

The return of newBufferedWriter(...) is BufferedWriter, a subclass of Writer. Every Writer has methods like write(String) that write strings to the stream. The following example uses this method:

```java
try ( Writer out = Files.newBufferedWriter( Paths.get( "out.bak.txt" ),
                                        StandardCharsets.ISO_8859_1 ) ) {
  out.write( "Knock! Knock! Who's there? Spell! Spell who? W-H-O..." );
  out.write( System.lineSeparator() );
}
catch ( IOException e ) {
  e.printStackTrace();
}
```

Listing 19.9 src/main/java/com/tutego/insel/stream/NewBufferedWriterDemo.java, main()

newBufferedReader()

BufferedReader provides two practical methods in addition to the simple inherited read methods of the Reader superclass:

■ String readLine(): Reads a line up to the end-of-line character (or end-of-stream). The return will be null if no new line character can be read because the end of stream has been reached. The end-of-line character isn't part of the string.

■ Stream<String> lines(): Returns a stream of strings, where each string represents one line (without the separator).

For example, the following program runs through all lines of a file:

```
try ( BufferedReader in = Files.newBufferedReader( Paths.get( "lyrics.txt" ),
                                          StandardCharsets.ISO_8859_
1 ) ) {
 for ( String line; (line = in.readLine()) != null; )
  System.out.println( line );
}
catch ( IOException e ) {
  e.printStackTrace();
}
```

Listing 19.10 src/main/java/com/tutego/insel/stream/
NewBufferedReaderDemo.java, main()

Example

With the Stream API, the code looks similar, as shown in the following example:

```
try ( BufferedReader in = Files.newBufferedReader( … ) ) {
  in.lines().forEach( System.out::println );
}
```

If an error occurs while reading over the stream, a RuntimeException of type Unchecke-dIOException will be thrown.

[Ex]

19

19.5.3   The Function of OpenOption in the Files.new*(…) Methods

If a file already exists, the contents of that file will be deleted when it is opened for writing, so to speak, and then rewritten; if the file doesn't exist, it will be created anew. However, this default option is a bit too restrictive, and therefore, OpenOption describes additional options. OpenOption is an interface implemented by the LinkOption and StandardOpenOption enumerations.

OpenOption	Description
java.nio.file.StandardOpenOption	
READ	Open for read access.
WRITE	Open for write access.
APPEND	New data is appended to the end. Atomic in parallel write operations.

Table 19.3 Constants from StandardOpenOption and LinkOption

OpenOption	Description
TRUNCATE_EXISTING	For writers, if the file exists, the length is set to 0 beforehand.
CREATE	Creates the file if it doesn't exist yet.
CREATE_NEW	Creates the file only if it didn't exist before. Otherwise, an error will be thrown.
DELETE_ON_CLOSE	The Java library tries to delete the file when it's closed.*
SPARSE	Hint to the file system to store the file in a compact manner because it consists of many zero bytes.**
SYNC	Every write access and every update of the metadata should immediately go to the file system.
DSYNC	Every write access should immediately go to the file system.
java.nio.file.LinkOption	
NOFOLLOW_LINKS	Symbolic links aren't followed.

* This option is useful, for example, when the main memory is too small and files are used as temporary storage for reading/writing. At the end of the operation, the file can be deleted.

** This option is interesting for Windows and NTFS file systems, see also *https://stackover-flow.com/questions/17634362/what-is-the-use-of-standardopenoption-sparse*.

Table 19.3 Constants from StandardOpenOption and LinkOption (Cont.)

The CREATE_NEW option can work only if the file doesn't exist yet, as clearly shown by the following example:

```
Files.deleteIfExists( Paths.get( "popi.herbert.tmp" ) );
Files.newOutputStream( Paths.get( "popi.herbert.tmp" ) ).close();
Files.newOutputStream( Paths.get( "popi.herbert.tmp" ) ).close();
Files.newOutputStream( Paths.get( "popi.herbert.tmp" ),
                       StandardOpenOption.CREATE_NEW ).close();
```

Listing 19.11 src/main/java/com/tutego/insel/nio2/ StandardOpenOptionCreateNewDemo.java, main()

In this case, the last line leads to "java.nio.file.FileAlreadyExistsException: popi.herbert.tmp."

The DELETE_ON_CLOSE option is useful for temporary files. The following example illustrates how that works:

```
Path path = Paths.get( "popi.herbert.tmp" );

Files.deleteIfExists( path );
System.out.println( Files.exists( path ) );    // false

Files.newOutputStream( path ).close();
System.out.println( Files.exists( path ) );    // true

Files.newOutputStream( path, StandardOpenOption.DELETE_ON_CLOSE,
                              StandardOpenOption.SYNC ).close();
System.out.println( Files.exists( path ) );    // false
```

Listing 19.12 src/main/java/com/tutego/insel/nio2/StandardOpenOptionDeleteOn-CloseDemo.java, main()

In the last case, the file is created, a data stream is fetched and immediately closed. Because of StandardOpenOption.DELETE_ON_CLOSE Java will delete the file by itself, which is shown by Files.exists(Path, LinkOption...).

19.5.4   Loading Resources from the Module Path and from JAR Files

The classpath/module path can contain resources, such as graphics or configuration files, in addition to the class files. Access to these files isn't implemented via Path or File because these files can be located within a Java Archive file (JAR file). For this reason, you can use getResourceAsStream(String) from the Class object:

```
final class java.lang.Class<T>
implements Serializable, GenericDeclaration, Type, AnnotatedElement
```

▶ InputStream getResourceAsStream(String name)
Returns an input stream to the file named name or null if no resource exists with the name in the class/module path.

Note
The method isn't about opening and reading a file from a different JAR file. You can only access files from inside your own JAR file.

Because the class loader finds the resource, it discovers all files entered in the class loader path. This rule also applies to JAR archives because everything from the class

19

loader is available there. Since the method doesn't throw an exception, a test about whether the return is not null is essential.

The following program reads a byte from the *onebyte.txt* file and outputs it to the screen:

```java
package com.tutego.insel.io.stream;

import java.io.*;
import java.util.Objects;

public class GetResourceAsStreamDemo {

  public static void main( String[] args ) {
    String filename = "onebyte.txt";
    try ( InputStream is = Objects.requireNonNull(
            GetResourceAsStreamDemo.class.getResourceAsStream( filename ),
            "File does not exist" ) ) {
      System.out.println( is.read() );  // 49
    }
    catch ( IOException e ) {
      e.printStackTrace();
    }
  }
}
```

Listing 19.13 src/main/java/com/tutego/insel/io/stream/GetResourceAsStreamDemo.java

The *onebyte.txt* file is located in the same path as the class and thus is located at *com/tutego/island/io/stream/onebyte.txt*. For example, if the resource is located in the root directory of the package, the notation is "/onebyte.txt". If a resource lies outside the module path, it can't be read. But one big advantage is that the method can tap all the resources accessible via the class loader, which is especially the case when the files come from JAR files. With JAR, no usual path in the file system is used; the program usually stops at the JAR file itself.

To use the getResourceAsStream(String) methods, a Class object is needed, which you can get in our case via *Typename*.class. This step is necessary because our main(String[ ]) method is static. Otherwise, getClass(), a method that each class inherits from the base class java.lang.Object, can also be used within object methods.

19.6   Further Reading

For files, the Files class provides a multitude of options, enabling such activities as reading the attributes, searching the file system, or listening for changes. The following Javadocs provide a good overview of all these options:

- *https://docs.oracle.com/en/java/javase/17/docs/api/java.base/java/nio/package-summary.html*
- *https://docs.oracle.com/en/java/javase/17/docs/api/java.base/java/nio/file/package-summary.html*

19

Chapter 20

Introduction to Database Management with JDBC

"What can be stored? Anything you'd like to extract."
—*National Security Agency presentation on the XKeyscore system (2008)*

Collecting, accessing, and managing information is a central pillar for any business in the "information age." Whereas information had been written on paper, information technology (IT) provides *databases* for this purpose. A database is managed by a *database management system (DBMS)*.

A database model determines the structure in which the *data* (i.e., information units) are related and organized. Different models of databases exist, the most common being the relational database, which is based on tables. In addition to relational databases, document-oriented databases, graph databases, and key-value databases may also be encountered. These kinds of databases are generally grouped under the term *NoSQL databases*. For Java, application programming interfaces (APIs) are available for all kinds of databases.

20.1 Relational Databases and Java Access

Relational databases have been around since the 1970s. The theoretical foundations were laid by Edgar F. Codd as early as the 1960s.

20.1.1 The Relational Model

The basis for relational databases are tables (also called *relations*) with columns and rows, which assign properties to what is called *entities*. Columns are indicated vertically; the rows, horizontally. A *row* (also referred to as a *tuple*) corresponds to an entry of a table, while a *column* (also referred to as an *attribute*) refers to an element of a table.

ID	Name	Address	Place of Residence
004	Prescott J. G.	4490 Oak Drive	Quincy
009	Home M.	4312 Wood Road	New York

Table 20.1 A Sample Table

ID	Name	Address	Place of Residence
011	Rheinwerk Publishing, Inc.	2 Heritage Drive	Quincy
013	Walters	145 Pearl Street	Albany
...	...	...	...

Table 20.1 A Sample Table (Cont.)

Each table corresponds to a logical view of the user. The rows of a relation represent the *database specification*, while the *database schema* describes the structure of the tables (i.e., the number, name, and type of columns).

To access to these tables to determine the characteristics of a database, you'll need to use several query options.

20.1.2   Java Application Programming Interfaces for Accessing Relational Databases

Let's imagine our database system is on one side, and our Java program is on the other side but wants to access the data. What you need is a uniform programming interface so that the functions of different databases can be used in the same way.

Different APIs at different levels are in operation here. At the lowest level, you'll encounter the following APIs:

- *Java Database Connectivity (JDBC)*
- *Reactive Relational Database Connectivity (R2DBC)*

JDBC and R2DBC abstract from relational databases through an API. As a result, as a developer, you don't need to learn different access methods for the databases of various manufacturers. Java developers are thus provided with methods that establish connections to databases, read data records, and compose new data records. Additionally, tables can be updated, and procedures can be executed on the server side.

Based on these concepts, more abstract APIs such as the *Jakarta Persistence API (JPA)* or *jOOQ* can make access more convenient and less error prone. We won't go into further details about these extensions, however.

20.1.3   The JDBC API and Implementations: The JDBC Driver

JDBC refers to a set of interfaces that can be used to address relational database systems from within Java. The API has been part of the standard API for 20 years, and the types are distributed between the java.sql and javax.sql packages.

To access a database via JDBC, you must install a driver that implements the JDBC API and mediates between the Java program and the database. Each driver is usually implemented differently because it must transfer the database-independent JDBC API to the database. Each database has its own protocol (and possibly its own network protocol), but the implementation is known only to the database driver.

JDBC has an advantage in that access to databases always looks the same, and every relational database can be accessed by Java. What's required is only a corresponding driver. The manufacturers of DBMSs usually deliver a JDBC driver themselves, which you would include as a JAR file in the module path. In this case, a search engine offers quick help. With the right driver, even CSV files (see *https://github.com/simoc/csvjdbc*) or Excel files can be addressed via JDBC.

20.1.4 H2 Is the Tool in Java

Before you can address a database with Java, you must start up the database system (in this chapter, the most difficult part). A large number of commercial, free, and open-source DBMS are available, but for simplicity, this tutorial is limited to H2.

The H2 Database

The sample query from Section 20.2 is based on H2 (*https://www.h2database.com*) because the DBMS is nice and simple and doesn't require administrator rights. H2 can run in standalone mode or embedded and has several nice features. H2 has a web interface for configuration and queries and supports all major SQL features, such as triggers and joins, as well as secured connections and a full text search. H2 also keeps memory consumption low. In addition, an Open Database Connectivity (ODBC) driver (from PostgreSQL) can use H2 as a database for Windows programs (such as Microsoft Access).

Since JDBC abstracts from databases, the Java program code can basically run on any database, and you are welcome to use other databases.

The H2 Database and the JDBC Driver

With H2, the DBMS and the driver are bundled together in a single Java archive. Thus, you can easily put a dependency in our Maven Project Object Model (POM) file and reference H2, as shown in the following example:

```
<!-- https://mvnrepository.com/artifact/com.h2database/h2 -->
<dependency>
  <groupId>com.h2database</groupId>
  <artifactId>h2</artifactId>
  <version>2.1.214</version>
</dependency>
```

Listing 20.1 pom.xml (Supplement)

20.2 A Sample Query

To become familiar with the JDBC API, let's start with an example.

20.2.1 Steps to Query the Database

The following steps are required to access a relational database with JDBC:

1. Including the JDBC database drivers in the module path
2. Possibly logging in the driver classes
3. Connecting to the database
4. Creating SQL statements
5. Executing SQL statements
6. Retrieving the result of the statement and possibly iterating over the result (in the case of result sets)
7. Closing the database connection

In the following sections, we'll limit our work to establishing a connection to the free DBMS H2. Access for other relational database will be similar—except for the JDBC URL itself.

20.2.2 Accessing the Relational Database with Java

Our program needs to use a database called *TutegoDB*, which we'll create as an empty database at the beginning. In JDBC, we'll enter the name of this database in the JDBC URL, but the exact syntax is slightly different for each JDBC driver. H2 will try to locate the database as a file in the user directory, and so an example JDBC URL might look like jdbc:h2:**file**:~/TutegoDB. You can also specify absolute paths, such as jdbc:h2:file:C:/ *TutegoDB*. H2 reads the data from the file at the first start, manages it in the memory, and writes it back to a file at the end of the program. If the database as such hasn't been created yet, H2 will create it automatically.

```
String url = "jdbc:h2:file:~/TutegoDB";
try ( Connection con = DriverManager.getConnection( url, "sa", "" );
section
      Statement stmt = con.createStatement() ) {

  // CUSTOMER table is missing? Then create
  if ( ! con.getMetaData().getTables( null, null, "CUSTOMER", null ).next() ) {
    String[] sqlStmts = {
      "CREATE TABLE CUSTOMER(ID INTEGER NOT NULL PRIMARY KEY,FIRSTNAME VARCHAR(2
55),"
      + "LASTNAME VARCHAR(255),STREET VARCHAR(255),CITY VARCHAR(255))",
```

```
      "INSERT INTO CUSTOMER VALUES(0,'Laura','Steel','429 Seventh Av.','Dallas')
",
      "INSERT INTO CUSTOMER VALUES(1,'Susanne','King','366 -
 20th Ave.','Olten')",
      "INSERT INTO CUSTOMER VALUES(2,'Anne','Miller','20 Upland Pl.','Lyon')" };
    for ( String sql : sqlStmts )
      stmt.executeUpdate( sql );
    System.out.println( "Table created and data inserted." );
  }

  // Query table
  try ( ResultSet rs = stmt.executeQuery( "SELECT * FROM CUSTOMER" ) ) {
    while ( rs.next() )
      // Access to FIRSTNAME, LASTNAME, STREET
      System.out.printf( "%s, %s %s%n", rs.getString( 1 ),
                        rs.getString( 2 ), rs.getString( 3 ) );
  }
}
catch ( SQLException e ) {
  e.printStackTrace();
}
```

Listing 20.2 src/main/java/com/tutego/insel/jdbc/FirstSqlAccess.java, main()

At the first start, the program checks if tables already exist in the database. If not, a new table is created, and three records are inserted.

20.3   Further Reading

Developers should ask themselves whether this simple and raw access to a database is necessary and useful in the first place. Java developers should usually think in terms of objects, and database tables are on a different level of abstraction. The good news is that object-relational mappers can mediate between the object-oriented (OO) world and relations. The next step for developers after learning about JDBC is to explore the *Jakarta Persistence API* and alternatives like Spring Data JDBC. The Java tutorial from Oracle gives a broader introduction into JDBC: *https://docs.oracle.com/javase/tutorial/jdbc/TOC.html*. A book with great detail on Jakarta Persistence is High-Performance Java Persistence by Vlad Mihalcea.

Chapter 21

Bits and Bytes, Mathematics and Money

"There are only 10 types of people in the world.
Those who understand binary code and those who don't."

This chapter takes a closer look at the representation of the numbers and explains how binary operators operate on these values. Once we've examined integers in more detail, a detailed presentation of floats will follow, in turn followed by basic mathematical functions such as max(...), sin(...), and abs(...), which are implemented in Java by the Math class.

21.1 Bits and Bytes

A *bit* is an information carrier for the statement "true or false" and thus has two states. By combining individual bits, larger sequences are created such as the *byte*, which consists of 8 bits, for example, 00010011_{bin}. Since the number mentioned could well be a decimal number due to the digits 0 and 1, we place a small $_{bin}$ after the number to avoid misunderstanding.

If 8 bits = 1 byte is used as a basis, 256 different numbers can be formed by different assignments. If no bit of the byte is set, the number is 0; if every bit is set, the number is 255. Each bit at a position in the byte can be 0 or 1, and this results in a value at which position 0 or 1 appears in the sequence. In this case, we're focused on what's called *positional notation* (or *place-value notation*, or *positional numeral system*), where the position of a digit is crucial because 12 is not equal to 21 and 10_{bin} is not equal to 01_{bin}. Now, the only question is how bit numbering is done because the bit with the lowest place value could be on the left or on the right—usually, it's on the right, and the bit with the highest place value is on the left.

In the *binary system*, we have the digits 0 and 1. The value of a binary number is obtained by adding the digits 0 or 1, each of which is previously multiplied by its place value 2^i. The value assignment for the number 19 is calculated from 16 + 2 + 1 since it's composed of terms of the sum of the form 2^i: $19_{dec} = 16 + 2 + 1 = 1 \times 2^4 + 0 \times 2^3 + 0 \times 2^2 + 1 \times 2^1 + 1 \times 2^0 = 10011_{bin}$.

Bit	7	6	5	4	3	2	1	0
Value	2^7=128	2^6=64	2^5=32	2^4=16	2^3=8	2^2=4	2^1=2	2^0=1
Assignment for 19	0	0	0	1	0	0	1	1

Table 21.1 Value Assignment

To modify bits, Java provides two kinds of tools:

- Bitwise operators
- Bitwise shift operations

We'll now look at these tools next.

21.1.1 The Bit Operators: Complement, AND, OR, and XOR

Bit operators can be used to perform binary operations on operands, for example, to set a bit of a byte. Bit operations include the complement of an operand and links to other values. These bitwise operators allow individual bits to be queried and manipulated.

Operator	Name	Task
~	Complement (bitwise NOT)	Inverts each bit: 0 becomes 1, and 1 becomes 0.
|	Bitwise OR	For a | b, each bit of a and b is individually linked via OR.
&	Bitwise AND	For a & b, each bit of a and b is individually linked via AND.
^	Bitwise exclusive OR (XOR)	For a ^ b, each bit of a and b is individually linked via XOR; do not confuse this construction with a to the power of b.

Table 21.2 Bit Operators in Java

The complement is a unary operator; the others are binary operators. Let's generally consider the binary link a # b. With the binary bitwise AND operation with &, the following applies to each bit: If any bit is set in the operand a and at the same position also in the operand b, then the bit is also set at the position in the result. With the OR operation with |, only one of the operands must be set, so that the bit in the result is set. With an exclusive OR (XOR), the result is 1 if only exactly one of the operands is 1. If both are 0 or 1, the result is 0, which corresponds to a binary addition or subtraction.[1]

---

[1] You can basically do without XOR because it can be expressed by the other operators: a ^ b is like (a & ~b) | (~a & b).

Let's summarize the result once again in a table:

Bit 1	Bit 2	~Bit 1	Bit 1 & Bit 2	Bit 1 | Bit 2	Bit 1 ^ Bit 2
0	0	1	0	0	0
0	1	1	0	1	1
1	0	0	0	1	1
1	1	0	1	1	0

Table 21.3 The Bit Operators in a Truth Table

Let's consider two integers, for example:

	Binary	Decimal
Number 1	010011	16 + 2 + 1 = 19
Number 2	100010	32 + 2 = 34
Number 1 & Number 2	000010	19 & 34 = 2
Number 1 | Number 2	110011	19 | 34 = 51
Number 1 ^ Number 2	110001	19 ^ 34 = 49

Table 21.4 Binary Operation of Two Integers

21.1.2 Representation of Integers in Java: Two's Complement

The computer stores data in the states 0 and 1 and must be able to represent positive as well as negative numbers. For this purpose, different encodings exist, such as one's complement or two's complement, the latter being common for modern programming languages. The nature of *two's complement* defines the following encoding for positive and negative integers:

- The sign of a number determines a bit that is 1 for negative numbers and 0 for positive numbers.

- To represent a 0, no bit is set.

- For negative numbers, you must take the absolute value of the number, invert the bit pattern, and add 1 to the result.

Example

Let's test this scenario on the number –1: The absolute value is 1, the bit pattern (for 16 bits) is 0000 0000 0000 0001. The negation results in 1111 1111 1111 1110. If we add 1, 1111 1111 1111 1111 will follow.

Java Integer Data Types in Two's Complement

Java always encodes the integer data types byte, short, int, and long in the two's complement (the data type char doesn't define negative numbers). With this encoding, there exists one more negative number than positive number because no positive or negative 0 exist in the two's complement, only a "positive" 1 with the bit mask 0000...0000.

Decimal	Binary	Hexadecimal 0
–32,768	1000 0000 0000 0000	80 00
–32,767	1000 0000 0000 0001	80 01
–32,766	1000 0000 0000 0010	80 02
	...	
–2	1111 1111 1111 1110	FF FE
–1	1111 1111 1111 1111	FF FF
0	0000 0000 0000 0000	00 00
1	0000 0000 0000 0001	00 01
2	0000 0000 0000 0010	00 02
	...	
32,766	0111 1111 1111 1110	7F FE
32,767	0111 1111 1111 1111	7F FF

Table 21.5 Representations of Two's Complement in the short Data Type

So, for all negative integers, the top bit is set to 1.

> **Note**
>
> Two's complement and complement (bitwise NOT) have an interesting relationship. ~0 inverts all bits, which results in -1. In general, ~a is equal to -(a+1). So, for example, ~5 is equal to -(5+1) = -6. This rule is also true when negated: ~-5 is equal to -(-5+1) = 4. And ~-~-~-~-5 is 1.

21.1.3 The Binary, Octal, and Hexadecimal Place Value Systems

The literals for integers can be specified in four different place value systems. The most natural value system is the *decimal system* (also called the *base-ten system*), where the literals consist of the digits 0 to 9. Additionally, the *binary, octal*, and *hexadecimal systems* write the numbers in base 2, 8, and 16, respectively. Except for decimal numbers, numbers in other formats begin with a special prefix.

Prefix	Place Value System	Base	Representation of 1
0b or 0B	Binary	2	0b1 or 0B1
0	Octal	8	01
None	Decimal	10	1
0x or 0X	Hexadecimal	16	0x1 or 0X1

Table 21.6 The Place Value Systems and Their Notation

A hexadecimal value starts with 0x or 0X. Since 10 digits aren't sufficient for 16 hexadecimal numbers, a number for base 16 additionally consists of the letters a to f (or A to F). The hexadecimal system is also referred to as the *sexadecimal system*.[2]

An octal value starts with the prefix 0. With base 8, only the digits 0 to 7 are needed for octal values. The name comes from the Latin *octo*, which means "eight" in English. The octal system was a common representation choice since individual bits no longer had to be considered separately, but 3 bits were combined into a group—with 3 bits you can express numbers from 0 to 7. The octal system is still popular in communications electronics but doesn't play any role elsewhere.

For binary numbers (i.e., numbers with base 2), you'll use the prefix 0b or 0B. Only the digits 0 and 1 are permitted.

[Ex]

21

Example

The following examples output decimal, binary, octal, and hexadecimal numbers:

```
System.out.println( 1243 );          // 1243
System.out.println( 0b10111011 );    // 187
System.out.println( 01230 );         // 664
System.out.println( 0xcafebabe );    // -889275714
System.out.println( 0xCOBOL );       // 49328
```

In Java programs, octal numbers should be used with caution. If you fill a number left-justified with the 0 for reasons of readability, you'll experience a surprise:

```
int i = 118;
int j = 012;                         // Octal 012 is decimal 10
```

2 The prefix "octo-" in "octal system" comes from Latin. The word "hexadecimal" contains two components from two different languages: "hexa-" comes from Greek and "decem" (ten) from Latin. The alternative designation *sexadecimal* (not sexagesimal, which is base 60) is derived purely from Latin. You can find more about the origin of the word "hexadecimal" at *https://en.wikipedia.org/wiki/Hexadecimal#Etymology*.

21.1.4   Effect of Typecasting on Bit Patterns

Typecasting sometimes results in the upper bits of integers being simply cut off. When adjusting floats to integers, rounding is performed. This section will demonstrate what exactly happens.

Explicit Typecasting for Integers

When converting a larger integer type to a smaller one, the upper bits are truncated. An adjustment of the sign does *not* take place. The representation in bits shows this scenario clearly:

```
int   ii = 123456789;    // 0000011101011011_11001101_00010101
int   ij =   -123456;    // 1111111111111110_00011101_11000000

short si = (short) ii;    //                 11001101_00010101
short sj = (short) ij;    //                 00011101_11000000

System.out.println( si ); // -13035
System.out.println( sj ); //   7616
```

Listing 21.1 src/main/java/com/tutego/insel/math/TypecastDemo.java, main()

si becomes a negative number because the 16th bit at int ii was set and now shows the negative sign at short. The number after ij doesn't have a 16th bit set, and so, the short sj becomes positive.

Converting short and char

Like char, short has a length of 16 bits. But this conversion is not possible without explicit casting. because of the sign of short. Characters are by definition always unsigned. If a char with a last set bit of the highest value were converted to a short, the result would be a negative number. Likewise, if a short denotes a negative number, the top bit in the char would be set, which is undesirable. The explicit conversion always produces only positive numbers.

The loss in typecasting from char to short occurs, for example, in the character encodings for Chinese, Japanese, or Korean characters because, in these cases, the first bit is set in Unicode, which must give way to the unset sign bit when converting to a short.

Typecastings of int and char

The print*(...) method is overloaded with the types char and int, and typecasting results in the desired output, as shown in the following examples:

```
int  c1 = 65;
char c2 = 'A';
```

```
System.out.println( c1 );                    // 65
System.out.println( (int)c2 );               // 65
System.out.println( (char)c1 );              // A
System.out.println( c2 );                    // A
System.out.println( (char)(c1 + 1) );        // B
System.out.println( c2 + 1 );                // 66
```

You can output an integer value in an int as a character, just as you can output a char variable as a numeric value. Note that an arithmetic operation on char types results in an int. For this reason, the following expression doesn't work for char c:

```
c = c + 1;
```

The correct version would be the following example:

```
c = (char)(c + 1)
```

Different Value Ranges for Floats and Integers

Of course, the conversion between double ⟷ long can't be without loss of information. How could that be possible? While both a long and a double have 64 bits for data storage, a double can't store an integer as efficiently as a long and has some "overhead" for large exponents. When implicitly converting a long to a double, some information-carrying bits may be missed, as illustrated by the following example:

```
long   l = 1111111111111111111L; // 1111111111111111111
double d = l;                     // 1111111111111111170 (1.11111111111111117E18)
long   m = (long) d;              // 1111111111111111168
```

Java permits the conversion of a long into a double without explicit adaptation and also into an even smaller float, which is perhaps even stranger since float has a precision of only 6 to 7 digits, while long has 18 digits. Consider the following example:

```
long  l = 1000000000000000000L;
float f = l;
System.out.printf( "%f", f );     // 999999984306749440,000000
```

Loss of Material Due to Overflows*

Overflows in calculations can lead to serious errors, as in the crash of Ariane 5 on June 4, 1996, exactly 36.7 seconds after launch. The European Space Agency (ESA) had launched the unmanned rocket, which carried four satellites, from French Guiana. Fortunately, no lives were lost, but the material damage amounted to about $500 million. The project also involved development costs of around $7 billion. The reason for the crash was a rounding error in the Ada program when converting a 64-bit float (the horizontal velocity) to a signed 16-bit integer. Unfortunately, the number was larger than $2^{15} - 1$ and the conversion wasn't secured because the programmers hadn't assumed this range of numbers. An exception occurred, and, as a consequence, the guidance system broke down, and the self-destruct mechanism was triggered as the engines threatened to stall. The really stupid thing about this story is that the software wasn't essential for the flight and only served for launch preparations. In the event of an interruption during the countdown, the program could have been quickly terminated. Some program parts had been copied, unchanged, from the Ariane 4 software via copy/paste, but the Ariane 5 flew faster.

21.1.5   Working without Signs

Except for char, all integral data types in Java are signed and encoded in the two's complement. With a byte, 8 bits are available for the coding of a value; however, actually only 7 bits are available because 1 bit is used for encoding the sign. The value range is from –128 to +127. A workaround enables you to exhaust the full range of values and pretend that Java has unsigned data types.

Using Byte as an Unsigned Data Type

An important property of explicit typecasting for integer types is that the excess bytes are simply truncated. Let's look at typecasting in this case with an example:

```
int  l =        0xABCD6F;
byte b = (byte) 0xABCD6F;
System.out.println( Integer.toBinaryString( l ) ); // 101010111100110101101111
System.out.println( Integer.toBinaryString( b ) ); //                  1101111
```

If a number is in the range from 0 to 255, a byte can basically store it by its 8 bits. However, Java must be forced, by explicit typecasting, to ignore the sign bit. Only then will the number 255 correspond to 8 set bits because assigning it with byte b = 255; doesn't work.

For further processing to be successful, another property must be taken into account. Let's look at the following example:

```
byte b1 = (byte) 255;
byte b2 = -1;
System.out.println( b1 );   // -1
System.out.println( b2 );   // -1
```

The bit pattern is the same in both cases, and all bits are set. But the fact that the console output is negative involves another Java feature: Java converts the signed byte to an int during further processing (the parameter type in the method is toBinaryString(int)). In this conversion process, the sign moves on from the byte to the int. The following example illustrates this conversion process with a binary output:

```
byte b = (byte) 255;
int  i = 255;
System.out.printf( "%d %s%n", b, Integer.toBinaryString(b) );
// -1   11111111111111111111111111111111
System.out.printf( "%d %s%n", i, Integer.toBinaryString(i) );
// 255                    11111111
```

The assignment of the lower 8 bits of byte b and int i is identical. But whereas with int the top 3 bytes are really zero, Java also fills up the top 3 bytes with 255 by automatically adjusting the sign when converting from byte to int in the two's complement. If the calculation is to be continued without a sign, this conversion is disruptive. Java always makes this automatic adjustment when calculating with byte/short, not just when a method requires the data type int, in our example.

To get a data value between 0 and 255 during further processing (i.e., to see the byte of an int unsigned), we'll cut out the lower 8 bits with the AND operation—all other bits thus remain excluded:

```
byte b = (byte) 255;
System.out.println( b );          // -1
System.out.println( b & 0xff );   // 255
```

Note that the AND operation leads to the target type int.

Library Methods for Unsigned Treatments

Always putting a & 0xff to an expression to hide the top bytes isn't much work, but it's not pretty either. Methods like toUnsignedInt(byte) are much nicer since their names clearly document what's actually happening.

The following methods in Byte may be useful:

- static int toUnsignedInt(byte x)
- static long toUnsignedLong(byte x)

Similarly, the following methods in Integer may be useful:

- static long toUnsignedLong(int x)
- static String toUnsignedString(int i, int radix)
- static String toUnsignedString(int i)
- static int parseUnsignedInt(String s, int radix)
- static int compareUnsigned(int x, int y)
- static int divideUnsigned(int dividend, int divisor)
- static int remainderUnsigned(int dividend, int divisor)

The following methods in Long may be useful:

- String toUnsignedString(long i, int radix)
- static String toUnsignedString(long i)
- static long parseUnsignedLong(String s, int radix)
- static int compareUnsigned(long x, long y)
- static long divideUnsigned(long dividend, long divisor)
- static long remainderUnsigned(long dividend, long divisor)

Finally, the following methods in Short may be useful:

- static int toUnsignedInt(short x)
- static long toUnsignedLong(short x)

In addition to simple toUnsigned*(...) methods in wrapper classes, methods can be added that also allow the conversion of numbers to a string and the parsing of a string. New methods can also be read for integer and long, which perform unsigned comparisons, division, and residual value calculation.

Conversions from byte to char

With a similar way of working, you can also solve the question of how to convert a byte whose int value is in the minus range into a char. The first approach via typecasting (char) byte is wrong, and only a rectangular box or a question mark will appear in the output, as shown in the following example:

```
byte b = (byte) 'ß';
System.out.println( (char) b );          // Output is  ?
```

Again, the dilemma is the incorrect sign matching. When the byte is used, it's first converted to an int. The character ß then becomes –33. In the next step, this –33 is then converted into a char. That results in 65,503 and is beyond what we wanted. The problem can be solved by considering only the lower 8 bits of b, performed again by hiding some bits via the AND operator. The following notation is correct:

```
char c = (char) (b & 0x00ff);
System.out.println( c );                  // Output is ß
```

As a rule, such an explicit adaptation will rarely occur in the code because Java provides extra classes for the conversion of character encodings.

21.1.6 The Shift Operators

In Java, three *shift operators* can be used to shift the bits of a value by a certain number of positions:

- n << s: Left shifting of the bits of n by s positions
- n >> s: Arithmetic right shifting by s positions with signs
- n >>> s: Logical right shifting by s positions without signs

These binary shift operators move all bits of a data word (the bit pattern) to the right or left. In the case of the shift, the number of positions by which the shift takes place is written after the binary operator (i.e., in the right operand). Although only two directions are possible, you still must consider whether or not the sign is observed when shifting to the right. This decision is referred to as *arithmetic shift* (sign remains) or *logical shift* (sign is filled with 0).

n << s

The bits of the operand n are shifted s times to the left, taking the sign into account (multiplied by 2 at each step), which results in 2 to the power of s. The bit space that becomes free on the right is always filled with 0. However, the sign changes as soon as a 1 is shifted from position *MSB – 1* to *MSB*. (MSB stands for *Most Significant Bit*, that is, the bit with the highest significance in the binary representation.)

> **Note**
>
> Although the data type of the right operand is first an int or long with full value range, only values up to 31 are meaningful for int and up to 63 bits for long as shift positions (width) because only the last 5 or 6 bits are considered. Otherwise, the shift is always performed by the value that results from dividing by 32 or 64 as the remainder, so that x << 32 and x << 0 are also equal. Consider the following examples:
>
> ```
> System.out.println( 1 << 30 );  // 1073741824
> System.out.println( 1 << 31 );  // -2147483648
> System.out.println( 1 << 32 );  // 1
> ```

n >> s (Arithmetic Right Shift)

When shifting to the right, a 1 or a 0 is inserted from the left, depending on whether the sign bit is set or not. So, the left sign bit remains untouched.

[Ex]

Example

Observe how the bits are shifted to the right:

```
Consumer<Integer> printBinary = value -> {
  String s = String.format( "%32s", Integer.toBinaryString( value ) );
  System.out.println( s.replace( ' ', '0' ) );
};
printBinary.accept( 0b10000000_00000000__00000000_00000000 >> 0 );
printBinary.accept( 0b10000000_00000000__00000000_00000000 >> 1 );
printBinary.accept( 0b10000000_00000000__00000000_00000000 >> 2 );

printBinary.accept( 0b10000000_00000000__00000000_00000000 >>> 0 );
printBinary.accept( 0b10000000_00000000__00000000_00000000 >>> 1 );
printBinary.accept( 0b10000000_00000000__00000000_00000000 >>> 2 );
```

The result is the following output:

```
10000000000000000000000000000000
11000000000000000000000000000000
11100000000000000000000000000000
10000000000000000000000000000000
01000000000000000000000000000000
00100000000000000000000000000000
```

[»]

Note

A bit that has been pushed out is lost forever! Consider the following examples:

```
System.out.println( 65535 >> 8 );  // 255
System.out.println(   255 << 8 );  // 65280
```

In this case, 65,535 = 0xFFFF, but after right shifting 65,535 >> 8, we get 0x00FF = 255. If we now shift to the left again (i.e., 0x00FF << 8), the result is 0xFF00 = 65,280.

For the integer data types, taking into account the always present sign, a signed integer division by 2 follows for normal right-shifts.

n >>> s (Logical Right Shift)

The >>> operator doesn't take into account the sign of the variable, so an unsigned right-shift is performed. Thus, only zeros are inserted on the left, at the place of the most significant bit; the sign is also shifted.

> **Example**   [Ex]
>
> You can use shift operators to easily extract the individual bytes of a larger data type, such as a 4-byte int, as in the following example:
>
> ```
> byte b1 = (byte)(v >>> 24),
>      b2 = (byte)(v >>> 16),
>      b3 = (byte)(v >>>  8),
>      b4 = (byte)(v        );
> ```

For a positive number, this shift has no effect, and the behavior is the same as for the >> operator.

> **Example**   [Ex]
>
> For negative operands, the following output is particularly exciting:
>
> ```
> System.out.println(  64 >>> 1 );  // 32
> System.out.println( -64 >>> 1 );  // 2147483616
> ```

A <<< operator makes no sense since the left-shift only inserts zeros to the right anyway.

21.1.7   Setting, Clearing, Reversing, and Testing a Bit

You can use bit operators together with shift operators to set a bit or to determine whether a bit has been set. Let's consider the following methods that set, query, invert, and clear a particular bit:

```
static int setBit( int n, int pos ) {
  return n | (1 << pos);
}

static int clearBit( int n, int pos ) {
  return n & ~(1 << pos);
}

static int flipBit( int n, int pos ) {
  return n ^ (1 << pos);
}

static boolean testBit( int n, int pos ) {
  int mask = 1 << pos;
```

21

```
  return (n & mask) == mask;
  // alternativ: return (n & 1<<pos) != 0;
}
```

21.1.8   Bit Methods of the Integer and Long Classes

The Integer and Long classes provide a set of static methods for bit manipulation and for querying various bit states of integers. The notation int|long indicates by int the static methods of the Integer class and by long the static methods of the Long class.

```
final class java.lang.Integer|Long
extends Number
implements Comparable<Integer|Long>
```

▶ static int Integer.bitCount(long i)
▶ static int Long.bitCount(long i)
  Returns the number of set bits.

▶ static int Integer.reverse(int i)
▶ static long Long.reverse(long i)
  Reverses the order of the bits.

▶ static int Integer.reverseBytes(int i)
▶ static long Long.reverseBytes(long i)
  Sets the bytes in the reverse order (i.e., the first byte to the last position, the second byte to the penultimate position, and so on).

▶ static int Integer.rotateLeft(int i, int distance)
▶ static long Long.rotateLeft(long i, int distance)
▶ static int Integer.rotateRight(int i, int distance)
▶ static long Long.rotateRight(long i, int distance)
  Rotates the bits by distance positions to the left or to the right.

▶ static int Integer.highestOneBit(int i)
▶ static long Long.highestOneBit(long i)
▶ static int Integer.lowestOneBit(int i)
▶ static long lowestOneBit(long i)
  The result is i, where all bits are cleared except the bit with the highest/lowest value. In other words, they return a value where only the highest (leftmost) or lowest (rightmost) bit is set. So, only 1 bit is set at most; of course, no bit is set with argument 0, and the result is also 0.

▶ static int Integer.numberOfLeadingZeros(int i)
▶ static long Long.numberOfLeadingZeros(long i)

▶ static int Integer.numberOfTrailingZeros(int i)

▶ static long Long.numberOfTrailingZeros(long i)

Returns the number of zero bits before the highest or after the lowest set bit.

As an example, Table 21.7 shows some applications of the static bit methods on the Long class.

Static Method of the Long Class	Method Result
highestOneBit(0b00011000)	16
lowestOneBit(0b00011000)	8
numberOfLeadingZeros(Long.MAX_VALUE)	1
numberOfLeadingZeros(Long.MIN_VALUE)	0
numberOfTrailingZeros(16)	4
numberOfTrailingZeros(3)	0
bitCount(8 + 4 + 1)	3
rotateLeft(12, 1)	24
rotateRight(12, 1)	6
reverse(0x00FF00FFF0FF000FL)	$\text{f000ff0fff00ff00}_{16}$
reverseBytes(0xFEDCBA9876543210L)	$\text{1032547698badcfe}_{16}$
reverse(Long.MAX_VALUE)	−2

Table 21.7 Static Methods of the Long Class

21.2   Floating Point Arithmetic in Java

Numbers with periods are called *floating points*, *floats*, or *fractions* (fraction numbers). The term "float" originates from the fact that sliding (shifting) the decimal point represents a change in the number defined as a product of a digit and a power of 10. Let's consider the speed of light at 299,792.458 kilometers per second as an example: $299.792,458 = 29.979,2458 \times 10^1 = 2.997,92458 \times 10^2 = 299,792458 \times 10^3 = 29,9792458 \times 10^4 = 2,99792458 \times 10^5$.

For floats, Java supports the types float and double, which follow the *Institute of Electrical and Electronics Engineers (IEEE)* 754 specification. This standard has been in existence since the mid-1980s. A float has a length of 32 bits, while a double has a length of 64 bits. Related *arithmetic* operations are defined in the *IEEE Standard for Floating-Point Arithmetic*.

Note

Be aware that the accuracy of float is actually not that great. Inaccuracy can quickly grow, as shown in the following example:

```
System.out.println( 2345678.88f );   //  2345679.0
```

21.2.1 Special Values for Infinity, Zero, and Not a Number

The double and float data types can store not only "standard numbers," but they can also accept a positive or negative zero. Furthermore, Java defines special values for the following numbers:

- Both positive and negative infinity
- Not a number (NaN)

Positive and Negative Zeros

A positive zero (+0.0) and a negative zero (–0.0) appear with an underflow (the result of a calculation is too small to be represented).

Example

The following example generates underflows:

```
System.out.println( 1E-322 *  0.0001 );  //  0.0
System.out.println( 1E-322 * -0.0001 );  //  -0.0
```

With the comparison operator ==, positive zero is equal to negative zero, so 0.0 == -0.0 returns the result true. As a result, 0.0 > -0.0 is also wrong. However, the bit mask is distinguishable, as shown by the comparison Double.doubleToLongBits(0.0) != Double.doubleToLongBits (-0.0).

Another small difference is evident when calculating 1.0 / -0.0 and 1.0 / 0.0. Due to the limit value, the result goes towards negative infinity and towards positive infinity, respectively.

Infinity

The overflow of a mathematical operation results in a positive or negative infinity.

Example

The following examples multiple two really large values and divide some values by zero:

```
System.out.println(  1E300 * 1E20 );    //  Infinity
System.out.println( -1E300 * 1E20 );    // -Infinity
System.out.println( 1. /  0. );         //  Infinity
System.out.println( 1. / -0. );         // -Infinity
```

For these values, the Java library declares two constants in Double and Float. Together with the largest and smallest representable floats, these values can be represented by the following constants:

Value for	Float	Double
Positive infinity	Float.POSITIVE_INFINITY	Double.POSITIVE_INFINITY
Negative infinity	Float.NEGATIVE_INFINITY	Double.NEGATIVE_INFINITY
Smallest value	Float.MIN_VALUE	Double.MIN_VALUE
Greatest value	Float.MAX_VALUE	Double.MAX_VALUE

Table 21.8 Special Values and Their Constants

The minimum for double values is about 10^{-324}, and the maximum is about 10^{308}. In addition, Double and Float declare constants for MAX_EXPONENT/MIN_EXPONENT.

Note

The display of overflow/underflow and of undefined results is only available for floats, not for integers.

[«]

21

```
public final class java.lang.Float|Double
extends Number
implements Comparable<Float|Double>
```

▶ static boolean isInfinite(float|double v)
  Returns true if v is either POSITIVE_INFINITY or NEGATIVE_INFINITY.

▶ static boolean isFinite(float|double d)
  Returns true if d is a finite number.

The Number That's Not a Number

NaN is often an error indicator for the result of undefined arithmetic operations, such as 0/0.

[Ex] **Example**

The following examples result in NaN when calculating the root of a negative number and performing a division by zero:

```
System.out.println( Math.sqrt(-4) );      // NaN
System.out.println( 0.0 / 0.0);           // NaN
```

NaN is declared as a constant in the Float/Double classes. The static method isNaN(...) tests whether a number is NaN.

```
public final class java.lang.Float|Double
extends Number
implements Comparable<Float|Double>
```

▶ static final float|double NaN = 0.0 / 0.0;
  Declaration of NaN for Double and Float

▶ static boolean isNaN(float|double v)
  Returns true if the passed number is v NaN.

▶ boolean isNaN()
  Returns true if the current Float|Double object is NaN.

The implementation of isNan(float|double v) is simple: return v != v.

Everything in Order*

Except for the value NaN, a total order is defined on all floats; that is, they can be enumerated from the smallest number to the largest. At the edge is negative infinity, followed by negative numbers, negative zero, positive zero, positive numbers, and positive infinity. The only thing remaining is the single unsorted number, NaN. All numerical comparisons, such as <, <=, >, and >= return false with NaN. A comparison with == is false if one of the operands is NaN. != behaves the other way round; true is returned if one of the operands is NaN.

[Ex] **Example**

The following example puts NaN through some equality tests:

```
System.out.println( Double.NaN == Double.NaN );      // false
System.out.println( Double.NaN != Double.NaN );      // true
```

Since NaN isn't equal to itself, the following construction, which is usually an infinite loop, is simply skipped with d as Double.NaN:

```
while ( d == d ) { /* Never executed */ }
```

A NaN value adjusted to an integer, such as `(int) Double.NaN`, results in 0, and no exception is thrown.[3]

Quiet NaNs*

A problem in floating point arithmetic is that no exceptions indicate errors. NaNs of this kind are also called *quiet NaNs* (*qNaNs*). Thus, as a developer, you must always determine yourself if the result is correct during a calculation. An average numerical processor distinguishes between a qNaN and a *signaling NaN* (*sNaN*).

21.2.2 Standard Notation and Scientific Notation for Floats*

Two notations exist for representing floating point literals: standard and scientific. The *scientific notation* is an extension of the standard notation. In scientific notation, the decimal places are followed by an E (or e) with an exponent to the base 10. The part before the separator may be introduced by a + or - sign. Also, the exponent can be positive or negative[4] but must be an integer. Table 21.9 contains three examples.

Standard	Scientific
123450.0	1.2345E5
123450.0	1.2345E+5
0.000012345	1.2345E−5

Table 21.9 Notations of Floats

Example

Scientific notation is used in the following examples:

```
double x = 3.00e+8;
float  y = 3.00E+8F;
```

21.2.3 Mantissas and Exponents*

Internally, floats consist of three parts: a sign, an integer *exponent*, and a *mantissa*. While the mantissa determines accuracy, the exponent indicates the magnitude of the number.

---

3 *https://stackoverflow.com/questions/5876369/why-does-casting-double-nan-to-int-not-throw-an-exception-in-java*

4 LOGO uses the letter N instead of E for negative exponents. In Java, E is followed by a unary plus or minus sign.

The calculation for floats from the three elements looks basically as follows: *Sign ×*
Mantissa × 2 ^ Exponent, where the *sign* can be –1 or +1. The mantissa *m* is not a number
with an arbitrary value range but is *normalized*, which means the value is in the range
of $1 \le m < 2$. Therefore, a float that starts with 1 is therefore also called *1-plus-form*.[5] The
initially signed exponent is also not stored directly, but as a *biased exponent* in an IEEE-
encoded representation. Depending on the accuracy, +127 (for `float`) and +1,023 (for
`double`) gets added to the exponent. After the calculation, an integer always exists in the
representation. The values 127 and 1,023 are referred to as *bias*.

The sign always costs 1 bit, and the number of bits for exponents and mantissas
depends on the data type, as listed in Table 21.10.

Data Type	Number of Bits for the Exponent	Number of Bits for the Mantissa
float	8	23
double	11	52

Table 21.10 Number of Bits for Exponents and Mantissas

[Ex]

Example

The following examples are encodings for the number 123,456.789 as a `float` and as a
`double`. The # separates sign, exponent, and mantissa:

```
0#10001111#11100010010000001100101
0#10000001111#1110001001000000110010011111101111100111011011001001
```

To get from this representation to the number, you can write the following:

```
BigInteger biasedExponent = new BigInteger( "10001111", 2 );
BigInteger mantissa = new BigInteger( "11100010010000001100101", 2 );
int exponent = (int) Math.pow( 2, biasedExponent.longValue() - 127 );
double m = 1. + (mantissa.longValue() / Math.pow( 2, 23 ));
System.out.println( exponent * m );  // 123456.7890625
```

The exponent (without bias) of a float is returned by `Math.getExponent(...)`; thus,
applied to our number, the result is 16.

Access to the bit pattern is provided by the methods `long doubleToLongBits(double)`
and `int Float.floatToIntBits(float)`. The reverse methods are `double Double.longBits-`
`ToDouble(long)` or `float Float.intBitsToFloat(int)`.

---

5 An exception occurs due to denormalized numbers, but this topic doesn't matter for our understanding of the concept.

Example

Print an alternative representation of double and float floating point numbers:

```
double x = 123456.789;
float  y = 123456.789f;
out.printf( "%016x%n", Double.doubleToLongBits( x ) ); // 40fe240c9fbe76c9
out.printf( "%08x%n", Float.floatToIntBits( y ) );     // 47f12065
out.println( Long.toBinaryString( Double.doubleToLongBits( x ) ) );
out.println( Integer.toBinaryString( Float.floatToIntBits( y ) ) );
```

Note

Since floats can only be represented as approximations for periodic binary fractions, the result is often not "precise." Thus, 0.1 corresponds to a periodic mantissa in IEEE format.

21.3   The Members of the Math Class

The java.lang.Math class is a typical utility class that declares only static methods and class variables for constants. The private constructor can't be used to create instances of Math. All operations take place strictly according to the IEEE-754 specification.

History Lesson

Between Java 1.2 and Java 16, the Java compiler supported the strictfp keyword. The distinction was supposed to allow the JVM to not strictly follow the IEEE-754 specification and thus execute Java programs more quickly on local hardware. However, for the last 20 years, all processors have supported IEEE-754, and the distinction has become irrelevant—all mathematical operations performed by the JVM are as described in the IEEE-754 standard. With the removal of strictfp, the StrictMath class also became irrelevant.

21.3.1   Object Variables of the Math Class

The Math class has two public class variables:

```
class java.lang.Math
```

▶ static final double E
   The Euler number[6] e = 2.7182818284590452354.

▶ static final double PI
   The number pi[7] = 3.14159265358979323846.

---

6 The irrational number e is named after the Swiss mathematician Leonhard Euler (1707–1783).
7 A bit of trivia: The one billionth digit of pi after the decimal point is a 9.

21.3.2   Absolute Values and Signs

The two static abs(...) methods return the amount of the argument (mathematical amount function: $y = |x|$). If a negative value is passed as an argument, abs(...) converts it to a positive value.

A special method is also copySign(double, double). It determines the sign of a float and transfers it to another number.

---

class java.lang.**Math**

▶ static int abs(int x)

▶ static long abs(long x)

▶ static float abs(float x)

▶ static double abs(double x)

▶ static double copySign(double magnitude, double sign)

▶ static float copySign(float magnitude, float sign)
   Returns magnitude, but with the sign of sign.

[»]

> **Note**
>
> For exactly one value, Math.abs(int) can't return a positive, and the result is truly negative: −2,147,483,648. This number is the smallest representable int number (Integer.MIN_VALUE), while +2,147,483,648 doesn't fit into an int at all! The largest int number that can be represented is 2,147,483,647 (Integer.MAX_VALUE). What should abs(-2147483648) actually result in?

Querying Signs

The static method signum(value) returns a numeric return for the sign of value, namely, "+1" for positive, "−1" for negative numbers, and "0" for 0. The method isn't quite logically distributed between the classes Math for floats and Integer/Long for integers. Consider the following examples:

■ java.lang.**Integer**.signum(int i), java.lang.**Long**.signum(long i)

■ java.lang.**Math**.signum(double d), java.lang.**Math**.signum(float f)

21.3.3   Maximums/Minimums

The static max(...) methods return the larger of the passed values. The static min(...) methods return the smaller of two values.

---

class java.lang.**Math**

▶ static int max(int x, int y)

▶ static long max(long x, long y)

▶ static float max(float x, float y)

▶ static double max(double x, double y)

▶ static int min(int x, int y)

▶ static long min(long x, long y)

▶ static float min(float x, float y)

▶ static double min(double x, double y)

These methods aren't declared with varargs, and no min-max methods exist that can take three or more arguments. If arrays are present, a different solution must be chosen, such as using Arrays.stream(value).min().getAsInt().

21.3.4 Rounding Values

To round values, the Math class provides five static methods:

---

class java.lang.**Math**

▶ static double ceil(double a)

▶ static double floor(double a)

▶ static int round(float a)

▶ static long round(double a)

▶ static double rint(double a)

Rounding Up and Down with ceil(double) and floor(double)

The static method ceil(double) rounds a value up and returns the next higher integer (but as a double, not a long) if the number isn't already an integer. The static method floor(double) rounds down to the next lower integer. Consider the following examples:

```
System.out.println( Math.ceil(-99.1) );     // -99.0
System.out.println( Math.floor(-99.1) );     // -100.0
System.out.println( Math.ceil(-99) );     // -99.0
System.out.println( Math.floor(-99) );     // -99.0
System.out.println( Math.ceil(-.5) );     // -0.0
System.out.println( Math.floor(-.5) );     // -1.0
System.out.println( Math.ceil(-.01) );     // -0.0
System.out.println( Math.floor(-.01) );     // -1.0
System.out.println( Math.ceil(0.1) );     // 1.0
System.out.println( Math.floor(0.1) );     // 0.0
System.out.println( Math.ceil(.5) );     // 1.0
```

```
System.out.println( Math.floor(.5) );      //     0.0
System.out.println( Math.ceil(99) );       //    99.0
System.out.println( Math.floor(99) );      //    99.0
```

Listing 21.2 src/main/java/com/tutego/insel/math/Rounding1Demo.java, main()

These static methods have no effect on integers.

Commercial Rounding via round(...)

The static methods round(double) and round(float) round to the nearest integer of type long or int. Whole numbers aren't rounded up. This is called *commercial rounding.* You can use round(...) as a counterpart to the typecasting (long) doublevalue, as in the following examples:

```
System.out.println( Math.round(1.01) );    // 1
System.out.println( Math.round(1.4) );     // 1
System.out.println( Math.round(1.5) );     // 2
System.out.println( Math.round(1.6) );     // 2
System.out.println( (int) 1.6 );           // 1
System.out.println( Math.round(30) );      // 30
System.out.println( Math.round(-2.1) );    // -2
System.out.println( Math.round(-2.9) );    // -3
System.out.println( (int) -2.9 );          // -2
```

Listing 21.3 src/main/java/com/tutego/insel/math/Rounding2Demo.java, main()

[»]

Internal Affairs

The Math.round(int) and Math.round(long) methods are programmed into Java. They add 0.5 to the current parameter and pass the result to the static floor(double) method.

```
public static long round( double a ) {
  return (long) floor( a + 0.5 );
}
```

Listing 21.4 java.lang.Math, round(double) (Slightly Shortened)

Fair Rounding with rint(double)

rint(double) is comparable to round(...), except that rint(double) is "fair," meaning that rint(double) rounds up or down at 0.5 depending on whether the adjacent number is odd or even.

```
System.out.println( Math.round(-1.5) );    //    -1
System.out.println( Math.rint( -1.5) );    // -2.0
```

```
System.out.println( Math.round(-2.5) );    //    -2
System.out.println( Math.rint( -2.5) );    // -2.0
System.out.println( Math.round( 1.5) );    //     2
System.out.println( Math.rint(  1.5) );    //  2.0
System.out.println( Math.round( 2.5) );    //     3
System.out.println( Math.rint(  2.5) );    //  2.0
```

Listing 21.5 src/main/java/com/tutego/insel/math/Rounding3Demo.java, main()

With a consistent rounding up or down, errors naturally propagate more awkwardly than with this 50/50 strategy.

Example

The static rint(double) method can also be used when numbers should be rounded to two decimal places. If d is of type double, the expression Math.rint(d*100.0)/100.0 returns the rounded number.

```
class Round2Scales {
  public static double roundScale2( double d ) {
    return Math.rint( d * 100 ) / 100.;
  }

  public static void main( String[] args ) {
    System.out.println( roundScale2(+1.341 ) );    //  1.34
    System.out.println( roundScale2(-1.341 ) );    // -1.34
    System.out.println( roundScale2(+1.345 ) );    //  1.34
    System.out.println( roundScale2(-1.345 ) );    // -1.34

    System.out.println( roundScale2(+1.347 ) );    //  1.35
    System.out.println( roundScale2(-1.347 ) );    // -1.35
  }
}
```

Listing 21.6 Round2Scales.java

If you use round(...) instead of rint(double), the number 1.345 won't be rounded to 1.34, but to 1.35 instead. You can test how the format string %.2f rounds with printf(...).

21.3.5   Remainder of an Integer Division*

Besides the remainder operator %, which calculates the remainder of the division, a static method named Math.IEEEremainder(double, double) can also calculate the remainder.

```
double a = 44.0;
double b = 2.2;
System.out.println( a / b );                       // 20.0
System.out.println( a % b );                       // 2.1999999999999966
System.out.println( Math.IEEEremainder( a, b ) ); // -3.552713678800501E-15
```

Listing 21.7 src/main/java/com/tutego/insel/math/IEEEremainder.java, main()

The second result is almost 2.2 with the mathematical inaccuracy, but slightly smaller, so the algorithm couldn't subtract another 2.2. The static method IEEEremainder(double, double) returns a result close to zero (–0.000000000000000035527136788005), which is better because 44.0 can be divided by 2.2 without a remainder, so the remainder would actually be 0.

---

class java.lang.**Math**

▶ static double IEEEremainder(double dividend, double divisor)
  Returns the remainder of the division of the dividend and divisor, as required by the IEEE-754 standard.

A separate static method that sometimes returns better results—with the values 44 and 2.2 being actually 0.0—is shown in the following example:

```
public static double remainder( double a, double b ) {
  return Math.signum(a) *
         (Math.abs(a) - Math.abs(b) * Math.floor(Math.abs(a)/Math.abs(b)));
}
```

21.3.6   Division with Rounding toward Negative Infinity and Alternative Remainders*

Integer division in Java is simple: convert the integers to floats, perform the division, and truncate everything after the decimal point. For example, 3 / 2 = 1 and 9 / 2 = 4. If the result is negative, either because of a negative dividend or because of a negative divisor, the same thing happens: -9 / 2 = -4 and 9 / -2 = -4. Let's look at rounding these numbers.

If the result of a division is positive and has a decimal part, the result is made a little smaller by truncating the decimal places (i.e., by rounding down). If 3 / 2 would be 1.5 for floats, it's 1 for an integer division rounded down. With negative results of a division, the reverse is true because, by truncating the decimal places, the number becomes slightly greater. Thus, -3 / 2 is, strictly speaking, –1.5, but in integer division, it is -1. But -1 is greater than –1.5, and therefore, Java applies a procedure that rounds to zero.

The floorDiv(...) Method to Round to Negative Infinity

Three methods don't round to zero if the result of a division is negative but instead round to negative infinity (i.e., also in the direction of the smaller number, as is the case with positive results).

```
class java.lang.Math
```

▶ static int floorDiv(int x, int y)

▶ static long floorDiv(long x, long y)

▶ static long floorDiv(long x, int y)

In practical terms, 4/3 = Math.floorDiv(4, 3) = 1, but where -4 / 3 = -1, in contrast, Math.floorDiv(-4, 3) = -2.

The floorMod(...) Method to Round to Negative Infinity

The division also appears indirectly in the calculation of the remainder. Remember: The relationship between the division a/b and the remainder a%b (a is called *dividend*, b *divisor*) is (int)(a/b) * b + (a%b) = a. A division exists in the equation, but with two kinds of divisions (a / b and floorDiv(a, b)), consequently, two kinds of remainders must also exist, which differ if the signs are different. For this reason, besides a % b, the library method floorMod(a, b) is available, and the relationship between floorMod(...) and floorDiv(...) is floorDiv(a, b) * b + floorMod(a, b) == b. A transformation of the equation is followed by floorMod(a, b) = a - (floorDiv(a, b) * b). The result is in the range -abs(b) and abs(b), and the sign of the result is determined by the divisor b (for the % operator, the dividend a).

The Javadoc for floorMod(...) shows an example with the values 4 and 3 with different signs.

floorMod(...) Method	% Operator
floorMod(+4, +3) == +1	+4 % +3 == +1
floorMod(+4, -3) == -2	+4 % -3 == +1
floorMod(-4, +3) == +2	-4 % +3 == -1
floorMod(-4, -3) == -1	-4 % -3 == -1

Table 21.11 Results of Different Ways to Calculate a Remainder

If the signs for a and b are identical, the results of floorMod(a, b) and a % b will also be the same. The examples in the table also demonstrate the difference in the result sign, which comes once from the dividend (%) and once from the divisor (floorMod(...)). The completely different events (apart from the sign) in the pairs (+4, –3) and (–4, +3) simply result from different results of the division.

---

class java.lang.**Math**

▶ static int floorMod(int x, int y)
▶ static long floorMod(long x, long y)
▶ static long floorMod(long x, int y)

The implementation is relatively simple with x - floorDiv(x, y) * y.

21.3.7   Multiply-Accumulate

The mathematical operation $a \times b + c$ occurs frequently in calculations, so that processors today can perform this calculation in an optimized way, that is, faster and with a higher accuracy. Math has the fma(...) method for the *fused multiply-accumulate function* from the IEEE-754 standard.

---

class java.lang.**Math**

▶ static double fma(double a, double b, double c)
▶ static float fma(float a, float b, float c)
   Performs $a \times b + c$ using RoundingMode.HALF_EVEN. Compared to a simple a * b + c, fma(...) takes into account the special features (i.e., infinity and NaN).

21.3.8   Square Root and Exponential Methods

The Math class also provides methods for calculating the square root and other exponential methods:

---

class java.lang.**Math**

▶ static double sqrt(double x)
   Returns the square root of x; sqrt stands for *square root*.
▶ static double cbrt(double a)
   Calculates the cube root of a.
▶ static double hypot(double x, double y)
   Calculates the square root of $x^2 + y^2$, also called *Euclidean distance*. Could be rewritten as sqrt(x*x + y*y), but hypot(...) provides better accuracy and performance.
▶ static double scalb(double d, double scaleFactor)
   Returns d times 2 to the power of scaleFactor. Can in principle also be written as d * Math.pow(2, scaleFactor), but scalb(...) provides better performance.

▶ `static double exp(double x)`

Returns the exponential value of x to the base e (of the Euler number $e = 2.71828...$), for instance, e^x.

▶ `static double expm1(double x)`

Returns the exponential value of x to the base e minus 1 (i.e., $e^x - 1$). Calculations near zero can express `expm1(x) + 1` more precisely than `exp(x)`.

▶ `static double pow(double x, double y)`

Returns the value of the power x^y. No separate method for integer values exists.

The Question of 0.0/0.0 and 0.0^0.0*

As you've learned, 0.0/0.0 results in a straightforward NaN. In contrast to the integer values, however, we don't get an exception in this case because the special number NaN has been introduced especially for this purpose. You might ask what exactly results in `(long)(double)(0.0/0.0)`. The Java Language Specification (JLS) states[8] that converting a floating point value NaN to an int 0 or to a long results in 0.

Another exciting question concerns the result of $0.0^{0.0}$. To calculate general powers, the static function `Math.pow(double a, double b)` is used. From your school days, you may recall that we take the square root of a number when the exponent b is exactly ½. But now we want to know what happens if a = b = 0. The JLS requires that the result is always 1.0 if the exponent b is equal to −0.0 or 0.0. Thus, in this case, base a doesn't matter at all. In some algebra books, 0^0 is treated as undefined. However, it makes perfect sense to define 0^0 as 1 since otherwise numerous special treatments for 0 would be required.[9]

21.3.9 The Logarithm*

The logarithm is the inverse function of the exponential function. The exponential function and the logarithm are related by the following relationship: If $y = a^x$, then $x = \log_a(y)$. The logarithm calculated by `Math.log(double)` is the natural logarithm to base e. In mathematics, this relationship is indicated by *ln* (*logarithmus naturalis, natural logarithm*). Logarithms with base 10 are referred to as common logarithm or *Briggsian logarithm* and are abbreviated as *lg*, while logarithms with base 2 (*binary logarithm, dual logarithm*) are abbreviated as *lb*. In Java, the static method `log10(double)` exists for the brig logarithm lg, but not for the binary logarithm lb, which must still be emulated. In general, the following conversion applies: $\log_b(x) = \log_a(x) \div \log_a(b)$.

21

---

8 *https://docs.oracle.com/javase/specs/jls/se17/html/jls-5.html#jls-5.1.3*

9 R. Graham, D. Knuth, and O. Patashnik, authors of the book *Concrete Mathematics* (Addison-Wesley, 1994) write the following: "Some textbooks leave the quantity 0^0 undefined because the functions x^0 and 0^x have different limiting values when x decreases to 0. But this is a mistake. We must define x^0 = 1 for all x, if the binomial theorem is to be valid when x=0, y=0, and/or x=-y. The theorem is too important to be arbitrarily restricted! By contrast, the function 0^x is quite unimportant."

Example

In the following example, a custom static method calculates the logarithm for base 2:

```
public static double lb( double x ) {
  return Math.log( x ) / Math.log( 2.0 );
}
class java.lang.Math
```

▶ static double log(double a)

Calculates the logarithm of a to the base *e*.

▶ static double log10(double a)

Returns the logarithm of a to the base 10.

▶ static double log1p(double x)

Returns log (*x*) + 1.

21.3.10 Angle Methods*

The Math class provides some angle-related methods and their reversals. In contrast school mathematics, the angles for sin(double), cos(double), and tan(double) are passed as radians (2ð corresponds to a full circle), not in degrees (360 degrees corresponds to a full circle).

```
class java.lang.Math
```

▶ static double sin(double x)

▶ static double cos(double x)

▶ static double tan(double x)

Returns the sine, cosine, and tangent of x, respectively.

Arc Methods

Arc methods implement the inverse functions to trigonometric methods. The argument is not an angle, but, for example with asin(double), a sine value between –1 and 1. The result is an angle in radians, approximately between $-\pi/2$ and $\pi/2$.

```
class java.lang.Math
```

▶ static double asin(double x)

▶ static double acos(double x)

▶ static double atan(double x)

Returns the arc sine, arc cosine, or arc tangent of x, respectively.

▶ static double atan2(double x, double y)

Returns the angle *theta* (i.e., a component of the polar coordinate tuple), when converting rectangular coordinates to polar coordinates. The static method takes into account the sign of the parameters x and y, and the free leg of the angle is in the correct quadrant.

Hyperbolic functions are provided by the Java methods sinh(double), tanh(double), and cosh(double).

Conversions from Degrees to Radians

Two static methods exist for converting an angle from the degree measure to the radian measure, and vice versa:

```
class java.lang.Math
```

▶ static double toRadians(double angdeg)

Converts an angle from degrees to radians.

▶ static double toDegrees(double angrad)

Converts an angle from radians to degrees.

21.3.11 Random Numbers

Positive random floats between greater than or equal to 0.0 and truly less than 1.0 are returned by the static method Math.random(). The return value is double, and a type conversion to int always leads to the result 0.

To have values in a different range of values, a simple solution is to expand the random numbers from Math.random() to the desired range of values by multiplication (scaling) and shift them appropriately by addition (an offset). To obtain random integer numbers between min (inclusive) and max (inclusive), you can write the following code:

```java
public static long random( long min, long max ) {
  return min + Math.round( Math.random() * (max - min) );
}
```

Listing 21.8 src/main/java/com/tutego/insel/math/RandomIntInRange.java

A custom implementation isn't necessary because the Random class—and its subclasses—provide several useful object methods like nextInt(n). The implementation is not in the Math class itself, but in Random, which we'll take a closer look at in Section 21.5.

21

21.4   Accuracy and the Value Range of Type and Overflow Control*

Data types in Java always have a certain number of bytes, and thus the value range is known. However, an operation can run beyond this range of values.

21.4.1   The Largest and Smallest Values

For each primitive data type, a separate class in Java is available with various methods and constants. The classes Byte, Short, Integer, Long, Float, and Double have the constants MIN_VALUE and MAX_VALUE for their minimum and maximum value ranges. The Float and Double classes also have the important constants NEGATIVE_INFINITY and POSITIVE_INFINITY for negative and positive infinity as well as NaN (undefined).

[»]
> **Note**
>
> Integer.MIN_VALUE represents the smallest value the integer can assume: −2,147,483,648. However, Double.MIN_VALUE represents the smallest *positive* number (best approximation to 0) that a double can represent (4.9E-324).

When we speak of "double precision," especially when hearing the word double as opposed to float, you must be careful because double provides more than twice as precise a mantissa, at least according to the number of bits. However, this precision doesn't say anything about the number of decimal places.

[Ex]
> **Craft Task**
>
> Ask yourself the question, "Why are the expenses the way they are?" when considering the following example:
>
> ```
> double d1 = 0.02d;
> float  f1 = 0.02f;
> System.out.println( d1 == f1 );          // false
> System.out.println( (float) d1 == f1 ); // true
>
> double d2 = 0.02f;
> float  f2 = 0.02f;
> System.out.println( d2 == f2 );          // true
> ```

21.4.2   Overflow and Everything Entirely Exact

For some mathematical questions, you must determine whether operations (such as addition, subtraction, or multiplication) may go beyond the valid number range (i.e., leave the integer range of an integer of 32 bits, for example). If the result of a calculation doesn't fit into the value range of a number, this error won't be displayed by Java by default; neither the compiler nor the runtime environment will report this problem. Also, no exception is raised since no built-in overflow control is available in Java.

Example   [Ex]

Mathematically, $a \times a \div a = a$ is correct, so, for example, 100,000 × 100,000 ÷ 100,000 = 100,000. In Java, the result is different because overflow occurs in int at 100,000 × 100,000. Consider the following example:

```
System.out.println( 100_000 * 100_000 / 100_000 );      // 14100
```

This statement prints 14100. If we increase the data type to long by placing an L after 100_000, we're still safe with this multiplication since a long can store the result, as in the following example:

```
System.out.println( 100_000L * 100_000 / 100_000 );     // 100000
```

Multiplying int Integers

The * operator doesn't perform any data type matching on int, so multiplying two ints again returns int. But the product can quickly run beyond the acceptable value range, thus causing an overflow. Even if the product is written to a long variable, the conversion from int to long doesn't occur until after the multiplication. Consider the following examples:

```
int  i = Integer.MAX_VALUE * Integer.MAX_VALUE;
long l = Integer.MAX_VALUE * Integer.MAX_VALUE;
System.out.println( i );     // 1
System.out.println( l );     // 1
```

If two ints must be multiplied without overflow, one of the two factors must be adjusted to long so that the calculation leads to the correct result (4611686014132420609), as in the following example:

```
System.out.println( Integer.MAX_VALUE * (long) Integer.MAX_VALUE );
System.out.println( (long) Integer.MAX_VALUE * Integer.MAX_VALUE );
```

Because this typecasting can be quickly forgotten and isn't particularly explicit, the Math class provides the static method long multiplyFull(int x, int y), which performs the typecasting for you using (long)x * (long)y.

Multiplying Long Integers

No primitive data type has more than 64 bits (8 bytes), so the result of long * long with its 128 bits only fits completely into a BigInteger. However, one method allows you to query the upper 64 bits of a long multiplication separately, using the multiplyHigh(long x, long y) method in Math.

21

Example

Example of multiplying large numbers:

```
BigInteger v = BigInteger.valueOf( Long.MAX_VALUE )
                      .multiply( BigInteger.valueOf( Long.MAX_VALUE ) );
System.out.println( v );  // 85070591730234615847396907784232501249


long lowLong = Long.MAX_VALUE * Long.MAX_VALUE;
long highLong = Math.multiplyHigh( Long.MAX_VALUE, Long.MAX_VALUE );
BigInteger w = BigInteger.valueOf( highLong )
                      .shiftLeft( 64 )
                      .add( BigInteger.valueOf( lowLong ) );
System.out.println( w );  // 85070591730234615847396907784232501249
```

Detecting an Overflow

All the methods listed below in Math provide overflow detection:

```
class java.lang.Math
```

▶ static int addExact(int x, int y)

▶ static long addExact(long x, long y)

▶ static int subtractExact(int x, int y)

▶ static long subtractExact(long x, long y)

▶ static int multiplyExact(int x, int y)

▶ static int multiplyExact(long x, int y)

▶ static long multiplyExact(long x, long y)

▶ static int toIntExact(long value)

▶ static int incrementExact(int a)

▶ static long incrementExact(long a)

▶ static int decrementExact(int a)

▶ static long decrementExact(long a)

▶ static int negateExact(int a)

▶ static long negateExact(long a)

All methods throw an ArithmeticException if the operation isn't feasible—the last one, for example, if (int)value != value. Unfortunately, Java doesn't declare subclasses like UnderflowException or OverflowException and only reports anything of type ArithmeticException with the error message "xxx overflow," even if it's actually an underflow.

[Ex]

Example

As shown in the following example, subtracting 1 from the smallest integer using `sub-tractExact(...)` leads to an exception:

```
subtractExact( Integer.MIN_VALUE, 1 );    // ☠ ArithmeticException
```

[«]

Comparison with C#

C# behaves the same way as Java and doesn't respond to an overflow by default. However, special `checked` blocks can report an `OverflowException` when an overflow occurs in basic arithmetic operations. The following code raises this exception: `checked { int val = int.MaxValue; val++; }`. Such `checked` blocks don't exist in Java. If you require this special overflow control, you must use the methods and then also rewrite a `val++` to `Math.addExact(val, 1)` or `Math.incrementExact(val)`.

21.4.3   What in the World Does the ulp Method Do?

The `Math` class provides special methods if you're concerned about computational (im)precision and may work with numerical approximations.

The distance from one float to the next isn't always the same due to the internal structure. The exact distance of a number to the next possible one is shown by `ulp(double)` or `ulp(float)`. This funny method name is an abbreviation for "unit in the last place." The exact next higher/lower number is determined by the methods `nextUp(float|double)` and `nextDown(float|double)`, which use `nextAfter(...)`.

[Ex]

Example

Ask yourself the question, "What comes after and before 1?" when considering the following example:

```
System.out.printf( "%.16f%n", Math.nextUp( 1 ) );
System.out.printf( "%.16f%n", Math.nextDown( 1 ) );
System.out.printf( "%.16f%n", Math.nextAfter( 1, Double.POSITIVE_
INFINITY ) );
System.out.printf( "%.16f%n", Math.nextAfter( 1, Double.NEGATIVE_
INFINITY ) );
```

The result is the following output:

```
1.000000119209289
0.9999999403953552
1.0000001192092896
0.9999999403953552
```

21

nextUp(d) is an abbreviation for nextAfter(d, Double.**POSITIVE_INFINITY**), and next-Down(d) is an abbreviation for nextAfter(d, Double.**NEGATIVE_INFINITY**). If the second argument of Math.nextAfter(...) is larger than the first, then the next larger number will be returned; if the second argument is smaller, then the next smaller number will be returned. In case of equality, the same number comes back.

Method	Return
Math.ulp(0.00001)	0.00000000000000000000001694065895
Math.ulp(-1)	0.0000000119209228955078125
Math.ulp(1)	0.0000000119209228955078125
Math.ulp(2)	0.000000023841857910015625
Math.ulp(10E30)	1125899906842624

Table 21.12 As the Numbers Get Bigger, the Jumps Also Get Bigger

A Quantum of Inaccuracy

The usual mathematical floating point operations have a ulp of ½, which is as accurate as possible. The Javadoc will indicate how much in ulps Math methods can deviate from the real result. Calculation errors can't be avoided, especially with complex methods. Thus, sin(double) may have a possible inaccuracy of 1 ulp; atan2(double, double), an inaccuracy of at most 2 ulps; and sinh(double), cosh(double), tanh(double), inaccuracies of 2.5 ulp.

The ulp(...) method is interesting for testing because you can always implement deviations in the appropriate order of magnitude. For small numbers, a difference of perhaps 0.001 makes sense; for larger numbers, the tolerance may be larger.

Java declares three special constants in the Double and Float classes, which can be illustrated via nextAfter(...). Let's look at some examples using Double:

- MIN_VALUE = nextUp(0.0) = Double.longBitsToDouble(0x0010000000000000L)
- MIN_NORMAL = MIN_VALUE/(nextUp(1.0)-1.0) = Double.longBitsToDouble(0x1L)
- MAX_VALUE = nextAfter(POSITIVE_INFINITY, 0.0) =
    Double.longBitsToDouble(0x7fefffffffffffffL)

21.5 Random Numbers: Random, ThreadLocalRandom, and SecureRandom

The Math class provides a simple method for random numbers: random(). Internally, however, this method based on a different class that you can also use directly, thus enabling you to ask for more than just random numbers between 0 and 1.

The usual random numbers of Java are actually *pseudo-random numbers* because they are generated by a mathematical algorithm. Good "random values" are repeated only after exceedingly long sequences, have no obvious context, and are generated quickly. Perfect random numbers would never be predictable: The probability for each number would always be the same—regardless of the preceding values—and the sequences would never be repeated.

21.5.1   The Random Class

The Random class in the java.util package implements a generator for pseudo-random numbers. Unlike Math.random(), Random doesn't provide any static functions but does provide a set of next*(...) methods. The static function Math.random() uses a Random object internally.

Creating Random Objects with a Seed

Every Random object needs an initial value for the calculation. The initial value for each random number is a 48-bit seed. "Seed" indicates that, in the generation of random numbers, as with plants, a seed leads to offspring. From this initial value, the random number generator then determines the following numbers by linear congruences. (Thus, the numbers aren't really random but instead obey a mathematical procedure.)

At the beginning, you'll need an instance of the Random class. This instance is initialized with a random value (data type long), which is then used for the subsequent calculations. This initial value shapes the entire sequence of generated random numbers, although how the sequence behaves isn't obvious. One thing is certain: Two Random objects created with the same initial values also return the same sequence of random numbers, namely: If the seed is the same, of course, the sequence of random numbers is always the same. For testing, this similarity isn't bad at all. The parameterless constructor of Random initializes the start value with the sum of a magic start value and System.nanoTime().

```
class Random
implements RandomGenerator, Serializable
```

▶ Random()
Creates a new random number generator.

▶ Random(long seed)
Creates a new random number generator and uses the seed parameter as a start value.

▶ void setSeed(long seed)
Resets the seed. The generator subsequently behaves in the same way as a generator freshly created with this seed value.

Generating Single Random Numbers

The Random class generates random numbers for four different data types: int (32 bit), long (64 bit), double, and float. Four methods are available for this purpose:

- int nextInt()
- long nextLong()

  Returns the next pseudo-random number from the entire value range (i.e., between Integer.MIN_VALUE and Integer.MAX_VALUE or between Long.MIN_VALUE and Long.MAX_VALUE).

- float nextFloat()
- double nextDouble()

  Returns the next pseudo-random number between 0.0 and 1.0.

- int nextInt(int range)

  Returns an int pseudo-random number in the range 0 to range.

The Random class has a special method for generating a series of random numbers all at once: the nextBytes(byte[]) method. The parameter is a byte array, which is completely filled with random numbers.

All methods for generating random numbers are based on the next(int bits) method. This method is implemented in Random, but due to its protected visibility, the method is only visible from an inheriting class. Subclasses are possible because Random is a normal public non-final class.

Pseudo-Random Numbers in the Normal Distribution*

Via a special method, you can obtain random numbers that satisfy a normal distribution: nextGaussian(). This method works internally according to the polar method and generates two normally distributed numbers from two independent pseudo-random numbers. The midpoint is 0, and the standard deviation is 1. The values returned by nextGaussian() are double numbers and often approximate 0. Larger numbers are rather rare.

```
class java.util.Random
implements Serializable
```

▶ double nextGaussian()

  Returns the nearest random number in a Gaussian normal distribution with 0.0 as the midpoint and a standard deviation of 1.0.

Generating a Stream of Random Numbers*

If several random numbers are required, a loop with repeated calls of next*() isn't necessary. Instead, two varieties of methods in Random return a bunch of random numbers.

The first approach uses an array:

- void nextBytes(byte[] bytes)
  Fills the bytes array with random bytes.

Other methods provide a stream of random numbers:

- IntStream ints(…)

- LongStream longs(…)

- DoubleStream doubles(…)

Example [Ex]

The following example returns ten random numbers that are probably prime numbers:

```
LongStream stream = new Random().longs()
                    .filter( v -
> BigInteger.valueOf( v ).isProbablePrime(5) );
stream.limit( 10 ).forEach( System.out::println );
```

The methods ints(...), longs(...), and doubles(...) come in four flavors, as shown in Table 21.13.

Parameterization	Explanation
IntStream ints()	Returns an infinite stream of random numbers in the entire range of values of the primitives.
LongStream longs()	
DoubleStream doubles()	
ints(long streamSize)	Returns a stream with streamSize random numbers.
longs(long streamSize)	
doubles(long streamSize)	
ints(int randomNumberOrigin, int randomNumberBound)	Returns an infinite stream of random numbers with values in the range from randomNumberOrigin (inclusive) to randomNumberBound (exclusive).
longs(long randomNumberOrigin, long randomNumberBound)	
doubles(double randomNumberOrigin, double randomNumberBound)	

Table 21.13 Stream Methods of the Random Class

21

Parameterization	Explanation
`ints(long streamSize, int randomNumberOrigin, int randomNumberBound)`	Returns a stream with `streamSize` random numbers with values in the range from randomNumberOrigin (inclusive) to randomNumberBound (exclusive).
`longs(long streamSize, long randomNumberOrigin, long randomNumberBound)`	
`doubles(long streamSize, double randomNumberOrigin, double randomNumberBound)`	

Table 21.13 Stream Methods of the Random Class (Cont.)

[Ex]

Example

The following example outputs five random floats in the range from 10 to 20:

```
new Random().doubles(5, 10, 20).forEach( System.out::println );
```

21.5.2   ThreadLocalRandom

The `ThreadLocalRandom` class is a subclass of `Random` and overrides central methods because `Random` has a safeguard against concurrent access that `ThreadLocalRandom` doesn't have—an object of this class should only ever be used in the same thread. For this reason, a `ThreadLocalRandom` isn't created via `new`, but a static factory method returns the object associated with the respective thread.

[Ex]

Example

The following example determines two random numbers between 1 and 10:

```
Random threadLocalRandom = ThreadLocalRandom.current();
System.out.println( threadLocalRandom.nextInt( 1, 10 + 1 ) );
System.out.println( threadLocalRandom.nextInt( 1, 10 + 1 ) );
```

21.5.3   The SecureRandom Class*

The `Random` class is in a dilemma: producing good and random numbers, on one hand, but also calculating quickly on the other hand. `Random` doesn't generate cryptographically decent numbers; for this scenario, the implementation would need more effort (which costs more time). Still, such advanced random numbers are not generally necessary in everyday life.

Random numbers that are cryptographically more sound are provided by java.security.SecureRandom, a subclass of Random. This subclass provides the same set of next*(...) methods, but the quality of the random numbers is better. This isn't due to SecureRandom itself because the class doesn't implement any algorithms, but to the referenced replaceable random number providers. An implementation is provided by SecureRandom.getInstanceStrong() or by the parameterless constructor as well. In this case, however, the SecureRandom object doesn't necessarily have to be "strong," that is, it doesn't have to meet the highest cryptographic standards. The difference exists because new SecureRandom().getAlgorithm().toString() returns SHA1PRNG, and SecureRandom.getInstanceStrong().getAlgorithm().toString() returns Windows PRNG.

21.6 Large Numbers*

The fixed length of the primitive data types int and long for integer values, and float and double for floating point values, isn't sufficient for various numerical calculations. Arbitrarily large numbers in cryptography and precise resolutions in financial mathematics are particularly desirable. For such applications, two classes in the math package are available: BigInteger for integers and BigDecimal for floats, as shown in Figure 21.1.

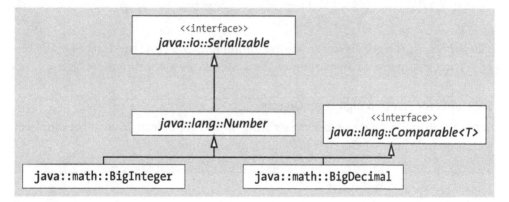

Figure 21.1 The Inheritance Relationship of BigInteger and BigDecimal

21.6.1 The BigInteger Class

The BigInteger class enables you to create and manage integers of any accuracy for use in calculations. BigInteger objects are always as long internally as the corresponding results take up space (*infinite word size*). The calculation options go far beyond options using primitive types and furthermore offer many static methods of the Math class. Extensions include modular arithmetic, the determination of the greatest common divisor (GCD), pseudo-prime tests, bit manipulation, and more.

[Ex]

Example

The square of a number consisting only of 1s yields an interesting result, namely, a number that is both a palindrome[10] and also counts up (to the middle) in the manner of 1234, etc. Consider the following example:

```
BigInteger ones = BigInteger.ONE;
for ( int i = 0; i < 20; i++ ) {
  System.out.println( ones + "^2 = " + ones.pow( 2 ) );
  ones = ones.multiply( BigInteger.TEN ).add( BigInteger.ONE );
}
```

Listing 21.9 src/main/java/com/tutego/insel/math/BigIntegerDemo.java, main()

The result of the loop is the following output:

```
1^2 = 1
11^2 = 121
111^2 = 12321
1111^2 = 1234321
11111^2 = 123454321
...
11111111111111111111^2 = 1234567901234567901209876543209876654321
```

Like strings, `BigInteger` objects are always immutable. The same rule is true for `BigDecimal`. Thus, mathematical operations on these objects always return new objects.

Constants for Selected BigInteger Objects

In our small example, we used some existing `BigInteger` objects to create new objects with their help. In total, the class provides four constants:

```
class java.math.BigInteger
extends Number
implements Comparable<BigInteger>
```

▶ static final BigInteger ZERO

▶ static final BigInteger ONE

▶ static final BigInteger TWO

▶ static final BigInteger TEN

---

10 A word that reads the same from front to back as vice versa.

Creating BigInteger Objects

For creation, several constructors and a factory method are available. No parameterless constructor exists because an empty immutable BigInteger object isn't especially useful.

```
class java.math.BigInteger
extends Number
implements Comparable<BigInteger>
```

▶ static BigInteger valueOf(long val)
A static factory method that constructs a BigInteger from a long.

▶ BigInteger(String val)
Creates a BigInteger from a string of digits with an optional sign.

▶ BigInteger(String val, int radix)
A string with an optional sign is translated into a BigInteger object. The constructor uses the specified base radix to interpret the characters of the string as digits. For radix > 10, the letters A-Z or a-z are used as additional "digits."

▶ BigInteger(byte[] val)
A byte array with a two's complement representation of a BigInteger number in big-endian format (array element with index 0, contains the bits with the highest values) initializes the new BigInteger object.

▶ BigInteger(byte[] val, int off, int len)
Like BigInteger(byte[] val), only a subfield is considered.

▶ BigInteger(int signum, byte[] magnitude)
Creates a BigInteger object from a big-endian amount or sign representation. signum specifies the sign and can be assigned –1 (negative numbers), 0 (zero), and 1 (positive numbers).

▶ BigInteger(int signum, byte[] magnitude, int off, int len)
As the previous constructor, but with a subfield.

In addition to constructors that initialize the object with values from a byte array or string, an object can also be created with a random assignment. The class BigInteger uses the java.util.Random class. Likewise, BigInteger objects can be created that are pseudo-primes.

▶ BigInteger(int numbits, Random rnd)
Returns a random number from the value range 0 to $2^{numBits-1}$. All values are equally probable.

▶ BigInteger(int bitLength, int certainty, Random rnd)
Creates a BigInteger number with bit length bitLength (>1), which is a prime number with some probability. The certainty value determines how probable an incorrect

21

judgment might be. With probability $1/(2^{\text{certainty}})$, the generated number is not a prime number after all. The larger certainty is (and the less probable a misjudgment), the more time the constructor takes.

In case of incorrect strings, the constructor with a string parameter will throw a NumberFormatException.

Example

Let's say we have a string that encodes a binary sequence of zeros and ones. Then, an object of the BigInteger class can be used to convert this string into a byte array. In a second step of the following example, an output is made:

```
String s = "11011101 10101010 0010101 00010101".replace( " ", "" );
byte[] bytes = new BigInteger( s, 2 ).toByteArray(); // [158,261,69,69]
System.out.println( Long.toBinaryString( ByteBuffer.wrap( bytes ).getInt() )
);
// 11011101101010100010101000010101
System.out.printf( "%04X", new BigInteger( 1, bytes ) ); // 6ED51515
```

The first output uses ByteBuffer.wrap(bytes).getInt() as a trick to assemble the bytes of a (small) array into an int. However, the call only works if the array for an int is exactly 4 bytes in size—in addition to getInt(), you can also use getShort() and getLong() for arrays of size 2 and 8. For our example, getInt() is OK because we actually have 4 bytes. The second output shows yet another use case for BigInteger, namely, to produce hex outputs; the byte array can be of any length. The fact that it's called new BigInteger(1, bytes) instead of new BigInteger(bytes) is important because we don't want a sign for the hexadecimal output if the first bit in the byte array is set and usually indicates a negative number. The format string %4X fills the output on the left with zeros if necessary.

Internal Representation*

The implementation represents a BigInteger object internally as well as the primitive data types byte, short, int, and long in the two's complement. The other operations also correspond to the integer operations of the primitive data types, such as division by zero, which throws an ArithmeticException.

Internally, a BigInteger increases the range of values, if necessary, so that some operations aren't transferable. For example, the shift operator >>> can't be taken over because, in a right-shift, we have no sign bit in the BigInteger. Since the size of the data type is always expanded if necessary and no overflow is possible due to this internal adjustment of the internal buffer, users may have to include their own overflow test in their programs if they need to limit the value range.

An interpretation of the values must also be made for logical operators. For operations on two BigInteger objects with different bit lengths, the smaller value is matched to the larger one by replication (repetition) of the sign bit. You can use special bit operators to set individual bits. As with the BitSet class, the "infinite" size allows bits to be set even if the number doesn't require that many bits. Bit operations can't change the sign of a number; if necessary, a new sign bit with the original value is added before the number.

Methods of BigInteger

The first category of methods replicates arithmetic operations for which there would otherwise be an operator character or method from Math:

```
class java.math.BigInteger
extends Number
implements Comparable<BigInteger>
```

▶ BigInteger abs()
Returns the absolute value, similar to Math.abs(...) for primitive data types.

▶ BigInteger add(BigInteger val)

▶ BigInteger and(BigInteger val)

▶ BigInteger andNot(BigInteger val)

▶ BigInteger divide(BigInteger val)

▶ BigInteger mod(BigInteger m)

▶ BigInteger multiply(BigInteger val)

▶ BigInteger or(BigInteger val)

▶ BigInteger remainder(BigInteger val)

▶ BigInteger subtract(BigInteger val)

▶ BigInteger xor(BigInteger val)
Creates a new BigInteger object with the sum, AND-operation, AND-NOT-operation, division, modulo, product, OR-operation, remainder, difference, and XOR-operation of this object and the other one.

▶ BigInteger[] divideAndRemainder(BigInteger val)
Returns an array with two BigInteger objects. In the array, the return object, position 0 contains the value for this / val, followed by this % val at position 1.

▶ BigInteger modInverse(BigInteger m)
Creates a new BigInteger by inverting the current BigInteger (equivalent to 1/this) and then taking it modulo m.

▶ BigInteger modPow(BigInteger exponent, BigInteger m)
Takes the current BigInteger to the power of exponent modulo m.

▶ `BigInteger negate()`
Negates the object and thus returns a new `BigInteger` with reversed sign.

▶ `BigInteger not()`
Returns a new `BigInteger` whose bits are negated.

▶ `BigInteger pow(int exponent)`
Creates this to the power of `exponent`.

▶ `int signum()`
Returns the sign of the custom `BigInteger` object.

▶ `BigInteger sqrt()`
Returns the square root and `ArithmeticException` if the number is negative.

▶ `BigInteger[] sqrtAndRemainder()`
Returns an array with two elements. In the first position is the square root (see `sqrt()`); in the second position is the difference between the current value and the product of `sqrt()`.

[Ex]

Example

The wrapper classes `Integer` or `Long` don't provide methods for determining a greatest common divisor or for checking for a prime number. Using `BigInteger` in this case may pay off. For example, what is the GCD of 855 and 99? Answers will be `BigInteger.val-ueOf( 855 ).gcd( BigInteger.valueOf( 99 ) ).longValsueExact()` with 9.

The next category of methods is closely related to the bits of the number:

▶ `int bitCount()`
Counts the number of set bits of the number that's in the two's complement.

▶ `int bitLength()`
Returns the number of bits necessary to represent the number in the two's complement without a sign bit.

▶ `BigInteger clearBit(int n)`

▶ `BigInteger flipBit(int n)`

▶ `BigInteger setBit(int n)`
Returns a new `BigInteger` object with the nth bit deleted, flipped, or set, respectively.

▶ `BigInteger shiftLeft(int n)`

▶ `BigInteger shiftRight(int n)`
Shifts the bits by n places to the left or right.

▶ `int getLowestSetBit()`
Returns the position of the bit that is set furthest to the right in the representation of the number.

▶ boolean testBit(int n)
   true if the bit n is set.

The following methods are of particular interest for cryptographic procedures:

▶ BigInteger gcd(BigInteger val)
   Returns the greatest common divisor from the current object and val.

▶ boolean isProbablePrime(int certainty)
   Determines if the BigInteger object with probability certainty is a prime number.

▶ BigInteger nextProbablePrime()
   Returns the next integer after the current BigInteger, which is probably a prime number.

▶ static BigInteger probablePrime(int bitLength, Random rnd)
   Returns a prime number of length bitLength with a certain probability.

Furthermore, several extraction and conversion methods are available:

▶ double doubleValue()

▶ float floatValue()

▶ int intValue()

▶ long longValue()
   Converts BigInteger to a double, float, int, or long. These methods are implemented methods of the abstract superclass Number. If the value ranges don't fit, they'll be made to fit. Conversion errors due to lack of accuracy aren't noticed by mistake.[11]

▶ long longValueExact()

▶ int intValueExact()

▶ short shortValueExact()

▶ byte byteValueExact()
   Converts the value of BigInteger to the desired primitive data type. If the accuracy isn't sufficient, an ArithmeticException will follow. The *ValueExact() methods follow the construction of the *Exact() methods from Math, which throw an ArithmeticException if the value range is exceeded during operations (addition, multiplication...).

▶ byte[] toByteArray()
   Returns a byte array with BigInteger as two's complement.

▶ String toString()

▶ String toString(int radix)
   Return the string representation from this BigInteger to base 10 or to any base.

---

11 Some performance issues may arise with the conversion of some values. Thus, in the OpenJDK reference implementation of doubleValue(), it says return Double.parseDouble(this.toString()); "Somewhat inefficient but guaranteed to work."

Example

The following example uses byteValue() and byteValueExact() in comparison:

```
System.out.println( BigInteger.TEN.pow( 3 ).byteValue() );
BigInteger.TEN.pow( 3 ).byteValueExact();
```

While the former returns the output −24, the latter is followed by a "java.lang.Arith-meticException: BigInteger out of int range" because of course 1,000 doesn't fit into a byte.

The last group of methods are comparison methods:

▶ BigInteger max(BigInteger val)

▶ BigInteger min(BigInteger val)
  Returns the larger or smaller of the BigInteger objects.

▶ boolean equals(Object x)
  Compares whether x and the current BigInteger object take on the same value. Over-rides the method from Object.

▶ int compareTo(BigInteger o)
  Since the BigInteger class implements the java.lang.Comparable interface, any BigInteger object can be compared to another BigInteger. This method is useful because, in this way, BigInteger objects can be easily placed into sortable data struc-tures.

21.6.2 Example: Quite Long Factorials with BigInteger

In our next example, the program should calculate the factorial of a natural number. The number must be positive:

```
import java.math.*;

public class Factorial {
  static BigInteger factorial( int n ) {
    BigInteger result = BigInteger.ONE;

    if ( n > 1 )
      for ( int i = 1; i <= n; i++ )
        result = result.multiply( BigInteger.valueOf(i) );

    return result;
  }

  public static void main( String[] args ) {
```

```
      System.out.println( factorial(100) );
  }
}
```

Listing 21.10 src/main/java/com/tutego/insel/math/Factorial.java

In addition to this iterative variant, a recursive variant is also conceivable. However, two reasons warn against its use. First, memory requirements are high because, for the calculation of *n*!, *n* objects are necessary. Unlike the iterative variant, however, all intermediate objects must be kept in the memory until the recursion is resolved. This memory requirement results in the second weakness: a longer runtime. For academic reasons, however, this path should be mentioned because it's interesting to observe how this recursive implementation can eat up memory. The problem wouldn't be so bad if the heap could no longer store new objects, but unfortunately, the stack of the current thread is impacted:

```
public static BigInteger factorial2( int i ) {
  if ( i <= 1 )
    return BigInteger.ONE;

  return BigInteger.valueOf( i ).multiply( factorial2( i - 1 ) );
}
```

Listing 21.11 src/main/java/com/tutego/insel/math/Factorial.java, factorial2()

21.6.3   Large Floats with BigDecimal

While BigInteger takes care of the integers of arbitrary accuracy, BigDecimal takes care of the floats. Again, these objects are immutable, and three constants exist: BigDecimal.ZERO, BigDecimal.ONE, and BigDecimal.TEN.

Creating BigDecimal

BigDecimal provides parameterized constructors for various types, including long, double, and String, and initializes a BigDecimal object with them.

Note

Care must be taken with double. Consider the following example:

```
new BigDecimal( 1.000000000000000000000000000000000000000000000000000000000001 )
```

The compiler takes the literal to the range valid for double (1), as in the following example:

```
new BigDecimal( "1.000000000000000000000000000000000000000000000000000000000001" )
```

21

This number is precise. The same phenomenon can be observed with `System.out.println(new BigDecimal(Math.PI));`, which outputs the following value:

3.141592653589793**115997963468544185161590576171875**

The output suggests high accuracy; however, the correct version is the following value:

3.141592653589793**238462643383279502884197169399375**

Methods instead of Operators

With the `BigDecimal` objects, you can now perform calculations known from `BigInteger`. The main methods are the following:

```
class java.math.BigDecimal
extends Number
implements Comparable<BigDecimal>
```

▶ BigDecimal add(BigDecimal augend)

▶ BigDecimal subtract(BigDecimal subtrahend)

▶ BigDecimal divide(BigDecimal divisor)

▶ BigDecimal multiply(BigDecimal multiplicand)

▶ BigDecimal remainder(BigDecimal divisor)

▶ BigDecimal abs()

▶ BigDecimal negate()

▶ BigDecimal plus()

▶ BigDecimal max(BigDecimal val)

▶ BigDecimal min(BigDecimal val)

▶ BigDecimal pow(int n)

Rounding Mode

A special feature is the `divide(...)` method, which can additionally get a rounding mode and optionally a number of valid decimal places. Let's first look at the method without a rounding mode indicated, as in the following example:

```
BigDecimal ten = new BigDecimal( "10" );
BigDecimal two = new BigDecimal( "2" );
System.out.println( ten.divide( two ) );          // 5
```

If the result is an integer or the result is exact, the lack of rounding isn't a problem:

```
System.out.println( BigDecimal.ONE.divide(b) );  // 0.5
```

However, if the result isn't exact, divide(...) can't be used. The expression new BigDecimal(1).divide(new BigDecimal(3)) results in the runtime error "java.lang.ArithmeticException: Non-terminating decimal expansion; no exact representable decimal result."

At this point, various rounding modes specify how the last digit of a rounding should be determined. A rounding mode can be specified via an enumeration, java.math.Submit RoundingMode. The following constants exist:

Constant in RoundingMode	Meaning
DOWN	Rounding toward 0
UP	Rounding away from 0
FLOOR	Rounding toward negative infinity
CEILING	Rounding toward positive infinity
HALF_UP	Rounding to nearest neighbor and away from 0 if both neighbors are equidistant
HALF_DOWN	Rounding to nearest neighbor and towards 0 if both neighbors are equidistant
HALF_EVEN	Rounding to the nearest neighbor and to the even neighbor if both neighbors are equidistant
UNNECESSARY	No rounding; operation must be exact

Table 21.14 The Meanings of RoundingMode Constants

ROUND_UNNECESSARY may only be used if the division is exact; otherwise, an ArithmeticException will be thrown.

```
BigDecimal one   = BigDecimal.ONE;
BigDecimal three = new BigDecimal( "3" );

System.out.println( one.divide( three, RoundingMode.UP ) );     // 1
System.out.println( one.divide( three, RoundingMode.DOWN ) );   // 0
```

Listing 21.12 src/main/java/com/tutego/insel/math/DivideRoundingMode.java, main()

Now, the number of decimal places can be determined, as shown in the following examples:

```
System.out.println( one.divide( three, 6, RoundingMode.UP ) );   // 0.333334
System.out.println( one.divide( three, 6, RoundingMode.DOWN ) ); // 0.333333
```

[Ex]

Example

BigDecimal provides the useful setScale(...) method, which can you can use to set the number of decimal places, which is quite useful for rounding. In our example, 45 liters of gasoline are supposed to be paid at 1.399:

```java
BigDecimal petrol = new BigDecimal( "1.399" ).multiply( new BigDecimal(45) );
System.out.println( petrol.setScale( 3, RoundingMode.HALF_UP ) );
System.out.println( petrol.setScale( 2, RoundingMode.HALF_UP ) );
```

Listing 21.13 src/main/java/com/tutego/insel/math/RoundWithSetScale.java, main()

The expenses are 62.955 and 62.96.

```
class java.math.BigDecimal
extends Number
implements Comparable<BigDecimal>
```

▶ BigDecimal divide(BigDecimal divisor, RoundingMode roundingMode)

▶ BigDecimal divide(BigDecimal divisor, int scale, RoundingMode roundingMode)

▶ BigDecimal setScale(int newScale, RoundingMode roundingMode)

21.6.4   Conveniently Setting the Calculation Accuracy via MathContext

An object of type java.math.MathContext conveniently specifies the calculation accuracy (not the decimal places) and the rounding mode for BigDecimal. As the previous example showed, this information was given to the individual calculation methods. Now, this one object can be easily passed to all calculation methods.

The state is set with the constructors because MathContext objects will be immutable afterwards.

```
class java.math.MathContext
implements Serializable
```

▶ MathContext(int setPrecision)
  Creates a new MathContext object with specified precision as rounding mode HALF_UP.

▶ MathContext(int setPrecision, RoundingMode setRoundingMode)
  Creates a new MathContext with specified precision and a given rounding mode of type RoundingMode. The declared constants of the enumeration are CEILING, DOWN, FLOOR, HALF_DOWN, HALF_EVEN, HALF_UP, UNNECESSARY, and UP.

▶ MathContext(String val)

Creates a new MathContext object from a string. The structure of the string corresponds to the formatting of MathContext toString().

▶ toString()

Returns a string representation, for example, precision=34 roundingMode=HALF_EVEN for MathContext.DECIMAL128.

For the usual cases, four ready-made MathContext objects are available as constants of the class: DECIMAL128, DECIMAL32, DECIMAL64, and UNLIMITED.

Once the MathContext object has been created, it will be passed within the constructor of BigDecimal.

```
class java.math.BigDecimal
extends Number
implements Comparable<BigInteger>
```

▶ BigDecimal(BigInteger unscaledVal, int scale, MathContext mc)

▶ BigDecimal(BigInteger val, MathContext mc)

▶ BigDecimal(char[] in, int offset, int len, MathContext mc)

▶ BigDecimal(char[] in, MathContext mc)

▶ BigDecimal(double val, MathContext mc)

▶ BigDecimal(int val, MathContext mc)

▶ BigDecimal(long val, MathContext mc)

▶ BigDecimal(String val, MathContext mc)

Even with each calculation method, the MathContext object can now be passed:

▶ BigDecimal add(BigDecimal augend, MathContext mc)

▶ BigDecimal subtract(BigDecimal subtrahend, MathContext mc)

▶ BigDecimal divide(BigDecimal divisor, MathContext mc)

▶ BigDecimal remainder(BigDecimal divisor, MathContext mc)

▶ BigDecimal divideToIntegralValue(BigDecimal divisor, MathContext mc)

▶ BigDecimal abs(MathContext mc)

▶ BigDecimal plus(MathContext mc), BigDecimal negate(MathContext mc)

▶ BigDecimal pow(int n, MathContext mc)

▶ BigDecimal round(MathContext mc)

▶ BigDecimal sqrt(MathContext)

21

21.6.5 Calculating even Faster with Mutable Implementations

The two data types `BigInteger` and `BigDecimal` are immutable, which leads to runtime losses in many calculations. Alternatives are available in the open-source world, such as *https://github.com/bwakell/Huldra*, which implements other algorithms in addition to changeability. However, `BigInteger` is also continuously optimized by Oracle.

21.7 Money and Currency

Numbers require context. A number alone without a unit and without context isn't usable. Numbers always must describe something: an age, a tree height, a turnover, or more generally "life, the universe, and everything."

21.7.1 Representing Amounts of Money

For money amounts, no specific data type exists in Java, and so the storage of money values can look different, depending on the program. The following data types are suitable:

- `BigDecimal`: Its advantages are precise calculations and selectable roundings.
- A pair of `int` or `long`: Enables separate storage of the digits before and after the decimal point.
- `int` or `long`: Instead of separate dollar and cent amounts, everything is stored in cents.

[»]

Note

The primitive data types `double` and `float` aren't recommended because of their inability to correctly represent multiples of 0.01—rounding errors can quickly occur.

Money and Currency API

In Java Specification Request (JSR) 354 "Money and Currency API," a separate data type for amounts of money is defined. Originally, the types were supposed to be included in Java Platform, Standard Edition (Java SE), but this inclusion hasn't happened yet. Nevertheless, these types are interesting, and the reference implementation *Moneta* is worth a look: *http://javamoney.github.io/ri.html*. Besides monetary amounts, this small library permits conversions, formatting, and custom currencies.

21.7.2 ISO 4217

Currencies are described by currency codes, and their definitions can be found in the ISO 4217 standard.

ISO-4217 Code	Currency/Unit	Country
EUR	Euro	Countries of the Economic and Monetary Union of the European Union
CNY	Renminbi	China
DKK	Crown	Denmark
GBP	Pound	United Kingdom
INR	Rupee	India
USD	Dollar	USA, Ecuador, etc.
XAU	Troy ounce of gold	

Table 21.15 Some ISO 4217 Codes

The last entry in the table reveals that there are also ISO codes for precious metals and even funds. A numeric code is defined for each abbreviation.

21.7.3   Representing Currencies in Java

Java represents currencies through the `java.util.Currency` class. Instances of the class are requested by the factory method `getInstance(String currencyCode)` or selected from an enumeration.

Example

The following example outputs all the currencies registered in the system with some additional information:

```
Currency.getAvailableCurrencies().stream()
        .sorted( Comparator.comparing( Currency::getCurrencyCode ) )
        .forEach( c -> System.out.printf( "%s, %s, %s, %s%n",
                                        c.getCurrencyCode(), c.getSymbol(),
                                        c.getDisplayName(), c.getNumericCod
e() ) );
```

The result is the following output:

```
ADP, ADP, Andorran Peseta, 20
AED, AED, VAE Dirham, 784
AFA, AFA, Afghan Afghani (1927-2002), 4
AFN, AFN, Afghan Afghani, 971
ALL, ALL, Albanian Lek, 8
...
```

21.8 Further Reading

Apart from classes to support large ranges of values, the Java library doesn't provide many other algorithms often needed for mathematical problems. The few available methods include solveCubic(...) and solveQuadratic(...) from the CubicCurve2D and QuadCurve2D classes, and even those aren't without errors.[12]

On the (free) market, however, a large number of extensions are available, for example, for fractions, polynomials, and matrices. Let's briefly look at a small selection of extensions:

- *Eclipse January* (*https://projects.eclipse.org/projects/science.january*): an Eclipse Foundation project for large *n*-dimensional fields and matrices. Emulates the NumPy library known in Python. The goal is to define standard interfaces.

- *Commons Math: The Apache Commons Mathematics Library* (*https://commons.apache.org/proper/commons-math/*): includes statistics, linear algebra, complex numbers, and fractions, among others.

Another problem area is dealing with calculation inaccuracies, but these problems are simply in the nature of things. Other problems exist as well, which the paper "How Java's Floating-Point Hurts Everyone Everywhere" (*https://people.eecs.berkeley.edu/~wkahan/JAVAhurt.pdf*) covers in great detail.

---

12 *https://bugs.java.com/bugdatabase/view_bug.do?bug_id=4645692*

Chapter 22
Testing with JUnit

"There's no reason why you should have a computer at home."
—Ken Olson, President of Digital Equipment Corporation, 1977

In this chapter you'll learn to write unit tests for Java applications with the JUnit testing framework.

22.1 Software Tests

To gain as much confidence as possible in one's own codebase, software tests are a good idea. Tests are small programs that run automatically over the codebase without user control and use rules to show that sections of the code behave as specified. Of course, software can't show the absence of errors, but a test case always shows whether a program meets the requirements of the specification.

Figure 22.1 Test, Test, Test, but Please Have a Plan!

Although software testing is extremely important, it's not terribly popular among software developers. One reason is that tests cost time, which must be spent in instead of pursuing actual development work. If the actual software needs changing, test cases often must be modified as well, so ultimately, you're managing two construction sites at once. Since developers should always complete a feature as soon as possible, testing is often dropped from the agenda. Another reason is that some developers think they are infallible coding gods, who consider all their program code (after a few hours of debugging) to be absolutely correct, performant, and delightful.

How can such a skeptical group now be convinced to write tests after all? A big advantage of automated testing is that, when major changes are made to the source codebase (i.e., refactoring), your test cases automatically tell you if everything has been changed correctly. After refactoring, for example, for a performance optimization, the tests report an error, something has probably been "optimized" in the wrong way. Software is subject to permanent change and is never finished, a sufficiently compelling argument for testing because, when software has reached a certain size, what effects changes to the source codebase will have is unpredictable. In addition, another reason exists for dealing with tests: One positive side effect of testing is that the generated software is significantly better by design because writing testable software, although tricky, almost inevitably results in better design. And a better design is always desirable because it increases comprehensibility and makes customizing the software later much easier.

22.1.1 Procedure for Writing Test Cases

The focus of software testing is on three characteristics: automatic, repeatable, and traceable. These characteristics require a library that must support two things:

- Test cases always look the same and consist of three steps. First, a scenario is developed, then the method or a combination of methods to be tested is called, and finally the specific application programming interface (API) of the testing framework determines whether the executed program has shown exactly the desired behavior. This process is taken over by some sort of "is it true that" methods that match the desired state with the actual state and throw an exception if a conflict exists. In the event of an error, the tests should document exactly what went wrong.

- The testing framework must run the tests and issue a message in the event of an error. This part of the testing framework is referred to as the *test runner*.

In the following sections, we'll focus on the description of *unit tests*. These tests examine individual *units*. In addition, other tests will be required, such as load tests, performance tests, and integration tests, but these topics don't play a major role for the purposes of our book.

22.2 The JUnit Testing Framework

Oracle doesn't define a general standard framework for defining unit test cases, nor does it provide a runtime environment for test cases. Testing frameworks fill this gap;

the most popular in the Java area is the free open-source *JUnit* (*https://junit.org/junit5/*). More than 60% of all open-source projects on GitHub reference this library.

22.2.1 JUnit Versions

Kent Beck and Erich Gamma started developing the JUnit framework in 2000. Its current state is the result of contributions from various developers. The original JUnit 3 branch doesn't use any annotations. This lack of annotations changed in 2006 with the release of JUnit 4, which currently has the largest user base. Because JUnit 4 is a monolithic library, JUnit 5 was written, and modularization was implemented. JUnit 5 consists of three parts: *JUnit Platform*, *JUnit Jupiter*, and *JUnit Vintage*. For the remainder of our discussion about JUnit, we're always referring JUnit 5.

22.2.2 Integrating JUnit

Since JUnit isn't part of Java Platform, Standard Edition (Java SE), you'll need to integrate libraries in the classpath. You can, of course, download the JAR files manually and include them in the classpath, but an easier and faster approach uses Maven and an integrated development environment (IDE). First, we'll add the following dependency to the Project Object Model (POM) file:

```
<dependency>
  <groupId>org.junit.jupiter</groupId>
  <artifactId>junit-jupiter-engine</artifactId>
  <version>5.8.2</version>
  <scope>test</scope>
</dependency>
```

Listing 22.1 pom.xml (Supplement)

Most standard IDEs provide wizards that you can use to easily create test cases from existing classes. Test cases can be processed at the touch of a button, and a colored bar instantly shows whether or not our job has been done well.

22.2.3 Test-Driven Development and the Test-First Approach

Let's develop our JUnit example using a specific approach called the *test-first approach*. In this case, the test case is written before the actual implementation. The sequence with the test-first approach (somewhat extended) can be described in the following way:

1. Consider which class and method to write. Create source code for the class and for the variables, methods, or constructors so that the compilation unit can be compiled. The code blocks are empty, but sometimes contain a return statement with return, so the types and methods or constructors are "there" but have no functionality.

2. Write the API documentation and document the function and meaning of parameters, returns, and exceptions.

3. Test the API on an example that shows whether the class feels "natural" with its members. If necessary, go back to step 1 and adjust the properties.

4. Implement a test class.

5. Implement the logic of the actual program.

6. Determine if the implementation introduces new things that a test case should test. If yes, extend the test case.

7. Run the tests and repeat from step 5 until everything runs error free.

The test-first approach has a great advantage of forcing overly hasty developers to start thinking again. These developers, without thinking much, may grab the keyboard and implement and change everything again in 20 minutes. Major changes cost time and therefore money, and the test-first approach reduces the need for later changes. Because when developers invest time in API documentation and write test cases, they already have a clear idea of how the class works, and major changes are less likely.

The test-first approach is an application of *test-driven development (TDD)*, which is a matter of defining testability right away as a goal in software development. This omission of testing was a problem with earlier development models, such as the well-known *waterfall model*, which placed testing at the end (i.e., after analysis, design, and implementation). A consequence of this old sequence was often a large chunk of program code that was impossible to test, which with TDD should no longer happen. Today, for every architecture, design, and class, developers should think about how to test the result right from the start. Research has shown that, with TDD, designs are significantly better.

On the question of when to test, only one thing can be said: as often as possible. This recommendation is sound because, the sooner a test fails due to an incorrect program change, the sooner the error can be corrected. Therefore, the best times for testing are before and after major design changes and definitely before committing to version control. In the modern development process, a computer may run *continuous integration* software. These systems integrate a build server that automatically checks out sources from a version control system, compiles them, and then runs test cases and other metrics. This software then carries out an *integration test*, which is where all the modules of the software are assembled into a whole, highlighting problems that may not show up in isolated tests on the developer machines.

22.2.4   Test, Implement, Test, Implement, Test, Rejoice

So far, Java doesn't provide a simple function that reverses strings. Our first JUnit example is therefore wrapped around a new `Strings` class with a static `reverse(String)` method.

Writing a Class to Be Tested

Based on the TDD approach, you can implement a class with a method so that a correct interpretation is possible, but everything is initially without functionality. (The example doesn't include the complete API documentation.)

```java
public class Strings {

  /**

   * @param string input.

   * @return reversed string

   */

  public static String reverse( String string ) {
    return null;
  }
}
```

Listing 22.2 src/main/java/com/tutego/insel/junit/util/Strings.java, Strings

The name and parameter type "feel" right, and against this custom API, a test case can now be written.

Writing a JUnit Test Case

Now, you may think that an empty reversed string also results in an empty string and that the string "abc" therefore results in "cba." Our goal is to get the best possible *coverage* of all cases. If you suspect case distinctions in the program code, you should try to find enough test cases that all these case distinctions are covered. Special cases or limits in value ranges are always interesting to test. (Our method doesn't offer much in this context, but for a substring functionality, for instance, you can quickly find many tests that could be interesting.)

```java
package com.tutego.insel.junit.util;

import org.junit.jupiter.api.Test;
import static org.junit.jupiter.api.Assertions.*;

class StringsTest {

  @Test
  void reverse_non_null_string() {
    // given
    String emptyString = "";
```

```
  // when
  String reversed = Strings.reverse( emptyString );

  // then
  assertEquals( "", reversed );
  assertEquals( "cba", Strings.reverse( "abc" ) );
  }
}
```

Listing 22.3 src/test/java/com/tutego/insel/junit/util/StringsTest.java

The class reveals five code patterns:

- The test class ends with the suffix Test, but this rule is only a convention and is not mandatory. Usually, the classes are package-visible.

- The methods that take on individual scenarios and test the classes or methods have the annotation @Test. Usually, the test methods are package-visible.

- Different authors use different naming practices for test methods, and no mandatory naming convention exists. In our case, we chose a notation where the prefix names the method to be tested, followed by what the test actually checks, which is the reversal of non-empty strings. To improve readability, an underscore separates the segments, thus leading to the method name reverse_non_null_string(). A traditional naming convention is that the method containing the test begins with the prefix test and ends with the name of the method it tests. Following this blueprint, our method could be called testReverse().

- JUnit provides a set of assert*(...) methods that compare the expected state with the actual state. If discrepancies are found, an exception will be thrown. assertEquals(...) internally performs an equals(...) comparison of two objects. Accordingly, if Strings.reverse("") returns the empty string "", all is well, and the test continues.

- The static import of all static members of the class org.junit.jupiter.api.Assertions shortens the notation, so that instead of Assertions.assertEquals(...), only assertEquals(...) can be written in the program.

22.2.5   Running JUnit Tests

You can execute test cases in several different ways, including the following:

1. In a development environment, the tests can be easily executed. Eclipse or IntelliJ, for example, displays the results in a JUnit view and provides direct visual feedback through a green or red bar.

2. JUnit can run the tests from the command line via the *Console Launcher*.[1]

---

1 More details on this topic are available at *http://junit.org/junit5/docs/current/user-guide/#running-tests-console-launcher*.

3. A test run in the IDE is useful in development. However, in a professional build infrastructure, tests are triggered using Maven or Gradle. In Maven, the test run is part of
a phase in the lifecycle.

Revising a Custom Implementation

In our example, the test run will fail because we lack a working implementation of the
reverse(...) method. So far, the body reads:

```
public static String reverse( String string ) {
  return null;
}
```

Let's change this method body with the following code:

```
public static String reverse( String string ) {
  return new StringBuilder( string ).reverse().toString();
}
```

No error will occur in the next test run.

22.2.6   assert*(...) Methods of the Assertions Class

Assertions is a class with various assert*(...) methods that raise an Assertion-
FailedError whenever a current value doesn't meet expectations. The JUnit Runner
catches all AssertionFailedErrors and stores them for statistics. With three exceptions,
all methods of the Assertions class start with the prefix assert: two are called fail(...),
and one is called isArray(...). The assert*(...) methods are available either with a
test message, which appears when JUnit is to specify an extra message, or without,
when no extra message is requested. The messages can also be supplied via a Sup-
plier<String>, but this string isn't included in the following documentation.

Is Something True or False?

Actually, the assertTrue(boolean condition) method should be sufficient for testing. If
the condition is true, then everything is fine. If not, an internal AssertionFailedError
will occur, which is a subclass of java.lang.AssertionError, which is itself a subclass of
java.lang.Error.

---

class org.junit.jupiter.api.**Assertions**

▶ static void assertTrue(boolean condition)

▶ static void assertTrue(String message, boolean condition)

▶ static void assertFalse(boolean condition)

▶ static void assertFalse(String message, boolean condition)

▶ assert[True|False](BooleanSupplier booleanSupplier)

Is Anything Null?

To make testing a bit more convenient for developers, JUnit provides six categories of helper methods. First, assertNull(...) and assertNotNull(...) can test whether the argument is null or not null, respectively. Calling assertNull(Object object) is then nothing more than assertTrue(object == null):

▶ static void assertNotNull(Object object)

▶ static void assertNotNull(String message, Object object)

▶ static void assertNull(Object object)

▶ static void assertNull(String message, Object object)

Are Objects Identical?

The next category tests whether an object is identical to another object, and not just equal:

▶ static void assertNotSame(Object unexpected, Object actual)

▶ static void assertNotSame(String message, Object unexpected, Object actual)

▶ static void assertSame(Object expected, Object actual)

▶ static void assertSame(String message, Object expected, Object actual)

Are Objects Equals?

Instead of a reference test, the following methods perform an equals(...) comparison:

▶ static void assertEquals(Object expected, Object actual)

▶ static void assertEquals(String message, Object expected, Object actual)

Are Primitive Values Equal?

Basically, only three methods can test primitive data types: one for the data type long (everything "small" is automatically type-matched), one for float, and one for double:

▶ static void assertEquals(long expected, long actual)

▶ static void assertEquals(float|double expected, float|double actual, float|double delta)

▶ static void assertEquals(String message, long expected, long actual)

▶ static void assertEquals(String message, float|double expected, float|double actual, float|double delta)

When comparing floats, assertEquals(...) must be supplied with a delta value within which the result must range. This delta value takes into account the fact that perhaps two numbers look the same in the screen output but aren't equal bitwise, for example, if small calculation errors have accumulated. However, if the floats are wrapped in a wrapper, such as a `double`, `assertEquals(...)` passes the test only to the `equals(...)` method of the wrapper class, which of course doesn't consider a delta.

Are Arrays Equal?

Other methods compare array contents (`BCSIL` stands for `byte`, `char`, `short`, `int`, and `long`):

▶ `static void assertArrayEquals(BCSIL[] expecteds, byte[] actuals)`

▶ `static void assertArrayEquals(String message, byte[] expecteds, BCSIL[] actuals)`

▶ `static void assertArrayEquals(String message, long[] expecteds, long[] actuals)`

▶ `static void assertArrayEquals(String message, Object[] expecteds, Object[] actuals)`

In addition to the `assertEquals(...)` methods, negations for some variants exist, such as the following:

▶ `static void assertNotEquals(long unexpected, long actual)`

▶ `static void assertNotEquals(float unexpected, float actual, float delta)`

▶ `static void assertNotEquals(double unexpected, double actual, double delta)`

▶ `static void assertNotEquals(Object unexpected, Object actual)`

▶ `static void assertNotEquals(String message, long unexpected, long actual)`

▶ `static void assertNotEquals(String message, float unexpected, float actual, float delta)`

▶ `static void assertNotEquals(String message, double unexpected, double actual, double delta)`

▶ `static void assertNotEquals(String message, Object unexpected, Object actual)`

Is All This True or False?

JUnit declares the `org.junit.jupiter.api.function.Executable` type, which can be used to express any block of code. `Assertions` takes on this type via the following methods:

▶ `static void assertAll(Executable... executables)`

▶ `static void assertAll(Stream<Executable> executables)`

▶ `static void assertAll(String heading, Executable... executables)`

▶ `static void assertAll(String heading, Stream<Executable> executables)`

An executable is a functional interface with a `void execute() throws Throwable` method. The useful thing about `assertAll(...)` is that it executes all blocks even an error on only one block occurs. A `@Test` method will typically abort in that case. An exception only terminates the current execute(), and Assertions.assertAll(...) catches this exception and reports the error while processing the test code, but otherwise continues.

22.2.7   Testing Exceptions

During implementation, things often stand out that the actual implementation doesn't yet take into account. Then, immediately, this newfound knowledge should be incorporated into the test case. In our example, we haven't so far clarified what should happen in the case of a null argument. So far, a NullPointerException is perfectly fine, but in a test case, a NullPointerException may not actually follow. This question puts the focus on a testing aspect that's often forgotten because test writers must not only concentrate on what the implementation is supposed to do correctly—the test must also check whether, in the event of an error, this error is also reported correctly. If not in the specification, incorrect values must not be corrected under any circumstances: Incorrect values must always result in an exception or result in another well-defined behavior.

Let's extend our example so that reverse(null) throws an IllegalArgumentException. Two ways to test whether the expected IllegalArgumentException really occurs are available.

Try and fail(...)

Let's look at the first variant of testing IllegalArgumentException, as in the following example:

```
@Test void reverse_null_string_1() {
  try {
    Strings.reverse( null );
    fail( "reverse(null) should throw IllegalArgumentException" );
  }
  catch ( IllegalArgumentException e ) { /* Ignore */ }
}
```

Listing 22.4 com/tutego/insel/junit/utils/StringsTest.java, reverse_null_string_1()

If reverse(null) leads to the exception, as intended, then the catch block will simply catch and ignore the IllegalArgumentException. Then, the test function will move on to other things. If no exception follows, the code after the reverse(...) call gets executed, and that's fail(...). This method triggers a JUnit exception with a message, signaling that something was wrong in the test.

assertThrows(...)

A second option provided by JUnit is to use assertThrows(...), as in the following example:

```
@Test void reverse_null_string_2() {
  assertThrows( IllegalArgumentException.class, () -> {
    Strings.reverse( null );
  } );
}
```

Listing 22.5 com/tutego/insel/junit/util/StringsTest.java, reverse_null_string_2()

In total, the Assertions class has the following methods for testing exceptions:

▶ static <T extends Throwable> T assertThrows(Class<T> expectedType, Executable executable)

▶ static <T extends Throwable> T assertThrows(Class<T> expectedType, Executable executable, String message)

▶ static <T extends Throwable> T assertThrows(Class<T> expectedType, Executable executable, Supplier<String> messageSupplier)

22.2.8   Setting Limits for Execution Times

After major refactoring, software may functionally pass its tests but also become slower. Then, the question arises whether the software is still correct in the sense of the requirements catalog. A previously performant program can run like a snail after a change.

To introduce runtime changes as a validity criterion, the test can be set in an assertTimeout(...) or assertTimeoutPreemptively(...). Both methods expect an Executable or ThrowingSupplier after a given Duration.

```
@Test
void reverse_execution_time_below_1ms() {
  assertTimeout( Duration.ofMillis(1), () -> {
    Strings.reverse( "abc" );
  } );
}
```

Listing 22.6 com/tutego/insel/junit/util/StringsTest.java, reverse_execution_time_below_ 1ms()

If the test method is then not executed within the limit, the test is considered a failed test, and JUnit will report an error.

22.2.9   Labels with @DisplayName

Earlier, we used the method name reverse_non_null_string, for example, to make it easier to read later when running the test. However, tests can get their own labels for output via @DisplayName. Consider the following example:

```
@Test
@DisplayName( "reverse a non null string" )
void reverseNonNullString() { … }
```

Thus, if desired, a method name can be inserted according to the usual naming convention.

22.2.10   Nested Tests

If programmers choose the approach of writing exactly one @Test method for each method to be tested, a large number of assert*(...) methods will be required for different areas. This option is thus confusing and not ideal because the entire test method will abort if an error occurs.

A good solution to bundle tests of an operation or method under test is to use nested tests. JUnit implements this kind of testing with nested classes annotated with @Nested. The annotation @DisplayName isn't mandatory but pretty useful, as in the following example:

```
class StringsTest {

  @DisplayName( "reverse(string)" )
  @Nested class reverse {

    @Test void reverse_non_null_string() { … }

    @Test void reverse_null_string_2() { … }
  }
}
```

Listing 22.7 com/tutego/insel/junit/util/StringsTest.java (Snippet)

If other methods exist in the utility class besides reverse(String), nested classes could exist for each of them. Basically, the levels could go as deep as required.

22.2.11   Ignoring Tests

Restructuring source code may mean that test code is no longer valid and must be removed or rebuilt. To prevent a test case from being executed, you don't to commented it out. (One added disadvantage is that refactoring, for example in the course of renaming identifiers, won't affect areas that have been commented out.) Instead, another @Disabled annotation can be set to the method, as in the following example:

```
@Disabled @Test
void reverse_non_null_string()
```

22.2.12 Canceling Tests with Methods of the Assumptions Class

While the assert*(...) methods lead internally to an exception in case of a failure and thus indicate that the test has found something that isn't correct, JUnit provides Assumptions.assume*(...) methods that enable you to discontinue the tests. This cancelation is useful if test execution isn't possible, for example, because the test computer doesn't have a graphics card, the network doesn't respond, or the file system is full. The point in this case is not to test how the routine behaves in the absence of a network—of course, that functionality also needs to be tested. But if the network isn't available, then logically no tests can run that require the network.

Two of the dozen or so assume*(...) methods include the following:

```
class org.junit.jupiter.api.Assumptions
```

▶ static void assumeTrue(boolean assumption)

▶ static void assumeFalse(boolean assumption)

The assume*(...) methods don't raise an exception but instead abort the test execution.

22.2.13 Parameterized Tests

In test cases, the methods to be tested are often fed with different values. Earlier, we used such a case:

```
assertEquals( "",    Strings.reverse( "" ) );
assertEquals( "cba", Strings.reverse( "abc" ) );
```

Unfortunately, this test approaches code duplication, which can be reduced by means of parameterized tests.

org.junit.jupiter:junit-jupiter-params Dependency

Because parameterized tests aren't part of the JUnit core, you must add a new dependency in the Maven POM, as shown in the following example:

```
<dependency>
  <groupId>org.junit.jupiter</groupId>
  <artifactId>junit-jupiter-params</artifactId>
```

```
  <version>5.8.1</version>
  <scope>test</scope>
</dependency>
```

Listing 22.8 pom.xml (Snippet)

@org.junit.jupiter.params.ParameterizedTest

Let's return to the Java code. For parameterized tests, methods are no longer annotated with @org.junit.jupiter.api.Test, but instead with @org.junit.jupiter.params.ParameterizedTest.

Next, valid input values must be determined, which can be done in several ways. Let's look at two options next.

The first option is to specify a collection of values via @ValueSource. Various data types are possible, including numeric values, strings, and Class objects. JUnit runs through the collection and submits each value to the test method via the method parameter. You can then process these parameters and pass them to the method under test, as in the following example:

```
@ParameterizedTest
@ValueSource( strings = { "", "   ", "abc" } )
void reverse_will_not_throw_exception_with_non_null_inputs( String input ) {
  Strings.reverse( input );
}
```

Listing 22.9 com/tutego/insel/junit/util/StringsTest.java (Snippet)

What you can't do with @ValueSource is include expected results along with the given values. Instead, you can use @CsvSource, as in the following example:

```
@ParameterizedTest
@CsvSource( { "a,a", "ab,ba", "abc,cba" } )
void reverse_non_null_inputs( String input, String expected ) {
  assertEquals( expected, Strings.reverse( input ) );
}
```

Listing 22.10 com/tutego/insel/junit/util/StringsTest.java (Snippet)

One warning: you can't take a "," for the empty string; otherwise, an IllegalArgument-Exception will follow. By default, the delimiter is a comma, but this delimiter choice can be changed.

22.3   Java Assertion Libraries and AssertJ

The problem with the simple tests is that they always end up being simple truth tests. Let's construct an example. Suppose we want to check whether a collection contains two desired elements. We could write the following test:

```
assertTrue( collection.contains(elem1) && collection.contains(elem2) );
```

If the test fails, some questions will remain unanswered:

- Was the first or the second element not in the collection? So, which was present, and which was missing?
- What's in the collection in total?

Of course, these questions can be answered by your own implementation, but various JUnit supplements can help, including *AssertJ* (*https://assertj.github.io/doc*), *Truth* (*https://truth.dev/*), or *Hamcrest* (*http://hamcrest.org/JavaHamcrest*). These supplements allow tests to be written more declaratively, so that they be read almost like English sentences.

22.3.1   AssertJ

AssertJ is a popular add-on to JUnit. Let's briefly contrast the API for AssertJ with JUnit's API. JUnit uses simple assert*(...) methods with one, two, or three parameters for a test. In AssertJ, assertThat(xxx) forms the basis for a property xxx to be tested. This property can be a primitive type, a collection, a file, a database connection, or anything else. After assertThat(...) follows an assertion of the desired properties via the fluent API.

assert*(...) in JUnit	assertThat(...) in AssertJ
Object o = new Object(); assertNotNull(o);	Object o = new Object(); assertThat(o).isNotNull();
assertEquals("", Strings.reverse(""));	assertThat(Strings.reverse("")). isEqualTo("");

Table 22.1 Comparison of the assert*(...) and assertThat(...) Methods

The essential difference can be seen in the table: In the assertThat(...) methods of AssertJ, the argument always contains the value that should be examined for characteristics. With the assert*(...) methods of JUnit, the first argument is what JUnit should expect as correct and then the query for the page effect.

Including AssertJ

JUnit doesn't include AssertJ, so the first step is to include a Java archive in the class-path. Maven users would write the following code:

```
<dependency>
  <groupId>org.assertj</groupId>
  <artifactId>assertj-core</artifactId>
  <version>3.21.0</version>
  <scope>test</scope>
</dependency>
```

Listing 22.11 pom.xml (Snippet)

Sample Program

Let's return to our opening example: testing whether certain elements are contained in a collection and others aren't. Let's start with the following setup:

```
List<String> letters = new ArrayList<>();
Collections.addAll( letters, "a", "b", "c", "d", "e" );
letters.removeAll( Arrays.asList( "b", "d" ) );
```

The list first contains the letters "a" to "e," then "b" and "d" leave the list. AssertJ allows us to check different things, as shown in the following example:

```
assertThat( letters ).hasSize( 3 );
assertThat( letters ).contains( "a" ).contains( "c" );
assertThat( letters ).contains( "a", "c", "e" ).doesNotContain( "b", "d" );
```

You can clearly recognize the fluent API because of the cascading of method calls. Different parameter types of assertThat(…) lead to different return types. For our list, assertThat(letters) returns type org.assertj.core.api.ListAssert. If we had the parameter type int, the return type would be org.assertj.core.api.AbstractIntegerAssert; if a string, the return type would be org.assertj.core.api.AbstractStringAssert.

Let's change the collection a bit and create an error by removing "b" and "e" instead of "b" and "d." The output message is meaningful:

```
java.lang.AssertionError:
Expecting:
 <["a", "c", "d"]>
to contain:
 <["a", "c", "e"]>
but could not find:
 <["e"]>
```

22.4 Structure of Large Test Cases

So far, we've been dealing with individual, complete test cases and have not really covered how to organize a large number of tests.

22.4.1 Fixtures

An important property of tests is that they are independent of each other. The assumption that a first test, for example, creates some test data that the second test can then draw on is wrong. Consequently, you should consider that each individual test method must assume to be the first test method and thus must establish its initial state itself. However, unnecessary source code duplication would result if each test method would now build this initial state by itself. The initial state is referred to as a *fixture* (roughly "fixed inventory"), and JUnit provides four annotations in this context (which have changed from version 4 to version 5). The following example shows how they work:

```java
package com.tutego.insel.junit.util;

import java.util.logging.Logger;
import org.junit.jupiter.api.*;

public class FixtureDemoTest {

  static final Logger log = Logger.getLogger( FixtureDemoTest.class.getName() );

  @BeforeAll
  public static void beforeClass() { log.info( "@BeforeAll" ); }

  @AfterAll
  public static void afterClass() { log.info( "@AfterAll" ); }

  @BeforeEach
  public void setUp() { log.info( "@Before" ); }

  @AfterEach
  public void tearDown() { log.info( "@After" ); }

  @Test
  public void test1() { log.info( "test 1" ); }

  @Test
  public void test2() { log.info( "test 2" ); }
}
```

Listing 22.12 com/tutego/insel/junit/util/FixtureDemoTest.java, FixtureDemoTest

The annotations refer to two use cases:

- @BeforeAll and @AfterAll: Annotates static methods that are called once when the class is initialized for testing or when all tests for the class have been completed.
- @BeforeEach and @AfterEach: Annotates object methods that are always called before or after a test method.

When our sample program runs, the (shortened) output will therefore look as follows:

```
INFO: @BeforeAll
INFO: @Before
INFO: test 1
INFO: @After
INFO: @Before
INFO: test 2
INFO: @After
INFO: @AfterAll
```

The @BeforeAll methods usually contain what is expensive to build, such as a database connection. The resources are then released again in the symmetric method @AfterAll; for example, database connections will be closed again. Since no artifacts should remain from the test case after a test, good @AfterAll/@AfterEach methods perform "undo" operations, so to speak.

[Ex]

Example

If a System.setProperty(...) sets "global" states or overrides predefined properties, @BeforeAll is a good time to take a snapshot and restore it later at @AfterAll. Consider the following example:

```
private static String oldValue;
@BeforeAll public static void beforeClass() {
  oldValue = System.getProperty( "property" );
  System.setProperty( "property", "newValue" );
}
@AfterAll public static void afterClass() {
  if ( oldValue != null ) {
    System.setProperty( "property", oldValue );
    oldValue = null;
  }
}
```

22.4.2 Collections of Test Classes and Class Organization

If the tests become more numerous, the question of their ideal organization arises. A proven tactic is to put the test cases in the same package as the classes under test but to physically separate the source code. Development environments can use different source code folders that are physically and visually separated but ultimately result in class files and resource located within in the same package. According to the Maven default directory layout, these locations are *src/main/java* and *src/test/java*. The advantage of having types in the same package is that package visibility is often sufficient, and thus, you don't need to make private members public just for testing.

In IntelliJ and Eclipse, you can simply go to a branch and then select **Run** from the context menu; this step will run all tests in the subpackages as well. Test suites do not replace this feature yet because suites are executed outside the IDE.

22.5 Good Design Enables Effective Testing

Static methods with the pattern "parameter provides the input, return value provides the result" are easy to test. These methods don't change any environment, and states don't exist. The test case merely examines the return, which is easy. Testing gets more complex when the thing to be tested entails extensive system changes: Has a file been created? Are things in the database as desired? Has the cluster mirrored the data to other servers? Does an external program provide the expected return? Does a native method really return what it promises, without crashing the JVM?

If things suddenly become untestable, then a bad design has been revealed. This problem often happens because a class has too many responsibilities. As an example, let's look at a class that writes business cards in the vCard format (file extension *.vcf*).[2] To keep the source code lean, the VCard class doesn't use setters and getters.

```java
public class VCard {

  public String formattedName;
  public String email;

  public void export( String filename ) throws IOException {
    StringBuilder result = new StringBuilder( "BEGIN:VCARD\n" );
    if ( formattedName != null && ! formattedName.isEmpty() )
      result.append( "FN:" ).append( formattedName ).append( "\n" );
    if ( email != null && ! email.isEmpty() )
      result.append( "EMAIL:" ).append( email ).append( "\n" );
    Files.write( Paths.get( filename ),
            Collections.singleton( result.append( "END:VCARD" ) ) );
  }
}
```

Listing 22.13 com/tutego/insel/junit/util/vcf/v1/VCard.java, VCard

---

2 More information about this file format is available at *http://en.wikipedia.org/wiki/VCard*.

For example, if the application set the variable formattedName to Powerpuff Girls and email to powerpuff@townsville.com, then the export(...) method would create a file with the following content:

```
BEGIN:VCARD
FN:Powerpuff Girls
EMAIL:powerpuff@townsville.com
END:VCARD
```

The main task of the class is to correctly create the output format according to the vCard standard. The class can be tested in principle, but the test won't be nice. First, different vCard properties would have to be set, then the vCard would be written to a file, then the file would be opened, the content would be read, and finally it would be checked for correctness—not a really pleasant method! The VCard class wasn't designed to be test oriented. Why not? Besides the fact that such a test could take quite a long time because of the file access required, you can basically state that the export(...) method combines two responsibilities, namely, the output in the special vCard format and the output to a file. If the design had been based on the TDD principle, we would have separated the parts *Format* and *Output*. By having a separate method for formatting the files, say in a string, the test would only need to call this method and would not need to write to a string. Let's improve the class in the following way:

```java
public class VCard {

  public String formattedName;
  public String email;

  public void export( Writer out ) throws IOException {
    out.write( toString() );
  }

  public void export( String filename ) throws IOException {
    try ( Writer writer = Files.newBufferedWriter( Paths.get( filename ) ) ) {
      export( writer );
    }
  }

  @Override public String toString() {
    StringBuilder result = new StringBuilder( "BEGIN:VCARD\n" );
    if ( formattedName != null && ! formattedName.isEmpty() )
      result.append( "FN:" ).append( formattedName ).append( "\n" );
    if ( email != null && ! email.isEmpty() )
      result.append( "EMAIL:" ).append( email ).append( "\n" );
```

```
        return result.append( "END:VCARD" ).toString();
    }
}
```

Listing 22.14 com/tutego/insel/junit/util/vcf/v2/VCard.java, VCard

This variant brings about two improvements at the same time:

1. The toString() method now returns the string prepared according to the vCard standard. The test now only must build a VCard object, set the variables, call toString(), and test the string for correctness without any file operations. For the client, however, the API doesn't change; it continues to write export(...).

2. Writing directly to files is no longer really up to date. This fact is taken into account by the class that provides an overloaded version of export(...) with a generic Writer. If, for example, a vCard is to be sent over the network, no problem arises. Only a suitable Writer for the network target must be passed. Previously, this task would have been rather cumbersome (create file, read file, and send string).

The bottom line is that the payoff is big. The test is more performant, and the design leads to better source code—a win-win situation.

This approach shows how to proceed with implementations that communicate with external resources in particular. These resources must be extracted as far as possible, if necessary also using a new type, which can then be injected as a test implementation.

22.6   Dummy, Fake, Stub, and Mock

Systems with a design based on good object orientation are characterized by high interaction with other objects. Ideally, a class decomposes a problem only to the point where it can make use of another class that solves the simpler problem. Where things get tricky is when a custom class references another complex class, and the object only works meaningfully if the referenced object is there and responds in a way that makes sense. This dependency is unfavorable because the goal of a good test is to be local (i.e., to test the actual class and not all referenced classes around it at the same time).

In practice, three helper constructs can enable the locality of tests:

- **Fake objects**
  These objects are a valid implementation of an interface. For example, if a repository goes to the database, a fake implementation can store records in a data structure. The behavior is replicated and simplified, but functional. Thus, instead of customers from the database, a fake repository always provides the same *n* prebuilt customers. Fake objects are also useful when, for example, a graphical user interface (GUI) application is programmed that's developed with the fake objects instead of real database data, thus displaying only demo data. If one team builds the GUI and another team

22

builds the service, both groups can work independently, and the GUI team doesn't need to wait for the implementation first.

- **Stub objects**

  Stub objects implement a specific protocol so that they can always give the same answers for the test case. For example, if an email service provides an isTransmitted() method, the stub can always return true. Stubs therefore have no behavior, but the body of the methods is quasi-empty and minimal. These objects exist only for test cases.

- **Mock objects**

  Mock objects are "charged" by a test case and then show the desired behavior—so they don't always return the same result as stubs. Usually, mock objects are created automatically at runtime by libraries such as *Mockito* (*https://site.mockito.org*) or *EasyMock* (*https://easymock.org/*).

We can summarize these three types under the generic term *dummy object*. In general, however, the four terms aren't used in a uniform manner.[3]

[Ex]

Mockito Example

Let's assume everything from org.mockito.Mockito.* is statically imported, and we want to create a java.util.List. For this goal, Mockito must first build something that behaves like List, as in the following example:

```
List<?> mockedList = mock( List.class );
```

The next step is to determine the behavior of the special list, as in the following example:

```
when( mockedList.get(0) ).thenReturn( "tutego" );
```

Now, the list is ready for use, so let's display it with the following code:

```
System.out.println( mockedList.get(0) ); // tutego
```

To avoid having to call the mock(...) method manually, a JUnit 5 test case can be annotated with @ExtendWith. Then, all object variables provided with @Mock can be initialized automatically. Consider the following example:

```
@ExtendWith( MockitoExtension.class )
class MyTest {
  @Mock private MyType mock;
  @BeforeEach private void setUp() {
    when( mock.… ).thenReturn( … );
  }
}
```

---

3 Discussion of how these terms are used is available at *http://xunitpatterns.com/Mocks,%20Fakes,%20Stubs%20and%20Dummies.html*.

22.7 JUnit Extensions and Testing Add-Ons

The *JUnit* framework itself is quite compact, but as can be seen from AssertJ, you'll need convenient testing methods that simplify typical and frequently recurring testing tasks. Not only does this include methods that test whether an element exists in a data structure, but also support for tests with database accesses, REST calls, or GUI tests.

22.7.1 Web Tests

Two methods are used for testing web applications. One is a tool-assisted recording of web interactions and automatic playback of the consequences for testing, and the other one is the programmed solution. For recording, the free tool *Selenium (https://www.selenium.dev)* or integration in Chrome and Firefox with the *Selenium IDE (https://www.selenium.dev)* is suitable. To program tests, you can find a good basis with *REST Assured (https://github.com/rest-assured/rest-assured)*.

22.7.2 Testing the Database Interface

The database is usually accessed via *repository classes* (also called *DAO classes*). If a service accesses a database, the service always goes through the repository. Testing the service is simplified by using a repository dummy instead of a database repository implementation. The question remains, however, of how you can test the repository classes.

Testing can take a long time because interactions with a database are often the slowest steps in an entire business application. One approach is to run the tests in your local Docker container in main memory; here you can make use of the *test containers* framework (*https://www.testcontainers.org/*).

Another task is filling the database with test data. The open-source software *DbUnit (http://dbunit.sourceforge.net/)* can help with this task. External data is written in XML and can be easily imported into the database beforehand, so that the test works on this sample data. The sample data is then inserted into the in-memory database, if possible, or into a local development database. However, for advanced testing (especially to estimate runtimes), tests must also be run with a copy of the real business data. Enterprise frameworks such as *Spring* also provide options for easily importing test data prior to a test run.

22.8 Further Reading

Application testing and TDD are hot topics, and more on JUnit and Mockito is to find in the book *Practical Unit Testing with JUnit and Mockito* by Tomek Kaczanowski. For AssertJ it's useful to study the very good examples that are available online: *https://*

github.com/assertj/assertj-examples/tree/main/assertions-examples/src/test/java/ org/assertj/examples.

Another worthwhile task might be to review a more critical look at TDD, for example, inspired by "TDD Harms Architecture" *(https://blog.cleancoder.com/uncle-bob/2017/ 03/03/TDD-Harms-Architecture.html).*

Chapter 23
The Tools of the JDK

"Success should always be only the consequence, never the goal of action."
—Gustave Flaubert (1821–1880)

This chapter introduces the most important programs of the Java Development Kit (JDK). Since most programs are command-line-oriented, we'll show you their calling syntax as well.

23.1 Overview

Programs of the JDK include the following tools:

Tool	Description
javac	Java compiler for translating *.java* to *.class* files
java	Java interpreter for running Java applications
javaw	Like java, but no console window opens
javap	Displays the bytecode of a class file
jdb	Debugger to run through a program
javadoc	Utility for generating documentation
jar	Archiving tool that combines files into one Java Archive file (a JAR file)
jconsole	Java Monitoring and Management Console
jcmd	Sends diagnostic commands to the Java virtual machine (JVM)
jdeps	Lists module dependencies
jdeprscan	Java Deprecated API Scanner, which lists deprecated application programming interfaces (APIs)
keytool, jarsigner	Programs for working with certificates
serialver	Generates a constant serialVersionUID for serializable classes

Table 23.1 Some Tools of the JDK

Although other call parameters may be involved depending on the version, we've only listed those officially mentioned in the current documentation. In general, most tools are executed via build tools like Maven and rarely purely from the command line.

23.1.1   Structure and Common Switches

Command-line programs have options (also called *switches*) that thus define different functions and behaviors. Many switches are available in a short version and a long version. The short version starts with exactly one hyphen, such as `-cp`, and the long version with two minus signs, such as `--class-path`.

Although these tools serve different functions, several commonalities exist. For example, the following switches occur quite frequently:[1]

- `-help`, `--help`, or `-?` outputs the help.
- `--module-path` or `-p` specifies the module path.
- `--version` or `-version` outputs the version.
- `-v` or `--verbose` outputs more messages.
- `-Xmn` and `-Xms` specifies the heap size.

23.2   Translating Java Sources

A Java compiler translates Java source code files into bytecode. The Java compiler *javac* ships with the JDK by default.

23.2.1   The Java Compiler of the Java Development Kit

The *javac* compiler translates the source code of a file into Java bytecode. Each type declared in a file is translated by the compiler into a separate class file.

A general call of the compiler can be written in the following way:

```
$ javac [ options ] filename(s).java
```

In Maven, the `compile` stage performs the translation, while calling `javac` in the background, with the following command:

```
$ mvn compile
```

23.2.2   Native Compilers

An application written in Java can first be executed only with a Java Runtime Environment (JRE). However, some manufacturers have developed compilers that create

---

1   See *https://openjdk.java.net/jeps/293*

executable programs directly on Windows or another operating system. These compilers that generate the machine code of the respective architecture from Java source code—or Java bytecode—are referred to as *native* or *ahead-of-time compilers (AOT)*. The result is a directly executable file that doesn't require a JRE. Depending on the use case, the program may be more performant, but no guarantee of better performance can be made. Startup times are generally shorter, and the program is much more difficult to decrypt with regard to reverse engineering.[2]

Existing runtime environments now achieve sufficient speed, reasonable memory consumption, and acceptable startup times. To reduce startup times even further, *GraalVM Native Image* enables you to create native images. Details about this project are available at *https://www.graalvm.org/reference-manual/native-image/*.

23.3   The Java Runtime Environment

The Java interpreter *java* executes the Java bytecode in the runtime environment. For this task, the interpreter looks for the special static main(String[]) method in the class file passed as a parameter. A general call of the interpreter can be written in the following way:

```
$ java [ options ] class name [ arguments ]
```

If the class is declared in a package, the name of the class must be fully qualified. For example, if the Main class is located in the package com.tutego (i.e., in the subdirectory com/tutego), the class name must be com.tutego.Main. The runtime environment must be able to find the required classes. Like the compiler, the JVM evaluates the CLASSPATH environment variable and allows the classpath to be specified by the -classpath option.

23.3.1   Switches of the Java Virtual Machine

Various switches are possible for the JVM runtime environment, for instance, the following:

Option	Meaning
-client	Selects the *Java HotSpot Client VM*, which is the default.
-server	Selects the *Java HotSpot Server VM*.
-cp *classpath*	A list of paths within which the compiler can find the class files. This option overrides the CLASSPATH environment variable that may be set and doesn't add to it. The semicolon (Windows) or colon (Unix) separates multiple directories.

Table 23.2 Options of the java Interpreter

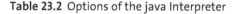

2   That is, converting unstructured binary code back into source code.

Option	Meaning
-DProperty=value	Sets the value of a property, such as -Dversion=1.2, which can later be queried by System.getProperty(..).
-help or -?	Lists all available options.
-ea	Enables assertions that are disabled by default.
-jar	Starts an application from the JAR file if a class with a main-method is named in the manifest file. However, the main class can still be specified.
-verbose	Provides further information about the runtime environment: ■ -verbose:class provides information about loaded classes. ■ -verbose:gc provides information about garbage collection calls. ■ -verbose:jni provides information about native calls.
-version	Displays the current version.
-X	Displays non-standardized options.
-Xdebug	Starts with the debugger.
-Xincgc	Turns on incremental automatic garbage collection.
-Xms*n*	Initial size of the memory area for allocating objects (in MiB); the default is 2 MiB.
-Xmx*n*	Maximum available memory area for the allocation of objects. As a simple number, n describes the bytes or kilobytes with an appended k or megabytes (appended m), for example, -Xms128m.
-Xnoclassgc	Turns off the garbage collector for classes that have been loaded but are no longer needed.
-Xrs	Reduces internally the use of Unix signals by the runtime environment. This switch may result in worse performance, but better compatibility with various Unix/Solaris versions.
-Xss*n*	Sets the size of the stack.

Table 23.2 Options of the java Interpreter (Cont.)

[»]

Note

The longer Oracle's JVM exists, the longer the list of options will become. The standard JVM documentation at *https://docs.oracle.com/en/java/javase/17/docs/specs/man/java.html* briefly lists all the available options.

Classpath Wildcard

The -cp option extends the classpath by Java Archive files (JAR files, with the *.jar* extension) and individual class files (with the *.class* extension). The classpath wildcard * allows even easier specification of JAR files. We advise enclosing the specifications in quotation marks so that the shell doesn't perform any expansions, unless expansion is desired.

Example [Ex]

The following example loads the *log.jar* and all JAR files in the *lib* directory to the classpath:

```
$ java -cp "log.jar;lib/*" MainClass
$ java -cp "log.jar:lib/*" MainClass
```

Windows separates paths with a semicolon, while Unix separates them with a colon.

Additional Options

The -X option can set further switches and then send additional statements to the runtime environment, for example, about the maximum memory to be used. An interesting switch is -XshowSettings, which prints the states of the default properties. This switch is quite useful, for example, to read which paths have been set. If you apply this switch to the program NinetyNineBottlesOfBeer from Chapter 1, Section 1.8.1, you'll get the following output:

```
$ java -XshowSettings NinetyNineBottlesOfBeer
VM settings:
    Max. Heap Size (Estimated): 3.95G
    Using VM: Java HotSpot(TM) 64-Bit Server VM

Property settings:
    file.encoding = Cp1252
    file.separator = \
    java.class.path = .
...
```

Note [«]

In addition to these simple -X options, other special HotSpot options are set with -XX. But the use of these switches is quite rare.

23.3.2 The Difference between java.exe and javaw.exe

In a Windows installation, two executables in the Java JDK exist for the interpreter: *java.exe* and *javaw.exe*. Mostly, *java.exe* is used. The difference is that an application started via a graphical user interface (GUI) with *java.exe* displays a console window, unlike *javaw.exe*. Without a console window, *javaw* also doesn't show any output via `System.out/err`.

Usually, a program with a GUI uses *java* during development and then *javaw* in production operation.

23.4   Documentation Comments with Javadoc

The documentation of software systems is an important but often neglected part of software development. Unfortunately, because software is generally read more often than written. During the development process, developers must invest time in the description of each component, especially when additional developers make these components available to other developers in a public library for reuse. To understand the classes, interfaces, enumerations, and methods as well as class/object variables fully, they must be described carefully. Important elements in a description include the type name, the method name, the type and number of parameters, the effect of the methods, and the runtime behavior. Since creating external documentation (i.e., a description outside the source code file) is error-prone and therefore not terribly exciting, special documentation comments are introduced into the Java source code. A special program generates description files (generally HTML) with the desired information from the comments.[3]

23.4.1   Setting a Documentation Comment

Documentation comments (also called "Javadoc") are used in a particularly excellent comment environment. The comment environment extends a block comment and is common before all types (classes, interfaces, enumerations) as well as methods and variables. In the following example, Javadoc provides comments for the class, for class/object variables, and for methods:

```
package com.tutego.insel.javadoc;

/**
 * This class models a room with a given number of players.
 */
public class Room {

  /** Number of players in a room. */
  private int numberOfPersons;
```

---

3 This idea isn't new. In the 1980s, Donald E. Knuth used the WEB system to document TeX. The program was converted to a Pascal program and a TeX file using the *weave* and *tangle* utilities.

```java
/**
 * A person enters the room.
 * Increments the number of persons.
 */
public void enterPerson() {
  numberOfPersons++;
}

/**
 * A person leaves the room.
 * Decrements the number of persons.
 */
public void leavePerson() {
  if ( numberOfPersons > 0 )
    numberOfPersons--;
}

/**
 * Gets the number of persons in this room.
 * This is always greater than or equal to 0.
 *
 * @return Number of persons.
 */
public int getNumberOfPersons() {
  return numberOfPersons;
}
}
```

Listing 23.1 com/tutego/insel/javadoc/Room.java

Comment	Description	Example
@param	Parameter description.	@param x coordinate.
@see	Reference to another package, type, or member.	@see java.util.Date @see java.lang.String#length()
@version	Version.	@version 1.12
@author	Creator.	@author Christian Ullenboom
@return	Return value of a method.	@return Number of elements
@exception/@throws	Exceptions that can be thrown.	@exception NumberFormat-Exception

Table 23.3 The Most Important Documentation Comments at a Glance

Comment	Description	Example
{@link reference}	Built-in reference in text in code font; same parameters as for @see.	{@link java.lang.Thread}
{@linkplain reference}	Like {@link}, but in normal font.	{@linkplain java.lang.Thread}
{@code Code}	Source code in code font, also with HTML special characters.	{@code 1 is < 2}
{@literal literals}	Masks HTML special characters. No code font.	{@literal 1 < 2 && 2 > 1}

Table 23.3 The Most Important Documentation Comments at a Glance (Cont.)

[»]

> **Note**
>
> The documentation comments are structured in such a way that the first sentence appears in the listing of methods and state variables and the rest in the detail view. Consider the following example:
>
> ```
> /**
>  * A short sentence that will be in the Method Summary section.
>  * The following is a detailed description, which can later be found in the
>  * Method Detail section, but not in the overview.
>  */
> public void foo() { }
> ```

Because a documentation comment /** starts with /*, it's a typical block comment for the compiler. Javadoc comments are often visually enhanced by putting an asterisk at the beginning of each line—Javadoc ignores this.

23.4.2   Creating Documentation with the javadoc Tool

An external program generates the target documents from the source code with comments. The JDK provides the console program *javadoc* to which is passed a filename of the class with comments as a parameter. Of course, description files can't be created from compiled files. Like the Java compiler, Javadoc is usually deployed via a build tool such as Maven. You have two options: You can either use a plugin configuration in the Project Object Model (POM) file or you can directly deploy Javadoc with the following command:

```
$ mvn javadoc:javadoc
```

Javadoc runs through the source code, parses the declarations, and pulls out the documentation. From this process, the tool generates a description, which is usually an HTML page.

> **Note**
>
> Visibility plays an important role in Javadoc. By default, Javadoc only includes public things in the documentation.

23.4.3 HTML Tags in Documentation Comments*

HTML tags can be used in the comments, for example, `<b>bold</b>` and `<i>italic</i>`, to set text attributes. These tags are transferred directly to the documentation and must be correctly nested so that the output displays correctly. Heading tags `<h1>...</h1>` and `<h2>...</h2>` shouldn't be used, however, because Javadoc uses these tags to organize its own output and assigns style sheets to these tags.

In Eclipse, the **javadoc** view previews the result of the documentation comment.

23.4.4 Generated Files

For each public class, Javadoc creates a HTML file. If classes aren't public, a switch must be specified. The HTML files are additionally cross-referenced to the other documented classes. In addition, Javadoc creates other files, such as the following files:

- *index-all.html*: An overview of all classes, interfaces, exceptions, methods, and fields in an index.
- *overview-tree.html*: Displays the classes in a tree structure so that the inheritance is clearly visible.
- *allclasses-frame.html*: Lists all documented classes in all subpackages.
- *deprecated-list.html*: A list of deprecated methods and classes.
- *serialized-form.html*: A list of all classes that implement `Serializable`. Each class/object variable appears with a description in a paragraph.
- *help-doc.html*: Shows a short description of Javadoc.
- *index.html:* Javadoc creates a view with frames. Thus, this file is the main file that references frames on the right and on the left. The left frame is the *allclasses-frame.html* file. In the frame on the right, the first class is displayed if the package description is missing.
- *stylesheet.css*: A style sheet for HTML files in which, among other things, colors and fonts can be specified, which are then used by all HTML files.
- *packages.htm*: An obsolete file that references the new files.

23.4.5   Documentation Comments at a Glance*

Some Javadoc comments must be isolated after the main description, like @param (description of parameters) or @return (description of returns). These tags are called *block tags*. Other tags may appear in the text, such as {@link} to set a reference to another type or method. These tags are called *inline tags*. The Javadoc tool recognizes the following tags, among others:

- **Block tags**: @apiNote, @author, @deprecated, @exception, @implNote, @implSpec, @param, @return, @see, @serial, @serialData, @serialField, @since, @throws, and @version
- **Inline tags**: {@code}, {@docRoot}, {@inheritDoc}, {@link}, {@linkplain}, {@literal}, and {@value}

Examples

You can specify an external additional source in the following way:

```
@see <a href="spec.html#section">Java Spec</a>.
```

Thus, we can reference a method that is related to the method described in the following way:

```
@see String#equals(Object) equals
```

Several variants of @see are available, such as the following:

```
@see #field
@see #method(Type, Type,...)
@see #method(Type argname, Type argname,...)
@see #constructor(Type, Type,...)
@see #constructor(Type argname, Type argname,...)
@see Class#field
@see Class#method(Type, Type,...)
@see Class#method(Type argname, Type argname,...)
@see Class#constructor(Type, Type,...)
@see Class#constructor(Type argname, Type argname,...)
@see Class.NestedClass
@see Class
@see package.Class#field
@see package.Class#method(Type, Type,...)
@see package.Class#method(Type argname, Type argname,...)
@see package.Class#constructor(Type, Type,...)
@see package.Class#constructor(Type argname, Type argname,...)
@see package.Class.NestedClass
@see package.Class
@see package
```

While documenting a variable, you can specify a reference to a method, as in the following example:

```
/**
 * The X-coordinate of the component.
 *
 * @see #getLocation()
 */
int x = 1263732;
```

A deprecated method that references an alternative is indicated in the following way:

```
/**
 * @deprecated  As of JDK 1.1,
 * replaced by {@link #setBounds(int,int,int,int)}
 */
```

Instead of using HTML tags like <tt> or <code> for source code, {@code} is much easier, as shown in the following example:

```
/**
 * Compares this current object with another object.
 * Uses {@code equals()} an not {@code ==}.
 */
```

Other useful tags include @index, @hidden, @provides, @uses, and @summary.

23.4.6   Javadoc and Doclets*

The output of Javadoc can be customized to meet your needs by using *doclets*, which is a Java program based on the Doclet API and writes to an output file. The program reads source files like the well-known Javadoc tool and creates any output format from them. This format can be chosen and implemented by yourself. Thus, if you want to create Framemaker files (MIF) or RTF files besides the standard doclet for HTML files provided by JavaSoft, you must program your own doclet, or you can use doclets made by different vendors. For example, the (somewhat dusty) website *http://www.doclet.com/* lists doclets that generate DocBook or include Unified Modeling Language (UML) diagrams.

In addition, a doclet isn't only used for interface documentation. A doclet can also show whether documentation exists for each method and whether each parameter and return value has been correctly described.

23.4.7   Deprecated Types and Members

During the development stage of a software, method signatures change again and again, or methods are added or dropped, which may occur for many reasons such as the following:

23

- Methods can't really be programmed to be platform independent but were once offered that way. Now, the method should no longer be supported (an example is the method `stop()` of a thread).

- The Java naming convention should be introduced, and older method names should be discontinued. This reason primarily concerns special `set*(…)`/`get*()` methods that were available from version 1.1. Thus, you'll find many examples of inconsistencies with the Abstract Windowing Toolkit (AWT). Now, for example, instead of `size()` in a graphical component, you would use `getSize()`.

- The program authors were mistaken about the method name. So, in `FontMetrics`, it was previously called `getMaxDecent()`, and now it's `getMaxDescent()`, and in `HTMLEditorKit`, `insertAtBoundry(...)` becomes `insertAtBoundary(…)`.

Simply deleting methods is now inconvenient because compiler errors will occur. For this reason, one solution is to declare the method or constructor as deprecated. `@deprecated` is a separate documentation comment. The following excerpt from the `java.util.Date` class illustrates its use:

```
/**
 * Sets the day of the month of this <tt>Date</tt> object to the
 * specified value. …
 *
 * @param   date   the day of the month value between 1-31.
 * @see       java.util.Calendar
 * @deprecated As of JDK version 1.1,
 * replaced by <code>Calendar.set(Calendar.DAY_OF_MONTH, int date)</code>. */

public void setDate(int date) {
  setField(Calendar.DATE, date);
}
```

Listing 23.2 java.util.Date.java (Snippet)

The `@deprecated` identifier indicates that a method or constructor should no longer be used. Robust commentary will also point out alternatives if any are available. One alternative is using the `set(...)` method from the `Calendar` object. Since the comment is included in the generated API documentation, the developer can easily recognize that a method is deprecated.

> **Note**
>
> That a method is marked as "deprecated" doesn't necessarily mean that the method will be deleted in the next Java version. This marker is only an indication that the method should no longer be used and that support is no longer provided.

Compiler Messages for Deprecated Methods

The compiler displays a small message on the screen for deprecated methods. Let's test this feature on the OldSack class:

```
package com.tutego.insel.tool;

//@SuppressWarnings( "deprecation" )
public class OldSack {
  java.util.Date d = new java.util.Date( 62, 3, 4 );
}
```

Listing 23.3 src/main/java/com/tutego/insel/tools/OldSack.java

Now, let's call the compiler as usual:

```
$ javac com/tutego/insel/tool/OldSack.java
Note: com\tutego\insel\tool\OldSack.java uses or overrides a deprecated API.
Note: Recompile with -Xlint:deprecation for details.
```

As shown in the following example, the compiler indicates that the -deprecation switch provides additional hints:

```
$ javac -deprecation com.tutego.insel.tool.OldSack.java
com\tutego\insel\tool\OldSack.java:5: warning: [
deprecation] Date(int,int,int) in Date has been deprecated
  java.util.Date d = new java.util.Date( 62, 3, 4 );
                 ^
1 warning
```

The output provides exactly the line with the deprecated code; the compiler doesn't mention any alternatives. However, interestingly, the compiler looks into the documentation comments even though it should ignore comments. Finally, to evaluate the special comments, there is an extra tool called *javadoc* and it has nothing to do with the Java compiler.

> **Note**
>
> Classes can also be marked as deprecated (see, for example, java.io.LineNumberIn-putStream). However, you rarely find this marker in the Java library, and with custom types, you should avoid its use.

The @Deprecated Annotation

Annotations are a kind of additional modifier. The @Deprecated annotation (capitalized) is standard and allows things to be marked as deprecated. For this purpose, the annotation is placed before the return type, like a usual modifier for methods, for example. Oracle has marked the setDate(...) method with this annotation, as the following snippet shows:

```
/** …
 * @deprecated As of JDK version 1.1,
 * replaced by <code>Calendar.set(Calendar.DAY_OF_MONTH, int date)</code>.
 */
@Deprecated
public void setDate(int date) { … }
```

One advantage of the @Deprecated annotation over the Javadoc tag is that the annotation is also visible at runtime. If you have a @Deprecated tester before a method call, it can report the deprecated methods at runtime. With the Javadoc tag, the compiler translates the program into bytecode and outputs a message at compile time, but no hint exists in the bytecode itself.

The annotation type @Deprecated has two annotation attributes:

- String since() default "": Documents the version when the element became obsolete.
- boolean forRemoval() default false: Indicates that the element should be deleted in the future.

[Ex]

Example

Consider the following example from the Thread class:

```
@Deprecated(since="1.2", forRemoval=true)
public final synchronized void stop(Throwable obj) {
   throw new UnsupportedOperationException();
}
```

[»]

Deprecated Libraries

A large number of deprecated elements have accumulated over time. An overview is provided by *https://docs.oracle.com/en/java/javase/17/docs/api/deprecated-list.html*.

23.4.8   Javadoc Verification with DocLint

The Javadoc tool can detect errors in the Javadoc comments; this check can be activated via the Xdoclint switch. DocLint detects the following groups of errors, which can also be specified as options:

Group	Description
accessibility	Checks for documentation accessibility issues, for instance, checking that tables always have summaries.
html	Detects HTML errors, such as missing closing angle brackets.
missing	Checks for missing elements, for example, if a comment or @return is missing.
reference	Checks all references in the Javadoc tags, for example, at @see, or checks for invalid names at @param.
syntax	Checks common syntax errors such as unmasked HTML characters like <, >, or & and non-existent Javadoc tags.

Table 23.4 Possible Groups with Javadoc and the DocLint Tool

For more options for the Javadoc extension, see *https://docs.oracle.com/en/java/javase/17/docs/specs/man/javadoc.html*.

23.5 The JAR Archive Format

The JAR file format is an archive format similar to ZIP. As usual for an archive format, JAR also packs several files together. However, "packed" doesn't necessarily mean that files must be compressed; they can simply be bundled in a JAR. An unpacking program like 7-Zip can unpack JAR files. You may consider whether a program like 7-Zip should be associated with the *.jar* file extension or whether the default behavior should be retained with the JRE installed: On Windows, the *.jar* file extension is associated with the JRE that launches the main class of the archive.

23.5.1 Using the jar Utility

jar is a command-line utility that provides several options to create, unpack, and view archives. Rarely, the jar tool is used on the command line or in a shell script. Usually, build tools like Maven or Gradle build a JAR file at the end of the compilation process. In a Maven project, the following command creates a Java file:

```
$ mvn package
```

23.5.2 The Manifest

Without the output showing it, jar automatically inserts a manifest file named *META-INF/MANIFEST.MF* when creating an archive. A manifest contains important additional information for an archive, such as the signature listed for each file.

[Ex]

Example

Consider the following excerpt from a manifest file for the H2 database management system:[4]

```
Manifest-Version: 1.0
Implementation-Title: H2 Database Engine
Implementation-URL: https://h2database.com
Implementation-Version: 1.4.200
Build-Jdk: 1.7
Created-By: 1.7.0_80-b15 (Oracle Corporation)
Main-Class: org.h2.tools.Console
Automatic-Module-Name: com.h2database
Bundle-Activator: org.h2.util.DbDriverActivator
Bundle-ManifestVersion: 2
Bundle-Name: H2 Database Engine
Bundle-SymbolicName: com.h2database
Bundle-Vendor: H2 Group
Bundle-Version: 1.4.200
…
```

The entries in the manifest are reminiscent of a property file because in this case too are always keys and values separated by a colon.

23.5.3   Launching Applications in Java Archives: Executable JAR Files

The fact that files are bundled together in one archive has an advantage in that developers no longer must deliver a whole bundle of class and resource files to a customer; only a single file needs to be sent. Another advantage is that an operating system like Windows or macOS associates the JRE with the *.jar* extension by default, so double-clicking on a JAR file starts the program right away.

Main-Class in the Manifest

So that the runtime environment knows which class has the necessary main(String[]), a small note with the Main-Class key in the manifest file is necessary, which you would write in the following way:

```
Main-Class: fully.qualified.class.name.of.class.with.main
```

Since the manifest file is generated, the entry must be generated by the build tool. For Maven, for example, this generation process is documented at *https:// maven.apache.org/shared/maven-archiver/examples/classpath.html#Make.*

---

4 *https://repo1.maven.org/maven2/com/h2database/h2/1.4.200/h2-1.4.200.jar*

Launching from the Command Line or via Double-Click

JAR files with the Main-Class entry can also be easily launched from the command line via the JVM in the following way:

```
$ java -jar JarFile.jar
```

If Java was brought to the hard drive via an installer, then executable JAR files can be launched with a double-click because the file extension *.jar* causes javaw -jar to be executed with the file name. If you've only unpacked the ZIP archive for the Java "installation," then simply launching it won't work.

> **Note**   [«]
>
> java (or javaw) ignores the information about -cp or entries in the environment variable CLASSPATH, if a Java program is started with -jar.

Instead of referencing many small JAR files, another option is to first unpack all the JAR files and then pack them back together into a new large JAR file that java -jar can launch. With Maven, this process can be implemented via the *Apache Maven Shade plugin*.[5] The result is also called a Fat-JAR.

23.6   Further Reading

The Oracle website *https://docs.oracle.com/en/java/javase/17/docs/specs/man/index.html* describes these utilities extensively and should be read carefully. We recommend learning right away how the tools are rum from Maven; the switches for setting it up are usually the same as we've seen from the command line tools.

23

---

5 *https://maven.apache.org/plugins/maven-shade-plugin/index.html*

The Author

 **Christian Ullenboom** is an Oracle-certified Java programmer and has been a trainer and consultant for Java technologies and object-oriented analysis and design since 1997.

Index

B

C

G

H

M

S

X

Y

Z